A "blank wall" for J. Robert Oppenheimer
Supreme Court outlaws school segregation

1955 The Davy Crockett craze
Enter the beat generation
Formosa resolution
Geneva summit
Ike's heart attack

1956 Grace Kelly becomes a princess
Hungary, Suez, and Ike's reelection
Montgomery bus boycott

1957 Little Rock
Russia launches its first sputnik
The Edsel disaster
U.S. rocket fiasco at Cape Canaveral

1958 Hula hoop craze
Eisenhower Doctrine in Mideast
Nixon mobbed in Caracas
Sherman Adams's vicuña coat
John Birch Society founded

1959 Charles Van Doren unmasked
Nixon in Moscow; Khrushchev in U.S.

1960 FDA approves Enovid — the Pill
Black sit-ins start in Greensboro, N.C.
U-2 incident; Geneva summit collapses
Kennedy elected President by an eyelash

1961 Alan Shepard's fifteen minutes in space
Freedom riders in Dixie
The Bay of Pigs
Kennedy vs. Khrushchev in Vienna
LBJ visits Saigon, pledges support
Taylor-Rostow mission to Vietnam

1962 Grossinger's first Singles Only weekend
John Glenn orbits earth
James Meredith at Ole Miss
SDS organized
Cuban missile crisis

1963 *Who's Afraid of Virginia Woolf?*
Beatles tour U.S.
Birmingham and Bull Connor
Wallace stands in the schoolhouse door
March on Washington
Diem brothers assassinated in Saigon
Death in Dallas

1964 Tonkin Gulf
The first of the long hot summers
Mario Savio and the Free Speech Movement

Civil rights murders in Mississippi
LBJ vs. Goldwater
Dr. Strangelove

1965 Dr. Zhivago
Medicare; the "Xerox Congress"
LBJ commits U.S. ground troops in Vietnam
Herald Tribune coins "credibility gap"
Selma march; Watts
Electricity blackout blankets Northeast

1966 Nudity becomes chic
America scarred b̶   ̶ce riots
                        klash
                        y
                        d Junction

RFK and Martin Luther King die
Columbia campus blows
Jacqueline Kennedy remarries
My Lai
Nixon elected in a cliffhanger

1969 Apollo 11 lands on moon
Woodstock
Chappaquiddick
Charles Manson
M Days for peace
Chicago Seven trial

1970 Women's Lib and hotpants
Cambodia and Kent State
Judge Carswell rejected
X-rated movies sweep country
Angela Davis and George Jackson
Postal strike
White House hires Plumbers

1971 U.S. ping-pong players visit China
"Mayday Tribe" in Washington
Pentagon Papers leaked
A second-story job on Dr. Fielding
ITT, Vesco, and the milk fund
Phase One and Phase Two
Attica

1972 Bobby Fischer and Clifford Irving
Nixon in Peking and Moscow
Giap's offensive
Watergate and cover-up
McGovern: a disaster for the Democrats
Kissinger: "Peace is at hand"
Saturation bombing and a cease-fire
Dead ahead: Watergate exposure

THE GLORY AND THE DREAM

A Narrative History
of America

1932-1972

WILLIAM MANCHESTER

THE GLORY AND THE DREAM

A Narrative History of America

1932-1972

VOLUME TWO

LITTLE, BROWN AND COMPANY
BOSTON — TORONTO

Acknowledgments of permission to reprint excerpted material appear on pages 1641–1643.

Portions of this book were first published in slightly altered form in the *New York Times Magazine* and *New York* magazine.

Published simultaneously in Canada by Little, Brown & Company (Canada) Limited

PRINTED IN THE UNITED STATES OF AMERICA

Contents

PART II
Sacrifice and Transformation
1941–1950

PART III
Sowing the Wind
1951-1960

VOLUME TWO

PART IV
Reaping the Whirlwind
1961-1968

PART V
Nixon, After All
1969-1972

THE GLORY
AND THE
DREAM

A Narrative History
of America

1932-1972

Twenty-one

MR. CHAIRMAN, MR. CHAIRMAN

LATER THE SPECTER of Dienbienphu would loom ever larger in the American consciousness, but at the time it was something that was happening to somebody else. Its downfall wasn't the only major event of 1954, or even one of the top stories. That was a newsy year in the United States. In January the world's first atomic submarine, *Nautilus*, was launched in Groton, Connecticut. Six weeks later in Detroit six leaders of the Communist Party in Michigan were found guilty of conspiring to overthrow the U.S. government. Confronted by indisputable evidence of an approaching recession, the President decided in his March 12 cabinet meeting to call it a "rolling readjustment."

The Easter 1954 issue of *McCall's* introduced "togetherness," a concept which quickly became so popular that it took on overtones of a social crusade and became almost a national purpose of the 1950s. The Air Force Academy was created on April 1; its first class was sworn in at Lowry Air Force Base, Denver, Colorado. Rejecting a lower British bid, Secretary of Defense Charles E. Wilson awarded contracts for construction of the Chief Joseph Dam in the state of Washington to an American firm, and both houses of Congress approved the St. Lawrence Seaway.

Julius and Ethel Rosenberg had been executed after a demonstration outside the White House in which picketers protesting the sentence were accosted by noisy young demonstrators bearing placards which read TWO FRIED ROSENBERGERS COMING RIGHT UP. Admiral Robert B. Carney, Chief of Naval Operations, contributed to cold war tensions by telling reporters that he and his staff expected a Chinese Communist attack on the offshore islands of Quemoy and Matsu within a month. "They have information I do not have," said the President. Nevertheless, he warned that any assault on Formosa "will have to run over the Seventh Fleet." The cabinet was elated at its July 23 meeting to learn that economic indicators would soon turn upward, ending the rolling readjustment. August's Hurricane Carol blew down the steeple of Boston's historic Old North Church. Other hurricanes named Edna and Hazel followed in September.

Eisenhower and Churchill conferred in Bermuda on world peace. The Atomic Energy Commission on October 5 approved a contract under which a West Memphis power plant would be built for the TVA by a southern utility group headed by Edgar H. Dixon and Eugene A. Yates. President Eisenhower described his administration's political philosophy as "dynamic conservatism," then as "progressive, dynamic conservatism," then as "progressive moderation," then as "moderate progressivism," and then as "positive progressivism." On December 21, 1954, Dr. Samuel H. Sheppard, a Cleveland osteopath, was convicted of murdering his wife Marilyn on July 4. Sir Edmund Hillary, conqueror of Mount Everest, was thrilling lecture audiences in the Middle West, and nationwide circulation was given to the first authoritative reports linking cigarette smoking and heart disease.

Playboy was selling for fifty cents, competing on newsstands with such other publications of the decade as *Flair* (fifty cents), *Confidential*, "Uncensored and Off the Record" (a quarter), *Mad* (a dime), and, at fifteen cents, the most successful periodical of the 1950s, *TV Guide*, which by the end of the decade would be running fifty-three regional editions for seven million subscribers.

America's drug culture lay far in the future, but the roots of its idiom could be heard at bebop sessions where one heard the esoteric jazz of such maestros as Miles Davis and Thelonious Monk. They called money bread and girls chicks. To understand was to flip; something which in the past had been fabulous was now crazy. Superlatives of crazy were cool, groovy, the end, and far out (later to become out of sight). To be appreciative was to be hip, and someone who was so hip that he had passed into an ecstatic trance would soon be called a hippy.

Better known then, and a source of amusement in intellectual circles throughout the decade, was advertising cant. As society became more aware of advertisers, and as they became more clever, their instant clichés briefly became part of the language. In 1954 the reigning platitude was the suffix "wise," meaning "with regard to," "in respect of," or "in the manner of." Battered by overuse, it became an all-purpose word. Instead of saying "This year's cars are all chrome," you said, "Stylewise, this year's cars are all chrome." Moneywise, a tycoon was rich. Sequencewise, a loser was last. Agewise, a girl was young; clotheswise, she might be chic; and personalitywise, she would be attractive. Boozewise, you might have a big night. Headwise, you would feel terrible in the morning, but jobwise, you would make it to the office.

On the other side of the island from Madison Avenue lay Tin Pan Alley, and there sovereignty still rested in the clammy hands of the balladeers. The biggest hit of 1954 was Kitty Kallen's "Little Things Mean a Lot." Runners-up included Perry Como's "Wanted," Frank Sinatra's "Young at Heart," and the Crew Cuts' (only classical musicians wore their hair long then) "Sh-Boom." Archie Bleyer's "Hernando's Hideaway" was another memorable ditty that year. The Four Aces' "Three Coins in the Fountain" was from the motion picture of the same name, a Cinemascope production in De Luxe Color starring Dorothy McGuire, Clifton Webb, and Jean Peters. Waterfront corruption in New York was a running story throughout 1954— on April 15 Albert Anastasia was deprived of his citizenship—and the Academy of Motion Picture Arts and Sciences awarded its Oscar for the best picture of the year to *On the Waterfront*. Other honored films were *The Caine Mutiny, The Country Girl, Seven Brides for Seven Brothers, Sabrina, Executive Suite, Dial M for Murder, Rear Window*, and Disney's *20,000 Leagues Under the Sea*. Movies still weren't making much money, but for the time being the big talent was staying in Hollywood.

Variety listed as 1954's most popular television programs *I Love Lucy, Dragnet*, and the mixed bags of Groucho Marx and Ed Sullivan. The only really bright hour of TV comedy, Sid Caesar and Imogene Coca's Saturday evening *Your Show of Shows*, folded in 1954 after 160 performances; the network blamed lack of audience interest. Above all, 1954 was the year of the quiz show: *I've Got a Secret, Stop the Music, Place the Face, Name That Tune*, and *What's My Line*. The big money quiz programs, *Twenty-one* and

The $64,000 Question, were in the wings. TV spectaculars—long, lavish, one-performance extravaganzas—were more interesting. *Amahl and the Night Visitors,* a Christmas Eve opera written for television by Gian-Carlo Menotti in 1951, had been acclaimed everywhere. As it happened, 1954's chief spectacular, *Satins and Spurs,* was so terrible that its star, Betty Hutton, retired from show business. Next year promised to be much better, though. Contracts were out for Mary Martin's superb *Peter Pan,* to be telecast March 7, 1955.

Obviously television was having an immense impact on American mores, but defining the nature of the impact was difficult. Some thought the networks were too wide-open, too permissive. TV fare was more violent than radio, and franker about sex. Plunging necklines, an exciting development of the early 1950s, left little doubt that female performers were mammary and proud of it. When Desi Arnaz impregnated his wife and costar, Lucille Ball, the producers of *I Love Lucy* took it as an opportunity; each week's episode offered late bulletins on Lucy's condition, and Desi was even depicted suffering from sympathetic morning sickness.

In reality TV was merely noting a trend here, one whose implications would not emerge until another decade. The medium itself would never be a pace-setter. Like the life-styles of the 1950s of which it was so faithful a mimic, it was bland, innocuous, noncontroversial. Its most familiar themes were charming but irrelevant to real issues: the bromides Loretta Young read at the end of each program, Dave Garroway's "Peace," and the "Ho-Ho Song" to which Red Buttons danced offstage.

Commercial? Absolutely: the profit motive was as sacred as togetherness. Sneering at it was almost prima facie evidence of subversion. Everybody was selling something, and Americans approved; the diversity of their marketplace was the marvel of the world. A confidential survey made for the Republican National Committee by Batten, Barton, Durstine, and Osborn reported that foreign policy was the number one issue for American voters, with Communist infiltration in the U.S. second, but it was untrue. The agency was telling its clients what they wanted to hear. Prosperity was what Americans wanted, and they had it, were getting fat with it, and enjoyed reading the scales. It was a bull market that was going to get bullier. Detroit was counting on Chevrolet's Dinah Shore to be especially alluring in 1955. The automotive industry's confident—and justifiable—expectation was that nearly eight million cars would be sold, nearly a million more than in any previous year. In February 1954 over 7,500 Republicans descended on Washington to eat fried chicken box lunches in the Ellipse and observe Lincoln Day by singing "God Bless America." The President came out for a few brief remarks. At the moment he wasn't toying with "moderate progressivism" or any of that; he used the simple term "conservative," paused, then added firmly: "And don't be afraid to use that word." They cheered. Middle-class Republicans were feeling their oats. They were proud to be conservative, prosperous, conformist, and vigilant defenders of the American way of life, and they wanted no truck with crackpots, Reds, heretics, Bohemians, radicals, nuts, Bolsheviks, loonies, pinkos, fellow travelers, galoots, geezers, or screwballs. Eggheads were subjects of particular scorn. No wild-eyed college professors were going to be allowed to gum up the works. On April 13, 1954, James Reston reported in the *New York Times* that the Atomic Energy Commission, at the direction of President Eisenhower, had withdrawn the security clearance of Dr. J. Robert Oppenheimer pending an investigation of charges that he had, among other things, "worked tirelessly from January 21, onward, to retard the United States H-bomb program."

The accusation had been lodged five months earlier by William L. Borden, former executive secretary of the Joint Congressional Committee on Atomic Energy and senior assistant to Senator Brien McMahon. Borden had written J. Edgar Hoover on November 7, 1953, that "more probably than not J. Robert Oppenheimer is an agent of the Soviet Union." A bill of particulars followed, including charges that prior to April 1942 "He was contributing substantial monthly sums to the Communist Party," that "His wife and younger brother were Communists," and that "He had no close friends except Communists."

Borden's motives are obscure. He had nothing new. The government had long known that Oppenheimer had been a freewheeling left-of-center ideologue in the 1930s. It hadn't affected his work. Lately he hadn't had much to do with Washington anyhow. At one time he had been a member of no fewer than thirty-five government committees, but in July 1952 he had resigned as chairman of the AEC General Advisory Commission, and since the beginning of the Eisenhower administration he had been devoting most of his energies to the Institute for Advanced Study in Princeton, of which he was the director. As a government consultant he retained his top-secret Q clearance, but he never used it. At the time of Borden's accusations Oppenheimer wasn't even in the country. He had been chosen to deliver the BBC's prestigious Reith Lecture for 1953, and while he was in Britain Oxford decided to award him his sixth honorary degree. It was a question of who was more honored by the occasion, Oppenheimer or Oxford. By this time America's most eminent scientist had been elected to every learned society in Europe. Prizes, awards, and foreign decorations had been showered upon him. At home he had been chosen for everything from the American Academy of Arts and Sciences to the *Popular Mechanics* Hall of Fame.

Now Borden said he was a Russian spy. What is far more likely is that he was a victim of scientific politics. A savage dispute was raging between nuclear physicists belonging to two schools of thought named for America's two great nuclear laboratories, Los Alamos and Livermore. The Los Alamos group, comprising Oppenheimer's colleagues and protégés, held that nuclear missiles should be only one of many kinds of weapons in the American arsenal. This was called "finite containment." The Livermore, or Teller, group believed that the nation's security depended upon the unlimited development of nuclear striking power. That was "infinite containment." Most scientists took the finite view, but an administration that advocated "massive retaliation" was plainly thinking in infinite terms. The Livermore men were in power, and this, in fact, was one reason Oppenheimer had withdrawn to Princeton. But that wasn't enough for his adversaries. The debate had turned some men of science into fanatics—which is not really surprising, since the issue could determine the future of the human race—and certain admirers of Edward Teller were determined to discredit Oppenheimer. Almost certainly they were behind Borden.

Borden, however, merely wrote a letter. Washington desks were covered with such letters then. There was no reason why an official should pay attention to a new smear, unless, of course, he thought there was something in it. That was true in this instance. J. Edgar Hoover had been suspicious of J. Robert Oppenheimer for a long time. In 1947 Hoover had done all he could to tag Oppenheimer as a security risk. The *Herald Tribune* reported that the FBI file on Oppenheimer was four feet six inches high. Borden could hardly have sent his letter to a more receptive addressee, and the chances are that he knew it.

Hoover spent the next three weeks preparing an inch-thick digest of the Oppenheimer file. On November 30 he sent it to the White House. Copies went to Lewis A. Strauss at the Atomic Energy Commission and Charlie Wilson at the Pentagon. After reading his, Wilson phoned the President; he wanted Oppenheimer barred from all military installations at once. Eisenhower called it "very disturbing" (which of course it was, however you felt about Oppenheimer) and called an emergency meeting to weigh the charges. Had the scientist ever been confronted with them? he asked. Told he hadn't, Ike ordered a hearing. Meantime, he said, he wanted a "blank wall" put between Oppenheimer and all government secrets. It was an arresting phrase, and although only Wilson, Strauss, Brownell, and Robert Cutler of the National Security Council had been present, word of the decision reached the Washington gossips and, through them, the Capitol Hill home of Senator Joseph R. McCarthy.

Upon returning from England Oppenheimer found a message to call Admiral Strauss. Strauss urged him to come to the capital at once; the matter was pressing and couldn't be discussed over the telephone. On the afternoon of December 21 the scientist entered the AEC's gleaming marble building on Constitution Avenue, and in room 236, the admiral's large, paneled office, he found Strauss in conference with Major General Kenneth D. Nichols, the commission's general manager. They asked him to join them at a conference table. There, after an exchange of pleasantries and news of mutual friends, Strauss told Oppenheimer, as gracefully as you can tell a man such a thing, that he was suspected of treason. Eisenhower's directive was explained to him, and then the possibility of a graceful exit was discussed. Oppenheimer refused to take it.

On Christmas Eve a special indignity was visited upon him. Security men from the AEC arrived in Princeton to confiscate all classified material in his possession. The hearing was then scheduled for April. Reston knew of it. He intended to publish nothing until a decision had been reached, but since McCarthy was planning to announce it in the Senate to claim that he had forced the administration's hand, Reston went ahead. The news was sensational, and the determination to avoid further sensationalism gave the subsequent hearing a furtive air. The sessions, closed to the press and public, were held in temporary building T-3, a shabby relic of OPA's wartime bureaucracy. To hoodwink any reporters who might learn of the location, Oppenheimer used a back door. The trial—for that is what it amounted to—was held in T-3's room 2022, a 24- by 12-foot office which had been converted to its temporary purpose by an arrangement of tables, chairs, and a seedy old leather couch. Oppenheimer used the couch; afterward a participant would recall that the scientist "leaned back lazily, sometimes as though his thoughts were elsewhere, on the sofa which had been turned into a dock for the occasion."

A bench had been set up at the opposite end of the room. There sat Oppenheimer's judges: Gordon Gray; Thomas A. Morgan, a retired industrialist; and Ward V. Evans, emeritus professor of chemistry at Northwestern. The AEC was represented by Robert Robb, counsel to its Personnel Security Board. Robb contributed to the inquisitional aura by adopting the abrasive manner of a prosecuting attorney. His attitude toward Oppenheimer was one of contempt. A stranger entering room 2022 would never have guessed that the man under interrogation had been director of the laboratory that had perfected the atomic bomb. Robb used all the timeworn trial tricks, including keeping the sunlight in the defendant's eyes by putting his own back to a window. The 992-page transcript of the hearings bristles with his disdain.

Periodically Oppenheimer's disembodied voice would be heard over a portable public address system—recordings of wartime G-2 telephone taps which had been made without his consent or even knowledge. It was humiliating; at times it was almost unbelievable. When André Malraux read the record of the proceedings he expressed astonishment that Oppenheimer, who after all was a free man, had remained to hear Robb's studied insults. Malraux said, "He ought to have stood up and shouted, 'Gentlemen, *I* am the atomic bomb.'" But Oppenheimer was too diffident, too introverted for that, and he had suffered much brooding over the destruction of Hiroshima; he felt, as he told a friend, that "We did the devil's work."

After taking testimony from forty witnesses, the tribunal retired to write its opinion. The allegation that Oppenheimer had been an enemy agent was rejected: "We have given particular attention to the question of his loyalty and we have come to the clear conclusion, which should be reassuring to the people of this country, that he is a loyal citizen." Indeed, the panel observed, "It must be said that Dr. Oppenheimer seems to have had a high degree of discretion reflecting an unusual ability to keep to himself vital secrets." Evans, the only scientist on the tribunal, wanted to restore Oppenheimer's security clearance, but Gray and Morgan wouldn't go that far. They didn't like some of Oppenheimer's friends. It was their opinion that his "associations have reflected a serious disregard for the requirements of the security system." Then there was his troubling lack of enthusiasm for the superbomb:

> We find his conduct in the hydrogen bomb program sufficiently disturbing as to raise a doubt as to whether his future participation, if characterized by the same attitudes in a government program relating to the national defense, would be clearly consistent with the best interests of security.

Oppenheimer appealed the two-to-one decision to the AEC, which upheld it in a four-to-one vote. Commissioner Henry D. Smyth urged the others to see that Oppenheimer's "loyalty and trustworthiness emerge clearly," that in the light of his distinguished attainments "his services could be of great value to the country in the future," and that "the security system has . . . neither the responsibility nor the right to dictate every detail of a man's life." But it was precisely there that the others parted company with him; a man of great achievements might be forgiven much, and the commissioners were less rigid than the Gray board in passing judgment on Oppenheimer's mixed feelings about thermonuclear weapons, but failure to repudiate friends and relatives with unorthodox political persuasions could not be overlooked.

Ironically, the effect of purging Oppenheimer was the exact opposite of what his enemies had intended. In martyrdom he acquired new stature. Teller, on the other hand, became something of an outcast. The plotters had expected him to become the new wise man of nuclear physics. Instead he was ostracized. The only established scientist who had spoken against Oppenheimer, he was looked upon as an FBI informer, a turncoat who had betrayed both a fellow scientist and science itself. At scientific meetings he was snubbed by the others; when he protested they walked away. Eventually he came to be tolerated, but he was never really trusted again; in panel discussions and conversations his fellow physicists were formal and guarded. He appealed to Enrico Fermi, now near death, and the great Italian scientist supported him in an article in the magazine *Science,* but to Teller's critics this was just one more breach of ethics. They put him down as a publicity seeker and continued to ignore him. In the world of science his Dr. Strangelove image had already formed.

Meantime the human condition which would be symbolized by Strangelove had been brought into focus by a chance wind in the western Pacific Ocean, giving Americans a brief but terrible glimpse of what they were doing to themselves and to the world. On March 1, when Robb was preparing his case against Oppenheimer, the AEC had exploded its second hydrogen bomb on Bikini atoll, just east of Eniwetok. Outstripping all expectations, it ripped open the coral reef with a force of some 18 million to 22 million tons of TNT—the equivalent of 900 to 1,000 Hiroshima bombs. Then the wind picked up the fallout. Meteorologists had predicted a stiff breeze to the north. Instead, it blew southward until, 120 miles from Bikini and far from the danger zone marked by the bomb testers, it dropped clouds of radioactive dust on a Japanese trawler grimly misnamed the *Lucky Dragon No. 5.* The startled Japanese fishermen at first thought themselves to be in the world's first tropical snowstorm. By the time they reached their home port of Yaizu, the ghastly truth had begun to emerge. All twenty-three of them were sick and had to be hospitalized. Subsequently one, the wireless operator, died. Meanwhile sensitive devices had picked up traces of radioactivity from rainfall in Japan, Australia, the United States, Europe, and even in the oil in airliners which had been flying over India.

This brought a new term to the vocabulary of death: strontium 90, or radiostrontium, a heavy radioactive isotope of strontium with a half-life of 25 years. That was what had been in the lethal blizzard which had struck the *Lucky Dragon No. 5.* Deposited in the bones, like calcium, and combined with radioactive iodine, which had been discovered in the thyroid glands of the fishermen, strontium 90 was a cause of cancer. It was further believed to threaten posterity, though its impact there could not be measured for several generations. Admiral Strauss called the scientists who warned of these dangers, "appeasers" and "alarmists." He dispatched his own teams of technicians around the world, and their findings appeared to justify his name for the project, "Operation Sunshine." Other investigators were gloomy. A. H. Sturtevant, emeritus professor of

biology at Cal Tech, said that "the bombs already exploded will ultimately result in the production of numerous defective individuals."
Curt Stern, professor of genetics at Berkeley, said, "By now everyone in the world harbors in his body small amounts of radioactivity
from past H-bomb tests," and physicist Ralph Lapp, a consultant
for the Bikini tests and head of the Office of Naval Research nuclear branch, predicted that at some time in the 1970s the buildup
of radioactive material in the stratosphere would exceed the maximum permissible amount and begin to affect the health of everyone on earth.

At the distance of twenty years this issue may seem to transcend
all others of that spring—the uproar over the Bricker amendment,
the crisis in Indochina, the fall of Oppenheimer—but at the time it,
like them, was overshadowed by a question so absurd, so petty, so
devoid of significance or even seriousness as to cast grave doubts
upon the ability of democratic institutions to survive the challenges of the second half of the twentieth century. Incredible as it
seems now, for thirty-five days the nation was engrossed in a
dispute which began as a quarrel over who had granted a routine
promotion, from captain to major, to a left-wing Army dentist
named Irving Peress.

"Who promoted Peress?" Senator McCarthy demanded over and
over. He never found out, and the truth is that he wasn't much interested. Peress merely gave him an excuse to wade into the Army.
Actually the dentist's majority had come to him not because any
of his superiors approved it, but because he was entitled to it under automatic provisions of the Doctor Draft Law, a measure meant
to correlate military pay with civilian earnings—and one which Mc-
Carthy had approved. Peress had entered the Army in October 1952.
He received his bronze oak leaves a year later. Next it developed
that he had belonged to the American Labor Party, then tanta-
mount to being a Communist. In testifying before McCarthy's subcommittee at Camp Kilmer, New Jersey, on January 30, 1954, he
invoked the Fifth Amendment. The Office of the Adjutant General
had already instructed the First Army to discharge him, and three
days later it did, but that wasn't good enough for the junior senator
from Wisconsin. McCarthy thought the Army should have court-
martialed Peress. He took its failure to do so as proof that Com-

munists had infiltrated the Department of the Army, a situation which he meant to remedy by his investigative powers.

McCarthyologists reasoned that there must be more to it than that, and in fact there was much more. To be sure, as a nihilist Joe McCarthy was opposed to the Army for no better reason than that it represented established authority. His first appearance as a Washington mischief-maker, predating his discovery of Communism, had pitted him against the Army. During the Battle of the Bulge seventy-three SS troopers had murdered 150 captured American GIs at Malmedy. After the war they had been sentenced to death, and in 1949 Joe had taken up the SS cause. The furor had brought the senator the sort of headlines he craved (MCCARTHY HITS BRUTAL-ITY; MCCARTHY HINTS AT MYSTERY WITNESS; MCCARTHY CHARGES WHITE-WASH). The Germans' lives had been spared, and nothing that had happened since then suggested that he would be reluctant to take on the Pentagon again. Yet he bore it no grudge. There was no conflict between his interests and the Army's. In early 1954 he had stronger motives for attacking other institutions. The decision to attack the Army was not really his; it was made for him by two remarkable young men, two members of McCarthy's staff who might be called the Leopold and Loeb of the 1950s. Their names were Roy M. Cohn and G. David Schine.

Cohn typified young political militants of his generation, just as Mario Savio and Mark Rudd would later typify theirs. Short, dark, insensitive, and haughty, he also possessed a photographic memory. His drooping eyelids and his curiously sensual mouth gave him a sullen, vulpine expression. Like McCarthy, he loved a quarrel for its own sake. The fact that Cohn always kept his dark hair combed was just about the only sign that he came from a good family. His father—a Democrat—was a judge in the appellate division of the New York Supreme Court. Roy's mother worshipped him. Once in his childhood, when he was invited on an excursion to be supervised by the father of one of his friends, the father had a phone call from Mrs. Cohn. She said, "You're in for a great treat. Roy's going with you. He's such a smart boy and knows so much about so many things. I'm sure you'll get a lot of pleasure out of him and probably learn a lot from him, too."

Certainly he was precocious. At twenty he was graduated from Columbia Law School; he had to loiter around Manhattan waiting to turn twenty-one before he could be admitted to the bar. On that day he was sworn in as an Assistant U.S. Attorney. He became a specialist in what was called subversive activities, working on, among other cases, the Remington and Rosenberg trials. At twenty-three he was an inside source for Walter Winchell and George Sokolsky, and while he was scratching their backs, they scratched his with flattering references which gave him a start on his next goal: appointment as special assistant to U.S. Attorney General James McGranery. He reached it in September 1952. Cohn's first day in Washington was a portent: he was sworn in in McGranery's private office, although no new oath was necessary; he held a press conference to announce his duties but forgot to reveal his title, held a second press conference to correct the oversight, demanded a private cable address and a private telephone line to his former boss in New York, and was turned down both times but somehow managed to have three other junior lawyers evicted from the office they shared so that it could become his private office. In December he prepared the indictment which charged Owen Lattimore with perjury. That case collapsed, but by then Cohn didn't care; on January 14, 1953, he had resigned from the Justice Department to become chief counsel for Senator Joseph R. McCarthy's Permanent Investigations Subcommittee.

Schine was the sleeker of the two, a fair, languid youth with the face and physique of a fledgling Greek god. Born to wealth, he was a graduate of Andover and Harvard, '49. In Cambridge he had been conspicuous for his valet and his big black convertible with a two-way phone-radio. The Harvard *Crimson* took note of his way of arriving at parties:

> This consisted of phoning from his car and saying, "This is G. David Schine. I'm now driving through Copley Square. Could you direct me a little further," and then later, "This is G. David Schine. I'm now at Kenmore Square. Could you give me more directions please."

Like Cohn, he became interested in Communism. In school he wrote a paper about it which he afterward published as a six-page pamphlet, *Definition of Communism*. After Schine became famous *Time* called it "remarkably succinct." The *New Yorker*, more critical, reported that "It puts the Russian Revolution, the founding of the Communist Party, and the start of the First Five Year Plan in years when these things did not happen. It gives Lenin the wrong first name. It confuses Stalin with Trotsky. It confuses Marx with Lenin. It confuses Alexander Kerensky with Prince Lvov. It confuses fifteenth-century Utopianism with twentieth-century Marxism." By then copies of it had become extremely rare, but when it first appeared, *Definition of Communism* could be found beside the Gideon Bible in every Schine hotel—the Roney Plaza in Miami Beach, the Ten Eyck in Albany, the Ambassador in Los Angeles, the Ritz Carlton in Atlantic City, and the Boca Raton in Boca Raton. One guest who read it with pleasure was a certain Rabbi Benjamin Schultz, the director of something called the American Jewish League Against Communism. Rabbi Schultz sought Schine out and introduced him to George Sokolsky. Through Sokolsky, Schine met Cohn, and through Cohn he met McCarthy.

Putting a multimillionaire on the subcommittee payroll would have been ridiculous. Besides, Schine didn't have any qualifications, as the word is understood on Capitol Hill. Early in 1953 Cohn persuaded McCarthy to appoint his new friend chief consultant on psychological warfare. There was no such position. Cohn made it up. Schine was delighted to serve without pay. In New York the two young men set up temporary headquarters in the Waldorf Towers, where Schine had a permanent suite, and there they planned an ingenious investigation of the Voice of America. Voice employees were quietly urged to put the finger on fellow workers with odd ideas or habits—it was these informants McCarthy had in mind when he talked of his "Loyal American Underground"—and after televised hearings under klieg lights there was general agreement in the press that the Senator's exuberant protégé had demoralized the Voice program. Cohn and Schine were still only twenty-six. There was no limit to how far they might go.

They flew to Europe, surfacing in Paris on Easter Sunday, April 4. Eighteen days of madness followed: in-and-out trips to European capitals during which they strutted and posed for the press and exercised, to the greatest possible degree, their rights and prerogatives as representatives of the U.S. Congress. And wherever they went they were trailed by a gleeful corps of correspondents who chanted:

> *Positively, Mr. Cohn!*
> *Absolutely, Mr. Schine!*

Or sang:

> Oh, the Cohn Schines east!
> The Cohn Schines west!
> McCarthy knows
> Where the Cohn Schines best!

By late 1953 McCarthy's hostility toward the White House was apparent to all around him. Two days before Thanksgiving he made it public. In a November 16 broadcast Harry Truman had referred scathingly to "McCarthyism." Joe had demanded equal time to reply. Like the administration, the networks were trying desperately to appease him, and the request was granted. But after the first few minutes the senator turned his wrath from Truman to Eisenhower. At a press conference the week before Ike had said he didn't know what McCarthyism meant. He would soon find out, Joe said ominously. Ike had also expressed confidence in his ability to rid the government of security risks; in next year's congressional elections, he said, the issue would be a dead one. Far from it, the senator told his radio and television audience. The "raw, harsh, unpleasant fact" was that "Communism is an issue and will be an issue in 1954."

Of course, he said patronizingly, the Republican administration was doing "infinitely" better than the Democrats in this respect. But there were "a few cases where our batting average is zero—we struck out." As always he got down to cases: names, dates, figures, dossiers—the wrong ones, though his listeners couldn't tell that. Joe said that was shameful, it was disgraceful, it made McCarthy sick way down deep inside. But there was worse. Despite admonitions from him, Eisenhower, like Truman before him, persisted in adhering to mutual aid treaties with Britain while the British insulted the memory of American boys who had fallen in Korea by trading with Peking. McCarthy's voice rose nasally:

"Are we going to continue to send perfumed notes? . . . it is time that we, the Republican Party, liquidate this blood-stained blunder . . . we promised the American people something different. Let us deliver—not next year or next month—let us deliver now. . . . We can do this by merely saying to our allies and alleged allies, 'If you continue to ship to Red China . . . you will not get one cent of American money.'"

Eisenhower was furious. C. D. Jackson and Paul Hoffman urged him to repudiate McCarthy as a Republican at the next presidential press conference. Hagerty agreed; so did Bryce Harlow and four other presidential assistants. But Nixon said the real victim in such a showdown would be the Republican party. It was decided that Dulles should answer McCarthy at his own press conference on December 1 with a statement that Eisenhower would approve word by word. McCarthy, the secretary said, had attacked "the very heart of U.S. foreign policy." That policy was to treat other nations as sovereign, not to pick their trade partners or "make them our satellites." As a real anti-Communist hard-liner—unlike McCarthy— Dulles observed that the United States must always be prepared "to retaliate with a devastating blow against the vitals of Russia," and that it retained the capacity to do this "only because we share the well-located bases of other friendly countries."

McCarthy was now on favorite turf. He liked nothing better than a slugging match with a Secretary of State, and he hadn't had one for nearly a year. Besides, this was an exceptionally good time to do mischief. Eisenhower was about to confer with Churchill in Bermuda. An emotional televised appeal to the American people on the eve of the conference could go a long way toward sabotaging it and embarrassing the President. And that was in fact Joe's next move. On the evening of December 3, as Ike was leaving for the meeting, McCarthy took the air to cry out against Englishmen who fattened their bankrolls by dealing with the murderers of U.S. soldiers. He implored "every American who feels as I do about this blood trade with a mortal enemy to write or wire the President . . . so he can be properly guided." Five days later the White House acknowledged that over fifty thousand messages had been received. No one in Washington had been deceived by the moonshine about guidance. This was a straight-out contest between the two men, and the presidential spokesman who reported the mail count did not pretend otherwise. McCarthy won among letter writers, he announced, while Eisenhower held the edge among those who had sent telegrams. Since the White House receives comparatively few wires, this was an artful way of saying that the senator had overwhelmed the President.

It was at this point that it became fashionable in Washington to describe McCarthy as the second most powerful man in the country. Certainly any demagogue who could trigger that sort of response had become formidable. There were other indications that McCarthyism was approaching a new crest. In the next month, January 1954, Gallup reported that public approval of the senator had risen sixteen percentage points in the past six months. Fewer than three Americans in every ten disapproved of him. It is improbable that one in ten knew what a mountebank he was, so dexterous had he become in his manipulation of the press, but if the reactions of the man on the street can be put down to ignorance—and they probably can—those of the U.S. Senate cannot. Nowhere else was his wickedness so well known, yet in February, when the time came to vote on a $214,000 appropriation for his permanent subcommittee, the membership of the Senate was reduced to quivering jelly. Exactly one senator, Fulbright of Arkansas, had the courage to vote against it. Among those who did not find it possible to join Fulbright were Kennedy of Massachusetts, Johnson of Texas, Humphrey of Minnesota, Kefauver of Tennessee, Mansfield of Montana, Magnuson of Washington, Russell of Georgia, Long of Louisiana, Williams of Delaware, Kuchel of California, Douglas of Illinois, Lehman of New York, and Margaret Chase Smith of Maine. All were resolute, their characters were strong, they were enormously popular with their constituents. But they had never before encountered a prodigy like Joseph R. McCarthy.

Who believed him? Where was his strength? Who were the hardcore McCarthyites? They were Legionnaires, Minute Women, Texas millionaires, and people who felt threatened by fluoridation of public reservoirs and campaigns for mental health. They belonged to organizations like the DAR, the Sons of I Shall Return, We the Mothers Mobilize, the Nationalist Action League, and the Alert Council for America. They were anti-eggheads like Louis Bromfield, John Chamberlain, Max Eastman, James Burnham, and William F. Buckley Jr. ("McCarthyism," Buckley wrote, ". . . is a movement around which men of good will and stern morality can close ranks.") They were fugitives from lost battles against Roosevelt legislation, the alliance with western Europe, the United Nations, the communications revolution, anti-anti-Semitism, the egalitarian passion, racial equality, the great internal migration of the 1940s, and social upheavals which were destroying the lines between the classes and the sexes, and widening those between the generations. At McCarthy rallies they sang reedily, "Nobody Loves Joe but the People," and politicians were convinced that dark masses of troubled voters stood behind them. It was believed on Capitol Hill, in the winter of 1953–54, that eight men in the Senate owed their presence there to McCarthy support.

As the second year of the Eisenhower administration began, the junior senator from Wisconsin stood on an awesome pinnacle, and Roy M. Cohn was right up there with him. G. David Schine was missing. He had been drafted. His absence was thought unimportant in Washington. Schine wasn't bright, like Cohn. In fact, McCarthy had secretly found him a pain in the neck. He hadn't mentioned this to Cohn, because McCarthy needed Cohn. What he was just discovering was that Cohn needed someone, too. Cohn needed Schine.

Schine's greeting from the Army had arrived in July. Apparently the blow was unexpected; he seems to have forgotten that he had even registered. Until then he and Cohn had been busy having a lively time—adjoining rooms in the Statler from Monday to Friday, merry weekends in Manhattan, and the anticipatory pleasure of planning antic forays into stodgy bureaucratic agencies. Joe, a lazy demagogue, had left the running of the subcommittee to them. They had felt, and had seemed to be, invulnerable. If no one in the capital dared strike back at them, who would? The answer was Schine's Gloversville draft board. There was irony here. The good citizens of Gloversville were too far from the power structure to know of Schine's mighty friends. They were also safe from a political fix: the one thing Washington feared more than McCarthy was a selective service scandal.

Cohn's first thought was that his friend should be commissioned immediately. It was impossible; the Army, Navy, and Air Force in turn rejected Schine as unqualified. Cohn then summoned to his office Brigadier General Miles Reber, the Army's chief of liaison on the Hill. Later Joseph N. Welch, special Army counsel, was to question Reber about that.

WELCH: Were you actually aware of Mr. Cohn's position as counsel for this committee?

REBER: I was, Mr. Welch.

WELCH: Did that position . . . increase or diminish the interest with which you pursued the problem?

REBER: . . . I feel that it increased the interest.

WELCH: Disregarding the word "improper" influences or pressure, do you recall any instance comparable to this in which you were put under greater pressure?

REBER: . . . I recall no instance in which I was put under greater pressure.

The Pentagon hadn't taken this lightly. Indeed, to outsiders the most remarkable aspect of the Schine case was not the pressure from Cohn, but the favoritism which the military establishment had voluntarily displayed over a rich young McCarthy protégé who was, after all, only one of nearly a half-million Americans to be drafted that year. Schine's situation had been studied by the Secretary of Defense, the Secretary of the Army, two Army chiefs of staff, a vice chief of staff, the adjutant general of the Army, the commanding general of the Transportation Corps, the Air Force major general directing legislative liaison, and the judge advocate of the Navy.

At the direction of Secretary of the Army Robert T. Stevens, a New York textile manufacturer whose role in the affair would soon grow, two full colonels and a lieutenant colonel were ordered to reconsider the possibility that Schine might be officer material. Meanwhile the young applicant himself had begun to take an interest in the matter. The first time General Reber interviewed him, Schine was ready to raise his right hand and be sworn in as an officer right there. He was put out when Reber explained that there was more to it than that. As the general later testified, "he apparently felt that the business of filling out forms and going through with the processing was an unnecessary routine step."

On November 3, 1953, Schine went into uniform, and after fifteen days of temporary duty in New York ("to complete committee work") he was assigned to Company K, Fort Dix, New Jersey, for four weeks of basic training. Thanks largely to Cohn's persistence, the case remained open. Indeed, it grew even more interesting. The Army cannot be said to have been inflexible. Unlike other recruits, Schine was given a pass almost every weekend. His limousine was allowed inside the camp to pick him up and bring him back. He was released from drill for no fewer than 250 long-distance telephone calls. One rainy day, when everybody else was on the rifle range, Company K's commander found Private Schine goldbricking. Schine threw a comradely arm over the captain's shoulder and explained that he had been studying logistics "to remake the military along modern lines"—an excuse which actually was accepted. Schine's unusual ideas about how he might serve his country might, in fact, have been taken more seriously had not McCarthy, in his own talks with the Pentagon, let it be known that he did not share Cohn's unqualified enthusiasm for Schine. In a monitored call to Stevens the senator asked the secretary, as a "personal favor," not to assign

"Dave . . . back on my committee." He said that Schine was "a good boy but there is nothing indispensable about him . . . it is one of the few things I have seen Roy completely unreasonable about."

John G. Adams, counselor for the Department of the Army, was now receiving the brunt of Cohn's anger. In his phone conversations with Schine, at the camp, Cohn would learn of little ways in which his friend's life might be made easier. He would then call Adams at any hour. Once he phoned Amherst College, where Adams was speaking, in an effort to have Schine relieved from KP duty the following day. If his suggestions were rejected, he became cross. During a heated discussion in New York he ordered Adams out of his car in the middle of three lanes of traffic, at Park Avenue and Forty-sixth Street, and on January 14, 1954, when Adams told him that Schine, like 90 percent of all inductees, would probably draw overseas duty, Cohn said this would "wreck the Army" and cause Stevens to be "through as Secretary of the Army."

By now the bizarre situation was being whispered about. In mid-December Drew Pearson ran an account of the Schine story. The following week the *Baltimore Sun* carried a long piece about it, and a *New York Post* article appeared in January. At the same time, McCarthy's view of the Army was darkening. Goaded by Cohn, wrathful over the discharge of Peress, and spurred, perhaps, by his need for daily victories, he erupted at a subcommittee hearing in New York on February 18. The unlucky witness at the time was Brigadier General Ralph W. Zwicker, a hero of the Bulge and the commanding officer of Camp Kilmer in New Jersey. McCarthy told Zwicker that he was "not fit to wear that uniform," that he should "be removed from any command," and that he did not have "the brains of a five-year-old child." When word of this reached the Pentagon, Stevens, under pressure from Ridgway, told the press that McCarthy would not be given the names of officers answerable for the discharge of Peress. Stevens deplored the "humiliating treatment" and "abuse" of Zwicker. He ordered the general not to appear before the subcommittee again, and said that he would testify instead. The secretary promptly received a phone call from McCarthy. "Just go ahead and try it, Robert," the senator said menacingly. "I am going to kick the brains out of anyone who protects Communists! . . . You just go ahead . . . I will guarantee you that you will live to regret it."

This was followed on February 24 by what became celebrated as "the chicken luncheon" in Dirksen's Senate office, an attempt by senior Republicans to close the widening breach between Mc-Carthy and the Army. Stevens found himself facing McCarthy, Dirksen, Karl Mundt and Charles Potter; Nixon was in an adjoining office. The secretary, as one reporter put it, was like a goldfish in a tankful of barracuda. Believing himself safe in the hands of these genial, sympathetic fellow Republicans, Stevens lowered his guard. All he wanted, he said, was to live and let live. Sure, he would be glad to put his name on a statement to that effect. He then did. The next thing he knew, the doors opened to admit a crowd of newspapermen. Mundt waded into them, distributing copies of the "memorandum of understanding," which was what Stevens, disarmed by the senatorial bonhomie all around him, had just signed. Now in anguish he found that in neglecting to read the fine print he had capitulated to virtually all McCarthy's demands. Among other things, the memorandum stipulated:

> There is complete agreement that the Secretary . . . will give the committee the names of everyone involved in the promotion and honorable discharge of Peress and that such individuals will be available to appear before the committee. If the committee decides to call General Zwicker . . . General Zwicker will be available.

In the Pentagon next morning officers greeted one another by waving handkerchiefs. "Private Schine," said one of them, "is the only man left in the Army with any morale." The *Times* of London commented that "Senator McCarthy achieved today what General Burgoyne and General Cornwallis never achieved—the surrender of the American Army." Herblock depicted Eisenhower whipping a white feather from a scabbard and saying to McCarthy, "Have a care, sir!" Palmer Hoyt of the *Denver Post* telegraphed Sherman Adams: FROM HERE IT LOOKS AS THOUGH STEVENS' COMPLETE CAVE-IN HAS SPATTERED MORE MUD ON THE U.S. ARMY UNIFORM THAN HAVE ALL OUR ENEMIES IN ALL OUR WARS. A story going the rounds in Washington went, "Stevens didn't mean to surrender to the senators. He just thought they wanted to look at his sword," and McCarthy, brutal in triumph, told a reporter that Stevens could not have yielded "more abjectly if he had got down on his knees."

For the next two weeks matters drifted. Republicans were huddling all over the capital. National Chairman Leonard W. Hall, having called McCarthy a "great asset" less than a month earlier, now criticized his conduct with Stevens. The President praised Zwicker at his March 3 press conference and said his administration would not stand having any official "submit to any kind of personal humiliation when testifying before congressional committees or elsewhere." Extraordinary efforts continued to be made in the hope of accommodating Joe. All that was required of him at this point was that he show the same spirit of compromise. He wouldn't do it. Instead he taunted the Pentagon, calling Peress the "sacred cow of certain Army brass" and saying that his investigation of the case had established "beyond any possibility of a doubt" that "certain individuals in the Army have been promoting, covering up, and honorably discharging known Communists."

"Just damn tommyrot," Defense Secretary Wilson replied. McCarthy was ridiculed in the Senate for the first time, by Ralph E. Flanders of Vermont: "He dons his warpaint. He goes into his war dance. He emits his warwhoops. He goes forth to battle and proudly returns with the scalp of a pink Army dentist. We may assume that this represents the depth and seriousness of the Communist penetration in the country at this time." Senator John Sherman Cooper of Kentucky congratulated Flanders, and the President wrote to him: "I was very much interested in reading the comments you made in the Senate today. I think America needs to hear from more Republican voices like yours." Attacking McCarthy still took courage, but it had begun, and the Army took heart. The senator's impact on the military had been fearful, Hanson Baldwin wrote in the *New York Times:* "Its morale is depressed; discipline and efficiency leave much to be desired." Now it was ready to go over to the counteroffensive, and the weapon it chose was the Schine affair. A strong case could be made that McCarthy and Cohn had been punishing the Army for allowing Cohn's friend to be drafted; it was probably true, and in any event it was the weakest spot in Joe's armor. On March 11 the Army leaked (through a Democrat) a chronology of the Schine case, including Cohn's threat to "wreck the Army."

Next day McCarthy countercharged that the Army had attempted to "blackmail" him into calling off his "exposure of Communists" by holding Schine as a "hostage." Plainly a full-dress congressional investigation was needed to hear both sides. The White House hoped it would be made by the Senate Armed Services Committee —McCarthy influence was relatively weak there—but the chairman, Leverett Saltonstall of Massachusetts, was up for reelection in November and wanted no part of it. A mazurka of parliamentary moves followed. The Democrats tried to have it assigned to the full Senate Committee on Government Operations; their own senators there, with Margaret Chase Smith, would outnumber McCarthy's men. The Republicans wouldn't stand for that, however, and the only solution acceptable to all parties was foolish: the conduct of McCarthy and Cohn was to be investigated by their own subcommittee. McCarthy agreed to step down as chairman; Mundt, one of his most ardent admirers, would preside. Cohn was similarly unqualified to serve as chief counsel. The task of finding a successor for him seemed insurmountable; what was needed was an able attorney who had not expressed an opinion about McCarthy. Dirksen came up with Ray Jenkins, a Knoxville, Tennessee, trial lawyer. Procedural questions followed. Dirksen protested against public hearings, but Lyndon Johnson successfully demanded televised sessions, and McCarthy won the right of cross-examination—one he had adamantly denied to witnesses when he sat in the chair.

The hearings opened in the floodlit Corinthian splendor of the Senate Caucus Room shortly after 10:30 on the morning of April 22, 1954. Everything seemed to be in order. Jenkins was at the microphone. The gavel was in Mundt's hand. McCarthy sat far to his left, at the very end of the coffin-shaped table. Nine months earlier Democratic members of the committee had begun boycotting its meetings in protest against McCarthy's tactics, but now they were back with their minority counsel, twenty-eight-year-old Robert F. Kennedy, then known chiefly for his hostility to Cohn. Mundt exchanged banalities with John McClellan of Arkansas, the ranking Democrat;* then he rapped for order. Mundt said, "Our counsel, Mr. Jenkins, will call the first witness." Jenkins opened his mouth—it was enormous—but before he could speak there was an interruption. The record reads:

McCARTHY: A point of order, Mr. Chairman; may I raise a point of order?

According to H. M. Robert's *Rules of Order*, a chairman may be interrupted on a point of order, provided that the question is one

* McClellan followed details of the privileges which had been extended to Private Schine with great interest. He had lost two of his three sons in World War II.

of propriety under the rules. McCarthy had something else in mind. His resonant voice rose.

> McCARTHY: I have heard from people in the military all the way from generals with the most upstanding [sic] combat records down to privates recently inducted and they indicate they are very resentful of the fact that a few Pentagon politicians attempting to disrupt our investigations are naming themselves the Department of the Army. . . . The Department of the Army is not doing this. It is three civilians in the Army and they should be so named.

An impartial chairman would have gaveled McCarthy into silence the moment it became clear that, far from raising a procedural matter, he was making a speech. Mundt let him make it. Placidly he agreed to a preposterous McCarthy proposal: that judgment be withheld on whether the Secretary of the Army represented the Army. With that as an opening, McCarthy interrupted to make the same speech again. "Mr. Chairman, Mr. Chairman," he sang out in that tight whine. Mundt looked down the table and nodded, and Joe made his point again:

> McCARTHY: I maintain it is a disgrace and a reflection upon every one of the million outstanding men in the Army to let a few civilians who are trying, trying to hold up an investigation of Communists labelling themselves as the Department of the Army.

McClellan quietly pointed out that the 46 countercharges against the Army had been signed for the subcommittee by "Joe McCarthy, Chairman," but Mundt ruled in favor of the Wisconsin senator. A pattern was forming. Joe would dominate the hearings as surely as though he were in the chair. Between his "points of order" and his cross-examinations, he would say everything he wanted to say. Mundt was his man, and so, it developed, was Ray Jenkins. Chosen for his supposed impartiality, the subcommittee's special counsel openly encouraged McCarthy's excesses, swearing him in and asking him to explain "just what the set-up of the Communists is." To the dismay of those who had been through this so many times before, Joe produced maps mounted on easels and a pointer. At the end of his lecture he said, "There are many people who think that we can live side by side with Communists." Eagerly Jenkins said, "What do you say about that, sir?" The answer consumed most of that afternoon. Even so, Jenkins was not done with encouraging Joe:

JENKINS: Senator McCarthy. . . . it is about closing time. . . .
Now, while you have an audience of perhaps twenty or thirty
million Americans . . . I want you to tell . . . what each individual American man, woman and child can do . . . to do their bit
to liquidate the Communist party.

McCarthy's critics were in despair. The senator seemed invincible.
Nothing, not even the U.S. Army, was a match for him. By the force
of his personality he was turning each session into a McCarthy melo-
drama, with doctored photographs, phony FBI reports, memoranda
lifted from Pentagon files by the Loyal American Underground, and
savage little McCarthy homilies, such as the bit of advice he attributed to one of his childhood mentors, someone called Indian
Charlie, to the effect that "if one was ever approached by another
person in a not completely friendly fashion, one should start kicking
at the other person as fast as possible below the belt until the other
person was rendered helpless." The moment any testimony unfavorable to him began to get interesting he would rumble into the
record with one of his vibrant calls for "A point of order," or "Mr.
Chairman, Mr. Chairman," and then he would be off with a digres-
sion about how "sick and tired" he was of "sitting down here" and
hearing all these "packs of lies." So one-sided were the hearings becoming that the Caucus Room audience, which had come to see a
fight, grew restive and cheered Symington just for having the courage to talk back to Joe: "You said something about being afraid.
I want you to know from the bottom of my heart that I'm not afraid
of anything about you or anything you've got to say any time, any
place, anywhere."

No one else around the table seemed prepared to go farther than
that, and of all of them the man who appeared least likely to bell
the McCarthy tiger was the Army's special counsel. Tall, portly, and
birdlike, Joseph N. Welch was sixty-three, a lifelong Republican and
a senior partner in the eminently respectable Boston firm of Hale
and Dorr. He had undertaken this assignment for no fee. And that,
said reporters, must have been why he had been chosen. Hour after
hour he sat quietly with an elbow on the table, his chin in the palm
of his hand or his fingers tracing the furrows on his forehead. He
might have been another spectator. He let McCarthy browbeat his
client, Stevens, without an objection. The few remarks he did make
were almost comic in their grave courtesy. With his green bow ties,
his fussy manner, and his high-pitched voice, Welch seemed more
like a Dickensian solicitor than a successful American trial lawyer.

Rarely had the capital seen a man whose appearance was more deceptive. He knew the impression he conveyed and was content; at times, he had found, it was useful to be underestimated. Life on Beacon Hill and Boston Common had not prepared him for the Mc-Carthy demimonde of bluster, intimidation and transparent lies, so Welch cocked his head and listened. His hands deep in his pockets, his toes pointed outward, he could be seen during recesses lurking on the fringes of groups, taking everything in. And when he spoke up at the hearings, as in time he did, the contrast between him and McCarthy could not have been greater. As Michael Straight put it in his *Trial by Television,* "McCarthy never forgot the vast audience. Welch seemed not to remember it. McCarthy spoke with contempt for the mob. Welch seemed to be conversing respectfully with one individual, and so he gained the audience's devotion to the end."

Bit by bit those watching Welch for this first time sensed the steel in him. He and McCarthy were the real duelists here, and their first significant encounter came on the ninth day of the hearings, when Welch cross-examined the senator over a confidential FBI letter which had found its way into McCarthy's hands. Along the way it had been retyped, an important point because under the law the retyping of a classified document amounted to publication. Joe crouched over the microphone, tense and swarthy. Under the klieg lights a roll of flesh beneath his dark eyebrows gave his upper eyelids a slanted, demonic expression. Welch let him wait awhile. The Bostonian lolled almost puckishly on an elbow, finger crooked on the purplish veins of his cheek, his brow wrinkled as though he were looking for the first time at something which was quite incredible. Now he was ready.

WELCH: Senator McCarthy, when you took the stand you knew of course that you were going to be asked about this letter, did you not?

McCARTHY: I assumed that would be the subject.

WELCH: And you, of course, understood that you were going to be asked the source from which you got it.

McCARTHY: . . . I won't answer that. . . .

WELCH: Have you some private reservation when you take the oath that you will tell the whole truth that lets you be the judge of what you will testify to?

McCARTHY: The answer is that there is no reservation about telling the whole truth.

WELCH: Thank you, sir. Then tell us who delivered the document to you!

McCARTHY: The answer is no. You will not get the information.

Jenkins came to the senator's rescue with the amazing opinion that McCarthy's position was justified because he was a "law enforcing officer . . . ferreting out crime," and the committee members turned to other matters. Only gradually did they and their audience realize what Welch had done. He had exposed McCarthy as an outlaw. In acknowledging his possession of the purloined letter the senator had violated a federal statute, and by refusing to answer Welch's questions he had put himself in contempt of Congress. There was something else. His defiance of the Boston attorney had been somehow familiar. Comparing impressions at the end of that session they realized why. For four years the country had watched McCarthy bully witnesses who refused to respond to his own interrogations. He had held these people up to public scorn as "Fifth Amendment Communists," reducing the Bill of Rights to an epithet. Now he was behaving in the same way.

Demagogues are conspicuously vulnerable to ridicule, but masters of derision are rare. Since the emergence of Cohn and Schine there had been speculation over whether their relationship was an unusual one, but no one could think of the right way to touch upon this very delicate subject. Welch found a way to do it. He had been honing the rapier of his wit since the hearings began, waiting to thrust it under McCarthy's bludgeon. The opportunity arose in an exchange over a cropped photograph. Cohn had given Jenkins, in proof of an obscure point, what appeared to be a picture, taken at McGuire Air Force Base, of Stevens beaming at Schine. Then the original turned up. In it Stevens was smiling at someone else, who had been cropped out to produce the fake. There was a thoughtful silence in the Caucus Room. Cohn strenuously denied knowing that this picture had been cropped. He said he didn't even know where it had come from. Welch innocently asked the witness at the time, another member of McCarthy's staff, "Do you think it came from a pixie?"

There was a rumbling at the end of the table. The bludgeon was being raised. McCarthy asked, "Will the counsel for my benefit define—I think he might be an expert on that—what a pixie is?"

Welch's rapier flashed: "Yes, I should say, Mr. Senator, that a pixie is a close relative of a fairy."

The chuckles were suppressed, but the giant had been wounded. From that moment forward McCarthy reserved his most venomous tones for Welch and searched for a way of retribution. On June 9, in the eighth week of testimony, he thought he had it. Cohn was in the chair at the time. Welch was asking him about the subcommittee's hunt for subversives among Army Signal Corps employees at Fort Monmouth in New Jersey.

> WELCH: Mr. Cohn, if I told you now that we had a bad situation at Monmouth, you'd want to cure it by sundown if you could, wouldn't you?
>
> COHN: Yes, sir.
>
> WELCH: May I add my small voice, sir, and say whatever you know about a subversive or a Communist or a spy, please hurry! Will you remember these words?

McCarthy's voice rose, tense and vibrant.

> McCARTHY: Mr. Chairman, in view of that question—
>
> MUNDT: Do you have a point of order?
>
> McCARTHY: Not exactly, Mr. Chairman, but in view of Mr. Welch's request that the information be given once we know of anyone who might be performing any work for the Communist Party, I think we should tell him that he has in his law firm a young man named Fisher . . . who has been for a number of years a member of an organization which was named, oh years and years ago, as the legal bulwark of the Communist Party. . . .

Welch looked stricken. A hush had fallen over the table. Smiling, licking his lips, his words freighted with sarcasm, McCarthy went on:

> McCARTHY: . . . Knowing that, Mr. Welch, I just felt that I had a duty to respond to your urgent request. . . . I have hesitated about bringing that up. But I have been rather bored with your phony requests to Mr. Cohn here that he personally get every Communist out of government before sundown. Therefore we will give you the information about the young man in your own organization. . . .

And he did, while Welch, obviously desolate, sat with his head in his hands, staring at the table before him. By now it was clear that something had gone wrong. Cohn, still at the microphone, was staring at the senator and shaking his head in silent entreaty. If anything, he seemed more distressed than Welch. But McCarthy went on to the end, shredding the reputation of someone whose very existence had not been a matter of public knowledge until now.

MCCARTHY: . . . Whether you know he was a member of that Communist organization or not I don't know. I assume you did not, Mr. Welch, because I get the impression that while you are quite an actor, you play for a laugh, I don't think you have any conception of the danger of the Communist Party. I don't think you would ever knowingly aid the Communist cause. I think you are unknowingly aiding it when you try to burlesque this hearing in which we are trying to bring out the facts, however.

He snickered. In that silence it was eerie. The room awaited Welch's reply. It was long in coming; once while McCarthy was still speaking the Bostonian's lips had formed the mute word "stop," but now he seemed to be groping for words. To Mundt he said, leaning forward, "Mr. Chairman, under these circumstances I must have something approaching a personal privilege." Mundt said quickly, "You may have it, sir. It will not be taken out of your time." He, too, was upset. Everyone at the table appeared to be affected, with the exception of McCarthy, who was talking loudly to one of his aides. Welch had to begin three times before he could attract the senator's attention. "I can listen with one ear," McCarthy said to him. "This time," said the Bostonian, "I want you to listen with both." McCarthy ordered the aide to bring a clipping showing that Frederick G. Fisher had belonged to the Lawyers Guild, the proscribed organization. "I think," said the senator, "that should be in the record."

WELCH: You won't need anything in the record when I have finished telling you this. Until this moment, Senator, I think I never really gauged your cruelty or your recklessness. Fred Fisher is a young man who went to the Harvard Law School and came into my firm and is starting what looks to be a brilliant career with us.

He then told the television audience what insiders at the hearings already knew. Welch's one misgiving about coming to Washington had been the possibility that because of him, someone at Hale and Dorr might be slandered. In talking to the two young assistants he had planned to bring to the capital with him he learned that one of them—Fred Fisher—had briefly belonged to the Lawyers Guild after leaving law school.* On learning more about it, he had resigned. Welch had left Fisher in Boston, and McCarthy and Cohn, who knew of him, had agreed not to mention his name. In 1954 few worse things could happen to a man than being identified over national television as a subversive. That was what McCarthy, to pay off a score, had done to Fisher. Welch now told the full story. At the end of it he turned back to the senator.

> WELCH: . . . Little did I dream you could be so reckless and so cruel as to do an injury to that lad. It is true he is still with Hale and Dorr. It is true that he will continue to be with Hale and Dorr. It is, I regret to say, equally true that I fear he shall always bear a scar needlessly inflicted by you. If it were in my power to forgive you for your reckless cruelty I would do so. I like to think that I am a gentle man, but your forgiveness will have to come from someone other than me.

McCarthy afterward told a friend that as Welch spoke he could feel knots in his stomach. It wasn't contrition. He was probably incapable of that. What he grasped was that he had stumbled badly, that Welch had outwitted him again. Trying desperately to regain his footing, he growled that Welch had no right to mention cruelty because he had "been baiting Mr. Cohn here for hours."

> WELCH: Senator, may we not drop this? We know he belonged to the Lawyers Guild, and Mr. Cohn nods his head at me.

Cohn, in evident agony, was indeed nodding at Welch. He was also biting his lips and trembling visibly.† He had crushed too many witnesses himself not to see what Welch was doing to McCarthy. To Cohn Welch said: "I did you, I think, no personal injury, Mr. Cohn."

> COHN: No, sir.
> WELCH: I meant to do you no personal injury and if I did I beg your pardon.

* The other was James D. St. Clair, who became counsel to President Nixon during the House of Representatives impeachment inquiry twenty years later.
† Writing in the February, 1968, *Esquire,* Cohn revealed that McCarthy had consented not to bring up Fisher if Welch promised not to explore Cohn's lack of a military record. Welch had kept his word. Thus Cohn had reason to be concerned over his leader's violation of the agreement.

Again Cohn nodded. Again McCarthy tried to shape a reply, and again Welch turned him away.

WELCH: . . . Let us not assassinate this lad further, Senator. You have done enough. Have you no sense of decency, sir, at long last? Have you no sense of decency?

The senator stared into his lap, looked up, and tried one more time. He tried to ask Welch if it was not true that Fisher had been his assistant. This time the Bostonian silenced him with superb disdain.

WELCH: Mr. McCarthy, I will not discuss this with you further. You have sat within six feet of me and could have asked me about Fred Fisher. You have brought it out. If there is a God in heaven it will do neither you nor your cause any good. I will not discuss it further. I will not ask Mr. Cohn any more questions. You, Mr. Chairman, may, if you will, call the next witness.

But there would be no more testimony that day. The audience was struggling to its feet, cheering Welch. Even Mundt was with them. He put down his gavel, and six policemen, who had been told at the opening of each session to eject anyone who applauded, stood impassive. McCarthy's face was grim; he was breathing hard. Welch moved toward the door, and a woman there touched his arm and then began to cry. As he stepped into the hall the press corps surged after him. Suddenly everyone broke for the door. It was as though someone had yelled, "Fire!" They couldn't wait to get out, and presently McCarthy, who had not left his chair, was left with the guards and the television technicians. He looked around, stretching his neck, trying to catch someone's eye. At first no one would look at him, then one man did. The senator turned his palms up and spread his hands. He asked, "What did I do?"

After thirty-six days of testimony the Army-McCarthy hearings ended on June 17. The subcommittee then studied the 7,400 printed pages of testimony and issued a report blaming both sides. At first the extent of the damage done to McCarthy was unknown. He had been exposed before and had recovered quickly each time. His physical stamina was unimpaired, he retained the loyalty of eight to ten key senators, his influence with the Republican legislative leadership continued to be great, and with his customary vigor he announced new investigations of Communists in the Army, the defense industry, and the CIA.

All died stillborn. New voices were being heard in the land on the subject of McCarthy, and old voices spoke in different tones. From Nebraska, Republican leader Jim Schramm wrote Sherman Adams that every member of the Republican State Central Committee felt that GOP candidates had been hurt by the "public spectacle" of the hearings. In Colorado Palmer Hoyt said, "It is now time for the Republican party to repudiate Joe McCarthy before he drags them down to defeat," and in Ohio conservative Republican congressman George Bender, campaigning for Taft's Senate seat, declared that "McCarthyism has become a synonym for witch-hunting, star-chamber methods, and the denial of those civil liberties which have distinguished our country in its historic growth." Cohn, it was generally agreed, had been discredited. With every subcommittee member except McCarthy against him, he resigned July 19. ("A great victory for the Communists," Joe said bitterly.) Since the first open rupture between the senator and the Army, at the beginning of the year, poll takers had been observing a vast change in the public's view of McCarthy. By late August some 22 percent of the adult population had revised their opinion of him downward. Over 24 million Americans now looked upon him with disfavor.

Ralph Flanders didn't wait until all the evidence was in. Two days after McCarthy's disastrous attack on Fisher, the Vermont Republican introduced a resolution calling on the Senate to strip its junior member from Wisconsin of his chairmanships. McCarthy said, "I think they should get a net and take him to a good quiet place." The measure was given little chance then. Knowland denounced it next day at a hurriedly called press conference, and southern Democrats let it be known that they were wary of a precedent which might threaten the seniority system. Debate opened on Friday, June 30. That evening Flanders, shifting tactics, substituted a simple motion of censure: "Resolved, That the conduct of the Senator from Wisconsin, Mr. McCarthy, is contrary to senatorial traditions, and tends to bring the Senate into disrepute, and such conduct is hereby condemned." Knowland proposed that it be referred to a select committee of three Republicans and three Democrats. That seemed safe. The members, chosen by Knowland and Lyndon Johnson, were all conservatives. Their chairman was Utah Republican Arthur V. Watkins. The McCarthy men felt they had won.

They misjudged Watkins. Determined to avoid another carnival, the chairman banned television from the new hearings and laid down strict ground rules. Even smoking was forbidden. Either Joe or his attorney would be allowed to cross-examine witnesses, but not both. Since McCarthy was a poor courtroom lawyer, this meant that he had to yield the center of the stage. At the first session he tested Watkins with cries of "Mr. Chairman, Mr. Chairman." The chairman's gavel came down like an executioner's ax. He said crisply, "The Senator is out of order. . . . We are not going to be interrupted by those diversions and sidelines. We are going straight down the line." McCarthy bolted into the corridor, where the television crews were waiting, and spluttered into a microphone, "I think this is the most unheard of thing I ever heard of." Unimpressed, the select committee reported out the Flanders resolution with the recommendation that McCarthy be censured, and the full Senate agreed 67 to 22—this in a chamber which had produced exactly one anti-McCarthy vote, Fulbright's, the previous January.

Vice President Nixon, exercising his prerogative as presiding officer of the Senate to alter the title of a measure, struck out the word "censure," changing it to "Resolution relating to the conduct of the Senator from Wisconsin, Mr. McCarthy." He was trying to help Joe, and McCarthy's admirers sought semantic solace in that. McCarthy himself was undeceived. "Well," he told reporters, "it wasn't exactly a vote of confidence." He said, "I'm glad to have this circus ended so I can get back to the real work of digging out Communism, crime, and corruption." In the White House Eisenhower greeted his cabinet with a slow grin. "Have you heard the latest?" he asked. "McCarthyism is McCarthywasm."

So it was. Missing the stimulus of Cohn, Joe became listless, flabby, and easily depressed. His devoted followers had formed a Committee of Ten Million Americans Mobilizing for Justice, with a retired rear admiral as "chief of staff," to protest the censure; they delivered to the Capitol, in an armored truck, a petition bearing 1,000,816 signatures. In New York thirteen thousand attended a "Who Promoted Peress?" rally. Its sponsors included Governor Bracken Lee of Utah, Alvin M. Owsley of the American Legion, Mrs. Grace Brosseau of the DAR, a former governor of New Jersey, and a former ambassador to Russia. A high school band played "On, Wisconsin." A rock singer intoned that he would "shake, rattle, and roll" for their leader, and Cohn told the crowd that "Joe Mc-

Carthy and I would rather have American people of this type than all the politicians in the world." But Joe himself wasn't there. He had hurt his arm shaking hands with a voter. In what some saw as a symbolic act, the other man had inadvertently shoved Joe's elbow through a glass table top. The senator went into Bethesda Naval Hospital and emerged with a sling.

McCarthy's successor as chief Republican campaigner was Richard Nixon. The Democrats said they couldn't see much difference. Nixon charged that their party was "bending to the Red wind." When Adlai Stevenson observed that the American economy appeared to be in the doldrums, Nixon accused him of "spreading pro-Communist propaganda." If the Democrats endorsed by Stevenson were elected, he said, "the security risks which have been fired by the Eisenhower administration will all be hired back," and he urged patriotic Democrats to "put their party in their pocket and vote for an Eisenhower Congress" because "we recognize the Communist menace and this administration is determined to crush that menace." The Communist party, he warned, was battling "desperately and openly" against Republicans because "the candidates running on the Democratic ticket are, almost without exception, members of the Democratic party's left-wing clique which has been so blind to the Communist conspiracy and has tolerated it in the United States."

"By golly," said Eisenhower, "sometimes you sure get tired of all this clackety-clack." Nixon was weary of it, too; "I'm tired, bone tired, my heart's not in it," he told a friend. Barnstorming the country seemed particularly fatiguing this time, but the President's decision not to campaign actively left Nixon as the party's highest-ranking politician, and he believed that much was at stake. "The election of a Democratic Eighty-fourth Congress in November," he told the Ohio Republican state convention in Columbus, "will mean the beginning of the end of the Republican party. It is that simple." To stave it off he delivered 204 speeches, held over a hundred press conferences, flew 26,000 miles, and visited 95 cities in 31 states. By the end of it he had become the country's second most controversial figure. "McCarthyism in a white collar," said Stevenson of his tactics. Walter Lippmann went further. He described the Vice President as a "ruthless partisan" who "does not have within his conscience those scruples which the country has a right to expect in the President of the United States."

It was characteristic of the 1950s that even Eisenhower's adversaries were anxious to believe the best of him, and he was not held responsible for Nixon's speeches. How he could have avoided knowing about them was unexplained. The *Herald Tribune*, whose most loyal subscriber he was, played them on its front page. Somehow it was felt, as James Reston wrote, that the President would never imply that the Democrats had winked at treason, "but things are done in his name he knows not of." To be sure, Nixon's style was not Eisenhower's style. Ike wanted to be regarded, he said, as "President of all the people," and invective wasn't his forte anyway. Nevertheless, he wanted the candidates of his party to win, believed Nixon was helping them, and cheered him accordingly.

Both men had hoped that Republicans could stow campaign rhetoric and run on the administration's record. "The time, the right time to start winning the 1954 elections is *now,*" Nixon had told the cabinet in April 1953. Eisenhower believed that his 1954 legislative accomplishments were worth boasting about. It had been a good session, despite the sideshow in the Senate Caucus Room. He had signed into law bills extending the federal housing program and reciprocal trade agreements, liberalizing the Atomic Energy Act, broadening unemployment insurance and social security, simplifying customs procedures, establishing a new farm program, authorizing two billion dollars for federal highways, and providing more than a billion dollars in tax relief. He calculated that his "batting average" had been .830 and was delighted. The *Congressional Quarterly*, figuring differently, put it at .646; even so, he had done well, and Democratic predictions that a Republican administration would bring back the Depression—as irresponsible, in their way, as Nixon's Red issue—had been exposed as myth.

But the twenty-year trend toward Democratic voter registrations had given the party out of power the same advantage that the Republicans once had. All other things being equal, the man in the middle tended to favor the Democrats. Eisenhower and Nixon were also fighting history; the party in power has nearly always lost strength in off-year elections. Furthermore, postwar prosperity had paused to catch its breath. There were no breadlines in 1954, but farm prices had taken a downward lurch, and the recession had given some employers the jitters.

In view of the hurdles ahead, party councils had decided that a Republican hatchet man was needed. The Vice President had been chosen because he handled hatchets well, because using this one would endear him to the rank and file of his party, and because, as Eisenhower pointed out, it would add to his fame. Nixon was game —"Every campaign has to have someone out front slugging," he said —but he was also unenthusiastic. It wasn't pleasant to return to Whittier as commencement speaker, which he did in the spring of 1954, to find that two reception lines had been set up, one for students who didn't want to shake his hand. His wife liked strife even less than he did, and in mid-February, after a long talk, they had discussed the possibility of his retirement from public life when his present term ended in 1956. According to Murray Chotiner, Nixon weighed the relative merits of opening his own law practice and joining an established firm while flying back to Washington on election eve. As the plane entered its glide pattern he handed Chotiner seven pages of notes. "Here's my last campaign speech," he said. "You may want it as a souvenir, I'm through with politics."

The results of the election were perplexing. The Democrats did regain control of Congress, whereupon Nixon had to admit that the survival of Republicanism hadn't been at stake after all. McCarthy called it "a bad defeat" and held the administration responsible for waging "jungle warfare among those of us who were trying to expose and root out Communists." But it wasn't bad at all. The Republican edge in the 83rd Congress had been so slight that realists had conceded its loss in advance. After the dust had cleared the Democrats had recaptured twenty House seats—they had expected fifty —and in the Senate they had won just two. "The administration," the *Washington Post and Times-Herald* concluded two days later, "has experienced neither victory nor overwhelming defeat at the polls."

Nixon interpreted the returns for the cabinet that same day. What they showed, he said, was "really a dead heat." He thought he knew a way to improve performance. The key to future campaigns, he said, was a good public relations program. The American people had to be "sold." The party with the best image would win elections; the secret to control of 1600 Pennsylvania Avenue would lie not on Main Street or Wall Street, but on Madison Avenue. Parties would invest in catchy jingles, not pretentious campaign songs. How a candidate looked on the television screen would be as important as what he had to say. It would all be one big package, Nixon told them, and he offered to show them the gist of it. Reaching into his pocket he drew out a mechanical toy drummer, wound it up, and sent it clattering down the polished table past the astonished President and his secretaries. The Vice President said, "Just keep beating that goddamned drum."

The most memorable singing commercial of that year, as evocative of the Army-McCarthy hearings as Joe's sonorous "Mr. Chairman, Mr. Chairman," went:

> When the values go up, up, up,
> And the prices go down, down, down,
> Robert Hall this season
> Will show you the reason,
> Low overhead, low overhead!*

Robert Hall, clothier, was a precursor of the discount houses which had begun to rise, like vast gymnasiums, on the outskirts of metropolitan areas and in suburban shopping centers. The first of them, E. J. Korvette, had opened its doors in 1948. It had been an instant success. In the past, discounting had been largely confined to shabby little factory annexes, difficult to find and seldom clean. Labels had been removed from wares; the wholesaler didn't want the retailer to know that he was competing with him. Now an entirely new approach to merchandising was emerging. Businessmen had begun to grasp the implications of America's automotive economy. In the 1930s and 1940s, when the greater part of customers had arrived on buses and streetcars, downtown streets lined with retail stores had made sense. But now public transportation had begun to atrophy. The typical urban shopper of the 1950s came in a car and had no place to put it. Downtown parking had become almost impossible. Millions of meters were being installed, but the results were disappointing; as often as not a Main Street merchant, blind to his own interests, would allow his clerks to occupy the spaces in front of his store and feed the meters every hour while potential customers cruised up and down.

Shopping centers were the obvious solution. Planners provided them with ample parking facilities, great tracts paved with ma-

* Copyright 1946, 1954, 1963, and 1972 by Robert Hall Clothes, Inc. Reprinted by permission.

cadam. Nationwide firms began erecting discount wonderlands: Korvette's, Topp's, Bradlee's, Grant's, King's, etc. By selling directly to the consumer there, manufacturers avoided the retailers' overheads. Those Main Street merchants who could afford suburban annexes built them. The rest joined a long, slow decline into what sociologists began to call "inner-city blight."

Meantime the discount marts were acquiring problems of their own. Shoplifting grew to epidemic proportions, encouraged by the discounters' practice of substituting checkout counters for aisle clerks. After hours, shopping center parking areas were often inhabited by restless teen-agers. Mobile like their parents, they needed a place to rendezvous. Unfortunately, police discovered, the paved expanses became staging areas for gang fights and drag racing.

Fueled by affluence, the teen subculture continued to develop its separate identity in the 1950s, with its own customs, status symbols, stigmata, rites, and fads—the ducktail haircuts and sleeves rolled up to a prescribed length for boys, and, for girls, poodle cuts and pop-it necklaces that could be changed from chokers to waist-length. Long hair and peculiar modes of dress lay a decade away, but the new language which would go with them was already developing. Like the bop musicians they admired, teen-agers frequently used the term cool, though for them the emphasis was different; it meant pretty much what keen, neat, swell, snazzy, or smooth had meant twenty years earlier. "Like" had become an all-purpose pauseword and modifier.

Scram had been replaced by blast-off, and a drip was now a drag. The draggiest were variously described as spastics, turkeys, nerds, yo-yos, or—the most popular of all pejoratives—square. A teen-ager would say, "She's a ——," switching to mimicry and drawing a square in the air with his index finger. It was considered tactful, if the square was present, to refer to her obscurely as an "L7" (because the letter and the numeral could form a crude square). The ultimate in squares was the cube. Wits would say that he was so square he could block his own hat. That might elicit a grudging laugh, but as a rule joking with teen-agers of that period was a risky business; they would often riposte with a withering "Hardeeharhar."

Every adolescent familiar with the facts of life, as they were still called, knew that a drive-in movie was a passion pit. Admittance to these arenas of foreplay was restricted, of course, to those with automobiles (wheels), but almost every boy in the great middle class either had wheels or knew someone who could get them; the Allstate Insurance Company found that nationally 75 percent of all high school juniors had driver's licenses and nearly 60 percent had access to the family car for "social purposes." The auto was so fundamental a part of the subculture that teen-age argot was often almost indistinguishable from hot-rod slang (also called jive), though subtle distinctions could be detected. To a pure hot-rodder, drag, for instance, had nothing to do with social acceptability; it was a race, from a standing start, between motor vehicles powered by souped-up engines. The hot-rod itself was also known as a hack, a stormer, a bomb, a screamer, or a draggin' wagon. Substantial alterations, a sure way to acquire greater prestige within the peer group, were chopping (lowering the roof) and raking (lowering the front end). Tires were skins; whitewalls, snowballs. Driving around for the sheer joy of the trip was bombing or spooking.

That was for lovers of speed, which did not then mean amphetamines. The vast majority of adolescents were much more interested in exploring sexual diplomacy. Unless he had been grounded—enjoined from the use of the family car—a young male who had taken his date to the passion pit would attempt to make out (the equivalent of the long-gone pitching woo) under cover of darkness. The eternal scourge of seducers and the most common of all female complaints was still known almost universally as the curse, or the monthly, though girls' boarding schools in New England clung to the more proper, and more engaging, "off the sports list." This could be frustrating for the fledgling roué, unless the date was a blind one and had been revealed to him, during a moment under a strong light, as a dog, or a beast. Of course, the girl also had discriminatory rights. If she reached the conclusion that her escort was a drag, she might incinerate him with "DDT" (drop dead twice). That was the ultimate insult. His position would then be extremely uncomfortable, or, to use his word for it, hairy.

Teen-agers and their younger brothers and sisters were emerging as a major target group for national advertisers. They not only had their fashions; increasingly they had a voice in what their parents bought. David Riesman observed: "One must listen to quite young children discussing television models, automobile styling, or the merits of various streamliners to see how gifted they are as consumers . . . their influence in family councils must not be underestimated." Eugene Gilbert, who was then establishing a consulting firm to advise businessmen on marketing policies for young customers, told his clients:

> An advertiser who touches a responsive chord in youth can generally count on the parent to finally succumb to purchasing the product. . . . It is not to be denied that a parent subjected to requests from the youngster who thinks he is in dire need of an item, witnessed on television, may find it easier to "give in" rather than dispute rationally with a highly emotionalized child.

A survey found that 94 percent of the mothers interviewed said that their children had asked them to buy goods they had seen on television. Testers of small children discovered that they could recognize the word "detergent" before they could even read. Exposed to TV while still in their playpens and then put in front of the tube to keep them quiet, they looked upon the world of goods with a sophisticated awareness new to their generation. *American Girl*, the magazine of the Girl Scouts, noted that their subscribers "use their first lipstick, wear their first nylons and first bra sooner than girls ten years ago." Brassiere styles for twelve-year-olds were named Allowance, Freshman, Little Angel and Littlest Angel—"the bra that expands as a girl develops." Bernice Fitz-Gibbon, merchandising consultant for *Seventeen* magazine, told advertisers attending a "fashion clinic" that "Your fashion department is the wooing chamber. Get the teen-age fly to come into your parlor and little by little the web will be spun. Then when the girl marries you haven't lost a customer. You've gained a goldmine." Miss Fitz-Gibbon advised her audience to lure "the teen tycoons, not in the sweet by-and-by, but in the much sweeter now-and-now." She described young girls as "women of means."

Often they were women of very substantial means. *Teen Times*, the magazine of the Future Homemakers of America, put weekly spending by seventh-graders at 30 cents to $8.50 and by high school seniors at $1.65 to $19.50, but in some cases it was much more. In a pictorial essay *Life* described the expenditures of a suburban seventeen-year-old girl who was given $4,000 each year. Among her budget items were $1,300 for bedroom decorations, $1,500 for clothes (including seven bathing suits), and $500 for entertainment, not counting "a jaunt to Hawaii for having survived high school." *Life* noted that "more and more teen-agers will be moving into Suzie's bracket." It ended on what was meant to be a cheerful note:

"Her parents' constant indulgence has not spoiled Suzie. She takes for granted all the luxuries that surround her because she has had them all her life."

National statistics on this emerging leisure class of youth were awesome. As the flood of war and postwar babies approached puberty the new market expanded until there were between eighteen and twenty million of the new consumers in the country. Their annual purchases rose to 10 billion dollars, then to 25 billion. Gilbert reported that girls between fourteen and seventeen were spending 773 million dollars on "back to school" outfits alone. In one year of the 1950s, *Teen Times* found, the average American adolescent spent $555 "for goods and services, not including the necessities normally supplied by their families."

Entire industries retooled to accommodate the young. The phonograph record business offered them two lines, "singles" (45 rpm) for subteens and "albums" (33⅓ rpm) for the teen-age market. Together they bought 43 percent of all records sold in the United States. Adolescent purchases accounted for 53 percent of movie admissions, 44 percent of camera sales, 39 percent of new radios bought, and 9 percent of new automobile sales. Each year the fifteen-to-nineteen group was spending 20 million dollars on lipstick, 25 million on deodorants, and 9 million on home permanents. The total spent annually on toiletries by teen-agers of both sexes was almost a third of a billion dollars.

Some parents raised in the austere 1930s were becoming accustomed to such phenomena as a twelve-year-old daughter's weekly trip to the hairdresser, or a fourteen-year-old son engrossed in a brochure on retirement insurance written for his age bracket. In certain places the younger generation had its own credit accounts, with such enticing names as the 14 to 21 Club, the Campus Deb Account, and the Starlet Charge Account. They might order merchandise over Princess phones in their own rooms, or exchange Going Steady rings ($12.95, "nothing down, payments of 50 cents a week") with boyfriends or girlfriends. In California one firm built a $2,500,000 teen-age shopping center, with six stores, a milk bar, a swimming pool, an ice-skating rink, and a bank.

On the evening of December 15, 1954, Walt Disney touched off a children's craze that showed the whole country how very young consumers could be successfully wooed. *Disneyland* was then the high point of Wednesday TV for 40 million viewers, most of them youngsters and their parents, and that week's program was the first in a series on Davy Crockett. As played by twenty-nine-year-old Fess Parker, a hitherto unknown actor, Davy was a hero of irresistible charm. Mesmerized by his folksiness, tiny America was easy prey for hawkers of Crockett pseudomemorabilia. By the following spring every playground and supermarket seemed to be populated by five-year-olds wearing coonskin caps. The price of coonskins jumped to $8 a pound. Before the boom ended the following summer 100 million dollars' worth of coons had been marketed, not to mention Davy Crockett sweat shirts, sleds, blankets, snowsuits, toothbrushes, school lunch boxes, swing sets, playhouses, sandboxes, stools, toy guns, and bicycles. An entrepreneur overstocked with 200,000 pup tents stenciled "Davy Crockett" on them and sold them all in two days. Some adults were pushed past endurance; a department store buyer said, "The next person who says Davy Crockett to me gets a Davy Crockett flintlock over his head," and it was a rare mother who didn't want to stop her ears after the thousandth rendering of Fess Parker's "Ballad of Davy Crockett," which sold four million copies during his six-month hegemony:

> *Born on a mountain top in Tennessee,*
> *Greenest state in the Land of the Free,*
> *Raised in the woods so's he knew ev'ry tree,*
> *Kilt him a b'ar when he was only three.*
>
> *Davy, Davy Crockett,*
> *King of the wild frontier!*

Fred M. Hechinger of the *New York Herald Tribune* feared that a "passion for possession" might be putting a spiritual blight on youth. In that regard two forms of entertainment introduced in 1954 were troubling. The new music of Bill Haley and the Comets, billed as "the first R 'n' R Pop Smash," gave rise to fears that the children of the new prosperity, like those of the Twenties, might be seduced into a mindless hedonism. To this Stanley Kramer's *The Wild One* added a prophecy of savage violence. Marlon Brando played the title character, Johnny, the apelike "president" of a scruffy motorcycle club whose members wore skin-tight jeans and black leather jackets with a skull and crossbones painted on the back. In the film Brando's gang rides into a quiet town on a lazy Saturday afternoon and, for want of anything else to do, takes the place apart. Obviously the movie was an indictment, but of what? Youth? Permis-

siveness? Disrespect for law and order? Most critics wrote that
Kramer was showing a seamy side of postwar opulence, of crass
acquisitiveness run amuck. Some, repelled by the movie's brutality—
in that gentler time it *was* rough—suggested that such censure might
be carried too far.

One small group of youthful Bohemians thought that no indictment of materialism could be strong enough. To them affluence was
an outrage. They had grappled with it and lost. Now they conceded
that they were beaten, or, more succinctly, beat. The beat generation first surfaced in the early 1950s amid the peeling billboards
and crumbling stucco of Los Angeles's seedy Venice West. Nur-
tured in dimly lit coffeehouses there, the movement then leaped 350
miles north and found a Mecca at 261 Columbus Avenue in San
Francisco, soon to be famous throughout the movement as the City
Lights Bookshop. The store's colorful co-owner was Lawrence Ferlinghetti, a bearded native of Paris who had served in the Navy,
worked at *Time* as a mail boy, and taken degrees at Columbia and
the Sorbonne. In 1953 he and Peter D. Martin founded their em-
porium as the first all-paperback bookstore in the United States.
Ferlinghetti took the name from the Chaplin film. Expanding, he
established City Lights Books, a publishing house. The first poet
on its list was himself. The title of one of Ferlinghetti's poems, "Ten-
tative Description of a Dinner to Promote the Impeachment of
President Eisenhower," gives some idea of how far he was from
the typical merchant of the 1950s.

The City Lights Bookshop served as an address for certain authors who had no fixed address of their own. They were unusual,
even in their profession. Gregory Corso had been captured in 1946
for trying to seize New York City by carrying out a series of elaborate robberies with his friends; when arrested, Corso was attempting to coordinate the attempt with a walkie-talkie. After three years
in prison he educated himself in Harvard's Widener Library and
wrote such poems as "Marriage," in which he advised a young man
planning an evening with his fiancée:

> Don't take her to movies but to cemeteries tell all about
> werewolf bathtubs and forked clarinets then desire her
> and kiss her and all the preliminaries and she going just
> so far and I understanding why not getting angry saying
> You must feel! It's beautiful to feel!

The ages of beat writers put them in the swing generation, though they had now opted out of it. As social prophets they advocated spontaneous expression, travel, Oriental mysticism, singing folk ballads, playing the guitar, the blues, sex in all its forms, and their version of the American dream. Some of them became celebrities. The most famous was a husky French-Canadian who had played football at Columbia, served as a merchant seaman during World War II, and taught at the New School for Social Research in the late 1940s. Born Jean-Louis Kerouac, he changed his first name to Jack for his first book, *The Town and the City*, in 1950. Kerouac rebuked commentators who called him and other new renaissance authors negative. He insisted that they were in fact passionately affirmative. On television Ben Hecht asked him why he didn't write more about "what's wrong with this country." Kerouac wrote afterward:

> . . . all he wanted me to do was speak out my mind AGAINST people, he sneeringly brought up Dulles, Eisenhower, the Pope, all kinds of people like that . . . No, I want to speak FOR things, for the crucifix I speak out, for the Star of Israel I speak out . . . for sweet Mohammed I speak out, for Lao-tse and Chuang-tse I speak out, for D. T. Suzuki I speak out . . . why should I attack what I love out of life. This is Beat. Live your lives out? Naw, LOVE your lives out. When they come and stone you at least you won't have a glass house, just your glassy flesh.

His *On the Road* was written in three weeks. Truman Capote said of it, "It isn't writing at all—it's typing." Yet it told people something they wanted to hear; they bought 500,000 copies. *On the Road*'s wenching episodes were dull, the visions of the characters were puerile, and for all their expeditions back and forth across the country they never seemed to get anywhere or find anything, not even themselves. But perhaps that was the point. At least Kerouac's people were looking; they refused to be encapsulated by things they owned. The Beats were honest men offended by the sterile myths of their decade. Allen Ginsberg, a more powerful writer than Kerouac, was devastating on the cold war:

> *America you don't really want to go to war.*
> *America it's them bad Russians.*
> *Them Russians them Russians and them Chinamen. And*
> *them Russians.*

The Russia wants to eat us alive. The Russia's power mad.
She wants to take our cars from out our garages.
Her wants to grab Chicago. Her needs a Red Reader's Di-
gest. Her wants our auto plants in Siberia. Him big bu-
reaucracy running our fillingstations.
That no good. Ugh. Him make Indians learn read. Him
need big black niggers. Hah. Her make us all work six-
teen hours a day. Help.
America this is quite serious.
America this is the impression I get from looking in the
television set.
America is this correct?
I'd better get right down to the job.
It's true I don't want to join the Army or turn lathes in pre-
cision parts factories, I'm nearsighted and psychopathic
anyway.
America I'm putting my queer shoulder to the wheel.

Ginsberg wasn't really demented, but a year of psychotherapy had changed his life. That was in 1954 and early 1955. It ended his career as a fledgling market research consultant. Coming off the couch he turned out "Howl" in a nonstop frenzy. San Francisco policemen confiscated it as obscene, but a judge found "redeeming social importance" in the long poem, and Ginsberg joined Kerouac, Corso, Ferlinghetti, and other stars in the beat firmament.

No sooner had they arrived than prim admirers tried to sanitize them. Entranced English teachers averted their eyes from Ginsberg's homosexuality and Kerouac's amorality. Beat, they said, was short for "beatitude"; these poets were blessed. The beats were understandably nettled. Whatever the intrinsic value of their work, and it is probably slight, they did succeed in their social purpose of raising doubts about thoughtless conformity. Denying them would have turned them into literary eunuchs. But there was little chance of the attempt succeeding; the continuing uproar over them assured that.

Twenty years later the only odd aspect of their movement would be that it had been so controversial. It was never revolutionary. Its poets were yea-sayers and minstrels, not challengers of the social order. They broke no windows, planted no bombs, profaned no faiths, and were no threat to the establishment—a word which, in its later sense, did not then exist in the American language. Kenneth Rexroth, at fifty their senior citizen, did declaim sardonically, "I write poetry to seduce women and overthrow the capitalist system." In reality, however, Rexroth was married, the father of two children, the proud holder of several literary awards, and, as a former popcorn salesman, something of an entrepreneur. So, in fact, was Kerouac; in *The Subterraneans* he ingenuously describes the hero's disappointment and frustration when he learns that another beat writer has received a larger publisher's advance than his own. Elsewhere Kerouac said, "We love everything—Billy Graham, the Big Ten, Rock and Roll, Zen, apple pie, Eisenhower—we dig it all." They didn't, of course, and he didn't expect to be taken seriously, but the beats were incapable of militance. The thought of them marching on the Pentagon or stoning National Guardsmen is ludicrous. They would have been startled by anyone who called policemen pigs, and the closest any of them came to a demonstration was Ginsberg wearing a sandwich board that said SMOKE POT.

But that was enough to affront convention then. Smoking marijuana was believed to be wicked beyond imagining. In addition, beats were known to use foul language, sometimes in public. It was an intolerant time. Exotic life-styles were suspect. The mere fact that members of the movement said they were different put them beyond the pale. "Beatnik" was coined as a term of opprobrium. Male beatniks wore khaki trousers, sandals, and beards. (Their hair, however, was short.) The movement's females could be distinguished by their tousled hair and black leotards. Though they scorned lipstick, they put so much make-up around their eyes that they were sometimes called "raccoons." Beatniks were said to live in what they called "pads," surrounded by unwholesome books and records. They didn't pick up after themselves. The beds were unmade—did not, in fact, have proper bedclothes. Reportedly they slept naked on bare mattresses and did disgraceful things in the dark, even when they weren't married. Some had actually advocated bearing children out of wedlock.

Eisenhower's America was horrified. Fathers told daughters that they could not date beatniks. Ronald Reagan told jokes about football players in sandals. Slick magazine writers described beatnik debauchery. Commuters exchanged stories about beatnik orgies. Hollywood cranked out morality tales with beatnik villains. Even Helen Trent acquired a beatnik character. In Middletown, Connecticut, teen-agers in a convertible tried to run down a bearded man on a bicycle because they thought that such a defier of conventions must be beat. And at the bottom of all this commotion was nothing more sinister than a few romantic poets who recoiled from the prevailing life-style. They were individualists, and in that sense their claim to be the real Americans was valid. They asked only to secede from the majority, and they expounded nothing more than the eternal bohemia, as in this passage from *On the Road:*

> . . . they danced down the street like dingledodies, and I shambled after as I've been doing all my life after people who interest me, because the only people for me are the mad ones, the ones who are mad to live, mad to talk, mad to be saved, desirous of everything at the same time, the ones who never yawn or say a commonplace thing, but burn, burn, burn like fabulous yellow roman candles exploding like spiders across the stars and in the middle you see the blue centerlight pop and everybody goes "Awww!"

That was what passed for nonconformity then. The alarm next time would be triggered by the real thing.

Montage: The Mid-Fifties

DAISY: You the policeman?
JOE: Yes ma'am (Shows ID) My name's Friday.
This is Frank Smith.
FRANK: Hello.

not a recession, said the White House, but a "rolling readjustment" . . . .

Best actress of 1955: Anna Magnani in The Rose Tattoo

And here is the best part
You have a head start
If you are among
The very young
At heart

The Man With the Golden Arm   Bad Day at Black Rock   East of Eden
Mister Roberts   Diabolique   The Desperate Hours

She's the sweetest little rosebud that Texas ever knew
Her eyes are bright as diamonds, they sparkle like the dew
You may talk about your Clementine and sing of Rosalee
But the yellow rose of Texas is the only girl for me

"*Sincerity*," said Vice President Nixon, "*is the quality that comes through on television.*"

AFL, CIO TO MERGE

See the U.S.A. in your Chevrolet

Better dead than Red

According to Nancy Mitford, "England" is ·U and "Britain" non-U, and "dentures" is non-U for false teeth.

"A Classic"
— Brooks Atkinson
New York Times

KURT WEILL'S

THE THREE-PENNY OPERA

MARTY (in a low, intense voice): *You don't like her. My mother don't like her. She's a dog, and I'm a fat, ugly little man. All I know is I had a good time last night. I'm gonna have a good time tonight. If we have enough good times together, I'm going down on my knees and beg that girl to marry me.*

English adaptation of book and lyrics by
MARC BLITZSTEIN

McCALL'S
The magazine of Togetherness

When it seems that everything is lost
I will smile and never count the cost
If you love me, really love me,
Let it happen, darlin', I won't care

Original text by
BERT BRECHT

THEATRE DE LYS
121 Christopher Street
WAtkins 4-8782

BEST SELLERS: Nonfiction
Gift from the Sea by Anne Morrow Lindbergh
Life Is Worth Living by Fulton J. Sheen
MacArthur 1941-1951 by Major General Charles A.
 Willoughby and John Chamberlain
Call to Greatness by Adlai E. Stevenson
The Scrolls from the Dead Sea by Edmund Wilson

EINSTEIN DEAD

Best actor of 1954: Marlon Brando in On the Waterfront

Best actress of 1954: Grace Kelly in The Country Girl

BEST SELLERS: Fiction
Not As a Stranger by Morton Thompson
Marjorie Morningstar by Herman Wouk
Andersonville by Mackinlay Kantor
The Man in the Gray Flannel Suit by Sloan Wilson
Something of Value by Robert Ruark

"In the opinion of the Joint Chiefs, MacArthur's strategy would involve us in the wrong war, at the wrong place, at the wrong time and with the wrong enemy."

Seven Brides for Seven Brothers   Three Coins in the Fountain
Twenty Thousand Leagues Under the Sea   Dial M for Murder
Executive Suite   Rear Window   Mr. Hulot's Holiday

two doctors working together, Gregory Pincus of the Worcester Foundation for Experimental Biology and John Rock of the Reproductive Study Center in Brookline, Mass., have discovered a drug which, when taken as a pill by a woman, interrupts the process of ovulation.

Hey there you with the stars in your eyes
Love never made a fool of you
You used to be too wise

Better Red than dead

Mama   Make Room for Daddy   Our Miss Brooks   Mr. Peepers

Burns and Allen Show   December Bride   Leave It To Beaver

Father Knows Best   The Phil Silvers Show   Ozzie and Harriet

Dobie Gillis   The Honeymooners   *Goodnight, Mrs. Calabash*

Twenty-two

WITH ALL
DELIBERATE SPEED

THE AVERAGE AMERICAN MALE in 1954 stood five feet nine inches tall and weighed 158 pounds, according to Dr. George Gallup's Institute of Public Opinion, a diligent collector of such Americana. The average female was five feet four and weighed 132. Husbands thought the knack of running a smooth, orderly household was more important in a wife than anything else, and most of them—55 percent—felt that American women were spoiled.

In announcing these and other results of an elaborate study of American life, the institute observed that "Throughout history, races and nations have sometimes been remembered for their small human quirks rather than for their great deeds and battles. Here," it said, "are some of the small things that 'homo Americanus' may be famous for in 1,000 years' time." In fact they have become of interest after only twenty years' time, and although some are frivolous, it is interesting, and sometimes even significant, to know the little details of everyday life—what people thought of themselves and others, what they worried about, and how they lived. Already some of the findings of this survey seem quaint.

No audible voices protested the traditional distinctions between the sexes. Wives believed that men drank too much and that one of the chief faults of husbands was "just not paying enough attention," but nothing was said about chauvinism. The typical woman said she preferred marriage to a career. She wanted the word "obey" taken out of the wedding ceremony—it is rather astonishing that it was still there—but in other ways she accepted the double standard. For example, 61 percent of all women agreed that a wife should never open her husband's mail, even if a letter arrived in a scented envelope addressed in feminine handwriting, and when asked, "Should a wife's adultery be more condemned than a husband's?" an overwhelming majority of women—four out of every five—replied, "Yes, of course it should."

Most people listed money as their greatest worry; only 21 percent checked "the threat of world war, keeping the peace." Confidence in the United States and pride of country ran high. Generosity was voted the most conspicuous American characteristic, followed by friendliness, understanding, piety, love of freedom, and progressivism. The American faults listed were petty: shallowness, egotism, extravagance, preoccupation with money, and selfishness.

There were still enough farmers for them to be treated as a separate category. They were the first to rise in the morning; 69 percent of them were out of bed before 6 A.M. The typical American, on the other hand, got up at 6:30 A.M. weekdays and 8 A.M. Sundays. (Women, surprisingly, rose a bit later than men.) The average bedtime was 10 P.M. weekdays and 11 P.M. Saturdays. The typical breakfast was served at 7 A.M., the typical lunch at noon, and the typical supper or dinner at 6 P.M. The postwar custom of a fifteen-minute coffee break was catching on, but less than half of the population enjoyed it; to the question, "At your place of work are employees given time off for coffee, refreshments, or rest?" 51 percent checked "No." Farmers suffered more from the well-named common cold than any other group. The peak month for colds was February, when 15 percent of the adult population, or 15 million people, had them. The low point was July, but even then 5 percent, or five million, were coughing and sneezing and generally miserable.

Even without a war or scandal to divide the country, living was a strain. Every other adult complained of trouble getting to sleep. It was a greater problem for women than men, worse for the unmarried than the married, greatest for the divorced and the widowed. The main cause given was "nervous tension." Sedatives had not achieved wide acceptance; most insomniacs just tossed and turned. Among other complaints, one American in three said his feet hurt, one in five had trouble hearing, two in seven were worried about being overweight, and two out of three wore glasses, half of them all the time.

By gourmet standards their eating habits were dull. If allowed to order anything for dinner, regardless of cost, they said they would choose fruit cup, vegetable soup, steak and french fried potatoes, peas, rolls and butter, apple pie à la mode, and coffee. Three million Americans were vegetarians. Nearly six in ten drank wine, beer or liquor, but they didn't drink much; fewer than one in five had something every day. Their favorite sport was bowling. A startling eight million bowled at least once a week, and there were three occasional bowlers for every golfer or ping-pong player, the second and third most popular recreations. Only 52 percent of all adults knew how to swim, a reflection of the fact that opportunities for swimming were fewer then, for vacations were shorter and less frequent. Over 15 million, or 15 percent of all adults, had not been more than 250 miles from home—the equivalent, then, of one day's ride in an automobile. After Sunday dinner half of all families with cars took an afternoon pleasure ride, but they didn't go far. One American in four had not seen either the Atlantic Ocean or the Pacific.

Nine out of ten adults had been on a train, and four in ten had spent at least one night on a Pullman sleeper. Trips by air, though rising in frequency, were still preferred by a minority. Cars were used for short trips, but traffic was lighter than it has since become. One reason was that there were about 50 million fewer people living in the country. Farmers excluded, the average worker lived two miles from his job, and he could get there in about eighteen minutes. One man in three went home for lunch. Less than one-third of all families said grace at meals, but 95 percent said they believed that prayer helped "in one way or another," 94 percent believed in God, and 68 percent in life after death; 69 percent were in favor of adding the phrase "under God" to the pledge of allegiance, which was done on June 14, 1954. The highest proportion of Bible readers was in the South, the lowest in New England and the Middle Atlantic states. America's two favorite mottoes were "Do unto others as you would have them do unto you," and "Live and let live."

In winter the average family with a house kept it heated at 70 degrees in the daytime and 60 degrees at night. The smallest amount of money a family of four needed to get along in an average U.S. community was $60 a week. (In 1937 it had been $30 a week.) The impression fostered by movies and television was that twin beds had become increasingly popular, but only one couple in eight had them; the rest still slept in double beds. Men preferred showers to bathtubs. Women favored tubs, three to one. The average family had a pet, with dogs outnumbering cats two to one. Most Americans said they liked and trusted their neighbors. Prudence with money, instilled during the Depression, was habitual. If suddenly given $10,000, the average American said, he would buy a home. The next largest group would pay off debts, put the money in a bank, or invest in securities. Only a few said they would take life easy, travel, or go on a spending spree. A twenty-three-year-old Chicago stenographer replied that she would get married right away. Another working girl answered that she would move to California, "where there are plenty of men."

On the whole, America remained a nation of optimists. In spite of grousing about high taxes and high prices—though even then they were considered high—a clear majority said they believed they were better off than their parents had been. The average American wanted to live to be a hundred, and more men than women wanted it, though women, with their longer life expectancy, had a greater chance of reaching it. Asked to single out the age he would most like to live over again, the typical adult chose twenty-one. Nearly half of all those polled had a pet superstition. The superstitions named most often were knocking on wood, avoiding black cats when walking, and throwing spilled salt over the shoulder. Women were more superstitious than men.

Most people thought the ideal family had three youngsters. Mothers felt that the first child should not arrive until the second year of marriage. Parental opinions of 1954's young people were high; they were regarded as more sensible and level-headed than the parents had been at that age. But the children were more critical: only one in five had no complaints about his father or mother. Nearly all adult Americans felt that a child ought to have an allowance, even though fewer than three out of ten parents had had one when young. While disturbed about juvenile delinquency, which had been rising since World War II and was already a source of anxiety, most adults took the position that parents, not youngsters, were chiefly to blame for it. Typical parents of that time thought a girl should not begin dating until she was sixteen.

Mixed marriages, a term which then meant marriages between Christians of different religious faiths, were a subject of lively discussion. Slightly more than half the people—54 percent—approved of them, but only one American in four believed they had much chance of turning out successfully. Marriages between Gentiles and Jews were statistically insignificant. Unions between whites and Negroes, as blacks were then called, were unknown to the great middle class. Their possibility wasn't even discussed.

Negroes still did not exist as people for mainstream America. In popular entertainment they were more like pets. Stepin Fetchit, Hattie McDaniel, Butterfly McQueen, and Eddie Anderson—these were good for the nudge and the guffaw but they weren't looked upon as human beings. If Hollywood wanted to portray human feelings in a man with a black face, it put burnt cork on the face of somebody like Al Jolson. Black America was unnoticed by white America. "I am an invisible man," cried the hero of Ralph Ellison's 1953 novel. ". . . I am invisible, understand, simply because other people refuse to see me. I can hear you say, 'What a horrible, irresponsible bastard!' And you're right. . . . But to whom can I be responsible, when you refuse to see me?"

Now, after three centuries of black submission and black servitude, "the long habit of deception and evasion," as Ellison once called it, was about to end. The Supreme Court of the United States had pondered the matter and concluded that Negroes were real people after all, and that as such they must become visible to their white compatriots and treated as equals everywhere, beginning in the public schools.

By the U.S. Supreme Court clock it was 12:52 P.M., May 17, 1954. A concealed hand parted the red velour draperies at the front of the Court's magnificent chamber, and nine men robed in black, stepping past the gleaming Ionic columns, seated themselves in the leather chairs at the long mahogany bench. Editors all over the world were awaiting what was already being called the greatest moment in the Court's history since the Dred Scott decision of 1857. Associate Justice Robert Jackson, who was convalescing from a heart attack, had left his hospital bed that morning so that the full Court, including its three southerners, would be present for the occasion. In a departure from custom, newsmen had not been given advance copies of the decision. They had no inkling of which way it would go. The new Chief Justice had been on the bench only six months. At the time of his appointment lawyers had been appalled by his total lack of judicial experience, and few in Washington had been willing to predict how he would stand in this case of Brown v. Board of Education of Topeka. Earl Warren was no racist, but he had the reputation of being a staunch believer in states' rights.

Wire service reporters who cover Court sessions scribble bulletins in longhand at the press table, just below the bench, and send them on their way in pneumatic tubes. At 12:57 the Associated Press A wire came alive:

Chief Justice Warren today began reading the Supreme Court's decision in the public school segregation cases. The Court's ruling could not be determined immediately.

Delivery of an opinion by the Chief Justice meant that he sided with the majority. This was Warren's first important ruling, and for a while all that spectators could be sure of was that he was taking an unconscionable amount of time to say what the decision was. Instead of delivering a brisk text he was meandering, stopping to cite such psychologists and sociologists as Kenneth Clark and Gunnar Myrdal on the mental development of Negro children. At 1:12 the exasperated AP correspondent dispatched a second bulletin. Warren was clearly opposed to segregation on principle, he said, but "the Chief Justice had not read far enough in the court's opinion for newsmen to say that segregation was being struck down as unconstitutional."

The decision's constitutional pivot was the Fourteenth Amendment: "Nor shall any state deny to any person the equal protection of the laws . . . ," but there was no judicial precedent for this application of it. The Supreme Court had never ruled on the issue of school segregation. In 1896 it had laid down a "separate but equal" doctrine in a case involving segregation of train passengers. Since then it had found against segregated housing and railroad transportation and ordered Negro students admitted to graduate schools of six southern and border state universities. Now at 1:20 P.M. Warren came to the climax of the ruling:

To separate [Negro children] from others of similar age and qualifications solely because of their race generates a feeling of inferiority as to their status in the community that may affect their hearts and minds in a way never to be undone . . . We conclude that in the field of public education the doctrine of "separate but equal" has no place. Separate educational facilities are inherently unequal.

Segregation in schools, then, was unconstitutional: against the law. And the decision was unanimous, a special triumph for the National Association for the Advancement of Colored People and its scholarly counsel, Thurgood Marshall, himself a graduate of Jim Crow schools. Acknowledging that compliance would take time, the Court said it would withhold further instructions until its fall term. Meanwhile all sides were asked to prepare arguments on when segregation should be abolished and who—a special master or the federal district courts—should establish and enforce the terms under which it would end.

In the white South there was gloom. No greater blow to its social structure could be imagined. In seventeen states and the District of Columbia public school segregation was required by law, and four other states permitted it. Altogether, schools with a total population of twelve million children were affected. The first reactions of the authorities responsible for them varied according to their geographical location. In Kansas and Oklahoma, border states, officials were calm; they predicted that the change would be made with little commotion, if any. In Austin Governor Allan Shivers said Texas would submit, though he warned that full compliance might "take years." After studying the full opinion, Virginia's Governor Thomas Stanley told the press: "I shall call together . . . representatives of both state and local governments to consider the matter and work toward a plan which will be acceptable to our citizens and in keeping with the edict of the court."

The Deep South was more hostile. South Carolina's Governor James F. Byrnes, now seventy-five, said he was "shocked." He could scarcely claim to be surprised. In the hope of intimidating the Court, South Carolina had amended its constitution to allow for abandonment of the public school system. The question now was whether it would carry out its threat. Georgia had taken the same step, and its leaders were fiercer. Senator Richard Russell argued that racial matters were in the jurisdiction of the legislative, not the judicial, branch of government, and he accused the Warren Court, as some were already calling it, of "a flagrant abuse of judicial power." Governor Herman Talmadge delivered a diatribe: "The United States Supreme Court . . . has blatantly ignored all law and precedent . . . and lowered itself to the level of common politics . . . The people of Georgia believe in, adhere to, and will fight for their right under the U.S. and Georgia constitutions to manage their own affairs." They would, he said, "map a program to insure continued and permanent segregation of the races."

By autumn there was a lot of that sort of rhetoric as local candidates in southern elections fell to quarreling over who would be the greater defender of white supremacy. The Court, wary of civil disorder, set no rigid schedule for compliance. At the same time the justices let it be known that having laid down the law, they meant to see that it was enforced. Federal courts and local school districts were directed to evaluate their situations and study administrative problems. Then they were to take steps toward a "prompt and reasonable start" in carrying out the decision with "all deliberate speed" as soon as was "practicable."

President Eisenhower was troubled by all this. He knew there was a certain inevitability in it—that the end of European colonialism in Africa and Asia was bound to be matched in the United States by rising protests against discrimination, and that Americans were increasingly aware that the country's position of world leadership was being jeopardized by racism at home. Still, his innate conservatism distrusted sudden change. Privately he called the Warren appointment "the biggest damfool mistake I ever made." While believing in eventual integration, he argued that "if you try to go too far too fast . . . you are making a mistake." Nixon disagreed. He said that he felt strongly that "civil rights is primarily a moral rather than a legal question." But Ike remained reticent on this very delicate issue. To one of his advisers he said emphatically: "I am convinced that the Supreme Court decision set back progress in the South at least fifteen years. . . . It's all very well to talk about school integration—if you remember you may also be talking about social *dis*integration. Feelings are deep on this, especially where children are concerned. . . . We can't demand perfection in these moral questions. All we can do is keep working toward a goal and keep it high. And the fellow who tries to tell me that you can do these things by force is just plain nuts."

Still, as an old soldier he knew that orders must be obeyed. The Court had interpreted the Constitution; the chief executive had to carry out its instructions. At his direction all District of Columbia schools were integrated at once. He ended segregation on all Navy bases where it was still practiced—Truman had abolished it on Army posts—and overnight, literally over one night, the COLORED and WHITE signs over drinking fountains and rest room doors disappeared from naval installations. Lois Lippman, a Boston Negro, became the first black member of the White House secretarial staff; a few months later another Negro, E. Frederic Morrow, was appointed an administrative assistant to the President. Hagerty saw to it that all these facts reached the press; no one would say that Eisenhower wasn't practicing what he expected of others.

Over the next several months Oklahoma, Texas, Kentucky, West Virginia, Maryland, Tennessee, Arkansas, and Delaware reported partial integration in 350 school districts. Elsewhere the picture was less encouraging. Legislatures in Virginia and the Deep South passed complex measures designed to lead to long, involved court battles and circumvent the Supreme Court's ruling. Their governors were speaking stubbornly of "state sovereignty," "nullification," and the "interposition" of state authority to balk enforcement of federal laws—antebellum expressions which had not been heard since the death of John C. Calhoun. Encouraged by the warlike stance of their leaders, southerners on the lower rungs of the social ladder were reviving the Ku Klux Klan and organizing White Citizens' Councils to resist integration. Tempers were short throughout the white South.

But there could be no turning back now. Blacks had tempers, too. Over a century earlier de Tocqueville had predicted that once Negroes "join the ranks of free men, they will be indignant at being deprived of almost all the rights of citizens; and being unable to become the equals of the whites, they will not be slow to show themselves their enemies." That was the alternative to substantial integration. The Court had stirred hope in Negro hearts, and it is hope, not despair, that is the fuel of social action. J. Edgar Hoover reported to the White House that the sale of small arms had increased all over the South. In some communities it was up by as much as 400 percent. The most volatile rhetoric was coming from whites, but it was also notable that throughout the winter of 1954–55 the Black Muslims, with their gospel of inverted racism and retaliatory violence, were expanding rapidly.

Americans found, to their consternation, that they were rapidly moving into an era of racial incidents. Given the deeply held convictions at either end of the spectrum, such episodes were unavoidable. Militant whites vowed to defend the racial status quo, which the NAACP and the new Negro organizations springing up around it were bound to challenge. As often as not the officials in the middle simply came apart. With Thurgood Marshall as her adviser a twenty-six-year-old black woman, Autherine Lucy, announced her intention to enroll at the University of Alabama. The university trustees were distraught. After three days of unruly crowds at Tuscaloosa, during which her car was stoned and pelted with rocks, Miss Lucy reached the registrar's office, only to be handed this telegram from the trustees: FOR YOUR SAFETY AND THE SAFETY OF THE STUDENTS AND FACULTY MEMBERS OF THE UNIVERSITY, YOU ARE HEREBY SUSPENDED FROM CLASSES UNTIL FURTHER NOTICE. Marshall led her to a court, which lifted the suspension. The trustees then met that night, accused Miss Lucy of making "false, defamatory, impertinent, and scandalous charges" against the university authorities—and ordered her permanent expulsion.

Frustration ran high on both sides in such episodes. With the power of the federal courts behind her, Autherine Lucy was bound to win in the end, and the trustees knew it. Only a bullet could stop her—a haunting possibility. Not only were guns and gunmen all around; it was possible, and indeed in some cases probable, that such a killer would go free. The same Constitution which required desegregation entitled a defendant to trial before a jury of his peers. His peers, in large areas of the South, were likely to acquit him. This happened. The first such incident occurred in Greenwood, Mississippi, in August 1955. Emmett Till, a fourteen-year-old black youth from Chicago, was visiting relatives there. Rumor spread that he had insulted a white woman, and three white men dragged him from his relatives' home and drowned him. Witnesses identified two of the three killers to federal agents, but an all-white jury acquitted them. The two—they were half-brothers—were then charged with kidnapping by a U.S. attorney, but a grand jury refused to indict them, and the FBI, which had painstakingly assembled irrefutable evidence, reluctantly closed its file.

By the first anniversary of the Supreme Court decision, racism lay like an ugly blight across much of the South. Rabble-rousers stirred up mobs which frightened, and sometimes attacked, blacks insisting on their constitutional rights. The cruelest incidents were in the grade schools, where children, most of them too small to understand the savage struggle being waged over them, were subjected to intimidation and outright terror. The return to school each September is a familiar American ritual. Mothers dress youngsters in new clothes, brush their hair, give them pencil cases, and send them off to their new classrooms. It is at precisely this time that boards of education introduce whatever changes in regulations there are to be—such as desegregation. Beginning the year after the Supreme Court decision and extending to the end of the 1950s, American front pages each fall carried accounts of ghastly demonstrations in front of bewildered pupils. Sometimes there was violence.

Two representative incidents erupted almost simultaneously in one week of 1956. In Clinton, Tennessee, mob hysteria was whipped up by John Kasper, a racist zealot from Washington, D.C. (He saw no irony in his charge that desegregation was the work of "outside agitators.") Until Kasper arrived, Clinton had been a quiet backwater town of four thousand people, where twelve black students were preparing to enroll in the local high school. Goaded by him, a thousand Clinton citizens disrupted the school, blocked traffic, battered the cars of Negroes who happened to be passing through, and then threw themselves on the eight-man Clinton police force shouting, "Let's get the nigger lovers! Let's get their guns and kill them!" After a night of fear 100 state troopers, 633 National Guardsmen, and seven M-41 tanks put down what looked like an incipient revolution. That was a lot of law enforcement for one township, but the country was learning how vulnerable to hotheads schools were. Mansfield, Texas, with a population of 1,450, was even smaller than Clinton. There a federal district court had ordered the integration of three blacks with three hundred white high school students. On registration day four hundred men barged into the school waving placards that read DEAD COONS ARE THE BEST COONS and $2 A DOZEN FOR NIGGER EARS. The three Negro students quickly withdrew. A fourteen-year-old white girl told a reporter: "If God wanted us to go to school together He wouldn't have made them black and us white."

It was easy for Americans outside the South to be scornful of it, but it wasn't necessarily fair. The fact that racist vigilantes could disrupt the peace did not make them a majority. In the aftermath of the Clinton disorders the town looked like a stronghold of bigotry. Kasper, arrested on charges of instigating a riot, was freed. In a current election campaign the White Citizens' Council there nominated its own candidate for mayor. Bumper stickers urging his election seemed to be everywhere. In the school students wearing Confederate flags sewn on their sweaters stoned black boys, shouted

"Nigger bitches" and "Dirty nigger whores" at black girls, and poured ink over the blacks' books. On the morning of election day a white minister attempting to escort the Negro children past a mob outside the school was badly beaten; so were two people who tried to come to his assistance. The principal expelled a thirteen-year-old white boy for assaulting a black girl and then, after he himself had been threatened, announced that the school was being closed "because of lawlessness and disorder." At that point, just as Clinton seemed lost to decency, the tide shifted. On orders from Attorney General Brownell, the FBI arrested sixteen of the mob's ringleaders. Fifty white high school students, led by the seventeen-year-old football captain, asked people to comply "with the federal court order to provide an education for all the citizens of Anderson County who desire it." Then came a surprise, even to those who thought they knew the town well. The polls closed, the votes were counted—and every segregationist candidate for local office was defeated by a margin of nearly three to one.

That year a new phrase was on the lips of public speakers: "the winds of change." The expression came out of Morocco, where French troops transferred from Vietnam were fighting another losing battle against anticolonialists, but it also seemed applicable to the United States. The Warren Court in particular appeared to be a storm center for winds of change. In time its reinterpretations of the Constitution would bar prayer from classrooms, expand defendants' rights to counsel (notably in Miranda v. Arizona), extend freedom of speech and freedom of the press to moviemakers, strike the bonds of censorship from pornographers, and lay down guidelines for legislative apportionment in the states.

Diehard conservatives dug in. IMPEACH EARL WARREN billboards went up all over the South. The Chief Justice had become the most controversial figure in the government since Franklin Roosevelt; all turmoil and racial tensions were laid at his door. Yet the Supreme Court was but one of many federal institutions which were acting to alter the system. Congress was fashioning the first of what would eventually be five civil rights acts. The Civil Service Commission was speeding up the advancement of black workers, and federal regulatory agencies were taking a sudden interest in charges of discrimination. One of them, the Interstate Commerce Commission, was weighing a proposal to forbid the interstate segregation of travelers on trains, buses, and in waiting rooms when a black seamstress in Montgomery, Alabama, anticipated it.

Her name was Rosa Parks, she was forty-two years old, and on Thursday, December 1, 1955, she was very tired. She found a seat on a Montgomery bus, but when the bus filled up the driver told her to stand so a white man could sit there. It was an old southern custom for Negroes to surrender their seats to whites. It was also against the law for anyone to disobey a bus driver's instructions. Mrs. Parks thought about it for a moment and then said she wouldn't move. At that moment, Eldridge Cleaver later wrote, "somewhere in the universe a gear in the machinery had shifted."

Arrested at the next stop, she was charged with a misdemeanor, found guilty, and fined ten dollars. That made Mrs. Parks's friends angry, and she was a popular woman; within forty-eight hours mimeographed pamphlets being distributed in Negro neighborhoods called for a one-day boycott of all city transportation. The boycott was so spectacular a success that leaders of Montgomery's black community started asking one another larger questions. The city's 25,000 blacks accounted for 75 percent of the bus company's patronage. Suppose they extended the boycott and set terms for an end to it? Eventually the management would either yield or go bankrupt.

That was how it started. The company was told that it would have no more black passengers until Negroes were seated on a first come first served basis and allowed to keep their seats. In addition the Negro leaders demanded that drivers be ordered to treat blacks courteously and that black drivers be hired for buses in Negro districts. The management replied that white drivers would be polite, but that was all. So the passenger strike continued. It was 95 percent effective, and as the weeks passed with no compromise on either side, the determination of the blacks simply increased. The rest of Alabama began to watch Montgomery; then the rest of the country; and then the world. The segregationists were led by W. A. Gayle, Montgomery's mayor. Gayle and his fellow members of the city commission ceremoniously joined the local White Citizens' Council. Then he declared that the city would never capitulate to the boycotters. He said, "We have pussyfooted around long enough and it has come time to be frank. There seems to be a belief on the part of the Negroes that they have the white people hemmed in a corner and they are not going to give an inch until they can force the white people of the community to submit to their demands."

Gayle's chief adversary, the leader of the blacks, was Martin Luther King, an unknown twenty-six-year-old clergyman. King had come to Montgomery the year before to become pastor of the Dexter Avenue Baptist Church. The white South paid grudging respect to black clergymen, but King was one of the new Negroes, and he lay outside the southern white experience. He was a Ph.D., a product of Harvard, and a genuine scholar. In his sermons he dwelt less on the river Jordan than on the wisdom of Socrates, Aristotle, Shakespeare, Galileo, and Toynbee. Writing in his small white Montgomery bungalow to the soft accompaniment of classical music, he had fused Christianity, Hegelianism, and Gandhiism into a philosophy teaching strength through struggle and harmony out of pain. Gandhi's satyagraha—passive resistance and noncooperation as a way of opposing mistreatment—had become King's "soul force." He showed his congregation films of the Indian mahatma and said of the boycott:

> This is not a tension between the Negroes and whites. This is only a conflict between justice and injustice. We are not just trying to improve Negro Montgomery. We are trying to improve the whole of Montgomery. If we are arrested every day; if we are exploited every day; if we are triumphed over every day; let nobody pull you so low as to hate them.

He taught the Dexter Avenue church's worshippers the meaning of "victory over your enemies through love," and he inspired them with rousing old Baptist hymns and camp-meeting tunes, sometimes with new words:

> *Deep in my heart,*
> *I do believe*
> *We shall overcome*
> *One day.*

Hard-core segregationists were derisive. One described King as "just another rabble-rouser the Communistic N-double-A-C-P is sending down here to stir up our decent Nigras." Not all whites felt that way. Mayor Gayle was discovering that families accustomed to Negro help were giving rides to their cooks and handymen or paying their taxi fares. He protested that the domestics "are fighting to destroy our social fabric just as much as the Negro radicals who are leading them," and he said, "The Negroes are laughing at white people behind their backs. They think it's very funny that whites who are opposed to the Negro boycott will act as chauffeur to Negroes who are boycotting the buses."

After three months of deadlock the city attorney produced a 1921 state anti-labor law enjoining restraint of trade. Under it a grand jury indicted King and 114 other black leaders. "In this state," the indictment read, "we are committed to segregation by custom and law; we intend to maintain it." The defendants were fingerprinted and freed on $300 bond each. Late in March King became the first of them to come to trial on the charge of conspiring "without a just cause or legal excuse" to hinder a company in its conduct of business. Black witnesses testified that they certainly did have just cause. One told how a bus driver had shut the door on her blind husband's leg and then stepped on the accelerator. A second described a Negro being forced from a bus at pistol point because he did not have correct change. A third said his pregnant wife had been compelled to surrender her seat to a white woman, and a fourth said a driver had called her an "ugly black ape."

King, who had waived a jury trial, pointed out that the boycott had begun spontaneously and that he had become its spokesman only after it was in full swing. The judge nevertheless found him guilty; he was ordered to pay $1,000 in fines and court costs and released on bond pending appeal. If the verdict was meant to intimidate Montgomery's Negroes, its effect was the exact opposite. They promptly held a rally on the lawn outside the courthouse. One black shouted, "We ain't going to ride the buses now for sure." A middle-aged woman pushed through the crowd to tell King, "My heart and my pocketbook are at your disposal." A mass prayer meeting was scheduled for that evening. One man called to the others, "Are you going to be there?" They called back, "Yes!" He asked, "Are you going to ride the buses?" and they roared, "No!"

And they didn't. Spring passed, summer passed, and still the spirit of the blacks showed no signs of flagging. The mayor confided to friends that he had never dreamed that Negroes could be this determined. The bus company sank into debt. Drivers drifted into other jobs or left the city. The Negroes showed every sign of being able to survive without them. Some had become accustomed to walking to work, some had bicycles, and for the others King had organized a vast car pool with two hundred automobiles. The mayor announced that this was illegal. In the twelfth month of the customer strike King and the other black leaders were arrested for running a business enterprise without a franchise. They were on trial in state circuit court when electrifying news arrived. The Supreme Court, which had already overturned the "separate but equal" doctrine for recreational facilities as well as in schools, had now killed it in public transportation. Discrimination on buses was now a violation of federal law. Martin Luther King was free. He was in addition a world celebrity. The unprecedented boycott had dealt Alabama segregation a devastating blow. American Negroes everywhere had found new hope, and the young black preacher had been catapulted into the first rank of the struggle for civil rights.

King did not gloat. He advised his flock to act with dignity and without pride. He said, "We have been going to the back of the bus for so long that there is danger that we will instinctively go straight back there again and perpetuate segregation." At the same time, he continued, "I would be terribly disappointed if any of you go back to the buses bragging, 'We, the Negroes, won a victory over the white people.' If you do, our struggle will be lost all over the South. Go back with humility and meekness."

He would have been less than human if he hadn't ridden a bus himself when the boycott ended, 381 days after Rosa Parks had started it. The driver said to him, "Is this the Reverend?" The clergyman said, "That's right. How much?" It was fifteen cents—up a nickel from the year before—and putting the coins in the slot he took a front seat. He said afterward, "It was a great ride." Most Montgomery whites were relieved to have it all over, and some were in good humor. A bank teller wryly told a reporter, "They'll find that all they've won in their year of praying and boycotting is the same lousy service I've been getting every day." On one bus a white man said to nobody in particular, "I see this isn't going to be a white Christmas." A nearby black smiled. "Yes sir," he said. "That's right."

Long after an event has passed, its place in the scheme of things becomes clear, but at the time it often seems insignificant. Doubtless the driver who told Mrs. Parks to stand merely thought he was dealing with one uppity Nigra; had he known that his own grandchildren would one day study the incident in school, he might have been more circumspect. Presidents are more conscious of history than bus drivers, but they, too, may be blind to the consequences of their decisions. Dwight Eisenhower was above all a man of peace. That and his respect for congressional prerogatives had caused him to stop other members of his administration from making unwise commitments on Indochina. Yet in the same year that Rosa Parks altered destiny, Ike took the country a step down the long road toward madness in Vietnam.

It was not the first such step. Any assessment of the growth in presidential war-making powers should note the precedents set by Franklin Roosevelt in 1941 and 1942. Before then, congressional authority in this area was intact. It was shakier afterward; FDR, with his brilliant display of political legerdemain, had used executive agreements to create a situation in which the Axis powers were virtually compelled to attack the United States. Then came Korea. Cabell Phillips, Harry Truman's biographer, observes that "His decision to intervene in Korea . . . came close to pre-empting the right to declare war . . . all Presidents are now armed with the Truman precedent to strike swiftly on their own, wherever and with whatever force is necessary, when they believe the national interest demands it."

The last steps in the erosion of congressional authority, and the accompanying executive ascendancy, were to be taken by Lyndon Johnson and Richard Nixon against the backdrop of Southeast Asia, but each link in the chain of precedent deserves notice. The Formosa resolution of 1955 was one of them. It was a special consequence of the cold war, but its implications for the future were broad and grave.

Dean Acheson had wanted to wait "until the dust has settled" in China before formulating a new policy there. By 1955 it was as settled as it would ever be, yet the eastern edge of the picture remained murky. The Communists controlled the mainland and the Nationalists Formosa, but the status of Formosa Strait, which separated them, was unresolved. Here and there the 115-mile-wide sound was sprinkled with tiny, barren islands whose only real significance, in 1955, was as a bone of contention between the Peoples Republic of China, on the one hand, and Chiang and his American allies on the other.

The islands varied in size and proximity to larger land masses. One group of sixty-four islets, the Pescadores, was thirty miles from Formosa and was considered a part of it; the White House let it be known that any attack on the Pescadores would be interpreted as preliminary to an invasion of Formosa and as such would be resisted by the Seventh Fleet. Congressional approval was not needed for a defense of the Pescadores because they had been captured from Japan in World War II; under international law the United States was entitled to protect them. The situation on the far side of the strait was different. The islands there were Quemoy, Matsu, and the Tachen group, each of which was more than a hundred miles from Formosa and within five to ten miles of the mainland. As Adlai Stevenson pointed out, they lay "almost as close to the coast of China as Staten Island does to New York," had "always belonged to China," and were properties to which neither the U.S. nor the Nationalists on Formosa had any legal claim. Walter Lippmann underscored the implications of this: ". . . were we to intervene in the offshore islands, we would be acting on Chinese territory in a Chinese civil war."

Nothing would have given John Foster Dulles greater satisfaction. He was ready to fight for the offshore islands any time, and he complained to Sherman Adams about the inability of the British and other U.S. allies to understand "the tremendous shock that a retreat from Quemoy and Matsu would be to the free people of East Asia." That was how Dulles saw the world. He conjured up visions of mass meetings in places like Sumatra and Tibet, with millions of stern peasants gathered under banners reading FREE PEOPLE OF EAST ASIA UNITE and SUPPORT COLLECTIVE SECURITY. The Chinese Communists knew of Dulles's intractability and liked to twit him. While he was in Manila signing the Southeast Asia Treaty Organization protocols in September 1954 they had bombarded Quemoy, and the following January 18 they occupied the islet of Yikiang in the Tachens. Since Yikiang was so microscopic that it wasn't even shown on State Department maps, and since the Tachens were two hundred miles north of Formosa, the threat to Chiang's Nationalists was obscure. Nevertheless, the Joint Chiefs went into emergency session. A majority was hawkish. Admiral Radford, Admiral Carney, and General Nathan F. Twining felt that it was time to take a stand against the Communists and bring about a showdown once and for all.

General Ridgway was the lone dissenter. He advised the President that "Such an action would be almost impossible to limit. It would bring us into direct conflict with the Red Chinese. It could spread to full and all-out war, employing all the terrible weapons at our command." Even if China were conquered, Ridgway went on, the situation would still be highly unsatisfactory; the United States would have created "by military means a great vacuum. Then we would have to go in there with hundreds of thousands of men to fill that vacuum—which would bring us face to face with Russia along a seven-thousand-mile frontier."

With Ridgway the only dove, the Joint Chiefs voted to move against the Reds. Dulles agreed; so did Senator Knowland. But Eisenhower concluded that Ridgway was right. Once again he refused to be drawn into a war on the Asian mainland. The war fever abated. Nevertheless, Dulles did succeed in persuading Ike that face was involved. After the seizure of Yikiang the Peking radio had declared that the thrust showed a "determined will to fight for the liberation of Taiwan." If under these circumstances America did nothing, Dulles warned, Asians would conclude that the U.S. was a paper tiger. The President agreed to do something. He would ask Congress for a resolution.

His message of January 24 was unprecedented in American history. Ike was asking Congress for something more and something less than a declaration of war. He wanted it to let him decide when and where America would fight. He said:

> The situation has become sufficiently critical to impel me, without awaiting action by the United Nations, to ask the Congress to participate now, by specific resolution, in measures designed to improve the prospects for peace. These measures would contemplate the use of the armed forces of the United States, if necessary, to assure the security of Formosa and the Pescadores.

The President then suggested that whether or not a Chinese attack off the offshore islands invited retaliation depended upon the character of the assault. If they just wanted Quemoy and Matsu he might let them have it. If they had a leap toward Formosa in mind, he might not. He wanted Congress to let him read the Communist mind and take whatever action he thought appropriate.

For a measure which was meant to remove doubts, this one bewildered a lot of people. Liberal Democrats contended that Ike already had authority to take the steps he had in mind. As champions of Roosevelt-Truman foreign policy, they were believers in a strong Presidency. His constitutional power as commander in chief, they insisted, permitted him to deploy American military might any way he wished. Some of the arguments spun that winter make curious reading today. Vietnam was destined to become the graveyard of many U.S. policies, none more so than this one. As in the struggle over the Bricker amendment, conservatives wanted to keep the prerogative of making great decisions abroad on Capitol Hill, while liberals insisted that it belonged in the White House. The absolutist nature of the liberal position was most clearly stated by Richard H. Rovere. On March 19, 1955, he wrote that:

> . . . the President's power to defend Formosa does not rest on the hastily composed resolution that Congress passed in January. As President of the United States he has the right to take whatever action he deems necessary in any area he judges to be related to the defense of this country, regardless of whether it is related to the defense of Formosa or anything else.

Eisenhower himself was uncertain over whether he was giving Congress something or taking it away. Before sending the message to the Capitol he made one change. It had read, "The authority I request may be in part already inherent in the authority of the Commander-in-Chief." He crossed this out and wrote in its place, "Authority for some of the actions which might be required would be inherent in the authority of the Commander-in-Chief." Congress was no surer of itself than he was. The most common interpretation there was that the administration was looking for a way to get off the hook on the offshore islands.

Hubert Humphrey tried in vain to tack on an amendment which would have restricted the grant of power to Formosa and the Pescadores. Others in Congress were worried that the United States might be trapped into a war over some obscure place that had nothing to do with American security. Senator Ralph E. Flanders went further. "We have had intimations from the highest quarters," he said, "that it would be militarily advisable to prevent the massing of troops and equipment gathered for the purpose of making an assault on the islands. Put in plain English, this is preventive war. And it is seriously proposed as a possible action pursuant to the purposes of this resolution."

Opposition receded when Senator George threw his great weight behind the bill, saying, "I hope no Democrat will be heard to say that because the President of the United States came to Congress he is thereby subject to criticism." The resolution passed the Senate 85 to 3 and the House 410 to 3. Eisenhower signed it on January 29. That happened to be George's seventy-seventh birthday, and a great fuss was made over the senator when he arrived for the ceremony. Yet in less than a month the Seventh Fleet seemed to show how pointless the whole debate had been by evacuating fourteen thousand Chinese Nationalist troops from the Tachens. So much for the Formosa resolution, Washington said, assuming that it would now become a meaningless scrap of paper. But one man saw it differently. Adlai Stevenson observed that the President had asked for, and had received from Congress, a "blank check." That is precisely what it was. One day Eisenhower or another occupant of his office could present it for payment without consulting Congress further. The delicate balance of constitutional powers had shifted again; another restraint on the chief executive had been removed.

Eisenhower's greatest foreign policy coup, which came six months later, was a public relations triumph. To achieve it he had to all but run over John Foster Dulles. For ten years the Republican Old Guard had resolutely opposed any meeting with the Soviet leaders. Winston Churchill had been proposing a top-level meeting for some time—he called it a "summit"—but for American conservatives the mere suggestion that an American President might clink cocktail glasses with the Russians was like a Pavlovian bell. It set them to protesting against another Yalta or Potsdam, to them synonyms for sellout. Dulles agreed; as an anti-Communist fundamentalist he recoiled from any bargaining with men as steeped in sin as the Soviets.

He couldn't come right out and say that, because the President had repeatedly declared that he would meet anyone, anywhere, in the name of peace. Therefore Dulles tried to establish impossible prerequisites for such a meeting. Before it could be seriously considered, he said, Moscow must show by its deeds that the Soviet Union belonged to the comity of nations and would cooperate in settling differences. When pressed for an example of such a deed, he would reply with vague generalities. He gave the impression that he might be impressed by a withdrawal of all Russian troops from eastern Europe, say, or free elections throughout Russia under U.N. supervision. Sometimes he implied that he would expect handsome apologies from them, too, for their transgressions in the past.

To mollify him and the Republican ultras, Eisenhower called in key senators and congressmen and promised them that he would not be party to "another Yalta." He assured them that no commitments would be made without their approval. Dulles, who was there, said he wouldn't put it past the Russians to make some grandstand play in the name of world peace. He would be on the lookout for it, he said grimly.

Eisenhower had said nothing when Dulles spoke scornfully of dramatic peace proposals. Inwardly, however, he must have been troubled. He himself had that very thing in mind. Nothing definite had been decided, but the draft of a fresh approach to disarmament lay on his desk. In March the President had appointed Nelson Rockefeller chairman of a panel of experts in arms control and psychological warfare. He had given Rockefeller office space at the Marine Corps base at Quantico and asked him to come up with new recommendations which might be produced at a summit meeting. Dulles heard about the task force, but he didn't know its mission. All the same, he was suspicious. To Sherman Adams he said of Rockefeller, "He seems to be building up a big staff. He's got them down at Quantico, and nobody knows what they're doing."

They were studying European opinion surveys. People in the NATO nations, they learned, were weary of the alliance, unenthusiastic about the American bases on the continent, and in favor of banning nuclear weapons. That was disturbing. Lacking Russia's huge standing army, America needed the bombs and the bases as a deterrent. Some way must be found to keep them and still convince Europeans that the U.S. was seeking peace. The Quantico group's answer was a proposal for aerial inspection—in a felicitous phrase, "Open Skies." The idea was not new. Aerial inspection had been suggested as early as 1946 in a Bernard Baruch plan for the international control of atomic energy, and later it had appeared in the report of a U.N. disarmament commission and an Acheson plan for "international disclosure and verification" of all armed forces and weapons. Until now, though, it had been overlooked. Eisenhower thought it both appealing and practical. He hadn't made up his mind over whether to present it at the summit, but on the way to the *Columbine*, his plane, he stuffed it in his briefcase.

The *Columbine*'s destination was Geneva. There he unpacked in the fifteen-room Château Creux de Genthod, which the wife of a Swiss perfume tycoon had placed at his disposal. Meantime Plane No. 001 of the Ilyushin fleet landed and discharged down its ramp Stalin's two successors, Nikita Khrushchev and Nikolai Bulganin, the first looking like a labor union boss and the second bearing an uncanny resemblance to Colonel Sanders, the fried chicken magnate of the early 1970s. Later that afternoon, Anthony Eden and French Premier Edgar Faure arrived to complete the roster of participants in the Big Four talks, or, in the neat Swiss phrase, the Conférence à Quatre. Already the Spirit of Geneva, the newsmen's name for it, was casting a magic spell, attracting crowds of tourists and some celebrities. Pastor Martin Niemöller was there to hold a press conference, and an American clergyman, Billy Graham, was presiding over a revival in the Parc des Eaux-Vives.

In the Palais des Nations Dulles looked disconsolate. Ike, by contrast, was in fine form. At first he tried to match Dulles's stony expression, agreeing with the secretary that it would be unwise to raise false hopes that might be quickly dashed if the meetings were unfruitful. But Eisenhower was too genial, too optimistic, too bursting with good spirits to stay gloomy. He allowed himself to tell the press that "a new dawn may be coming," and in chairing the opening session on Monday, July 18, he spent the first quarter-hour greeting Marshal Zhukov.

The Russians, for their part, seemed more relaxed than at any time since the war. Khrushchev assured his listeners that "neither side wants war," and back home *Pravda* and *Izvestia* were telling the Russian people the same thing—a major shift in the party line, which until now had held that the rest of the world was implacably against them. Khrushchev, Bulganin, and Zhukov rode around Geneva in open cars and took long walks without bodyguards, something of an embarrassment to the Americans, because Eisenhower's every move was screened by Secret Service details and monitored by men in helicopters overhead.

Nevertheless, it was Ike who dominated the Conférence à Quatre. His smile, his candor, and his obvious concern for all mankind captivated the Europeans. *Le Monde* of Paris, usually anti-American, observed that "Eisenhower, whose personality has long been misunderstood, has emerged as the type of leader humanity needs today." Addressing himself to the Soviets, he said earnestly: "The American people want to be friends with the Soviet people. There are no natural differences between our peoples or our nations. There are no territorial or commercial rivalries. Historically, our two countries have always been at peace." He then proposed freer communications between East and West, disarmament, and a united, democratic Germany.

Despite their better manners, the Russians were still Russians when the chips were down. They had a few favorable words to say about peaceful coexistence, but in exchange for it they wanted nothing less than the dissolution of NATO. They dusted off and presented a plan which all those present had heard before: America, Russia, and China would each limit itself to 1,500,000 soldiers; Britain and France would have 650,000 each; and all nuclear weapons would be banned. When they laid that on the table the talks bogged down. After a two-hour huddle of the Americans in the château, Stassen went off to draw up a general disarmament proposal while the President himself drafted an Open Skies presentation. He continued to be undecided about submitting it; he wanted to hear what Bulganin had to say in the morning. Bulganin said nothing new. Not much was expected from Ike, either; this was the fourth day of the conference, and the others assumed that he had already spoken his mind. His first words were familiar: the United States was "prepared to enter into a sound and reliable agreement making possible the reduction of armaments." Then he paused, squared his shoulders against the high windows looking out over Lake Geneva, took off his glasses, and laid them down. He said:

I should address myself for a moment principally to the delegates from the Soviet Union, because our two great countries admittedly possess new and terrible weapons in quantities which do give rise in other parts of the world, or reciprocally, to the fears and dangers of surprise attack.

I propose, therefore, that we take a practical step, that we begin an arrangement, very quickly, as between ourselves—immediately. These steps would include:

To give each other a complete blueprint of our military establishments, from beginning to end, from one end of our countries to the other; lay out the establishments and provide the blueprints to each other.

Next, to provide within our countries facilities for aerial photography to the other country—we to provide the facilities within our country, ample facilities for aerial reconnaissance, where you can make all the pictures you choose and take them to your own country to study; you to provide exactly the same facilities for us and we to make these examinations, and by this step to convince the world that we are providing as between ourselves against the possibility of great surprise attack, thus lessening danger and relaxing tension.

Likewise we will make more easily attainable a comprehensive and effective system of inspection and disarmament, because what I propose, I assure you, would be but a beginning. . . .

The United States is ready to proceed in the study and testing of a reliable system of inspections and reporting, and when that system is proved, then to reduce armaments with all others to the extent that the system will provide assured results.

The successful working out of such a system would do much to develop the mutual confidence which will open wide the avenues of progress for all our peoples.

During the translation a blinding flash of lightning filled the room, thunder rolled across the lake, and all the electricity in the Palais des Nations went dead. Ike chuckled. He said, "I didn't mean to turn the lights off." They flickered on again, revealing a dumbfounded Russian delegation. The Soviet Union was still in the grip of Stalinist paranoia. Diplomats in Moscow were shadowed, foreign correspondents were limited in their movements, the telephones of foreigners were tapped, and any Soviet citizen seen in conversation with them was closely questioned. The idea of providing the Americans with detailed maps of their military bases and then allowing U.S. photographers to fly over and take all the pictures they liked was stupefying. Khrushchev and his fellow delegates didn't know what to say. They just stared.

The Europeans were overjoyed. They hailed the proposal as a diplomatic masterstroke. Premier Faure said, "I wish the people of the world could have been in this conference room to hear the voice of a man speaking from great military experience. Had this been possible, they would believe that something had changed in the world in the handling of this question of disarmament. I am sure that this conference has scored its first victory over skepticism." Next morning newspaper editorials all over western Europe echoed Faure. Opening the skies was something everyone could understand. It was simple and direct, and only a President whose country had nothing to hide could have proposed it.

In practice it was impossible, as out of the question for Americans as for Russians. Ike's military advisers knew that. They had read the fine print he had skipped in his extemporaneous delivery—Open Skies was described there as a suggestion to "instruct our representatives in the Subcommittee on Disarmament in discharge of their mandate from the United States to give priority effort to the study of inspection and reporting"—and they had concluded that he was talking about a distant goal, something that could become practical only after a great many other agreements had been reached and tested. The Pentagon was not paranoid, but it did have a great many hoops through which anyone must jump before he could look at classified material. A government that withheld data from J. Robert Oppenheimer wasn't going to turn it over to the NKVD. This was still the McCarthy era. The senator might be discredited, and the country might be willing to forgive the promoters of Peress, but that was a far cry from filling the sky over Los Alamos with MIGs.*

At the end of the conference Bulganin drew the President aside and said, "Don't worry—this will come out all right." Ike left Geneva convinced that the Soviet leaders, especially Zhukov, were persuaded that he had been sincere. In the following months they treated Open Skies gingerly, mindful, perhaps, of the enthusiasm which had greeted it elsewhere. As late as March 1, 1956, Eisenhower was writing Bulganin to propose the merger of Open Skies and another plan, for the peaceful use of atomic energy. By then, however, Bulganin was being shouldered aside by Khrushchev, who wasn't interested in conciliatory gestures. He preferred to deliver speeches about "wars of national liberation." The Spirit of Geneva was dead. There had been no detente. The conference had achieved nothing that lasted, and is now remembered only for the warmth of Ike's grin and the density of the ice which it didn't melt.

Mercifully, disillusionment was slow to emerge. As the President flew home, Geneva was being acclaimed as a thundering success. Gallup reported that 84 percent of the American people could not think of a single thing in the Eisenhower administration that deserved criticism. The *Columbine* brought the President home in the early hours of Sunday, July 24. It was still dark, the Washington National Airport was drenched in rain. Nevertheless, people were there to cheer him as he descended the ramp, and others lined the roads to the White House. It was a peak in his Presidency, one of the great moments of the 1950s. He had left determined to lessen world ten-

---

* Assuming, that is, that the Russian photographers would have been in Russian planes. They could have been carried in American transports while the American photographers flew over the Soviet Union in Russian planes. Eisenhower hadn't made that clear, and no one asked him. Perhaps even elated Europeans knew in their hearts that Open Skies were too redolent of BBD&O.

sions, he was returning in apparent triumph, and now he looked forward to a long golfing vacation in Denver.

On September 23, 1955, President Eisenhower awoke early on Byers Peak Ranch outside Denver, where he was the guest of Aksel Nielsen, a Colorado banker, and cooked his own breakfast: beef bacon, pork sausage, fried mush, and flapjacks. He stopped off at the stucco administration building at Lowry Air Force Base, spent two intensive hours working with aides, and then drove to the Cherry Hills Country Club for eighteen holes of golf. He shot 84, which was better than it seemed because twice his game had been interrupted by urgent phone calls, one of them from Dulles about the Soviet responses to Open Skies.

The President lunched on hamburger and raw onions, then golfed another nine holes. On the eighth hole he paused, frowning, and rubbed his chest. To the club pro he said, "Maybe I can't take those onions any more. They seem to be backing up on me. I seem to have a little heartburn." The rest of his afternoon was spent in the basement of his mother-in-law's Lafayette Street home painting; he was copying a photograph of an Argentine woman in the July 11 issue of *Life*. Then George and Mary Allen arrived for dinner. Over roast lamb, potatoes, and vegetables Ike mentioned being troubled by the onions earlier, but then he appeared to forget it. At 10 P.M. he retired to his second-floor bedroom. Mamie's bedroom was directly across the hall.

She awoke at 2:30 A.M. and heard him tossing about. Crossing the corridor, she found him asleep but restless. "What's the matter, Ike?" she asked. "Are you having a nightmare or something?" No, he mumbled; he was fine; she left. But he wasn't fine. And he couldn't get back to sleep. Suddenly an agonizing pain gripped his chest. He rose and crossed the hall to her. He couldn't speak; he rubbed his chest to show where it hurt. Remembering the onions, she gave him milk of magnesia. She was troubled. This was something new; he had never complained of a pain there before. Picking up the phone, she called Major General Howard McC. Snyder, the President's personal physician, at Lowry's bachelor officers' quarters four miles away. She told him what was happening and said, "You'd better come over."

Snyder didn't need to be told. Those symptoms would alarm any doctor. Flinging his clothes over his pajamas, he told his driver,

"Seven-fifty Lafayette Street, and step on it." They raced through red lights all the way; at 3:12 the doctor was at the President's bedside. Ike was flushed, sweating, and in extreme discomfort. His pulse was rapid and his blood pressure was high. Listening to his chest with a stethoscope, Snyder reached a diagnosis within minutes. The President had been stricken by a coronary thrombosis. His heart had been damaged; how much, Snyder could not tell. He administered amyl nitrate, papaverine hydrochloride to dilate Ike's arteries, and morphine for shock. Then he gave him a shot of heparin to prevent clotting. At 3:45 he administered a second injection of morphine. Ike fell into a deep sleep. His crisis was passing, but Snyder decided that for the time being he would tell no one of it, not even Mrs. Eisenhower. There was nothing they could do, and the commotion of an alarmed household would only decrease the President's chances.

For nearly four hours the doctor sat alone by the bed. A little before 7 A.M., when others in the gray brick house began to waken, he sent for Ann Whitman. The President was indisposed, he told the secretary; it was a digestive upset. At 10:30 this word was given to the press and flashed around the world. By then, however, Snyder knew he couldn't withhold the truth much longer. He quietly informed Mrs. Eisenhower of it and called the chief of cardiology at Fitzsimons General Hospital, just outside Denver, asking him to bring an electrocardiograph. Ike awoke at 11:45. He was conscious but feeble. The tracing of the electrocardiograph, when spread out on Mrs. Doud's dining room table, confirmed the diagnosis, and Snyder told Ike what had happened. He said, "We would like to take you to Fitzsimons." Then he said that an ambulance would not be necessary. The President nodded and asked him to inform the Secret Service. Assisted down the stairs and into a limousine waiting in the driveway, Ike was driven nine miles to the hospital. There a wheelchair took him to a special suite and an oxygen tent.

At 2:30 P.M. a press aide at Lowry told the White House correspondents there: "The President has just had a mild anterior—let's cut out the word 'anterior'—the President has just had a mild coronary thrombosis. He has just been taken to Fitzsimons General Hospital. He was taken to the hospital in his own car and walked from the house to the car."

His last words were drowned by pandemonium.

In Washington, where it was 4:30 P.M., Jim Hagerty had returned from vacation that morning. Informed by phone of the heart attack shortly before the announcement to the press in Denver, he immediately put through a call to Vice President Nixon's white brick home in Washington's fashionable Spring Valley neighborhood. The Nixons had just returned from a wedding, and the Vice President was reading the *Washington Evening Star*'s brief account of Eisenhower's digestive upset. Hagerty asked him, "Dick, are you sitting down?" Nixon said he wasn't, and then the President's press secretary, speaking very slowly, told him what happened. He said, "The press will be told about it in a half-hour or so." Nixon said, "My God!"

Hanging up, the Vice President walked into his living room in a daze and sat down. According to his later recollection, he said nothing for at least five minutes. After the shock had worn off he phoned William Rogers, then deputy attorney general, and asked him to come at once. By the time Rogers's taxi drew up, the news had been broken in Denver. Nixon's phone was ringing constantly. Outside, a crowd was gathering: neighbors, reporters, photographers. Determined to say nothing to newspapermen, Nixon remained inside as long as he could. By the time he had finished dinner, however, the din outside had become alarming, and he decided to hide out in Rogers's Bethesda home. It was like a movie escape. Rogers called his wife and told her to come and park a block away, keeping the motor running. Then, while nine-year-old Tricia Nixon distracted the crowd on the lawn, the two men darted out a side door, raced down an alley, and jumped into the car.

In Prestwick, Scotland, the weather was cold and drizzly as Sherman Adams, the assistant to the President, checked into headquarters of the U.S. base there with Colonel Andrew J. Goodpaster. Adams had just completed a four-week tour of U.S. installations in Europe; he was meeting General Gruenther for a return flight to Washington that night. Before they could exchange a word the commanding officer of the base darted up and told them that he had just learned the President had been hospitalized in Denver with a heart attack. No details were available. Fleetingly Adams wondered whether Denver's elevation of five thousand feet would be good for a mending heart. Then it occurred to him that if Eisenhower had to be ill, this was a good time for it. Congress was in recess, Ike had no pending obligations as head of state, presidential duties were at a minimum, and planning for the coming year's program, then in its early stages, would not require the President's attention for some time.

Wall Street did not know that. The stock market, which is a kind of fun-house mirror exaggerating ups and downs in the American mood, opened nervously Monday morning as the plane bearing Adams approached the U.S. coast. Then stocks dove. The Dow Jones average plummeted to 444.56; losses were estimated at twelve billion dollars; it was the Street's worst day since the Crash.

The extent of Ike's illness was the only topic of conversation at 1600 Pennsylvania Avenue that noon when Adams arrived in time to lunch with Nixon, Rogers, and Jerry Persons. Halfway through the meal a call came from Denver. Dr. Paul Dudley White, the eminent Boston heart specialist, had completed his first examination of the President and was surprisingly optimistic. Ike's condition was satisfactory, he said, and his morale was good. He would be able to meet a light schedule in two weeks if all went well, and could probably return as a full-time President within a few months. Indeed, Dr. White said, barring the unforeseen, Eisenhower ought to be able to run for reelection. The stock market, delighted with this prognosis, surged back on Tuesday, and administration leaders lunched again, this time in the office of Secretary Humphrey in the Treasury Building, to consider ways of carrying on in the chief's absence.

All that week Washington buzzed with rumors of mistrust and misunderstandings on the highest levels of the government, and all of them were false. Eisenhower's much maligned staff system worked smoothly while he himself lay on a hospital bed 1,551 miles away. On Thursday the cabinet met with Nixon presiding. He read the morning bulletin from Denver—the President had had an excellent night, his first one out of the oxygen tent—and after a review of the diplomatic fronts by Dulles, Brownell led a discussion on the delegation of powers. As things worked out in the days ahead, Nixon signed some papers "in behalf of" the President while Adams really ran the office. Once a week during the rest of Eisenhower's convalescence Adams flew to Denver to report on meetings of the cabinet and the National Security Council. Only urgent problems were brought to the President's bedside. There were few of those; the one topic of substance was the coming State of the Union message, and that wasn't due until January.

In Adams's opinion, "the real key figure in the government" that autumn was Paul Dudley White. By the end of September Dr. White had become the most famous physician in the country. His candid medical briefings reassured the press and the country, and with his encouragement—sometimes, in fact, at his insistence—presidential aides overcame their reluctance to burden the hospitalized chief executive. "Look," White said to Hagerty, "he's not so much of an invalid as he is the President of the United States lying in there. He wants to do his job." On October 14 Ike told Adams he felt fine. "Funny thing," he said. "If the doctors didn't tell me differently, I would think this heart attack belonged to some other guy."

That was his sixty-fifth birthday, and sacks of congratulatory mail were piled high in the hospital auditorium. Over and over the President told visitors how moved he was by them; to Mamie he said, "It really does something for you to know that people all over the world are praying for you." The White House correspondents gave him his gayest moment of the day. Their gift was a suit of fire-engine red pajamas with five tiny gold stars embroidered on each collar tab and "Much Better, Thanks" embroidered over the breast pocket. To complete the gaudy costume, Merriman Smith of the United Press and Laurence H. Burd of the *Chicago Tribune* had contributed a 39-cent black cowboy tie tricked out with silver sequins. Ike was delighted. He told Dr. White these were the most marvelous pajamas he had ever owned. The doctor encouraged him to wear them as often as possible. They were more important than they seemed, White privately told the presidential staff; one of the worst aspects of a heart attack was the depression that accompanied recovery.

For a time it seemed that Ike might be spared that. Discharged from Fitzsimons after a fluoroscopic examination, he returned to Washington on November 11 for a long White House weekend, and on November 14 he drove to his Gettysburg farm with Mrs. Eisenhower. Seven thousand Pennsylvanians greeted him there, waving placards saying GLAD YOU'RE HOME, IKE and WELCOME HOME, IKE AND MAMIE. On November 22 he presided over a cabinet meeting, his first since the attack, at Camp David. All of those present noticed that he had lost weight, but his spirits appeared to be fine. He had seen an editorial expressing surprise that the cabinet could work well without him, he said. In fact, he said with a smile, there were hints that it had worked better. Adams noted: "He was quick, decisive, and keen. I could see that the Cabinet liked what they saw. Some of them were openly astonished by the President's fast recovery and all of them were agreeably surprised."

Then, back in Gettysburg, gloom struck. December was dark, cold, and wet; the putting green at the farm was brown and soggy. Cooped up indoors, he faced, as Hagerty put it, "the sheer, God-awful boredom of not being President." For five terrible weeks he stalked around the farmhouse using a golf club as a cane, suffering in that special hell known only to victims of severe depression. In the two months since his coronary neither he nor anyone close to him had seriously supposed that he might run for another term. Now he began to have second thoughts. Paul Dudley White saw no reason why he shouldn't stay in the White House. It was, the President told those around, something to think about.

Newspapermen raised the question on January 8, 1956, at a Key West press conference. Ike had flown down for a few days of work and exercise. After a thirty-minute stroll he faced the reporters and was asked about his political future. He replied: "All the considerations that apply to such things are complicated. Naturally I will want to confer with my most trusted advisers." He noted that the Presidency was probably the most tiring job in the world but that "it also has, as I have said before, its inspirations." Afterward newsmen asked one another what that had meant. By a margin of nearly five to one they concluded that Ike would retire at the end of this term.

The minority wasn't so sure; they were picking up persistent rumors that the President was scheduling a meeting to weigh that very question. It was true, and the meeting was held that same week. Puckishly Ike called it for the evening of Friday, January 13, and made out place cards for exactly thirteen men. Mrs. Eisenhower joined them for dinner in the Mansion's state dining room and retired when they withdrew into the second-floor Trophy Room. Sitting with his back to the fireplace, Ike explained that he wanted each of them to speak out frankly on the question of whether he should try for another term and why. There was, of course, little doubt about which way the wind would blow. As Adams dryly observed afterward, "I don't imagine that the President expected to get a cross-fire of pro-and-con arguments from a group like that one. . . . If Eisenhower was looking for cogent reasons for leaving his office, he would have hardly sought them from his own appointees."

Adams, Humphrey, Dulles, Hagerty, Summerfield, Lodge, Persons, Len Hall, Brownell, Howard Pyle, Tom Stephens—one by one they told him how indispensable he was. Then Milton Eisenhower, who didn't want his brother to run again, summed up the arguments on both sides. The President made no decision then. He appeared to be undecided as late as February 13. That morning he reminded a cabinet meeting that he had wanted to put into his inaugural address his intention of remaining in office for only one term. He had been dissuaded, he said, and now he regretted it. Adams, however, was already proceeding on the assumption that they would be in the White House for another four years. While the President had been in Key West his chief assistant had called in government carpenters to shorten the office of the presidential appointments secretary, thereby creating a small room adjacent to the office large enough for a cot and a lounging chair—a retreat where Ike could rest before lunch, as Paul Dudley White had recommended. Adams counted on continuing strong support from the doctor for a second term, and he wasn't disappointed; on February 14, in his last medical briefing, White was able to remove the last traces of doubt about his patient's stamina. X-rays of his heart now and before the attack were almost identical, showing that there had been no enlargement of it since he had resumed normal activity in January. If the President ran again, White said, he would vote for him.

The following day the President flew to Secretary Humphrey's Georgia plantation and tested his strength golfing and hunting. He felt fine, and that convinced him: he was going to run. At 4 P.M. Tuesday he told Adams, Nixon, Persons, and Hall, and at 10:37 A.M. on Wednesday, February 29, he announced the news to the press in the Indian Treaty Room. If asked to make the race again, he said, "My answer will be positive, that is, affirmative."

The radio networks broadcast their first bulletin at 10:52, and in the next moment a House Armed Services subcommittee was given a startling glimpse of the postwar revolution in communications. A witness there was reciting a long list of statistics. Congressmen were dozing, reporters doodling. Only Chairman F. Edward Hebert of Louisiana was bright-eyed. Suddenly he whacked his gavel and cried, "Gentlemen, the President has just announced his candidacy for reelection!" After the excitement had died down a colleague from Illinois asked Hebert how he had known. The telephone hadn't rung, no notes had been passed, no one had entered the room.

Shamefacedly, Hebert confessed; instead of listening to the witness he had been tuned in to one of the tiny new transistor radios, tucked inside the pocket of his coat and hooked up with an earphone that looked like a hearing aid.

In a telecast that evening from the oval office Ike told an audience estimated at 65 million: "I wanted to come into your homes this evening because I felt the need of talking to you directly about a decision I made today after weeks of the most careful and devoutly prayerful consideration. . . . I have decided that if the Republican party chooses to nominate me I shall accept the nomination. Therefore, if the people of this country should elect me I shall continue to serve them in the office I now hold. I have concluded that I should permit the American people to have the opportunity to register their decision in this matter."

Beforehand, he had been chatting with television adviser Robert Montgomery when a network assistant asked him about an inch-high plaque on his desk bearing the Latin motto *Suaviter in Modo, Fortiter in Re,* and the translation "Gently in Manner, Strongly in Deed." The President chuckled and said, "Maybe I'd better hide that; it proves I'm an egghead."

The country's ranking egghead was also in a witty mood. Asked about the President's decision, Adlai Stevenson said, "The real reason Eisenhower is running again is that he can't afford to retire to his farm at Gettysburg while Benson is Secretary of Agriculture."

In the high summer of 1956 the corn stood tall from Mount Rushmore to the panhandle. America seemed to have returned, momentarily at least, to the frivolous 1920s, to wonderful trivia, hot music, placid politics, glamorous athletes, and automobile worship. General Motors president Harlow Curtice was *Time*'s Man of the Year. The compact Rambler was Detroit's current success; Republicans were wondering whether George Romney of American Motors might make a future President.

President Eisenhower's contribution to the American landscape, the interstate highway system, was just getting under way; ultimately it would provide 41,000 miles of new roads—high-speed, limited access, nonstop travel arteries. It was going to be the biggest public works project in the nation's history; the cost was expected to run somewhere between 33 and 41 billion dollars. (It came to 76

billions.) Landlocked cities in the Middle West would be opened to
new commerce. The driving time between Chicago and Indianapolis
alone would be cut from six hours to three. Roadside services would
become a billion-dollar industry, and people and goods would move
quickly and safely across the country on well-engineered ribbons of
concrete.

It was appropriate that in 1956 Oregon miler Jim Bailey was
clocked at 3:58.6, the first under-four-minute mile run in the United
States. Americans were not only moving toward new horizons; they
could hardly wait to get there. The Gross National Product was 400
billion dollars' worth of goods and services that year, and inflation
was still negligible, though a warning of what lay ahead came
when, after a quarter-century of unchanged postal rates, first-class
mail went from three cents to four and airmail from six cents to
seven.

Businessmen pointed with pride to the increase in productivity,
and sermons and editorials viewed with alarm the frantic pace of
American life. Popular misconceptions to the contrary, however,
America did not lead the world in suicides. According to the World
Health Organization, the U.S. suicide rate was 10.8 per 100,000 (16.1
for men and 4.3 for women), which put it far down the list, below
Denmark (24.1), Austria, Switzerland, Japan, Sweden, West Germany, Finland, France, and England and Wales. Of course, psychiatric help was now more available for Americans, and beginning in
1956 jittery executives could find peace with meprobamate, an exceptionally effective tranquilizer better known by its trade name,
Miltown. *Time* called Miltown "Don't-Give-a-Damn Pills." Their first
big markets were Madison Avenue and Hollywood. In Hollywood,
a drugstore at Sunset and Gower pasted a huge red sign across its
display window: "Yes, we have Miltown!" Milton Berle said, "I'm
thinking of changing my name to Miltown Berle." It was a poor year
for humor.

Popular athletes of the 1940s were entering the cruel twilight of
their trade: Joe DiMaggio was in his forties, and now that Floyd
Patterson was heavyweight champion, Joe Louis, overweight and
slow, was stumbling into the oblivion of professional wrestling. Jackson Pollock died and Liberace arrived, accompanied by his
ubiquitous mother. Grace Metalious and Françoise Sagan also
emerged, edifying nobody, and so did a new minstrel of youth

whose voice seemed to be everywhere, singing, "Hi luh-luh-luh-luv yew-hew," or

> *Awopbopaloobop! alopbamboom!*
> *Tutti Frutti! Aw rutti!*
> *Tutti Frutti! Aw rutti!*

Elvis Aaron Presley made his movie debut that fall in *Love Me Tender*. He sang four songs in a secondary role, and his curious amalgam of rock 'n' roll, bluegrass, and boogie dominated the show. All year he toured the South and West, fighting off hysterical teen-agers in pedal pushers and boosting his first LP album—it went straight to the top of *Billboard*'s weekly ratings—and such singles as "Don't Be Cruel" and "Heartbreak Hotel," each of which sold over a million copies.

Presley shocked the parents of young girls. Drape-suited and tight-panted, his petulant eyes glassy and his pouting lips hanging open, he would grip the microphone, crouch, and then buck his hips against his dangling guitar. Television producers refused to show him below the waist. They called him lewd, and they were right; that was the secret of his appeal. Teen-aged girls carved his name on their forearms with pen knives while older women bestowed gifts upon him and tried to lure him away. In Amarillo a reporter asked him if he was contemplating marriage. He replied, "Why buy a cow when you can get the milk through the fence?"

Offstage Presley could be refreshingly straightforward. Unlike Liberace, Presley had no musical pretensions. He recalled that he had been given a guitar when he was twelve. "I beat on it for a year or two," he said. "Never did learn much about it." Tired of driving trucks, he had taken the guitar to a recording studio. "It sounded like somebody beatin' on a bucket lid," he said, "but the engineer at this studio had a recording company called Sun, and he told me I had an unusual voice, and he might call me up sometime." When Presley records started to sell, he acquired a manager who said, "He may not sound like a hillbilly, but he gets the same response."

The pervasive vulgarity of Elvis the Pelvis was part of his appeal. He liked to spend hours at amusement parks riding dodgem cars, wore $10,000 gold lamé suits, and bought a fleet of Cadillacs painted in pastels. Obsessed with his hair—it was turning prematurely gray —and guarded by a ratpack of muscular young men who doubled as companions, he settled down in a garish estate ringed with sentry boxes. When he wanted to go nightclubbing word would be phoned ahead, so that precautions could be taken. Like royalty, he carried no cash. Then, like G. David Schine, he was drafted. In Germany, where he was stationed, he received much attention from the local press, in which he was identified as a symbol of American culture.

Presley in the flesh wasn't much different from the comic opera roles he played on the screen. In this he was supremely a man of the time. There was little room in the ambiance of 1956 for genuine tragedy. Sober events were ignored or externalized. It is significant that on July 20, 1956, one of the most important dates in American history, headline writers were enthralled by the fact that Eisenhower had at last balanced a budget. None noted that on that day, according to the Geneva agreement of 1954, free elections were to be held in Vietnam. The failure to hold them would produce the Viet Cong, civil war, and American intervention; but commentators had no time for its implications then.

The catastrophes that did attract attention were explicit, obvious; the kind that tabloids feed on. It was a time of sensations. Victor Riesel, a New York labor columnist, was blinded by a man who threw acid in his face. Dr. Jesús de Galíndez disappeared outside a Manhattan subway station; presumably he was kidnapped by henchmen of Rafael Trujillo, the dictator of the Dominican Republic, and murdered. On Parris Island, South Carolina, a Marine Corps drill instructor led 74 recruits into a treacherous tidal stream; six of them drowned. In Boston the FBI solved a $2,775,000 Brink's robbery, and the great Hungarian uprising was encouraged by Radio Free Europe in an act of criminal irresponsibility.

In June of 1956 Phyllis Brown, an editor at the Research Institute of America, entertained Wisconsin bankers at their annual convention with a charming little talk on the innate frailties of her sex. Never tell a woman she is being illogical, she said: "The average woman starts off on the premise that the way she feels about something is itself a most compelling argument." Miss Brown further recommended that they praise women more than men and remember that women always take things personally.

Time reprinted this Aunt Tom's remarks with a manly good humor. In another issue *Time*'s editors put a woman of intellectual pretensions in her place by reporting that "Like many of her sisters in what she bitterly refers to as the Second Sex, France's Simone de Beauvoir would rather talk than eat." Women's magazines, edited by men, treated their subscribers with similar condescension. A *Ladies' Home Journal* editor explained to a writer, "If we get an article about a woman who does anything adventurous, out of the way, something by herself, you know, we figure she must be terribly aggressive, neurotic." At the peak of feminine achievement the *Journal* introduced to its readers a Texas housewife who had her face made up an hour after breakfast and could say, "By 8:30 A.M., when my youngest goes to school, my whole house is clean and neat and I am dressed for the day, I am free to play bridge, attend club meetings, or stay home and read, listen to Beethoven, and just plain loaf."

There were signs, for those who could read them, that not all of her sisters were satisfied with bridge or club meetings. In 1956 *McCall's* published an innocent little piece called "The Mother Who Ran Away" and was dumbfounded to find that it drew more readers than anything they had ever carried. Later *Redbook* ran an article on "Why Young Mothers Feel Trapped." Young mothers who felt that way were encouraged to write in—and more than twenty-four thousand of them did. But the notion that a woman should aspire to become something other than a fetching housewife was too heretical to take hold. The altar remained the only acceptable destination for single girls, and those who managed to reach it with a prize groom in tow became celebrities. Memorable brides of 1956 included Mrs. E. Clifton Daniel Jr., née Margaret Truman, and the former Odile Rodin, who became the fifth wife of Porfirio Rubirosa. (Her predecessors were Danielle Darrieux, Doris Duke, Barbara Hutton, and the daughter of Rafael Trujillo.) The ultimate prize, however, was won that year by a pretty actress from Philadelphia who, after being wooed by dress designer Oleg Cassini and actor Jean-Paul Aumont, hooked the most eligible bachelor in Europe: Prince Rainier III of Monaco. How Grace Kelly did it was a secret to be pondered by the wives of America as they loaded their automatic washing machines and scoured the blades of their husbands' electric carving knives. All her father would say was: "Grace met him when she was on the French Riviera. She went there to make a picture called *To Catch a Thief*—and look what she came back with."

The father, a Philadelphia contractor and politician who had been national sculling champion and therefore something of a catch himself, recalled that when the prince first called at the Kelly mansion, "I was under the impression he was going to stay just a couple of hours. But he stayed and stayed and stayed." Kelly was wary. ("I don't generally approve of these oddballs she goes out with.") Then Rainier asked for Grace's hand. This being too important a matter for her, she was sent off while the menfolk conferred. In a speech which might be memorized by every American tycoon whose daughter is being courted by a sovereign, Kelly warned Rainier to beware the occupational weaknesses of his class: "I told the prince that royalty didn't mean a thing to us. I told him that I certainly hoped he wouldn't run around the way some princes do, and I told him that if he did, he'd lose a mighty fine girl." Mrs. Kelly sold her as-told-to memoirs to Hearst (*My Daughter Grace Kelly, Her Life and Romances*). The *Chicago Tribune*, in an allusion to Monaco's Monte Carlo, complained, "She's too well-bred a girl to marry the silent partner in a gambling parlor." Aristotle Onassis, who virtually owned Monte Carlo and would continue to pay no French taxes if Grace presented her husband with an heir, cried, "I am mad with joy," and gave the Monaco Red Cross a million francs.

The Kelly-Rainier wedding was an MGM press agent's dream, one reason being that the MGM publicity department had a hand in it. On April 12 the American Export liner *Constitution* hovered off the French coast and set Grace on the deck of the prince's white yacht *Deo Juvante II*. Accompanying her were 80 wedding guests, 24 columnists, four trunks, 20 hatboxes, 36 other pieces of luggage, and the bride's black French poodle, Oliver. Overhead, an aircraft from Onassis's private squadron bombarded the yacht with red and white carnations. From the shore came a din: klaxons, sirens, rockets, and cannon firing 21-gun salutes. The dock was literally black with newspapermen—1,500 of them from all over the world, more than had covered the Geneva summit the year before. Ashore and with Grace beside him in his green Chrysler Imperial, Rainier discovered that his way was temporarily blocked by fifty photographers. Everyone seemed to be in Monaco except the ones the couple most wanted: Europe's more famous crowned heads. Elizabeth II had declined to come, and other members of European royalty had followed her example. England was represented in Monaco by a minor diplomat and Randolph Churchill, who yelled in a moment of pique, "I didn't come here to meet vulgar people like the Kellys."

If Elizabeth was wary of being exploited by the world press, others with famous names didn't mind at all. President Eisenhower was represented at the wedding by Conrad Hilton, the hotel magnate. The Aga Khan was there with his begum. Somerset Maugham led Monte Carlo's literary contingent, and former King Farouk of Egypt, now obese and besotted, distressed the wedding marshals by waddling up the central staircase of St. Nicholas Cathedral, supposedly reserved for the bridal party. He was whisked aside and the principals arrived. Grace said "*Je veux*," thereby becoming twice a princess, four times a duchess, nine times a baroness, eight times a countess, four times a marchioness, and once a viscountess. Her wedding gifts included a quarter-million dollars in diamonds alone. Pickpockets at the festivities made off with $150,000, but to Onassis, who kept picking up tabs, it was all worth it. In August Rainier disclosed that his wife was pregnant. Monaco celebrated the announcement with fireworks, trumpets, bonfires, and dancing in the street and the *New York Daily Mirror* used a line it had been saving almost a year: MONACO WEATHER FORECAST: A LITTLE RAINIER IN FEBRUARY.

In the four years since Farouk had fled Cairo, taking his priceless collection of pornography with him, Egypt had become the stronghold of a military clique. Lieutenant Colonel Gamal Abdel Nasser emerged in June 1956 as the leader of the junta. John Foster Dulles believed he had Nasser's number, and he decided to teach him a lesson. The upshot was a minor war and, ironically, a tremendous boost for President Eisenhower in his campaign for reelection.

As a neutral in the cold war, Nasser was naturally anathema to Dulles. The United States had been trying to coax Egypt into the western camp. With that in view, Washington had told Cairo the previous winter that it would loan the Egyptians 56 million dollars for their three-mile Aswan High Dam on the Nile. But Nasser was ungrateful. He recognized Red China, tried to break up the Baghdad Pact, announced plans to visit Moscow, and traded 200 million dollars' worth of cotton for Czechoslovakian guns. Thereupon Dulles, on July 19, publicly canceled the American loan. Foreign service officers on the State Department's Middle Eastern desk had warned that Nasser might seize the Suez Canal in retaliation. He did. He cried, "I look at Americans and say: may you choke to death on your fury!" He said, "We shall build the high dam as we desire. The annual income of the Suez Canal is 100 million dollars. Why not take it ourselves?" Then: "We shall rely on our own strength, our own muscle, our own funds. And it will be run by Egyptians! Egyptians! Egyptians!"

The full weight of this blow fell not upon the United States, but on Britain and France. At the urging of anticolonialists in Washington, the British had withdrawn the last of their troops from Suez in June. Now Nasser had cut Anglo-French industry off from its chief source of petroleum. Of the 1.5 million barrels of oil that passed through the canal each day, 1.2 million went to western Europe. Suez provided two-thirds of the fuel the continent needed for heat and production, and the other third came overland through pipes that could easily be sabotaged by the Arabs. Therefore this was a real crisis for London and Paris. It would have taxed the gifts of a Disraeli, and the householder at 10 Downing Street was no Disraeli. He was Sir Anthony Eden, once Churchill's great foreign secretary and now worn to a shadow. The office of prime minister was simply too much for him. Struggling along with less than five hours sleep a night, he became addicted to amphetamines. Years later medical scientists discovered that amphetamines could rob a sensible man of his good judgment, and that was what happened to Eden in 1956.

Blaming Dulles for their plight, Eden and Guy Mollet, the French premier, turned their backs on Washington. They decided to tackle the problem in their own way—or, to be precise, in the way advocated by David Ben-Gurion. To the Israeli premier, this seemed a perfect time to settle accounts with the hated Egyptians. Russia was preoccupied by a developing crisis in Hungary, the United States was in the middle of a national election, and the British and the French, furious at Nasser, were spoiling for a fight. Ben-Gurion reminded them that under certain circumstances an Anglo-French expeditionary force could act in the Middle East under a cloak of legitimacy. The Tripartite Declaration of 1950 provided that Britain and France could reoccupy the Suez Canal if war erupted between Israel and Egypt. Ben-Gurion said he would be delighted to provide that excuse, and Eden and Mollet endorsed the plan.

In the last week of October the CIA received troubling reports. Israel was mobilizing. More than 100,000 Israeli troops were poised along their border with Egypt, and Israeli tanks were in position for a lunge westward. Whitehall and the Quai d'Orsay had lapsed into a studied silence. To Washington the very correctness of their behavior was puzzling. They were like men building up an alibi. It was hard to believe that they could be plotting with Jerusalem, though. Eisenhower, who was in Walter Reed for a physical checkup on Sunday, October 28, rejected the idea. Drafting notes to Ben-Gurion between trips up and down hospital corridors for tests, Ike said wryly, "Israel and barium make quite a combination."

The Israelis struck the next day. At 3 P.M. Washington time teletypes chattered out the first bulletin: Israeli forces were crossing into Egyptian territory. Eden and Mollet now had their justification. They went through the motions of sending ultimatums to Jerusalem and Cairo demanding that both sides lay down their arms. In the House of Commons Eden said, "We have asked the Egyptian government to agree that Anglo-French forces should move temporarily into key positions." If the request was ignored, he said, British and French troops would intervene in Suez "in whatever strength may be necessary."

Eisenhower had left the hospital to campaign in the South. Now he rushed back to Washington. At 7 P.M. that Monday, as dusk began to gather in the capital, his limousine entered the southwest gate of the White House grounds. After conferring with Adams, Radford, Persons, and the Dulles brothers, he authorized a statement from Hagerty: "At the meeting the President recalled that the United States, under this and prior administrations, had pledged itself to assist the victim of any aggression in the Middle East. We shall honor our pledge."

On Wednesday British bombers based in Cyprus attacked Egyptian airfields. Ike said, "I just don't know what got into those people. It's the damnedest business I ever saw supposedly intelligent people get themselves into." But: "We cannot subscribe to one law for the weak, another for those allied with us." In a Wednesday telecast he told the American people just that. The British and the French, who held Dulles responsible for the whole mess, were furious. Eden let it be known that he would reject any U.N. cease-fire proposal. On Saturday Dulles, exhausted and distraught, collapsed; an ulcer had penetrated his abdominal wall; he was taken to Walter Reed for two and a half hours of surgery. The world seemed very near war that weekend. On Sunday the White House learned that British and French troops were boarding transports at Cyprus for an invasion of Suez. Early Monday British paratroopers began landing on the north end of the canal. That evening Bulganin warned Eden,

Mollet, and Ben-Gurion that unless they withdrew immediately they would become targets for Red missiles loaded with nuclear warheads. At the same time Bulganin proposed to Eisenhower that the United States and the Soviet Union form an alliance to stop the invasion. Ike was indignant. To an aide he said, "Those British—they're still my right arm!" He told Bulganin that Russo-American intervention was "unthinkable" and accused the Soviet premier of trying to divert attention from Hungary, where the Red Army "at this very moment is brutally repressing the human rights of the Hungarian people."

This was more than cold war rhetoric. Ike was right: the Russians were also guilty of atrocities that week. Afterward the Communists would remember Suez while the West remembered Hungary; in fact the two were equally ugly. On Wednesday, the day of the first RAF raids on the canal zone, anti-Soviet rioters in Budapest had made Imre Nagy premier of Hungary. By Saturday the entire country had risen. Nagy denounced the Warsaw Pact, which made Hungary a Soviet satellite. Russian troops withdrew from Budapest and then regrouped to crush the revolt. The streets were carpeted with the bodies of Budapest's martyrs, Joseph Cardinal Mindszenty took refuge in the besieged American embassy, and the Hungarian delegation to the United Nations begged the U.N. to intervene. Lodge introduced a measure which would do that. The Russians vetoed it. Eisenhower spent twenty million dollars in Mutual Security funds on food and medicine for Hungary. He ordered that 21,500 Hungarian refugees be admitted to the United States and told his staff to see to it that the administration found homes and jobs for them, and he sent protests to Bulganin. The Soviet premier coldly replied that Russia and Hungary would settle their differences without outside help.

On the morning of Tuesday, November 6, 1956, French infantry seized the east side of the canal, Russian troops captured Nagy, the U.N. General Assembly condemned Soviet aggression, and 61,-616,938 Americans went to the polls. War was on everyone's mind, and the country's most famous general was on the ballot. The conclusion that the voters put the two together is inescapable. Perhaps they were right to do so. Certainly Ike retained his poise throughout that terrible week. Adams was with the President in his oval office when Eden phoned. Eisenhower said heartily, "Well, Anthony, how *are* you?"

It was a question, Adams dryly observed, which, "it seemed to me at the time, would have required a long and involved answer."

Afterward there is a certain inevitability to political landslides, and this one was no exception. Eisenhower would have been re-elected if Nasser had kept his hands off Suez and Hungary had remained servile. No Democratic candidate could have driven him from office, and to those who enjoy hindsight it may seem surprising that a man as intelligent as Adlai Stevenson didn't realize that. Gallup figures showed that the President retained the confidence of better than seven out of every ten Americans. In his first term he had accomplished much that had seemed unattainable four years earlier. The Korean War had been ended, and without a depression. McCarthy had been routed. The Bricker amendment was a dead issue. Knowland stood isolated in the Senate. The Republican party was now committed to the United Nations, and except for Styles Bridges no Republican with a safe seat was advocating the invasion of China or a preventive war against Russia. Furthermore, Ike's management of domestic problems suggested that he was a wiser politician than he appeared to be. His federal highway program was outspending the WPA. Inflation had been checked. Labor was getting a larger share of the national income. Social security had been extended. The administration had built a sound antitrust program, and its soil bank, by appeasing farmers, had robbed the Democrats of a major issue.

The President had still other assets, less tangible but very real, which could be redeemed at the polls. His personality was gilt-edged political capital. Joseph Alsop wrote that "Eisenhower's greatest single contribution has been bringing us back to a sense of the true American style—setting the style, in fact, by his own example and in the most trying circumstances," and Richard H. Rovere concluded that "when Eisenhower has spoken for the nation, he has . . . in general appeared before the world as a not unworthy successor to those few American presidents whom the world has known and respected."

This account is, of course, incomplete. If those had been the only issues, the Democrats would not have battled so hard for the nomination. To them the administration seemed highly pregnable. The GOP was more than ever the party of big business. The schism between liberal Republicans and the Old Guard continued to be unsightly. Dulles's performance abroad had been less than brilliant, as the mess in the Middle East demonstrated. Apart from these, there were three overriding major points at issue: the President's health, Vice President Nixon, and the eloquence and charm of the Democratic nominee.

Hopes for Dwight Eisenhower's longevity were at best precarious. If reelected he would be seventy before he left office. Only a year ago he had suffered a massive heart attack, and he himself had observed that the Presidency was the most demanding job in the world. Moreover, there was worry about more than his heart. Less than ten weeks before the national conventions he was stricken with another ailment, taken from the White House in an ambulance, and subjected to a two-hour ordeal on the operating table.

At first the Denver scenario seemed to be repeating itself. In the small hours of June 9 Dr. Snyder was awakened in his Connecticut Avenue apartment by an anxious Mamie Eisenhower. The President was tossing and turning. He complained of stomach pains. What should she do? Milk of magnesia was ineffective, and Snyder hurried to the Executive Mansion. After breakfast Hagerty issued a brief statement: "The President has an upset stomach and headache. Dr. Snyder has been with him since early this morning. There is nothing wrong with his heart." But that was far from reassuring. The Denver crisis had also begun with a "digestive upset." A second statement was more specific: "The President has had an attack of ileitis (inflammation of the lower portion of the small intestine)." As a "precaution" he was entering Walter Reed Hospital.

It was a wretched day for Hagerty. He kept telling reporters that ileitis wasn't serious while appearances indicated that it was. The ambulance left the Mansion behind a screen of motorcycles with screaming sirens. Paul Dudley White appeared. ("They wanted me on hand in case anything needed to be done," he said.) Another specialist was stopped by state policemen in South Carolina and hurried aboard a jet trainer for a supersonic trip to Walter Reed, where a dozen surgeons were examining the lower part of the President's digestive system. Surgery was necessary—without it the condition could lead to gangrene of the bowel—but Hagerty had been right, there was nothing to worry about. Afterward Dr. Leonard D. Heeton, the leading surgeon, was asked whether he thought Ike should decline to run for reelection. He said, "I certainly do not." Of the President's life expectancy Snyder said, "We think it improves it." The physicians estimated that he would be back on the job in four to six weeks, and headlines across the country read OKAY FOR IKE TO RUN SAY DOCTORS.

Kenneth S. Davis, Stevenson's biographer, believed afterward that the frailty of Eisenhower's health, "far from being a hazard to his reelection, was probably a political asset. Having passed through the valley of the shadow of death, he was now a greater hero, more beloved of the populace than before." Davis thinks this was due to Ike's personal qualities, "to the perfection with which he expressed the dominant mood of the country and to the warm affection he personally inspired." Democrats were aware of Eisenhower's appeal and treated him gingerly.

Nixon was another matter. The leaders of the party out of power had noted with grim pleasure that he had reconsidered and decided to run again. They took it as an article of faith that the rest of the country despised the Vice President as much as they did, and they went for him with sandbags. Stevenson called the Vice President "shifty," "rash," "inexperienced," and a "man of many masks," and in Minneapolis on November 5 he told listeners that Nixon "has put away his switch-blade and now assumes the aspect of an Eagle Scout." The Vice President, he reminded them, had recently declared in their city that there would be no war in the Middle East. Like many other Democrats, Stevenson honestly thought that a Nixon succession to the Presidency would be a catastrophe.

Nixon could ignore the opposition, and he did. The critics in his own party were more serious. Ironically, the GOP leader of the "Dump Nixon movement," as it was called, was Harold Stassen, Nixon's first political idol. Not without reason, Stassen believed that the President wouldn't be heartbroken if the movement succeeded. To an adviser Ike expressed doubts about Nixon's stature and then said: "Well, the fact is, of course, I've watched Dick a long time, and he just hasn't grown. So I just haven't honestly been able to believe that he is presidential timber."

At that point the party's rank and file took a hand. Republican voters, always strong for Nixon, let their wishes be known; in the New Hampshire and Oregon primaries 52,202 of them wrote his name in under Ike's. That impressed Nixon, if not Stassen. On April 26 the Vice President asked for an appointment with the President and told him he would be happy to make the race again. Eisenhower rang for Hagerty, who came in to find the two running mates of 1952 grinning at each other. According to Hagerty's recollection, the President said, "Jim, Dick just told me he would be happy to be on the ticket, and he has made up his mind that he would like to run again with me." Adams and Persons came in, and after they had the news Ike said to Hagerty, "What do you think we ought to do on the announcement?" The press secretary suggested that Nixon make it to White House correspondents right now. Eisenhower nodded and said, "Jim, you go with him, and after he finishes his announcement, you say I was delighted to hear this news from the Vice President."

That was the end of serious attempts to dump Nixon in 1956, and for all practical purposes it was the end of Harold Stassen's political career. His arguments had convinced only one delegate, an eccentric Nebraskan named Terry Carpenter who had been identified with the Coughlin-Townsend fringe in the 1930s. In the roll call of states Carpenter expressed his displeasure with Nixon by casting one vice-presidential vote for a mythical "Joe Smith," thereby providing the San Francisco convention with one of its two memorable moments. The other one came when Eisenhower paused in his acceptance speech to berate liberal columnists. That brought the delegates to their feet, roaring. For as long as they could remember they had suffered the barbs and quips of publicists who had small use for them and their party, and now their President gave them a chance to get a little of their own back. Next day the political writers filled columns with passionate defenses of freedom of the press. In the long run it made no difference. The resentment of political journalists was in the open now, and in a later Republican administration Nixon and his own Vice President would build it into a major issue.

Four years earlier Governor Stevenson had won the admiration of the commentators by his dignity and grace in defeat. This was his second time round, and it was too much to expect that he could repeat that sparkling performance. He didn't. He dulled the memory of it. Musing over the tactics which had won in 1952, the Democratic standard-bearer succumbed to the fatal charms of the media manipulators. He allowed himself to be drawn into discussions of the relative merits of the "old" Stevenson and the "new" Stevenson, as if there were two of him running around, and there was a lot of mindless chatter in his entourage about the "blurring" of his "image."

"The campaign of 1956 was curious and special," a veteran Democrat later told Emmet John Hughes. "It was nearly a classic of its kind. For it's almost impossible to recall anything you people did wrong—and nearly as hard to remember anything we did right." The worst thing was Truman's emergence from retirement. Trying to secure the nomination for Governor Averell Harriman of New York, he drew Stevenson into a wasting intraparty fight for political survival, and when he found he couldn't rule the convention he seemed bent upon ruining Stevenson's hopes. In his anger the former President gave the Republicans ammunition beyond their wildest hopes. He called Stevenson a "conservative" who followed the "counsel of hesitation" and lacked "the kind of fighting spirit we need to win."

Stevenson had other handicaps. He should have been dueling with Eisenhower, not Truman and Nixon. But the President had taken a lofty stance above the battle. Like President Roosevelt, he wouldn't let his opponent come to grips with him. When not preoccupied with the deepening crises abroad, he ran serenely on the GOP's bland campaign slogan, "Peace, Progress, Prosperity." Nixon, meantime, had discovered what would later become one of his most familiar political stratagems. Confronted by alternatives, he would choose the popular one while insisting that it was really the harder of the two. It would be "easy," he said, for him to endorse an end to hydrogen bomb testing, as Stevenson was urging. Then, his voice vibrating, the Vice President announced that his conscience compelled him to defy public opinion and call for continuing tests. Actually it was Stevenson who was taking the hard road; few votes were lost that year by demanding bigger and better bombs. Nixon was having it both ways, pleasing the majority while winning marks for audacity.

The professionals in Stevenson's camp warned that the testing issue would alienate large blocs of Democrats, especially in ethnic and blue-collar neighborhoods. He knew it, and his decision to plunge ahead anyway, insisting that what he had to say needed saying, was an example of true political courage. In such moments the gallant candidate of 1952 could still be seen. He hadn't lacked heart then and didn't now. His difficulties were with shrewdness and native cunning—small virtues, perhaps, but essential in a political leader.

To laymen, Eisenhower's testing argument—that improved bombs must be built so that the U.S. could "negotiate" from a "position of strength rather than weakness," that "the only way to win World

War III is to prevent it"—sounded persuasive. While time would later vindicate Stevenson, elections are not won by such moral victories. The cold war was still a formidable reality in 1956. Stevenson misjudged its impact, and not only on the question of testing. In the middle of one address he declared that it was time to take a "new look" at American defenses and to consider "ending the draft." So many voices were raised in protest that he was thrown on the defensive, never a good stance for the challenger.

As November approached, Stevenson's campaign became wobbly. He was tired, he was careless, and in his election eve telecast he was guilty of bad taste. Repugnant as the matter was, he said, "I must say bluntly that every piece of scientific evidence we have, every lesson of history and experience, indicates that a Republican victory tomorrow would mean that Richard M. Nixon would probably be President of the country within the next four years." It was true. Saying it in a nationwide broadcast was another matter. It jarred Stevenson's followers, and it was an unhappy note upon which to end a brave battle against odds.

The dimensions of the second Eisenhower avalanche were awesome. He won 457 electoral votes to Stevenson's 72, amassing a triumphant margin of nearly ten million votes. For the first time in a quarter of a century, Negroes were voting Republican. The President had won two-thirds of the nonunion labor vote and 45 percent of the votes of union members. He had swept all the new suburbs. His plurality was 16 percent, just two points behind Hoover's in 1928.

This time Eisenhower celebrated in the presidential suite of Washington's Sheraton Park. By 9 P.M. what little suspense there had been was over. Sherman Adams was sitting on the floor staring rapturously at a small TV tube. Jerry Persons called out in his Alabama accent: "I want all of you to know that the cradle of the Confederacy—Montgomery, Alabama—has just voted for a Republican for the first time in its history!" Ike led the cheering. To Emmet Hughes he said, "There's Michigan and Minnesota still to see. You remember the story of Nelson—dying, he looked around and asked, 'Are there any of them still left?' I guess that's me. When I get in a battle, I just want to win the whole thing . . . six or seven states we can't help. But I don't want to lose any more. Don't want any of them 'left'—like Nelson. That's the way I feel."

All in all it had been a tedious election. Yet there had been one exciting moment at the Democratic convention. Declining to select his running mate, Stevenson had announced that the delegates would make the choice, and in the ensuing turmoil the watching nation had been given a glimpse of the future.

The scramble was between Estes Kefauver, Albert Gore, Robert Wagner, John F. Kennedy, and—the only man who had come to Chicago as an avowed vice-presidential candidate—Hubert Humphrey. Kefauver won, but Kennedy, in nearly beating him, had made a greater impression on the watching audience. The nomination had seemed to be in his grasp after Senator Lyndon Johnson came out for him, shouting tremulously, "Texas proudly casts its vote for the fighting sailor who wears the scars of battle," but at that moment Missouri switched from Gore to Kefauver. Next day the *New York Herald Tribune*'s convention story began, "The famous Kennedy luck ran out today." Actually, losing the vice-presidential nomination was the luckiest thing that had ever happened to Kennedy. He had appeared on the rostrum to make a short, charming speech of concession, and his winning manner had created an instant Kennedy constituency. The country was now aware of him. As James MacGregor Burns noted, "Kennedy's near-victory and sudden loss, the impression he gave of a clean-cut boy who had done his best and who was accepting defeat with a smile—all this struck at people's hearts in living rooms across the nation."

That was half of it. The other half was that since he hadn't made the ticket, its subsequent defeat couldn't be blamed on him or, more especially, on his Catholicism, which had been regarded as a crushing political handicap since Hoover's rout of Al Smith in 1928. Shortly after the election Kennedy was told that he would easily win the vice-presidential nomination in 1960. "I'm not running for Vice President any more," he said crisply. "I'm now running for President."

Twenty-three

THE PURSUIT OF HAPPINESS

THE EISENHOWER SIESTA, as it may be called, extended from the Korean armistice in 1953 to the autumn of 1957, when Americans who had assumed that their technical supremacy would never be challenged were dismayed to learn that rocketeers in the Soviet Union had stolen a long march on them. After that, the country's self-confidence was never the same. Ahead lay a frantic hundred-billion-dollar scramble to reassert the U.S. technological lead by exploring the stars while, year by year, disheartening developments on earth were causing a new and different erosion of American pride. To those who had cherished it, the 1953–57 breather would come to be remembered as an uncomplicated, golden time, mourned as lost childhoods are mourned and remembered, in nostalgia, as cloudless.

If it was never that splendid, neither was it as flatulent as its intellectuals made it out to be. In their view these were dreary, complacent years of an all-out, pedal-to-the-floor materialistic binge in which mass society bred alienation, conformity, facelessness, and moral emptiness; a frivolous boredom and a joyless vulgarity; a time of rootlessness, when small-town hotels were being replaced by 41,-000 motels, at the more pretentious of which you could, for a quarter, lie on a bed and have your erogenous zones jiggled. The disillusioned saw America as a country in which religion had been reduced to Dial-a-Prayer, *Modern Screen*'s series on "How the Stars Found Faith," and prepackaged sixty-second solutions for every spiritual problem. In this judgment the mid-1950s were entirely lacking in merit, with status being represented by the key to the executive washroom, virility by the Mennen After-Shave Club, democracy by a vote for Miss Rheingold, decor by the knotty pine rumpus room, and economics by You Auto Buy Now.

There *were* a lot of gadgets. Technological change had never held a greater fascination for Americans. Men talked wonderingly of transistors, those slivers of germanium or silicon no bigger than a shoelace tip which, when not running tiny radios like Congressman Hebert's, were powering hearing aids so small that they could fit in the frames of spectacles and lightening the load of fighter planes by 1,500 pounds. But all the gadgetry wasn't necessarily bad. Only an ascetic crank could despise the Simmons Company for promoting king- and queen-sized Beautyrest mattresses. If it was absurd to find strips of paper across motel toilet seats reading "This seat has been sterilized for your protection," the fact remained that too much cleanliness was preferable to too little. And after Los Alamos and all that it was rather engaging to find that American technologists were now making life more comfortable.

There was nothing inherently wrong with the innovations, though their sheer number was sometimes bewildering: central vacuuming, vinyl flooring, push-button phones, stereo FM sets, washer-dryers, automatic transmissions, drive-in shopping malls, air-conditioned buses, electric blankets, electric floor polishers, electric pencil sharpeners, electric can openers, and electric floor waxers, to name only the most conspicuous. One by one they appeared, were assimilated into the general experience, and became a part of the average middle-class American's routine. And little by little the more practical innovations altered everyday existence. At one time or another in the mid-1950s millions of men and women of the swing generation realized that in countless little ways life had become easier, more tolerable, more convenient, more interesting—in a word, more livable. At about the same time they remembered the Depression. With a sense of awe they realized: *It's gone.*

And so it had. Evidence of a surge to abundance was everywhere. The boom arose from many springs; natural resources, global politics after World War II, demography, the altered economy of Western Europe, and Americans' love of work. The United States was producing half of the world's goods. Since the war the Gross National Product had doubled. (By the early 1970s it would double again.) U.S. investment abroad had increased from twelve billion dollars to eighty billions. The budget of one firm, General Motors, had grown to the size of Poland's.

The consequence of all this was a standard of living beyond the comprehension of the rest of the world. Nearly 60 percent of all American families were reporting wages in the middle-class brackets. Just since the late 1940s the median family income had risen from $3,083 to $5,657; even when corrected for inflation this meant a rise of 48 percent. America, in Adolf A. Berle's phrase, was in the throes of "galloping capitalism." The proletariat was being transformed. Assembly line workers with working wives were driving expensive new automobiles and buying stocks. *Fortune* in May 1954 suggested that it was "time to change the stereotype of the American middle-class consumer. He is not, and has not been for some years, a small landlord or drugstore proprietor. If any stereotype at all is meaningful, it might be the machinist in Detroit."

No sooner had the Depression survivor comprehended the new prosperity than he became obsolescent. Economic prosperity had been the impossible dream of his youth. His fiscal instincts were timid, defensive; if he could get a hundred dollars together, he squirreled it away. But thrift had suddenly become old-fashioned. Americans who had come of age since World War II, who had no memory of the lean years, were spending every cent they could lay their hands on together with other income they wouldn't earn for a long time to come. "Big spender" became a term of approbation. The spenders were living on credit and buying on margin like the speculators of 1929, except that they were acquiring consumer goods, not securities. Life for them was life on the installment plan. Between 1952 and 1956 consumer debt in the United States increased from 27.4 billion dollars to 42.5 billions, or 55 percent. Installment credit grew 63 percent and that for automobiles almost 100 percent. Though these were boom years, disposable income for individuals increased by merely 21 percent. The new Americans were in hock to the future, and they were plainly enjoying it. They spoke with easy confidence of "debt consolidation" and revolving credit plans. A new profession, debt counseling, sprang up to advise them on ways of handling their credit.

Even the big earners among the new suburbanites saved little. In both Long Island's Levittown and Illinois's Park Forest, the average bank deposit was about $300. Accustomed to tax withholding and packaged mortgages, the young couples were indifferent to rates of interest. Installment buyers asked of a new purchase only the size of the monthly payments. They actually seemed to find security in the entrapment of bank loans, in the obligations of coupon books with specified payments and debts. And the banks were delighted to oblige them. "Instead of merchandising the idea of saving," William H. Whyte Jr. observed, they were providing "the apparatus of it."

Grasshoppers, their scandalized parents called them. Older brothers and sisters were also shocked. Over and over one heard couples in their thirties say of those in their twenties, "When we were that age we wouldn't have dreamed of going into debt." But in the past Americans had lacked the protection of such institutions as hospital insurance and expanded social security. There were fewer reasons for nest eggs now. In a short-term emergency the new people could always float another loan. That clearly violated the precepts of rugged individualism—what Max Weber called the Protestant ethic—but it was individualism, the young hedonists in the developments pointedly replied, which had led to the Depression. In ads one noted a decline in the very vocabulary of the Protestant ethic: such verbs as "compel," "force," "climb," and "control" had become unfashionable. Spending was not only more fun, the young argued; it was more sensible. Some thought it more patriotic, too. One radio station recorded a five-voice choir singing a jingle which ended, "Buy, buy something that you need today" and played it seventy times a day.

Even if you didn't need what you bought, you were still fueling the boom. Any tendency to go the other way was considered alarming. One New York newspaper reported that a "rise in thrift" was "disturbing the administration." Madison Avenue quoted Samuel Butler—"All progress is based upon a universal desire on the part of every organism to live beyond its income"—and a researcher for the J. Walter Thompson agency came up with an indulgent quotation from, of all people, Benjamin Franklin: "Is not the hope of being one day able to purchase and enjoy luxuries a great spur to labor and industry? . . . May not luxury therefore produce more than it consumes, if, without such a spur, people would be, as they are naturally enough inclined to be, lazy and indolent?" (In the ad citing this reflection the agency said that it "appears to be a mature afterthought, qualifying his earlier and more familiar writings on the importance of thrift.")

John Kenneth Galbraith maintained that talk of customer sovereignty had become nonsense. Demand was managed; consent was engineered; the public was being subjected to organized bamboozlement. This was consumership, as essential to an understanding of the evolving new economy as Dullesship was to an understanding of American policy abroad. In the packaged suburbs it was called the "good life." It meant the gratification of acquisitive desires—the split-level home, two cars in the two-car garage, a boat, a place at the beach, more new possessions as old ones wore out or became unfashionable (which was often, thanks to the wizards of planned obsolescence), and, somewhere in the nebulous future, college educations for the children, who would then begin to repeat the process. But the prosperity psychology was not confined to the suburbanites. It was meant to include everyone in the growing middle class. It had to be; mass production assumed mass consumption. Farther down the status ladder, Americans whose lower incomes would not permit a move to the Park Forests, Park Merceds, and Drexelbrooks (that is, an income below $4,800 to $5,200) participated by buying other wares, notably those hawked in television commercials: beers, dentifrices, pain-killers, rinses, cake mixes, laxatives, detergents, razor blades, skin conditioners, cigarettes, and—the big purchase for most families—new cars. In the relentless propaganda for goods in general, viewers were ceaselessly urged to be on the lookout for advertised brands, to get them, to incur debt with approved finance companies if that was necessary, and to participate in the huckstered vision of the good life or risk the loss of everything they prized, including their own sense of identity.

The concepts of consumer exploitation and manipulation were not new to the mid-1950s, but widespread awareness of them was. Motivational research, with all it implied, was becoming highly sophisticated. Its seductive presence was felt in virtually every walk of life. The candor of advertising's chief legerdemainists was sometimes breathtaking. They gloried in building empires on the smell of soap, the texture of its suds, the whiteness of textiles. At their wish, they boasted—and they had polls and sales figures to confirm them—buyers from Oregon to Cape Cod switched to Marlboros, discarded their undershorts for jockey shorts by Fruit of the Loom, or made pilgrimages to the loan companies so their wives and daughters could answer affirmatively the famous question which, Philip Wylie had said, was inherent in all ads beamed at American women: "Madam, are you a good lay?"

Of the creative pitchmen A. C. Spectorsky said:

> These people, God save us all, set the styles, mold the fashions, and populate the dreams of the rest of the country. What they do will be done, a few weeks or months later, by their counterparts in Lake Forest and Santa Barbara and on the Main Line. What they decree, via such esoteric channels as the "People Are Talking About . . ." feature in *Vogue*, will all too often be picked up and actually talked about, in Beverly Hills, Grosse Pointe, and Sewickley. What they tell us to buy, by God, we buy.

Spectorsky was fascinated by these transactions. Others were more judgmental. The deliberate encouragement of irrational behavior and impulse buying constituted an invasion of privacy, they said; people were being victimized. The creation of wants was a form of enslavement, and the critics believed that they could detect symptoms of profound disturbance beneath the prosperous surface of Eisenhower America. The figures on alcoholism and addiction to the new tranquilizers were alarming. By 1957 drug sales had increased sevenfold since the end of the war. There was much more shoplifting. In one Illinois community the average shoplifter was not, as might be expected, a figure of destitution or even want. She was, the chief of police said, a housewife married to a junior executive making $8,000 a year; she was a churchgoer, active in the PTA, a member of a bridge club, and a consumer with about $50 a week to spend.

Galbraith was troubled by society's double standard: "Anything which increases production from given sources is good and implicitly important; anything which inhibits or reduces output is, *pro tanto*, wrong." The prophets of self-indulgence and accumulation applauded private goods but recoiled from public services—education, public health, crusades against urban blight. According to that reasoning, Galbraith contended, it was "unquestionably more rewarding, in purely pecuniary terms, to be a speculator or a prostitute than a teacher, preacher or policeman." The younger generation was being "prevulgarized," Louis Kronenberger wrote, "as materials are said to be preshrunk." Edmund Wilson wrote: "Production, consumption and profit have come to play the role that religion played in our grandfather's generation." Such things, he said, could not even be discussed, since "they have taken the place of the Book of Genesis and the divinity of Jesus Christ." To some observers the admen seemed to be stockbrokers in neuroses. Walter Lippmann scorned them as "new barbarians," and Galbraith, in a striking passage, indicted consumerism and at the same time provided later writers with a bench mark against which to measure the very different society of the late 1960s and early 1970s:

These are the days in which even the mildly critical individual is likely to seem like a lion in contrast with the general mood. These are the days when men of all social disciplines and all political faiths seek the comfortable and the accepted; when the man of controversy is looked upon as a disturbing influence; when originality is taken to be a mark of instability; and when, in minor modification of the scriptural parable, the bland lead the bland.

An understanding of the social revolt that came fifteen years later is impossible without some grasp of the 1950s life-style which arose from the new prosperity. Here, as elsewhere, the character of the time is most easily discerned in the new suburbs. They were not representative of all America (hardly anyone ever died there, for example, and there were almost no unmarried adults) but they did represent what America was becoming. It was there that junior executives unwound after each day, there that their wives honored what Betty Friedan would call the "feminine mystique"—and there that future hippies and straights roamed the community playgrounds.

The vast internal migration of the early 1940s had continued, in a somewhat lower key, in the postwar period. Throughout the 1950s over a million farmers were leaving their farms each year—17 million altogether for the postwar era by the 1960s. At the same time the centers of the cities, once so splendid, were being deserted—to become ghettos of the poor and bastions of the rich. The rest fled and camped outside. Even in so settled a prewar suburb as Stratford, Connecticut, commutation tickets had doubled and then tripled, and in the new cities the figures comprised virtually the entire male population. Every weekday morning now hundreds of thousands of white-collar workers rode or drove into Manhattan; every evening they returned home. At the end of the 1950s the population of the island south of City Hall was over a million by day—and about two thousand at night. During the decade more than a million New Yorkers left the city to live in the postwar communities ringing it. The suburbs, John Brooks wrote, were "draining downtown of its nighttime population, except for night watchmen and derelicts; it was becoming a part-time city, tidally swamped . . .

when the cars and commuter trains arrived and abandoned again at nightfall when the wave sucked back—left pretty much to the thieves, policemen, and rats."

It was the same in all American metropolises. Of the thirteen million new homes which were built in settled areas in the ten years before 1958, about eleven million—85 percent—were outside the inner cities. Refugees from both the farms and the central cities were converging on townships which hadn't even existed on V-J Day. The loss of metropolitan vigor was especially significant. In the past it had served as a magnet for the young and ambitious. Now it was flowing into the rising communities on the perimeters of the cities, to the curving superblocks, garden duplexes, and red brick labyrinths and manicured lawns of suburbia. There stood the dormitories of the new people, the swing generation and its younger cousins. In these developments the new life-style flourished.*

Its most conspicuous quality was a tremendous emphasis on social skills. Rural and small-town America had been strongholds of what David Riesman called "inner-directed" men and women. The source of their direction—he compared it to a gyroscope—was planted early in life by parents and never wavered afterward. The classic example of inner direction was the Englishman who dressed for dinner in the jungle. In the suburbs an entirely different type was gaining ascendancy: the "other-directed Americans." Their impetus came from an insatiable need to be liked. Riesman likened this to radar picking up impulses. The response was an adjustment to what the group wanted. In the Hillendales and Gardenvilles the accolade was to be called "well-adjusted."

These characteristics were not new to the postwar United States. Seymour Martin Lipset argues persuasively that Americans, with their lack of an autocracy and their emphasis on egalitarianism, have always been other-directed, and Alexis de Tocqueville found supportive evidence more than a hundred years ago. Though Americans took great pride in talking about their individualism, he noted, their special genius—and the source of their greatest potential weakness —lay in their ways of cooperation with each other. If America ever lost that drive, he predicted, it would be through strengthening social virtues at the expense of all others, creating a dictatorship of the majority. "In times of equality," he wrote, "no matter what political

---

* The word "development" has since come to mean a publicly financed housing project. Here it is used in its earlier sense, as a tract of developed land.

laws men devise for themselves, it is safe to foresee that trust in common opinion will become a sort of religion, with the majority as its prophet." The danger in this was that the individual might be "overwhelmed by the sense of his insignificance and weakness."

This is precisely what such critics as William Whyte thought they saw emerging in the suburbs of the 1950s. The great stress on behavior acceptable to the team was inhibiting to the individual, they believed; it was thwarting natural leaders and creating a new breed of yes-men. In some ways that was inevitable. Small business was going under everywhere. Americans increasingly were employed by bureaucracies, both private and public. In 1956 the country passed a milestone as important, in its way, as the closing of the frontier in 1890: the number of blue-collar workers (people producing things) was surpassed by that of white-collar workers (in middle-class, service occupations). Increasingly the representative wage earner became the pencil pusher working for a large, impersonal entity. In the newly developed areas it sometimes seemed that everyone was employed by a vast floating cooperative. The swing generation had become a generation of technicians, of interchangeable parts. Its members knew it—and for the most part they liked it.

To be sure, they often spoke of life as a treadmill, but their despair was a mock despair; if they felt imprisoned, their prison was the most comfortable in history, as they would have been the first to point out. Paternalism had become benevolent. The most modest example was RCA's issuance of company neckties. Other corporations went farther. Richfield Oil erected model homes and IBM built country clubs; Reynolds Tobacco engaged company chaplains and Eastman Kodak and Du Pont employed staff psychiatrists. To junior executives who spent their weekdays in such corporate wombs, a carryover of organizational principles in the home neighborhood was only natural.

"It seemed to me," John Steinbeck wrote of the newly organized, "that they looked at me for a place to insert a coin." That was unfair. There was nothing inherently wrong in Park Merced's employment of uniformed attendants to cut the grass, or in Drexelbrook's annual Christmas decoration contest for its 1,223 garden apartments, in which the rivalry between garden courts became so imaginative that a hundred thousand Philadelphians drove out every year to see it. Life in the developments was in many ways an improvement over the life its dwellers had known as children in the 1930s, and not just because everyone was now prosperous. Even as modern business kept all ways of advancement open in order that any junior executive might graduate one day to Westchester, Bull Valley, or Bloomfield Hills, so were the new suburbs free, unstructured, and genuinely hospitable to anyone from any background except blacks, whose time had not yet come. Families moving in found that their new neighbors were eager to help them unpack, take care of their children, and feed them until they had settled down. Even William Whyte conceded that the young suburbanites had achieved "a pretty high quotient of kindliness and fundamental decency."

They owned their own homes, and that was important; it satisfied an old American yearning. Their sense of community was rooted in the American past, too; the pioneers had also been generous and hospitable. The new people were relaxed and informal, almost to a fault. Sport shirts and denim pedal pushers replaced collars and hose. Mother wouldn't have dreamed of going downtown without dressing; now her daughter went with her hair in curlers, and if anyone thought the kerchief over it suggestive of the babushkas worn by the peasant women of eastern Europe, she didn't care. Her concern was the attitude of the other girls in her neighborhood. They did the same thing and would have been disappointed in her if she had done anything else.

Children in the developments exchanged toys and clothes almost as though they were community property, which they almost were. If little Bobby had outgrown his playsuit, it went to little Billy across the way. It wasn't unusual for a mother to recognize a familiar garment on a strange child long afterward; since she had given it away it had passed through several households. Bikes and scooters were also exchanged. Front doors were unlocked; neighbors felt free to enter without knocking. Doors inside were disappearing. So were the massive overstuffed chairs of the Thirties, the heavy rugs and the inside walls; the formal dining room mother had dusted every day and used only for big meals had been replaced by a single living-dining-kitchen area, and the suburbanites saw little reason to mourn its loss, even when guests came. The sitdown dinner had been succeeded by casserole dinners, served buffet style. Sometimes they were awkward, but no one seemed to mind. This way a hostess could enjoy her own party.

The host usually mixed the drinks beforehand, which in 75 percent of the dwellings were martinis. If there was an uprising in the nursery he hurried off to suppress it. Suburban fathers took a livelier interest in their children; home had become a place for companionship and recreation. Nearly two-thirds of all American husbands were helping with housework by 1954, and in the developments the percentage was higher. In addition, and to a degree which often amazed their own parents, the young fathers there were pitching in to help with the dishes, the cooking, and the diapering of the babies. Russell Lynes complained that the young wives were beginning to treat their husbands as part-time servants or as the latest new appliance, but to the new men there was nothing emasculating about stopping at the supermarket for extra groceries on the way home from work, or filling in at the laundromat, or pushing the stroller around the block. They believed it was good for them and good for their families. Spock was the grandfather clock by which the new fathers set their watches, and he approved, and that made it right.

Suburban mothers, in the togetherness vanguard, seemed very young and often were. During the 1950s the age at which U.S. women married dropped from twenty-two to twenty and into the teens. High school marriages became an accepted phenomenon. Children began going steady in junior high school. Girls began thinking about their weddings then or even earlier; a *New York Times* advertisement for a child's dress said, "She Too Can Join the Man-Trap Set."

Being a successful man-trap entailed being desirable—a good lay, in Wylie's phrase; ideally, a great lay. To achieve this happy state females of all ages invested in wardrobes, cosmetics, and exotic perfumes whose makers claimed that they incited rape. Since 1939 the average woman had shrunk three or four sizes. Instead of shopping for a dress her size, she now found one she liked and then dieted to fit it. Metrecal made its appearance and found an eager mass market. So did a new Clairol slogan: "If I have only one life, let me live it as a blonde." Some social scientists and aging suffragettes worried about women's reckless haste to abandon their hard-won independence, but their voices were muffled. *Life* applauded the mass movement of girls into the home, and in a cover story on the suburban wife *Time* reported that wives were "having too good a time . . . to believe that they should be unhappy." The truth, Carl N. Degler wrote, was that "American society in general, which includes women, shuns like a disease any feminist ideology."

By the late 1950s the U.S. birth rate was approaching India's. The number of U.S. mothers who had given birth to three or more children had doubled in twenty years. The increase was most spectacular among college women; they were abandoning careers to bear four, five, and six or more children. The percentage of females in the American college population (35 percent) was lower than that in any European country and smaller than the prewar figure on U.S. campuses (40 percent). Nearly two-thirds of matriculating girls dropped out before graduation, while more than half the men stayed. Many coeds left the classroom to take menial jobs, supporting their partners, who remained on campus; this was called the degree of "Ph.T." (Putting Husband Through). Other women quit because they had *not* acquired spouses. Deans' offices found that coeds were leaving at the end of the first year or two because they had found the pickings slim and wanted to try their luck elsewhere.

To ambitious junior executives hanging their hats in Levittown and casting covetous eyes on Westchester, the right spouse was as important as a hearty chuckle and a sincere necktie. Corporations set up training programs to show company wives what they should and should not do, and *Fortune* found in interviews that the wives, especially the young ones, approved of the idea. They felt that women should become gregarious if they were shy, and, if they were smarter than men, learn to hold their tongues. Several movies of the time dramatized their situation, among them *Executive Suite* and *Woman's World*. The theme in each was a corporation's search for the right man to fill a big job and how a wise mate could help her man by wearing the right dress, hiring the right interior decorator, choosing the right friends, and serving the boss his favorite menu when he came to dinner.

The very anonymity of the big corporation served to sap confidence and independence in men and women dependent on it. So did their own lack of roots. In the front office, where employees were so many pins on a map, personnel chiefs seemed to move them about with reckless abandon. Each relocation meant farewells to friends and the search for new ones elsewhere. The *Wall Street Journal* reported that a Montgomery Ward executive and his family had been moved twenty-eight times in twenty-six years of marriage. Growing mobility was a fact of suburban life. According to Atlas Van Lines, the average corporate manager now moved fourteen times in his lifetime, once every two and a half years. For him the ability to adjust to new circumstances was important to a degree beyond the comprehension of men who live their lives in one place. Though the premium on socialization in the developments sometimes became excessive, the alternative—a family dependent upon its own emotional resources—was considered worse.

Suburbia was superbly equipped to meet the needs of newcomers. Its inhabitants had little reason to feel lonely. The American compulsion to join every association on sight found its ultimate expression there. Meetings were scheduled by one organization or another at every hour from breakfast to late in the evening. Partners were always available for bridge, canasta, poker and bowling. Camera, bird-watching, gun, embroidering, archery, and ping-pong clubs flourished; so did PTAs, the League of Women Voters, the ADA, the Minute Women and, beginning in 1958, the John Birch Society.

Many Americans who would later rise in public life began to acquire their political expertise in suburbia's constant shuffle of adjustment. Here they were likelier to be Republican than in their old neighborhoods. Socially ambitious couples arriving from the inner cities switched their party affiliations—much as they abandoned other lower-class ways. Their parents had contributed to the Democratic party's huge great urban majorities. They didn't. Now that they had made it, they wanted to pull the ladder up behind them. In Europe the postwar expansion of labor unions was leading to the formation of a large, militant, class-conscious force. Not here; although eighteen million industrialized U.S. workers were now unionized, their craving for middle-class status, and the frequency with which it was being satisfied, created instead a large new middle group. Uneasy in their new roles, distrustful of liberalism, and deeply hostile toward further social reforms, they constituted a neoconservative force which would become increasingly significant as the old Roosevelt coalition faltered.

The most common indictment of suburbia's life-style was that it was oppressive. Its passion for informality was so intense that preference for privacy was treated almost as a sign of malaise. Picture windows became windows for looking in. Couples who wanted to lock out the neighbors occasionally were expected to provide an explanation afterward. The group felt it had a right to know everything—"Did you have your period yesterday?" or "Who was that woman you were talking to at Stop and Shop?" or "Your Roger was looking daggers when he left for the office this morning. What's his problem?"

The term "polite society" fell into disuse because society wasn't polite any more. The increasing use of first names was extraordinary. Once it had been limited to family and friends. Then it was extended to colleagues at work and the neighborhood. At office parties and neighborhood cocktail parties finding out who you were talking to became increasingly difficult. Last names were used only in introductions; afterward everyone was Al, Debby, Chuck, or Beth. Eventually the circle of first-namers widened to include virtually everyone who knew who you were: doctors, tradesmen, the children of others, etc. The suburbanite who arrived home to find her bathroom being used by a strange boy might be greeted, "Hi, Doris." In suburbia this was looked upon as just friendliness. Any objection to it would be regarded as snobbish and resented.

One option closed to the suburbanite was scolding someone else's child—in the idiom of earlier generations, "correcting" him. Any correction had to come from his own parents, and there wasn't much of it. Children were special people in the new communities. Whether or not they benefited from their status was a question which would later be debated nationally. Certainly they weren't neglected. Permissiveness took time and patience, and the parents in the developments were among the most permissive in the country. Children made other demands on their time. A mother was expected to plan her youngster's activities and then chauffeur him to them. At times this required the energy and ingenuity of a Grossinger's social director, for suburbia's children were busy all the time. Sociologists were struck by the remarkable degree to which their lives were organized for them. After school and on Saturdays, hurrying station wagons crisscrossed suburbia, carrying their charges to dancing lessons, Little League practice, tennis lessons, sailing lessons, play groups, parties, piano lessons, Cub Scouts, dramatic school—schedules which returned them home just in time for dinner and evenings in front of the television set. So occupied were they, Henry A. Murray protested in *Daedalus*, that their chances of growing into individuals were being curtailed sharply, if not crushed altogether; "parents make their babies play with other babies," he wrote, "as soon as they can toddle." The swing generation wasn't much interested in individuality. Though older executives still paid lip service to it, their juniors were more anxious to raise children who, as they put it, could "get along with other people." They admired that quality in one another, sought to develop it in themselves, and saw it becoming the key to success in the next generation.

The upshot was that millions of pupils approached the age of awareness equipped with marvelous radar but no gyroscopes. They were well instructed about society's need for morale but hadn't been told what it produced; they knew a great deal about achieving popularity but very little about achieving anything else. "Give me a boy for the first seven years and he will be a Catholic for life," a prelate had said. The apostles of adjustment had more than seven years, and it is doubtful that even the church could have done a more thorough job than they did. First mothers instilled in children the necessity for wooing their peers. Next came practice workouts in sandboxes and on swing sets. Activities followed: Brownies, Little Leagues, etc. The propaganda for good fellowship was relentless. Sunday schools in the modern churches taught that God was really just a pal; that religion was fun, like the movie nuns who played softball and rode around in helicopters. Any fledgling Luther who felt inclined to cultivate his own identity was exhorted not to by the mass media, while the last layers of goodguymanship polish were zealously applied in the new suburban schools.

The character and quality of classroom instruction in America varied from one community to another. In some, McGuffey readers and rote memorization were still prevalent. One-teacher public elementary schools were on the way out, however; their number dropped from 143,391 in 1932 to 59,652 in 1950, and at the end of the Eisenhower era they would be down to 20,213. The leaders in the profession, honored at teachers' conventions and teachers colleges and extolled by the National Education Association, were advocates of what was called progressive education. It wasn't really progressive. It had been that, in its beginnings as a movement, when it was dedicated to freeing the imaginative child from lockstep classroom discipline and encouraging him to develop his own individuality. Then, as educators became more enthusiastic about developing social skills, teachers replaced the old stress on intellectual attainments with the even greater constraints involved in turning a child into what Gesell profiles suggested he should be.

Pupils in these schools were not told what they must learn. They were asked to choose their own electives. To avoid fixed standards of performance ("straitjackets," they were called), grades were often limited to "satisfactory" and "unsatisfactory." Courses in "family living" replaced algebra, geometry, grammar, and foreign languages. At times the attitude of the new educators toward the traditional academic disciplines bordered on outright hostility. Eric Baber, superintendent of the Park Forest, Illinois, high school, which in 1954 was chosen one of the five winners in the "All America Schools" contest of the National Municipal League, deplored the stubbornness with which college admissions offices clung to entrance requirements. "The so-called 'bright student,'" he said, "is often one of the dumbest or least apt when he gets away from his textbooks and memory work. This is evidenced by the fact that many $20,000-to-$100,000 jobs in business, sales, sports, radio . . . are held by persons with I.Q.s of less than ninety."

Alert to signs of what was denigrated as "maladjustment," teachers in schools participated in their pupils' choices of friends, their games at recess, their very fantasies. Instead of visiting national monuments, classes visited dairies or grocery stores. Learning to become consumers, they gathered information that, they were told, would be useful to them in later life. In such "doing" sessions, supervisors explained at PTA meetings, pupils were participating in actual situations. Abjuring what was called "elitism," they were concentrating not on what changes might be made in life, but how to make them "without upsetting human relationships." "Ours is an age of group action," Dr. Baber told a teachers' workshop, stressing the need to emphasize the extroverted side of their pupils' nature. So the children were taught, and so they learned to be "well-rounded"—people who understood that the goals of the individual and the goals of society were identical. If uncertain about a problem, they polled one another.

Some parents objected. They wanted to bring back Latin, chemistry, integral calculus—courses that colleges and universities also wanted. Smiling principals shook their heads and replied, "We teach the child, not the subject." They believed that in preparing pupils for participation in the consumer world they were taking a practical, realistic, hardheaded approach which would be vindicated by the future.

On October 4, 1957, Tass, the Soviet news agency, had an interesting item for the American public. "The first artificial earth satellite has now been created," it announced. "This first satellite was successfully launched in the USSR . . . Artificial earth satellites will pave the way for space travel and it seems that the present generation will witness how the freed and conscious labor of the people of the new socialist society turns even the most daring of man's dreams into reality."

To grasp the full impact of this announcement, it must be remembered that in 1957 the United States was still regarded as the home of scientific innovation. It was a running joke of the postwar years that from time to time Moscow would announce that this or that Russian—usually some Ivan or Ilya no one had ever heard of—was responsible for a discovery which everyone outside the Soviet Union knew had been made in the United States. Americans had grown up believing they held a virtual monopoly on technological ingenuity. Now the proud were fallen. In addition they were mortified. Nikita Khrushchev was crowing, "People of the whole world are pointing to the satellite. They are saying that the U.S. has been beaten." And so they were. Tass called the space vehicle a *sputnik;* literally a "traveling companion" or, more appropriately, a "fellow traveler." It instantly won the attention of the world. To the United States it came as a shock on the order of the Crash.

Montage: Eisenhower At Flood Tide

Best actor of 1956: Yul Brynner in The King and I
Best actress of 1956: Ingrid Bergman in Anastasia

Stevenson, Stevenson
If you vote for Stevenson
He will be, easily,
President next year
Help him win, get him in
Now the fight's begun
Gotta be, gotta be, gotta be
Believe in Stevenson!

Dear <u>Modern Screen</u>:
I think you had a hand in the reconciliation of the Dean Martins. You wrote on "open letter" in <u>Modern Screen</u> telling Dean and Jeanne how silly they were to stay apart when they really love one another. I read your words, and I bet they did, too.
And after this fling   Maria, New York
Who could blame Mr. Bing
If he shipped Madam Callas to Dallas?

Shortly after 8 o'clock on Sunday night, Staff Sergeant Matthew C. McKeon limped into the barracks of Platoon 71 at the U.S. Marine Corps Recruit Depot, Parris Island, S.C. . . . The 74 boots of Platoon '71 followed him toward the salt tidal marshes of Parris Island, where death was waiting.

ALTHEA GIBSON WINS WIMBLEDON TROPHY

La Strada

SCOTT paper has WET STRENGTH

A white sport coat and a pink carnation
I'm all dressed up for the dance
A white sport coat and a pink carnation
I'm all alone in romance

The wedding day burst fair and warm; Margaret Truman walked out of the 91-year-old house a last time on the arm of her ever-punctual, this time solemn father. "She looks beautiful, Mr. Truman," called a voice from the crowd. "Thank you, thank you very much," said the father of the bride. "I think so, too."

YOUTHFUL INSURGENTS ATTACK BATISTA'S PALACE: 46 DIE

BEST SELLERS: Fiction
Don't Go Near the Water by William Brinkley
By Love Possessed by James Gould Cozzens
The Last Hurrah by Edwin O'Connor
Auntie Mame by Patrick Dennis
Peyton Place by Grace Metalious

Around the World in 80 Days

U.S. INTERSTATE HIGHWAY SYSTEM TO BE LAUNCHED

PLEASE INFORM EUROPE AND THE AUSTRIAN GOVERNMENT . . . THEY OPENED FIRE ON EVERYBODY . . . A FEW HUNDRED TANKS ATTACKED BUDAPEST . . . THERE IS HEAVY FIGHTING . . . I STAY OPEN AND CONTINUE WITH THE NEWS . . . WE SHALL INFORM THE WORLD ABOUT EVERYTHING. LONG LIVE HUNGARY AND EUROPE. THE RUSSIANS ARE USING PHOSPHORUS BULLETS. ANY NEWS ABOUT HELP? QUICKLY, QUICKLY, WE HAVE NO TIME TO LOSE. NO TIME TO LOSE. I AM RUNNING OVER TO THE WINDOW IN THE NEXT ROOM TO SHOOT BUT I WILL BE BACK. WE WILL HOLD OUT TILL THE LAST DROP OF BLOOD. GOOD-BYE FRIENDS. GOOD-BYE FRIENDS. GOD SAVE OUR SOULS. THE RUSSIANS ARE TOO NEAR. The Edsel performs fine, rides well, and handles good.

The Catered Affair

WEST SIDE STORY

Book by Arthur Laurents
Music by Leonard Bernstein
Lyrics by Stephen Sondheim

✦

WINTER GARDEN
Just walking in the rain gettin' soaking wet
Torturing my heart by trying to forget
Just walking in the rain so alone and blue
All because my heart still remembers you

Standing on the corner watching all the girls go by
Standing on the corner watching all the girls go by
Brother you don't know a nicer occupation
Matter of fact neither do I
Than standing on the corner watching all the girls
watching all the girls watching all the girls
go by

Try Zest — the soapless soap

BEST SELLERS: Nonfiction
Arthritis and Common Sense by Dan Dale Alexander
Kids Say the Darndest Things by Art Linkletter
The Search for Bridey Murphy by Morey Bernstein
Profiles in Courage by John F. Kennedy
Too Much, Too Soon by Diana Barrymore and Gerold Frank

Make me feel real loose
Like a long-necked goose
Oh, baby, that's what I like

You ain't nothin'
but a hound dawg
My baby
rocks me
with a
steady roll

Bus Stop

Where there's life — there's BUD

By ABIGAIL
VAN BUREN

DEAR ABBY

The funniest questions, and the wittiest and wisest answers, from the famous "Dear Abby" column

Twenty-four

BEEP BEEP

T HE FIRST WORD that a Russian sphere the size of a beachball was circling the earth once every 96.2 minutes, traveling at a speed of 18,000 mph and emitting beeping sounds as it did so, had reached Washington, quite by chance, during a cocktail party in the Soviet embassy at 1125 Sixteenth Street. Scientists from twenty-two countries were observing 1957–58 as an International Geophysical Year, or IGY as they called it—a general sharing of data—and Russian diplomats were entertaining fifty IGY luminaries that historic Friday evening when one of the guests, Walter Sullivan of the *New York Times*, was called away for an urgent telephone call. At the phone he learned of the Tass announcement. He hurried back and whispered to an American scientist, Dr. Lloyd Berkner, who rapped on the hors d'oeuvre table until the hubbub quieted. "I wish to make an announcement," he said. "I am informed by the *New York Times* that a satellite is in orbit at an elevation of 900 kilometers.* I wish to congratulate our Soviet colleagues on their achievement."

The room burst into applause. Eminent scientists are indifferent to national loyalties, and the Americans there were particularly generous. Dr. Joseph Kaplan, chairman of the U.S. IGY program, called the Russian achievement "tremendous" and added, "If they can launch one that heavy, they can put up much heavier ones." The White House, however, was momentarily speechless. The advent of the first sputnik astounded U.S. intelligence even though the So-

* Approximately 559 miles.

viets had made no great secret of their satellite plans. At an IGY planning conference in Barcelona Russian delegates had spoken openly and confidently of their plans to launch a space vehicle. As early as November 1954, Defense Secretary Wilson had been asked whether he was concerned over the possibility that the USSR might win the satellite race. He had snorted, "I wouldn't care if they did."

That continued to be the Republican line now that Sputnik was an accomplished fact. Administration spokesmen seemed to suggest that the press was making molehills out of molehills. Hagerty issued a statement describing the satellite as a matter "of great scientific interest" but adding that "we never thought of our program as one which was in a race with the Soviet's." Wilson, now in retirement, called the Russian feat "a nice technical trick." Rear Admiral Rawson Bennett, chief of the Office of Naval Research, wondered why there was so much fuss over a "hunk of iron almost anybody could launch." White House adviser Clarence Randall described the space vehicle as "a silly bauble"—thereby infuriating the President—and Sherman Adams said disparagingly that the government wasn't interested in "an outer-space basketball game." (In his memoirs Adams regretted this. "I was only trying to reflect the President's desire for calm poise," he wrote, "but I had to admit on reflection that my observation seemed to be an overemphasis of the deemphasis.")

Others in Washington were in no mood to dismiss Sputnik so lightly. Trevor Gardner, who as former Assistant Secretary of the Air Force had tried to mediate interservice quarrels over who should run the American space program, said bitterly, "We have presently at least nine ballistic missile programs, all competing for roughly the same kind of facilities, the same kind of brains, the same kind of engines and the same public attention." Electronics and airframe experts recalled Wilson's casual attitude toward space research. "The basic reason we're behind the Russians," a major defense contractor said, "is that we haven't gone all out." One of the President's closest aides said he felt an urge to "strangle" Budget Director Percival Brundage. Knowland privately warned Ike that the worldwide impact of the Soviet accomplishment had all but nullified the value of America's Mutual Security program, and some publicists were actually suggesting a negotiated peace with the Russians "before it is too late."

The Democrats, predictably, were indignant. Senator Henry Jackson of Washington wanted the President to proclaim "a week of shame and danger." Missouri's Symington demanded a special session of Congress. Fulbright of Arkansas said, "The real challenge we face involves the very roots of our society. It involves our educational system, the source of our knowledge and cultural values. And here the Administration's program for a renaissance of learning is disturbingly small-minded." Majority Leader Johnson saw cosmic implications in the Russian success. "The Roman empire controlled the world because it could build roads," he said. "Later—when men moved to the sea—the British Empire was dominant because it had ships. Now the Communists have established a foothold in outer space. It is not very reassuring to be told that next year we will put a 'better' satellite into the air. Perhaps," he concluded sarcastically, "it will even have chrome trim—and automatic windshield wipers."

This was more than partisan oratory. Periodically Americans feel a need to agonize over why the country has gone soft. The last time it had happened had been in the spring of 1940, when France was falling and the older generation thought American youth too engrossed in swing to hear the Nazi jackboots. Now, as then, the press was aroused. "It is downright terrifying with [Sputnik] staring down at us," the Portland *Oregonian* said, and *Time* said that "the U.S. takes deep pride in its technical skills and technological prowess, in its ability to get things done—first. Now, despite all the rational explanations, there was a sudden, sharp national disappointment that Americans had been outshone by the Red moon." John Kenneth Galbraith had been awaiting publication of *The Affluent Society*. Neither he nor his publishers had expected much of a sale. "Then, in the autumn of 1957," he wrote in an introduction to the second edition, "the Soviets sent up the first Sputnik. No action was ever so admirably timed. Had I been younger and less formed in my political views, I would have been carried away by my gratitude and found a final resting place beneath the Kremlin Wall. I knew my book was home."

Americans were learning humility—and humiliation. They had become an international laughingstock. At a scientific conference in Barcelona Leonid I. Sedov, Russia's chief space scientist, taunted a U.S. colleague: "You Americans have a better standard of living than we have. But the American loves his car, his refrigerator, his house. He does not, as we Russians do, love his country." Anti-Americans were derisive. RUSSIANS RIP AMERICAN FACE, read a headline in Bangkok's *Sathiraphab*, and a Beirut professor said dryly of his students, "You would have thought they launched it themselves." The editors of London's *Economist* saw the Russians scoring a brilliant psychological triumph in the Afro-Asian world. French journalists saw the catch, the price the Soviet masses had paid. Thierry Maulnier wrote in *Le Figaro*, "The Russian people can . . . see in the sky a brilliant star which carries above the world the light of Soviet power, thanks to millions of pots and shoes lacking," and *Combat* commented: "We ourselves would like it if the Russians would put some of their pride into the evolution of a better world—an end to the world of concentration camps." But in all Europe only the London *Express*, faithful to Britain's old ally, predicted that somehow the United States would muddle through: "The result will be a new drive to catch up and pass the Russians in the sphere of space exploration. Never doubt for a moment that America will be successful."

Americans themselves had plenty of doubts, and the more they knew about the implications of the Soviet achievement the more apprehensive they became. In those first days virtually all the details about the man-made star came from Tass and *Pravda;* the Smithsonian Institution was building an astrophysical observatory in Cambridge to track precisely this sort of phenomenon, but it was unfinished and unable even to correlate visual observations being phoned to it by widely scattered moonwatchers. The Russians disclosed that their first sputnik was a polished steel ball twenty-two inches in diameter, weighing 184.3 pounds and equipped with four radio antennas. Its orbit was higher than U.S. scientists had thought possible. Because of that height it would avoid the atmosphere and could keep circling the earth for years. Sputnik's weight was also stunning; the directors of America's Vanguard Project, still in the theoretical stage, had been hoping to send a 21.5-pound Navy Viking research projectile to a maximum of 300 miles. That would have required 27,000 pounds of rocket thrust. The Russian catapult had used 200,000 pounds—an incredible figure, clearly indicative of a new source of power.

As new data came in and were digested by MIT computers, American appreciation of Soviet technical virtuosity soared. The orbit was stunning. It was elliptical, of course, carrying the sputnik from an apogee 583 miles above the earth to a perigee 143 miles down, but since both of these distances were added to the radius of the earth (3,960 miles) the ellipse was almost a circle, showing that the Russians had precise control as well as power. Moreover, the launch had been daring. The simplest way to orbit the satellite would have been to aim it eastward from the equator, taking advantage of the earth's rotation to give the object about 1,000 mph of free speed—in effect, a tailwind. Vanguard's planners had expected to do this; according to their calculations the Viking rocket, rising due east from Florida, would have had a 914 mph boost. But Vanguard rocketeers working under lights those first nights were astounded to learn that the Russian course was 65 degrees the other way. That indicated that they had power to burn. It had another significance. Vanguard's course would have kept it south of Europe and most of Russia. Sputnik's journey took it over most of the inhabited earth, meaning most of the world's peoples could see it, as well as hear it and read about it—a propaganda coup in itself.

Americans would be among the last to have a clear view of it, owing, perhaps, to a sly bit of Muscovite humor. The launch had been timed so that during its first weeks the satellite would pass over the United States during the day, when it would be invisible against the glare of the sun, or at night, when the shadow of the earth would hide it. The curious—and there were tens of thousands of them—had to peer up at daybreak and twilight, when the object could be briefly glimpsed against the gray sky. That would change. The orbit was shifting around the earth at four degrees a day, Dr. Joseph A. Hynek of the Smithsonian observatory explained; on about October 20 the sputnik would come into view overhead for those with binoculars or small telescopes. But Americans, impatient as always, wanted to know everything now. They had been huddling over their radios and television sets since that Friday night when an NBC commentator had told them, "Listen now for the sound which forevermore separates the old from the new." Then they had heard it for the first time, alternating between 20 and 40 megacycles—an eerie A-flat beeping from outer space.

It was generally assumed in those early days that the object was sending back signals in cipher, and CIA cryptographers worked in shifts to break the code. A man who could enlighten them happened to be right there in Washington; he was General Anatoly Arkadievich Blagonravov, chief of the three-man delegation Moscow had sent to the IGY conference. There was no code, the general said. The designers had put the beeps in to track the sputnik and reassure themselves that the satellite was still out there. There was nothing in the steel ball except the transmitter and the batteries. The power of the signal was one watt—just about enough for a conversation between hams in Australia and the United States. In about three weeks the batteries would be exhausted, Blagonravov said, and the beeping would stop. A likely story, Americans snorted. Who could trust a Russian general? There was something fishy about those signals. "Many believe that the whole story has not been told," *Time* noted darkly. The CIA had better get to the bottom of it, the man on the street muttered, or the U.S. taxpayer would know the reason why.

Sputnik I dealt the coup de grace to Ford's fading Edsel, which had been introduced to the public the month before, and which was now widely regarded as a discredited symbol of the tinny baubles Americans must thrust aside. There were other scapegoats. The administration was one. It was M. Robert Bendiner who suggested that until now the Republican idea of a scientist had been a man who tore and compared cigarettes on television. Public education was another conspicuous target and did, in fact, have much to answer for. American parents were angered to learn that while their children were being taught "life adjustment," Russian education had been acquiring a reputation for being tough and competitive, ruthlessly winnowing out mediocrities beginning in the fourth grade and awarding to outstanding students the laurels which, in the United States, were reserved for athletes and baton-twirling, tail-twitching cheerleaders.

Parental wrath would grow with the publication of John Gunther's *Inside Russia Today*, then in galleys. Gunther reported that "In the schools which prepare for college, the Soviet child must absorb in ten years what an American child gets in twelve—perhaps more." Russian pupils, he said, went to school six hours a day, six days a week, attending classes 213 days a year as against 180 in the United States, and in the last two years of schooling four hours of homework were assigned each day. Gunther continued:

> . . . the main emphasis is on science and technology, for both boys and girls, and herein lies the greatest challenge to our system. In addition to ten solid years of mathematics, every child must take four years of chemistry, five of physics, six of biology. By contrast, only about half of American high schools have *any* physics, and

only 64 percent have *any* chemistry. An American authority told me that the average Soviet boy or girl graduating from the tenth grade (our twelfth) has a better scientific education—particularly in mathematics—than most American college graduates!

Emphasis on science came early in Soviet schools; pupils began studying optics and quantum theory in grade school. By the mid-1950s the USSR was graduating twice as many scientists and engineers as the United States, and in a sixty-four-page report the National Science Foundation estimated that 14 percent of all Soviet scientists were allowed to pursue basic research—that is, inquiries which may or may not have practical significance. Such work often seems pointless at the time, but it is the restless search for answers by the laboratory man with insatiable curiosity which makes possible the technological miracles of the next generation. Thomas Edison could not have developed the incandescent lamp without Henry Cavendish and Michael Faraday; the atomic bomb became a reality because in 1905 Albert Einstein had published an obscure volume setting forth the proposition, then wholly inapplicable, that energy is encompassed in every bit of matter; and the H-bomb was created by men who had been studying the stars. Charles E. Wilson thought basic research ridiculous. As Secretary of Defense he had once mocked it as finding out "what makes grass green and fried potatoes brown," a remark scientists now remembered and quoted bitterly. The number of Americans in long-range studies was fractional, and the funds allotted to them—about 450 million dollars a year—represented only one-tenth of one percent of the national income.

Now scientists were beginning to speak up. Norbert Wiener had something to say about science and society. Wiener blamed the tight lid government had clamped on research, beginning with radar and the Manhattan Project. The consequence, he said, was that the individual scientist was often not only unaware of the vast problem he was dealing with, but even worse, that his scientific inquisitiveness was frequently discouraged. Physicists pointed out that the Soviets had an 8.3-billion electron-volt particle accelerator (atom smasher), better than America's best, the University of California's betatron, and UCLA's Joseph Kaplan, the U.S. IGY chairman, said, "In oceanography, meteorology, and upper-atmosphere physics, the indications are that they are certainly as good as we are."

Edward Teller also spoke up. Though still a pariah among most of his fellow physicists, Teller remained a brilliant and prescient scholar. His Pentagon friends pointed out that in last April's issue of *Air Force* magazine, six months before the first beep, he had gloomily written: "Ten years ago there was no question where the best scientists in the world could be found—here in the U.S. . . . Ten years from now the best scientists in the world will be found in Russia." In the Soviet Union, he had pointed out, science was almost a religion; its ablest men were singled out and treated as a privileged class while their underpaid American colleagues lacked status in their society and could offer few incentives to bright protégés. His appeal for respect for the dignity of scientific inquiry was well taken. The number of cartoons about mad scientists dropped sharply. There were also fewer jokes about them. And it was extraordinary how quickly the word egghead dropped out of the language.

For some time Walter Lippmann had been urging his countrymen to consecrate themselves to a national purpose. Few had grasped what he had in mind, but now they knew: the national purpose was to rescue education and, with it, America's next generation. Suddenly Rudolf Flesch's *Why Johnny Can't Read—and What You Can Do About It*, which had come out in 1955 without making much of a dent, was on everyone's best-seller list. Hardly anyone had a good word for schools as they were except people like Dr. Ruth Strang of Teachers College, Columbia, and she and TC were in disgrace. Social critics' heaviest guns trained on just such educators, or, as they were derisively christened, "educationists." Chancellor Lawrence A. Klimpton of the University of Chicago explained how the Strangs and the William Heard Kilpatricks had distorted and misrepresented the ideas of John Dewey. Dewey had held that thinking begins in an interest, or a concern. But this had been twisted into an insistence that teachers must amuse, or entertain, pupils.

Herbert Hoover said that the Communists "are turning out twice or possibly three times as many" scientists "as the U.S." He scorned the "too prevalent high-school system of allowing a thirteen- or fourteen-year-old kid to choose most of his studies." That same week another distinguished engineer from whom more would be heard on this score observed in Detroit that one root of the trouble lay in the "misconception of the worth" of the American high school. "We have always overvalued it," said Rear Admiral Hyman G. Rickover, the man responsible for America's atomic submarines. "It comes out," he continued, "that we have many more children in high school and in college than [Europeans] have in secondary schools and universities, and this makes us proud. But all these comparisons are meaningless because the European secondary school graduate has learned more than most of our college graduates. As to the high school diploma," he added heavily, "the less said about it the better."

Even resolute Republicans were uneasy. Clare Boothe Luce, in other ways a steadfast defender of the status quo during the Eisenhower years, found complacency on this issue impossible. She called the sputnik's beep an "outer-space raspberry to a decade of American pretensions that the American way of life is a gilt-edge guarantee of our national superiority." Her husband was also troubled by heretical thoughts. "Turning to Washington for reassurance," *Time* said nervously, "the U.S. saw administrative confusion, sensed a crisis in leadership and demanded action." The stock market tobogganed dizzily downward that week, and with Russia's man-made moon flashing across the skies all America seemed depressed. A contagion of black humor cropped up—proposals to change Project Vanguard's name to Project Rearguard and a story about a Washington reporter who called the U.S. Space Agency, asked how the program was going, and was asked by the girl on the phone, "Sir, are you calling *for* information or *with* information?"

Sputnik I's beeps died away in the last week of October, as General Blagonravov had predicted. It was still there and could be tracked, but at least you couldn't hear it any more. Then, just as Americans had begun to catch their breath, Sputnik II went up on November 3. In some ways it was a more breathtaking achievement than its predecessor. The new satellite weighed 1,120.29 pounds— making it six times as heavy as Sputnik I—and its orbit carried it 1,056 miles away from the earth. "The unfathomed natural processes going on in the cosmos," Moscow radio proclaimed, "will now become more understandable to man." It was true; American scientists were envious. A space vehicle that large would house a maze of instruments radioing back data on cosmic rays, solar radiation above the atmosphere, atmospheric temperature and composition, the danger of meteors, the earth's gravitation, its magnetic field, its electric charge, and the cloud patterns of its weather. The Russians had another surprise. There was a little dog of the *laika* breed aboard, strapped with contrivances which would provide other information about the ability of fauna to survive in space.

It was another luckless day for administration image makers. Ideally news of the event should have found the leaders of the government at their desks furiously striving to catch up. As it happened, Eisenhower was just returning from a West Point class of '15 reunion and homecoming football game, while a Big Ten game had taken Charlie Wilson's successor, the new Secretary of Defense, Neil McElroy, to Columbus.

The United States was in an uproar. The presence of the dog in Sputnik II clearly meant that eventually the Russians intended to put a man on the moon. Most people in the U.S. were determined to beat them there, and they were becoming impatient with the composure of their President. *Time* said: "The storm showed promise of being the most serious that Dwight Eisenhower had ever faced." A headline in the *Pittsburgh Press* begged: SHOOT THE MOON, IKE.

Ike wasn't going to do it. He refused to be stampeded. Unlike the three Presidents who followed him in the White House, he had grave doubts about the wisdom of investing the national resources in space exploration. He was General Eisenhower now, pondering what he saw as a military threat. He knew he was falling in public esteem. To Gallup's question, "Do you approve of the way Eisenhower is handling his job as President?" only 57 percent now answered affirmatively. Previously the figure had rarely dropped below 71 percent. The present decline was greatest in the South, where it had dropped from 72 percent the previous January to an all-time low of 36 percent.* No President enjoys an erosion of popularity, and Ike valued public esteem more than most. But on matters of national security he was the expert, and he had regarded rocketry from the first as a military matter. He suspected his opinion was shared in the Kremlin, and from mid-October on he was certain of it, largely thanks to a remarkable interview with Nikita Khrushchev by James Reston of the *New York Times*.

The first secretary of the Soviet Communist party was in an expansive mood. Elated by the triumphs of his scientists, he boasted that the space satellites were only the beginning of Russia's rocket

---

* Much of the loss here was attributable to the Little Rock crisis. See pages 978–91.

wonders. "When we announced the successful launching of an Intercontinental Ballistic Missile," he gloated, "some American statesmen did not believe us. Now that we have successfully launched an earth satellite, only technically ignorant people can doubt this. The U.S. does not have an intercontinental ballistic missile; otherwise it would also have easily launched an earth satellite of its own." The West, he said, might as well scrap its B-52s and abandon its airfields: "If you study our latest proposals you will no longer find any mention of control posts at airfields* . . . It is useless to create control posts to watch obsolete airplanes." In another interview that same week with two visiting British M.P.s he said even more vividly: "Bombers are obsolete. You might as well throw them on the fire. You cannot send human flesh and blood to fight things like that." A few days later the Russians announced that they had successfully tested a new hydrogen warhead for a guided missile. To General Eisenhower there could be but one interpretation of all this. The skeptics of Russian advances in rocketry had been wrong. Khrushchev had to be believed now. Manned bombers might not yet be obsolete, but they were becoming obsolete. The Soviet Union had in fact developed the dreaded ICBM. The touch of one button in Moscow and Washington would vanish.

The danger then confronting the United States is evident in retrospect:

June 5, 1957 An Army Jupiter travels over 1,500 miles from Cape Canaveral, the first successful flight of an intermediate range weapon (IRBM) for the United States.

August 26, 1957 The USSR reports that it has successfully tested a multistage ICBM.

November 28, 1958 An American Atlas completes a 6,325-mile flight from Cape Canaveral to Ascension Island, the first full-range flight for a U.S. ICBM.

Thus Soviet rocketry held a clear lead for fifteen perilous months. The U.S., to be sure, was hardly defenseless. Despite Khrushchev's jeers at bombers, at every hour of the day and night the vigilant Strategic Air Command had fleets of B-52 jets in the air in a state of readiness with nuclear warheads on board, and the Jupiter IRBMs, poised on NATO bases ringing the Soviet Union, were a powerful deterrent to Russian aggression. Nevertheless, the fact re-

---

* Control posts: radar installations.

mained that America had fallen behind in the vital ICBM race and would remain there for well over a year.

In the seclusion of the presidential mansion, Ike was very different these days from the cool-headed, almost tranquil chief executive who exasperated the White House press corps. "Although Eisenhower maintained an official air of serenity," Sherman Adams later wrote, "he was privately as concerned as everybody else in the country by the jump ahead that the Russians had made in scientific enterprise." Even before the ascent of Sputnik II he had ordered McElroy, sworn in only the day before, to undertake an immediate, urgent review of the country's missile program, and when Emmet John Hughes suggested to him that popular concern could be an advantage, winning support for new programs, the President quickly replied, "Oh, absolutely. Anything that will get us out of this complacency—and make this next Congress realize how serious things are—that's all to the good."

His problem was more complicated than that. If he had revealed the real stakes in this contest with the Russians, Congress and the people would not only have lost their complacency, they might very well have lost their perspective, or even their minds. The previous spring the President had asked H. Rowan Gaither Jr., then chairman of the board of the Ford Foundation, to evaluate the nation's state of defense readiness with the cooperation and guidance of the National Security Council. The results were submitted in November, just after Sputnik II went into orbit. They were so shocking that the President decided to suppress them. The Gaither Report endorsed a proposal for a nationwide nuclear bomb shelter program. The shelter plan was financially impossible, Ike concluded, and he saw no point in publication of a text which would merely terrify the people without offering any hope of a solution.

He believed a solution could be found, however. The answer was to draw ahead, or at least abreast, of the Soviet missile achievements. As he saw it, that was the task before the country, not exploits in outer space. It was as great a challenge as any President had ever faced, and because of it he had no difficulty in keeping his eyes off the stars, though not many in the country, or even in his own administration, could resist the fascination of space travel. Knowland couldn't; Ike had to tell him curtly that he had no intention of being "pushed into an all-out effort in every one of these glamour performances without any idea of their eventual cost." The

President's determination to keep all rocket programs in the Defense Department, at least for the present, was also challenged, by Vice President Nixon and President James R. Killian of MIT, whom Ike appointed special assistant to the President for science and technology on November 7. Eisenhower said to both that the mechanics of launching space rockets and long-range missiles were virtually the same; a costly duplication of effort made no sense to him. Killian was doubtful, and Nixon, supporting Killian, argued that America's image abroad would be more favorable if the peaceful aspects of space exploration were handled by an agency without ties to the country's military establishment. The President, less concerned with image than with survival, replied that he would rather have "one good Redstone nuclear-armed missile than a rocket that could hit the moon." He added pungently, "We have no enemies on the moon."

His wisdom is apparent to a generation accustomed to nuclear weapons housed in hardened silos, Polaris submarines, and fail-safe mechanisms—all the horrid realities of the future from which Ike flinched but which he nevertheless faced. ICBMs, which the Russians had, and the inferior IRBMs, which America had, had not yet found their way into the language. Even the sophisticated had not come to terms with the implications of joining H-bomb warheads to unmanned missiles capable of traversing oceans and continents at speeds even greater than Sputnik I's 18,000 mph. All that was beyond the mind of the average American in 1957. A paragraph in the October 28 *Time* gives some idea of the innocence of the well-informed then. It was headed "What About Armed Satellites?" and it might have been written by Jules Verne:

Many imaginative military planners have dreamed of satellite fortresses armed with nuclear missiles to shoot at the earth below. All space vehicles must be lightly built to conserve weight. They would therefore be vulnerable, and since they are forced to move on predictable orbits, they should not be too hard to shoot down. One suggested method of dealing with a hostile satellite is to shoot a modest rocket into its orbit, but moving in the opposite direction. The warhead would burst and fill the orbit with millions of small particles. Any one of these, hitting the satellite with twice its orbital speed (36,000 mph) would have the effect of a meteor, punching a hole and sending a blast of flame and shock into its interior.

That was in 1957, with a Soviet projectile in orbit and fresh information about the phenomenon accumulating hourly. Another five months would pass before *Time* reported: "A word coming more and more into Pentagon usage is 'overkill'—a blunt but descriptive term implying a power to destroy a military target many times more than necessary." By then the country was learning fast. But when Eisenhower had taken office the very theory of guided missiles had been almost as remote as the atomic bomb concept when Einstein's famous letter reached FDR's desk in October 1939. During the eight years after V-J Day government spending on long-range ballistic missile projects had averaged less than a million dollars a year. In 1954 American physicists advised Washington that they now believed they could design a hydrogen warhead small enough to be carried in the nose of a missile. The administration then gave the green light to ballistic missile development. But the United States was already behind—the Russians had decided to push on with missile research without knowing whether one would ever be capable of carrying a warhead—and the lag grew greater after a fateful recommendation of the U.S. IGY committee.

In 1954 Wernher von Braun, the Nazi V-2 scientist who was to become a naturalized U.S. citizen the following year, had persuaded the Army and the Navy to share in a joint venture under his leadership. Von Braun planned to soup up the Army's tested Redstone missile with booster rockets and send a tiny (five-pound) satellite into orbit. The endeavor was christened Project Orbiter. It was coming along nicely until October of that year, when an International Geophysical Year panel meeting in Rome proposed earth satellite launchings during the IGY—from July 1957 to December 1958. The Americans on the panel agreed. They recommended that the United States undertake a satellite project as part of the country's IGY contribution. The White House consented. At the same time certain administration policy makers insisted that any appearance of using an IGY undertaking for military purposes must be avoided. Their reasoning was the same as that set forth three years later by Killian and Nixon; neutral governments might misunderstand and become offended. It made sense to the National Security Council, which thereupon separated satellite research from military ballistic work. This decision, ending von Braun's Project Orbiter, was reached in mid-1955, when, as it happened, up in Dearborn the

Ford Motor Company was deciding to produce the starcrossed Edsel.

After Sputnik I went up, I. M. Levitt, director of Philadelphia's Fels Planetarium, called the separation of the rocketeers and the missilemen an "astonishing piece of stupidity." Army projectile engineers echoed him. In 1955 progress on their Jupiter IRBM had been sufficiently advanced for it to launch a satellite; in September 1956 a modified Jupiter-C reached a height of 650 miles, higher than Sputnik I's orbit, and sailed on for a distance of 3,500 miles. There was no appeal from the National Security Council, however. Orbiter's rocket men were transferred to Project Vanguard, its successor. Vanguard was then assigned to the Navy on the ground that the Navy's Vikings and Aerobees represented greater advances in high-altitude missile research than similar enterprises in the other services. There Vanguard had languished. As a first step under the new management, Director John P. Hagen, the Canadian astronomer now at the helm, announced his intention of launching a 20-pound satellite—one-eighth the weight of Sputnik I—late in 1954. But then there were snags, delays, postponements. Hagen issued a revised schedule, under which the first 21½-pound satellite would go up in the spring of 1958, provided the 27,000-pound thrust of its Viking launcher worked perfectly. Hagen and his colleagues were still working on this when Soviet scientists began hurtling Red moons across the skies.

In Eisenhower's mind the distinction between scientific inquiry and military necessity continued to be sharply defined, and he drew it in his first press conference after the launching of Sputnik I. Vanguard was a scholarly undertaking, he said, "merely an engagement on our part to put up a vehicle of this kind." It was all very well in its way; if the ambitions for it were realized, mankind's knowledge would be enriched with information about "temperatures, radiation, ionization, pressures." But it had nothing to do with any race to the moon, and he didn't know where that idea had started, and he wished someone would tell him.

The launching of the sputnik, Ike said, was something else again. It meant Soviet possession "of a very powerful thrust in their rocketry, and that is important." Unfortunately the figures he had received up to now were militarily meaningless: "I don't know anything about their accuracy, and until you know something about their accuracy, you know nothing at all about their usefulness in warfare." He acknowledged that he was deeply concerned: "I wish we were farther ahead and knew more as to accuracy and to the erosion and to the heat-resistant qualities of metals, and all the other things we have to know about. I wish we knew more about it at this moment."

It was Russian weaponry, he explained, that was the source of his anxiety. The administration had spent $110 million on its satellite project and would spend more. All the same, missile research and development would continue to have priority over it. Almost disdainfully he said: "So far as the satellite itself is concerned, that does not raise my apprehensions, not one iota."

Over at the Vanguard offices, Dr. Hagen and his staff appeared to be equally tranquil. They acknowledged some obstacles, some disappointments, but that was always the way of things on the drawing boards and in the labs. Nodding and puffing thoughtfully on his pipe, the soft-spoken Hagen conceded that his launching vehicle was still undergoing tests, but neither he nor his colleagues admitted to any sense of failure. They had promised to put a satellite in orbit before IGY's end, and that was over a year away. Time, they gently reminded journalists, has little meaning in basic research.

fau-bus (faw-bus), v.i.; FAUBUSED, FAUBUSING. 1. To commit an error of enormous magnitude through malice and ignorance. 2. To make a serious error, to commit a fault through stupidity or mental confusion. Syn. Blunder, err, bollix.

Thus Jack Mabley of the *Chicago Daily News* proposed, in October 1957, that the name of Arkansas Governor Orval Faubus be added to the language. The suggestion never caught on, partly because Faubus's period of notoriety, though great, was brief, and also because under it all he was really quite colorless. If Faubus had not existed it would not have been necessary to invent him. All over the South white politicians were campaigning against the Supreme Court's three-year-old decision striking down the concept of separate but equal education. In Alabama alone four gubernatorial candidates were pledging unyielding opposition to school integration, one of them vowing he would go to jail for segregation and another going one better by swearing that he would die for it. The difference between them and Faubus was that he was already in office and therefore able to attract and hold national attention by official action. In that tumultuous fall he moved in counterpoint with the momentous developments at Cape Canaveral and in outer space, his parochialism juxtaposed against their promises of glory.

There was never any doubt about Faubus's motives. In Arkansas he faced an uphill fight for reelection. The state had a strong tradition against a third-term governor, and his popularity was waning; he had offended liberal constituents by approving rate increases for utilities and railroads and disillusioned others by raising taxes. His strategy was to build a new base in red-neck, racist eastern Arkansas. On August 20, 1957, he made his first move, calling on Deputy Attorney General William Rogers in Washington to ask what the government would do to prevent violence when Little Rock schools opened in September. This was the first time anyone had intimated that violence might come to Little Rock. All the signs indicated that integration would proceed smoothly. On the initiative of Mayor Woodrow W. Mann the city had worked out a model seven-year integration program, carefully picking black pupils likely to do well. Startled by Faubus's question, Rogers replied that local disorders were usually handled by local police.

To be certain that federal officials were still abreast of developments there, the deputy attorney general sent the head of the Justice Department's civil rights division to Little Rock. The official, himself a native of Arkansas, explained to Faubus how federal injunctions could pinion conspirators. He asked the governor why he expected trouble. Faubus's answer was evasive; his evidence, he said, was "too vague and indefinite to be of any use to a law-enforcement agency." Back in Washington, the official reported that he believed the governor intended to play racial politics with schoolchildren.

Faubus's next step confirmed him. On August 29 the governor asked a state court to block the city's integration schedule on the ground that it would lead to bloodshed. The local judge gave him his injunction and was promptly overruled by U.S. District Judge Ronald Davies. The board of education proceeded with its integration arrangements. They were modest enough; nine black pupils were to be enrolled with the two thousand whites in Little Rock's Central High School. There were still no signs of unrest, but to be safe Mayor Mann and his 175-man police force worked out tactics for controlling possible demonstrations.

It was a waste of time. The governor had no intention of consulting the mayor. His plan was rather to call out the National Guard and order it to stop the nine Negro children from registering. Getting wind of this on September 1, Arkansas's most famous citizen, Winthrop Rockefeller, hurried to the statehouse and for two hours begged Faubus not to do it. The governor refused. He said, "I'm sorry, but I'm already committed. I'm going to run for a third term, and if I don't do this, Jim Johnson and Bruce Bennett"—racists who would oppose him in the primary—"will tear me to shreds." At 9 P.M. on September 2, the evening before schools would reopen, National Guardsmen carrying M-1s with fixed bayonets set up a perimeter defense around Central High while their leader, a major general in the Air National Guard, set up his command post in the principal's office. An hour later Faubus appeared on Little Rock's KTHV-TV and announced that he had called out the militia "to maintain or restore the peace and good order of this community." The city, he said, was on the brink of riot: "the evidence of discord, anger, and resentment has come to me from so many sources as to become a deluge!"

Little Rock was astonished. The mayor said, "There was no indication whatever. We had no reason to believe there would be violence." The governor had said that the city's stores were running out of knives (sold "mostly to Negro youths"), but an FBI check of 100 stores revealed that the sale of knives and guns was below normal. The only weapons in sight were those of the National Guard. There had been every reason to believe that the capital of the state would follow the pattern of three other Arkansas communities—Fort Smith, Ozark, and Van Buren—which were quietly integrating that same day. Now the nine black youngsters, arriving at Central High in a group, were turned away by National Guardsmen who said, "Governor Faubus has placed this school off limits to Negroes." One fifteen-year-old black girl tested the perimeter. The Guardsmen raised their rifles against her, and as she retreated a spectator called out, "Go home, you burr head"; then the white-haired wife of a teacher shielded the child and led her to a bus stop. That was the extent of Faubus's "violence," and Judge Davies denied a new petition for further delay of integration.

At the judge's request, fifty FBI agents had roamed Little Rock, looking once more for signs of racial tension. Their 500-page report disclosed not a shred of evidence to support the claim that the peace was threatened. Accordingly, Davies summoned the governor to appear in court September 20 and show cause why he should not be enjoined from interfering with the school board's program. Faubus had retired to the salmon-pink gubernatorial mansion and ringed it with Guardsmen, but a U.S. marshal easily penetrated this screen and handed him the summons on the executive lawn. For the first time the governor looked worried. He wired President Eisenhower, complaining that he was being investigated by federal agents, that his telephone was being tapped, and that he had learned of a scheme to take him "into custody, by force." He asked for a presidential assurance of "understanding and cooperation." Eisenhower replied, "The only assurance I can give you is that the federal constitution will be upheld by me by every legal means at my command."

Representative Brooks Hays, Little Rock's congressman, thought Eisenhower and Faubus ought to sit down together and talk things over. It was arranged; on September 14, the eleventh day of the crisis, they met at the summer White House in Newport, Rhode Island. Sherman Adams's impression of Faubus was that "he would not be unreasonable or difficult to deal with," and Eisenhower thought Faubus seemed confused about the course he should take. Both were wrong. The governor continued to stonewall, and the situation was unchanged six days later when Judge Davies called from his bench, "Civil case no. 3113 on a Motion for preliminary injunction." He was handling the hearing like any other, but it was historic. The governor of a state was being brought to justice in a federal court.

Faubus himself was not there. Ever since calling out the National Guard he had dodged questions about his evidence of violence by promising to produce it in open court, but the evidence wasn't there, either. In place of it were three Arkansas lawyers representing him. They filed motions asking first that Davies disqualify himself because of personal bias, and second that charges against the governor be dismissed here because they should be heard by a three-judge court. Davies quietly overruled them. Speaking from notes, their chief counsel then said, "The position of the respondent, Governor Faubus, and his military officers must be firm, unequivocal, unalterable: that the governor of the state of Arkansas cannot and will not concede that the United States in this court or anywhere else can question his discretion and judgment."

The attorney asked if he and his colleagues might be excused from the hearings, the judge nodded, and they walked out. The governor's defense had rested without summoning a witness. His argument was that federal courts had no jurisdiction over him in Arkansas. That issue had been raised in 1861 and presumably settled in 1865.

The U.S. attorney had planned to call nearly two hundred witnesses. Now eight were enough. They included the mayor, the police chief, and the superintendent of schools. All testified to the city's racial peace. Summing up the evidence afterward, the judge said it showed that the school board's integration program had been "thwarted by the governor of Arkansas by the use of National Guard troops," adding, "It is equally demonstrable from the testimony here today that there would have been no violence in carrying out the plan of integration." He thereupon issued orders that Faubus and the National Guard were to stop their interference. Asked to comment, Faubus scrawled a statement for reporters. He noted that his attorneys had not been present, omitting the fact that they had left on his instructions. He declared: "Now comes the crucifixion. There will be no cross-examination, no evidence presented for the other [his own] side. So now, by the use of carefully selected witnesses, the Justice Department's case can be continued. The results are a foregone conclusion." That night he issued a milder statement, attacking Davies's "unwarranted action" but saying that he would comply with the court order until its "certain reversal on appeal." The militia was withdrawn from Central High, and as the troops marched away Faubus and his wife Alta left Little Rock for a Southern Governors' Conference in Sea Island, Georgia. On the way they stopped to see a Georgia-Texas football game in Atlanta. Afterward a fellow governor told the press, "He's really lapping up the glory. There were 33,000 people at the game, and every time they cheered a play, Faubus got up and bowed."

That evening he was the cynosure of all eyes in the Silver Room of Sea Island's Cloister Hotel, signing autographs, drinking bourbon and Seven-Up, and dancing. His partners included Mrs. James Karam, who was accompanying the governor's party. Her husband had been unable to make the trip. "Jimmy the Flash" Karam, as he was known in Little Rock, was one of the governor's closest friends. A former football player and professional strikebreaker, Karam was now head of the Arkansas State Athletic Commission. As such he had intimate knowledge of the world of locker rooms, sparring partners, and bullyboys. That was what was keeping him home. He had a special assignment from the governor, and it began at daybreak the following morning. While the Faubuses and his wife lay asleep in Sea Island recovering from the festivities in the Silver Room, Karam was deploying a force of husky young men outside Central High, whispering here, nodding there, and ducking in and out of a filling station phone booth.

At 6 A.M. seventy Little Rock policemen arrived swinging nightsticks and erected sawhorse barricades around the school. Three weeks earlier that would have been enough to keep the peace, but now the crisis had been building too long; Faubus's prediction of trouble was about to become self-fulfilling, especially with Karam there to rally faint hearts. Afterward the mayor blamed what happened on "professional agitators" and an assistant police chief said that "half the troublemakers were from out of town." Civic pride kept them from pointing out that many of the leaders were figures in Little Rock sports and therefore friends of the policemen. Some cops, sympathetic with them, were defensive about being here. "Do you think I like this?" one of them told spectators. "I'm just trying to do my job."

At 8:45 the Central High class bell sounded. In the next instant a yell went up: "Here come the niggers!" These blacks weren't schoolchildren. They were four Negro newspapermen who had arrived together. Retreating, they were pursued by about twenty bullyboys, who cut them off and began systematically beating them. One cop climbed on a car to get a better look. Others moved in to stop the mayhem, and as they did Jimmy Karam cried angrily, "The niggers started it!" A powerfully built youth hurried up to him and said, "Get me five or six boys and get them over there where the nigger kids came in last time." Karam rounded up five of the biggest and led them there. He was too late; while the mob had been watching the attack on the black reporters, the nine Negro children had arrived in two cars and walked into the school. Once there, they seemed safe. Most of the white students looked at them curiously. Some made friendly overtures. None appeared to be hostile.

Nevertheless, the position of the newcomers was untenable. The scene outside was rapidly deteriorating. Radio and television descriptions of the melee had attracted toughs from surrounding towns. The throng doubled and redoubled, until nearly a thousand men were milling around, spoiling for a fight. The ineffectual police response to the assault on the Negro newsmen had taught them that hooliganism would go unpunished. Looking for new targets, they settled on white journalists. Three *Life* men were mauled. Every reporter without a southern accent was in danger. So were the policemen and the state troopers who had answered their appeals for help. In the turmoil the sawhorse barricades were demolished. Surging toward Central High, the crowd was at its very doors when, at 11:50 A.M., Mayor Mann capitulated and ordered the black children withdrawn from the school. The toughs dispersed, chortling. Jimmy Karam darted into the filling station booth and put through a call. Shortly afterward Governor Faubus called a press conference in Sea Island. "The trouble in Little Rock," he said, "vindicates my good judgment."

President Eisenhower was in Washington that morning, speaking before the International Monetary Fund. All that week he had been depressed by the growing crisis in Arkansas. He told Sherman Adams that he was well aware that the Warren Court's resolution of Brown v. Board of Education was "cutting into established customs and traditions in such communities as Little Rock," and "You cannot change the hearts of people by law." Later in the week he would tell four moderate southern governors, "I have never said what I thought about the Supreme Court decision—I have never told a soul." He added, "But how I feel about it is immaterial. The fact is that it is the law, and as the President of the United States I have the responsibility of seeing to it that it is enforced." He had been about to leave the Monetary Fund meeting after speaking when he received an urgent call from Brownell. The attorney general gave him a terse account of the disorders outside Central High. The President then approved a tough statement:

> The federal law and orders of a United States District Court . . . cannot be flouted with immunity by any individual or any mob of extremists. I will use the full power of the United States including whatever force may be necessary to prevent any obstruction of the law and to carry out the orders of the Federal Court.

He was hoping to shake some sense into Faubus. But it was too late. He had barely returned to Newport when a second call from Brownell came in over the maximum-security telephone in his personal quarters. Reports from U.S. marshals in Arkansas disclosed that law enforcement had broken down on both the state and local levels. A mob had ruled at Central High. Moreover, Little Rock was asking Washington to intervene; School Superintendent Virgil Blossom had just called the Justice Department and said, "Mayor Mann wants to know who to call to get federal help." He had been put through to Brownell, who, after hanging up, had drafted a proclamation setting forth the traditional authority and responsibility of the President, reaching back to 1795, to use troops to enforce the federal law. If approved by Eisenhower, it would open the way to sending in the Army. Ike listened to it over the phone. He said, "I want you to send up that proclamation. It looks like I will have to sign it, but I want to read it."

He studied it that evening on the sun porch of his living quarters and went to bed leaving it unsigned. The prospect appalled him, he told Adams; using U.S. soldiers against U.S. citizens would never be "a wise thing to do in this country." But events in Little Rock had acquired a momentum of their own. It is doubtful that even Orval Faubus and Jimmy Karam could have controlled them now. Only strict obedience of the court order would keep the Army out, and a crowd which has successfully defied policemen obeys nobody. Walking to his Newport office just before eight o'clock the following morning, Ike squinted at the horizon and said, "There's a cold wind blowing up." It was an omen. In less than an hour Brownell was on the line again with bad news from Central High. The mob was even bigger today; pushing and shoving, it jeered cops who tried to break it up. The nine Negro students had stayed home. In the opinion of the U.S. marshals, only their absence had saved the school from an invasion. This time Mayor Mann had sent Washington a telegram formally requesting presidential intervention. Eisenhower hung up and signed the proclamation, and that evening he went on national television to explain: "The very basis of our individual rights and freedoms rests upon the certainty that the President and the executive branch of government will support and insure the carrying out of the decisions of the federal courts, even, when necessary, with all the means at the President's command. Unless the President did so, anarchy would result."

That morning, responding to the proclamation, Secretary of Defense Wilson had placed the Arkansas National Guard in federal service, beyond the reach of Governor Faubus, and General Maxwell Taylor, the Army chief of staff, had assigned the 327th Battle

Group of the 101st Airborne Division to bring peace to Central High. Eight C-130 and C-123 transport planes had carried the paratroopers from Fort Campbell, in Kentucky, to Arkansas. As Eisenhower spoke to the nation the first trucks drew up in front of the school. For the first time since Reconstruction days southern intransigence on the issue of race had brought Army rule.

The difference between these troops and the militia was striking. Both wore the same uniform, but the resemblance ended there. The National Guard was made up of weekend soldiers, easygoing, casual in dress, and slow to obey. The 101st Airborne was a crack outfit, professional in all ways. While salty officers carrying swagger sticks barked commands, disciplined men spilled out of the trucks and formed ranks on the school grounds. Jeeps were parked just so, in a line. Immaculate tents, each the same distance from the others, rose in a field beyond Central High's tennis courts. Field telephone wires were strung from oaks in the school yard, and before dawn walkie-talkies crackled with the code names of communications men: "Hello, Defiance, this is Crossroads Six. Come in, Roadblock Alpha."*

Roadblock Alpha was the scene of the day's most dramatic incident. The barrier had been thrown up in an intersection a block east of Central High. There, in the first olive moments of Tuesday morning, ringleaders began organizing their men. A lanky, lantern-jawed major watched them from beside a sound truck. His voice rasped over the loudspeaker: "Please return to your homes or it will be necessary to disperse you." They didn't budge. "Nigger lover," one of them muttered, and another called, "Russian!" A man in a baggy brown suit shouted to the others, "They're just bluffing. If you don't want to move, you don't have to."

The major ripped out a command. Twelve paratroopers with fixed bayonets formed a line and braced their rifle butts against their hips in the on-guard position for riot control; it brought each bayonet on a line with the crowd's throats. Again the major snapped an order, and the soldiers moved forward. The mob retreated. The man in the brown suit held his ground until the last moment; then he broke and ran. He didn't run far, however. The Army had won the

---

* The officer responsible for this impressive display, the 101st's commander, was Major General Edwin Walker. Later he was retired for circulating John Birch Society material among his men; later still, he was on the wrong side in a racial incident and was arrested. He retired in Dallas, where he flew the American flag upside down. In Little Rock his conduct was above reproach.

first skirmish, but the showdown was yet to come. The black children hadn't even reached the school.

That moment arrived in a crisp, swiftly executed maneuver. Central High's 8:45 bell rang. Simultaneously the barricade at Park Avenue and Sixteenth Street opened to admit a lead jeep, an Army station wagon, and a rear guard jeep. They braked together in front of the school, and the Negro children emerged from the station wagon as three platoons of paratroopers ran up on the double with rifles at port arms and formed a semicircle, shielding the children with a hedge of bayonets. A fourth platoon, lining up on either side of the black students, escorted them up the steps. The crowd watched in stunned silence. Then a woman cried brokenly, "Oh my God! The niggers are inside!" Others shouted, "They're in! They're in!" Another woman screamed and tore at her hair. The crowd shifted, tilting forward.

At Roadblock Alpha the throng had thickened. Again the major said harshly, "Let's clear this area right now. This is the living end! I'll tell you, we're not going to do it on a slow walk this time." Nothing happened, and he ordered the paratroopers to resume their advance. As they came on, the crowd recoiled, hopping, to the front lawn and then to the veranda of a private home, all the time yelling that this was private property, that the troopers had no right to come after them on it. The soldiers didn't miss a step. Up on the porch they came, and then across it as the mob scrambled backward from the bayonets.

Those who hesitated were being methodically pushed off the piazza when one of them struck back. He was C. E. Blake, a Missouri-Pacific switchman who had been among the most active agitators during the past two days. Blake seized a soldier's rifle barrel and dragged him down. As they sprawled together another paratrooper reversed his M-1 and clouted the switchman's head with the steel butt. Blood streaming from his scalp, he crawled away on all fours shouting at photographers, "Who knows the name of that lowlife son of a bitch who hit me?" Without a glance in his direction the troopers continued to move out while a stony-eyed sergeant called, "Keep those bayonets high—right at the base of the neck."

Back from Sea Island, Orval Faubus joked with the press ("I feel like MacArthur. I've been relieved of my job") and asked the networks for equal time to answer President Eisenhower. ABC-TV gave it to him; the other two turned him down because he refused to answer questions afterward. In the Faubus version of what had happened, Blake had been "a guest in a home." Troopers had run wild with "wholesale arrests." High school girls had been "taken by the FBI and held incommunicado for hours of questioning while their frantic parents knew nothing of their whereabouts." Young white southern womanhood was very much on the governor's mind; he held up a photograph for just a moment and said, "Evidence of the naked force of the federal government is here apparent in these unsheathed bayonets in the backs of schoolgirls." Again, he cried that he had returned from Georgia to find paratroopers "bludgeoning innocent bystanders, with bayonets in the backs of schoolgirls, and the warm, red blood of patriotic Americans staining the cold, naked, unsheathed knives." At the end he cried: "In the name of God, whom we all revere, in the name of liberty which we hold so dear, which we all cherish, what is happening in America?"

What was happening in Little Rock bore little relationship to his speech. Blake, of course, had been no one's guest. Only eight arrests had been made; four of the men had been fined for loitering, and the other four had been released at the police station. The FBI hadn't questioned anyone; J. Edgar Hoover said the governor was "disseminating falsehoods." As for the bayonets in girls' backs, the picture, which Faubus had quickly whipped out of sight, was of girls walking—and giggling—past a group of soldiers.

Those were the facts, and they testified to the good judgment of the troops from Fort Campbell. It continued to go unrecognized by Faubus. Two weeks later he descended to what the *Washington Post and Times-Herald* called "the lavatory level," charging that troopers were entering the girls' locker room at Central High and staying to leer at their nudity. Reporters asked Faubus for eyewitness accounts or documentary proof. He replied, "I do not choose to release them at this time." Actually he never produced evidence to support any of his accusations. In November the Army withdrew all but a token force from the school, and the black children began attending Central High unescorted. By the following May the incident belonged to history. It had been a skillful if expensive use of force; keeping the nine Negro students in school had cost the federal government $4,051,000.

But the country paid another, far higher price for the events that autumn in Arkansas. The real significance of Little Rock lay in its impact on the white South. Deep in the southern consciousness lay tales of the Civil War and its aftermath, told to them in childhood by their grandparents, and the trouble at Central High evoked the martyred ghosts of that terrible era. On this subject they were beyond the reach of reason. Their reaction was compounded of the Stars and Bars, the strains of "Dixie," Jackson at Bull Run, Lee at Appomattox, and the dead on the field at Antietam. It rendered them blind to Faubus's clumsy lies. Northern soldiers on southern soil meant just one thing to them—an evil, loathsome presence to be attacked in righteous wrath, sounding a rebel yell that drowned out voices of sanity. Senator Richard Russell of Georgia accused Eisenhower of "applying tactics that must have been copied from the manual issued to the officers of Hitler's storm troopers."* Senator Olin Johnson of South Carolina said, "If I were Governor Faubus, I'd proclaim an insurrection down there, and I'd call out the National Guard, and I'd then find out who's going to run things in my state." Senator James O. Eastland of Mississippi charged, "Eisenhower has lit the fires of hate," and Senator Herman Talmadge of Georgia said, "We still mourn the destruction of Hungary. Now the South is threatened by the President of the United States using tanks [sic] and troops in the streets of Little Rock. I wish I could cast one vote for impeachment right now." Alabama's Governor James E. "Kissin' Jim" Folsom promised that he would disband his state's National Guard before he would let Eisenhower federalize it, and Governor James Bell Timmerman of South Carolina resigned his U.S. Navy reserve commission so he could not be called into service.

They were the leaders. In a thousand ways private southerners made it known that they regarded Faubus as their hero and the President as their enemy. Gallup found that while only 10 percent of the people in northern and western states thought Eisenhower had been wrong in sending the troopers to Central High, only a third of the southerners thought he had been right. In Jacksonville, Florida, an Air Corps veteran mailed his four Air Medals and six battle stars to the White House for distribution among the paratroopers. In Marshall, Texas, a speaker at a Kiwanian luncheon said,

* The President, indignant, wired Russell: "I must say I completely fail to understand your comparison of our troops to Hitler's storm troopers. In one case military power was used to further the ambitions of a ruthless dictator; in the other to preserve the institutions of free government."

"This is the darkest day in Southern history since the reconstruction"; the Kiwanians then refused to pledge their allegiance to the flag. Near Dover, Delaware, two Negroes in business suits were ordered to leave a Howard Johnson restaurant by a waitress who said, "Colored people are not allowed to eat in here," thereby embarrassing the State Department; one of the men was the finance minister of Ghana, who had entertained Richard Nixon in his home, and the other was his secretary. As always in the South, the raising of the racial issue was accompanied by intimations of terror. In Albany, Georgia, night riders put a college for Negroes to the torch, and at the height of the Little Rock crisis six Alabamans trapped a black named Judge Aaron on a lonely country road, took him to a deserted shack, castrated him with a razor blade, and poured turpentine into the wound. None of them had known Aaron; one of them said afterward, "We just wanted some nigger at random."

The subsequent career of Orval Faubus was a measure of southern feeling. The governor had played his role in full view of Arkansas voters. Elsewhere biased reporting may have clouded the judgment of readers, but not in Faubus's home state; one of the bravest chapters in American journalism was written by Harry Scott Ashmore of the *Arkansas Gazette*, who won a Pulitzer Prize for his superb coverage of the turmoil at Central High. Not all of his subscribers were appreciative. Ashmore's phone rang around the clock with threatening calls; Faubus denounced him as "an ardent integrationist"; Little Rock's racist Capital Citizens Council called him the state's "Public Enemy No. 1," and a statewide boycott cost the *Gazette* 3,000 subscriptions. He continued to print the truth, whereupon the people of Arkansas swept Faubus back into the statehouse in 1958 for a third term—he received 255,086 votes; the man who ran second got 56,966—and continued to reelect him by massive majorities in subsequent elections. In 1967, after twelve years in the executive mansion, he retired.

Outside the South, and indeed beyond the United States, was another matter. The struggle to put the nine black children in Central High had global ramifications. Little Rock, an editor wrote at the time, had become "a name known wherever men could read newspapers and listen to radios, a symbol to be distorted in Moscow, misinterpreted in New Delhi," and "painfully explained in London." Americans solicitous of good opinion in foreign capitals were chagrined. They recognized the principles at stake in Arkansas, and saw them being flouted; and they felt shame.

And yet they had virtually nothing to say about the human dimensions of the episode. In perspective that silence is deafening. The voice of the American Negro was still unheard. The word southerner meant white southerner. There was no term for the South's blacks, and U.S. newspapers there and elsewhere seldom carried day-by-day news about them. The true meaning of the Howard Johnson episode was that a victim of racial discrimination had to be a cabinet member in a foreign country before the country's conscience was stirred, and even then it regretted not the wrong done, but the damage to America's image.

Black adults, bred to passivity, accepting the system because for so long there had been no alternative, turned inward as they always had, transmuting what should have been righteous anger into despair. For every American Negro who felt elation when the 101st Airborne triumphed in Arkansas there were dozens who feared—justifiably—the rage of aroused whites; who read of Judge Aaron and knew that there, but for the grace of God, went they. But their children reacted differently. Coming after the Montgomery bus boycott and the Supreme Court decisions outlawing discrimination, the confrontation at Central High confirmed the hope that the stereotypes of the past might be broken. It was in this sense, in the fall of 1957, that Little Rock left a profound impression on such young blacks as Stokely Carmichael, who was sixteen; Cassius Clay, fifteen; H. Rap Brown, thirteen; and Angela Davis, twelve.

In the first fortnight of November those who thought it their duty to cheer up America examined the bleak clouds that had been gathering, and in search of silver linings concentrated on repairing the havoc that had been wreaked upon U.S. morale by the sputniks. Von Braun told the press that the United States could launch a satellite with equipment already available. To the surprise of everyone, including those who had been working on it, Secretary McElroy announced that Vanguard was back on schedule. Emissaries from *Time*, dispatched to take soundings in 33 cities, found stout hearts in the president of the Kansas City Stock Yards Company, a Florida congressman, a group of bankers in Lincoln, Nebraska, and a Los Angeles sales engineer ("Six weeks ago I'd walk into an aircraft plant and it would look as if everybody from the chief engineer to the draftsmen was taking a coffee break at once. When I made my rounds this week, the recreation rooms were empty. Everybody was working.")

"Upward" was the inspirational title of a *Reader's Digest* article by Beirne Lay Jr., who suggested that "a Supreme Being" was America's silent ally in the space quest. By then the administration was responding to aroused public opinion. Rocket crews worked feverishly at Cape Canaveral, and at Nixon's urging the President reluctantly agreed that he must do something more to brighten the country's mood. After his appointment of Killian as special assistant for science and technology (to Ike's annoyance the press changed this to "missile czar") he named a Pentagon coordinator to crack down on interservice rivalries. Then he decided to deliver a series of five presidential TV talks. Much was expected of these, and the first went well. In it he displayed the four-foot nose cone of a retrieved Jupiter. He explained: "One difficult obstacle on the way to producing a long-range weapon is that of bringing a missile back from outer space without its burning up like a meteor . . . This one here in my office is the nose cone of an experimental missile. It has been hundreds of miles into outer space and back. Here it is, completely intact." It was his conviction, he said, that "as of today the overall military strength of the free world is distinctly greater than that of the Communist countries." ICBMs were on their way. Meantime SAC's B-52 jet bombers stood vigil.

The mail response was encouraging. His second chat was equally successful, and he set to work on a draft of the third, to be telecast from Cleveland. It was slow going; he had a lot on his mind. The seasonal load of the Presidency is always at its heaviest between Labor Day and Christmas. On December 16 he was scheduled to preside over a NATO meeting in Paris. Before then he had to complete his legislative program for the coming year and explain it to the congressional leadership. The massive federal budget for the coming fiscal year demanded presidential attention, the new State of the Union address would be due in January, and it now appeared that the country was entering a major recession.

Still, restoring the nation's self-confidence was the most urgent issue before the President, and he was determined to complete the remaining TV talks. He didn't do it. On November 25, 1957, for the third time in twenty-six months the President of the United States was in bed, prostrate, unable to meet the simplest of his obligations. Dr. Snyder diagnosed his illness as a "vascular spasm." To the rest of the country it was a stroke.

That Monday before Thanksgiving, awaiting the arrival of Morocco's King Mohammed V on a state visit, the President had stood bareheaded in a raw autumn wind at Washington National Airport. Back in his White House office, Ike said he felt a chill coming on. He was afraid he might be catching the flu. It was graver than that. Dictating to Ann Whitman, his secretary, he was dismayed to find that the words wouldn't come. Near tears, she went to Sherman Adams. "The President has gone back to the house," she said. "He tried to tell me something but he couldn't express himself. Something seemed to have happened to him all of a sudden. And just now he gave up and went home. I can't imagine what's wrong with him."

In the presidential apartment upstairs, Adams found the President in pajamas. Snyder, on his way, had telephoned instructions for his patient to go to bed. Eisenhower smiled at his assistant. He said, "I suppose you are dis—" He couldn't finish it. Hesitating, he stammered: ". . . talking about the dinner tonight." Frustrated and angry over his inability to talk about plans for entertaining the African king, he struggled to say, "There's nothing the matter with me! I am perfectly all right!" But plainly he was having trouble forming words. As he continued to falter, he repeatedly came out with a word or syllable that had no relation to the word that was in his mind. In dismay Mrs. Eisenhower said to Adams, "We can't let him go down there in this condition." Adams agreed. He told the President that Nixon could take his place at the dinner. Ike shook his head violently. He managed to say, "If I cannot attend to my duties, I am simply going to give up this job. Now that is all there is to it."

Then the doctor arrived. On hearing a single word from Eisenhower—"international," which came out "internatt-nl"—Snyder reached his diagnosis. Ike's stroke had affected the speech center of the brain. He was suffering from aphasia, an impairment of the power to use words as symbols of ideas. It was impossible to say whether the lesion would heal, and if it did, how quickly. The doctor called Walter Reed and Adams called Nixon, who agreed to preside at the banquet. For the time being nothing was said to the press. Hagerty was in Paris advancing the NATO trip. When word of the President's illness reached him there, he wept.

But it was not an occasion for grief after all. Eisenhower's recovery was both speedy and miraculous. His improvement was noted in a matter of hours. Even as a Hagerty assistant briefed reporters on the findings of four neurological specialists ("an occlusion" accompanied by "slight difficulty in speaking"), the President was back in the White House watching Wyatt Earp on television. The next morning he awoke at 7:40 A.M., showered, and made his own breakfast. He painted awhile, picking up where he had left off on a portrait of Britain's Princess Anne. Feeling much better, he received his aides and the Moroccan king, worked on state papers for a half-hour, and signed or initialed a dozen of them. On Thursday, Thanksgiving, he went to church and shrugged off the helping hand of the pastor. In the Mansion he carved a forty-pound Thanksgiving turkey. Then, with Snyder as their house guest, the Eisenhowers drove to the Gettysburg farm. Saturday they watched the Army-Navy game. With Snyder's approval, Ike planned to return to a full schedule on Monday and preside over a cabinet meeting. The doctor told the press, "The President's progress continues to be excellent."

At Cape Canaveral, Vanguard scientists looked forward to giving the convalescing President's spirits a boost by putting an American sputnik in orbit on December 6. Everything seemed ready that Friday morning. The tall, three-stage, black-and-silver Navy Test Vehicle 3, or TV-3, stood in a spider-web gantry. Sunlight sparkled on a rime of frost crystals from its liquid oxygen fuel. TV-3 had been hurried along on orders from Washington; it was expected to throw into outer space a U.S. satellite the size of a small bowling ball—not much, to be sure, but a symbol of fine workmanship and American determination to enter and then win the space race. To reap a propaganda harvest the administration had made certain that the entire world knew what was coming. Although the Martin rocket had never been tested before, its performance was expected to be flawless. Pentagon PR men had kept 127 American and foreign journalists posted on latest developments, including details on the countdown, usually highly classified information. U.S. READY TO FIRE SATELLITE, said a *New York Times* head. The *Pittsburgh Sun-Telegram* predicted: MOON—MINUTES TO GO. The Associated Press distributed an advance story to member papers for release the moment the satellite went into orbit. In a thousand press rooms it was in type, ready to go:

Cape Canaveral, December 6 (AP)—The radio-signalling baby moon circling the earth is the U.S.'s reply to Russia that it too can stake a claim to the space frontier.

After several postponements because of valve leaks, Cape Canaveral hoisted the red ball signifying that Vanguard blast-off was imminent. Observation planes—two old World War II B-17s and a new Cessna—took off and rose swiftly to gain altitude. They looked down on a multitude of spectators. None were allowed within three miles of the launching pad, but enormous crowds were watching from the barriers there. Children had been dismissed from schools throughout Florida's Canaveral peninsula; factories and offices had let their workers out; the streets, yards, and public beaches were dense with anticipative Americans awaiting the historic event.

At 10:42 A.M. the gantry was wheeled away; it was wheeled back fifty minutes later and then at last rolled away for good. The last cable connecting TV-3 to the disconnect pole dropped away at 1:44. Within seconds the first whiffs of white-hot vapor emerged from the rocket's base. In Washington the voice of Vanguard's deputy director, J. Paul Walsh, could be heard over an open phone. He called: "Zero! . . . Fire! . . . First ignition! . . ."

The massive rocket stirred and rose cumbersomely from the pad a foot, then two feet, then three. At that point, two seconds after launch time, it appeared to stand motionless, fixed in space. Suddenly Walsh cried, "Explosion!" A long orange flame spurted from beneath the doomed rocket, shot downward, and then surged upward in a billowing sheet of fire that enveloped TV-3's right side. Overhead one of the B-17 pilots was shouting: "There it goes! There is an explosion! Black smoke is now over the entire area—We do not see the rocket that is carrying our satellite—The rocket may not have gotten off—There is a very large black smoke cloud—a very large black area around the location that the explosion occurred."

The smoke was caused by streams of water and carbon dioxide from automatic extinguishers. As it drifted away the rocket's nose cone could be seen leaning against the disconnect pole. Here and there fires continued to burn. The charred and mutilated tail jutted into the pad. One part of the assembly was intact: the coconut-sized satellite had been thrown clear and lay on the ground, sending steady signals on its assigned frequency, 108 megacycles.

It was a public relations disaster. The scientists protested in vain that this had only been a test. Having summoned the world's attention in anticipation of its applause, the United States now had to endure its scorn and derision. Grinning Russians at the U.N. advised Americans to apply for Soviet technical assistance to backward nations. In London a calypso balladeer sang over the BBC, "Oh, from America comes the thought/ Their own little Sputnik won't go off," and the wits of five continents rechristened TV-3 the flopnik, sputternik, goofnik, dudnik, oopsnik, puffnik, stallnik, and kaputnik. Lyndon Johnson wailed in the Senate, "How long, how long, oh God, how long will it take us to catch up with Russia's two satellites?" Confronting a gloomy press conference in Washington, Vanguard's Dr. Hagen, had a one-word comment: "Nuts." Editorial writers sought a new scapegoat—they settled on the public relations men, who joined the progressive educators in disgrace—and a professor in Pittsburgh said, "It's our worst humiliation since Custer's last stand."

In the age of instant communications the debacle seemed to be worse than it was. The fallen rocket wasn't the only one in the U.S. arsenal. Within a month, as soon as Cape Canaveral's launch pad could be repaired, the Navy would be ready for another satellite shot. The very week of the TV-3 fiasco the Air Force successfully retested Thor and Atlas missiles, and by March the Army would have eight Jupiter-Cs ready for the space program, each of them larger and more dependable than the Vanguard. The President had ordered the Jupiters withheld from civilian scientists because of military testing's absolute priority, but now he rescinded that order. Soon the people would forget the shame of December 6. The politicians would not forget, however. To them the risk of another such public roasting was unthinkable. From this point forward a succession of adminstrations would be committed to staying in the space race until it was won. No excuse for dropping out would be acceptable. Other calls upon the nation's resources, whatever their urgency—and by the late 1960s the need for some of them would be desperate—would have to wait until the Stars and Stripes had been firmly planted on the moon.

Portrait of an American

THE EDSEL

CONCEIVED IN 1948, the car was meant to solve a problem, not to become one. Satisfied Ford owners who grew more prosperous were ignoring the firm's Mercurys and trading up instead to Buicks, Pontiacs, and Oldsmobiles. "We have been growing customers for General Motors," said a Ford executive. Six years later company planners began investing a quarter-billion dollars on a new medium-price ($2,400 to $4,000) automobile. They knew they had to sell at least 200,000 in the first year to make money, but they were confident they could do it.

Lacking a name, they called it the E-Car, the E standing for "Experimental." Nothing was spared in its development. The mid-1950s were the salad days of motivational research, and among the advisers to the E-Car's stylists was the Columbia University Bureau of Applied Social Research, which appraised the "personalities" of other medium-priced cars, concluding, among other things, that the Buick was the wife of a professional man and the Mercury was sexy. After poring over this data, one of the Dearborn executives wrote: "The most advantageous personality for the E-Car might well be THE SMART CAR FOR THE YOUNGER EXECUTIVE OR PROFESSIONAL FAMILY ON ITS WAY UP," and added in explanation, "On Its Way Up: 'The E-Car has faith in you, son; we'll help you make it!'"

On August 15, 1955, the corporation's general staff, headed by Henry Ford II and Ernest R. Breech, witnessed the unveiling of a full-size clay model of the car, with tinfoil substituted for aluminum and chrome. They applauded. The stock market was booming that summer, and so was the medium-price market. Times seemed propitious for the E-Car. It already had the external features which were to become famous: the flaring gull-wing tail and the pinched-in oval radiator grille. Inside, it was to be what one designer called "the epitome of the push-button era."

After the motivational people had turned up 6,000 possible names, all of them alphabetized and cross-referenced, Breech christened it the Edsel, after Henry II's father, on a hunch. E-Day was set for September 4, 1957. On E minus 51 the first Edsels began rolling off assembly lines, but only a few people, all carefully screened, were allowed to see them. A tremendous aura of mystery was created by the car's promoters. Ads showed it as a blur, or as a shapeless hulk beneath canvas. Edsel buildings were fitted with special locks that could be changed in fifteen minutes should a key fall into the hands of Chrysler or General Motors spies. In July word was leaked that a model had been conveyed in a closed truck to Hollywood, where Cascade Pictures photographed it in a locked studio while armed guards patrolled outside. ("We took all the precautions we take for our AEC films," a Cascade spokesman said.) Ford's test track was encircled by barbed wire and camouflaged sentry boxes. In Dearborn telescopes kept watch on nearby roofs and hills for any competitors' agents who might be lurking there.

Business Week called the launching of the Edsel the most expensive such venture in the history of commerce. The stakes were enormous. Ford's Edsel division had its own plant, with 800 executives and 15,000 workers; 60 highly paid copywriters were turning out advertising copy, and nearly 1,200 auto dealers across the nation had surrendered profitable franchises for other makes to sell Edsels. They would become rich if it proved popular—and would lose their shirts if it failed.

In the last week of August Ford spent $90,000 on a three-day press conference at which 250 newsmen were shown the four main Edsel lines, which would be available in eighteen models. The affair was not an unqualified success. Daredevil drivers at the wheels of souped-up Edsels scared the daylights out of the reporters, and the music stands of a band hired for the occasion bore, in memory of Glenn Miller, the initials GM. These matters were slight but ominous. The new car appeared to be unlucky. Still, the public's curiosity was undoubtedly aroused. By the weekend that followed E-Day, almost three million people had entered dealers' showrooms to see what all the fuss was about. On E-Day itself, over 6,500 had bought Edsels. Dearborn was elated. If just one in fifteen of the remainder signed up, the car would finish its first year in the black.

It didn't happen. For one thing, the golden age of the medium-price car had begun to wane. In July the stock market had broken sharply, signaling the onset of the 1957–58 recession; *Automotive News* reported that dealers were experiencing the second worst season for sales in the history of the industry. More important, on E plus 30—October 4, 1957, a date which will live in infamy at the Ford Motor Company—the Russians sent their first sputnik into orbit. Styles Bridges's thundering rhetoric in the Senate was typical of the American reaction: "The time has clearly come to be less concerned about the depth of pile on the new broadloom rug or the height of the tailfin on the new car and to be more prepared to shed blood, sweat, and tears." In this new climate of opinion *Business Week* called Dearborn's latest spawn "a nightmare." *Consumer Reports* said it represented "the many excesses" with which Detroit was "repulsing more and more potential car buyers," and *Time* wrote that it was "a classic case of the wrong car for the wrong market at the wrong time" and "a prime example of the limitations of market research, with its 'depth interviews' and 'motivational' mumbo-jumbo."

But there was more to it than that. The Edsel was a failure by other standards. The oval grille set vertically in the front end, with the aluminum letters EDSEL emblazoned in it, was not a success. Its designer had adopted the idea from contemporary European automobiles in the hope that it would give the car cachet. It didn't, partly because it was inconsistent with the rest of the front design, and the public's negative reaction to it was the first blow against the auto's success. One writer likened it to an egg. Others described it as a horse collar, Bugs Bunny, and—this may have been inspired by malicious counter public relations of General Motors or Chrysler—a toilet seat.

Even worse, fully half of the first Edsels to go on the market were lemons. Brakes failed, push buttons didn't work, oil pans fell out, trunks wouldn't open, hoods stuck, transmissions froze, paint peeled, hubcaps fell off, batteries died, doors wouldn't close—the list of defects seemed to have no end.

On E plus 3 the theft of an Edsel occurred in North Philadelphia. There were virtually no others. It was a sign of the car's diminishing glamour that it didn't even seem to be worth stealing. After the bloom wore off nationwide sales plummeted until the sales chart in Dearborn resembled a ski slope. Dealers were selling fewer than one-fifth of the number necessary if they were to break even. The promotion became defensive, frantic:

1959 Edsel. Looks right! Built right! Prices right! Makes history by making sense. Exciting new kind of car! A full-size practical beauty. Roomy without useless length. Soundly engineered. Powered to save. And priced with the most popular three!

On January 14, 1958, the Ford Motor Company merged its Edsel and Lincoln-Mercury departments. The new car had lost 400 million dollars. It was finished, and the entire country knew it. The time had come to throw in the towel. Unfortunately that was not yet possible. Just as new cars need a long lead time, so does a cessation of production. The Edsel's new models had been designed long ago; the steel dies had been cut, and the 1959s were plonking down at the end of their assembly lines. Finally, having sold fewer than 1 percent of the cars bought during their time on the market, the Edsel's manufacturers discontinued manufacture on November 19, 1959. Viewers of *Wagon Train*, a Western TV series sponsored by the car's advertising agency, were invited to participate in a contest. The purpose was promotional, but the prizes weren't Edsels. They were ponies.

Twenty-five

THE CRUSADE FALTERS

I N 1958 Mike Todd's *Around the World in Eighty Days* entered its third year as the movie industry's greatest box office sensation since the arrival of the tube. Part of its appeal lay in the realization that in the late 1950s, as in Jules Verne's early 1870s, transportation was big news. The globe was growing noticeably smaller, and not only because of the satellites. British Overseas Airways Corporation introduced jet airliners for trans-Atlantic flights on October 4, 1958, and two months later, on December 10, U.S. jetliners made their first domestic appearance on the National Airlines New York to Miami run. The St. Lawrence Seaway was opened to traffic on April 25, 1959. U.S.S. *Wisconsin*, at that time the U.S. Navy's last battleship, was put in mothballs as Mamie Eisenhower christened N.S. *Savannah*, the first atom-powered merchant ship. Nuclear submarines surpassed Verne's wildest, 20,000-leagues-deep dream, circling the globe underwater and crossing the North Pole by passing beneath the Arctic ice cap. In June 1959 the 110-million-dollar sub *George Washington* slid stern first into the Thames River at Groton, Connecticut, carrying solid-fuel Polaris missiles, a guarantee that Russia could never level all U.S. nuclear bases in a sneak ICBM attack.

The American Telephone and Telegraph Company now had 100 million telephones in service, half the world total. Direct distance dialing (DDD), which had been introduced in Englewood, New Jersey, on November 10, 1951, was now being extended to overseas calls. Ocean telephone cables, radiophone, and over-the-horizon radio—soon to be joined by Telstar, the Bell System's first experimental communications satellite—linked Americans with 190 nations and territories overseas. Mark Cross, manufacturer of alligator handbags, provided some insight into the global character of modern American business when it announced a grant of financial aid to Zululand for the propagation of the crocodile species. At the same time, shrinking trade routes brought American auto dealers new competition from abroad. Foreign cars were accounting for 10 percent of all automobile sales in the United States. The leaders were West Germany's Volkswagen (1958 sales were 102,035), France's Renault (47,567), Italy's Fiat (23,000), and Britain's Hillman (18,663). Japan, Sweden, and Holland were about to enter the American market with other small cars, and Detroit, in a gesture toward reality, at last prepared to make little American autos. To distinguish them from automobiles made overseas they were to be called "compacts."

Asked what Americans might expect to find when they reached the moon, Edward Teller replied grimly, "Russians." In early January 1959 the Soviets launched Lunik I, a spectacular 3,245-pound satellite that came within 5,000 miles of the moon. Their head start in space exploration continued to be a tremendous advantage, though the United States had begun to take the first steps toward catching up. Cape Canaveral crews finally put a tiny American satellite in orbit with an Army Jupiter-C rocket. The National Defense Education Act of 1958 provided federal aid for improved teaching in science, mathematics, and foreign languages. In 1958 Congress also created the National Aeronautics and Space Administration (NASA). To test human endurance in space, Air Force Captain Joe Kittinger took the longest parachute jump in history, bailing out at 76,400 feet, falling twelve miles before a barometric device on his parachute blew it open, and landing safely in the New Mexican desert. Front pages on April 10, 1959, introduced the country to a new category of celebrities—the Project Mercury astronauts. All were veteran test pilots aged thirty-two to thirty-seven. Their names were Alan Shepard, Walter Schirra, Virgil Grissom, John H. Glenn Jr., Scott Carpenter, Gordon Cooper, and Donald Slayton. Each was white, a father, a native of small-town America, and a Protestant. Six of the seven had crew cuts.

The oceans on either side of the United States, which had been so comforting to isolationists in the 1930s, seemed at times to have shrunk to fordable streams. In August 1958 scientists debating the threat of fallout agreed that the bones of all Americans could be affected to some extent by any nuclear explosion anywhere on earth. Remote Indochina became less remote on July 10, 1959, when two American military advisers were killed and a third wounded at Bien Hoa, Vietnam, twenty miles north of Saigon. They had been watching a Jeanne Crain film, *The Tattered Dress,* on a home projector in a mess hall. Terrorists had surrounded the building, and when a sergeant switched on the lights to change reels, they had opened fire.

The first Eisenhower administration now belonged to the past, and some notable figures had vanished with it. Joe McCarthy died of drink on May 2, 1957. ("He was discouraged," George Sokolsky wrote. "He regarded himself as betrayed. He particularly felt that he was betrayed by Vice President Nixon, whom he had always trusted.") His widow, Jean Kerr McCarthy, continued to live in Washington; four years later she married a member of the Civil Aeronautics Board. Frank Lloyd Wright died at eighty-nine, leaving a time bomb of controversy over his last major work, New York City's three-million-dollar Solomon R. Guggenheim museum. Deaths in the entertainment world included Errol Flynn, Mario Lanza, Maxwell Anderson, and Lou Costello. John L. Lewis resigned as president of the United Mine Workers. Dave Beck of the Teamsters went to jail, leaving his successor, Jimmy Hoffa, locked in a desperate struggle with John F. Kennedy, a member of a Senate investigating committee, and Robert F. Kennedy, the committee's chief counsel. Maria Callas, thirty-five, left an Italian millionaire, Giovanni Meneghini, for the shipping czar Aristotle Socrates Onassis. Some gossips thought that at fifty-three Onassis was too old for her.

Increasingly the decade was being compared with the 1920s. Zany as they were, the 1950s had witnessed nothing comparable to the ukulele or flagpole sitting until 1958, when the deficiency was spectacularly remedied by two young toymen in San Gabriel, California. Richard Knerr and Arthur Melin, co-owners of an enterprise called the Wham-O Manufacturing Company, had started making slingshots after World War II with less than $1,000 capital. In 1957 they had racked up their first big score with Frisbees, light plastic saucers which could be skimmed slowly through the air from one thrower to another. At a New York toy fair in March 1958 an acquaintance told them that large wooden hoops had achieved swift and startling popularity in Australia; children rotated them on their hips. Back at Wham-O, Knerr and Melin went into production with wooden hoops. After twenty or so they stopped; they didn't like wood and wanted to experiment with plastics. In May they had what they wanted: three-foot hoops of gaudy polyethylene tubing which could be marketed at ninety-three cents each, representing a 16 percent gross profit. Wham-O's new toy was christened the hula hoop.

Patenting the hoops was impossible and by Labor Day a dozen other firms were turning out imitations under other trademarks. Even so, by early September Wham-O had sold two million hula hoops for a net profit of over $300,000. Then adults started using them for calisthenics. Wham-O's bookkeeper couldn't keep up with the production figures. Workers went into three shifts. Counting the copiers at home and abroad, hula hoop sales that autumn were reckoned in the tens of millions. So widespread was their use that European medical journals warned of injuries which might be sustained by enthusiasts. It was a long list. In Leiden, Holland, a Dutch woman was being wheeled into surgery for removal of her appendix when her physician found that what was really wrong with her was a torn abdominal muscle, the result of strenuous gyrations inside a hoop. In England, where a quarter-million hulas had been sold, the British Medical Association cautioned, "No one with a known heart disease should try it, and anyone who is out of training should not go hard at it right away." Japanese emergency wards were filling up with hoopers suffering from slipped discs and dislocated backbones. After a child was killed chasing a runaway hula the hoops were banned from Tokyo streets. Nevertheless sales there passed the three million mark. Lines of Japanese waiting to buy more stretched down the Ginza for blocks, and Premier Nobusuke Kishi received one as a gift on his sixty-second birthday.

Queen Mother Zaine of Jordan, returning from a visit to Europe, included a hula in her luggage. That should have been a guarantee of respectability, but some toymakers were nervous just the same. One of hooping's attractions for adult spectators was its suggestiveness on some hips. An unexpected pleasure at football games that autumn was a view of winsome drum majorettes pumping their loins in a frenzy of excitement as thousands cheered. A French manufacturer of hoops, Jacques de Saint-Phalle, was afraid the church might notice and object. Saint-Phalle had a reputation to safeguard; in hoopless times he made his living manufacturing plastic tubing for hospitals and laboratories. To protect himself he persuaded French celebrities to be photographed hooping. Finland solved the same problem by staging marathons in which participants had to keep three hulas going, at the neck, hips, and knees.

Elsewhere the American fad swept on, whatever watchers with coarse minds thought. In Germany it was popularized by the prize-fighter Max Schmeling and his wife Anny Ondra. Germans who had no children, and therefore no easy explanation for buying toys, avoided embarrassment by having stores deliver them, wrapped, at night. A party of Belgian explorers leaving for the South Pole disclosed that twenty hoops were in their baggage; the expense was charged to morale. In some countries hoop shortages were serious. Correspondents in Johannesburg, where hulas were retailing at sixty-five cents, reported that only white customers could afford them; the natives were restless until charitable organizations started distributing free hoops. *Het Vrije Volk* of Amsterdam noted that Dutch industries requiring plastic tubing were at a standstill, and in Warsaw a weekly newspaper for young Poles observed, "If the Ministry of Light Industry and the Chamber of Artisans do not embark upon the production of hoops, we will be seriously delayed in hula hoop progress, especially on the international level." The ministry and the chamber continued to be dilatory, so hulas were smuggled in through East Germany.

The craze receded as quickly as it had spread. By the summer of 1959 discarded hoops had begun to pile up in city dumps, but the rage had been a singular illustration of how great a grasp even the trivia of American mass culture had on the rest of the world.

In Europe, Whitehall and the Quai d'Orsay had blamed Dulles for the Suez disaster; in Washington, a number of members of the Eisenhower administration were inclined to agree with them. Given the Mideast as it was after Suez, however, there were no two minds about what Washington's next move should be. It was an article of cold war faith that every desirable part of the world must belong to either the Communist world or the Free World. Sherman Adams wrote in 1961:

> The defeat of the attempt by Britain and France to settle the Suez Canal controversy by military force temporarily destroyed the prestige and political power of those two nations in the Middle East

. . . Unless the United States undertook to fill the vacuum and made
clear to the world the intention to do so, the President said, the Soviets could be counted upon to move into the Middle East and we
would find ourselves in an intolerable situation.

The President told the congressional leadership, "I just do not believe that we can leave a vacuum in the Middle East," and to a
joint session on the Hill he asked for authority to use U.S. troops
there "to secure and protect the territorial integrity and political
integrity and political independence of . . . nations requesting such
aid against overt armed aggression from any nation controlled by
International Communism." This was the Eisenhower Doctrine. Like
FDR's undeclared war of 1940–41, Truman's decision to send American soldiers to Korea without consulting Congress, and the Formosa
resolution of 1955, the doctrine was another long step toward presidential authority to use U.S. armed forces anywhere.

Adams put his finger on one weakness in the Eisenhower Doctrine. "The difficulty in any American attempt to stop the spread of
Communism abroad," he wrote, "was in trying to prove that an
internal upheaval which posed as a nationalist struggle was really
under the direction of Moscow." The resolution supporting the doctrine passed the House easily but ran into trouble in the Senate.
As in the Formosa resolution debate, critical senators were divided.
Some believed the White House was trying to share responsibility
for what should be an executive decision; others thought Eisen-
hower was asking for the right to make war. Richard Russell of
Georgia and Fulbright of Arkansas were particularly apprehensive.
Russell told Dulles, "We are being asked to buy a pig in a poke."
Dulles replied that the issue was one of loyalty. He said to Russell,
"If we are going to pinpoint everything, if Congress is not willing
to trust the President . . . we can't win this battle."

But where was the battle? Britain and France having laid down
their arms, the only Mideast danger spots were disputes between
Arabs and Israel in the Gaza Strip and the Gulf of Aqaba. After two
months of debate the Senate approved the resolution 72 to 19. "During the following year," Adams wrote, "there were a series of
explosive developments in Jordan, Syria, and Lebanon, and all involved, directly or indirectly, the application of the Eisenhower
Doctrine." In reality they mostly involved its inapplicability. Trouble in Jordan arose in a classic Mideastern form: anti-Israel Arabs
rocked Amman, forcing the resignation of young King Hussein's

premier. The king then appealed to Eisenhower, claiming that the crisis was "the responsibility of international Communism and its followers." Dulles endorsed this motion, and the President sent the Sixth Fleet to make a whiff-of-grape demonstration in the eastern Mediterranean. In the shadow of the guns Hussein selected a loyal government. The rioters having dispersed, the new premier survived. There is no evidence that the outcome would have been different without the warships.

The Syrian blowup came next, and it had an *opéra bouffe* air. Dulles was eager to show the flag in Damascus, but the Syrians weren't buying that. The government favored the Soviet Union; the opposition consisted of anti-American officers; each preferred to be left alone with the other. King Saud of Saudi Arabia assured Eisenhower that ideology had nothing to do with the feud, that no true Arab could be a Communist. The President replied that he had heard that one before; de Gaulle had told him that "no true Frenchman could be a Communist." "Obviously, the turmoil was Communist-inspired," Adams wrote, "but, in contrast to the situation in Jordan, the Syrian government wanted nothing to do with any assistance from the West, and there was therefore little that Eisenhower could do about it. This was an example of the weakness of the Eisenhower Doctrine."

On the morning of July 14, 1958, Washington awoke to learn that the Middle East was in the throes of one of its periodic convulsions. During the night pro-Nasser Arab nationalists in Iraq had seized the Baghdad radio station, post office, cable office, and the bridges over the Tigris River. Advancing on the royal palace, they put the king and the crown prince to the sword. Premier Nuri as-Said tried to escape disguised as a woman, but he, too, was captured and slain. This knocked out the central prop holding up Dulles's Baghdad Pact, which was only six months old.[*] It also panicked President Camille Chamoun of Lebanon. Earlier Chamoun had accused Arab Communists of a massive infiltration of his regime. Secretary General Dag Hammarskjöld had personally led a United Nations observation team investigating the charge. They had found no evidence supporting Chamoun's fears. Now, convinced that he was next

[*] Citing the Eisenhower Doctrine, Dulles had assured member countries that the United States would shield them from subversion with a "mobile power of great force." After the Baghdad coup the alliance was re-created, omitting Iraq, as the Central Treaty Organization (CENTO), with headquarters in Ankara, Turkey.

on Nasser's list, he formally requested the dispatch of American troops to Beirut. Eisenhower consented.

This was 1930s isolationism turned on its head, the far swing of the interventionist pendulum. By no stretch of the imagination could American security be said to be in jeopardy. After 9,000 U.S. Marines had been put ashore under the watchful eye of 70 Sixth Fleet warships and 420 fighter planes, until then the greatest concentration of American armed might ever assembled in peacetime, the President issued a statement explaining that "The mission of these forces is to protect American lives—there are about 2,500 Americans in Lebanon," but there was not a shred of proof that any Americans (or Lebanese, for that matter) were in danger. Moreover, by raising that issue the President in effect conceded that the Eisenhower Doctrine was irrelevant. Dulles tried to convince the congressional leadership that it was. If the United States did not act on Chamoun's request, the Secretary of State warned, "our prestige is gone; nobody will take our word again—ever. If we get there first, there might not be Communist intervention." Fail to act, he said, and the free world would lose not only the Mideast and nearly three-fourths of the free world's oil reserve with it, but also Africa and non-Communist Asia. This catechism was to be recited by cold-warriors as a justification for the use of force in every international crisis down to and including Vietnam. Eisenhower had resisted it in 1954. This time resistance came from the leaders on the Hill. They made it plain that they wanted no share in the responsibility for the Lebanese move.

To all intents and purposes, that was the end of the Eisenhower Doctrine. Four months later Chamoun was replaced by a neutralist president and premier, and at their request the marines were withdrawn. The episode had been "a frustrating and unhappy experience for Eisenhower," Adams concluded. Its implications were graver than they seemed at the time; the President had warned the senators and representatives that he might have to risk war in the Mideast without prior discussion in Congress—"In this case," he said, "if there has to be a public debate about the course of action, there would be no use in taking it at all"—thereby adding to the sanction of precedent under which presidential power to make war was expanding.

Gunboat diplomacy on the other side of the globe was something new for the United States. It suggested an imperial presence, and that is precisely what such Europeans as Reiner Hellman, author of *Amerika auf dem Europäischen Markt,* and J.-J. Servan-Schreiber of *Le Défi Américain (The American Challenge)* believed they saw rising on the western rim of their horizon. To prewar Europeans the old America had appeared to be a land of affluence and bally-hoo, where everyone looked like Gary Cooper and Ginger Rogers and had children like Mickey Rooney and Ann Rutherford. That U.S.A. had been idealistic and innocent, the wonder and secret envy of the world. Except in time of natural disasters, when Americans were Good Samaritans, they had played virtually no role in world affairs.

Now they were all over the globe. Missionaries of Point Four, ECA, and technical assistance programs had fanned out across Africa and Asia. Congress had chartered the Development Loan Fund for underdeveloped countries, Fulbright scholarships, and Smith-Mundt exchanges for forty-two countries not covered by the Fulbright program. The number of American tourists abroad was increasing 12 percent annually; there were more than two million U.S. tourists in far lands in the late 1950s, and they were spending more than two billion dollars a year there.

It was not always spent wisely and gracefully. For every European who said with Churchill, "I love these Americans. They have behaved so generously," there was one or more who shared the contempt of Jean-Paul Sartre: *"Les Américains ne comprendront jamais rien à existentialisme."* Defenders of older cultures on the continent and in Asia felt threatened by the spread of Americanization. They were alarmed by the appeal of America's teen-age culture, especially its music, for the world's youth. Jazz could be heard almost everywhere. The young king of Thailand was writing songs for a Broadway musical called *Peep Show,* and the king of Cambodia taught himself to play a hot saxophone. And then there were the American soft drinks. In Bangkok the prime minister was the Coca-Cola concessionaire and the police chief had the Pepsi-Cola franchise; Adlai Stevenson called their rivalry "the ice cold war." Coke was ahead there and everywhere else. The sun never set on it. Every day people abroad consumed fifty billion bottles of it, enough Coke to float a light cruiser.

"What we are faced with," Servan-Schreiber wrote, "is not classic imperialism driven by a desire for conquest, but an overflow of power due to the difference in 'pressure' between America and the rest of the world." U.S. industry was in the process of investing 57.5 billion dollars in overseas plants, with a gross output of about 100 billion dollars a year. "One by one," Servan-Schreiber warned, "American firms are setting up headquarters to coordinate their activities throughout Western Europe."

As the American giants grew larger and stronger, Europeans, Asians and Africans became more curious about the quality of life in the United States. Not everything they heard was accurate and balanced. Admirers of the Soviet Union and the new China came down hard on racial discrimination, picturing the Montgomery bus boycott and Little Rock as race riots. Most accounts of American society emphasized the high standard of living; it was becoming a source of bitterness. The gap between the American standard and that of the rest of the world, particularly in the emerging countries, was steadily widening. In 1950 Premier Liaquat Ali Khan of Pakistan said on a visit to the United States: "As I let myself ponder over this, I suddenly see the United States of America as an island—a fabulously prosperous island. And all around this island I see the unhealthy sea of misery, poverty, and squalor in which millions of human beings are trying to keep their heads above water. At such moments I fear for this great nation as one fears for a dear friend."

U.S. embassies, USIS libraries, and cultural centers around the globe became targets in forty major riots. Spontaneous attacks on the American flag were now a common phenomenon, the reason in most cases being a long-smoldering anti-Americanism among the demonstrators which, for one reason or another, had reached the flash point. There were five such disturbances in Indonesia alone. They were by no means confined to nations whose leaders were critical of the United States. Demonstrations occurred in neutral capitals—Algiers, Cairo, and Khartoum among them—and even in those of U.S. allies, including Rio de Janeiro, Athens, Saigon, Taipeh, and Panama City.

Americans were puzzled. They had thought of themselves as being generous with foreign aid programs, unaware that, as Leon Keyserling wrote, the actual percentage of America's Gross National Product that flowed into international economic cooperation and assistance was "so imperceptible that one blushes to mention it." The American man in the street suspected that the rioters had been misled by agitators. If they understood the benefits of free enterprise, he thought, they would want it, too. In his naiveté he omitted the many other factors that made the U.S. mix so successfully, natural resources and the temperate climate being among them. He thought that if men in other lands only knew how prosperous the U.S. was, they would cheer the Stars and Stripes, not defile it. It never occurred to him that documenting that prosperity would be regarded as intolerable gloating.

It didn't occur to his leaders, either. In boning up for visits abroad, Vice President Nixon memorized charts and graphs showing how much better off Americans were than less fortunate people. After one of the visits he described how, in discussions with citizens in host countries, he had awaited an opening and then rammed his points home:

> I cited figures to show that the 44 million families in America own 56 million cars, 50 million television sets, 143 million radio sets, and that 31 million of those families own their own home. Then I made the point that so many people overlook. What these statistics dramatically demonstrate is this: that the United States, the world's largest capitalist country, has from the standpoint of the distribution of wealth come closest to the ideal of prosperity for all in a classless society.

By midpoint in the second Eisenhower administration, a considerable number of people overseas had heard this line of reasoning. President Eisenhower had taken to sending Mr. and Mrs. Nixon abroad a lot. In the interests of international good will the Vice President had endured diarrhea in Indonesia, Afghanistan, and Ethiopia, picketing in Burma, insults in Casablanca, and a sweaty hour trapped in a defective Mexico City elevator.

These efforts were to be capped, in the spring of 1958, by a strenuous eighteen-day tour of South America with stops in Uruguay, Colombia, Argentina, Paraguay, Bolivia, Ecuador, Peru, and Venezuela. It was to be a neighborly gesture, and Nixon expected it to be boring. Afterward he wrote: "Of all the trips I made abroad as Vice President the one I least wanted to take was my visit to South America in 1958—not because I thought it would be difficult but because I thought it would be relatively unimportant and uninteresting compared with the assignments I had in Washington at that time." The CIA had assured him that the trip would be uneventful. To newspapermen who were hesitant about covering it he said that they would probably miss little if they stayed home.

There wasn't much in the beginning. South Americans of the ruling classes, who welcomed the Nixons to Montevideo, Buenos Aires, Asunción, and La Paz, were accustomed to North American policy makers taking them for granted. Under Assistant Secretary Henry Holland, who kept watch on Latin America for Dulles, the State Department fought all proposals for U.S. loans to countries there on the ground that if liberals came to power they might try to regulate businessmen, thus depressing business morale. The elite in the first countries Nixon visited knew that, appreciated it, and had no intention of rocking the boat.

Here and there on street corners intense young men held up signs calling the *yanqui* Vice President "Racist," "Imperialist," and "Son of a Dog." One placard advised him to "Go back to the U.S.A. where you enjoy the lynchings of Negroes and massacres of Indians." As a forthright politician, he paused wherever possible to explain that he wasn't a racist, an imperialist, or a son of a dog; that he didn't enjoy lynchings or massacres and had not, in fact, participated in any of them. But these incidents didn't amount to much. The number of pickets at his early stops were so few he didn't notice them. For every hostile placard there were greeters to welcome him with the Latin *abrazo,* a good-natured bear hug. He heard some students chanting *"Fuera Nixon."* His translator told him it meant "Go home, Nixon." He said smilingly that he didn't want to go; people were much friendlier here.

No one later could remember exactly when and where the chants changed to *"Muera Nixon"*—death to Nixon. He was jeered in Buenos Aires on the fifth day and booed in Asunción on the sixth, but on the whole the crowds remained cordial. Bolivians showered him with flying confetti; there were no visible signs of danger there. Actually he had been lucky. An attack on him had been narrowly averted in Bolivia by blowing up a railroad track to isolate a mining town where protesters wearing bandoliers of dynamite sticks had assembled. Elsewhere police vigilance had turned away men bent on violence. Such good fortune couldn't favor the Nixons all the way, and it didn't. Their first inkling that disaster might lie ahead came in Lima, Peru, on Wednesday, May 7, their eleventh day away from home.

The reception at Lima Airport was gracious, but as the motorcade entered the city Nixon observed that there were not many people on the streets and most of those who were there "did not seem to be aware" of who he was. The Peruvian official in his car explained that the motorcade route had not been published, to avoid "incidents." This, Nixon was to recall, was "somewhat disquieting since I had not anticipated any incidents in friendly Peru."

Little is known about the leaders of the mobs which were to confront Nixon there and later in Venezuela. They are shadowy figures, made more so by Nixon's later insistence that all his troubles could be traced to a centrally controlled Communist conspiracy. Upon his arrival at Lima's majestic Grand Hotel Bolívar, he wrote afterward, the extent of the plot was revealed to him: "It was apparent that the Communists, after the failure of their efforts to disrupt my tour in Uruguay, Argentina, or Bolivia, had decided to make an all-out effort to embarrass me and the United States at San Marcos University, an institution so well known throughout Latin America that whatever happened there would be front-page news everywhere." Watching the demonstrators, he thought, "How are they able to stir the people up to this pitch? Then I realized as this was going on that right here was the ruthlessness and the determination, the fanaticism of the enemy that we face. That was what I saw in the faces of the mob. This is really Communism as it is." Noting the youth of the crowds, he wrote, "My reaction was a feeling of absolute hatred for the tough Communist agitators who were driving children to this irrational state."

This is largely conjecture. Undoubtedly there were Communists in the forces which were forming against him in Peru and Venezuela, and clearly people were inflamed by the *Tribuna Popular*, the Communist weekly, which ran a front-page picture of him retouched so that his teeth looked like fangs and his expression was that of a madman. But to infer from this that all the Latin-American demonstrators protesting his trip were being manipulated and coordinated by agents of the Cominform is, to put it mildly, rich. The CIA was far from omniscient in these years—the agency had been caught napping by the Iraqi coup—but it is hard to believe that it would have missed something that big. A more reasonable interpretation is that poor people, regarding themselves as victims of injustice, saw an opportunity to express their hatred of the wealthy and—understandably—took it. Communists and extremists of other persuasions then added fuel to the flames of anti-American rage that had sprung up on their own.

The mobs in Lima were ugly, but there was a respite for the vice-presidential party afterward. Four days in Ecuador and Colombia provided an opportunity to regain the strength needed for the last and most risky stop: Caracas. The situation in Venezuela was volatile, the mood in the streets was ugly, and the ruling junta, which had been in power less than four months, had not taken the vigorous measures needed to suppress the troublemakers. Unwilling to acknowledge its helplessness, the new government responded to periodic inquiries from the American embassy with assurances that it foresaw no serious incidents for the Vice President and that it was prepared to deal with any which might arise.

Caracas was the one city in which Communist plotting against Nixon was probably a factor. South American Communists are proud of their ability to organize, and the Venezuelan mobs awaiting him had been well prepared. As the vice-presidential aircraft entered its glide pattern over Maiquetía Airport on the morning of Tuesday, May 13, five crowds took up strategic positions. One was at the air terminal. Three others lay in wait for the motorcade on the twelve-mile road between the airfield and the Panteón Plaza in the center of Caracas, where Nixon was scheduled to lay a wreath on the tomb of Simón Bolívar. The last and largest of the crowds, in the plaza itself, was armed with Molotov cocktails. At one place or another, the ringleaders expected Nixon to be torn to pieces and burned. In Venezuela that is regarded as the most degrading death possible. The previous January it had been the fate of policemen defending the outgoing regime, and the fresh memory of that doubtless accounts for the reluctance of surviving police officers to come to Nixon's aid.

Official laxity went beyond that, however, and some aspects of it are still puzzling. American correspondents covering the Vice President's tour landed before he did and found that five hundred anti-Nixon teen-agers had been bused to the airfield and deployed on the terminal's observation deck. Obviously they were there to make trouble. Already they were shaking fists and shouting insults at the plane overhead. Yet when Secret Service agents asked the Venezuelan security chief to make them move, he refused, saying, "They are harmless. They have a right to demonstrate." He then

ordered the motorcade to form in the street beyond the terminal
instead of at the customary place on the field. That meant the Nixons would have to walk another hundred yards, through demonstrators. His subsequent explanation—that the sleek motorcade
limousines would have detracted from the splendor of the honor
guard—was preposterous.

Other suspicious figures that day included the bandleader at the
airport, who knew that whenever he struck up the American or
Venezuelan national anthem the Vice President would have to stand
at attention, and the authorities responsible for safeguarding the
motorcade route. These last were the most derelict of all. They told
Americans responsible for the Vice President's safety that all traffic
on it had been halted an hour before his arrival. This was untrue;
heavy traffic on it continued. In addition, men and material for the
three ambushes had been assembled at points where even a casual
inspection would have revealed them. Junta complicity in the plot
is unthinkable, but hope for a newsworthy episode is not. Latin
American editors had noted that the disorders in Lebanon and elsewhere had attracted American attention and aid. If shaking the Vice
President up would end U.S. complacency about its southern neighbors, they implied it would not be wholly deplorable. Nixon later
found this explanation for the poor security persuasive. He noted,
with commendable restraint, that those responsible cannot have
known much about mobs.

In descending an airplane ramp he customarily sized up a crowd
to see what kind of reception he might expect. One glance at these
shrieking youths told him, as he put it afterward, that "here was
one place where we would have an altogether different situation
than we ever had in any country I visited." The interpreter said,
"They aren't friendly, Mr. Vice President." Nixon didn't have to understand Spanish to know that; the din was so great that he could
scarcely hear the national anthems and the 19-gun salute for him.
Before the last 105 shells had been fired he decided to skip the
other airport formalities, notably the greeting to him and his response. To the interpreter he said, "Look, we're not going to do
the mike scene," and to Venezuela's foreign minister, Oscar García
Lutín, "Let's dispense with the customary speeches here and go directly to our cars. No one could possibly hear what we said over
the noise of this mob."

It was then that he missed the limousines. He turned to where they should have been and discovered instead that the red carpet ran all the way to the terminal building, through it, and out the other side. There in the distance the cars gleamed. In between angry teen-agers were forming ranks and brandishing gamy fruit and other refuse. The bayonets of the honor guard might have been useful, but their commander was nowhere to be found.

The situation was rapidly deteriorating when the Americans found unexpected allies: thirty aircraft mechanics at the field. They cheered him as the others booed, making themselves so conspicuous that they briefly distracted the crowd. That gave the Americans time to slip into the terminal building. Coming out of it, Nixon and his wife were just below the observation deck when the bandleader decided to replay the Venezuelan national anthem. The Nixons froze. The Vice President had what he afterward called "the sensation that rain was falling"; then he realized that it was spittle. The saliva was coming from the crowd overhead, and some of it, from tobacco chewers, fell on the new red suit Pat Nixon had bought for the trip, staining it with splotches of a dirty brown. A rubber noisemaker struck Nixon on the face. The music ended. He took Pat's arm and they waded into the throng, toward the cars, following a flying wedge of Secret Service agents and Americans from the embassy.

With a sudden lurch the wedge shoved the Vice President into the first car and Pat into the second. Secret Service agents and interpreters followed. As they rapidly rolled up windows and wiped the saliva from their faces and clothes, they were joined by their host and hostess, Foreign Minister García Lutín in Nixon's limousine and Señora García Lutín in Mrs. Nixon's. Both were mortified. García Lutín, a gentle, mild-mannered man, tried to clean the worst of the spittle from the Vice President's suit. "Don't bother," Nixon said sharply. "I am going to burn these clothes as soon as I can get out of them." The foreign minister then tried to explain. He said, "The Venezuelan people have been without freedom so long that they tend now to express themselves more vigorously perhaps than they should. In our new government we do not want to do anything which would be interpreted as a suppression of freedom." Nixon replied, "If your new government doesn't have the guts and good sense to control a mob like the one at the airport, there soon will be no freedom for anyone in Venezuela."

The ride into Caracas was hair-raising. Led by a police escort and a press truck, they were going 40 mph on the Autopista, a modern dual-lane highway, while demonstrators on motorcycles and motor scooters zigzagged in and out of the motorcade, shouting, spitting, and throwing rotten fruit at the lead car. The windows had to remain closed. The air inside—there was no air-conditioning —became stifling. Approaching the city, Nixon noticed that the sidewalks were deserted and the shops locked and shuttered. He was about to remark that this was ominous when he heard a dull thud. Momentarily he thought the driver had hit a pothole. Then he heard another thud and then another; the car was being hit by flying rocks. Simultaneously the chauffeur slammed on his brakes and skidded to a halt. They had reached the city limits and the first ambush. A tattered mass of people of all ages and descriptions came boiling out of a dingy alley nearby and rushed into the street hurling heavy stones. The roadblock here was unfinished, and the driver found a way around it, but a few minutes later he braked again. On a slope where the Autopista curves into the city and becomes the lower end of the Avenida Sucre, a six-lane roadway with a center divider, it bisects one of the poorest neighborhoods in Caracas, and the second trap was there. A huge dump truck and several buses and cars had been parked in the street and abandoned. Another ragged throng carrying placards and clubs came howling down on the stalled motorcade. There were more rocks here, and several wild-eyed demonstrators flung themselves at Nixon's limousine.

Here, too, a detour was found, and the motorcade raced on, tense and silent, until, in the very center of Caracas and almost at their destination, the way was blocked by the most elaborate barricade yet. Three banks of buses, trucks, and automobiles had been parked directly in the path of the motorcade. The chauffeur could not cross the center island because there the traffic was one-way, toward them, and it was hopelessly jammed anyhow. For a few seconds nothing happened. The silence was eerie. Then Agent Jack Sherwood said under his breath, "Here they come."

Later estimates of this mob put it between two and five hundred. Running full tilt and spitting as they came, the demonstrators brandished axes, poles, and sections of pipe. Watching from the motorcade's press car, Earl Mazo of the *New York Herald Tribune* thought the spectacle looked "like a scene from the French Revolution." This was the ultimate in mobs, a killer mob. The saliva stream-

ing down the windshield was so thick that the driver turned on
the windshield wiper. The leaders rode pickaback, shouting instructions and leading the chant: "Muera Nixon! Muera Nixon!" Their
obvious aim was to get the Vice President and drag him out, by
opening the doors if possible, by smashing the windows if not. A
large stone hit one window and stuck in the special glass, spraying
splinters from it into García Lutín's face. He cried, "It's in my eye!
My eye!" Another window, the one by the interpreter, was hit by
a length of iron pipe. It did not give way entirely, but pieces of
it struck the interpreter's mouth. Sherwood, hit, began to bleed.
Fragments struck Nixon in the face. Another piece of pipe, thrust
through the opening, wobbled toward him.

The foreign minister, almost hysterical, sobbed, "This is terrible,
terrible." Nixon looked out the back window. As he remembered
afterward, he was relieved to see that Pat was chatting away with
Señora García Lutín, "as though the trouble was no worse than an
afternoon traffic jam on the Hollywood Freeway." Her driver had
showed presence of mind by pushing his front bumper against the
front limousine, so that the mob couldn't get at the Vice President
through the rear window. The demonstrators, Nixon saw, were not
interested in Pat's car. Those were the only bright spots, however.
The violence had continued here for twelve minutes, and now it
seemed that it could have but one outcome.

Inside the limousine they heard one of the pickaback commanders
outside shout an order. The car began to rock. To those who knew
the ways of mobs—as all here did—this was the most frightening
development yet. Rioters unable to get in an automobile rock it,
trying to turn it over and set it afire, cremating the occupants. The
window beside Nixon gave way. Sherwood and another agent, in
the front seat, drew their guns.

At that moment, about 12:45 P.M. on May 13, 1958, Richard Nixon's chances of surviving the afternoon were even slighter than he
knew. Four blocks away at the Bolívar Tomb an American scouting
party, which included a Secret Service agent, the embassy's military
attachés, and the Vice President's administrative assistant, had arrived early to appraise the situation for the wreath-laying ceremony.
They were aghast. Between six and eight thousand angry people
were milling around. Here, as at the airport, police protection had
disappeared. In the place of law officers, surly demonstrators were

waiting at strategic corners on the Avenida Sucre. Their hostility toward Americans was obvious. The attachés being in uniform, they were kicked, spat upon, and manhandled, and a window in an embassy station wagon was broken. Thoroughly alarmed, the scouting party sent back three separate warning messages in code over a prearranged radio network centered at Caracas police headquarters.

At the third barricade the motorcade was disintegrating. Drivers behind the leading cars who could find a way clear were wheeling out of line and racing away down side streets, leaving the embattled American Vice President and his escorts to their fate. So chaotic had the situation become that to this day there is confusion over how Nixon escaped. According to his recollection, the driver of the truck carrying the correspondents who were covering the tour "somehow . . . edged his way into the oncoming lane of traffic, clearing a path for us like a football blocker leading a ball carrier. Our driver took us down the wrong side of the street with Mrs. Nixon's car following behind us." Mazo of the *Herald Tribune* was on that truck, however, and in his memory, just as the violence seemed to be reaching a murderous climax, "some Venezuelan soldiers showed up. They made a narrow opening in the traffic tie-up. Mrs. Nixon's car followed close behind."

The limousines at that time were still headed for the Panteón Plaza. In the last block before reaching it the Vice President told the chauffeur to swerve down an alley and take off in the opposite direction. The foreign minister cried, "We can't leave our protection!" Nixon said, "If that's the kind of protection we're going to get, we're better off going it alone." Once they were safe on another main boulevard he ordered a stop so that he could talk to Pat and take stock. The lead car was a wreck; all its windows were broken and its fenders smashed, and everyone in it had been scratched or cut. At the same time, no one had been seriously injured. The ladies were unhurt and the way ahead was clear. They drove directly to the U.S. embassy residence, located on the top of a steep, easily defensible hill in Caracas's exclusive Las Lomas neighborhood. Nixon took his first nap in twelve years of public life, sleeping the sleep of the exhausted; the rest of the men turned the hill into a fortress. The embassy's marine detachment and the Secret Service agents were reinforced by sixty American military men who were in the country as instructors of the Venezuelan armed forces. All messages, packages, and letters coming to the embassy were screened by security men. Plans were secretly drawn to leave Caracas at 3 P.M. the following day, nine hours ahead of schedule, and at Maiquetía Airport other guards prepared to defend the vice-presidential aircraft against possible attack.

Meanwhile, back in Washington, orders had been cut for a fantastic rescue mission. Lacking information about the Nixon party and warned to expect the worst, President Eisenhower had dispatched to Venezuela six destroyers, a guided-missile cruiser, and an aircraft carrier equipped to land marines by helicopter. A thousand marines and paratroopers were suiting up at Guantánamo Bay and on Puerto Rico, and Air Force fighters and bombers had been alerted to stand by. Nixon himself knew nothing of this. Dulles had cabled him the details, but this message, like the others that day, never reached its destination. The Nixons were dining alone in the privacy of their room at the embassy when the ambassador interrupted them. Word of the sensational new development had just reached him via a news report. The Pentagon had announced it at 6:05 P.M., explaining in a communiqué that "The movement is being undertaken so these troops will be in a position to cooperate with the Venezuelan government if assistance is requested."

This was an unexpected propaganda gift to the Venezuelan extremists responsible for the mobs. They had been in disgrace, but now they were almost forgotten as all Latin America protested the armada, which awakened in them the worst fears of North American imperialism. Nixon and the ambassador quickly issued a joint statement explaining that everyone was safe and there was no need for outside help. Next morning, when communications had been restored, the President was able to telephone the Vice President, who reassured him.

At Washington National Airport fifteen thousand people cheered Nixon as he came down the ramp. Eisenhower was there, accompanied by his entire cabinet. Nixon spoke briefly, saying that the best part of going away was coming home and that most of the people he had seen in his South American travels had been friendly.

Lima and Caracas had tested the Vice President and tempered him, but the effect of the incident on Nixon's popularity was as brief as it was immense. In June 1958, a month later, the Gallup poll showed him leading Adlai Stevenson for the first time and running a dead heat with Kennedy. It was the high point of his popularity in the 1950s. By the end of autumn it would be a memory. The Republicans were in trouble, and as their ranking politician he was, too.

Society knows few greater satisfactions than the discovery of a puritan caught practicing what he has preached against, and rarely does it happen so startlingly as in the month after Richard Nixon's return from Venezuela. The scandal was accompanied by a symbol as memorable as any in the influence-peddling 1940s. For 1958 not only produced the hula hoop, the big TV quiz shows, and Alec Guinness in neighborhood theaters showing the Japs how to build that bridge over the River Kwai; it was also the year of the vicuña coat. Before that summer possibly one American in ten thousand could have told you that the vicuña is a small fleet-footed hoofed mammal found in the Andes from Ecuador to Bolivia and much hunted for the wool of its fine lustrous undercoat, which is woven into fine cloth. By July 4 every taxpayer knew that a vicuña topcoat was to men what mink was to women—warm, handsome, stylish, and a status symbol. The taxpayer knew, if for no other reason, because every Democrat running for office was telling the vicuña story.

It is a curious fact that no one ever cleared up the question of how much vicuña wool there was in the vicuña coat, although that was one reason the government had brought the manufacturer, Bernard Goldfine, to book; he had been putting a "90% wool, 10% vicuña" label on cloth that actually contained some nylon. This and all other aspects of the story were eclipsed by testimony that the White House had intervened in Goldfine's behalf and that he, in appreciation, had seen to it that one of his top-quality, five-hundred-dollar coats hung in the closet of the assistant to the President of the United States, the former governor of New Hampshire, Sherman Adams. Other expressions of Goldfine's gratitude had included the gift to Adams of a $2,400 Oriental rug from Macy's and picking up the tab on twenty-one occasions between 1955 and May 1958 when members of the Adams family had stayed at Boston's elegant Sheraton Plaza Hotel, running up bills totaling $3,096.56. He had also paid for Adams's stays at the Waldorf Astoria in Manhattan. Goldfine had then claimed all of these expensive favors as business expenses on his tax returns.

They were deductible, under Internal Revenue regulations, pro-

vided some "ordinary and necessary" benefit or advantage had
flowed to Goldfine businesses from the expenditure. It had, and he
could prove it. The two men were very close. Subpoenaed telephone
records were to reveal that over a six-month period Goldfine had
placed 43 long distance calls to Adams, about one every four days.
Adams had made countless others to the textile manufacturer and
in his behalf. On December 30, 1953, the President's chief of staff
had called Federal Trade Commission chairman Edward F. Howrey
—who owed his appointment to Adams—to ask the source for the
complaint against Goldfine for mislabeling textiles. On April 14,
1955, when the manufacturer was again under investigation for the
same charge, Adams used his influence to get Goldfine an appointment with Howrey. During it, Goldfine wielded the name of his
friend in a heavy-handed manner. "Please get me Sherman Adams
on the line," he ordered a secretary in a voice loud enough to be
heard in the next office. "Sherm, I'm over here at the FTC," he said
on the phone. "I was well treated over here."

The following year Adams had asked Gerald Morgan, the White
House special counsel, to ask Security and Exchange lawyers for
confidential information about an SEC investigation of Goldfine's
East Boston Company—a violation of the commission's rules. Later
John Fox, publisher of the *Boston Post*, was an especially damaging
witness. He testified that Goldfine regarded his friendship with the
President's assistant as a license to make deals. "He told me," Fox
said in one of his less plausible moments, "that as long as he had
Sherman Adams in his pocket he could do it." Fox further testified,
"I asked Mr. Goldfine just what his trouble . . . was and he told
me they had accused him of mislabeling." Later, "as a matter of
idle curiosity," Fox asked if Adams had taken care of the FTC matter, and Goldfine "told me that he had."

On that rare afternoon in June when the first choice Adams-
Goldfine revelations were entered into the record of the House Special Subcommittee on Legislative Oversight, the presidential aide
was delivering a baccalaureate address to the Holderness School
for boys in New Hampshire on "the questions the Bible tells us
shall be asked on Judgment Day." Adams had long been interested
in what was going to happen to sinners on that Day. Democrats
knew him as the stern moralist who had decried minks, freezers,
and influence peddling during Truman's tenure, calling that administration an "Augean stables" in a memorable January 1952 speech

and promising that Eisenhower would end such corruption. "Here is the man to do it," he said. "The kind of people with whom he has surrounded himself is answer enough for that."

Conservative Republicans also resented Adams. They remembered his accusations that Taft was stealing GOP delegate votes in Texas. "Thou shalt not steal," he had cried, wagging a finger at them. To them he was the man who had delivered a ruthless judgment against Air Force Secretary Harold Talbott because he had solicited business for his efficiency-engineering firm on official Air Force stationery. One of the bitterest ironies of the Goldfine disclosures was that White House secretaries, one of whom worked within seventy-five feet of President Eisenhower's desk, had accepted cash gifts from the textile manufacturer ranging from $35 to $150. Until now that would have been enough to bring instant dismissal from Eisenhower's chief of staff, who had warned them to be on the lookout for improper requests for influence. Now they could not even be reprimanded. In the West Wing of the White House members of the President's staff moved on tiptoe and spoke in whispers, as though someone in the First Family were gravely ill.

How had it happened? All his life Adams had been, as his eighty-two-year-old father put it, "sound as a dollar and square as a brick." His wife Rachel fondly called him "the Great Stone Face." In the White House he scrupulously paid for office stamps he put on personal letters and insisted that he be billed for personal phone calls. Until recently he had still used stationery headed "Sherman Adams, Governor of New Hampshire," with "ex-" typed in. He was always at his desk by 7:30 in the morning—that had been true in New Hampshire, too, where he had been known to wade through blizzards to get to work on time—and any member of the staff who came in after the office had opened would hear his sharp call: "You're late to work this morning!" In using the telephone he refused to waste valuable time saying "Hello" or "Good-bye." He began talking the instant the other person picked up the receiver, and when he had said his piece he promptly hung up, cutting off the other fellow in mid-sentence. No man had ever been more trusted by a President. He checked out every piece of paper, every visitor, and every decision headed for Eisenhower's desk, giving Ike clear options for choice, as in a short list of men eligible for a cabinet post. "Whatever I have to do," the President had told a press conference, "he has in some measure to do." Adams had never betrayed that enormous trust. How, then, had he wound up in the sticky embrace of a man like Bernard Goldfine?

Much of the answer lies in the fact that there were two Bernard Goldfines. One of them was a cheap, devious manipulator, always in and out of trouble with the government and capable of exploiting any relationship. That was the Goldfine who had attracted the interest of the House committee. But Adams had never met that man. The Goldfine he had known ever since the war was a self-made, humble, eager-to-please immigrant, a diamond in the rough eager to use his wealth in good causes. In Adams's words he was "an upright and honest citizen, trustworthy and reliable." The suggestion that he would stoop to underhanded practices was absurd. He didn't need to be underhanded; he was already rich. The Goldfine empire consisted of six textile mills in Maine, Vermont, New Hampshire, and Massachusetts and two real estate firms, East Boston Company and the Boston Port Development Company. Each year he gave $50,000 to charities. He, his wife, and his four children lived in a fashionable home in Boston's Chestnut Hill suburb.

Adams had been introduced to him by Norris Cotton, U.S. Senator from New Hampshire, as a public-spirited millionaire who refused to follow other textile manufacturers in the exodus south to cheap southern labor and taxes. Adams made inquiries and found that Goldfine was known to be a sound businessman with a good reputation in his trade; he treated his employees well, paid good wages, and had never been in trouble with the textile union. Once he had held a good-will conference between representatives of labor and management. It had been attended by the governors of Maine, New Hampshire, Vermont, and Massachusetts. His friends and admirers included Cotton, Senator Frederick Payne of Maine, Speaker of the House John McCormack, Mayor John Hynes of Boston, and John Steelman and Maurice Tobin of the Truman administration.

The congressional investigation of Goldfine's manipulations revealed that some of these friendships had seamy sides. He owned the house in which Cotton lived, and he had made Payne's purchase of a home possible by lending him $3,500 for a down payment without interest, which had never been repaid. His relationship with Fox had begun when he had taken the extraordinary step of extendng $400,000 credit to the *Post* in exchange for an editorial endorsement of Massachusetts Governor Paul A. Dever's campaign for reelection. Recently the Goldfine-Fox friendship had soured, which may account for the incriminating passages in Fox's testimony.

Goldfine and Adams had become and remained steadfast friends. Rachel Adams and Charlotte Goldfine were also close to one another. The four of them often spent weekends together—in his memoirs Adams describes Goldfine as "a man with a lot of good fun in him"—and when young Solomon Goldfine almost failed at Dartmouth, "Uncle Sherm" sternly lectured him and put him on the right track. In this context the gifts become more understandable. They went both ways; the Goldfines had an oil painting from Rachel, and Goldfine wore a gold Le Coultre wristwatch inscribed "To B.G. from S.A. Jan. 20, 1953." Adams was startled to learn that Goldfine had deducted the hotel bills on his tax returns. He had been under the impression that the suites were rented permanently by one of Goldfine's companies and would have been empty if Adams hadn't used them. As for the favors he had done for Goldfine, they weren't at all improper, he said. He hadn't guided him. Nor had he known that he had violated an FTC rule by making information available to his friend. In any event, that had been the extent of the accommodation. He would have done the same for any businessman bewildered by Washington bureaucracies.

White House correspondents hammered at Hagerty: "Does this indicate a departure from the administration's previous attitude toward freeloading by high officials?" He ducked: "I don't know what you mean by that. . . . This is a personal friend, if that's what you're talking about." They relentlessly pursued him: "It's all right for a personal friend?" He dodged again: "I stick with the letter that the governor issued. The facts are as they are."

The presidential assistant's failure to grasp the interpretation which others might put on his relationship with Goldfine stemmed in part from an inability to see himself as others might see him. Adams knew Adams to be honest; that was that. So was his friend; it couldn't be otherwise. Those close to the former governor believed that he had been flattered by the admiration of the Lithuanian immigrant who had followed the Horatio Alger course to the top. Adams's bedrock New England upbringing prevented him from being free with his own money, but he could not resist the lavish attentions of an openhanded big spender. Thus he had drifted thoughtlessly across a line.

Testifying before the subcommittee on June 7, a full week after the disclosure of his relationship with Goldfine, Adams acknowledged that he had been "imprudent." He said, "If . . . I have in any way so conducted myself as to cast any semblance of doubt upon such conduct, I can only say that the error was one of judgment and certainly not of intent." The question was whether that concession from him was adequate now. He had made it only after he had found that it was not enough to sit behind the White House gates and issue a statement attacking the "unwarranted and unfair insinuations" of his accusers. Newspaper editors, vigilant as always on the issue of morality in public servants, were reminding their readers that on May 4, 1956, President Eisenhower had said:

> If anyone ever comes to any part of this government . . . claiming some privilege . . . on the basis that he is part of my family or of my friends, that he has any connection with the White House, he is to be thrown out instantly . . . I can't believe that anybody on my staff would ever be guilty of an indiscretion. But if ever anything came to my attention of that kind, any part of this government, that individual would be gone.

Now, two years and fifty-five days later, Eisenhower faced 257 reporters in the Indian Treaty Room and doggedly declared that "Anyone who knows Sherman Adams has never had any doubt of his personal integrity and honesty. No one has believed that he could be bought." Adams had been accused of imprudence, and he had used that word himself. Ike said, "Now, the utmost prudence must necessarily be used by everyone attached to the White House . . . Carelessness must be avoided." But a valuable presidential aide should not be lost because he had skidded once, especially in these circumstances:

> I personally like Governor Adams. I admire his abilities. I respect him because of his personal and official integrity. I need him.
>
> Admitting the lack of that careful prudence in this incident . . . I believe with my whole heart that he is an invaluable public servant doing a difficult job efficiently, honestly, and tirelessly.

Ike had gone over the statement with Hagerty, who had approved it, believing that it would take the pressure off Adams. Only afterward did the presidential press secretary see the three damaging words leap from the pages: *I need him.* In a stroke the President had allowed his critics to depict him as a weak old man who could not govern without the help of an indispensable man and had permitted an exception to the White House rule that anyone on his staff involved in improper conduct should be fired.

The President, then, had gone bail for Adams's faith in his friend and benefactor Bernard Goldfine. Much would now depend upon the manner of the man with whom he had been imprudent. That came next and it destroyed Adams. The ensuing sessions on Capitol Hill turned into a burlesque. It began when Goldfine strode into the hearing room of the House subcommittee brandishing a twenty-five-page introductory statement. He had already angered the committee by releasing the text to the press at 7 A.M., three hours before he was scheduled to testify. Unperturbed and jaunty in a dark blue suit, wearing a blue silk tie initialed BG, he took the chair to read it. Then he removed his gold watch and passed it to the committee-men ("providing I get it back"), explaining, "The watch I am wearing now, on the back of it is written 'to B.G.'—that means Bernard Goldfine—'from S.A.'—that's Governor Sherman Adams—dated 'Jan. 20, 1953,' and we all know that date. That is the inauguration date President Eisenhower was inaugurated." In the visitors' section Rachel Adams winced. She had just realized that that was how their friend had been introducing himself to strangers, including federal officials, all these years.

In the spectacle that followed, the star millionaire was assisted by a worshipful secretary named Mildred Paperman; an entourage of lawyers headed by Roger Robb, who had been the heavy-handed cross-examiner of J. Robert Oppenheimer; Tex McCrary, a Manhattan press agent; and a press headquarters in Washington's Sheraton-Carlton Hotel featuring caviar, free whiskey, and "Press Receptionist" Bea Duprey, a Boston Venus whose most conspicuous activity was urging reporters to get her measurements (35-22-35) right. There was also a New York flack named Jack Lotto, who identified himself as "a former ace reporter for INS" and who, in his press releases, spelled his client's name "Bernard Goldfein." Late one night Lotto caught two spies bugging the office from the next room. One of them was a private detective, Baron (name, not title) Ignatius Sacklette, who had been working for the subcommittee. He was instantly dismissed. The other was Drew Pearson's leg-man, Jack Anderson. Pearson refused to fire Anderson. He said, "I need him."

On the first page of Goldfine's opening statement McCrary had printed in block letters the message: YOU WILL BE GREAT! In reality Goldfine was awful. McCrary had also underlined words to be emphasized. Instead of stressing them, Goldfine yelled them. Periodically McCrary had written "Glass of water." Unfortunately he had neglected to check out the committee room. There were no glasses there, only floppy paper cups, with the result that from time to time his client peered around in confusion. But neither McCrary nor any of the others was responsible for the devastating impression Goldfine made. He appeared to be a sleazy, amoral, double-shuffle con man because he was, in fact, a sleazy, amoral, double-shuffle con man.

His voice rasping and his tone belligerent, he told how he had clawed his way upward in New England's savage textile and real estate world. It was a world of which Eisenhower and Adams knew little. Whenever they thought of a businessman they thought of George Humphrey. Goldfine was of a different breed. Waving the watch and calling Fox a character assassin, he backpedaled frantically when committee counsel questioned him about his troubles with federal regulatory agencies. No, he had no records; "Paperwork has been out of my line." Ask his secretary; "After all, I'm not a bookkeeper. She is." Loyal Miss Paperman, seated a few feet away, piped up at this point in an attempt to explain why there were no records, and Robb snarled, "Keep quiet, keep quiet, keep *quiet!*" Begging the congressmen for understanding, Goldfine explained that Adams had merely given him directions to "these giant federal agencies where a little man gets lost without some kind of guidance from a friend."

At this juncture the subcommittee trapped him in a lie. In his opening statement he had flatly said, "The first difficulty that any of my mills ever had with the Federal Trade Commission was in November . . . 1953. Neither I nor anyone else in our companies had had prior experience with the FTC in matters of this type." His point, essential to his case and Adams's plausibility, was that when the FTC charged him with mislabeling in November 1953 he was so mystified that he needed Sherman Adams to explain what it was all about. Now subcommittee investigators produced proof that Goldfine had been inundated in 1942 and every year thereafter with FTC complaints accusing him of using labels that made his products appear to be of a higher quality than they were. At the hearing he answered weakly that this was just more paperwork and, besides, that they were "minor matters" and therefore not likely to get to his level. The congressmen didn't challenge him. They knew what else was coming.

Among the topics that Goldfine and Paperman were keeping quiet about, on the ground that they had no files, was a sum of $776,879.16, all of it in treasurer's checks and cashier's checks dating back to 1941 and, as of May 8, 1958, still uncashed. People in shady enterprises like money that way because, among other things, such checks have no time limit. Also, the name of a bank official, not that of the person footing the bill, appears on them. Finally, public officials fearful of cashing them because of the possibility of scandal may put them up as prime collateral for loans.

Goldfine refused to answer questions about his treasurer's and cashier's checks, saying that they were irrelevant. The committee counsel countered that they could hardly be called that, inasmuch as thirty of those which had been cashed had been given to legislative aides on Capitol Hill. The names of men close to John McCormack and Styles Bridges entered the transcript. Goldfine replied: "At Christmas time these are all checks that we have sent at different times to some of the poor workers who work in different offices at Christmas time. If that is something that is bad, I would like to be told about it."

He was told that it was bad to ease in and out of firms through dummy organizations and straw men, bad to match loans, bad to disregard federal and state regulations designed to protect the public, bad to subsidize a pack of big and little politicians who thus became indebted to him, and bad to build an incredible record of litigation, including 89 lawsuits in the Boston area alone. It was bad, and it was also criminal, to plunder his own companies, thereby defrauding fellow shareholders, and there had been a lot of that.

As the hearings progressed, Goldfine played more and more to the gallery, blustering and shouting his answers. He tried to argue that his infractions of the law had been insignificant, that he was the victim of legalisms—neglecting to file an annual report with the Vermont secretary of state, in one instance, and failure to take up his legal responsibilities as a company officer in others. As in most cases of financial skulduggery, the path of guilt was sometimes hard to follow, but plenty of Goldfine swindles were easy to understand. Operating through his secretary, who held key posts as treasurer and director in his firms, he repeatedly helped himself to generous sums of stockholder money. The pretenses for taking it varied. It would be called a loan, a sales commission, or repayment for non-existent expenses ($25,475 in the case of a local firm dealing in real estate). Sometimes there was no excuse at all. The cash just disappeared. Neither he nor Miss Paperman could account for some $89,000 taken out in the late 1940s. She blandly suggested that the bank had "made mistakes in the past, and these can be an error." It was hard to pin down exchanges because she and her employer were dealing every day with hundreds of thousands of dollars in liquid assets. In one respect ominous for Goldfine, however, the particulars didn't matter. Whatever had happened, he clearly owed the government far more than he had claimed on his tax returns.*

Afterward Adams wrote of his relationship with Goldfine that "I knew little or nothing about the details of his business dealings. I did not learn of his tax arrears until some of the facts began to unravel as a result of the hearings by the Legislative Oversight Committee; nor did I know about his troubles with his East Boston Company's financial operations." No one, of course, had suggested that he had. The question was one of judgment. The unavoidable conclusion was that Eisenhower's chief of staff had been gulled and the office of the Presidency demeaned. He would have to step down. It was both a public and a private tragedy. Adams had brought a rare talent to the White House, and one wonders how he could have fashioned an enduring social relationship with a cheat. Goldfine's indifference to the implications of his conduct is astonishing. Even after Adams had set up his appointment with the chairman of the FTC, he let matters drift until three of his firms had been slapped with "cease and desist" orders for label violations. His concept of friendship appears to have been a lopsided swap. In return for a rug, a coat, and payment of some $3,000 in hotel bills, he had compromised Adams's honor. A friend said of Goldfine, "He's a name dropper and a Scotch drinker, and he had a weakness of talking too much, dropping too many names and things." Now he had set in motion a chain of events which could only end in the dropping of Adams's name from the White House roster.

---

* Goldfine was sentenced to a year in jail and fined $1,000 for contempt of Congress following the 1958 hearings. The sentence was suspended and he was placed on probation.

It didn't happen at once. Ike's executive officer was too valuable; he wouldn't give him up without a struggle. Another member of the White House staff explained, "Adams has been with the President since 1952, and he knows how he thinks better than any other man. He has talked with the President about policy more than any other man. The governor has got tucked away in his head all the policy decisions the President has ever made, all the policy questions that have been laid aside for the right time, all the questions that have been rejected. It would be impossible for any new man to operate like Adams operates. And the new man could never accumulate the knowledge that Adams has."

After the second week of the crisis—for that is what it amounted to—Ike and Adams persuaded themselves that the problem would go away. The President told Hagerty to announce meaningfully that "the Governor is back at his desk at White House business." In other words, Adams was staying.

Then came the Goldfine circus. When the House of Representatives voted August 13 to cite Adams's friend for contempt, the governor was through. A vast army of editorial writers and cartoonists, led by those who had supported Eisenhower in his two presidential campaigns, was waging an all-out war on him, and as the summer waned it grew more intense. That was the noisiest threat to Adams. It was secondary, however. The heart of the problem was political.

Democratic indignation was almost ritualistic—"I am tired of pious preaching from Sherman Adams," Adlai Stevenson said— but Republican censure came as a surprise to Eisenhower and Adams. It shouldn't have. This was an election year. Knowland, fighting a desperate battle for the California governorship, suggested that the President "should carefully weigh as to whether Adams has so hurt his usefulness that it might be harmful." Arthur Watkins of Utah was more blunt. "In the light of the record as measured by the high standards of ethics set by both the President and Mr. Adams," he said, "there seems to be no other possible conclusion than that Mr. Adams' usefulness is seriously impaired, if not completely destroyed."

The first test at the polls in 1958 came on September 8, when Maine voted. The Democratic slogan there was "Payne of Maine is mainly on the wane." If that was so, it was important; the results would be regarded as a measure of voter reaction to Goldfinian

ethics. The Maine senator had never provided a convincing explanation of how he had acquired the $3,500 from Goldfine six years
earlier, and his opponent, forty-four-year-old Governor Edmund S.
Muskie, had made that the chief issue. The results made terrible
reading in the White House. An incredible 20,000 registered Republicans had stayed home. Not only did Muskie become Maine's
first popularly elected Democratic senator; his plurality was twice
as large as he had predicted. The GOP slate had gone down with
Payne. The Democrats had captured the statehouse, two of Maine's
three congressional seats, and twelve seats in the state legislature.
Senator Margaret Chase Smith said, "We took a shellacking." Hagerty said, "The President views it as I do. We took a beating," and
Meade Alcorn, Republican national chairman, said that the results
should "alert every Republican in the land to the urgency of an all-
out effort on November 4."

Mainly it inspired them to redouble their insistence that Eisenhower dismiss Adams. "As Maine goes, so goes Adams," the Washington press corps prophesied. Alcorn's phone rang constantly.
Goldwater said he was afraid that "the harm has already been
done." Knowland, lagging now in the opinion polls, declared that
Ike's assistant should resign "immediately," and New York's Congressman Kenneth Keating, running for the Senate, added that "the
good of the country" required it.

Adams was a marked man, and he knew it. The pressure became
intolerable, and he took a few days off for a fishing trip in southeast
Canada with Rachel and Jerry and Alice Persons. They were up
there in the stark beauty of the Miramichi valley when the boom
was lowered upon him.

Nixon had called upon Ike with a painful message from virtually
all Republicans running for Congress; Adams, they felt, was a sea
anchor dragging them down. The President had promised to reconsider the subject. Then Alcorn reported that the party's big
donors were keeping their checkbooks closed until "the Adams
mess" had been cleaned up. The Republican National Committee was
meeting in Chicago. Eisenhower asked Alcorn to make one more
appraisal of party opinion. When the chairman returned shaken—
Richard Simpson of Pennsylvania was threatening to lead a mutiny
if Adams stayed another week—the President capitulated. He called
it "the most hurtful, the hardest, the most heartbreaking decision"
of his Presidency, and he refused to do the firing himself. He told

Alcorn, "You've got to handle it. It's your job, the dirtiest I can give you."

Adams, meantime, was finding that not even the lonely Miramichi country was remote enough to hide him; Canadian reporters were asking him when he would resign. It seemed to be the only question people asked him any more. Then Gerry Morgan phoned from the White House and, according to Adams's recollection, said "he thought I ought to come back to Washington because Nixon and Meade Alcorn . . . wanted to talk with me." He knew why: "So I went." At 8 A.M. the following day he was at his desk, ready for the blindfold and the last cigarette.

Nixon told him that most Republican candidates and political leaders would, as a matter of self-preservation, repudiate him, and that would make his position impossible. Alcorn spoke for an hour, mostly about GOP contributions drying up and the incipient revolt within the National Committee. Adams sat impassively in his great leather chair, his head thrown back, staring at the ceiling and nibbling a stem of his glasses. Then, with a weary nod, he agreed to go.

In *Six Crises* Nixon recalled how the 1958 election served "to virtually erase the public memory of my success in Caracas and put in its place an image of failure with which my name was associated." Friends urged him to avoid the campaign, since a Republican defeat was inevitable; Dewey said, "You have done enough for Republican candidates." But Eisenhower told him, "I would give a year of my salary if we could win either the House or the Senate." The President, "by personal and political inclination," did not want to become enmeshed in political battles which could destroy his ability to work constructively with Congress, Nixon wrote; therefore, "if anyone was to carry the major load for political cross-country campaigning, I was the one who had to do it."

> I could not stand aside and see my fellow Republicans go down to disastrous defeat. I had to risk my political prestige to avoid a disaster, if possible, knowing full well, as in 1954, we would probably lose, and I would be the big-name target for the defeat. . . . I ended up stumping more than 25,000 miles in twenty-five states.

What this account omits is the character of the Republican campaign and the zeal with which the President joined it in the last two weeks. Nixon's line of attack was narrow and highly partisan. The Democratic party, he warned, was a haven for "socialism" and "left-wing extremists." He accused the Democrats of "retreat and appeasement," scorned "the Acheson foreign policy" that "resulted in war," and rejoiced in the "military strength and diplomatic firmness" of the Republican administration. The President, appalled at first, told White House correspondents that he deplored "this kind of thing." That stirred up conservative protests, which turned him around so completely that he publicly praised his bellicose Vice President: "No one can do this more effectively than you." By the end of October Ike was sharing Nixon's mood. He vowed that "there will be no appeasing Communist aggression while I am President," declared that "the so-called missile gap is being rapidly filled," and called the Democrats "political radicals" and "self-styled liberals" with "the irresistible impulse . . . to squander money—your money."

On November 4 the roof fell in on the Republicans. They lost twelve seats in the Senate, forty-eight seats in the House, and thirteen of the twenty-one contests for governor. Knowland went down, and so, unexpectedly, did John Bricker in Ohio. Even rock-ribbed Republican Vermont was lost; for the first time in one hundred and six years a Democrat would represent it in Congress. Nixon summed up the nationwide results: "It was the worst defeat in history ever suffered by a party having control of the White House."

Three races were of national interest. In Massachusetts John F. Kennedy's margin was 874,608—the largest ever for a candidate for any office in the state, and the largest in any senatorial race in 1958. Barry Goldwater ran against the Democratic tide in Arizona and was reelected decisively. And Rockefeller, even more impressively, rolled up a landslide plurality of a half-million votes. A TV commentator observed, "The big winner in this election is Nelson Rockefeller; the big loser, Richard Nixon." On November 9 New York's Governor-elect flew south to rest on his Venezuelan estate. At Maiquetía Airport, where the Nixons' baptism of Caracas spit had begun six months earlier, reporters asked him about Nixon. Rockefeller replied, *"No tengo nada que ver con Nixon"*—"I have nothing to do with Nixon."

Late Fifties Montage

Best actor of 1958: David Niven in *Separate Tables*
The Horse's Mouth   *The Inn of the Sixth Happiness*
The Long Hot Summer   *The Brothers Karamazov*

Come and click with Dick
The one that none can lick
He's the man to lead the U.S.A....
So let's all click with Dick

CRISIS IN FRANCE FADES AS DE GAULLE TAKES HELM

Best actor of 1959: Charlton Heston in *Ben-Hur*
Best actress of 1959: Simone Signoret in *Room at the Top*

Just you wait, 'Enry 'Iggins, just you wait
You'll be sorry, but your tears will come too late
You'll be broke and I'll have money
Will I 'elp you? Don't be funny
Just you wait, 'Enry 'Iggins, just you wait

THE STATUS SEEKERS

An exploration of class behavior in America and the hidden barriers that affect you, your community, your future
VANCE PACKARD
Author of *The Hidden Persuaders*

Now — Zenith brings you portable TV's biggest picture.... 21" Super Screen

Babies are FRAGILE — Handle with JOHNSON'S

The Apartment   *Inherit the Wind*   *Sunrise at Campobello*
I'm All Right, Jack   *Hiroshima, Mon Amour*

GET RID OF TIRED BLOOD!
Take Geritol. It builds iron power in your blood fast.

MAXWELL HOUSE coffee:
TASTES as good as it *SMELLS*

DURKEE'S Instant Minced Onion

BEST SELLERS: Nonfiction
The Rise and Fall of the Third Reich by William L. Shirer
Only in America by Harry Golden
Born Free by Joy Adamson
How I Made $2,000,000 in the Stock Market by Nicholas Darvas
Aku, Aku by Thor Heyerdahl

Best actor of 1960: Burt Lancaster in *Elmer Gantry*
Best actress of 1960: Elizabeth Taylor in *BUtterfield 8*

"Funniest Musical in Years" —*N.Y. News*

BYE BYE BIRDIE
CHITA RIVERA   DICK VAN DYKE

54th Street Theater
150 West 54th Street

K-E-Double-N-E-D-Y
Jack's the nation's favorite guy
Everyone wants to back Jack
Jack is on the right track

BEST SELLERS: Fiction
Doctor Zhivago by Boris Pasternak
Exodus by Leon Uris
Advise and Consent by Allen Drury
The Ugly American by William J. Lederer and Eugene Burdick
Lolita by Vladimir Nabokov

BAN *takes the worry out of being close*

little old wine-maker me

Hang down your head, Tom Dooley
Hang down your head and cry
Hang down your head, Tom Dooley
Poor boy, you're bound to die

MOSCOW, NEW YORK START JET PASSENGER SERVICE

POWER FAILURE HITS 500,000 NEW YORKERS: ANOTHER BIG BLACKOUT IS TERMED UNLIKELY

noisiest potato chips in the world

1ST CLASS POSTAGE UP FROM 3¢ to 4¢

	1950	1960
U.S. homeowners	23,600,000	32,800,000
Powers mowers sold	1,000,000	2,600,000
Automatic washing machine sales	1,700,000	2,600,000
Children five to fourteen	24,300,000	35,500,000
Little Leagues	776	5,700
Girl Scouts, Brownies	1,800,000	4,000,000
Bowling lanes	52,500	108,000
Gallons of gin	6,000,000	19,000,000
Gallons of vodka	100,000	9,000,000
Pounds of aspirin	12,000,000	18,000,000

Things Go Better with Coke
Buy Beech-Nut, by Gum.
Any thirst you can get 7-UP can quench
REAL GUSTO In a Great Light Beer SCHLITZ

Twenty-six

TATTOO FOR THE GENERAL

H L. MENCKEN once observed that journalism is an inexact science. The last years of the Eisenhower era were rich in proof of it.

Six weeks after the Democrats' off-year sweep a special Arkansas legislative committee disclosed that it had "definitely proved that there was Communist influence" in the Little Rock integration dispute. The chairman, Representative Paul Van Dalsen, said that the committee's three-day public hearing had alerted Arkansas to the threat of Communism, and a colleague of Van Dalsen confidently predicted that American Negroes would reject invitations to join any new demonstrations instigated by the National Association for the Advancement of Colored People and "backed by the Communist Party." Racial peace, he said, lay dead ahead.

Clark Kerr, newly installed as the president of the University of California, took a close look at college students in 1959 and said, "The employers will love this generation. . . . They are going to be easy to handle. There aren't going to be any riots."

That November the Roman Catholic bishops of the United States, in opposing the use of federal money to promote artificial birth control at home and abroad, ridiculed the assertion that American Catholics would gradually come to accept contraception.

NBC, looking for a clean-cut young American to counterbalance Elvis Presley, chose Charles Van Doren, a $4,400-a-year Columbia University instructor who had just won $129,000 in fourteen spectacular weeks on the network's biggest quiz show, *Twenty-one*.

Hired at $50,000 a year as an NBC consultant and *Today* show commentator, he edited an inspirational anthology, *Letters to Mothers.* In his own mail, three of every four letters were from parents or teachers grateful to him for the shining example he was setting for the country's youth. Late in 1958, when a New York County grand jury began looking into charges that quiz shows were rigged, reporters converged on his smart Greenwich Village home. He scorned the idea. "I never got any kind of hint or help," he said, "and as far as I know, nobody else ever did on the program." When they persisted he said sternly, "It is an insult to keep asking me these questions."

Whereupon Negroes, college students, Catholics, and Charles Van Doren proceeded to surprise those who thought they knew them.

The hope that black militancy would go away died a sudden death on February 1, 1960, when four black students at the North Carolina Agricultural and Technical College entered an F. W. Woolworth store on South Elm Street in nearby Greensboro, made several small purchases, took seats at the lunch counter, and ordered coffee. In conformity with the southern laws and tradition requiring segregation, the management ignored them. They stayed in silence until closing time, and the next morning they appeared at the counter again, this time with five black friends. They called it a sit-in. Each succeeding day there were more of them. Calm and well-behaved, ignoring catcalling white youths who dangled Confederate flags in front of them and flipped cigarette butts at them, the young blacks let it be known that they were going to stay until they got their coffee.

If it had been up to the store's Greensboro employees, they would never have been served. But Woolworth is a nationwide chain, and that was what they were counting on. In North Carolina the movement spread to Durham, Winston-Salem, Charlotte, Raleigh, and High Point, and outside the state lunch counters were occupied in Nashville, Chattanooga, Tallahassee, Richmond, and Rock Hill, South Carolina. Over the next fortnight blacks staged Woolworth sit-ins in fifteen cities, and in Boston four hundred students from Harvard, Brandeis, Boston University, and MIT picketed twelve Woolworth stores. That pleased the Greensboro blacks. What happened next astonished them and the country. Demonstrators appeared at Walgreen, S. H. Kress, W. T. Grant, and Liggett lunch counters. Englewood, New Jersey, sympathizers took up a collection to back the demonstrators. Yale Divinity School students marched through downtown New Haven in support. Exasperated dime store managers raised their coffee prices to a dollar a cup for Negroes, unscrewed the seats, and threatened to close the lunch counters. Nothing worked; the demonstrators met them at every turn with new forms of passive resistance. Then the movement leaped from the stools to every segregated facility in society. There were sleep-ins in motel lobbies, play-ins in parks, read-ins in public libraries, watch-ins in movie theaters, bet-ins in bingo halls, sweat-ins in Turkish baths, and, when spring approached, swim-ins on restricted beaches.

On May 10 the blacks scored their first victory when lunch counters were desegregated in six Nashville stores, the first such general action in any southern state except Texas. All spring battles of attrition were fought throughout the South, with the color bar moving a foot here, a yard there, and pressure on the diehards mounting. On June 5 the blacks' Southern Regional Council reported desegregated counters in nine scattered border cities; there had been no violence in any of them, and none of the merchants had been hurt by the threat of retaliatory boycotts by angry whites. Virginia felt the opening wedge on June 23, when its Hot Shoppes were opened to Negroes. Knoxville stores ended lunch counter segregation July 18. July 25 was a day of black jubilation; the Woolworth and Kress stores in Greensboro, where it had all started six months earlier, were integrated. That same day four Virginia stores in the Norfolk-Portsmouth area also ended discrimination. After that the going was rougher. The never-say-die Deep South was digging in. On October 19 Atlanta policemen arrested fifty-one sit-in demonstrators led by Martin Luther King. They refused to put up bail and were jailed. The great sit-in blitz of 1960 was over, and the blacks paused to consolidate their gains. But even the Arkansas legislature now knew that the respite would only be temporary. A Negro nation of 18,-871,831 was stirring. American blacks were becoming visible at last.

The future was revealed to Clark Kerr on the cloudless afternoon of Friday, May 13, 1960. The House Committee on Un-American Activities, still tenaciously investigating California Communists after all these years, was holding hearings in San Francisco's rococo city hall. Among those subpoenaed were several public schoolteachers and a Berkeley sophomore, all of them rumored to be active leftists. Several busloads of Berkeley students arrived to give them moral support. No demonstrations had been contemplated; in that innocent day few undergraduates knew how to demonstrate. They merely wanted seats in the hearing room. But the building was already crowded. Policemen barred the door at the top of the steps. Somebody started to push. One cop lost his footing; afterward it was said that he was beaten. Nightsticks appeared, and then hoses. At the end of a wild half-hour twelve people were casualties and fifty-two were on their way to jail. Jessica Mitford of Oakland reported in the *Nation* that "the current crop of students has gone far to shake the label of apathy and conformity that had stuck through the Fifties." She predicted that in the coming decade they would be dedicated to "shaping the future of the world." One beaten undergraduate told a reporter, "I was a political virgin, but I was raped on the steps of city hall." To the country's 3,610,000 students the message from Berkeley was a challenge. Impatient faculty members had long been goading them to make a political commitment. Now they knew how to do it.

During those same tumultuous months, as black pride and collegiate political awareness grew, the curtain was rising on another instrument of social change. On May 9, 1960, the U.S. Food and Drug Administration announced that it had approved an oral contraceptive as safe.* The Pill was Enovid, made by G. D. Searle & Company, Chicago, which said it had proved to be 100 percent effective in a four-year test by 1,500 women. Twenty pills a month, obtainable by prescription, would provide assurance against pregnancy at a cost of $10 to $11 a month. This chemical form of birth control, combined with the new intrauterine devices and an increase in the acceptance of surgical birth control, offered women escape from the fear of pregnancy, the restraint that had inhibited their sexual activity since the beginning of time. Now, it seemed, they could go to bed as freely as men. Physicians and pharmaceutical houses were overwhelmed by the demand from millions of women for the Pill. Never had so many people taken a potent drug regularly for any purpose other than the control of a disease. And the Roman Catholic bishops were dismayed when Monsignor Irving A. LeBlanc, director of the National Catholic Family Life Bureau,

---

* The *New York Times* carried the story on page 75 of its May 10 issue.

reported that Catholic women were taking it as regularly as non-Catholics. As recently as November 1959 the bishops had reproved "some representatives of Christian bodies"—Protestant clergymen —for not practicing continence. Now even Catholic priests, and indeed some sisters in holy orders, were reappraising their vows in the light of the altered facts of life.

The clay figure of Charles Van Doren began to crumble in August 1958, when one Herbert M. Stempel, a CCNY student who had won $49,500 on *Twenty-one* before losing to Van Doren, took his troubled conscience to Manhattan District Attorney Frank Hogan and the *New York World-Telegram and Sun*. Stempel told them that the show was a fake. He said that contestants were given the answers in advance until their popularity began to wane; then they had to take a dive. He had been ordered to lose to Van Doren, who, like him, had been coached in facial expressions, lip-biting, brow-mopping, and stammering as he agonized over a question in the glass-walled isolation booth on camera. Rehearsed by the show's producer, Van Doren had then amazed 25 million televiewers by such feats as naming the only three baseball players to have collected more than 3,500 hits ("Ty Cobb, Cap Anson and . . . Tris Speaker!"), identifying the singer of the aria "Sempre libera" in *La Traviata* ("She sings it right at the end of the party given by . . . What's her name! Soprano. Her name is . . . Violetta!"), and spitting out the names of the Seven Dwarfs ("Sleepy, Sneezy, Dopey, Happy"—pause—"the grouchy one—ah, Grumpy—Doc—ah, the bashful one—Bashful!").

Stempel and other contestants on *Twenty-one* and CBS's *The $64,000 Challenge* told their story to a New York grand jury. Van Doren denied it under oath, and Judge Mitchell Schweitzer, deeply offended by the slandering of a contemporary American folk hero, impounded the record on the ground that it contained accusations which had not been proved. Outside the jury room, Van Doren told the press that he was "sad" and "shocked" by the lies about him. He repeated that he had played "honestly. . . . At no time was I coached or tutored."

The trouble with perjury is that those who commit it have no way of knowing whether there is someone who can prove they were lying. There is always the possibility that a Whittaker Chambers has the truth socked away in a pumpkin, and that is what happened to Van Doren. One James Snodgrass, an artist and a *Twenty-one* winner, produced registered letters that he had mailed to himself one to three days before the programs he was on, containing the questions and answers involved. These were then opened by the House Subcommittee on Legislative Oversight, the same stern tribunal which had been Bernard Goldfine's, and thus Sherman Adams's, downfall. The letters confirmed Snodgrass, and the committee, taking up where the Manhattan grand jury had left off, began building a trap of testimony and exhibits for that winning, handsome, loose-limbed, Ivy-clothed son of a distinguished literary family named Charles Van Doren.

They sprung it in October 1959. Van Doren, playing the outraged patrician like Hiss before him, wired the subcommittee a categorical denial of all the charges maligning him, declaring that he had not been "assisted in any form" and that he would be "available" to the subcommittee whenever it wished to question him. Back came a telegram inviting him to appear before the congressmen voluntarily, at which time he vanished. A formal subpoena was issued, but the process server could not find him. For six days the American people did not know whether he was alive or dead. On the seventh day, October 14, he materialized by prearrangement in New York's Roosevelt Hotel, accepted the subpoena, and confronted a packed press conference. He read a prepared statement. "Distressed" by the course of events, he said, he had taken a leave of absence from Columbia and gone with his wife to New England, "to gather my thoughts . . . in the October beauty of the region." He hadn't known he was wanted. The reporters boggled. How could he have been unaware of the subpoena when it was the lead story in every newspaper and news broadcast? Smiling wanly, he said out of respect for the U.S. Congress he would have no further comment until he appeared in the "appropriate forum," which was to say, its hearing room.

He surfaced there next on November 2, conservatively dressed and obviously tense as he confessed. "I would give almost anything I have to reverse the course of my life in the last three years. . . . I've learned a lot about good and evil. They are not always what they appear to be. I was involved, deeply involved, in a deception . . . I was almost able to convince myself that it did not matter what I was doing because it was having such a good effect on the national attitude toward teachers, education, and the intellectual life."

In time he became "terribly uncomfortable," he continued, and "very much afraid." He begged the producers "several times" to let him lose. They replied that it would have to be done in "a dramatic manner." At last a glamorous blonde lawyer became a contestant, and one of the producers "told me that . . . I would be defeated by her. I thanked him." When the public began to learn that the show had been a fraud, Van Doren said, he had been "horror-struck. . . . I simply ran away. . . . Most of all, I was running away from myself." There was "one way out which I had, of course, often considered, and that was simply to tell the truth." But "emotionally" this was not "possible." Then the subpoena was served upon him. ". . . it was a small thing that tipped the scales. A letter came to me from a woman, a complete stranger, who had seen me on the Garroway show and who said she admired my work there. She told me that the only way I could ever live with myself, and make up for what I had done—of course, she, too, did not know exactly what that was—was to admit it, clearly, openly, truly. Suddenly I knew she was right." Next morning, Van Doren went on, he summoned up the courage to phone his lawyer, who, when he had heard all, said, "God bless you." And that was the end of his statement. Putting it down, he turned to the attorney and smiled at him.

It was preposterous. It was the subpoena, not an unknown woman, which had forced him to own up. Furthermore, if he had really been "terribly uncomfortable" on the show there had been no need to plea for release from the producers; all he had to do was give a wrong answer to one question on the air. A Republican member of the subcommittee, Steven B. Derounian of New York, saw through Van Doren's fraudulence. He said to him, "I don't think an adult of your intelligence ought to be commended for telling the truth." But that was just what the other congressmen proceeded to do. Chairman Oren Harris said he wanted to "compliment" him on his candor. Representative William E. Springer of Illinois expressed the hope that Columbia would not "prematurely" dismiss him from its faculty, and Representative Peter F. Mack of Illinois said he trusted that NBC would forgive him. Others said they wanted to "commend" him for his "fortitude," and for the "forthrightness" of his "soul-searching" statement. Five hours later Columbia, seeing things differently, announced that it was dispensing with Van Doren's services; NBC discharged him the next day. But that was not a popular reaction. The crowd at the hearing had been with Van Doren, applauding him and his admirers on the subcommittee and greeting Congressman Derounian's comment with stony silence. Columbia students held a rally to protest his ouster. A poll showed that three of every four Americans felt that faced with the same situation "most people" would have done what he had done, and NBC's mail favored him, five to one.

No sooner had Van Doren and thirteen other celebrities been indicted in New York for perjury than the Harris subcommittee turned up new evidence of TV fraud. Dick Clark, the number one disc jockey in the teen-age subculture, admitted that he chose records in which he had a financial interest. This was called "payola." Chairman John C. Doerfer of the FCC in effect defended it. Nobody was harmed by it, he argued, and any attempt at regulation would "tamper with our cherished freedom of speech." At that point it was discovered that Doerfer himself had accepted payola from one of the big broadcasters he was supposed to be watching. Eisenhower accepted his resignation, but here, too, the public seemed to be indifferent. It is not surprising that viewers who showed no concern over any of this should have accepted the networks' tasteless programming in 1960. If 1959 had been the Year of the Quiz Show, *Variety* suggested, 1960 was the Year of the Western. There were eight such programs on CBS, nine on NBC, and eleven on ABC—a total of twenty-four and a half hours of prime viewing time every week.

After seven years of basking in Eisenhower sunshine, the nation's opinion makers, including those who had supported the President, were becoming restless. As early as 1958 the *Chicago Daily News* had asked, "Things are in an uproar. But what is Eisenhower doing? All you read about is that he's playing golf. Who's running the country?" Subscribers, however, remained apathetic. While the President was in Europe, the Vice President scored a personal triumph in negotiating the end of a 116-day steel strike. Opinion polls were virtually unaffected; the public hadn't been watching. The newly freed Congo was bleeding in a tragic civil war, and rebellious Laotian soldiers led by Captain Kong Le overturned the pro-Western government of Premier Tiao Samsonith; the average American couldn't have found either country on a map. At home a newspaper strike halted publication of all New York papers, there was a rash of prison riots, and another of bombs smuggled aboard airliners, including one planted by a greedy youth who thereby blew up his airborne mother, with everybody else on the flight, for her insurance. A survey reported that front pages were unread; readers preferred the comics and sports. When Caryl Chessman was executed in California after eight reprieves, opponents of capital punishment objected, but there were comparatively few of them, and the general lethargy seemed to be unaffected by a series of particularly brutal, senseless killings. One of them at this time was the murder of a Kansas farmer named Herbert Clutter with his wife, son, and daughter. *Time*'s account of the crime appeared in the news magazine's November 30, 1959, issue. Its headline was "In Cold Blood," and its readers included a writer named Truman Capote.

The instant cliché that year was the use of the word "bit" as an all-purpose verbal punctuation mark. Greensboro's blacks were doing "the protest bit." Romance was "the love bit," Metrecal "the diet bit," and Alfred Hitchcock's *Psycho* "the thrill bit." The commonplace cropped up almost everywhere, but it was never applied to one department of the federal government. No one ever said John Foster Dulles was doing "the diplomacy bit." It would have been unseemly, and it would also have been inappropriate, for Dulles belonged to an earlier age, to a craft of statesmanship fashioned by foreign ministers in cutaways and striped pants. His haughty moralizing and simplistic "massive retaliation" had been outmoded by the statistics of Soviet rocket thrust, and in the early months of 1959, as he hobbled back and forth to Walter Reed Hospital in the agony of his last illness, he seemed to realize that the rigidity of the East-West posture which he had done so much to perpetuate was about to become obsolete. He defended it to the last. Grimacing with pain as he left Washington on his final journey to Europe, he told a friend, "If it isn't cancer, then I feel the trip is too important to be put off. If it is cancer, then any additional discomfort doesn't fundamentally matter anyway."

It was cancer. Blasted daily by million-volt X-rays in Walter Reed Hospital or resting in the Florida sun on Jupiter Island, the secretary became preoccupied with his desperate, losing battle with death, and as he struggled the reins of statecraft slipped at last from his hands. Outwardly the world's balance of power was unchanged. The United States was still committed by treaty to the defense of forty-two nations, and Dulles, to use another emerging cliché, was still a man with tremendous clout. American editorial writers paid tribute to the "wise counsel" and "single-minded strength" of this "indispensable man." Whitehall sent him word that it was "extraordinarily sorry," the Quai d'Orsay expressed concern over "the greatest possible loss for the West," and Bonn regretted that "a spoke" had been "torn from the wheels of Western policy making." But that was all diplomatic cant, and Dulles must have known it. Although he kept in close touch with the White House and his own office by telephone, alert for any sign of cold war heresy, to those who could read the signs—and he was one who could—it was clear that moves toward a detente between Washington and Moscow awaited only his departure from the scene. "The clenched fist of Dulles," Emmet John Hughes wrote, was about to be replaced by "the outstretched hand of Eisenhower."

In the aftermath of the GOP's off-year election defeat, Hagerty had put together a long memorandum looking toward the 1960 election, in which Eisenhower, campaigning for a Republican successor, would stand on his record as a man of peace. Based on conversations with the President, it set forth as goals everything Dulles had resisted in his six years at Foggy Bottom. Its frank assumption was that the time had arrived for diplomatic flexibility. The President must take the center of the international stage, the Eisenhower-Hagerty memo held, as a peacemaker. Continuing, it declared that he must play this role in appearances at the United Nations, in journeys to the far corners of the world, including neutral India, and in a hospitable attitude toward suggestions that he participate in summit conferences and conversations with Russia's Khrushchev.

The Soviet premier was ready for such overtures. In welcoming Premier Anastas Mikoyan home from a U.S. tour on January 26, 1959, Khrushchev had said that "the possibility of a thaw" in Russo-American relations was "not excluded." "Everything possible" must be done to improve relations between the two superpowers, he said, for thermonuclear war was unthinkable; those in the West who said that Khrushchev was "more frightened of war than anyone else" were absolutely correct. As always, Dulles had replied that any meeting would have to be preceded by Soviet demonstrations of good faith, and that he doubted that there would be any, for the USSR, in his opinion, was committed to winning the cold war, not ending it. But this time another administration spokesman had expressed a different view. Vice President Nixon said that the United States also wanted a thaw, "because we realize that if there is none we will all be eventually frozen in the ice so hard that only a nuclear bomb will break it."

On May 24 the death watch at Walter Reed ended with the bulletin: MR. JOHN FOSTER DULLES DIED QUIETLY IN HIS SLEEP AT 7:49 E.D.T. THIS MORNING. Already Undersecretary Christian A. Herter was running the State Department. His first priority was the most recent of the long, dreary series of crises over Berlin. Khrushchev had delivered an ultimatum to the western powers: if they weren't out of the city in six months, the Red Army would throw them out. The characteristic Dulles response would have been a counter ultimatum and a show of strength, forcing a showdown on the brink of war. Eisenhower had taken a different tack. The President read a careful statement to a press conference declaring that if there was any shooting in Berlin it would be "to stop us from doing our duty. We are not saying that we are going to shoot our way into Berlin. We say we are just going to go and continue carrying out our responsibilities to those people. So that if we are stopped, it will be somebody else using force." Herter treated the ultimatum as a maneuver in presummit bargaining, and that, it developed, was exactly what it was.

Once Dulles was in his grave, events moved with almost unseemly haste. Five weeks later, on June 28, Soviet Deputy Premier Frol R. Koslov led a delegation of Russian officials to New York to open a Soviet Exhibition of Science, Technology, and Culture. On July 11 Eisenhower personally drafted an invitation to Khrushchev to visit the United States. And on July 23, two months to the day after Dulles's death, the Vice President of the United States was in Moscow to open an American National Exhibition in Sokolniki Park, thus paying what Eisenhower called a "return courtesy" for the New York visit of the Soviet officials.

What followed can hardly be called a contribution to the slackening of East-West tensions, but it did provide some insight into the combative instincts of Nikita Khrushchev and Richard Nixon. The exhibition's most interesting display was a six-room model ranch house with a central viewing corridor, permitting visitors to see all its furnishings. The Soviet leader had worked himself into a rage over it. It touched a sensitive nerve; Russia's sputniks had been built at the expense of consumer products and services. The opening of the fair was being televised in the USSR, and Khrushchev felt that he had been somehow outmaneuvered. He was spoiling for a fight. Nixon was the man to give it to him. The ceremony was to appear on American television, too. He expected to be the Republican presidential nominee next year, and whatever Hagerty's views on campaign strategy, Nixon had plans of his own which did not include allowing himself to be bullied on TV by an angry Communist. The result was what the press called the "kitchen debate" or the "Sokolniki Summit."

It began when they paused at the model home's sleek, gadget-stocked kitchen. Nixon declared that this was a typical American house, and that almost any U.S. workman could afford it or one like it. The Soviet premier bridled.

KHRUSHCHEV: You think the Russians will be dumbfounded by this exhibit. But the fact is that all newly built Russian homes will have this equipment. You need dollars in the United States to get this house, but here all you need is to be born a citizen. If an American citizen does not have dollars he has the right to . . . sleep on the pavement. And you say we are slaves of Communism!

NIXON: . . . We don't think this fair will astound the Russian people, but it will interest them just as yours interested us. To us diversity, the right to choose, the fact that we have a thousand different builders, that's the spice of life. We don't want to have a decision made at the top by one government official saying that we will have one type of house. That's the difference—

KHRUSHCHEV (cutting in): On political differences, we will never agree. If I follow you, I will be led astray by Mikoyan. He likes spicy soups and I don't. But that doesn't mean we differ.

NIXON: Isn't it better to be talking about the relative merits of our washing machines than the relative strength of our rockets? Isn't this the kind of competition you want?

KHRUSHCHEV (pushing his thumb against Nixon's chest): Yes, that's the kind of competition we want, but your generals say they are so powerful they can destroy us. We can also show you something so you will know the Russian spirit. We are strong, we can beat you. But in this respect we can also show you something.

NIXON (wagging his finger at Khrushchev): To me, you are strong and we are strong. In some ways, you are stronger than we are. In others, we are stronger. . . .

Pausing at a table of California wines, they scored their final points. Khrushchev proposed a toast "To peace and the elimination of all military bases on foreign lands."

NIXON (*without raising his glass*): Let us just drink a toast to peace.

A RUSSIAN BYSTANDER: One hundred years to Premier Khrushchev!

NIXON: I will drink to that. We may disagree with your policy, but we want you to be of good health. May you live to be one hundred years old.

KHRUSHCHEV (*after the toast*): At ninety-nine years of age we shall discuss these questions further. Why should we be in haste?

NIXON (*he has the last word*): You mean that at ninety-nine, you will still be in power, with no free elections?

It was a curious exchange, less a debate than a quarrel between two aggressive men, each of them determined to impress the audience as more peaceful than the other. Both suffered from a self-imposed handicap. In a thousand speeches, the Soviet leader had created a crude stereotype of the typical capitalist politician as a Wall Street lackey, and Nixon didn't fit it. Nixon's handicap was a mirror image of Khrushchev's. His archetype of the evil Communist boss had as much substance as a man of straw, as much life as a Sunday supplement demon. The American Vice President had scored more forensic points, but the Russian premier had come across as warm, direct, and perhaps as better suited to his role. Nixon emerged as a man who liked ideas, Khrushchev as one who loved his people and would go to great lengths to champion them. As if to confirm that, he overlooked Nixon's insolence—plainly he regarded it as that—and accepted Eisenhower's invitation to visit America once Nixon had returned home. "I am prepared to turn out my pockets to show that I am harmless," he said in his disingenuous way. "In the old times people used to leave their weapons in the hall when they went in to talk peace. We should do that now, and there should be no saber rattling." With that, he quietly scuttled his Berlin ultimatum.

One reason Dulles had given for opposing such summitry had been his concern that U.S. allies might feel that they were being abandoned. To reassure them, the President flew to Europe at the end of August for two weeks of talks with Konrad Adenauer, Harold Macmillan, and Charles de Gaulle. It was an amazing trip. In

Washington it was easy to forget the tremendous affection Europeans felt for Dwight D. Eisenhower. Their feeling for him was unclouded by partisanship or ideology. To them he was the kindly, straightforward, low-key American general who had led the victorious crusade to free them from Nazi rule. The Germans seemed as grateful as the British and French. As Eisenhower's Mercedes-Benz entered Bonn an estimated 315,000 people, twice the population of the city, lined the route, cheering him and holding up banners proclaiming, WE TRUST YOU and WE RELY ON YOU. In London his car was a dove-gray Rolls-Royce. There the shouts—from a crowd numbered in the hundreds of thousands—were "Glad to see you, Ike," and "Good for you, Ike," and as the motorcade entered Grosvenor Square, from which General Eisenhower had directed the coalition of armies that had routed Hitler, reporters saw tears in his eyes.

De Gaulle, now entering his difficult period, would have preferred that Parisians show more restraint, but it was impossible. At Le Bourget Airport the two generals-become-presidents exchanged tributes; then the throng's cry of "Ike!" which in French came out "Eek!" drowned out everything else. It never died out completely during Eek's two days in Paris, not even when he placed a wreath of pink lilies and red roses on the tomb of France's unknown soldier, beneath the Arc de Triomphe, or during his response to the continuing ovation at the Hôtel de Ville: "When the heart is full, the tongue is very likely to stumble. I have one small French phrase that, I think, expresses my feelings—*Je vous aime tous*." Obviously it was impractical to conduct serious talks against such a background. De Gaulle did press his plan for a NATO guided by a three-power directorate. Eisenhower warded him off with a promise to keep in closer touch over the transatlantic phone. ("I know he's a stubborn man," Ike told an aide, "but as long as he's stubborn on our side, everything's all right.") After a weekend at Scotland's Culzean Castle, where he occupied a nine-room apartment given to him by the Scottish people after V-E Day, the President flew home September 7. There he told a welcoming crowd: "I am quite certain that for the moment, at least, everything is going splendidly."

Nikita Khrushchev's barnstorming of the United States was to be the next stage in the slackening of world tensions. On September 15, at Andrews Field in Maryland, Soviet Ambassador Mikhail Menshikov called to a ramp, "Nikita Sergeyevich, I salute you on American soil," and as American spectators blinked in disbelief, down the steps he came, short, bald, and stocky, wearing three small medals on his black suit and accompanied by his shy wife, Nina Petrovna, his daughters Julia and Rada, his son Sergei, and a retinue of sixty-three Russian bureaucrats. President Eisenhower formally welcomed them, and then they were off on a two-week guided tour of the United States with U.N. Ambassador Henry Cabot Lodge as their host.

On the whole it was a successful journey. Americans are partial to curmudgeons, and this one was as salty as Thomas Edison and Henry Ford. In speeches before American businessmen, tours of rural Iowa, and luncheons with Mayor Robert Wagner of New York and Mayor Norris Poulson of Los Angeles, Khrushchev came on as shrewd, eccentric, and unscrupulous, but very human and determined to live in peace with his neighbors. Inevitably there were incidents. Khrushchev won an argument with Sypros P. Skouras, president of Twentieth Century–Fox, and lost one to Walter Reuther and his six union vice presidents. (He then denounced them as "agents for capitalists" and was puzzled when Reuther laughed.) After a Hollywood troupe had performed a cancan for him, the premier revealed a priggish streak, calling the dance "immoral" and adding, "A person's face is more beautiful than his backside."

At Camp David, the presidential retreat on Maryland's Catoctin Mountain, Khrushchev was on his best behavior. He said nothing offensive. In fact, he said almost nothing beyond vague generalities. His concept of discretion seemed to preclude getting down to brass tacks. Midway in the second day of their talks Eisenhower turned to him with a personal appeal: "You have the opportunity to make a great contribution to history by making it possible to ease tensions. It is within your hands." But the Russian leader refused to be pinned down. He praised American roast beef, enjoyed a western movie with Ike, and, after a helicopter hop to Gettysburg, admired the President's prize herd of Black Angus cattle. For the time being, that was going to be the extent of his contribution to a detente.

After their third day together the two leaders issued a joint statement. They had agreed that general disarmament was the most important question facing the world, that negotiations on the Berlin issue should be "reopened with a view to achieving a solution which would be in accordance with the views of all concerned and in the interest of the maintenance of peace," that "all outstanding international questions should be settled not by the application of force but by peaceful means through negotiation," and that President Eisenhower would visit the Soviet Union next year.

For a while the newspapers made much of "the spirit of Camp David." Briefly it seemed almost as substantive as the Roosevelt-Churchill Atlantic Charter. A turning point, men thought, had been reached in U.S.-USSR relations at last. It was all illusion. The President and the premier hadn't even touched upon the basic and critical problems arising from different views over the future of Germany and the world. The benign mood eventually turned out to be evanescent. In time it soured and was succeeded by disenchantment. Among the participants who resolved that a firmer groundwork should be prepared before any new conferences with the Russians was Richard Nixon.

Nixon did not, however, feel that the disappointing outcome vindicated Dulles's implacable opposition to meetings at the top. The world's statesmen had embarked on what *Time* called "the new global game of personal diplomacy," and none of them wanted a return to the arctic past. Their orchestrated journeys were now following a definite plot leading toward a desirable ending. The next step would be what was being called the "Western Summit," a kind of semifinal conference whose participants would be Eisenhower, Macmillan, Adenauer, and De Gaulle. These four would renew their vows to keep Berlin free and hammer out a joint approach for the final conference, which would be between them and Khrushchev.

The semifinal was held in Paris in December. Eisenhower was not going to limit the December trip to France, though. The ventures in personal diplomacy, made endurable by the new Boeing 707 jet airliners, were encouraging. The rousing welcome given him in the capitals of western Europe had given rise to a naive hope that the enthusiasm of the crowds that cheered motorcades could somehow be transformed into enduring good will and better international relations. With this in mind, and with Hagerty's memorandum before him, the President decided that as long as he was abroad he might as well call on the rulers of Italy, Turkey, Pakistan, Afghanistan, India, Iran, Greece, Tunisia, Spain, and Morocco. Before leaving on this 19-day, 19,500-mile trip to eleven nations on three continents, he delivered a televised report to the country. "During this mission of peace and good will," he said, "I hope to promote a better understanding of America and to learn more of our friends abroad."

Whether it led to a greater understanding is moot. It did provide staggering new evidence of the President's popularity, however. In Italy, where Romans stood in drenching rains for a glimpse of him —here "Ike" came out "Eekay"—a journalist wrote in *Corriere Della Sera*, "We welcome this man who speaks to us with the accent of Kansas farmers who cultivate fields of wheat as vast as seas, of pioneers who went West not long before his birth. He speaks without rhetoric before the imminent peril as he calls for 'Peace, peace.'" Turkey was next. Eisenhower himself called his welcome to Ankara "the most stupendous I have ever seen." Over 750,000 Pakistanis welcomed him to Karachi, and in New Delhi he said he was "completely overwhelmed" by the crowds, as well he might have been: a million shouting Indians held aloft banners acclaiming him as, among other things, "Eisenhower, Prince of Peace," and they threw so many flowers at his open car that he stood a foot deep in blossoms. It was the same in every country. There were 750,000 cheering Iranians in Teheran, where he addressed a joint session of the Shah's parliament; 500,000 enthusiastic Athenians outside when he spoke to Greece's Chamber of Deputies; 500,000 Spaniards when Generalissimo Francisco Franco welcomed him to Madrid, and 500,000 to greet him in Casablanca.

It was numbing, and it was also rather baffling. Applause in western Europe could be traced back to World War II, but the only nation on this trip to have been in the war was Italy, and the Italians had been on the other side. Why should Indian untouchables walk forty miles to see the American President, or Afghan tribesmen spend days weaving floral tributes to lay before the wheels of his limousine? Part of the explanation seemed to lie in the recurring chants, in every tongue, of "Peace, peace." War was recognized everywhere as mankind's greatest scourge, even among peoples that had never heard gunfire. But that wasn't all that lay behind these awesome demonstrations. Clearly America was more beloved than Americans knew. Anti-Americans made more noise, but the vast majority in these countries seemed to admire and trust the United States.

Eisenhower returned home on December 22. That Christmas was a high point in his Presidency and in the history of U.S. diplomacy. In his annual Christmas message to the nation—beamed overseas this time in twenty-eight languages—he said of his journey: "My purpose was to improve the climate in which diplomacy might work more successfully; a diplomacy that seeks . . . peace with justice for all men." The test of his accomplishment lay less than five months away, when he and the three leaders of western Europe would confront Khrushchev in the summit of summits. It was scheduled to open on May 16, 1960, in Paris.

From time to time in the later 1950s subscribers to the *New York Times* read, under the byline of Herbert L. Matthews, captivating accounts of bearded young Cuban revolutionaries hiding out in the tangled jungles of that island's Sierra Maestra range. Their leader was a hulking, verbose lawyer in his early thirties, Fidel Castro Ruz. Castro had landed in Cuba on Christmas of 1956 with just twelve men. Taking to the hills before dictator Fulgencio Batista's soldiers could seize them, they unfurled the red and black flag of their 26th of July movement, so named for a desperate attack led by Castro on Santiago Batistianos on July 26, 1953, and called on Cuban lovers of freedom to join them.

In those early years Castro's movement was very popular in the United States. Batista's Cuba was a police state run by terrorists and corrupt bureaucrats who made fortunes in prostitution, gambling, and raids on the public till. Havana University was padlocked to suppress mutinous students; dissenters were murdered; their corpses were dismembered and sent to their parents, or dumped in gutters like garbage. Washington was elated at the prospect of a truly democratic Cuba. As early as March 1958 all deliveries of U.S. arms to Batista were halted. American correspondents like Matthews wrote sympathetic stories depicting Castro and his *barbudos*, or bearded rebels, as selfless Robin Hoods who wanted to give their countrymen liberty and justice. The reporters erred, but the error was common then, and it was shared by most members of the Cuban middle class and a great many influential Cuban army officers who were fed up with Batista. That was Batista's undoing. Castro had fewer than two thousand *barbudos* to put against forty thousand superbly equipped Batistianos, but businessmen and landowners were financing him, and the middle class was acclaiming the rebels, who were, for the most part, middle-class themselves—young professional men and intellectuals like Fidel, his brother Raul, and

Major Ernesto "Che" Guevara, the Argentine physician who had become Castro's Trotsky.

In the last weeks of 1958 Guevara routed three thousand government troops in the province of Las Villas, one hundred and fifty miles from the capital, and captured the provincial capital, Santa Clara. A trainload of troops sent by Batista refused even to get out of the railroad cars. The old regime was through, and Batista knew it. On New Year's Day he flew off into exile. Castro then began a seven-day, six-hundred-mile march of triumph down Cuba's Central Highway. Fidel's men fired their pistols and tommy guns at the sky. In affection they called their leader "El Caballo," the horse. He was Gargantuan, a charismatic figure before the concept became popular. His personal life was ascetic. There were no women in it. Except for fifty-cent Montecristo cigars, he never indulged himself. Getting him to change his grimy green field jacket was next to impossible.

"Power does not interest me, and I will not take it," Castro said. "From now on the people are entirely free." He restored Cuba's lost pride, gave it a national identity, rooted out corruption, and launched vast programs to educate Cuba's children and inspire their parents. When whispering voices tried to spread reports that he was a Communist, the general reaction was scorn. Reactionaries always called reformers Reds; men like Matthews of the *Times* could remember their doing it in Spain twenty years earlier and they said so.

To demonstrate that he was a good neighbor to the United States, Fidel flew to Washington with a hundred cases of good-will rum. He lunched on steak and champagne with Acting Secretary of State Christian Herter—he wore his field jacket even there—and talked to eighteen congressmen in the Senate Foreign Relations Committee room. "The July 26 movement is not a Communist movement," he told them. "Its members are Roman Catholics, mostly." Asked about American investments in Cuba, he replied, "We have no intention of expropriating United States property, and any property we take we'll pay for." He was charming. To be sure, there was one sour note. After a three-hour conference with Castro, Vice President Nixon wrote a twelve-page confidential memorandum for distribution to the CIA, the State Department, and the White House, in which he said that he was convinced that Cuba's new leader was "either incredibly naive about Communism or under Communist discipline." But the CIA pigeonholed it, State ignored it, and Eisenhower waved it away. The administration was getting a little tired of Nixon's seeing Communist bogeymen everywhere.

The rude awakening of the Americans, and the subsequent deterioration of U.S.-Cuban relations, came in that spring and summer of 1959. Castro's hatred of dictators vanished, it seemed, when the name of the dictator was Castro. His indifference to power also disappeared. With a ruthlessness that would have startled Batista, Fidel suspended habeas corpus, established military tribunals all over the island, and decreed an end to the right of convicted defendants to appeal their sentences. By September he was careening leftward. He recognized Red China, called the United States a "vulture . . . feeding on humanity," renounced Cuba's 1952 military pact with the U.S., and dared the *yanquis* to invade Cuba.

The idealists and visionaries of the 26th of July movement had been betrayed. When they realized it, all Cuba rocked with their thwarted rage. Over a hundred of them were jailed, and the others fled north to Florida. Manuel Ray, a radical young engineer who had commanded Castro's Havana underground, was one. Two were famous liberals: Mio Cardona, whom Castro had chosen to be the first premier of his new government, and Manuel Urrutia, also hand-picked, the regime's first president. Others who felt that they had been sold to the Reds included brave officers like José Peréz ("Pepe") San Román, Erneido Oliva, and Huber Matos, one of the 26th of July heroes of the Sierra Maestra. Some were incredulous when they first heard of Castro's treachery. They said they wouldn't believe until they saw it. Some literally witnessed it. Dr. Manuel Francisco Artime, the brilliant young manager of Oriente province, heard Castro himself outline his plan to communize Cuba within three years. "I realized," Artime later said, "that I was a democratic infiltrator in a Communist government."

Such men could not compromise with what they regarded as total evil. If they wanted to call their souls their own, they had to escape through what American reporters were calling "the cane curtain" in the hope that one day they could reclaim their homeland. Cubans have a certain style about them, and some of their escapes were dashing. Artime's was one. He wrote a personal note to Castro declaring that he was quitting the movement because he had "heard from your lips the complete plans to communize Cuba." Dressed as a priest and carrying a pistol inside a missal, he walked into the

American embassy. There he was introduced to a certain man called "Williams," who saw to it that he sailed north in a secret compartment on a Honduran freighter. On the Tampa pier Artime was met by a tall American who identified himself as "Mr. Burnett, a friend of Williams." In Miami, which soon had so many refugees that it took on the air of a Cuban city, other friends of Williams and Burnett appeared and introduced themselves as "Jimmy," "Sonny," "Seabee," "Don," etc. All of them, Artime eventually discovered, were operatives of the United States Central Intelligence Agency.

They did not identify themselves as CIA agents, of course. Neither did they admit it if asked. Their cover story was that they were employed by a great American corporation which was determined to solve the Cuban problem. Their leader was particularly anxious to preserve this facade. He was tall and expensively dressed, and he was the only agent with a first and last name: "Frank Bender." "Remember, Manolo," Frank kept reminding Artime, "I am not a member of the United States government. I have nothing to do with the United States government. I am only working for a powerful company that wants to fight Communism." Later the Americans tried to give the impression that a Cuban millionaire was backing them. The Cubans winked at one another and joked that the "millionaire" was named "Uncle Sam." "At that time we were so stupid," one of them said long afterward. "We thought that Uncle Sam was behind us. He wanted to do this secretly. That was all right because he was Uncle Sam, and he is strong." The CIA agents solemnly told them that they all risked jail if the FBI found out what was going on. That, they explained, was why they could not disclose their real names. It was also given as the reason for a great deal of such hokey-pokey as blindfolds, passwords, and countersigns. The Americans were haunted by the fear that the operation might be penetrated by double agents. The Cubans were required to submit to lie detector tests, Rorschach tests, and lengthy interrogations by a genial, bespectacled psychiatrist with a heavy German accent. (He was "Max.") Those who passed were dispatched on mysterious errands—typically, one of them entailed flying to New York, registering at the Statler Hilton as "George L. Ringo," and following telephoned instructions from a series of callers—until their hosts' suspicions were allayed.

Those who had passed muster were divided into two groups. The younger men, who would do the actual fighting, were recruited for a brigade—La Brigada, as it was henceforth known. In Miami the older group formed a united political front, the Frente, which would eventually replace Castro's government. As an effective apparatus the Frente was a sieve, but it couldn't reveal much about its young soldiers because it wasn't told much. Not that that would have mattered. Had Fidel been told the strength of the tiny force to be sent against him, he wouldn't have believed it. He assumed it must have about 20,000 men. As late as November 1960 the actual figure was 450, and it never exceeded 1,200. To deceive the enemy if prisoners were taken, serial numbers began with 2500. When one recruit died in training, the brigade took its name from his number, 2506. Its emblem was the figure 2506 superimposed on a cross. They wore this on their uniforms and on a battle flag.

Later, after the agents' cover had been blown, it turned out that the operation had been guided by orders from the highest levels in Washington. Day-by-day supervision was the responsibility of the CIA's director, Allen Dulles; overall planning came from what was called "the special group"—a high command of officials from the White House, the Department of State, the Joint Chiefs of Staff, and the CIA. President Eisenhower did not attend their meetings, but he knew of them, and when Castro rejected the administration's last attempt to reach an understanding on March 17, 1960, the President approved a recommendation that the Cuban exiles be trained for possible use against Castro.

Many of La Brigada's operational details might have been lifted from one of Ian Fleming's bizarre spy novels about James Bond, which were then coming into vogue. The American officers who supervised the training of the exiles were borrowed from the Army and Marine Corps more or less on an old boy basis; frequently decorated in World War II and Korea, they tended to be high in personal courage and low in good judgment. Selecting sites for the training seems to have been almost haphazard. At first one of the Cubans used CIA money given to him by Frank Bender to lease the resort island of Useppa in the Gulf of Mexico; the Cubans were comfortably billeted at the Useppa country club, and the golfers among them improved their strokes. Next a C-54 transport plane flew them to the U.S. Army jungle warfare training camp at Fort Gulick in the Panama Canal Zone. They weren't supposed to know

where they were, but one of their CIA instructors left a Panama
City newspaper around, and the canal itself was clearly visible from
a hill in the camp.

After eight weeks of lessons in guerrilla warfare—skills which,
they were told, they would teach to a Cuban liberation army—they
were transferred again, this time to Guatemala. Here, too, it was
intended that they would be kept ignorant of their location. Leaving
Panama, they were given only the code name of their destination,
"little farm." But they knew what it meant soon after the two buses
carrying them left Guatemala's San José Airport. The level of
trainee sophistication was high. Many of them had traveled widely.
The cobblestone streets and dirty adobe buildings in the Indian villages bespoke Central America, and the profusion of signs of American influence—Coca-Cola and Pepsi-Cola signs along the highway,
and the number of filling stations selling Texaco, Shell, American
or Esso gasoline—could only mean Guatemala. Soon the buses began climbing through the tropical foliage of the surrounding mountains, the Sierra Madre ridge on the Pacific coast of Guatemala.
They were on their way to a vast coffee plantation, a *finca* belonging
to Roberto Alejos, the brother of the Guatemalan ambassador to
Washington. Alejos had given CIA operatives permission to use part
of it for training after Miguel Ydígoras, the president of Guatemala,
had agreed to look the other way. (In a sordid epilogue to the
operation, Ydígoras would insist that the United States had agreed
to press his claim for territory in British Honduras; Washington
would vehemently deny it.) The camp there was christened Base
Trax. It was characteristic of the operation that it was in the least
desirable part of the *finca*. The volcano Santiaguito, still active,
could be seen from base headquarters, and the camp's soil was vol-
canic ash. In some places the ash was six feet deep. Rainfall turned
it into a thin porridge. The rains that year were the heaviest in
memory. Much of the time the Cubans wallowed around in slime.

At this point some of them began to wonder aloud about the
CIA's omniscience. They were hooted down by the others. The majority's trust in their *yanqui* advisers was complete. Surely, they reasoned, the mighty conquerors of Nazi Germany and Imperial Japan
must know what they were doing. They agreed that La Brigada's
strength was slight, but Castro, after all, had started his 26th of
July movement with only a dozen guerrillas. At that time the parallel between them and him could be justified; their CIA advisers

were planning to divide them into small guerrilla bands, each of which would be trained to infiltrate one of Cuba's six provinces. They were to be ready to go before the American presidential election; the deadline was September 19. It might have worked. Even if it hadn't, the consequences would have been bearable. Defeated bushfighters can usually fade away; small stigma is attached to their failure. Castro would be hard put to prove that the United States was behind them, and they might return to fight another time.

In August the special group in Washington began to doubt the wisdom of establishing guerrilla forces in the new Cuba. Castro's troops were far more formidable than Batista's had been. State Department figures put them at about 400,000 troops and militiamen, ten times his strength. A long bushwhacker campaign directed from the Sierra Maestra no longer seemed feasible. Moreover, Castro's men had been superbly equipped by his new friends in Moscow and Peking; the State Department study estimated that they had sent him 28,000 tons of military supplies. On top of all this, the vigilance and disposition of his coast watchers and aircraft spotters indicated that he had profited from Batista's mistakes in that regard, so that supplying guerrilla forces by airdrops now would be exceedingly difficult.

If these reasons were sound—and events the following year were to prove that they were, eminently so—then it would seem that they ought to have discouraged *any* military expedition. Not so; the men directing the operation from Washington began weighing the advantages of an amphibious landing by the Brigada with tactical air support provided by Cubans in American warplanes. Ship-to-shore invasions had been very effective in Europe and the Pacific in World War II, it was pointed out, and MacArthur had ravaged the North Korean supply lines by landing the 1st Marine Division at Inchon. No one appears to have pointed out to the group that La Brigada was the size of an American infantry battalion, and that no major amphibious operation had been attempted with fewer than nine battalions backed by artillery, air supremacy, and an armada of warships—1,200 of them at Okinawa, World War II's last ship-to-shore attack.

Confident that the key to victory had been found, Washington abandoned plans for guerrilla activity, certain that once La Brigada had established a bridgehead all Cuba would flock to its standard. In a long cable to Base Trax, CIA headquarters in Langley, Vir-

ginia, ordered that the number of bushfighters be reduced to sixty;
the agents in Guatemala were to "use conventional arms and training for everyone else." The Cubans took this to mean that once they
were ashore an American army would land behind them, that being
the only circumstance, they reasoned, which could justify the
change. Their CIA advisers not only failed to correct them; "Frank
Bender," the leader, told Pepe San Román and his fellow Cuban
officers that they were "going to have protection by sea, by air, and
even from under the sea." All the CIA operatives were enthusiastic
about the new plan, and from that day forward they made it plain
that they looked upon expression of doubt that it would succeed
as a sign of weakness. Frank Bender came to believe that it super-
seded his loyalty to the President of the United States. He told Pepe
San Román that powerful figures in Washington were trying to call
off the invasion, and that it was conceivable that orders to that end
might arrive from the White House. "If this happens," he said, "you
come here and make some kind of show, as if you were putting
us, the advisers, in prison, and you go ahead with the whole plan,
even if we are your prisoners." To make sure that the amazed Cuban understood him, he became more specific. He explained that
they would have to put an armed member of La Brigada at the
door of each CIA adviser, cut communications with Washington,
and go ahead with the invasion. He would tell them when and how
to leave Base Trax for the staging area. He laughed and said, "In
the end we will win."

Doubtless Frank's superiors in Washington knew nothing of this.
Like everyone else who was involved, they couldn't piece together
the whole picture until long afterward. To varying degrees it was
a muddle to Dwight Eisenhower in the White House, Fidel Castro
in Havana, Allen Dulles in Virginia, Frank Bender in Guatemala,
the Joint Chiefs in the Pentagon, the Frente in Miami, and the brave
men drilling on the coffee plantation beneath the Sierra Madre.
Communication was faulty. The special group had neglected to tell
Eisenhower of the switch from guerrilla tactics to plans for an amphibious landing. The Cubans in La Brigada continued to believe
that they would constitute only the first wave of an invasion, and
the Frente had understood the Americans to say that no attack
would be mounted with fewer than five thousand men.

The CIA was trying to recruit as many fighters as possible. Wages
were paid—$175 a month for a man, $50 for his wife, and $25 for

each child. In this situation it was inevitable that security would be compromised. The word was out, and it was out everywhere. Castro was regularly predicting the imminent arrival of the "mercenaries," but his people didn't need him to tell them it was coming. The lowliest *guajiro* cutting sugar cane knew that counter-revolutionaries were on their way. Articles about La Brigada appeared in the city of Guatemala in *La Hora* and had been reprinted in most of the Spanish-language press, including some newspapers circulating in Cuba. Militiamen of the new Cuba slept with their rifles, and artillerymen beside their guns.

Americans could read accounts in English in the *Miami Herald* and the *New York Times,* though on the whole people in the United States were less than Cubans in the coming battle. They knew that something was going on down there, but they were distracted by other matters. It was not their country which was going to be invaded. They were likelier to be preoccupied by the dramatic struggle for the Democratic presidential nomination and the approaching climax to Eisenhower's White House years—the great Paris summit, to be followed by his tour of the Soviet Union. Advance parties of Secret Service men were already checking security arrangements in the Elysée Palace when, on May 1, sixteen days before the conference was to begin in France, a strange aircraft appeared high in the skies over Sverdlovsk, an industrial complex in the Ural Mountains some 1,200 miles inside Russia. Like the brigade in Guatemala, the flight was part of a CIA operation; the airplane had been built to CIA specifications by Lockheed. Its official designation was U-2. Presently the entire world would know it as "the spy plane."

Long and black, with a high tail, wide wings, and a single turbojet engine, the U-2 was piloted from a one-man cockpit. In the strict sense of the word, it was not a warplane. There were no guns. Instead it was equipped with sensitive infrared cameras aimed through seven portholes under the fuselage. They could photograph a strip of earth 125 miles wide and 3,000 miles long, producing prints in 4,000 paired frames. The detail was almost unbelievable. Photo interpreters studying huge enlargements could actually read a newspaper headline that had been nine or ten miles below the aircraft. Other instruments could test the air for evidence of secret nuclear tests and measure the efficiency of Russian radar. The U-2's protection was its height. Efficient cruising performance at very high altitudes had been achieved by careful aerodynamic and structural details; it was believed to be beyond the reach of Soviet radar. All in all it was the most sophisticated espionage device the world had ever seen. Its pilot that May Day was named Francis Gary Powers.

Powers was one of a new breed of soldiers of fortune. He flew, not for love of country, but for money. It was a job to him, and a good one; he was earning $30,000 a year as against an $8,400 combined income for him and his wife before he went to work for the CIA. That had been four years earlier, when he had been a twenty-seven-year-old Air Force first lieutenant. Beefy, thickset, and with a crew-cut, he looked like a professional football player—a defensive tackle, perhaps, with diligence and reliability, but little imagination.

He was not stupid, however. Earlier in the year he had asked an intelligence officer, "What if something happens and one of us goes down over Russia? That's an awfully big country and it could be a hell of a long walk to a border. Is there anyone there we can contact? Can you give us any names and addresses?" According to Powers this was the first time the question had been asked, despite the fact that Operation Overflight, as it was called, was about to enter its fifth year. The reply was "No, we can't." He persisted: "All right, say the worst happens. A plane goes down and the pilot is captured. What story does he use? Exactly how much should he tell?" It is Powers's recollection—and no one has corrected him— that the intelligence officer's exact words were: "You may as well tell them everything because they're going to get it out of you anyway."

The lack of a well-rehearsed cover story is by no means the least credible aspect of the affair. Sherman Adams had been in the White House when Operation Overflight began in 1956, and he knew that none of the flights were made without the President's approval. Visiting Eisenhower after the Powers debacle, he asked him about it. "You're right," Ike said. "I made the decision, just as I have known about and personally approved every one of those flights. When they brought me the plan for this particular flight over Russia, I approved it as one among several within an intelligence policy already adopted. I had no thought of it having any possible bearing upon the summit meeting or on my forthcoming trip to Moscow.

Except for unforeseen circumstances, it would not have had any."

Doubtless Eisenhower believed that, but it is untrue. The circumstances were foreseeable, or, at any rate, sufficiently within the range of possibilities to be weighed carefully. Powers's last trip was not routine. It was the first of two overflights after a long period without any, and it was the first attempt to cross the entire Soviet Union. From an American base in Peshawar, Pakistan, Powers was to fly 3,800 miles to Bodo, Norway. Taking off from one country and landing in another required two ground crews. That, too, was unprecedented. It was judged to be worth chancing because, by going deeper into Russia than ever before, the U-2 would pass over important targets never before photographed.

There was considerable speculation among the U-2 pilots over the timing of the mission. One theory was that the Russians were on the verge of a missile guidance breakthrough and that the CIA was trying to crowd in as many targets as possible beforehand. Another was that Eisenhower wanted the latest available data before sitting down with Khrushchev, and still another that an approaching detente with the Russians would make any covert operations unwise in the future. The fliers were well aware that they were part of a shady business. The suspicion had been growing among them that Soviet radar had been developed to the point where it was possible to track them. The possibilities of mechanical failure were also discussed. "One loose screw, in just the right place," as Powers put it, "could bring an aircraft down." In fact, this had happened. A U-2 had crash-landed near Tokyo the previous autumn. A Japanese journalist had inspected it, concluded that its mission was espionage, and reported that finding at length in the next issue of his magazine.

The designers of the plane had known it would run unusual risks, and they had equipped it with timed destruction mechanisms. Later the "granger," a device designed to throw off radar, had been installed as a further precaution. Despite the intelligence officer's rather casual answer to Powers's question about contingency planning, some thought had been given to forced landings. Colonel William M. Shelton, the Air Force officer commanding the Operation Overflight unit, told Powers that if he found he was running low on fuel over the Soviet city of Landalaksha, in the Murmansk region, he could take a shortcut to alternate landing fields in Finland

and Sweden. He added, "Any place is preferable to going down in the Soviet Union."

The CIA had even considered the advantages of suicide for a downed pilot. Apparently the agency hadn't been able to make up its mind. The decision had been left with the fliers themselves. Cyanide tablets were available for those who wished them, and later they were shown a small device that looked like a good-luck charm. It was a silver dollar with a metal loop that permitted it to be fastened to a key chain or a chain around the neck. The loop unscrewed. Inside there was a straight pin, which in turn was a sheath that could be removed to expose a thin needle. Toward the end of the needle were tiny grooves. In the grooves was a sticky brown substance—curare, one prick of which brought instant death. Most of the pilots, including Powers, had decided against carrying either cyanide or curare, but when Colonel Shelton asked him during preparations for his last flight, "Do you want the silver dollar?" he changed his mind. He thought the deadly needle might make an effective weapon. "O.K.," he said, and slipped it into the pocket of his outer flight suit. He also carried a shaving kit, civilian clothes, a half-smoked packet of filter cigarettes, pictures of his wife, some German marks, Turkish liras, and Russian rubles; some gold coins, watches, and rings (to be used for bribery or barter if in need of help); about a hundred dollars in U.S. currency, some U.S. postage stamps, a Defense Department I.D. card, a NASA certificate, instrument rating cards, U.S. and international driver's licenses, a Selective Service card, a social security card, and an American flag poster that had "I am an American" printed on it in fourteen languages, including Russian. Long afterward Powers recalled that when he got into trouble he was asked whether he was an American. "It seemed," he said, "pointless to deny it."

The CIA facilities in Pakistan were surprisingly primitive; the airmen slept on folding cots and cooked their own food from rations. But they weren't there much. Most of the time they played poker and loafed at the U.S. Air Force base near Adana, Turkey. (A favorite topic in bull sessions was the coming summit meeting and how it could dispel world tension.) By March of 1960 they were champing at the bit. The number of flights had been drastically reduced now for nearly two years, and the fewer there were, the more apprehensive they became over the next one. Then, after a long pause, the two 1960 flights had been scheduled for April. Powers was the backup pilot for the first, April 9. It went smoothly. The second was to be his.

Things started to go wrong when, on arriving in Pakistan, he was told that the U-2 which had been reserved for this flight—it was the best they had—would be unavailable, having been grounded for a maintenance check. In its place he would fly a substitute, U-2 No. 360. This was bad news; No. 360 was a lemon; a "dog," they called it. There was always something going wrong with it. Its most recent malfunction was in the fuel tanks. Sometimes they wouldn't feed fuel to the engine. Colonel Shelton had them in mind when he authorized Powers to land in Finland or Sweden if necessary.

If the tanks behaved, and everything else went well, Powers's course would resemble a huge zigzag. Taking off from Peshawar, he would cross Afghanistan and the Hindu Kush, an extension of the Himalayas, and enter the Soviet Union near Stalinabad. Then he would pass over the Aral Sea, the Tyuratam Cosmodrome, Chelyabinsk, Sverdlovsk, Kirov, Archangel, Kandalaksha and Murmansk on the Kola peninsula; after Russia would come the Barents Sea and the northern coast of Norway to Bodo—some of the bleakest land in the world. The flight would take about nine hours. Three-fourths of it, 2,900 miles, would be inside the USSR. After the take-off he would break radio contact with the Mobile Control Officer. The rest of the trip would be made in complete silence. It was, Powers said, "a lonely feeling."

For three agonizing days it seemed that the flight would never get off the ground. Washington was hemming and hawing over last-minute instructions. Thursday, April 28, was fixed as the departure date when Colonel Shelton, Powers, and eighteen other specialists and crew members flew down to Peshawar from Turkey. Powers went to bed at 4 P.M. Wednesday. At 2 A.M. Thursday he was awakened and told that the takeoff had been postponed twenty-four hours. The next night was the same. This time he was up and "on the house"—breathing oxygen—when word came of another twenty-four-hour wait. Saturday there was a third twenty-four-hour delay. Somebody at 1600 Pennsylvania Avenue couldn't make up his mind.

At last, at 5:30 A.M. Sunday, May 1, Powers climbed into the plane for the preflight check. There the delay continued. The scheduled departure time was 6 A.M. It came and went without the signal to go. The cockpit was fiercely hot; his long underwear was drenched with perspiration when Colonel Shelton came out to explain. They were awaiting final approval from the White House. This had never happened before. Presidential approval had always come through before the pilot was locked in his seat and ready to go. The wait lasted twenty excruciating minutes. Then Powers was given the green light. He roared off and, once up, completed his flight log entries: the aircraft number, 360; the sortie number, 4154, and the time. It was 6:26 A.M. local time, 1:26 Greenwich mean time, and 8:26 P.M. in Washington. In Moscow it was 3:26 A.M.

Crossing into Russia the cloud cover was solid. That didn't matter here; the CIA wasn't interested in this area. The sky cleared over the Aral Sea, and glancing down he glimpsed the condensation trail of another single-engine jet plane, moving parallel to his course but in the opposite direction. Shortly afterward he saw another contrail, this one moving in the opposite direction. Probably it was the same machine. He assumed that Soviet spotters had spotted him on their radar screens and were sending up scouts. He wasn't worried. The trails were so far below him that the Russian pilot couldn't possibly see him.

Some thirty miles to the east he passed over the Tyuratam Cosmodrome, Russia's Cape Canaveral, and looked down on the pads from which the Soviet sputniks and ICBM's had been launched. He flipped switches, turning on the cameras. The cloud cover thickened again; he switched them off. Fifty miles south of Chelyabinsk the skies cleared, giving him a good view of the snow-topped Ural mountain range, once considered the dividing line between Asia and Europe, and at that point the aircraft started giving him trouble. The autopilot had gone haywire; the U-2 was pitching nose-up. He turned the autopilot off, drove the plane manually for a while, and turned the autopilot on again. Again it pitched. He considered turning back to Pakistan—in an abort situation the decision was up to the pilot—but he had already crossed 1,300 miles of Russia and the visibility ahead was excellent. He decided to continue, flying manually. Passing over an enormous oil storage area and an industrial complex, he zigged toward Sverdlovsk, the Soviet Ruhr. There, at an altitude of 65,000 feet, he made a 90-degree turn for a zag northward. He was making log entries of the altitude, time, speed, exhaust-gas temperature and engine instrument readings when he felt a dull thud. The plane bucked forward, and a blinding flash of orange light flooded the cockpit.

It was about a half-hour after midnight in the White House. In the Kremlin it was 7:30 A.M. Powers thought: "My God, I've had it now!"

Out of control, the machine started to go down. He reached for the destruction switches and changed his mind; he wanted to get into position to use the ejection seat first. He couldn't quite make it. The metal canopy rail was pinning his legs. Ejecting in this position, he would lose both legs, each severed about three inches above the knee. He was down to 34,000 feet and losing altitude fast. Fleetingly he thought of the destruction switches again, but first he wanted to release his seat belt. He did, and the force of gravity pulled him halfway out of the plane. Now the oxygen hoses were holding him back. He had forgotten to unfasten them. Near panic, he kicked and squirmed away from them. He floated free and was thinking about pulling the parachute ripcord when he felt a tremendous jerk. At 15,000 feet it had opened automatically. Suddenly his plane passed him; it was intact, and hurling downward. He thought of the silver dollar. Unscrewing the loop of it, he slipped out the suicide needle and considered pricking himself. Then he dropped it into his pocket. He wanted to live.

That was on a Sunday. The following Thursday Nikita Khrushchev addressed the Supreme Soviet for three and a half hours. His remarks on the U-2, coming at the end, set off two weeks of pandemonium.

USSR	U.S. AND ALLIES
MAY 5 Khrushchev says: "I am duty bound to report to you on the aggressive acts . . . by the United States of America." Announces Russian gunners have shot down a U.S. aircraft over Soviet territory but does not say where. Charges that the mission of the operation was "one of aggressive provocation aimed at wrecking the summit conference." Is careful to exonerate Eisenhower of blame.	U.S. Aeronautics and Space Administration reports that a weather observation plane is missing over Turkey after pilot reported oxygen trouble. NASA says the pilot may have strayed over the Russo-Turkish border.

USSR	U.S. AND ALLIES

MAY 6

Lincoln White, State Department spokesman: "There was absolutely no—N-O—deliberate intention to violate the Soviet air space, and there has never been." NASA identifies the "weather" pilot as Francis G. Powers. This is what Khrushchev has been waiting for.

MAY 7 Khrushchev tells the Supreme Soviet that Powers has been captured "alive and kicking," that a Russian rocket brought the U-2 down from an altitude of 65,000 feet, and that at that time the plane was 1,300 miles from the Soviet-Afghan border. Powers, he says, has made a complete confession.

State Department admits it lied yesterday. Says these "surveillance" flights date from Soviet rejection of Ike's "open skies" proposal at Geneva in 1955.

MAY 8

Consternation among allies over timing of flights, the fact that U.S. has been caught in lie, and the implication that the President has been unaware of something so important.

MAY 9 Khrushchev warns that Soviet rockets will attack countries that allow U.S. spy planes to use their territory.

Secretary of State Herter says Ike approved the program but specific flights are not subject to presidential approval. U-2 flights will continue.

MAY 10 Soviet formally protests U-2 operation and states that Powers will be tried.

MAY 11

President Eisenhower assumes personal responsibility for the U-2 flights.

USSR | U.S. AND ALLIES

Speaking at a display of the U-2 wreckage, Khrushchev says, "The Russian people would say I was mad to welcome a man who sends spy planes over here."

MAY 12

Eisenhower tells congressmen that he still plans to fly to Moscow unless the invitation is withdrawn.

MAY 14 Hopes that the summit can be retrieved rise when Khrushchev, arriving in Paris, pledges himself to work for its success.

MAY 15 Khrushchev says he will not participate in the summit talks unless U.S. ends all U-2 flights, apologizes for past "aggressions," and punishes those responsible for the flights.

Eisenhower says the flights have been suspended and will not be resumed.

MAY 16

Khrushchev, Eisenhower, President de Gaulle, and Harold Macmillan meet in Elysée Palace in Paris for the opening session of the conference. The atmosphere is frigid.

Khrushchev takes the floor. He is curt and rude. He suggests that the summit be postponed for six months, accuses Ike of "treachery" and "bandit" acts, and cancels the invitation for the reciprocal Eisenhower visit to Russia.

Ike, grim, says that the overflights are over, but that Khrushchev's "ultimatum" is unacceptable to the U.S.

USSR	U.S. AND ALLIES
Khrushchev stalks from the palace, leaving behind the shambles of Ike's hopes for a detente and world conciliation.	Eisenhower returns to the U.S. embassy in Paris shaking with rage.

MAY 17

Khrushchev boycotts the meeting. One of his aides telephones the Elysée Palace to ask whether Ike is ready to apologize for the U-2 and punish those responsible.	De Gaulle and Macmillan make last-ditch efforts to save the conference. At 3 P.M. Eisenhower, de Gaulle, and Macmillan meet for the conference's first business session.
	Eisenhower: no apologies, no punishment.

5 P.M.: *The summit ends.*

MAY 18   In a chaotic press conference attended by 3,000 people, Khrushchev denounces the U.S. as "thief-like," "piratical," and "cowardly." The Soviet Union will now solve the Berlin problem by signing a separate treaty with Communist East Germany.

MAY 25

General Thomas D. White, the U.S. Air Force chief of staff, says that the U-2 gamble was needless and that had he known about it he would have recommended suspension of the overflights before the summit.

On the way home Eisenhower landed in Lisbon; he had chosen this peculiar time to honor Antonio de Oliveira Salazar, Portugal's septuagenarian dictator. While strolling through the formal gardens of Queloz Palace he came upon an American reporter who was idly tossing French coins into a fountain. Wearily the President asked, "That how you're keeping busy?"

"No, sir," said the reporter. "This is just for luck."

Turning away, Eisenhower said, "Then you'd better throw some in for all of us."

But the President was not rid of the U-2 jinx. Japan, America's strongest Asian ally, was to be the last destination in his odyssey of personal diplomacy. Had the summit gone well, it would have been a triumphal tour. Now it became a desperate opportunity to patch up presidential prestige. Even that was denied him. Japan was known to be the Asian base for U-2 overflights. Three of the now notorious spy planes were there, and Japanese leftists, taking their cue from Khrushchev, made them an excuse for rioting. On June 11 Jim Hagerty landed at Tokyo's Haneda Airport to make arrangements for the visit. Like Nixon in Caracas, he was lucky to escape with his life. For over an hour a mob of twenty thousand kept him and Ambassador Douglas MacArthur II imprisoned in their automobile. They had to be rescued by a marine helicopter.

Eisenhower was in Manila when the Japanese cabinet, meeting in emergency session, asked him to stay away for the sake of his own safety. Humiliated, he went to Formosa instead, convoyed by six warships and 100 aircraft of the Seventh Fleet. The ships raced through the water at speeds exceeding thirty knots, not because they didn't want to keep Chiang Kai-shek waiting but as a precaution against unfriendly submarines. On the Chinese mainland Radio Peking was denouncing the President as a "god of plague." To give him some idea of how they felt, they battered the offshore island of Quemoy with its heaviest shelling in years. It could be heard aboard his Seventh Fleet armada. Wry correspondents said that he was the only chief of staff ever to get an eighty-thousand-gun salute.

When Eisenhower landed back in Washington on June 27, his travels were over. In eighteen months he had covered 60,000 miles in pursuit of peace, and he had come home empty-handed. Surveying the wreckage and looking for the cause, he said wanly, "After all, Communists will act like Communists." Emmet John Hughes wrote sorrowfully:

All the gleam of political promise in his fantastic global journeys now was gone beyond recapturing. He had given unstintingly of his energy and his personality. He had been repaid in popular coin—the voices of millions yelling lusty ovations, the hands of millions waving gaudy banners. He had invested all this amassed political capital in the two great chances—one in Paris, one in Tokyo. Now it was spent —all of it.

The cold war was closing in again on all fronts. Travel to the Soviet Union became difficult. There were incidents at Checkpoint Charlie in Berlin. After the summit debris had been swept away, a ten-nation East-West disarmament conference, which had been going well all spring, resumed in Geneva; it, too, collapsed when Valerian A. Zorin, the chief Soviet delegate, denounced the West for ninety minutes and walked out. In July the Russians shot down an American RB-47 reconnaissance plane over international waters and vetoed a United States-sponsored U.N. resolution calling for an impartial investigation of it.

Then, in August, during the lull after the Democratic and Republican national conventions in the United States, Americans relived the mortification of the U-2 when Francis Gary Powers was convicted of espionage in Moscow. Powers had landed on a large state farm. Taking his pistol away from him, the farmers had held him at gunpoint until officers of the KGB—the Committee for State Security, the secret police—arrived to take him into custody. He told the Soviet court that he understood that the summit conference and Eisenhower's planned visit to the USSR had been called off because of his flight and that it had increased world tension. "I am sincerely sorry that I had anything to do with this," he said. He was sentenced to ten years in prison.*

During his last months in office the President became reflective. Government spending by his administration made Franklin Roosevelt's pump priming seem puny—the total cost of government, including state and local expenditures, was now 170 billion dollars, almost one-third of the Gross National Product—and he was chagrined by his party's failure to convert young independent voters who had supported him into Republicans. "What happened," he asked Sherman Adams when his former assistant returned to 1600 Pennsylvania Avenue for a visit, "to all those fine young people who sailed balloons and rang doorbells for us in 1952?"

He had one final word for his constituents, and he gave it the following January, three days before he left the White House. During the 1950s the Pentagon, and especially the Air Force, had fostered a growing band of corporations whose leaders were retired generals and admirals. Eisenhower warned of the dangers in this.

---

* After seventeen months the Russians exchanged him for Colonel Rudolf Abel, a Soviet spy who had been convicted in an American court. Lockheed gave Powers a job as a test pilot until 1970, when he was laid off.

In his farewell radio and television address to the American people he observed that "Disarmament, with mutual honor and confidence, is a continuing imperative. Because this need is sharp and apparent, I confess I lay down my official responsibilities in this field with a definite sense of disappointment." He continued, "I wish I could say tonight that a lasting peace is in sight. Happily, I can say that war has been avoided." He spoke of the prodigious growth of companies manufacturing munitions. Then:

"This conjunction of an immense military establishment and a large arms industry is new in the American experience. . . . We recognize the imperative need for this development. Yet we must not fail to comprehend its grave implications. . . . In the councils of government we must guard against the acquisition of unwarranted influence, whether sought or unsought, by the military-industrial complex. The potential for the disastrous rise of misplaced power exists and will persist."

It was a remarkable speech, but forces favoring an arms race between the United States and the Soviet Union were too strong. Despite their many differences they were, in essence, the world's two largest industrial nations. By 1966 the size of the American military-industrial complex, and its dependence on congressional appropriations, would become staggering. In that year Boeing and General Dynamics sold 65 percent of their output to the government; Raytheon sold 70 percent, Lockheed sold 81 percent, and Republic Aviation sold 100 percent. As Galbraith admonished readers of *The New Industrial State* six years later, a company developing a new generation of fighter aircraft, to cite but one example, was "in an admirable position to influence the design and equipment of the plane. It can have something to say on the mission for which it is adapted, the number of planes required, their deployment, and, by implication, on the choice of the enemy toward which it is directed."

The presidential election of 1960 shaped up as a classic duel. Both nominees were from the swing generation and had been young naval officers in World War II, each had entered public life in the months after World War II, and both were now vigorous men in their forties. Richard Nixon believed at the outset, in January 1960, that the coming race would be the closest presidential election in America up to that time. It was; but that was just about the only prediction about it which proved correct.

The United States was not the same country that Dwight D. Eisenhower and Adlai E. Stevenson had stumped in 1952, and it was even less like the country that had gone to war in Korea two years before that. By 1960 the wave of migrants to the new suburbia was at floodtide. The nation was richer. Washington, the new census revealed, had become the first American city with a black majority—54 percent as against 35 percent in 1950. By 1960 40 million American families, or 88 percent of them, owned at least one television set. Fully aware of the hundred million viewers, the two candidates were pondering ways to beguile them. Afterward it was widely believed that the tube helped Kennedy most. Marshall McLuhan thought he knew why. Kennedy, he said, had projected the image of a "shy young sheriff" in a TV western, while Nixon resembled "the railway lawyer who signs leases that are not in the best interests of the folks in the little town." What McLuhan overlooked was that as Americans became more prosperous they were increasingly conservative; more of them were investing in the railway, and were therefore on the lawyer's, not the sheriff's, side.

Each candidate followed a strategic plan. Kennedy appealed to the young, to the blue-collar vote, and to the liberal constituency which Roosevelt had drawn into the Democratic party in the 1930s. The two great Kennedy bases were the Democratic South—holding it was to be the task of his running mate—and the industrial northeast. His campaign would be largely directed at nine big states: Massachusetts, California, New York, Texas, New Jersey, Illinois, Ohio, Michigan, and Pennsylvania. If they could be carried, they would give him 237 of the 269 electoral votes he needed to be elected. His techniques included the mass registration of seven million unregistered voters—seven of every ten new registrants now were Democrats—the articulation of ideas from an Ivy League brain trust—Schlesinger, Galbraith, et cetera—and the brilliant tactics of his young Irish-Americans from Massachusetts, led by Lawrence F. O'Brien and Kenneth O'Donnell.

Kennedy's built-in advantages were support from organized labor, his father's great wealth, his Pulitzer Prize, a friendly press corps, his charisma—reporters were beginning to call it the Kennedy "style"—and his membership in the majority party.

His disadvantages were long memories of his father's support of appeasement twenty years earlier, his youth—forty-three to Nixon's forty-seven—his inexperience, and the widely held conviction, dating from Al Smith's candidacy in 1928, that a Roman Catholic could not be elected President.

Kennedy meant to run as hard as he could as far as he could as long as he could. Nixon took a different tack. He believed that a political campaign had high tides and low tides, and that to ignore them was to risk boring, and therefore alienating, the electorate. The object, in his view, was to "peak" a campaign—to bring it to a climax—on election day. Like Kennedy, Nixon planned to zero in on key states, seven of them in his case: New York, California, Michigan, Texas, Pennsylvania, Ohio, and Illinois. He also promised to campaign in each of the other forty-three states—a pledge he later regretted. He had no brain trust; now, as always, Nixon was a loner, a solitary, brooding introvert. While the theme of Kennedy's drive was that American prestige was slipping and that Americans must move ahead, the Republican nominee preached the virtues of free enterprise, individual responsibility, hard-nose anti-Communism, and Eisenhower peace with prosperity.

Nixon's built-in advantages were support from big businessmen, his greater experience (for example, in the steel strike settlement during the President's illness, and in his kitchen debate with Khrushchev), his strong middle-class roots, and Eisenhower's occupancy of the White House.

His disadvantages were recollections of Hoover in the White House, still vivid in the minds of older voters; his reputation as a dirty fighter—the "old Nixon"—the bad luck which was to plague him throughout this campaign, and his membership in the minority party.

Each year there were fewer Republicans in the United States. GOP candidates had won 49 percent of the votes cast in the off-year elections of 1950. In 1954 the figure was 47 percent; in 1958, 43 percent. A Gallup poll published in 1960 traced the decline of Republican loyalties in various occupational groups over the past eight years. Asked which party "best served" their interests, 28 percent of the farmers had said the Republicans in 1950. In 1960 only 18 percent said so. Among white-collar workers the drop had been even sharper, from 44 to 29 percent. Everybody liked Ike in the White House, but that affection wasn't transferable to Republicans playing supporting roles, and the rate of attrition among the party's lesser figures was alarming.

Eisenhower's effect on the 1960 race was further blurred by his equivocal feelings about his Vice President. He clearly preferred him to Kennedy, whom he regarded as a young upstart ("that boy," he called him), but he had told too many people that "Dick just isn't presidential timber"; the word was out. Eisenhower's insensitivity in this regard was puzzling. He slighted Nixon again and again. Discussing possible successors in his second term, he came down hard in favor of his last Secretary of the Treasury, Robert Anderson —"Boy, I'd like to fight for him in 1960!" Making a mental list, he added "some good new other fellows," including Attorney General William Rogers. He loyally included Sherman Adams, "although he'll be sixty-one in 1960, and that's pretty old for this job." Only at the end did he say, ". . . and Dick Nixon." On August 24, 1960, Eisenhower dealt Nixon the worst blow in the campaign. He was asked in a press conference, "What major decisions of your administration has the Vice President participated in?" The President's almost unbelievable reply was, "If you give me a week, I might think of one." Nixon wrote in *Six Crises* that Eisenhower had telephoned to apologize, saying that he had merely meant to be "facetious." The justification is odd, and he never offered any public explanation.

In a trial heat taken by Gallup after the 1958 off-year election, the voters chose Kennedy over Nixon, 59 to 41 percent. Just before the Vice President's visit to Moscow in July 1959, it was Kennedy 61 to Nixon 39—a greater margin than Eisenhower over Stevenson in 1956. After that trip the figures were Kennedy 52 to Nixon 48. In November 1959 Nixon moved ahead for the first time, 53 to 47. On the eve of the first presidential primary on March 8 that six-point margin held steady.

Between New Hampshire and the Democratic national convention in Los Angeles four months later, Kennedy captured the Democratic nomination by proving himself unbeatable. Other Democrats who had pursued it were Hubert Humphrey, Lyndon Johnson, Stuart Symington and—his last hurrah—Adlai Stevenson. Humphrey had led the challengers in the primaries. Kennedy bent Humphrey's lance in Wisconsin on April 5, taking 56 percent of the vote, and then destroyed him in supposedly anti-Catholic West Virginia on May 10, outpolling him three to two. At that point Humphrey quit; he had run out of money. Then the Kennedy bandwagon picked up momentum, winning in Maryland, in Indiana, and Oregon. By June 27, when Kennedy addressed the Montana legislature, in search of support, he had 550 of the 761 delegate votes needed for the nomination.

On the eve of the Democratic convention, Gallup had him leading Nixon 52 percent to 48 percent.

When he moved into his Los Angeles command post, suite 8315 of the Biltmore Hotel, the young Irish-American senator from Massachusetts had 600 delegate votes. Like all Democratic conventions, this one was boisterous, and rich in political talent. Chicago's retiring boss, Jake Arvey, was there with his successor, Dick Daley, and the most eloquent speech was that of Senator Eugene McCarthy, nominating Stevenson. Eleanor Roosevelt was for Stevenson; so was Marian Schlesinger. (Bob Kennedy scrawled a note to her husband: "Can't you control your wife—or are you like me?") The Stevenson people were well organized. They had packed the galleries, and their placard carriers were numerous on the convention floor; included among them was one whose sign delighted her candidate: an enormously pregnant woman, she carried a placard reading, STEVENSON IS THE MAN.

The Stevenson movement was exciting, at times it was even gallant, but it altered nothing. John F. Kennedy was nominated on the first ballot with 806 votes; Wisconsin's 15 had put him over the top. He chose Lyndon Johnson for the bottom of the ticket—no two men who were there can agree exactly how it was done, but Kennedy knew he needed November support in the South, and Johnson was the man likeliest to give it to him. In his acceptance speech Kennedy spoke of "a New Frontier—the frontier of the 1960s—a frontier of unknown opportunities and perils—a frontier of unfulfilled hopes and threats." He warned, "the New Frontier of which I speak is not a set of promises—it is a set of challenges. It sums up, not what I intend to offer the American people, but what I intend to ask of them." At the end he said, "Now begins another long journey, taking me into your cities and homes all over America. Give me your help"—the crowds cheered—"give me your hand"—they cheered again—"your voice and your vote"; they gave him a standing ovation, cheering on and on.

Gallup figures after the Democratic convention showed Kennedy leading 55 to 45.

After Nixon's nomination at the Republican national convention the following week, he took the lead in Gallup's report, 51 to Kennedy's 49. The week after that he lengthened the load, 53 to 47. Late in August the two were running neck and neck. In September the number of undecided voters pushed both candidates below the 50 percent mark, but Nixon remained in front, 49 to Kennedy's 46.

This was the low point in the Democratic campaign. Lyndon Johnson, convinced that he would be the party's nominee, had scheduled a special session of Congress in which he expected to shine. Kennedy was now trapped in it while Nixon jubilantly opened his first tour in Atlanta on August 26. Six days later the special session ended and Kennedy took off for Maine. Gallup's new figures were Nixon 50, Kennedy 50.

Luck now intervened. On the third day of his southern trip Nixon struck his right kneecap on an automobile door in Greensboro, North Carolina. The injury did not heal. At Walter Reed Hospital he was told that it had become infected with hemolytic *Staphylococcus aureus*. Unless he remained at Walter Reed for two weeks of intensive antibiotic treatment, he was told, the cartilage of the joint would be destroyed. Thus he lay on his back from August 29 to September 9 with his leg in traction, wretched at the thought of the lost time. Back in action, he caught cold in St. Louis. His voice grew hoarse. To compound his misery, the religious issue emerged at this time under the worst possible circumstances for him.

Nixon had repeatedly instructed his staff not to discuss Kennedy's religion with anyone, under any circumstances. Unfortunately he could not control Dr. Norman Vincent Peale, the best-known Protestant clergyman in the country and a Nixon friend. Dr. Peale led a group of ministers issuing a statement expressing doubt that a Roman Catholic President could free himself from the influence of the church hierarchy in Rome. Nixon couldn't attack Dr. Peale, though he came close to it on that Sunday's *Meet the Press* program. Kennedy, meanwhile, had seized the chance to deal with this most delicate of issues, one that he had known he must confront sooner or later. The Greater Houston Ministerial Association had just invited him to discuss his faith on September 12 in Houston's Rice Hotel. He accepted. With dignity and lucidity he told them that he firmly believed in the complete separation of church and state, and that if he could not solve a conflict between his conscience and his office, he would resign. They applauded.

Two weeks later Gallup announced that voter preferences were again narrowing. The figures were Nixon 47 and Kennedy 46, with 7 percent undecided.

The race was approaching the critical period. In two September weeks both candidates stumped the country from coast to coast. Nixon had now traveled fifteen thousand miles in twenty-five states, addressing crowds exceeding two million voters, but he realized, as he later put it, that "no matter how big the crowds or how extensive the local coverage, it was a drop in the bucket: the effect up to September 25 would be infinitesimal compared with the first joint debate for all-network coverage the next evening, Monday, September 26."

There were to be four debates—the others were on October 7, October 14 and October 21—but the first one was the most important. It drew the largest audience, some seventy million Americans, twenty million more than the others, and it was a Kennedy triumph. That was dismaying for Nixon, and it came as a surprise. He was a skillful debater. Watching Kennedy's acceptance speech on television—unaware that Kennedy was exhausted—he had thought that his rival spoke too rapidly, that his voice was too high-pitched, and that his concepts were too complicated for the average American. That was why Nixon had accepted the challenge of the debates. Both men had crammed for the first debate as though they were boning up for a bar exam. In words and ideas it was a standoff. But that in itself was a victory for Kennedy. Until that evening Nixon had been the more famous of the two, holding as he did the higher office. But here they stood toe to toe with Howard K. Smith as referee, and Kennedy held his own. More important, he *looked* better. Those who heard them on radio thought both did well, but the larger television audience saw the senator as tanned and fit. Nixon, on the other hand, had lost five pounds in Walter Reed. He was haggard, and he wore a shirt collar a half size too large for him. He slouched, his expression was grim, and his complexion was pasty, a consequence of ill-advisedly coating his face with Lazy Shave, a pancake make-up meant to hide afternoon beard growth.

Gallup's new poll showed that Kennedy had moved ahead 49 to 46; 5 percent were undecided.

Drinking four chocolate milk shakes a day on his doctor's instructions, Nixon regained his lost weight. In subsequent debates he looked as fit as his rival. He scored more debating points, too. It was all to no avail; millions had seen all they wanted, and their minds were made up.

After the last debate, and before Nixon's last-minute surge, Gallup's findings were Kennedy 51, Nixon 45; 4 percent were undecided.

Two key incidents affected the Negro vote as the campaign approached the home stretch. Speaking in Harlem on October 12, Lodge, without consulting anyone, said: ". . . there ought to be a Negro in the Cabinet . . . It is part of our program and is offered as a pledge." Nixon angrily denied that it was part of any program of his—which unfairly but inevitably offended blacks. A week later, on October 19, a Martin Luther King sit-in once more collided with Georgia law. Arrested in an Atlanta department store for refusing to leave the store restaurant, King was sentenced to four months at hard labor. When reporters asked Nixon for an opinion, he answered that he had none. Privately he thought that King's constitutional rights had been violated, and he called Attorney General Rogers to ask for a Justice Department inquiry. Rogers agreed, but Eisenhower wanted no part of it and the matter was dropped. The Kennedys had reacted differently. The Democratic candidate put through a person-to-person call to Coretta King telling her of his sympathy and his desire to help in any way he could. Next he conferred with his brother. Bob phoned the Georgia judge who had sentenced King, and on the following day the black clergyman was out on bail. At the time the press was unaware of all this, but Mrs. King told other black leaders about it. They spread the word, which undoubtedly contributed to the tremendous majorities Kennedy rolled up in northern cities on November 8. One of the voters who switched was Martin Luther King's father. He told reporters that he never thought he could cast his ballot for a Catholic, but a call from his daughter-in-law had won him over. Kennedy murmured, "Imagine Martin Luther King having a bigot for a father." Then he added, "Well, we all have fathers, don't we?"

In the last days of October Gallup concluded that the race was too close for prediction. The Elmo Roper, Lou Harris, and Claude Robinson polls agreed, and Lawrence O'Brien told Kennedy that it was "a toss-up." It wasn't a dead heat all the way, though. Political writers and politicians on both sides agree that two trends counterbalanced in October. A decided shift toward Kennedy two weeks before the election was followed by a last-minute surge to Nixon. Nixon subsequently took this to be confirmation that Kennedy had "peaked" too early, but there is another interpretation. The switch in momentum accompanied President Eisenhower's entry into the campaign. Neither the U-2 nor the Japanese humiliation had diminished Ike's tremendous popularity in the country, but Nixon's relationship with him had continued to be difficult, which explains the Vice President's failure to ask for his help until Monday, October 21. The President plunged in then and turned the campaign around. Conceivably another week or even a few more days could have reversed the result.

Toward the end the election seemed to blur into a montage of sights and sounds: Kennedy reminding audiences in his cool clipped accents that Castro had put Communists "eight jet minutes from Florida," Nixon saying that America could not afford to use the White House "as a training ground for a man who wants to learn how to be President, at the expense of the United States of America," Kennedy repeating over and over, almost as an incantation, "This is a great country. But I think it can be greater. I think we can do better. I think we can make this country move again," Truman's profanity and Nixon's response, vowing never to sully the Presidency by using blasphemy while in the White House, Eisenhower reciting Republican accomplishments in the last eight years: a 48 percent increase in personal income, a 45 percent growth in the Gross National Product, the expansion of social security, the St. Lawrence Seaway, 41,000 miles of interstate highways—"My friends, never have Americans achieved so much in so short a time"—the teen-age girl "jumpers" in motorcade crowds, bobbing up for a glimpse of the candidate, the Vice President promising that a Nixon administration would never allow Red China into the U.N., thus giving "respectability to the Communist regime which would immensely increase its power and prestige in Asia, and probably irreparably weaken the non-Communist governments in that area," the enthusiasm on college campuses when Kennedy spoke of the years ahead, "the challenging, revolutionary Sixties," Nixon favoring a resumption of atom bomb tests, Kennedy's calloused hand bursting with blood near the end when a Pennsylvania admirer squeezed it too hard, Nixon charging that Kennedy, by declaring that American prestige was at an all-time low, was "running America down and giving us an inferiority complex," the smiles of the women whenever Kennedy mentioned his pregnant wife, and Nixon urging audiences: "Vote for the man you think America and the world needs in this critical period. Whatever that decision is, it is the one that I know will be best for America. It is one that we will all abide by; one that we will all support."

Abruptly it was over. Bright weather and the closeness of the contest brought forth the largest turnout in history—68,832,818 votes, 11 percent more than 1956. After voting, Nixon relaxed by driving three friends down the California coast and showing them Tijuana, the Mexican border town; Kennedy spent the day playing touch football in the family compound in Hyannisport. Elaborate electronic gear had been installed on the sun porch of Bob Kennedy's home there, and it was there that the Democratic candidate watched the results that night and Wednesday morning.

An IBM-CBS computer enlivened the early evening by predicting, on the basis of data available at 7:15 P.M., that Nixon would win—its incredible odds were 100 to 1—with 459 electoral votes to Kennedy's 68. Then, as hard figures poured in, the country appeared to be going Democratic in a landslide. Kennedy took Connecticut, always the first state with complete returns, by 90,000. He was winning New York City by a huge margin and carrying Philadelphia by 331,000, 68.1 percent of the vote. Cook County, under the watchful eye of Dick Daley, was giving the Democratic ticket a lead that seemed to place it beyond the reach of downstate Republican Illinois. At 10:30 Kennedy's popular vote plurality was 1,500,000. He was then being projected as the winner by 4,000,000 or 5,000,000. The IBM-CBS machine was giving him 311 electoral votes; NBC's RCA-501 computer was putting it at 401. Viewers in the eastern United States were switching off their sets and going to bed, believing that it was all over. Jacqueline Kennedy whispered to her husband, "Oh, Bunny, you're President now!" He replied quietly, "No . . . no . . . it's too early yet."

It was indeed. Kennedy's high-water mark came shortly after midnight. His margin then exceeded 2,000,000, and the first returns from Los Angeles County indicated that he might carry California by 8,000,000. It was at precisely that point that the ticket began to run into trouble. Something unexpected was happening on the far side of the Appalachians. In the swing county of Lexington, Kentucky, for example, Kennedy was running behind Stevenson in 1952 and far behind Truman in 1948. Early Kansas returns put Nixon ahead or abreast of Eisenhower in 1956. Over the next two hours the picture cleared. It was not reassuring to the watchers in Hyannisport. The GOP ticket was sweeping: Kansas by 60.4 percent, South Dakota by 58.3, North Dakota by 55.4, Nebraska by 62.1. Wisconsin, conceded to Kennedy in all the polls, was going Republican by over 60,000 votes and the Democratic lead in California was disappearing as returns came in from the Los Angeles suburbs. Nationally, Kennedy's popular vote margin dwindled to 1,700,000 to 1,600,000 to 1,100,000. Plainly it was going to be less than a million. It might vanish altogether.

By 3 A.M. the country knew that Nixon was going to carry more states than Kennedy. That was small comfort to the Republicans, though; their ticket had virtually no chance of winning the 269 electoral votes needed for a Nixon triumph. The larger question was whether Kennedy would make it. Four big states hung in the balance: Illinois (27 electoral votes), Michigan (20), California (32), and Minnesota (11). Nixon could become President only if he carried all four, at that point a very remote possibility. Any two would cinch the election for Kennedy. But if he took only one of them, he would fall short. His triumph would be thwarted by 14 or 15 Dixiecrat electors, and the winner would be chosen by the House of Representatives.

By dawn everyone in Hyannisport had gone to bed except Bob Kennedy, who kept vigil over the teletypes, the television sets, and the telephone. (The Kennedy phone bill for that night was $10,000.) At 9:30 Michigan's Republicans threw in the towel, having concluded that Kennedy's 67,000 vote lead there would hold. The ticket was also carrying Minnesota and Illinois. That was good enough for U. E. Baugham, chief of the U.S. Secret Service. Baugham put through a call from Washington to a team of sixteen of his agents registered at Hyannis's Holiday Heath Inn, and they moved in on the Kennedy compound. The campaign belonged to history. Kennedy was now President-elect Kennedy.

Official returns in December gave him 34,226,925 to Nixon's 34,-108,662—a margin of 112,881, less than two-thirds of one percent of the popular vote. For Nixon it was a heartbreaker. A change of a half-vote per precinct would have given him the decision. He had run nearly five percentage points ahead of GOP congressional candidates, and of the country's eight geographic regions—New England, the mid-Atlantic states, the South, the farm states, the Rocky Mountain states, the industrial Midwest, the five Pacific states, and the border states—he had carried all but the first three. Some of his advisers wanted him to challenge the outcome. There was sufficient evidence of fraud in Illinois and Texas, among other states, to suggest the possibility of a turnaround. He was tempted, but decided against it. The barriers were too formidable. In Cook County, for example, a recount would have taken a year and a half, and there was no recount procedure at all in Texas. Meantime the country would have to be governed.

In January the U.S. Constitution played a cruel trick on this intense, driven man. Article II, Section 2, provides that after the presidential electors have cast their ballots, "the President of the Senate shall, in the presence of the Senate and House of Representatives, open all the certificates and the votes shall then be counted." The President of the Senate is the Vice President of the United States. Once before, in 1861, a Vice President, then John C. Breckinridge, had to attest thus to his defeat, then at the hands of Abraham Lincoln. Nixon solemnly announced the result, 303 to 219, with 15 Dixiecrats for Harry Byrd. He took the occasion to deliver a short, graceful speech congratulating Kennedy and Johnson and paying tribute to the stability of the American political process. In response the Congress gave him an ovation.

After he left an inaugural day luncheon at the F Street Club, his chauffeur gently reminded him that this was the last day that he, as Vice President, would have a limousine at his disposal. That evening Nixon rode to Capitol Hill. In the darkness the city seemed briefly deserted. He later wrote, "I got out of the car and looked once again down what I believe is the most magnificent vista in the world—the Mall, now completely snow-covered, with the Washington Monument and the Lincoln Memorial in the distance."

Here, as so often in his life, he found comfort in sententious reflections. "Defeat is a greater test of character than victory" was one. Another was in a handwritten letter from Robert O. Reynolds, the former Stanford All-American and Detroit Lions star who went on to become one of the owners of the Los Angeles Rams. "Sometimes one loses a battle to win the war," Reynolds wrote Nixon. Quoting one of his college professors, he explained:

> . . . defeats are poison to some men. Great men have become mediocre because of inability to accept and abide by a defeat. Many men have become great because they were able to accept and abide by a defeat. If you should achieve any kind of success and develop

superior qualities as a man, chances are it will be because of the manner in which you meet the defeats that will come to you just as they come to all men.

Nixon liked that, and he remembered it while packing to go home to California and start all over again.

IV

REAPING
THE
WHIRLWIND
1961–1968

Twenty-seven

A NEW GENERATION
OF AMERICANS

BITTER COLD had set in that week of Richard Nixon's farewell to Washington, and on Thursday, January 19, the day before Kennedy's inauguration, new snow began to fall. By late afternoon, when the government offices let out, streets and pavements were covered. Softly through the long blue winter twilight it sifted down in great powdery layers, and by 8 P.M., when the President-elect and his wife attended a concert in Constitution Hall, the District lay frozen under a thick coverlet which dismayed even hardy New Frontiersmen. Still it continued to fall, speckling the pink faces of soldiers using flamethrowers to melt the caked ice around the inauguration stand on the east side of the Capitol, deepening in the Capitol's many squares and circles, stitching the eaves of the Executive Office Building and the federal triangle complex with the same shimmering thread. Open fires were lit along the Mall in an attempt to keep it clear for traffic, but the flames had to be kept too low to help much, for the snow was accompanied by a wind that howled in from the Potomac and the Tidal Basin, sending the hard white silt scudding before its raw gusts. Shortly after 3:45 A.M., when the President-elect returned to his Georgetown home, the snow died away, but the cold continued to hold the city in its frigid grip. Drifts hung in the alleys of the Negro ghetto in northeast Washington, and there was an epidemic of broken oil burners in Cleveland Park.

At noon Friday the temperature was twenty degrees above zero; the winds were still punishing. Twenty minutes later the shivering crowd saw the new President appear on the stand and cheered, hoping to hear his speech soon. It didn't for a while. Instead it shivered some more while Richard Cardinal Cushing honked his way through an invocation that seemed endless. Like so many other chapters in John Kennedy's life, the inaugural was beginning in disarray. As the cardinal finished, smoke began to curl up from a short circuit in the wires under the lectern. Momentarily the horrified chief of the Secret Service envisaged the whole stand going up in flames. Three times he started to order it cleared and checked himself. Then the smoke stopped, only to be succeeded by another setback. Rising to read a poem, Robert Frost was blinded by the sun glaring on the snow; he had to put it away and recite a poem from memory. At last Chief Justice Warren administered the oath at 12:51. And with that, everything changed. Hatless and coatless, his voice frosting in the air, and his starchy vowels redolent of Boston, the vigorous young President set the tone of the new administration:

"Let the word go forth from this time and place, to friend and foe alike, that the torch has been passed to a new generation of Americans . . . tempered by war, disciplined by a hard and bitter peace, proud of our ancient heritage."

"That speech he made out there," Sam Rayburn said afterward, "was better than Lincoln." It was an occasion for extravagant remarks. After the tranquil, healing years under Eisenhower, the capital was witnessing the commencement of an innovative administration, the first since Franklin Roosevelt's. Now, as then, the accent was on youth. The new First Lady, who had been born the year of the Crash, was a young woman of stunning beauty. Joining her husband in the Capitol after his speech, she softly touched his face and said in her breathy way, "Oh, Jack, what a day!"

Subsequent days in those first weeks were equally radiant. Writing of Kennedy years afterward in a memoir on the swing generation, Joan Swallow Reiter said, "He was *our* President, the first born in our century, the youngest man ever elected to the office and, we were sure, certain to be one of the best." Among New Frontiersmen that faith was absolute: never had men picked up the symbols of command with greater confidence.

John Fitzgerald Kennedy had been chosen President by 34,221,-463 Americans, or 49.7 percent of those who had voted. After his death in November 1963 a nationwide poll reported that 65 percent recalled casting their ballots for him, which meant that over ten million of his constituents had altered their memories of that election day. But they had been changing them even before he went to Dallas. In June 1963 another poll had found that 59 percent said they had voted Democratic three years earlier.

The phenomenon was not an accident. Kennedy had entered office determined to broaden his support in the country. During the interval between his election and his inauguration he had read Richard E. Neustadt's scholarly *Presidential Power,* in which Neustadt wrote that the public's impression of a chief executive "takes shape for most constituents no later than the time they first perceive him being President (a different thing from seeing him as a candidate)." Kennedy was determined that the first time Americans saw him as President he would be at the post and pulling away.

Noticing that there were no blacks among the Coast Guard cadets in the inaugural parade, he started an official inquiry on the spot. The next morning he was in his bare office early, witnessing the swearing in of his cabinet, pumping Harry Truman's hand—Truman was in the White House for the first time since his last day as tenant —and firing off Executive Order No. 1, to double the food rations of four million needy Americans. In the weeks which followed the new President continued to vibrate with energy. He would pace corridors while dictating rapidly, read on his feet, dart out for brisk constitutionals, and return in a fast walk that was almost a sprint, restlessly snapping his fingers. "He did everything today except shinny up the Washington Monument," James Reston wrote of one of those typical early days.

The rest of Washington was expected to keep pace with him. In the Kennedy administration, said Arthur J. Goldberg, the new Secretary of Labor, "the deadline for everything is day before yesterday." Charles E. Bohlen said, "I never heard of a President who wanted to know so much." Some members of the government were so hard-pressed by the new chief executive that routine work suffered. A committee chairman from the Hill complained, "*He* may have two hours to spend, but *I* don't," and Llewellyn Thompson, ambassador to Russia, who had seldom been alone with Eisenhower for more than ten minutes, had four two-hour sessions with Kennedy. The talk wasn't small talk. "When you see the President," a senator remarked, "you have to get in your car and drive like blazes back to the Capitol to beat his memo commenting on what you told him."

One day a hundred people were counted entering his West Wing office. One meeting there produced seventeen separate directives, and two months after taking the oath Kennedy had issued thirty-two official messages and legislative recommendations (Eisenhower had issued five in his first two months) while delivering twelve speeches, promulgating twenty-two executive orders and proclamations, sending twenty-eight communications to foreign chiefs of state, and holding seven press conferences. Reporters were fascinated: more of them came than for the press conferences of any other President before or since. A Washington wit observed that the new President seemed determined to be not only his own Secretary of State but his own Mrs. Roosevelt too. No detail seemed too small for him. At one early press conference he answered in a knowledgeable way a question about a proposal to ship $12,000,000 in Cuban molasses to the United States—information which had appeared four days earlier near the bottom of a departmental report. Noting that Army Special Forces troops had been deprived of their green berets, he ordered that they be returned. Conferring with generals about strategy in Southeast Asia, he tested the carbines being shipped to Vietnam, and as his first presidential spring approached he even detected crabgrass on the greening White House lawn and told the gardeners to get rid of it.

He was out to expand his all-important base. The people he needed were watching him, and he wanted to be sure they liked what they saw. The hatless, coatless vigor helped. Americans approve of self-starters. It was useful for reporters to report that the new President was very much in charge; useful, for example, to let the word get around that Dean Acheson had been given just four days to hammer out a detailed NATO report. The first televised sessions with the White House press corps were, of course, crucial. One of them—the third—was watched by some sixty-five million people in twenty-one and a half million homes. These performances were live. Kennedy had to be not only his own Mrs. Roosevelt but also his own Robert Montgomery. He did it; McLuhan acclaimed him as a virtuoso. And presently the wisdom of the Neustadt approach was reflected in studies by opinion samplers. Kennedy's racing start had converted an enormous segment of the electorate. These were Nixon voters who had changed their minds and would soon convince themselves that they had been for Kennedy all along. It was something of a political miracle: the new chief executive's base was as big as Ike's.

"Presidents, like great French restaurants, have an ambiance all their own," Douglass Cater observed. The Kennedy image was forming, an amalgam of, among other things, Jacqueline Kennedy's camellia beauty, three-year-old Caroline's Kate Greenaway charm, the elegant rhetoric of the President's speeches, the football on the attorney general's desk, and the new idealism. Gone were the former administration's flannel phrases—"bigger bang for a buck," "rolling readjustment," "agonizing reappraisal." Instead, the country learned, there was to be a dynamic policy of action, typified by the new Secretary of Labor, who settled a strike during his first twenty-four hours in office. Like the harassed senator, everyone in the new cabinet appeared to be driving like blazes, working twelve-hour days and displaying signs of Kennedy hypomania. It was mostly illusion, of course, and later there was bound to be some disillusion, but at the time it was undeniably impressive. One secretary was observed simultaneously signing his mail, carrying on a telephone conversation, and relaying instructions to an aide by crude semaphore; a second was said to be training himself to carry on with only six hours of sleep; and a third member of the cabinet, Robert McNamara, startled Pentagon guards by showing up at 7:30 each morning.

Restoration of green berets to the Special Forces reflected Kennedy's belief in excellence. Later David Halberstam would write of those first days that the members of the Kennedy team "carried with them an exciting sense of American elitism"—elitism was not yet a term of opprobrium—"a sense that the best men had been summoned forth from the country to harness this dream to a new American nationalism, bringing a new, strong, dynamic spirit to our historic role in world affairs." Examples abounded, particularly in the recruiting of distinguished scholars. An astonishing number of them came from Cambridge, Massachusetts; a mot of the time offered a new definition of a failure: a Yale man driving an Edsel with a Nixon sticker on it. Asked how he happened to be chosen Secretary of Agriculture, Orville Freeman said, "I'm not really sure, but I think it had something to do with the fact that Harvard does not have a school of agriculture." Freeman did indeed lack a Harvard degree, but what was more important in this administration was that at Minnesota he had been graduated magna cum laude and elected to Phi Beta Kappa. A Mauldin cartoon depicted a Phi Beta Kappa key as the new key to the capital. Disdain and even contempt for intellectuals, so conspicuous in Washington eight years earlier, had vanished. In cultivating this image, New Frontiersmen soft-pedaled certain inconvenient facts—their President loved golf, for example, and his two favorite songs, "Bill Bailey" and "Heart of My Heart," were anything but classical. Yet picturing him as a Brahmin was not inaccurate. As Truman had admired generals and Eisenhower tycoons, Kennedy turned to academics. Among his advisers were fifteen Rhodes scholars, led by the Secretary of State, and four professional historians. The Secretary of Defense, the Commissioner of Internal Revenue, the chairman of the Civil Service Commission, and the ambassadors to India, Japan, and Yugoslavia were former college teachers. The President's expert on gold was a professor. Even the President's military adviser, General Maxwell D. Taylor, came to him from the Lincoln Center for the Performing Arts, and for the first time in history the White House had a cultural coordinator.

The Best and the Brightest, Halberstam would later call them in a bitter reckoning of their foreign policy failures. His appraisal came eleven years later and was largely an indictment of their role in Vietnam. Unquestionably that was the worst of their handiworks, but it was not their only disaster, a fact to be weighed in putting the Kennedy years in perspective. The new administration had stumbled earlier. The responsibility for their first outstanding nonsuccess was far from theirs alone. They were executing a plan drawn up by the outgoing administration. Nevertheless, they should have been more skeptical of it. The fact that they were not is illustrative of how fallible the cleverest politicians can be. Their error lay in confusing image and reality. Looking back on those first weeks in power, Robert Kennedy would observe almost wistfully, "Those were the days when we thought we were succeeding because of the stories on how hard everybody was working." Their discovery of their mistake was a spin-off of one of American history's most farcical misadventures, which took its name from Cuba's Bahía de Cochinos, the Bay of Pigs.

Of that debacle Halberstam was to write: "How a President who seemed so contemporary could agree to a plan so obviously doomed to failure, a plan based on so little understanding of the situation, was astounding." Afterward Kennedy himself asked Ted Sorensen, "How could I have been so far off base? All my life I've known better than to depend on the experts. How could I have been so stupid, to let them go ahead?" Again and again, Arthur Schlesinger noted, the remorseful President would "recur incredulously to the Bay of Pigs, wondering how a rational and responsible government could ever have become involved in so ill-starred an adventure."

All that, of course, was after the fact. In the beginning the scheme had not seemed so harebrained. President-elect Kennedy had first learned of it from Allen Dulles on November 29, 1960. Two days after the inaugural, Dulles and General Lyman Lemnitzer, chairman of the Joint Chiefs, briefed the leading members of the new administration—Rusk, McNamara, Robert Kennedy. On January 28 the President called the first White House meeting to discuss the future of La Brigada. Schlesinger observed that Kennedy was "wary and reserved in his reaction." The CIA men told their new chief not to worry. There were no loose threads, they assured him; every base was covered.

Kennedy at that time had been President one week. He wanted time to mull the thing over, but the CIA said he couldn't have much of it. For La Brigada it was now or never. Castro was about to receive crated MIGs from Russia. By June 1 enough of them would be assembled and in service, piloted by Cuban fliers who were being trained in Czechoslovakia, to wipe out the brigade on the beaches. In addition, President Ydígoras said the trainees couldn't stay in Guatemala after April. By then the rainy season would turn the Sierra Madre into one vast bog. Further training there would be impossible. The CIA reported that La Brigada was fit and eager to fight. The liberation of Cuba awaited a word, a single word, from the President.

Still he hesitated. The pressure mounted. Allen Dulles bluntly put it to him: either he approved the plan or he would be refusing to allow freedom-loving exiles to deliver their homeland from a Communist dictatorship, encouraging Cuba to undermine democratic governments throughout Latin America, and creating an ugly '64 campaign issue as the disbanded, disillusioned brigade toured the United States under Republican auspices, revealing how Kennedy had betrayed them and the cause of anti-Communism. Dulles asked the President whether he was ready to tell this "group of fine young

men" who asked "nothing other than the opportunity to try to restore a free government in their country" that they would "get no
sympathy, no support, no aid from the United States?"

Kennedy asked what the chances of success were. Dulles reminded him that in June 1954 the CIA had overthrown Guatemala's
Marxist government. He said, "I stood right here at Ike's desk, and
I told him I was certain our Guatemalan operation would succeed,
and, Mr. President, the prospects for this plan are even better than
they were for that one." The Joint Chiefs unanimously endorsed it.
Late in February Kennedy asked for a second opinion from the
Chiefs. They sent an inspection team to the Guatemalan base. After
reading the report and studying La Brigada's tactical plan, General Lemnitzer again predicted that it would succeed, and Admiral
Arleigh Burke, chief of naval operations, seconded him. Looking
for still another opinion, the President ordered to Guatemala a veteran Marine Corps colonel with a brilliant combat record. The result
was this evaluation:

> My observations have increased my confidence in the ability of
> this force to accomplish not only initial combat missions, but also the
> ultimate objective, the overthrow of Castro. The Brigade and bat-
> talion commanders now know all details of the plan and are enthusi-
> astic.* These officers are young, vigorous, intelligent and motivated
> by a fanatical urge to begin battle. . . .
> They say they know their own people and believe that after they
> have inflicted one serious defeat upon the opposition forces, the
> latter will melt away from Castro, whom they have no wish to sup-
> port. They say it is a Cuban tradition to join a winner and they have
> supreme confidence they will win against whatever Castro has to
> offer.
> I share their confidence.

At that, Kennedy yielded, conceding that there was some logic
in the argument that an administration which was prepared to send
U.S. troops to fight Communism in Laos, on the other side of the
world, could not ignore an aggressive Communist regime ninety
miles south of Florida. Yet even then he expressed misgivings.
Schlesinger later believed that if one senior adviser had spoken out
against the expedition, it would have been canceled. Only he and
Senator William Fulbright protested. (Chester Bowles and Edward

---

* The record shows that at that point the CIA had not shown any of them the
plan.

R. Murrow knew of it and were against it, but as their sources of information were unofficial, they couldn't appeal to the White House.) Schlesinger asked Kennedy, "What do you think about this damned invasion?" Kennedy replied dryly, "I think about it as little as possible."

On Monday, April 10, the brigade was moved by truck to its point of embarkation, Puerto Cabezas, in Nicaragua. Thursday the men boarded the boats. On Friday their CIA leaders told them their objectives: the capture of three beaches in the Bay of Pigs, with brigade paratroops seizing key points in the great marshy swamp— Cienaga de Zapata—that lay between the island proper and the sea. At noon Sunday the expedition passed the point of no return. The rebels, their armada, and their tiny air force were committed.

The real nature of that commitment and the plan Kennedy thought he had approved were not the same thing, however. The President had been assured that the brigade comprised 1,400 elite troops who had been trained as guerrillas. Their objective in the Bay of Pigs, he—and they—had been told, was a remote, abandoned beach whose only signs of habitation were deserted resort houses. Landing at night, the briefers explained, the rebels' presence would be unknown to Castro. CIA intelligence further assured the President that the Cuban dictator would be unable to act for at least seventy-two hours. Even then he would be bewildered; to divert him, 168 brigade commandos would make a diversionary landing on the coast of Oriente province over three hundred miles away.

Dulles, Richard Bissell—chief architect of the CIA plan—and their advisers, including E. Howard Hunt Jr., were confident that enough Cubans were disillusioned with Castro to guarantee the success of the main landing. They reported that 2,500 of them belonged to resistance organizations, that another 20,000 sympathized with the resistance, and that 25 percent of the population, at the very least, was prepared to give the insurgents active support. This was essential, for both in private and in public Kennedy had emphasized that the American military would play no part in an assault on Castro. He was locked in on this. At an April 12 press conference he said that "there will not be, under any conditions, any intervention in Cuba by United States forces, and this government will do everything it possibly can—and I think it can meet its responsibilities— to make sure that there are no Americans involved in any actions inside Cuba . . . The basic issue in Cuba is not one between the United States and Cuba; it is between the Cubans themselves."

Should the exiles fail to establish a beachhead in the Bay of Pigs and hold it, he was told, they would break off the action and "melt into the hills." With that, the President thought that all bets had been covered. Believing such a diversion would alter the plan from one for a spectacular amphibious assault to a low-key infiltration, he felt that any chance that U.S. credibility and prestige might be damaged had been eliminated.

He was mistaken. The CIA to the contrary, none of the exiles had received any instruction in guerrilla warfare since November 4, 1960, at which time their force had numbered just 300 men. Many of the more recent recruits were not fit for an arduous jungle campaign. Only 135 members of the brigade were really soldiers. The rest were clerks, lawyers, bankers, physicians, geologists, teachers, cattlemen, newspapermen, musicians, draftsmen, engineers, artists, and mechanics. Three were Catholic priests and one was a Protestant clergyman. Crack troops should be young, in their late teens or early twenties. The average age of these men was twenty-nine; some of them were in their sixties, and some of the late arrivals had not learned to fire a rifle.

That was only the beginning of Kennedy's misapprehensions. Actually the question of how the rebels would fare in the hills was never tested, because, incredibly, the nearest range was the Escambray Mountains, eighty miles inland and separated from the Bay of Pigs by a hopeless tangle of swamps. Being Cubans, the exiles might have pointed that out. The difficulty was that nothing had been said to them about the possibility of melting away there or anywhere else. On its own, without consulting either the President or the Joint Chiefs, the CIA had decided to withhold the alternative plan from the insurgents. Its reasoning was that if the exiles knew of it, their determination to fight might be weakened; they might be tempted to abandon their beachhead while they still had a good chance of winning.

Everything possible was done to build up the insurgents' morale, and that included making promises that could not be kept. Frank Bender said to them: "You will be so strong, you will be getting so many people to your side, that you won't want to wait for us. You will go straight ahead. You will put your hands out, turn left, and go straight into Havana." Furthermore, the CIA agents assured the exiles that if they foundered Americans would rescue them. Long afterward their leader, José Pérez San Román, learned of the option, the last resort of flight to the hills. He said bitterly, "We were never told about this. What we were told was, 'If you fail *we* will go in.'" In Miami, Manuel Ray of the Frente believed that U.S. troops would come in as a second wave. He said later, "We were told that the landings would be followed up by all necessary support. We were even told that ten to fifteen thousand men would be available."

The first setback came in the air, and it was crucial. CIA appraisals of the Cuban air force had been scornful. Its combat efficiency was rated "almost nonexistent," its planes "for the most part obsolete and inoperative," and its leadership "entirely disorganized." Castro had fifteen B-26 bombers, ten Sea Furies, and four fast T-33 jet trainers. To knock them out, the CIA scheduled a strike against Cuban airfields on Saturday, April 15, two days before the landing. Eight exiles were to fly World War II prop-driven B-26s; afterward two of them would identify themselves in Miami as defectors from the Cuban air force. It wasn't good enough. Castro, after all, knew who was deserting from him and who wasn't, and to assure confusion among the Americans a *real* defector chose this awkward time to land in Jacksonville. The lumbering B-26s were slow, unwieldy, and plagued by engine trouble. Saturday evening Frank Bender sent a message to Pepe San Román. The bombing mission had been a success, he said; nearly all Castro aircraft had been destroyed on the ground—twelve at his Santiago de Cuba airfield, six to eight at Ciudad Libertad, and eight to ten at San Antonio. This would have been marvelous if it were true, but it wasn't; the Cuban air force had been left with six B-26s, two Sea Furies, four fighters and, most important, two T-33 jets. Unaccountably, both the CIA and the Joint Chiefs had assigned no value to the T-33s because they were trainer planes. They were jets all the same, and as such could fly circles around the insurgents' B-26s. Armed with 50-caliber machine guns, they would hop on the tails of the B-26s. Moreover, the bombers were particularly vulnerable to attack from the rear. As flown in World War II, B-26s had been defended by tail gunners, but the CIA had eliminated tail guns in these planes to put in extra gas tanks, giving the fliers more time in the air over Cuba. Now the exiled fliers were doomed. Air mastery would belong to Castro. Always important in an amphibious operation, this was especially so for this one because of another CIA error. For reasons which have never been explained, the agents had ordered all the supplies for the first ten days of fighting—the ammunition, gasoline, food, hospital equipment—loaded on one ship.

The name of the vessel was the *Río Escondito*. It was one of five hulking old World War II troop transports and two escort ships bearing the cover name García Line for this operation, and in a way it was a symbol of the entire undertaking. Unpainted and covered with rust, its engines temperamental and its hold reeking of foul odors, the *Río* listed like *The African Queen*. The exiles were appalled by it. One of them, Enrique Ruiz-Williams, a mortarman with some knowledge of the sea, was shocked—it gave him what he later described as "a cold feeling"—and Erneido Oliva felt "a great deception when we got over to the ships. It was something we didn't expect. That was not what we were waiting for." The idea that such a boat had been chosen for a mission of stealth was ludicrous. Its hoists and winches shrieked when used. Its rust-caked loading machinery was even noisier. The *Río* was already in trouble. Moving down the Mississippi to the Gulf of Mexico, one of its propellers had struck a log. Brigade frogmen found it completely bent. Its maneuverability sharply limited, it limped onward on its way to a duel with enemy aircraft.

Kennedy's understanding that young Cuban patriots would be landed quietly on an isolated coast were first jarred by a Manhattan public relations firm. Without a word to the White House or anyone else, including the Cuban Frente, whose authority was being preempted, the CIA had hired Lem Jones Associates to issue press releases in the name of the "Cuban Revolutionary Council." The bulletins were being telephoned to Jones's Madison Avenue office by CIA agents and then distributed to the press. One, "for immediate release," reported: "The principal battle of the Cuban revolt against Castro will be fought in the next few hours. Action today was largely of a supply and support effort." At the end it called for "a coordinated wave of sabotage and rebellion."

In Washington administration insiders were beginning to wonder whether it wasn't the exiles who were being sabotaged. Everything was going wrong for them. The landing craft assigned to their assault waves turned out to be fourteen-foot open boats with no protection for those aboard. The 50-caliber machine guns on them were improperly sighted and aimed in the wrong direction. The boats were powered by outboard motors; at the peak of the coming action one of the invaders, jumping from his ship, struck a pilot and knocked him overboard, leaving the landing craft to drift in aimless circles. There were other mishaps; aboard the transport *Atlántico* three insurgents were practicing with a 50-caliber machine gun when it tore loose from its mounting and fired wildly in all directions, killing one of their comrades and wounding two others. More ominous for the outcome of the operation, the force of rebel commandos who were supposed to draw Castro's mission away from the Bay of Pigs by a feint in Oriente province never reached the shore. Twice they boarded their landing craft and twice returned to reembark on their ship, *La Playa*. The CIA agents accompanying them sent back word that the diversion had been "aborted primarily because of bad leadership." The leaders had been chosen by the CIA.

The Oriente landing was to have been part of a cunning design meant to throw Castro off balance. Even more important were plans for a general uprising in Cuba by the anti-Castro underground. President Kennedy had been told that the underground movement was vital to the success of the mission. The Joint Chiefs had agreed. The behavior of the CIA, however, had been curiously ambivalent. The underground was part of the overall strategy. Agents had been in touch with Rogelio Gonzáles Corso, the almost legendary leader of the movement, known throughout Cuba under his code name, "Francisco." He and his men were on the alert. At the proper time they were to be told to create disorders and create a general air of insurgency which would then be capitalized upon by Radio Swan, the exiles' propaganda station; Radio Swan broadcasts would tell the populace how to help La Brigada, how to join its ranks, how to blow up power stations, and so on. This looked fine on paper, but in practice it raised a basic question of priorities. The difficulty was one of timing. The uprisings conflicted with the air strike meant to wipe out Castro's air force. Whichever one came first would alert him to the other. Command of the air was judged to be more important. It came first and it failed. The following night Radio Swan broadcast orders for the underground to rise. They were in code and lyrical in the most florid Howard Hunt prose:

Alert! Alert! Look well at the rainbow. The first will rise very soon. Chico is in the house. Visit him. The sky is blue. Place notice in the tree. The tree is green and brown. The letters arrived well. The letters are white. The fish will not take much time to rise. The fish is red.

The strangest thing about this message was that it seems to have beamed toward the wrong people. It was picked up by the Columbia and National broadcasting networks and by several Florida stations, none of which could fathom its meaning. But although it was repeated over and over, it reached none of the listeners for whom it was intended—the brigade, the commandos, the Frente, the infiltration teams, and the saboteurs in Cuba. In reality it didn't much matter, though. Castro, warned by the air attack the day before, had ordered a roundup of all Cubans whose loyalty to him was suspect. Instantly, in the words of nineteen-year-old Félix Rodríguez, one of those who was waiting to revolt, "The roads were closed, the houses were surrounded, and they were arresting thousands of people. I cried." In Havana alone more than two hundred thousand men and women were arrested and lodged in baseball parks, public buildings, theaters, and auditoriums. Thus the underground audience wasn't tuned in. It was being held at gunpoint. On the next day, D-day, Monday, April 17, 1961, Francisco himself was found guilty of treason and executed.

At 7:45 P.M. the previous evening the five rusty cargo ships and two escorts of the exiles' task force had arrived in the Bay of Pigs and cast anchor. One by one the subplots meant to support the insurgents on board had failed—the Oriente deception, the sabotage, Radio Swan's instructions, the rising of the underground—and now the amphibious landing would go in with as little subtlety as at Anzio. The men didn't know that. Like assault troops in all wars, they had been told as little as possible. They waited below deck dressed for combat, dozing fitfully. At 11 P.M. Pepe San Román, their commander, came topside for a breath of air. What he saw stunned him. The shore, which he had been told would be forsaken, glittered with lights. His briefers had described the Bay of Pigs as it had been three years earlier, before Castro seized power. Since then the government had decided to turn this strip of coast into a public park. Modern roads now crossed the swamps, which the CIA thought were still impassable. Three tourist centers were in advanced stages of construction. One of them dominated the brigade's first objective, the town of Girón. Motels, snack bars, and bathhouses—nearly two hundred buildings altogether—were almost ready; they would accommodate a thousand Cubans at a time. The grand opening was scheduled for May 20, less than five weeks away. Every weekend since Three Kings' Day in January sightseers by the thousands had been driving down from Havana to inspect the progress. This being a Sunday, the last cars had left only a few hours before the brigade's transports sighted land. There were still people moving around on the beach; construction workers putting the finishing touches on the new buildings were living in Girón with their families. It was as though Russian conspirators had planned a hostile landing on Coney Island or Jones Beach. When Kennedy found out he was openmouthed. He remembered that Eisenhower had been in the White House when this venture was planned, and he said, "My God, the bunch of advisers we inherited. . . . Can you imagine being President and leaving someone like all these people there?"

That may have been the worst of it, but it wasn't all. If there was one kind of operation the American military had mastered in the past twenty years, it was the amphibious landing. From North Africa to Normandy, from Guadalcanal to Inchon, fighting men had been put ashore with practiced skill. Tide tables, underwater obstacles, undertow, surf, riptides—all obstacles had been overcome by brilliant seamanship, special landing craft, and ingenious amphibious techniques. Veterans of those operations were now CIA strategists. If they remembered anything, it should have been that no American commander in those battles had been foolhardy enough to increase the odds against him by scheduling a landing at night. Yet that was what they had laid out for the Cuban exiles. In addition, they had neglected to note a vital feature of the Bay of Pigs: every approach to it was guarded by sharp coral reefs just beneath the surface.

The first insurgents to go in were frogmen, former officers in the Cuban navy whose job was to place landing lights. (Despite Kennedy's order to the contrary, Americans were leading them.) Coming upon the reefs, they realized that they would have to chart a way through. At midnight their first flashing beacon, a guide to the troops who would be coming ashore, was placed beside a concrete pier. No sooner had it been switched on than the headlights of a jeep appeared on the beach. It was a militia patrol. The jeep swerved and stopped, its lights on the frogmen. They opened fire on it. Next a truck carrying armed Castro militia raced up to join the jeep. Gunners aboard one of the troopships, the *Blagar*, silenced that threat, but it was small comfort; the first wave of exiles hadn't even left the transports and already the element of surprise—the sole justification for a night landing—had been lost.

Now the frogmen set to work in earnest trying to find lanes through the coral for LCVPs and the wider, tank-bearing LCUs. In some cases it was impossible. Men halted as far as 150 yards from the shore, waded through surf carrying weapons and radios which became inoperable in the salt water. The reefs knocked propellers off some boats. Impatient soldiers who leaped into deep water sank like stones because of heavy equipment lashed to them; comrades dragged them to safety. Some men yearned for dawn and even prayed for it, but daybreak, it became apparent, would only increase the odds against them. The officer who discovered that was Erneido Oliva. At 2:30 A.M., Oliva later testified, he reached the shore. The first building he saw was a shack with the antenna of a microwave station on top. He captured it at once, but as he said afterward, "You could see that they had transmitted from there recently." At 6 A.M. two more microwave stations had been discovered in Girón. In each the equipment was still warm. The failure of CIA intelligence to warn of them was one of the greatest oversights in the entire operation. Because of those sets, Castro knew they were here. Now he would be coming after them.

At 3:15 A.M. the bearded dictator had been roused in Havana and told that the enemy was landing troops at Girón and nearby Playa (beach) Larga. Wary of a trap, he asked for details. Operators at the microwave stations replied that they were under attack from naval gunfire, 50-caliber machine guns, bazookas, and recoilless cannons. Then they went off the air, obviously overrun. A beachhead had been established; at any moment a provisional government might be landed and recognized by the United States, creating a political problem. Castro was determined to throw the rebels into the sea.

It says much for the state of his defenses throughout Cuba that he had in that area, ready to march, a sufficient force to repel a landing much larger than this: a battalion commanded by Osmani Cienfuegos, his minister of public works; a battalion of militia armed with three mortar batteries; an infantry battalion; three battalions of reserves to guard the roads through the swamps, and several detachments of armed militia. Altogether 20,000 men barred the exiles' way out of the Zapata peninsula. In addition Castro still had his air force. At sunrise he ordered his six B-26s, each carrying a full bomb load, to take off from San Antonio de Los Baños airfield with a fighter escort and attack the ships at anchor in the Bay of Pigs.

There was a great deal of confusion on the beachhead that morning, part of it arising from the error of exiles on the ground who opened fire on their own planes. When Castro's pilots arrived over the beach the most vulnerable unit beneath them was La Brigada's heavy gun battalion. The frogmen had finished mapping a route through the coral at 6 A.M., and at 6:25 these big weapons began to come ashore. It was slow going, and it stopped altogether when the enemy swooped down from above. Briefly the action shifted to dogfights in the sky—the brigade's fliers were up there, too—but the T-33 jet trainers chased away the rebel aircraft. Then Castro's bombers zeroed in on the rusty cargo ships. The first to be lost was the *Houston*, loaded with ammunition and gasoline; twenty-six of her men drowned. Then came the *Río Escondido* and the ten days of supplies aboard her. A Sea Fury fighter put a rocket in the *Río*, which simply disintegrated in a blinding sheet of flame. That was enough for the task force commander. His crews, mostly Cubans with no strong political loyalties, were on the verge of mutiny. He notified Pepe San Román that although less than 10 percent of the brigade's ammunition had been unloaded, he and the surviving vessels were leaving now, immediately, at flank speed. He promised to come back that night.

In Washington the conflicting stories coming from Cuba at first seemed very far away. Cuba dominated the news that morning, however. In the United Nations Raúl Roa, Castro's foreign minister, had charged that in Saturday's air raid by rebel pilots in B-26s he detected the fine hand of the Central Intelligence Agency. Adlai Stevenson, disturbed, sent a query to Harland Cleveland. Cleveland called the Bureau of Inter-American Affairs, which called the CIA, which solemnly denied the charge, thereby betraying America's most respected spokesman in foreign affairs. On the strength of that, Stevenson told the U.N. that the President had vowed "to make sure that no American participates in an action against Cuba." He then read from a bogus statement by a phony defector in Miami, which Stevenson believed to be true. He said, "These pilots and certain other crew members have apparently defected from Castro's tyranny." He added: "No United States personnel participated. No

United States aircraft of any kind participated. These two planes, to the best of our knowledge, were Castro's own air force planes and, according to the pilots, they took off from Castro's own air force fields."

He held up a picture of one of the B-26s and said, "It has the marking of Castro's air force on the tail, which everyone can see for himself. The Cuban star and the initials F.A.R., *Fuerza Aerea Revolucionaria,* are clearly visible." Roa replied that anyone could have painted the insignia on, which of course was what had happened. The American ambassador assured him: "Steps have been taken to impound the Cuban planes and they will not be permitted to take off for Cuba."

There were to be no such steps. Already the CIA's cover story was becoming unstuck, leaving a humiliated Stevenson to extricate himself from the tangle of lies as best he could. As Robert F. Kennedy said afterward, "Things were beginning to surface." By Monday evening the worst was known. Kennedy's admirers abroad were dismayed. "In one day," said the *Cordiere della Sera* of Milan, "American prestige collapses lower than in eight years of Eisenhower timidity and lack of determination." The *Frankfurter Neue Presse* declared that "Kennedy is to be regarded as politically and morally defeated." In the U.N. General Assembly diplomats from African and Asian countries, remembering John Foster Dulles's charges that neutralism was immoral, were having a field day. Stevenson said dryly that he wasn't sure who was attacking Cuba, but he knew who was attacking the United States.

The 6 P.M. edition of Monday's *Miami News* bore the headline: CUBAN NAVY IN REVOLT; INVASION FORCE MOVES IN. The story disclosed that the navy's mutiny bore the imaginative code name "Bounty," and that the exiles were slicing up Castro's disintegrating forces with gigantic pincer attacks. "Various accounts" were cited as sources for the claim that the invaders had "hit the beaches in four of Cuba's six provinces, sparing only Havana Province and Camaguey in Eastern Cuba." The accounts were all wrong. There was no operation called "Bounty"; the navy remained loyal to a man; and the only action was on the shores of the Bay of Pigs, where the 20,000 defenders of Castro's regime had the exiles trapped with their backs to the sea.

Deserted by their ships, the invaders were in a hopeless position. Yet they were fighting magnificently. The paratroopers, though they had been dropped in the wrong place, were beating back militia attacks. Outnumbered thirteen to one or more, facing an enemy with heavy artillery and tactical air support, the brigade had lost fewer than a hundred men that first day while holding every position. Oliva's command, just 370 rebels, had thrown back 2,100 Castro soldiers and twenty tanks. They had sustained fewer than a hundred casualties while inflicting on the government—the figures are from a Castro doctor—five hundred dead and over a thousand wounded.

They were exultant. Their overall plight was known only to their leaders, who clung to hope because they were being encouraged by radio messages from CIA agents on the dispersed troopships. ("Hello, Pepe. I want you to know that we will never abandon you, and if things are very rough there we will go in and evacuate you.") Afterward there was much controversy about these exchanges. There can be no doubt that by heartening the men on the beach the agents prolonged their resistance and thereby added to the bloodshed. It was generally believed by CIA critics that strategists in the agency had convinced one another that Kennedy wouldn't let the invasion fail, whatever his earlier position—that once he realized that American prestige was at stake he would intervene with U.S. might. Here, as in so many other ways, they were wrong. He meant what he had said. "What is prestige?" he asked those around him in the White House that day. "Is it the shadow of power or the substance of power? We are going to work on the substance of power. No doubt we will be kicked in the can for the next couple of weeks, but that won't affect the main business."

Most Americans seemed to understand, and to sympathize. The bitterness which was to divide them later in the 1960s lay ahead. The country had not yet split into hostile camps. As Robert F. Kennedy was to write afterward in *Thirteen Days,* "We had virtual unanimity at the time of the Bay of Pigs." Editor John Fischer expressed the general view when he observed in *Harper's* that "Every President needs about twelve months to get his executive team organized, to feel his way into the vast and dangerous machinery of the bureaucracy. . . . While [Kennedy] was still trying to move in the furniture, in effect, he found the roof falling in and the doors blowing off." The Gallup poll showed that 82 percent of his countrymen approved of the way he was handling his job. "It's just like

Eisenhower," Kennedy said dourly. "The worse I do, the more popular I get."

To be sure, opinion wasn't unanimous. On the right were such hard-liners as Richard Nixon, who was to reveal in the November 1964 *Reader's Digest* that he had advised Kennedy to "find a proper legal cover and . . . go in." But that was expected. What was surprising was the emergence at this time, and on this issue, of an abrasive New Left. Schlesinger noted that many "on the left, more than one would have thought, now saw full vindication of their pre-election doubts about Kennedy." Their placards demanded "Fair Play for Cuba." They filled Manhattan's Union Square with demonstrators. Norman Mailer joined them. Outside the White House a sandwich board worn by a tall woman poet reproached the First Lady: JACQUELINE, VOUS AVEZ PERDU VOS ARTISTES. The Fair Play movement found recruits on many campuses, especially in the humanities and the social sciences; H. Stuart Hughes, a member of the Harvard history department and an early New Left militant, led seventy college teachers who signed an open letter to the President demanding that the administration "reverse the present drift towards American military intervention in Cuba." Barrington Moore Jr., a sociologist, predicted "a militarist and reactionary government that covers its fundamental policies with liberal rhetoric," and from a hospital bed C. Wright Mills, author of *The Power Elite*, telegraphed a Fair Play rally in California:

> Kennedy and company have returned us to barbarism. Schlesinger and company have disgraced us intellectually and morally. I feel a desperate shame for my country. Sorry I cannot be with you. Were I physically able to do so I would at this moment be fighting alongside Fidel Castro.

Actually Castro wasn't fighting. It wasn't necessary. At the Bay of Pigs his subordinates had the situation well in hand, and he stood to one side, a spectator for once, while they relentlessly reduced the perimeter of the rebel beachhead. Latin America had never seen weapons like those of the government troops. Monday morning four batteries of their Soviet 122-mm howitzers started to rake the beach; the exiles who had been in the target area stumbled around in a daze. Rebel tank commanders fought gallantly, but the Russian T-34 tanks outgunned them. By Monday evening the exiles were desperately short of ammunition. "The night came and we were expecting

the ships," Pepe San Román later told Haynes Johnson. "Everybody
turned their faces to the sea waiting for the ships. We knew that
without the ships we could not make it." Midnight came and there
was nothing. In despair Pepe boarded an open boat with his radio
operator and cruised six miles out, trying to reach the CIA boats
with his signal. Then he returned to his command post and sent
another officer out to keep trying to reach the captains, whose mutinous crews had rendered them impotent. Hour after hour the message went out from the open boat: DOLORES. THIS IS BEACH. DOLORES.
THIS IS BEACH. I AM TRYING TO FIND YOU. WE NEED YOU. WE NEED YOU.

At dawn Tuesday six of La Brigada's remaining B-26s tried to
bomb the Cuban air force planes at San Antonio de Los Baños.
Castro's luck held; cloud cover blanketed the field; there was no
damage. On the ground at Girón, massed T-34s stood in a solid
line, firing point-blank into the beachhead. Within the narrowing
perimeter all omens were bad. The lack of air cover had been the
exiles' undoing. Now they couldn't even be evacuated without it.

In the White House Tuesday evening the President was called
away from the Mansion's annual congressional reception. Incongru-
ously dressed in white tie and tails, he stood over a map in his
office while Rusk, McNamara, two of the Joint Chiefs, and Richard
Bissell of the CIA told him that only the U.S. air force could save
the brigade from Castro's kangaroo courts. He compromised, authorizing a flight of six unmarked jets from the carrier Essex, on
duty in the Caribbean off the Bay of Pigs. For one hour—from 6:30
A.M. to 7:30 A.M. Wednesday—the U.S. planes would keep the sky
over the beachhead clear of Castro planes while the rebels' remaining B-26s attacked the government troops on the perimeter.*

The last act of the Bay of Pigs tragicomedy followed. The rebel
fliers' base was at Puerto Cabezas in Nicaragua, a three-hour-and-
twenty-minute flight from Cuba. They were exhausted by their previous missions; only two of them had the strength for another effort.
Four American advisers, believing that jets from the Essex would
protect them, volunteered to pilot the other B-26s. They then made
the last and least plausible of all the CIA mistakes in the blunder-
studded operation. Nicaragua and Cuba are in different time zones.
The pilots forgot to reset their watches. They arrived over Girón

* In *Give Us This Day* E. Howard Hunt Jr. has the effrontery to charge that
Kennedy's failure to fill the sky with American warplanes was to blame for the
failure of the Bay of Pigs expedition.

an hour early, while the jets which were to shield them were still on the flight deck of the *Essex,* Castro's T-33s swarmed up and made short work of them; the four Americans were killed.

Only the final agony was left now. Pleas from Girón for reinforcements, tanks, and ammunition became fainter. Messages were terse: FIGHTING ON BEACH. SEND ALL AVAILABLE AIRCRAFT NOW. And: IN WATER. OUT OF AMMO. ENEMY CLOSING IN. HELP MUST ARRIVE IN NEXT HOUR. The last stand began Tuesday night. Encircled by Castro's artillery and tanks, the exiles' leader sent his last message at 4:32 P.M. Wednesday: AM DESTROYING ALL MY EQUIPMENT AND COMMUNICATIONS. TANKS ARE IN SIGHT. I HAVE NOTHING TO FIGHT WITH. AM TAKING TO THE WOODS. I CANNOT WAIT FOR YOU.

The woods could provide only temporary shelter. Lacking the fallback plan, the rebels stumbled into enemy hands one by one. Castro's triumph was complete. He had broken the invasion in less than seventy-two hours, turning it into what Haynes Johnson in his excellent study of the battle calls "perhaps the most heavily publicized of the many bungled, poorly planned operations since the Light Brigade charged into oblivion at Balaklava." Ahead for the survivors in the brigade lay the humiliation of a public trial in Havana's Sports Palace and an imprisonment which was not to end until Christmas 1962, when Robert F. Kennedy and James B. Donovan led a successful movement to ransom them.

In the mid-1960s contemporary historians tended to believe that in the long run the Bay of Pigs was really a blessing; that because of it Kennedy became disillusioned with experts and was better equipped to face the Cuban missile crisis eighteen months later. Seen from the 1970s, the debacle at Girón, and his reaction to it, have a very different look. On Thursday of that week, the day after the invasion collapsed, the President spoke before the American Society of Newspaper Editors at the Statler-Hilton Hotel in Washington. He took a fighting stance. He was letting Castro go this time, he said, but he wanted the record to show that "our restraint is not inexhaustible." The United States was ready to act, "alone, if necessary," to "safeguard its security," and he warned Moscow that "should that time ever come, we do not intend to be lectured on intervention by those whose character was stamped for all time on the bloody streets of Budapest."

This was cold war rhetoric at its most bleak. Implicit in it was the assumption that the only danger to America lay outside the country's borders. The country's one adversary was monolithic international Communism, whose forces were "not to be underestimated in Cuba or anywhere else in the world." The governments and peoples of the Western Hemisphere were exhorted to "take an ever closer and more realistic look at the menace of external Communist intervention and domination in Cuba," for it was "clearer than ever before that we face a relentless struggle in every corner of the globe that goes far beyond the clash of armies and even nuclear armaments."

The great liberal turning of the 1960s still lay ahead then. Once it had been taken, the threats to the nation would be viewed as internal—racism, militarism, pollution, technology, bureaucracy, the population explosion, "the establishment." But in the Kennedy years all that lay ahead. The liberal hero of the hour, who in the 1930s had been the angry young workman, in the 1940s the GI, and in the 1950s the youth misunderstood by his mother, had become, in the early 1960s, the dedicated Peace Corpsman battling hunger, disease—and Communism—with tools of peace. As an American liberal of the time, Kennedy believed that the basic reasons for the revolutionary movements in underdeveloped countries were poverty and ignorance, which were being exploited by Communists for their own ends. He was sure that once those conditions had been changed by Point Four programs, the appeal of Communism would vanish. That was what the appeal of the Alianza was all about. A Latin America allied with the United States in pursuit of progress, it was held, would reject overtures from the Comintern.

These beliefs were deeply held. There was, perhaps for the last time, a liberal conviction that man would be able to solve his problems. The young idealist of the early 1960s was a pragmatist, to use a word much in vogue then. The hour of Ralph Nader, the liberal model of the next decade, had not yet struck. In the Kennedy years liberals believed, as they had believed since the years of Franklin Roosevelt, that the remedy for social wrongs lay in big government and stronger presidential powers. Later their disenchantment would shake the very foundations of the republic.

Kennedy's speech in the Statler-Hilton that Thursday might have been delivered in the Eisenhower years, perhaps even by John Foster Dulles. There were many differences in style, but not much in substance. Like all cold warriors Kennedy invoked the name of Munich toward the end, reminding his listeners of its meaning: that democracies which failed to stand up to totalitarian dictators were doomed; that "our security may be lost, piece by piece, country by country, without the firing of a single missile or the crossing of a single border." He intended "to profit by this lesson," he said, and he concluded: "History will record the fact that this bitter struggle reached its climax in the late 1950s and the early 1960s. Let me then make clear as the President of the United States that I am determined upon our system's survival and success, regardless of the cost and regardless of the peril."

Thus one of the worst guesses ever of what history would say. That address was Kennedy's public response to the Bay of Pigs. Back at the White House he took another, more symbolic step. McGeorge Bundy's status as national security adviser was sharply upgraded. He was moved from the relatively humble Executive Office Building, on the other side of West Executive Avenue, to the West Wing. There, much closer to the President's oval office, Bundy began presiding over regular morning meetings of his National Security Council staff. In addition he extended his sway over the White House war room, with its huge maps and brightly colored telephones. Next time the forces of world Communism plotted a blow at the free world, the United States would be on guard. If they dared subvert the anti-Communist government of another weak little country anywhere, they would meet a firmer will. The White House was ready. Bundy was ready. The war room was ready. The hot lines were plugged in. The aggressors would be taught a lesson they would never forget.

Among the thoughtful readers of reports from Cuba was Nikita Sergeyevich Khrushchev. The Chairman wasn't much impressed by cold war oratory, having delivered a lot of it himself. What interested him was that the new President, young and inexperienced, had stumbled badly. Kennedy seemed unsure of himself. This looked like a good time to pounce on him.

The White House knew that in the Kremlin this would be the interpretation of the debacle. It was the chief reason for Washington's dismay after taking stock of the wreckage of confidence left by the Bay of Pigs. In February a meeting between Kennedy and Khrushchev had been scheduled for early June, in Vienna. On May 12 the Chairman wrote that the invitation was still open. Kennedy thought of suggesting a postponement. But that, he decided, would be interpreted as a further sign of weakness. Better the summit, he said, than the brink. Instead of staying away he would redouble his preparations for the Vienna conference. He had been told that the Chairman had been disdainful of Eisenhower's failure to bone up on his homework before his two summits with Khrushchev; whenever a tough question came up, Ike had had to turn to aides for answers. Kennedy decided that the important talks there would be just the two of them and an interpreter.

Like him, Khrushchev was under pressure from hard-liners at home, Stalinists who believed that the only way to get what you wanted from the other side was to demand it, to grab it, to be coarse and abusive and intimidating. There was a lot of this in Khrushchev himself. Stalin had admired it in him. It was what gave him his aura of primitive power. The previous autumn he had provided the U.N. General Assembly with a memorable demonstration of it. The Congo in these years was a graveyard for the reputations of geopoliticians. Khrushchev, already frustrated by the U-2 incident, the aborting of the Geneva summit with Eisenhower, and the end of his hopes for a Soviet-American detente, had been maddened at fresh humiliations in Katanga. He had blamed Dag Hammarskjöld, calling him a tool of colonial powers. Demanding that the post of secretary general of the U.N. be abolished, he had proposed that it be replaced by an executive body of three men representing the three groups of nations, western, Communist, and neutral. He had called it a "troika," after the Russian wagon drawn by three horses abreast. For emphasis, he had removed his shoe and pounded his desk in rhythm. The General Assembly was in an uproar. Trying to restore order, the Irishman who was presiding at the time banged the gavel so hard that he broke it. The chaos delighted the Chairman. Returning to Moscow, he crowed, "How shaky the United Nations is! It's the beginning of the end."

On January 6, 1961, Khrushchev countered the American liberals' policy toward underdeveloped countries—a dual plan of economic aid, with military intervention if necessary—with what was to be Communism's great challenge of the 1960s: "unlimited support" to "peoples fighting for their liberation" in "just" wars. Six weeks later Patrice Lumumba, his Congolese ally, was murdered in Katanga. The infuriated Russian called the assassination "the crowning achievement of Hammarskjöld's criminal activities" and again demanded the secretary general's immediate removal.

The Russian right had other grievances for which Khrushchev was the spokesman. Laos, which had appeared to be about to drop into their lap, was veering toward a neutral course. Red Army hardliners wanted a resumption of nuclear tests, suspended in the Soviet Union since the fall of 1958; they now had 20-, 30-, 50-, and 100-megaton weapons, and were eager to try them out. These were daily irritants, symptoms of the cold war which kept the diplomatic climate chilly without creating a world crisis. But for them one issue was vital, and transcended the others. Khrushchev had variously described it as a "bone stuck in the throat," "a sort of cancerous tumor requiring a surgical operation," and a "Sarajevo" likely to lead toward another world war. It was divided Berlin.

For fifteen years the Russians had regarded the presence of the West in the former German capital as unbearable. Stalin had tried to evict Allied troops in 1948 and had been thwarted by the great airlift. When the first sputnik raised Soviet stock, Khrushchev had seized the opportunity to demand that Berlin be made a demilitarized "free city." He had given the Allies a six-month deadline then, and he had postponed it only when Eisenhower had made that a condition of Khrushchev's trip to the United States. Ike had made certain concessions. He had agreed that the Berlin situation was "abnormal." He had offered to negotiate the size of the western garrison there and the extent to which the city would serve as a base for West German propaganda and intelligence activities.

Now Khrushchev was stalking Kennedy with the same issue. In his wars-of-liberation speech the Chairman had come down hard on Berlin. He had openly threatened Kennedy. If "the imperialists" refused "to take into consideration the true situation," he had said, the Soviet Union would "take firm measures" and "sign a peace treaty with the German Democratic Republic." Thus Kennedy faced the demon Eisenhower had exorcised. Khrushchev made it clear that such an agreement would include guarantees that any "violation" of East Germany's frontiers would be considered "an act of aggression" against all members of the Warsaw Pact—meaning that the West would have to forsake Berlin or go to war. Did he mean it? Charles de Gaulle was doubtful. He urged the President to hold firm (*"tenir le coup"*). If Kennedy held fast and made plans for a new airlift, he said, the Chairman would back off. Looking to Vienna, Averell Harriman agreed, though he recommended different tactics. Khrushchev, he predicted, would be fierce. He would try to frighten the young President. The best response would be to turn him aside, but it should be done gently. And Kennedy mustn't overestimate his adversary. Khrushchev would be nervous too, Harriman said. The Chairman's only other trip to the West had failed. Furthermore, American Kremlinologists agreed that he had never forgotten his lowly origins. Inevitably there would be tension in Vienna. The Chairman would be offensive as only he knew how to be. The President, Harriman suggested, should rise above it and laugh it off.

This advice reached Kennedy in Paris, on the eve of his flight to Austria. The French leg of the trip had turned into a triumph for the young First Lady. Eleven years earlier, she had been a student here at the Sorbonne. Now she arrived with two truckloads of luggage, a blinding array of jewels, and a retinue that included Europe's leading hairdresser. De Gaulle could scarcely take his eyes off her. The French press cried *"Ravissante!"* *"Charmante!"* and *"Apothéose!"* Arriving at a press conference, the President said, "I do not think it altogether inappropriate for me to introduce myself. I am the man who accompanied Jacqueline Kennedy to Paris."

Vienna was different. Mrs. Kennedy teased Khrushchev—"Oh, Mr. Chairman, don't bore me with statistics"—but the gloomy pall was too heavy to be laughed away, even by her. Almost from the moment Khrushchev's black, Russian-built Chaika drove past the barbwire and up to the massive stone and stucco building that served as the U.S. embassy residence in the Austrian capital, the mood was as ugly as the weather. To an aide Kennedy described his adversary as a combination of external jocosity and "internal rage." During the two days of talks the rage was external, too. James Reston had asked to interview the President after the final encounter. Kennedy was wearing a hat that day, and as he entered the room where the reporter was waiting and sank down on a couch, he pushed the hat over his eyes and uttered a great sigh. Reston thought he seemed in a state of semi-shock. He asked the President, "Pretty rough?" Kennedy replied, "Roughest thing in my life."

Afterward Reston wrote:

> He [the President] came into a dim room in the American Embassy shaken and angry. He had tried, as always, to be calm and rational with Khrushchev, to get him to define what the Soviet Union would and would not do, and Khrushchev had bullied him and

threatened him with war over Berlin. . . . Kennedy said just enough in that room to convince me of the following:

Khrushchev had studied the events of the Bay of Pigs; he would have understood if Kennedy had left Castro alone or destroyed him; but when Kennedy was rash enough to strike at Cuba but not bold enough to finish the job, Khrushchev decided he was dealing with an inexperienced young leader who could be intimidated and black-mailed.

In their talks, Kennedy told Reston, the Chairman had been rude, savage; at times he had seemed to be about to lunge at Kennedy. On only one issue was he reasonable: Laos, which he regarded as unimportant. In discussing everything else his manner was vicious, sneering. Hammarskjöld had to go, he insisted; he must be replaced by the troika. Similarly, three executives from the world's three political camps would be needed to administer any disarmament agreement between the United States and the USSR. In vain Kennedy argued that an arrangement would be rendered impotent by a veto—"Even the Russian troika has but one driver." On the matter of Berlin Khrushchev delivered an ultimatum. The bone, he said, must be removed from the Soviet throat. With or without an American agreement, he would sign a treaty with East Germany before the end of the year. If the United States wanted to go to war on this question, there was nothing he could do about it. Madmen who sought war deserved only straitjackets.

During their last private meeting, held at Kennedy's request, the President desperately tried to dissuade him from so rash a step. Khrushchev bluntly refused. "I want peace," he said, "but if you want war that is your problem." His treaty decision was irreversible. He would sign it in December. As they parted Kennedy said, "It will be a cold winter."*

To Reston Kennedy said: "I've got two problems. First, to figure out why he did it, and in such a hostile way. And second, to figure out what we can do about it. I think the first part is pretty easy to explain. I think he did it because of the Bay of Pigs. I think he thought anyone who was so young and inexperienced as to get into a mess like that could be taken, and anyone who got into it,

* In *Khrushchev Remembers* the Chairman commented: ". . . I was genuinely pleased with our meeting in Vienna. Even though we came to no concrete agreement, I could tell that he was interested in finding a peaceful solution to world problems. . . . He was a reasonable man, and I think he knew that he wouldn't be justified in starting a new war over Berlin."

and didn't see it through, had no guts. So he just beat hell out of me. So I've got a terrible problem. If he thinks I'm inexperienced and have no guts, until we remove those ideas we won't get anywhere with him. So we have to act."

Khrushchev's credibility would be watched, too, and he knew it. Returning to Moscow, he ordered publication of the two aides-mémoire he had handed the President on nuclear testing and Berlin. Sharp eyes in the State Department saw that here there was no time limit attached to the Berlin demands, but it hardly mattered now. The whole world knew of the Russian ultimatum. Since then Khrushchev had increased the Soviet military budget by 3.144 billion rubles and had delivered a series of chauvinistic speeches.

Kennedy escalated with him. On June 25 he made a telecast report to the American people. "If war breaks out," he said, "it will have been started in Moscow and not in Berlin. . . . Only the Soviet government can use the Berlin frontier as a pretext for war." He asked Congress to approve authorization of $3,247,000,000 for the Pentagon, calling up reserves, tripling draft calls, raising the ceiling for combat troops, and reconditioning planes and ships which were in mothballs. Dean Acheson wanted him to declare a state of emergency, and Vice President Lyndon Johnson agreed. Kennedy preferred to leave the door open to negotiations. He hesitated to make an atomic bluff because it might be called. His chief fear, he told an editor of the *New York Post*, was that the Chairman "wants to rub my nose in the dirt," in which case "it's all over."

Pressure built up for both leaders. To reassure Germans in the old capital that they would not be abandoned, Kennedy sent his Vice President there with General Clay, the hero of the airlift. Khrushchev warned the world that the USSR could now create a bomb with an explosive power equal to 100 million tons of TNT and had rockets capable of delivering it. As though to prove his point, a second Soviet astronaut, Major Gherman S. Titov, was launched into orbit and circled the earth seventeen times. Kennedy urged Americans to build bomb shelters. Meanwhile Berlin was in an uproar. During July, 30,444 refugees flowed into the western part of the city. In the first ten days of August another 16,500 crossed. On the twelfth alone 4,000 were counted, among them a high proportion of physicians, technicians, and skilled workers—the very people necessary for the Five-Year Program of the First Secretary of East Germany's Communist party, Walter Ulbricht.

At a half-hour past midnight on August 13, sirens screamed down the dark and deserted streets as squat tanks—T-34s and T-54s— led East German military convoys to the twenty-five-mile border that separated the western part of the city from the east. Trucks of steel-helmeted Vopos, East Berlin policemen, took up positions in the major intersections. Troops unloaded wooden horses, concertinas of barbed wire, concrete posts, stone blocks, and picks and shovels. Four hours later, at sunrise, the beginning of a wall was visible. Four days later it was complete, imprisoning the Germans who remained in East Berlin.

The western powers had been caught off balance. Kennedy was away from Washington. It took the State Department four days to deliver a formal protest in Moscow. Then, on September 1, Khrushchev gave the screw another turn. U.S. seismographs recorded unmistakable evidence that the Russians had resumed testing. Kennedy and Macmillan appealed to the Chairman to stop, citing the extent and toxicity of the new fallout. Khrushchev ignored them. Detection devices picked up a second test, and a third. Over the next month the Soviets detonated thirty major devices, nearly all of them in the atmosphere. At the end of the series the Russians had become responsible for more radioactive poison in the air than the Americans, the British, and the French combined. In a speech before the Communist Twenty-second Congress the Chairman announced the imminent explosion of a 50-megaton bomb—2,500 times as large as the one which had been dropped on Hiroshima and five times the size of all high explosives used in all the wars in history. He drew laughter from the delegates at the next session when he told them that the resulting blast "proved somewhat bigger than the 50 megatons that the scientists had calculated," but that they would not be punished for the "mistake."

Kennedy decided that if this constituted Khrushchev's only answer to western proposals for an atmospheric test ban, he had to authorize a resumption of U.S. tests, though he approved only those underground, which had no fallout. In view of the acts of the Soviet government, he said, "we must now take those steps which prudent men find essential." It was now September 8, the peak of the crisis. The wall was complete, a corral of brick and jagged cement cutting through the heart of Berlin. Since August 22 all but one of the crossing points had been closed to the Allies, and there the Vopos insisted upon inspecting soldiers' papers. Any approach to the border closer than 100 meters (110 yards) was prohibited. Next notes to Paris, Bonn, and Washington formally demanded that West German leaders be forbidden to enter Berlin by plane. At that, the West stiffened. On September 8 Khrushchev's insistence that West German flights into Berlin should be controlled was curtly rejected. Ten days later, when Kennedy was about to leave Hyannisport to return to Washington, he was handed a grim note. Dag Hammarskjöld had been killed in a Congolese plane crash which has never been clearly explained. War had not seemed so close since V-J Day.

Two weeks later Khrushchev began to back away from the brink. To the Belgian diplomat Paul-Henri Spaak, who was visiting Moscow, he said, "I realize that contrary to what I had hoped the western powers will not sign the peace treaty. . . . I'm not trying to put you in an impossible situation; I know very well that you can't let yourself be stepped on." The bone in the throat wasn't intolerable, after all. "You know," he continued to the Belgian, "Berlin is not such a big problem for me. What are two million people among a billion Communists!" Nor was there any hurry now. He had given Kennedy an ultimatum—"by the end of the year"—but to Spaak he said, "I'm not bound by any deadline." Having built his wall, he now appeared to be trying to wring concessions from the West which would allow him to save face. He made several gestures intended to ease tensions, including generous comments about Kennedy's maturity and evident wisdom. When there was no response to them, he threw in his hand anyhow. Speaking once more to the Communist Party Congress, he declared on October 17, "The western powers are showing some understanding of the situation and are inclined to seek a solution to the German problem and the issue of West Berlin." He concluded, "If that is so, we shall not insist on signing a peace treaty absolutely before December 31, 1961."

With that, the confrontation ended. It seemed to be a victory for the Americans. Later the real price paid began to emerge. Given the attitude of Moscow, the Berlin question, and the resumption of nuclear testing, Schlesinger would write, "the President unquestionably felt that an American retreat in Asia might upset the whole world balance." Kennedy believed that there he must provide his adversaries with additional proof of fearlessness and backbone. To James Reston he observed that the only place where Communists were challenging the West in a shooting war was in Indochina, so "now we have a problem in trying to make our power credible, and Vietnam looks like the place."

This was a cheerless time for Lyndon Johnson. The year before, he had been the mighty majority leader of the U.S. Senate, and now, as Vice President, he occupied the emptiest, most exasperating position in the government. Every day Johnson's relative insignificance was driven home to him in countless ways. He was allowed only one parking place at the White House, and just one White House phone extension. (Attorney General Robert Kennedy had three.) His wife had never seen the inside of the presidential aircraft. He himself had been aboard, though not by invitation. Three times Kennedy aides had found him poking around its cabins alone. Inasmuch as they had been there because the President was about to use the plane, they had been obliged to ask him to leave. Each encounter should have been daunting, but he kept returning, fascinated, it seemed, by the symbols of real power.

Kennedy men treated Johnson people as outsiders. With the exception of Walter Jenkins, members of the vice-presidential staff were total strangers to the glamorous presidential advisers. Several lacked credentials to enter the White House and had seen it only as tourists. The obscurity even enveloped Secret Service agents assigned to the Johnson detail. Officially they were full equals of the men who guarded the President. In practice they were ostracized by the White House detail—excluded from their cars, their offices, their social functions. Most of them were philosophical about it. They knew there was nothing personal about the snubs. They had been banished by the elite because the man they were guarding was—there is no other word for it—unimportant.

Kennedy was largely unaware of this. Like most Presidents he kept the man next in line at arm's length. The occupants of America's first and second elective offices have never been congenial, for reasons rooted in historical precedent and, perhaps, in human nature. Some Vice Presidents who have been close to their chief executives in earlier years have been hurt to find friendship replaced by icy aloofness. They forget that to a President a Vice President is a daily reminder of his own mortality. He is more. Though individuals may contemplate the grave serenely, they are not constantly shadowed by understudies. Those who expect Presidents to provide Vice Presidents with detailed briefings rarely weigh the implications of it. To grasp it, one must understand the meaning of the Presidency, the legacy the second man stands to inherit. The head of a family may make out his will without flinching, but he would blanch if told that the man next door would, in the event of his death, become father to his children and husband to his wife.

Beyond this institutional difficulty lies another. It is a fact of political life that presidential campaign tickets are "balanced" by pairing two candidates from different parts of the country who appeal to different constituencies and whose make-ups may be antithetical. The husband, in short, must choose as his possible replacement a man who doesn't look like him, dress like him, talk like him, or share his values. Franklin Roosevelt and Harry Truman bore only the faintest resemblance to one another. The same was true of Eisenhower and Nixon, and of Kennedy and Johnson. To Kennedy, Johnson was a marvelous and often comical prodigy. His self-aggrandizement was shameless and exuberant; on trips abroad he would telephone his Washington office daily for reports on how his activities were being played in the American press. He was always campaigning—"My God!" gasped an American doctor in Pakistan. "He's shaking hands with a leper!"—and his decision to transform a Karachi camel driver into an ambassador of good will delighted the country. "We have come to see you and your camel," he told the astonished Bashir Ahmed. "Our President wants to see your camel. He has plans to make things better for you." He had no such thing, and the stunt seemed certain to backfire. Yet in the end it didn't. Ahmed's trip to the United States was an enormous success. Kennedy was impressed. "If it had been me," he said, "I'd have wound up with camel shit on the White House lawn."

Knowing how unhappy the Vice President was, the President went out of his way to honor Johnson and invent missions abroad for him. Later some of them became important. It is ironic that the two which appealed to him the least in advance loom largest in retrospect. The first was to Berlin. He was glum before it, but he spoke well there and was on hand to greet the first U.S. reinforcements to enter the city. His hosts believed that his visit was a turning point for the beleaguered city, and he returned home deeply affected.

The other trip, that May, was to Saigon. In the end it was of even greater significance, although that wasn't apparent then. The journey was a tour of southern Asia. The Vice President was expected to bolster the confidence of non-Communist regimes. He was not, as he had been in Berlin, a symbol of America's resolve to fight alongside them. At that time U.S. commitments there had not gone that far. Nevertheless, his pledge to Saigon was very strong. Greatly taken with Ngo Dinh Diem, he publicly hailed him as "the Winston Churchill of south Asia." After the party had left Vietnam, Stan Karnow, a writer for the *Saturday Evening Post*, asked him whether he really believed that. "Shit, man," the Vice President replied, "he's the only boy we got out here."

The Winston Churchill of south Asia was a dark, stubby, chain-smoking bachelor whose most striking trait was his seeming inability to end a conversation. Survivors would emerge from his big yellow stucco Freedom Palace after nonstop Diem monologues that were said to last six, seven, even twelve hours. But he didn't have many other weaknesses. At sixty he was decisive, dedicated, and firm in purpose. Diem was an archetype of the strong man in power. His title was president, yet he didn't think much of democracy. He was more of an Oriental despot, or at any rate an aloof mandarin who firmly believed that it was the duty of his people to respect and to obey him. His rivals were sent to concentration camps. Under him there was no freedom of the press and no real reform. Army officers were political appointees, chosen for their loyalty, not their ability, and though Diem himself was honest, the halls of his palace swarmed with the corrupt and the ambitious. Rigid and inflexible, he seemed to feel that Roman Catholics should be privileged for no other reason than that he himself was a Catholic. To an astonishing degree, his responsibilities were undelegated—company commanders couldn't move their men without his permission, and until late in his regime, no passport was valid unless it bore the signature of Diem himself. With each passing month he held the reins of authority more tightly, consulting only a few trusted aides and the members of his family, particularly an aggressive brother, Ngo Dinh Nhu and Nhu's lovely, venomous wife, known to American foreign correspondents as "the Dragon Lady." "If we open the window," Madame Nhu once said, explaining the Ngo philosophy of government, "not only sunlight but many bad things will fly in."

Little went in and not much came out. This was especially true of information. The lack of hard facts explains one of the two great mysteries about the Vietnam War: why it became a graveyard for the reputations of experts from the West. Rarely in history have so many eminent men been so singularly wrong about such an important event. Right down to October 1972, when Henry Kissinger fell flat on his face by prematurely announcing a settlement of it, soldiers and statesmen misjudged the character of the war and its probable course. On April 6, 1954, a New England senator had diverted his colleagues by reciting some earlier appraisals of it: "the military situation appears to be developing favorably" (Dean Acheson, 1952), "In Indochina we believe the tide now is turning" (Assistant Secretary of State Walter Robertson, 1953), a French victory "is both possible and probable" (Secretary of Defense Charles E. Wilson, 1954), and "the French are going to win" (Admiral Radford, 1954). The French lost, having sacrificed 19,000 Frenchmen in seven years.* That would seem to have vindicated the skeptical New England senator, who was John F. Kennedy. Then Kennedy, too, became trapped. In the White House his policy toward Vietnam came to be based on such Lewis Carroll appraisals as a 1960 Senate committee report which predicted that "on the basis of the assurances of the head of the military aid mission in Vietnam . . . the U.S. military . . . can be phased out of Vietnam in the forseeable future," and early in 1961 President Kennedy approved an aid plan based on the assumption that the war would be won in eighteen months.

The second Vietnam mystery is why Americans of so many persuasions, including four Presidents, two Republican and two Democratic, felt obliged to rescue the Saigon government. The country was, after all, in Asia, over seven thousand miles away, a primitive land of rice paddies and dense jungle curled around the remote Indochinese peninsula. Yet for over a decade administrations in Washington battled desperately to keep questionable men in power in there, even at the risk of domestic tranquillity at home. The American effort in Vietnam was ill-starred from the outset. Kennedy should have seen that. He was one of the few who had diagnosed the trouble in the beginning. As a congressman, he had toured Vietnam in 1951. "Without the support of the native population," he had said on *Meet the Press* on his return, "there is no hope of success in any of the countries of Southeast Asia." Later he, too, fell

---

* Compared with 45,882 Americans lost between 1961 and 1972. The usual figure given for French casualties is 92,000, but that includes Foreign Legionnaires, Africans, and Vietnamese who fought under the French flag. France, unlike the United States, sent no draftees to Vietnam.

under the spell of cold war rhetoric. America had "lost" China, cold-warriors held; now it must not "lose" Indochina.

The original American commitment to Saigon had been made in 1954 and renewed in 1957. In a letter to Diem after the Geneva agreements had been signed, President Eisenhower pledged U.S. support "to assist the Government of Viet-Nam in developing and maintaining a strong, viable state, capable of resisting subversion or aggression through military means." Ike made this agreement with the understanding that it would be accompanied "by performance on the part of Viet-Nam in undertaking needed reforms." The purpose of his assurance was to "discourage any who might wish to impose a foreign ideology on your free people."

"Ike has made a promise," Lyndon Johnson would say of Vietnam during his years in the White House. "I have to keep it." But he didn't. This wasn't a pact. The Senate had nothing to do with it. It lacked even the legitimacy of an executive order. Yet both Johnson and Kennedy felt bound by it. To have withdrawn U.S. support, Theodore C. Sorensen wrote, would have caused "the world to wonder about the reliability of this nation's pledges." Arthur Schlesinger went further:

> Whether we had vital interests in South Vietnam before 1954, the Eisenhower letter created those interests. Whether we should have drawn the line where we did, once it was drawn we became every succeeding year more imprisoned by it. Whether the domino theory was valid in 1954, it had acquired validity seven years later, after neighboring governments had staked their own security on the ability of the United States to live up to its pledges to Saigon. Kennedy . . . had no choice but to work within the situation he had inherited.

"The cause in Vietnam," Theodore H. White wrote in *The Making of the President 1968*, was "the cause of America for half a century, a cause made clear to the world. . . . If there is any fragile form of world order today, 400,000 American battle deaths in four wars in this century have created that world order." President Johnson argued that to "cut and run," would have been to "say to the world in this case that we don't live up to our treaties and don't stand by our friends." *Time* explained to those who felt otherwise that:

> . . . South Vietnam must be defended at all costs. . . . If the U.S. cannot or will not save South Viet Nam from the Communist

assault, no Asian nation can ever again feel safe in putting its faith in the U.S.—and the fall of all of Southeast Asia would only be a matter of time.

The consequences of such a withdrawal were considered unthinkable. In support of sending American draftees to Vietnam, Robert McNamara and the Joint Chiefs of Staff flatly declared that the alternative was serious deterioration throughout that part of the world. General Lyman L. Lemnitzer, speaking for the Chiefs, predicted that in the event of a Viet Cong victory, "We would lose Asia all the way to Singapore," and General Maxwell Taylor, confident of success against the guerrilla enemy—North Vietnam was "extremely vulnerable to conventional bombing," he said—told President Kennedy that a "U.S. military task force" was "essential."

There was no sense in any of this. If the Kennedy administration hadn't felt bound to evacuate the Cuban brigade from its doomed beachhead, then it owed Diem nothing. Furthermore, the Eisenhower letter had no validity now because Diem had openly flouted the obligation of introducing "needed reforms." He had also refused to hold all-Vietnam elections in 1956. For him to have invoked the sanctity of treaties would have been absurd, even if the United States had been bound to him by a treaty, which of course it wasn't.

The real pressures binding Washington to Saigon were political. McCarthy was dead, but both Democrats and Republicans were haunted by the nightmarish possibility that Diem might become a second Chiang Kai-shek. It is all the more ironical, then, that they repeated the very mistake Americans counseling Chiang had made; though the problem was political there, too, the aid they gave was military. One reason for their error was the attitude of powerful figures on Capitol Hill who had great faith in the Joint Chiefs and little trust in the political officers on the State Department's Asian desk. Another explanation lay in the character of the two cabinet members advising the White House on Vietnam in the early 1960s. McNamara was decisive and forceful, Rusk was timid and vague; inevitably the more persuasive voice came from the Pentagon.

Vietnam had been comparatively placid in the latter Eisenhower years. Eight hundred U.S. military advisers and three hundred million dollars in military aid a year had sufficed to preserve the status quo. Then, in December 1960, the month before Kennedy's inaugural, Diem's adversaries announced the formation of a National Liberation Front. In Freedom Palace their rivals christened the NLF the Viet Cong (literally, "Vietnamese Communists"). Diem wasn't worried by it at first. The previous autumn he had easily turned back an attempted coup, and when Vice President Johnson asked him if he wanted some American soldiers, he said he didn't. But though ground troops weren't necessary then, he admitted needing some help. President Kennedy approved the dispatch of a 400-man Special Forces group (the Green Berets) for training missions. For the first time the American commitment included troops.

Early in May 1961 a new U.S. ambassador, Frederick E. Nolting Jr., arrived in Saigon. His predecessor had tried to reason with Diem, and as a result had become, in effect, *persona non grata.* Nolting was resolved not to repeat that mistake. By now Viet Cong depredations were so obvious that even the mandarin president had to acknowledge them. The situation in the countryside was deteriorating. Guerrilla bands roamed at will, assassinating village chieftains. A U.S. intelligence estimate reported that an "extremely critical period" lay "immediately ahead" and warned that the Saigon regime's "reliance on virtually one-man rule" and "toleration of corruption" led many to "question Diem's ability to lead in this period."

In Washington the White House was being urged to step into the Vietnamese breach of its various bureaucratic constituencies. Deputy Undersecretary of State U. Alexis Johnson asked Kennedy to accept "defeat of the Vietcong" as a "real and ultimate" objective. The Joint Chiefs assured the President that 40,000 U.S. troops would "clean up the Vietcong threat," and that another 128,000 would be enough to turn back possible North Vietnam or Chinese Communist intervention. Roswell W. Gilpatric, McNamara's deputy at Defense, proposed talks with Diem on the "possibility of a defensive security alliance," and William P. Bundy, also in the Pentagon at that stage, urged "early and hard-hitting" American intervention in the war. Bundy gave it a 70 percent chance of success.

Kennedy authorized further studies, agreed to expand the 685-man U.S. military advisory group in Saigon, and approved plans to equip and pay 20,000 more Vietnamese troops for Diem (for a total of 150,000). Like Ike, he wanted aid contingent upon domestic reforms and mobilization of South Vietnamese resources against the Viet Cong, but he wasn't emphatic about it. He was preoccupied with Berlin and nuclear testing at the time. Schlesinger doubts that he ever gave Vietnam "his full attention." Observers attuned to the cold war continued to be baffled by Vietnam. "The situation gets worse almost week by week," Theodore H. White wrote in August 1961. White found that "guerrillas now control almost all the Southern delta—so much so that I could find no American who would drive me outside Saigon in his car even by day without military convoy." He reported a "political breakdown of formidable proportions." Then he wrote: ". . . what perplexes hell out of me is that the Commies, on their side, seem to be able to find people willing to die for their cause." The revolutionary spirit has often perplexed those not imbued with it.

The following month guerrillas captured a provincial capital and executed the governor. Diem's troops were in retreat everywhere. Reluctantly he summoned Nolting and asked for a bilateral defense treaty. Washington was in a responsive mood. All summer support had been coalescing around the Lyndon Johnson approach to Southeast Asia. The Vice President was voicing the classic liberal position: the real enemies in Vietnam, he had written on his return from there, were "hunger, ignorance, poverty, and disease." He believed that Americans "must—whatever strategies we evolve—keep those enemies the point of our attack, and make imaginative use of our scientific and technological capacity."

The President responded by sending to Saigon a high-level mission comprising two of his most trusted advisers, General Maxwell Taylor and Walt W. Rostow. Thus a general and a militant civilian —for Rostow, first to last, was the most uncompromising of the hawks—were to be the President's eyes and ears in Vietnam at this critical juncture. The absence of any American diplomat of stature was significant. It reflected, as Sorensen later wrote, "the State Department's inability to compete with the Pentagon." The result was further emphasis on military objectives at the expense of political considerations.

The Taylor-Rostow report marked one of the great turning points in the Vietnam War. To arrest the decline in Diem's fortunes, Kennedy was urged to send him a large contingent of American advisers, and—more important—American infantry: 8,000 at once and more as needed. Taylor, the dominant member of the team, wanted Vietnam to be the subject of a major presidential telecast. Some of his arguments for intervention were curious. In coming down hard on the side of an expeditionary force, for example, he compared Vietnam with Korea, "where U.S. troops learned to live and work without too much effort." Actually Korea and Vietnam were very different. The first was a conventional struggle, with enemy formations crossing a border and engaging Americans in fixed battles on terrain relatively familiar to U.S. soldiers. The second was irregular warfare in dense tropical jungle. Most important of all, the native population in South Korea wanted the Americans there. In Vietnam they didn't; Vietnamese villagers tended to regard U.S. Caucasian troops as successors to the French, and the Viet Cong as heroes.

Some members of the administration subcabinet—Chester Bowles, George Ball, and Averell Harriman among them—were appalled by this recommendation. The only senior man to question it, however, was Kennedy himself. He refused to go to the people on TV because that would confer upon Vietnam the status of Berlin. He also noted pointedly that Taylor and Rostow, unlike the Joint Chiefs, were optimistic about the effectiveness of U.S. intervention only if the North Vietnamese were prevented from infiltrating South Vietnam, and that they had no ideas for accomplishing that. What dismayed him most was the proposal to send soldiers. Sorensen wrote: "All his principal advisors on Vietnam favored it, calling it the 'touchstone' of our good faith, a symbol of our determination. But the President in effect voted 'no'—and only his vote counted." Kennedy told an aide: "They want a force of American troops. They say it's necessary in order to restore confidence and maintain morale. But it will be just like Berlin. The troops will march in; the bands will play; the crowds will cheer; and in four days everyone will have forgotten. Then we will be told we have to send more troops. It's like taking a drink. The effect wears off, and you have to take another."

Nevertheless, he was being manipulated. He vetoed U.S. troops but yielded on other points, and a buildup of U.S. strength in Vietnam began in December 1961. Like Eisenhower seven years earlier, the President affirmed the arrangement in a public exchange of letters with Diem. It wasn't all one-way; Diem conceded the need for reforms and acknowledged the need for more leadership and better morale in his army. But no limits were set for the amount of U.S. assistance or when it would end, other than when the Viet Cong had been pacified and the North Vietnamese driven out. Taylor saw no great peril in that. "The risks of backing into a major Asian war by way of South Vietnam," he cabled the President from the Philippines, "are present but not impressive." George Ball, on the other hand, was apprehensive. Diem wouldn't stop pressing until he got the administration to send infantrymen, he said. That was what Diem really wanted; it would allow him to stabilize his regime while the Americans did his fighting for him. Ball predicted that if that commitment was made it would not stay small. Within five years, he told the President, there would be 300,000 U.S. troops in Vietnam. Kennedy laughed and said, "George, you're crazier than hell."

One factor in the coming acceleration—which would vindicate Ball and then some—was the character of the Americans making decisions in Saigon. From early 1962 until the end of Kennedy's thousand days in power the two key figures were Ambassador Nolting and General Paul D. Harkins, the new head of the U.S. Military Assistance Advisory Group (MAAG), who reached Vietnam in February. The choice of both was tragic. Nolting, a member of an old Virginia family, was a traditionalist who knew nothing about Asia. His appointment had been recommended by the anti-Communist hard-liners in the State Department. In any crisis he would back Diem, and when Kennedy really needed him he would be found to be off cruising on the Aegean Sea on an extended vacation. Harkins was worse. He was the maverick son of a cultivated Boston family, a high school dropout who had risen in the Army solely because he was a good cavalryman, a spirited polo player, and a horsy companion for George S. Patton when Patton wanted to relax. In World War II Harkins had been Patton's deputy chief of staff; his nickname then had been "the ramrod" because of the way he drove Patton's orders home. Like Patton, he sometimes had trouble taking orders himself. This was to be particularly true when his instructions required him to send the President candid reports on how the war was going. Kennedy had made it plain that he wanted to know everything, the good news and the bad. But Harkins didn't like to relay bad news. He thought it might reflect on him. Instead he acted as though his mission were to make things look good on the surface. When he arrived in Saigon he told American correspondents that he was an optimist and liked to have optimists around him. Henceforth, he disclosed, the daily situation appraisal for Washington would be called "The Headway Report." He intended to leave no doubt that under him the fight against the Viet Cong would be making headway.

Nolting and Harkins agreed that Diem was the answer to all problems, that nothing could be done without him, and that since criticism of his regime would only anger him, there would be none of it. In the phrase of Homer Bigart of the *New York Times*, this became the policy of "Sink or Swim with Ngo Dinh Diem." Diem quickly realized that there was no limit to the ways he could take advantage of these two Americans.

The first drive against the Viet Cong after Harkins's arrival was called, appropriately, Operation Sunrise. Harkins told reporters that he was planning construction of a chain of fortified "strategic hamlets" which would be manned by home defense units; his co-planner was the Vietnamese president's brother Nhu. The next thing Washington knew, strategic hamlets were a thundering success, with over one-third of the total rural population living in them. The war seemed to be turning around. All the reports from Saigon were good. Skeptics could check Harkins's appreciations with those from Nolting, which also glowed.

In reality the experiments with the fortified hamlets were a failure. Nothing had changed except the men at the top. They were waging war through public relations releases. Reports from the field were being rewritten by Harkins, with pessimism and unwelcome information deleted and outright fiction substituted. Colonels and majors who objected—and some did, most memorably Lieutenant Colonel John Paul Vann—were transferred to unwelcome assignments with notations in their records that ended their military careers. When another general, junior to Harkins, toured the front and found a situation very different from that being depicted in the MAAG commander's self-serving dispatches, he gave Harkins an appraisal telling the truth about the war. Harkins scribbled in the margin—"Lies," "Lies," "More lies"—and stuck it in the back of a file cabinet. The real lies were his own, but the only sources to contradict him were the stories in American newspapers cabled back from correspondents in Vietnam. Harkins explained them away by calling the reporters sensation-mongers or, worse, traitors. When occasional reverses were acknowledged it was because Harkins had an ulterior motive. He wanted more men, more guns, more choppers. Failure to supply them, he warned, would mean that civilians were letting down the army, and anybody who remembered China knew what *that* would mean.

Had there been a Tet offensive or any other eruption in Viet Cong activity, this press-agentry might have been exposed in the beginning. As it happened, there was a drop in guerrilla activity. That was all the manipulators of news needed. Operation Sunrise, they declared, had brought blue skies over the battlefield. They were elated, and in Washington their elation was infectious. Maxwell Taylor said he sensed "a great national movement" in Vietnam to crush the Viet Cong. McNamara said, "Every quantitative measurement we have shows we're winning this war." President Kennedy, surprised and pleased, authorized an expansion of the Saigon command from 2,000 men to 16,000, and the U.S. Military Assistance Advisory Group (MAAG) was upgraded to the Military Assistance Command, Vietnam (MACV).

Montage: The Early Sixties

Michael row the boat ashore
Hal — le — lu —— jah
Michael row the boat ashore
Hal — le — lu —— jah

NEWBURGH MAYOR CUTS RELIEF TO MAKE UNEMPLOYED FIND JOBS

Are you smoking more and enjoying it less?

The Twist's origins are obscure, according to *Billboard*. It is said to have grown out of a dance called the Madison which originated in Philadelphia and was based on Rock 'n' Roll music. Nineteen-year-old Chubby Checker and twenty-two-year old Joe Dee are often considered the fathers of the Twist.

Margaret Mead, commenting on Mary Quant dresses which actually climb *above* the knee, observed, "We are going through a period of extreme exhibitionism."

bug out

Good night, David
Good night, Chet

VOTE HERE FOR MISS RHEINGOLD!
You gotta shake, rattle, 'n' roll

Maximilian Schell
in
JUDGMENT AT NUREMBERG

David Niven   Anthony Quinn
in
THE GUNS OF NAVARONE

FICTION
Advise and Consent, Drury
Hawaii, Michener
The Last of the Just, Schwarz-Bart
Decision at Delphi, MacInnes
The Agony and the Ecstasy, Stone
To Kill a Mockingbird, Lee
The Winter of Our Discontent, Steinbeck
Mila 18, Uris
The Carpetbagger, Robbins
A Burnt-Out Case, Greene.

HAL — LE — LU —— JAH

NONFICTION
The Rise and Fall of the Third Reich, Shirer
The Waste Makers, Packard
The New English Bible
A Nation of Sheep, Lederer
Born Free, Adamson
The Snake Has All the Lines, Kerr
Nobody Knows My Name, Baldwin
The Making of the President 1960, White
The Politics of Upheaval, Schlesinger
The Conscience of a Conservative, Goldwater

I like your thinkin'

You still using that greasy kid's stuff?

the *way* people get information, rather than the information itself, is the key fact in history; the *medium* is the message.

The river Jordan is deep and wide
Hal — le — lu —— jah

LORD'S PRAYER BANNED IN SCHOOLS

CUBA SI, YANQUI NO   ## ROCKY'S SON LOST IN NEW GUINEA

2,990,513 JOBS IN FEDERAL GOVT.

Hey, fun-ny

Just think how much you're going to be missing. You won't have Nixon to kick around any more, because, gentlemen, this is my last press conference.

ASTRONAUT PROBES SPACE IN A B. F. GOODRICH SUIT

And today motoring is safer than ever before because the tubeless tire, originated by B.F. Goodrich, provides protection against bruise blowouts.

Elizabeth Taylor and Richard Burton
WHO'S AFRAID OF VIRGINIA WOOLF?
from the play by Edward Albee
Directed by Mike Nichols

scrambles back to pass he's in trouble
always use Gillette. Closest, fastest, safest razor you can buy
doctor coming on the field
Gillette gives you your money's worth
bringing out a stretcher
So act sharp, feel sharp
with Gillette blue blades
I mean he's really hurt

This land is my land
This land is your land

LA DOLCE VITA
HAL — LU — LU — JAH
making out
Hey, getcha cold beah!
Hey, getcha Ballantine!

Twenty-eight

NOW THE TRUMPET
SUMMONED US AGAIN

I N 1961 the troubled years of the decade lay in the future. The
disorders at home would not begin until the summer of 1964,
eight months after President Kennedy's death. Later this would encourage the myth that if only he had lived none of it would have
happened. In fact, his responsibility for the coming turmoil was substantial. The Vietnam buildup was one of two major steps he took
toward it. The second step was his decision to mount a program
aimed at putting a man on the moon before the end of the 1960s.
Because Kennedy committed the country to the spending of vast
sums on space exploration—over 56 billion dollars before Apollo 11
reached the moon, and even that wasn't the end of it—successive
administrations lacked the resources to provide imaginative, far-
reaching responses to the ghetto upheavals which rocked the nation from Watts to Harlem. Those riots, combined with anguished
demonstrations against the U.S. role in Vietnam, weakened the
fabric of American society to an extent unknown since the Civil
War a hundred years earlier.

Kennedy agonized over both the Vietnam and space issues. In
the first of them he may even have been on the verge of withdrawing from Indochina. Kenneth O'Donnell, his chief of staff, has said
that he planned to get out in his second term, and before flying to
Texas on his last journey the President had issued an order to bring
back the first 1,000 U.S. military advisers. (According to O'Donnell,
Lyndon Johnson quietly rescinded the order after the return from

Dallas.) There are other signs that Kennedy was moving toward disengagement. David Halberstam, who cannot be called a friendly critic on this issue, believes that Kennedy had made up his mind but "did not want to rush too quickly, to split his administration unnecessarily. There was always time."

Space exploration is another matter. Here there are no extenuations. Whatever the glory or lack of it attending that decision, all must go to Kennedy, and with each passing year the scales tip farther against him. By 1961 the space race no longer had any bearing on national security. Paradoxically, the very fact that the Russians had larger rockets was evidence of their technological inferiority. Americans had found a way to design H-bomb warheads which were only a fraction of their former size and weight. Therefore they had no need of powerful rockets to send them toward their targets. Soviet scientists required enormous boosters—over 800,000 pounds of thrust—because their H-bombs remained crude and big. That meant that in this early phase of space exploration they had power to burn, charges which could hurl much heavier satellites into orbit, but that was all it meant, and it wasn't much. In later phases the superiority of American technology would pay off. Everyone in the White House knew it; so did everyone in the Kremlin.

The man on the street did not know it. As far as he could see, the Russians were showing America their heels, and somehow that was menacing to the free world. It was useless to explain to him that three out of every four satellites now in orbit were American, that in contrast to the clumsy Sputniks and Luniks the United States had launched whole families of Vanguards, Discoverers, Explorers, Pioneers, Samoses, Tiroses (weather), Transits (navigational), Midases (infrared detector of missiles), and Echos (communications). What counted in the public's eye was that the Russians were more spectacular. They had been first in orbit, the first to hit the moon and then to photograph it, the first to put a satellite in orbit around Venus with devices to radio back information about it. It was now clear that they were going to beat U.S. scientists to manned space flight. They had already put dogs into orbit, and now the first vehicle to put a man up was standing by on a launch pad near the Aral Sea, the site Francis Gary Powers had been trying to photograph on his ill-starred flight the year before.

This had nothing to do with either American security or the pursuit of knowledge. It was a matter of face or, as someone unkindly called it, of astropolitics. Given Kennedy elitism there was probably no question that the United States would have risen to the challenge anyhow, but the cold war had a lot to do with it. Like Acheson and Dulles—and Richard Nixon—Kennedy believed that the whole world was watching the rivalry between the two superpowers, and that destiny hung on the outcome of every contest between them. The thought that the Soviet Union might be more admired by the emerging nations in Africa and Asia was unbearable. In some vague way the freedom of mankind was at stake. This is clear from the memoirs of Theodore C. Sorensen. To Kennedy, Sorensen writes, the "space gap" which the new administration had inherited symbolized the country's lack of "initiative, ingenuity, and vitality."

> He was convinced that Americans did not fully grasp the worldwide political and psychological impact of the space race. With East and West competing to convince the new and undecided nations which way to turn, which way was the future, the dramatic Soviet achievements, he feared, were helping to build a dangerous impression of unchallenged world leadership generally and scientific preeminence particularly.

In this view, the fact that the United States had superior weapons systems didn't count for much, because they didn't *seem* superior: "Other nations . . . assumed that a Soviet space lead meant a missile lead as well; and whether this assumption was true or false, it affected their attitudes in the cold war." Here, surely, was the triumph of image, the notion that in the huts and villages of the Third World peasants, weighing which way they would turn, were awaiting the latest word from outer space. The extraordinary implication was that Soviet rocketeering feats, if unchallenged, would be a greater blow to American prestige than anything else—greater, say, than oppressed American Negroes wrecking the centers of U.S. cities in riots of frustration.

This wasn't much of an improvement on the fantasies of John Foster Dulles, and Sorensen makes it clear that in this instance, unlike that of Vietnam, Kennedy was no reluctant convert: "The President was more convinced than any of his advisers that a second-rate, second-place space effort was inconsistent with this country's security and with the New Frontier spirit of discovery." Like Cuba, this had been one of his major themes in 1960. Campaigning in Manhattan, he had said: "These are entirely new times, and they require new solutions. The key decision which this [Eisenhower's] administration had to make in the field of international policy and prestige and power and influence was their recognition of the significance of outer space. . . . The Soviet Union is now first in outer space." In Pocatello, Idaho, he had charged: "They [other nations] have seen the Soviet Union first in space. They have seen it first around the moon, and first around the sun. . . . They come to the conclusion that the Soviet tide is rising and ours is ebbing. I think it is up to us to reverse that point." And in Oklahoma City five days before his election he had cried: "I will take my television black and white. I want to be ahead of them in rocket thrust."

On Monday of the second week in April, UPI began to move a story on the persistent Moscow rumor that Soviet rocketeers had sent a man into space and recovered him. Although that was premature, Tuesday evening the CIA reported that the flight was scheduled for that night. As Washington slept, Moscow's radios greeted the new day there with the slow, moving strains of the Russian patriotic anthem, "How Spacious Is My Country." It was followed by the momentous announcement: "The world's first spaceship, *Vostok*, with a man on board, has been launched on April 12 in the Soviet Union on a round-the-world orbit." To follow it, Russian children were released from classrooms, clerks from shops, workmen from factories. In the beginning they were silent, stunned. It seemed incredible that somewhere above them a fellow countryman could be soaring past the stars at 18,000 mph.

His name was Yuri Alekseyevich Gagarin, a twenty-seven-year-old Soviet major who had been chosen to be Russia's first "cosmonaut." Gagarin had been launched at 9:07 A.M. Moscow time—1:07 A.M. in Washington—and at the time his niche in history appeared to be somewhat greater than it was. There are events whose chief significance lies in the popular response they evoke at the time. The reaction to the Orson Welles Martian broadcast of 1938 was one; so were the Wanna-Go-Home riots of 1946 and the support for the Bricker amendment in the early 1950s. Now people, and not just Russian people, were hungry for heroes. The Soviet Union gave them Gagarin. After 108 hours of flight, 89 of which were spent actually in orbit, he descended from his altitude of 188 miles to become a prized propaganda asset. Standing on the tomb of Lenin, he received a twenty-gun salute. A Moscow square was named after him, then a glacier. Soviet artists set to work designing a commemorative stamp bearing his picture. In Russian newspapers his name was printed in red. Adoring Soviet journalists christened him Gaga. One wrote breathlessly of him that "his eyes were shining as though still reflecting spatial starlight." In Red Square Khrushchev made a speech comparing him to Columbus. A nationwide Soviet radio broadcast carried a conversation between Khrushchev and the cosmonaut, whose most improbable revelations were "While in outer space I was thinking about our party and our homeland," and "When I was going down, I sang the song, 'The Motherland Hears, the Motherland Knows.'"

Americans gnashed their teeth. "Kennedy could lose the 1964 election over this," a space administrator said, and a NASA scientist said, "Wait until the Russians send up three men, then six, then a laboratory, start hooking them together and then send back a few pictures of New York for us to see." At Cape Canaveral a bitter astronaut told a reporter, "We could have got a man up there. We could have done it a month ago if somebody at the top two years ago had simply decided to push it." At four o'clock that afternoon Kennedy faced a tumultuous press conference in the new State Department auditorium. He was asked: "Mr. President, a member of Congress said today he was tired of seeing the United States second to Russia in the space field. I suppose he speaks for a lot of others. . . . What is the prospect that we will catch up with Russia and perhaps surpass Russia in this field?" The reply was defensive: "However tired anybody may be, and no one is more tired than I am, it is a fact that it is going to take some time [to catch up] . . . We are, I hope, going to go in other areas where we can be first, and which will bring perhaps more long-range benefits to mankind. But we are behind." Columnist Hugh Sidey commented that this "seemed hardly in the spirit of the New Frontier." One news magazine reported that the nation's mood was one of "frustration, shame, sometimes fury," and predicted: "Only a spectacular and extremely difficult bit of rocketeering, say a manned trip around the moon, will top Russian spacemen in the eyes of the world."

In fact, Kennedy learned that evening, it had to be the moon or nothing; on lesser objectives the Soviet lead was too great to overcome. The President had called a 7 P.M. meeting in the Cabinet Room to search for alternatives. One by one his advisers spoke up—Jerome Wiesner; James Webb, NASA head; Dr. Hugh Dryden,

Webb's distinguished deputy; David Elliot Bell, director of the Bureau of the Budget; and Sorensen. The scientists had Kennedy at a disadvantage. Space was not his forte. He knew less about this issue than any other, hadn't been briefed on the projects at Cape Canaveral, and lacked the science background necessary to sort out scientific options and priorities. After Wiesner, Webb, and Dryden had spoken the President muttered gloomily, "We may never catch up." He said, "Now let's look at this. Is there any place we can catch them? What can we do?" He did know that three half-built U.S. rockets would produce over a million pounds of thrust each when finished. He asked of them: "What about Nova and Rover? When will Saturn be ready? Can we leapfrog?"

Dryden told him there was only one hope, and it would take a crash program similar to the Manhattan Project. That might put an American on the moon in ten years. It would be a gamble, though. And it would cost at least twenty billion dollars—perhaps twice that. The President was silent. Then he said, "The cost, that's what gets me." He looked hopefully at Bell, but there was no comfort there; Bell said that exploring space was a very expensive business. Kennedy asked, "Can't you fellows invent some other race here on earth that will do some good?" But nothing else had the fascination of a flight to the moon, and after drumming his fingernails on his teeth he asked Wiesner and the NASA men to take another look at the figures. Rising to go, he said, "When we know more, I can decide if it's worth it or not. If somebody can just tell me how to catch up. Let's find somebody—anybody. . . . There's nothing more important."

Three weeks later the American people showed that their judgment confirmed his. After twenty-eight months of delays and breakdowns, the first vehicle in NASA's Project Mercury rose from the gantries at Cape Canaveral. As a hundred million viewers held their breath, a tall, slender white Redstone rocket slowly climbed into the sky, emitting a widening vapor trail. Its passenger was naval Commander Alan B. Shepard Jr. The country was elated. On turnpikes and freeways drivers pulled over to the shoulder and turned up their car radios. An Indianapolis judge declared a recess so everyone in the courthouse could watch the picture on a television set which police had seized as part of a burglar's booty. The nation was eavesdropping on the exchanges between *Freedom 7*, as Shepard's space capsule was called, and his control in Florida. He was in outer space for fifteen minutes. His flight was nothing like Gagarin's complex trajectory, but for the moment Americans didn't care. As his capsule descended beside the carrier *Lake Champlain*, swinging widely beneath its parachute, the sailors cheered wildly. "It's a beautiful day," were his first words back on earth. "Boy, what a ride!" His ride to glory had only begun. New York gave him its biggest ticker tape welcome in history as of then. A new school in Deerfield, Illinois, was named for him. Greeting cards went on sale for admirers to send Shepard. Derry, New Hampshire, his home town, with a population of 6,987, staged a parade in his honor. People came from all over New England to march in it; Army, Navy, Marine Corps, Air Force, and National Guard troops passed in review while jet fighters roared overhead. Senator Styles Bridges in an eloquent speech described New Hampshire's pride in the new hero. Legislators debated renaming Derry "Spacetown, U.S.A."

None of this was lost on the White House, just then smarting from the Bay of Pigs defeat. On May 25 the President stood before Congress with a special message on "urgent national needs," his second State of the Union address in four months. He wanted "an estimated seven to nine billion dollars additional over the next five years" for the space program. He knew he was asking a lot, he said, but "These are extraordinary times. We face an extraordinary challenge." To him the issue was a matter of patriotism: "I am here to promote the freedom doctrine." He said: "I believe that this nation should commit itself to achieving the goal, before this decade is out, of landing a man on the moon and returning him safely to earth."

Congress approved by a thundering margin. Simultaneously ground was broken for expansion of facilities at Cape Canaveral and a mission control center in Houston. The aerospace industry was on its way.

In July, Air Force Captain Virgil I. Grissom completed a flight similar to Shepard's. The Russians sent Major Gherman S. Titov whirling around the earth seventeen times in August, and in November NASA orbited a male chimpanzee and recovered him after two trips around the earth; while up, the chimp responded to various lights by pulling levers which released sips of water or banana-flavored pellets. NASA then announced that the pilot of the first U.S. human orbital flight would be the oldest of the seven astronauts who had been chosen from 110 candidates, Marine Lieutenant

Colonel John H. Glenn Jr. By then the tremendous popularity of the Mercury Project had been established. It was evident that if Glenn made it back he would be America's first aerospace superstar, a second Lindbergh. Teams of journalists explored his childhood in the tiny hamlet of New Concord, Ohio, and returned with reams of data which captivated the nation. As a boy he had been an avid reader of *Buck Rogers*. He had admired Glenn Miller and had played a loud trumpet himself in the New Concord band. As strict Presbyterians the Glenns had held that cigarettes were sinful, and New Concord was a Presbyterian stronghold; boys from surrounding towns called it "Saint's Rest." Glenn and his chums had taken a pledge never to use profanity. Once while singing "Hail, Hail, the Gang's All Here," one besotted boy, throwing caution to the winds, had recklessly continued with the phrase, "What the hell do we care?" Now, a quarter-century later, the blasphemer told eager journalists how the future astronaut had rounded on him: "Johnny came up to me, white-faced and righteous, and told me to stop. I think he was ready to knock my block off." In 1962 Glenn's faith remained strong; he assured interviewers that he believed in "a power greater than I am that will certainly see that I am taken care of."

After ten frustrating postponements he lifted off the pad at 10 A.M., Tuesday, February 20, 1962. His departure was like Shepard's, but magnified many times. A great spurting gout of yellow-white flame licked out from the Atlas D rocket, casting weird shadows on the flat, sandy scrubland of Cape Canaveral. For four incredible seconds the rocket just hung there, balanced over its gantry. Then it ascended, gaining in momentum until it disappeared into the deep blue overarching sky. Glenn said, "Lift-off. The clock is operating. We're under way." From the Project Mercury Control Center the deep, calm voice of Lieutenant Colonel John "Shorty" Powers, NASA's public affairs officer, explained the next step to the country. It was the separation of the rocket and the capsule, *Friendship* 7, at the precise angle which would put Glenn in orbit. As it happened Glenn cried: "Capsule is turning around. Oh, that view is tremendous! I can see the booster doing turnarounds just a couple of hundred yards behind. Cape is go and I am go."

The temperature in the capsule had risen to 108 degrees, he noted, but the air-conditioning in his suit kept him cool. He had been instructed to explain his every sensation—the audience, after all, was paying for the trip—and he began by reporting that he had no feeling of speed. It was "about the same as flying in an airliner at, say, 30,000 feet, and looking down at clouds at 10,000 feet." Over the Atlantic he spotted the Gulf Stream, a river of blue in the gray sea. Over the West Coast he made out California's Salton Sea and the Imperial Valley, and he could pick out the irrigation canals near El Centro, where he had once lived. His first twilight was awesome: "As the sun goes down it's very white, brilliant light, and as it goes below the horizon you get a very bright orange color. Down close to the surface it pales out into a sort of blue, a darker blue, and then off into black." The stars were spectacular. "If you've been out on the desert on a very clear, brilliant night when there's no moon and the stars just seem to jump out at you, that's just about the way they look." Approaching Australia he radioed, "Just to my right I can see a big pattern of light, apparently right on the coast." From a tracking station below, Astronaut Gordon Cooper explained to him that this was the Australian city of Perth. Its 82,000 inhabitants had turned on all their light switches, to welcome him and test his night vision. Glenn replied, "Thank everybody for turning them on, will you?"

Glenn made other tests himself, exploring his weightless state. He swallowed some nutritious tablets and some applesauce which he squeezed out of a tube. No problems there, he reported: "It's all positive action. Your tongue forces it back in the throat and you swallow normally. It's all a positive displacement machine all the way through." He jiggled around as best he could to see if he could bring on giddiness or space sickness. There was none of it; "I have no ill effects at all from zero G. It's very pleasant, as a matter of fact. Visual acuity is still excellent. No astigmatic effects. No nausea or discomfort whatever." An amateur photographer, Glenn had brought a camera along. Instead of putting it on a shelf after he had taken some pictures through his window, he just stuck it out in the air, and there it stayed, suspended. Changing rolls, he let the film slip. He quickly reached for it, but as he explained to the enchanted millions, "instead of clamping onto it, I batted it and it went sailing around behind the instrument panel, and that was the last I saw of it."

Sometimes he ran out of words. "I don't know what you can say about a day in which you have seen four beautiful sunsets," he said. It was at that point that he forgot his travelogue commentary. So did his listeners. He was having trouble. As he passed over Mexico a small jet, meant to keep his capsule steady, developed a malfunction. He reported to the control center that the vehicle "drifts off in yaw to the right at about one degree per second. It will go to 20 degrees and hold at that." That was the end of the tests; the flight now commanded his entire attention; he had to take over the controls and fly it himself. That wasn't the end of his difficulties. During his second pass over the Pacific, his gyroscopes went out. The capsule began "rolling"—turning on its horizontal axis. Glenn eliminated that by skillful handling of the controls. Then, in his second orbit, he developed what looked like real trouble. An ominous light flashed on the control board at Cape Canaveral. It meant that *Friendship 7's* fiberglass heat shield had come ajar. If the shield came off at any time before the capsule reentered the atmosphere, Glenn would be instantly incinerated. As it turned out, the fault was in the warning light, not the shield, but neither the astronaut nor his mentors on the ground knew that then. They made adjustments to change the reentry procedure, retaining the vehicle's retro-rockets—which were to be jettisoned—in the hope that their metal bands might help keep the shield in place. Then they prayed.

Glenn knew that this was the moment of maximum peril. His braking rockets were fired in sequence, and he braced himself. As the pressure on him mounted, *Friendship 7* shimmied. He gasped, "It feels like I'm going clear back to Hawaii." The G forces were mounting, squeezing him against his contour couch. He was coming down, and the heat shield was disintegrating, breaking up into glowing fragments. Later he said, "You could see the fire and the glow from them—big flaming chunks." He couldn't explain it at the time because he had lost radio contact. That was to be expected; he was in the delicate process of reentering. The blackout lasted seven minutes and fifteen seconds. As it ended he could be heard shouting, "That was a real fireball!" At 2:43 P.M. the glowing capsule hit the waters of the Atlantic and was instantly enveloped in clouds of sizzling steam. At 3:01 the destroyer *Noa* rescued Glenn. A steward handed him a glass of iced tea. Glenn said, "It was hot in there."

Idolatry awaited him. His footprints on the carrier deck were traced in white paint for later exhibition in the Smithsonian Institution. Cameramen recorded the fact that his eyes were full at the moment of reunion with his wife and children, and after he had wiped his eyes the handkerchief was set aside so it, too, would be preserved. As he fielded questions from the press, reporters noted that in speaking of himself and *Friendship 7* he often said "We"— just like Lindy at Paris's Le Bourget Field thirty-five years earlier. Vice President Johnson was there to greet him. Johnson said, "In my country we'd say you're pretty tall cotton. Were you very tense at takeoff?" Glenn replied that he supposed so. LBJ said, "You were about as near the Lord's end as a person ever is."

At Cape Canaveral one banner read: WELCOME TO EARTH. There the Vice President was replaced by the President, who had just flown over from Palm Beach. There was a bit of byplay as Glenn tried to put a hard hat on Kennedy and failed—JFK had once seen a picture of Calvin Coolidge in an Indian headdress and had vowed never to pose in a funny hat—and then the country's first astronaut was off to address a joint session of Congress. "Usually the honor is reserved for heads of state," Johnson told him, "but in this case the whole country has elected you." A gala parade in New York was next, featuring Glenn, the other six of the original astronauts, and a star-studded cast of big-name scientists. After that Glenn flew abroad to tour other continents, telling America's allies and the un- committed peoples that truly great achievements were possible in a free society. *Time* commented: "In terms of national prestige, Glenn's flight put the U.S. back in the space race with a vengeance, and gave the U.S. and the entire free world a huge and badly needed boost."

"This is a new ocean," said Kennedy, "and I believe the U.S. must sail on it." At Cape Canaveral American rocketeers, confident once more, talked enthusiastically of launching two-man capsules by 1964; of giant, solid-propellant boosters to lift great payloads off the earth; and of plans for Project Apollo, aimed at putting three men on the moon and bringing them back, perhaps as soon as 1968. A passionate interest in space travel took on the proportions of a national rage. It was the theme of that year's Century 21 Exposition, in Seattle. "Orbit" entered Madison Avenue's vocabulary as a noun and as a verb. Small boys launched water-propelled toy satellites that landed in trees, like kites before them. Wernher von Braun, whose skills had played a major part in the success of the Atlas, be- came a national celebrity. ("He aimed for the stars," Mort Sahl said of his earlier years, "and often hit London.") Europeans of all convictions were tremendously impressed. Even Pablo Picasso, no Americanophile, said of Glenn, "I am as proud of him as if he were

my brother." Presently all sorts of people were launching satellites
—American Tel & Tel, for example, put up Telstar, and even the Canadians sent a small vehicle into orbit.

In August the Soviet Union's second cosmonaut, Major Gherman
S. Titov, circled the earth seventeen times. This was seized upon as
a new evidence for the need to mobilize America's industrial and
technological might in a great effort to surpass the Russians once
and for all. By now there were some dissenters, particularly on the
campuses and in the U.S. intellectual community. The President
answered them in September. Speaking at Rice University in Houston he said:

"But why, some say, the moon? . . . And they may well ask, why
climb the highest mountain? Why, thirty-five years ago, fly the Atlantic? Why does Rice play Texas? . . . Many years ago the great
British explorer George Mallory, who was to die on Mount Everest,
was asked why did he want to climb it, and he said, 'Because it is
there.' Well, space is there, and . . . the moon and the planets are
there, and new hopes for knowledge and peace are there."

The black problem was also there, however, and it was much
closer. In retrospect Kennedy's underreckoning of it seems astonishing. He was, after all, a northern liberal and an admirer of Martin
Luther King. But the liberals, and even King, were about to be
pressed hard by militant young northern blacks. While America's
eyes had been turned upward toward the stars, they had been
searching for ways to distract the country. The first attempt, and
it was memorable, came in the spring of 1961. On May 4, three
weeks after Gagarin's flight, seven black and six white members of
the Congress of Racial Equality (CORE) left Washington by bus
for an expedition through the Deep South. Their purpose was to
challenge segregation in interstate bus terminals in defiance of local
custom—in waiting rooms, restaurants, and toilets. They called themselves freedom riders.

The course they had charted zigzagged across Dixie: south
through Virginia, North Carolina, and South Carolina; southwest-
ward to Atlanta; westward through Alabama, and then on across
Mississippi and down to New Orleans. It was bound to be a memorable trip. Their flouting of the customs of the region was breathtaking. After four years Little Rock was all but forgotten, and
Arkansas was a border state anyway. Here in the real southland the

relationships between the races were still very precise and had scarcely changed in the ninety years since the departure of the last carpetbagger. In that respect there were almost no southern liberals as the term was understood above the Mason-Dixon line. The WPA guidebook to Alabama, written by native New Dealers in 1941, pictured the sort of welcome wayfarers might expect in Montgomery, one of the state's three largest cities:

> The atmosphere of measured dignity tempered by cordiality is matched nowhere else in Alabama. A Negro boy—his face wreathed in smiles—usually accosts the traveler with, "You don't have to tote that grip, boss man; I'll do it cheap"; and a resident will willingly give directions and accompany the stranger a block or more to set him on the right road.

That was not an accurate description of the greeting awaiting the freedom riders, a fact so obvious that they can be fairly said to have been looking for trouble. The nature of their sponsorship was less clear. Under the leadership of James Farmer CORE was an independent, self-supporting organization and had been active since 1942. But in the seething days ahead many southern leaders and southern editorials would charge that the administration ("the Kennedys") was behind them or had at least encouraged them to come. The truth was that no one in the government had known of their journey until they had left on it. CORE had sent an advance copy of a press release about the trip to the Department of Justice, but it had wound up on the desk of Burke Marshall, chief of the Civil Rights Division, who was out with the mumps. Newspaper accounts of the departure had been buried on the inside pages. The White House first heard of it when the story erupted on front pages, and then its reaction was anger—directed at the riders.

From the administration's point of view, the timing was dreadful. Not only had the Russians just won the race for the first manned space flight to encircle the earth; the week after that the Cuban brigade had been overwhelmed on the beach. On June 3, less than a month away, Kennedy would meet Khrushchev in Vienna. The new President needed a victory or, if that was impossible, the absence of a fresh defeat. The last thing he wanted was an ugly racial incident. The Russians were still exploiting Little Rock for propaganda directed at the Third World, portraying America as racist. Any episode which could be interpreted as evidence of that would be a humiliation for the United States. That was how the White House first regarded the rides—as an embarrassment. Later John Kennedy, and particularly Robert Kennedy, would see the civil rights struggle as a moral imperative, but in their first months in office it was not yet that. An understanding of their position then is important, because it was shared by most liberal Democrats, including some who thought themselves to be very advanced.

Their commitment to end prejudice was total. It was a wrong, and they were determined to right it. It was intolerable to them that the Negro condition should be unchanged in the world's oldest and greatest democracy. Throughout that campaign John Kennedy had reminded audiences that "The Negro baby born in America today, regardless of the section of the nation in which he is born, has about one-half as much chance of completing high school as a white baby born in the same place on the same day, one-third as much chance of completing college, one-third as much chance of becoming a professional man, twice as much chance of becoming unemployed, about one-seventh as much chance of earning $10,000 a year, a life expectancy which is seven years shorter, and the prospects of earning only half as much." As President he had pledged himself to support programs aiming at correcting that injustice. What more could the blacks ask?

The first thing they asked was that liberals stop thinking of blacks as statistics. After that they expected an end to gradualism. They realized that the spring of 1961 was an awkward time for the government to deal with the freedom riders. Every season for the past century had been awkward, and so they had waited and waited and waited. What they expected their white sympathizers to understand was that to the new Negro, freedom for his people was more important than any issue in Vienna—or in Vietnam, or Cuba, or outer space.

In 1961 it was considered political bravery just to endorse equality before the law in front of an audience of southern whites. That was what Robert Kennedy did in his first major speech as attorney general, and he did it in Athens, Georgia, on May 6, two days after the departure from Washington of the freedom riders, of whose existence, however, he was still unaware. The occasion was Law Day at the University of Georgia. He went to explain to them that it was his sworn duty to uphold the law, a circumstance of which one might suppose law students would already be aware, but on this issue, in this part of the country, nothing could be assumed. "We are maintaining the orders of the courts," he told them. "We are doing nothing more nor less. And if any one of you were in my position, you would do likewise, for it would be required by your oath of office. You might not want to do it, you might not like to do it, but you would do it." This was hardly a passionate affirmation of the rights of an oppressed race, and there was even a hint in it that on this issue Robert Kennedy might be doing his duty against his better judgment, but there were no weasel words at the end: "Our position is clear. We are upholding the law. . . . In this case—in all cases—I say to you today that if the orders of the court are circumvented, the Department of Justice will act. We will not stand by or be aloof. We will move."

In civil rights, as in the Third World, liberals of the early 1960s believed in the eventual triumph of right. This perhaps more than anything else sets the Kennedy years apart from what lay ahead and makes them seem almost naive now. Send surplus wheat to an emerging nation, send Peace Corpsmen, send a Chester Bowles as the American ambassador, the catechism read, and you will have a bright new democracy, a credit to the free world and a potential ally in the eternal struggle against the powers of darkness in Moscow. So at home: strong leadership and the fundamental sense of decency in the American people would overcome the bigotry implanted by generations of ignorance. Integration was just good sense, and Americans were above all sensible; it was just a matter of showing them the light; if Eisenhower had taken a stand he could have accomplished it in the 1950s.

The notion that there were dark places in the American mind was illiberal and therefore rejected. The liberal vision had no explanation for the phenomenon of the McCarthyism, the most recent instance in which decency and good sense had been scorned by masses of Americans, but in 1961 nobody talked about McCarthy any more. Optimism was almost a requirement on the New Frontier. General Harkins had the right idea, his body counts were certainly encouraging, and why couldn't those American correspondents in Saigon join the team? On the domestic front good liberals would fight the good fight until the Negro baby born in America had just as much chance of completing his education as the white baby, no more chance of becoming unemployed, as much chance of earning $10,000 a year, and the same life expectancy.

However, these things took *time*. They mustn't expect it all *now*. But the freedom riders wanted it all now.

Richmond, Petersburg, Lynchburg—here they stopped, stretched their legs, had a bite together at lunch counters under signs reading "White" and ignored the toilets designated "Colored" with no more than a few ugly looks and muttered obscenities from bystanders. Then stories about the trip began appearing in the newspapers of cities farther along on their route. They weren't big news yet, not important enough to attract the attention of an attorney general or a governor; all they warranted was a couple of sticks, a squib or two, something to wrap around the ads. But that was enough to alert gas station attendants leafing through the inside pages in search of the comics, enough for ticket clerks in the bus terminals, for sheriff's deputies passing by and the kind of men who hang around stations and depots waiting for something to happen.

The first incident was in Charlotte, North Carolina: a black freedom rider strolled into the bus station barbershop and refused to leave. He was arrested for trespassing and the others proceeded without him. It wasn't much, but the word was sent ahead, passed on as such news is always passed, by a phone call, or another driver, or police radio. It doesn't matter. It was inevitable and they expected it; that was why they had come. Still, the tension on the bus grew. When they saw the crowd at the station in Rock Hill, South Carolina, they knew the violence had begun to escalate. Three of them were beaten; then the Rock Hill police intervened. Again in Winnsboro, thirty-seven miles to the south, police stepped in before anything could start and arrested two riders. Next came another quiet stretch: Sumter and Camden, South Carolina; Augusta and Atlanta, Georgia. Atlanta was an important stop. They divided there into two groups for the ride to Birmingham, one going on a Trailways bus and the other by Greyhound. There was no trouble here—Georgia troopers were everywhere—but after Rock Hill and Winnsboro they were on page one of every newspaper in the South. It was a Sunday, the day papers are read most. They assumed that the population of Alabama would know all about them. It did.

Today travelers between Atlanta and Birmingham cruise easily across eastern Alabama on Interstate Route 20, but in 1961 that was still under construction, and they had to follow the tortuous curves of U.S. 78 through a succession of remote crossroads communities virtually untouched by postwar change. This was "upcountry" Alabama, an untamed region clothed with scrub pine—mostly high, with elevations of nearly 1,800 feet in the Raccoon and Lookout ranges, the southernmost spurs of Appalachia. Coming down off their slopes to the Cumberland plateau, the road descended to fields soybean farmers had reclaimed after the devastations of the boll weevil, to the coal region, and, beyond, to the Black Belt. Cleburne County, Calhoun County—these were an old breeding ground of wool-hats and red-necks, the strongholds of the camp meeting and the revival, and it was here, six miles from Anniston on U.S. 78, that a gang of Ku Klux Klansmen armed with blackjacks, clubs, and tire chains ambushed the Greyhound bus. A rock sailed through one window, followed by an incendiary bomb. As it burst into flame the riders fled. Twelve of them were being methodically beaten when policemen arrived and fired pistols into the air. Ambulances carried away the injured. Then Birmingham blacks who had heard of the battle arrived in cars and rescued the others.

The riders on the Trailways bus escaped the Klan trap, but in Anniston eight young toughs boarded the bus, dragged them into the aisles, and began punching them. Anniston cops drove them off. Birmingham, the destination of the bus, was worse. A crowd of men carrying lengths of pipe had surrounded the Trailways terminal at Nineteenth Street and Sixth Avenue North. An informer had warned the FBI about them. Incredibly, the FBI had not relayed the information to Burke Marshall's Civil Rights Division or to the attorney general's office. Instead it passed the tip along to the Birmingham police, whose chief, Police Commissioner T. Eugene "Bull" Connor, pigeonholed it. Although Connor's headquarters were only two blocks from the terminal, he sent no one over. The hoodlums there dragged the riders into the station and clouted them for thirty minutes, injuring three seriously enough to require hospitalization. The next morning the *Birmingham News*, which had denounced the *New York Times* the year before for saying that fear and hatred stalked the streets of Birmingham, now admitted that "fear and hatred did stalk Birmingham's streets yesterday." But Alabama officials had no apologies. Governor John Patterson said, "I cannot guarantee protection for this bunch of rabble-rousers," and Bull Connor said, "Our people of Birmingham are a peaceful people, and we never have any trouble here unless some people come into our city looking for trouble." Asked why there had been no policemen at the terminal, Connor said he had been shorthanded because it was Mother's Day. It was a joke.

The Sunday beatings brought the freedom riders to the attention of the Justice Department for the first time, and Burke Marshall called Bob Kennedy at home to tell him of it. Bob thought he might be able to resolve the situation with a phone call. He knew Patterson, who had been the first southern governor to support John Kennedy for President and had stayed with him even after his delegation had gone over to Lyndon Johnson. He called the governor Monday morning and asked him to protect the buses. Passengers on them had a right to travel between the states, and local authorities had a clear responsibility to guarantee their safe passage. Patterson agreed. Then he called back and said he had changed his mind. He had been elected with Klan support, and now the Klansmen were cashing in their credit.

This was the first of several strange long distance exchanges the two Kennedy brothers were to have with southern governors on the race issue, and like the others it was exasperating. Bob tried to phone Patterson again. He was told that the governor couldn't come to the phone. He tried again on Tuesday, on Wednesday, and on Thursday. Each time aides expressed their regrets. The most they could do, they said, was take a message, and they couldn't guarantee that it would reach the governor. They couldn't be sure, but they thought he was "out on the Gulf"—unreachable in any case. Meanwhile the situation in Birmingham was deteriorating. The original group of freedom riders, battered and frightened, had flown on to New Orleans, but their places had been taken by volunteers from Fisk University in Nashville, from Martin Luther King's Southern Christian Leadership Conference, and from the younger civil rights organizations, one such newcomer being a cool nineteen-year-old immigrant from Trinidad named Stokely Carmichael. In Washington, Attorney General Kennedy issued a statement asking for restraint from both the freedom riders and their opposition. He said, "In order to insure that innocent people are not injured, maimed, or even killed, I would call upon all people who have paramount interest in the future of our country to exercise restraint and judgment over their activities in the next few weeks or the next few days." There was a sense of unreality in this. He seemed to be trying to play the role of an impartial arbiter between two equally responsible, equally strong adversaries. The riders solemnly promised not to attack Alabamans; the Alabamans said nothing. Then Kennedy issued another statement saying, "What is needed now is a cooling-off period." A CORE spokesman tartly commented that what was needed was an end to cooling off, that black Americans had been cooling off for a hundred years. By Friday, when the new freedom riders prepared to continue the journey that the others had started, it was clear that they would be heading into fresh trouble. At his brother's request, President Kennedy put in a call to Governor Patterson. He was told that the governor was "out of town and still unreachable." He did get through to the lieutenant governor, who after several hours said he could arrange a meeting between the governor and a personal representative of the President.

The Kennedys chose John Seigenthaler, a handsome and brave young Tennessean and the attorney general's best friend. Seigenthaler was on a plane within an hour. At first his mission seemed successful. After he and Patterson had conferred for two hours they phoned Bob Kennedy. While Patterson listened and nodded Seigenthaler reported that he had been assured that Alabama had, as Patterson put it, "the means, ability, and the will to keep the peace without outside help." The governor said that he could protect everyone in the state, both Alabamans and visitors, in the cities and on the highways, and he said he would do it. Bobby then called Floyd Mann, the chief of Alabama's highway patrol, who backed up the governor's guarantee. With that, a biracial group of twenty-one students voted to board a Birmingham to New Orleans bus in the morning. An unexpected hitch developed when no driver could be found. Getting one required a long, abrasive phone conversation between the attorney general and George E. Cruit, the Greyhound representative in Birmingham, but in the end Cruit produced a man and the riders departed for Montgomery, which turned out to be even worse than Birmingham.

The trip there was uneventful. Mann's Highway Department did its part; both U.S. 65 and U.S. 31 were clear. The FBI had alerted the Montgomery police to the arrival of the bus, and when it was about fourteen miles from the city Mann radioed a second warning to Montgomery's police commissioner, Lester B. Sullivan. But Sullivan was no more ready than Connor to run interference for uppity blacks and renegade whites. He ignored the messages, and there were no policemen when the bus arrived at the Union Bus Terminal to confront a throng estimated at between a thousand and three thousand. The attorney general's office had a blow-by-blow account of what happened next because John Doar, second in command to Burke Marshall in the Civil Rights Division, was in the U.S. Attorney's office across the street from the terminal.* Doar had just put through a call to Kennedy when the bus drew up at the terminal. Kennedy and his deputy attorney general, Byron White, heard him say:

"The bus is in. The people are just standing there, watching. . . . Now the passengers are coming off. They're standing on a corner of the platform. Oh, there are fists, punching! A bunch of men led by a guy with a bleeding face are beating them. There are no cops. It's terrible. It's terrible. There's not a cop in sight. People are yelling, 'Get 'em, get 'em.' It's awful. . . . The cops are there now."

They were state troopers, not Montgomery policemen. ("We have no intention of standing police guard for a bunch of troublemakers coming into our city," Sullivan told reporters.) And the troopers were too few to be effective. Mann saved one black by pulling his pistol, but the rest of the riders were beyond help. So were several bystanders who were unconnected with them, and who seem to have been attacked on general principle. One boy's leg was broken. A group of young whites poured inflammable liquid on another boy and set him on fire. One Montgomery woman held up her child so that he could reach out and beat on a black man with his fists. Other women swore at two white girls who had been among the riders and then slapped them with their purses. The girls begged a passing motorist for help. He said, "You deserve what you get. I hope they beat you up good." Another man in a rented car pulled over. "Come on, I'll help you," he called to the girls, "I'm a federal man." Before he could do anything, however, he was dragged to the pavement and slugged. He was John Seigenthaler, the President's personal envoy to the governor of Alabama, and he lay unconscious in his own blood on the sidewalk for twenty-five minutes before an ambulance arrived. Commissioner Sullivan later explained that no ambulance had been called for Seigenthaler because "every white ambulance in town reported their vehicles had broken down."

Bob Kennedy, livid, put Byron White on the next plane to Mont-

* On December 21, 1973, Doar became legal adviser to the House Judiciary Committee's inquiry into the possibility of impeachable offenses by President Nixon.

gomery with Jim McShane, U.S. marshal for the District of Columbia. After Little Rock, Attorney General William P. Rogers had instituted riot training for U.S. marshals and their deputies to provide a federal law enforcement force other than the Army. At Maxwell Air Force Base outside Montgomery, Byron White now assembled four hundred men who had been so trained—revenue agents, border patrolmen, and guards from federal prisons—and who could be swiftly deputized for the occasion. Meanwhile Doar appeared in U.S. District Court and obtained an injunction enjoining the Ku Klux Klan and the National States' Rights Party, the two organizations most heavily represented in the mob, from interfering with interstate travel by bus. Governor Patterson then appeared at long last to protest that these moves were unconstitutional. Besides, he said, federal officers were unnecessary. On that he was simply proved wrong.

That Saturday afternoon the most famous civil rights activist, Martin Luther King, flew into Montgomery. At the home of the Reverend Ralph Abernathy he announced that he would speak that evening to a rally in the First Baptist Church. This presented the Ku Kluxers and their allies with a prize beyond their most vicious dreams. For a while King didn't seem to be an insurable risk. Byron White was supervising the preparations of the marshals when he received a startling phone call: Governor Patterson had called a meeting of Alabama law enforcement officers and was instructing them to arrest any federal men who broke state laws. White went to the meeting alone. It was open to the press, which took down the tense exchange between him and the governor. Patterson asked the deputy attorney general to share the government's information about CORE. "No," said White. Then the governor asked for information about the freedom riders. "No," White said again. Then:

PATTERSON: You know where some of these freedom riders are, don't you?

WHITE: Yes, in the hospital.

PATTERSON: Do you know where the others are?

WHITE: No, I don't.

PATTERSON: If you knew where some of these people are, would you inform us?

WHITE: I will never know where these people are.

At that moment they were in the First Baptist Church with Martin Luther King. By nightfall some fifteen hundred Birmingham Negroes had arrived for the rally. It had scarcely begun when an ugly crowd began to gather in a park across the street. Learning that the local police were again absent, White dispatched his marshals by every conveyance he could find—postal delivery trucks, private automobiles, and a prison truck. They were wearing business suits and brassards and were armed with pistols, nightsticks, and tear gas guns. About a hundred of them had formed a skirmish line outside the church when the mob charged, hurling stones and broken bottles. With that, the governor declared marshal law. The marshals' skirmish line held until crucial reinforcements arrived: Floyd Mann at the head of his troopers, and Henry Graham, a National Guard major general, with a detachment of his men. Even so, before the attack of the mob was blunted the marshals had to fire several volleys of tear gas. The gas seeped into the hot, overcrowded church. At times the blacks there were close to panic. If the church had been put to the torch, which was the mob's intention, undoubtedly the loss of life would have been great. As it was, they were well shielded by the mixed force of state and federal law enforcement officers.

Governor Patterson phoned Attorney General Kennedy to protest that Alabama was being invaded.

"John, John," Bob said quietly. "What do you mean, you're being invaded? Who's invading you, John? You know better than that."

Patterson accused him of sending the freedom riders into the state and blamed him for the violence.

"Now John," Bob said. "You can say that on television. You can tell that to the people of Alabama, but don't tell me that. Don't tell me that, John."

Nevertheless Patterson did it again, repeating every word. Then he said that the National Guard would defend the church and the congregation inside, but could not guarantee the safety of King.

"I don't believe that," said Kennedy. "Have General Graham call me. I want to hear a general of the United States Army say he can't protect Martin Luther King."

By now the governor was yelling. He shouted shrilly that he was giving his opinion, not the general's. He cried that sending federal marshals had created "a very serious political situation" and shrilled, "You're destroying us politically!"

"John," Kennedy said in the same quiet tone. "It's more important that these people in the church survive physically than for us to survive politically."

That ended the threat of violence against the freedom riders. In the north, Patterson was regarded as the heavy loser in the episode. Southerners took a different view, however. Lost causes have had a special appeal to them since Appomattox. They rallied to his side, sent him money and encouragement, and promised to join the fight against integration. That was ominous; it committed them. Keeping the vow became a matter of honor, and by June it had been taken publicly by virtually every politician in Dixie, including George Corley Wallace, who the following year was elected to succeed Patterson.

Nevertheless, as such things go, the freedom riders were counted a success. No one had been killed, and Jim Crow had been routed. Enforced segregation in interstate travel, theoretically outlawed by the Supreme Court in 1950, now ended in fact. Bob Kennedy petitioned the Interstate Commerce Commission to issue regulations requiring desegregation in all interstate terminals, including airports and train depots, and four months later, on September 22, it did. A few cities cited local laws as an excuse for not complying; the Justice Department brought suit against them. By the end of 1961 Negroes could travel coast to coast without seeing "White" or "Colored" in waiting rooms.

Countless bastions of segregation remained, of course, and the most formidable of them were in Mississippi. In 1931 H. L. Mencken and Charles Angoff ran a two-part series in the *American Mercury* ranking the states from good to bad, "from civilized to barbaric." Their criteria included wealth, literacy, education, entries in *Who's Who in America*, symphony orchestras, crime, voter registration, infant mortality, transportation, and availability of medical attention. In the final standing Mississippi was last, behind the rest of the Deep South, and its situation hadn't changed in 1962; indeed, when John Bererdt repeated the Mencken-Angoff survey for the magazine *Lifestyle* ten years later, in November 1972, Mississippi was again on the bottom, just below Alabama.* The average Mississippian had less than nine years' schooling. Over a third of the people were poor, as the Department of Commerce *Statistical Abstract of*

* In 1931 Massachusetts was first. In 1972 Connecticut had replaced it.

the United States defines poverty. One in four households lacked plumbing and 29 percent telephones; only 24 percent read a daily newspaper and only 3 percent a news magazine. "The Closed Society," Professor James W. Silver of the University of Mississippi called the state in 1964, and it became clear as the 1960s progressed that an astonishing number of its people, white and black, were actually unaware of the civil rights movement. There were no attacks on the freedom riders there because the state police didn't allow them the freedom of movement necessary to be mobbed. Their buses were met at the Alabama border and escorted to Jackson, and when they ignored the discriminatory signs in the terminal there, they were arrested and led to jail. Eventually federal courts overturned their convictions, but the rulings meant little to individual prisoners, who had served their time by then.

Burke Marshall, almost alone in the Justice Department, understood the inflexibility of Mississippi white supremacy. He knew that its prophets regarded the present period as a second Reconstruction. If they were just as single-minded in their resistance to it as their great-grandfathers had been, they thought, the federal challenge would fail and the problem would go away. But in 1961 most of the rest of the Justice Department (with the exception of Doar) wasn't on Marshall's wavelength. At the end of the year the attorney general submitted a report to his brother, the President, on civil rights progress. It almost sang with hope, and in a Voice of America broadcast a week after the confrontation at the First Baptist Church, Bob declared that racism was ebbing in the United States. He actually predicted that a black man could be elected President before the end of the century.

A brief conversation with one Mississippi black, James Meredith, would have tempered his optimism. Meredith was a nine-year veteran of the Air Force and one of ten children of a farmer in the midstate town of Kosciusko. Inspired by President Kennedy's inaugural address, Meredith had written to the University of Mississippi the same evening he heard it, requesting an application for admission. He returned the completed form with an explanatory note: "I am an American-Mississippi-Negro citizen. With all of the occurring events regarding changes in our educational system taking place in our country in this new age, I feel certain that this application does not come as a surprise to you. I certainly hope that this matter will be handled in a manner that will be complimentary to the University and to the state of Mississippi."

Ole Miss, as the university at Oxford was known throughout the South, rejected him for complex academic reasons, but Meredith wasn't discouraged that easily, and he found a powerful ally in Medgar Evers, the state director of the NAACP. In June 1961 NAACP lawyers filed suit for Meredith in the federal district court, charging that he had been turned down solely because of his race. The litigation which followed is unique in the history of American jurisprudence. A district court judge ruled against Meredith twice. In June 1962 the court of appeals for the Fifth Circuit reversed the judge; then Judge Ben Cameron of the Fifth Circuit reversed the reversal. The appeals court vacated Cameron's order, but he promptly issued another. This went on until, after his fourth stay, he had made it clear that he intended to continue along this line indefinitely. The NAACP appealed for sanity to Supreme Court Justice Hugo Black. In September Black, a native Alabaman, upheld the court of appeals and ordered the university to admit Meredith at once. "Never!" cried Governor Ross Barnett, and two days later he went on statewide television to declare: "We will not surrender to the evil and illegal forces of tyranny."

Apart from his age—he was sixty-four in the autumn of 1962— Ross Barnett was more like Meredith, whom he was about to engage in a duel by proxy, than he would have acknowledged. Like him he had been one of ten children, and had come to manhood in the hardscrabble clay wasteland of central Mississippi, the barren soil familiar to explorers of Yoknapatawpha County, the creation of William Faulkner, whose nephew Murry Falkner would play a key role in the unfolding crisis just ahead. Like Meredith, Barnett was also a prisoner of the past, a fundamentalist who took the Old Testament to be the literal truth and believed it proscribed racial "mixing." In another time, under other stars, the two men might have become friends. Barnett would have liked that, for he was naturally warm and gentle, ready to do almost anything for someone in distress, including Negroes. But if the man was black he had to know his place. On the strength of his vow to keep the Merediths of Mississippi where they were, Barnett had been elected governor two years earlier with the endorsement of the state's White Citizens' Councils. As an elector in the last presidential election, he had bolted the Kennedy-Johnson ticket to vote for Harry Byrd. He was,

in short, representative of his kind and his region: charming, ignorant, friendly, suspicious, blindly loyal to the lost Confederacy,
appalled by the present and frightened of the future. Martyrs are
made of just such stuff, and only one trait kept Barnett from becoming one. He was a coward. Under great pressure he would look for
a way out, a deal. His tragedy, which became Mississippi's, was that
he just didn't know how to find or make one.

If Barnett resembled Meredith, his antithesis was Robert F. Kennedy, who completely misread him. On the strength of the fact that
Mississippi's highway patrol had effectively convoyed the freedom
riders to safety, Bob assumed that the authorities there believed in
law and order. He mistook the patrol's commander, the felicitously
but inaccurately named Colonel T. B. Birdsong, for another Floyd
Mann. All the situation seemed to need was a plan, and Bob was
very good at plans. On Saturday, September 15, he called Barnett
and explained crisply how it would all be managed. He understood,
of course, that as a southern governor Barnett would have to offer
token resistance. Therefore Meredith would be escorted by several
marshals brandishing court orders. The governor could throw up
his hands and the university officials, bowing to the inevitable,
would then enroll Meredith. Kennedy asked if Barnett understood,
if there were any questions. In what should have been recognized
as a sign of how far apart they were, the governor said, "That will
take about a year."

It took just five days. The following Thursday Meredith, accompanied by the marshals, appeared in Oxford to register. He was met
by Barnett, who was attempting to shield the university administration by appearing himself in the role of a "special registrar." While
two thousand white students chanted, "We want Ross, we want
Ross," and "Glory, glory, segregation," the governor read a decree
barring Meredith from the campus "now and forevermore." Then
he handed it to him and said, "Take it and abide by it." One of the
men from the Justice Department said, "Do you realize you are
placing yourself in contempt of court?" Barnett said, "Are you telling me this or does it take a judge?"

His legal position, and he thought it unassailable, was what is
called interposition—interposing himself, as a representative of the
states' rights, between the administration in Washington and the
people of Mississippi. He had asked his legislature to give him that
authority, and it had complied. When American historians learned

of that, they were incredulous. Interposition had been discredited as a doctrine before the Civil War. In fact, when John C. Calhoun had tried to invoke it in 1832, the Mississippi legislature of that time had rejected it as "a heresy, fatal to the existence of the Union . . . contrary to the letter and spirit of the Constitution and in direct conflict with the welfare, safety and independence of every state." Now, one hundred and thirty years later, the governor was trying to breathe life into the same dead dogma. The Fifth Circuit in New Orleans, undeceived and unwilling to recognize Barnett as a special registrar, ordered university officials to appear the following Monday and show cause why they should not be cited for contempt. Barnett protested bitterly to the press at the speed of the courts. Mississippi's Senator James Eastland phoned Bob Kennedy to say, "The governor thinks you can back down a little, and I think so, too." Bob replied, "You don't really believe that, Senator. You've been in the Senate too long to believe that."

In court the university officials promised to admit Meredith by 4 P.M. the next day. Barnett still refused to budge. Saying that he was "shocked" at the officials' "surrender," he announced that anyone from the Department of Justice who interfered with Mississippians doing their duty would be arrested and jailed. Kennedy phoned him to point out that the people of Mississippi, including their governor, were citizens of the United States of America and subject to its laws. Barnett said, "I consider the Mississippi courts as high as any other court and a lot more capable. . . . Our courts have acted too, and our legislature has acted too. I'm going to obey the laws of Mississippi!" His attorney general, Joe Patterson, then issued a statement saying that freedom had been dealt "a staggering blow. . . . The constitutional rights of over 5,000 students have been ignored to gratify the pretended constitutional rights of one."

Meredith made his second attempt to register the next day in Jackson, at the office of the university trustees. John Doar and Jim McShane were with him. They were met by Barnett, Colonel Birdsong, and a jeering crowd of onlookers. The university officials couldn't keep the commitment made yesterday in New Orleans, the governor said, because they had been subpoenaed by a legislative committee investigating un-Mississippian activities. Doar tried to serve court papers on the governor; Barnett put his hands in his pockets. Doar asked, "Do you refuse to let us through that door?" Courtly as always, the governor said, "Yes, sir, I do so politely."

1160   REAPING THE WHIRLWIND: 1961–1968

Doar said, "And we leave politely." The crowd was not polite. As Meredith and his escort departed there were cries of "Go home, nigger," and "Communists!"

Bob Kennedy had been trying to keep Barnett's name out of the court proceedings because he remembered how Faubus had made political capital in Little Rock, but this was too much. The successive failures to admit Meredith were conveying the impression, in Mississippi at least, that the white supremacists were winning. Kennedy decided to ask for a Fifth Circuit order showing the governor in contempt. He phoned Barnett to tell him he was going to do it. He said further that Meredith would appear in Oxford in the morning, ready to attend classes. Barnett was aggrieved. Didn't that boy know when he wasn't wanted? As governor he had other duties, he said; he couldn't keep "running all over the State of Mississippi" for one Mississippian, and a Negro at that. Kennedy thought Meredith's enrollment would work. He said, "Why don't you try it for six months and see how it goes?"

"It's best for him not to go to Ole Miss," Barnett said.

Bob replied softly, "But he likes Ole Miss."

On campus alarmed faculty members noted a growing swell of visitors from all over Dixie, hard-bitten men with brush-fire eyes who were often armed and who asked, "Where will the nigger come from?" Their leader was General Edwin A. Walker, now of Dallas. On Wednesday, September 26, the day before the confrontation in Jackson, the general had issued a somewhat incoherent radio appeal to those who shared his convictions: "It is time to move. We have talked, listened, and been pushed around far too much by the anti-Christ Supreme Court. Rise to a stand beside Governor Barnett at Jackson, Mississippi. Now is the time to be heard. Ten thousand strong from every state in the union. The battle cry of the republic. Barnett, yes; Castro, no. Bring your flags, your tents, and your skillets. . . . The last time in such a situation I was on the wrong side. . . . This time I am out of uniform and I am on the right side and I will be there."

That day Barnett went into temporary seclusion. When Meredith and his escorts approached the campus in Oxford they were turned back by Lieutenant Governor Paul Johnson, backed by detachments of state troopers and county sheriffs. This time there was some jostling as the federal men tried to walk around Johnson in the hope that, having resisted, he would bow to the inevitable. He didn't bow. It was clear that force would be required to get past him. The marshals had been told to stop short of that, and there weren't enough of them anyway. Meredith was turned back again.

By this point every civil rights leader in America and most of official Washington thought that the Justice Department was being too patient, that the dignity of the federal government was in jeopardy. Robert Kennedy knew it, but he had sensed fear in Ross Barnett. The governor, he thought, would welcome an opportunity to save face; he seemed to be learning the peril of continuing to defy a federal court. On the phone the next morning, Thursday, Bob suggested that they explore the possibility of finding a way out. He had been right; the governor instantly agreed. If he had been as able a politician as George Wallace, the crisis might have been resolved then. But he wasn't able. His sense of timing (or Bob's timing in waiting this long to close with him) was wrong; too many hopes of total victory had been raised in diehard segregationists, emotions were running too high, too many Mississippians were calling for resistance "regardless of the cost in human life"—a phrase heard everywhere there. Most important, the governor didn't know how to strike a bargain. He knew he would have to sacrifice something to make peace, but he couldn't decide how much he would give up, how much resistance he could show for the sake of appearances and still remain below the flash point of violence.

Their first attempt to reach an understanding ended in ludicrous failure. They talked of Barnett and Lieutenant Governor Johnson at the campus gate, flanked by unarmed state troopers, facing McShane and thirty marshals. McShane would draw an unloaded pistol. The Mississippians would then step aside, and Meredith would pass through the gate and be registered. Barnett said one revolver wasn't enough. He wanted all thirty marshals to draw; that way, he could say he yielded to avoid bloodshed. Bobby proposed that the other marshals just slap their holsters. That wasn't sufficiently realistic for the governor, and so it was settled that all thirty guns would be drawn.

Earlier in the week this might have been enough, but now it would be dangerous. The fact that the troopers were unarmed was irrelevant; they would be counterbalanced by the guns carried by General Walker's followers in Oxford. In addition, Barnett was the only man on his side who knew of the deal. He might be the only one to step aside. The realization of this came to him while he was waiting for Meredith at the campus gate. The black Air Force veteran was then proceeding toward him in a thirteen-car convoy which was in radio contact with Washington. At 3:35 P.M. Mississippi time, 5:35 in Washington, Barnett called Kennedy to say that he couldn't control the crowd, it was too big and in too ugly a temper. That ended the showdown scenario. The convoy turned back. Meredith had been denied registration four times now, and that evening at the university white students held a wild demonstration.

But there would be no more failures. Bob Kennedy was conferring with General Maxwell Taylor, chairman of the Joint Chiefs, and his principal commanders, General Earle G. Wheeler and Major General Creighton W. Abrams. At the Justice Department an assistant attorney general was drafting documents for President Kennedy's signature putting Mississippi's National Guard in federal service, alerting U.S. infantry units at Fort Benning for action, and warning civilians in the streets of Oxford to go home and stay there. Another assistant attorney general was flying down to assume command of a growing force of marshals. From New Orleans came word that the Fifth Circuit had found Barnett guilty of contempt, ruling that if Meredith were not registered by Tuesday—it was now Friday—the governor would be fined $10,000 a day; for Lieutenant Governor Johnson, if Johnson took his place, it would be $5,000 a day.

The only card the government hadn't played was presidential prestige, and that was committed Saturday afternoon when the White House put through a call to the statehouse in Jackson. President Kennedy had already requested television time at 8 P.M. to lay the matter before the American people. He canceled it when Barnett proposed that Meredith be admitted secretly in Jackson on Monday while the governor was diverting the mob in Oxford. His manner didn't inspire confidence, however; hanging up, the President turned to the others and asked in wonder, "Do you know what that fellow said? He said, 'I want to thank you for your help on the poultry program.'"

At ten o'clock that evening the lack of confidence was justified. Barnett phoned the Justice Department to say that he had changed his mind. The agreement was off; he wouldn't go through with his part of it. Again the President requested television time, for 7:30 the following evening, Sunday, September 30. Sunday morning the governor called Robert Kennedy. It was another fruitless, frustrating conversation, and in the middle of it Bob lost his temper. He said his brother was going on TV to tell the country how Barnett had reached an agreement "with the President of the United States" and had then broken his word.

Alarmed, the governor said in a high-pitched voice, "That won't do at all."

"You broke your word to him."

"You don't mean the President is going to say that tonight?"

"He is."

Barnett, breathing hard, suggested flying Meredith in "this afternoon."

That seemed to be the end of it. Meredith, it appeared, would be enrolled that same day, and without bloodshed. He would be admitted quietly while state troopers kept the peace. Afterward Barnett would issue a furious statement saying that it had been done behind his back, that he was yielding to irresistible force but would fight it in the courts. Deputy Attorney General Nick Katzenbach flew down to supervise the details. At 5 P.M. Mississippi time, accompanied by Colonel Birdsong, he led four hundred marshals onto the Ole Miss campus, now almost deserted, through the little-used west gate. Meredith was taken quietly to Baxter Hall, at one end of the grounds, while Katzenbach and the marshals established a command post at the other end in the lovely old red brick Lyceum Building, the university's administration building. The President delayed his television address until 10 P.M. in the belief that the crisis would be all over by then. But this Sunday, like every other day in the Meredith case, seemed jinxed. Almost at once communications with Washington broke down, and they remained out until Monday morning. Even after Army units arrived on the scene, the Signal Corps was unable to establish a link to the White House. Throughout this, the height of the crisis, with the eyes of the nation and much of the world on Ole Miss, the President of the United States and the attorney general, his brother, received crucial reports from Katzenbach, who was dropping dimes into a pay phone in a campus booth.

As the sun sank over Mississippi it became evident that somehow word of what had happened was spreading in Oxford. A crowd of about a thousand quickly gathered outside the Lyceum. Meredith's whereabouts were unknown to them; throughout the coming nightmare he remained concealed a mile away, guarded by twenty-four marshals who had doffed their white helmets and orange vests so that they, too, would be inconspicuous. There can be little doubt about what would have happened to him, and possibly to them, if his presence in Baxter Hall had become known to the mob. Like Richard Nixon in Caracas, he was in very real danger of being torn apart. The marshals (all of whom were white southerners themselves) were being taunted with "Kill the nigger-loving bastards," "Go to Cuba, nigger lovers," and a chant: "Two-four-one-three, we hate Kennedy!" The evening deepened. The crowd doubled, and redoubled. Its shouts became obscene. The marshals were pelted with stones, then rocks, then lighted cigarettes. A Texas newsman and his wife were beaten by men swinging pieces of pipe. Many of the state troopers on the scene were unhelpful. Some stood aside with folded arms and did nothing.

It was 7:30 P.M. in Mississippi when the FBI monitored a radio signal ordering the state troopers to withdraw entirely and leave Meredith and the marshals to the mob. Later efforts to find out who had sent it were unsuccessful. Katzenbach phoned Bob Kennedy to tell him of it. In the background Bob could make out the ragged sounds of riot. Then—it was at 7:58—he heard that thumping sound of gas grenades. Katzenbach said, "Bob, I'm very sorry to report we've had to fire tear gas. We had no choice."

In Washington the President went on television unaware of the latest developments. To the best of his knowledge then, Barnett was keeping his word to maintain order with the troopers. He explained to the national audience that Meredith was on the campus, explained the need to enforce court order, spoke glowingly of the heroism of Mississippi men in the country's wars, and appealed to Ole Miss undergraduates: "The honor of your university and state are in the balance. I am certain that the great majority of the students will uphold that honor."

In Oxford the students watching him jeered. General Walker was moving among them purposefully. A fire engine and a bulldozer were seized by men who used them to try to crash through the line of marshals and into the Lyceum; well-lobbed grenades drove them off. The attackers hurled Molotov cocktails fashioned from Coca-Cola bottles. Campus benches were demolished to make jagged concrete projectiles, iron bars and bricks from construction sites were thrown, and here and there the crack of rifles could be heard as invisible snipers zeroed in on the Lyceum. Two men were killed, a French foreign correspondent and an Oxford spectator. Over a third of the marshals—166—were injured, and 28 were wounded by snipers' bullets. The marshals carried sidearms; they were under fire; it seemed right to return it. They repeatedly asked for permission to do so, and Katzenbach relayed the requests to Washington. The Kennedy brothers rejected the appeals. There would be no federal use of live ammunition, they ruled, unless Meredith was in danger. The marshals, exhausted and bloodied, held out with only their black, stubby tear gas guns to protect them.* Edwin Cuthman was in the Lyceum, on the phone with Bob Kennedy. Bob asked, "How's it going down there?" Ed answered, "Pretty rough. It's sort of like the Alamo." Bob said, "Well, you remember what happened to those fellows."

At ten o'clock in Oxford, Katzenbach reluctantly told Washington that troops were necessary. In three-quarters of an hour the first unit arrived, sixty National Guardsmen of Troop E, 108th Armored Cavalry, under the command of Captain Murry C. Falkner. Before daybreak sixteen of them would become casualties, among them Captain Falkner, two of whose bones were broken by a brickbat. To the exasperation and then the fury of the Kennedys, nearly five hours passed before regular Army contingents, who had been alerted, reached the scene. Three times the marshals almost ran out of tear gas. When the soldiers did arrive, they had to fight their way to the campus. Forty of them were hit by missiles or shotgun blasts. Most of the attackers vanished in the night. The 503rd Military Police Battalion, arriving with the main body of troops from Memphis, arrested over two hundred members of the mob, including General Walker. Only twenty-four of them were students; the others came from all over Dixie—Georgia, Alabama, Louisiana, Tennessee, and Texas, as well as Mississippi. At dawn the campus was seen to be littered with chunks of cement, tear gas canisters, wrecked vehicles, rocks, smashed window glass, and green chips from thousands of pulverized Coke bottles. Governor Barnett blamed the riot on "inexperienced, nervous, trigger-happy" marshals.

* "One would remember them," Ed Guthman wrote nine years later, "in the racial riots and wild campus demonstrations of the latter half of the 1960s and at Kent State and at Jackson State universities in 1970, when lawmen, with far, far less provocation and injury than the marshals endured, gunned people down."

Shortly before eight o'clock Monday morning Jim McShane and two other marshals accompanied Meredith to the battered Lyceum. There, at last, he was admitted by Robert Byron Ellis, the stony-faced registrar. There was no resistance in the administration building, only resignation and studied courtesy. Meredith listed his academic goal as a degree in political science. With credits from extension courses already taken he would graduate in three semesters. As he left the Lyceum another student yelled, "Was it worth two lives, nigger?"

Booked and fingerprinted, Major General Edwin A. Walker was charged with assaulting an officer, resisting arrest, insurrection, and conspiracy. The charges were dropped three months later after he had been given a psychiatric examination at Parkland Memorial Hospital in Dallas, and on an April evening three months after *that* a sniper standing on his lawn and aiming a cheap mail order rifle tried to kill him. In December 1963 ballistics experts found that the owner of that rifle, and presumably the man who had fired it, was Lee Harvey Oswald, who, among other things, had become since then an active supporter of the Fair Play for Cuba Committee and the assassin of John F. Kennedy. The confusion of the radical left and radical right is puzzling unless one grasps that President Kennedy, supremely a man of the center, was hated by both. Their feelings for him had begun to harden at the time of the Bay of Pigs, when one extreme denounced him for backing the invasion of Castro Cuba while the other condemned him for not going all the way and wiping Castro out. By the end of his second year in office it was clear that among those at either end of the political spectrum Kennedy had become the most scorned President since Franklin Roosevelt.

The New Left had begun to organize for the long pull in June 1962, when forty-five quiet, neatly dressed young people met at an old UAW-CIO summer camp at Port Huron, Michigan, to found the Students for a Democratic Society. The SDS then was but a shadow of its future self. The principal activity at the meeting was discussion of a moderate, sixty-two-page manifesto drafted by a weedy, pock-marked twenty-two-year-old University of Michigan undergraduate named Tom Hayden. Hayden cited, as the two greatest challenges to society, racism and "the enclosing fact of the cold war, symbolized by the presence of the Bomb." He proposed "that we as individuals take the responsibility for encounter and resolution."

There was nothing new in the diagnosis or the prescription for cure: "We would replace power rooted in possession, privilege, or circumstances by power and uniqueness rooted in love, reflectiveness, reason and creativity." Hayden specifically renounced what would later become an SDS trademark—violence as catalyst for change —on the ground that it "requires generally the transformation of the target, be it a human being or a community of people, into a depersonalized object of hate."

The right was much farther along. The John Birch Society, the SDS's mirror image, was four years old and flourishing. His membership in it had been the reason for General Walker's dismissal from the Army, and the Kennedy brothers had increased its fame by damning it, the attorney general calling it "ridiculous" and the President warning that it was an inept adversary of Communism. Robert Welch, "The Founder," as he called himself, continued to mastermind Birch activities from a two-story brick building in the Boston suburb of Belmont. He seemed to enjoy publicity and was doubtless aware that it helped recruit new Birchers. The basic unit in the society was the chapter, which was frankly based on the Communist cell. (Welch was fascinated by Communism and imitated it slavishly.) Each chapter numbered between ten and twenty members. By the early 1960s there were reported to be chapters in thirty-four states and the District of Columbia with a total membership of about one hundred thousand. Birch ranks were increased by what The Founder called "fronts," such as the Patrick Henry Society, the Sons of the American Revolution, and the Minute Women and Minutemen. In many communities the Birchers were treated as a joke, but it was no joke in places like Shreveport, Tampa, Houston, and Dallas, where, as the *New York Times* reported, "businessmen, management executives, physicians, lawyers, and other 'solid' people have joined chapters."

As the decade grew older the New Left would emerge as the greater threat to democratic institutions, but that was not apparent in the Kennedy years. The resources of the right overshadowed anything at the other extreme; during the Kennedy Presidency outlays by ultraconservative organizations rose from five million dollars a year to over fourteen million, while the national budget for a liberal enterprise like the Americans for Democratic Action ran to a mere $150,000. The worst the left could do then was an occasional ill-tempered remark—C. Wright Mills was reported to have said on his deathbed that he was "ashamed to be an American, ashamed to have John F. Kennedy as his President"—while Senator Fulbright uncovered a working political arrangement between ultraconservative organizations and career officers in the regular Army. When Fulbright held hearings to bring it to light, he was all but drowned out by charges that he was trying to "muzzle the military."

Among the more conspicuous activities of the ultras in those years were Dallas's National Indignation Convention, first convened in 1961 and again in 1963. In its first session the 1,800 delegates to the convention roared their approval of a speaker who protested that the chairman was becoming moderate—"All he wants to do is impeach Warren—I'm for hanging him." Two years later the convention counteracted United Nations Day by holding a "United States Day"—an event blessed by Governor John B. Connally Jr. with an official proclamation.

Under the ultra umbrella were gathered such groups as the Reverend Billy James Hargis's Christian Crusade and Dr. Fred Schwarz's Christian Anti-Communism Crusade. The farthest reaches of the right wing were dismissed as a refuge for impotent crackpots. It is true that George Lincoln Rockwell's American Nazi Party never threatened American liberties, but elsewhere ultras were both respectable and influential. C. D. Jackson, publisher of *Life*, bore reluctant witness to this. After an issue of his magazine had treated Schwarz with disdain the flak from powerful advertisers was so great that Jackson flew to a Schwarz rally in the Hollywood Bowl to eat crow: "I believe we were wrong, and I am profoundly sorry. It's a great privilege to be here tonight and align *Life* magazine with Senator Dodd, Representative Judd, Dr. Schwarz and the rest of these implacable fighters against Communism."

Extremists of both left and right were characterized by what Benjamin DeMott has called "the Spirit of Overkill." Susan Sontag wrote in the *Partisan Review* that "the white race is the cancer of history." The *Berkeley Barb* flatly declared, "The professors have nothing to teach. . . . We can learn more from any jail than we can from any university." An off-Broadway cast chanted, "The middle class/ Are just like pigs . . . The middle class/ Are just like pigs," and in 1961 Bertrand Russell said, "We used to call Hitler wicked for killing off the Jews, but Kennedy and Macmillan are much more wicked than Hitler. . . . They are the wickedest people who ever lived in the history of man and it is our duty to do what we can against them." On the opposite horizon The Founder of the Birchers said of the United States that "the whole country is one vast in-

sane asylum and they're letting the worst patients run the place,"
while Dean Noebel, a Christian Crusade prophet, maintained that
agents in the bowels of the Kremlin had formed a "Commie-Beatle
Pact"—"the Communists have contrived an elaborate, calculating,
and scientific technique directed at rendering a generation of American youth useless through nerve-jamming, mental deterioration,
and retardation. . . . The destructive music of the Beatles . . . re-
inforces . . . mental breakdown."

John Kennedy was very much aware of both varieties of irrecon-
cilables. At Seattle in November of 1961 he suggested that it was
the very insolubility of the day's problems which engendered a
yearning for simple answers. "There are two groups of these frustrated citizens," he said. "It is a curious fact that each . . . resembles
the other. Each believes that we have only two choices: appeasement or war, suicide or surrender, humiliation or holocaust, to be
either Red or dead." When possible he pricked them with wit. At a
White House gathering, E. M. "Ted" Dealey of the morning *Dallas
News* said, "We need a man on horseback to lead this nation, and
many people in Texas and the southwest think that you are riding
Caroline's tricycle." The editor of the evening paper in Dallas, the
Times Herald, wrote Kennedy to say that Dealey did not speak for
Texas. The President wrote back, "I'm sure the people of Dallas are
glad when afternoon comes."

Ultra humor tended to be black humor. In milder versions it was
innocuous. The sign on the marquee outside a Georgia theater showing *PT-109,* the story of the President's World War II heroism, read,
"See How the Japs Almost Got Kennedy." A riddle ran, "If Jack,
Bobby, and Teddy were on a sinking boat, who would be saved?"
The answer: "The country." A mimeographed, widely circulated
leaflet set forth plans for a Kennedy monument in Washington: "It
was thought unwise to place it beside that of George Washington,
who never told a lie, nor beside that of F. D. Roosevelt, who never
told the truth, since John cannot tell the difference."* It continued:

Five thousand years ago, Moses said to the children of Israel: "Pick
up thy shovels, mount thy asses and camels, and I will lead you to
the Promised Land." Nearly five thousand years later, Roosevelt
said: "Lay down your shovels, sit on your asses, and light up a

* Many Roosevelt haters believe that there is an ostentatious FDR monument
in the capital. In fact, Roosevelt had requested only that after his death a small
plaque be placed on a rock outside the National Archives building on Pennsylvania Avenue, and that it bear simply his name and the dates of his birth and
death. This was done in 1965. It is modest; few passersby notice it.

Camel; this *is* the Promised Land." Now Kennedy is stealing your shovels, kicking your asses, raising the price of Camels, and taking over the Promised Land.

From there to the outer limits of the lunatic fringe, however, ultra wit became increasingly unprintable. As in the Roosevelt years it was often preoccupied with unusual sexual practices, and it involved not only the Kennedy men and women, but also their children and even their pets. The sons of men who had mimicked FDR's upper-class accent now mimicked JFK's while telling stories about hot lines running from the Pope's toilet and the sewers of Rome to the White House, about the strange ways he spent his father's money, about a woman who claimed to be his first wife—Joe Kennedy was supposed to have bought an annulment—and even about his illnesses. Arthur Schlesinger noted that virtually every aspect of Kennedy fed resentment: "His appearance, his religion, his wealth, his intelligence, his university, his section of the country, his wife, his brothers, his advisers, his support of the Negroes, his determination to de-emotionalize the cold war, his refusal to drop the bomb." The ultras simply hated everything they read about the President.

That was a lot. News of the First Family and its various affiliates at times seemed to have preempted the attention of the communications industry. Kennedy lore was featured in films, on television, on the Broadway stage, and in musical tributes. Every bookshop had its department of Kennedy books, of which by 1962 there were already over a hundred; book collectors were paying small ransoms for signed copies of *Profiles in Courage*. The fact that Lord David Cecil's biography of Melbourne was the President's favorite book was enough to turn what had been a book of limited appeal into a best seller; a report that Kennedy had enjoyed Ian Fleming's *From Russia With Love* made Fleming a millionaire. Caroline Kennedy's picture was on the cover of *Newsweek*, and three screen magazines adopted the rule that *every* cover, every issue, must feature a photograph of Caroline's mother.

Once it became known that the President had learned to read 1,200 words a minute at a speed-reading course, the number of such courses increased tenfold. Courses at hairdresser schools gave instruction in how to imitate the First Lady's bouffant coiffures. Because her husband usually appeared bareheaded, Danbury, Connecticut, the center of the hatting industry, entered a severe recession. The White House press revealed that his favorite cocktail was a daiquiri; suddenly bottled daiquiri mixes appeared on the shelves of package stores. Jackie believed it was smart to have small dinner parties at home. As a result, the names of the great party givers of the Eisenhower years—Pearl Mesta, Gwen Cafritz, etc.—went into eclipse. The word went out that busy as they were, such key figures in the administration as Robert McNamara and General Taylor were finding time to improve their minds at "Hickory Hill University," the evening and weekend seminars at Robert Kennedy's Virginia home. The idea spread to Alexandria and Arlington, to Georgetown and Cleveland Park, and presently such firms as Johnson & Johnson were offering self-improvement courses for their executives.

The Kennedys were very outdoorsy. Not since Theodore Roosevelt had so ardent an advocate of the strenuous life lived in the White House. There was touch football, and sailing off Hyannisport, and Jackie's water-skiing. One or another of them was enthusiastic about nearly every sport: tennis, swimming, horseback riding, badminton, golf, softball, isometrics, skiing at Aspen, and hiking before breakfast. The fact that Pierre Salinger, the White House press secretary, had a stocky build which was growing stockier made him an apostate, almost un-American, and the President tried to redeem him by challenging him to push-up matches. With Pierre in mind, Kennedy at one time asked everyone on his staff to lose five pounds each. The President himself faithfully went through special back exercises in the miniature White House gym, in hotel rooms on trips, and on the floor of *Air Force One*.

At times the preoccupation with keeping fit became obsessive. The Hyannisport version of touch football was a rough sport; catching a pass in the rose bushes could be dangerous; Jackie quit playing after she broke a leg. When Kennedy appointed Red Fay Undersecretary of the Navy, Red, a balding friend from PT days, toured Navy bases taking on gobs in push-up contests. Guests at Hickory Hill were expected to play at least one set of tennis before breakfast, and after the President saw his Green Beret guerrilla fighters master an almost unbelievable obstacle course at Fort Bragg, he told his three middle-aged military aides that he wanted them to do it, too.

The most memorable physical education exploit of those days became known as the Great Hike. It began with General David M.

Shoup, commandant of the Marine Corps and a Kennedy favorite. Shoup unearthed a 1908 Theodore Roosevelt directive which had required Marine Corps company officers to march fifty miles in twenty hours, double-timing the last seven hundred yards. He sent a memo about it to the President, who after a little research wrote back: "President Roosevelt laid down such requirements not only for the officers of the Marine Corps but, when possible, for members of his own family, members of his staff and Cabinet, and even for unlucky foreign diplomats." Kennedy then challenged the Marine Corps. He asked Shoup whether today's marines could do as well as the marines of 1908. They could and did, but that was only the start of it. Robert Kennedy hiked the length of the C & O Canal path; assistant attorneys general and Justice Department secretaries followed him. The story reached the papers and engendered a craze. Walking long distances became the latest thing. People who seldom strolled farther than the distance from the armchair to the martini pitcher were on the road. Alarmed physicians pointed out that over-enthusiasm in exercise was dangerous. At their behest the President warned against overdoing it, and Salinger, who had rashly agreed to lead the White House press corps fifty miles, gratefully backed down.

Salinger was pitched into the Hickory Hill swimming pool fully dressed at the end of an uproarious lawn party there, and on impulse Ted Kennedy dove in after him. When stories of the incident found their way into print the frowns on the faces of Kennedy haters deepened. For some reason the episode seemed particularly decadent to them. Private swimming pools were an affront to the Protestant ethic anyhow; entering them wearing anything except a bathing suit was almost a perversion. But those who felt that way received an even ruder shock. June 17, 1962, was the attorney general's twelfth wedding anniversary. He and Ethel gave a party to celebrate it. Tables were set around the pool; Ethel was at a table that teetered on an impromptu catwalk which actually crossed the pool. Arthur Schlesinger and a partner decided to dance between courses. That was a mistake. Their weight on the catwalk tilted it. The hostess's chair started to slide, and, splash, there was Ethel, in the drink. Schlesinger, mortified, plunged in after her. They put on dry clothes and the party continued, but that wasn't the way the Kennedy haters told it; in their accounts the cavorting around the pool had stopped just shy of Babylon. For the next year Ethel had to set new guests straight on what had really happened, and sometimes she had the uneasy feeling that they didn't believe her.

Like FDR, President Kennedy came to realize that the very intemperance of those who spread malicious stories about him and his family was a political asset. It offended decent Americans and thus redounded to his advantage. He expected Barry Goldwater to run against him in 1964, and he wanted to be sure that the country understood the difference between his centralism and Goldwater's extremism. In a speech he never lived to deliver—it was in his pocket when he died—he scorned those who confused "rhetoric with reality" and assumed "that vituperation is as good as victory." And earlier he had said of them:

> They look suspiciously at their neighbors and their leaders. They call for a "man on horseback" because they do not trust the people. They find treason in our churches, in our highest court, in our treatment of water. . . . Unwilling to face up to the danger from without [they] are convinced that the real danger is from within.

Despite C. Wright Mills and H. Stuart Hughes, Communism was then a threat to American security, and despite Robert Welch and the Christian Crusaders, the threat came from the Soviet Union and not fluoridated water. The tensions of the cold war were powerful enough to generate one more convulsion of terror. It would bring the country and the world to the very brink of nuclear oblivion, and it came, anomalously, in a month of unsurpassed autumnal glory, October 1962.

Ordinarily Senator Kenneth Keating of New York was not a suspicious man, but reports from Cuban refugees reaching Florida that summer had troubled him. Fidel Castro's brother Raúl, Cuba's war minister, was known to have been in Moscow on July 2. Late in that same month activity in Cuban harbors picked up sharply; large numbers of Soviet freighters from the Black Sea began arriving at Mariel, a deepwater port on the northern coast of Pinar del Río province. Their cargoes were unknown, and puzzling. The ships rode high in the water and were distinguished by very wide hatches. Equally odd, each vessel brought with it large teams of Soviet technicians.

By the end of August more than five thousand Russians were in Cuba, and refugees being questioned at the CIA interrogation center at Opa-Locka, Florida, reported seeing truck convoys hauling long tubular objects swathed in tarpaulins. A CIA agent reaching Opa-Locka from Cuba had seen the tailpiece of one object and had a sketch of it. That same week Castro's personal pilot boasted in a Havana bar that Cuba now had long-range missiles with atomic warheads. On October 3 word reached Opa-Locka of activity "probably connected with missiles" in Pinar del Río. How much of this information reached Senator Keating is unknown, but in a series of speeches that month he warned of a Soviet military buildup. On October 10 he said that according to his informants, who had been "100 percent reliable," six intermediate-range missile sites were being constructed on the island.

The administration was skeptical. The Soviets had never put missiles in other countries, not even in bordering eastern European satellites bound to them by the Warsaw Pact. On both sides of the Iron Curtain Castro was regarded as an unstable leader and an unreliable ally. It was inconceivable that Khrushchev would entrust such a man with weapons which could destroy the world. The Kremlin had not recognized Cuba as a member of the Soviet bloc, though Castro had so proclaimed it. Cuba was far from the Soviet Union; transportation and communication lines between them could be quickly cut by the United States. Finally, the Russians could be sure that any such move would trigger a violent reaction in Washington.

At 3 P.M. Sunday, October 14, McGeorge Bundy was interviewed on television by Edward P. Morgan and John Scali of the American Broadcasting Company. As the President's special assistant for national security, he was asked to comment on Keating's charges. He replied: "I know there is no present evidence, and I think there is no present likelihood, that the Cubans and the Cuban government and the Soviet government would, in combination, attempt to install a major offensive capability." That was the opinion of almost everyone in the CIA. Keating, they thought, was being had. Cuban informants were notoriously unreliable. The tubular objects were doubtless SAMs—surface-to-air missiles of the kind that shot down Francis Gary Powers's U-2 twelve hundred miles within the Soviet Union. The Russians had provided Egypt and Indonesia with them, and other SAMs were known to be on their way to Castro. They were defensive weapons, nothing to worry about.

One man disagreed with the majority: John A. McCone, the CIA director. Returning to the capital after a wedding trip, McCone learned that there had been no aerial reconnaissance of western Cuba for a month. The reason was that SAM installations had been discovered there. No one had been willing to risk the loss of another U-2 to SAMs. McCone said that the gamble would have to be taken. On October 4 he called for the immediate photographing of the entire island, with special vigilance over its western end. After various delays because of clouds over the target areas and instructions for new U-2 pilots, October 14 dawned cloudless, and two Air Force majors took off for western Cuba. They had been told to expect ground fire, but the SAM crews were either absent or dozing; their sweep was a milk run. On their return their film magazines were dispatched to Washington and developed at processing laboratories. At the interpretation center in the Pentagon skilled specialists began studying enlargements of each frame.

By Monday afternoon they had seen enough to vindicate Keating. A field near San Cristóbal had been laid out in a trapezoidal pattern which until now had been seen only in U-2 photographs of the Soviet Union. There were SAM sites at each corner of the field, guarding a launch pad. No ballistic missiles were in sight, but the analysts had identified missile transporters, erectors, and the launchers. The evidence was not conclusive, but it certainly required immediate attention on the highest levels of the American government. Secretary McNamara had left the Pentagon earlier than usual—he was attending a seminar at Hickory Hill University—so the commanding general at the Defense Intelligence Agency put through a hot-line call to the Washington apartment of Deputy Secretary of Defense Roswell Gilpatric. It was a few minutes after 7 P.M., Monday, October 15, 1962.

Gilpatric, dressing for dinner and overdue at General Taylor's Fort McNair quarters, decided that he would be even later than he had expected. He said he wanted to see the photographs. Two analysts brought them. After looking at them and issuing appropriate orders he continued on to the general's dinner, where the principal guests were already being called to the telephone, one by one, and given whispered information which, they were cautioned, could not be shared with their wives. Reports for the President would be channeled through McGeorge Bundy, who was giving another dinner for Charles E. Bohlen, the newly appointed ambassador to France. Bundy received his call, from the deputy director of the

CIA, at 8:30. He decided not to tell the President until the next day. There was nothing Kennedy could do that was not already being done except lose a night's sleep. "So," he explained to the President in a subsequent memo, "I decided that a quiet evening and a night of sleep was the best preparation you could have in the light of what you would face in the days ahead."

Dean Rusk, presiding at a third formal dinner on the eighth floor dining room at the State Department, was chatting with his guest of honor. Foreign Minister Gerhard Schroeder of West Germany, when he was called to a phone in the butler's pantry. The caller was Assistant Secretary of State Roger Hilsman. Rusk listened a moment, then said, "Do you, personally, think this is it?" Hilsman replied, "There has only been a preliminary analysis, but from what I can get over the phone there doesn't seem to be much doubt." Any unusual behavior by the Secretary of State would set loose a flood of rumors. Rusk, though wretched, saw no alternative to observing the amenities. He returned to his guest, and the thirteen-day crisis began the next morning.

Tuesday, October 16, 1962

Analysts have been up all night reexamining the photographs of San Cristóbal; McNamara sees them at 7:30 A.M., Bundy at eight. Bundy goes directly to the President's bedroom, where Kennedy is reading the morning papers, and breaks the news: "Mr. President, there is now hard photographic evidence, which you will see a little later, that the Russians have offensive missiles in Cuba." The President directs Bundy to summon key members of the administration to an 11:45 A.M. meeting in the Cabinet Room. Then he calls his brother.

In addition to the Kennedys, those present at the 11:45 meeting, or subsequent sessions of it, include Gilpatric, Bundy, McNamara, Rusk, O'Donnell, Lyndon Johnson, McCone, Maxwell Taylor, General Marshall Carter of the CIA, Sorensen, George Ball, Gilpatric's counterpart at the State Department; Secretary of the Treasury Dillon; Edward Martin, Assistant Secretary of State for Latin America; Ambassadors Bohlen, Llewellyn Thompson, and Adlai Stevenson; U. Alexis Johnson, Paul Nitze, and three men no longer in the government: Dean Acheson, John J. McCloy, and Robert A. Lovett. These men will enter history as the Executive Committee of the National Security Council, or simply the Ex Comm.

Reports from technicians indicate that the San Cristóbal site will be ready for firing in about ten days, and that completion will cut the warning time for an attack on the United States from fifteen minutes to between two and three minutes. Robert Kennedy makes a note of the dominant feeling: "shocked incredulity." There is a general awareness that any American response might worsen the situation, but that not challenging Khrushchev would be the worst course of all.

The President orders a sharp increase in U-2 overflights. Other Ex Comm members will investigate possible choices—in Rusk's phrase, they will "box the compass." The State Department will explore the chances of support from Latin America and U.S. allies in Europe; the Defense Department will investigate the time factor, the kinds of units, and the number of men necessary for various military alternatives. At this point a majority feels that there is only one option: an air strike against the missile sites. Robert Kennedy passes a note to his brother: "I now know how Tojo felt when he was planning Pearl Harbor."

Wednesday, October 17

To maintain an appearance of calm, the President keeps a promise to campaign for Democratic candidates in Connecticut. He is away from the capital until midnight. The Ex Comm meets all day and most of the evening in George Ball's conference room on the seventh floor of the State Department. There is new U-2 evidence, and it is chilling. The Soviet technicians are working around the clock. Missiles are now visible in the photographs. Sixteen, and possibly thirty-two, sites may be ready for firing within a week. In addition to definite proof of medium-range missiles (1,000 miles) at San Cristóbal, there are intermediate-range sites (2,200 miles) in the Guanajay area, between San Cristóbal and Havana, and at Remedios in eastern Cuba. The intermediate-range weapons will be ready by December 1. They are what the military call "first-strike" weapons. With them, the U.S. Intelligence Board estimates, the USSR will be able to fire an initial salvo of forty nuclear warheads on targets in the United States as far west as Montana.

In the absence of his brother, Bob Kennedy emerges as the Ex Comm discussion leader. Majority opinion still favors an air attack—the euphemism for it is a "surgical operation." Bundy and Acheson are its chief advocates. McNamara proposes an alternative: a naval blockade of Cuba. Bombing and blockading are both acts of war, but the blockade has the advantage of avoiding bloodshed, at least in its first stages. An air strike would kill about 25,000 Cubans and an undetermined number of Soviet technicians. If Russians die, total war with the Soviet Union will be almost inevitable.

During the day six options, or "tracks," are pondered. Track A is to do nothing now. Track B would send an emissary to Khrushchev and try to settle matters quietly. Track C would hale the Russians before the U.N. Security Council. (Unfortunately Valerian Zorin of the USSR is chairman of the council this month.) Track D, known in the Ex Comm as "the slow track," is the blockade, Track E the air attack, and Track F an invasion of Cuba. Track F is put aside for restudy later; it cannot be weighed now because it must be preceded by elaborate preparations. However, these are under way.

Thursday, October 18

The U.S. intelligence community estimates that the weapons now in Cuba constitute about half the ICBM capacity of the entire Soviet Union. Photo analysis indicates that they are being aimed at specific American cities. If they are fired, eighty million Americans will be dead within a few minutes. According to the latest Intelligence Board reports, presented at the 11 A.M. session of the Ex Comm, the first missiles could be ready for launching in eighteen hours. The President says to Acheson, "This is the week I better earn my salary." While he is meeting with the Ex Comm, General Shoup says, "You are in a pretty bad fix, Mr. President." Kennedy replies swiftly, "You are in it with me."

The President has an appointment of long standing to receive Andrei Gromyko. He keeps it, talking with Gromyko for over two hours, giving him every opportunity to bring up the matter of missiles, but Gromyko misses all his cues. (Later there will be doubt that Gromyko knew what had been happening in Cuba.) Meanwhile, Rusk is suggesting to the Ex Comm that it regard Tuesday, October 23, as the deadline for action. If by then missile pads are still being built, he says, force should be used to remove them.

Air Force Chief of Staff Curtis LeMay joins the group and argues forcefully that a military attack is essential. The President asks LeMay what the Russian response might be. LeMay assures them that there would be none. Kennedy is skeptical: "They, no more than we, can let these things go by without doing something. They can't, after all their statements, permit us to take out their missiles, kill a lot of Russians, and then do nothing. If they don't take action in Cuba, they certainly will in Berlin." McNamara continues to build support for a blockade. A legal adviser from the State Department recalls Franklin Roosevelt's "quarantine-the-aggressor speech" and suggests it might be better if the blockade were called a quarantine. The weight of opinion is moving toward this option. Robert Kennedy is strongly in favor of it. With the memory of Pearl Harbor, he says, the United States cannot launch a surprise air attack in which thousands of innocent people would die. For a hundred and seventy-five years we have not been that kind of country, he says; surprise raids are not in the American tradition.

The evening session of the Ex Comm is held directly beneath a Rusk dinner for Gromyko on the eighth floor of the State Department Building. Reporters seeing the Secretary of Defense and the director of the CIA arriving sense something unusual. They are led to believe that McNamara and McCone are going to the dinner. To avoid another confrontation with the press, at the end of the meeting nine Ex Comm members—whose cars bear easily recognized license plates—pile into the attorney general's limousine. Their destination is the White House, where the President learns that the trend toward a blockade is continuing. Deputy Attorney General Katzenbach, a former professor of international law, is told to explore the legal basis for a blockade of Cuba.

Friday, October 19

Because the security lid is still on tight, the President leaves Washington again to honor an obligation, this time a commitment to campaign in Chicago. In the capital the Joint Chiefs put the Atlantic and Caribbean commands on alert at 1:20 P.M. The Pentagon announces that McNamara has asked the Chiefs to remain in Washington for six weeks to consult on "budget planning." Katzenbach reports that in his opinion a unilateral order for a blockade can be legally justified under the circumstances. The President decides to make a televised report to the American people Monday evening —the earliest time possible if all necessary steps are to be taken first.

The Ex Comm is in continuous session all day Friday and all Friday night. Now that there is a clear majority for the blockade,

Acheson withdraws. The others split into groups to write out their recommendations and then exchange papers. Out of this the outline of a definite plan begins to emerge. The most important of Friday's developments is the decision to ask for an endorsement of the blockade by the Organization of American States (OAS). A two-thirds majority of twenty voting American republics will be necessary. If achievable it will be invaluable, the Kremlinologists believe, because the Russians are impressed by legalisms. As an adjunct to this, Ball gives the bare facts of the crisis to Don Wilson, deputy to ailing Edward R. Murrow at the United States Information Agency. Wilson asks a Bell Telephone executive to clear lines to Spanish-language radio stations without telling the stations why.

Saturday, October 20

Robert Kennedy phones his brother at the Sheraton Blackstone Hotel in Chicago: the Ex Comm is ready with a plan of action. The President summons Salinger to the presidential suite at the Sheraton Blackstone and hands him a slip of paper: "Slight upper respiratory [infection]. 1 degree temperature. Weather raw and rainy. Recommended return to Washington." At 9:35 Chicago time Salinger makes the announcement to the press. Aboard *Air Force One* he asks Kennedy, "There's nothing wrong with your health, is there, Mr. President?" Kennedy replies, "If you know nothing about it, you're lucky."

Robert Kennedy meets the presidential aircraft at Andrews Field. The afternoon session of the Ex Comm begins at 2:30 in the oval study on the second floor of the Executive Mansion. The President makes the final decision in favor of the blockade. The last small lingering doubt in his mind is removed when the commanding general of the U.S. Tactical Air Command tells him that even a major surprise air attack could not be certain to destroy all the missile sites and nuclear weapons in Cuba.

Adlai Stevenson, down for the day, suggests a deal. He proposes that the President tell the Russians that if they withdraw their missiles from Cuba, the United States will withdraw its missiles from Turkey and give up the American naval base at Guantánamo Bay. The general reaction is vehemently negative, a bitter aftertaste of which will stay with Stevenson until his death.

Elsewhere progress is smooth. Alexis Johnson has turned out a master scenario schedule of everything which must be done before the President's 7 P.M. speech Monday—instructions to U.S. embassies abroad, congressional briefings, etc. Acheson, recalled, agrees to tell Macmillan, de Gaulle, and Adenauer. Edward Martin prepares for the OAS meeting. As detailed arrangements are made and legal justifications marshaled, however, more and more government officials are brought into the discussions. As a consequence, word that something big is coming has begun to seep through to the press. Too many trips have been canceled, too many announcements made for odd reasons, too many lights have been burning late in unexpected places, too many high officers in the government have failed to appear at dinner parties or, having appeared, have left, murmuring excuses. James Reston of the *New York Times* and Alfred Friendly, managing editor of the *Washington Post,* have begun to stalk the truth, and Reston has most of the essential facts. At the President's personal request, both agree to publish less than they know until Tuesday.

The Navy has deployed 180 ships in the Caribbean. The B-52 bomber force has been ordered into the air fully loaded with atomic weapons; as one plane lands, another immediately takes its place in the air. Late Saturday night the 1st Armored Division begins to move out of Texas headed for embarkation ports in Georgia. Five other divisions are placed on alert.

Sunday, October 21

A golden fall day. In the State Department forty-three letters to heads of government and to Mayor Willy Brandt, mayor of West Berlin, are drafted for the President's signature. In addition, the President is writing a letter to Khrushchev; it will be delivered with a copy of his speech. American embassies and consulates abroad are warned to prepare for demonstrations and riots. U.S. ambassadors will receive explanatory telegrams at 6 P.M. tomorrow, an hour before Kennedy speaks. The U.S. Passport Office opens on a Sunday for one traveler—Dean Acheson's passport must be validated.

The secret won't keep much longer. An air of crisis hangs over Washington. The entire press corps now knows that something is afoot. The *New York Herald Tribune* spikes the story at McNamara's request, but other papers may be expected to divulge it at any time; the British embassy has found out what is coming, and the rest of the diplomatic corps have begun checking rumors. Sunday evening Dean Rusk advises his staff to get some sleep. "Gentlemen," he says, "by this time tomorrow we will be in a flaming crisis."

Monday, October 22

At noon Salinger announces that the President will speak on television at 7 P.M. The topic will be "of the greatest urgency."

Lawrence F. O'Brien phones twenty congressional leaders of both parties; the President wants to see them at 5 P.M. Those who can't make it by commercial airlines are picked up by Air Force planes—in some cases, jet fighters. The meeting turns out to be the most difficult of the crisis for Kennedy. The leaders condemn the quarantine-blockade as too weak. He leaves the room in a rage. Later, with his brother, he is more philosophical, recalling that though the congressional reaction is now more militant than his, it is close to what his was when he first learned of the missiles six days ago.

The diplomatic orchestration is flawless. Following the master scenario, separate briefings are given to forty-six allied diplomats, to Latin American ambassadors, and to envoys from the emerging nations. De Gaulle tells Acheson, "It is exactly what I would have done." At 6 P.M. Rusk sees Dobrynin, the Soviet ambassador; twenty-five minutes later Dobrynin emerges grim and shaken. (U.S. officials will come to believe afterward that Dobrynin had not known of the missiles in Cuba.) In France Acheson lays the matter before the NATO leadership. Adlai Stevenson delivers to Zorin of the USSR a request to convene a special meeting of the Security Council to deal with "the dangerous threat to the peace and security of the world by the secret establishment in Cuba" of missiles "capable of carrying thermonuclear warheads to most of North and South America."

The initial response to these moves is heartening, even among the governments of neutral nations. The Russians appear stunned. Only one allied leader is suspicious of the Americans: John Diefenbaker of Canada.

Kennedy's speech begins at 7 P.M. on all TV channels and on the Spanish language network:

"Good evening, my fellow citizens. The Government, as promised, has maintained the closest surveillance of the Soviet military buildup on the island of Cuba. Within the past week, unmistakable evidence has established the fact that a series of offensive missile sites is now in preparation on that imprisoned island. The purpose of these bases can be none other than to provide a nuclear strike capability against the Western Hemisphere."

He recites the Russian assurances, now revealed as "deliberate deception," and pledges that it will be his "unswerving objectives" to remove the nuclear menace. The quarantine, he says, is only an initial step; it will be followed by stronger measures if that is necessary. The Organization of American States is meeting in emergency session to consider the threat, and U-2 flights over Cuba are being intensified. He warns Khrushchev: any missile launched from Cuba will be regarded as an attack by the Soviet Union on the United States, requiring full retaliatory response against the USSR. Any vessels attempting to run the blockade will be sunk by the U.S. Navy.

After his speech he is handed a confidential report from McNamara listing the resources being marshaled for further military action: warplanes capable of flying 2,000 sorties against targets in Cuba, 90,000 marines and paratroopers forming an invasion force, and 250,000 troops backing them up. An estimate of American casualties in the event of invasion puts the expected figure at over 25,000.

Unexpectedly, there is a light note in this. The Pentagon reports to the President that the Russians and Cubans have inexplicably lined up their planes wing tip to wing tip, ready to be destroyed, like the American planes at Pearl Harbor twenty-one years earlier. Kennedy asks General Taylor to put a U-2 photographic mission over the U.S. air bases in Florida. "It will be interesting if we have done the same thing," he says. We have. The Air Force hastily disperses them.

Tuesday, October 23

George Ball, who has spent the night in troubled sleep on his office couch, awakens to see Dean Rusk looking down on him, smiling for the first time in a week. "We have won a considerable victory," Rusk says. "You and I are still alive." The worst fears have not, in fact, materialized. The Russians have not bombed U.S. bases in the Middle East, blockaded Berlin, or moved to close the Dardanelles. Soviet strategy, whatever its intended thrust, has been checked by the President's challenge.

In Moscow there is no reaction for thirteen hours. Then the American ambassador there is handed a note accusing the United States of "piracy" and denying that the missiles in Cuba are intended for military purposes. The note is interpreted as betraying uncertainty; Khrushchev, caught off guard, appears to be playing for time to think things through. Even so, there is little time for maneuver. President Kennedy has signed the blockade proclamation; it will go into effect tomorrow morning. In it, contraband is defined as covering offensive missiles, their warheads and electronic equipment, and bomber aircraft. Already the Navy is tracking Russian submarines in the Caribbean. The twenty-five Soviet merchant ships on the way to Cuba have not changed course. They are receiving an extraordinary number of coded messages from Russia.

The Organization of American States meeting opens at 9 A.M., with Dean Rusk in the United States chair. The resolution supporting the quarantine must win fourteen Latin American votes, a two-thirds majority. Edward Martin believes that it will get exactly fourteen. The Secretary hopes that his participation will widen the margin. It does—a few minutes after five o'clock the measure carries unanimously, 18-0, with only Uruguay abstaining. The Russians are reported to be astounded. At the same time, American ambassadors in Jamaica and Trinidad, Guinea, and Senegal report success in excluding the possibility that Soviet warheads might be flown to Cuba; their host governments have agreed to deny landing rights for Soviet bloc planes on their way there. Still another encouraging word comes from the U.N.: Stevenson has the support of seven of the eleven nations on the Security Council.

At the President's request, Robert Kennedy calls on Ambassador Dobrynin at the Russian embassy. Dobrynin spreads his hands; as far as he knows, there are no missiles in Cuba. Back at the White House, Bobby learns that the President has shortened the line of interception for the quarantine from eight hundred miles to five hundred miles, giving the Russians more time. McNamara phones from the Pentagon—the latest U-2 photographs show work continuing on the sites in Cuba.

President Kennedy has begun to show the tension. He talks rapidly, in staccato bursts, and his eyes are screwed up tight, as though he is squinting at the sun. A telegram arrives from Bertrand Russell:

YOUR ACTION DESPERATE. . . . NO CONCEIVABLE JUSTIFICATION. WE WILL NOT HAVE MASS MURDER. . . . END THIS MADNESS. Kennedy replies, "I think your attention might well be directed to the burglars rather than to those who have caught the burglars."

Wednesday, October 24

Ten A.M.: the blockade line is drawn. Since Monday afternoon an American fleet, designated Task Force 136, has been racing at flank speed—27 knots—to close off all five navigable channels through which ships from the mid-Atlantic can approach Cuba. Now they have reached their stations in a great arc five hundred miles out to sea from the eastern tip of Cuba. On the forward picket line there are thirteen destroyers; then two cruisers, each flanked by two more cruisers—nineteen ships altogether. Bearing down on them are the twenty-five Russian merchantmen, each of which has been spotted by Navy reconnaissance planes. Two of the vessels, the *Gagarin* and the *Komiles,* are within a few miles of the picket line. A Russian submarine has moved into position between them. In Washington the Ex Comm awaits the first interception, probably before noon.

Aerial photographs from special low-level reconnaissance missions of Cuba, supplementing the U-2s, show that feverish work continues on the ground there. Eight to ten bases are situated near the cities of San Cristóbal, Remedios, Guanajay, and Sagua la Grande. Each base has about four launchers. At least thirty missiles with nuclear warheads are in Cuba, and there are over twenty crated IL-28 (Ilyushin) jet light bombers capable of delivering nuclear bombs on American or Latin American cities. In the new photos the launching pads, the missiles, and the nuclear storage bunkers are clearly defined. Within a few days several of the launching pads will be ready for war.

At the U.N., Secretary General U Thant sends identical letters to Kennedy and Khrushchev urging suspension of the blockade and arms shipments for two to three weeks. Kennedy refuses to negotiate until the Russians agree to dismantle and remove the missile bases. In Moscow William Knox, an American industrialist, is invited to the Kremlin, where he finds Khrushchev in a state of near-exhaustion. The Soviet premier says he has a message for Washington. He looks like a man who has not slept all night; at times he is almost incoherent; the message is unimportant.

On his way to an Ex Comm session President Kennedy says to

his brother, "It looks really mean, doesn't it? But then, really there was no other choice. If they get this mean on this one in our part of the world, what will they do on the next?" Bob tells him, "I just don't think there was any choice, and not only that, if you hadn't acted, you would have been impeached." The President says, "That's what I think—I would have been impeached."*

The first sign of hope comes at 10:32 A.M. Twenty Russian ships have stopped dead in the water. Six, then twelve, turn around. Rusk nudges Bundy and says softly, "We're eyeball to eyeball and I think the other fellow just blinked."

Thursday, October 25

At 8 A.M., twenty-two hours after the quarantine proclamation, the first interception of a Russian ship occurs at sea. She is the tanker *Bucharest*. Identifying herself by radio and declaring that her only cargo is petroleum, she is allowed to proceed through the line of American warships. At 8:35 A.M. the East German passenger ship *Völkerfreund*, carrying twenty students, also passes. The President has ordered that the captain of each vessel must be permitted sufficient time to consult Moscow.

The situation is still grave. In Cuba work on the missile sites continues at an extraordinarily rapid pace. The IL-28 bombers are also being uncrated and assembled. Kennedy keeps the pressure. To all offers of compromise he replies that the missiles and bombers must be removed; nothing else will do.

In the U.N. Security Council, Valerian Zorin makes the mistake of challenging Adlai Stevenson to produce evidence of the missiles. As millions of Americans watch—it is during the dinner hour—Stevenson turns on him with superb scorn. He says he has proof, but first he asks Zorin to deny that the missiles are there. "*Yes* or *no?*" he snaps. "Don't wait for the translation, *yes* or *no?*" Zorin says

---

* In *Thirteen Days* Robert Kennedy wrote that this Wednesday and the following Saturday were the worst days of the crisis. Of that moment when they were awaiting the naval confrontation at sea on Wednesday, Bob wrote: "I think these few minutes were the time of gravest concern for the President. Was the world on the brink of a holocaust? Was it our error? A mistake? . . . His hand went up to his face and covered his mouth. His face seemed drawn, his eyes pained, almost gray. We stared at each other across the table. For a few fleeting seconds, it was almost as though no one else was there and he was no longer the President. Inexplicably, I thought of when he was ill and almost died; when he lost his child; when we learned that our oldest brother had been killed; of personal times of strain and hurt."

he is not in an American courtroom. Stevenson says, "You are in the courtroom of world opinion right now and you can answer *yes* or *no*." Zorin, retreating, says, "You will have your answer in due course." Stevenson closes in: "I am prepared to wait for my answer until hell freezes over, if that's your decision. And I am also prepared to present the evidence in this room." With that, he unveils easels which have been shrouded, revealing blown-up photos of the sites.

Friday, October 26

At 7 A.M. the American destroyer *Joseph P. Kennedy Jr.*, hails the freighter *Marulca* in the open sea about 180 miles northeast of Nassau. The *Kennedy* hoists the international signal "Oscar November," meaning "Heave to," and the *Marulca* does so. In less than an hour an armed boarding party of American sailors is searching her. There is no contraband; the ship is allowed to continue. The inference, which is encouraging, is that Moscow has instructed Soviet captains to submit to searches.

Nevertheless the Ex Comm is glum. In Cuba the Russians continue to work feverishly. The first missiles will be ready for firing in a matter of hours. At a White House press conference Salinger takes note of this and observes that the Soviet technicians are clearly trying to achieve "full operational capability as soon as possible." A State Department spokesman says ominously that if this continues, "further action" by the President "will be justified." Robert Kennedy tells Ambassador Dobrynin that the President cannot hold off more than forty-eight hours.

The first real break in the crisis comes at 1:30 P.M. It is highly unconventional. John Scali, a TV commentator who covers the State Department for the American Broadcasting Company, receives a telephone call from an acquaintance at the Soviet embassy. The caller is Alexander S. Fomin, a counselor at the embassy who is believed to be a colonel in the KGB, the Soviet secret police. Scali says he is busy. Fomin, highly agitated, says, "It's very important. Meet me at the Occidental in ten minutes." At the Occidental Restaurant on Pennsylvania Avenue, Fomin says he wants to know whether the State Department would discuss an agreement with three provisions: the removal of the missiles in Cuba under U.N. supervision, a promise from Castro to accept no offensive weapons in the future, and an American pledge not to invade Cuba. Scali says he will find out. At 7:35 the two men meet again in the coffee shop of the Statler Hilton. Scali, having talked to Rusk, informs the Russian that the United States government is definitely interested. Fomin rushes off.

At 6 P.M. (1 A.M. in Moscow) a long, emotional letter from Khrushchev starts coming through over the teletype linking the State Department with the American embassy in Moscow. The Soviet premier acknowledges for the first time that there are Russian missiles in Cuba. His proposal, he says, is this: no more weapons will go to Cuba, and those within Cuba will be either withdrawn or destroyed if Kennedy agrees not to attack Cuba. Essentially, these are Fomin's terms. At 10 P.M. the Ex Comm meets to consider the offer. The decision is to accept it as though it were a formal note and reply in the morning, pending a careful examination during the night by Kremlinologists at the State Department. The Fomin conditions will be studied at the same time. For the first time in ten days the President goes to bed believing that a peaceful solution may be found.

Saturday, October 27

The height of the crisis. Even as the reply to Khrushchev is being drafted, Radio Moscow broadcasts a second Khrushchev letter to Kennedy. This one is unacceptable. As a condition for withdrawal of the missiles he demands that NATO missile bases in Turkey be dismantled. The Ex Comm has already weighed the possibility of such a swap and rejected it. Though the bases in Turkey now have little military value (and will, in fact, be phased out soon), the Turks regard them as symbols of the American commitment. To bargain away the weapons of an ally in exchange for the security of the United States would, it is believed, shake, and perhaps shatter, the western alliance. This second letter is different in more than content; it lacks Khrushchev's style, and reads as though drafted by a committee. The FBI reports that Soviet diplomats in New York are preparing to destroy their documents. The bridges to sanity seem to be crumbling. On top of this there is another blow. An American U-2 pilot is shot down over Cuba, meaning that the SAM bases on the missile sites are operational; the missiles themselves will be next. The Joint Chiefs join the Ex Comm meeting. They recommend an air strike Monday, to be followed by an invasion of Cuba. With one exception the Ex Comm believes that there is no other course. The exception is the President. He says: "It isn't the first step that concerns me . . . but both sides escalating to the fourth and fifth step—and we don't go to the sixth because there is no one around to do so. We must remind ourselves we are embarking on a very hazardous course."

Robert Kennedy sees a way out. He proposes that they ignore the second letter and answer the first. Various drafts along these lines are submitted by Dean Rusk, George Ball, McGeorge Bundy, and Llewellyn Thompson. Bob doesn't like any of them. His brother tells him, "If you disagree so violently, go draft one yourself." Bob and Ted Sorensen leave the meeting to do just that. By choosing the terms they like best in each of the two letters and in the Fomin proposal, they agree to a proposal Khrushchev never made. The President approves it, sends it to Khrushchev at 8:05 P.M.—and tells the world he has accepted the Russian conditions. Bob then phones Dobrynin and asks him to come to the Justice Department. He tells the Soviet ambassador that they are running out of time. Only a few hours are left. The President must have a reply the next day. Dobrynin is pessimistic; the Kremlin, he says, is deeply committed to Castro.

At the White House the President remarks that the outcome seems to him to be touch and go, that it can now go "either way." McNamara, glancing at the sky on his way back to the Pentagon, wonders aloud how many more sunsets he will see. Thompson tells his wife that if he does not come home, he will let her know where she and the children will join him should the capital be evacuated.

Sunday, October 28

Another magnificent October day. A few minutes before 9 A.M. (4 P.M. in the Russian capital) Radio Moscow announces that an important announcement will be broadcast on the hour. This is the very last chance for peace. If Khrushchev rejects Kennedy's terms the American attack will go in. McNamara's estimate of U.S. casualties is now 40,000 to 50,000.

The Soviet announcer begins reading the Russian answer. The key to it is in the third paragraph:

> In order to eliminate as rapidly as possible the conflict which endangers the cause of peace . . . the Soviet government . . . has given a new order to dismantle the arms which you described as offensive, and to crate and return them to the Soviet Union.

Castro, who has not been consulted, declares that he has been betrayed, that he will ignore the settlement. But while he can delay the end of the crisis, he cannot stop it; though the missiles are on Cuban soil, they are in Russian hands, and there are no Cubans who know how to fire them anyhow. At 1:30 P.M. the Joint Chiefs signal Task Force 136: there will be no more boarding of ships, no show of force. The Ex Comm is jubilant, but the President speaks of how difficult it must have been for Khrushchev to back down; he warns them that there must be no claims of an American victory. He writes the Soviet premier a careful letter ending:

> I think we should give priority to questions relating to the pro-liferation of nuclear weapons, on earth and outer space, and to the great effort for a nuclear test ban.

That evening the Kennedy brothers review the thirteen days of crisis. At the end the President says, "Maybe this is the night I should go to the theater." Both of them laugh uproariously. Then Bob says, "If you go, I want to go with you."

Portrait of an American

PETER CARL GOLDMARK

BORN IN BUDAPEST on December 2, 1906, he was one of that genera-tion of brilliant Hungarian scientists which included Edward Teller, John von Neumann, and Eugene Paul Wigner. But while they dedi-cated their talents to the technology of death, he became a leader in the communications revolution. They gave America the Bomb. He gave it the long-playing record, color television, and the promise of a whole new world of sight and sound.

His was a creative family. One great-uncle, Karl Goldmark, was one of the nineteenth century's most gifted composers of opera. Another great-uncle, Joseph Goldmark, discovered red phosphorus, essential to the manufacture of kitchen matches. Joseph defied the government of Austria-Hungary, fled to America, fought in the Civil War, and contributed to the defeat of Lee by inventing a new kind of percussion cap for the Union Army.

Peter was a precocious child. Showing the Joseph in him, he exasperated his parents by taking over the family bathroom for his experiments, and before the onset of adolescence he had assembled a huge motion-picture projector. Later in his youth he told his teachers that he had found a mistake in a paper by Britain's most celebrated physicist, Ernest Rutherford. They were amused—until he reconstructed the experiment for them and proved himself right.

In a magazine he read an article by an eccentric Scotch stocking salesman, John Logie Baird, who devised a primitive television system in the early 1920s, convinced the Royal Society that it would work, and talked the BBC into transmitting experimental broadcasts. The article told how to assemble a receiver and advertised a kit. Peter sent for one. Years afterward he described the result: "The picture came through in postage-stamp size. You could hardly make it out, it flickered so. It was also in color—all red. But it was the most exciting thing in my life."

It remained so. He took an engineering degree at the Berliner Technische Hochschule and a doctorate in physics at the University of Vienna, where he displayed the Karl Goldmark in him at a series of concerts in which he performed as a pianist and cellist. But Baird had captured his imagination; his dissertation, "A New Method for Determining the Velocity of Ions," which he read before the Academy of Science in Vienna, laid much of the groundwork for television projection. When his faculty advisers urged him to continue as a physicist, he politely declined, packed his cello, and sailed for England.

Hired by Pye Radio, Ltd., in Cambridge, he built a mechanical TV transmitter. Although it worked, the Pye studios seemed indifferent to its possibilities, and after two years he left Cambridge with savings of $250 and boarded a boat for New York. There he applied for American citizenship and a job at RCA. To the subsequent chagrin of David Sarnoff, Sarnoff's underlings at NBC turned the slight Hungarian scientist away. CBS then hired him.

The next thing Peter's new superiors knew, he was glimpsed atop the Chrysler Building putting up a television antenna. Four relatively fallow years followed. Then, while visiting Canada in the spring of 1940, he happened to drop in at a theater showing the

Technicolor *Gone With the Wind*. Stunned by the beauty of the color, he said later, he came away with "an inferiority feeling about television in black and white." He developed color television in just three months.

His color system was built around a revolving disc with transparent color segments of green, blue, and red. The disc spun in front of the camera tube. When a picture representing, for example, the green in a scene was being sent out, the green transparency was in front of the camera; in the viewer's set another spinning disc, synchronized with the one in the camera, turned the picture into the right color, and the colors followed each other so rapidly that the viewer's eye mixed them together. In August 1940 Peter put on a demonstration for CBS executives. They saw an experimental set project, in succession, a lovely zinnia, black-eyed Susans, red sails in a sunset, a brunette with a red scarf, a blonde chasing a colorful beach ball into surf, and at the end—like a vaudeville show—an American flag waving in a spanking breeze.

Then war intervened. Peter led a team of engineers making devices to jam Nazi radar. In 1945 he turned again to color television. When the FCC held trials at the end of the decade, his pictures were beautiful, while RCA's, to the humiliation of David Sarnoff, showed green monkeys eating blue bananas. The FCC adopted the CBS system. Sarnoff hired a hundred expensive technicians, gave them a budget of 130 million dollars, and told them to develop better color. Meanwhile Peter came up with an improvement of his own called the shadow-mask tube. The FCC approved of RCA color, but RCA needed the shadow-mask tube for proper color projection—and had to pay CBS royalties for it. Later the Soviet Union and NASA's Apollo flights used Peter's original system.

One postwar evening he and several friends were listening to a record of Horowitz playing Brahms. "Suddenly," as he recalled afterward, "there was a click. The most horrible sound man ever invented, right in the middle of the music. Somebody rushed to change records. The mood was broken. I knew right there and then I had to stop that sort of thing."

After three years he had the 33⅓ rpm microgroove record as we know it, stamped from Vinylite to reduce surface noise. The old 78 rpm records had from 85 to 100 grooves to an inch; Peter increased this to from 224 to 300, which meant that 45 minutes of music could be played on the two sides of a 12-inch record—a whole concerto, or an entire symphony. Sarnoff announced that RCA had a 45-rpm record and ridiculed the notion that a slower speed was needed. But Columbia's first LP album was a tremendous success, offering everything from Bach to Harry James at prices ranging from $2.85 for a 10-inch popular disc to $4.85 for one of its 12-inch Masterworks, and RCA's challenge failed.

By Peter's fiftieth birthday CBS had assigned one executive to be his full-time factotum. (He was known as the "Vice President in Charge of Peter.") Then Peter was designated president of CBS laboratories, and the network built a workshop for him on a grassy knoll overlooking a Stamford thoroughfare not far from his home. Stanton later said, "The smartest thing we ever did was to build Peter a lab in the country to play with." From it CBS acquired patents on over a hundred of his inventions. One was the Reverbatron, which reproduces the vibrations of a large concert hall, adding depth to sound. Others included a record player for the blind and a miniature color television camera to transmit pictures for surgeons from inside the stomach, developed by Peter in one of his several roles—professor of medical electronics at the University of Pennsylvania. Perhaps his most extraordinary creation was EVR (Electronic Video Recording), a tiny device enabling the viewer to play programs on his home set without commercials—a seven-inch reel of tiny film covering a half-hour of color or an hour of black-and-white that would drop in place like a phonograph record and rewind automatically when finished.

In suburban Connecticut legends about him accumulated: stories of his musical evenings with Benny Goodman, a neighbor; his chess playing; his fantastic LP library; the speakers cunningly concealed about his house which could convert it into a church, with a choir singing in every corner. If a secretary came to work late and said her car was defective, Peter would repair it on the spot. Fastidious about his own Mercedes-Benz, he would clean up after the filling station attendants who serviced it. And he worked all hours, calling assistants at 3 A.M. or 5 A.M., saying, "Just thought of something, meet me at the lab," and hanging up.

There were tales about his temper, too. Yet he was one of the few scientists of his time with a social conscience, finding work for jobless blacks, heading the Stamford antipoverty office, and putting in long hours crusading for the use of educational television in public schools. He gave Stamford's Riverview Elementary School a complete television studio. Thanks in part to his efforts, by the time he retired in 1971 the teachers in nearly one-third of American schools were using film strips, projectors, or other visual teaching aids.

It was a measure of Peter's genius that CBS was very nervous about his retirement. The network offered him $75,000 a year for ten years to do nothing. He refused. Instead he threw his vast energies into a scheme for establishing as many as forty coast-to-coast TV channels by uniting domestic satellites and cable television. In his vision of the future there were nationwide chains of movie theaters of the air, free TV access to the voters for campaigning politicians, home instruction for students, and national facsimile newspapers delivered through television sets.

Once in the late 1960s a radio interviewer asked him whether he thought mental telepathy would ever replace TV. Peter paused, adjusted his glasses, and said it was conceivable that undiscovered radiation from the brain might be used someday. He added: "But that's a long way off."

There was a protracted silence in the studio. With Peter you couldn't be sure.

Twenty-nine

DON'T LET IT BE FORGOT

N OW IN THE THIRD YEAR of the Kennedy Presidency a fundamental change loomed in the character of the civil rights
movement. Beginning with the Montgomery bus boycott in 1955
and extending through Little Rock, the freedom rides, and Oxford,
Mississippi, the struggle for racial equality had been in the form of
a serial drama, with whites in the role of bullies and blacks as martyrs. The conscience of the nation's great white middle class had
been aroused, and its indignation had become a solvent eroding
barriers of law and custom which had endured for generations. But
that era was about to end. Angrier, fiercer, more headstrong blacks
were fighting their way to the center of the stage. The established
black leadership was discovering that young Negroes were approaching the end of their patience. The emergence of the eye for
an eye trend foreshadowed a new, darker period in the struggle for
integration, but first there were a few more episodes in the serial
to be played out. The bully who made black martyrs best was the
police commissioner of Birmingham, T. Eugene "Bull" Connor, who
had first come to the nation's attention during the freedom rides.
Two years had passed; he was about to assume a star role.

Martin Luther King had called Birmingham "the most segregated
city in the United States." Connor liked to quote him on that; he
wore his bigotry like a badge of pride. For twenty-three years the
commissioner had used terror and brutality to cow Negro leaders,
always with success. Not only were Birmingham's schools completely segregated; so were its public toilets, drinking fountains,
theaters, parks, playgrounds, restaurants, and even churches. Fed-

eral rulings prohibiting discrimination did not intimidate Bull Connor. To him they were just contrivances for disrupting law and order in Birmingham and, as such, opposition to be ruthlessly crushed. Until the spring of 1963 civil rights leaders tried to stay clear of him; he was running for mayor, and racial demonstrations would merely give him more white votes. In April the election was over. He had lost, which made him meaner, but they were ready for him.

King's campaign opened April 2 with sit-ins and marches. Connor retaliated swiftly, arresting over four hundred Negroes on charges of parading without a permit, loitering, or trespassing. King then sent groups to worship in white churches, defying the police to seize them there. Connor refused to be drawn. He counted on Birmingham's white Christians to draw the color line, and most of them did; four churches admitted the Negroes, seventeen turned them away. King called for a protest march on Good Friday, April 12. Connor obtained an injunction forbidding it. Burke Marshall urged the black leaders hold off until the inauguration of Albert Boutwell, the moderate mayor-elect. Little could be expected from Arthur Hanes, the outgoing mayor, who said of Robert Kennedy, "I hope that every drop of blood that's spilled he tastes in his throat, and I hope he chokes on it," and of King, "This nigger has got the blessing of the Attorney General and the White House." But the black leadership had no choice. Their people were ready to march without them. The demonstrations were held in defiance of the injunction, and the inevitable arrests, including King's, followed.

On May 2 about five hundred Negroes were locked up—high school students, most of them, carried to jail in school buses. Other students paraded in protest the next day. White spectators pelted them with brickbats and bottles. King held a mass meeting in the New Pilgrim Baptist Church to protest; a thousand blacks came, and Connor threw police lines around the church. There were no incidents then, but when twenty-five hundred Negroes surged into downtown Birmingham the following day in another demonstration, Connor met them with police dogs and fire hoses. The dogs were trained to rip clothing with their teeth, and the hoses, with 700 pounds of pressure, smashed the blacks against buildings or to the ground. On May 4 newspaper readers around the world were shocked by a brutal photograph showing a huge, snarling dog lunging at a frightened Negro woman. President Kennedy said the picture made him "sick," and he said, "I can well understand why the Negroes of Birmingham are tired of being asked to be patient." An ADA delegation asked him to intervene, but at this point there was little he could do under the Constitution. He did send Burke Marshall down to open the channels of communications. In quiet talks with Birmingham businessmen Marshall negotiated a fragile truce which lasted five days. On May 11 the home of a Negro leader and a desegregated hotel were bombed. The next day, Mother's Day, enraged blacks again erupted into the streets, and this time they were too much for the policemen, the dogs and the hoses. After a night of riots and fires Connor asked the new governor, George C. Wallace, for reinforcements.

This was the first the rest of the nation heard of Wallace. He had been expecting something of this sort, and he was ready with a motley force—seven hundred deputy sheriffs, game wardens, liquor agents, and highway patrolmen. Shouting threats, they stomped around the city shoving blacks into doorways and snapping the safety catches of their guns menacingly. The blacks weren't surprised. They distrusted Wallace, and with good reason; he had already told the press that he would use the power of his office to suppress King. Of Marshall's truce he said that he would not be party to any "compromise on the issues of segregation." It was his avowed purpose to sabotage Marshall, and the only thing that stopped him was the decision of President Kennedy to fly three thousand troops to an air base near Birmingham. "This government," the President said, "will do whatever must be done to preserve order, to protect the lives of its citizens, and to uphold the law of the land." Any misuse of force by the governor's officers now would bring in an overwhelming counterforce. Mayor Hanes denounced "bayonet brotherhood." Wallace, furious, filed suit with the Supreme Court, charging that the President's action was "unconstitutional and void." The governor said, "This military dictatorship must be nipped in the bud." The Justice Department quietly replied that as commander in chief of the nation's armed forces the President could move troops to any base he wished.

Marshall reconciled the black and white leaders once more, and this time a lasting peace returned to the littered but integrated streets of Birmingham. The outcome was clearly another triumph for Martin Luther King. Its implications were discernible far beyond the city; again the conscience of the country's white middle class had been stirred, and elsewhere protesting Negroes were marching in Selma, Alabama; Albany, Georgia; Cambridge, Maryland; Raleigh and Greensboro, North Carolina; Nashville and Clinton, Tennessee; Shreveport, Louisiana; Jackson and Philadelphia, Mississippi; and, in the north, in Chicago. "The fires of frustration and discord," the President said, "are burning in every city . . . where legal remedies are not at hand." In a phrase which would be remembered, Ken O'Donnell predicted "a long, hot summer." Before autumn ended fourteen thousand demonstrators would be in southern jails.

The next chapter in Wallace's burgeoning gubernatorial career put him in the path of Attorney General Kennedy. Robert Kennedy didn't want the conflict, and in the beginning he thought it might be avoidable. He had come to believe that the Mississippi crisis might have ended differently if he had cultivated Ross Barnett earlier. He hoped to do better with Wallace, though the prospects could hardly have been called auspicious. Not only had Wallace been elected as a racist; it had been, and still was, his only issue. In his campaign he had repeatedly vowed to stand in the doorway of any white Alabama school to drive away Negro children, and he had ended his florid inaugural address with the incendiary passage: "In the name of the greatest people that have ever trod on this earth, I draw the line in the dust and toss the gauntlet before the feet of tyranny. And I say: Segregation now! Segregation tomorrow! Segregation forever!" Still, Bob Kennedy thought a man-to-man exchange with him might prevent future grief. The fact that he thought that is curious. Demagogues have never been responsive to the voices of reason, and Bob's manner did not encourage moderation in those who differed with him. But he never saw himself as others saw him. He thought he might bring George Wallace around to his way of thinking.

His suit bogged down from the very beginning. Like his predecessor in Montgomery's executive mansion, Wallace was almost impossible to reach from Washington by telephone. Intermediaries arranged a meeting, and Bob did everything he could to make it seem casual, even scheduling other appointments in Alabama to make it seem one of many calls there. But Wallace had other ideas. He wanted his constituents fully informed about his battles for white supremacy, and to that end he did everything but greet the attorney general at the airport with a band playing "Dixie." The statehouse was ringed by state troopers. Pickets carried placards reading: CHRISTIANS AWAKE, "COME OUT FROM AMONGST THEM AND BE YE SEPARATE," and KOSHER TEAM: KENNEDY KASTRO KHRUSHCHEV. The place where Jefferson Davis was sworn in as President of the Confederacy was marked by a fresh wreath, and a Daughter of the Confederacy clad in spotless white stood guard there with folded arms, presumably to prevent Kennedy from defiling it. Inside, Wallace greeted him by turning on a tape recorder "as a precaution." It was a waste of electricity; nothing of substance was said. The most urgent racial problem in Alabama, which Bob hoped Wallace would share with him, arose from court orders ruling that the state university must admit black applicants. Over and over he told Wallace that the law must be enforced, that it was their sworn duty to do so; over and over Wallace said that this would mean violence and that the blood would be on Kennedy's hands. At the end of the conference the governor called in the press to announce that nothing which had been said altered his vow to stand in the schoolhouse door. Kennedy said he hoped local authorities would discourage mob violence. Ed Guthman, who was with him, thought that "Bob was dumbfounded by Wallace's attitude. It was the closest I ever saw him come to throwing up his hands in despair."

The Kennedys were determined to prevent another Oxford. They had the campus photographed with the same reconnaissance planes which had been used over Cuba, and troop commanders used the photos to map maneuvers. Flying down to Muscle Shoals, the President spoke from the same platform as Wallace and elliptically warned him not to defy the law. Again the governor told reporters that his mind was unchanged. They were moving rapidly toward confrontation. Under the terms of a court order three Negroes had been declared eligible for the university's summer term, beginning June 10, one of them to an extension course and two to the main campus at Tuscaloosa. These two, Vivian J. Malone and Jimmy A. Hood, were in the same situation as James Meredith twenty months earlier. Wallace, more audacious than Barnett, announced that he intended not only to bar Hood and Miss Malone from the Tuscaloosa campus; he also meant to force federal officers to arrest Alabama's governor. After a U.S. District Court enjoined him with interfering with their enrollment, he declared: "The action I am going to take involves even my personal freedom, but I intend to carry it out, regardless of what risk I take."

As Bob Kennedy's deputy, Nick Katzenbach was again cast in his difficult Oxford role, leading the federal officers at Tuscaloosa. In the name of states' rights Wallace had mobilized his seven hundred deputy sheriffs, game wardens, liquor agents, and state troopers, plus several National Guard companies. Unlike Barnett, Wallace wasn't taking university administrators into his confidence. They didn't know whether he planned to seal off the campus, issue guns, or what. The situation had comic aspects. The administrators reported to Katzenbach that Al Lingo, the state patrol chief, had painted a white line on the pavement in front of Foster Auditorium, where students would register. Wallace was occupying an office just inside the entrance. He had installed two air-conditioners, and there, as the sweating deputy attorney general tried to guess what he was up to, the bantam governor of Alabama sat coolly reading the *Montgomery Advertiser*. In the White House the President and his brother listened to Katzenbach's running analysis on an open telephone line and watched events develop on television.

They decided to let Wallace have his show. Katzenbach's plan, which was adopted, was to make the governor look ridiculous by robbing his doorway stand of meaning. Katzenbach would drive Miss Malone and Hood to the campus. Parking the car and leaving them in it, he would confront Wallace himself, telling the governor that going through the door was unimportant, that the government considered the two students enrolled, and that they would begin classes in the morning. The President would federalize the 31st National Guard division if Wallace continued to obstruct them.

That is more or less what happened. Katzenbach told the press that the two blacks would arrive at 10 A.M. Wallace appeared at 9:53 escorted by towering state policemen in combat gear—helmets, side arms, gas guns, and truncheons. When Katzenbach and the two Negroes drove up, accompanied by marshals in mufti, Wallace's public relations man darted out with a lectern and put it in front of the white line. The temperature was almost 100 degrees. The heat seemed to rise from the pavement in waves, and reporters and troopers tried to crowd in the building's shadow as Wallace took his stand. He raised his right arm like a traffic policeman. Katzenbach walked up with a marshal on either side and halted in front of him. He said, "I have a proclamation from the President of the United States ordering you to cease and desist from unlawful obstructions." Wallace replied by reading a proclamation of his own excoriating "the unwelcome, unwarranted and force-induced intrusion upon the campus of the University of Alabama of the might of the central government." He concluded: "Now, therefore I, George C. Wallace, as governor . . . do hereby denounce and forbid this illegal and unwarranted action by the central government."

Arms folded, Katzenbach answered mildly that all this was about two students who simply sought an education—"a simple problem scarcely worth this kind of attention." He asked the governor to reconsider, and, when Wallace refused to reply, he returned to the car and drove the two Negroes to dormitories which the administration had already assigned to them. Four hours later a brigadier general in the National Guard drove up. He saluted Wallace, who saluted back; he told him that the Guard had been federalized and asked him to "please stand aside so that the order of the court may be accomplished." After a last bitter volley at Yankee justice Wallace walked away.

The Kennedys thought he had been made to look ludicrous, and that the country would see his posturing for the absurdity it was. Millions of Americans agreed, and since more than three hundred blacks enrolled in the university after Hood and Malone without incident—indeed, without a word or even a glance from the statehouse—it appeared that the governor had been outwitted. George Wallace didn't see it that way, however, and neither did his admirers. He declared, "I stood eyeball to eyeball with them and they turned back." So they had, on television; all that viewers of the news had seen was the exchange of statements between him and Katzenbach and Katzenbach's departure. The registration of the two blacks had occurred off camera, and Wallace, then an underrated politician, had seen that in the eyes of the easily manipulated, his show in apparently staring down a federal official would carry more weight. In his book *Wallace* Marshall Frady wrote that the Alabama governor had "discovered a dark, silent, brooding mass of people whom no one—the newspapers, the political leaders, the intellectuals—no one but Wallace had suspected were there."

The race issue had emerged as one of the great themes of the 1960s. Already the civil rights movement was being described as revolutionary. In a televised speech on the evening of that June 10, the day of the Wallace-Katzenbach confrontation, President Kennedy called it "a moral issue"—"as old as the Scriptures and . . .

as clear as the American Constitution." "A great change is at hand," he said, "and our task, our obligation, is to make that revolution, that change, peaceful and constructive for all." To that end he was asking Congress to enact a broad, sweeping civil rights bill committing it to the premise "that race has no place in American life or law."

Medgar Evers was returning that night to his home in Jackson, Mississippi, after attending a civil rights rally in a church. As the NAACP field secretary in that state, Evers had been James Meredith's friend and adviser, and that had marked him for Klansmen and the state's White Citizens' Councils. As he walked from his car he was murdered by a sniper lying in ambush. Discouraged and gloomy, the President said to Arthur Schlesinger, "I don't understand the South. I'm coming to believe that Thaddeus Stevens was right. I had always been taught to regard him as a man of vicious bias. But when I see this sort of thing I begin to wonder how else you can treat them."

When civil rights leaders told him that they were planning an enormous peaceful demonstration in Washington, he was appalled. "We want success in Congress," he said, "not just a big show." He was afraid it might get out of hand, or create "an atmosphere of intimidation." A. Philip Randolph, head of the Brotherhood of Sleeping Car Porters, answered him. The march was Randolph's idea. He had proposed it to Franklin Roosevelt twenty years earlier, and Roosevelt, equally apprehensive, had promised to establish a federal Committee on Fair Employment Practices if Randolph would call it off.* That had been the end of it then, but this time Randolph was determined to go ahead. "The Negroes are already in the streets," he said. "It is very likely impossible to get them off." He argued that it would be better that they be led by responsible leaders than by others who would exploit them and encourage violence.

The March on Washington, held on August 28, was a high point for those who believed that the grievances of the blacks could be redressed by working within the system. "We subpoenaed the conscience of the nation," Martin Luther King said. Nothing like it had ever been seen in the country—over two hundred thousand Americans, the largest crowd ever to gather in the capital, and all of them orderly. Most were Negroes, but thousands of whites came, too, led

* See Vol. I, page 297.

by Walter Reuther. They sang hymns and spirituals, and "We shall overcome," and they carried placards reading: EFFECTIVE CIVIL RIGHTS LAWS—NOW! INTEGRATED SCHOOLS—NOW! DECENT HOUSING—NOW!

Their self-discipline was a marvel. The District's fifty-nine hundred policemen had nothing to do but direct traffic; four thousand soldiers and marines who were standing by were never called. While the march was in progress the President received its leaders—among them King, Randolph, Reuther, Roy Wilkins, Whitney M. Young, Jr., Chairman John Lewis of the Student Nonviolent Coordinating Committee, and Floyd B. McKissick of CORE. Kennedy said he had been "impressed with the deep fervor and the quiet dignity" of the demonstration. They left and he watched the rest of it on television. The most memorable moment came when Martin Luther King spoke at the Lincoln Memorial:

"I have a dream that one day this nation will rise up, live out the true meaning of its creed: 'We hold these truths to be self-evident, that all men are created equal.' I have a dream that one day on the red hills of Georgia sons of former slaves and the sons of former slaveowners will be able to sit down together at the table of brotherhood. I have a dream that one day even the state of Mississippi, a state sweltering with the heat of injustice . . . will be transformed into an oasis of freedom and justice. I have a dream that my four little children will one day live in a nation where they will not be judged by the color of their skin but by the content of their character."

"Dream some more!" cried his delighted listeners. Yet there were other Americans who were not delighted. Ward leaders in the great ethnic neighborhoods of the northern cities, keystones in the Democratic coalition Roosevelt had built, were stirring angrily. The Poles, the Irish, and the Italians, all of whom had given Kennedy wide margins in the election three years earlier, had struggled up from the bottom without the help of the government. Negroes, they argued, should do the same. They pointed out that congressmen who urged integration had withdrawn their own children from Washington classrooms and put them in private schools, and that a California study reportedly showed that outspoken liberals privately opposed Negroes in their schools and neighborhoods. A Lou Harris survey revealed that the administration's handling of the race issue had alienated over four million Democrats. In the South, naturally, the deterioration was greatest. "K.O. the Kennedys" was a political slogan in Mississippi. The governor of moderate North Carolina said that if an election were held then, Kennedy would lose it, and in Birmingham a Lubell poll found only one white voter who had supported Kennedy and didn't regret it.

The tragic fact is that this was a reaction to what had been, on the whole, exemplary black behavior. White Americans who were offended by the rhetoric of Martin Luther King and who thought James Meredith uppity were in for a shock. The same Negroes they regarded as upstarts were being called Uncle Toms by some black audiences. In Harlem young Negroes threw eggs at King, and in Chicago they booed Meredith. Their new heroes were Muslim leaders Jeremiah X, Malcolm X, and Elijah Mohammed, who preached the innate wickedness of the white race and dismissed nonviolence as folly. "The day of nonviolent resistance is over," Malcolm X told them. "If they have the Ku Klux Klan nonviolent, I'll be nonviolent. If they make the White Citizens' Councils nonviolent, I'll be nonviolent. But as long as you've got somebody else not being nonviolent, I don't want anybody coming to me talking any nonviolent talk."

The first administration figure to encounter the new blacks was Robert Kennedy. He was impressed by a James Baldwin article in the *New Yorker* in which Baldwin wrote of the Negro's past of:

> . . . rope, fire, torture, castration, infanticide, rape; death and humiliation; fear by day and night, fear as deep as the marrow of the bone; doubt that he was worthy of life, since everyone around him denied it; sorrow for his women, for his kinfolk, for his children, who needed his protection, and whom he could not protect; rage, hatred and murder, hatred for white men so deep that it often turned against him and his own and made all love, all trust, all joy impossible.

Baldwin believed that "the price of the liberation of the white people is the liberation of the blacks," and he quoted a Negro spiritual: *"God gave Noah the rainbow sign:/ No more water, the fire next time!"*

The comedian Dick Gregory suggested to Burke Marshall that the attorney general ought to meet Baldwin. Marshall passed the recommendation along, and the two men had breakfast together at Hickory Hill. Their talk was brief but amiable, and Kennedy proposed that they continue it in New York the next day in his father's

Manhattan apartment. Burke Marshall would be with him. They wanted opinions about what the government should be doing, and they hoped that other blacks would join them. Baldwin said he would bring Kenneth B. Clark, the psychologist; Lorraine Hansberry, the writer; Lena Horne, Harry Belafonte, and Jerome Smith, a twenty-four-year-old CORE chairman who had been beaten and jailed during the freedom rides. Kennedy expected a serious discussion, the kind of talks he had had with Roy Wilkins and Martin Luther King. The first thing he got was a tirade from Smith, who said that being in the same room with Bob Kennedy made him feel like vomiting. From then on the meeting deteriorated.

Kennedy tried to explain what the government had done and was doing, and what its new bill would do. They didn't care. Baldwin didn't even know that a presidential civil rights message was before Congress. He said that the only reason the President had acted in Alabama was that a white man had been stabbed, and when Marshall protested that he had consulted Martin Luther King, they burst into laughter. This went on for three hours. Bob said afterward, "It was all emotion, hysteria. They stood up and orated. They cursed. Some of them wept and walked out of the room." Toward the end of it a young black said that he would not fight for the United States, and when Bob asked how he could say such a thing the youth repeated it.

The irony was that Bob's reason for coming to New York was to confer with several chain store executives over ways to end Jim Crow in their southern stores. That didn't impress the angry blacks either, and another attorney general might have become disenchanted with them. This one was different. He was resentful at the time; back in Washington, repeating the remark about refusing to defend the country, he added wonderingly, "Imagine anyone saying that." But later in the week he said thoughtfully, "I guess if I were in his shoes, if I'd gone through what he's gone through, I might feel differently about this country." It was the beginning of his real conversion to the movement, the realization that a rage that deep must have profound origins, and that if nothing was done about it the consequence would in fact be a fire next time.

On May 29 the President became forty-six years old. His staff had planned a surprise birthday party for him, getting him to it on the pretext that a call awaited him on the scramble phone in the situation room, but not much surprised this President, and he was grinning broadly when Mac Bundy led him into the White House mess. Pierre Salinger, the emcee, handed Kennedy a speech. "We know you usually write your speeches, Mr. President," he said, "but here is one written by a ghost writer, and we would like you to read it." It began, "Twoscore and six years ago there was brought forth at Brookline, Massachusetts . . ." Kennedy was handed a satellite model with a card reading, "Hope you have a good trip, Barry," and Jackie, teasing her husband over his pride in the new flower garden outside his office, gave him an enormous basket of dead grass. "From the White House Historical Society," the card read, "Genuine Antique Grass from the Antique Rose Garden." The evening was lovely. They spent it cruising down the Potomac in the presidential yacht, the *Honey Fitz*.

It was high tide for the Kennedy regime, but they didn't know that. They thought they had another five years in the White House, and when the President moved out he planned to start a new Washington newspaper. It would be a great one; the best newspapermen in the country would want to work for it. But that was a long way off, and they were not of an age to brood about the future. Youth continued to be a dominant theme in the administration. Their life-style in many ways was that of what were then called "the young marrieds." The three Kennedy wives, Jackie, Ethel, and Joan, were all pregnant that spring. Baby carriages and playpens had become familiar furniture in the homes of senior government officials who, in other years, would have been in their late fifties or sixties. That was part of the Kennedy era; like the Peace Corps it reminded young Americans that this was their President. To be sure, he had other constituencies, the intellectual community among them. Celebrating the end of his six-year term as a member of Harvard's board of overseers, he gave a stag dinner at the Executive Mansion for distinguished Harvard men. But even then he was conscious of his age. "It is difficult to welcome you to the White House," he said, "because at least two-thirds of you have attended more stag dinners here than I have."

His popularity, like that of any President, fluctuated. After the missile crisis in 1962 Gallup reported that 83 percent of the people approved of him; over the next ten months the figure fell to 61 percent and then 59. In September 1963, when the Senate ratified the nuclear test ban treaty with the Russians, the Gallup curve turned up. He had predicted that. The right-wingers, he believed, were misreading the country's mood. They made much of what they called a swing to conservatism on the campuses. They held that Admiral Lewis Strauss spoke for millions when he said, at the test ban hearings, "I am not sure that the reduction of tensions is necessarily a good thing," and that Edward Teller was reflecting the alarm of the entire middle class when he said at the same hearings, "If you ratify this treaty . . . you will have given away the future safety of this country." Kennedy didn't accept that. At Billings, Montana, and at Salt Lake City—in the very heart of what was thought to be Goldwater country—he was given standing ovations when, at midpoint in prepared speeches, he left his text to speak of his pride in the test ban. To friends he said that the treaty was the essence of his foreign policy; if he lost to Goldwater next year he would be willing to pay that price.

The signs of the coming detente were now unmistakable. The test ban, and the expressions of approval Kennedy heard across the country when it became an accomplished fact, had been possible because in Cuba the Russians had finally accepted the principle of verifying missile sites. The world had heard the last of the troika. In East Berlin Khrushchev said that the Wall had diminished the need for a separate German peace treaty. He had learned to live with the bone in his throat. Then Kennedy, speaking at American University on June 20, held out an olive branch to the Russians: "Our problems are man-made; therefore they can be solved by man . . . Some say that it is useless to speak of world peace . . . until the leaders of the Soviet Union adopt a more enlightened attitude. I hope they do. I believe we can help them do it. But I also believe that we must reexamine our own attitude."

The speech was largely ignored in the American press—his civil rights address, which came the following evening, preempted editorial attention—but the *Manchester Guardian* called it "one of the great state papers of American history," and Khrushchev, genuinely impressed, later told Harriman that it was "the greatest speech by an American President since Roosevelt."

On August 30 the Department of Defense announced that a hot line linking the White House and the Kremlin had gone into operation that same day. In October, when Russia's rift with China came into the open, Khrushchev said he did not share Mao's willingness to sacrifice millions of lives in a nuclear showdown with the West.

Kennedy then authorized a sale of surplus wheat to the Soviet Union as "one more hopeful sign that a more peaceful world is both possible and beneficial to all."

The radical right was furious, but he relished its fury. He delighted in building a record as a liberal President. Kennedy chuckled when Ike, baffled by Keynesian economics, cried out in a magazine article: "What can those people in Washington be thinking about? Why would they deliberately do this to our country?" What Kennedy was doing to the country's economy, with the help of Douglas Dillon and Walter Heller, was producing the longest peacetime expansion in history, resulting in an annual increase in the Gross National Product of 5.6 percent a year. And if Congress would go along with his recommendation for a tax cut, he believed, there would be no recession in 1964, either.

That was by no means certain. The 88th Congress was mulish. The President was far ahead of its conservative instincts with his liberal program calling for Medicare, massive grants to encourage the rebuilding of decaying urban slums, a more sensible farm plan, the development and conservation of national resources, improved social security, his broad civil rights bill, and a growing commitment to the Alianza. At the time, critics gave him low marks in his struggle for legislation. Looking back, it is surprising that he did as well as he did. Of 107 recommendations he had sent to the 87th Congress, 73 had been enacted into law, and the early legislative victories of his successor were programs Kennedy had sent to the 88th.

Addressing the Irish Parliament in June, he recalled a line from George Bernard Shaw's *Back to Methuselah:* "You see things; and you say 'Why?' But I dream things that never were; and I say 'Why not?' "* That was the Kennedy outlook at its best, a blend of social prophecy and political vision. He was not always on that plane. At times he seemed to be looking toward wrong horizons. A decade later his pledges to support manned space flight and supersonic transport would be seen as dubious ventures. But even his errors of exuberance seemed preferable to the stagnation of the 1950s. Like Franklin Roosevelt he was using politics to expand the limits of the possible at home and abroad. In that context his triumphant ten-day tour of Europe five months before his death, of which the Irish visit was a part, is important to an understanding of him. More

* Later this was attributed to him, and then to Robert Kennedy. But it was Shavian.

than anything else he resembled the statesmen of the European left, and they knew it. In him they saw their own idealized self-images. Willy Brandt in Germany, Gaston Defferre and Pierre Mendès-France in France, Harold Wilson in Britain, Pietro Nenni in Italy—all of them praised him, quoted him, and to some extent patterned their political styles after his. "Nenni, the old firebrand Socialist, cannot now contain his praise for Kennedy," Anthony Sampson wrote in the London *Observer*. ". . . There is hardly a word of anti-Americanism, except on the far right." As a liberal, Kennedy had, among other things, no patience with those who thought men should wear blinders to shield them from evil. Jailing students who wanted to see Castro's Cuba seemed to him absurd. "Why shouldn't they go?" he asked. "If I were twenty-one years old, that's what I would like to do this summer." And in Amherst on October 26, 1963, he spoke words which would be cherished by historians of his period:

"It may be different elsewhere. But democratic society—in it, the highest duty of the writer, the composer, the artist is to remain true to himself and to let the chips fall where they may. In serving his vision of the truth, the artist best serves his nation."

At such times John Kennedy seemed inevitable. But there was another aspect of him. Astronomers are familiar with the phenomenon of the dark star, a star so feebly luminous as to be invisible, one which follows another star and eclipses it sporadically. Kennedy had a dark star, a shadow of imminent tragedy which was never far from him and those he loved and which would intervene unexpectedly to obscure their most splendid moments. It happened now. In early August Jacqueline Kennedy gave birth to a second son, who arrived five and a half weeks prematurely and with a lung ailment. Christened Patrick Bouvier Kennedy, the baby struggled for thirty-nine hours before expiring. The President, desolate, tried to lift the little coffin at the services to carry it to the grave; then Cardinal Cushing gently drew him away.

To lift his wife's spirits Kennedy suggested that she accept an invitation from Aristotle Onassis, the Greek shipping tycoon, for an Aegean cruise on his majestic yacht, the *Christina*. Later she would remember early October as an unreal time, two dazzling weeks of sunshine between the loss of Patrick and the catastrophe that awaited in November. Dispatches from the Mediterranean traced her progress from Istanbul to Lesbos, Crete, Delphi, Marrakesh, and to an island in the Ionian Sea that Onassis owned. Royalty, beginning with the king and queen of Greece, entertained her and her sister Lee Radziwill; they toasted her, admired her, and gave her exotic gifts. When she returned to the White House on October 17, one member of the White House staff said, "Jackie has stars in her eyes—Greek stars." The President asked her if she would join him for a short campaign trip. She said fine, and she asked where, and he said Texas.

If there was any one place where things had seemed to be going exceptionally well for Kennedy earlier in the year, it was Saigon. Opening his State of the Union message on January 14, 1963, the President had reported: "The spearhead of aggression has been blunted in Vietnam." A Pentagon spokesman announced that "we have turned the corner in Vietnam," and General Harkins said that the war would be won "within a year." On April 22 Rusk said that the American effort in Saigon was "producing excellent results," and Ngo Dinh Diem and the Republic of Vietnam were "on their way to success." U. Alexis Johnson, Rusk's deputy undersecretary for political affairs, was particularly encouraged by "the intangible knitting together of government and people" in Vietnam and by the strategic hamlet program, which he called "the most important reason for guarded optimism."

Afterward this seemed puzzling. The fact that these prophets had been wildly wrong was bad enough; why had they been so eager to put themselves on the record? The answer was that they were trying to drown out other members of the government who were convinced that President Ngo Dinh Diem and everyone with him was doomed. The terms hawk and dove were not yet fashionable, but the administration was split along those lines. The chief hawks, or advocates of American involvement in the war, were the generals, including Maxwell Taylor, and McCone of the CIA, Rusk, Rostow, Ambassador Nolting in Saigon, and at this point McNamara, who was impressed by the force and precision of the reports from Saigon. Ranged against them were Robert Kennedy, George Ball, Averell Harriman, Roger Hilsman, Michael Forrestal, Richard Helms at the CIA, the American colonels in the field with Vietnamese troops, and American war correspondents, who sang to the tune of "Twinkle, Twinkle, Little Star":

> *We are winning, this we know.*
> *General Harkins tells us so.*

In the delta, things are rough.
In the mountains, mighty tough.
But we're winning, this we know.
General Harkins tells us so.
If you doubt this is true,
McNamara says so too.

As the third year of the Kennedy Presidency opened, no one could be said to be winning the war, because hardly anyone was fighting it. The Viet Cong was husbanding its strength, waiting to pounce, and the Republic of Vietnam's overcautious commanders had no intention of stirring them up. The calm was deceptive. The country was seething with resentment, and not all of Diem's critics were in the Viet Cong. Because he represented what might be called the Vietnamese establishment, the conservative, upper-class mandarins who spoke French and worshipped God as Roman Catholics, his natural adversaries in the non-Communist community were the young Buddhist priests and monks, who were poor, militant, middle- and lower-class, radical, and distrustful of everything western. Their religious faith was that of the majority, and they bitterly resented the privileges accorded the Catholics. Both sides were in a belligerent mood, needing only an incident to kindle a struggle between them.

It came in early May 1963. The Buddhists were celebrating Buddha's 2587th birthday in the ancient imperial city of Hue when officers commanding government troops ordered a group of them to disperse. They refused and the soldiers fired into the crowd, killing nine. Diem refused to express regrets—he said privately that he would lose face—and on June 11 a Buddhist monk, Quang Duc, protested with a spectacular demonstration of self-immolation. Sitting on the pavement, he waited patiently while his fellow monks drenched him with gasoline; then he struck a match and went up in flames. Other suicidal Buddhists followed his example, providing the press (which was notified in advance each time) with outstanding photographs. The newspaper-reading American public was appalled, but the government in Saigon was unmoved President Diem at this point was almost entirely under the influence of his brother, Ngo Dinh Nhu, who was usually under the influence of opium. Madame Nhu demonstrated the ruling family's genius for public relations by telling reporters that she gaily clapped her hands each time one of these "so-called holy men" put on a "barbecue show."

Under great American pressure Diem tentatively agreed on June 15 to meet some of the Buddhist demands. Almost immediately it became clear that he had no intention of following through. On June 30 the Buddhist demonstrations were renewed. Students rioted in Vietnam schools, and American correspondents who were writing about the turmoil were attacked in the streets and beaten. This was too much for President Kennedy. The cold war thaw had provided him with a new incentive for wanting the shooting in Vietnam stopped. A truce was necessary before he could offer the world what he had called a "strategy of peace" at American University: "Not a *Pax Americana* enforced on the world by American weapons of war . . . not merely peace for Americans, but peace for all men; not merely peace in our time but peace for all time."

Apart from other considerations—such as corruption and ineffectuality—the rigid anti-Communism of Diem and the Nhus had no place in these plans for a new foreign policy. Kennedy wanted to take a strong hand with them, and when he discovered in early July that Nolting was absent on a two-month cruise in the remote Aegean, he decided that his first step should be to dispatch a new envoy to Saigon. Rusk picked the man, Henry Cabot Lodge. It was an excellent choice. Liberals in the administration were uneasy at first, fearing that as a patrician Lodge might favor South Vietnam's aristocracy. They didn't understand that as a Boston Brahmin Lodge expected the well-born to be gentlemen, which Diem and Nhu definitely were not. Among other things, gentlemen do not betray their friends. Whatever else may be said of Nolting's tenure, he had been a good friend to Diem, and they were about to repay him with an act of shocking treachery.

In a farewell speech at the airport Nolting spoke of bonds between the two countries: "humility and tolerance, respect for others and a deep sense of social justice." Correspondents thought these strange words in Vietnam, but Nolting believed them to be justified; the South Vietnamese president had just given him his word that there would be no more attacks on the Buddhists. Six days later Diem sent his secret police out on a midnight raid to seize the pagodas, arrest the priests and monks, and terrorize their followers. The raiders tried to camouflage their identity by wearing regular army uniforms, but the truth emerged forty-eight hours later after Madame Nhu, in a reference to a gang of cutthroats, which had been rooted out several years before, said that the sally had brought her "the happiest day in my life since we crushed the Binh Xuyen in 1955."

Lodge arrived in Saigon the following evening. He saw the raid as a studied act of scorn for the Americans. It was, in fact, a new low for Diem, and it marked the beginning of his isolation from other Vietnamese conservatives. His foreign minister quit in protest and shaved his head like a Buddhist monk. In Washington Madame Nhu's father, South Vietnam ambassador to the U.S., disowned his daughter. The Voice of America placed the blame for the storming of the pagodas squarely on the Nhus. Diem's generals, wanting no part of the atrocity, began plotting against him. Lodge cabled Washington that the plotters wanted to know what the American attitude would be if a coup was successful. What should he tell them?

The answer said much about the fissure in the Kennedy administration over the Vietnam question. It was August 24, a Saturday. The President was in Hyannisport. McNamara and McCone were on vacation, Rusk was out of town, and General Taylor could not be reached. Their key deputies were Gilpatric in the Pentagon, Helms at the CIA, and Ball at State, all critics of the regime in Saigon. The cable they approved was drafted by Ball, Harriman, Hilsman, and Forrestal, and it bluntly told the American ambassador that the Nhus must go. Afterward, when everyone was back in Washington, there were bitter recriminations, but when the President decided to put everyone on record no one was willing to take the responsibility for repudiating it.

The generals now had a green light from Lodge. On August 29 he cabled Rusk, "We are launched on a course from which there is no respectable turning back: the overthrow of the Diem government." Everything seemed set for it. Days passed, and then weeks, with no coup. The plotters appeared to have lost their nerve. The crackdown on the pagodas had cramped their style, sidelining several of their leaders, and Diem had tightened his control of the troops around Saigon. The State Department asked Lodge what was the matter with the generals. He said, "Perhaps they are like the rest of us, and afraid to die."

Encouraged by Diem's survival, the hawks in the administration took on new life. The need now, McNamara said at a council of war on August 31, was to reopen conversations with Diem. Rusk agreed, saying that this much was clear: the American presence must remain in Vietnam until the Viet Cong war was won, and the United States could not approve of a coup. General Taylor said they were both right. George Ball and Averell Harriman thought that this was absurd. Autumn was approaching, and each day the division between the two camps in Washington was wider. It became an abyss in September, when the National Security Council sent another fact-finding mission to Saigon. The investigators were Major General Victor H. "Brute" Krulak of the Marine Corps and, from the State Department, Joseph A. Mendenhall, a senior foreign service officer of comparable rank with experience in Vietnam. On their return President Kennedy reconvened the National Security Council, and each presented his report. General Krulak said that the war was being won and Diem's performance could hardly be improved upon. Mendenhall said that the Diem regime was at the point of collapse. There was a silence. Then the President said, "Were you two gentlemen in the same country?"

During all this the relationship between Lodge and General Harkins in Vietnam was deteriorating. Both were from Boston, and their families were old friends, but now they scarcely spoke to one another. Late in September McNamara and General Taylor arrived in Saigon on one more attempt to find out what was going on. At the airport Lodge, determined to reach McNamara first, detailed two of his men to obstruct Harkins's way. ("Please, gentlemen! Please let me through to the secretary!") Apart from that, Harkins was as cheerful as ever. His optimism was reflected in the opening paragraph of the subsequent McNamara-Taylor report, which declared that Diem's army "has made great progress and continues to progress." Because Diem's troops were victorious on all fronts, the appraisal continued, the first thousand American soldiers could be withdrawn before Christmas, and all of them would be home by the end of 1965. At the same time the report dealt a glancing blow to the heretical suggestion of Robert Kennedy that the Americans pull out now. McNamara and Taylor took what would be the Pentagon line to the bitter end:

> The security of South Vietnam remains vital to United States security. For this reason, we adhere to the overriding objective of denying this country to Communism and of suppressing the Vietcong insurgency as promptly as possible.

But this view was now definitely losing support in the administration. The President himself was moving away from it. Interviewed on CBS-TV by Walter Cronkite on September 2, he had said pointedly that if the Republic of Vietnam was to be successful in its struggle against the Viet Cong it needed "changes in policy, and perhaps in personnel." He had then said: "I don't think the war can be won unless the people support the effort, and in my opinion, in the last two months the government has gotten out of touch with the people. . . . In the first analysis, it is their war. They are the ones who have to win it or lose it. We can help them, we can give them equipment, we can send our men there as advisers, but they have to win it, the people of Vietnam."

Early in October a ten-million-dollar-a-month program for Diem was quietly suspended. He and the Nhus angrily denounced Kennedy, and Madame Nhu arrived in California to open a lecture tour of the United States, condemning Kennedy with the support of right-wing groups. From the outset the trip was a fiasco. Official Washington boycotted her. When she attempted to call on her estranged father, Tran Van Chuong, she found the door locked and bolted; the ex-ambassador was in Manhattan speaking on what he called "the trail of stench" left by his daughter. She tried to follow him. At La Guardia Field she was met by a city official who curtly denied that he was greeting her; "I'm just here to see that the lady has sufficient police protection," he said. Madame Nhu snapped that she didn't need protection. "God is in my corner," she said. She never did find Tran. Speaking at Harvard, she was picketed by about five hundred students carrying such signs as NHU DEAL IS NHU DIEM GOOD. They pounded on the door of the lecture hall, spattered the side of the building with eggs, and rattled the windows as she spoke. After Cambridge, her crowds dwindled. Apart from ultraconservative claques, virtually the only people who turned out to see her were reporters.

Back in Saigon the government seemed to be losing its grip on reality. Nhu was threatening to form an alliance with Hanoi to drive the Americans out of the country. Diem's secret police, having purged the Buddhists, were attacking the country's schools. In a series of incomprehensible raids they jailed college students, then high school pupils, and finally children in the elementary schools. Even Catholics weren't safe from persecution. Vietnamese of all faiths and persuasions were appealing to General Duong Van Minh, "Big" Minh, the most prestigious officer in the army, begging him to oust Diem and Nhu. Minh approached John Richardson, the

CIA station chief, and asked him for his advice. Bypassing General Harkins, Richardson arranged a meeting between Minh and Lodge. The ambassador told Minh that the Americans would do nothing to impede a coup, and that if it was successful U.S. aid would go to another anti-Communist government. This position was relayed to the White House, which approved it. Everyone in Washington and Saigon seemed to be aware of the coming revolt except Diem, Nhu, and General Harkins, who assured the President that there would be no coup, that it was all talk, that he had checked the rumors and found them to be groundless. Nothing could happen, Harkins said, without his knowing of it. It could, though. David Halberstam of the *New York Times* and another reporter had already received slips of paper with the message, "Please buy me one bottle of whisky at the PX"—the signal that the uprising was imminent.

Diem's hour struck at 1 P.M. Vietnamese time (1 A.M. in Washington) on Friday, November 1, All Saints' Day. In Saigon it was siesta time on a day of stupefying heat. The president and his brother had retired to their bedrooms in Gia Long palace, where they were presumably protected by the palace guard and seven-foot fences topped by barbed wire. But as they slept, truckloads of rebel marines wearing red kerchiefs had already launched an attack on their defenses while other soldiers threw up roadblocks at key intersections. The insurgents quickly seized the airport, the police station, navy headquarters on the banks of the Saigon River, and the government radio station, which broadcast a declaration in the name of fourteen generals and seven colonels: "Soldiers in the army, security service, civil defense force, and people's force! The Ngo Dinh Diem government, abusing power, has thought only of personal ambition and slighted the fatherland's interests. . . ."

That evening the siege of the palace began with a mortar and artillery barrage. In the early hours of the next morning a force of eighteen tanks began blowing holes in the fences. At 6:15 A.M. a rebel general ordered a five-minute cease-fire and called on Diem and Nhu to surrender. A white flag appeared in a first floor window, but Diem and Nhu were not there. They had fled through a secret tunnel to the Chinese suburb of Cholon, from which they sent word to the victorious junta that they were ready to open negotiations. Exactly what happened after that is unknown. Reportedly they accepted offers of safe conduct out of the country, but it was a ruse; they who had deceived so many were now betrayed themselves.

Picked up by rebel soldiers, they were killed, on orders from the generals, in the back of an armored personnel carrier. Their bodies were found there, riddled with bullets and dressed in Roman Catholic priests' robes in which they had hoped to escape if nothing else worked. Diem had also been stabbed repeatedly.

Awakened with the news in the Beverly Wilshire Hotel in Beverly Hills, Madame Nhu sobbed that President Kennedy was to blame. The President was in fact shaken, depressed for the first time since the Bay of Pigs; whatever Diem's faults, he said, he had not deserved to be slain. Elsewhere in the administration the news was accepted with resignation, even relief. There was one significant exception. Vice President Johnson was bitter. The Vice President had given Diem his hand, had been his friend, and in Johnson's view the friendship had symbolized the American commitment to Diem. The same officials who had been Diem's critics in the administration were also critical of the Vice President. He knew it, and knew who they were, and he had long since come to despise them and everything about them, right down to their Cardin shirts and PT-109 tie clasps. On other issues Johnson admired Kennedy, but not here.

The people of Saigon did not share Johnson's view. They had turned the day into a holiday, dancing in the streets; statues of Diem, his brother, and his sister-in-law were smashed and posters of them were torn down, until the only likeness of the late President in the capital was on one-piaster coins. The triumphant generals were showered with confetti everywhere they went, and Lodge became the first American within recent memory to be cheered in public. Hope was running high in the U.S. embassy; the factions which had been united against the ruling family seemed popular enough to give the country a stable government.

A week passed, and then two weeks; the autumn days grew shorter, and President Kennedy's spirits rose. The McNamara-Taylor report, dated October 2, was still on his desk, but he felt no sense of urgency about the need to deal with it. As David Halberstam later wrote:

> He knew Vietnam was bad and getting worse, that he was on his way to a first-class foreign policy problem, but he had a sense of being able to handle it, of having time, that time was somehow on his side. He could afford to move his people slowly; too forceful a shove would bring a counter-shove. It was late 1963, and since 1964 was an election year, any delay on major decisions was healthy; if the Vietnamese could hold out a little longer, so could he.

On November 13 he summoned a conference of his chief strategists for the coming campaign. Meeting in the Cabinet Room late that Wednesday afternoon, they agreed that prospects for a landslide victory against Goldwater were encouraging. The economy was flourishing. The annual Gross National Product had grown 100 billion dollars since his inaugural; its rate of growth was greater than that of either Russia or Europe. The huge new Saturn rocket, which would be launched next month, would at last put the United States ahead of the Soviet Union in the manned spacecraft race. Except for Vietnam the world was calm, and to get more perspective on that the President cabled Ambassador Lodge suggesting that he come home for a long talk. Lodge replied that he was making arrangements to leave Saigon as soon as possible. That would be on Thursday, November 21.

Richard M. Nixon, then an attorney representing Pepsi-Cola, left Dallas, Texas, aboard American Airlines Flight 82, bound for New York, at 9:05 A.M. on November 22, 1963, thus missing President Kennedy's arrival there aboard *Air Force One* by about two and a half hours. Mr. Nixon had spent the past two days at a Pepsi-Cola Bottlers Association meeting. He was just beginning to learn the ropes as a corporation lawyer. He had filed a petition for admission to the New York State bar only last Friday, and his name was not yet on his office door, because he would not become a full partner in the law firm of Mudge, Stern, Baldwin & Todd until January 1, 1964.

It was expected to remain there a long time. Earlier in the week during a televised interview Dwight Eisenhower had spoken of Nixon's chances in the next presidential election, but his remark is chiefly memorable as vintage Eisenhowerese: "Now, if there should be one of those deadlocks, I would think he would be one of the likely persons to be examined and approached, because he is, after all, a very knowledgeable and a very courageous type of fellow." Hardly anyone agreed with Ike. Certainly the American Broadcasting Company didn't. Not only had the network called a broadcast about him *The Political Obituary of Richard M. Nixon;* the program, filmed the year before, had featured an interview with, of all people, Alger Hiss. Two companies tried to cancel their advertising contracts with ABC because of it, but FCC Chairman Newton N. "Wasteland" Minow turned them down with the cold observation that broadcasting must be free from censorship by "those few, fearful advertisers who seek to influence the professional judgment of broadcast newsmen." President Kennedy said he agreed. Those were golden days for effete snobs.

Aboard Flight 82 a stewardess offered her distinguished passenger a selection of current periodicals, and if one could return in time from the mid-1970s to that fateful Friday, one of the differences to be noted in the American scene would be the wider choice of magazines, *Look, Life,* and the *Saturday Evening Post* then being alive, well, and on the stands. (The long retreat from mass circulation was already well advanced among newspapers, however, and four weeks earlier, on October 16, the *New York Mirror* had folded. Before the end of the decade 163 magazines and 160 daily newspapers, including the *Indianapolis Times,* the *San Francisco News-Call-Bulletin,* the *Boston Traveler,* the *Portland Reporter,* and the *Houston Press* would end publication.)

Nixon may well have picked *Time,* for he knew he would be in it. The first news page carried an informal picture of him—he was fifty and looked a young forty then—and in an accompanying interview he was quoted on the political consequences of the Saigon coup: "If this Viet war goes sour, Viet Nam could be a hot issue next year. If all goes well, it won't be. It's strange to me, when we are fawning over Tito, catering to Kadar, accommodating Khrushchev, we don't even have the decency to express our sympathy to a family which was a real foe of Communism."

Barry Goldwater, who rarely fawned over Communists, was the front runner for the 1964 Republican presidential nomination, Nelson Rockefeller having diminished his chances by marrying Happy Murphy the previous May. In that third week of November Goldwater had just scored a fresh triumph with one of his natural constituencies by telling a Better Business Bureau banquet in Chicago that the New Frontier had produced "1,026 days of wasted spending, wishful thinking, unwarranted intervention, wistful theories, and waning confidence."

Each time the Arizona senator tore into Kennedy reporters asked the President to reply. "Not yet," he would say, grinning; "not yet," but plainly he relished the prospect of running against him.

Among his valuable campaigners this time would be the First Lady. The Secret Service hoped Mrs. Kennedy could persuade her husband to be more careful in crowds. Eschewing SS advice the week before the Texas trip, he had ordered his driver to leave his car's motorcycle escort and detour through crowded downtown Manhattan. While the presidential limousine was halted at the traffic light an amateur photographer had darted up and fired a flash bulb at Kennedy's side of the car. A New York police official had told reporters, "She might well have been an assassin."

It was a year of technological innovations. Kodak introduced the Instamatic camera and Polaroid brought out color packs. Polyethylene appeared. Detroit's fall models featured sleekly sloping rear windows—"fastbacks," they were called; the one on the Sting Ray was particularly dramatic. On July 1, 1963, the Post Office Department, while announcing an increase in first-class postage from four cents to five, sprang the zip code system on a stunned and resentful public. The triumph of the digits moved one step closer with the conversion of the White House telephone number from NAtional 8-1414 to 456-1414. On the Bell systems' master map the hatched areas indicating switchovers to direct distance dialing were spreading like a vast cancer; DDD reached 44.2 million Bell subscribers in 1963. Students at liberal arts colleges displayed decals reading, "I Am a Human Being—Do Not Fold, Spindle, or Mutilate."

The sale of Barbie dolls reached its initial peak in 1963, and Barbie, who had acquired a boyfriend, Ken, two years earlier, was now joined by her "best friend," Midge. (Barbie's "black is beautiful" friend, Christie, would not appear in the Mattel sales line until 1968. In 1963 black beauty, like black power, was waiting to be discovered.) The question of how lifelike female dolls should be was still sparking lively debates among toymakers. A considerable number of parents objected to Barbie's firm little breasts. The public attitude in such matters remained comparatively conservative. In the matter of premarital intercourse it continued to hold that "Nice girls don't," although Gael Greene, researching *Sex and the College Girl* in 1963, was finding that more and more nice girls *did*. (A memorable passage in Miss Greene's book, startling at the time, described a sorority girl pretending to climb a wall in mock agony while crying out in frustration, "You don't know how long it's been since I got screwed.")

Few of collegiate America's mothers had any idea how casually some of their daughters were accustomed to being bedded. Parents would later rise up in righteous indignation to protest coed dorms, only to reel back when confronted by the new facts of campus life.

One stunning fact was in a report of the infirmary at the University of California in Berkeley to the effect that venereal disease had become a serious health hazard among female undergraduates. Integrated dormitories was one answer to a problem which had other solutions. But in 1963 that belonged to the future. *Playboy* was then averaging fifty applications a week from young women whose aspiration was to appear on its gatefold in the altogether and who, in the judgment of the editors, were qualified to do so, yet even *Playboy* had to trim its sails somewhat to public opinion; for example, it did not yet dare show its Playmates' pubic hair. (It did, however, create an uproar in 1963 with a topless photo of a model who was an almost perfect double for the nation's First Lady.) Hard-core pornography was neither chic nor legal; in November 1963 a three-judge Manhattan court ruled that *Fanny Hill* was obscene and therefore forbidden. "While it is true that the book is well-written, such fact does not condone its indecency," the court found. "Filth, even if wrapped in the finest packaging, is still filth." It is startling to reflect that Linda Lovelace, who would rocket to fame ten years later as the superstar of *Deep Throat*, was then a twelve-year-old girl sucking lollipops in Bryan, Texas.

Among the names not in the news were Gloria Steinem, Kate Millet, Germaine Greer, and Bobby Riggs, then an executive for the American Photograph Corporation. Betty Friedan's *The Feminine Mystique* had just been published, but Women's Lib was, so to speak, still in the uterus. "Nobody," reported that November 22 issue of *Time*, "is more noisily dissatisfied these days than that symbol of stability—the fortyish housewife with teen-age children and a reasonably successful husband," but by the audiometers of the early 1970s the noise was almost imperceptible. The Seven College Conference, which had set up vocational workshops for college women "who are now ready for activity outside the home," had found just fifty such women. None described males as porcine. The vocations were largely limited to education, library science, social work, and—this was regarded as a breakthrough—public relations. Anne Cronin, director of the conference, fielded questions about what men might think with the defensiveness bluestockings had shown since the fall of the Claflin sisters. "In only one or two cases," she told a newspaperman, "have husbands gotten stuffy about their wives' going back into careers. For the most part, they're serious and understanding. We're not breaking up any homes that wouldn't break up anyway."

The fashions of the gentle sex were neither bold nor forward. There were no pantsuits, not even for toiling airline stewardesses. Styles were set by Jacqueline Kennedy—the pillbox hat, the shoes with very pointed toes and very slender heels, the hair length just below the ears and softly curled or bouffant. Skirts were a little below the knee, and the waistless sheath was popular. It was all very feminine. Male supremacy was riding high. No protests followed the showing, as a late movie, of Cary Grant and Myrna Loy in *Mr. Blandings Builds His Dream House*—nobody wondered what *Mrs.* Blandings might want in *her* dream house—and the author of a magazine profile of Dorothy Kilgallen, describing her race around the world as a journalistic stunt in 1936, was allowed to say: "Just like a woman, Dorothy came in late." In the summer of 1963 Ian Fleming's *The Spy Who Loved Me* appeared in paperback with this choice passage:

> All women love semi-rape. They love to be taken. It was his sweet brutality against my bruised body that had made his act of love so piercingly wonderful. That and the coinciding of nerves completely relaxed after the removal of tension and danger, the warmth of gratitude, and a woman's natural feelings for her hero. I had no regrets and no shame. . . . all my life I would be grateful to him, for everything. And I would remember him forever as my image of a man.

The *New York Times Magazine* carried a report on the campus mood that third week of November 1963. In it, undergraduate editors generally found their fellow students to be detached, determined to succeed, and concerned less with issues than with security and their personal lives. In their hours of relaxation Tarzan movies were the current thing. The University of Chicago was trying to revive football. Two Cornell fraternity teams had just played a thirty-hour touch football game; the final score was 664-538. LSU coeds had staged a "drawers raid" on a men's fraternity—all college residences were male or female, of course. Berkeley students, ever in the sexual vanguard, had asked the dispensary there to dispense contraceptives. They weren't militant about it, however; the demand was negotiable and was in fact ignored.

Camelot had ended its Broadway run in January 1963. *Tom Jones* was awarded the Academy Award as the best picture of the year. Sidney Poitier was voted the best actor for his performance in *Lilies of the Field;* Patricia Neal for hers in *Hud.* Films drawing big audiences in November 1963 were *Mary, Mary* and *It's a Mad, Mad, Mad, Mad World.* Popular television shows were *Dr. Kildare, Andy Griffith, My Three Sons, Perry Mason, Hazel, Lucy, The Beverly Hillbillies,* and *Twilight Zone.* NBC's Monday movie scheduled for November 25—it would not be shown—was *Singing in the Rain.*

That year was the high point of the Ajax White Knight and White Tornado ("Cleans like a white tornado!") commercials, according to Harry McMahan of *Advertising Age.* Piel's Beer was presenting the Return of Bert and Harry. Maxwell House Instant Coffee offered a Cup and a Half. The Chevrolet commercial had a car riding on the water of a Venice canal, and Hertz commercials were dropping people into convertibles. Songs which were popular were "Go Away Little Girl," "Dominique," "If I Had a Hammer," "Puff the Magic Dragon," and "Blowing in the Wind."

Best-selling fiction included Mary McCarthy's *The Group,* Morris West's *The Shoes of the Fisherman,* James Michener's *Caravans,* and Helen MacInnes's *The Venetian Affair.* Best-selling nonfiction included James Baldwin's *The Fire Next Time,* Rachel Carson's *Silent Spring,* from which the ecology movement may be said to date, and two books which would be affected by the events of the coming weekend, Jessica Mitford's *The American Way of Death* and Victor Lasky's *J.F.K.: The Man and the Myth.* The first of these acquired historical significance because Robert Kennedy, who had read it, was guided by it in choosing a coffin for his brother's funeral. The Lasky book, which led the nonfiction best-seller lists, was a hatchet job and it would be withdrawn from the bookstores by its publisher.

In sports, Texas was ranked college football's number one. Darrell Royal's marvel that season was a shoeless field-goal kicker named Tony Crosby. The weekend before President Kennedy flew to Dallas, Crosby booted one 42 yards to beat TCU. Among the pros, Jimmy Brown of the Cleveland Browns was at the height of his remarkable powers. The New York Giants and the Chicago Bears were headed for a collision at the end of the National Football League season; Chicago would win the championship 14 to 10. In the American Football League finale, the San Diego Chargers would take the Boston Patriots 51 to 10. There was no superbowl. In hockey the big noise was Gordie Howe of the Detroit Red Wings. Having played 1,132 games in which he had lost twelve teeth and sustained wounds requiring 300 stitches, Gordie scored his 545th goal against the Montreal Canadiens in November 1963; it was a record. In basketball Bob Cousy of the Boston Celtics had hung up his jockstrap at the end of the 1962 season. As a consequence the Celts had been expected to be pushovers, but when Kennedy left the White House for the last time the 1963 season was two months old and the Celtics had lost only one game—by one point. Center Bill Russell was the big (six feet ten inches) reason.

Among the places not in the news that year were Woodstock, Watts, East Village, Grant Park, Wounded Knee, People's Park, My Lai, Khe Sanh, Kent State, Biafra, Lincoln Park, Bangladesh, Attica, the Ho Chi Minh Trail, Chappaquiddick, Bimini, Botswana, Qatar, and Watergate, though the Watergate office-and-apartment complex was under construction beside the State Department in Washington; President Kennedy's funeral procession would pass it. Haight-Ashbury was a drab working-class district in San Francisco. No one living in the Haight, as it would later be known, was then familiar with the hippy terms acid-zap, freak out, superstar, mind-blowing, bummer, joints, munchies, turn on, tune in, rip off, drop out, commune, horse, crash pad, steam, zonked, love-in, be-in, share-in, flower power, trash, Panhandle Park, acid-American Dayglo art, role-playing, bunch-punching, past-blasting, guerrilla theater, psychedelic Satanism, and Christ vibes.

The *New York Times* carried a dispatch from its London bureau about "a group of four male pop singers now highly popular in Great Britain and the cause of numerous teen-age riots." They were the Beatles. In November 1963 they were on their way to the United States, preceded by recordings of their first three hits: "She Loves You," "Wanna Hold Your Hand," and "Standing There."

The Vietnamese generals who had staged the Saigon coup, David Halberstam reported, wanted to see General Harkins replaced, but the Pentagon expressed confidence that Harkins would fulfill his promises to beat the Viet Cong. Any suspicion that the United States might not be able to find a military solution in Vietnam was challenged by Deputy Secretary of Defense Roswell Gilpatric in an address to the Business Council in Hot Springs, Virginia. The U.S. had such lethal power, Gilpatric said, that defiance of it would be an act of self-destruction.

Nicole Alphand, the wife of the French ambassador, was on the cover of the November 22 *Time*. Jimmy Hoffa was being indicted. Charles de Gaulle was vetoing Britain's entrance into the Common Market. Governor Ross Barnett was endorsing the findings of a grand jury which blamed the federal government for the recent disorders that had accompanied the admission of James Meredith to the state university in Oxford. Richard Burton and Elizabeth Taylor, having fallen in love during the filming of *Cleopatra,* were divesting themselves of their spouses and planning an early wedding. The Mona Lisa was in the United States, heavily chaperoned.

In 1963 there were 189,242,000 Americans (in 1973 there would be 209,000,000), of whom 70,000,000 were employed (1973: 80,-627,000). Five percent were unemployed. The population center of the United States lay four miles east of Salem, Illinois, having moved fifty-seven miles to the west in the 1950s, the greatest westward drift since the 1880s. World War II was no longer the paramount experience of most Americans. Because of the huge number of war babies, the median age was 29.5.

A startling figure came from organized labor: between 1960 and 1962 unions had lost about a half-million members. The percentage of workmen belonging to them had dropped from 24.4 percent in 1955 to 22.2 percent in 1962, and Murray Kempton, no enemy of unions, was talking about the "twilight" of the labor movement.

One reason for this was the passage of time. Fewer and fewer workers could remember the heroic strikes of the 1930s. At the same time, the character of the work force was changing. In the years since V-J Day the number of blue-collar workers had decreased by four million while the number of white-collar workers—managers, professionals, salesmen, office workers—had grown by nearly ten million. •

Furthermore, the blue-collar of November 1963 would hardly have been recognized as a fellow worker by his oppressed father of the 1930s. In June 1963 the weekly pay of the average production worker for slightly more than forty hours' work passed $100—four times the Depression wage for the same job. About 40 percent of all families now earned more than $7,000 a year. John Brooks pointed out that the word "proletarian" had virtually disappeared from the language. "People think that prices are going up," Caroline Bird wrote, "but it is their own standard of living that is rising."

The best place to measure the long-range impact of boom was in the classroom. In his comprehensive study of economic development, Edward F. Denison put education at the very top of factors contributing to economic expansion. Between the Crash in 1929 and the end of the Kennedy Presidency, America's investment in education increased tenfold, to 39 billion dollars a year.

The sociological implications of this can hardly be exaggerated. In 1900 only 4 percent of Americans of college age were enrolled in a college or university. In 1957 the figure was 32 percent; when Kennedy took office it was 40 percent, and when he died it was 50 percent. Andrew Hacker calculated that between 60 and 70 percent of all Americans now belonged to the middle class. It was, in fact, swiftly becoming the only class, the values of which were those which had once belonged to a small, highly educated upper middle class.

"The American economy has become so big," a European diplomat said, "that it is beyond the imagination to comprehend." U.S. editorial writers marveled at West Germany's *Wirtschaftswunder*, but a far greater economic miracle had been taking place at home. A few figures suggest its scope. Approximately 90,000 Americans were now millionaires—as against 27,000 in the early 1950s—and each year now the figure grew by 5,000. Since World War II American investments abroad had leaped from 12 billion dollars to 80 billion. The annual sales of a single corporation, General Motors, were 17 billion dollars, almost equal to a third of the Bundesrepublik's Gross National Product. The *increase* alone of the U.S. Gross National Product in the first four years of the 1960s would be greater than the *entire* GNP of Germany in one year, 1964—122 billion dollars to 100 billion. The value of New York Stock Exchange investments had grown from 46 billion dollars to 411 billion since the war; Wall Street's public relations men spoke glowingly of a "people's capitalism," and with considerable justification—the stocks listed on the Big Board were held by some twenty million Americans.

Social prophets of the time regarded this as an unmixed blessing. Some, like John Kenneth Galbraith, thought that profits should be distributed differently, but the assumption that affluence was benign was virtually unchallenged. Lenny Bruce was just an obscene comic one jump ahead of the law in 1963; Ralph Nader was an obscure lecturer in history and government at the University of Hartford. The New Left notion that the country was threatened not by international Communism but by technology and the sheer magnitude of American institutions—that the immensity of U.S. corporations and the Washington bureaucracy was mere obesity—lay quiet in the womb of time. The faith of liberals in big government was still strong.

"Change is the biggest story in the world today," James Reston said at Columbia University in 1963. Nowhere was this more evident than in the growing mobility of American society. The great internal migration of the early 1940s had continued in the postwar years, fueled by the conclusion of southern blacks that a better life awaited them in the northern cities and by technological innovation. American agriculture in 1963 produced 60 percent more food than in 1940, while the number of hours needed to do the nation's farming dropped from twenty million to nine million. As a consequence, by 1963 the number of Americans living in urban and suburban communities had reached 75 percent. The "farm bloc" no longer struck fear in the hearts of congressmen. The Grange had lost its political potency.

Even the vehicles of change were changing. The railroad depot was becoming one of the loneliest places in metropolitan America; for every passenger mile crossed on trains three were crossed on airplanes. (In 1973 the ratio would be one to thirteen.) Ninety percent of local transport was by auto; altogether, car traffic amounted to nearly 800 billion vehicle miles in 1963. The U.S. Department of Commerce reckoned that there were now 17,000 automobile graveyards in the United States, and with the completion of President Eisenhower's nonstop, limited-access, high-speed interstate highway system, the great American traffic jam was beginning to sprawl across state lines.

Across the street from the flyblown train depots the lights in the old mansard-roofed city hotels were darkening. Over 4,000 of them had shut down completely since V-J Day. The travelers who bypassed them were staying instead at motels, which had been evolving from shabby prewar "tourist cabins" into lush pavilions offering all the traditional services of hotels and a few new ones. Black-and-white television had become standard equipment in all but the grubbiest motels (color TV was still a novelty). There were now 56.4 million television sets in the United States. That fact, combined with the discovery of 1960 census takers that only 8.5 percent of the population lacked radios, meant that a communications system of unprecedented magnitude was ready to report any news flash of national importance. In the early afternoon of November 22 the source for all information would be two wire service reporters clutching commandeered telephones at Dallas's Parkland Memorial Hospital. An investigation conducted the following winter by the National Opinion Research Center of the University of Chicago found that by 1 P.M. Dallas time, a half-hour after the shooting, 68 percent of all adults in the United States—over 75 million people—knew about it. Before the end of the afternoon 99.8 percent knew. Even those without television or radio had ready access to those with it.

On September 2, 1963, the CBS *Evening News* increased its nightly news show to thirty minutes and NBC followed its example on September 9, developments which were to have the most profound implications for the Vietnam War; to fill the extra time, networks would run footage showing, among other things, American soldiers lopping off Viet Cong ears. In November 1963 it had not come to that. There weren't even any television commentators in Saigon then. That year just seventeen Americans were killed in Vietnam and 218 were wounded. The most interesting story from Saigon in the third week of November 1963 was a report on Colt's new M-16 rifle. It was smaller and lighter than the M-14. An Army spokesman explained it was one of the reasons anti-Communist forces were wiping out the Viet Cong so effortlessly in guerrilla warfare.

Polls in foreign countries, tabulated by the United States Information Agency, showed U.S. prestige to be very high in 1963. Other stories from abroad were a report from Katanga, which was ending its two-year secession from the Congo, and an appraisal of Sir Alec Douglas-Home's new Tory government in London. It was shaky; the country was still in a state of shock over Lord Denning's report on the Profumo scandal, starring Christine Keeler, that year's most eminent British prostitute.

At home the Dow Jones industrial average hovered around 732. A Roman Catholic prelate excommunicated New Orleans segregationists who refused to bow to the church's endorsement of integration. None of them had heard of the Fathers Berrigan. Other names not in the news included Daniel Ellsberg, Clifford Irving, William Calley, Jimi Hendrix, James Earl Ray, Jeb Stuart Magruder, Angela Davis, Andy Warhol, Arthur Bremer, Vida Blue, Archie Bunker, Myra Breckenridge, and Spiro T. Agnew, who was then in the second year of a four-year term as a local official in Baltimore County.

No one had heard of Jesus freaks, the *Whole Earth Catalog, Crawdaddy, Screw, Money*, hotpants, waterbeds, *Sesame Street, Love Story*, the Black Liberation Army, or Gay Lib.

The November 1963 issue of the *Reader's Digest* anticipated the future with an article reprinted from *Good Housekeeping:* "Sleeping Pills and Pep Pills—Handle with Extreme Caution!" In the November 24, 1963, *New York Times Magazine*, which was fated to be one of its least read issues, Mary Anne Guitar analyzed some new expressions in subteen slang: "rat fink," "triple rat fink," a "real blast" (party), "fake out," "tough toenails," "the straight skinnies," "Jeez-o-man," "hung up," "hairy," "wuzza-wuzza," and "gasser." Of the preteens, who would become the college generation of 1973, Miss Guitar said that their coinages were no worse, and sometimes more imaginative, than their elders': "According to reliable reports, 'terrific' is the word on the New Frontier."

Among the living, in addition to President Kennedy, were Attorney General Robert F. Kennedy, Martin Luther King, Mary Jo Kopechne, Fred Hampton, Malcolm X, George Lincoln Rockwell, and 45,865 young American men who would die violently in Vietnam over the next nine years.

On November 12, 1963, Mrs. John F. Kennedy played hostess to two thousand underprivileged children on the White House lawn. It was her first official appearance since the death of Patrick the previous August, and while she supervised the distribution of two hundred gallons of cocoa and ten thousand sugar cookies among her guests, a detachment of Scotland's Black Watch Regiment strutted and skirled for them. Hearing the tunes and liking them, the President came out of his oval office to watch the performance. Ten days later she would remember his pleasure and ask them to play again, at his funeral.

Nearly every day now impressions were being imprinted on her memory, to be recalled, brooded over, relived, savored, or regretted after Dallas. The day before the Black Watch appearance for the children, the President took young John, not quite three, to Veterans Day ceremonies at Arlington National Cemetery. To the indignation of some, who thought the occasion should be solemn, the little boy was allowed to toddle into the procession and disrupt it. His father was delighted, and while he beamed down at the child, cameramen put the scene on celluloid. There were those who thought that Kennedy had brought the boy along with that in mind. *Look* was coming out with an exclusive spread of John Jr. pictures; it would have been like the President to stage something for photographers who would feel left out by it.

The admiring spectators at Arlington included Major General Philip C. Wehle, commanding officer of the military district in Washington. Twelve days later he would look down on Kennedy's body on the autopsy table at Bethesda Naval Hospital and recall A. E. Housman's lines "To an Athlete Dying Young":

> *Today, the road all runners come,*
> *Shoulder-high we bring you home*
> *And set you at your threshold down,*
> *Townsman of a stiller town. . . .*

Mrs. Kennedy had many recent recollections which would put the tragedy in context; General Wehle had one. Most Americans hadn't any. To them the blow that fell in Dallas came out of nowhere. They didn't even know that the President was in Texas. His visit was only of local interest there; he had come down to make peace between two feuding Democrats, Senator Ralph Yarborough, the liberal, and Governor John B. Connally Jr., the deviate. Non-Texans were unaware of the trip until the first incredible bulletin reached them with the news that the President had been gunned down by a sniper while riding in a downtown motorcade.

Afterward Americans, giving a shape to their grief, reconstructed the events there. They came to know the grid of downtown Dallas streets; the location of the Texas School Book Depository, from which the shots had come, and Parkland Memorial Hospital, to which the President and Governor Connally, who had also been wounded, had been rushed; and the identity of each figure in the tragedy and the part each had played. In time the country forgot its terrible ignorance in the first hours after the assassination, and how they had learned about it.

Merriman Smith of UPI had been riding in the press pool car, four cars behind the presidential limousine in the motorcade. Moments after the sound of the gunfire, at 1:30 P.M. Washington time, he dictated the first bulletin to his local bureau over the pool car's radiophone: "Three shots were fired at President Kennedy's motorcade in downtown Dallas." That went out on UPI printers at 1:34, two minutes before the presidential car reached the hospital. At 1:36 Don Gardiner of the ABC radio network cut into local programs with it. At 1:40 CBS-TV interrupted *As the World Turns,* a soap opera; viewers beheld a distraught Walter Cronkite relaying Smith's report of the three shots and adding, "The first reports say that the President was 'seriously wounded.'" At 1:45 NBC-TV scuttled another soap opera, *Bachelor Father,* to switch to Chet Huntley. That put the three networks on the air with the news, and they would remain there, with no interruptions for commercials, for three days and three nights, until the President had been buried in Arlington National Cemetery.

Some people first heard about the shooting from those early broadcasts and telecasts. One watcher in Fort Worth was Marguerite Oswald, the assassin's mother; she was tuned to WFAA-TV. In Irving, a Dallas suburb, her daughter-in-law Marina was another viewer. Elizabeth Pozen, the wife of a government official, was listening to WGMS over her car radio in Washington. One of her passengers was Caroline Kennedy, who was going to spend the night with a Pozen child, and when Mrs. Pozen heard the announcer say ". . . shot in the head and his wife Jackie . . ." she instantly switched it off. But most people did not learn what had happened that directly. The news reached them third or fourth hand, from a passing stranger, or a telephone call, or a public address system, or a waiter in a restaurant—often from sources which were so unlikely that a common reaction was utter disbelief. To make sure that it was false, they gathered around transistor radios, car radios, and television sets in bars—whatever was available—and there they learned that it was true after all.

(Some of the reports were inaccurate or misleading, however. At 2:18 Washington time the Associated Press circulated an unconfirmed report that Lyndon Johnson had been "wounded slightly," and at 3:14 Washington time AP teletypes chattered that "A Secret Service agent and a Dallas policeman were shot and killed today some distance from the area where President Kennedy was assassinated." This seemed to support theories of an elaborate plot. It wasn't corrected until 4:33 P.M.)

At 2 P.M. Washington time Kennedy was pronounced dead. The announcement was delayed until Lyndon Johnson could get away from the hospital. In that first hour it was wisely assumed that the gunman had been part of a larger conspiracy. The new President left for the airport at 2:26 P.M. Six minutes later UPI quoted Father Oscar Huber, the Dallas priest who had performed the last rites, as saying, "He's dead, all right." Confirmation by the President's acting press secretary followed, and at 2:35 Washington time—an hour earlier in Dallas—UPI bells chimed on teletype machines around the world:

FLASH

PRESIDENT KENNEDY DEAD

JT135PCS

Meantime attention had shifted to another part of Dallas. Lee Harvey Oswald, having left his rifle in his sniper's nest on the sixth floor of the book depository, had caught a bus outside, ridden in it for seven blocks, and then switched to a taxi. He stopped at his rooming house for a pistol. At 2:15 he committed his second murder in less than a hour, gunning down J. D. Tippit, a Dallas policeman who tried to question him. Oswald was seized thirty-five minutes later in a nearby movie theater. The homicide squad then learned that its new prisoner worked as a stockman in the book depository and was, in fact, the only depository employee missing at the building. The net of circumstantial evidence began to build.

At 3:38 P.M. Lyndon Johnson took the presidential oath of office on *Air Force One* with a stunned and bloodstained Jacqueline Kennedy standing beside him. Nine minutes later the plane took off for Washington's Andrews Field. The flight took less than two and a half hours. Johnson made his first televised statement as President at Andrews Field and was then taken by helicopter to the White House. The Kennedy party followed the coffin to Bethesda and the autopsy, which continued through most of the night. It was 4:34 A.M. when the casket, now covered by an American flag, was carried into the White House and placed upon the catafalque in the East Room. Mrs. Kennedy knelt beside it and buried her face in the flag's field of stars.

The next three days passed in a blur. Saturday was accompanied by drenching rains and high winds in the capital. The groggy country would later remember it as a gap between days, between the shock of Friday's assassination and the murder of the assassin on Sunday. The University of Chicago study indicated that the average adult spent ten hours in front of his television set on Saturday, the weekend's peak, but the watchers didn't learn much. The body remained in the East Room; Kennedy's family, his friends, and senior members of the government called to pay their respects there. On Sunday the coffin was carried up Pennsylvania Avenue on a horse-drawn caisson led by a riderless horse with reversed boots in the stirrups, the symbol of a fallen chieftain. At the same time word of a new, unbelievable outrage came from Dallas. Lee Harvey Oswald, in the process of being transferred to another jail, was mortally wounded by a Dallas night club owner named Jack Ruby. The killing occurred in the presence of seventy uniformed Dallas policemen. Because NBC was televising the transfer, it was also television's first live murder. The President's widow was told about it when she returned to the White House. She called it "one more awful."

On Monday the coffin was taken on the caisson to St. Matthew's Cathedral for a funeral mass and thence to Arlington. Delegations from ninety-two nations, led by Charles de Gaulle, had come to participate in the funeral. Afterward they attended two receptions, one at the State Department and another, much smaller, at the White House; Mrs. Kennedy received them there. That was the end of it, though in a sense that weekend never ended; years later men would still be trying to fathom its meaning. It had been the greatest simultaneous experience in the history of this or any other people. Long afterward Americans would tell one another how they had first heard the news from Dallas, how they felt about the eternal flame Mrs. Kennedy had requested for the grave, and young John's saluting of his father's coffin, and the rest of it. David Brinkley concluded that the assassination was beyond understanding: "The events of those days don't fit, you can't place them anywhere, they don't go in the intellectual luggage of our time. It was too big, too sudden, too overwhelming, and it meant too much. It has to be separate and apart."

Nevertheless, people couldn't stop attempting to incorporate it into their lives. The most obvious approach was to name something after the President. Cape Canaveral was rechristened Cape Kennedy. Idlewild International Airport was renamed. The National Cultural Center was changed to the John F. Kennedy Center for the Performing Arts. The Treasury began minting fifty million Kennedy half-dollars—and couldn't keep them in circulation because they were being hoarded as souvenirs. In every part of the country committees and councils were voting to honor the President by altering local maps. Presently Jacqueline Kennedy was wondering whether she would be driving "down a Kennedy parkway to a Kennedy airport to visit a Kennedy school." The impulse reached abroad. Canada had its Mount Kennedy—the first man to climb it was Robert Kennedy—and the climax was reached when England set aside three acres of the historic meadow at Runnymede, where the Magna Carta was signed, as a Kennedy shrine. In May 1965 Queen Elizabeth presided at the ceremony, dedicating the tract to the President "whom in death my people still mourn and whom in life they loved." Mrs. Kennedy replied that it was "the deepest comfort to me to know that you share with me thoughts that lie too deep for tears."

The hundreds of thousands of letters which Americans sent to Mrs. Kennedy then were often touching precisely because they were emotive and unashamedly demonstrative. To David Bell the fallen President was "a warrior-king"; to Natalie Hemingway "a dear godfather"; and John Steinbeck wrote the widow of "this man who was the best of his people" and who "by his life, and his death, gave back the best of them for their own."

Buried in the bales of envelopes was another memorable letter which was found and answered long afterward:

Richard M. Nixon
810 Fifth Avenue
New York, N.Y. 10021

November 23

Dear Jackie,

In this tragic hour Pat and I want you to know that our thoughts and prayers are with you.

While the hand of fate made Jack and me political opponents I always cherished the fact that we were personal friends from the time we came to the Congress together in 1947. That friendship evidenced itself in many ways including the invitation we received to attend your wedding.

Nothing I could say now could add to the splendid tributes which have come from throughout the world to him.

But I want you to know that the nation will also be forever grateful for your service as First Lady. You brought to the White House charm, beauty and elegance as the official hostess for America, and the mistique [sic] of the young in heart which was uniquely yours made an indelible impression on the American consciousness.

If in the days ahead we could be helpful in any way we shall be honored to be at your command.

Sincerely,

DICK NIXON

How many roads must a man walk down
Before they can call him a man
How many seas must a white dove sail
Before she sleeps in the sand
How many times must a cannonball fly
Before they're forever banned
The answer my friend is blowin' in the wind
The answer is blowin' in the wind

There was only one catch and that was Catch-22, which specified that a concern for one's own safety in the face of dangers that were real and immediate was the process of a rational mind. . . . Orr would be crazy to fly more missions and sane if he didn't, but if he was sane he had to fly them. If he flew them he was crazy and didn't have to; but if he didn't want to he was sane and had to. Yossarian was moved very deeply by the absolute simplicity of this clause of Catch-22 and let out a respectful whistle.

"That's some catch, that Catch-22," he observed.

"It's the best there is," Doc Daneeka agreed.

DISORDERS IN CANAL ZONE CAUSE U.S.-PANAMA DIPLOMATIC BREAK

TFX DEFENDED BY MCNAMARA

—— Pall Mall ——

WINSTON TASTES GOOD *LIKE A CIGARETTE SHOULD*

Best actor of 1963: Sidney Poitier in *Lilies of the Field*
Best actress of 1963: Patricia Neal in *Hud*

— What do you want: good grammar or good taste?

Tom Jones   *The Great Escape*   *How the West Was Won*   *The Leopard*
Cleopatra   *The L-Shaped Room*

Blacks have to fashion a world where they can live with dignity and restraint. I am not interested in being a murderer, but then I am not interested in being a dier, either. I am not going to kill you, but I am not going to let you kill me, said LeRoi Jones

BEST SELLERS: Nonfiction
The Warren Commission Report on the Assassination of President Kennedy
The Fire Next Time by James Baldwin
The American Way of Death by Jessica Mitford
Silent Spring by Rachel Carson
The Kennedy Wit edited by Dill Adler

SCHAEFER the one beer to have *when you're having more than one*

SEVEN STEEL COMPANIES INDICTED FOR PRICE FIXING

LBJ: U.S. WILL DESTROY 480 B-47s IF RUSSIANS WILL GUT 480 TU-16s

HOOVER DEAD AT 90

— AJAX — **MACARTHUR DEAD AT 84**

fruiti-juici, fruiti-juici, say, pal, how 'bout a nice HAWAIIAN PUNCH!

HOOTENANNY!

Gone was the glow of blue velvet
But in my heart there'll always be
Precious and warm a memory
through the years
And I still can see blue velvet through my tears

SUB THRESHER LOST WITH 129 ABOARD

BEST SELLERS: Fiction
The Shoes of the Fisherman by Morris West
The Group by Mary McCarthy   **GO-GO-GOODYEAR**   *Big John*
The Venetian Affair by Helen MacInnes
The Spy Who Came In from the Cold by John le Carre
Herzog by Saul Bellow   *Big Bad John*

We demand that no more American youth be sent to fight in a war that is helping neither them nor the Vietnamese people. We have learned lessons from Nazi Germany, and will not go along with the aggressive war-making policies of any government even if it happens to be our own

EXILES BOMB CUBAN REFINERY

LINK PHILBY TO MACLEAN, BURGESS

Dr. Strangelove   **U.S. MOSCOW EMBASSY BUGGED**

MOURN POPE JOHN

CASTRO'S DEFECTING SISTER AIDED CIA

Thirty

THE LONG ARM

O N AN AUGUST AFTERNOON in 1964 Dwight Eisenhower described to this writer Lyndon Johnson as he saw him in the Executive Office Building that rainy Saturday, the day after the assassination:

"I'd known him for a long time. He was, as he always is, nervous —walking around and telephoning everyone. . . . I would mention someone in the conversation and he would snatch up the receiver and call the person. He asked my advice about many matters, including the tax cut. I told him that he had to show what he was going to do with his own budget. We also discussed foreign affairs. As far as I could see at that time, Lyndon Johnson's only intention was to find out what was going on and carry policy through. He suggested nothing new or different. He wanted to talk about Laos, Cuba, and so forth. He did seem to be less informed about foreign policy than about domestic policy."

"Lyndon," said the new President's wife, "acts as if there is never going to be a tomorrow." He himself defined his philosophy of leadership with his favorite Biblical quotation, from Isaiah 1:18: "Come now, and let us reason together, saith the Lord," but he confessed that he liked to "show a little garter" while doing it, and in practice he persuaded other men to join what he called his "consensus" less by reasoning with them than by imploring, bullying, and begging them, and he was not above outright extortion. As Senate majority leader he had become one of the greatest manipulators in the history of Capitol Hill; his arm-twisting had been highly regarded there. One of his problems as President was that he never understood that the same wheeler-dealer reputation was a handicap in the White House. Eric Goldman called him "a Machiavelli in a Stetson." The public might endorse his legislative goals, but his manner of reaching them was another matter. The pollster Samuel Lubell found that many Americans planning to vote for Johnson in 1964 were nevertheless suspicious of him. They had a feeling: he was a wheeler-dealer; you had to watch his hands; he was a master politician, useful at times, no doubt, but not entirely trustworthy. His admirers, and he had many of them, protested that this was unjust. While there was much to be said for this, the skepticism was not entirely unjustified. There is no blinking the fact that until early 1966 he deliberately misled the country about the extent of the American commitment in Vietnam, or that three of his closest associates—Bobby Baker, Walter Jenkins, and Abe Fortas—were involved in scandals during his administration.

Yet there was nothing dishonorable about Johnson himself, and nothing petty. At times in that first year he seemed to be everywhere at once, turning out the White House lights and cutting Kennedy's budget to display economy with garter; declaring war on poverty, lobbying personally for Medicare, conferring with the chiefs of state of six American allies ("my prime ministers," he explained to one journalist), settling the U.S.-Cambodian dispute (if only temporarily), offering to destroy 480 B-47 bombers if the Russians would demolish the same number of TU-16s, arranging a U.S.-USSR reduction in the supply of atomic materials, touring Appalachia, persuading the Republican presidential nominee to join him in a moratorium on the race issue during the 1964 campaign, intervening with armed force in the Dominican Republic, and, in a speech on October 31, 1964, envisioning "the Great Society." Everything about the man was gargantuan. As he stepped down from an address to a congressional joint session, a senator congratulated him. "Yes," said Johnson, "I got applause eighty times." The senator checked the record, which confirmed the President; he had been counting the house as he spoke.

In both the oval office and in his bedroom three television sets stood side by side, permitting him to watch commentators on CBS, NBC and ABC at the same time. His telephone console had forty-two buttons; he could put that many callers on hold and deal with them in turn or talk to all of them at once. To sign three bills he used 169 pens, a record. He liked to drive fast. In Texas he took four women reporters for a hair-raising ride, going ninety miles an hour while describing in graphic detail the sex life of a bull. One of his passengers looked at the speedometer and gasped; the President whipped off his five-gallon hat and covered the dashboard with it. His appeals to patriotism were shameless; asked what had happened during a jawbone session about a railroad strike, a labor leader said, "Lyndon has a flag in the corner of his office. He picked it up and ran around the room with it." He spoke of "my army," "my government," and "my taxes." To make certain that no one forgot who he was, he had the presidential seal emblazoned on his cuff links, his boots, his twill ranch jackets, even on plastic drinking cups. He ordered a 44-foot portrait of himself for the Democratic national convention in 1964, and he scheduled the convention for the week of his birthday, August 27, so that the party faithful could present him with the biggest cake of all time. He wanted to roll up the greatest landslide in the history of American politics that November, and he pulled out all the stops. Entering a new city at night, he would cruise through its neighborhoods shouting into a bullhorn, "Howdy, folks! Come to the meetin'! Come to the speakin'!" Jack Gould of the *New York Times* called him "the Y. A. Tittle of handshakers." Once in Los Angeles a pickpocket reaching into a pocket found his hand grasped by that of the President of the United States.

That year the White House press corps entertained themselves by drawing up a list of what could be the shortest books ever written. The top three were *Italian War Heroes*, the *Polish Who's Who*, and *Mistakes I Made*, by Lyndon Baines Johnson. Many of those who knew the President best believed that he never searched his own soul because he never felt secure enough to do it. His problem certainly wasn't a lack of intelligence. Eric Goldman, a Princeton professor who became a Johnson aide, wrote: "After years of meeting first-rate minds in and out of universities, I am sure I have never met a more intelligent person than Lyndon Johnson—intelligent in terms of sheer IQ's, a clear, swift, penetrating mind, with an abundance of its own type of imagination and subtleties." The difficulty appeared to be rooted in the realization that his youth had been culturally deprived. The high school he attended hadn't even been accredited by the easygoing standards of its region.

In a revealing outburst he once said to Hugh Sidey of *Time*, "I don't believe that I'll ever get credit for anything I do in foreign affairs, no matter how successful it is, because I didn't go to Harvard." That was absurd, though his suspicion of intellectuals was not. Their contempt for him—there is no other word for it—was a shocking phenomenon of the 1960s. They jeered at him for pulling the ears of his beagles, as though that mattered. Buttons worn on campuses read, "King Lyndon the First," "Sterilize LBJ: No More Ugly Children," "Hitler Is Alive—in the White House," and—most unforgivable of all—"Lee Harvey Oswald, Where Are You Now That We Need You?" They applauded *MacBird*, which in depicting him as an assassin was in far worse taste than any lapse of his, and they justified their conduct as an expression of mourning for Kennedy—unwilling or unable to realize that Kennedy had chosen Johnson as his Vice President precisely because he was so able. Theodore White noted that "Political jokes were resurrected from as far back as the days of Herbert Hoover and pinned on Johnson; bedroom jokes of the President's life with Lady Bird were of a pornography to match those about Franklin Roosevelt's life with Eleanor." The Secret Service reported that crank letters attacking the President jumped from a hundred a month to over a thousand.

Johnson's speaking manner did not help. He suppressed his natural warmth and earthiness and tried to appear solemn and humble instead. What came through on the TV tube was unction and sanctimony. Instinctively people realized that whatever the real Lyndon Johnson was like, this one was a fake. The feeling that he was a mountebank was heightened by his inability to cast aside the extravagant style of the southern politician, so alien to a nation which had become accustomed to Kennedy understatement. Johnson was derisively christened "Uncle Cornpone," and to some extent he deserved it. Addressing the nation over television after settling the railroad strike, he read a letter he had received from a seven-year-old child in Park Forest, Illinois, named Cathy May Baker. "My grandmother lives in New York," Cathy had written. "She is coming to see me make my first Holy Communion. Please keep the railroads running so that she can come to see me." The President said, "So Cathy's grandmother can now go to see her." As a senator he had been able to get away with this sort of thing, but no more; within twenty-four hours the country learned that the letter was ten days old. Cathy's grandmother had visited her, witnessed the Communion, and returned to New York. Johnson never learned to abandon such stratagems. Later, when the issue was Vietnam, his habitual stretching of the truth would be much more damaging.

Liz Carpenter, one of his devoted Texans, wrote: "When I think of Lyndon Johnson, I always seem to see a Long Arm—reaching out to pick up a telephone, to grab a sheaf of papers, to shake hands, to embrace, to comfort, to persuade, sometimes even to shove —but always to include, yes, always to include." But not everybody. Johnson excluded Robert F. Kennedy. They brought out the worst in each other. It was the strong, irrational dislike of two proud and sensitive men, and it had been evident long before the tragedy in Dallas. Robert Kennedy had opposed his brother's choice of Johnson in Los Angeles, and Johnson at times seemed to oppose the younger Kennedy's very existence. Johnsonians could be very bitter about their predecessors. Liz Carpenter wished her President had been given "some public words of encouragement from the bereaved family after the assassination . . . He never mentioned it, but being a woman and a partisan, I was conscious of the silence . . . the Kennedys looked at the living and wished for the dead and made no move to comfort the country."

Undoubtedly grief for the slain President made Johnson's task harder, but it was not confined to the Kennedy family. Shortly after the assassination Congressman Clarence Cannon of Missouri predicted that "Everything will be Kennedy for a while. Then people will forget." But they did not forget. Magazines issued JFK memorial editions which were quickly sold out. The demand for Kennedy books grew ever more insatiable. Collectors of Americana discovered that holographic Kennedy letters were as valuable as Lincoln letters. An autographed copy of *Profiles in Courage* brought $375. To point up the Kennedy-Johnson transition, the presidential staff took to distributing pictures of both Presidents during Johnsonian trips, but the practice was soon discontinued; for every Johnson picture the public took ten of Kennedy. The Secret Service raged when the new chief executive rebuked an agent for wearing a Kennedy PT boat tie clip, but Johnson's resentment was understandable. He was being shadowed by a ghost.

It must have sometimes seemed to him that he was encountering Kennedys whichever way he turned. He sent Bob and Ethel Kennedy off on a tour of the Far East and the tour was on every front page. Ted Kennedy was hurt in a plane crash and the accident obscured Johnson's announcement that U.S. military might was greater than the combined strength of all the armies and navies in the history of the world. Above all there was Jacqueline Kennedy, whose most trivial remark or appearance could eclipse a statement by the President. Gallup reported that the First Lady, in a break with tradition, was only the second most admired woman in the United States; her predecessor was still first. In July 1964 Mrs. Kennedy moved to New York, and there was hope in the White House that the country's idolatry of her might diminish. It didn't; the mere fact that she continued to prefer bouffant hairdos to hats was enough to do to the women's hat industry what her husband had done to the men's.

Francis B. Sayre, dean of the Episcopalian Washington Cathedral and a Kennedy friend, rose in the pulpit to call Johnson "a man whose public house is splendid in its every appearance but whose private lack of ethic most inevitably introduces termites at the very foundation." The *Washington Star* commented that Sayre's "harsh pronouncement, we suspect, sums up the real mood of a great part of the electorate." Even harder for the President to bear were the vicious rumors that he was implicated in his predecessor's death. A commission headed by Chief Justice Earl Warren found that Kennedy had been murdered by Lee Harvey Oswald, who had acted alone, and the Kennedy family did everything possible to encourage acceptance of the commission's findings, but irresponsible attacks on the Warren Report continued throughout Johnson's years in the White House, sometimes in respectable society. The *New York World Journal Tribune* commented that "Out of respect for the memory of a martyred President, we think it is time to ask the ghouls, the buck-chasers, the sensation-mongers and the character assassins to desist—to shut up until or unless they can put up, as so far they have so notoriously failed to do." It was wasted ink; assaults on the report continued, and reached a high-water mark when the British Broadcasting Company paid a discredited critic $40,000, a record price, for a two-hour film which proved nothing.

The "Bobby problem," as it was called in the White House, became a major headache for Johnson. The new President had been in office less than six months when Washington became aware that the previous President's brother was building a government-in-exile. Comprised of New Frontiersmen who had left the government, the Kennedy people met at Jacqueline Kennedy's Georgetown residence that spring and, after she left Washington, at the attorney general's home, Hickory Hill. They were united in hostility to Johnson. None of them believed that he had been responsible for the tragedy in Dallas, of course, but they did feel that the younger Kennedy had a right to become Johnson's Vice President. They had lost touch with reality. There was never any possibility that the two men might run on the same ticket. In one of his milder comments on Bob Kennedy, President Johnson said, "That upstart's come too far and too fast. He skipped the grades where you learn the rules of life. He never liked me, and that's nothing compared to what I think of him." Johnson people called Bob a former McCarthyite and a "liberal fascist"; they said he was "Rover Boy, without birth control," and that he supported "God and country—in that order, after the Kennedys."

At 1 P.M. on Wednesday, July 29, 1964, the President summoned Attorney General Kennedy to the oval office and told him that he would not be his running mate. Johnson said that he approved of the young Kennedy's ambition and thought it would be fine if Bob ran the country some day. But not yet. He offered him his choice of any other post in the government and asked him if he would run Johnson's coming presidential campaign, as he had his brother's. Bob declined. The manner of announcing the end of Kennedy's vice-presidential ambitions this year was left undecided. Kennedy left believing that the meeting had been confidential. Evidently Johnson didn't think so, for he invited three Washington correspondents to lunch the next day and told them about it. That was bad enough; what was worse was that he couldn't resist using his considerable talents as a mimic to show them how Kennedy had taken it. Bob hadn't said a word at first when he had been told, the President said. He had just gulped. Johnson showed how he had gulped. When the story reached Kennedy he was furious. He confronted the President and accused him of a breach of confidence. Johnson said he hadn't told anyone about the meeting, and when Bob bluntly called him a liar he said, well, maybe there was some conversation he had forgotten; he would have to check his records and his calendar.

The President wanted Kennedy to announce that he wouldn't be on the ticket. Bob wouldn't do it. That left Johnson with a dilemma. He didn't want to offend the national Kennedy following. On the other hand, he felt he couldn't risk leaving the question open; the delegates to the coming Democratic national convention in Atlantic

City were Kennedy people, quite capable of choosing Bob themselves. His solution was bizarre and typically Johnsonian. On July
30 he announced: "With reference to the selection of the candidate
for Vice President on the Democratic ticket I have reached the conclusion that it would be inadvisable for me to recommend to the
convention any member of my Cabinet or any of those who meet
regularly with the Cabinet." He gave no reason. It didn't make
sense. In a stroke he had doomed the vice-presidential ambitions
not only of Robert Kennedy but also of McNamara, Stevenson,
Shriver, Rusk, and Orville Freeman. Johnson said, "Now that damn
albatross is off my neck." Bob said, "I'm sorry I took so many nice
fellows over the side with me."

In *The Making of the President 1964* Theodore H. White wrote
of a historic encounter that summer: "The deft response of American planes to the jabbing of North Vietnam's torpedo boats in the
Gulf of Tonkin had been carried off with the nicest balance between
boldness and precision." So it seemed then. Later, when disenchantment with the Vietnam War was metastasizing through the country, the events in Tonkin Gulf turned out to be shadowy, imprecise,
and, most disturbing, a consequence of deliberate American provocation.

The key to understanding what happened in those waters off
North Vietnam during the first week of August 1964 is a U.S. plan
for clandestine operations against the Communist forces there
whose code designation was 34A. White had never heard of 34A;
neither had the American people; neither had Congress, which on
the strength of events for which it was responsible was asked to
commit, and did commit, the country to a disastrous escalation of
the Asian war. To some extent the Gulf of Tonkin incidents may
have been misinterpreted and distorted by chance, but those errors
would have been inconsequential if men in Washington had not
been playing a deeper game. The chief intriguer was President
Johnson. He in turn may have been deceived and manipulated by
high officers in the Pentagon. All that can be said with certainty
is that Congress was maneuvered into supporting hostilities.

Plan 34A was conceived in December 1963, the month after the
assassination of President Kennedy. Secretary of Defense Mc-
Namara, in Saigon on one of his many inspection trips, liked what
he heard of the scheme for stealthy actions against the North Viet-

namese. He put General Krulak in charge of it. Back in Washington he described it to President Johnson, who was equally enthusiastic. In execution 34A proved disappointing, however. The attacks by South Vietnamese guerrillas, parachutists, and frogmen were well organized, but the population in North Vietnam liked the Hanoi regime; the saboteurs were betrayed every time. General Harkins and McGeorge Bundy, who were masterminding 34A, switched to commando raids on Communist shore installations by South Vietnamese torpedo boats. Hanoi regarded these as more an annoyance than a threat, but radio intercepts revealed a growing demand for retribution among Communist naval officers commanding the raided North Vietnamese bases.

On Thursday, July 30, 1964, the day that Johnson eliminated Attorney General Kennedy and the rest of his cabinet from the Vice Presidency, a flotilla of South Vietnamese PT boats sailed from Da Nang on a 34A errand. The U.S.S. *Maddox*, an American destroyer, was headed for the same waters; its task was to goad the shore installations into using their radar and then to plot the radar—the naval equivalent of spotting enemy artillery positions so that they can be destroyed by counterbattery fire. On August 1 the destroyer passed the PTs coming the other way; they had just completed their torpedo attack and were returning home. The destroyer entered the combat zone and began its task of provoking radar operators on the coast. North Vietnamese officers there assumed that the *Maddox* and the PT boats were part of the same mission. This assumption was clear to Americans who were monitoring radio messages from three North Vietnamese torpedo boats sent out to investigate the destroyer, and their report to that effect was sent back to the Pentagon. There it was filed in the back of a deep drawer without comment. In its report to the White House the Pentagon merely said that the three Communist PT boats had attacked the *Maddox*, which had responded by sinking one of them.

In the laundered version which was given to the public, the destroyer was said to have been thirty miles from the coast, peacefully sailing through international waters. There was no mention of its assignment, and nothing at all about the South Vietnamese boats. President Johnson ordered the *Maddox* to continue its activities, and a second destroyer, the *Turner Joy*, was told to join it. Thus the stage was set for a second Tonkin Gulf incident. The night of August 4, one sailor said later, was "darker than the hubs of hell."

Captain John Herrick, the commander of the destroyer patrol, radioed back that it was clear from interceptions of the North Vietnamese radio that they continued to believe that the American vessels were part of a 34A attack. Like its predecessor, this message was suppressed in the Pentagon. The public was told that American vessels had been the target of a second act of unprovoked aggression, this time when they were sixty-five miles from the coast.

Considering the gravity of the actions based upon it, the evidence in this second episode was surprisingly thin. The Senate Foreign Relations Committee did not hear the full story until three and a half years later. To their astonishment, the senators then learned that there may have been no encounter at all. Blips had appeared on the *Turner Joy's* radar screen; the destroyer had opened fire. The *Maddox* did, too, although its radar screen was clear. Both ships took evasive action. The captain of the *Maddox* noticed that his signalmen reported torpedoes each time the destroyer turned sharply. After three hours of this Herrick radioed back: "Review of action makes recorded contacts and torpedoes fired appear doubtful. Freak weather effects and overeager sonar man may have accounted for many reports. No actual visual sightings by *Maddox*. Suggest complete evaluation before further action." There were certainly North Vietnamese torpedo boats in the vicinity—destroyer gunfire and carrier-based aircraft sank two of them—but the American vessels were undamaged, and there was a very real doubt over which side had fired the first shot. Fourteen hours after the first reported contact the Pentagon was still asking the destroyers for the names of witnesses, their reliability, and the size, type, and number of attacking North Vietnamese forces.

Lyndon Johnson hadn't waited. On his orders American warplanes were already taking off from the carriers *Ticonderoga* and *Constellation*; their targets were four North Vietnamese torpedo boat bases and an oil depot. The next morning the country learned that thirty-five North Vietnamese boats and 90 percent of the depot had been damaged or destroyed. Johnson appeared on television to report that "aggression by terror against the peaceful villages of South Vietnam has now been joined by open aggression on the high seas against the United States of America." The response, he said, was "limited and fitting. We Americans know, although others appear to forget, the risks of spreading conflict. We seek no wider war."

Possibly his reaction to these brief clashes between small vessels would have been different if he had been facing another opponent in that election year. Three weeks earlier the Republicans had nominated Barry Goldwater in the San Francisco Cow Palace, and was accusing the administration of "timidity before Communism." He brought his admirers to their feet, roaring, with the charge that "the Good Lord raised up this mighty republic to be a home for the brave . . . not to cringe before the bullying of Communism . . . Failures cement the wall of shame in Berlin. Failures blot the sands of shame at the Bay of Pigs. Failures mark the slow death of freedom in Laos. Failures infest the jungles of Vietnam."

By exploiting the events in Tonkin Gulf, Johnson could break the back of that Goldwater issue. All he needed to do was to wrap himself in the flag and ask Congress to give him a free hand to deal with the North Vietnamese pirates. To this end he called the congressional leaders to the White House and asked them for a resolution authorizing him to deal decisively with such challenges. What he wanted, he said, was a joint resolution similar to the ones Congress had given Eisenhower to oppose Communist threats in Formosa in 1955 and the Middle East in 1957. Bill Bundy had already drafted a version for him. The President asked Senator Fulbright, chairman of the Foreign Relations Committee and an old Johnson friend, to be the resolution's floor manager. To his subsequent sorrow, Fulbright agreed.

The cold war was still frigid in 1964; few men on the Hill were ready to urge a soft answer to Communist wrath. But there was one: Wayne Morse of Oregon. On the night after the second Tonkin Gulf incident Morse had a call from someone in the Pentagon. The caller had heard that the senator was going to fight the President's resolution. He suggested that the senator ask two questions. First, he should insist upon seeing the *Maddox*'s log; it would show that the destroyer had been much closer to the shore than civilians realized. Second, he should demand to know the ship's mission; it had been far from innocent.

The next morning Morse studied the wording of the resolution and concluded that it was unconstitutional. Only Congress could declare war, he pointed out to Fulbright. This measure would give blanket approval to the waging of war by the chief executive with no war declaration. Fulbright reminded him of the Formosa and

Middle East resolutions. Morse said they had been unconstitutional, too, but they had been more justifiable than this one. The crises which inspired them had been subject to quick solutions. Not so this one; the struggle in Vietnam seemed interminable, and this open-ended license would allow the President to intervene any time he saw fit. The wording was far too general, Morse said. He implored Fulbright to hold hearings. Impossible, said Fulbright; this was an emergency. Morse denied it, and he was right; but Fulbright had decided to ask for instant passage, making the issue one of senatorial patriotism. That isolated Morse and Ernest Gruening of Alaska, the only colleague to side with him. The measure passed the House 414 to 0, after just forty minutes of discussion. The Senate took longer—eight hours of debate—but that, as one observer later commented, was "less time than the Senate usually took to amend a fisheries bill."

There were few critical comments at the time. The move was seen as a logical extension of a line of thought reaching back to the decision, after Munich, never again to appease aggressors, relying instead on collective security. If we and SEATO's other signatories came to South Vietnam's rescue now, the reasoning went, they would help us if California found itself threatened by Ho Chi Minh, or by Ho and Mao. Dean Rusk flatly stated that to do less would put the United States in "mortal danger." Later there were hoots at this, but there was no derision at the time. The Rusk position was that of practically all public men in both parties; among the senators who voted for the resolution were Eugene McCarthy, George McGovern, Birch Bayh, Albert Gore, Jacob K. Javits, John Sherman Cooper, Frank Carlson, George D. Aiken, and Frank Church. The *New York Times* commented: "The nation's united confidence in the Chief Executive is vital." The *Washington Post* said: "President Johnson has earned the gratitude of the free world." Lou Harris reported that whereas 58 percent of the nation had been critical of Johnson's handling of the war in July, 72 percent now approved. Harris wrote: "In a single stroke Mr. Johnson has turned his greatest political vulnerability in foreign policy into one of his strongest assets." Even Walter Lippmann approved, believing that the President was telling the country that bombing would be the outer limit of American involvement in Vietnam, that he would never send troops. The friends of the administration, which in 1964 meant most of the nation, were jubilant. It was much later that Morse's prophetic words were recalled:

> I believe that history will record that we have made a great mistake in subverting and circumventing the Constitution of the United States . . . by means of this resolution. As I argued earlier today at great length, we are in effect giving the President . . . warmaking powers in the absence of a declaration of war. I believe that to be a historic mistake.

Johnson signed the document the day it was passed, August 7. Eight months later he told a group of visitors with a grin, "For all I know our Navy was shooting at whales out there."

In the summer of 1963 Eliot Janeway, the syndicated economic columnist, speculated about what might happen if black and white workmen found themselves competing for the same jobs. He suggested that the white workers might become resentful of the civil rights movement, and he gave the reaction a name: "backlash." During the winter after Dallas "backlash" acquired a political meaning. Specifically, it was applied to racist support for the presidential primary campaigns of Governor George C. Wallace of Alabama. After displays of strength in Indiana (where he won 30 percent of the vote on May 5) and in Maryland (43 percent on May 19), Wallace's national following dwindled. His popularity seemed to suffer from the dignified demeanor of most blacks, who were still turning their cheek to injustice. In July Wallace quit the race. Yet even as he withdrew, blacks in New York were making history by declining to turn a cheek. As a consequence, headlines began conveying news which was bound to stimulate backlash.

On July 16, the day the Republican presidential candidate accepted his party's nomination in San Francisco, a Manhattan janitor was hosing the sidewalk outside a building of luxury apartments at 215 East Seventy-sixth Street, near the edge of Harlem. Noticing three Negro youths lounging across the street, he impulsively turned the hose on them. That was unwise. To the boys the hose was reminiscent of Bull Connor and Birmingham. Infuriated, they attacked the janitor, holding trash can lids as shields and hurling missiles. A bottle hit him; he fled. One of the boys, James Powell, fifteen, went after him with a knife. At this point an off-duty police lieutenant, Thomas R. Gilligan, arrived on the scene. Gilligan drew his pistol and ordered Powell to drop the knife. Instead the boy lunged at the licutcnant, slashing his right forearm. Gilligan discharged one warning shot and then fired for keeps, killing him instantly.

Young Powell's death aroused all Harlem. For three days the Negroes' rage smoldered. On the third evening, a Saturday, CORE held a protest rally on West 123rd Street. Goaded by an impassioned speaker, a black mob marched to the nearby 29th Precinct station and demanded Gilligan's immediate suspension. When it wasn't forthcoming they rioted, throwing bottles and debris at the policemen. The riot spread and continued for five nights. Dying down there, it then broke out in the Bedford-Stuyvesant section of Brooklyn, and when the violence subsided in Brooklyn it erupted in Rochester, New York, three hundred miles away. On Sunday, August 2, Jersey City blew. Paterson and Elizabeth were next, then Dixmoor, a Chicago suburb, and finally Philadelphia. Hundreds had been injured, and nearly a thousand arrested. A thousand stores were damaged; losses were placed at several million dollars.

The FBI declared that there was no pattern to the riots, that they were "a senseless attack on all constituted authority, without purpose or objective." The report continued: "While in the cities racial tensions were a contributing factor, none of the . . . occurrences was a 'race riot' in the accepted meaning of the phrase." Essentially chaotic, the disorders were nevertheless far from lacking form and significance. Until 1964 whites had always been the aggressors in major American interracial disturbances, of which there had been thirty-three since the turn of the century. Now the situation was reversed; the initiative had passed to the blacks. The race riots of the 1960s shared other characteristics. They came in the summer, in ghettos marked by an absence of contact between the slum population and those who made the key decisions concerning it, and they were sparked by hostility between the Negroes and white policemen.

"Watch out," said Negro Congressman Adam Clayton Powell, often a shrewder man than his critics, black or white, knew. The "black revolution," as he called it, would, he said, have two phases. The first was southern and concerned with "middle-class matters": sitting on buses and at lunch counters, using public toilets, going to the same schools as whites—issues of status. The second phase was northern. It was just beginning, and it was going to be very different, he said. Powell called it "proletarian," and he predicted that it would be "rough." Northern Negroes had always had the rights their counterparts in the South sought. Their concern was what Powell called the "gut issue of who gets the money." They were in a mutinous mood, and they were not moved by Martin Luther King's appeals for nonviolence. Their war cry was: "Burn, baby, burn!"

Although no one knew it at the time, 1964 marked the beginning of a cycle which would devastate the northern cities within three years. In addition to the tumult in New York there were scattered disorders that summer in New Jersey, Philadelphia, Chicago, and St. Augustine, Florida. Race was becoming the country's overriding domestic issue. In northern schools it was the year of the boycott; black parents in New York and Cleveland, dissatisfied with the treatment of their children, kept them at home. Malcolm X formed the Black Nationalist Party in 1964. The consciences of the North had at last been aroused by the injustices in the South. That spring Mrs. Malcolm Peabody, the seventy-two-year-old mother of the governor of Massachusetts, was arrested for participating in the St. Augustine protests, and the declaration of a mistrial in the Medgar Evers murder case, which only a few years earlier would have been accepted passively by Negroes, stimulated recruitment for the most important civil rights program of the year, the Mississippi "Freedom Summer" of 1964.

The immediate importance of the events in Mississippi lay in their impact on the ghettoed blacks in the North. Until 1940, some 75 percent of American Negroes had lived in the South. The long emigration of southern Negroes northward and the coming of age of the children born in their new homes had created a new, militant generation of blacks. Washington, D.C., and Newark now had Negro majorities, and Cleveland, Baltimore, St. Louis, and Detroit were more than one-third Negro. The black birth rate—approximately 40 percent higher than that of whites—had replaced immigration as the U.S. population's expansional factor. The urban slums of the North were swarming with black youths. More than half the country's Negroes were now below the age of twenty-two, and great masses of them lacked parental supervision. Fully 30 percent of the black families in big cities were headed by women who lacked husbands; in New York City alone there were 100,000 illegitimate Negro children in 1964. The revolution in communications meant that TV news programs provided this volatile audience with vivid reports of civil rights developments in the South. "Amid all the sad statistics poured forth about the ghettoes," the *Economist* of London reminded its European readers, "it is worth remembering that . . . some 88 per cent of black American families have television sets."

The Freedom Summer was sponsored by the Council of Federated Organizations (CFO), principally SNCC and CORE. None of the participants expected a graceful reception from white Mississippians. Memories of James Meredith and Medgar Evers were still fresh, and the red-necks and wool-hats of the South were known to be resentful over the Civil Rights Act of 1964. Introduced by John Kennedy and shepherded through Congress by Lyndon Johnson, it extended the bans against discrimination into many new areas. CFO cast its recruiting nets on the campuses of northern colleges and universities, chiefly among white students whose consciences were troubled by injustices to Negroes. A thousand of them volunteered to participate in a drive to register as many voters as possible among Mississippi's 900,000 blacks. They were trained in Oxford, Ohio. On June 19 the first group of 200 left for the South, and on June 21 they reached Jackson.

Almost immediately—it was the following day—three of them were reported missing. They were Michael H. Schwerner, twenty-four, of Brooklyn; Andrew Goodman, twenty, of New York, and James E. Chaney, twenty-one, of Meridian, Mississippi. Schwerner and Goodman were white; Chaney was black. The three were traveling in a 1964 Ford station wagon, and they had been arrested for speeding in Neshoba County, in east central Mississippi. Sheriff Lawrence Rainey and his deputy, Cecil Price, said the youths had disappeared after paying a fine in Philadelphia, the county seat. The station wagon was found the next day fifteen miles northeast of Philadelphia. It had been burned.

The FBI, local law officers, and Navy men stationed in Mississippi conducted a massive search for the missing youths. Rivers and creeks were dragged; helicopters and a photoreconnaissance jet hovered overhead. At the request of the President, Allen Dulles flew down to confer with Governor Paul B. Johnson Jr. A considerable part of the state's white population believed that the three were in Cuba or, as one report had it, in a Chicago bar, drinking beer and laughing at the baffled lawmen looking for them. The prevailing opinion in white Mississippi was that the searchers had no expectation of finding the youths. They were there, the story went, to win Negro votes for President Johnson in the North.

Meanwhile the rest of the CFO volunteers were encountering

oefore being

ıoba County
was accused
ι lynch mob,
en, and one
that any of
seemed un-
:ral Joe Pat-
ges; in their
ınd jury in
ıst eighteen
1870 statute
: slain men,
had helped
: recent oc-
ıimpanzees.
le.

ımissed the
charges to
iff, his dep-
ıe awarded
reporters it
:roes. Con-
;; one huge
across the
ıled by re-
t reversed
·n the con-
: observers
ıe accused
ɔlainly en-
vers called
st to good
he jury of
ro venire-

led forty-
no crin
y of C

pi Delta their meetings with local
-the Klan Air Force: private planes
ɔped satchels of explosives. After
lemolished in McComb, in south-
te men were arrested; with them
igh-powered rifles, several carbines
nbs, a five-gallon can of explosive
:s, and several thousand rounds of

ed handbills in Belzoni, Mississippi,
minal syndicalism," and held in the
ɔre out a wall in the home of the
mised blacks equal protection under
ced men who burned churches, and
ı. As the summer waned the leaders
ıent drew up a list of their casualties.
en beaten. Three had been wounded
ıgs. Over a thousand had been ar-
rches and thirty-one homes had been
there were several unsolved murders
to be attributable to hostility toward

NAACP that the federal government
ve police action in the state; it was
constitutional. J. Edgar Hoover went
he deplored what he called an "over-
said his men "most certainly" would
vith protection. At the suggestion of
resident sent more FBI agents to the
t on the top two floors of a new office
au's Mississippi headquarters. Governor
: assistance in the search for the three
Predictably, that call was unheeded,
y $30,000 in reward money brought in-
ıers. With it, agents rented excavation
a newly erected earthen dam on a farm
: of Philadelphia. They found the bodies
r the base of the 25-foot-high red clay dam
25o-foot length. They had been shot to death,

and Chaney, the black, had been beaten savagely
murdered.

On December 4 the FBI arrested twenty-one Nes
men, including Sheriff Rainey and Deputy Price. Price
of arresting the three youths and turning them over to
which he then joined. Most of the men were Klansn
was the local Klan leader. Civil rights leaders doubte
them would be convicted, and for a while it certainly
likely. Governor Johnson and Mississippi Attorney Ger
terson announced that the state would not prefer char
opinion the evidence was inadequate. A federal gr
Meridian, Mississippi, did hand down indictments aga
of the men, charging them with violating an obscure
by conspiring to violate the constitutional rights of th
but the U.S. District Judge was W. Harold Cox, who
delay due process in the James Meredith case. On or
casion Cox had compared black voter applicants to
He was not expected to give the defendants any troul

In the beginning he didn't. In February 1965 he d
felony indictments against the accused, reducing the
misdemeanors. For a time it even appeared that the she
uty, and a Philadelphia justice of the peace might
damages against the government by a local jury. To
seemed that the defendants were widely regarded as h
federate flags were displayed outside the federal buildin
one was run up each morning at the barbershop directl
street. Television and wire service cameramen were ma
sentful bystanders. Although the U.S. Supreme Cou
Judge Cox, ruling that the accused men must stand trial
spiracy charges brought by the Justice Department, mo
believed that the case was as good as dead. Certainly
thought so. Freed on bond during the trial, they were
joying their local fame. A battery of twelve defense law
114 witnesses, most of them to provide alibis or to att
character. One lawyer called the informers "traitors."
seven women and five men was all white; eighteen Ne
men had been eliminated by defense challenges.

John Doar, prosecuting for the Justice Department, c
one witnesses. They revealed that the murders had bee
of passion. Schwerner, who had preceded the main boc

volunteers, had been marked for death by the Klan nine days before he was killed for having eaten and slept in the homes of Negroes. He and his two companions had been seized after a wild chase and taken to a lonely dirt road. One of the klansmen had spun Schwerner around and asked him, "Are you that nigger lover?" Schwerner had replied, "Sir, I know how you feel." Those had been his last words. Goodman, too, had been swiftly murdered. One Klansman had been disappointed because the two white volunteers had been put to death before he could fire. He had shot Chaney, saying, "At least I killed me a nigger."

One day after retiring to consider the evidence the jury reported that it was hopelessly deadlocked. Judge Cox refused to accept the stalemate. Instead he issued new instructions, among them the so-called "dynamite charge" which had been upheld by the Supreme Court in 1898 as a way to jolt a deadlocked jury into a decision. Under it jurors in the minority were urged to "carefully examine and reconsider" their opinions, weighing the feelings of the majority. The judge also told them that he would approve a mixed verdict. During a recess at this point Deputy Price and another defendant, Wayne Roberts, a salesman of automobile trailers, blundered. They told spectators in the federal building corridors that they were going to fix the judge. Roberts was heard to say, "Judge Cox gave the jury the dynamite charge. Well, we have some dynamite for him ourselves." Word of this reached the judge. Ordering them to the bench, he said, "If you think you can intimidate this court, you are sadly mistaken. I'm not going to let any wild man loose on any civilized society." With that, he ordered them locked up and denied them bail. On October 20 the jury found seven of the men, including Price and Roberts, guilty. Sheriff Rainey and seven others were acquitted. Over three years had passed since the crime, but the Justice Department was jubilant. The verdict had made history; for the first time, a federal jury of white Mississippians had convicted white defendants in a civil rights case. On December 29 Judge Cox sentenced the seven to jail terms ranging from three years to ten—the maximum.

It was the year of Goldwater. In seven consecutive national conventions of the past, beginning with the nomination of Landon in 1936, Republican conservatives had suppressed their yearning for a presidential candidate from their own ranks. This time they did not suppress it. This time they turned to $Au + H_2O = 1964$. They wanted A Choice, Not an Echo, as their placards proclaimed, and on July 15 they nominated Barry Morris Goldwater, Arizona's senior senator and a denizen of deep right field.

The fact is that the party felt desperate. George Gallup had discovered that during the past quarter-century the GOP had lost a third of its members; the number of Americans who regarded themselves as Republicans had diminished 13 percent, while the number of Democrats had increased 11 percent. Goldwater and his people had an explanation for this. The GOP, their argument went, had been choosing "me too" candidates—moderate Republicans who merely repeated Democratic promises. Their conclusion was that because the Democrats were originals and the Republican moderates mere carbon copies, the GOP had been repeatedly defeated, voters tending to prefer the real thing.

Here the skating reached thin ice. Polls indicated that a majority of the electorate favored the middle of the road. The Republican right-wingers denied it. They were convinced that out in the country there was a hidden conservative majority. It was, they insisted, the key fact in American politics. Lacking a home, these disgruntled conservatives had scorned both parties. On election days they went fishing or stayed home. To them the result was a matter of no consequence; either way they were going to be stuck with liberals, leftists, socialists, "collectivists," "bleeding hearts." Nominate a genuine conservative, said the Goldwater ideologues, and this hidden majority would come swarming into the streets and elect a real American.

Although President Kennedy had been convinced that Barry Goldwater would be the Republican nominee in 1964, Goldwater himself wasn't so sure, and other GOP leaders were slow in taking him seriously. The struggle over who would become the standard-bearer turned into an odd one. The Arizonan had announced his candidacy from his sun-drenched Scottsdale, Arizona, patio on January 3. The next Republican to throw a hat in the ring had been a woman, Margaret Chase Smith. The first primary, in New Hampshire, was won with write-in votes by a man who hadn't announced at all, Henry Cabot Lodge. Nelson Rockefeller then divulged that he was available; next William Scranton of Pennsylvania said *he* was.

Until the last of the big primaries, in California on June 2, almost everyone seemed to believe that someone would take it away from Goldwater. The likeliest one was Rockefeller. Then, on May 30, a Saturday, the second Mrs. Rockefeller gave birth to Nelson A. Rockefeller Jr.—thereby reminding California Republicans of the New York governor's recent divorce. Overnight he lost seven percentage points in the Lou Harris poll. On Tuesday Goldwater received 51 percent of the primary vote and Rockefeller 49 percent. At the convention the Arizonan's well-organized legions then deflected all opposition and took the prize with an overwhelming 883 delegate votes on the first ballot. Thereupon the nominee deepened the division in the party by giving the moderates the rough side of his tongue in a memorable passage: "Extremism in the defense of liberty is no vice! And . . . moderation in the pursuit of justice is no virtue!"

Barry Goldwater was fifty-five years old, a man of absolute integrity, and one of the most charming politicians ever to run for the Presidency. Handsome, leonine, silver-haired, with the black horn-rimmed spectacles which were his trademark, he had become one of the most celebrated public men in the nation and certainly the best-known conservative. Goldwater represented a love for the best of the past and defiance toward the worst of the present. In his crisp, low southwestern drawl he reminded the country of American maxims and ethical certitudes which had lost their validity but not their fascination. It was his special talent that he could make them seem both plausible and relevant.

Away from the Senate he was a mishmash of anachronisms. For all his summoning of the legends of the past, he was a major general in the Air Force reserve, a hot jet pilot, and a tremendous admirer of sophisticated technology. (In San Francisco he buckled himself into the cockpit of his private jet and zoomed back and forth over the Cow Palace while his name was being placed in nomination.) He was an expert radio ham; he maintained expensive sending and receiving sets in his suburban Phoenix home and his Washington apartment, and he brought a third to the San Francisco convention. He was also a superb photographer; a volume of his desert studies had been issued. Perhaps his most significant acquisition was the twenty-five-foot flagpole at his Arizona home. It was equipped with a photoelectric device which automatically raised the colors when the dawn light reached it and lowered them as twilight deepened, thereby assuring a display of patriotism even when no one was home.

"*Viva olé! Viva olé!*" chanted his faithful followers. They were passionate, they were exuberant, and sometimes they were frightening. One unforgettable moment came in the Cow Palace when Nelson Rockefeller took the rostrum to urge the adoption of minority resolutions which had been drafted by the platform committee. The galleries, packed with Goldwaterites, booed him and shouted, "We want Barry!" Some men would be daunted by this, but Rockefeller relished it. "This is still a free country, ladies and gentlemen," he taunted, and as their fury mounted and they roared with rage, he described some of the tactics which had been used against him in the California primary: "These things have no place in America, but I can personally testify to their existence, and so can countless others who have also experienced midnight and early morning telephone calls, unsigned threatening letters, smear and hate literature, strong-arm and goon tactics, bomb threats and bombings, infiltration and take-over of established political organizations by Communist and Nazi methods."

By this time there were people in the galleries who were all but lying on the floor and drumming their heels. Chairman Thruston B. Morton vainly gaveled for order while the Goldwater delegates on the floor—aware that this demonstration of ferocity was hurting their man in the eyes of the television audience—pleaded for quiet. The storm of abuse continued unabated, and Rockefeller, grinning, delivered another thrust: "Some of you don't like to hear it, ladies and gentlemen, but it's the truth."

It was part of the truth. Goldwater and his managers permitted no little old ladies in tennis shoes in their organization. Indeed, one of the weaknesses of their campaign was that it was too disciplined, too lacking in spontaneity. After the convention the senator sent two of his very straight young men, Dean Burch and John Grenier, to take over the Republican National Committee, Burch as chairman and Grenier as executive director. They spent five full weeks putting it in order—five weeks when they should have been campaigning. The day after the election in November Goldwater's finance chairman elatedly announced that his books were in the black.

A shrewder politician would have used his acceptance speech to woo the losers. He might even have visited the vanquished, as Eisenhower had done with Taft in 1952. But Goldwater had been angered by dirty tricks, too, and for all his generosity of spirit he wasn't a healer. In mid-August, much too late, he sat down in Hershey, Pennsylvania, with the party's elders—Rockefeller, Eisenhower, Nixon, Scranton, and George Romney—in an effort to bind up wounds and plan a master election strategy. It was a wasted day. They lacked a conciliatory spirit, and none had any useful campaign ideas. Mostly they complained. It was after this meeting, and in part as a consequence of it, that Republicans running for other offices began avoiding the presidential standard-bearer, even declining to share the same platform with him.

IN YOUR HEART YOU KNOW HE'S RIGHT, read the Goldwater billboards, pins, and bumper stickers. There was some truth to it. In his three books and eight hundred newspaper columns he had tackled many sacred cows which deserved it. Over the past half-century the federal bureaucracy had grown to something in the order of fifty or sixty times its original size. Its officials were often arrogant and overbearing, and some of the practices that the government either employed itself or encouraged in others had plainly outlived their usefulness—among them labor featherbedding, depletion allowances, farm price supports, and subsidies to peanut growers. Senator Goldwater was trenchant on the subject of these, and here millions of Americans knew in their hearts—or at any rate believed—that he was right.

The difficulty was that he had said, done, and written so many other things, some of them bizarre. He had offered to sell TVA for a dollar. He had said that he wished it were possible to saw off the eastern seaboard and let it float out to sea. He had depicted all of America's great cities as sin-steeped Babylons. At various times he had advocated the elimination of rural electrification, the replacement of the National Labor Relations Board, and a new U.S. Supreme Court. Here Americans knew in their hearts that he was wrong.

His opponent was one of the most masterful politicians in the history of the country; as a result, the flaws in Goldwater's armor were deftly exposed, over and over, so that he was put on the defensive and remained there. Atomic warfare was a particularly devastating issue. Speaking in Hartford on October 24, 1963, Goldwater had said that he believed the size of the American military presence could be reduced by as much as a third if NATO "commanders" were authorized to use tactical nuclear weapons in a crisis. That put the Bomb in the campaign, and it remained there to the end.

As exploited by Rockefeller in New Hampshire's January campaign, it was a legitimate campaign issue. The Democrats probably went too far in what became known as their "Daisy Girl" television spot, first shown on September 7. NBC's Monday Night at the Movies that evening, *David and Bathsheba*, starring Gregory Peck and Susan Hayward, was interrupted for an idyllic picture of a child pulling the petals off a daisy and counting them; as she did, the picture dissolved into a mushroom cloud. The Republicans were understandably incensed. Yet Goldwater had failed and continued to fail to clarify his Hartford remarks. At the very least his manner of referring to nuclear weapons was disturbing. A candidate for the Presidency of the United States ought not to speak of "lobbing one into the men's room at the Kremlin." On one occasion when Goldwater was supposed to be exorcising the shadow of the Bomb, Charles Mohr of the *New York Times* counted almost thirty such phrases as "push the button," "atomic holocaust," and "nuclear annihilation." That was not the way to reassure the people. IN YOUR HEART, the Democrats said in a wicked thrust, YOU KNOW HE MIGHT.

Another issue digging graves for Republican hopes was social security. Here the trouble had begun on January 6 in New Hampshire. In reply to a question, Goldwater said that he favored improving social security by making contributions voluntary. The next day's Concord, New Hampshire, *Monitor* carried the head, GOLD-WATER SETS GOALS: END SOCIAL SECURITY. The senator protested, but plainly that would be the consequence of voluntary participation; payments to retired workers must come from young workers, who are no more eager than anyone else to pay taxes if they can get out of it. In the Democrats' TV spot on this, two hands tore up a social security card. Since social security affects a hundred million Americans, it would have been hard to find a theme of greater interest.

Goldwater had other problems; he had voted against the nuclear test ban treaty and—the previous June—the Kennedy-Johnson civil rights bill. The consequences of his record became clearer and clearer as one conservative newspaper after another endorsed Johnson, and ultimately even the Republican candidate could see it. Poll figures had never been so lopsided; Gallup had Johnson over

Goldwater 65 to 29 percent. After the election the Arizonan remarked that he should have realized that it was all over in San Francisco, before the campaigning had even begun. As it was, he said, he knew in August that it was hopeless. That had the ring of hindsight. As late as October he was giving lip service, at least, to confidence in victory. Whatever his expectations, though, he never tried to improve his chances with low blows. He admonished audiences that hissed Johnson ("Don't boo the office of the Presidency"). When F. Clifton White, one of his advisers, produced a documentary film called *Choice*, exploiting the ghetto riots with shocking scenes of marauding Negroes, Goldwater called it racist and suppressed it. And he refused to capitalize on, or even to discuss, reports of an impending scandal in the Johnson campaign—the arrest of the President's chief aide on a charge of committing sodomy in a public toilet.

The aide was Walter Jenkins, who, exhausted by overwork, had yielded to temptations he might otherwise have suppressed. Jenkins had left the White House for a few hours on October 7 to attend a cocktail party celebrating the occupancy of new offices by *Newsweek*'s Washington bureau. After several drinks he left and walked two blocks to the Washington YMCA. The basement men's room was known to him as a trysting place for homosexuals. Unfortunately the Washington police knew it, too, and at about 7:30 P.M. Jenkins and an elderly army veteran were arrested by an officer who had been watching them through a peephole. They were taken to a police station, where it was discovered that five years earlier Jenkins had been arrested on the same charge. Newspapermen were reluctant to make this public, but they had no choice once Dean Burch called attention to "a report sweeping Washington that the White House is desperately trying to suppress a major news story affecting the national security"—an early instance of incautious use of this phrase by the Republican right. Once the report was public, Jenkins entered a hospital with a diagnosis of "extreme fatigue." Burch and many of Goldwater's other advisers begged him to avail himself of this opportunity to hammer away at what they called a shocking example of immorality on the highest level of the administration. He declined.

Johnson anxiously commissioned an Oliver Quayle survey to find out how many votes the disaster would cost. None to speak of, was Quayle's surprising conclusion, and the sad incident swiftly faded from public memory. Goldwater's compassion was only part of the explanation for this. Another part was that just as people had begun talking about Jenkins they were rocked by three startling developments in foreign affairs. Within forty-eight hours on October 15–16, Khrushchev was stripped of power and deposed, Communist China announced that it had exploded its first atomic bomb, and Sir Alec Douglas-Home's Conservative government fell. The White House press corps talked of Johnsonian luck. He was having a lot of it; when Lady Bird Johnson headed south with a group of southern administration wives on a sixteen-car train christened "The Lady Bird Special," they were met by hecklers—the one reception sure to win sympathy, and votes, elsewhere.

Johnson met the Lady Bird Special in New Orleans, where he then delivered his finest speech of the campaign. It was risky—a fiery appeal for civil rights, delivered against the advice of Senator Russell Long—and that alone would have made it memorable. The last line, however, made it unforgettable. After appealing for an end to bigotry he said that he was going to enforce and observe the Civil Rights Act of 1964 ("I'm not going to let them build up the hate and try to buy my people by appealing to their prejudice"), and then he told how, when Sam Rayburn first went to Congress, he had had a long talk with an ailing southern senator who said he wished he felt well enough to take one more trip home. "I would like to go back down there and make them one more Democratic speech," Johnson quoted the senator as saying. "I just feel I've got one more in me. Poor old state, they haven't heard a real Democratic speech in thirty years. All they ever hear at election time is *nigra, nigra, nigra.*" The audience gasped, recovered, and gave him a five-minute standing ovation.

The record of other LBJ campaign highlights does not always read so well. This is particularly true in regard to Vietnam. Accusing Goldwater of loose talk and loose thinking about nuclear weapons was powerful political medicine. The Democrats couldn't resist ever stronger doses of it. The "Daisy Girl" TV spot was followed by another on September 17 which was so outrageous that it was run but once; it showed a lovely child eating an ice cream cone while a voice told of strontium 90 poisoning the air and reminded viewers that Goldwater had voted against the test ban treaty. The senator's suggestion that atomic bombs might be used to "defoliate" the Ho Chi Minh Trail was cited as an example of his irresponsibility and militarism. But this was a dangerous topic for Johnson. It reminded voters that Americans were in a hot war in Vietnam and that Goldwater hadn't put them there. To keep the momentum of the peace issue, therefore, the President made certain pledges to the country which would not be forgotten.

In Eufaula, Oklahoma, on September 25 he said: "We don't want our American boys to do the fighting for Asian boys. We don't want to get involved . . . and get tied down in a land war in Asia."

Then in Manchester, New Hampshire, on September 28: "I have not thought we were ready for American boys to do the fighting for Asian boys. What I have been trying to do, with the situation that I found, was to get the boys in Vietnam to do their own fighting with our advice and with our equipment. . . . Now we have lost 190 American lives. . . . I often wake up in the night and think about how many I could lose if I made a misstep. . . . It is not any problem to start a war. . . . I know some folks who think I could start one mighty easy. But it is a pretty difficult problem for us to prevent one, and that is what we are trying to do."

In Akron, Ohio, on October 21: ". . . we are not about to send American boys nine or ten thousand miles away from home to do what Asian boys ought to be doing for themselves."

And in Pittsburgh on October 27: "There can be and will be, as long as I am President, peace for all Americans."

In a bitter joke a year later a girl said, "I was told if I voted for Goldwater we would be at war in six months. I did—and we were." Surely a voter whose sole motive was the preservation of peace, and who carefully followed accounts of speeches in the newspapers, would have voted for Johnson and against Goldwater in November 1964. Later he would feel betrayed, as many did. In El Paso during the campaign the President said, "I pledge you here today I will go to any remote corner of the world to meet anyone, any time, to promote freedom and peace," but the fact was that as long as he believed that American forces could impose a military solution on the Communists he rejected all gestures, including some promising ones, from the Viet Cong and the North Vietnamese. The issue during the campaign had seemed clear-cut. Goldwater recommended the dispatch of U.S. soldiers and aircraft to the support of South Vietnam, and Johnson accused him of reckless warmongering. The President appeared to be sincere. Yet it is difficult to think of any military proposal by Goldwater which Johnson had not taken, despite his vows to the contrary, by the following summer.

On November 3 Lyndon Johnson won election to a full term in the White House. He and Hubert Humphrey carried forty-four states and the District of Columbia, with an aggregate of 486 electoral votes. Goldwater and Congressman William E. Miller took Arizona, Mississippi, Alabama, South Carolina, Louisiana, and Georgia, with 52 electoral votes. The Democrats also swept the congressional races. They won 28 of the 35 senatorial seats, giving them 68 to the Republicans' 32, and picked up 41 House seats. They now dominated the House by better than a two-thirds majority, 295 to 140. The Republicans did make a net gain of one statehouse, but they still had only 17 governors to 33 for the Democrats.

GOLDWATER FOR HALLOWEEN jeered one campaign bumper sticker that had been popular in Washington. Not all the cars displaying it had been owned by Democrats. On election day this writer lunched with Earl Warren in his chambers. The most vivid memory of that occasion was the vehemence with which the Chief Justice expressed the hope that Goldwater would be beaten soundly. Like many another GOP moderate, Warren wanted to see a total rout of the Goldwater conservatives. When disaster befell them the Republicans confirmed a theory of long standing, that their feuds are far more savage than those among Democrats. The conservatives had not only lost an election; in many cases they found themselves being cut dead by members of their own party.

Perhaps Richard Nixon best expressed the frustration and confusion among Republican regulars. Two days after the election he excoriated Nelson Rockefeller, charging that Rockefeller's refusal to help the Goldwater campaign had cost it votes. He called the New York governor a "divider." By the following Tuesday Nixon was having second thoughts. He urged his fellow Republicans to reject "right-wing extremism" while finding a place for all "responsible viewpoints," from liberal to conservative. Yet Nixon's observations were no longer compelling, even among his fellow Republicans. Unlike Rockefeller, he had campaigned tirelessly for the ticket, and apparently it had been a wasted effort. He had collected a lot of IOUs, but it was highly unlikely that they would ever prove valuable.

These were quiet years for Nixon, and in many ways they were good ones. He was making a lot of money. He had time to read and reflect. Except when he was speaking he saw as much of his family as fathers in private life. On the Sunday of that week that the campaign opened, Checkers, the little black and white cocker spaniel that he had turned into a political asset in 1952, died at the age of twelve, and he was there to comfort his daughters. (In October, while he was campaigning in Iowa, he was given another cocker and urged to call it Checkers II, but he gave it away; there was only one Checkers.) Eight weeks after the election his daughter Tricia led the parade at the International Debutante Ball in New York. He escorted her. Next day, the last day but one in 1964, he put a headstone over the grave of Checkers. To many it seemed symbolic.

Until November 1964 Lyndon Johnson had presided in the shadow of President Kennedy, but now he had been elected President in his own right. The hold of the Kennedy legend on the American imagination was still powerful—two of the most charismatic men on Capitol Hill were Robert Kennedy, the new senator from New York, as he now was, and Senator Edward M. Kennedy of Massachusetts, who had been swept back into office by over 900,-000 votes—but Johnson was now number one, and the city began to reflect it. Among the songs heard most frequently in bars were "The Eyes of Texas" and "The Yellow Rose of Texas." Middle-aged men wearing cowboy boots and five-gallon hats with their business suits milled around in the lobby of the Washington Hotel on Fifteenth Street, beside the Treasury Building. Washington began to remind visitors of a frontier town, but then, so did the country; the wide-open, anything-goes 1960s were under way.

In 1964 Rudi Gernreich, the California designer, introduced the topless bathing suit, which led to all sorts of things. On a certain level of night club entertainment "topless" women employees became a feature attraction and then a commonplace; in the tawdry Washington cabarets down by the National Archives, as in other American metropolises, waitresses strode about with naked breasts swinging. Next Mary Quant created the miniskirt in London. Girls and many women wore skirts which shrank inch by tantalizing inch as the decade grew older, until, when the microskirt arrived, they had ceased to be tantalizing; all but the most handsome legs had lost their appeal.

Nudity was becoming fashionable in the theater, and as the mid-1960s wore on, seminudity became chic in society. Transparent, or "see-through" dresses were the new thing. Yves Saint Laurent brought out gauze shifts with coy sequins guarding the nipples and the crotch. In Italy the couturier Forquet created a South Seas skirt slung precariously on the hips; for a blouse he substituted a string of beads. Timid women wore either a flesh-colored something called a body stocking underneath, or "fun-derwear"—flashy, gay-colored undergarments to be glimpsed through gauze—but the more daring (and better-endowed) flaunted the works. Naked midriffs reached higher and lower. When the Smithsonian Institution acquired some of the more fantastic new gowns, Republican Congressman H. R. Gross of Iowa rose in the House to protest.

Both sexes in the rising generation insisted upon their right to say whatever they thought "relevant," relevance, like commitment, being one of the new things. Berkeley witnessed the rise of the Free Speech Movement, or the FSM, as it was known in California. That in turn led to the first great student-administration confrontation of the 1960s. The FSM, a coalition formed in the late summer of 1964 by undergraduates, graduate students, and junior faculty, ran the gamut ideologically from Goldwaterism to Maoism. All were united against a university prohibition of on-campus solicitation for political or civil rights demonstrations to be mounted off campus. Mobilizing under the leadership of Mario Savio, a twenty-two-year-old philosophy major from New York, the FSM reached the remarkable conclusion that the university's board of regents was trying to convert the campus into a concentration camp. The purpose of the conspiracy, as they saw it, was to make Berkeley a vast trade school turning out white-collar technicians useful to the establishment—industry, banks, publishing houses, the military, conservative labor unions. Savio cried, "The time has come to put our bodies on the machine and stop it!"

On September 14, 1964, a week before the opening of fall classes, the disorders began, and neither Berkeley nor any other American university would ever be the same. Those who called the FSM Communistic missed the point. It was anarchic, and it scorned all dialectic. A research fellow who approved of the movement explained, "All the old labels are out; if there were any orthodox Communists here, they would be a moderating influence." The movement's contempt for rationalism was at times ludicrous. When police dragged Savio and eight hundred of his followers out of Sproul Hall, the epicenter of the revolt, he cried, "This is wonderful! We'll bring the university to our terms!"

One lazy day the following March a barefoot, long-haired youth paraded through the main gate of the Berkeley campus holding aloft a placard emblazoned in blue with a single four-letter word. He wasn't a student. His name was John J. Thompson, and he was an unpublished poet, a member of Berkeley's so-called "hidden community"—unknown writers and political militants who would be blamed for much of the unrest there later in the decade. The following day a dozen other youths appeared carrying signs with similar messages; one shouted his cherished word into a campus microphone; another read a passage from *Lady Chatterley's Lover* aloud to an arresting officer. No one in the movement went bail for him and his friends. The campus newspaper deprecated this "filthy speech movement." To use another phrase which was entering the language, they suspected the odd crusaders of putting them on.

Yet both their demonstrations and the new uses of taboo words appear to have been aspects of a general revolt against constraints which characterized the 1960s. Thompson and his friends may have been pulling the FSM's leg, but many serious writers were in earnest about their right to use language which until now had been proscribed. They believed that the Supreme Court agreed with them (they were right), and in the long run their impact on society may prove to be more lasting than Savio's civil disobedience. Appearing in print, locker room language was next heard on the stage —for example, in *Who's Afraid of Virginia Woolf?*, which after 664 performances on Broadway became a film in 1966—and then in mixed company, among the sophisticated at first, swiftly followed by the young. In what had once been called polite society one heard, frequently from the loveliest lips, short Anglo-Saxon words formerly limited to unmixed company. The effect on the inhibited older generation was often electrifying.

Like the Pill and the new nudity, this reflected an evolving life-style and a new morality. To many in the older generation it seemed to be no morality at all, and they came to identify it with excessive hair and communes. But the forbidden fruit was just as tasty on the palate of Goldwater's admirers in the Young Americans for Freedom. YAF members never marched in antiwar demonstrations or read *Ramparts*, but when the lights went out they were as active as the most erotic hippy. One survey of casual adulterers found that a majority were short-haired and politically conservative. A Los Angeles entrepreneur who dealt with a community of conservative hedonists told a reporter, "This is the America you don't hear about. It's clean-cut people who don't wear sandals and beards—guys and girls living very normal lives. It's almost blasphemous how American it is."

Colleges had long provided grounds suitable for pairing off, but until the mid-1960s finding a member of the opposite sex off campus who was attractive, agreeable, and prurient had been time-consuming and rather expensive. Now that, too, was changing. Two years before the Johnson-Goldwater race, Grossinger's Hotel in the Catskills held its first weekend for singles only. It was the beginning, though no one knew it then, of another movement. In 1964 a lonesome ensign named Michael G. O'Harro, stationed in Arlington, Virginia, established the beginning of a fortune and a way of life by throwing a party for other young unmarried people—officers, professional men, airline stewardesses, teachers, models, secretaries, and career girls. Three years later O'Harro was back in civilian life and president of an organization called the Junior Officers and Professional Association, with thirty thousand members, twelve local chapters, and a staff of fifty. By then it was possible to vacation at resorts for singles only, take Bahaman cruises or European tours in groups which accepted only bachelors and unmarried girls, and read such singles-only magazines as O'Harro's JOPA *Niteletter*. And O'Harro had competitors. In San Francisco the lonely could meet at Paoli's; Chicago had The Store, Dallas the TGIF (Thank God It's Friday), and Manhattan Mr. Laff's and Friday's.

The logical consequence of all this was the construction of apartment complexes in which the unmarried could rent apartments and visit one another at all hours, and that was what happened. In part it was a reflection of the balkanizing of generations—the tendency of people in one age group to go off by themselves, thus engendering misunderstandings and what would soon be known as "gaps." The first to do it were the elderly, not the young. The earliest "retirement town" was built by Del Webb in Arizona in 1960. Like O'Harro's enterprise it was a tremendous success, inspiring imitators and, in 1965, the first singles community, the South Bay Club in the Los Angeles suburb of Torrance. South Bay's 248 apartments were all rented while it was still going up. Ultimately the firm built thirteen such complexes, including one in Phoenix, with eight thousand tenants who could play bridge, engage in round-table discussions, attend barbecues, stage masked balls, participate in wine tastings, and cohabit without encountering anyone else's husband or wife.

Understandably, a popular topic in the singles-only round-table discussions was birth control. Another was wedlock, often put as a proposition: "Marriage—Is It Defensible?" Matrimony was only one of many social institutions which were under attack in the mid-Sixties. Nothing was sacred any more; during Holy Week in 1966 *Time* asked on its cover, "Is God Dead?" thereby generating an intense theological debate and one memorable bumper sticker: GOD IS ALIVE AND HIDING IN ARGENTINA. People who read *Time*—or anything else—were belittled as old-fashioned and "linear" in Marshall McLuhan's *The Gutenberg Galaxy: The Making of Typographic Man* (1962) and *Understanding Media: The Extensions of Man* (1964).

The iconoclasm of the mid-Sixties did not always pay. Ralph Ginzburg published *Eros* in 1962; the post office ruled that it was smut and he was sentenced to five years in prison. In 1964 he brought out *Fact;* it contained material about Barry Goldwater which was not factual, and when Goldwater sued he was awarded $75,000. In 1967 Ginzburg issued *Avant-Garde;* it flopped. Another loser, though no one would have guessed it in the beginning, was Cassius Clay. After winning the world's championship by knocking out Sonny Liston in one minute flat, the fastest kayo in heavyweight title history, Clay confused fight fans by becoming a Black Muslim, changing his name to Muhammad Ali, refusing induction into the Army on grounds of conscience, and then, like Ginzburg, going to jail.

But anyone could stumble in this hazardous time. The Strategic Air Command, which as the guardian of the U.S. nuclear striking capacity was supposed to be discreet, scared the country, not to mention Europe, when one of its B-52s collided with a jet tanker and dumped four hydrogen bombs in Spanish waters. Norman Mailer was reputed to know something about the writing of fiction, yet in 1965 *An American Dream,* his first novel in ten years, was mercilessly panned by critics. Lyndon Johnson was said to be determined to suppress vulgarian tendencies in order to achieve presidential dignity, but after undergoing an operation he yanked out his shirt so news cameramen could photograph the scar. James Pike, Episcopal bishop of California, resigned when accused of heresy, took up spiritualism, wrote a book about it called *The Other Side*, got lost in the Judean desert, and was found dead in a kneeling position. Betty Grable and Harry James, after twenty-two years of being regarded as the happiest couple in Beverly Hills, were divorced in Las Vegas.

Nothing, it appeared, was as it seemed. In a gubernatorial election Alabamans voted "for Lurleen" to "let George do it." Black militants blamed black lawlessness on tension between the races, but in 1964 the toughest enforcers of the law in the Crown Heights area of Brooklyn were the Maccabees, an organization of middle-class Negro vigilantes. The belief that Americans go to college to make more money took its lumps when the *Wall Street Journal* complained that few Ivy League graduates were going into business; instead they were taking jobs in churches, labor unions, the Peace Corps, and civil rights organizations. Even the cold war wasn't what it had been. In 1966 the United States and the Soviet Union introduced direct air service between Moscow and New York with one round trip each week by Pan American and Soviet Aeroflot.

In 1964 *Dr. Strangelove* faded from the marquees, to be supplanted, in 1965, by *Dr. Zhivago*, which inspired fashion fads for huge fur hats, thigh-high boots, and coat hems that swept the ground. The skateboard became the successor to the hula hoop in 1965, when its manufacturers grossed a hundred million dollars; a skateboard meet at Anaheim, California, was televised by the three networks, and the circulation of the *Skateboard Quarterly* reached fifty thousand. Then the dippy boards faded as the next toy sensation, the super ball, bounced into view. Bicycles returned to what would be a more lasting popularity that same year, when six million were sold and the Long Island Railroad installed bike racks for commuters.

An Associated Press writer observed of 1965 that "the more things were out, the more they were in." There were demands for, among other unlikely articles, tasseled lamps, and sailor suits. Bell-bottoms came on strong. Peter Max, a twenty-five-year-old commercial artist, had a vision of "a huge monumental wave of youth—the youth revolution coming," and in anticipation of it he created psychedelic art. Within five years his designs on decals, posters, scarves, etc., would provide him with an annual income of two million dollars. Pop art masterpieces included a woman's girdle with an enormous eye painted on the back. "Camp" entered the language and was applied to such artifacts as feather boas, antimacassars, bubble gum cards. Shirley Temple photographs, and souvenirs of Atlantic City. Humphrey Bogart and Jean Harlow films enjoyed revivals, and for a while girls again tried to look like Harlow. Big films included *Lord Jim*, *The Agony and the Ecstasy*, and two broad farces: *Cat Ballou* and *What's New, Pussycat?*

Lou Harris reported a "growing disenchantment with television on the part of the affluent, better-educated section of the adult American public." All three networks appeared to be searching for the lowest common denominator in popular taste, and they were virtually tied in the Nielsen ratings. ("It was inevitable," observed the *New Yorker*. "It shines with the clarity of a mathematical law.") The debasement of network programming was particularly painful at CBS, which in the great days of Edward R. Murrow had appealed to intelligent viewers. Now, under James T. Aubrey Jr., CBS offered mystery dramas, rural comedies, and peepshow sex.

Adlai Stevenson and Winston Churchill died in 1965. J. Edgar Hoover was still alive and running the FBI, but he was becoming senescent. FBI figures indicated that the national crime rate was rising 11 percent a year, and the President's Commission on Law Enforcement and Administration of Justice concluded that possibly three times as much crime was committed as was reported. Social protest was a growing category for law infractions. The anti-Vietnam teach-ins, which began with a twelve-hour all-night seminar at the University of Michigan on March 24, 1965, were perfectly legal, but that was not always true of the nude-ins, lie-ins, and love-ins which followed. Leaders of the Brooklyn chapter of CORE threatened to spoil the opening day of the New York World's Fair on April 22, 1964, with a stall-in—snarling traffic by allowing thousands of cars to run out of gas in the middle of it. They succeeded in cutting the opening day crowd from about 250,000 to 92,646. Nearly three hundred were arrested, including James Farmer, national director of CORE.

The level of violence in the country continued to appall. In the summer of 1966 an itinerant worker named Richard Speck murdered eight student nurses in Chicago. Two weeks later Charles Whitman, an honor student at the University of Texas, climbed to the top of the university's twenty-seven-story tower in Austin and opened fire on passersby below, killing fourteen and wounding thirty, and three months after that an eighteen-year-old student entered the Rose-Mar College of Beauty in Mesa, Arizona, with a pistol and killed four women and a child. He told police he had been inspired by the Chicago and Austin killings. Like Speck and Whitman, he said, he wanted "to get known."

Two legislators from opposite ends of the ideological spectrum were in trouble. Adam Clayton Powell had called a Harlem widow "a bag woman for the police department"; she had been awarded damages, but he ignored the verdict and avoided New York. Senator Tom Dodd of Connecticut was censured by his colleagues for misuse of campaign funds and selling influence to an agent for West German business interests. A New York undercover policeman infiltrated a conspiracy to blow up the Statue of Liberty, the Liberty Bell, and the Washington Monument; the causes of the various plotters ranged from Quebec independence and admiration for Fidel Castro to Negro rights and support of North Vietnam. In New York a Vacation Exchange served as a contact for homeowners who wanted to swap houses during holidays, and from a small city in eastern Massachusetts came the first word of young married couples who swapped spouses. A travel agency advertised a judo tour of Japan: two sweaty weeks for $1,396. President Sarah Gibson Blanding of Vassar told her 1,450 girls that she expected them either to abstain from sexual intercourse or leave the campus. Jack Valenti told an audience of advertising men that "I sleep each night a little better, a little more confidently because Lyndon Johnson is my President."

The Dallas trial of Jack Ruby opened on February 17, 1964, and ended March 14 with a guilty verdict. His lawyer, Melvin Belli, screamed: "This was a kangaroo court, a railroad court, and everyone knew it." Ruby would die of cancer in jail on January 3, 1967. Senator J. William Fulbright delivered a major speech on foreign policy, warning that unless the United States "cut loose from established myths" he would break with the administration. Pope Paul VI spent an October day in New York and addressed the United Nations. Hubert Humphrey, the new Vice President, seemed determined to demonstrate superloyalty to Johnson; echoing an Avis car rental ad, he said, "I'm number two and I have to try harder." Some observers wondered whether the winning Democratic ticket was developing a sadomasochistic relationship. The President almost seemed to enjoy humiliating his Vice President. "Boys, I just reminded Hubert I've got his balls in my pocket," he told reporters.

In 1966 *The Sound of Music* became one of the greatest hits in movie history. People went around saying, "You better believe it." Televison was now almost 100 percent color during prime time. The two pro football leagues merged. *The Valley of the Dolls* and *How to Avoid Probate* were best-sellers. *Cabaret* and *Mame* were big on Broadway. David Merrick put $500,000 into *Breakfast at Tiffany's;* it failed. A clothing firm marketed disposable paper dresses which came in cans, cost a dollar or two, and were discarded when dirty. New male cosmetics included false eyelashes—called "Executive Eyelash"—and an after-shave powder puff—"Brass Knuckles." The summer of 1966 was spoiled for a lot of travelers by the longest and costliest airline strike ever; five major airlines were grounded for forty-three days. That fall the Dodgers lost four in a row—the World Series—to Baltimore. A wacky bumper sticker in California announced: MARY POPPINS IS A JUNKIE.

Labor troubles left New Yorkers without newspapers for 279 days in the mid-Sixties. The *World-Telegram, Journal-American,* and *Herald Tribune* merged into one paper, the *World Journal Tribune* —it was called the *Wijit*—which failed after nine months. After 190 years, superstition finally killed the two-dollar bill; the Treasury Department stopped printing the bills on August 10, 1966, citing "a lack of public demand."

The fall elections of 1966 marked a political turning point. Resentment against ghetto riots and civil rights demonstrations had finally coalesced, making white backlash a potent political force for the first time. Combined with inflation, high interest rates, a scarcity of mortgage money, and the rising cost of living, backlash provided Republican candidates with a powerful springboard. George Romney and Nelson Rockefeller were re-elected with huge majorities. Among the new Republican faces in the Senate were Howard Baker Jr. of Tennessee, Edward W. Brooke of Massachusetts, Mark Hatfield of Oregon, and Charles H. Percy of Illinois; new Republican governors included Ronald Reagan of California and Spiro T. Agnew of Maryland. Altogether the Republicans picked up three seats in the Senate, eight new governors, and 47 seats in the House of Representatives, more than they had lost in 1964.

But by then Johnson had lost interest in legislation. Increasingly, he had become preoccupied with the Vietnam War, believing that its outcome would determine his place in history. Nearly every night at 3 A.M., according to his brother, Sam Ealy Johnson Jr., he would "crawl out of bed, wearily slip on his robe and slippers, then go down to the Situation Room in the basement of the White House to get the latest reports coming in from Saigon."

He was increasingly isolated. Robert S. McNamara, Secretary of Defense in this administration as he had been in Kennedy's, was losing confidence in the ability of bombing to bring the enemy to his knees. McNamara was now engrossed in a fantastic scheme for building an electronic barrier across the waist of Vietnam to stop infiltration from the North. When he abandoned that, his faith in military technology would collapse. Soon the chief White House consultant on Vietnam would be Walt Rostow, whose relation to the embattled and lonely war President, said another aide, was "like Rasputin to a tsar under siege." The conservative 90th Congress would join Rostow in goading Johnson on, passing huge military appropriation bills, encouraging him to sink ever deeper in the Vietnamese mire.

By then it all seemed inevitable. Yet it hadn't been. After his rout of Goldwater, Johnson's consensus had been genuine. The nation had been behind him. His goals had been the country's goals. It had been a time of great hope for him and for the American people, and few gauged correctly the threat from "a raggedy-ass little fourth-rate country," as Johnson once called Vietnam. One member of the First Family was worried, though. "I just hope," Mrs. Johnson had said in the middle of 1965, "that foreign problems do not keep on mounting. They do not represent Lyndon's kind of Presidency."

Thirty-one

A DREAM OF GREATNESS— AND DISENCHANTMENT

PRESIDENT KENNEDY had devoted his inaugural address to foreign affairs; President Johnson's four-thousand-word inaugural—which was delivered so slowly and deliberately that one observer said it sounded as though the President were dictating to a stonemason—almost ignored events abroad. The same was true of his second State of the Union message; Vietnam was covered in exactly 131 words. Considering what was to come, the emphasis on economy was odd. ("Last year we saved almost 35 hundred million dollars by eliminating waste in the national government. [Applause.] And I intend to do better this year. [Louder Applause.]") Johnson said that he wanted to be remembered as "the education President and the health President." He intended to complete the unfinished business of the New Deal and the Fair Deal.

He was also going to keep faith with Kennedy. From the New Frontier he had inherited four big bills: civil rights, a proposed tax cut, Medicare, and federal aid to education. Priority went to the first two, but he shepherded all of them through Congress. The battle for Medicare was a spectacular confrontation between a President who was a master parliamentarian and the mighty American Medical Association lobby. In 1945 President Truman had appeared personally before a joint session of Congress to ask for a comprehensive medical insurance program; the AMA had beaten him soundly, and he had taken it hard. This time, five presidential administrations and sixteen congressional sessions later, the AMA doctors came forward with something called Bettercare, which was to be voluntary, handled by the private insurance industry—and wholly inadequate, for the number of Americans over sixty-five had more than doubled since the Truman years.

To battle Johnson the AMA employed twenty-three full-time lobbyists and spent $5,000 a day. The President countered with personal telephone calls and invitations to the White House. He twisted arms and he twisted hearts. On July 30, 1965, just 204 days after Johnson had asked for Medicare, he signed the bill in Independence with eighty-one-year-old Harry Truman beaming alongside. On July 1, 1966, Medicare eligibility came to 160,000 elderly hospital patients in the United States. A New Jersey embroidery worker named Eugene Schneider, sixty-five, entered Polyclinic Hospital in New York at 12:01 that Friday, and treatment for his eye was paid for by the Social Security Administration, making him and Mrs. Robert Avery of Napierville, Illinois, the first Medicare patients. An Associated Press survey indicated that the program had increased hospital occupancy by 3 percent—about 100,000 new patients a week.

Five days after his call for Medicare Johnson had sent Congress another historic message, "Toward Full Education Opportunity," asking a billion dollars for public and parochial schools. Providing federal money for Catholic education was a profound break with the past and a guarantee of searing debate in the House. But Johnson knew that of the forty million American children in school, about six million were in overcrowded parochial schools—schools which would have to be replaced with public money if the church abandoned them. Moreover, excluding them had alienated Catholic legislators on the Hill, who had retaliated by voting against federal funds for public schools. Johnson had decided to include all, and he let it be known that he wanted no amendments, no changing of so much as a comma. All things were possible for him in the 89th Congress—the "Xerox Congress," Goldwater was beginning to call it —and the measure went through both houses of Congress in eighty-seven days. Designating it "the most important bill I will ever sign," the President staged this signing ceremony in the one-room Texas schoolhouse he had attended as a child, with his teacher, now seventy-two and retired, beside him.

A voting rights bill was next, a response to the ever more insistent civil rights movement. The measure was ready for his signature August 6. By now a blizzard of Great Society legislation was sweeping through Congress—over forty bills for education alone, including 2.4 billion dollars for college aid, more education legislation than in all American history until then. There were Johnsonian programs to fight heart disease, strokes, cancer, water pollution, air pollution, roadside billboards, and auto junkyards. Congress established a Department of Housing and Urban Development, a National Foundation for the Arts and the Humanities, and an Administration on Aging. A High-Speed Ground Transportation Act opened the way to a study of mass transit problems. The immigration service was reformed. A big excise tax cut—4.7 billion dollars—was approved. Farm legislation and a Public Works and Economic Development Act gave the federal government a strong role in dealing with the changing face of the land for the first time since the 1930s.

Over 900 million dollars was set aside to deal with America's oldest rural slum, Appalachia. Under the ebullient leadership of Sargent Shriver, who had been the first director of the Peace Corps, the new Office of Economic Opportunity declared war on poverty. OEO programs included Job Opportunities in the Business Sector (JOBS), to provide special help in job placement for the hard-core unemployed; Head Start, for preschool children from poor families, which brightened the future for 1,300,000 of them in its first year; Volunteers in Service to America (VISTA), in effect a domestic peace corps; the Neighborhood Youth Corps, providing a half-million part-time jobs for teen-agers; Upward Bound, enrolling precollege youths in campus programs; the Community Action Program (CAP), coordinating local health, housing, and employment programs and offering the poor free legal advice; Foster Grandparents, to work with children without homes; and agencies to work with Indians, migrants, and seasonal workers.

Critics christened the Washington office building in which the OEO leased seven floors "The Poverty Palace." Republican Congressman Albert Quie of Minnesota said the OEO undertaking "could become not just a national disgrace but a national catastrophe." Richard Nixon said, "The war on poverty has been first in promises, first in politics, first in press releases—and last in performances." And even Shriver conceded that administration of the most successful of the OEO programs, Head Start, was marred in one state (Mississippi) by nepotism, conflict of interest, misuse of government automobiles, and payments to people who weren't even in the state.

But time would be kind to the OEO, as it was to Roosevelt's WPA. In five years the war on poverty programs would play a key role in lifting thirteen million people out of pauperism. Another part was played by Johnsonian prosperity. The Great Society appeared to be on its way, and Americans seemed appreciative; at the end of Johnson's second year in office the public opinion surveys reported that no other President in their thirty years of polling had received such strong, consistent support throughout the country.

His landslide triumph over Goldwater would have tempted another President to ride roughshod over Congress. Not Johnson; he remembered vividly how Roosevelt, after his great victory in 1936, had been humbled by the defeat of his plan to reorganize the Supreme Court. "I've watched the Congress from either the inside or the outside, man and boy, for more than forty years," he said in the aftermath of the 1964 election, "and I've never seen a Congress that didn't eventually take the measure of the President it was dealing with." Rather than aim for a spectacular Hundred Days, he said, he would send each bill to the Hill only when the legislators were ready for it. He explained: "It's like a bottle of bourbon. If you take a glass at a time, it's fine. But if you drink the whole bottle in one evening, you have troubles. I plan to take a sip at a time and enjoy myself."

The final result was stunning. When the first session of the 89th Congress rose on October 23, it had approved 89 major administration bills and rejected just two: home rule for the District of Columbia and repeal of Section 14(b) of the Taft-Hartley Act, permitting states to ban union shop contracts—and it had been by no means clear on the Hill that the President really wanted the Taft-Hartley change. He was entitled to rest on his laurels. He didn't do it. Ever dissatisfied, he kept casting about for new ways to dominate the news and convert his critics.

One of the oddest was a summit meeting with Soviet Premier Alexei N. Kosygin in Hollybush, the turreted stone home of the president of Glassboro State College in New Jersey. Glassboro was chosen because it was exactly halfway between Washington and U.N. headquarters in New York, where Kosygin was staying; neither leader would call on the other; the little campus was a compromise. The two leaders had no agenda—had, indeed, nothing specific to talk about. Afterward Johnson said, "It helps to try to reason together. That is why we went to Hollybush. Reasoning together was the spirit of Hollybush." There was little else to say, other than that "the exchange of views once more revealed profound differences between the United States and the Soviet Union." The President's popularity rating soared just the same. The very fact that the two men, with nuclear arsenals at their disposal, had talked together seemed to reassure people.

Yet there were many who were not reassured, who regarded Johnson with scorn and often with contempt. LBJ-haters continued to be found in large numbers among the creative communities in large cities and on university faculties. Visiting the United States in 1965, the British journalist Henry Fairlie wrote: "I have found nothing more strange or unattractive than the way in which American intellectuals take pleasure in reviling President Johnson." Fairlie noted that the strictures were "personal" and reflected a "fastidious disdain for the man. . . . He is a slob, one of them said to me. . . . Others say much of the same, if less briefly."

Dwight Macdonald, one of the most caustic of them, wrote of "tasteless, crude" Lyndon Johnson and minted a word, "midcult," to mock the President's middlebrow taste. Macdonald and others like him ridiculed Mrs. Johnson because her favorite television program was *Gunsmoke*. They despised LBJ for enjoying the New Christy Minstrels, telling photographers to "Use my left profile," disliking Peter Hurd's portrait of him, having a daughter who changed her name from Lucy to Luci, and calling the work of serious artists "artsy." Their discontent spread to the much larger number of Americans who were vaguely offended by Johnson's mountebank manner. Millions of others were susceptible because they had loved John Kennedy, grieved for him still, and irrationally felt that Johnson was a usurper. To all these, eventually, were added the vast mass of Americans who felt troubled or even threatened by the escalating violence in the Negro slums in large cities and the growing turmoil on campuses. Johnson's insistence that he was in charge made him an inviting target, and they let fly at him.

At the end of his unprecedented string of legislative successes on the Hill in 1965 he entered Bethesda Naval Hospital for the removal of a stone-obstructed gallbladder. Convalescing, he brooded about the newspapers, which had been baiting him, and his taunters, "those people out there." In exasperation he blurted out, "What do they want—what *really* do they want? I'm giving them boom times and more good legislation than anybody else did, and what do they do—attack and sneer! Could FDR do better? Could anybody do better? What *do* they want?"

Senator Eugene McCarthy, whose role in the collapse of Johnson's consensus would become crucial, found half of the solution to the riddle when he suggested that Johnson was a kind of anachronistic President, providing New Deal remedies—social welfare legislation—for a nation whose dilemmas were very different. It was arguable, for example, that affluence, not poverty, was the great domestic challenge of the 1960s. McCarthy said that the President completely misjudged the temper of the liberal intellectuals: "he keeps going to them with the list of bills he's passed—the laundry list—and he doesn't know that they aren't interested any more."

Johnson raged, "Don't they know I'm the only President they've got?" Sometimes he would add, "Don't they know there's a war on?"

They knew. That was the other half of the answer to the riddle.

After the Gulf of Tonkin incidents there was a lull in American activity in Vietnam until November 1, 1964, when five U.S. military advisers were killed and 76 wounded in a Viet Cong mortar attack on an air base at Bienhoa, twenty miles north of Saigon. On Christmas Eve the guerrillas struck again, planting a bomb at the Brink's Hotel in Saigon. American casualties there were two dead and 58 wounded, and Lyndon Johnson's patriotic instincts were aroused. He strode around the White House saying that he wasn't going to let them kill our boys out there, that they were firing on the flag, that he'd show them he wasn't any "Chamberlain umbrella man." Plainly the North Vietnamese were guilty of aggression. ("Aggression is when one country won't let another one alone. Everybody knows when that is happening.") But depending on the United Nations to act would be a mistake. ("It couldn't pour piss out of a boot if the instructions were printed on the heel.") He wasn't going to go down in history as the President who lost Vietnam. The United States had the power to teach these little-biddy, raggedy-ass Communists a lesson. The Tonkin resolution gave him the authority to use it, and if the Viet Cong didn't back off he would do just that.

The difficulty was in deciding which approach to take. This new enemy, being unconventional, resisted conventional military solutions. The mighty American martial establishment wasn't equipped to deal with their hit-and-run tactics. President Kennedy had sent to Vietnam a 400-man Special Forces group, experts in antiguerrilla warfare, but the Joint Chiefs were unenthusiastic about these husky elitists. At one time, of over a hundred American generals in MACV, not one had gone through counterinsurgency training at Fort Bragg, North Carolina. And of all of them, none was more of a traditional soldier than MACV's new commander, William Childs Westmoreland.

What the Chiefs wanted was heavy bombing of North Vietnam. That would bring the enemy to his knees, they told the White House, and it would also bring him to the negotiating table. Clearly the bombing mystique had a powerful hold on the Johnson administration. Why this was so is less obvious. Two influential Democrats, George Ball and John Kenneth Galbraith, had participated in the U.S. Strategic Bombing Survey after World War II. That study had found that Allied bombing had not only failed to cripple German war production; it had strengthened the morale of the German people. And Germany was highly industrialized. If the Air Force had failed there, certainly its chances against the economy of a backward Asian country were at best doubtful.

Not all of Johnson's advisers had faith in the bombardiers. Ball and Galbraith didn't, and they were far from being alone. Early in 1964 the State Department's Policy Planning Council had conducted an exhaustive survey of the bombing question. The conclusion was that bombing North Vietnam would be ineffective, that it wasn't even likely to boost spirits in South Vietnam. Pier de Silva, John Richardson's successor as CIA station chief in Saigon, thought bombs would be useless; so did Westmoreland. As West Point graduates, both men knew that if you brought in planes you would need troops to protect the landing fields—that the decision to bomb would therefore bring the United States in all the way. Early in 1965, CIA analysts in Saigon completed two lengthy new reports on the same issue. The gist of them was that unleashing the bombers would be worse than futile; there was a strong probability that it would boomerang by touching off a massive infiltration of North Vietnamese troops down the Ho Chi Minh Trail.

That should have given the White House pause. At the very least the President ought to have listened intently to the counsels of caution. But something mysterious was happening to the doves, as opponents of escalation were beginning to be known. There were fewer and fewer of them in the halls of power. In October of 1964, when George Ball at State submitted his first memorandum protesting further American involvement in the war, he had plenty of company. Then, one by one, his allies were transferred or eased out of key positions. Roger Hilsman, Averell Harriman, Michael Forrestal, Paul Kattenburg, William Trueheart—all were gone by the time of Johnson's inaugural. Ball stood alone. Maxwell Taylor, who had agreed with Ball about bombing, was still an insider, but Taylor had changed his mind. He now wanted a green light for the Air Force. He thought the U.S. troop level in Vietnam could be controlled and need never rise above 100,000.

Now only one major White House special assistant was still uncommitted. He was McGeorge Bundy, the President's national security adviser. On January 27, 1965, Bundy proposed that he visit Vietnam as the President's eyes and ears. McNamara concurred, and Johnson's security aide flew to Asia in the first week of February. It was a fateful trip. Bundy was brilliant and experienced, but he had never served in the field. All he knew of war was in memos and reports or on celluloid. The grime and the stench of combat were new to him, and when he encountered them he suffered a physical revulsion. Above all—and this would be decisive—he could not stand the sight of blood.

On the evening of February 5, while Bundy was being feted in Saigon, Spec. 5c Jesse A. Pyle of Marina, California, was taking up sentry duty in a foxhole outside a U.S. stronghold at Pleiku, a mountain town in Vietnam's central highlands. He was still there at 2 A.M. when he saw shadowy figures in black pajamas moving toward him through underbrush. Pyle opened fire; the Viet Cong guerrillas replied with a storm of grenades; Americans in their nearby barracks awoke and joined the fight. The Battle of Pleiku lasted fifteen furious minutes. At the end of it the guerrillas had demolished or damaged sixteen helicopters and six aircraft. Eight U.S. soldiers, Pyle among them, were dead. Another 126 were wounded.

At 2:38 P.M. in Washington, the first account of Pleiku reached the President. After a four-hour National Security Council meeting he ordered Navy jet fighter-bombers from three carriers to attack a Viet Cong staging area at Donghoi, forty miles north of the 17th Parallel. Whether or not the American combat role would grow, he announced, was a decision which "lies with the North Vietnamese aggressors." McNamara said, "I think it's quite clear that this was a test of will." But the most unexpected result of Pleiku was its impact on the President's national security adviser, who, being on the spot, visited the wounded and came away deeply moved. He flew home a hawk. "Well, they made a believer out of you, didn't they?" the President said to him. "A little fire will do that."

Ball was still opposed to the bombing. Vice President Hubert Humphrey was also against it, and he expressed himself so forcefully that Johnson, who now regarded such doubts as unmanly, excluded him from National Security Council meetings. The United States had entered the critical period of decision. McNamara later remarked that all the U.S. errors in Vietnam—and he conceded that there had been many—were committed by the late spring of 1965; after that, he said, there was no way out. In Washington it seemed that the Viet Cong was bent upon provoking the U.S. into massive intervention. Less than three days after Pleiku, black-pajamaed guerrillas blew up the Viet Cuong Hotel, a barracks for American soldiers in the Annamese port of Quinhon; 23 enlisted men were killed and 21 injured. Johnson, infuriated, gave orders for a three-hour bombing of Chanh Hoa and Chap Lee, military depots in North Vietnam.

On February 11 the Viet Cong hit Quinhon again. This time LBJ stayed his hand for forty-eight hours. When he did move, however, it was to take a long step down the road of escalation. Henceforth American reprisals from the air were not to be on a one-for-one, tit-for-tat basis. Instead Johnson ordered a sustained bombing campaign against the North, to be mounted without regard for provocation. Its code name was to be Operation Rolling Thunder. The justification for it was set forth in a sixty-four-page white paper, *Aggression from the North*, which, the State Department said, established "beyond question that North Viet Nam is carrying out a carefully conceived plan of aggression against the South." To defend Da Nang air base, fifty miles southeast of Hue, from which Rolling Thunder would be launched, General Westmoreland asked for two Marine Corps battalions. These 3,500 marines were the first U.S. ground troops to be committed to the war. On March 8 they splashed ashore under overcast skies at Nam O Beach, three miles from Da Nang. Awaiting them were ten smiling Vietnamese girls with flowers.

Elsewhere the landing was more controversial. In Moscow two thousand demonstrators hurled rocks and bricks at the American embassy; two western foreign correspondents were roughed up there. In the United States the teach-ins spread and reached a climax in Washington, where Bundy agreed to debate his critics on a program which would be broadcast to over a hundred campuses. (At the last minute he had to withdraw; the President needed him to deal with another foreign crisis in the Dominican Republic.) The administration sent a "truth team" to visit universities and reply to the charges of faculty doves. Dean Rusk caustically told the American Society of International Law, "I sometimes wonder at the gullibility of educated men and the stubborn disregard of plain facts by men who are supposed to be helping our young to learn—especially to learn how to think."

But the more the critics of the war learned about its South Vietnamese ally the stronger their reservations became. Half of U.S. aid, they learned, was going into the Saigon black market. Vietnamese youths from opulent families were buying their way out of the draft. The desertion rate in the South Vietnamese army was 15 percent. And the politicians in Saigon seemed to have a genius for bad timing. It seemed that at every critical moment in the conflict whatever government was in power would be overthrown by a new regime. Johnson, angered, told his staff that he wanted "no more of this coup shit," but he got it just the same. On February 21, 1965, Lieutenant General Nguyen Khanh was ousted and succeeded by Phan Huy Quat, a physician. (The secretary general of the junta behind Quat was Major General Nguyen Van Thieu, from this point forward a man to watch.) The Quat administration lasted exactly 111 days. When it toppled (the ninth change of government since Diem's assassination) the new prime minister was the colorful chief of the Vietnamese air force, Nguyen Cao Ky, and Thieu was deputy prime minister.

Each new sign of instability in Saigon increased the ranks of the doves, who were rapidly replacing the Republicans as Lyndon Johnson's most effective political opposition. Former Secretary of the Army Cyrus Vance said misgivings about the war were "threatening to tear the United States apart," and in the Senate Frank Church of Idaho, one of the first senatorial doves, warned: "There are limits to what we can do in helping any government surmount a Communist uprising. If the people themselves will not support the government in power, we cannot save it . . . The Saigon government is

losing its war, not for lack of equipment, but for lack of any internal cohesion."

That was not yet a popular position, however. When Johnson asked for a 700-million-dollar supplemental appropriation to finance the escalation, the House approved, 408 to 7, in twenty-four hours, and the Senate followed suit, 88 to 3, in another twenty-four hours. In the popular press a certain stigma was attached to disapproval of American participation in the war. When Majority Leader Mike Mansfield gloomily told the Senate that it might go on "for four, five, or ten years," an Associated Press writer called this an "extreme view." (It was to be eight years.) In its annual review of that year's news the AP, ordinarily the most impartial of institutions, also reported that opponents of the war were giving aid and comfort to enemies of the United States. And when Senator Fulbright held Vietnam hearings in April, providing a forum for such distinguished critics of administration policy as George Kennan and General James Gavin, twenty-four NBC-TV stations refused to carry their network's coverage of them, while CBS-TV blacked them out entirely.

The war was becoming steadily hotter for the Americans in Vietnam. On March 30 a Vietnamese driver parked a black Citroën in front of the U.S. embassy in Saigon and roared off on a companion's motorcycle. In the car were 250 pounds of explosive, which went off at 10:55 A.M., tearing a hole in the side of the building and killing seventeen embassy employees. The next day U.S. planes bombed six North Vietnamese radar installations. It was their fifteenth raid across the border between the two Vietnams since Pleiku. The Viet Cong countered with more explosives. A bicycle loaded with nitroglycerin was parked one evening on the bank of the Saigon River beside My Canh, a floating restaurant popular with foreigners. When it went off forty-four people, twelve Americans among them, were killed. Still the U.S. troop buildup went on. At the beginning of the year there had been some 25,000 American servicemen in the country; by the end of spring the number had tripled.

On June 9 the White House announced that General Westmoreland had been authorized to send U.S. soldiers and marines into battle "when other effective reserves are not available and when in his judgment the general military situation urgently requires it." Four days later Westmoreland decided that circumstances at Dong

Xoai, a district capital sixty miles north of Saigon, justified American intervention. After a clash in the night, 1,200 paratroopers of the U.S. 173rd Airborne joined 1,600 Vietnamese and Australians in aggressive pursuit of the guerrillas. Westmoreland called this a "search and destroy" mission, a phrase which would be used henceforth to describe the strategy, which evolved in these months, of seeking out and then wiping out Viet Cong bands. It was to be a costly and often frustrating process. The Dong Xoai melee was characteristic of the war; after the smoke had cleared it was impossible to say which side had come off best. All the commander of the 173rd could be sure of was that he had lost nineteen men. The casualty lists swiftly lengthened, for the Viet Cong were in the second month of their spring offensive. Long afterward Westmoreland would describe this as the time that the enemy won the war. No one knew it at the time, however. That same month Westmoreland asked Washington for forty-four fresh battalions and authority to use them as he saw fit, and he could not guarantee that even that would do the job.

It was in this period that Lyndon Johnson's deviousness and secretiveness began to shrivel public trust in him. Referring to it on May 23, a copyeditor on the *New York Herald Tribune* put the phrase "credibility gap" over a story by David Wise, the newspaper's White House correspondent. Then Murray Marder of the *Washington Post*, in an article analyzing the feeling, widespread in Washington, that the President was sometimes careless with the truth, wrote: "The problem could be called a credibility gap." Johnson's glittering peace promises in the 1964 campaign were being recalled and contrasted with his new martial stance. Marder noted a "growing doubt and cynicism concerning administration pronouncements in Washington." Reporters were particularly susceptible to it. Because the President had denounced Senator Goldwater for proposing the very policies he himself was now adopting, the press was becoming skeptical of new olive branches being extended by the White House.

Speaking at Johns Hopkins University on April 7, the President declared that the United States was ready for "unconditional discussions" leading toward a negotiated peace. The address was carried around the world by the U.S. Information Agency, and many of its details sounded new and exciting. He proposed that the nations of Southeast Asia, including North Vietnam, join in a crash

Marshall Plan, and he said, "For our part, I will ask Congress to join in a billion-dollar American investment in this effort as soon as it is under way." U.S. farm surpluses would be sent to hungry Asians. He would "shortly name a special team of outstanding, patriotic, distinguished Americans" to guide the United States in all this. An end to the Vietnam War would, of course, be "necessary for final success. But we cannot and must not wait for peace to begin this job." It was all very sensible. It made Asia sound like central Texas.

David Wise's suspicious article was written in the aftermath of this speech, when many flaws in the President's proposition had become apparent. His proposal for truce discussions did have a condition, after all; he ruled out participation by the Viet Cong, which guaranteed Hanoi's rejection of it. Nothing more was heard about the billion-dollar commitment by the United States or the offer of U.S. surplus crops, and the panel of distinguished Americans was never chosen. Within a month what had appeared to be an imaginative approach to the problems of Southeast Asia had taken on the aspect of a publicity stunt. Not only had the President failed to follow through on any part of it; he was showing his real Asian policy in ever more vigorous prosecution of what was fast becoming a major American war.

The first six weeks of Rolling Thunder had been a total failure. Bombing hadn't brought the enemy to his knees, to the negotiating table, or even to what the Johnson administration conceived to be his senses. The Viet Cong were as disrespectful of the American flag as ever. The President decided to raise the ante again. In the third week of April he flew to Honolulu for a two-day conference with Ky and Thieu. Afterward McNamara announced that U.S. aid to Saigon in 1965 would jump from 207 million dollars to 330 million. Another 40,000 American soldiers—"grunts," as they had begun calling themselves—were ordered to Vietnam. Senator Gruening asked Johnson how long winning the war would take, and the President's answer was six months. Hanoi wouldn't be able to stand the bombing longer than that, he said; the Viet Cong would be begging MACV for terms before Christmas.

George Ball was deeply troubled. Intelligence, he knew, pointed toward a very different conclusion. John McCone reported that the CIA concluded the bombs were neither crippling Hanoi nor frightening it. Instead the raids were strengthening the hand of the hard-liners there. One North Vietnamese regiment had already been identified in South Vietnam, and a second was forming at the border. McCone told the National Security Council that a higher American troop level would be met by increased infiltration from the North; the U.S. troop transports on their way to Saigon would be neutralized before the grunts could even be landed. The Pentagon replied that the Air Force was preparing to commit its eight-engine B-52s, designed for nuclear weapons, and that nobody could stand up to B-52s, Phantoms, and F-111s.

But the air war was no longer the only event, nor even the main event, for the Americans in Vietnam. The U.S. military role there was subtly changing. The objective of the American troops was not limited to the protection of airfields now. The grunts were going to intimidate the guerrillas, persuading them that Uncle Sam meant business. Americans at home were unaware of the shift. Afterward James Reston would comment that the President had escalated the war by stealth. Under Johnson, David Halberstam would write years later, the decision makers in Washington "inched their way across the Rubicon without even admitting it" while the task of their press officers became "to misinform the public rather than inform it."

The next quantum jump in Washington's MACV commitment came in July. McNamara returned from his sixth fact-finding tour of Vietnam to report "deterioration" and recommend pledges of more men and more money. Johnson summoned his generals and advisers to Camp David for the weekend of July 17 to find a consensus, though the word, as he used it, had lost its original meaning; for him it had come to mean a ritual of agreement with a decision he had already made—to raise the number of U.S. troops in Vietnam by 50,000. The Joint Chiefs concurred reluctantly. They had hoped for much more; their greatest fear was involvement in partial war. Some of the men at Camp David refused to go along. "Whatever we do," Clark Clifford said prophetically of the Communists, "they will match it." Mike Mansfield also objected, telling the President that he was opposed to sending any more troops, that he thought the war would divide the country. The others approved of the President's judgment; the domino theory, mutual security, containment, and the lesson of Munich still outweighed their misgivings.

After locking up the decision Johnson became furtive. He wanted no further debate. McNamara proposed a reserve call-up of 235,000 men. Instead the President doubled draft calls administratively, raising them from 17,000 to 35,000 a month, on the ground that it would attract less notice than a call-up. He also decided against asking Congress for more money. The new costs could be hidden in the Defense Department's huge budget. He said he didn't want to scare anyone, and for a time he considered making public only part of the increase in troops for Vietnam. Douglas Kiker of the *Herald Tribune* asked him about reports of the expansion. Rumors, Johnson assured him, nothing but rumors; he was just filling out a few units, and accounts predicting that U.S. troops in Vietnam would pursue the Viet Cong aggressively were also untrue. On July 28 he changed his mind and announced the full figure, together with the new, forceful nature of MACV's mission, thereby alienating Kiker and widening the credibility gap. "We did not choose to be the guardians at the gate," the President told an estimated 28 million Americans on noonday television, "but there is no one else."

Distrust was one evil crop he sowed that summer; another was eventual misunderstandings among those he was herding into consensus. The Joint Chiefs thought he was keeping the figures low until he could persuade the civilians that he must go higher; they were counting on an eventual force of a million men. Westmoreland, watching Hanoi reinforce at a faster rate than anyone dreamed possible and sending Washington reports of it, planned on between 640,000 and 648,000 Americans ultimately under his command, confident that when he needed them they would be there. His staff had a contingency plan under which the MACV force level could reach 750,000, a figure which it thought was both sensible and justifiable. But the assumption of the Secretary of Defense was the strangest of all. Years afterward it would still be comprehensible only to those who understood Robert McNamara's very orderly mind and his belief that disorderly events could be made to conform to it. McNamara arbitrarily decided in 1965 that the war would be over by June 30, 1967, the end of that fiscal year. It would be a perfect time for him, making his budget come out even, and he clung to it even after Westmoreland told him that it was impossible.

In one respect, however, McNamara and the Pentagon were more realistic than the White House. The Joint Chiefs urged the President to raise taxes. Their reasoning had nothing to do with economics. They wanted to see the country on a total war footing, and their textbook solution to civilian apathy was higher taxes. As it happened, the economists in the administration wholeheartedly agreed with them. Gardner Ackley, the Michigan professor who headed Johnson's Council of Economic Advisers, told the President that the administration could not have three things—prosecution of the war, continuance of his Great Society programs, and the absence of inflation—unless taxes were raised.

But this was the period in which Johnson was passing huge amounts of social legislation through Congress. If the true cost of the war were known, he feared, that process would come to a shuddering stop. "I don't know much about economics," he said to those around him, a confession that some of them later thought should be engraved on his tomb, "but I do know the Congress. And I can get the Great Society through right now—this is a golden time. We've got a good Congress and I'm the right President and I can do it. But if I talk about the cost of the war, the Great Society won't go through and the tax bill won't go through. Old Wilbur Mills will sit down there and he'll thank me kindly and send me back my Great Society, and then he'll tell me that they'll be glad to spend whatever we need for the war."

At this point he made the ultimate blunder. He fooled himself. Everything would come out all right, he reckoned, if victory could be bought cheap. Maybe that would happen; maybe Hanoi and the Viet Cong guerrillas would collapse. In that event, the estimates from the Pentagon would be overestimates. The wish became father to the thought, and when Ackley and his colleagues became insistent about the need for a 3 to 4 percent tax increase, the President responded by staging an extraordinary charade. Key Congressmen and leaders of the business community were invited to the White House and asked for their opinion about higher taxes. They in turn inquired about the cost of the war. He gave them phony figures. Thereupon they rejected the idea of a tax increase. Johnson then told the Council of Economic Advisers that a tax hike was impossible; he couldn't get it through Congress. Later Edwin Dale Jr., economic correspondent of the *New York Times*, called this the most single irresponsible presidential act in his fifteen years of covering Washington.

Johnson's decision against a tax raise, made in early 1966, was a stupendous blow to fiscal sanity. The federal deficit that year was 9.8 billion dollars. Even deeper vats of red ink lay ahead, for by then the war was costing between two and three billion dollars a month. The estimate the White House was putting out was 800 million dollars, and when Ralph Lazarus of the Business Council said the government's figure was much too low, he received an indignant call from Abe Fortas, who told him that his calculations were wrong and were upsetting the President. Actually Lazarus was right on target. The war cost 27 billion dollars that year, and the deficit was a catastrophic 23 billion dollars. Johnson's legerdemain had brought the beginnings of runaway inflation.

Of all the war's aspects, perhaps the most incomprehensible was the lack of real planning. David Halberstam would later find that "the principals never defined either the mission or the number of troops. It seems incredible in retrospect, but it is true. There was never a clear figure and clear demonstration of what the strategy would be." All that was apparent in 1965 was that the numbers were going ever higher. U.S. soldiers were pouring into Vietnam in August, and by September it was obvious that the troop level was going to top 200,000.

Checking reports of a battle near Saigon, Peter Arnett of the Associated Press drove out of the capital to find clouds of smoke in three colors, South Vietnamese troops in action—and no enemy. He was told that the soldiers were making a color movie for the United States Information Service, "to show how things really are here." Arguments over how things really were there were going full blast on all fronts, including the home front. Lyndon Johnson talked at times as though he were responding to a personal challenge from Ho Chi Minh, the two of them striding toward one another in a *High Noon* confrontation. Terrorist bombings seemed closer to the truth in Saigon, where the list of atrocities lengthened; at dawn on December 4 another truck loaded with 250 pounds of explosives went off, this time outside the Metropole, a hotel for American servicemen; eight were killed and 137 wounded.

Westmoreland's spokesmen often sounded preoccupied with the daily "body count," a singularly insensate phrase which was used to describe Viet Cong casualties. To correspondent Neil Sheehan the war was typified by the enormous casualties among innocent civilians resulting from indiscriminate shelling and bombing. Sheehan asked Westmoreland if it didn't bother him, and the general replied, "Yes, but it does deprive the enemy of the population, doesn't it?"

In 1965 Americans demonstrating against the war were still a relative oddity in most of the country. Few people wished to be counted in favor of immediate, unconditional U.S. withdrawal from Indochina. Even college faculties, one of the most dovish groups in the country, were to be evenly divided as late as 1967 on the issue. Nevertheless, the vigor of the peace movement was already phenomenal. On the weekend of October 15-16 a crowd estimated at 14,000 paraded down Manhattan's Fifth Avenue. Simultaneously another 10,000 marched on the Oakland Army Base—they were turned back at the city line by police—and 2,000 demonstrated in Berkeley. Elsewhere during this "weekend of protest," as it was heralded, fifty students from the University of Wisconsin tried to arrest the commanding officer at Truax Air Force Base as a "war criminal," and protesters staged a "lie-in" at a draft board office in Ann Arbor.

The Fifth Avenue Vietnam Peace Parade Committee declared:

> We demand that no more American youth be sent to fight in a war that is helping neither them nor the Vietnamese people. We have learned lessons from Nazi Germany, and will not go along with the aggressive war-making policies of any government, even if it happens to be our own.

That was reasonable, but elsewhere the rhetoric of the demonstrators, like the war itself, was becoming hateful. It was in Washington the Saturday after Thanksgiving that 20,000 of them first chanted, "Hey! Hey! LBJ! How many kids did you kill today?" Members of the May 2nd Movement (M2M), named for May 2, 1964, when they first took to the streets to protest American involvement in the war, trooped around the White House carrying Viet Cong flags and advertised "bleed-ins" at which blood was collected for North Vietnamese soldiers. In Berkeley the Free Speech Movement had been succeeded by the Vietnam Day Committee, which twice tried to halt troop trains by occupying cars and sitting on the tracks.

On October 15, 1965, a new feature was introduced in demonstrations when David J. Miller, a twenty-two-year-old volunteer in a relief program, mounted a sound truck in New York, announced, "Instead of the speech I prepared I'll let this action speak for itself" —and held a match to his draft card. Miller was arrested a few weeks later, but burning Selective Service cards enjoyed a brief vogue, despite congressional action on August 31 making it a federal offense punishable by a $10,000 fine or five years in jail. Acts of self-immolation continued to be the ultimate protest; a Quaker outside the Pentagon and a Catholic relief worker outside the United Nations turned themselves into human torches.

Counterpickets from the American Nazi Party carried jerricans and placards reading, "Free Gas for Peace Creeps." As usual, nobody wanted any part of them. The tone of most antiprotest protests was relatively mild. A girl in New York carried a sign reading, "I Wish I Had a Draft Card." Earnest demonstrations were organized by the Young Americans for Freedom, the American Legion, and the Veterans of Foreign Wars. "Bomb Hanoi" was the most belligerent sentiment on signs of most of them. Placards at a typical march in Florida read, "We Love America," "Love Our Country," "My Country—Right or Wrong," "Will We Let Them Bury U.S.?" and "No Glory Like Old Glory." Bob Hope told one audience that "If we ever let the Communists win this war, we are in great danger of fighting for the rest of our lives and losing a million kids." That was an extravagant statement, but it was hardly in the same category with accusing the President of murdering children.

The gravest charges lodged by those favoring the war were suggestions that the other side was disloyal. "We won't creep around in the dark with candles like these traitors do," said the police chief of Charlestown, West Virginia. "We'll march at high noon and let free people fall right in and march behind us." Some newspaper accounts of peace vigils in 1965 were inclined to hint broadly at Communist participation, and the FBI, which like Hope was shedding its nonpartisan reputation, virtually credited all such protests to the Kremlin. A government report said: "Control of the anti-Viet Nam movement has clearly passed from the hands of the moderate elements who may have controlled it at one time into the hands of the Communists and extremist elements who are openly sympathetic to the Viet Cong and openly hostile to the United States."

In fact the reverse was true. Despite the inflammatory language and provocative behavior of individual antiwar militants, each demonstration tended to be more respectable than the last. Middle-class conservative housewives and even servicemen in uniform were joining the movement. So, increasingly, were celebrities who felt a pull opposite to Bob Hope's. When stop-the-bombing marchers formed under cloudless skies in Washington on November 27, their number included, in addition to Norman Thomas and James Farmer, such strangers to political action as Dr. Benjamin Spock, cartoonist Jules

Feiffer, novelist Saul Bellow, sculptor Alexander Calder, and author
Michael Harrington.

That autumn dispatches from Vietnam reported that famous
American military units were being mauled in Vietnam. It was the
101st Airborne Brigade at An Khe in September, the Green Berets
at Plei Me in October, and, in November, the 1st Cavalry Division
in the Ia Drang Valley. The encounter at Ia Drang, a week before
the stop-the-bombing march in Washington, was of special significance; like the Viet Cong offensive the previous spring and the Tet
offensive of early 1968, it was a turning point in the war. Troopers
of the 1st Cav, pursuing enemy detachments in the aftermath of
the Plei Me engagement, met stiff resistance in the valley, near Chu-
pong Mountain, seven miles from the Cambodian border and two
hundred miles north of Saigon in Vietnam's central highlands. This
time the Americans faced not Viet Cong guerrillas, but the North
Vietnamese 66th Regiment.

The 66th, an elite unit of the North Vietnamese army, faced a
severe test. The 1st Cav was something new in military history, a
heliborne division, equipped to take maximum advantage of superior American firepower. The tactics of the Communists, who knew
all about the battlefield weapons designed by inventive Americans,
called for grappling with the grunts at the closest range, hand to
hand if possible, but at most within thirty-four yards, thus nullifying
U.S. artillery and tactical air support.

The implications of the Ia Drang fighting were bound to be great.
At the time of the Camp David conference in July there had been
just two North Vietnamese regiments in the South. Now MACV had
confirmed the presence of six regiments from the North, with two
more probable and another possible. Others were on their way;
General Vo Nguyen Giap, Ho Chi Minh's commander, was continuing to break up his battalions into companies and platoons and send
them down the trail faster than the Americans could bring in transports.

Both sides rushed reinforcements into the valley, and although
a 1st Cav battalion, flown in, was ambushed and badly chewed up,
when it was all over Westmoreland and his deputy, General William Depuy, claimed a victory. The figures seemed to support them;
the enemy, attacking in waves like the World War II Japanese and
yelling in English, "Kill GI!," had lost 1,200 to the Americans' 200.

But other observers, among them John Paul Vann, who had returned to Vietnam as a civilian, had reached a very different conclusion. The Communists were prepared to accept such losses indefinitely. ("It is," one Viet Cong soldier wrote in his diary, "the duty of my generation to die for our country.") But the U.S. toll in Ia Drang, although much smaller, was a record for Westmoreland's troops; it put American casualties in the war at 1,335 dead and 6,131 wounded. While MACV believed that Westmoreland had found the strategic key to triumph and was eagerly planning more Ia Drangs, Giap took the Vann view. The North Vietnamese general was convinced, and events were to confirm him, that the American people would not accept such casualties in an open-ended commitment. Giap regarded the new phase of the war as a contest between his manpower and Westmoreland's technology, with U.S. public opinion as the referee.

In December McNamara urged a bombing pause on Johnson. Objections came from Rusk, now one of the toughest of the hawks, but the President grounded the B-52s and sent out diplomatic scouts to key world capitals, spreading the word that Washington was ready for peace. Two Italian professors arrived in Hanoi to sound out Ho. At first negotiations seemed possible, but just as word reached Rusk that the Communists were in a conciliatory mood, Hanoi denounced the whole thing as "sheer, groundless fabrication." The Americans were taken aback. After Ia Drang, they thought, it should be obvious to Ho that he faced defeat. The marines were reminded of the tagline of an old Corps joke: "There's always some son-of-a-bitch who doesn't get the word."

In appealing to a joint session of Congress for the voting Rights Act of 1965, Lyndon Johnson concluded his speech with a phrase which had become hallowed by the blood and tears of a new generation of black Americans marching for justice. He said that their cause "must be our cause too. Because it's not just Negroes, but really it's all of us who must overcome the crippling legacy of bigotry and injustice. *And we shall overcome.*"

That was fine liberal eloquence, but at times during the year it appeared to be a doubtful prediction. The eleventh anniversary of the Supreme Court's ruling in Brown v. Board of Education passed on May 17, and racism seemed stronger than ever. C. Vann Woodward, Sterling Professor of History at Yale, said, "Negroes now have

less contact with whites in schools than they did a generation ago."
Between the middle of 1964 and the middle of 1965 the Ku Klux
Klan made its greatest membership gains ever, including the Reconstruction era. In October of 1965 a Birmingham black reportedly
bled to death because a white ambulance driver refused to take
him to a hospital. An Alabama businessman, speaking of civil rights
pickets, casually remarked to a *New York Times* correspondent,
"The niggers are going to be in trouble around here when this is
all over." The racial climate was not much better in the northern
cities; speaking in Marquette Park, on Chicago's South Side, Martin
Luther King Jr. said, "I have never seen such hate, not in Mississippi
or Alabama, as I see here in Chicago." The attitude of millions of
whites seemed symbolized in a lapel pin worn by Dallas County
Sheriff James G. Clark Jr. in Selma. It simply read, "Never." Never,
it appeared, would men like Clark, in the North as well as the
South, accept Negroes as equals.

Confronted by this prejudice, the black mood continued to
change. There was a splintering into various camps, many hostile
to one another. The assassination of Malcolm X by fellow blacks
in upper Manhattan's Audubon Ballroom on February 21, 1965, just
as he had reached the threshold of leadership, reflected the depth
of the division among the black militants. A sign of Negro despair
was the upsurge in groups advocating "repatriation"—a "return to
the African homeland." The Deacons for Defense were formed in
some fifty Black Belt communities to combat the KKK. Others followed the preaching of Le Roi Jones, who told them that "The
majority of American white men are evil"; and of James Forman,
who issued a Black Manifesto demanding that white churches and
synagogues (the very white institutions, ironically, which had been
most ardent in support of the civil rights movement) pay Negroes
500 million dollars in "reparations."

The Muslims became the most famous of the groups advocating
separatism, and in Oakland the first tiny pack of Black Panthers
emerged in 1966. Daniel Patrick Moynihan came forward in November 1965 with the Moynihan Report, a closely reasoned document
which argued that realistic approaches to internal problems in the
Negro community must first deal with the worst legacies of slavery:
Negro welfare dependency, a divorce rate 40 percent higher than
that of whites, and the appalling rate of illegitimacy, one black birth
in four being out of wedlock. Moynihan's facts were undisputed,

but such was the Negro agony that year, and so shattering the impact of events on Negro pride, that blacks could not face them. Their leaders therefore branded the report racist propaganda and denounced its author as a "fascist."

C. Vann Woodward wrote in 1965 that "insofar as federal laws are capable of coping" with segregation and prejudice, "Congress has just about fulfilled its role." The capstone of such legislation was the voting act of that year. In January Martin Luther King called a press conference to point out that three million of the five million blacks in the South old enough to vote were not registered, and to announce that he was launching an all-out registration drive. It would open in Selma, Alabama, where 325 of 15,000 potential black voters were registered, as against 9,300 of 14,000 whites. Typically, Dr. King led the first group of Negroes ever to stay at Selma's Hotel Albert, previously all-white, and typically he was punched and kicked by a white segregationist while signing the hotel register. His assailant was fined one hundred dollars and sentenced to sixty days in jail, which King thought was a good start toward respect for the law, but then the drive stalled. The blunt truth was that most of Selma's Negroes were indifferent to the right to vote. Something dramatic was needed to arouse them. It was provided—again, this was characteristic—by rural whites who murdered a black would-be voter in nearby Perry County. Local civil rights leaders counted on that, on Sheriff Jim Clark's short temper, and on Governor Wallace's showboating to revive their campaign.

They declared that on March 7 they would stage a protest march. Negro and white sympathizers would hike from Selma to Montgomery, fifty-four miles away, moving straight down the middle of route 80, the Jefferson Davis Highway. Wallace promptly banned the demonstration as a menace to commerce and public safety and sent a hundred state troopers to reinforce Sheriff Clark, who gave a sign of his allegiance to the past by rounding up a mounted posse. On March 7—which would enter Alabama history and folklore as "Black Sunday"—six hundred Negroes and a few white partisans of their cause defiantly marched from the Brown's Chapel African Methodist Episcopal Church to the Edmund Pettus Bridge, spanning the Alabama River. There they ran into Clark's horsemen and troopers wearing gas masks. When they ignored a two-minute warning to disperse, possemen waded into them swinging billy clubs and wet bullwhips. Yellow clouds of tear gas belched from the ranks of the troopers. Routed, the blacks stumbled and crawled back to the church. Accompanying them were television cameramen, whose footage guaranteed that Selma would become overnight a symbol of oppression.

Dr. King had been preaching in Atlanta on Black Sunday. Dropping everything, he flew to Selma, announced that he would lead a second march on Tuesday, and called on clergymen of both races to join him. Over three hundred white ministers, priests, and rabbis responded. Sympathy demonstrations were held in all the great cities of the North. Black activists staged sit-ins at the Department of Justice and the White House, and President Johnson issued a statement blaming Alabama officials for "the brutality with which a number of Negro citizens were treated." He sent John Doar and former Governor LeRoy Collins of Florida to Selma, and they succeeded in arranging a token march, back and forth across the bridge. Sheriff Clark and Dr. King agreed with many misgivings, which in King's case were justified. Militant black youths from SNCC accused him of Uncle Tomism. Coming off the bridge, they mocked him by singing the civil rights song "Ain't Gonna Let Nobody Turn Me Around."

King was turned around that same evening by the first of three murders arising from the Selma crisis, all of whites who sympathized with the civil rights movement. The Reverend James J. Reeb, a Boston Unitarian, was set upon by red-neck hoodlums as he left a Negro restaurant and beaten to death. James Forman of SNCC and five hundred of his followers then threatened to mutiny if Dr. King didn't take a bolder line. An angry crowd of fifteen hundred blacks held a rally in Montgomery's Beulah Baptist Church. King had encouraging news for them. A federal judge, Frank M. Johnson Jr. of Montgomery, had agreed to allow the march from Selma to Montgomery; although such a procession "reaches to the outer limits of what is constitutionally allowed," he had ruled, the mistreatment of the demonstrators had obviously surpassed "the outer limits of what is constitutionally permissible."

Governor Wallace, addressing a televised joint session of the Alabama legislature, condemned the imminent march as comparable to Communist "street warfare" that "ripped Cuba apart, that destroyed Diem in Vietnam, that raped China—that has torn civilization and established institutions of this world into bloody shreds." The state couldn't afford to protect all these outside agitators, he said, and he telegraphed the White House, calling upon the federal government to enforce the decision of the federal judge. That was exactly what Lyndon Johnson had been hoping he would do. The President now had an official request from Wallace to protect the demonstrators, and he complied by sending 1,863 federalized National Guardsmen, 250 U.S. marshals and FBI agents, two regular Army MP battalions, demolition experts to search the road and bridges ahead of those making the hike, and helicopters to hover overhead. In addition, the hikers were provided with huge tents for overnight stops, a 600-gallon water truck, latrine trucks, ambulances, trucks for rubbish, and scout cars to set up campsites in advance. Johnson was showing a little garter.

The march itself was a triumph. Veterans of the movement had become astute at providing TV cameramen with colorful material. Leading the procession were Dr. King, Ralph Bunche, a pretty coed, a sharecropper in overalls, a rabbi, a priest, a nun, and a one-legged marcher on crutches. (The white Alabamans along the way, hopelessly ignorant of how to cultivate a good image, made obscene gestures at the nun and guffawed while chanting, as a cadence for the man with one leg, "Left, left, left.") Although the Alabama legislature indignantly—and unanimously—fulminated against "the evidence of much fornication at the marchers' camps," behavior along the route was peaceful and orderly, a remarkable achievement in light of the number of people involved. Leaving Selma on March 21 there had been 3,200 in the procession; arriving in Montgomery four days later there were 25,000. Dr. King spoke to them on the grounds of the statehouse, which a century ago had been the capital of the Confederacy. He ended by crying four times, "Glory hallelujah!" They disbanded and heavy traffic carried them back on route 80 to Selma. A sullen clump of Ku Klux Klansmen watched them go. As the stream of cars thinned the Klansmen moved in for the second murder.

The victim was Viola Gregg Liuzzo, a red-haired Detroit housewife and the mother of five. Mrs. Liuzzo had told her husband, an agent for the Teamsters Union, "This is something I must do," and after the victorious rally on the statehouse lawn she volunteered to ferry Alabama marchers to their homes. On her last trip she was singing "We Shall Overcome" with her only passenger, a nineteen-year-old Negro barber, when a car full of Klansmen drew alongside on a lonely stretch of road. One of the white hoodlums, an auto mechanic, fired a 38-caliber pistol at her head. She collapsed with blood spurting from her temple; the car careened into a ditch; the terrified young barber hitchhiked into Selma for police help.

The third killing was of an Episcopalian seminarian from New Hampshire who was gunned down in a grocery. The killer, a part-time deputy sheriff, pleaded self-defense and was found innocent by a jury of twelve white Alabama men, though no weapon had been found on the seminarian and witnesses said there had been none. In the death of the Reverend Mr. Reeb, three men were charged a few hours after he had been battered to death. They, too, were acquitted; their jury deliberated just ninety-five minutes. The trial of Mrs. Liuzzo's murderers was the most interesting of the three. One of the Klansmen in the death car had in fact been an under-cover man for the FBI; he identified each of his companions, their weapons, and what they had done and said. They were defended in their first trial by Matt H. Murphy Jr., a third-generation Klans-man. Murphy's summation was one-hundred-proof racism: "When white people join up with them [blacks], they become white nig-gers. . . . God didn't intend for us to mix with the black race, I don't care what Lyndon Baines Johnson says." The FBI man, Murphy said, was a violator of his Klan oath, "as treacherous as a rattlesnake . . . purporting himself to be a white man and worse than a white nigger." That jury was hung (10 to 2 for con-viction of manslaughter), but Murphy had made his last bow; he was killed in an auto accident during the interval before a second trial. A biased judge presided at those proceedings, which ended in an acquittal, but then the federal government stepped in and tried the Klansmen for violating Mrs. Liuzzo's civil rights. That curious law, which had been the downfall of the Klan killers in Mississippi's Freedom Summer and of the slayers of a Negro Army officer in Georgia, worked once more here with another jury of twelve southern men, and the judge sentenced the defendants to ten years, the maximum.

Selma inspired the voting rights act—Johnson said as much in ask-ing Congress for it on March 15—and the country credited it to Dr. King. It proved to be the peak of his reputation. The events of the previous year in Mississippi having created the first serious doubts about nonviolence, the Alabama murders confirmed the suspicions of the new generation of black activists. These skeptics left Selma convinced that King had nothing more to teach them. The vast majority of the Negro people disagreed; in a subsequent CBS public opinion poll where anonymity was preserved, only 4 percent said they would give active support to Stokely Carmichael, 2 percent to the more militant H. Rap Brown, and 1 percent to Ron Karenga, the most militant of the three, while 40 percent backed the ideals of Dr. King. Nevertheless, the activists had correctly gauged a change in mood. The majority yearned for peace—a majority has always wanted it—but the country was entering a new period, and one of its most striking qualities would be an affinity for violence. In retrospect the death of President Kennedy and the murder of his assassin now seemed to have been omens. Once more a gear had shifted somewhere in the universe. Search and destroy, emerging in Vietnam during the same months in 1965, was one expression of the emerging mood, the Selma murders were another; still others would crowd upon one another in the succeeding months and years as Negro rage and frustration which had been repressed for a century now erupted.

The new inner city temper emerged in Los Angeles on Wednesday, August 11, 1965, in a shabby Negro district of low, faded stucco houses, suggestive of certain poor areas in Puerto Rico, which lay under the approaches to Los Angeles International Airport. Trash never seemed to be properly collected there. There was litter everywhere—broken glass, rusty cans, rotting chicken bones, empty Tokay bottles—and the quality of life was further diminished by the typical white policeman, also known locally as The Man, who had a way of stopping black citizens and demanding, "Let's see your I.D."

That August evening Lee Minikus, an officer of the California Highway Patrol, wanted a look at the I.D. of a young Negro named Marquette Frye; he intended to take him in on suspicion of drunken driving. A knot of people, gathering around, kidded both Minikus and his suspect. It all seemed low-key and harmless, but beneath the surface tension was building. Los Angeles was in the fourth day of a brutal heat wave. People were outdoors, ready to assemble quickly at the promise of excitement. The arrest was taking place at the corner of Avalon Boulevard and Imperial Highway, a busy L.A. intersection through which passed a constant stream of white drivers, often behind the wheels of expensive cars. Most inauspicious of all was the neighborhood. It was 98 percent black, with a population density of 27.3 people per acre (the figure was 7.4 for Los Angeles County as a whole). Negro immigrants had been arriving here in massive numbers since the early 1940s, when an average of 2,000 each month came to work in war industries. Now 420,000 of the 2,731,000 inhabitants of the city were black. Yet in this ghetto there were just five blacks on the 205-man police force. And every month in 1965 another 1,000 Negroes poured into these swarming warrens, often looking for jobs that no longer existed. The temptations of drugs and alcohol awaited their children, and when the children went wrong The Man came after them. These snares, not the inhabitants, were the real transgressors in this district, a region known locally as Watts.

At 7:45 P.M. that Wednesday, California Highway Patrolman Minikus took the Frye youth into custody. Almost immediately he was in trouble. Among those attracted by the winking red light of his squad car was the prisoner's mother. At first she rebuked her son. Then she turned on the police officer. As her manner became distraught and the murmurs of the spectators less good-humored, Minikus nervously radioed for reinforcements. Then he made two mistakes. He attempted to force Frye into the squad car and he turned his back on Frye's mother. She jumped on it. As other officers arrived they pried her loose, and when the crowd began to mutter indignantly they held it at bay with shotguns. Minikus got away with his man, but the price had been exorbitant. Already the use of force was beginning to inspire distorted accounts of what had happened, and with each passing hour the stories grew taller. Two versions were widespread. One had it that a cop had struck a pregnant woman in the belly with his club. In the other, a cop had pushed a woman against the patrol car and tried to choke her. Aroused, the crowd pelted policemen with stones and bottles. By 10 P.M. the spectators had been transformed into a mob which set upon passersby, overturned cars, and smashed shop display windows. The familiar stages of riot escalation now appeared. Police sealed off eight blocks at 11 P.M. Two hours later the rioters burst free and roved Watts, two thousand strong, waylaying strangers, breaking everything fragile, and looting the stores.

At 3 A.M. the level of violence fell—rioters must sleep, too—and police patrols imposed a semblance of order in the ghetto. In the morning shop managers called their insurance companies, clerks cleaned up the mess, and those who knew nothing about riots assumed this one was over. Their disillusionment began at 7:45 P.M. that Thursday, just twenty-four hours after the arrest of young Frye. At first it was all a repetition of Wednesday evening: youths pouncing on passing autos, pelting cops with bricks, breaking windows. The change came at 4 A.M. At that hour the day before, a peace of exhaustion had fallen over the ghetto. This time a second shift of rioters spilled into the streets. These men were older and more vicious. They were also armed. Dick Gregory toured Watts with a bullhorn, begging for order, and was shot in the leg. The ghetto violence was approaching the force of an insurrection, but the authorities didn't realize it yet; a flying wedge of policemen cleared Watts's darkened streets and then announced that the situation was under control.

The truth was revealed to them at 10 A.M., when two white salesmen were attacked in the first incident of daytime violence. At 11 A.M. a policeman wounded a black looter. Governor Edmund Brown, on vacation in Greece, read reports of the growing disorders and hurried home; his lieutenant governor granted a request from the L.A. police chief for National Guard troops. The first contingent of Guardsmen reached Watts Friday afternoon. Even as they were being briefed in an elementary school the version they heard was being outdated by new developments in the ghetto. More than 5,000 rioters now roamed a 150-block area, firing buildings with Molotov cocktails and ambushing firemen who answered the alarms. Watts claimed its first fatality, a sheriff's deputy mortally wounded in the stomach, at 9:40 P.M. Three other deaths quickly followed. National Guard soldiers entering the district with fixed bayonets saw looters, their way illumined by a hundred major fires, carrying guns, appliances, liquor, jewelry—everything of value—from the shops of the ghetto. Crudely lettered signs outside some stores read "Black Brother," "Soul Brother," "Negro Owned," and "Owned by a Brother." Some had been robbed anyway. One gang was trying to burn Oak Park Community Hospital, which was crowded with Negroes hurt in the disorders. Robert Richardson, a black *Los Angeles Times* reporter, wrote: "The rioters were burning their city now, as the insane sometimes mutilate themselves."

On Saturday snipers on rooftops began picking off soldiers and policemen. Firemen were issued bulletproof vests. The Guard force grew to 10,000 men, then to 14,000; a curfew was imposed on 40 square miles Saturday and on 46 square miles Sunday. Intermittent shoot-outs continued until the early hours of Wednesday, August 18, when officers seized 35 blacks after a gunfight at a Black Muslim mosque. That was the end of it. During the six days of madness 34 had been killed, 898 hurt, and over 4,000 arrested. Losses were put at 45 million dollars.

The Watts devastation was called the worst race riot since Detroit in 1943, but it was really in a class by itself. While the death toll was the same, the damage in Detroit had been less than a million dollars. There was trouble elsewhere, too. Coincident with Watts, the West Side of Chicago ran amok when a fire truck, answering an alarm in West Garfield Park on August 12, struck and killed a black woman. Negroes fought cops and 2,000 Guardsmen for two nights, looting and hurling bottles at whites. Over 100 were arrested and 67 hurt. And in Springfield, Massachusetts, far from the ghettos of the great cities, the arrest of eighteen blacks outside a nightclub gave rise to accusations of brutality against seven cops; Molotov cocktail bombings of stores owned by whites then led to mass arrests and, once more, the calling of the National Guard. A protest march by 4,000 Springfield Negroes ended at City Hall, where George Wiley, assistant national director of CORE, told them that "the civil rights struggle in the North" would be "longer, bloodier, and more bitter" than it had been in the South.

It was characteristic of the 1960s that each outbreak of violence was followed by the appointment of a commission to study it. Governor Brown picked a panel of eminent citizens led by John A. McCone to look into Watts. Their findings were published under the title *Violence in the City: An End or a Beginning?* By then everyone knew that Watts was only a beginning, but the searches for remedies followed various paths. The McCone Report came down hard on the need for law and order. Black militants protested that objection to laws oppressing Negroes was what Watts had been all about. Bayard Rustin called it "the first major rebellion of Negroes against their own masochism." Theodore H. White thought that television and radio reporting shared some of the responsibility. White charged that it had gone "beyond reporting and become a factor in itself," and he asked, "Can electronic reporting be curbed in the higher interest of domestic tranquillity?" Martin Luther King, touring the smoking ruins of Watts, received a mixed welcome. He was growing accustomed to this. The torch had been passed to the new generation of black leaders, and it had become a real torch.

If the summer of racial disorders had been hot in 1965, it had also been short. Until Watts burst into flame that second week in August there had been hope that the country might make it that year without a major riot. The next year was a different story. Again Los Angeles sounded the tocsin, but this time it was in March that a gang of Negro students stoned the auto of a white teacher there, attacked other whites, and turned to looting. Angeleno policemen had learned a lot the year before; this new threat was suppressed overnight with only two deaths. Yet if L.A. escaped with fewer scars, the rest of the nation did not. It almost seemed as though every large black community in the United States was in rebellion against society. In Washington, D.C., Negroes rose in April. By May three California cities were embattled. Cleveland erupted in late June, and Omaha, Des Moines, and Chicago two weeks after that. Next came Cleveland, and then in swift succession Brooklyn, Baltimore, Perth Amboy, Providence, Minneapolis, Milwaukee, Detroit, Dayton, Atlanta, San Francisco, and St. Louis; Pompano Beach, Florida; Cordele, Georgia; Cicero, Illinois; and Lansing, Muskegon, Benton Harbor, and Jackson, Michigan. By the end of the summer the toll was seven dead, over 400 hurt, some 3,000 arrested, and more than five million dollars lost to vandals, looters, and arsonists. By the end of 1966, America had been scarred by forty-three race riots that year.

In Cicero a Negro march for open housing ran into a counter-demonstration by hostile whites, who repeatedly tried to lunge past police to harm the blacks. Twelve were hurt; six officers were hit by missiles; 32 of the whites were arrested. Cicero was of special interest because it demonstrated that policemen, far from starting riots, often held together a fragile peace; when Negroes went after them it was often because the cops represented authority and were the only whites in sight. In working-class communities whites often matched, and more than matched, the black rage. The tension between the races was felt on both sides. It was in 1966 that backlash came into its own.

Originally the open housing demonstration had been in Cicero's Marquette Park and led by Martin Luther King. He called it off when a rock hit him and knocked him to his knees. Robert Lucas, Chicago chairman of CORE, defiantly sponsored the new march, explaining that "CORE wants to keep the pressure on." Lucas was one of the new militants, and 1966 was turning into their year, too. Floyd McKissick replaced the more moderate James Farmer as head of CORE and Stokely Carmichael succeeded John Lewis as chairman of SNCC. The development was not as auspicious for the movement as they thought. Carmichael had been in office just a month when an event that none of the civil rights leaders had taken seriously showed the extent of the divisions in their ranks.

On June 5 James H. Meredith announced that he was leaving Memphis to hike 225 miles to Mississippi's state capitol in Jackson. His motive was to prove that American Negroes were unafraid. The McKissicks and Carmichaels thought the idea impractical and visionary—"the silliest idea I ever heard of," one movement leader called it—and they decided to ignore him. Meredith was undaunted. Still guided by a feeling of "divine responsibility," as he had called it in *Three Years in Mississippi*, his account of his ordeal on the Ole Miss campus, he believed that destiny awaited him in his native state, and he was correct, destiny in this case being represented by a middle-aged, unemployed white Mississippian named Aubrey James Norvell. At 4:15 P.M. on the second day of the journey, Meredith and a convoy of FBI agents were striding along U.S. 51 just south of Hernando, Mississippi, when Norvell rose out of the bushes beside the road. "James Meredith!" he yelled. "James Meredith! I only want Meredith!" He fired three shotgun blasts. Doctors in a Memphis hospital found Meredith peppered with birdshot.

None of the wounds was serious. Norvell's real damage had been done to the notion that Meredith's walk needn't be taken seriously. The bursts of gunfire had turned it into a crusade, and everyone in the movement wanted to be part of it. Dick Gregory flew to Memphis to retrace Meredith's steps, and McKissick, Carmichael, and Martin Luther King headed south on foot from the stretch of pavement where Meredith had fallen. Dr. King, borrowing two thousand dollars to launch what he called the Meredith March for Freedom, ordered his Southern Christian Leadership Conference to mobilize resources for another Selma.

It wasn't possible. Selma had been an achievement of united Negro leadership advocating nonviolence. Now King's critics, and particularly those in SNCC, were out in the open. The day after Norvell's ambush Carmichael told a Memphis rally, "The Negro is going to take what he deserves from the white man." King deplored such demagoguery; Roy Wilkins of the NAACP and Whitney M. Young Jr. of the Urban League agreed. But the rhetoric of the young militants became more bellicose. In Philadelphia, Mississippi, where in the Freedom Summer of 1964 death had come to three members of the movement—two of them white—a white Mississippian was wounded by gunfire in the dark, and Ralph Featherstone of SNCC, far from regretting the incident, exulted that blacks were no longer meek, that "their reaction is shot for shot." Carmichael spoke up for the Black Panther political party. In Yazoo City young Negroes chanted, "Hey! Hey! Whattaya know! White folks must go —must go!" and that night in the Yazoo City fairgrounds Willie Ricks, a twenty-three-year-old member of SNCC known as "the Reverend" because of his evangelical style, mounted a flatbed truck and delivered a sermon of hate that made older Negro leaders shudder. He spoke of the blood of whites flowing and repeatedly described his goal in two explosive words: "Black power!"

In Greenwood, forty-five miles away, Carmichael was emerging from seven hours in jail. In a way his plight was a consequence of his militancy. White liberals, dismayed by it, were being far less generous with contributions than they had been at the time of Selma. Food and shelter were a problem, and Carmichael had been arrested while trying to erect tents on a Negro school playground. He heard about Ricks's speech just as he himself was climbing another flatbed truck to address a Greenwood rally. Using the repetition and question-and-response techniques which civil rights leaders had adopted so successfully from Negro preachers, he reminded his audience that he had been apprehended by police in a Negro schoolyard. "Everybody owns our neighborhoods except us. . . . Now we're going to get something and we're going to get some representing. We ain't going to worry about whether it's white— maybe black. Don't be ashamed. We . . . want . . . black . . . power!"

They shouted, "That's right!" and he took up the theme: "We . . . want . . . black power! We . . . want . . . black . . . power! We want black power! We want black power! That's right—that's what we want. . . . Now, from now on, when they ask you what you want, you know what to tell them. What do you want?"

"Black power!"

"What do you want?"

"Black power!"

"What do you want? Say it again!"

"Black power!"

What did it mean? Roy Wilkins had no doubts: "The term 'black power' means anti-white power . . . It has to mean going it alone. It has to mean separatism. We of the NAACP will have none of this." Wilkins called the phrase "the father of hatred and the mother of violence." Martin Luther King said much the same thing at first, though later, seeing that the coalition of civil rights groups was coming apart over the issue, he hedged, interpreting it as "an appeal to racial pride, an appeal to the Negro not to be ashamed of being black, and the transfer of the powerlessness of the Negro into positive, constructive power." McKissick saw it as an appeal to joint action: "Unless we can get around to unifying black power, we're going to be in bad shape." But Charles Evers, brother of the martyred Medgar Evers and the ranking NAACP worker in Mississippi, warned that "If we are marching these roads for black supremacy, we are doomed," and A. Philip Randolph, deploring the war cry as "a menace to racial peace and prosperity" said that "No Negro who is fighting for civil rights can support black power, which is opposed to civil rights and integration."

A nationwide *New York Times* survey reported that the dissension among civil rights leaders in Mississippi was reducing public support for the movement. An opinion poll found that 77 percent of whites felt the black power creed was hurting the black cause. James Meredith agreed. "There seems to be a good bit of show going on down there," he said in New York, where he was convalescing. Fully recovered, he rejoined the march and was embraced by King and the others. Nevertheless his doubts remained. "I think something is wrong," he said, and he spoke of "some shenanigans going on that I don't like."

An open break between the old leaders and the new was inevitable. It came at Canton, near the end of the Meredith March, on June 23, after police had refused to let them pitch their tents on another school playground. Refusing to disperse, twenty-five hundred blacks stood their ground. Carmichael cried, "The time for running has come to an end." It hadn't really—when the police charged with nightsticks and tear gas the people scattered—but when King turned down a proposal that they try to put up the tents anyway, the SNCC leadership deserted him. One of them said, "What we

do from now on we will do on our own." Then they proposed that
the NAACP be excluded from the climactic rally in Jackson on the
ground that its support of the march had been tepid. King and an
organization of volunteer doctors and nurses, who had provided
medical attention during the journey, opposed the resolution, but
SNCC, CORE, and two other groups representing young blacks
gave it a majority. Charles Evers said, "It's all right. I'll be here
when they're all gone." He observed caustically that marches did
nothing to register black voters. When the procession reached the
statehouse grounds in Jackson, with a band playing "When the
Saints Go Marching In," veterans of other civil rights demonstrations noted that the whites who had marched with King in other
years were not there.

That did not end the liberal commitment to justice for blacks,
of course. Nor did it block programs for Negro progress which were
already under way. That same month a six-month boycott of white
businesses in Fayette, Mississippi, ended with the hiring of black
clerks in Fayette stores, the closing of filling station toilets for colored people, and the swearing in of black policemen and deputy
sheriffs. Julian Bond, having been elected to the Georgia legislature
three times in twelve months, was finally seated by order of the
U.S. Supreme Court. In Selma Sheriff Jim Clark quietly removed
his "Never" button as his job went on the ballot. It didn't save him;
when Negro voters, registered under the voting act he had opposed,
went to the polls, he lost.

Once it had been enough for all blacks that a few blacks made
it. The entire race had been proud of the few. No more; typically,
Carmichael quoted a Negro woman as saying that September, "The
food that Ralph Bunche eats doesn't fill my stomach." The tool and
die maker and the three-dollar-a-day cotton picker wanted their
share, too. It was human and it was natural, but the militants' way
of going about it was hopelessly unrealistic. Negroes constituted
only 11 percent of the U.S. population. The talk of black revolution
—and there was a lot of it in 1966—was senseless, and SNCC's demand that blacks reject integration was absurd.

Philip Randolph, appalled by the violent confrontations between
slum blacks and policemen, suggested in September that "the time
has come when the street marches and demonstrations have about
run their course." He proposed a new approach, "a shift from the
streets to the conference table." In October he, Wilkins, Young,

Rustin, and three other veterans of the civil rights struggle signed a statement repudiating violence, rioting, and demagoguery, and concluding: "We not only welcome, we urge the full cooperation of white Americans." Martin Luther King, while approving in principle, declined to sign on the ground that he did not want to give the impression that he thought the spokesmen for black power were "conclusively and irrevocably committed to error."

For a time Carmichael took a conciliatory line, redefining black power as "black people coming together to form a political force and either electing representatives or forcing their representatives to speak their needs. . . . saying, 'Look, buddy, we're not laying a vote on you unless you lay so many schools, hospitals, playgrounds and jobs on us.'" It didn't last. Soon he was telling audiences that "If we don't get justice we're going to tear this country apart," and calling on Negroes to "fight for liberation by any means necessary." In Prattville, Alabama, he said, "We came here to tear this town up and we're going to tear it up." He called President Johnson a "hunky," a "buffoon," and a "liar." Increasingly he identified himself with the Panthers, whose "Power to the People" slogan meant power to black people and no one else. Then, like Danton being succeeded by Robespierre, Carmichael was replaced as SNCC's chairman by an even more violent racist, H. Rap Brown. When much of downtown Cincinnati went up in flames during five terrible days and nights of Molotov cocktails, Brown told reporters that there would be no peace "until the honky cops get out." Then he said: "SNCC has declared war."

The backlash vote in the 1966 elections was one response to the call for black power. Another was a shift in position by such sensitive politicians as Senator Everett Dirksen. Dirksen had supported civil rights legislation in 1964 and 1965 as "an idea whose time has come," but he scorned the 1966 bill, with Title IV, the "open housing" clause, as "a package of mischief," and that killed it. Curiously, it was a British periodical, the *Economist* of London, which took the most critical view of the new militants. "Many of these 'leaders' are of a lurid fascist type," said the *Economist*. It derided "liberal intellectuals" who "insultingly tell one another that the general anti-white mood among black Americans is similar to the anti-German mood among the French in 1943," observed that "robberies and assaults on white women" were being interpreted by some activists as "almost a noble act of black revolution," and predicted that "a temporary and rather extraordinary toleration by the American people of flamboyant violence is almost certainly about to turn to a harsh white intolerance of it."

Meantime the black racists were flourishing. The Panthers were acquiring what Tom Wolfe pungently called "radical chic" among some affluent urban liberals, and criminals whose notoriety would once have been limited to the police blotter were being seriously discussed as observers with fresh insight into the human dilemma. All were creatures of the ghettos, and the rise of some could be traced directly to the recent riots. Ron Karenga came from the depths of Watts; although he denied that members of US, his black nationalist organization, had engaged in riot activity, four of them had been so charged. Karenga's celebrity was a consequence of the Watts upheaval. The full bill for that convulsion, it was becoming clear, was incalculable. Some of the highest costs would be hidden for years. One item in the legacy of violence was a snub-nosed, eight-shot 22-caliber Iver-Johnson revolver, model 55SA, bought for protection by a frightened Angeleno for $31.95 late in August 1965 in the wake of the disorders. Later he gave it to his daughter, who passed it on to a Pasadena neighbor, who sold it to an employee in Nash's Department Store named Munir "Joe" Sirhan. Eventually Joe turned it over to his kid brother, Sirhan Bishara "Sol" Sirhan, who used it to assassinate Robert F. Kennedy in Los Angeles three years after Watts.

In the twelve-year cycle of the Vietnamese calendar, the Year of the Snake, 1965, gave way to the Year of the Horse, 1966, which in turn was followed by the Year of the Goat, 1967. The Horse was supposed to be lucky, second only to the Year of the Dragon in auspiciousness, but almost half of America's total Vietnam dead by the end of the first ten weeks of 1966—2,559 men—had fallen to Communist guns and bombs in those ten weeks, and that, it turned out, was only the beginning. That year's toll was 4,800 U.S. soldiers killed in action. In May of the following year the total of U.S. dead passed 10,000, and as the war grew older, it grew bloodier. Average weekly losses in the Year of the Goat ran 33 percent higher than in the Year of the Horse. More men died in 1967 than in all the war's previous years. And during that same period there were 53,000 civilian deaths, a matter of increasing concern to the war critics at home.

The toll didn't deter the Pentagon from proposing an ever more vigorous, aggressive policy. The Joint Chiefs kept pressing McNamara to recommend to the President the bombing of petroleum, oil, and lubricant supplies (POL raids, they were called) in North Vietnam. Admiral U. S. Grant Sharp of CINCPAC predicted that this would "bring the enemy to the conference table or cause the insurgency to wither." McNamara finally agreed in March 1966, though the CIA prophesied that POL strikes would not halt infiltration of men and supplies. The CIA was right; despite heavy losses in combat, the number of North Vietnamese soldiers coming down the 1,000-mile Ho Chi Minh Trail grew from 1,500 a month to 3,500 and then to 4,000. By the end of the year Giap was sending an average of 8,800 men a month to the South. Soon the annual replacement rate would be 100,000 men.

Defense Department study groups advised McNamara that despite the bombing the flow of guerrillas southward was "undiminished" and that the raids "had no measurable direct effect" on Hanoi's capacity to make war below the 17th Parallel. The secretary flew over to see for himself; it was his eighth on-the-spot inspection. Returning, he told the President that "pacification has if anything gone backward," and that the air war had not "either significantly affected infiltration or cracked the morale of Hanoi." He recommended a reappraisal of the bombing campaign. The Joint Chiefs strenuously objected to any suggestion of a cutback in the raids. In a memorandum to the President they contended that the military situation had "improved substantially over the past year" and called bombing "a trump card." General Westmoreland, flying home to address a joint session of Congress, reported: "I have never been more encouraged in my four years in Vietnam. . . . We have reached an important point when the end begins to come in view."

McNamara was not encouraged. By now he had seen too many optimistic forecasts go glimmering. In Saigon he had spent a gloomy session with one of his men there who told him that the official cheerfulness was false, that there was no light at the end of the tunnel; the informant was Daniel Ellsberg. In fact Westmoreland was in Washington not to report victories but to ask for more troops. He had ended 1966 with 375,000. By April of 1967 he had 480,000, more than in the Korean War at its peak. He wanted 680,000 men by June 1968, or at the very least 565,000. With the higher figure, he told Johnson, he could end the war in two years; with the smaller figure it would take three years. The President noted unhappily that the Communist force in the South was at a record high. He asked the general, "When we add divisions, can't the enemy add divisions? If so, where does it all end?" Westmoreland said that if Giap's infiltration rate went much higher his supply problems would become difficult. Anyhow, the grunts were killing North Vietnamese quicker than they could be replaced. Johnson asked what would happen if Giap asked for Chinese volunteers. The general replied, "That's a good question."

Already American involvement in the Vietnam War had lasted longer than World War II or the Korean War. The conflict seemed more than ever a struggle between whites and Asians. MACV christened the battles with colorful names which became reminders of agony in the jungle and growing bitterness among an increasingly divided people at home. There was operation Attleboro, and Leatherneck Square, and operations Masher, Double Eagle, and White Wing. Then Dak To, Hill 881 North, Loc Ninh, and operations Crazy Horse, Hawthorne, and Hastings—Hastings, the costliest engagement since Ia Drang. And then Hill 881 South, Khe Sanh, the three red hills of Con Thien, and Ashu. The Iron Triangle, a three-cornered region of abandoned rubber plantations and rain forest between the Saigon River and Route 13 twenty miles north of Saigon, had been a Communist stronghold for twenty years. Operation Cedar Falls in January 1967, an attack on the Triangle by 30,000 grunts, was the largest American drive of the war till then. But operation Junction City, a month later, was even bigger: 45,000 American troops thrusting into Zone C near the Cambodian border to wipe out a Viet Cong base. They did it—and then had to let the enemy reclaim it, because ARVN (Army of the Republic of Vietnam) forces couldn't hold it, even as garrison troops.

Congress, meantime, was making dissent from Johnson's war policies respectable. By later standards the protests were muffled; addressing Hanoi, sixteen senators who opposed the administration's conduct of the war warned that there were limits to their dissent, that they were "steadfastly opposed to any unilateral withdrawal of American troops." Yet the Hill was growing restive. At the request of the President, five senators led by Mike Mansfield spent thirty-five days in Vietnam. When they issued their report Johnson was dismayed; they had found that a year of U.S. campaigning had not altered the progress of the war and that America was becoming trapped in an "open-ended" conflict: "how open is dependent upon the extent to which North Viet Nam and its supporters are willing and able to meet increased force by increased force." Senator Robert F. Kennedy charged that the administration had "switched" from the policy of his brother, so that now, "We're killing innocent people . . . because [the Communists] are 12,000 miles away and they might get 11,000 miles away."

That was the highest level of protest. Senatorial doves might object to Johnson's course in Indochina, but they voted him funds to continue on it, and their language was polite. Fulbright, the most outspoken of them, was never uncivil; when Westmoreland told a New York audience that he was "dismayed . . . by recent unpatriotic acts here at home" and accused the perpetrators of giving aid and comfort to the enemy, Fulbright merely replied that Westmoreland's visit had been planned by the administration "to pave the way for escalation," which was of course true. One step down was Martin Luther King, who called the United States "the greatest purveyor of violence in the world today," and compared American experiments with new weapons in Vietnam, where they were killing peasants, to Nazi tests of "new medicine and new tortures in the concentration camps of Europe." Eartha Kitt used much the same rhetoric in attacking the war at a White House luncheon given by Lady Bird. So did Dr. Spock in telling peace demonstrators that "Lyndon Johnson is the enemy"; so did folk singer Pete Seeger, censored by CBS for a number called "Waist Deep in the Big Muddy," which dealt contemptuously with the President's war policy ("And the old fool says, 'Push on'"), and Captain Howard Brett Levy, a Brooklyn physician who refused to train medical corpsmen assigned to the Army's Special Forces—Green Berets—on the ground that under the Nüremberg Doctrine he would thereby become an accessory to war crimes. One of the charges against Dr. Levy at his court-martial in June 1967 was that he had called the war a "diabolical evil." He was found guilty, sentenced to three years in prison, and led off in handcuffs.

Colleges and universities continued to be the centers of heavier protest. Job recruiters for the CIA, the Dow Chemical Company—manufacturers of napalm, the incendiary jelly—and the armed forces were treated roughly and sometimes ejected from campuses. The revelation on St. Valentine's Day 1967 that $200,000 a year in CIA funds had been subsidizing the National Student Association (NSA), which represented student governments on over three hundred campuses, was enough to cripple the NSA. Students provided the leadership for "Stop-the-Draft Week" in October 1967, including a march to the steps of the Pentagon by more than fifty thousand demonstrators, and they were responsible for imaginative and sometimes shocking protests against the draft—pasting eight draft cards on the door of the American embassy in London, battling Oakland police for five days while attempting to block buses carrying draftees from an induction center to military bases, and seizing and holding the administration building at the University of Chicago for three days to dramatize opposition to the war.

It was not all selfless idealism. College students were of the age most vulnerable to conscription, and as monthly draft calls in 1966 were boosted nearly tenfold over the 1965 average of five thousand, blanket deferments for students became rarer. Resistance to the draft was being expressed openly on posters, buttons, and bumper stickers. The theme of a 1967 hit tune, Arlo Guthrie's "Alice's Restaurant," was draft evasion, and virtually every undergraduate dormitory had a collection of leaflets providing tips on how to get rejected at Selective Service physical examinations. ("Arrive high. If you want to go about the addiction scene in a really big way, use a common pin on your arm for a few weeks in advance.") General Hershey struck back by sending a directive to the country's 4,088 draft boards instructing them to reclassify the protesters 1-A. Congressmen objected that Hershey was exceeding his authority, and the American Civil Liberties Union charged that using the draft to punish dissidents was "outrageous," but Hershey wouldn't back away. One consequence was that the flow of draft evaders to Canada grew until there were some ten thousand young American expatriates there, making new homes with the help of such groups as the Students Union for Peace Action in Toronto.

As the polarization of the country grew, the hawks became more hawkish. In response to back-to-back antiwar speeches by Morse of Oregon ("The United States is leading mankind into World War III out of which will come no victory") and Gruening of Alaska (who called a new war appropriation bill "a blank check for unlimited escalation"), Russell B. Long of Louisiana wrapped himself in the flag in attacking those who "encourage the Communists to prolong the war." Long said, "I swell with pride when I see Old Glory flying from the Capitol . . . My prayer is that there may never be a white flag of surrender up there." Everett Dirksen predicted that if Vietnam fell, "the whole Pacific coastline" of the United States would be "exposed." Manhattan hawks staged Operation Gratitude, a two-day vigil at Battery Park. At the same time, motorists who believed in the war were asked to drive with lights on—and suddenly every highway offered a vivid demonstration of how badly divided the people were.

Lyndon Johnson characteristically said one thing while believing the exact opposite. "No American, young or old, must ever be denied the right to dissent," he declared in June 1966, putting on his white hat. "No minority must be muzzled. Opinion and protest are the life breath of democracy—even when it blows heavy." His deeper feeling was that those who quarreled with his conduct of the war were un-American, and that it was his duty to battle them with any weapon that came to hand. Presidential publicity was effective, and at various times he conferred with Asian allies at Guam, Honolulu, Manila, and Melbourne, staging the trips to coincide with antiwar events he wanted to drive off the front page. It didn't always work. In Australia he discovered that American students weren't the only ones capable of mounting antiwar demonstrations; Melbourne hecklers tossed two plastic balloons filled with paint at his limousine, smearing it red and green, the Viet Cong colors.

His true feelings about opponents of the war boiled over on May 17, 1966, at a Democratic fund-raising dinner in Chicago, when he upbraided "Nervous Nellies" who "will turn on their leaders and on their country and on our own fighting men." By the end of that summer he was avoiding the phrase "Great Society." He had come to prefer the company of political conservatives to that of "knee-jerk liberals" who were such "trouble-makers that they force politicians to the right." In the privacy of the White House he would flatly state that Americans in the antiwar movement were disloyal, that "the Russians" were "behind the whole thing." The FBI and the CIA, he confided to his staff, were keeping him posted on what was "really going on." The doves in the Senate were in touch with Soviet agents, he said; they lunched with them, attended parties at the Russian embassy, and encouraged the children of their aides to date Soviet diplomats in Washington and at the U.N. He asserted, "The Russians think up things for the Senators to say. I often know before they do what their speeches are going to say." In June 1966 the parents of one of the winners of a Presidential Scholarship, a gifted seventeen-year-old girl, turned out to be critics of the war. Word went out to the staff that the girl was to be deprived of her medal. Eric Goldman protested and the order was rescinded, but Goldman was told that before Presidential Scholars were nominated in the future, they and their families would be subjected to FBI checks.

Hawks, following Johnson's example, saw the stain of disloyalty spreading. In 1966 CBS-TV showed marines in the "Zippo squads"— as they called themselves—setting fire to peasant huts, and the Pentagon virtually accused the commentators of treason. When McNamara opposed the bombing of Hanoi in a Montreal speech, noting that the weekly bomb tonnage dropped on North Vietnam already exceeded that of all the bombings of Germany in World War II, he too came under suspicion. He decided to resign in November 1967, joining Mac Bundy, George Ball, Jack Valenti, George Reedy, Richard Goodwin, and Horace Busby in the exodus of trusted Johnsonian advisers from Washington. The departure of Bill Moyers hurt the President most, but it was Johnson's equivocations which had made Moyers's role as press secretary untenable. Reston wrote of him that he had been wounded at Credibility Gap, and Moyers himself said that the gap had become so bad that "we can't even believe our own leaks." The President, stung by his resignation, accused Moyers of ingratiating himself with the Kennedys and exploiting the White House, using it to better himself at the expense of the administration. He read the clippings, LBJ stormed, and he wasn't stupid; he saw what had been happening; the press secretary had been getting a good press for himself while Johnson's grew worse and worse.

He was right about his public image. By 1967 it was terrible. The Secret Service disclosed that the number of people arrested for threatening the life of the chief executive had increased by over 500 percent since Dallas. The number of people holding Lyndon Johnson responsible for the death of John Kennedy was growing. By May 1967 there were, Esquire estimated, some sixty different versions of the Dallas tragedy on sale. Early that year District Attorney Jim Garrison of New Orleans told the press, "My staff and I solved the assassination weeks ago." Subsequent events made it plain that Garrison belonged in a padded cell, not a courtroom, but a Harris poll that May indicated that the number of Americans who doubted the Warren Report had jumped from 44 percent to 66. Many believed Garrison "had something"; others simply came to distrust everything about President Johnson, including the way he entered the White House.

His popularity dropped until in March 1968 Gallup's figures indicated that only 36 percent of the country approved of his conduct of the Presidency. Like Richard Nixon five years later, Johnson responded by withdrawing into a self-imposed isolation. During his campaign against Goldwater three years earlier he had alarmed the Secret Service by his way of wading joyously into seas of humanity. Now his public appearances were confined to reliable audiences —meetings of business executives or service families on military bases, where he could trust his listeners to be respectful. The White House became embattled. Getting past the gates became much more difficult; credentials had to be just so, and dispatch cases were rigorously searched. The President's staff urged him to get out among the people. Even if crowds were hostile the nation would sympathize and admire his courage. Anything would be an improvement on this seclusion. The Secret Service objected. Given the country's ugly mood, they felt that appearances before unscreened groups would be risky, and this time Johnson obeyed them.

More and more he kept watch on his staff and cabinet, alert for further defections. Those who wanted to stay, or who needed his approval for advancement now and his endorsement for future positions, felt they had to display excessive zeal and unquestioning devotion to him. Hubert Humphrey became a superhawk. Larry O'Brien drafted the dead in support of the war, telling an audience in Lexington, Virginia, that if General George C. Marshall were alive he would "no doubt" back Johnson's Vietnam policy in every particular. Nick Katzenbach, appointed attorney general, held in testimony before the Senate Foreign Relations Committee on August 17, 1967, that Congress had authorized the President "to use the armed forces of the United States in whatever way necessary" when it passed the Tonkin Gulf resolution three years earlier, and that this was indeed sufficient warrant for any military commitment the President might make in Indochina, including the bombing of targets close to the Chinese border. This exchange followed:

SENATOR FULBRIGHT: You think it is outmoded to declare war?

MR. KATZENBACH: In this kind of context I think the expression of declaring a war is one that has become outmoded in the international arena.

It was enough, Katzenbach said, that the Senate had approved of American participation in regional defense treaties, in this case

SEATO. He intimated that a President could do whatever he liked with U.S. military power without consulting Congress. At that point a member of the committee rose and strode angrily out of the room muttering, "There is only one thing to do—take it to the country." The senator was Eugene McCarthy of Minnesota.

It was in May 1967, the third and ugliest year of black violence, that Stokely Carmichael resigned as chairman of the misnamed Student Nonviolent Coordinating Committee and flew off to tour Cuba and North Vietnam. "You'll be happy to have me back," he said, referring to his successor, H. Rap Brown, as "a bad man." The rise of Brown was a triumph for militants bent on the rejection of integration and the alienation of white liberals. "If you give me a gun I might just shoot Lady Bird," he said on July 26, and he told Detroit blacks, "The honky is your enemy."

Whites were barred from a national conference on black power in Newark the weekend of July 20–23. The delegates took their theme from Malcolm X: "The day of nonviolent resistance is over." Among the measures they endorsed were resolutions calling for the formation of a "black militia," for "a national dialogue on the desirability of partitioning the United States into two separate nations, one white and one black," and for recognition of "the right of black people to revolt when they deem it necessary and in their interests." Integration was dead, the nearly one thousand delegates declared; absolute segregation of the races was the new goal.

The August 14 issue of Brown's SNCC *Newsletter* denounced Zionism, attacked American Jews, and accused Israel of crushing Arabs "through terror, force, and massacre." That drove from SNCC membership such liberals as Harry Golden and Theodore Bikel and drew the fire of the Anti-Defamation League of B'nai B'rith. The militants were undaunted. To be sure white sympathizers got the message that they were unwelcome, CORE dropped "multiracial" from the constitutional description of its membership. Speaking for CORE, Floyd McKissick issued a Black Manifesto declaring that sit-ins, boycotts, and peaceful demonstrations belonged to the past. "The tactics and philosophy of the civil rights era can take us no further along the road to total equality," he said. "New methods must be found; a new era must begin." The long, hot summers of rioting, he suggested, might be remembered in the future as "the beginning of the black revolution."

Some honkies seemed to take an almost masochistic pleasure in their mortification. Perhaps the most vivid example was the National Conference for New Politics (NCNP), held in Chicago over Labor Day weekend in 1967. The conference was attended by three thousand delegates representing over two hundred groups with varied goals, among them an end to the Vietnam War, better treatment of the poor, and equity for black Americans. The number of votes represented by each delegate was determined by the number of active members in his organization back home. Women Strike for Peace, for example, had 1,000 votes; the Camden Citizens for Peace in Vietnam 31 votes. Negro groups had 5,000 votes. They wanted more. "Black people can't be a plank in someone else's platform," said McKissick. "They must be the platform itself." Forming a Black Caucus, the Negro delegates issued an ultimatum of thirteen points. Among them were a demand for 50 percent black representation on all committees, censure of the "imperial Zionist war," and approval of all measures passed by the Newark conference. They demanded that all this be accepted without change by 1 P.M. that Saturday. An editor of *Ramparts* suggested a modification of the language but withdrew it when a member of the Black Caucus shouted at him, "What right has a white man got amending the black man's resolution?"

After an elderly white woman explained that this was merely a test of the NCNP's "social barometer," the thirteen-point program was accepted by a three-to-one vote. The delegates then gave themselves a standing ovation. Then they received a jolt. The Black Caucus was still dissatisfied. The caucus groups wanted not the 5,000 votes they had been allocated but 28,498 votes—absolute control of the convention. Negro speakers explained from the podium that it was all a matter of trust; whites had to prove that they trusted blacks by adopting the proposal. "An extraordinary development took place," one of the white delegates said afterward. "The walls of the Palmer House began to drip with guilt." Adoption passed, two to one. Thereafter the fate of each resolution before the convention was determined by a young Negro in the front row of the Black Caucus holding a large pink card that represented 28,498 votes. In fact, not much was accomplished. A sizable number of whites had come hoping to nominate a presidential ticket, Martin Luther King for President and Dr. Spock for Vice President. It died stillborn: the Black Caucus regarded Dr. King as a black honky, and Dr. Spock, in his old-fashioned way, still used the word Negro.

Despite Brown-McKissick rhetoric, the flow of blacks into the middle class was increasing. Census figures would later show that the number of Negro families with annual incomes over $10,000 increased from 11 to 28 percent during the 1960s. The way was opening up spectacularly for talented blacks. In 1965 Benjamin O. Davis Jr. became a lieutenant general in the Air Force. Secretary of Housing and Urban Development Robert C. Weaver, U.S. Senator Edward W. Brooke, Bishop Robert Perry of the Catholic Church, and Judge Constance Baker Motley of the federal bench all reached their eminent offices in 1966. A survey by two private organizations revealed that 1,469 Negroes held public office. Thurgood Marshall was appointed to the Supreme Court in 1967; Air Force Major Robert H. Lawrence became the first Negro astronaut on June 30 (he was killed in December when his plane crashed on a training flight); Elizabeth D. Koontz was elected president of the National Education Association; Dean Rusk's daughter married a black, Guy Gibson Smith; Cleveland and Gary acquired Negro mayors, and Walter E. Washington was named commissioner of the District of Columbia. The very excesses of the black militants seemed to ease the way for some Negro moderates; James Meredith repeated his Mississippi march in 1967, and the only whites to interrupt him asked for his autograph or snapped his picture.

But backlash continued to deliver stinging blows elsewhere. In Boston Louise Day Hicks, a forty-four-year-old grandmother, became a popular figure, and later a congresswoman, on the strength of her stand against remedies for racial imbalance in schools. A black youth was murdered in Detroit's Algiers Motel while under police interrogation; the officer who shot him pleaded self-defense and was acquitted by an all-white jury, showing that such cases were not confined to the Deep South. Adam Clayton Powell was denied his seat in Congress. There was no doubt about his misconduct, but Thomas Dodd, it was noted, was merely censured by the Senate. Father James E. Groppi failed in his campaign for "open" (integrated) housing in Milwaukee. Lester Maddox was sworn in as governor of Georgia, and the winner of Mississippi's gubernatorial race was another racist, John Bell Williams.

But these developments were overshadowed by that summer's havoc in the metropolitan ghettos, bringing to a climax the Negro revolt which had begun two years earlier in Watts. In its fury and the desolation it left behind it was like a war, and indeed there were those who believed that it was a mirror image of the Vietnam violence which could be seen on the television screens in every living room now during the dinner hour. "The government is contradictory," said John Lewis, Carmichael's predecessor as chairman of SNCC, "telling oppressed black men not to be violent in the streets while it carries out the terrible slaughter in Vietnam and finances it with money it should be spending to get things right at home."

That year the first torches were lit on April 8. Nashville police ejected a Negro from a restaurant at Fisk University that evening. Two days of chaos followed, and during the next month Cleveland, Washington, Louisville, Montgomery, and Omaha exploded. May arrived, and June, and Molotov cocktails, looters' clubs, and snipers' rifles appeared with increasing frequency. Major cities hit were New York, Minneapolis, Tampa, Atlanta, Birmingham, Cincinnati, San Francisco, Buffalo, Dayton and Wichita. Then came the first weekend in July and the first real ghetto catastrophe of 1967.

It began according to the now established ritual, with policemen. Late that Friday afternoon squad cars were summoned to the Grove Hall welfare office in Roxbury, a black district in southeast Boston. An organization of women on relief was demonstrating against welfare policy. They wanted more money, and they wanted to be treated with greater civility. It was past closing time, but the women wouldn't leave, and they had locked arms at the doors to prevent the employees from leaving. The cops entered through the windows. A crowd of Negroes gathered. Bottles and stones were thrown. More police arrived with helmets and riot sticks. They charged the mob, as it now was, in a flying wedge. That broke it up, which turned out to be a mistake. Forming small bands, the Negroes roamed Roxbury smashing glass, looting, putting buildings to the torch, and clouting whites. Before dawn a thousand policemen were battling a thousand blacks, and by Sunday evening, when the riot was spent, seventy people had been injured and fifteen blocks of Blue Hill Avenue, a main artery between downtown Boston and the suburbs, were a vast junkyard.

The week after Roxbury was peaceful but tense; nothing in the past two summers encouraged complacency. Urbanists were watching Newark, New Jersey, with particular vigilance. Even in peaceful times Newark would have been considered volatile. In seeking Model Cities grants its administration had frankly described it as

"a basic training camp for the poor." Crowded and slummy, its very
air was polluted with offensive odors from its many factories. Newark had the country's highest rate of venereal disease, the most
crime, and the greatest percentage of condemned housing. Over
the past century it had been successively inhabited by Protestants,
Irish, Italians, and Jews, and by this time it was second only to
Washington as a major city with a black majority. In 1960 Newark's
population had been 62 percent white. Now it was 52 percent black
and 10 percent Puerto Rican. Most of the 208,000 blacks lived in
the shabby Central Ward. The unemployment figure there was
twice the national figure, and the black rate of joblessness was twice
the city's. In Washington the people at the new Department of
Housing and Urban Development whose job it was to watch such
things had long been worried about Newark. They thought the city
awaited only a police incident to erupt. It came on Wednesday,
July 12.

At 9:45 P.M. a black cab driver, arrested for a traffic violation,
was brought into the 4th Precinct station in the Central Ward. He
argued heatedly with two police officers and exchanged blows with
them. Word spread outside that the cabby had been beaten to death.
The customary spectators gathered, but nothing much happened
there; after they had left officers reported downtown that they had
been nothing more than "a bunch of roving kids" anyway. At dusk
the next day another crowd assembled, carrying signs but apparently in good humor. Then the first bottle was thrown, and the first
brick. The policemen broke up the throng with nightsticks. In twos
and threes the Negroes disbanded—and began looting stores. By 11
P.M. plundering was proceeding on a massive scale, snipers were
firing from roofs, and fires were blazing high. Newark's 1,400 police
couldn't handle it. By daybreak, when 2,600 National Guardsmen
and 300 state police arrived, the sun shone down on what Governor
Richard J. Hughes called "a city in open rebellion." Almost half of
Newark's twenty-four square miles was in the hands of the rioters,
and order was not restored until Monday, July 17. By then twenty-
seven were dead. The loss was put at ten million dollars. It was the
worst disorder since Watts.

Detroit blew the following Sunday after a police raid on a
Twelfth Street black nightclub which was selling liquor after 2 A.M.,
the legal closing time. The crowd milled around, the rumors of brutality spread—this time it was said that a boy wearing handcuffs

had been kicked down a stairway—and the crowd, scattered by police, wandered away in small groups and began looting. In some ways this outburst was unusual. Unlike Newark, Detroit had not been regarded as a potential trouble spot. The mayor, elected with Negro support, had introduced measures which, together with the booming automobile business, had helped create a large black middle class. That, in fact, was part of the trouble. The rioters, who had not made it, were as resentful of middle-class Negroes as of whites. Another difference was that looting was integrated in Detroit; blacks and whites ransacked stores side by side. The extent of the arson was almost unbelievable—1,600 fire alarms in eleven days. But the most remarkable aspect of the Detroit riot was its size. Henry Ford called it "the greatest internal violence since the Civil War." The death toll was forty-three. Over seven thousand were arrested. Eighteen blocks of Twelfth Street and three miles of Grand River Avenue were burned to the ground. Aerial photographs of the city resembled Berlin in 1945. Five thousand people were without shelter. And many were insanely jubilant. "Those buildings going up was a pretty sight," said one of the Detroit rioters. "I sat right here and watched them go. And there wasn't nothing them honkies could do but sweat to put it out." He was speaking, of course, of Negro homes.

President Johnson appointed a commission headed by Governor Otto Kerner of Illinois to study outbreaks and find a way to prevent more of them. Hearings were scheduled by the Senate's Subcommittee on Investigations and the House Committee on Un-American Activities—which was under the impression that subversives were responsible for the disorders. And still that summer's rage in the ghettos was unspent. Altogether rioters struck 114 cities in 32 states. The complete toll would never be known, but there were at the very least 88 deaths, more than 4,000 other casualties, and 12,000 arrests. Among the grimmest upheavals were those in Wilmington, Toledo, South Bend, Grand Rapids, Pontiac, Milwaukee, New Haven, Providence, Saginaw, Flint, Portland (Oregon), and Cambridge (Maryland).

The Cambridge uprising was of particular interest. It was one of the few episodes which justified the Un-American Activities Committee's suspicions, and it had an unforeseen impact on national politics. Backlash had been a major factor in Maryland's 1966 gubernatorial campaign; when a racist candidate won the Democratic primary, black voters had backed the Republican nominee, Spiro T.

Agnew, a moderate. Agnew's feelings about law and order were stronger than his views on race, however, and he was outraged when Rap Brown, an outside agitator if there ever was one, told a rally of Eastern Shore Negroes that "It's time for Cambridge to explode." Brown called a Negro school a firetrap which "should have burned down long ago." He urged them to "Get yourself some guns," said that the riots were a "dress rehearsal for revolution," and added that "Violence is as American as cherry pie."

Thereupon Cambridge exploded, the school was burned, and Agnew issued a warrant for Brown's arrest on charges of inciting to riot and arson. "Such a person," said the governor, "cannot be permitted to come into a state with the intention to destroy and then sneak away, leaving these poor people with the results of his evil scheme." Brown was arrested in Alexandria, Virginia, two days later. Afterward he faced other charges for carrying firearms across a state line while under indictment. Meanwhile Governor Agnew's resolute handling of the incident had attracted the attention of the Republican party's national leadership, winning him the admiration of, among others, Richard M. Nixon.

REAGAN FIRES CLARK KERR AS BERKELEY CHANCELLOR: SCORES "PERMISSIVENESS"

Get your head together

APATHY

GOD IS DEAD

U.S. POPULATION SEEN SURPASSING 200 MILLION MARK

KEEP THE FAITH BABY

U.S., U.S.S.R. CATAPULT VENUS PROBES

"LSD is Western yoga," Dr. Leary explained. "The aim of all Eastern religion, like the aim of LSD, is basically to get high; that is, to expand your consciousness and find ecstasy and revelation within."

off the pigs

WE LOVE YOU AND ARE WORRIED,

PLEASE CALL COLLECT,

NO PUNISHMENT

Hare Krishna, Hare Krishna
Krishna Krishna, Hare Hare
Hare Rama, Hare Rama
Rama Rama, Hare Hare

COMPUTER, SET TO SELECT IDEAL MATES, PICKS BROTHER, SISTER

SPEED KILLS

First you get a really strong sex urge. You get a fantastic rush — a feeling that you're speeded up, you think you can do anything. It opens up little doors to the channels in your mind so you actually believe you can do anything. After a while it induces acute paranoia.

Say it loud — I'm black and I'm proud

Bangs manes bouffants beehives Beatle caps butter faces brush-on lashes decal eyes puffy sweaters French thrust bras flailing leather blue jeans stretch pants stretch jeans honeydew bottoms eclair shanks elf boots ballerinas Knight slippers, hundreds of them, these flaming little buds, bobbing and screaming, rocketing around inside the Academy of Music Theater underneath that vast old mouldering cherub dome up there — aren't they supermarvelous!

3 ASTRONAUTS DIE; LAST PRAYERS TOLD

JACKIE VISITS CAMBODIA, LAUDS ORIENTAL CHARM

WARNING: YOUR LOCAL POLICE ARE ARMED AND DANGEROUS

IN COLD BLOOD: The show-place farm of Herbert Clutter, set in the peaceful, prosperous, picture-book country west of Garden City, Kans. (pop. 11,000), seemed the nation's least likely setting for cold-blooded, methodical murder.

LBJ, BIRD SET FOR LUCI VOWS

"There's no room for deathless prose in the novel," Miss Susann said.

DE GAULLE: "VIVE LE QUEBEC LIBRE"

BOOKS MUST GO!

BAN THE BRA

power to the people

GREEK COLONELS SEIZE CONTROL IN ATHENS COUP

The new 100-mm. cigarette, six-tenths of an inch longer than the traditional king-sized ones, had jumped from 2 percent of the market at the beginning of 1967 to 15 percent at the year's close — about $1 billion worth

TURN ON TUNE IN DROP OUT

BLACK IS BEAUTIFUL

I'VE GONE TO POT

BLACK POWER

Good grief, Charlie Brown

Thirty-two

UP AGAINST THE WALL

IN *The New Industrial State*, published in 1967, John Kenneth Galbraith noted "an interesting and widely remarked phenomenon of recent years," an "ill-defined discontent, especially among students and intellectuals, with the accepted and approved modalities of social thought." These, wrote Galbraith, "whether espoused by professed liberals or conservatives, are held to be the views of 'The Establishment.'"

Actually, by then, blacks, radicals, feminists, and just about everybody else who felt systematically cheated by organized society had taken to calling it and all its works the "establishment." Often the word was used so loosely as to render it meaningless—shoplifting was called a blow to the establishment; the establishment was blamed for poor television programming—but some applications of it indicated a profound instinct for the workings of the system. This was never truer than on the memorable night of Tuesday, November 9, 1965, when antiestablishmentarians felt vindicated, and others dismayed, by the extraordinary failure of one of society's essential services: electrical power.

The sun set over the eastern United States at 4:44 P.M. that afternoon, and the demand for electricity then began building toward its daily peak. Light switches were flipped on in homes and offices. Neon signs lit up. In places of business elevators came into maximum use as workers departed. Subways put on extra trains for commuters, farmers in the country beyond the skyline hitched cows to milking machines, and lighthouses commenced to flash. Children raced in from play and turned on TV sets, while their mothers started supper. The day being autumnal and the temperature 46, thermostats triggered millions of furnaces into operation. Greenhouse heating systems became more active, and reptile houses in zoos were provided with that extra margin of heat without which their vipers and crocodiles would perish. In bars, ice machines began hatching cubes for office workers pausing for that daily drink before setting out for home. On parkways and highways electrically powered gasoline pumps filled the tanks of homeward-bound cars.

All this was a matter of routine to Edward J. Nellis, a slender, balding man of sixty-two and a forty-one-year veteran employee of the Consolidated Edison Company of New York. Nellis was seated in the controller's chair of Con Ed's Energy Control Center at 128 West End Avenue, Manhattan, near Sixty-fifth Street. The center, the hub of the company's electronic universe, is a high-ceilinged, antiseptic, rather Orwellian room whose dials and switches, bathed in brilliant fluorescent light, were all visible to Nellis. By vigilantly scanning them, he could be sure that Con Ed was fulfilling its role not only here in the metropolis, but also as chief member of the Ontario, New York, and New England electric power pool, an area of 80,000 square miles inhabited by 30 million people. At any rate, that was the theory. It entered the realm of intense controversy at about 5:16 P.M., when Nellis, starting from his chair, saw that the needles on all the dials had begun to oscillate wildly.

At the time neither he nor anyone else knew what was happening, though Con Ed's senior engineers had often discussed the possibility of a massive electric failure. They predicted—correctly—what they called a "cascade effect," in which an enormous, unexpected demand for power by one member of the pool would suck up the electricity of all the others. If that occurred, every generator in the pool, also known as the Northeast Power Grid, would automatically shut off to avoid damaging the equipment. All 80,000 square miles would be plunged into instant darkness.

The swinging needles at 128 West End Avenue were the consequence of such a cascade. The trouble lay 315 miles north of Manhattan and four miles west of Niagara Falls, in a Canadian hydrogenerating installation called the Sir Adam Beck Station No. 2. A relay—a device no larger than a breadbox—had been set for 1963 requirements and never readjusted, though power loads had been expanding steadily ever since. At 5 P.M. that afternoon electricity for Toronto was flowing north over six of the Adam Beck plant's lines. At 5:16:11, instruments showed later, the load increased slightly—just enough to trip the incorrectly set relay. That in turn set a circuit breaker in motion, putting one of the six lines out of action. Its load was instantly picked up by the other five, but they couldn't handle it. Overloaded, they were then cut off by their own relays. Two disasters followed almost simultaneously. About 1.6 million kilowatts of energy, destined for Toronto but unable to get through the invalided Adam Beck station, surged southward on the grid's great electric superhighway into upper New York State and New England, knocking out generating plants as it went. That created a power vacuum. The areas stricken by it demanded current from Manhattan—more than Manhattan had. The second calamity swiftly followed. Protective devices were activated all over the Northeast Power Grid. The cascade, or "falling domino" effect as some called it, was taking areas out of the pool automatically. It was complete at 5:38 P.M., when Vermont and southern New Hampshire joined the states to the south. Except for hospitals and other institutions, with their own generators, scarcely a light shone between Niagara and the Hudson. The great blackout had begun.

New York City went out at 5:27 P.M. Nellis had just decided to push the eight buttons which would have cut the metropolis free of the grid, but he was too late. It was a forgivable error: one of the few things unchanged about the consumption of electricity since Thomas Edison invented the first practical incandescent lamp in 1879 is that it still travels at the speed of light. But the consequences were stupefying. Except for Staten Island and one small Brooklyn neighborhood, the power was gone—all of it: illumination, appliances, subways; the works. In unaffected Montclair, New Jersey, a woman looking out her picture window had been admiring the fairy-like spectacle of Manhattan alight. She called her teen-age son to share it with him, and when she turned back to the window the city had disappeared. Above Kennedy International Airport, Captain Ron George of Air Canada was entering his glide pattern. He looked down at the runway, glanced at his instruments, glanced back—and saw only Stygian blackness. The airport, too, had vanished.

Reactions in those first moments of the blackout varied, and to a certain extent they reflected individual fears. "The Chinese," thought a woman on Manhattan's East Side. "An attack from outer space!" cried a small boy in an apartment twenty stories above the East River. Two newspaper reporters were struck by the same thought

—that the antiwar movement had scored a real coup. Others were too preoccupied with unexpected crises to wonder who was responsible. In hospitals awaiting the ninety-second shift to emergency power, surgeons were continuing to operate by flashlight. The management of Schrafft's was worrying about $200,000 worth of ice cream. (It all melted.) Governor Rockefeller was climbing fifteen stories of stairs to his apartment. Over 800,000 people were trapped underground in the subways. Sixty of them would spend a harrowing night in an Astoria line BMT train in the Sixtieth Street tunnel under the East River. Far above them, on the Williamsburg Bridge over the river, 1,700 commuters were stranded on four trains. After five hours they would be led to safety.

In department stores, floorwalkers either led their customers out by flashlight or put them to bed in the home furnishing departments. Farmers reacquired the skill of milking cows by hand. Children, deprived of television, were learning to play on their own. Zoo keepers kept mammals alive with blankets and warmed their reptile houses with portable propane gas heaters. Not much could be done for motorists in need of fuel from the electrically operated gas pumps or housewives with cold electric stoves, however. Many who were suddenly idle were calling friends or relatives. The phones were working, and there was an 800 percent increase in local calls that evening. Others were doing other things. Nine months later to the day, all hospitals reported a sharp increase in births.

Thanks to transistors, radio broadcasts were getting through, but they cannot be said to have been much help to their bewildered audience. Breathless commentators spoke of "Canada in darkness . . . Cause unknown . . . worst power failure in the history of the world . . . President Johnson has summoned his emergency planning board . . . immediate investigation . . . sabotage feared." There were hints at war and nuclear holocaust until the Strategic Air Command in Colorado Springs reported "Condition Green," meaning normal. There were some local disturbances—looting in Springfield, Massachusetts, and a major riot at the Massachusetts state prison in Walpole—and a few tragic accidents. The body of one man was found at the bottom of a New York hotel elevator shaft, a burned-out candle in his hand.

In the early hours of that evening, virtually the only light in the grid was provided by candles, flashlights, automobile lights, and a full moon. Then the lights began returning, one area at a time. Vermont and southern New Hampshire came back after blackouts of thirty minutes to two hours. Connecticut had gone black at 5:30 and was slow to recover, but by 11:30 all but twelve of its towns were alight. Greater New York was the slowest of all. Brooklyn was back by 2 A.M. Wednesday, and thousands of sleepers there learned of it in a manner which would be repeated elsewhere; they had turned in leaving wall and lamp switches on, and were awakened when their bedrooms were suddenly flooded with light. Power returned to Queens at 4:20 A.M., to Manhattan and Westchester by 6:58 A.M., and to the Bronx at 7 A.M. Here and there stubborn pockets resisted the restoration of power. Pelham Manor in exclusive Westchester County didn't rejoin the grid until early Thursday. One Pelham Manor woman said afterward that she "burned a lot of candles," "kept the fireplace going," and "kept thinking about how people must have lived in Pelham Manor in the primitive days when there was no electricity."

The following Monday, November 15, 1965, six days after the power had failed, electrical engineers traced the blackout to the Beck plant. The Canadians were embarrassed; they had been insisting that the fault couldn't have been on their side of the border. American utilities spokesmen felt this proved that they had been blameless. But most of the public did not discriminate. They blamed the whole lot, Canadians and Americans alike. At the same time, the tales of their adventures during the blackout were improving in the telling. Eventually many forgot their anxieties at the time and were rejoicing in memories of the freedom from routine. Said a team of *New York Times* reporters:

> In every man there is a corner of rebellion against the machine. We were all delighted at the rediscovery of things that were not plugged into walls—things that were almost forgotten by us—most of all, the wonderful, wonderful candle. What a moment of triumph to know that the huge computers we really did not like and that we suspected really did not like us were lying massively idle and useless, but the old pencil sharpener still worked.

It was all illusion, as the *Times* men conceded. In the end all were "recaptured and brought back submissively to the prison farm of modern technology." The candle and the pencil sharpener were all very well for a hiatus of a few hours, but they would not have seemed wonderful much longer. They could not have transported commuters, or warmed homes, or provided light for reading, or provided any one of the countless services and necessities for which men had come to rely upon technology. The way of life in Pelham Manor in the primitive days when there was no electricity would have come as a savage shock to them. Many would have been unable to survive it. Some thought of what the *Times* writers called "the plugged-in society" as a prison farm, and some had worse names for it, but not many were so vehement about the huge computers that they were prepared to scrap them. There were, however, a few.

Taking their name from a half-witted Leicestershire worker who had attacked a machine a generation earlier, British handcraftsmen thrown out of work by the industrial revolution declared war on shearing frames and power looms in 1811. From a mythical retreat in Sherwood Forest they issued a nonnegotiable demand:

> We will never lay down Arms [till] The House of Commons passes an Act to put down all Machinery hurtful to Commonality, and repeal that to hang Frame Breakers. . . . We petition no more—that won't do—fighting must.
> Signed by the General of the Army of Redressers
>
>   NED LUDD   Clerk

Soreheads standing in the way of laborsaving devices have been known as Luddites ever since, and critics of America's increasingly technocratic society during the Johnson years were frequently accused of Luddism. In instances of rioting students this was sometimes justified. Professors' notes were destroyed, equipment was damaged, and a sign plastered on one Cambridge computer accused it of drawing high wages and fringe benefits at the expense of American workmen. That was as absurd as Ned at his most futile, but the case against technocracy was not entirely preposterous. Intelligent men and women were tired of receiving punch-card mail, riding on push-button elevators, standing in check-out lines, reading about a war being judged by body counts, listening to recorded voices over telephones, and being treated during political campaigns as pollster percentages. As Nicholas von Hoffman pointed out, the demonstrating students were rebellious at being "admitted, tested, and flunked by computers." There was something chilling about Human Inventory, Inc., the Los Angeles matchmaking service which had 6,000 clients and was headed by a former executive in an aerospace company. Everyone had his computer horror stories, and some were choice. An Albany hospital sent a woman a bill for "ritual circumcision." And in 1966 Mayor John F. Collins of Boston was favored to win reelection until, three days before the primary, the city computer, all by itself, prepared, addressed, and mailed 30,000 delinquent sewer tax bills. The mayor was defeated.

Erich Fromm warned: "A specter is stalking in our midst. . . . It is a new specter: a completely mechanized society . . . directed by computers; and in this social process, man himself is being transformed into a part of the total machine." Millions of Americans by the late 1960s were carrying as many as twenty multiple numbers in their wallets, some indicating their various identities, some necessary for daily business, and all tending to reduce them to random particles—zip codes, area codes, blood types, drivers' licenses, automobile licenses, social security numbers, army serial numbers, and numbers of charge accounts, checking accounts, book club memberships, insurance policies, passports, birth and marriage certificates, mortgages, and Veterans Administration claims. The author of *The Beast of Business* recommended playing "computer-card roulette" by closing holes with tape, cutting new holes with a razor blade, and exposing the code number to an electromagnet. When a California janitor received a $5,000 check for two weeks' work, everyone cheered except the aeroelasticity investigators, inertial systems engineers, superconductivity research specialists, and digital circuit design specialists—those, in short, whose great age this was.

John Mauchly, the builder of the first U.S. commercial computers, had predicted that "only four or five giant firms will be able to employ these machines usefully." He underestimated his prodigies. There were 1,000 computers in the United States in 1955. In 1960 government engineers suggested that 15,000 might be in use within five years. The time arrived and 25,000 were in use. By 1967 there were 40,000—some 2,000 for the federal government alone.

All this was disquieting to American humanists. Liberals in politics, they had become more and more traditional in their social attitudes. In the late 1940s they had been alarmed by *Nineteen Eighty-Four*. During the Eisenhower years a genteel shabbiness had acquired a certain cachet among them, for they were especially disturbed by the thing-oriented culture that had ridden in on the wave of technological advances. It appeared to them that the nation was becoming enslaved by manipulators of consumer appetites. Among the figures disgorged by the pullulating computers were analyses of what manipulation of the public was doing to consumer debt. Between 1956 and 1967 it increased 133 percent, to 99.1 billion dollars. Motor car paper alone was up 117 percent, to 31.2 billion dollars. It looked as though Will Rogers had been right; the country was going to the poorhouse in an automobile.

Autos would have been bad enough—thoughtful Americans were just beginning to learn what Detroit was doing to their environment—but the dismay of intellectuals over what was coming to be regarded as the blight of mass opulence went far beyond that. The voracity of the national vending machine seemed insatiable. Disposable personal income had almost doubled since the Eisenhower years, but the faith, so strong in the 1930s, that men would spend wisely if they just had the money, was in shreds. Then Edmund Wilson had written scornfully of "foods that do not nourish, disinfectants that do not disinfect," of "cosmetics that poison the face, lubricants that corrode your car," and "insecticides that kill your trees." But it was precisely these brands which were flourishing in the booming 1960s. At least in the Depression you hadn't been compelled to look at them in your own living room. Television commercials now spewed them forth in all their vulgarity—and in nauseous color to boot—until one wondered what the country was going to do with all the junk. An inspired Mobil commercial provided the answer during the 1969 American League baseball playoffs. With each $3 purchase it offered customers a plastic bag which would hold "22 pounds, four cubic feet" of trash. "You'll be glad you threw it away," said the commercial, and it was true.

Televised sport was a grievance in itself. It turned millions of men who ought to have been active outdoors—for their own health, if nothing else—into beer-drinking, flatulent spectators watching young athletes romp joyously in gilded playpens. The gaudiest pen of all was Houston's 32-million-dollar, air-conditioned Astrodome, with its 46,000 upholstered seats, 30,000-car parking lot, and a steel dome which eliminated the need to issue rain checks. So intent were the superstadium's designers upon making it playable in fog, rain, or darkness that they overlooked one possibility: the sun might shine. When that happened, they discovered to their horror, outfielders lost fly balls in the dazzling dome. Early games were played only on cloudy days, and even so the outfielders had to wear batting helmets. Then the skylights were painted gray—meaning that all games there would require lights, whatever the weather.

To skeptics of the new prosperity the Astrodome was a shrine of tastelessness and overconsumption. Its 53 private boxes, available for five-year leases, rented for $15,000 to $34,000 a season. Private clubrooms, for those bored with the game below, were outfitted with bars and TV and provided by decorators with such themes as "Tahitian Holiday," or "The French Hunt." Over fifty different uniforms were designed for Astrodome workers, depending on their tasks (ground crewmen wore space suits), and each was sent to school for three weeks to learn how to project the proper Astrodome image. The greatest spectacle in the stadium was a home run by the home team Astros. Fans never forgot it, and some visiting pitchers never recovered from it. The electric scoreboard went berserk. Rockets were launched and bombs exploded. Electric cattle wearing the American and Texas flags on their horns bucked wildly. Electric cowboys fired electronic bullets at them. An orchestra crashed through "The Eyes of Texas."

"When in doubt," went an advertising slogan that year, "buy the proven product." But the skeptics had no doubts. They recoiled from all mass merchandise. To them the marketplace was evil. The economic lessons they had learned in their youth had lost all relevance. "The essential mass problem had shifted," Eric Goldman wrote. It was "less food, housing and clothing than how to live with a weirdly uneasy affluence." Goldman described "a maldistribution no longer accepted by a significant section of the population." Certainly that section was highly articulate. Its polemics against maldistribution could be found in any bookstore. A common theme in them was that mass culture led to the garrison-prison state.

Some perceptive authors pointed out to intellectuals that they were not always logical. William H. Whyte Jr. remarked that it was "a retrograde point of view" which failed to recognize that a growth of Babbittry was "a consequence of making the benefits of our civilization available to more people." Caroline Bird noted that "People who are usually compassionate sometimes fail to see how the full employment of the 1960s is responsible for what they experience as a general decline in morals, competence, courtesy, energy, and discipline." John Kenneth Galbraith reminded liberal humanists that they could not pick and choose among technological advances. If they wanted some of them, they would have to put up with the rest. Nor could they accept the wonders of applied science and reject the special relationship between the state and industry which had made it possible: "It is open to every freeborn man to dislike this accommodation. But he must direct his attack to the cause. He must not ask that jet aircraft, nuclear power plants or even the modern automobile in its modern volume be produced by firms that are subject to unfixed prices and unmanaged demand. He must ask that they not be produced." Galbraith remained an eloquent advocate of a higher quality of life, but he told fellow critics that before dismissing the digital society entirely they should reflect that it has brought them much that they enjoy and take for granted; for example, "in the absence of automatic transmission of [telephone] calls, it would require approximately the entire female working force of the country to handle current traffic."

That was in 1967. Galbraith did not anticipate that within four years his assumption that all operators should be female would become fighting words. Yesterday's truism had become today's heresy. This, perhaps, was the overriding fact about the impact of science and technology on the United States. Its changes were convulsive, overwhelming. That was one reason for the jarring aspect of American life in the 1960s. Occupational skills became obsolete so rapidly that career planning was difficult and sometimes impossible for the young. In 1967, for example, the chemical industry calculated that half its business came from the sale of products which hadn't even existed ten years earlier. One of these, the contraceptive pill, played a crucial role in the dramatic revision of American female expectations. At the same time, life expectancy for white females was approaching 80 years (as against 75 years for white males). Science and technology was steadily altering the shape of the future. In 1968 Herman Kahn and the Hudson Institute issued a thousand-page study of what American life would be like in the year 2000. Their prediction was that by then the annual per capita income of Americans would be $7,500 a year. Seven-hour days and four-day weeks would be typical, the institute reported; so would thirteen-week annual vacations. With enjoyment replacing achievement as the goal of men and women, it appeared that the very reason for existence, and even existence itself, would be altered in ways which were now inconceivable.

But anticipating the future was not necessary to grasp what the technological revolution had already done to the United States. A glance backward could be breathtaking. In the early 1930s, when the now gray and balding swing generation was just approaching its teens, the largest category of Americans untouched by progress was the farm bloc—over 30 million people. In those days they lacked knowledge of even the fundamentals of conservation, which was one of the reasons for the devastating dust storms. Without rural electrification, farmers read by lamplight. Without electric power the typical farm wife had to carry as much as 28 tons of water each year from the pump or spring. Her butter churn was operated by hand. She did her laundry in a zinc tub and preserved meat in a brine barrel. Her husband's chores were even more backbreaking. After the morning milking he had two hours' work with the horses before he could set about whatever he had planned for the day. Horses and mules were his major source of locomotion—there were over 20 million of them in the country—and when he went to town he drove over dirt roads. Later his life would be sentimentalized by those who had no idea what it had really been like. Some of the most arrant nonsense would be written about the farm kitchen, when in fact, as Clyde Brion Davis pointed out in *The Age of Indiscretion*, "most of the cooking was frying—and not even in deep fat. The traditional American farmer . . . was scrawny-necked, flat-chested and potbellied from flatulent indigestion."

If the farmer's son was still living on the land a generation later, his world was entirely different. Trees planted by the CCC held the soil firm; strip-cropping and contour plowing made for greater yields and sturdier crops. Fifteen billion dollars in farm machinery had ended the tyranny of sweat and drudgery, and the 65 million acres once set aside for raising animal fodder were now used for produce. The development of hybrid corn had increased the nation's corn harvest 20 percent without boosting the acreage needed. Driven to abandon cotton by the boll weevil threat of the 1930s, southern farmers had learned to plant other crops—and had tripled their income. The new farmer in the new rural prosperity drove to market on macadam. And his wife, in a kitchen glittering with appliances, the brine barrel having been replaced by a commodious freezer, fed her family properly. Afternoons she had time to run into town herself. She went to the hairdresser regularly and wore the same synthetic fabrics as her city sisters instead of the gingham dresses and cotton stockings of her mother.

City toil had been transformed, too. The proletariat was disappearing. It was Norbert Wiener who had observed, in *Cybernetics;*

or, Control and Communication in the Animal and the Machine (1948), that "There is no rate of pay which is low enough to compete with the work of a steam shovel and an excavator." Already in the first half of the twentieth century automation had cut the number of common laborers from 11 million to 6 million. Over the next thirteen years the country's work force grew by ten million—to 70.6 million—but the number of laborers continued to dwindle. Blue-collar workers were a shrinking minority. During the Eisenhower years the automobile industry's production force dropped by 172,-000 while it turned out a half-million more cars each year. The stature of the once mighty trade unions diminished; machines can't strike. Labor leaders became conservative, suspicious of progress, and in some cases allies of their old foes, the corporations. Meanwhile, less need for male muscle was opening vast areas of employment to the women now entering the labor force, and the trend grew as the objectives of work changed. Instead of making goods, workers were joining the expanding service, amusement, and leisure industries. In the "new mass-consumption society," George E. Mowry wrote, "the old equation of man confronting materials and making something new of them had been changed to man confronting man and persuading him to act."

One masculine stronghold did not change. That was the executive suite. The Hudson Institute held out no hope that business executives might look forward to working less and loafing more in the year 2000. They could not be spared; too much depended upon them. This was a switch from the Roosevelt years. Executive illustriousness had been predicted in James Burnham's widely reviewed book of 1941, *The Managerial Revolution,* but Depression folklore had generally held bosses in contempt, and Depression novelists and dramatists had depicted them as knaves and fools. (Moviegoers may recall the character actor who portrayed this stock role most successfully. He was Edward Arnold.) Yet by the 1960s they were high in the saddle. To be sure, they had little in common with the piratical entrepreneurs of the past. "The Tycoon," said *Fortune,* "is dead." *Time* described the new businessmen as "the professional managers, the engineer-trained technicians" who "took over industrial societies so huge that the average owner"—stockholder—"seldom exercised more than theoretical control." Typically, they ruled not individually and by fiat but by committee, pooling information and expertise in what were variously called executive groups, task forces, assault groups, or, in the modish egalitarian spirit, "working parties." In *The New Industrial State* John Kenneth Galbraith called those who thus shared power the technostructure.

Bright, well-educated, and highly motivated, the men of the technostructure suffered, ironically, in one area to which they gave great attention: public relations. The problem here was refractory and institutional. American industry had always deceived itself and others about its true nature. Professing faith in Herbert Spencer went with the job, like the key to the executive washroom and membership in the Republican party. Executives insisted upon the viability of the profit motive, even though their own careers frequently gave it the lie; they continued to drive themselves although taxes took huge bites of their salaries. The name of John Maynard Keynes was ritualistically hissed even as they defected from Barry Goldwater, who not only criticized Keynes but actually meant it. They encouraged stockholders to think possessively about their corporation, yet the influence of corporate investors, always minimal, had declined even further by the 1960s, and anyone attending their annual meetings could quickly perceive that the decisions made by individuals there depended upon the information which the technostructure chose to provide them.

This masquerade had been noted by economists. Usually the duplicity had been dismissed as harmless. After all, political ethics were honored more often in the breach. The technostructural deceit was graver than it seemed, however. As the Johnson administration grew older with no resolution of the Vietnam conflict, American businessmen were astonished to find that demonstrators were turning on them and accusing them of committing monstrous crimes with products like napalm. They couldn't understand it; didn't these angry people know that management and government were natural antagonists, not co-conspirators? They believed that and thought it should be obvious to everyone. But of course it was untrue. The truth was that by the late 1960s the military-industrial complex which had alarmed Eisenhower at the opening of the decade had continued to grow until the United States had—there is no other name for it—a planned economy.

In 1967 Jean-Jacques Servan-Schreiber startled U.S. readers with such blunt assertions as "Federal agencies have been collaborating with American corporations in developing advanced technology ever since the end of the war," and "In the United States nearly

every major industry gets a substantial amount of federal assistance." It scarcely seemed credible. Roosevelt's heirs were still en-
trenched in Washington, scorning the economic royalists and the
moneychangers; presidents of the National Association of Manufacturers condemned Washington paternalism; speakers at the U.S.
Chamber of Commerce continued to explain that the government,
since it never *made* anything, was essentially parasitic, and that the
key to all economic progress was the businessman who was prepared to risk his capital in hope of gain.

This was perhaps true of the child's lemonade stand then being
acclaimed in full-page ads extolling free enterprise—though where
the child would be without paternal subsidies was unexplained—
but it had lost all applicability for the five hundred giant corporations which, by the 1960s, accounted for two-thirds of the nation's
industrial production. Where was the risk for the Rand Corporation,
whose total budget was underwritten by the U.S. Air Force? What
gamble did IBM run when it invested five billion dollars in the perfection of integrated circuits for its third generation of computers,
knowing that the Pentagon stood behind every dollar? How could
ITT's work on miniaturized electronic devices be called speculation
when NASA knew that a manned flight to the moon would be impossible without them? As technology became more sophisticated
and the lead time required for new developments lengthened, firms
which were asked to break new ground demanded long-term contracts. Industrial executives and government bureaucrats, sharing
the same goals, drew up budgets and reached decisions together.
If the finished products were useful in marketable wares, there was
nothing to stop the executives from cleaning up. Often they did.
Integrated circuits—microcircuits which eliminate a chain of linked
electronic parts: transistors, resistors, condensers, and tubes—are an
example. Huge space rockets could not get off the pad without
them. They made Polaris missiles and the swing-wing F-111 fighter
possible. Boeing SSTs required them. So did the European Con-
corde prototype; governments in Europe had not been so cooperative, and when the manufacturers there needed the microcircuits,
they had to deal with the only three firms making them, all American: Fairchild, Texas Instruments, and Motorola. The devices, they
found, were expensive.

It would be wrong to suggest that the American taxpayer had
been swindled in this process. The government was committed to

space travel; the electronic computer had become indispensable to the machinery of national strategy; improved methods of transport were in the public interest; national prestige benefited. Indeed, Servan-Schreiber was lost in admiration for the ingenious Yankees: "Behind most of their recent innovations is a huge reservoir of federal funds that have financed the most profitable investment any people ever made for itself." The byproducts of space research alone included tremendous and invaluable gains in understanding refractory metals and equipment for working in vacuums. Through federal guarantees of large outlays of capital, the Pentagon, NASA, the AEC and the Federal Aviation Administration made possible the creation of marvels which would otherwise have waited a generation. Between the invention of photography and the manufacture of cameras, 112 years passed, from 1727 to 1839. The gap was 56 years for the telephone and 35 for radio. By paying for technical development and assuring a market for the end result, Washington had cut the lag to six years for the atomic bomb, five years for the transistor, and three years for the integrated circuit. There is a case to be made against the process, but it is a case against progress. That many Americans would find it persuasive is doubtful.

What was not possible, however, was to argue that industry had maintained its sovereignty—that it remained free to oppose decisions made in Washington. With the administration spending 15 billion dollars a year on research and development, as against 6 billion from business and private agencies, the presumption of domination by the government was inescapable. In 1929 federal, state, and municipal governments accounted for about 8 percent of all economic activity in the United States. By the 1960s the figure was between 20 and 25 percent, far exceeding that in India, a socialist country. The National Science Foundation reckoned that federal funds were paying for 90 percent of research in aviation and space travel, 65 percent in electrical and electronic devices, 42 percent in scientific instruments, 31 percent in machinery, 28 percent in metal alloys, 24 percent in automobiles, and 20 percent in chemicals. Washington was in a position to hold the very survival of great corporations as a hostage. It never came to that, no one was that crude, the matter was never discussed. Nevertheless, big industry had surrendered a large measure of autonomy.

In another time this circumstance would have concerned few Americans and aroused even fewer. Johnsonian prosperity was being enjoyed on all levels of society. Except in times of great distress the United States has rarely been troubled by protesters swarming in the streets and damning the government. Most people have a stake in the system; radical movements have been historically frustrated in their search for American recruits. But the Johnson years were witnessing another significant innovation. Since the war the nation had acquired an enormous student population. At the time of Pearl Harbor about 15 percent of Americans of college age were so enrolled. By the fall of 1965, 40 percent were—over five million youths between eighteen and twenty-one. Within four years the figure would be 6.7 million. Nearly a half-million bachelor degrees were now being awarded each year. More than 30 billion dollars was being spent annually on formal education. Going to class had, in fact, become the largest industry in the United States, making students the country's biggest single interest group.

In the rest of the population this was a source of pride—education had become almost a secular religion, the proposed cure for all social ills—but undergraduates were becoming discontented and restless. Their futures were clouded by the Vietnam War, which grew more hideous and frustrating every day. Their dissatisfaction with the prosecution of the conflict was encouraged by thousands of the nation's 150,000 tenure professors—men shielded from external discipline, who could be removed from their chairs only by death or personal scandal. Finally, many students were troubled by the realization that much of society's enthusiasm for higher education stemmed from its market value. Just as other federal programs enhanced technology by creating microcircuits, so the huge grants to education served to train future technicians, executives, and customers. Undergraduates found that after acquiring a healthy skepticism, a university's greatest gift to them, they were expected to stifle it and become cogs in industrial and governmental bureaucracies. Millions of parents saw nothing wrong with that. Many of the children were beginning to take another view, however. They said to one another: "They are snowing us. They are burying us. We cannot put up with it any more. We're going to overthrow it."

American technology has always been an American strength, a source of wonder and, sometimes, of anxiety. In 1853 a periodical called the *United States Review* had predicted that within fifty years "machinery will perform all work—automata will direct them," leaving people free "to make love, study and be happy." But as the campuses of the 1960s trembled on the verge of upheaval, John Kenneth Galbraith was less sanguine. He sensed a "danger that our educational system will be too strongly in the service of economic goals."

In some way the great student upheavals of the 1960s were even more significant than they seemed at the time. Like the revolutionary fever that swept western Europe in 1848, they may never be fully understood. They cut across national orders and cultural barriers that had long intimidated older generations. Neither oceans nor even the Iron Curtain checked them; as Columbia exploded and Berkeley seethed, campuses erupted in England, Italy, Germany, Holland, Sweden, Spain, Belgium, Japan, Formosa, Poland, Hungary, Yugoslavia, and Czechoslovakia. Americans were preoccupied with the disorders at home, but in at least two foreign capitals, Prague and Warsaw, the damage was more extensive than anything in the United States.

Doubtless part of the explanation for the chain reaction lies in the speed and sophistication of modern communications. The sense of world community was real and growing. Each of the emerging continents was to some degree aware of what was happening on other continents. "Establishment," in its new sense, had been translated into the language of every industrial nation. Student activists, as the riots would demonstrate, hadn't much use for it. This feeling was global. The antipathy was just as strong in Asia or eastern Europe as beneath the elms of Old Wabash.

Nevertheless, the American role was special. The turmoil began in the United States, the world's most affluent nation and the one with the most strongly defined youth subculture. Undergraduates abroad were very conscious of events on American campuses ("What is happening at Columbia?" Sorbonne demonstrators eagerly asked American foreign correspondents in 1968), while U.S. students were largely indifferent to the frenzies overseas. In America, moreover, it was possible to trace the powerful currents which were stirring youth. As Tocqueville noted, Americans have always taken a distinctive, almost Rousseauistic view of youth, and they have turned naturally to education as the solution to every problem, public and private.

But now youth itself had become a problem, and a major one at that. A great source of anxiety was the new political militance. A conservative educator declared that the campuses were harboring "a loose alliance of Maoists, Trotskyites, Stalinists, Cheists, anarchists, utopians, and nihilists." Spiro Agnew made several memorable remarks on the subject. In St. Louis he called student demonstrators "malcontents, radicals, incendiaries, and civil and uncivil disobedients" and said, "I would swap the whole damn zoo for a single platoon of the kind of Americans I saw in Vietnam." On another occasion he described the universities as "circus tents or psychiatric centers for over-privileged, under-disciplined, irresponsible children of well-to-do blasé permissivists."

Parents denied that they were blasé or permissive, and those who disapproved of the demonstrations said they were the work of a minority. Gallup reported that 72 percent of all students had not participated in any of them; a *Fortune* poll concluded that just 12.5 percent of undergraduates held "revolutionary" or "radically dissident" views; SDS recruited just 7 percent. But Groucho Marx spoke for millions of older Americans when he remarked, "it's no good saying that the ones you read about are a minority. They're not a minority if they're all yours and you have to wait for the car to get home to know your daughter hasn't got pregnancy or leprosy."

The figures were deceptive anyhow. Extremists always attract a minority. A minority of northerners were abolitionists in 1861; probably a minority of colonists really wanted independence in 1776. Sympathies, not commitments, are the best indicator of a group's temper, and here the student pattern tells a different story. Gallup found that 81 percent of undergraduates were dissatisfied with college and university administrations. Another poll reported that more than 50 percent expressed major reservations about American foreign and domestic policies.

"The fear of being labeled radical, leftist, or subversive," Harvey Swados observed of academe in the early 1960s, "seems to have all but disappeared." Many, indeed, welcomed it. The undergraduates arriving on campus were often children of the middle-class liberals who had been most outraged—and in some instances had suffered most—during the McCarthy years. Their sons and daughters were determined not to be intimidated or repressed. They joined chapters of such organizations as SDS, Joan Baez's School for Nonviolence, the W. E. B. Du Bois Clubs, and the Young Socialist Alliance. They were in dead earnest but politically inept. Before the decade ended, the tactics of their New Left would offend virtually all potential allies, including their parents—which, some thought, might have been the point.

Yet in some areas they were highly skilled. Their demonstrations were often staged for TV news cameramen with a sense of what was good theater. The picketing in support of the Mississippi Freedom Party at the 1964 Democratic national convention was one example; the October 1967 march on the Pentagon was another. It is equally true that they frequently appeared to be shocking the country for the sake of shock. In 1965 SDS repealed its ban on admitting Communists and Birchers to membership. The New Leftists proclaimed that their sacred trinity consisted of Marx, Mao, and Herbert Marcuse, and they enthusiastically embraced Marcuse's "discriminating tolerance"; *i.e.*, the suppression of points of view which the New Leftists regarded as unsound or dangerous. Their campaigns against ROTC, the draft, and napalm were logical, and walking out on commencement ceremonies was valid protest, but when they advocated dynamiting public buildings, even Marcuse demurred. Some SDS leaders all but salivated over violence. Of the Sharon Tate murders SDS's Bernadine Dohrn said: "Dig it, first they killed those pigs, then they ate dinner in the same room with them, then they even shoved a fork into a victim's stomach! Wild!"

The New Leftists' view of society was essentially conspirational. They saw it as dominated by an establishment which was itself manipulated by a "power elite" of industrialists, military leaders, and corporate giants. They talked darkly of revolution, yet a real revolution starts with strengthening the power of the state—which they were dead set against. Like all movements, theirs had a glossary of special terms: "dialogue," "creative tension," "nonnegotiable demands," and "nonviolent" among others. But their meanings were often obscure. Nonnegotiable demands could be negotiated, for example, and throwing rocks and bottles at policemen was deemed nonviolent.

The alienation of the young militants, expressing itself in disdain for conventional careers, clothing, and politics, had begun at Berkeley in 1964. The next spring, when that campus began to tremble again, President Kerr said, "The university and the Berkeley campus really couldn't face another such confrontation." In fact four more years of turmoil lay ahead. Berkeley was to be but one of many disturbed campuses. In 1965 Berkeley fallout first rocked the University of Kansas when 114 students were arrested there for staging a sit-in at the chancellor's office to protest fraternity and sorority discrimination. Then, within a few days, colleges and universities were embattled from coast to coast.

Yale undergraduates demonstrated after a popular philosophy instructor had been denied tenure. After an anti-ROTC rally at San Francisco State, five were hospitalized. At Fairfield University, a Jesuit school in Connecticut, students broke into a locked stack to put forbidden books on open shelves. Brooklyn College undergraduates booed their president off a platform. At St. John's in New York, the nation's biggest Catholic college, students demanded an end to censorship of their publications. Michigan students demonstrated against higher movie prices, and three deans resigned at Stanford over reading erotic poetry in the classroom. At Fairleigh Dickinson in New Jersey students picketed as "an expression of general student discontent." The uproar continued through 1966 and 1967, with major riots at San Jose State College, Wisconsin, Iowa, Cornell, Long Beach State College, and, once again, San Francisco State. And all this was merely a buildup for the cataclysmic year of 1968. "Yesterday's ivory tower," said the president of Hunter College, "has become today's foxhole."

For all their ardor, the militant undergraduates achieved little. Students are by definition transients; once they are graduated new students arrive, and there is no guarantee that the newcomers may not take a different line—as in fact those in this movement did. SDS, inherently unstable, split into two groups at the end of the decade: Revolutionary Youth Movement I, also known as the Weathermen, and Revolutionary Youth Movement II, which condemned the Weathermen as "adventuristic." The students had other difficulties. One of their basic premises was absurd. "The fantasy," wrote Benjamin DeMott, lay "in the notion that if you're upset about Vietnam, racism, poverty, or the general quality of life, the bridge to blow is college."

A second handicap was the students' exaggerated sense of their own power. In 1966 they confidently challenged the gubernatorial campaign of Ronald Reagan. To their amazement, he won by a margin of almost a million votes. That same day the Republicans gained fifty congressional seats. "One of the most obvious casualties of the 1966 elections," Hunter S. Thompson noted, "was the New

Left's illusion of its own leverage. The radical-hippy alliance had been counting on the voters to repudiate the 'right-wing, warmonger' elements in Congress, but instead it was the 'liberal' Democrats who got stomped." Furthermore, analysts concluded that in California the New Left had actually boosted Reagan's vote by opposing him. Having found a popular issue, Reagan then capitalized on it, forcing Kerr's resignation on the ground that he had been too lenient with student dissidents and appointing Professor Samuel I. Hayakawa, a hard-liner, as president of San Francisco State.

Hostile reactions to politicized students were not confined to California. One Midwest legislature slashed over 38 million dollars from its state university's budget and raised tuition fees. Bills intended to stifle student dissent were introduced in most other legislatures, and eight of them were passed. "Americans," Oregon's Governor Tom McCall said of the demonstrators, were "fed up to their eardrums and eyeballs." Lou Harris reported that 62 percent of students' parents believed that it was more important for colleges to maintain discipline than to encourage intellectual curiosity. "Reduced to its simplest terms," *Life* commented, "the generations disagree on the most fundamental question of all: What is education for?"

Of course, they clashed over other issues, too. The demonstrations were one of the most visible manifestations of youth's subculture in the 1960s, but there was more to their subculture than that. Throughout the decade publicists wrote of "revolutions" in, among others, communications, sex, and drugs. Youth was active in all of them and was partly formed by them, if only because it had concluded that the election returns were what Hunter Thompson called "brutal confirmation of the futility of fighting the Establishment on its own terms." The generation gap had arrived, and it was an abyss.

"Don't trust anyone over thirty!" said the banners and buttons displayed by the most arrogant, and it was cruel; so many Americans over thirty wanted to be young again, to share the fads and enthusiasms of youth. They slipped discs dancing the Watusi and the Swim and the Cottage Cheese, hopped about chasing Frisbees, endangered their lives riding motorcycles, laughed at *The Graduate* and even played with Super Balls. The Beatles having introduced long hair, the kids picked it up, and presently the middle-aged were imitating that, too. Both sexes wore wigs to make them look younger. Often the hippies set fashions for adults. "I watch what the kids are putting together for themselves," said Rudi Gernreich. "I formalize it, give it something of my own, perhaps, and that is fashion." Older Americans caught the discotheque bug and asked children where the action was; young wiseacres told them the Vincent Van Gogh-Gogh and the Long, Long Ago-go. Women went to plastic surgeons for eyelid lifts ($350), nose jobs ($500), rhytidectomies—face lifts—($600), face peelings ($500), dermabrasions—removing acne scars—($275), bosom implants ($165), belly lifts ($500) and thigh lifts ($650). "Being young was *right*," *Life* observed in a special issue on the 1960s; "as everybody once wanted to be rich, now everybody wanted to be, or seem to be, young. Fashion, films, books, music, even politics leaned toward youth."

Early in the decade half the U.S. population was under thirty. Then half was under twenty-seven, and then it was half under twenty-five, with 40 percent seventeen years old or younger and those under eighteen increasing four times as fast as the rest of the population. Even so, there were many who took a saturnine view of what one called youth's "vinyl-mini-inflatable Disneyland of pop culture." Defenders of the young reminded them that Socrates had written: "Our youth now loves luxury. They have bad manners, contempt for authority, disrespect for their elders. Children nowadays are tyrants." The implication was that since the Greeks were vexed by kids that long ago, today's worriers were making an issue over nothing. Grace and Fred M. Hechinger countered that real questions should be, "What happened to Greece? Or to Rome? Or to any civilization once it substituted self-indulgence for self-discipline?"

At times in the 1960s it almost seemed that America was becoming a filiarchy. Adolescence, wrote the Hechingers, had "evolved into a cult, to be prolonged, enjoyed, and commercially catered to as never before." In the new suburbs, especially, the young appeared to have been reared on a philosophy of instant gratification. Agnew, Billy Graham, and Al Capp distorted the issue, but it did exist and was debatable. "Self-expression" and "child-centered" were part of the permissive jargon; in the schools the trend frequently led to a system of "elective" subjects for pupils too young to know what they were electing. The teacher was to be regarded as a pal, not a superior being. Elementary school teachers were required to work with limited vocabularies, sometimes twenty words or less repeated endlessly. (The result was summed up in the deathless line attributed to a teacher who rammed a tree with her car: "Look look look, oh oh oh, damn damn damn.")

Children told that they were equal to their parents in every way believed that decisions in the home should be put to a vote. This was called "democratic living." Often it meant chaotic living. Writing in *Daedalus*, David Riesman noted the effect on a stranger: "As in the home of a poor peasant which is shared with goats, chickens, and other livestock, guests here may face the hazard of children who are treated as pets and who are not put away with a babysitter when company comes."

Henry A. Murray, another Harvard contributor to *Daedalus*, pointed to one unexpected consequence. Most teen-age aggregates, he observed, were "bound together by an anti-authoritarian, anti-father compact." It was a strong man who could command respect in his own house. Society seemed to be conspiring against him. One of the greatest offenders was television. TV fathers were pitiful weaklings. *Make Room for Daddy*'s ineffectual daddy let his wife dominate him simply because she talked the loudest. Uncle Bentley in *Bachelor Father* was systematically humiliated by his niece and his servant, and Mr. Anderson, the antihero of a series sardonically called *Father Knows Best*, invariably responded to the strange antics of his children by saying, "Let's keep out of it and see what happens."

Advertisers were wary of offending youth; the nation's teen-agers were spending 25 billion dollars a year. It was ironic that student militants should take so vigorous a stand against materialism; their own generation was the most possession-conscious in history. In *The Lonely Crowd* Riesman wrote that in America "children begin their training as consumers at an increasingly young age," that "middle-class children have allowances of their own at four or five," and that the allowances "are expected to be spent, whereas in the earlier era they were often used as cudgels of thrift."

Advertisers courting them addressed teen-agers as "the Now Generation," the "New People," the "Pepsi Generation," and the "Go Anywhere, Do Anything Generation." John Brooks pointed out that they were the most conspicuous beneficiaries of Johnsonian prosperity: "American youth, like everybody else but more spectacularly, was getting rich. A combination of burgeoning national wealth and the settled national habit of indulging the young was putting unprecedented sums of cash in their hands." Keeping them solvent wasn't always easy. In 1964 the Harvard class of '39, hardly indigents, reported that providing their children with money was the chief paternal problem for 78 percent of them. Only 6 percent said that instilling moral values in them was as hard. And they weren't all that moral. For $12.50 a boy could buy a girl a "Going Steady" ring which looked just like a wedding band; certainly no motel manager could tell the difference. If they felt guilty next day, in some places they could pray for forgiveness at teen-age churches. The Emmanuel Hospital in Portland, Oregon, even had a teen-age wing. It was described by Frank J. Taylor in a *Saturday Evening Post* article, "How to Have Fun in the Hospital." Patients enjoyed "unlimited snacks, jam sessions, and wheel-chair drag races." Priggish nutritionists kept their distance; the teen-agers were allowed to "eat hot dogs and hamburgers day after day for lunch and supper."

Literature for the young included *How to Be a Successful Teenager*, by one William C. Menninger. In a chapter on "How to Live with Parents" Menninger described techniques of handling mothers and fathers who tried to dictate to them: "One of the best ways to maintain family peace and insure cooperation is by holding family councils periodically about important matters." There were plenty of other sources of advice for youth. The *Chicago Daily News* carried a column of adolescent gossip called "Keen Teens"; the *Ladies' Home Journal* a department, "Profile of Youth." Pulps for adolescents included *Confidential Teen Romances, Teen Times, Hollywood Teenager, 16 Magazine, Teen World, Teen Parade, Modern Teen,* and *Teen Screen.* Among their magazines were *Ingenue, Calling All Girls,* and *Seventeen,* which observed its seventeenth year of publication in 1961 with a breathless editorial, "It's Our Birthday"—"*Seventeen* is 17 . . . Isn't Everybody?"

I Was a Teen-Age Frankenstein was one of the more memorable films produced for the adolescent trade. The editor of *Teen Magazine,* Charles Laufer, said that "the music market for the first time in history is completely dominated by the young set." They were the most musical generation ever, and their taste, at its best, was very good; the swing generation could hardly improve on the Beatles, Joan Baez, Bob Dylan, and forty-four-year-old B. B. King, whom the youth of the 1960s discovered after he had been ignored by his contemporaries for twenty-one years. Unfortunately the youngsters had other idols who belonged aesthetically with Andy

Warhol's Brillo boxes and Campbell soup cans, among them the ruttish Presley. Presley's voice and appearance were at least his own. That wasn't true of most rock stars. To a striking degree they were all alike—short youths, running to fat, who were prepared for public consumption by strenuous dieting, nose surgery, contact lenses, and luxurious hair styles. And they couldn't sing. Most couldn't even have made themselves heard in the back of a theater. Their voices were amplified in echo chambers and then created on tape, a snippet here and a snippet there, destroying false notes. When they appeared in public, they would mouth the words while the records were being played over the loudspeakers. Wiggling their hips and snapping their fingers, their features always fixed in a sullen expression, they would desecrate good songs: "I loved, I loved, I loved yuh, once in si-ilence," or "The rain, yeah! stays mainly in the puh-lain."

"What I mean to kids," said Janis Joplin, shortly before she killed herself with whiskey and drugs, "is they can be themselves and win." John Lennon of the Beatles said, "We're more popular than Jesus now." Their listeners may have tuned such things out. They were, after all, accustomed to meaningless words—"Learn to forget," said a writer in *Crawdaddy*; it was one of the wiser apostrophes directed to that rock magazine's readers. Purdue polled two thousand teen-agers on the gravest problem facing American youth. A third of them said acne.

Policemen would have disagreed. Over the previous ten years arrests of the young had jumped 86 percent. "Teen-Agers on the Rampage," proclaimed a *Time* head after a single week which had seen violence "among high schools from California to Maine." Professor Ruth Shonle Cavan published the first sociology textbook to deal with upper- and middle-class delinquency, including what she called "alcohol-automobile-sex behavior." Felonies were almost commonplace in some neighborhoods which had once been serene. The FBI reported that Americans aged eighteen or younger accounted for almost half of all arrests for murder, rape, robbery, aggravated assault, burglary, and auto theft—and in the suburbs it was more than half. Beginning in 1960 suburbs began setting up teen-age codes of conduct, but they had no legal status, compliance was voluntary, and their chief value was evidence that parental authority was bankrupt. "Mit dose kids society is nix," said the cop of the Katzenjammer kids, and it often was. Gallup found a startling difference between the values of parents and those of their children. Three out of four youngsters said they knew that cheating on examinations was common. It didn't bother them, Gallup reported.

The first evidence of widespread teen-age drug parties in the paneled rumpus rooms of the affluent was turned up in 1960 by the Westchester County vice squad. After the shock had passed parents said that at least it wasn't liquor. Then police on Santa Catalina Island, the southern California resort, announced that drunkenness had become common among thirteen- and fourteen-year-old children in wealthy families, and in the future they would charge the parents $2.50 an hour to babysit teen-age drunks till parents came to take them home. Nationally the number of adolescents who drank regularly was put at between 50 and 66 percent. In Yonkers, New York, where it was 58 percent among high school juniors and seniors, 64 percent said they drove the family car while doing it. Parents in Rose Valley, a Philadelphia suburb, allowed children to bring their own bottles to parties. Their fathers did the bartending. One wondered what Clarence Day's father would have thought.

Among the recurring news stories of the 1960s—the ghetto disorders, the annual anniversary of Dallas, the war moratoriums—were accounts of rioting at the Newport Jazz Festival and at Fort Lauderdale, the watering places of the young. Yet the extent of teen-agers' drinking ought not to have been surprising. In a sense they were expressing their social role. Opulence, the lack of genuine responsibility, and a position outside the unemployment pool gave them all the attributes of a leisure class.

In their ennui or their cups, youths of the 1960s frequently turned destructive. A brief item from Hannibal, Missouri, gave melancholy evidence of the revision of a cherished American myth. At the foot of Hannibal's Cardiff Hill stands a famous statue of Tom Sawyer and Huckleberry Finn, barefoot and carrying fishing poles; a plaque explains that this is the neighborhood where Tom and Huck "played and roamed at will." But any boys who attempted to emulate them after dark in the late 1960s would have risked arrest. Because of the rise in adolescent vandalism, loitering by the young on Cardiff Hill—and indeed anywhere in Hannibal—was forbidden after 10 P.M.

It was a harsh but necessary law; the vandalism was a real problem, in Missouri and elsewhere. During one week in February 1968 thirty New Haven high school students were arrested in the wake of china-smashing cafeteria riots, five hundred boys in the Chicago suburb of Maywood battled police at a rally protesting the selection of a homecoming queen, and nearly three thousand students at Chicago's Dunbar High left classes to pelt rocks at cars. In a typical suburban incident, an Alexandria, Virginia, gang, the children of government officials, did between $7,000 and $8,000 in damage by smashing automobile windshields with baseball bats. When arrested, they said they had done it "for fun." Another widespread expression of violence was party crashing. For a time there was a rash of such incidents each weekend in Westchester, Fairfield, Rockland, and Bucks counties—the exclusive suburbs ringing New York. Characteristically, six or eight uninvited youths would arrive at the height of a party, break open the parents' liquor cabinet, and destroy glassware and furniture.

Sometimes invited guests were worse. They would rival one another in seeing how much they could damage their host's home. One memorable debutante party celebrated the coming out of blonde Fernanda Wanamaker at her stepparent's thirty-room mansion in Southampton, Long Island. Over eight hundred children of what Vogue was then calling "the beautiful people" were invited. After the band had left, a hundred and twenty-seven of them wrecked the mansion, smashing windows, tearing down curtains, swinging on chandeliers, ripping out phones, breaking lamps, carting off appliances and throwing most of the furniture on the beach. The cost of the mischief was estimated to be somewhere between $3,000 and $10,000.

Affluent youths were often the worst offenders, but disorders could break anywhere. On one Independence Day five hundred drunken youths in Arnolds Park, Iowa, hurled rocks, beer bottles, and pieces of concrete at policemen; the tumult was set off when one of them yelled at the police chief, "Hey, punk, we're going to take over this place." In Chicago a free rock concert series—arranged by municipal officials to build camaraderie with youth—had to be canceled. At the first performance the audience rose up swinging tire chains and clubs; 135 were injured, including 65 policemen.

North Dakota University was one of the quietest, best-behaved campuses in the country until the Student, its undergraduate newspaper, proposed a weekend of fun in the nearby town of Zap. Zap's Mayor Norman Fuchs, delighted, wrote to all neighboring colleges promising "Zap-Burgers with special seasoning" and lots of "good,

clean, beer-busting, food-munching, tear-jerking, rib-tickling fun."
He acquired a sweatshirt with the legend "Zap, N.D. or Bust" and
announced that the occasion would be called a "Zap-In." There was
talk of Zap becoming the Fort Lauderdale of the North. The mayor
could scarcely have understood the implications of all that. His town
had a population of three hundred. By the evening of Friday, May
9, 1969, nearly a thousand students, 90 percent of them male, had
arrived in Zap from five states. The town's three taverns were
packed. When the thermometer dropped below freezing the students started a bonfire in the street, ripping out tables and booths
from the taverns for firewood. Then they began breaking into stores
and houses. Fistfights followed. A fire truck arrived; they seized it
and dismantled it. Before five hundred National Guardsmen could
arrive, the visitors had done $10,000 worth of damage.

The Fort Lauderdale of the South was never confronted with
precisely that problem, freezing temperatures never having been
recorded there in May. But Florida was afflicted with youthful fire-
bugs that year just the same. Over a fifteen-month period an incredible number of unexplained fires (120) broke out on the University
of Florida campus in Gainesville. Fire marshals thought it possible
that the entire campus might be razed. The crisis was resolved when
residents in Hume Hall confessed they had done it. Students in the
east and west wings had been competing to see which could attract
the most fire trucks. What made the incident particularly striking
was a circumstance which would have been unthinkable in earlier
generations. Hume Hall was a girls' dormitory.

Men's rooms in genteel establishments had long displayed a sign
over urinals: PLEASE ARRANGE CLOTHING BEFORE LEAVING WASHROOM.
Well-brought-up boys didn't need to be reminded; they had been
taught never to fasten the flies of their trousers in public. They were
therefore startled when Françoise Dorleac, in the 1966 film *Where
the Spies Are*, emerged from a dressing room, reached for her crotch,
and casually zipped up her slacks in the presence of her costar, David Niven. It was one of those moments which served as reminders
that the delicate balance between the sexes had been altered, probably forever. Women were moving into jobs which had always been
considered masculine: telephone linemen, mining engineers, ditch
diggers, truck drivers, Secret Service agents. More of them were
sharing men's vices, too: public drunkenness, juvenile delinquency,

and assault and battery. Women's Liberation leader Ti-Grace Atkinson called marriage "slavery," "legalized rape," and "unpaid labor," and disapproved of love between the sexes as "tied up with a
sense of dependency." The Women's Lib movement was not confined to the United States; in 1970 Bernadette Devlin was designated Ireland's Man of the Year by her admirers, and 1,162 pregnant
Norwegian women sailors, who had conceived while on the high
seas, claimed and were granted compensation from their government. But it was in America that women took to the streets at the
end of the 1960s in massive rallies: 3,000 in Chicago, 2,000 in Indianapolis, 2,000 in Boston, and 50,000 in Manhattan, striding down
Fifth Avenue with their breasts, unencumbered by brassieres, swaying visibly.

The disappearance of bras among members of the movement was
but one of many changes in fashion. When Mia Farrow cropped her
hair girls flocked to hairdressers so they, too, could look like boys.
They crowded Army-Navy stores buying pea jackets, petty officer
shirts, and bell-bottom trousers. Square-toed, low, heavy shoes became popular among them, and so many coeds were using after-
shave lotion as perfume that the business journal *Forbes* protested
that the sexes were beginning to smell alike. In 1966 Twiggy, the
Cockney model, weighed in at ninety-one pounds, and women
dieted to look like her, angularity being considered antifeminine.
The idea was to look tough. Shiny plastic came into vogue, and
hard, metallic fabrics. Pantsuits appeared—not cute slacks but man-
nish, tailored slacks. The zippers or buttons were no longer on the
side; they went straight down the front, like Françoise Dorleac's,
and some girls reportedly made them to go all the way through and
up the back, so they could stand at urinals. Barbara Tuchman protested that too many women were beginning to look like Lolitas or
liontamers. A Woman's Lib leader called her an Aunt Tom.

At the very top of the movement there was some female homosexuality and bisexuality; Kate Millett said she sometimes slept with
women, and Joan Baez acknowledged that she had once had a les-
bian affair. There was considerable resentment in the movement
over being considered "sex objects"; girls objected to being whistled
at and featured in fetching ads designed to appeal to males. Most
girls in the movement preferred boys, however; Gloria Steinem, a
heterosexual Lib leader, said, "Men think that once women become
liberated, it will mean no more sex for men. But what men don't

realize is that if women are liberated, there will be more sex and better." Betty Friedan attested to "the mounting sex-hunger of American women," and David Riesman noted that "millions of women" had become "knowing consumers of sex" and "pioneers, with men, on the frontier of sex." Elderly Americans, who had called aggressive women "bold" or "forward," couldn't grasp what was happening. Attending his granddaughter's commencement in 1967, General Eisenhower told miniskirted girls: "Ankles are nearly always neat and good-looking but knees are nearly always not." The girls, of course, knew that what interested boys was higher up.

Certainly more girls were on the prowl, often roaming the streets in pairs or appearing at weekends, available, on college campuses. Bachelors dropping in for a drink at Chicago's dating bars in the Rush Street district—The Jail, The Store, The Spirit of '76—would be propositioned by girls who offered to "ball" them and tried to arouse them with a new gesture—the feminine hand, slipped between the man's thighs, squeezing him there. Over a third of the coeds at a New York university admitted to one-night affairs with total strangers. Nationally, during the 1960s, the number of girls reporting premarital intercourse in surveys more than doubled; in a five-year period it rose 65 percent. European surveyors found that twice as many boys as girls there volunteered to describe their sexual experiences; in the United States it was the other way around. The number of coeds reporting the petting of male genitals soared. High school girls tried to achieve a licentious air. To that end, *Seventeen* discovered, the number of its subscribers using mascara had jumped from one in five during the late 1940s to nine in ten. Rudi Gernreich said that twenty years earlier girls tried to look sweet and innocent; now, "before they are seventeen years old they cultivate a wild, consciously sexy look." Demure women all but vanished. Obscene language no longer shocked them; they used it themselves. If they wanted coitus they said so. In the film *All the Loving Couples*, a jaded wife waiting to be swapped said thickly, "When do we get laid?"

Presently she was in the throes of sexual intercourse, on camera, with another woman's husband. The movies, once straitlaced, were exploring all the visual possibilities of the sex act. Under the leadership of Jack Valenti, who left the White House to become president of the Motion Picture Association of America, Hollywood adopted a rating system for films in 1968. Those in the G category would be family movies; the others would be M (suggested for mature audiences), R (restricted to persons sixteen or older unless accompanied by a parent or guardian), or X (no one under sixteen admitted under any circumstances).

In the late 1960s each season's X movies went farther than the last. Even the movie ads in newspapers become something to put out of reach of children. *I Am Curious (Yellow)* was thought shocking when it appeared, showing nudity and coitus, but new productions rapidly made it obsolescent. Ads for *The Minx* said it "makes Curious Yellow look pale," and it did. Then *The Fox* depicted lesbians kissing passionately and a naked woman masturbating in front of a full-length mirror. A beast had intercourse with a woman in *Rosemary's Baby. Bob and Carol and Ted and Alice* was a comedy about wife swapping. *Blow-Up* provided a glimpse of a girl's pubic hair; it was thought daring at the time, but presently ingenious close-ups showed the genitals in intercourse from unusual angles—some from the bottom—and actresses masturbating actors to climax. The ultimate, or so it seemed at the time, was *Deep Throat,* a tremendous hit about cunnilingus and fellatio. At the conclusion of it the heroine took a man down to the hilt of his phallus, displaying a talent which the *New Yorker* compared to that of a sword swallower. The action was photographed at a range of a few feet, and when the man reached orgasm, so did the girl. Technicolor revealed her full body flush.

Dallas District Attorney Henry Wade said: "I wouldn't be too surprised to see a sex circus in the Cotton Bowl." On Manhattan's Forty-second Street, in the block between Seventh and Eighth avenues, a policeman said: "If a little old lady wants to buy the *Times,* she has to climb over three rows of *Screw* to get it." *Screw, Suck, Desire, Gay,* and *Coq*—all the smut magazines competed for circulation by trying to show more flesh of models in lewder poses than the others. In Miami, Bunny Dania, one of the more experienced models, said that when she began posing photographers would show nudes playing volleyball or swimming. "Now," she said, "you've got to have wife swapping and sadism and girls making out with girls. It's moved indoors."

On stage a performer named Jim Morrison described his latest sexual adventure; it had occurred five minutes before curtain time. *Oh! Calcutta!* was billed as "elegant erotica"; its sketches ranged in theme from wife swapping to rape. *Che!* provided a hundred minutes of faked sex acts. Those who preferred the real thing could find it in New York's "Mine-Cini Theater," or in San Francisco taverns where a boy and girl would strip, climb on the bar, and there engage in what was drolly called the act of love. Some spectacles shocked the most hardened observers. A reporter told of going backstage in one Manhattan show and seeing chorus girls, naked, shooting heroin into the backs of their knees while their illegitimate toddlers watched.

Sex became an issue in strange places. After searching his conscience for five years on contraception, Pope Paul rejected it in a 7,500-word encyclical entitled *Humanae Vitae* (*Of Human Life*) on July 29, 1969. Millions of American Catholics were furious. A study by the Urban Life Institute of the University of San Francisco, a Jesuit school, disclosed that 70 percent of them approved of birth control. The vast majority of young priests agreed (though over 90 percent of the older priests did not). In Washington several rebellious priests staged a sit-in, and a hundred and forty-two others sent a letter of protest to the head of their archdiocese, Patrick Cardinal O'Boyle. When the cardinal began a sermon on obedience in St. Matthew's Cathedral, two hundred members of the congregation rose from their pews and stalked out. Seven Buffalo priests were dismissed from a seminary for mutinous remarks. Still the revolt spread. The following year the former auxiliary bishop of the St. Paul-Minneapolis archdiocese married a New York divorcée. Soon stories about priests marrying—often to nuns who had leaped over the wall—lost their novelty.

A lot of carnal knowledge was being acquired in laboratories, observed by scientists in white coats holding stopwatches and other things. The most famous of them were Dr. William H. Masters and Virginia E. Johnson, who eventually married one another. Their findings at the Reproductive Biology Research Foundation in St. Louis were invaluable, but fastidious critics were appalled by the measuring and photographing of copulation; it smacked to them of charcoal filters and flip-top boxes. The most remarkable piece of Masters-Johnson equipment was an electrically powered plastic penis with a tiny camera inside and cold light illumination to allow observation and recording of what was happening inside the vagina. The size of this artificial phallus could be adjusted, and the woman using it could regulate the depth and speed of the thrust. Inevitably it inspired several novels. The best of them was Robert Kyle's *Venus*

Examined (1968). At the end of it a disillusioned heroine returns to the sex laboratory, demolishes the plastic phallus, and is electrocuted.

All this was a great strain for the young. Previous generations had been protected from early sexual entanglements by social custom, the fear of disgrace, and the possibility of venereal disease or pregnancy—a catastrophe for the girl. Now mores had changed spectacularly; society took a tolerant view of premarital affairs. Venereal infection had vanished. (Late in the decade it would reappear as a nationwide epidemic, a consequence of the new promiscuity.) "If it feels good, I'll do it," read a pin popular among college students. Intercourse felt good, and they did it a lot, protected by the Pill, or diaphragms, and various intrauterine devices, loops and coils.

Late in the decade, when abortions became easier to obtain, girls felt even safer. But improved contraceptives were not responsible for the increase in pushovers. It preceded them. Illegitimate births doubled between 1940 and 1960, and 40 percent of the mothers were in their teens. The Hechingers found that in some sophisticated communities a girl was expected to begin sexual intercourse with her steady boyfriend on her sixteenth birthday; if she refrained, she lost status. Pregnancy was so common in an Oakland high school that girls were allowed to attend classes until their confinement. A New York hospital on the privileged East Side reported that the number of unwed mothers jumped 271 percent in six years, and the *New York Times* quoted Dr. Margaret L. McCormack as saying that pregnancy, "once a college problem, is now a high school and junior high school problem." One New York junior high, she said, had 240 pregnancies in one year. The Pill came into widespread use during the winter of 1961–62, and by 1967 the illegitimacy rate among schoolgirls was on the decline. But no one suggested that coitus had lost its popularity.

The sex-drenched state of American culture was undoubtedly responsible for much of the increase in premarital and extramarital intercourse. Sexiness was everywhere—on paperback book racks, television, in ads, magazines, popular songs, plays, musicals, and everyday conversation. Betty Friedan cited a psychological study which found that references to sex in mass media increased by over 250 percent in the 1960s. The *New York Times Book Review* noted the popularity of books about "love" affairs between animals and human beings. Complaints to the U.S. Post Office about smut doubled within six years, to 130,000 in 1965.

"Be Prepared!" proclaimed a poster showing an enormously pregnant girl, smiling broadly, in a Girl Scout uniform. The Scouts asked for damages; the court threw out the case. "Use Contraceptives: Take the Worry Out of Being Close," said a Planned Parenthood ad. The New York Hilton, Manhattan's largest hotel, was renting rooms by the hour. Frustrated persons (or couples) took out ads in the personal column of the *Saturday Review*, or in underground newspapers, soliciting new partners. Everybody knew about key parties for swapping couples; the men threw their house keys on a table and the wives picked them up at random, each then going to bed with the owner of whatever key she had.

Nicholas von Hoffman described a game, manufactured by the Diplomat Sales Company of Los Angeles, which provided "a safe, nicely structured way for two or three couples to end an evening naked, drunk, out of their minds, and lascivious as hell." Called Bumps and Grinds, it was played by the light of one candle (which was included). Players moved around a board like the one used in Monopoly, drawing "Tomcat" and "Pussycat" cards. These advised them to "Take one drink," or "Strip one article of clothing," and so on. The game was rigged for the girls to wind up nude and drunk first. Subsequent moves decided who was going to stagger to the bedroom with whom.

If wife swapping was permissible for the middle-aged, youths argued, what was wrong with wife testing for them? Some communities, troubled by the question and aware of the temptations which prompted it, tried to ward off the great landslide of sex with local regulations. For a while wearers of bikinis on some public beaches were required to have two inches of cloth on each hip. Then President Kennedy's widow was photographed in a three-ring bikini, and the regulations collapsed. Thus clad, or unclad, the young could caress 95 percent of each other's bodies with suntan lotion in public. And as they thus excited one another, transistor radios alongside broadcast suggestive lyrics: "This girl is a woman now/ She knows what it's all about," or "If somebody loves you, it's no good unless she loves you/ All the way," or:

> Don't you know the facts of life,
> You've got a lot to learn;

I'd like to teach you all,
And get your love in return.

"There is," said a University of Michigan coed, "nobody saying 'No.'" So many were saying yes that it was a wonder one-third of female college undergraduates remained virgins. In some instances, parents actually regarded the absence of coital experience as troubling. All things being equal, they would have preferred that their daughters remained maidens. But in this generation everything else was unequal. A teen-age girl who lacked a normal interest in sex could be in the toils of another new snare for the young. She was possibly—and in some communities probably—a user of heavy drugs.

Early developments in mid-century chemotherapy were benign. The sulfa drugs had arrived in the late 1930s. Then came penicillin (1943), streptomycin (1945), cortisone (1946), ACTH (1949), terramycin and aureomycin (1950), the Salk vaccine (1955), the Sabin vaccine (1960), and the tranquilizers, led by Miltown and Librium, which cut the length of the average mental hospital stay in half. All these were called "miracle drugs" when they first appeared. Because of them, diseases which had afflicted men since the dawn of history were tamed and, in some cases, eliminated. In 1959 over 579 *tons* of tranquilizers were prescribed, which gives some idea of the need they met. As recently as the early 1950s polio terrorized parents during the summer months; 57,000 cases were reported in 1952. Now that was merely a memory.

The first inkling that the drug revolution had a dark side came in 1962, when eight thousand European women who had been taking a new tranquilizer called Thalidomide gave birth to limbless babies. Thanks to Dr. Frances O. Kelsey of the Food and Drug Administration, Thalidomide had not been licensed for general use in the United States. Nevertheless, a few Thalidomide-deformed babies had been born to expectant mothers who had been taking the blue tablets on an investigative basis. If a drug could do that, anything was possible. And the amount of medication in American medicine cabinets was unprecedented. Doctors were now writing nearly two billion dollars' worth of prescriptions each year for pills which included new barbiturates and amphetamines, hypnotics, and antidepressants. In addition, an enormous black market was flourishing. Of the eight billion amphetamines, or pep pills, manufactured each year, about four billion were being sold illegally. Laymen might call the pep pills and barbiturates "soft" drugs and heroin, morphine, and cocaine "hard," but pharmacologists knew it should be the other way around; the older drugs calmed addicts, but the new ones created dangerous, unpredictable moods. Some became part of the culture, familiar enough to have popular nicknames. Among them were "bluejays" (sodium amytal), "redbirds" (seconal), "yellow jackets" (nembutal), and "goofballs" (barbiturates laced with benzedrine).

The most widely discussed of the new compounds was d-lysergic acid diethylamide—LSD. First isolated in 1938 by Dr. Albert Hofmann in the Sandoz Research Laboratories in Basle, Switzerland, it lay around his lab for five years, unappreciated, its properties awaiting discovery. That occurred on April 16, 1943. Absorbing some LSD through the skin of his fingers, Hofmann began hallucinating. His scientific curiosity aroused, he then deliberately took 250 micrograms of it—an amount about the size of a grain of salt. In his diary he explained the effect: "With closed eyes, multihued, metamorphizing, fantastic images overwhelmed me . . . Sounds were transposed into visual sensations so that from each tone or noise a comparable colored picture was evoked, changing in form and color kaleidoscopically." In short, he had taken a trip.

Dr. Humphrey Osmond of the New Jersey Neuropsychiatric Institute neologized a new name for LSD. He called it a psychedelic and said it meant mind-expanding. At the start of the 1960s, the colorless, odorless, tasteless drug was still unknown to the public. Then two Harvard psychologists, Timothy Leary and Richard Alpert, began experimenting with colleagues, writers, artists, clergymen, and volunteer prisoners. Leary and Alpert were dismissed from Harvard in 1963, but by then LSD had achieved its reputation. Taking a trip, or turning on, had come to convey status on campuses. Alarmed, the FDA warned college presidents that taking it was an "insidious and dangerous activity." Sandoz Laboratories stopped making it. Laws barring it in any form were passed in Michigan, New Jersey, Nevada, and California. None of that made any difference; the use of it continued to spread.

LSD became a household word in 1966. Even recluses knew what was meant by tripping, freaking out, and blowing one's mind. Priests and pastors held a conference on the religious aspects of LSD. In discotheques—and also in art galleries and museums—films, slides, and flashing colored lights suggested the impact of an LSD experience. Chilling stories, some of them apocryphal, were told to scare those who were tempted to take a trip. A youth high on LSD was said to have taken a swan dive into the front of a truck moving at 70 mph. Teen-agers under its influence reportedly lay in a field staring at the sun until they were permanently blinded. That was exposed as a lie, but the Associated Press verified the case of a young man who turned himself in to police saying he had been flying on LSD for three days and asking "Did I kill my wife? Did I rape anyone?" and was then charged with the murder of his mother-in-law.

Users described feeling depressed, even homicidal, and told how they had turned themselves into ravens, or Jesus Christ, or tiny people six inches tall. Distraught parents told what had happened to their children: "My boy is on drugs. He went to St. Louis because it's the astrological center of the universe. He has met Hitler and Lincoln." And "Our son came home for Christmas. He looked awful. He rode his little sister's bicycle barefoot through the snow. The neighbors took their children in. People are afraid of him."

But the users of LSD—they called it acid—described their trips as ecstatic. "Who needs jazz, or even beer," wrote a contributor to the *New York Times Magazine*, "when you can sit down on a public curbstone, drop a pill in your mouth, and hear fantastic music for hours at a time in your own head? A cap of good acid costs $5, and for that you can hear the Universal Symphony, with God singing solo and the Holy Ghost on drums."

The Beatles sang "Yellow Submarine," which was a euphemism for a freakout, and another song freighted with LSD meaning, "Strawberry Field." Elementary school children dismayed their mothers by coming home chanting, to the tune of "Frère Jacques":

> *Marijuana, marijuana,*
> *LSD, LSD,*
> *College kids are making it, high*
> *   school kids are taking it,*
> *Why can't we? Why can't we?*

At times it seemed that an entire generation was turning on to drugs. In fact, the hippy movement, or counterculture, which sprang from the self-medication and narcotics, was at first smaller than it appeared to be. It was really an extension of the beat generation of the 1950s. In the early 1960s the beatniks moved into San Francisco's Haight-Ashbury district. A musical combo called the Jefferson Airplane was then playing the first acid rock in an obscure night spot called the Matrix. Their group and the Grateful Dead were being entertained by Ken Kesey and his band of Merry Pranksters at La Honda, Kesey's forest home fifty miles south of San Francisco. It was at La Honda that Kesey and the Pranksters served their guests Kool-Aid spiked with LSD, and there that he wrote *One Flew Over the Cuckoo's Nest* (1962) and *Sometimes a Great Notion* (1964).

Listening to the driving, drowning acid rock, the Pranksters experimented with light and color, wore spectacular clothes, and evolved a life-style which would later become familiar in virtually every American community and in many abroad. It wasn't popular then. The dances at which the Airplane and the Dead played were thinly attended. Most customers still preferred the Charlie Parker brand of jazz. The new musicians painted posters depicting the visual impact of an LSD trip. Few admired them. At first they gave away these early examples of psychedelic art, then they sold them for a dollar each. A *Ramparts* editor said the printing was "36-point illegible," but by 1967 some of the originals would be selling in the best San Francisco art galleries for $2,000.

By then a reporter for the *San Francisco Chronicle* had christened the new bohemians "hippies," and the movement had become first a national and then an international phenomenon. Hippy communes were flourishing in New York, Boston, Chicago, Los Angeles, and Atlanta, and hippy enclaves had been established in Mexico, Canada, London, Rome, Tokyo—even in Laos. By then many charter members of the movement had quit, disgusted by the exhibitionists who were giving colorful interviews to newspapermen and television commentators. "The best year to be a hippy was 1965," said Hunter S. Thompson, the Ernie Pyle of the movement, "but then there was not much to write about, because not much was happening in public and most of what was happening in private was illegal. The real year of the hippie was 1966, despite the lack of publicity, which in 1967 gave way to a nationwide avalanche."

Fortunes were made in the 1967 "Summer of Love" from the sale of DMT, mescaline, methedrine, LSD, and the even more popular —and safer—marijuana to the disillusioned children of the middle and upper middle class who flocked to hippy communes, leaving what they regarded as a stifling straight life to Do Their Thing. Pot, boo, maryjane, grass, or Mary Warner—the various names under which marijuana was known to them—sold in Mexico for $35 a kilogram (2.2 pounds). Smuggled into the United States, a kilo brought $150 to $200. Meted out in 34-ounce bags, it went for as much as $25 an ounce, or $850 the kilo. Joints—marijuana cigarettes—sold on the street for a dollar each. The heroin racket was even more lucrative. Undercover chemists made $700 for every kilo of morphine converted to heroin in Marseilles. Manhattan entrepreneurs paid $10,000 for it and sold it on the street in plastic bags, each containing just 5 percent heroin cut with sugar or quinine powder. In that form the original 2.2 pounds earned $20,000. And the market was expanding rapidly. The Federal Bureau of Narcotics estimated that 68,000 Americans became addicted in a single year.

In literally scores of cities there were share-ins, be-ins, and love-ins. As in the case of the beatniks ten years earlier, San Francisco was the focal point of the movement. The San Francisco *Oracle*, the leading underground newspaper, was published there, and there the original band of Diggers—named for a seventeenth-century English brotherhood that raised food for the poor on land which had been uncultivated—became beggars in order to feed indigent hippies. The distribution was in what was called Panhandle Park; it was known as the Politics of Free.

The issue of how many youths participated in the counterculture depends entirely on definitions. If smokers of marijuana are counted, the number is enormous. Dr. Henry Brill, chairman of the American Medical Association's committee on drug dependence, estimated that the number of Americans who tried pot went from a few hundred thousand in the early 1960s to eight million at the end of the decade, most of them in their teens. That was by far the most conservative of the estimates; the U.S. Public Health Service put the figure at 20 million. A *Playboy* survey reported that 47 percent of the nation's college students admitted smoking marijuana, though only 13 percent said they used it frequently. Members of families with high incomes smoked it most often. Just 2 percent acknowledged injecting methedrine, or speed—liquid amphetamines—directly into their veins, and a mere 1 percent were addicted to other narcotics.

The great year of the hippy may be said to have begun on Easter Sunday, March 26, 1967, when ten thousand boys and girls assembled in New York Central Park's Sheep Meadow to honor love. They flew kites, tossed Frisbees, joined hands in "love circles," painted designs on each other's faces, and chanted: "Banana! Banana!" after a current hoax, that banana scrapings had psychedelic properties. On the other side of the country that Sunday fifteen thousand youths in San Francisco cheered Dr. Leary's Pied Piper spiel: "Turn on to the scene; tune in to what's happening; and drop out—of high school, college, grade school . . . follow me, the hard way."

What came next was a nightmare for tens of thousands of mothers and fathers. With the memories of their Depression childhoods still vivid, the parents of the late 1960s could not grasp that the country had become so prosperous it could afford to support tramps, or that their own children would want to be among the tramps. "The kids looked like bums, often acted like bums," the Associated Press reported, "but they were no ordinary bums. Most had spent their lives in middle-class surroundings, finishing high school, often graduating from college—the American dream." Now their photographs, forwarded by their parents and accompanied by pathetic messages pleading for news of their whereabouts, were hung on bulletin boards in police stations. The pictures weren't much help. Taken when the youngsters were straight, they bore little relation to their new life-style.

The police did what they could. The Salvation Army opened a coffee house in East Village called The Answer, where flower children in their early teens were urged to return home. Runaways in Haight-Ashbury were sheltered at church-sponsored Huckleberry's while mothers and fathers were contacted. A physician opened a free clinic for hippies in San Francisco. Almost immediately he was overwhelmed by pregnancies, cases of venereal disease, and hepatitis caused by dirty syringes. Virtually every hippy in Hashbury had a cold or the flu. Many had tried sleeping in Golden Gate Park, unaware that a hidden sprinkling system automatically started up at dawn.

The greatest health hazard, of course, was the drugs. The hippies had no way of knowing what they were buying; Dr. Louis Lasagna found that many were getting veterinary anesthetics or even plain urine. In that summer many were experimenting with STP, a new compound named for a gasoline additive used in the Hell's Angels motorcycles. Between 5,000 and 10,000 STP capsules were given away. The flower children, liking it, christened it "the caviar of psychedelics." Doctors discovered that it was extremely dangerous;

when taken in combination with chlorpromazine, an LSD antidote, STP could prove fatal. The "speed freaks" or "meth monsters," as other hippies called them, were taking methedrine; when high, they were capable of almost anything. Meantime, in Buffalo, Dr. Maimon M. Cohen announced that preliminary findings in an investigation of LSD and chlorpromazine indicated that mixed together the two could result in chromosome damage, spontaneous abortions, or deformed infants.

That summer tourist buses were routed through Haight-Ashbury to provide a glimpse of the strange scene there. (Sometimes a hippy would run alongside the bus, holding up a mirror.) There, and in East Village, part-time flower children, or "plastics," as they were known—straights who were in effect slumming—were spending their weekends as hippies, returning to their jobs on Monday morning conservatively dressed and well groomed. The attitude of the New Left toward the flower children was equally ambivalent. In the beginning, when Leary succeeded Mario Savio as youth's demigod, New Left writers praised the hippies for their candor and spontaneity. After the Reagan landslide the situation changed. Many disillusioned militants tossed in the sponge, abandoned hope, and chose instead to stay stoned for days at a time. Flower power, they said, was nonpolitical. Stung, New Leftists retorted that the hippies lacked "stability" and "energy," that they were "intellectually flabby," and that they were really "nihilists" whose idea of love was "so generalized and impersonal as to be meaningless." Of course, the hippies replied; that was their thing, and they were going to do it, and up yours.

The immediate threat to the flower children was not from parents, policemen, tourists, or New Leftists. It came from lower-class ethnic groups into whose neighborhoods they had moved. Haight-Ashbury was a working-class district; New York's East Village was inhabited by Italians, Negroes, Poles, Jews, Puerto Ricans, and Ukrainians, all of them trying to climb into the lower middle class. The spectacle of idle youth scorning the class status to which the ghetto inhabitants aspired for their own children infuriated them. The AP quoted a twenty-year-old porter who had just been laid off: "These cats want to drop out. How do you think that makes a guy feel who is just trying to get in?"

"We hippies love people," a flute player protested; "we certainly aren't bigoted." The ethnics, he said wonderingly, thought of his neighborhood as "their turf." They did indeed. A black grumbled that the flower children had "taken over" Tompkins Square Park. The park had belonged to him and his; they didn't have much, but that, at least, had been theirs, and now these maddening, uninvited kids insisted on sharing it. The inevitable happened. Violence, always a menace in ghettos, erupted against the defenseless hippies. On Memorial Day of that year ethnic boys attacked a twenty-nine-year-old flower girl in Tompkins Square and stripped her naked. In Central Park a fifteen-year-old and her seventeen-year-old lover (characteristically she did not know his name; to her he was simply "The Poet") were attacked by blacks; she was raped and he was beaten insensible. In California a seller of drugs was murdered and his right forearm hacked off. A few days later another peddler was killed, stuffed into a sleeping bag, and left hanging from a cliff.

Clearly something ghastly was happening to that summer. Exploiters and predators were also stalking the young. In *The Family* Ed Sanders compared the flower movement to "a valley of plump rabbits surrounded by wounded coyotes." He wrote: "One almost had to live there to understand the frenzy that engulfed the Haight-Ashbury district of San Francisco in the spring and summer of 1967. The word was out all over America to come to San Francisco for love and flowers." But more awaited them in Hashbury than that. "The Haight attracted vicious criminals who grew long hair. Bikers tried to take over the LSD market with crude sadistic tactics. Bad dope was sold by acne-faced methedrine punks. Satanist and satanist-rapist death-freaks flooded the whirling crash pads. People began getting ripped off in the parks. There was racial trouble." In the midst of it, haunting Grateful Dead concerts in the Avalon Ballroom, was a bearded little psychotic who liked to curl up in a fetal position right on the dance floor, and whose secret ambitions were to persuade girls to perform fellatio with dogs and gouge out the eyes of a beautiful actress and smear them on walls. Later he would be well remembered in Hashbury. His name was Charles Manson.

Hippiedom would survive in one form or another, as beatism had —the bohemian strain runs wide and deep in America—but the movement as it had been known that year was doomed. All that was lacking was a final curtain. That came on the night of Saturday, October 8, 1967. A generation earlier, on June 8, 1931, the death of a New York girl bearing the singularly poetic name of Starr Faithfull had symbolized the magic and the depravity of an era then ending; John O'Hara had based *Butterfield 8* on it. Now the squalid Manhattan murder of another genteel girl ended the hippy summer of 1967. Her name was Linda Rae Fitzpatrick. She was eighteen, a blonde, the daughter of a wealthy spice and tea importer. Her home of record was her parents' mansion in Greenwich, Connecticut, but on Sunday, October 9, her naked corpse was found in a boiler room of a brownstone tenement at 169 Avenue B on the Lower East Side.

It was not a good address. Flanked by a flyblown junk shop and a dingy bar and grill, the boiler room reeked of dog excrement and rotting garbage. One naked light bulb shone down on peeling paint, decaying plaster, whitewashed bricks crawling with cockroaches, and a filthy mattress. Linda had come to this noisome trysting place with a tattooed drifter named James "Groovy" Hutchinson. As detectives and the police surgeon put the story together, she had stripped and sprawled on the mattress. At that point Linda and Groovy had discovered that they were not alone. This room was often used as an exchange point for the sale of drugs, and four speed-freaks, all of them flying, decided to share Groovy's girl with him. She refused. When Groovy tried to defend her, his face was bashed in with a brick. After Linda had been raped four times, her face was smashed, too. The bodies had been left face up; her black lace pants were found in a corner.

Three Negro men were swiftly arrested, but the public was more interested in the girl than in her victimizers. Linda had apparently led two lives. In Greenwich she had been the sheltered, well-bred child of an upper-class home. Like her parents she had been an Episcopalian; her favorite relaxation had been riding on the red-leafed bridle paths of the exclusive Round Hill Stables. The previous August, her father recalled, he had expressed his abhorrence of hippies, and her comments had been "much like mine." Her mother recalled that "Linda was never terribly boy crazy. She was very shy." Over Labor Day weekend she had told her mother that she didn't want to return to Oldfields, her expensive boarding school in Maryland. Instead she wanted to live in New York and paint. "After all," her mother said afterward, "Linda's whole life was art. She had a burning desire to be something in the art world." Her parents agreed to her plan when she told them she had a room in a respectable Greenwich Village hotel. Her roommate, she said, was a twenty-two-year-old receptionist of a good family called Paula Bush.

"*Paula* Bush?" said the desk clerk. "Sure, I remember Linda, but there wasn't no Paula Bush. It was *Paul* Bush." In East Village she had consorted with many men, her family learned, and she had used money sent from Greenwich to buy drugs for them and herself. Late in September she thought she was pregnant, and she had confided to another girl that she was worried about the effect of LSD on the baby. Saturday evening, three hours before she died, she had told a friend that she had just shot some speed and was riding high. The cruelest part of the sequel for her parents was the discovery that her East Village acquaintances were indifferent to her death. One hippy girl said that though they mourned Groovy, "The chick wasn't anything to us."

In San Francisco's Golden Gate Park that same week hippies burned a gray coffin labeled "Summer of Love." In it were orange peels, peacock feathers, charms, flags, crucifixes, and a marijuana-flavored cookie. The ceremony was called "The Death of Hip." After the mourners had watched the fire while singing "God Bless America" and "Hare Krishna," they shouted, "Hippies are dead! Now the free men will come through!" Violence had crippled the movement, and so had commercialism. Tourists were crowding craft shops in both the Haight and East Village. Hippies hungering for money were acting in *Indian Givers,* a full-length psychedelic western, in which the sheriff was being played by, of all people, Dr. Timothy Leary. Ron Thelin, proprietor of San Francisco's Psychedelic Shop, said dolefully, "The spirit is gone"; then he went out of business, and Roger Ricco, a veteran member of The Group Image, said, "It isn't the same any more. Where have all the flowers gone?"

Portrait of an American

KARL HESS III

EITHER/OR.

As Karl Hess saw it, every serious man was obliged to take an unyielding stand at one extreme or the other.

Either he was a Minuteman or a Weatherman, a hard-core,

better-dead-than-Red ultraconservative or a New Left militant, a Klansman or a Black Panther, an anti-Semite or a gunman of the Symbionese Liberation Army. If you didn't want the SAC to lob one into the men's room at the Kremlin, you must advocate blowing up the Pan Am Building. There was no middle ground, just one faith and one enemy of the faith, one way to save the world and one way to destroy it. Society was not marvelously complex; it was magnificently simple. One must merely choose between absolutes, between the black and the white, the good and the evil.

In 1954, as a sleek, well-paid spokesman of the ultraconservative right, he wrote in *The American Mercury:*

> It would not be America really if it did not produce men who suddenly tire of palaver and reach for the rifle on the wall, to use themselves or to hand to the underdog who needs it.

In 1970, as a bearded, ragged oracle of the SDS and the Black Panthers, he proudly displayed an announcement of his appearance on the University of Texas campus:

> Union Speakers Comm. (the people who brought you Abbie Hoffman) present: Karl Hess, farout freak, militant, commie, anarchist, pervert!!! Currently assoc. editor of *Ramparts.*

He never saw that the two poles were really one. Superficially it seemed that he had swung from one to the other. In fact he had not budged an inch. He ended where he had begun—at the farthest possible distance from the political center.

Born on a great Philippines estate in 1923, he was molded not by his father, a flamboyant millionaire, but by his mother, a former Washington, D.C., working girl. When strong-minded Thelma Hess discovered that her husband was a philanderer, she left him, returned to Washington with young Karl, and went to work as a switchboard operator rather than accept alimony. She made a rule: before her little son could have a toy, he must read a book. Entering kindergarten, he had finished H. G. Wells's *Outline of History.*

By the time he reached adolescence the husky young Hess had read more than his teachers, and they bored him. To him education was an organized bureaucracy. Already, at fourteen, he had identified the system as his enemy. He fought it by enrolling in two high schools, filing the transfer papers of each at the other. Lying about his age—he looked older than his years—Hess got a job at the Mutual radio network. He was writing news programs when he borrowed his boss's car one day. A policeman gave him a ticket, his true age was discovered, and he was fired. The system had won. It always would, but he would never quit struggling.

Next, as a copyboy on the *Alexandria Gazette*, he became fascinated with politics; that, too, would be a lifelong obsession. The Democrats repelled him. He became a right-wing Republican because the ultraconservatives championed individual liberty. Whatever the merit of his views, there was no questioning his ability. By his twentieth birthday he was a rising star on the *Washington Daily News*. Then the editor phoned him at home to say that FDR had died and he was assigned to the story. Hess replied that Roosevelt's obituary wasn't worth getting out of bed; he was fired.

He became news editor of *Aviation Week*, author of a children's book on natural science, editor of *Fisherman Magazine*, and, between 1950 and 1955, press editor at *Newsweek*. Had he been able to shuck his ideological yoke, he might have had a distinguished journalistic career. As it was, he became increasingly preoccupied with right-wing doctrine, writing an anti-Communist column for the conservative weekly *Pathfinder*, editing *Counter-Attack* and H. L. Hunt's *Facts Forum*, and founding the *National Review* with, among others, William F. Buckley Jr. At the same time he was contributing regularly to the *American Mercury*. In its pages he denounced Robert Oppenheimer, the United Nations, and critics of the National Rifle Association, in which he held a lifetime membership. ("If everybody in Latin America had a pistol, they would have democracy.") The National Guard, he declared, was the country's greatest protection against federal dictatorship. He believed in order, deference to military rank, and the "discipline that comes from respect of an obedience to authority."

By 1960 Hess's lyrical praise of rugged individualism had brought him a sinecure as assistant to the president of Ohio's vast Champion Paper and Fibre Company. He lived in an expensive suburban home with a wife, two children, and seventeen custom-made suits. His job at Champion was to discourage aggressive union organizers and instill loyalty to the company in employees. From time to time the firm loaned him to right-wing think tanks. He compiled *The Conservative Papers* for Congressman Melvin Laird. In 1960 he wrote policy papers for Richard Nixon, and in 1964, as Barry Goldwater's chief adviser, he dashed off the speech in which the senator accepted his party's nomination. Goldwater, he said, offered "a choice, not an echo."

Then something snapped. Lyndon Johnson not only won the election; he won it with contributions from the very big businessmen who had been Hess's heroes. Hess discovered that the backer of one of his right-wing publications had been enriched by federal agricultural subsidies. Most traumatic of all, the magnitude of the Goldwater defeat had made Hess a pariah in GOP circles. By custom, men who have served ably in a losing campaign may expect a job in the service of other members of the party who are still in office. On Capitol Hill he went from door to door, hoping for a place on some Republican payroll. He found none. No one wanted him in any capacity. By the following spring he was broke and desperate, ready to settle for a place as a Capitol elevator operator. Even that was closed to him. He wound up welding bulldozers on the night shift in a Washington machine shop.

That was the year of Johnson's first big Vietnam build-up. Hess was appalled by it. This was the system run amok. He perceived his error, and concluded that "my enemy was not a particular state —not Cuba or North Vietnam, for example—but the state itself." As he saw it, the anti-Communist zeal of ultraconservatives had led them into a tragic error. They had trusted federal power, and had reaped the triumph of bureaucracy. His new heroes were the Panthers, who called for power to the people, and the Weathermen: "The SDS is raising essential political questions, and the police are beating them down for it." He began to read anarchist literature and to recommend resistance to authority—flouting of the law, draft resistance, hiding of political prisoners, refusing to move if the government condemns your house.

Slowly his life-style changed. He left his wife and grew a beard. The custom-made suits were left in the closet; he now wore a Castro cap, tennis shoes without socks, a tattered field jacket, and faded green denims. Because he refused to pay his taxes, he wasn't allowed to own property. He lived on the Anacostia River, in a houseboat belonging to a girlfriend. To a reporter he said, "I splice lines, paint the deck, and plot against the state." His plotting was limited to lecturing on campuses, exhorting Panther rallies, and writing for *Ramparts* and *Hard Times*, but the FBI was watching him carefully.

His old friends, who were now running the government under Nixon, were dumbfounded. In the corridors of power they whispered stories about him. He was poaching on federal property. He had competed in a motorcycle race and broken a leg. He was seen in the company of known felons, trotting around the District with a knapsack on his back. He had advocated the expropriation of all public and corporate wealth, was carrying an IWW membership card, had been arrested in an antiwar riot, had been gassed in a march on Fort Dix, had spoken at a radical rally from a stage dominated by an enormous black flag, had won a *Playboy* award for the best nonfiction article of the year—a paean to libertarianism.

Aboard the houseboat *Tranquil* the soft-voiced, beefily handsome Hess continued to scheme away. Mounted on the fore bulkhead was his beloved rifle, representing his everlasting belief in the right of a man to protect himself from the bureaucrats who would enslave him. Papers surrounded him: drafts of speeches, notes for an autobiography, pamphlets, the manuscript of a book on the wickedness of the capitalist state. He lamented as "tragic, very tragic" the fact "that Goldwater has now taken his stand on the side of established authority." He had heard that the senator refused to talk about him, but he understood that. "I wouldn't be surprised," he said reflectively, "if Barry thinks I'm crazy."

Thirty-three

THE YEAR EVERYTHING WENT WRONG

I T WAS THE YEAR of the Hong Kong flu and *Hair*. The hundred-and-twenty-one-year-old Pennsylvania Railroad and the hundred-and-fourteen-year-old New York Central merged, and service was twice as bad. First-class postage went from five cents an ounce to six. Helen Keller, Edna Ferber, and John Steinbeck died. Mia Farrow divorced Frank Sinatra. The American ambassador to Guatemala was assassinated.

In Washington the Willard Hotel, where at least seven Presidents, beginning with Franklin Pierce, had been guests at one time or another, went bankrupt. Red China, as it was still called then, exploded its seventh atom bomb, France its first hydrogen bomb. Hitler's bones turned up in Russia. A U.S. Strategic Air Command B-52 crashed in Greenland, near Thule, spilling wreckage contaminated with plutonium-235 over miles of ice, the thirteenth such accident. Biafra starved.

Some things went right. Barbra Streisand was marvelous in *Funny Girl*. Julie Nixon married David Eisenhower. Network censors cut Pete Seeger singing an antiwar song from a Smothers Brothers show, but six months later they changed their minds and let him do it. It was a big year for heart transplants, although only one patient in four lived more than six months. The *Washington Daily News* reported that one out of every eight Americans was getting social security benefits. Tiny Tim tiptoed into the limelight. The American Civil Liberties Union decided to support draft evaders.

Laugh-In provided some lively graffiti: "Little Orphan Annie—call the eye bank," "This is your slum—keep it clean," "Forest fires prevent bears," and "George Wallace—your sheets are ready." Publishers issued John Updike's *Couples,* Charles Portis's *True Grit,* and Peter De Vries's *The Cat's Pajamas and Witch's Milk.* It was also the year of Allen Drury's *Preserve and Protect.* "When," asked *Time,* "will Drury cease and desist?"

The general thrust of events was suggested by the disclosure that the Defense Department budget this year would be 72 billion dollars, a record and a depressing one. (Roosevelt's *entire* annual budget, when he was accused of sending the country into the poorhouse, had been 8.8 billion dollars.) New Jersey Congressman Charles S. Joelson, told that the gun control bill had been watered down and that he would have to live with the new version, replied that "tens of thousands of Americans can die with it." The great American traffic jam became denser with the announcement, by the U.S. Bureau of the Census and Public Roads Administration, that 99.9 million automobiles were now registered in the United States, that 78.6 percent of all families owned at least one car, and that every fourth family owned two or more. If a man was younger than twenty-one the chances were that he had sideburns and wore bellbottoms. The young expressed approval of something by calling it "tough" or saying it had "soul" or was "out of sight," and if you didn't agree you were either straight or sick.

That year Dancer's Image won the Kentucky Derby, was disqualified on charges that he had been drugged, and then, to confuse everyone, was designated the official winner—while losing the purse to the runner-up.

In West Virginia the Consolidated Coal Company's No. 9 mine blew, entombing seventy-eight men. The U.S. submarine *Scorpion* was lost with ninety-nine men, which would have been the greatest naval disaster of the year had it not been overshadowed by the spectacular fate of another U.S. ship in the waters off North Korea.

The U.S.S. *Pueblo* was labeled an "environmental research ship" by the Pentagon, but she was really an electronic snoop, bristling with antennas and complicated radar gear which enabled her to cruise slowly through the Sea of Japan, taking readings of what was happening to North Korean electronic devices on land. This was perfectly legal, provided she stayed twelve miles out. The North

Koreans knew all about her. During the first two weeks of her first mission in 1968 they had tried to distract her with patrol boats and, overhead, low-flying MIGs. Her crew was therefore not surprised when, on January 23, a fleet of PTs sailed out and began circling her. Then one of the small boats signaled: "Heave to or I will open fire on you." That was new. Commander Lloyd M. Bucher, the *Pueblo*'s captain, replied, "I am in international waters." The PT said: "Follow in my wake." Bucher ignored that until another boat began backing toward him. Seeing that its fenders were rigged with rope mats and rubber tubes to cushion a collision, Bucher radioed his base in Japan: "These fellows are serious." Before the boarding party could arrive, he ordered his men to destroy as much of his intelligence ship's secret equipment as they could, shredding codes and wrecking the gear with sledgehammers, axes, and hand grenades.

The news that a U.S. Navy vessel had been captured—the first since the British seized the U.S.S. *Chesapeake* in 1807—stunned the United States. Dean Rusk said it was "a matter of the utmost gravity" and an "act of war." Republican Senator Wallace F. Bennett of Utah demanded that American ships storm Wonsan harbor, recapture the *Pueblo*, and free her crew. Democratic Senator Thomas J. Dodd wanted the Navy to seize all ships flying the North Korean flag "wherever they may be found on the high seas." Most of Washington took the advice of Rusk to remain calm, however. North Dakota's Karl Mundt, no appeaser, pointed out that "We have enough war worries on our hands without looking for another one." Others on the Hill said that belligerence would merely doom the *Pueblo*'s crew. Two appeals to Russia, asking the Soviet Union to act as mediator, were rejected. Arthur Goldberg, the former Supreme Court justice who was now U.S. ambassador to the United Nations, tried to get the U.N. Security Council to review the incident. He failed.

In the end the case was taken up by American and North Korean negotiators in the tin-roofed Panmunjom shed where the armistice between their armies had been negotiated fifteen years ago. Meanwhile the North Korean Central News Agency was broadcasting what was called a confession by Commander Bucher, saying that he had committed a "criminal act" and "an act of sheer aggression" for which he had "no excuse whatever." An open letter from the commander and his crew said that they were being "provided with all the necessities of life," but the letter was stilted, almost in pidgin English, and therefore not reassuring. In the United States bumper stickers appeared reading, "Remember the *Pueblo*," as though it were possible to forget.

Exactly one week after the seizure of the *Pueblo*, the North Vietnamese launched their most spectacular offensive of the war three thousand miles to the south. General Westmoreland was expecting it, and he thought he knew where it would come: at the big U.S. Marine Corps base at Khe Sanh. Khe Sanh was in many ways like Dienbienphu, the bottom of a red clay, shell-pocked bowl of hills athwart the Communist enemy's chief infiltration route to the south. "This is the cork," an American major explained to reporters. "If they can get past us, they can tear up the countryside way over to the coast."

The bowl was in fact an enemy objective, and was invested by 20,000 North Vietnamese troops. It was to remain under siege for seventy-six days before Operation Pegasus, a force of 30,000 American troops, could break the siege. But Khe Sanh wasn't the chief target of General Nguyen Vo Giap. Giap planned instead to attack almost every population center of any size in South Vietnam.

Tet, the lunar New Year, was observed with a kind of fatalistic gaiety in South Vietnam's cities on the evening of Tuesday, January 30. The next day would be the first of the Year of the Monkey, the most inauspicious of them all. It was going to be worse than they dreamed. Evidence of that was around them, had they known how and where to look. One sign was the large number of husky young strangers arriving in the towns by sampan, scooter, and bicycle. Another was the incredible number of funerals, celebrated with the traditional gongs, flutes, firecrackers, and coffins—coffins packed, it would later be learned, with things other than corpses. Shortly after midnight, when those who had celebrated Tet were fast asleep, the strangers—all members of elite Viet Cong units—assembled and assaulted key points in the capital and a hundred other cities from one end of the country to another: police stations, military bases, government buildings, radio and power stations, and foreign embassies, including that of the United States, which had just been rebuilt after the last terrorist raid at a cost of two and a half million dollars.

Altogether some 60,000 Viet Cong were being committed to the

Tet attack. After twenty-five days of the offensive they controlled large areas of the countryside, including most of the Mekong Delta. Inch by inch American and South Vietnamese troops drove them from the large population centers. The biggest battle was for the ancient imperial city of Hue, where 70 percent of the homes were in ruins. It was of Ben Tre, after air and artillery strikes there had routed the Communists, that an American officer made the memorable comment: "It became necessary to destroy the town to save it." After counting enemy bodies and finding that there were many more of them than of Americans and South Vietnamese, U.S. commanders triumphantly announced that they had won. President Johnson told a press conference that in military terms the Viet Cong drive had been "a complete failure." On television Secretary McNamara said, "It is quite clear that the military objective . . . has not been achieved."

"If this is failure," said Senator George D. Aiken of Vermont, "I hope the Viet Cong never have a major success." Robert F. Kennedy of New York warned against "the delusion" that the Tet campaign constituted "some sort of victory," and Eugene McCarthy of Minnesota said that "if capturing a section of the American embassy and several large cities constitutes complete failure, I suppose by this logic that if the Viet Cong captured the entire country, the administration would be claiming their total collapse." Another senator probably spoke for the largest number of Americans when he asked in bewilderment, "What happened? I thought we were supposed to be winning this war." Certainly that was what the country had been told. Only two months ago General Westmoreland had reported that he could see light at the end of the tunnel. And now this.

As David Halberstam later pointed out, the real casualties of the Tet offensive were "the credibility of the American strategy of attrition" and "the credibility of the man who was by now Johnson's most important political ally"—Westmoreland. If Westmoreland was no longer believable on the war, neither was Johnson. His administration began to come unstuck. John Gardner resigned as Secretary of Health, Education, and Welfare. Goldberg quit the U.N. McNamara left the Pentagon and was replaced by Clark Clifford.

By April 19, 1968, the American force level in Vietnam had risen to 549,000 troops. U.S. combat deaths reached 22,951, and on Sunday, June 23, the war became the longest in American history, surpassing the War of Independence. Both of President Johnson's sons-in-law were there, which in another time would have elicited sympathy for him. But bitterness over the war was too intense now. Draft evaders and Army deserters were forming colonies in Canada and Sweden. Then, as summer and the national conventions of 1968 approached, two events swelled the ranks of the protesters: General Westmoreland asked for 206,000 more men and his headquarters announced that "the Khe Sanh base in Quang Tri province is being inactivated." So much for the cork. All those Marine Corps casualties, all that bravery, and now the general didn't even want it.

On April 10 the White House announced a change in command for U.S. troops in Vietnam. On June 30 the new chief would be a West Point classmate of Westmoreland's, General Creighton Abrams. ("A tough, plain-speaking New Englander," *Time* called him, ". . . who could inspire aggressiveness in a begonia.") What was needed was a man who could preside over an orderly withdrawal, for it was increasingly evident that it would come to that sooner or later. For a time there was hope that it might be soon. In May Hanoi proposed peace talks in Paris. They were scheduled to begin May 10 in the old Hotel Majestic, with Averell Harriman facing Xuan Thuy, who had retired as Ho Chi Minh's foreign minister three years earlier.

But nothing had changed. Six weeks of tortuous diplomacy were required before delegations could be brought into the same room, and then they quarreled about the shape of the table. Meantime enemy attacks had made May the bloodiest month of the war, with 2,000 Americans killed. President Johnson told American Legion and VFW conventions that there could be no truce until the Viet Cong showed some "restraint." Harriman advised him that that seemed unlikely. Clark Clifford toured Vietnam and reported that the Communists were "refitting, regrouping, and rearming" for another blitz. General Abrams studied Westmoreland's plans for a new campaign. They bore the code name Operation Complete Victory.

Angered by Nick Katzenbach's brusque claim that the Tonkin Gulf resolution was sufficient authority for waging war in Vietnam, Senator Eugene McCarthy was further aroused, in October 1967, by Dean Rusk's remark that the real threat to American security was "a billion Chinese." Afterward McCarthy said, "At this point,

I thought I would call a halt." Urged by Allard K. Lowenstein, the leader of an antiwar campaign in search of a candidate, the Minnesota senator filed for the New Hampshire presidential primary. The polls predicted he would get at most 20 percent of the Democratic vote, but two factors increased his chances: the Tet offensive and the support of thousands of college student workers who shaved, scrubbed, and dressed to be "clean for Gene."

On March 12, the day of the primary, McCarthy electrified the country by polling 42 percent of the vote to Johnson's 48 percent. If Republican crossovers were counted, he almost defeated the President, with 28,791 to Johnson's 29,201. Suddenly LBJ looked beatable. The most important immediate consequence of the vote was its impact on Robert F. Kennedy. Kennedy hadn't entered the primary, and as recently as January 20 he had said, "I would not oppose Lyndon Johnson under any foreseeable circumstances." He had explained then that he hesitated because his campaign would divide the party "in a very damaging way." Now he declared that he was "reassessing" his position, and on the Saturday after the New Hampshire primary he elated his admirers—and infuriated McCarthy's—by declaring: "I am announcing today my candidacy for the Presidency of the United States."

The next big primary was in Wisconsin, and the news from there was bad for Johnson. His organization was disintegrating; even the sons and daughters of loyal Democratic politicians there were stumping for McCarthy. Kennedy wasn't entered there, but each day's newspaper brought fresh evidence of his growing strength. Theodore Sorensen, Kenneth O'Donnell, and Arthur Schlesinger had joined his team, and Lawrence F. O'Brien had resigned as postmaster general to manage it. With that as background, President Johnson went on television March 31. He had ordered a reduction in the bombing of Vietnam, he said, and he spoke of the strife in the country, with "all of its ugly consequences." The nation needed unity, he said. Then:

"I have concluded that I should not permit the Presidency to become involved in the partisan divisions that are developing in this political year . . . I do not believe that I should devote an hour or a day of my time to any personal partisan causes . . . Accordingly, I shall not seek, and I will not accept, the nomination of my party for another term as your President."

Once the impact of Johnson's withdrawal had worn off, it became clear that the contest for the Democratic nomination was going to be a three-way race between McCarthy, Kennedy, and, once he was ready to declare, Vice President Humphrey. Of the three, only McCarthy was on the Wisconsin ballot; he had been running against Johnson there. It was too late to take the President's name off the ballot; McCarthy took 57.6 percent of the Democratic primary vote while Nixon, whose most serious opponents had been George Romney and Nelson Rockefeller, polled 81.3 percent of the Republican vote.

Humphrey announced his candidacy on April 27. Except for Oregon, in which McCarthy won narrowly, the rest of the primaries were all Kennedy. His strongest stands were against the war and for the poor and underprivileged. The leaders of the black movement were his natural allies. This was especially true of Martin Luther King, who had reached the conclusion that Vietnam was the largest serious obstacle to progress for his people; Negroes provided more than their share of combat troops, and money which should have been spent in the ghettos was going into the war. King said: "No one can pretend that the existence of the war is not profoundly affecting the destiny of civil rights progress."

In April 1968 King was in Memphis, supporting a two-month-old strike by 1,300 garbage men, most of them black. Newspapers had taunted him for staying at a plush Holiday Inn, paying $29 a night there, so he moved to a $13-a-night room in the Negro-owned Lorraine Motel. Before dinner on April 4 he was leaning on the second-floor iron railing outside room number 306 talking to fellow workers below. In a nondescript rooming house across the street a sniper crouched with a scope-sighted 30.06 Remington pump rifle. He fired one shot. It penetrated King's neck and exploded against his jaw, cutting his spinal column. He fell away from the rail and against the motel's wall, his hands rigid, reaching for his head.

Martin Luther King had been the greatest prophet of nonviolence since Gandhi, and it was the final irony of his life that the end of it should touch off the worst outburst of arson, looting, and criminal activity in the nation's history. In all, 168 cities and towns were stricken. Washington was the worst hit. An incredible 711 fires were set there. "Get your gun," Stokely Carmichael told blacks, and many did. There were ten deaths in the capital alone, one of them a white man who was dragged from his car and stabbed. President Johnson ordered the flag at half-mast on all federal buildings, the first time this had been done for a Negro, but the terror continued. Buildings within a few blocks of the White House were put to the torch. Nationwide, 2,600 fires were set, 2,600 people were arrested and 21,270 injured. To restore order 55,000 soldiers were required—ten times the number of marines defending Khe Sanh.

Accompanied by the music of spirituals and the tolling of church bells, Martin Luther King's coffin was transported to the grave on an old farm cart drawn by two mules. An estimated 120 million Americans watched the funeral march on television. There were between 50,000 and 100,000 marchers, including most of the nation's leaders, among them Robert Kennedy, Eugene McCarthy, Nelson Rockefeller, and Hubert Humphrey. Governor Lester Maddox of Georgia did not attend, although the funeral was in his state. Maddox refused to close the schools and protested lowering the flag to half-staff. But the man he refused to honor could never again be hurt by bigotry. The words of his epitaph, hewn in his tomb of Georgia marble, were from an old slave hymn; he had used them to close his oration at the Washington march five years before:

> Free at last, free at last;
> Thank God Almighty, I'm free at last.

John Willard, the name the sniper had used in renting the room from which he fired the shot, was an alias for Eric Starvo Galt, which also turned out to be an alias. Witnesses at the scene of the assassination had seen him race off in a white Mustang bearing Alabama license plates and Mexican tourist stickers. The car was found abandoned in Atlanta, Georgia. The FBI learned that he had bought it for $2,000—cash—using the Galt name. A fugitive now, sought by police around the world, he fled to Toronto. There he adopted a new alias, Ramon George Sneyd, and acquired a Canadian passport by the only procedure necessary—swearing that was his name. Buying a $345 excursion ticket to Europe, he spent two days in Portugal before flying to London. There he vanished, no doubt he thought for good.

But he had made one irrevocable error. His fingerprints had been found in the Memphis rooming house. After a fifteen-day search in the 53,000 prints of wanted men in the Department of Justice, the FBI identified him as James Earl Ray. He had a long record of convictions for forgery, car theft, and armed robbery. In April

1967 Ray had escaped from the Missouri state penitentiary. Now Canadian Mounties picked up his trail from the FBI, and customs officials throughout Europe were alerted to be on the lookout for Ramon G. Sneyd. On June 8 he was picked up at London's Heathrow Airport. Extradited and handcuffed, he was flown back wearing a bulletproof vest, his legs encased in armored trousers; no one wanted another Oswald. He was transported to the Memphis jail in a six-and-a-half-ton truck. Heavy steel plates blocked his cell window. He pleaded guilty and was sentenced to ninety-nine years. The source of his money was never discovered.

Almost two months to the day after Martin Luther King was struck down, and the same week that Ray was arrested, another act of mindless violence cut down the front runner for the Democratic presidential nomination. "An assassin never changed the course of history," Robert Kennedy had said after his brother's death in Dallas, but it wasn't true; that one had, and now his did, too. He had beaten Eugene McCarthy in the Indiana primary, 42 percent to 27, and in Nebraska 51 to 31. On this day, Tuesday, June 4, 1968, he had defeated both Hubert Humphrey—in Humphrey's native state, South Dakota—and McCarthy in the biggest of all the primaries, California.

Kennedy had spent that morning on a beach near Los Angeles with six of his ten children and his wife Ethel, who was pregnant with their eleventh. He followed election reports in suite 512 of the city's Ambassador Hotel. At midnight he took the elevator down to his headquarters in the hotel's Embassy Room and spoke briefly to the elated volunteers there. At the end he said: "So my thanks to all of you and it's on to Chicago, and let's win there." Friends and members of his immediate entourage mimicked his accent, saying: "And it's on to The Factory," that being the name of the popular discotheque where they were going to celebrate with him. But first he had to say a few words in the press room. The crowd was so dense between the rostrum and the Embassy Room's entrance that one member of the party suggested that they leave by a back passageway. Bill Barry, the former FBI agent who was Kennedy's bodyguard, objected. He didn't like the idea. But the senator said, "It's all right," and they stepped into a hot, smelly corridor. Kennedy paused there to shake hands with a seventeen-year-old busboy, Jesus Perez, and answer a question about Humphrey: "It just goes back to the struggle for it—"

He never finished. A Pasadena reporter saw an arm and a gun come out of a knot of spectators. The assassin propped his right elbow on a serving counter and fired at Kennedy, just four feet away. He pumped off all eight shots in the snub-nosed Iver-Johnson revolver before Rafer Johnson, an Olympic champion and a Kennedy friend, could knock the pistol out of his hand. Six men lay bleeding on the floor of the hall, five with slight injuries. The sixth, Kennedy, was wounded mortally. One of the two bullets which had hit him was relatively harmless, but the other had pierced his skull and entered his brain. Ethel knelt beside him. Bobby asked for water. Then he asked, "Is everybody safe?" The busboy gave him a crucifix. Bobby's fingers held the beads, and Ethel prayed, and Roosevelt Grier, the three-hundred-pound Los Angeles Rams' lineman, held the slight, dark assassin in a bear hug.

"Why did you do it?" one member of the party yelled. The killer screamed, "I can explain! Let me explain!" Jesse Unruh, leader of California Democrats, shouted at him, "Why him? Why him?" The gunman answered: "I did it for my country." That seemed preposterous. Then the truth began to emerge. In his psychotic way he really believed he was being patriotic. To everyone else in Los Angeles this had been the day of the California primary, but to Kennedy's murderer it was the first anniversary of the Israeli-Arab six-day war. His name was Sirhan Bishara Sirhan, he was a native of Jordan, and he hated Israel, which Kennedy admired. On the surface that appeared to be the only motive the swarthy little Arab had.

The dying Kennedy was first taken to the Central Receiving Hospital and then to the larger Good Samaritan Hospital. Kept alive by adrenalin injections and by cardiac massage, he underwent surgery almost at once. But it was hopeless. At 1:44, after a few flutterings of life, he died. Lyndon Johnson denounced the country's "insane traffic" in guns. Then he sent a presidential jet to bring the body home, and once more the Kennedys and their friends flew eastward with a coffin in a Boeing 707. The United Nations lowered its flag to half-mast, an unprecedented tribute to one who had never been a chief of state. When the plane arrived in New York ten thousand people had already lined up outside St. Patrick's Cathedral to say goodbye. Candles were placed at each corner of the catafalque, and friends took turns standing vigil. Ted Kennedy, the surviving Kennedy brother, acted as paterfamilias, delivering the eulogy in a trembling voice.

Richard Cardinal Cushing presided. Andy Williams sang "The Battle Hymn of the Republic"; the choir, the Hallelujah Chorus. Then the motorcade proceeded to Pennsylvania Station, where a special train waited, drawn by two black engines. Its destination was Washington, but the crowds standing by the tracks along the way were so great that the trip took eight hours. By then it was night in the capital. With only streetlamps as illumination, the cavalcade wound past the city's huge dark government buildings and across the Potomac, to Arlington. There Bob's grave waited, a dark scar beneath a magnolia tree a few feet from his brother's tombstone. After a brief, simple service there the flag was folded in a triangle and presented to Ethel. The band played:

> *America! America!*
> *God shed his grace on thee!*
> *And crown thy good with brotherhood,*
> *From sea to shining sea!*

Between January 1 and June 15 of 1968 there were 221 major demonstrations, involving nearly 39,000 students, on 101 American campuses. Buildings were dynamited, college presidents and deans were roughed up, obscenities were painted on walls and shouted at policemen, sometimes by well-bred daughters of good families at the ivied Seven Sister colleges for women. Among the institutions of higher learning disrupted by student violence during those months were Temple in Philadelphia, the State University of New York in Buffalo, Oberlin, Princeton, Duke, Chicago's Roosevelt University, Southern Illinois University, Boston University, Marquette, Tufts, Stanford, Colgate, Howard, the University of Oregon, Northwestern, Ohio State, Barnard, Mills College, the University of Connecticut, Trinity, Tuskegee, the University of Chicago, Bowie State in Maryland, UCLA, the University of Miami—

And, of course, Columbia.

Until the third week after the assassination of Martin Luther King the newsiest event on the Morningside Heights campus was its reversal of a decision, made the year before, to accept a gift of royalties from the leasing of a new cigarette filter invented by Robert Strickman, an industrial chemist. That had brought much unwelcome publicity, but the Columbia uprising of April 1968 was much worse. It was the biggest campus confrontation since the Berkeley turmoil four years earlier, and in a way it was more significant, for it marked the emergence of the Students for a Democratic Society. Until then SDS was known to the public as merely one more campus political student organization. After eight years it had 5,500 members, chapters at 200 colleges, and a characteristic student distaste for centralization. In the mid-1960s SDS had become committed to militancy, however. Its leaders were avowed enemies of oppression, racism, and imperialism, all three of them as defined by SDS. It held that American universities had become corrupted by them, and that Columbia was especially wicked.

A college marching song popular among undergraduates on Morningside Heights in merrier days went:

> *Who owns New York?*
> *Who owns New York?*
> *Why, we own New York!*
> *Why, we own New York!*
> *Who?*
> *C-O-L-U-M-B-I-A!*

The SDS reminded fellow students that in fact the university did own 230 million dollars' worth of real estate in Manhattan, including the land under Rockefeller Center, and that much of it was occupied by deteriorating Harlem tenements nearby, making Columbia, in effect, a big slumlord. Six years earlier the university had unwittingly provided the fuel for an eventual explosion by leasing from the city an additional 2.1 acres of nearby Morningside Heights Park's thirty acres. The idea was to build a magnificent 11.6-million-dollar gymnasium there. Negroes living in the adjacent, bottle-strewn Harlem slum would be welcome to enjoy a free gym and swimming pool on the ground floor; the university's department of physical education would use the upper floors. Since the neighborhood was at present infested with prostitutes and drug addicts, with one of the highest crime rates in the city, Columbia's trustees assumed that every resident with a spark of civic pride would embrace the project. They were wrong.

Protesting tenants called the plan "a land grab," and "a desecration of a public park." At that point the university's administration blundered. An architect's conception of the gym was published showing an elaborate, expensive entrance facing the campus and a small, plain door facing Harlem. Leaders of the community group denounced the "separate but unequal facilities," the chairman of the Harlem CORE angrily charged that "This community is being raped," and one hundred and fifty demonstrators shouting "Gym Crow must go!" marched to the gymnasium site and tore down a section of fence. White participants included Mark Rudd, the chairman of Columbia's SDS, and as many followers as he had been able to muster.

Rudd was the kind of New Leftist that J. Edgar Hoover dreamed about. Hoover had just described the SDS as "a militant youth group which receives support from the Communist Party, and which in turn supports Communist objectives and tactics." Columbia students said sarcastically, "The Communists can't take over SDS—they can't find it." It did in fact have few members there. However, their penchant for outrageous words and for outrages themselves gave them, in a phrase of the time, a high profile. Rudd was particularly noisy. On the day that the balloon went up over Morningside Heights he had just returned from a three-week visit to Castro's Cuba. As if to confirm Hoover, he praised it as an "extremely humanistic society."

His opposite number was Columbia's president, sixty-four-year-old Grayson Kirk, aloof, frosty, and a poor administrator. Later a commission headed by Archibald Cox would conclude that under Kirk the administration conveyed "an attitude of authoritarianism and invited mistrust." Kirk had been unresponsive earlier in April when SDS collected 1,500 signatures to a petition demanding that Columbia withdraw from the Institute for Defense Analysis (IDA), an organization of researchers working for the Pentagon on twelve campuses. SDS charged that IDA projects were "aimed at the oppression of the people in Vietnam" and included "riot equipment to commit mass genocide against black people" in the United States.

Leaving the downed fence at the putative gym site that Tuesday, Rudd and his band marched on ivy-covered Hamilton Hall, the headquarters of Columbia College. There, to their surprise, they were met by a conciliatory acting dean, who said that although he had "no intention of meeting any demands under a situation such as this," both the gym and IDA membership were negotiable issues. SDS wasn't interested in that now. Having tasted victory, the insurgents retained momentum by imprisoning the acting dean and two other officials for twenty-six hours. The siege of Columbia had begun.

During the first night the white students discovered something else: black power. The sixty Negro students among them demanded that the whites leave. SDS, they said, wasn't militant enough for them. One version had it that the blacks were carrying guns and planned a shoot-out with policemen. Their white soul brothers didn't think the gym was as bad as that. Some of them felt hurt. "Why should they run this thing?" one of them asked. "There's enough division and polarization in this country as it is." In any event, at 6 A.M. on the second day, Wednesday, April 24, Rudd announced that the whites weren't wanted in Hamilton Hall. Leaving it to the blacks, he and his honkies took over Low Library, where they put up a notice: "Liberated Area. Be Free to Join Us." President Kirk's office was in the library. They broke into it and ransacked it, photographing letters and documents, throwing others away, smoking his cigars, and drinking his sherry. And they had just begun. To reporters they said that they believed they were right in disrupting the university. They cited principles established at the Nuremberg trials of Nazi war criminals. Columbia's administration under Kirk, they said, was as bad as the Nazis.

There were seven hundred of them now. On Thursday a hundred seized Fayerweather Hall, the social science building. Another hundred took over Avery Hall, the architecture center, and on Friday a fifth hall was invaded. Over the balcony of that one they hung a banner: "Rudd Hall, Liberated Zone No. 5." They set up a command post and mimeographed proclamations. One demanded amnesty for all of them, but Kirk refused, saying that failure to take disciplinary action would "destroy the whole fabric of the university community." For a while it looked as though another group of students, the athletes, would evict the rebels. ("If this is a barbarian society," a wrestler said, "then it's survival of the fittest—and we're the fittest.") Kirk wanted no more violence, and he restrained them. He also made a concession: all work on the gymnasium was suspended. Not enough, the demonstrators shouted from the halls; they demanded secession from IDA and a lot of other things they had just thought up. Runners brought them food, blankets, and jars of vaseline. They wanted the vaseline because they had heard that it was protection from Mace. They expected Mace, fired by police.

They were right about the police coming. When the first detachment arrived on Morningside Heights, thirty members of Columbia's junior faculty barred the entrance to Low Hall. It was a deadlock. But then the university's trustees voted "to affirmatively direct" Kirk "to maintain the ultimate disciplinary power over the conduct of students." Thereupon he made what he later called "the most painful" decision of his life, to clear the buildings with force, if necessary—a thousand policemen in flying wedges. Hamilton Hall came first. The Negro students were docile. Black lawyers were there to represent them, and black police officers supervised the operation. After the Negroes left quietly, the building was found to be tidy.

The buildings occupied by whites were another matter. Whatever the provocation, the cops there clubbed, kicked, and punched the students, hurling them down concrete stairways. The police had assured spectators—there were several thousand of them—that they would be safe if they remained behind police barricades, but when it became clear that the spectators were prostudent, they, too, were charged and beaten. All in all, 698 were arrested. Rudd and 72 other students were suspended for a year. Cox was asked to investigate the disorders. After twenty-one days of testimony from seventy-nine witnesses, he and four colleagues issued a 222-page report which was highly critical of both the university administration and the police. While holding no brief for the student ringleaders, the report found that their behavior "was in no way commensurate with the [police] brutality," which had "caused violence on a harrowing scale." Kirk and his staff had "regularly put the students at the bottom" of their priorities, the commission found, concluding that the gym and the IDA issue had in fact been mere surface manifestations of deep student dissatisfaction with the Vietnam War and racism in the United States.

According to a *New York Times* survey, the militant whites in campus riots at Columbia and elsewhere typically came from well-to-do homes in suburbia, had parents who were politically liberal, were students in the humanities rather than the sciences, were brilliant in class, and were predominantly Jewish. An example was Ted Gold, twenty-one, with Rudd a leader in the Columbia uprising and an SDS chairman. Gold said to reporters: "We are working, not just for a revolutionary Columbia, but for a revolutionary America."

At some point in the 1960s a man who had never run a stop sign did it. He was careful, nothing was coming; it was a silly statute, he reasoned; only robots obeyed it. He ran another; in a month he was doing it without qualms, and in another month he was running red lights if they turned red just as he was approaching an intersection. Though he overlooked the connection, he was annoyed because the attendant at his favorite filling station no longer checked his oil and cleaned his windshield unless asked. He switched filling stations; it was the same there. At about the same time a door in his new car developed a hideous rattle; he dismantled it and found that some anonymous worker on a Detroit assembly line had left a Coke bottle in it.

These were little things, but there were others. One morning you found a notice in your milk box. No more milk; the company had stopped deliveries; you had to go to the store. The postal system was a disgrace. Everybody had his horror story about the mails. Waitresses brought you somebody else's order. Cab drivers couldn't find your destination. Your evening paper wasn't delivered. The druggist filled the wrong prescription. The new washer-dryer was a lemon. Deliverymen double-parked and wouldn't move. By the end of the Johnson years it was a national joke. People displayed little signs:

PLAN AHEAD

The building industry was disgraceful; you were lucky if the job was done six months after the date promised. Airliners were late taking off; because they didn't reach your destination on time you had to wait, stacked over it, and when you did land you discovered that your baggage had gone on to another airport. This was so common that frequent travelers bought luggage expressly designed to fit under their seats. Bus and train timetables were fictive. Nearly everyone was dunned at one time or another for bills that were already paid. Nothing, it seemed, functioned any more. From the plumbing and the television to the F-111 swing-wing jet, all was snafu. A New York woman, billed for transatlantic telephone calls she hadn't made, picked up her phone to protest and heard violins playing; a Muzak line had crossed hers. Rex Reed, the writer, tried to use a credit card and was arrested on the ground that Rex Reed was dead. *Time* reported a man who had emptied a pistol firing at a vending machine.

Repairmen and salesclerks were as bad, or worse. The fault was difficult to pin down, but it was everywhere. People didn't seem to care whether things worked any more. The discipline that knits a society together was weakening and at some points giving way altogether. John Kenneth Galbraith attributed it to prosperity. Richard Nixon blamed it on permissiveness.

Jean-Jacques Servan-Schreiber likened the student demonstrators to General Giap in Vietnam, finding them different expressions of the same phenomenon. Clearly the war had something to do with it. Young men from the upper stratum of American society were evading the draft without guilt, encouraged by their parents and often with letters from physicians who lied about their health, also without guilt. Millions sympathized with the draft evaders and deserters making new lives in Toronto and Stockholm. Because the first four to arrive in Sweden had jumped ship from the aircraft carrier *Intrepid*, they were known as the "Intrepid Four." No one there thought the name ambiguous. One member of the colony, a nineteen-year-old South Carolinian, said: "We fall into two categories. There are those who are convinced the United States will blow up the world. There are others who think the United States can be saved before this catastrophe happens."

The war was only part of it. Not since Prohibition had so many people, concluding that some laws were senseless, proceeded to break them. Marijuana was an example. Unlike other drugs it was not habit-forming, unlike tobacco it was not harmful to the user, and unlike alcohol it was not dangerous to society. To the young it was often a matter of status; youths of the better families were known to be smoking it. For a time in 1969 police made a habit of "busting" —another new word—the sons and daughters of the famous.

Looters in the summer riots weren't arrested; you could see them helping themselves on the television news programs; policemen watched them and did nothing. "It seems to me," said Kenneth Clark, the Negro psychologist, "a high-policy decision was made to trade goods and appliances for human lives." Certainly it appeared that an arrest was determined by the identity of the person and place as much as by the act. In mid-May Ralph Abernathy, Martin Luther King's successor, set up a "Resurrection City," which King had planned, on the hallowed ground between the Lincoln Memorial and the Washington Monument. He led a thousand poor people on it, and the government not only failed to take any of them into custody; it gave them portable latrines, phone booths, power lines, showers, and even a zip number: 20013. Late in June, Alvin Johnson, the camp's chief security officer, resigned in anger, saying, "There are rapes, robberies, and cuttings every day, and there is nothing we can do about it." The National Capital Parks Police remained aloof.

In a previous generation Calvin Coolidge had won national recognition, and ultimately the Presidency, by breaking the Boston police strike of 1919. He said that there was "no right to strike against the public safety by anybody, anywhere, any time." In 1937 Franklin Roosevelt had called a strike by civil servants "unthinkable and intolerable." Since then the principle had been embodied in the Taft-Hartley Act and, in the states, by such laws as New York's Condon-Wadlin Act. Nevertheless, on January 1, 1966, Mike Quill led his Transport Workers Union in a strike that paralyzed downtown Manhattan by depriving the city, in effect, of 165 miles of subways and 530 miles of bus routes. When Quill was served with a court order to lead them back, he tore it up in front of television cameras. The city was forced to accept mediation and compromise with him.

Walkouts against the public interest in 1968 included that of the Memphis sanitation workers which Martin Luther King endorsed in his final hours. Another that same year left New York littered with a hundred thousand tons of reeking garbage on the streets before Governor Rockefeller capitulated and granted the garbage workers a $425 pay raise which Mayor Lindsay had rejected earlier. Next, New York policemen picketed City Hall, shouting "Blue power!" They reported "sick" with imaginary ills or watched languidly while drivers left their cars parked at bus stops and in other no-parking zones. The head of the firemen's union bargained by telling his men to ignore such routine tasks as inspecting buildings and fire hydrants. On three separate occasions in the autumn of 1968 a majority of New York's 58,000 teachers walked out. Then air traffic controllers, alarmed at the dense stack-ups overhead, conspired in a deliberate slowdown.

The climax to defiance of public service came at the end of the decade, when over 200,000 of the country's 750,000 postmen decided to stop delivering the mail for pay that started at $6,176 a year and reached $8,442 after twenty-one years. Despite the urging of their leaders, who reminded them that federal law threatened them with a $1,000 fine, a year in prison, the loss of pensions, and blacklisting from other government jobs, the 6,700 members of the Manhattan-Bronx local of the AFL-CIO National Association of Letter Carriers voted to walk out. Soon they were joined by the rest of greater New York's mailmen. The strike spread to Akron, Buffalo, Cleveland, Chicago, Denver, St. Paul, and San Francisco.

It was the first walkout in the history of the U.S. Postal Service, and it was devastating. On an average day New York's post office moves about 25 million letters and packages; the national average is 270 million. Many firms had to suspend operations. New York banks couldn't receive their daily average of 300 million dollars in deposits, 400,000 welfare clients couldn't get their checks, and brokerage firms had to hire armored trucks to move securities on Wall Street. On the sixth day the National Guard began handling the New York mail, and on the eighth day the mailmen resumed their appointed rounds. Like other civil servants who had struck, they profited from their illegal walkout. Congress voted them an 8 percent raise, retroactive to the month before, and established an independent U.S. Postal Service which, among other things, was meant to be more attentive to their grievances.

Among the things that went wrong in 1968 was the choosing of a new Supreme Court Chief Justice. Earl Warren still felt vigorous, but he decided to retire because of his age; he had turned seventy-seven on March 19. On the morning of June 19 he telephoned President Johnson and told him. It was a historic moment. No Court had played a greater role in determining the direction of its time. Under Warren's leadership, the Court had led the way on school desegregation, school prayers, the rights of Communists, pornography, the arrest and conviction of defendants, and the "one man, one vote" ruling ordering legislative reapportionment. Warren had presided over fifteen Court terms. And now Lyndon Johnson, who wanted to do everything as President, could choose a new chief judge. He named Associate Justice Abe Fortas and picked Texas Congressman Homer Thornberry to take Fortas's place.

Both men were old friends of the President. Fortas was as close to the President as any man; the President had put him on the Court three years earlier. Johnson, being Johnson, had to make the new selections complicated. He would not accept Warren's resignation until the Senate had confirmed his choice of Fortas. Then, with Fortas securely in office, Thornberry could move into his old spot.

But the Republicans, believing that they would capture the White House in November, were mulish. They called Fortas and Thornberry "lame duck" nominations and tarred Fortas as a "crony" of the President.

Senator Robert P. Griffin of Michigan emerged as the leader of seventeen hostile Republicans. In the beginning it seemed a lost cause. Everett Dirksen of Illinois, the minority leader in the Senate, called the "cronyism" and "lame duck" arguments "frivolous." "You do not go out looking for an enemy to put him on the Court," he said, and he remarked that Presidents Lincoln, Truman, and Kennedy had appointed friends. Rebuking Griffin, Dirksen said, "It's about time we be a little more circumspect about the kind of language we use." Even when the Senate Judiciary Committee decided to hold hearings—the first time for any nominee to the post of Chief Justice—Fortas seemed safe. The opening witness, Attorney General Ramsey Clark, pointed out that there was ample precedent for the President to keep Warren on the Court until Fortas's confirmation; many lesser federal judges were chosen while their predecessors remained in office.

The problem now was Fortas himself. He spent four terrible days being grilled. Under the Constitution he could not discuss his decisions while on the stand; that would be an outright violation of the principle of separation of powers. Nevertheless, opposition senators spent much of the time reading aloud liberal decisions in which he had participated. Then they questioned him about certain aspects of his conduct as an associate justice. That too was a matter of the separation of powers, but here it hurt him. As a member of the Court he was supposed to remain aloof from the executive department, and he hadn't been. He acknowledged that he had participated in White House meetings about the war and the ghetto riots, and that he had phoned Ralph Lazarus, the Columbus department store tycoon, to give him a tongue-lashing because of Lazarus's statement that Vietnam was affecting the economy.* Fortas protested that there was ample precedent for justices advising Presidents, but here, as always with Johnson, there was the nagging feeling that something shady was going on. One straw was needed to break the camel's back now, and it came when the committee learned that Fortas had accepted $15,000 as the fee for teaching a series of sum-

* See above, pages 1290–1291.

mer groups, the money coming from businessmen who might figure in cases coming before the Court.

The judiciary committee approved the appointment 17 to 6, but the Republican and southern senators staged a filibuster. A two-thirds vote of the Senate was required to end it, and at that point Dirksen pulled the rug from under Fortas. He would not support the move to stop the filibuster, he said, and he wasn't even sure he would vote for the nomination; a Court ruling overturning the death penalty for the killing of a Chicago policeman angered him. The vote on cloture was 45 yes and 43 no, far short of the two-thirds needed. Fortas asked Johnson to withdraw the nomination. The President agreed "with deep regret" and said he would make no appointment at all. The following May *Life* revealed that Fortas had accepted another, $20,000 fee from the family foundation of Louis Wolfsen, whose conviction for stock manipulation had come before the Court. Although he had returned the money, Washington was shocked, and when still other revelations loomed, he resigned. With Fortas and Goldberg gone, and with a Republican in the White House, clearly the future Court would be less liberal.

Americans have a way of anointing and consecrating their heroes, putting them on pedestals that are impossibly high, and then knocking them off. In the autumn of 1968 it was the turn of a heroine: Jacqueline Bouvier Kennedy, who wanted neither the adoration of the past nor the calumny of the present, but merely privacy. She was a woman of beauty and charm. For one terrible weekend in its history the United States needed a presidential widow with those gifts and something else: a histrionic talent. Eleanor Roosevelt was a greater First Lady, but she could not have done that. Jackie Kennedy had given the country's grief dignity and nobility. No woman could have improved on it. But afterward she needed to be alone, and as long as she remained a widow that seemed to be impossible. In Washington tourist buses paused outside her home, and when she moved to New York cabbies recognized her and honked.

To avoid gossip she went out only with happily married public men. Arthur Schlesinger Jr., Robert S. McNamara, and Leonard Bernstein were familiar escorts. Lord Harlech, who as David Ormsby-Gore had been the British ambassador to the United States during the Kennedy years, was now a widower. The press suggested him as a new husband. Movie magazines proposed an elderly Greek shipping magnate, and the fans laughed.

They stopped laughing on October 17, 1968, when Jackie's mother announced: "My daughter, Mrs. John F. Kennedy, is planning to marry Mr. Aristotle Onassis"—the elderly shipping magnate. The son of a Smyrna tobacco merchant, Onassis had acquired a fortune which was estimated at 500 million dollars. Among other things he owned 100 ships, Olympic Airways, several corporations, a 325-foot yacht, the *Christina*, and the Greek island Skorpios. Those who believed the report—who weren't convinced that either the bride's mother was out of her mind or the announcement was a monstrous practical joke—speculated over what to give the couple. The New York Stock Exchange, the Taj Mahal, the *Queen Elizabeth 2*, and the De Beers diamond mines were among the suggestions.

JACKIE, HOW COULD YOU? asked the headline in the *Stockholm Expressen*. Onassis was two inches shorter and could have been her father—he was either twenty-three or twenty-nine years older, depending on which birth date you accepted. Onassis was divorced, which meant that Jackie could not hope for the church's blessing. Worst of all was the groom's total lack of a social conscience, the very heart of the Kennedy creed. He once said that his idea of the perfect home would be in a country without taxes. The taxes he did owe were outstanding in several different nations, including the United States. "She's gone from Prince Charming to Caliban," one former Kennedy appointee commented. Bob Hope said, "Nixon has a Greek running mate, and now everyone wants one." It was widely remarked that she wouldn't have done it if Bobby were alive.

The marriage was celebrated on October 20 in a tiny Chapel of the Little Virgin on Skorpios. Tulips had been airlifted from Holland by the tycoon's private jet fleet. The bride wore a lace Valentino original. Her two children were pages. The groom's children were witnesses. The Greek Orthodox ceremony took forty-five minutes; then the couple took communion from one chalice and were crowned with garlands of lemon blossoms, a sign of fertility and purity. After kissing the New Testament they circled the altar in a ritualistic dance. Afterward there was a reception on the white-hulled yacht. The Greek navy and Onassis's own patrol boats kept reporters off the island. His present to her was a ring with a huge ruby surrounded by big diamonds, with matching earrings—a gift worth 1.2 million dollars.

That was only the beginning. According to the veteran journalist Fred Sparks, the pair spent about twenty million dollars their first year together, and their expenditures then continued at the rate of about $384,000 a week. Onassis had given his new wife five million dollars in jewelry alone. And since he was making about fifty million dollars a year, he wasn't even dipping into capital. Keeping out of the newspapers was another matter. Mrs. Kennedy, as she still was, had agreed to hold one press conference on the eve of the wedding. She said then, "We wish our wedding to be a private moment in the little chapel among the cypresses of Skorpios, with only members of the family and their little children. Understand that even though people may be well known, they still hold in their hearts the emotion of a simple person for the moments that are the most important we know on earth—birth, marriage, and death."

Nevertheless, reporters stalked them. They were news and had to be covered. Photographers were worse. One, an Italian, managed, with telephoto lenses, to get a picture of her sunbathing in the nude. But the greatest blow to her new role came not from the secular press but from the Vatican's *L'Osservatore della Domenica*. Branding her "a public sinner," it reported that she would be denied church rites. In Boston Cardinal Cushing protested that "Only God knows" who sins and who doesn't; he pleaded for "love, mutual respect and esteem." Nevertheless, the canon lawyers in the Vatican held fast. In sharing Onassis's bed, they ruled, the wife of America's first Catholic President was profane in the eyes of God.

Richard Nixon's second presidential campaign had begun the previous February in Nashua, New Hampshire, when he registered at a Howard Johnson motel as Mr. Benjamin Chapman. Shortly thereafter pseudonyms became impossible, for his picture was back on front pages, and when he received 79 percent of the vote in the New Hampshire primary, he became the Republican front runner. Thereafter his campaign was one string of triumphs. George Romney was beaten early, after he had said he had been "brainwashed" into supporting the Vietnam War. Nelson Rockefeller dropped out, then came back after Johnson declared that he wouldn't run again, but the only effect of Rockefeller's in-out-in candidacy was to alienate an early supporter of his, Governor Spiro Agnew of Maryland.

Until Nixon chose him to share the ticket, Agnew was unknown outside his state. His name, as he conceded, was "not a household word." A few hours after his name went before the convention a reporter stopped pedestrians in downtown Atlanta and said, "I'm going to mention two words to you. You tell me what they mean. The words are Spiro Agnew." One Atlantan replied, "It's some kind of disease." Another said, "It's some kind of egg," and a third, a little closer to the mark, said, "He's a Greek that owns that shipbuilding firm."

Agnew's credentials, said *Time*, "are not convincing." But they had impressed Nixon. He wanted a running mate who would take the low road and thus serve the purpose he had served for Eisenhower. It was hard to assess Agnew's impact on the electorate, because his opposite number in the campaign turned out to be not the Democratic vice-presidential nominee, Senator Edmund Muskie of Maine, but a third-party candidate, Governor George Wallace of Alabama. Agnew denounced "phony intellectuals who don't understand what we mean by hard work and patriotism"; Wallace attacked "pointy-headed" newspapermen, "scummy anarchists" and "pseudo-intellectuals." Wallace said that if policemen "could run this country for about two years, they'd straighten it out." At the same time, Agnew was saying in Detroit, "If you've seen one ghetto area, you've seen them all." Agnew called a Nisei reporter a "fat Jap" and called Poles "Polacks." His manner was so graceless that a picket greeted him with a placard reading: APOLOGIZE NOW, SPIRO. IT WILL SAVE TIME LATER. Other pickets met Wallace with: IF YOU LIKED HITLER, YOU'LL LOVE WALLACE and WALLACE IS ROSEMARY'S BABY.

One reason the also-rans were so newsy in the early weeks of the campaign was the dreariness of the Republican convention, which came first. "Richard M. Nixon rode to victory," the Associated Press commented, "in a tedious ritual at Miami Beach." Theodore H. White wrote, "Boredom lay on the convention like a mattress." Glee clubs sang. Bands played. John Wayne gave an inspirational reading on "Why I am proud to be an American." Other celebrities supporting Nixon were equally dreary: Art Linkletter, Connie Francis, Pat Boone, Lawrence Welk. The arid speeches of the politicians seemed to go on forever. The only interesting moments came on the periphery of the convention. Senator Edward W. Brooke was reportedly barred from a reception because he was a Negro. Miami blacks rioted; the television commentators said that seventy policemen with shotguns entered the riot area, and the news later was that four Negroes had died. Nixon scribbled away a speech on the yellow legal-length pads which he soon would make famous. In it he called for a return to America's "lift of a driving dream."

The AP reported that the Republicans' security precautions were "the tightest in the memory of convention goers." The second Kennedy assassination had scared the Secret Service, which Johnson at that time had made responsible for the protection of all serious candidates. Agents in helicopters hovered over the convention city. Other agents with rifles and binoculars scanned the crowd from rooftops. A thirty-man riot squad was held in reserve, and the 1,333 delegates had to submit all packages and purses to inspection each time they entered the convention. Some Democrats said it was overdone. Two weeks later their own delegates assembled in Chicago.

The violence that lay ahead in Chicago was not inevitable, but all the ingredients were there. The Committee to End the War in Vietnam, an umbrella organization coordinating over eighty peace groups under David Dellinger, came to jeer at the Chicago police. Hippies, Yippies, peace pickets, McCarthy workers, disillusioned liberals—altogether, they predicted there would be 100,000 of them, and they would march on the convention in the International Amphitheater. Mayor Richard J. Daley took them seriously. He turned Chicago into an armed camp. Manholes around the amphitheater were sealed with tar. A chain link fence seven feet high, with barbed wire on top of it, was thrown around the hall. The city's 11,500 policemen were put on twelve-hour shifts, 5,500 National Guardsmen were alerted, and 7,500 troops of the U.S. Army, airlifted from Fort Hood in Texas on White House orders, were ordered to stand by. Despite the extravagant forecasts, only about 10,000 to 12,000 demonstrators came to confront them.

In the convention, the reason for all this, Humphrey was nominated on the first ballot; McCarthy and George McGovern of South Dakota lagged far behind him. The only real contest was over how the peace issue should be handled in the party platform. The administration plank, the more hawkish of the two, won with 1,567¾ to 1,041¼ for the dovish substitute plank. The figures reflected the depth of the division in the party on the war. Four years earlier Lyndon Johnson had been nominated by acclamation and had won in a landslide. The Chicago convention had been scheduled for the week of his sixtieth birthday, which came that Tuesday. Now he couldn't even come. The Secret Service advised him that it was too risky.

"Stop the war!" shouted the youths in the galleries. (The next day, in a ludicrous change, municipal employees took all the seats and waved banners reading WE LOVE DALEY.) But the most dramatic moment of the week was an outside echo of events inside the hall. Delegates were watching what was happening downtown on television screens, and Senator Abe Ribicoff, looking down from the rostrum on the Illinois delegation fifteen feet in front of him, condemned "Gestapo tactics in the streets of Chicago." Daley and his aides were on their feet, shaking fists and yelling obscenities at him —lip-readers watching television could identify the oaths—and Ribicoff said calmly, "How hard it is to accept the truth."

The full truth about what was happening was complicated. If the policemen had matched the courage and discipline of the U.S. marshals on the Ole Miss campus, their record would have been clean. At the same time, it is fair to point out that some of them were provoked. Afterward they displayed over a hundred weapons they had taken from those they arrested: switchblade knives, studded golf balls, clubs with nails embedded in them, bats with razor blades in the ends, chunks of concrete, and plain rocks.

The sequence of events which eventually erupted beneath the very hotel windows of the major candidates had begun on August 3, the Thursday before the convention, when the Youth International Party—the Yippies—arrived in Chicago with Pigasus, the 125-pound hog they announced they were going to nominate for President. Conspicuous in their beads, sandals, and beards, the Yippies and hippies settled down in Chicago's 1,185-acre Lincoln Park on the North Side. Over the weekend they played guitars, read poetry, and gave speeches. At 11 P.M. Saturday, curfew time, a dozen were arrested. None resisted. Sunday there were 2,000 of them. At 5 P.M. they asked police for permission to take a truck into the park and use it as a bandstand. The cops refused. They then arrested the Yippy leader Jerry Rubin. The crowd, incensed, chanted, "Hell, no, we won't go," "Oink, Oink!" and "Ho-Ho-Ho Chi Minh." Tom Hayden of the New Left explained to the officers that this last meant nothing; it was an international student chant which began in Germany. They ignored him. At curfew time they charged through the park swinging nightsticks. They did the same Monday night, except that this time they were tougher. The evicted demonstrators raced away through the North Side traffic.

On Tuesday seventy priests and ministers erected a ten-foot cross. The demonstrators sang, "We Shall Overcome" and "The Battle Hymn of the Republic." That evening three hundred policemen charged them with tear gas. Choking youths threw stones and bottles, shouting, "Shoot me, pig!" and "Hit me, pig!" The climax came on Wednesday. Demonstration leaders had announced that the protesters would march from the Grant Park band shell to the amphitheater as a show of the solidarity of their opposition to the war. "This is a nonviolent march," Dellinger told an audience of eight thousand. "If you feel you can't respond nonviolently, please leave us." Many did. Nevertheless a Chicago official said, "There will be no march today."

And there wasn't. Instead there was what an investigatory commission later called a "police riot." Policemen with bullhorns shouted, "This is a final warning. Move out now." The crowd did, to a narrow strip of Grant Park across Michigan Avenue from the Conrad Hilton. As they moved they mocked the police with "Oink! Oink!" "Sieg Heil!" and other rude chants. At the intersection of Michigan and Balboa avenues a double line of cops awaited them. The scene was brightly illuminated by TV lights on trucks and the eaves of the Conrad Hilton Hotel, headquarters for the three candidates. As the crowd tensed and then surged back and forth taunting the officers, daring them to attack, the police swooped down on them in two flying wedges, nightsticks swinging, dragging individual demonstrators toward waiting wagons. Hundreds of girls in the throng screamed. The mayhem continued for eighteen mad minutes. What was happening, in a very real sense, was a battle between the upper middle and lower middle class. A journalist said, "Those are our children in the streets, and the policemen are attacking them." But of course the policemen had parents, too.

Apart from the major encounters there were skirmishes all week between patrolmen and demonstrators, and some between patrolmen and nondemonstrators. On Monday evening alone twenty-one newspapermen were hurt. At various times spectators, clergymen, and at least one cripple were clubbed. Hugh Hefner, the publisher of *Playboy*, was walloped, and Mrs. Anne Kerr, a British Labourite, was Maced outside the Conrad Hilton and thrown into a cell. Hotel guests in the lobby were also beaten and jailed. The hotel's air-conditioning shafts sucked up tear gas and wafted it into suite 2525A, where Hubert Humphrey was watching himself being nominated on television. On Friday policemen said they were being pelted by objects from windows above—sardines, herrings, beer cans, ashtrays, cocktail glasses, and ice cubes. They thought—they couldn't tell—that the missiles were coming from the fifteenth floor, corner suite 1505A and 1506A: McCarthy's command post. Without writ or warrant, they ran into the hotel, took elevators up, and clouted the occupants of the suite.

Bloodshed might have been averted in Chicago if Mayor Daley had consented when the demonstrators asked permission to sleep in the meadows and glens of Lincoln Park. Then the policemen could have guarded the fringes of the park until the protesters got bored and left. As it was, by enforcing the curfew the mayor made confrontation inevitable, and under the worst possible circumstances. "The whole world is watching," the youths had chanted at Michigan and Balboa. The world wasn't, but most of the country was—an estimated 89 million, including, at Key Biscayne, an elated Richard Nixon.

In Chicago, Theodore H. White had written in his notes at 8:05 P.M. Wednesday, "The Democrats are finished." Certainly it looked like it, and when Humphrey's campaign began with a sickening lurch his admirers despaired. Among his major handicaps were the alienation of Democrats whose hearts had been captured by McCarthy and who now wore blank campaign pins, lack of money, an inefficient organization, and his inability to free himself from the toils of Lyndon Johnson. Johnson wasn't helping. His attitude toward Humphrey was scornful. He seemed to regard him as contemptible. Asked to comment on him, Johnson said curtly, "He cries too much."

In those early autumn weeks he had something to cry over. Inadequately prepared, Humphrey swung through New Jersey, Delaware, Michigan, Louisiana, Texas, Pennsylvania, Colorado, and California, speaking as often as nine times a day, a sign of his energy —and the lack of judgment on the part of his staff. Advance men served him poorly; crowds were small and tepid. In Philadelphia, Joey Bishop, a local boy accompanying Humphrey, got more applause than Humphrey. There were hecklers at virtually every stop. In Boston an antiwar crowd booed Humphrey and Edward Kennedy off a platform. Humphrey, said one of his workers, "went to Chicago with one albatross," meaning Lyndon Johnson, "and came out with two," meaning Johnson and Daley.

His treasury was all but empty. His rhetoric, which could soar, was laced with bromides. At one point he actually said, "Government of the people, by the people, and for the people is as American as apple pie." Johnson seemed to be sabotaging him; when in September Humphrey said that the withdrawal of U.S. troops could begin at the end of the year, the President said that "no man can predict" when departure might start. Not counting Wallace votes, in August Gallup had Nixon leading by 16 points, and Harris put Nixon's margin at 40 to 31. Even Humphrey was discouraged. He said, "I have pursued impossible dreams before and maybe I am now."

Nixon's campaign was all the other way. He had plenty of money and exultant optimism. His schedule harmonized with deadlines of the network news programs, even allowing them plenty of time to develop their film. He dodged challenges to debate, and Republican senators filibustered a measure to allow public service TV debates without Wallace. He appealed to the "forgotten American"—the man who paid his taxes, didn't riot or break the law, went to church and raised his children to be "good Americans" who would wear the country's uniform with pride as "watchmen on the walls of freedom around the world."

Joe McGinniss described the advertising techniques used by the Nixon people in *The Selling of the President 1968*. One writer observed that to Nixon politics were "products . . . to be sold the public—this one today, that one tomorrow, depending on the discounts and the state of the market." Frank Shakespeare Jr., a Nixon aide, was tremendously excited by the Russian invasion of Czechoslovakia. "What a break!" McGinniss quoted him as saying. "This Czech thing is perfect! It puts the soft-liners in a hell of a box!"

Nixon said he had a plan to end the war; he couldn't divulge it now because it might disturb the peace talks going on in Paris. He promised to restore law and order by appointing a new attorney general, and he attacked the Supreme Court for being "patently guilty" of freeing defendants on technicalities. He favored approval of the nuclear nonproliferation treaty, but not now, because of Soviet treatment of the Czechs. Business would improve, he said, because he would give businessmen tax credits and other incentives which would create jobs and reduce the number of people on welfare. America, he said, became great, "not because of what government did for the people but because of what people did for themselves."

In October Humphrey began to gain.

He had put Chicago behind him, and as he forgot it, so did his audiences. He dismissed his mockers as "damned fools," introduced the clown, Emmett Kelly, as "Nixon's economic adviser," and accused Nixon of dodging issues. He backed the Supreme Court and the nonproliferation treaty. Union audiences were reminded of what Democratic administrations had done for them. Nixon was "Richard the chicken-hearted"; Wallace and General Curtis LeMay, his running mate, were the "bombsy twins." Humphrey developed a technique of naming the Democratic presidential champions— Roosevelt, Truman, Stevenson, Kennedy—and then, just as the applause started to build, slipping in the name of Lyndon Johnson. Meanwhile his running mate was savaging Agnew. Muskie would say, "Mr. Agnew tells us that we lack a sense of humor," and add dryly: "I think he is doing his best to restore it."

Salt Lake City was a pivot. When Humphrey declared there that he would stop the bombing in Vietnam as "an acceptable risk for peace," the tide started to turn. On October 21 Gallup reported that Humphrey had cut Nixon's lead in half. Fading memories of Chicago was part of it. The habit of voting Democratic for a generation was another part. That June Gallup had found that 46 percent of the people considered themselves Democratic, 27 percent said they were independents, and 27 percent Republicans. (In 1940 it had been 42, 20, and 38 percent, and in 1950 45, 22, and 33.) Liberals who had yearned for Robert Kennedy or McCarthy awoke to the fact that the choice was between Humphrey and Nixon, their bogey for the past twenty years. McCarthy himself, who had been pouting on the Riviera, announced his support of the Democratic ticket five days before the election. Finally there was the difference between the demeanor of the two candidates. Humphrey was at the top of his form; Nixon had begun to sound uncannily like Thomas E. Dewey.

On the afternoon before the election Gallup had 42 percent for Nixon, 40 for Humphrey, 14 percent for Wallace, with 4 percent undecided. Since September Humphrey had gained 12 percent to Nixon's 1 percent, both at the expense of the fading Wallace. That same Monday Harris had Humphrey in the lead with 43 percent over Nixon's 40 percent; Wallace had 14 percent and 4 percent were undecided.

Tuesday night was a spellbinder. Nixon had asked the electorate for a "mandate to govern." What he got was a surge of Humphrey votes which, in the opinion of many analysts, would have won the election if the campaign had lasted another day or two—as it would have, the Democrats reflected grimly, if they hadn't postponed their convention so that it would coincide with the week of Lyndon Johnson's birthday. The figures flashing on the networks' electric scoreboards showed the lead changing hands several times. It seemed at one point that the two leaders were, as the Associated Press put it, "trading state for state." Shortly after midnight Humphrey was leading by 33,000 votes. At dawn it appeared that although he couldn't win in the electoral college, he might win in the popular vote, and there was a distinct possibility that he could thwart a Nixon majority in electoral votes, throwing the election into the House of Representatives, where the Democrats had a majority.

The final electoral results were Nixon 301, Humphrey 191, and Wallace 45. The popular vote was 31,770,222 for Nixon (43.4 percent), 31,267,744 for Humphrey (42.7 percent), and 9,897,141 for Wallace (13.5 percent). The distance between the two leaders was less than .7 of one percentage point. Moreover, the Democrats had retained control of Congress. Nixon would be the first President in one hundred and twenty years to begin his administration with the opposition ruling both Houses on the Hill.

Campaigning in Ohio, Nixon had seen a thirteen-year-old schoolgirl holding a sign which read: "Bring Us Together." That, he said in his moment of triumph, had "touched me most." Did he mean it? With this complex man one could never be sure. "Watch what we do, not what we say," John Mitchell, his attorney-general designate, told a group of thirty southern black leaders. Later, during the Watergate scandals, James Reston would write of Nixon that "There is scarcely a noble principle in the American Constitution that he hasn't defended in theory or defied in practice." But in the pause after his election his credit was strong. Most Americans wanted to believe him, to persuade themselves that he knew how to leave the swamps of the 1960s for higher ground. He had promised to extricate the troops from Vietnam. Since 1961 there had been 24,291 American deaths in the war; it was an immense relief to know that soon the dying would end. The country needed a rest. Now partisan politics could be shelved.

From his windows on the thirty-ninth floor of Manhattan's Pierre Hotel, the President-elect could look out across the wooded sweep of Central Park and see America twinkling in the distance. Not since the pit of the Depression had the country been so torn. Between those whose bumper stickers said LOVE IT OR LEAVE IT and those who said CHANGE IT OR LOSE IT yawned a chasm so broad that no reconciliation was possible now; finding common ground would have to wait until outstanding issues had been resolved, the war being the first of them. In the matter of social questions as liberal a commentator as Eric Sevareid found himself drifting to the right. He looked at the long list of crimes for which Black Panthers had been convicted and was appalled. He watched on television as a Baltimore girl, the mother of seven illegitimate children, furiously blamed society for her plight, and shook his head; he watched black women hurrying to reach home before sunset and said: "I just don't believe that 'law and order' are code words, except for a few. This issue is survival itself."

To those on the left side of the divide, the aroused young ideologues, nothing seemed to be sacred: not the American flag, God, motherhood, knowledge, honor, modesty, chastity, or simple honesty. In 1968 insurance actuaries reportedly discovered that the group in society which failed most often to repay its debts was the young collegians who owed tuition loans; a college president wrote to one defaulter who had just graduated, and back came a photograph of the new alumnus naked and in a cave. It was almost possible to believe that for some middle-class youths the Boy Scout pledge which their fathers had recited had become inverted: they strove to be untrustworthy, disloyal, unhelpful, hostile, discourteous, unkind, disobedient, cheerless, wasteful, craven, dirty, and irreverent.

The campuses of venerable institutions of learning had often become disagreeable and even dangerous places. The one at Wesleyan, a little ivy college in Connecticut, had to be floodlit at night; crossing it was unsafe; there had been an epidemic of muggings there. Universities were confronted with a new disciplinary problem: how to cope with the undergraduate who was putting himself through college by peddling dope to fellow students who had become drug addicts. Crime became commonplace in peculiar places. One respected physician in New England entertained dinner party guests by telling how he and his wife had started shoplifting as children, still did it, and in fact had stolen the centerpiece on the table only three days ago. An assistant dean explained in great detail the information he had given, to a recent undergraduate drafted into the tank corps, on the best way to sabotage a tank. And a July 1967 issue of the *New York Review of Books* carried on its front page a large drawing showing how to make a Molotov cocktail, with a rag soaked in gasoline as the stopper, a fuse of clothesline rope, and instructions to use as fuel a mixture two-thirds gas and one-third soap powder and dirt.

The election of Richard Nixon to the Presidency was a reaction against all this, and a healthy one. The nation wanted no more visionaries for the present. What was needed was a genuine conservative administration, another Eisenhower era. Such a government would resist temptations to cut taxes and try, insofar as possible, to balance the budget, assuring a sound dollar and no inflation. Hostilities in Indochina would be ended as soon as possible, and all foreign policies would be evaluated solely in terms of the national interest of the United States. At home the role of the federal government would be sharply limited and congressional prerogatives restored, and ties would be strengthened between the generations, the races, the wealthy and the impoverished, the different regions in the country, and the religious faiths.

Nowhere was America's exhaustion in 1968 more evident than in the ghettos, which were calmer that year than anyone had prophesied. "We will have a bad summer," Lyndon Johnson had said in the spring. "We will have several bad summers before the deficiencies are erased." Nixon foresaw "war in the streets." The Justice Department had become so sophisticated on the subject of inner city disorders that it had established standards for a major riot. It had to be violent, had to have more than 300 participants, had to last at least twelve hours or more, and had to include gunfire, looting, arson, and vandalism. (A mere "serious disturbance" involved 150 people for three hours.) The Army had trained 15,000 men in seven task forces to cope with civil uprisings, and black leaders predicted that by spring they would be needed, that the biggest eruption ever lay ahead.

Certainly the leaders were setting an example. They taught courses in guerrilla warfare and house-to-house fighting. CORE joined SNCC and Martin Luther King's SCLC in a militant shift to the left, advocating compulsive separation of the races. Eldridge Cleaver's *Soul on Ice*, a best seller of 1968, described Cleaver as a "full-time revolutionary in the struggle for black liberation in America." James Baldwin called the United States the "Fourth Reich," and the disciples of Malcolm X observed the third anniversary of his death with a lack of restraint beyond anything he had advocated. Even black celebrities were taking a hard line. Black sprinters Tommie Smith and John Carlos obscured the glory of American victories at the Olympic games in Mexico City by bowing their heads during the playing of "The Star-Spangled Banner" in honor of their victories and raising black-gloved clenched fists in a defiant gesture. When Cleveland blew in July, the general reaction was here-we-go-again. A tow truck, called to the scene of an accident, was fired upon by snipers. Policemen called to the scene became targets of the riflemen. Within thirty minutes three officers and four blacks were dead, and eight policemen were wounded. The National Guard was summoned, and losses from looting and burning were put at 1.5 million dollars. In the brick canyons of other ghettos police braced themselves for what seemed inevitable.

It didn't come. There were half as many riots as expected and none of the other big cities experienced the havoc of the past three years. "In terms of racial conflict," the AP reported, "it was the coolest summer in five years." There were just nineteen deaths, shocking by pre-Watts standards but nothing like the eighty-seven of the year before. One reason was that the most inflammatory of the inciters weren't in the streets any more. They were in jail, or fugitives. H. Rap Brown had been put away. Cleaver disappeared in late November when his parole was revoked. Huey P. Newton was tried in Oakland for killing a policeman; a jury with a black foreman found him guilty. "If Huey goes, the sky's the limit," said his black-jacketed followers, threatening to terrorize all whites, but when he was sent away for two to fifteen years for manslaughter, nothing happened.

Another reason for the comparative tranquillity was that blacks had realized they themselves were the chief victims of the riots. *Their* stores were looted, *their* cars were destroyed, *their* homes burned, and *their* children endangered. Dr. Hiawatha Harris, a

Watts psychiatrist, said that "the rioting phase, where we burn down businesses in our own areas, is over. The whole movement is in another direction—toward implementing black power and finding our dignity as a people." Measured by education, wages, public service —"by every traditional index of progress," Theodore H. White wrote —American blacks were already moving forward. The change was evident in little ways. The television screen was one. Integration had become a reality there. Almost every serial had a black player now. The neurosurgeon in Peyton Place was a Negro—and one black, "Julia," was a heroine.

A new and more effective way to protest was put forward in Chicago by a Negro minister, Jesse Jackson, who forced white businessmen to hire blacks by telling his congregation to boycott their products. A & P made jobs for 970; Jewel Tea for 661. Operation Breadbasket, as Jackson called it, also persuaded businessmen to open accounts in two Negro banks, increasing their deposits from five million dollars to twenty-two million. Blacks had economic muscle to flex now. The Bureau of the Census later found that the number of Negro families making more than ten thousand dollars a year had risen in the 1960s from 11 percent to 28 percent. They were finally beginning to move into the middle class.

Montage: The Late Sixties

INTERSTATE HIGHWAY SURFACED
—— MILEAGE PASSES 42,500 MARK ——

HONOR U.S. HERO

Among the honors conferred upon General Westmoreland during his brief visit home were the USO Distinguished Service Award, a citation from the South Carolina Legislature, an honorary degree from the University of Buffalo, and the Boy Scout Silver Buffalo Award

Our battalion managed to retake the town by daybreak. When we moved in only one person was left alive in the place: a small boy who was badly wounded

This is the dawning of the Age of Aquarius, The Age of Aquarius

for EXPERT white collar girls ... get the Kelly Girl habit

The U.S. birth rate dropped to 17.9 births, the lowest on record, breaking a mark of 18.9 set in the Depression years of 1933 and 1938

Our motto comes from the novelist Hermann Hesse: "We are in a magic theatre, a world of pictures not reality/ Tonight at the magic theater for madmen only/the price of admission is your mind."

Take it off, take it all off

NIXON'S THE ONE

U.S. TELSTAR RELAYS TV
PIX ACROSS ATLANTIC

Picture yourself in a boat on a river
With tangerine trees and marmalade skies
Somebody calls you, you answer quite slowly
A girl with kaleidoscopic eyes
Cellophane flowers of yellow and green

A boo-boo

"I'm for anything that gets you through the night — booze or religion," Mr. Sinatra said.

How does it feel, how does it feel
To be without a home
Like a complete unknown
Like a rolling stone?

frug

No strain

SUPPORT OUR BOYS IN VIETNAM

No problem

GOD IS
LOVE IS
I AM

psychedelic, adj. Of, pertaining to, or generating hallucinations, distortions of perceptions, and, occasionally, states resembling psychosis.

People try to put us down
Just because we get around
Things they do look awful cold
Hope I die before I get old

What the world needs now Is love sweet love

COURT, 8-1, OKAYS STOP, FRISK

WOW! DIG ALL THE BEAUTIFUL FREAKS!

No sweat

Put silver wings on my son's chest
Make him one of America's best
He'll be a man they'll test one day —
Have him win the green beret

Had any lately?

GIVE A DAMN

MAKE LOVE NOT WAR

YOU FIGHT AND DIE BUT CAN'T DRINK AT 18

DON'T TRUST ANYONE OVER 30

Poor People's Campaign 1968

WE SHALL OVER KILL

Student Power

POWs never have a nice day

No way

HIPPY POWER

DROP

Have a nice day

monkey

STONED

PEACE

GOD IS ON A TRIP

Would you believe fifty?

V

NIXON, AFTER ALL

1969–1972

Thirty-four

THE RISE OF
THE SILENT MAJORITY

RICHARD NIXON'S HEROES included a Democratic President, Woodrow Wilson, and upon learning that President-elect Wilson had announced all his cabinet choices at once in 1913, the President-elect of 1968 decided to do the same thing, on television. The ceremony was held in the Palladium Room of Washington's Shoreham Hotel on December 11, 1968. Nixon asked that each secretary-designate be accompanied by his wife; loyal helpmates, he explained, deserved to share in reflected glory—a condescension which was branded sexist by infuriated feminists. The wives of the new cabinet members seemed to enjoy the occasion, but the national audience was another matter. For viewers the thirty-minute production was flat—one critic rudely called it "a political *What's My Line?*"—and many noted that the star kept repeating himself. Each of the twelve secretaries-designate was identified by Nixon as a man who understood not only his specialty but psychology as well. This was called an "extra dimension," a phrase which the President-elect used no fewer than ten times.

In fact, the incoming cabinet was conspicuous for its lack of dimension. Its members were all affluent, white, male, middle-class, and Republican, and seven of them lived west of the Alleghenies, territory which had been the chief source of Republican votes. Nearly all were businessmen, with three—Walter Hickel (Interior), Winton Blount (postmaster general), and John Volpe (Transportation)—from the construction industry. The lack of breadth was not altogether Nixon's fault. He had tried for more diversity. Earlier he had pledged the formation of "a government made up of Republicans, Democrats, and independents," consisting of "the very best men and women I can find in the country, from government, from labor, from all the areas." But the principal areas of Democratic strength had not responded to his overtures. Three blacks, for example, had bluntly turned him down: Whitney Young Jr., Senator Edward Brooke, and Mrs. Ersa Poston, president of the New York Civil Service Commission. So he had wound up with homogeneity instead of a cross section. The Nixon cabinet, a magazine writer commented, "seems to be constructed more of gray fieldstone than glinting steel and glass." But so was its architect. "The men suggest cool competence rather than passion or brilliance," *Time* said. Whatever their shortcomings, no one doubted their integrity.

The presence in the cabinet of such Nixon intimates as William Rogers (State), John Mitchell (Justice), and Robert Finch (HEW) was interpreted as evidence that the new President intended to give it more power than Johnson had; the demise of the kitchen cabinet as a presidential institution was predicted by columnists who did not yet know H. R. Haldeman and John Ehrlichman. To be sure, the President watchers granted, there would be exceptions. As presidential assistant for national security Henry Kissinger was already emerging as a key adviser. Rogers was reported to be reading Kissinger's books. What no one then foresaw was that Nixon's first Secretary of State would be keeping in touch with American foreign policy developments by reading transcripts of Kissinger's press conferences.

Six months after entering the White House the new President received a tremendous psychological boost when NASA's long voyage to the moon, begun eight years earlier on orders from John F. Kennedy, reached its destination. The mission was Apollo 11. It was the capstone of an extraordinary effort—20,000 contractors and 300,-000 workers had contributed to it—and while men could argue endlessly over whether it had been worth the cost, its success was undeniably an American triumph. In a proclamation Richard Nixon noted that while exploration had been "a lonely enterprise" in the past, "today the miracles of space travel are matched by miracles of space communication; even across the vast lunar distance, television brings the moment of discovery into our homes and makes us all participants." By "all" he meant more than Americans. The lunar landing was witnessed by the largest television audience ever, some 528 million people.

The possibility of failure was small. U.S. space science had come a long way since its first failures twelve years earlier. Between 1961 and 1966 the sixteen manned flights of the Mercury and Gemini series had demonstrated that man could live and function in space, and the Ranger, Lunar Orbiter, and Surveyor programs had sent back proof that the surface of the moon was safe for astronauts. There had been one dreadful setback. In January 1967 a flash fire in the Apollo 1 capsule had killed the three-man crew. After twenty-one months of delays manned Apollo command modules had gone up, however, and in late 1968 and early 1969 NASA had followed a rigid schedule, sending up an Apollo every two and a half months in hopes of meeting the Kennedy deadline of May 1961: to land a man on the moon and return him safely to earth "before this decade is out."

Apollo 11, with its 36-story-high Saturn 5 rocket, was fired at Cape Kennedy's launch complex 39A at 9:32 on the morning of July 16, 1969. Aboard were Neil A. Armstrong, the civilian commander, and two Air Force officers, Col. Edwin E. "Buzz" Aldrin Jr. and Lieutenant Colonel Michael Collins. The Saturn's third stage put them into an orbit at a height of 118 miles. After a two-and-a-half-hour check of all instruments systems, they refired the third stage. This gave them a velocity of 24,245 mph, sufficient to throw them beyond the earth's atmosphere and on their way to the moon, a quarter-million miles away.

At a distance of 50,000 miles from the earth Collins maneuvered the command vessel, which had been christened the *Columbia,* until it was nose to nose with the fragile lunar module, called the *Eagle* or simply the LM. Once the *Columbia* and the *Eagle* were hooked together, the Saturn's third stage was jettisoned. On Thursday, the second day of the trip, the men switched on *Columbia*'s engine just long enough to put them in a trajectory which would pass within 69 miles of the back side of the moon on Saturday. Friday afternoon, Cape Kennedy time, Armstrong and Aldrin crept through a tunnel connecting the two vessels and into the *Eagle,* and at the end of that day the astronauts entered the moon's field of gravity. They were now within 44,000 miles of it, and picking up speed.

Saturday afternoon they slowed to 3,736 mph and went into orbit around the moon. Mission Control, their radio link with NASA's

Manned Spacecraft Center in Houston, awoke them at 7:02 A.M. on Sunday, July 20, which was to be the day of the landing. In the *Eagle* Armstrong and Aldrin extended the four landing legs of the ungainly lunar module. "You're 'go' for undocking," Mission Control told them. Now the LM and the *Columbia* separated, and Armstrong said, "The *Eagle* has wings!" At 3:08 P.M. he fired the spacecraft's engine, and down they went, toward the moon's Sea of Tranquillity.

At a distance of 9.8 miles from the surface of the moon they went into a low orbit, sailing over an awesome lunar scape of mountains and craters. At this point a Houston computer started flashing warning lights on their instruments. Rather than turn back this close to their goal, they went forward on instructions from a young guidance officer in Houston, with Armstrong at the controls and Buzz Aldrin calling out speed and altitude readings from the instruments. They had a bad moment during their final descent. The *Eagle* was less than 500 feet from the moon when Armstrong realized that they were about to land in the large, forbidding West Crater, so called because it was four miles west of their target. He flew beyond it, but this unexpected extension of the journey meant that he was rapidly running out of fuel; he had to decide immediately whether to turn about there or risk crashing. In that instant two lights on the panel in front of him glowed. They read LUNAR CONTACT. The *Eagle* had made it.

"Houston, Tranquillity Base here," he said. "The *Eagle* has landed." It was 4:17:42 P.M. Eastern Daylight Time, Sunday, July 20, 1969.

After three hours of checking instruments, the two astronauts asked Houston if they might omit a scheduled four-hour break and disembark now. "We will support it," Houston answered. They put on their $300,000 space suits and depressurized the LM cabin; then Armstrong, moving backward, began his slow descent of a nine-rung ladder. On the second step he pulled a cord, opening the lens of a TV camera and thus allowing half a billion people to watch him move cautiously down to the stark surface.

His 9½B boot touched it, and he said: "That's one small step for a man, one giant leap for mankind." It was 10:56:20 P.M. He shuffled around. "The surface is fine and powdery," he said. "It adheres in fine layers, like powdered charcoal, to the soles and sides of my boots. I only go in a fraction of an inch, maybe an eighth of an inch, but I can see the footprints of my boots and the treads in the fine, sandy particles."

Armstrong put some of the powder in a pocket on the leg of his space suit. Then, nineteen minutes after his debarkation, Aldrin joined him, saying, "Beautiful, beautiful; magnificent desolation." Armstrong drove a stake in the lunar soil and mounted the TV camera on it. The spidery *Eagle* was sixty feet away, and in the middle of the television picture; behind it was the eternal night of outer space. Gravity here was one-sixth G, 16.6 percent of that on earth. Viewers saw the two men bounding about like gazelles and heard Aldrin say, "When I'm about to lose my balance in one direction I find recovery is quite natural and very easy." They planted a three-by-five-foot U.S. flag, the cloth held out from the staff by wires; Aldrin saluted it. They also deposited a container bearing messages from the leaders of seventy-six countries and a stainless-steel plaque reading, "Here men from planet Earth first set foot upon the moon, July, 1969, A.D. We came in peace for all mankind."

Gathering some fifty pounds of rocks for scientific study, they measured the temperature outside their space suits: 234 degrees Fahrenheit in sunlight and 279 degrees below zero in the shade. A strip of foil was set out to collect solar particles, and two instruments were erected, a seismometer to mark lunar disturbances, and a reflector to send readings to telescopes on earth. At midnight they returned to the *Eagle,* and after 21 hours and 37 minutes on the moon they fired their engine and departed. ("You're cleared for takeoff," Mission Control said. "Roger, we're No. 1 on the runway," said Aldrin.) Back in orbit, they rendezvoused with Collins in the *Columbia.* He rehooked the two vessels together. They crawled back through the tunnel to join him, and the *Eagle* was cast loose to float through space and, eventually, to crash on the moon.

At 1:56 A.M. Collins pointed the *Columbia* earthward and fired its engine, freeing the command module from the moon's gravity. The trip home would take sixty hours. That evening, via television, the astronauts sent the world a picture of itself taken at a distance of 175,000 miles. "It's nice to sit here and watch the earth getting larger and larger and the moon smaller and smaller," said Aldrin. Armstrong said, "No matter where you travel, it's nice to get home." On Thursday, moving at a speed of 24,602 mph, they reentered the earth's atmosphere 757 miles over the Pacific. During the crucial part of this phase the spacecraft's shield was scorched by 4,000-

degree heat. Clouds surrounded the command module, and radio contact was lost for three minutes.

Then radar aboard the waiting carrier *Hornet* picked up the descending *Columbia,* which was plunging down 13.8 miles away, beneath three 83-foot orange and white parachutes. The module splashed down in six-foot waves, capsized, and was righted when the three men inside inflated bags on the side. Helicopters from the *Hornet* hovered overhead, guiding the vessel to the spot. President Nixon was waving zoom binoculars on the bridge. The ship's band crashed into "Columbia, the Gem of the Ocean," and all over the United States, and in many foreign cities, church bells rang out, whistles blew, and motorists leaned on their horns.

Richard Nixon's greeting to the Apollo 11 astronauts came at the beginning of a nine-day presidential jet trip around the world. During it he visited six Asian nations: the Philippines, Indonesia, Thailand, South Vietnam, India, and Pakistan. His central purpose there was to drive home his determination to make sure there were no more Vietnams. Stopping overnight in Guam on his way to Manila, he spelled out the Nixon Doctrine for reporters: "Peace in Asia cannot come from the United States. It must come from Asia. The people of Asia, the governments of Asia—they are the ones who must lead the way." In Bangkok he said he wanted to speak plainly: "If domination by the aggressor can destroy the freedom of a nation, too much dependence on a protector can eventually erode its dignity."

That sounded unequivocal, but newspapermen were learning that often when the new President promised to make something perfectly clear, it was about to become opaque. So it was on this Asian swing. Even as he deplored America's overcommitment in Vietnam, he told U.S. troops there that he thought "history will record that this may have been one of America's finest hours," and he also pledged to the Thais: "The United States will stand proudly with Thailand against those who might threaten it from abroad or from within." Telling people what he thought they wanted to hear was an old Nixon weakness; if his hosts weren't elated by his assurances that he would send them some fragments of moon rock, it seemed, he was ready to hint that he might send a few divisions.

There was another explanation. This was a transitional period in his attitude toward Communism. Part of him was still the cold-warrior, ready to pick up any Red challenge, while another part believed that global stability depended on conciliation between Washington on the one hand and Moscow and Peking on the other. In this sense there was such a thing as a new Nixon. His flexibility emerged dramatically toward the end of this trip. He stopped in Bucharest to spend a day with Romanian President Nicolae Ceausescu, and as proof of his friendly feelings he rode through a downpour with the top of his car down. The crowd's response was amazing; people along the way not only cheered vigorously; they also vied with one another to pick up tiny paper American flags which fell to sidewalks, leaving flags of their own country where they lay.

In England Nixon paused for talks with Prime Minister Harold Wilson. This was his second European visit in five months; he had been in office only seventeen days when he had announced a trip to Belgium, Britain, West Germany, Italy, and France—"the blue-chip countries," as he called them. He had always believed that he had a special talent for foreign affairs, and he was certainly making friends among other chiefs of state, even though the most important of them, Wilson, Chancellor Kurt Kiesinger, and President Charles de Gaulle, were not to remain in office long. In that first year the new President was going out of his way to be cordial to a great many people at home and abroad, including some toward whom he had once been very chilly. He flew to Independence to give Harry Truman a grand piano which had once been in the White House and played "The Missouri Waltz" on it—Truman was too polite to tell him he had always hated the song—and he extolled retiring Chief Justice Earl Warren, as "a symbol of fairness, integrity, and dignity."

Even then Nixon kept his distance from the press, but most reporters were generous in their treatment of him. Hugh Sidey of *Life* wrote that the President had "devised a government in his own image—decent, thoughtful, competent, cautious." Although newsmen covering the White House felt that his public appearances were forced and contrived, they had a certain admiration for the pains he took for them, knowing how uncomfortable he was in such situations. They appreciated the diet he carefully followed to avoid appearing jowly, how he tried to stay tanned for television, and the time he spent choosing his wardrobe because he wanted his suits to give the public just the right impression of quiet good taste.

As his presidential image formed, he emerged as a thoughtful, rather lonely man who spent hours hunched over yellow legal tablets in various White House sanctuaries, notably a study off the Lincoln bedroom and a hideaway just across the street in the Executive Office Building. He liked paperwork more than Lyndon Johnson, and people less. The forty-two-button phone was removed from the oval office; Nixon needed only six buttons. He also appeared to be less interested in the news, even news about himself, than Johnson; the teletypes and the television sets of the previous administration were banished to an outer office. His favorite TV programs were Saturday afternoon football games in the autumn and winter, and he nearly always found time to watch them. "I know the job I have is supposed to be the most difficult job in the world," he said, "but it has not yet become for me that great, awesome burden that some have described it."

"Middle America" was a current journalistic phrase, and the new chief executive was its apotheosis. He liked the competitive spirit of Vince Lombardi, the music of Guy Lombardo, the novels of Allen Drury, the piety of Billy Graham, the wit of Bob Hope, and the sales techniques of J. Walter Thompson. Though most of his career had been spent in public service, he had the middle-class distrust of the federal bureaucracy; one of his first acts was to abolish the patronage system for selecting postmasters. (The following year Congress, at his request, established an independent U.S. Postal Service.) As a Middle American he believed in expert advice. The voices he listened to most were those of John Mitchell, Henry Kissinger, John D. Ehrlichman, and H. R. Haldeman. Sidey noted that although the President's programs were a little left of center on paper, "the men he named to high office leaned the other way—and in Washington experience suggested that in the end men would dominate blueprints." Doctrine seemed to mean little to Nixon himself anyway; he had Middle America's penchant for trying various approaches, zigging and zagging from the center, in hope of finding workable solutions. At various times in 1969 he proposed tax reform, tinkered with the ideological balance of the Supreme Court, reduced the troop level in Vietnam, returned Okinawa to Japan, tried to alter the welfare system, outlawed germ warfare, and made various attempts to restrain inflation. In that first year he also displayed Middle American modesty. When his advisers crowded around to congratulate him on his return from his first European journey, he called a halt. "Too soon, too soon," he said. "A year from now we'll know if it was a success."

He was not so modest as a spender. Like thousands of other American executives who had made it, the chief executive was over-extending himself to support an elaborate new life-style. He was earning $290,000 a year in salary and expenses. He had a home near the office and a retreat at Camp David, but he mortgaged himself to the hilt just the same. First he bought a pair of brick-and-stucco bungalows on Florida's Biscayne Bay. The cost was put at over $250,000. There the President could spend his leisure hours with an old friend, C. G. "Bebe" Rebozo—a onetime chauffeur and filling station operator who had made a fortune in real estate—aboard Rebozo's elaborate houseboat, the *Cocolobo*. Yet even that wasn't enough for Nixon. While gardeners were still putting in a ten-foot hedge around the Key Biscayne home, the President was in San Clemente, California, buying a $340,000 fourteen-room adobe villa, ordering a $100,000 swimming pool for it, and planning a four-hole golf course on adjacent land, each tee to be marked with a tiny presidential seal.

Although the facts were unknown at the time, Rebozo and an-other Nixon intimate, aerosol spray valve inventor Robert H. Abplanalp, held mortgages of about $500,000 on the two properties. At the same time, the government was laying out a staggering 10.5 million dollars on the two presidential estates and on houses fre-quently visited by the Nixons, such as Abplanalp's island in the Bahamas. Much of the money went for such necessities as helipads and military communications, but sums of money running to six figures were spent on landscaping, furniture, and heating systems.

That wasn't the end of it. Indeed, in terms of sheer cost it was only a beginning. Four years later *Fortune* would quote a former official of the Bureau of the Budget as estimating that the expense of President Nixon's household, as of then, had been approximately 100 million dollars. Lyndon Johnson, who was not thrifty, had main-tained three Boeing jetliners; when Lady Bird went shopping in New York, she had taken the Eastern Airlines shuttle. All Nixon's relatives, including his sons-in-law, traveled on government planes. At the President's exclusive disposal were five Boeing 707s, eleven Lockheed Jetstars, and sixteen helicopters. He installed an archery range, a swimming pool, and bowling alleys at Camp David; the annual operating costs of the camp went from $147,000 a year under Johnson to $640,000. In addition the chief executive was attended at his various homes by 75 butlers, maids, cooks, and caretakers, 21 gardeners and maintenance workers, 100 Secret Service agents, 300 guards, the crew of the presidential yacht, and the drivers of a fleet of official limousines. Under Richard Nixon the presidential style could only be called lordly.

In his first appearance as President he had appeared in the role of healer. "The greatest honor history can bestow is the title of peacemaker," he had said in his inaugural, and he had made it clear that he was not merely talking about Vietnam. "We find ourselves rich in goods, but ragged in spirit; reaching with magnificent precision for the moon, but falling into raucous discord on earth. . . . We are torn by division, wanting unity. We see around us empty lives, wanting fulfillment. We see tasks that need doing, waiting for hands to do them. To a crisis of the spirit, we need an answer of the spirit. And to find that answer, we need only look within ourselves. . . . We cannot learn from one another until we stop shouting at one another—until we speak quietly enough so that our words can be heard as well as our voices. For its part, government will listen."

It was a shrewd appraisal of the American dilemma, and during his first eight months in the White House Nixon's search for solutions was along those lines. He suppressed his own strong combative instincts, keeping his voice down, his profile low, and his ear to the ground. In seeking advice he cultivated an aura of responsible craftsmanship. He had promised a "small" White House staff in his campaign, and after he won had said that he would run an "open" administration with vigorous counsel from "independent thinkers." As Republicans, he and the members of his administration did not share the Johnsonian conviction that America's troubles could be traced to underprivilege and poverty, but they had their own guiding light. To them the national anguish arose from a loss of faith in religion, the family, the binding force of friendly neighborhood life, and *McGuffey's Reader* patriotism. These were the convictions of small-town America, the great keep of the Republican party. It was hardly their fault that most Americans no longer lived in small towns, or that the attack on the nation's most sacred institutions, from the flag to motherhood, had acquired an irresistible momentum. The furies of the 1960s were not yet spent. The period was still one of violent contention.

Yet some election results in 1969 suggested that backlash was turning the country rightward. Republicans won the Virginia statehouse for the first time in over eighty years and the New Jersey governorship after sixteen Democratic years. Barry Goldwater Jr. was elected to Congress by California's 27th District. Liberal Ralph Yarborough was in trouble in Texas; early the following year he would be toppled in the Democratic primary by a conservative challenger. In Minneapolis an astounding 62 percent of the voters swept Charles S. Stenvig, a previously unknown police detective, into the mayoralty on the strength of Stenvig's advocacy of tough law enforcement in black neighborhoods, and Los Angeles gave Sam Yorty, the closest thing to a racist mayor outside the South, a third term despite an appalling record of absenteeism, drift, strife, and the conviction, on charges of bribery, of three men Yorty had appointed city commissioners.

A trend toward the right did not explain some Nixon difficulties on the Hill. In a truly conservative climate the Pentagon would be sacrosanct, and in 1969 the Defense budget was in peril for the first time in twenty years. Ever since the North Koreans had crossed the 38th Parallel, astronomical annual sums had been appropriated for the military establishment, frequently without even a roll call. The Pentagon outlay had risen from eleven billion dollars to eighty-one billion, but now the generals were confronted by a balky Congress. Frustration over Vietnam was one reason; others included a scandal featuring senior Army noncoms who had been making fortunes through PX kickbacks, dissatisfaction with the excessive costs of Lockheed C-5A transport production, and the discovery that the Army's Chemical Warfare Service was transporting 7,000 tons of nerve and poison gas across the country and dumping it in the Atlantic Ocean. The immediate issue raising congressional hackles, however, was a matter of missilery. The Defense Department wanted to start work on an enormous antiballistic missile (ABM) system which could wind up costing the country as much as a hundred billion dollars.

The ABM was necessary, the Pentagon argued, to deprive the USSR of first-strike power—the ability to cripple U.S. ICBM installations with a single blow and therefore prevent American retaliation. Senate critics led by Edward M. Kennedy replied that the ABM would escalate the arms race, that it would waste money better spent on pollution and in slums, and that its radar and computers were too complicated to work. "History," one technical witness said dryly, "is littered with Maginot Lines." In the end an ABM appropriation passed the Senate by a single vote, but the victory was Pyrrhic. It laid the groundwork for future struggles over Defense programs and sowed seeds of bitterness between Congress and the new administration. Speaking at the Air Force Academy on June 4, President Nixon attacked the forty-nine anti-ABM senators as "new isolationists." Senator Fulbright replied: "The greatest threat to peace and domestic tranquillity is not in Hanoi, Moscow, or Peking but in our colleges and in the ghettos of cities throughout the land."

The split between the President and his adversaries on the Hill widened in two savage battles over Supreme Court nominees. Nixon's choice of Warren E. Burger to succeed Earl Warren as Chief Justice sailed through the Senate, but when he named federal Judge Clement F. Haynsworth Jr. of South Carolina to replace Abe Fortas he touched off a senatorial revolt. The AFL-CIO and the NAACP denounced Haynsworth as antilabor and racist. He might have survived that, but Birch Bayh of Indiana turned up evidence that the judge had ruled in favor of firms in which he held stock. The nomination was rejected 55 to 45, with seventeen Republicans, including Minority Leader Hugh Scott, in the majority. Nixon called the attacks on Haynsworth "brutal, vicious, and . . . unfair." Two months later he announced his second choice, federal Judge G. Harrold Carswell of Florida.

Carswell's chief qualification appeared to be that he wasn't rich and thus, unlike Haynsworth, couldn't be charged with conflict of interest in corporate verdicts. Unfortunately he had other liabilities. A reporter dug out a sentence from a 1948 Carswell speech: "Segregation of the races is proper and the only practical and correct way of life in our states." Confronted with the quotation, the nominee called it "obnoxious and abhorrent," but the NAACP came out against him anyway. Then it was revealed that Carswell had participated actively in a campaign to exclude blacks from a Tallahassee golf club, had insulted civil rights lawyers in his court, and had been often reversed on appeal. This last development inspired a well-meant comment by Senator Roman L. Hruska of Nebraska. He told a television interviewer that "even if he were mediocre, there are a lot of mediocre judges and people and lawyers. Aren't they entitled to a little representation and a little chance? We can't have all Brandeises and Cardozos and Frankfurters and stuff like that. I doubt we can. I doubt we want to."

Later Hruska was asked if he regretted saying it. "Indeed I do," he said, "indeed I do." A GOP floor leader remarked later, "Everywhere I go I hear that word—mediocre. If there was one single thing it was that. You could see the votes deserting in droves." Before Hruska said it, Senator Kennedy had forecast a maximum of 25 votes against Carswell, and Scott had predicted that the most the opposition could muster would be "in the 30s." In fact the ayes were 45 and the nays 51; "the nomination," said the presiding officer, Vice President Agnew, "is not agreed to." Two days later an angry President Nixon told newspapermen that as long as the Democrats controlled the Senate "I cannot successfully nominate to the Supreme Court any federal appellate judge from the South who believes as I do in the strict construction of the Constitution."

This was a far cry from the bring-us-together theme of his inaugural, but it was deliberate. Nixon was abandoning nonpartisanship and was counterattacking. The strategic shift had begun with a televised speech to the nation in response to the first in a series of new antiwar demonstrations which dramatized demands for peace in Vietnam. The President said they were unnecessary because he had "a plan . . . for the complete withdrawal of all United States ground combat forces and their replacement by South Vietnamese forces." He called this "Vietnamization." He said he believed it would succeed and asked for support from "the great silent majority of my fellow Americans." In a thrust at his critics he said: "Let us be united for peace. Let us also be united against defeat. Because let us understand: North Vietnam cannot defeat or humiliate the United States. Only Americans can do that."

Gallup reported that 77 percent of his audience approved of the speech—only 6 percent disapproved it—and Nixon, heartened, decided to send his Vice President into the breach with even more vivid rhetoric. This was to be what Agnew himself called the "politics of polarization," a deliberate effort to isolate the President's critics. He had won Nixon's warm congratulations for assailing the dissidents as "an effete corps of impudent snobs who characterize themselves as intellectuals" and their political supporters as "parasites of passion" and "ideological eunuchs." Because 70 million Americans watched television network news programs, and because the White House was unhappy with TV coverage of the President, Agnew made that his first target.

Speaking in Des Moines on November 13, he took out after "a small group of men, numbering perhaps no more than a dozen anchormen, commentators and executive producers," who "settle upon the twenty minutes or so of film and commentary that is to reach the public." This "unelected elite," he said, was "a tiny and closed fraternity of privileged men . . . enjoying a monopoly sanctioned and licensed by government." He accused it of distorting "our national search for internal peace and stability." A week later he zeroed in on the press, singling out the *New York Times* and the *Washington Post* and deploring "the monopolization of the great public information vehicles and the concentration of more and more power over public opinion in fewer and fewer hands." Both the networks and the newspapers reported a heavy run of mail supporting Agnew and condemning the "eastern liberal establishment." Washington wondered whether Agnew had been speaking for himself or for Nixon. Hubert Humphrey said "Anyone who thinks that the Vice President can take a position independent of the President or his administration simply has no knowledge of politics or government. You are his choice in a political marriage, and he expects your absolute loyalty."

His bombast identified Spiro Agnew as a man of the era, for it was a time of overstatement, of exaggerated gestures and posturing and hyperbole, when everything from eating grapes and lettuce to wearing (or not wearing) a brassiere carried political overtones, and CBS fired the Smothers Brothers, a comedy team, for encouraging guest stars to make flippant remarks about patriotism and the Vietnam War.

A number of courtrooms were preoccupied with political trials. James Earl Ray and Sirhan Sirhan, the assassins of Martin Luther King and Robert F. Kennedy, were being convicted, and in one of the most bizarre actions in American legal history, New Orleans District Attorney Jim Garrison was trying to convince a jury that Clay L. Shaw, a retired Louisiana businessman, had conspired to murder John Kennedy. The key witnesses were a former taxi driver who had vaguely incriminated Shaw while under hypnosis, a drug addict, a paranoid accountant, and a perjurer who ultimately confessed that he had invented his testimony. The trial lasted thirty-four days. The jury voted to acquit Shaw in less than an hour.

Norman Mailer ran for mayor of New York, Dr. Timothy Leary for governor of California. President Nixon appointed Shirley Temple Black, now forty-one, to the U.S. delegation to the United Nations ("because," someone said, "he wanted the world to have a happy ending"). Bernadette Devlin arrived from Ireland to ask New Yorkers for money that would be used for murdering British soldiers. At San Francisco State College, Timothy Peebles, black and nineteen, bungled while trying to set a crude time bomb and blinded himself. SDS Weathermen vowing to "Bring the War Home" rioted in Chicago; sixty were arrested and three shot. Over a five-month period in 1969 Manhattan terrorists bombed the Marine Midland Grace Trust Company, the Armed Forces Induction Center, the Federal Office Building, Macy's, a United Fruit Company pier, and the RCA, Chase Manhattan, and General Motors buildings. On the night of November 13 police arrested three young men and Jane Lauren Alpert, twenty-two, a brilliant Swarthmore student and the daughter of upper-middle-class parents, charging them with conspiring to bomb federal property. Miss Alpert's parents put up a $20,000 bond for her and forfeited it when she vanished.

Environmentalists were angry over the new jumbo jets, taxpayers over teacher strikes, cigarette manufacturers because they had been forbidden to advertise on television after the end of 1970. Honeymooners were irate because the water had been temporarily diverted from Niagara Falls. Believers in flying saucers were indignant at the Air Force, which concluded a two-year investigation of 11,000 reported sightings by declaring that the saucers did not exist. Squeamish theatergoers objected when the 1969 New York Drama Desk Award went to *Peace*, an antiwar play in which the God of War flushed nations down a huge toilet.

To millions of Americans the nation's abrasive new mood appeared to be symbolized when Mel Finkelstein, a *New York Daily News* photographer trying to photograph Jacqueline Kennedy Onassis as she left a Manhattan showing of *I Am Curious (Yellow)*, sprawled on the pavement outside the theater. He said she flipped him over her thigh in a judo maneuver; she said he slipped and fell. Whatever had happened, another cameraman snapped President Kennedy's widow striding away from Finkelstein and the Swedish blue movie. She was wearing a tight black leather miniskirt. In the background a sign advertised WINES AND LIQUORS. Camelot seemed very far away.

It was the roughest year yet on college campuses. Although Gallup found that 72 percent of the country's 6.7 million students had never joined a demonstration, and a *Fortune* poll reported that only 12.8 percent were "revolutionary" or "radically dissident," the minority disrupted or paralyzed institutions in every part of the country. San Francisco State was closed for three weeks. The home of San Mateo Junior College's dean was fire-bombed. A rally of a thousand students and two hundred faculty members forced the resignation of Rice's president, and desperate administrators summoned police to, among others, San Fernando State, Howard, Pennsylvania State, and the University of Massachusetts. At the University of Chicago Bruno Bettelheim said that "many of these kids are very sick—paranoid," and he compared them to German students who had backed Hitler. Their demands continued. Negroes sought more courses in black studies, whites called for an end to ROTC and Dow Chemical recruitment. And all wanted an end to the Vietnam War.

Campus clashes had a way of escalating rapidly, often reaching ugly proportions before authorities—or even some of the participants—clearly understood the issues at stake. At the University of Wisconsin an organization of Negro students, the Black People's Alliance, called a strike. Conservative students of the Young Americans for Freedom decided to cross the blacks' picket lines. Blows were exchanged, and in swift succession the governor called out 1,900 National Guardsmen, bayonets and tear gas were used on the Negroes, over five thousand whites marched on the state capitol to protest this use of force, faculty groups supported the black demands, and the Wisconsin legislature, lashing back, cut the university budget.

Puerto Rican students joined blacks at the City College of New York—CCNY, "the poor man's Harvard"—in locking themselves inside the South Campus and issuing a manifesto demanding that the college's enrollment reflect New York's racial balance, that a black studies program be introduced, and that they control it. Confronted by this threat to academic standards and consequently to the value of their diplomas, the white students mobilized. In the subsequent struggle an auditorium was burned. President Buell Gallagher closed the school twice and then resigned. The faculty senate then approved an almost unbelievable proposal under which 40 percent of the next freshman class would be blacks and Puerto Ricans who would not have to meet the academic requirements of CCNY, which as a consequence could no longer be called the poor man's Harvard.

Harvard itself blew on April 9, when undergraduates invaded University Hall, evicted the deans, and began rifling confidential files. President Nathan Pusey responded by calling on the state police, four hundred of whom fought their way into the building and arrested 197 students. Their classmates—six thousand of them—met in Harvard Stadium and voted to strike in protest. A faculty resolution asked that charges against the 197 be dropped. Pusey agreed, but the judge didn't; he fined them twenty dollars each for criminal trespass and sentenced a twenty-five-year-old graduate student to a year in prison for striking a dean. The university then formally endorsed a faculty resolution calling for agreement to the chief demand of the original group of demonstrators—an end to ROTC at Harvard.

Cornell was no more strife-torn than a dozen other campuses that spring, but a local aspect at Ithaca produced a sequence of photographs which shocked the world. Demanding an autonomous Afro-American college, two hundred and fifty Negro undergraduates took over Willard Straight Hall, the student union, on April 19. When rumors spread inside Willard Straight that a band of whites with guns was on its way, the Negroes acquired weapons themselves. That, said President James A. Perkins, made it "a whole new thing." He capitulated to every black demand, and the Negroes who had seized the building walked out—armed to the teeth, the newspaper pictures showed, with rifles in their hands and bandoliers of ammunition crisscrossed on their chests. The faculty rejected the president's settlement and then reversed itself. The university trustees announced an investigation and Perkins quit.

All this was being watched closely in Washington, where, as might be expected, the Nixon administration's sympathy was with everybody except the rebellious students. HEW Secretary Finch wrote to the head of every institution of higher learning in the country, pointing out that more than a million students were receiving aid which could be terminated if they abused their privileges. Nixon himself spoke out after Reverend Theodore M. Hesburgh, president of Notre Dame, warned his undergraduates that any who resorted to force would be expelled and charged with trespassing. In a "Dear Ted" letter, Nixon wrote Hesburgh, "I want to applaud the forthright stand you have taken," and asked him to forward his opinions on student unrest to Vice President Agnew, who was about to confer with the state governors. Hesburgh advised caution; "even the most far-out students," he observed, "are trying to tell society something that may be worth searching for today." His point was not lost on the governors, who rejected a proposal from Ronald Reagan for a federal inquiry into the student riots.

If Negro activists were busy on the campuses, they were lying low in most inner cities. For the second straight summer the ghettos were relatively quiet. The mood in the ghettos was changing. The turmoil of the mid-1960s had opened new lines of communication with the city halls, and big cities could now field well-trained, well-equipped riot police. The new emphasis among blacks was on political action. With the upsurge in Negro registrations, the election of Negro candidates had become a realistic alternative in many areas to open revolt against society. Howard Lee became the first black mayor of Chapel Hill, North Carolina, in 1969, and Charles Evers won the mayoralty of Fayette, Mississippi, with the slogan: "Don't vote for a black man. Don't vote for a white man. Vote for a good man."

Nixon called the role of the new administration in race relations a "middle course." By any term it was a slowdown in desegregation. The Johnson policy had been to end federal subsidies to schools which failed to integrate. Nixon rejected it, saying, "I do not consider it a victory for integration when the federal government cuts off funds for a school and thereby, for both black and white students in that school, denies them the education they should have." In one of his first press conferences in the White House he conceded that Negroes distrusted him, believing him, despite his earlier record, to be indifferent now to their cause. In his campaign he had made much of promises of help for "black capitalism." Nothing more was heard about it. Instead, in August 1969 Finch proposed a delay in Mississippi school integration.

This was widely regarded as a stratagem to court the South's white voters. It was thwarted late in October when the Supreme Court, in its first major decision since Warren Burger's appointment as Chief Justice, unanimously ruled that "the obligation of every school district is to terminate dual school systems at once and to operate now and hereafter only unitary schools." Nixon responded that he would make every effort to enforce the decree with "full respect for the law."

Although student riots were the work of a minority, American youths in much larger numbers were continuing to assert their separate identity by dressing, speaking, and behaving in ways alien to adult society. Their extraordinarily high visibility was in large part a result of their life-style, which was, and was meant to be, conspicuous and even outrageous. But there were also more of them to be seen. This was the inevitable sequel to the postwar baby boom. In 1960 there had been 27 million Americans between the ages of fourteen and twenty-four. Now there were 40 million of them, accounting for a full 20 percent of the population. Their numbers and their affluence guaranteed that youth's counterculture would grow in magnitude, and that if a sizable proportion of them flocked to any one event, its popularity would be tremendous. Such an event occurred on the weekend of August 15–17, 1969. It was a rock music festival, and it was called Woodstock.

Actually that was a misnomer. Originally the two twenty-four-year-olds who conceived and promoted the festival planned to stage it in the Hudson River village of Woodstock, New York, and it was so advertised. Zoning regulations and local opposition thwarted them there, however, and the event was moved to the six-hundred-acre dairy farm of one Max Yasgur in the Catskill town of Bethel, on White Lake, about seventy miles northwest of New York City. The promoters hoped the kids could find it. They were expecting to draw about 50,000 customers at seven dollars a ticket.

They grossly underestimated the festival's appeal. Max Yasgur's farm was stormed by a multitude of 400,000. Bethel briefly became the third largest city in the state. The surrounding road net was cluttered with abandoned cars, motorcycles, and microbuses decorated with psychedelic drawings. All adjacent exits from the Catskill highway were jammed. Collecting fees from so enormous a throng was impractical, and the promoters had to give up the idea, thereby losing two million dollars. That was one of two things which went wrong at Woodstock. The other was the weather. Two tremendous cloudbursts turned the farm into a swamp. The youths huddled in soggy sleeping bags and under plastic tents and lean-tos fashioned from blankets and pieces of clothing. The lack of normal supplies of food and water, or even of sanitation facilities, should have made Woodstock a disaster.

Instead it was a triumph. Looking out nervously over the huge crowd, one of the first performers said, "If we're going to make it, you had better remember that the guy next to you is your brother." They remembered. A police officer called the audience "the most courteous, considerate, and well-behaved group of kids that I have ever been in contact with in my twenty-four years of police work."

The most helpful hands came from their own ranks. A caravan of Ken Kesey's Merry Pranksters, who had driven all the way from Oregon, doled out a high-protein broth of raisins, oatmeal, and peanuts and set up a hospital tent; a hundred members of the Hog Farm, a Taos, New Mexico, commune, also provided essential services. What really made the event a success, however, was the magnet which had lured so many here: acid rock. The Jefferson Airplane, the Creedence Clearwater Revival, the Family Stone, Jimi Hendrix, Joan Baez, Janis Joplin—these were their folk heroes. They were here in person, and if they could not be seen, they could at least be heard from loudspeakers set atop eighty-foot scaffolds around the stage. And so, despite the rain and constant provocation, the youths in headbands, bell-bottoms, beads, and tie-dyed dungaree shirts made the festival so strong a symbol of generational unity that their future spokesmen would speak of them as the Woodstock Nation.

In an era of rapid change the strengthening of peer group bonds was inevitable. Woodstock was the most spectacular rock festival of 1969, but it was by no means unique. Others that year were held on a ranch near Tenino, Washington, after the state supreme court had overruled objections from the John Birch Society; at Lewisville, Texas ("This crowd is a lot better than Dallas football crowds," a security officer said, while the Lewisville mayor told reporters that the only problem was created by older Texans who came to stare at naked young swimmers in the Garza-Little Elm Reservoir); and at Prairieville, Louisiana, where the attractions included the Grateful Dead, Canned Heat, Country Joe and the Fish, and the Iron Butterfly.

The festival phenomenon was not confined to the United States. It being an American phenomenon, and this being the age of American dominance, the sounds of rock were echoing in western Europe, and particularly in England. HELP BOB DYLAN SINK THE ISLE

OF WIGHT, read banners over that English Channel island. Answering the appeal were 150,000 "oddly dressed people," as a local policeman put it, "of uncertain sex." Dylan himself arrived thirty-six hours after the music began; he wore a white suit, yellow shirt, and green boots. A young female admirer ripped off her clothes, danced nude, and screamed, "I just want to be free." Unlike Woodstock, the Isle of Wight concert wound up heavily in the black.

There was something anomalous here. Fortunes were being made by promoters and entertainers, yet the counterculture which supported them was aggressively antimaterialistic. Unlike swing music, rock was accompanied by an ideological strain. That was one reason many older Americans found it so objectionable. To them, the lifestyle and the social creed that went with it were unpatriotic, ungodly, immoral, and, if possible, worse. It was possible; their most hideous fears were realized when the ugliest murder of 1969 was committed by a band of hippies run amok. Those offended by the now generation saw it as a vindication of their direst predictions, and the failure of long-haired youth to accept responsibility for it merely deepened their rage.

The victims were actress Sharon Tate, honey blonde and pregnant, and four acquaintances. Their bodies, hideously mutilated and arranged in grotesque positions, were found one August morning in a Los Angeles mansion at 10050 Cielo Drive, overlooking Benedict Canyon. Four months later the killers—who had committed two other murders in the meantime—were found to be members of a commune on the fringe of Death Valley. Their leader was Charles Manson, a thirty-five-year-old ex-convict and, by all accounts, a sexual athlete. The slayers were his protégés: a demented Texas youth and three pretty girls who had been eager to do anything—literally anything—Manson required of them. Their days had been occupied with riding around in dune buggies fashioned from stolen Volkswagens and mounted with machine guns. (Manson had visions of war between the races.) At night they had explored unusual sexual activities—unless, of course, they had been busy stabbing strangers to death.

If Manson and his friends represented the dark side of hippy romanticism, the bright side was youth's social conscience. The best of young America was profoundly disturbed by man's abuse of his fellow man and his surroundings. The ecological issue was the least controversial; the need was obvious—pollution had become unconscionable. Gallup found that 70 percent of Americans put the environmental issue first among the country's domestic problems. Not only the younger generation but organizations on every level of society were awakening to the threat. The United Nations announced plans for a Conference on Human Environment. The President established an Environmental Quality Council. Governors and mayors appointed ecological committees. In Louisville, where a factory with ancient equipment was pouring eleven tons of dirt into the city's air each day, citizens wearing gas masks marched on City Hall bearing a protest petition with 13,000 signatures; the plant then installed new furnaces which cut the daily yield of soot to one hundred pounds.

That helped Louisville, but in the national view it hardly counted. There the dimensions of the problem were overwhelming. Combustion in the U.S. was disgorging 140 million tons of grime into the air every year. The automobiles in Los Angeles alone emitted each day 10,000 tons of carbon monoxide, 2,000 tons of hydrocarbons, and 530 tons of nitrogen oxides. Other pollutants rising into the great sewer in the sky over America were oxides of sulphur, sulphuric acid mists, fly ash, soot, and particles of arsenic, beryllium, cadmium, lead, chromium, and manganese. Annually they accounted for eleven billion dollars in property damage alone. Smog disintegrated nylon stockings, stripped paint from houses, turned other buildings a rusty orange, coated sidewalks with green slime, caused rubber to become brittle and crack, discolored clothing, etched windowpanes, attacked the enamel on teeth, induced pulmonary disease, and otherwise eroded, tarnished, soiled, corroded, and abraded man and his works.

All this had been going on for some time, but it was in 1969 that a combination of events forced the ecological issue into the forefront of the national consciousness. Nuclear power plants on the Hudson and Connecticut rivers on the East Coast, and the Columbia River in the West, were found to be killing fish by the ton with thermal pollution. DDT was also taking its toll of seafood and threatening the bald eagle, emblem of the nation, with extinction. Pedestrians in Manhattan were reported to be breathing air whose level of carbon monoxide was twice the danger level as determined by the federal government. And Everglades National Park in Florida and Sequoia National Park in California were threatened by plans for, respectively, a huge airport and an access road to a ski resort.

Construction of the airport was halted by nineteen groups of aroused conservationists who went to court. The Sierra Club also secured a court order stopping the building of the road by Walt Disney Productions, but the order was only temporary, and in other ways 1969 was a poor environmental year for the Golden State. Nature was partly to blame; three storms, dumping 52 inches of rain, hit the slopes of the San Gabriel Mountains in swift succession. Bridges were washed out and hundreds of homes literally slid down the hills—291 houses in Carpenteria alone, with a population of just 7,200. Life was also edgy along the San Andreas fault, which cuts across one corner of San Francisco and runs twenty miles east of Los Angeles. Tension had been building along the fault since the calamity of 1906; another earthquake was overdue. Californians faced the possibility good-humoredly. Bumper stickers declared, "California Deserves a Fair Shake," and a local best seller in 1969 was *The Last Days of the Late, Great State of California*, a fictional account of a quake. In reality only one tremor of any substance was recorded, on April 28, and its center was in uninhabited desert country.

That, however, was not the full story of the state's experience with geological faults that year. The stresses along another of them, combined with man's folly, provided the nation's ecological horror story of 1969. Late in January an oil drill which had been boring into a high-pressure pool of petroleum and gas 3,486 feet beneath the bottom of the Pacific Ocean was withdrawn for the replacement of a worn bit. Suddenly the well erupted, sending up oil bubbles 200 feet in diameter around the drillers' platform. Meanwhile pressure from the runaway well was being relayed along unmapped fissures in the sand and shale of the sea floor. This was catastrophic; drillers capped the original hole in eleven days, but oil continued to boil forth over a wide area.

Six miles east of the platform lay the immaculate beaches of Santa Barbara, where shore-front property had been selling at as much as $2,000 a foot. In the first week of February the white sands cherished by Santa Barbarans—forty miles of superb waterfront—began turning black. Hundreds of thousands of gallons of gummy crude oil coated yachts and fishing craft with a thick scum which could only be removed by live steam. A *Sports Illustrated* writer reported

that petroleum "lay so thick on the water that waves were un-
formed; they made a squishing sound. . . . The smell of oil followed me up the canyon to our house, a mile from the sea. . . .
The tideline was a broad black band that looked from the air like
something made on a map by a black crayon."

The most shocking aspect of the disaster was the destruction of
marine life. Mussels and rock lobsters died instantly. Porpoises and
sea lions disappeared. Pelicans dove straight into the oil and then
sank, unable to raise their matted wings, and the beaches were
studded with dead sandpipers, cormorants, gulls, grebes, and loons,
their eyes horribly swollen and their viscera burned by petroleum.
"A very sad-looking mess," said the Audubon Society; another spectator called it "a sickening sight." Residents held protest meetings,
picketed government offices with placards demanding BAN THE BLOB,
and joined a new ecological group called Get Oil Out (GOO).
Damage suits totaling a billion dollars were filed; the cost of the
cleanup was put at three million.

More than twelve thousand wires and letters went to Washington.
At first the government seemed responsive. The Department of the
Interior announced that in the future drills would have to be
sheathed in pipe below the depth of 239 feet, which had been the
previous requirement. Most important, drilling leases in the Santa
Barbara Channel were suspended. Then the petroleum industry began applying pressure. Large sums of money were at stake; the
leases, granting the right to drill in nearly one thousand square
miles of the Pacific, had been signed a year earlier with a dozen
firms which were paying 603 million dollars for the privilege. They
wanted the privilege back, and in September the Nixon administration gave it to them—in spite of dire warnings from geologists as
to other fissures, and in spite of continuing leaks from the original
runaway well.

Youthful participants were conspicuous in all the environmental
crusades, carrying petitions in Florida, marching on Louisville City
Hall in large numbers, and setting up "laundries" to clean and save
the California birds. How deep their convictions ran—to what degree they were merely caught up by the excitement of protest—
was, however, another question. In some ways they seemed to be
flagrantly inconsistent. Although vehemently opposed to pollution
of the environment, for example, they enthusiastically supported by
their patronage another form of pollution: the junk food industry.

Fast-food stands, peddling empty calories and little nourishment, had been a feature of the American roadside since the 1920s, but not until the 1960s did they impose a sameness on the landscape outside virtually all American cities by becoming the dominant force in the franchising business. Franchising itself—leasing the rights to a commercial name—was a sign of the times; among its creations were the Holiday Inns, Midas Muffler Shops, Citgo stations, and Howard Johnson's motels. These were conventional and sedate, however, when compared to the quick grill and ice cream shops. The going prices of top franchises in 1969 were $96,000 for a McDonald's ("Over 5 Billion Served") hamburger stand, $37,000 for an A & W stand, $24,500 for a Colonel Sanders ("Finger-Lickin' Good") Kentucky Fried Chicken stand, and from $7,500 to $30,000, depending on the location, for a Dairy Queen ice cream stand. Other emporia of the fatty snack, all of them drawing teen-agers by the millions, were doing business under the signs of Dunkin' Donuts, Bonanza, Hardee's, Burger King, Minnie Pearl's Chicken, Baskin-Robbins, Roy Rogers Roast Beef, and the International House of Pancakes.

If the young approved of these, they might have been expected to sanction another big financial phenomenon of the time, the conglomerates, of which the best known was ITT—the International Telephone and Telegraph Company—under whose banner hotels, car rental agencies, life insurance firms, bakeries, and manufacturers of communications equipment did business. But conglomerate was a dirty word among committed youths; it was associated with government contracts and therefore with the Vietnam War, which was an even greater enemy than pollution. Here passions ran highest, both for antiwar demonstrators and their critics, and here the rising generation was taking the stand for which it would be best remembered.

The word for protest that year was moratorium. The first M-day was scheduled for May 15. Richard Nixon said in advance, "Under no circumstances will I be affected whatever by it," thereby guaranteeing large turnouts to ring church bells, wear black armbands, carry signs and candles, and, above all, to march in thousands of American communities as proof of solidarity against the involvement in Indochina. That Wednesday there were 90,000 protesters on Boston Common, 20,000 in New York, and 22,000 in Washington. Some college campuses reported that half their students were gone. At Whittier College, whose most famous alumnus was in the White House, the wife of the acting president lit a flame which was to burn until the war was over.

November 15 fell on a weekend, and the New Mobe, as it was called, lasted for three days. This time the focus was Washington. Police put the crowd at 250,000; the New Mobe committee said 800,000 participated; there was really no way of reaching an accurate estimate, but certainly nothing like it had ever happened in America before. While the White House was announcing that President Nixon would stay inside, watching a football game on television, the first of 40,000 marchers passed by outside, each bearing a card with the name of an American who had died in Vietnam or the name of a Vietnamese community destroyed by the war. The marchers walked four miles, from Arlington to the Capitol, where the names were placed in huge, flag-draped coffins.

It was orderly. The Army had 9,000 troops in reserve to control unruly demonstrators, but they were not used, and praisers of the crowd's restraint included presidential aide Herbert G. Klein and Republican senators Hugh Scott and John Sherman Cooper. A minority view was expressed by Attorney General John N. Mitchell. Two minor episodes of violence had marred the weekend: an SDS band had attacked the South Vietnamese embassy, and a mob of Yippies had tried to rush the Justice Department building. Both had been turned back by tear gas. Taking note of them, Mitchell said that while "the great majority of participants" in the New Mobe had "obeyed the law," the march had been accompanied "by such extensive physical injury, property damage, and street confrontations that I do not believe that—overall—the gatherings here can be characterized as peaceful."

Spiro Agnew agreed. Washington was not surprised. By now it was clear that whatever other members of the administration might say, the attorney general and the Vice President would be pitiless with Americans who broke the law.

My Lai, which was to become the American Lidice, was a Vietnamese hamlet, too small to be known outside Quang Ngai province on the South China Sea until the hot, humid morning of Saturday, March 16, 1968, when it became an open grave for some 567 old men, women, and children. Even then the name was unfamiliar to most of its attackers, all members of Lieutenant William L. Calley

Jr.'s Americal Division platoon. They called it Pinkville because the area was colored pink on the military maps issued the night before at the platoon leader's briefing.

Calley and his men were members of Task Force Barker, named for Lieutenant Colonel Frank A. Barker Jr., who would die in a helicopter crash three months later, leaving his role in the events of March 16 forever obscure. The question of provocation was also nebulous; it was to be raised at Calley's court-martial. Charlie Company of the division's 11th Infantry Brigade, to which his unit belonged, had been in Vietnam three and a half months. During that time the company had lost almost half of its 190 men to booby traps and sniper fire. At the briefing the lieutenant was told that My Lai was held by the 48th Battalion of the Viet Cong. Captain Ernest Medina, the company commander, later said that he did not know any women and children were there. He told Lieutenant Calley to clean the village out, and Calley passed the word among his men. At daybreak they were helicoptered in, their M-16 automatic rifles loaded and ready.

On landing they found no Viet Cong. Instead there were only defenseless civilians, who, according to Private Paul David Meadlo, were herded by the American soldiers into the center of the hamlet "like a little island." There, where two trails crossed, the lieutenant ordered his men to shoot the inhabitants. Meadlo was one who obeyed—"I poured about four clips"—68 shots—"into them," he said afterward; "I might have killed ten or fifteen of them." Calley stood beside him, pumping automatic fire into the captives at point-blank range. Next the soldiers shoved seven or eight Vietnamese into one of the huts, or "hootches" as the grunts called them, and tossed a hand grenade in after them.

The third phase occurred in an L-shaped drainage ditch, which was to become infamous during the Fort Benning, Georgia, court-martial. There the mass murder took on aspects of an assembly line operation. "There was a variety of people there—men, women, and children," a rifleman testified at Fort Benning. ". . . There was being brought up small groups of people and they were being placed in the ditch and Lieutenant Calley was firing into it." Another witness told how the platoon leader had dealt with a Buddhist priest and a baby. The priest, who was wearing the flowing white robe of his office, held out supplicating hands as though in prayer. He kept repeating, "No Viet, no Viet." Calley, according to the testimony, smashed in the man's mouth with the butt of his M-16, reversed the rifle, "and pulled the trigger in the priest's face. Half his head was blown off." As for the infant, "Lieutenant Calley grabbed it by the arm and threw it into the ditch and fired."

Meanwhile, according to a Houston soldier named Herbert Carter, "We went through the village. We didn't see any VC. People began coming out of their hootches and the guys shot them down and then burned the hootches or burned the hootches and shot the people when they came out. Sometimes they would round up a bunch and shoot them together. It went on like this all day."

Sergeant Michael Bernhardt, whose comrades said he refused to participate, called it "point-blank murder." He said, "Only a few of us refused. I told them the hell with this, I'm not doing it. I didn't think this was a lawful order." Most of the firing had died away before Private Richard Pendleton reached My Lai, "but," he later said, "some guys were still shooting people. . . . There were big groups of bodies lying on the ground, in gullies and in the paddies." Only one American was a casualty—a soldier who had shot himself in the foot rather than take part in the killings.

Among the witnesses were two soldiers whose recollections would later carry special weight. Ronald Haeberle, an Army photographer, recorded the My Lai carnage on film with three cameras. One was official; he turned that in. The other two were his personal property, and he kept them. The second soldier was Warrant Officer Hugh C. Thompson Jr., a helicopter pilot. Thompson saw the L-shaped gully from the air and alerted his commanding officer. "I thought something was wrong out there," he said later, "because I couldn't foresee any way of how the bodies got in the ditch." Thompson returned to the village and rescued sixteen children there. The Army awarded him the Distinguished Flying Cross for "disregarding his own safety."

That was the only sign of official awareness that anything unusual had happened at My Lai. Twelve days later Colonel Barker filed a combat action report describing the attack as "well-planned, well-executed, and successful." In the words of a subsequent congressional report, "it can be reasonably concluded that the My Lai matter was 'covered up' within the Americal Division." Long afterward, when the cover-up had failed, the divisional commander, Major General Samuel Koster—who had gone on to become superintendent of West Point—was reduced in rank, and both he and the assistant divisional commander were censured and deprived of their Distinguished Service Medals. This could hardly have been foreseen then or for some time afterward, however. The first man to do something about My Lai hadn't been there that morning and didn't even hear about it until a month later. He was Ronald Ridenhour, who had been with Charlie Company earlier, in Hawaii; he learned about the massacre from his former comrades. A year later, as a returned veteran, Ridenhour wrote out an account of what had apparently happened and mailed twenty-three copies of it to President Nixon, key congressmen, and officials in the Pentagon and the State Department. He charged that "something rather dark and bloody did indeed occur sometime in March 1968 in a village called 'Pinkville' in the Republic of Vietnam."

That was on March 29, 1969. Within four weeks the Army opened a full-scale inquiry into the slaughter. Evidence was turned over to the provost marshal general on August 4; that same month the Pentagon received copies of photographer Haeberle's slides. On September 5, the day before Calley was scheduled to be discharged, he was accused of killing 109 Vietnamese civilians. Others were charged, including Medina, but only Calley was later found guilty, after a four-month trial which sent a shudder through the nation. Asked about the incident at a news conference when the story first broke, President Nixon said that it "was certainly a massacre," and that "under no circumstances was it justified." He continued: "One of the goals we are fighting for in Vietnam is to keep the people . . . from having imposed upon them a government which has atrocity against civilians as one of its policies."

When Calley was convicted in 1971 of murdering twenty-two Vietnamese and sentenced to life, however, an astonishing change swept the country, and the President's political antennae were quick to pick it up. A majority of Americans seemed to believe that the verdict was undeserved, either because the lieutenant was innocent or because he was being made a scapegoat. The mood, one observer said sardonically, was, "It didn't happen, and besides, they deserved it." Viking Press announced that it had paid $100,000 for Calley's memoirs, and in the first three days after his conviction a record on the Plantation label, "The Battle Hymn of Lieutenant Calley," sold 202,000 copies. After a saccharine voice-over about "a little boy who wanted to grow up and be a soldier and serve his country in whatever way he could," the song began:

My name is William Calley, I'm a soldier of this land,
I've vowed to do my duty and to gain the upper hand,
But they've made me out a villain, they have stamped me with a
    brand,
As we go marching on.

The White House reported that mail was running a hundred to one against the verdict and sentence. President Nixon ordered Calley released from the Benning stockade and moved to house arrest in his post apartment. Two days later the White House announced that "Yesterday the President made the decision that before any final sentence is carried out in the case of Lieutenant Calley the President will personally review the case and finally decide it." Later Nixon changed his mind, but at the time he seemed to be playing politics with a war crime. Indignant, the lieutenant's prosecutor, Captain Aubrey M. Daniel III, wrote the President that he was "shocked and dismayed at your decision to intervene in these proceedings in the midst of the public clamor."

Five weeks after Ronald Ridenhour put his My Lai statement in the mail, Secretary of the Navy John H. Chafee announced civilian intervention in the case of another embattled officer—Commander Lloyd M. Bucher of the *Pueblo*, back in the United States with his crew after the North Koreans had released them in exchange for an official American confession of espionage, an apology, and a promise that it would not happen again. Even as he handed it over at Panmunjom, Major General Gilbert H. Woodward said that the admission was false, that he had signed it "to free the crew, and only to free the crew." Still, the statement rankled in the Pentagon, and the Navy recommended a courtmartial for Bucher. Chafee vetoed it. The commander and his men, he said, "have suffered enough."

The locust years continued for the military, despite the change in Presidents. Campaigning in 1968, Richard Nixon had said of Bucher's lost ship, "Unless the United States reacts to these slights, you are bound to encourage bigger slights and you are going to have more *Pueblos*. In a new administration I say we've got to stop that kind of action . . . before it gets started." Less than three months after he entered the White House he was confronted by a similar humiliation, and he was as helpless in responding to it as Lyndon Johnson had been. This time the vehicle of mortification was an airborne *Pueblo*, a converted Lockheed Super Constellation which the Navy called an EC121. Unarmed, the EC121 carried thirty-one crewmen and six tons of electronic gear designed to monitor the communications of a potential enemy. On April 15 the North Koreans shot it down, killing all hands. This time there could be no question about the location of the incident. Russian vessels agreed that it had occurred in international waters, between 100 and 120 miles off the coast.

Nixon's first impulse had been to retaliate, but the more he pondered his options, the fewer he had. Short of risking nuclear war, there was little he could do. In the end he could only say, "I have today ordered that these flights be continued. They will be protected. This is not a threat. It is simply a statement of fact."

It was also a statement of frustration, heightened by the year's events in Vietnam. In Paris American negotiators were telling the North Vietnamese that the United States had ruled out hopes for a military solution in Indochina; in Saigon President Thieu was being told that unilateral American withdrawal, or the acceptance of terms amounting to a disguised U.S. defeat, was also unacceptable. What lay between was impotence.

Human kamikazes—Viet Cong with dynamite lashed to their bodies to blow up barbed wire—led attackers on Fire Base Russell, a Marine position just south of the demilitarized zone, and savage fighting erupted around the big U.S. base at Bien Hoa, fifteen miles from Saigon. The most controversial action of the year was the American assault on Apbia Mountain, christened Hamburger Hill by the grunts. Continuing its strategy of the Johnson years, the Army was subjecting the Viet Cong to what the Pentagon called "maximum pressure." Hamburger Hill began as a typical search-and-destroy mission. Nine battalions were set down by helicopters in the A Shau Valley, a corridor for infiltration from Laos. During the subsequent sweep, the 3rd Battalion of the 187th Regiment, 101st Airborne Division, ran into what the divisional commander, Major General Melvin Zais, called "a hornets' nest" of opposition. Pulling back, the battalion dug in and sent a company up to storm the hill.

The attack failed. Two companies then assaulted the crest. They too were thrown back. The next day the whole battalion charged the defenders and was repulsed. Three more battalions were called in. Meanwhile U.S. artillery and aircraft were battering the top of the hill; 2,000 shells and 155 air sorties defoliated the summit. Still the Viet Cong clung to it, sending the American attackers reeling backward each time in a tempest of rifle fire and exploding grenades. Ten successive U.S. charges were routed. On the eighth day 1,000 grunts and 400 South Vietnamese took the hill. General Zais called it "a great victory by a gutty bunch of guys." One week later an Army spokesman announced that Hamburger Hill was being abandoned. He said, "We feel we've gotten everything out of this mountain that we're going to get."

Senators reading the casualty lists—46 Americans had been killed on the slopes of Apbia, and 308 wounded—reacted angrily. Edward M. Kennedy called such assaults "senseless and irresponsible." He asked, "How can we justify sending our boys up against a hill a dozen times or more, until soldiers themselves question the madness of the action?" Some Republicans were also aroused. Aiken of Vermont, the ranking minority member of the Senate Foreign Relations Committee, proposed that the White House "immediately" start "an orderly withdrawal," to turn the war over to "its rightful owners"—the Vietnamese. Scott of Pennsylvania, the GOP whip, urged the withdrawal of "a substantial number" of U.S. soldiers.

Nixon was listening. During his first term he was sensitive to the mood on Capitol Hill. In speeches he remained the irreconcilable cold-warrior, earnestly asserting his belief in a Free Asia, the domino theory, and the rest of it, but his actions were something else. "Vietnam might or might not make us," one of his aides acknowledged, "but there is no question it could break us." The Johnsonian strategy was clearly bankrupt. By March 1969 the number of dead Americans had exceeded the 33,639 killed in Korea. The cost of the war, which continued to top 25 billion dollars a year, continued to generate irresistible inflationary pressure; a 1958 dollar was now worth about seventy-five cents, and economist Milton Friedman was predicting what sounded like a politician's nightmare: an "inflationary recession."

It was now clear that Nixon's most influential foreign policy adviser was not Rogers but Kissinger. Writing in *Foreign Affairs* as a private citizen, Kissinger had proposed two parallel lines of negotiation. Washington and Hanoi, he suggested, might schedule mutual troop withdrawals while the Viet Cong and the South Vietnamese forged a political solution. Now Secretary of Defense Melvin Laird returned from a visit to Saigon with another component of the new President's war policy. Laird believed that the combat efficiency of Thieu's troops could be improved to the point where they might be left on their own. The White House seized on this as a way to implement Vietnamization. Breaking the news to Thieu on Midway, Nixon announced the first cut, of 25,000 men, on June 8.

That same month Clark Clifford proposed in *Foreign Affairs* that the administration "reduce the level of combat" by scheduling the pullout of 100,000 U.S. troops by the end of 1969 and the elimination of "all ground combat forces" by the end of 1970. Clifford wrote: "Nothing we might do could be so beneficial or could so add to the political maturity of South Vietnam as to begin to withdraw our combat troops. Moreover, in my opinion, we cannot realistically expect to achieve anything more through our military force, and the time has come to begin to disengage." Annoyed, Nixon told a national television audience, "I would hope that we could beat Mr. Clifford's timetable, just as I think we've done a little better than he did when he was in charge of our national defense." Aides hastily explained that this was not a commitment, but in September the President announced that he expected to bring home all fighting men "before the end of 1970 or the middle of 1971." A *Life* writer observed at the end of the year, "Politically there did not seem to be much choice. Nixon had to get the U.S. out of Vietnam or face almost certain defeat in the presidential election of 1972."

In Vietnam General Creighton Abrams introduced tactics meant to lower U.S. casualties. Instead of large-scale search-and-destroy missions, tactics on a typical day entailed sending out as many as a thousand patrols of from one hundred to two hundred men each; their orders were to destroy enemy troops and supplies if possible, but to avoid bloodlettings. "Maximum pressure" had been replaced by "protective reaction"; an offensive stance had become defensive. This sounded more impressive in Washington than it really was, however. Two great armies remained in the field, each capable of maiming the other and each led by aggressive commanders. Only forty-six skirmishes were announced in the seven days ending Saturday, July 5, a typical week, but 155 U.S. soldiers were killed. And Abrams's conservative posture did not eliminate the possibility of a big battle, which could flare up at any time.

It happened in late August amid the rolling hills southwest of Da Nang, an area known as the Rice Bowl. A U.S. helicopter crashed there, killing the eight men aboard, and two companies of the 196th Light Infantry Brigade were ordered to recover their bodies. Simultaneously, a thousand North Vietnamese were forming up there to assault the district capital of Hiep Duc. The two forces stumbled into one another and the Communist troops withdrew into a labyrinth of bunkers and trench lines. When the Americans went after them, it was Hamburger Hill all over again. Reinforcements were sucked in until about three thousand Americans and South Vietnamese were pitted against the North Vietnamese Second Division. Both sides battled for possession of a hummock called Hill 102. The struggle ended when grunts of the 196th reached the top —and found it deserted. "It's the old story," a U.S. officer said. "Five days of fighting like hell and on the sixth day they give it to you for nothing." But there was a new story from the Rice Bowl, too, and it was ominous. Company A of the 196th had refused to obey direct orders to descend into the labyrinth and bring back the dead from the wrecked helicopter. Eventually the men did move out, but the specter of mutiny remained, one more dissonant note in the Vietnamese din.

Speaking of crime at home, the President held his hand at neck level and told reporters that the people "have had it up to here." It was in fact a lawless time in the United States; the FBI reported an increase in felonies of 10.6 percent over the previous year. Larceny was up 19 percent, forcible rape 16.8 percent, robbery 12.5 percent, and one offense went right off the chart: skyjacking, the hijacking of airplanes. Between 1950 and 1967 the airlines had reported an average of 2.3 attempted skyjacks a year. In 1969 there were 71, of which 58 went to Cuba—three times as many as the year before. On NBC-TV's *Tonight Show* Johnny Carson said, "There are so many hijackings that one airline changed its slogan to 'Up, up, and olé.'"

The airlines did try a lot of things. Signs in terminals warned that skyjacking was punishable by death, that passengers could be imprisoned just for carrying weapons aboard, and that they could be searched. The public was invited to offer some suggestions. Some memorable ones came in: stewardesses could be trained to seduce skyjackers, passengers should be required to travel naked, trapdoors could be built where the skyjackers would stand, the crew should play the Cuban national anthem over the public address system and then arrest everyone who stood up. Only one innovation worked. Although no U.S. airline scheduled regular flights to Cuba, every pilot flying over the South carried approach maps for Havana's José Martí Airport. With dismal regularity they were billed, through the Swiss government, for Cuban landing fees and incidental expenses.

That year's skyjacking climax came in November, when Captain Donald Cook of TWA's Los Angeles to San Francisco Flight 85 switched on the intercom and said, "There's a man here who wants to go some place, and he's just chartered himself an airplane. Drinks are on the house." The man was a twenty-year-old Marine Corps veteran of Vietnam, Raffaele Minichiello, and he was holding a pistol at the flight engineer's head. Minichiello was cagey about his destination. Cook said later, "Right away I suspected we would be heading south to pick up a few cigars, but that wasn't the way it was." The skyjacker ordered him to fly east.

After refueling at Bangor and Shannon, Ireland, they wound up over Leonardo da Vinci Airport in Rome. It seemed that Minichiello, a native Italian, was homesick. He ordered the control tower to park them in a far corner of the field; then he said he wanted an unarmed policeman as a hostage. Rome's police chief volunteered. The skyjacker made the chief drive him into the country and then released him. Several hours later Minichiello was arrested in a church. "Why did I do it?" he said. "I don't know." His sister said, "I think the war damaged my brother's mind." The Italian public appeared to regard him as a hero—he had, after all, established a skyjacking record: 17 hours in the air and 6,900 miles—but their government took another view. He was sentenced to six years and five months in prison.

Although the somewhat fey Minichiello was a comet in the world of crime, he was not the year's most famous miscreant. That distinction went to a motorist charged merely with leaving the scene of an accident without identifying himself. The misdeed became notorious because the culprit was a U.S. senator bearing a famous name—Edward M. Kennedy—and because the accident had tragic consequences. Until the night of July 18–19, 1969, Ted Kennedy had been the front runner for the next Democratic presidential nomination and a probable winner over Nixon and his minority party. Ted's eulogy at his brother Bob's funeral had moved the nation, and in January he had displayed his family's winning ways by blitzing Russell B. Long of Louisiana, beating him in a party caucus and thereby replacing him as the Senate's Democratic whip. The young Kennedy seemed to be on his way to greatness. Then came Chappaquiddick.

Among the many responsibilities Ted had inherited from his brothers was one for lifting the morale of the family's loyal campaigners. A cookout on July 18 was meant to do that. The hosts were Ted and several friends; their guests were six girls who had worked as volunteer drudges in the "boiler room"—back room—of Robert Kennedy's abortive presidential candidacy the year before. The place was Chappaquiddick Island, which lay just 250 yards off another island, Martha's Vineyard, on Cape Cod's Nantucket Sound.

According to Kennedy's testimony at the inquest six months later, he left the party in his Chrysler at about 11:15 P.M. with one of the girls, Mary Jo Kopechne. Mary Jo was attractive, twenty-eight, and known to her friends as "M.J." The senator said afterward that they were on their way to the two-car ferry which would have carried them back to Martha's Vineyard, where they were registered at different hotels, but the judge at the inquest didn't believe him, and neither did a lot of other people. Mary Jo left her pocketbook at the cookout. She told no one there she was departing, and she didn't ask her roommate for the key to their hotel room. When she and Ted drove off, they left behind ten people (including the Chrysler's chauffeur) who didn't intend to spend the night at the cookout and who, with the departure of the big car, were left with only one small rented auto, obviously inadequate for their return. Finally, and most compellingly, there was the question of the turn Kennedy took.

The blacktop road from the cookout to the ferry was the only surfaced road on Chappaquiddick. Ted left it for a bumpy gravel roadway that led to the beach. He said afterward that this was a mistake. But the turn was a hairpin curving back to the right, and the entrance to it was masked by bushes; you almost had to be looking for it to make it. The senator must have known the difference, the judge insisted; he had been driven over both more than once that day.

The bumpy way Ted and Mary Jo took was called the Dike Road, and a half-mile down it was the Dike Bridge, a narrow, humpbacked wooden structure. This span curved off the dirt road in a 25-degree angle to the left, rising to cross a slim channel in the dike which permitted sea water from the sound, on the right, to flow in and out of Poucha Pond. The bridge was their undoing. Ted didn't make the 25-degree turn. Instead the Chrysler plunged off the right side of the span, rolling as it fell, and hit the bottom of the ten-foot-deep channel wrong side up. At the inquest Kennedy testified that he didn't know he had turned on the wrong road until "the moment I went off the bridge."

> . . . the next thing I recall is the movement of Mary Jo next to me, the struggling, perhaps hitting or kicking me, and I at this time opened my eyes and realized I was upside down, that water was crashing in on me, that it was pitch black. . . . I can remember the last sensation of being completely out of air and inhaling what must have been a half a lung full of water and assuming that I was going to drown and the full realization that no one was going to be looking for us that night until the next morning and that I wasn't going to get out of the car alive, and then somehow I can remember coming up to the last energy of just pushing, pressing, and coming up to the surface.

Carried to the shore by the current, he waded back and dove into the ten feet of water for Mary Jo. He made seven or eight attempts to rescue her, he testified, but toward the end he was so out of breath that he could only hold his head under the water for a few seconds. For fifteen or twenty minutes he lay on the bank, coughing up water. Then, he said, he returned to the cookout, "walking, trotting, jogging, stumbling, as fast as I possibly could." There he told his story to two men, Joseph F. Gargan, a cousin, and Paul F. Markham, a Kennedy campaigner. Gargan and Markham returned to the scene with him and dove for Mary Jo without success. Like him, both men were lawyers, and they told him that this must be reported. He was deeply disturbed, they recalled afterward. He kept saying, "I just can't believe this happened."

At his request they drove him to the ferry slip. The lights of Edgartown, on Martha's Vineyard, lay just across the way. He told them to go back to the cookout but not to tell the girls what had happened. Then, he said, he "suddenly jumped into the water and impulsively swam across." As he crossed the narrow channel "the water got colder, the tide began to draw me out for the second time that evening, I knew I was going to drown." But he made it, rested on the far shore, and walked to the Shiretown Inn, where he was staying.

At the inn his behavior became increasingly incomprehensible. As he himself said later, "My conduct and conversations during the next several hours, to the extent that I can remember them, make no sense to me at all. I regard as indefensible the fact that I did not report the accident to the police immediately." He testified that he "just couldn't gain the strength within me, the moral strength to call Mrs. Kopechne at two o'clock in the morning and tell her that her daughter was dead."

What he did was to change into dry clothes and then complain to the hotel's co-owner that a party in the next room was keeping him awake. In the morning he discussed the weekend's yachting regatta with two couples. Then Gargan and Markham arrived and were aghast to learn that he hadn't reported the crash. He explained at the inquest: "I told them about my own thoughts and feelings as I swam across that channel and how I always willed that Mary Jo still lived." He also said that he wanted to make a telephone call, but apparently the phones in Edgartown wouldn't do; he passed two of them, both outdoors and both public. Taking the ferry back to Chappaquiddick, with Gargan and Markham accompanying him, he used a phone in the ferry-house on the other side. The ferryman asked them if they had heard about the accident. One replied, "We just heard about it." Only then, nearly eleven hours after the wreck, did Ted try to contact the Edgartown police.

Meanwhile the Chrysler had been discovered. At 7 A.M. two young men had crossed the bridge to fish in the surf; returning, they had noticed that the falling tide had exposed the wheel of a car. They had stopped to tell Mrs. Pierre Malm, who lived fifty yards away, and at 8:20 she had phoned Police Chief Dominick J. Arena. Borrowing trunks, the strapping Arena had come, dived down, radioed the automobile license number back for identification, and asked Fireman John Farrar to bring his scuba equipment. It was Farrar who found Mary Jo inside.

Arena's headquarters radioed back that the car was registered to Senator Edward M. Kennedy, and when the chief returned to Edgartown he found the senator waiting for him. Ted said: "I was driving. What do you want me to do? It has to be right." One thing he should do, Arena said, was make a proper report. Ted went into a back room with Markham and wrote one out; it was sketchy; he identified the victim as "one Miss Mary —, a former secretary of my brother Robert Kennedy," omitting the rest of her name because, he said, he didn't know how to spell it. (Markham didn't, either.) Markham asked the chief to keep the news from the press until Ted could phone Burke Marshall for legal advice. Arena agreed. He waited three hours. Having heard nothing further from Kennedy by then, he gave the newspaper the story and charged Kennedy with leaving the scene of the accident. Of the senator's strange trip that morning to use the Chappaquiddick phone the chief said, "If he had time to take the ferry over and back, he had time to see me." The medical examiner reported "a positive diagnosis of accidental drowning." Satisfied that there had been no foul play, he released the girl's body without an autopsy, and it was flown to her birthplace in Pennsylvania for burial—a move that brought criticism of the authorities later. In Hyannisport Ted went into seclusion. Seven days later he emerged to plead guilty in Edgartown's century-old courthouse. Judge James A. Boyle gave him the minimum sentence of two months in prison, suspended it, and took away his driver's license. That evening Kennedy went on nationwide television to explain the inexplicable. The speech was not a success. He answered questions which hadn't been asked, maintaining that he had not been "driving under the influence of liquor" and that there was "no truth, no truth whatever," to insinuations of "immoral conduct" by him and Mary Jo. He also seemed to imply that the damage to his career was more momentous than her death when he said that among his preoccupations the night after the accident had been "whether some awful curse actually did hang over all the Kennedys." The talk reminded some people of Nixon's Checkers performance in 1952. Like Nixon, Ted asked his constituents to help him decide whether he should continue in public life. Massachusetts being passionately pro-Kennedy, the response was favorable, and a week later he returned to his senatorial duties.

After the inquest reporters asked him about the judge's opinion that there was "probable cause to believe that Edward M. Kennedy operated his motor vehicle negligently," that "such operation appears to have contributed to the death of Mary Jo Kopechne," and that he found Ted's insistence that he and Mary Jo had been headed for the ferry incredible. Kennedy said: "In my personal view, the inference and the ultimate findings of the judge's report are not justified, and I reject them. . . . At the inquest I truthfully answered all the questions asked of me."

He also said: "I expect to be a candidate for the U.S. Senate in 1972, and I expect to serve out a full six-year term." The White House, taking no chances, was preparing to discredit him with the episode if he changed his mind and ran for President. Within six hours after the recovery of Mary Jo's body, presidential aides had sent a retired New York policeman to Chappaquiddick; according to John Dean, the man "posed as a newspaper reporter and always asked the most embarrassing questions at any press gathering." It was unnecessary. Temporarily, at least, Ted's national following had been diminished. He was no longer a charismatic figure on Capitol Hill. The following year he touched bottom there when Senator Robert C. Byrd of West Virginia challenged his right to continue as party whip. Kennedy had beaten Long 31 to 26. Now he lost to Byrd 31 to 24. Then, in the aftermath of a meeting at the White House, he was subjected to a new humiliation for a Kennedy: commiseration from Richard Nixon.

Portrait of an American

BENJAMIN McLANE SPOCK, M.D.

THE ELDEST OF SIX CHILDREN, born to a mother who wouldn't have a nurse, who wanted to do it all herself, he grew to love the idea of playing parent, feeding the others, even changing their diapers. He came naturally to think of children as very important, and—this from both his parents—was imbued with a New England hair-shirt conscience. Find a stern moral issue, they told him, and fight for it against all odds. He didn't want that. He decided to rebel. For a long time he thought he was going to succeed.

Hamden Hall Country Day School. Andover. Yale. Scroll and Key, and a flash of conventional glory as an oarsman in the 1924 Olympics. Aspiring briefly to becoming an architect, he fell into his parents' puritan mold while spending a summer as a counselor in a camp run by the Newington Crippled Children's Home near Hartford. He watched the orthopedic surgeon working with the children who had polio. Later he said: "I realized how much he was helping them and I decided that I wanted to be a doctor."

Columbia. An internship at New York's Presbyterian Hospital. A residency in pediatrics. Another in psychiatry. Six years of psycho-analytic training. His love for children grew and deepened, and they adored him. "The man with the gentle face and eyes," he was called. In his office toys were everywhere. He built a device for the shy ones—a small flight of steps led through a trap door to the ex-amining table. He wanted them to *want* to be examined, and they did. Years afterward he said: "One of my faults as a pediatrician has always been that I whoop it up too much with the children." But he never really tried to change.

The standard handbook for baby care was Dr. John B. Watson's *Psychological Care of Infant and Child,* published the year after Spock, then a second-year medical student, married Jane Cheney. Watson said: "Never, never kiss your child. Never hold it on your lap. Never rock its carriage."

Young Dr. Spock set himself against all that. While in the Navy during World War II he wrote his *Common Sense Book of Baby and Child Care.* Its opening words set the tone: "You know more than you think you do." Jane typed it from his longhand, and he indexed it himself, from abscess to Zwieback, because, he explained, he knew he would have "a better notion of what words mothers would look for in an index."

Over the next twenty-three years the book sold 22 million copies and was translated into thirty languages. He wrote a column for the *Ladies' Home Journal,* then for *Redbook;* his half-hour television program was seen Sunday afternoons over fifty-two stations of NBC-TV. And all the time Dr. Spock was rising in that most exact-ing of professions, the teaching of medicine. He taught psychiatry at Minnesota, child psychiatry and development at Pitt, child de-velopment in the psychiatry department at Western Reserve in Cleveland. His stand against Watson had made him the champion of indulgence. Troubled by the far swing of the pendulum, he re-wrote passages of *Baby and Child Care* in 1956, explaining, "I find that some uncertain parents are interpreting me as an advocate of extreme permissiveness, so in the revisions I'm making in the book, I'm having to emphasize the limits of permissiveness."

Then a deeper challenge stirred Spock's conscience. Raised a conservative Republican, he had been converted to Democratic liberalism by Franklin Roosevelt, and in 1960 he supported John F. Kennedy. But in March 1962, Kennedy resumed nuclear testing. Alarmed, Spock joined the National Committee for a Sane Nuclear Policy (SANE). He campaigned vigorously for Johnson against Goldwater and felt betrayed when, in February 1965, Johnson escalated the Vietnam War. Spock wrote the White House, protesting, and when that proved futile he took to the streets in demonstrations.

"*Excruciatingly* embarrassing," he said of this afterward, "like one of those bad dreams where suddenly you are downtown without any clothes on." Certainly he was unusually conspicuous—six foot four, with a strong craggy face, always wearing a suit with a vest and a watch chain—a grandfatherly figure articulating, with his taut Yankee twang, moral standards which other, younger demonstrators thought hopelessly old-fashioned. But he grew more militant, not less. His critics, and they were many and scathing in these years, ridiculed his concern as a new expression of permissiveness, which they were now presenting as a national bogey. To him the issue was simple decency and justice.

The National Mobilization Committee to End the War in Vietnam. The National Conference for a New Politics. Delivering 992 turned-in draft cards to a coldly furious functionary at the Department of Justice. Submitting to arrest for civil disobedience by crossing a police line at the armed forces induction center on Whitehall Street in Manhattan. Sitting on his long-legged stool at his drafting table, using a ballpoint pen to write—slowly and painfully, as always—"A Call to Resist Illegitimate Authority."

Authority finally struck back to salvage the pride of General Hershey, whose orders to draft antiwar demonstrators had been overruled by the Justice Department. Five antiwar leaders, virtual strangers to one another, were charged with conspiracy to subvert the draft law. They were not accused of committing a crime, just of plotting one. In a word, their offense was dissent. The most outstanding leader, literally towering over the other four, was Benjamin M. Spock, M.D.

The trial was held in Boston's District Court in May and June of

1968. The judge was eighty-five-year-old Francis Ford—rude, vain, and flagrantly partial. The verdict was guilty—"guilty," a juror explained afterward to a reporter, "as charged by the judge." The defendants were sentenced to two years in prison, and two of them, Spock and Chaplain William Sloane Coffin of Yale were fined five thousand dollars each.

Spock said: "There is no shred of legality or constitutionality to this war; it violates the United Nations Charter, the Geneva Accords, and the United States' promise to obey the laws of international conduct. It is totally, abominably illegal. . . . I intend to go on working against the war."

And he did. The U.S. Court of Appeals for the First Circuit threw out the convictions, citing Judge Ford's prejudice. Spock went on, and on. They were still killing his children in the endless night of Vietnam, murdering the generation whose mothers he had counseled, and the sense of duty instilled in his own childhood gave him no rest. Sometimes it almost seemed to him that he could hear the dying crying out across half the world for mercy. Dr. Watson would have turned a deaf ear. ("Never, never kiss your child.") Dr. Spock could not. And slowly, as the nation in its agony turned from the shibboleths of mindless anti-Communism toward the peace of exhaustion, the wisdom of his compassion became clear.

Jesus said, Suffer little children, and forbid them not, to come unto me; for of such is the kingdom of heaven.

But President Nixon called Dr. Spock a bum.

Thirty-five

NATTERING NABOBS

As AMERICA ENTERED the 1970s, the swing generation was in, or about to enter, its fifties, the age at which men begin to discover that the world they have loved is disintegrating. That year the impression carried special force, for there seemed to be an unusual number of reasons for feeling wronged, among them inflation, pollution, crime, the war, the stock market, the generation gap, immorality, riots, cyclamates, traffic, insulting bumper stickers and decals, strikes against the public, racism, and new skyjackings. Nothing worked as it once had. "Not only is there no God," said Woody Allen, "but try getting a plumber on weekends."

Hardly had three weeks of 1970 passed before a U.S. Navy ship set the tone for what was to come by tearing loose from its anchorage in a high wind and ripping a 375-foot hole in the Chesapeake Bay Bridge-Tunnel structure. To the superstitious it appeared that the new decade was off to an inauspicious start.

Nature appeared to be in a contrary mood elsewhere, too. After two hundred consecutive rainless days, Southern California was ravaged by the worst brush fires in its history, apparently caused by spontaneous combustion, denuding over 500,000 acres—an area nearly as large as Rhode Island. Eleven died in another fire of unexplained origin, in an eighty-five-year-old Minneapolis apartment building. All over the world natural disasters were besetting man; a Venice whirlwind left four dead, a cyclonic tidal wave in East Pakistan left 200,000 dead, and earthquakes in Peru, Turkey, and Iran left tens of thousands dead. Possibly God was angry with people like Woody Allen, who denied Him, or with the irreverent, like the flip college students who wore pins reading: "God Isn't Dead —He Just Doesn't Want to Get Involved."

Certainly religion wasn't the steady rock it had been. Christians who didn't regard God as a bigot were shaken by the new president of the Mormon Church, who said, "There is a reason why one man is born black and with other disadvantages, while another man is born white with great advantages. The Negro evidently is receiving the reward he merits." Episcopalians were agitated over the shelving, after three and a half centuries, of the King James Version of the Holy Bible for a New English Bible. Worst of all, from God's point of view, was the growing power of antichristianity—the worship of strange totems and even of Satan himself.

According to one reliable source, America was supporting 10,000 full-time and 175,000 part-time astrologers. Computers spewed forth ten-dollar horoscopes, a New York hairdresser employed a staff astrologer, a department store sold fifty-dollar annual subscriptions to a Dial-an-Astrologer service, and 300 newspapers with a combined circulation of 30 million carried a regular astrological column. Book clubs offered tarot cards as premiums. At the University of South Carolina 250 students were enrolled in a course on sorcery. Magazine advertisements inquired, "Tired of being on the outside of witchcraft looking in? Get in on the action yourself. Join our Diploma Course in Witchcraft and learn the age-old secrets, including raising power, meditation, prediction, fertility, and initiation rites." Mrs. Sybil Leek, a Houston sorceress who cast spells with a pet jackdaw named Hotfoot Jackson perched on her shoulder, calculated that there were "about eight million initiated witches in the world. I mean real witches, not Hollywood sex orgy, free-for-all types. I personally know of about four hundred regular covens in the United States. It is possible there are thousands of irregular ones."

If heaven was receiving insufficient respect, so were the authorities on earth. After one man had been killed and 105 wounded or injured during a People's Park riot in Berkeley, federal indictments were handed down accusing not the rioters, but ten deputies and two former deputies, who were charged with violating the civil rights of the demonstrators. ("This is the sickest operation any level of government was ever involved in," the sheriff raged.) Black Panthers seemed to be literally getting away with murder; juries or appeals courts threw out homicide charges against them in San Francisco, New Haven, and New York, and in Chicago a special federal grand jury criticized police conduct during the raid in which Panthers Fred Hampton and Mark Clark had been killed. Even the American Indians, who had been at the bottom of the status pyramid since the country was founded, were feeling feisty. The Senate didn't give the country back to them, but a bill did return New Mexico's Blue Lake and 48,000 surrounding acres to the Pueblo tribe.

It was a hard time for U.S. generals, and not just in Vietnam. The Russians arrested two of them on charges of violating Soviet air space. The commanding general of the European Exchange System was stripped of his rank for irregularities by subordinates, and Benjamin O. Davis Jr., who had retired from the Air Force as a lieutenant general, the highest rank ever held by a black, resigned as director of public safety in Cleveland because, he said, the city's black mayor was providing "support and comfort to the enemies of law enforcement." Anyone wearing a uniform was liable to be subjected to abuse by the tormentors of authority, though it did seem that President Nixon gave the White House police a special handicap. Impressed by the fancy uniforms of Romanian police, the President commissioned Jimmie Muscatello, a Washington tailor, to design new regalia for guards at the Executive Mansion. The result was a $16,000 joke—double-breasted white tunics with gold braid, brass buttons bearing the presidential seal, and black plastic Ruritanian hats. One guard muttered that if he had to wear such livery he wanted a bass drum to go with it. A designer said, "This is not the time for Gilbert and Sullivan at the White House." "You can't please everybody," said Muscatello, who hadn't pleased anybody, not even the President; the tunics stayed in service, but the hats were quietly shelved.

New York gravediggers struck in January. The air traffic controllers went out in April. Grounded passengers were bitter, but they may have been lucky; heavier-than-air transport wasn't at its most reliable in 1970. Air piracy continued, and an Arizonan named A. G. Barkley added a new wrinkle when he entered a TWA cabin with a gun, a razor, and a can of gasoline and announced that he wanted 100 million dollars. He was seized after a gun battle during which the pilot was wounded in the stomach. Boeing's 21-million-dollar jumbo jet, the 747, was off to a slow start, running as much as six hours behind schedule. Even a lunar flight, Apollo 13, broke down some 200,000 miles from home. The three astronauts aboard had to turn back.

Ironically, one of the most successful journeys of 1970 was a 3,200-mile ocean voyage by a papyrus boat, the Ra II, built and sailed by Norwegian explorer Thor Heyerdahl to prove that the ancient Egyptians could have crossed the Atlantic. At least the Ra II reached its destination, Barbados, and while it didn't make money, neither did many commercial carriers, including, most conspicuously, the biggest railroad in the United States. In bankruptcy court with 2.6 billion dollars in debts, the Penn Central was one of many American institutions which were having trouble balancing their books. Another was the motion picture industry; five major Hollywood studios were in the red, with total debts of over 100 million dollars. The great boom of the 1960s seemed to have ended with the decade, and the best evidence was in Wall Street, where the Dow Jones industrial average, which had been within striking distance of 1,000 in December 1968, sank to 631 on May 27.

The gallery at the New York Stock Exchange had been crowded with eager spectators in the years of the Johnson bull market. After the long slide of May 1970 it became a lonelier place. Indeed, the entire city of New York—which its mordant inhabitants now called Fun City—was less popular with tourists. There was the street crime, and there were other perils. On June 1 the city increased its towing fee for illegally parked cars from twenty-five to fifty dollars. That day a Springfield, Massachusetts, mother came to New York and took her children to a film. When she emerged her auto was gone and she owed the city fifty dollars plus a fine. The movie was *The Out-of-Towners*, dealing with the hazards of visiting Manhattan.

While 1970 was a year of doldrums on most California motion picture lots, a director named Russ Meyer finished his twenty-first successful movie that year. He had known from the outset that it would be big box office. None of its predecessors had lost money or grossed less than six figures, and one of them, *Vixen*, filmed for $72,000, had earned over six million. Meyer said: "I don't play games with an audience. In my films you know where you're at in fifteen seconds—the first fifteen seconds." Where you were at was in the middle of what the trade described as "erotica" and others called pornography. Peddling sex had become a big business in the United

States, netting over 500 million dollars a year, and the market seemed insatiable.

The merchandise came in various packages. Main Street theaters showed X-rated films; 1970 hits included *Sexual Freedom in Denmark, The Minx* ("Makes *Curious Yellow* look pale"—*New York Daily News*), and Allen Funt's *What Do You Say to a Naked Lady?* ("What *can* you say?" asked its ads. "We say wow"), which was grossing one San Francisco movie house $7,000 a week for round-the-clock showings. Manhattan was supporting two hundred "adult bookstores," and those in the twenty-four-hour-a-day block between Seventh and Eighth avenues displayed their goods like supermarkets, with overhead signs advertising the various departments—heterosexual, homosexual (male), bestiality, flagellation, lesbian, incest, fellatio and cunnilingus. Arcade machines offered skin flicks in color at a quarter a showing. Picture packets contained "Eight revealing poses! $2." Onstage in New York were *Grin and Bare It* with nine nudes in the cast, *The Boys in the Band,* which AP dramatic critic William Glover called "the most unabashed and forthright account of homosexuality yet seen in this era of growing artistic permissiveness," and *Futz,* which dealt with the problems of a yokel who enjoyed coupling with a sow. But the market was much bigger than Broadway. The Arcadian bachelor could resolve his frustrations by sending for obscene LP records; a lonely bachelor girl could purchase a vibrator in a hometown store or a plastic dildo through the mails, and as Professor Morse Peckham of the University of South Carolina observed, in the corner drugstore the public could now "buy for very little money pornographic works which a short time ago were unobtainable for any amount of money."

To Americans over the age of thirty the change was mind-boggling. In their childhoods the word "ass" had been forbidden in mixed company, and the swing generation could remember the uproar over the Hays Office decision to let Clark Gable say "Frankly, my dear, I don't give a damn" in *Gone With the Wind.* Now Jack Valenti approved "horseshit" and "Piss on you" in movies rated for the whole family. Part of the latitude studios now took could be traced to the Supreme Court's 1957 decision, in the case of Roth v. U.S., that to be obscene material must be prurient, offensive to community standards, and "utterly without redeeming social value." Another part of the new license was a byproduct of the new contraceptives, liberalized abortion legislation, and the consequent emancipation of women from the fear of unwanted pregnancy. And much of it, as William Glover had noted, was rooted in the era, in the sexual revolution and the mini-micro-bikini-topless-bottomless mood of the times. Curiosity about sex appeared to be insatiable; Nicholas von Hoffman wrote about a female reporter who, while collecting material for an article about prostitution, went to bed with a strange man for money and reported that the climax was "a moment of stunning pleasure." A mother in Braintree, Massachusetts, came home one afternoon to find her teen-age daughter and a girlfriend in bed naked, experimenting with Sapphic techniques. The word "indiscretion" in its sexual sense all but dropped out of the language, because hardly anybody was discreet any more. A Pennsylvania legislator opposing abortion legislation was unmasked as a hypocrite when a young woman came forward to tell the press that he had been her lover and had paid for her abortion. There had been a time when she would have kept that to herself.

All this was hard on children, who were exposed to it, were more precocious in their dating customs than their parents, and attained puberty at an earlier age. The remedy most often proposed was sex education in the schools. Gallup found that 71 percent of the people approved it, with 55 percent in favor of courses explaining birth control. Among the groups endorsing the teaching of sex were the AMA, the National Education Association, the Sex Education Association, and the Sex Information and Education Council in the United States (SIECUS). Dr. Mary Calderone, executive director of SIECUS, said sex should be taught "not as something you do but as something you are."

SIECUS issued no material; it merely offered professional advice to school systems. That point was obscured by the articulate minority, which was outraged by the very suggestion that reproduction might be discussed in the classroom. "Is the Schoolhouse the Proper Place to Teach Raw Sex?" asked Billy James Hargis's Christian Crusade, firing the opening gun in the ultraright's attack on sex education. The Reverend Billy called SIECUS the "pornographic arm of liberal education," and state boards of education in Oklahoma, California, and Utah rejected sound film strips because they had been approved by SIECUS.

Other organizations in the antisex coalition were the Movement to Restore Decency (MOTOREDE), a Birch front; Parents United

for a Responsible Education (PURE), the Mothers Organization
for Moral Stability (MOMS), Sanity on Sex (SOS), Parents Opposed to Sex Education (POSE), and Parents Against Unconstitutional Sex Education (PAUSE). "I doubt that one parent in a
thousand had heard about sex education a year ago," said a Birch
coordinator. "Now they've heard about it, and they don't like what
they hear." One group accused the schools of planning to "reveal
all the details of intercourse and masturbation to small children";
a school in Parsippany, New Jersey, was called an "academic whore-
house"; a PAUSE leader accused the schools of "undermining what
should be taught in the home." An eighth-grade mathematics
teacher was jailed for disseminating lewd materials, and a California
school superintendent was fired. Ultrarightists also won in Racine,
Wisconsin, after charging that sex education was a Communist plot
to undermine the morals of the pupils. One of the wilder battles
was in San Francisco over an innocuous book titled *A Doctor Talks
to Five-to-Eight-Year-Olds*. The ultras there printed a leaflet repro-
ducing an illustration from the book of one toad on another's back.
The book explained that it was a mother carrying her baby. The
leaflet lost sex education a lot of supporters by changing the caption
to "Mating Toads."

At the peak of the controversy sex education was an issue in
twenty-seven states. Toward the end of 1970 sanity triumphed and
the courses were introduced, to the bewilderment of the children,
who wondered what all the fuss had been about. Then, just as super-
intendents and school boards thought they could divert their professional attention to other matters, their presentation of sex came
under attack from an entirely different movement: Women's Lib.
Liberated women took it as an article of faith that all except physical differences between males and females were taught, not inherent. They believed that girls were trained to want motherhood and
cultivate domestic science, and they regarded the public schools
as a major training ground. Demanding that textbooks be revised
and teachers reoriented, they joined battle with their adversaries
in a struggle which was certain to endure as a major issue of the
1970s.

Millions of Americans had first become aware of the new fem-
inism when Robin Morgan, until then best known as a TV actress
in *I Remember Mama*, marched into the 1968 Miss America Pageant
pulling a train of blazing brassieres. She was there, she told startled

reporters, in her role as founder of the Women's International Terrorist Conspiracy from Hell (WITCH). Feminists paraded through metropolitan shopping districts on August 26, 1970, the fiftieth anniversary of ratification of the Nineteenth Amendment. All that year liberated women were demonstrating that they, like the members of other protest movements, understood the uses of publicity. "Take it off!" one of them yelled at a construction worker, and when she was asked if she meant his hard hat she said, "No, his jockstrap." One June Conlan won a ten-year court fight to become a day laborer digging ditches. Marlene Dixon wrote that "in all classes and groups, the institution functions to a greater or lesser degree to oppress women; the unity of women of different classes hinges upon our understanding of that common oppression." Abby Aldrich Rockefeller, a great-granddaughter of John D., denounced romantic love between men and women as "counterrevolutionary."

"I've had Women's Lib up to here," said Dr. Edgar F. Berman, a physician active in Democratic politics. Democratic Congresswoman Patsy Mink of Hawaii promptly accused Berman of being a sexist with the "basest sort of prejudice against women." As the year wore on, the rhetoric grew more heated. Margaret Mead said, "Women's liberation has to be terribly conscious of the danger of provoking men to kill women. You have quite literally driven them mad." One male spectator at the women's march in New York screamed at them, "All you pigs can't get a man!" while another stood silently by wearing a brassiere. "These chicks," said Hugh Hefner in a memo to his staff, "are our natural enemy. It's time to do battle with them. They are inalterably opposed to the romantic boy-girl society *Playboy* promotes."

Some of the women sounded as frivolous as Hefner. They devoted a great deal of energy to debates over whether they should be known as Mrs., Miss, or Ms.; to attempts to have chairmen called chairpersons, and to attacks on National Airlines for running ads of pretty stewardesses saying, "I'm Doris. Fly me." But the deeper questions they raised were anything but trivial. Over 23 million American women now held full-time jobs; another eight million had part-time jobs. Four of every ten married women were employed, 12 million of them with children at home under eighteen. Superficially this indicated a challenge to male supremacy in the job market, but the nature of the employment and the pay for it still reflected a society in which men, not women, were expected to support families. Men still dominated the most lucrative professions and brought home the bigger slices of bacon. Just 7.6 percent of America's 300,000 doctors, and only 1 percent of the surgeons, were women, while 90 percent of the phone operators and stenographers were female. The average woman was making $3 for every $5 made by a man with the same job. *Life* calculated that a woman needed a B.A. degree to earn as much as a man who left school after the eighth grade. The typical salesman made $8,549; the typical saleswoman $3,461.

By 1970 Women's Lib arguments for equality in employment and education were supported by many men. Demands for free abortions and free day-care centers for children were more controversial, and the masculine population seemed evenly divided on the proposed Twenty-seventh Amendment to the Constitution—the Equal Rights Amendment (ERA), ensuring women complete equality before the law. Yet within two years the Senate would approve ERA and send it to the state legislatures. Under it, women would no longer be required to change their names when they married; they would be given an equal voice in where the family would live; if the husband's job obliged him to move elsewhere, and his wife stayed behind, she would not be liable to a charge of desertion. On the other hand, should a marriage break up, the wife might have to pay alimony. Laws shielding women from danger and physical strain on the job and protecting them from certain sexual outrages would be void. (Rape was an exception.) In addition, women might be drafted and even sent into battle. A pro-ERA contributor to the *Yale Law Journal* argued:

> . . . the effectiveness of the modern soldier is due more to equipment and training than to individual strength. Women are physically as able as men to perform many jobs classified as combat duty, such as piloting an airplane or engaging in naval operations. . . . There is no reason to assume that in a dangerous situation women will not be as serious and well-disciplined as men.

It is doubtful that many housewives wanted to become machine gunners or BAR men, or identified with Elizabeth P. Hoisington, director of the Women's Army Corps, who became America's first female general in June 1970. Nevertheless, millions of American women—especially younger women—had been changed by the movement. There was a new spunkiness about them, a plucky defiance toward those who would manipulate them for selfish ends, and this was illustrated by the disaster which befell the new fashion known to readers of *Women's Wear Daily* as the longuette and to the rest of the country as the midi. Nearly a quarter-century earlier independent women had tried to lead a revolt against the long-skirted New Look, signing manifestos, forming LBK (Little Below the Knee) clubs, and demonstrating against the couturiers.* They had been routed then. Now the modistes were again turning out longer skirts. James Galanos said, "Long is where the direction is," Adele Simpson said, "It's good-bye thigh," and Leo Narducci said, "Women are definitely ready for a fashion change." All were confident that the female herd would grovel and buy their wares.

The first mutinous mutters came from Los Angeles, where one Juli Hutner, president of something called POOFF (Preservation of Our Femininity and Finances), told a reporter: "We're not going to let them pull the wool over our legs as well as our eyes. I know women who'd wear a tin box if Galanos said it was in. I think that's sick. All we ask is a choice." KEEP THE MINI ON THE MARKET and LEGS! LEGS! LEGS! said the placards carried by demonstrating members of Girls Against More Skirt (GAMS). Some of them suggested that the midi was a plot against Women's Lib, that the designers were trying to isolate the feminists by bringing femininity back; others blamed older matrons whose legs weren't sexy any more and who wanted to make nubile girls hide theirs. Gilman Ostrander, a social historian, said the falling stock market was responsible for the midi, and that it was bound to prevail: "The middle-aged, who like long skirts, determine social standards in times of depression or recession. And young people, who like short skirts, determine standards in times of prosperity."

By winter the stock market had gone up, however, and the fashion industry's enthusiasm for the midi had plunged. A *New York Times* survey found that while a few shop owners gallantly professed faith in the longer look ("It's here! Everybody's accepting and loving and buying it!"), most conceded that it had failed wretchedly: "Stores that last fall said they bought lots of midis are now saying they didn't really. What they did buy didn't sell very well. And women's knees are not yet obsolete." To be sure, more skirts covered the knee. But the dress designers had insisted that the midi was a specific length, measuring 44 to 45 inches from shoulder to hem, which put it at mid-calf for most women. The *Times*

* See Vol. I, pages 516–518.

found that only 20 percent of dresses sold at that length, and at the end of the year just 5 percent of the women were wearing them. The other frocks had been returned for shortening or left in the closet.

Bitter retailers said the style had "bombed," or "laid an egg"; one said it "certainly did fashion a disservice and didn't take as a look," and another told a newswoman, "Our customers didn't want it. . . . We were never really able to sell it." The massive attempt to push the calf-length hem did trigger an unintended sartorial shift, however. "The midi," said the *Times*, "virtually killed the dress . . . suddenly there were kickers, gauchos, and pants, pants, pants." Older women bought pantsuits, and their daughters kept their bare knees by donning very short shorts. Bergdorf Goodman called the shorts "cool pants." *Women's Wear Daily*, closer to the mood of the new women, gave them the name that stuck: hotpants.

The streak of violence which had blighted Johnson's administration continued under Nixon, growing, if anything, more lurid. The great metropolitan ghettos continued to be relatively quiet, but the assassin and the pyromaniac now moved with murderous stealth in the black neighborhoods of smaller cities. Six Negroes were shot to death in Augusta, Georgia. A boy was stabbed in an Oklahoma City racial incident. A church which had been used for civil rights meetings in Carthage, Mississippi, was bombed. And there were riots in East Los Angeles, Miami, Houston, Highland Park, Michigan; Michigan City, Indiana; New Bedford, Massachusetts; Asbury Park, New Jersey; South Melbourne, Florida; Aliquippa, Pennsylvania; Oxford, North Carolina; Hot Springs, Arkansas; River Rouge, Michigan; Cairo, Illinois; and three Georgia communities: Perry, Macon, and Athens.

In New York bomb threats were running at a thousand a month. Over a fifteen-month period 368 of the devices had actually exploded in the city, one of them in a second-floor men's room at police headquarters, and Commissioner Howard Leary told a U.S. Senate subcommittee that he could not guarantee the safety of visitors to precinct stations. At times it seemed as though an open season had been declared on American policemen. In 1970 the FBI reported 35,202 assaults on them, almost quadruple the number in 1960, and fifteen officers were killed, most of them by ambushers, in nine months of the year.

The Little Rock police chief said attacks on cops had become "practically a daily occurrence . . . It seemed everyone from school age on up is assaulting police officers." Commissioner Frank L. Rizzo of Philadelphia said, "We are dealing with a group of fanatics–psychopaths," and the director of public safety in Omaha suggested that "the problem being experienced by police departments throughout the nation gives all indications that there is a conspiracy. The timing gives another indication. We are piecing together all the information available and we hope to prove a conspiracy." He didn't do it, and most law enforcement officials thought it wasn't possible–"We look upon the assaults as separate and independent incidents," Leary said–but there was general agreement that at a time when authority was under widespread attack, cops were inevitable targets. As Quinn Tamm of the International Association of Chiefs of Police put it: "Attacks on police are becoming more and more violent as radical groups exhort their members to 'kill the pigs' . . . That blue uniform makes the wearer a highly visible representative of the establishment."

Hostility to the established order was responsible for the bombings. In some instances the bombers boasted about it. After blasts tore into the Manhattan offices of International Business Machines, the General Telephone and Electronics Corporation, and Mobil Oil, a group called Revolutionary Force 9 took credit for them, declaring that the firms were profiteering in Vietnam. In other cases the terrorists, not being skilled in the use of explosives, blew themselves up. Within a month of the IBM, General Telephone, and Mobil eruptions one revolutionist was killed and another gravely injured when their bomb factory fulminated in a tenement on New York's Lower East Side. In Baltimore two black militants, protégés of H. Rap Brown, died after one of their bombs detonated prematurely in their automobile. And on March 6 Greenwich Village was rocked by the most sensational bomb disaster of 1970, killing three young nihilists and involving the names of several wealthy families.

Cathlyn Platt Wilkerson was a recent graduate of Swarthmore; Diana Oughton and Kathy Boudin were Bryn Mawr alumnae; all three were Weatherwomen. Diana was the daughter of an ultraconservative, highly respectable Illinois multimillionaire whose extraordinary family estate had been visited by King Edward VII, then Prince of Wales, a century earlier. Kathy was the niece of I. F. Stone. Her father, Leonard B. Boudin, was a famous lawyer whose clients

included Paul Robeson, Judith Coplon, and Julian Bond; later he
would defend Daniel Ellsberg. Cathlyn's father owned a chain of
radio stations. He and his second wife were on holiday in the Caribbean that month. In his absence Cathlyn was entertaining Diana
and Kathy, Ted Gold, who had been active in Columbia's SDS chapter, and another young man—whose identity was to remain a mystery—in the elegant $100,000 Wilkerson town house at 18 West
Eleventh Street in Manhattan.

At noon on the day of the catastrophe the sky was clear and
sunny over New York, with just a suggestion of approaching spring
in the air. No one was in the house next door, which belonged to
Dustin Hoffman, the actor, and number 18 appeared to be quiet.
Inside, however, the young revolutionaries were busy. Two current
Weatherman slogans were "If you don't believe in guns and violence, then you aren't a revolutionary" and "Bring the war home."
On Monday one of the boys, dressed as a priest, had driven to
New Hampshire to buy two cases of dynamite. Now fifty-seven sticks
of TNT were strewn about in a makeshift basement workshop, together with friction tape, roofing nails, clockwork timing mechanisms, doorbell wire, thirty blasting tapes, and lengths of plumbing
pipe meant to contain the charges.

Probably no one will ever know exactly what went wrong, but
somebody bungled and set the lot off. It may have been Diana; her
body was the most mutilated—the head, both hands and a foot were
blown off, and the torso was riddled with roofing nails. Gold and the
unidentified youth were also dead. The first explosion ripped
through the living room wall of Hoffman's house, shattered windows across the street, and rocked a kitchen sixteen doors away.
Then the gas mains ignited, touching off two more blasts, and the
floors started to collapse.

Inside, stunned and bleeding, were Cathlyn and Kathy, one of
them naked and the other partially dressed. Two policemen and a
retired fireman—"the girls," John Neary wryly noted in Life, "would
have called them 'pigs'"—came to their rescue, and a neighbor gave
them the use of her shower and loaned them clothing. Then they
disappeared. At first firemen thought leaking gas was responsible
for the disaster. Then they found the dynamite, the blasting caps,
and stacks of SDS pamphlets. Suddenly they wanted to question
the survivors. New York authorities learned that Kathy and Cathlyn
were out on bail after indictment in Chicago for participating in the

Weathermen's Days of Rage the previous October. When they failed to appear there for trial March 16 the FBI joined the hunt. Their families said the girls had sent word that they were alive but gave no details.

On the other side of the country a weird blend of radical politics and witchcraft was blamed for the worst mass murder in California since the Manson killings. Sheriff's deputies on a routine patrol saw flames in the $250,000 home of Dr. Victor Ohta, an eye surgeon, overlooking Monterey Bay. They called firemen, who went to the Ohta swimming pool in search of water and there found the bodies of the surgeon, his wife, their two sons, and the doctor's secretary. All had been tied up with gaudy scarves and shot in the back of the head. Police found a scribbled message under the windshield wiper of the surgeon's car: "From this day forward anyone . . . who misuses the natural environment or destroys same will suffer the penalty of death. . . . I and my comrades from this day forth will fight until death or freedom against anything or anyone who does not support natural life on this planet. Materialism must die or mankind will stop." The signature was taken from tarot cards: "Knight of Wands, Knight of Cups, Knight of Pentacles, Knight of Swords." The signer, found living in a ramshackle hut a half-mile away, was a bearded youth named John F. Frazier. Frazier's lawyer said that his client had hurt his head in a car accident and had then "changed radically."

That year's most famous black advocate of revolutionary action in California was a dusky twenty-six-year-old beauty, Angela Davis. A daughter of the black middle class, she had been a Birmingham Girl Scout, apparently contented with society until four of her Negro girlfriends were killed in the September 1963 bombing of a church there. At Brandeis University, where she was elected to Phi Beta Kappa, she became an enthusiastic reader of Marx and Herbert Marcuse, and after graduate work at the Sorbonne and in Germany she became Marcuse's student on the San Diego campus of the University of California. There she joined the Black Panthers and the Communist Party. In one speech she told undergraduates that "the government has to be overthrown"; in another she said that "revolution must be tied to dealing with specific problems now, not a lot of rhetoric about revolution, but real, fundamental problems."

She participated in the storming of a campus building in San Diego and was arrested for refusing to leave a police station.

As an assistant professor on the university's Los Angeles campus she was teaching philosophy when, in April 1970, Governor Reagan's Board of Regents voted to fire her, citing a board resolution barring Communists from the faculty. Since both the California and U.S. Supreme Courts had held that Communist membership was insufficient reason to disqualify a professor from teaching in a state university, the board changed the grounds for dismissal to incompetence. A majority of students and UCLA faculty members took Angela's side. Her fellow professors adopted a resolution expressing "our shock, our dismay, our rage" at her removal. They voted to defy the regents by keeping her on the faculty, and the issue was unresolved when a new development put her case in an entirely different light.

As a black militant, Angela had been among those who were agitating for the release of the "Soledad Brothers"—three Negro prisoners, not actually related to one another, who had been charged with killing a white guard at Soledad Prison on January 16. The most interesting of the three was George Jackson, twenty-seven, who was serving five years to life for a 1961 filling station robbery. As the author of *Soledad Brother,* a collection of his prison letters, Jackson would become one of the most famous convicts in the country that fall. Some of the most moving notes in the book were written to Angela, who had first seen him during a hearing in a Salinas courtroom that May. In her own letters to him, and in a diary, she declared that she had "spontaneously" fallen in love with him. She called herself his "lifelong wife" and said she would dedicate her life to freeing him. She added that she didn't care what means she used, a passage which aroused much subsequent interest.

In the first week of August Angela was seen frequently in the company of Jonathan Jackson, George's seventeen-year-old brother. Three guns she owned found their way into Jonathan's possession; so did a twelve-gauge sawed-off shotgun she bought on August 5. That was a Wednesday. On Thursday she and Jonathan were driving around in a small, bright yellow enclosed Ford panel truck he had rented the day before. On Friday the van was parked in a lot outside the San Rafael courthouse, thirteen miles northwest of San Francisco. Minutes later Jonathan, slim and intense, entered a courtroom wearing a raincoat and carrying a small bag.

On the stand at the time was Ruchell Magee, a San Quentin convict who was testifying in the case of James McLain, a fellow prisoner accused of stabbing a guard. Another black inmate, William Christmas, was waiting to be called. Magee, McLain, and Christmas were powerfully built young men, and McLain, who was sitting at the counsel's table, was known at San Quentin as a firebrand, an agitator, and a Panther. Superior Court Judge Harold J. Haley was on the bench. The deputy district attorney was Gary W. Thomas, who was married to the judge's niece. There was a jury, but young Jackson was the only spectator. It was a boring case.

It became much livelier when Jonathan unzipped his bag, drew out one of Angela's revolvers, and slipped a 30-caliber carbine from under his raincoat. "This is it!" he yelled. "I've got an automatic weapon. Everybody freeze!" He ordered the unarmed bailiffs to unlock the handcuffs on McLain, Magee, and Christmas, and handed each of the three unshackled convicts a weapon. He gave the shotgun to McLain, who taped it around the judge's neck so that the muzzle hung a few inches from Haley's chin. The other prisoners tied Thomas and three women jurors together with piano wire. McLain commanded the judge to call the sheriff's office and direct him to give the inmates safe passage out. "I am in the courtroom," Haley said into the telephone on the bench. "There are a number of armed convicts here." McLain grabbed the phone and shouted into it, "You're going to call off your pig dogs. We're going to get out of here. Call them off!"

Herding the hostages before them, the blacks paused before the press room, fifty feet down the hall, but the door was locked. As they continued down the corridor McLain called, "We want the Soledad Brothers released by twelve-thirty today!" In the parking lot they shoved the five hostages into the Ford van. McLain slid behind the wheel; Jonathan gave him the keys; Magee took over the guarding of the judge, and they headed for U.S. 101, about two hundred yards away. Watching them were some hundred law enforcement officers, crouched behind other vehicles and the building. Suddenly a San Quentin guard darted in front of the panel truck and yelled, "Halt!"

The next minute was madness, with gunfire pouring into the panel truck and out from it. At one point the shotgun roared in the back of the van. That was the end for the judge; his jaw and part of his face were blown off. Thomas had a bullet in his spine; he would be paralyzed from the waist down for the rest of his life. One of the jurors was wounded in the arm. Magee had been shot in the chest but was still alive. McLain, Christmas, and Jonathan Jackson were dead.

Three hours later Angela Davis bought an airplane ticket at the San Francisco terminal. Then she vanished.

Under California law, anyone abetting a killer before the act is equally guilty of murder, and a warrant was issued for her arrest. Panther leader Huey P. Newton said he believed that she had been responsible for the courthouse shootings, was proud of her, and hoped others would follow her "courageous example." Charles Garry, a white attorney for the Panthers, cried, "More power to Angela Davis! May she live long in liberty." In fact she remained at large for over two months. On October 13 FBI agents arrested her in Manhattan after she had checked into a Howard Johnson's motel with David Rudolph Poindexter Jr., a wealthy Negro. Poindexter was charged with harboring a fugitive; Angela was extradited and lodged in a San Rafael prison less than five miles from George Jackson's cell in San Quentin.

Nearly a year later, on a hot August day in 1971, Jackson received a visit from his lawyer, Stephen Mitchell Bingham. Bingham was white, a Yale alumnus, and the grandson of Hiram Bingham, who had served Connecticut as governor and U.S. senator. Prison officials later became convinced that the younger Bingham, who had been active in the cause of minority groups, was on a smuggling mission that day. He was carrying two parcels which guards did not search: an expanding brown envelope and a small portable tape recorder. After he completed an hour-long session with Jackson and left, a guard noticed something different about the convict's Afro hairdo. Asked about it, the Negro yanked off a wig and pulled a small automatic pistol from it.

Terror and death followed. On Jackson's orders, twenty-seven prisoners, including the convalescing Ruchell Magee, were released. Then three white guards and two white trusties were murdered; two were shot in the back of the head, and the throats of the others were cut with a dull razor blade. The corpses were piled in a corner of Jackson's cell like bloody rugs. By now San Quentin's sirens were screaming. Still holding the pistol, Jackson bolted out a door and sprinted some seventy-five feet across an open courtyard before sharpshooters in the towers overhead cut him down.

Stephen Bingham was indicted for the murder of the guards and the trusties—the county district attorney said, "There is no way Jackson could have gotten the death gun except during his visit with Bingham"—but he disappeared without a trace, and by the following year authorities were suggesting that he might be dead: that black militants, having used him, may have then killed him. Law enforcement officers were embittered by the deaths of August 21. Negro activists were also outraged. Jackson became a martyr to them. His body was dressed in the Panther uniform—black leather jacket, black beret, and black shirt—and buried beside that of Jonathan. Julian Bond spoke of his "assassination" and of "the expected outcome of his constant attacks on a vicious system which was unable to crush his spirit or his body." California Assemblyman Willie Brown said, "The people in the street are saying this is an execution, that it's ridiculous Jackson could hide a gun in his hair," and Angela Davis wrote of "the loss of an irretrievable love."

Angela's trial in the late spring of 1972 was an international event. Her elegant profile, with the high cheekbones and vast Afro coiffure —she had cut it off while a fugitive, but it had grown back—adorned posters around the world. Militant slogans called her a "political prisoner" and demanded "Free Angela!" The prosecution, protesting that the proceedings had nothing to do with politics or race, that this was a criminal trial, submitted 201 exhibits and testimony from ninety-five witnesses. Three people identified her as Jonathan's companion at a gas station across the street from the courthouse the day before the escape attempt, and others put her with him on each of the three days beforehand.

The defense presented testimony from twelve witnesses (Angela chose not to take the stand) and ridiculed the idea that "a brilliant college professor" could have been implicated in such a harebrained scheme. She and Jonathan hadn't been together as often as some people claimed, her lawyers said. Admittedly she had given him the shotgun, but it had been with the understanding that he would use it only to guard the headquarters of the Soledad Brothers Defense Committee. She had kept the other weapons on a rack in her home for target practice by members of the Che-Lumumba Club. Jonathan had visited her there six days before the courthouse tragedy; probably he had stolen them then.

The attorney presenting the defense summation said that the only evidence against her was "that Angela was closely related to Jonathan Jackson, that her guns were used, that she expressed a desire to free the Soledad Brothers, that Angela expressed love for George Jackson, and that on August 7 Angela made herself unavailable to the authorities." The jury would have fled, too, the lawyer declared, if they had been Negro and had discovered that four guns they owned had been used in the escape attempt at the courthouse: "I say to you, when you look at the situation through the eyes of a black person, you would not wonder why she fled. You would only wonder why she allowed herself to be caught."

After thirteen hours of deliberation the panel found her not guilty. Turning her back on the jurors, Angela left the courtroom to address her admirers outside. A reporter asked her if she thought she had received a fair trial. She said she didn't. "The very fact of an acquittal," she said, "means that there was no fair trial, because a fair trial would have been no trial at all." Setting out on a triumphant tour of the country, she told her supporters: "Starting from this day forward, we must work to free every political prisoner and every oppressed person in this country and the whole world."

Four weeks after the Soledad murder, which had started the chain of events that culminated in Angela's fame, Chicago had witnessed the end of another remarkable trial. It had opened with eight defendants: Yippies Jerry Rubin and Abbie Hoffman; Rennie Davis, David Dellinger, and SDS's Tom Hayden, the three leaders of the National Mobilization Committee which had brought the antiwar demonstrators to Chicago; Bobby Seale of the Panthers; and Lee Weiner and John R. Froines. Before their arrests some of the defendants had scarcely known one another, and in fact the key complaint against them was not the conspiracy count, but the accusation that they had entered Illinois individually to incite a riot—"crossing state lines with a state of mind," said chief counsel William M. Kunstler, while Leonard I. Weinglass, their other attorney, called the statute—which had been passed as a rider to the 1968 Civil Rights Act—"the only federal law where the government can punish someone without the commission of an overt act." They were the first defendants to be indicted under it, though that fact and a great many others were forgotten during the circus into which the proceedings deteriorated.

Kunstler set the tone on the first day of the trial, when he moved for a mistrial because of the way Judge Julius J. Hoffman read the charges to the jury. "Your Honor sounded like Orson Welles reciting the Declaration of Independence," said the lawyer.

"I've never been compared to that great actor, Orson Welles," said the judge, "but I deny the motion."

Altogether, the defense would make more than a score of mistrial motions, and to a great degree the tempestuous character of the proceedings arose from the chasm between Kunstler, Weinglass, and their clients on the one hand, and Judge Hoffman and the state's attorneys on the other. "The trial," wrote Richard Ciccone of the AP Chicago Bureau, "was a collision of generations, ideologies, and life-styles." Judge Hoffman wore a vest; Abbie Hoffman wore love beads and buckskin, and during one uproarious session he and Rubin appeared in judicial robes. Rubin and Hoffman had beards. The defendants and their lawyers grew their hair long, a fact caustically noted by the well-barbered prosecutors, Thomas A. Foran and Richard G. Schultz.

At one point, when Allen Ginsberg was testifying for the defense, the witness showed how he had quieted antiwar Chicago demonstrators in 1968—with a ten-second grunt: "Ah-ooom!" Kunstler protested that the judge was laughing. His Honor denied it. "I just don't understand the language," he said. Ginsberg explained, "It's Sanskrit." The judge said, "That's one I don't know." The transcript shows that there was a great deal the court did not know, but Hoffman did have a clear concept of the decorum which should be observed in his courtroom. During the seventy-four years since his birth in a humble Chicago neighborhood he had come to expect respect from the people who came before him, and neither the Chicago Eight nor their defense staff gave it to him. The first signs of what lay ahead came during a pretrial hearing. Kunstler and Weinglass wanted to ask veniremen how they felt about protest demonstrations, American slums, and the Vietnam War. Judge Hoffman turned them down; he said they couldn't even ask prospective jurors their opinion of hippies and Yippies. The next defense request was for a postponement of the trial until Seale's attorney, Charles Garry, could recover from an operation. Hoffman rejected that, too, and when he followed it by denying Seale's appeal for the right to address the court, telling him that he would have to allow Kunstler to speak for him, he touched off judicial chaos.

"I can only see the judge as a blatant racist," Seale said. The dwarfish judge bounded to his feet. "Did you hear that?" he asked a

clerk in disbelief. The Panther leader was cautioned, then and repeatedly afterward, that interruptions would be "dealt with appropriately at some time in the future." Seale retorted, "What can
you do to me that hasn't been done to black people for three hundred years?" In the eighth week of the trial the judge started to respond to a series of Seale outbursts: "Look, young man, if you keep
this up—" Seale replied: "Look, old man, if you keep denying me
my constitutional rights you are being exposed to the world—" Hoffman said: "Mr. Seale, do you want to stop or do you want me to
direct the marshal—" Seale said: "I want to argue about this so you
can get an understanding of the facts."

His patience exhausted, the judge told the marshal, "Take that
defendant into the room there and deal with him as he should be
dealt with." After a recess the Panther was carried in gagged and
handcuffed to a metal folding chair. Even that didn't silence him.
He rattled his fetters against the chair and cried in a muffled voice,
"That means I object!" He was moved to a wooden chair and the
gag was tightened. At the next session he managed to work free of
the gag and shout at the bench: "You fascist dog, you rotten lowlife son-of-a-bitch!" Abbie Hoffman and Rubin jumped up, screaming, and Kunstler asked the court: "Your Honor, when are we going
to stop this medieval torture? This is an unholy disgrace to the law
. . . I feel so utterly ashamed at this time to be an American lawyer." Judge Hoffman, who had frequently said that he blamed
Kunstler and Weinglass for the misconduct of his clients, snapped:
"You should be." The following week he ordered the gag removed,
and when Seale persisted in his interruptions he sentenced him to
four years in prison for contempt. Now those left were christened
the Chicago Seven.

They weren't chastened. While Davis was on the stand he accused the judge of being asleep—His Honor warned him that his
insolence would be "dealt with appropriately at some time in the
future"—and Abbie Hoffman created pandemonium by coming into
the courtroom walking on his hands and calling Judge Hoffman a
"tyrant," a "Nazi," and "a disgrace to the Jews."

The sharpest exchanges were between the court and the chief
defense counsel. The judge explicitly directed Kunstler not to ask
in the presence of the jury that Mayor Daley—who had insisted the
trial be held despite Justice Department doubts—be declared a hostile witness. The attorney did it anyway, and he almost gave the

judge apoplexy by asking Daley point blank whether he had shouted an obscenity at Senator Abraham Ribicoff during the convention. At one point Abbie Hoffman raised his shirt. "Let the record show," the judge said, "that man bared his body in open court." Kunstler said, "Your Honor, I remember when President Johnson showed his stomach scar to a whole nation on television." "Maybe that's why he isn't President any more," His Honor replied. When the lawyer chuckled and was rebuked he said, "Come on, Your Honor, what's the harm in laughter? Sometimes we can't help ourselves." The judge said, "Oh yes, I can see that you can't help yourself."

Toward the end of the trial the court's hostility toward the defendants became flagrant. For two days Hoffman refused to let them use the toilet in the hall; the latrine in the jail, he said, was good enough for them. One day he said they would start a half-hour earlier the following morning. When Kunstler asked the reason he was told, "Because it will be at nine-thirty." The lawyer commented, "That's like a child saying, 'Because, because.'" The judge said, "Let the record show that, in the presence of the jury, Mr. Kunstler compared me to a child." The lawyer was effusive in court, often hilarious or in tears. Sometimes he hugged men, and he kissed Weinglass and one of the witnesses, the Reverend Ralph D. Abernathy. "Let the record show," Judge Hoffman said acidly each time, "that Mr. Kunstler kissed that man." As the end of the trial was to prove, his reasons for these insertions in the transcript were not frivolous.

Defense witnesses included Pete Seeger, William Styron, Judy Collins, Norman Mailer, Julian Bond, Reverend Jesse Jackson, Terry Southern, and Ginsberg, who at Prosecutor Foran's insistence read aloud some of his poems on homosexuality and masturbation, apparently because Foran thought they would offend the ten women jurors. Kunstler and Weinglass argued that Daley and the Chicago police had provoked the violence at the Democratic convention.

Most of the evidence against the Seven came from informers who had mingled with the antiwar demonstrators in Lincoln and Grant parks and had taken everything they heard literally. An undercover policewoman testified that Abbie Hoffman had yelled: "We need a lot of weapons. Get rocks, bricks, stones. Break the bricks in half—they're easier to conceal that way and the girls can carry them." An undercover policeman said the defendants had been determined to create violence as "the first step of the revolution." A Chicago official told the court that Abbie had said to him: "If the city was smart, it would give $100,000 to sponsor our festival. Better yet, give me $100,000 and I'll leave town." The official had construed this as attempted extortion.

After nearly five months of testimony and argument the jury retired and the judge, with obvious relish, began meting out sentences for contempt. It took him two days, with time out for the defendants' screams. As Kunstler heard his clients and his co-counsel being sent away—Weinglass was given two months—he staggered all over the courtroom and collapsed, sobbing, "My life has come to naught at your hands, Judge. Come to mine. Come to mine. Take me next, I don't want to be here any more." The judge took him last. Saying, "No lawyer has ever said the things to me that you said during this trial," he gave him four years and thirteen days in prison.

The jury acquitted all the defendants of conspiracy but convicted Davis, Dellinger, Hayden, Hoffman, and Rubin of crossing state lines to incite a riot. The judge sentenced each of them to five years in prison, fined each $5,000, and assessed them the costs of the prosecution—another $50,000. But the sentences didn't stand. Nearly three years later a U.S. Court of Appeals reversed the convictions. The appellate court found the controversial antiriot statute —the so-called Rap Brown Act—constitutional by a two to one vote but threw out the verdict, citing Judge Hoffman's "antagonistic" behavior and finding that his "deprecatory" attitude toward the defense was "evident in the record from the very beginning."

Indeed, far from vindicating the prosecution, the case of the Chicago Seven became the first of an unparalleled series of judicial disasters for the government. It was followed by the trials of the Harrisburg Seven, the Camden Seventeen, the Seattle Seven, the Kansas City Four, the Evanston Four, the Pentagon Papers case, and the Gainesville Eight. In each of them the defendants were heretics in the eyes of the established order, and in every case the accused were vindicated by a jury, a judge, or an appeals court. Hostility to informers and judicial bias were common threads in the findings. In addition, as Martin Arnold pointed out in the *New York Times,* "despite all evidence to the contrary, people generally believe that the government is competent, and it angers them when the government goes into court with a weak case, often incompetently presented."

The Vietnam War, the real fuel for the riots which had been blamed on the Seven, continued to divide and abrade the country in 1970. At the beginning of the year there had been hope for something better. During the first four months the news from Saigon had been mildly encouraging. U.S. troops under General Abrams were avoiding big battles with the Viet Cong and the North Vietnamese. Nixon was reducing American troops from 543,000 to 340,000, and he assured the country that another 60,000 grunts would be withdrawn by May 1. But an end to the war seemed as remote as ever. In Paris the Communists scorned a five-point Nixon peace proposal, saying, "Our rejection is firm, total, and categorical." David K. E. Bruce, the chief American negotiator, turned down a Communist plan, calling it "old wine in new bottles."

U.S. combat deaths, which had stood at 25,000 during the Chicago protests two years earlier, now passed the 44,000 mark. Barring a breakthrough, Washington let it be known, some 200,000 American soldiers would stay in Vietnam for years. War weariness was becoming increasingly evident in the United States, among the South Vietnamese, and in fighting units. Grunts in the 4th U.S. Division refused to go into battle until they had been persuaded by desperate officers; troops in another division reviled Nixon, shouting obscenities about him when they spotted a war correspondent; soldiers wore peace medals with their dog tags; estimates of marijuana use among U.S. servicemen ran as high as 80 percent, while deaths from overdoses of hard drugs almost tripled. Augmenting all this was an appearance of incompetence at the highest levels of the American military effort. U.S. paratroopers executed a daring raid on a POW camp at Son Tay, twenty-three miles from Hanoi; seventy to a hundred American fliers were believed to be imprisoned there. The raid would have been a success, but intelligence had blundered—all the POWs had been moved. That same week U.S. warplanes pounded North Vietnam for twenty-four hours. The Pentagon first said the sorties were part of a "protective reaction" operation, protecting unarmed American aircraft, then changed its story to acknowledge that supply bases were being attacked. In fact, the shocked nation later learned, the targets of the bombardiers had included hospitals.

Abandonment of the Saigon government was out of the question, the White House declared, because the Communists were said to have a list of three million Vietnamese who would be "dealt with" in a "blood bath." The existence of the list was a matter of some skepticism, and Americans in increasing numbers were ready to desert the regime of General Nguyen Van Thieu anyway. The South Vietnamese seemed unappreciative of their American ally, even hostile toward it. Saigon rioters burned Nixon in effigy, shouting "Down with the Americans" and accusing the United States of prolonging the war. Ominously, Buddhists with kerosene and matches were immolating themselves, as other bonzes had just before the overthrow of Ngo Dinh Diem. David Truong, the son of a South Vietnamese politician, toured the U.S. telling audiences that the grunts and the ARVN troops fighting beside them shared only a mutual hatred of each other.

Meantime the notion that Americans were fighting to defend an Asian democracy was becoming difficult to sustain. David's father ran against Thieu and was clapped in jail, becoming one of over 80,000 political prisoners of the Saigon government. Americans in the field reported the torture of the regime's critics and their convictions by kangaroo courts; the courts continued to sit even after Saigon's supreme court ruled that they were unconstitutional. And Thieu's demands for U.S. wealth appeared to be insatiable. After nearly a decade of unstinting support of Saigon by Washington, he continued to say that he needed more equipment from the United States, more time to train his troops, and a lot more money. Unless he got them, he said, he couldn't take responsibility for the consequences.

The last thing Americans wanted that year was a war in another Southeast Asian country, but that was what the administration gave them. Actually their Air Force had been hammering Communist bases in eastern Cambodia for over a year, though few of them knew it. On orders from the White House, B-52s had conducted 3,630 secret raids on jungle sanctuaries there. The Joint Chiefs had long wanted to send in the infantry. Nixon had demurred at that; he knew that Cambodia's ruler, Prince Norodom Sihanouk, would protest the violation of his country's neutrality. With double bookkeeping and tight security it was possible to suppress information about the B-52 sorties. Once U.S. troops lunged across the frontier that would be impracticable.

On March 18, however, the Cambodian situation was changed dramatically by a coup. Sihanouk, aware that his administration was threatened, was in Russia asking for Soviet help in his effort to get

40,000 Viet Cong and North Vietnamese troops out of his country, when Cambodian General Lon Nol took over the government. Lon Nol was a rightist; he wouldn't denounce a U.S.-ARVN expedition to drive out the Communist intruders. Six weeks after the coup Nixon went on television to tell Americans that an operation to do just that was under way. Its goal was to be the destruction of the Vietnam nerve center, base camps, and underground arsenals above the "Parrot's Beak" northwest of Saigon. "For five years," the President said "neither the United States nor South Vietnam has moved against these sanctuaries because we did not want to violate the territory of a neutral nation." He did not mention the clandestine bombing of Cambodia, which at that time had been in process for fourteen months.

The military value of the invasion of Cambodia was disputed. While it was still being mounted Nixon described it as "an enormous success—far exceeding expectations." Asked about Pentagon claims that the Viet Cong would need six to nine months to recover from it, Thieu said, "I say they will never recover. Cambodia from 1964 to 1969 was a second North Vietnam, a whole rear area." In Saigon, MACV claimed the seizure of 15 million rounds of ammunition, 7,250 tons of food, and 25,000 guns; the death of 11,285 enemy soldiers; and the capture of 2,156. Allied casualties were 1,138 killed and 4,911 wounded.

But now Cambodia had been drawn into the war. The Communist troops which had been squatting in the Parrot's Beak responded to the offensive by driving westward against Lon Nol's army, conquering half the country, threatening its capital, Phnom Penh, and establishing a new, secure supply route in the Mekong valley. Washington was now committed to a new regime which was even less defensible than Thieu's. And some of the expedition's Cambodian goals were unachieved because they had been wholly unrealistic. "American officials," Frances FitzGerald noted in *Fire in the Lake,* "spoke of plans to capture the enemy's command headquarters for the south as if there existed a reverse Pentagon in the jungle complete with Marine guards, generals, and green baize tables." No such command post was found because, of course, there had never been any.

The greatest damage wrought by the Cambodian adventure was its impact on the home front. So great was the public outcry against this new involvement that the Senate, stirring at last to invoke the congressional right to declare war, passed a measure demanding an evacuation of American troops from Cambodia and an end to air support there by July. On campuses the reaction eclipsed all previous protests. By the end of May 415 colleges and universities had been disrupted. It was the first general student strike in the country's history, and it was entirely spontaneous. At the end of the semester 286 schools were still paralyzed, and while 129 others in forty-three states had officially reopened, many classrooms were empty.

On the weekend of May 9–10, more than 100,000 students stormed Washington. The White House was transformed into an armed camp behind a bumper-to-bumper wall of transit buses. The President's first response was contemptuous; talking informally with some Pentagon secretaries, he called the protesters "bums." Then he decided to make a conciliatory gesture. On Friday night of that week he went to the Lincoln Memorial with his valet and Secret Service agents and tried to talk to students sleeping there. "I feel just as deeply as you do about this," he said to them. Trying to find common ground, he launched into a discussion of football and asked one of the students, a Californian, if he enjoyed surfing. "The two Americas," wrote a team of reporters for the London *Sunday Times*, "met and drifted apart in a state of mutual incomprehension."

Equally bewildering for the President was a letter to him from Secretary of the Interior Walter J. Hickel. Hickel had been a conservative businessman, but he was also the father of six sons. He protested that the administration was alienating youth. He was particularly incensed over attacks on the young by Vice President Agnew. Nixon's public response was propitiatory; he assured the secretary that members of the administration would cool their rhetoric. But Hickel had committed a cardinal sin. His letter had appeared in the newspapers before it reached the oval office. On Thanksgiving eve Nixon summoned him to the White House and fired him for lack of "mutual confidence." Within a few hours one of H. R. Haldeman's assistants arrived at the Department of the Interior with a list of men to be purged. Six senior officials were told: "We want your resignation, and we want you out of the building by five o'clock."

If that was tough, the actions on some campuses were rougher. A revolutionist's bomb tore out the sides of the University of Wisconsin's Army Mathematics Research Center, killing a physicist, wounding four, and doing six million dollars' worth of damage.* At predominantly black Jackson State, in Mississippi, an encounter between students and police in front of a dormitory ended tragically when officers opened fire with buckshot, machine gun, rifle and armor-piercing shells, killing two students and wounding nine. A presidential commission headed by former Pennsylvania Governor William W. Scranton called the 28-second fusillade "an unreasonable, unjustified overreaction," but a local grand jury blamed the students, declaring that "when people . . . engage in civil disorders and riots, they must expect to be injured or killed when law enforcement officers are required to reestablish order."

Mississippians weren't the only Americans in that troubled year to feel that students were fair game, and Negroes weren't the only victims. Flag-carrying hardhat Manhattan construction workers who marched into a crowd of antiwar demonstrators that May were enormously popular; when the White House commended them it was interpreted as smart politics. Hostility toward youth cut deep. Older Americans were offended by almost every facet of the youthful subculture: the long hair, the tie-dyed jeans, the loud music, the language, the gestures, the very names of the rock groups—the Cream, the Stones, the Grand Funk Railroad. Most objectionable of all were the heavy drugs. The college students, whom younger teen-agers slavishly aped, put up outrageous psychedelic posters of bleeding colors and distorted images; they spoke casually of getting spaced out, turned on, tuned in, getting it on, getting into it, getting funky or freaky or heavy from narcotics, and they lured adolescents away from parents with rock jamborees which appeared to be, and sometimes were, steeped in sin.

Woodstock had been the high-water mark for the rock bacchanals. According to John Morthland, assistant editor of the weekly *Rolling Stone*, of the forty-eight major festivals slated the following year, only eighteen were held. "The major reason," said Morthland, "is political. The day after a festival is announced, the city council and police come up with some emergency ordinance that makes it impossible to hold it." Authorities taking such steps were acting with the approval—often the entreaties—of residents who had seen

* In November 1973 Karleton Lewis Armstrong, twenty-seven, was convicted of the bombing and sentenced to twenty-three years in prison. His counsel was William Kunstler.

and heard enough of the subculture to know that they didn't want
it celebrated in their backyards. They felt vindicated and then some
by stories about 1970's most notorious rock gala: the Powder Ridge
festival in Middlefield, Connecticut.

Actually Powder Ridge was a nongala; it never went on as scheduled. Promoters had signed up twenty-five bands to play at the
three-hundred-acre ski area, but four days before the affair was to
begin a citizens' committee convinced a judge that the tiny community didn't have to endure the noise, the pot, the kids in the buff,
and the Viet Cong flags. He issued an injunction. That turned the
musicians away, but it was too late to stop the audience from gathering; the occasion had been advertised in underground newspapers
as far away as Los Angeles, the throng was already on its way,
and it arrived, 35,000 strong, on the Friday of that first weekend
in August. No entertainment awaited it, no food, no adequate
plumbing facilities. Powder Ridge was a disaster waiting to happen,
and it happened.

The heat was sweltering, and after pitching their colorful tents
the youths divested themselves of clothes. On the first day they
swam nude in a small pond beside the ski lodge, but so many of
them voided and defecated in it that on Saturday the pond was
declared a health hazard. Sanitation was a concern of Dr. William
Abruzzi, a bearded, bald physician who was there as a volunteer,
but it wasn't his chief worry; that was narcotics. Peddlers roamed
through the crowd hawking marijuana, cocaine, heroin ("only a
dollar-five-oh for magic magic"), barbiturates, speed, and LSD
("Acid here, the quality goes in before the name goes on"). State
police arrested seventy pushers leaving the crowd, one of them with
$13,000 in his pocket, but most of them got away. Kids who couldn't
afford the hucksters' prices could drink free from vast buckets of
"electric water," into which passers-by were asked to drop any drugs
they could spare. This ugly stew was blamed by Abruzzi for many
of the thousand bad trips he treated, more than the number at
Woodstock, where the multitude had been over ten times as large.
Every Middlefield resident had tales of what the doped youngsters
did. One of the more sensational scenes, attested to by several witnesses, occurred in a small wood near some homes. A boy and a
girl, both naked and approaching from different directions, met under the trees. On impulse they suddenly embraced. She dropped
to her knees, he mounted her from behind, and after he had

achieved his climax they parted—apparently without exchanging a word.

Obviously Powder Ridge had nothing to do with antiwar protest, but to its critics the subculture of the young was all of a piece; any one aspect of it reminded them of the others. The most memorable symbol of college backlash in the days after Nixon's announcement of the Cambodian invasion, the Kent State tragedy, didn't start as a protest. By all accounts the first phases of the disorders there would have occurred anyhow. Unlike Columbia and Berkeley, the university in Kent, Ohio, had no tradition of activism. Football was still big in Kent; after a triumph students would ring the Victory Bell on the Commons. There were proms and bull-and-beer joints in the town. Indeed, the trouble started with a beer bust that muggy Friday night.

Spilling out from a bar, students decided to dance in the street. An angry motorist gunned his engine as if to drive into them. Several young drunks climbed on the car, broke its windows, set fires in trash barrels, and smashed store windows. On orders from Mayor LeRoy Satrom, Kent policemen turned the roisterers out of the taverns. Driving them back toward the campus, they broke up the die-hards with tear gas. The next day Kent State's few political militants secured administration approval for a rally that evening. Out of an enrollment of nearly twenty thousand, about eight hundred students came. Shouting "One two three four, we don't want your fucking war!" at faculty members and student marshals, the crowd turned the rally into a demonstration. It got out of hand and disrupted a dance; lighted railroad flares were thrown through the windows of a one-story ROTC building facing the Commons. When firemen appeared, the demonstrators pelted them with rocks and chopped up their hoses with machetes. The building burned to the ground.

Without notifying the university administration, Mayor Satrom appealed for help from the National Guard. Governor James Rhodes responded by sending a five-hundred-man contingent equipped with M-1 rifles, Colt revolvers, and tear gas. Students greeted them by spraying trees with gasoline and setting them afire, but by midnight on Sunday the fires were out and everything seemed to be under control. Meantime Governor Rhodes had arrived on campus. On Tuesday Ohio Republicans were going to vote in a senatorial primary, and Rhodes was one of the candidates. He was trailing badly—in the event he would lose—but he was making a last effort to turn the tide. The situation in Kent seemed exploitable. Calling a press conference, he declared an emergency and said of the students, "We're going to use every weapon of law enforcement to drive them out of Kent . . . They're worse than the Brownshirts, and the Communist element and also the night riders and the vigilantes. They're the worst type of people that we harbor in America."

In fairness to Governor Rhodes, it should be pointed out that he was not the only student-baiter whose words reached the National Guardsmen. Attorney General Mitchell had attacked campus militants as rowdies; so had President Nixon and Vice President Agnew, who had been widely quoted as saying that "The troublemakers among the younger generation are only a bunch of hoodlums who don't deserve to bear the title of American youth." In Kent, Mayor Satrom was making inflammatory remarks, while Brigadier General Robert H. Canterbury of the Guard was virtually inciting to riot. Having sowed the wind, they reaped the whirlwind at noon Monday. Classes were resumed that day and the campus at first appeared to be quiet. Several students rang the Victory Bell at midday and about a thousand gathered for a peaceful demonstration on the Commons while another two thousand watched. Two jeeps appeared. Guardsmen in them shouted through bullhorns: "Evacuate the Commons area. You have no right to assemble." Students raised their middle fingers, flung some stones and yelled: "Pigs off campus! We don't want your war." Brigadier General Canterbury told reporters, "These students are going to have to find out what law and order is all about." Major General Sylvester Del Corso of the Guard, in full view of his troops, picked up several rocks and threw them back at students.

It was now about a quarter past twelve. Two skirmish lines of Guardsmen fired tear gas canisters into the crowd; a few students tossed them back, but they fell short. Other students fled, and a unit of about a hundred troopers chased some of them between two buildings. There the Guardsmen found themselves hemmed in, with a fence in front of them and rock-throwing students on either side. Their plight was not really serious; the rocks didn't come close enough to hit them, and many of the onlookers were laughing. At this point the troopers ran out of tear gas and began retreating up a hill, looking apprehensively over their shoulders. It was a dangerous situation. The Guardsmen were capable of savagery—over the weekend they had bayoneted three students—and their M-1 rifles were loaded with live ammunition. As a presidential commission headed by former Pennsylvania Governor William W. Scranton later put it, "all that stood between the Guardsmen and firing was a flick of a thumb on a safety mechanism and the pull of an index finger on a trigger."

There were suggestions afterward that a group of troopers decided to fire on their tormentors. Photographs show eight or ten of them gathered in what witnesses described as a "huddle." Another curious piece of evidence is a tape of the incident. On it, the fatal thirteen-second salvo is preceded by a single shot. This could have been fired, either as a signal or from fear, by Terence F. Norman, a spurious "freelance photographer" who was really an informer on the FBI payroll. (In addition he may have been in the employ of the university, which also had undercover men.) Norman had a gun, and some spectators say he drew it and fired it, either just before or just after the crucial moment. What is certain is that on reaching the top of the slope at 12:24 P.M. the troopers knelt, aimed at the students, who were hundreds of feet away, too far to harm them, and fired as though on command. (Brigadier General Canterbury, in their midst, managed to be looking the other way.) The fusillade was followed by an awful silence. Into it a girl screamed, "My God, they're killing us!"

Thirteen students had been shot, and four—none of them a militant and one an ROTC cadet—were dead. A stream of blood was gushing from the head of one youth, drenching the textbooks he had been carrying; another boy was holding a cloth against a friend's stomach, trying vainly to stem the bleeding. The troopers made no attempt to help their victims.

In the immediate aftermath none of them were prosecuted for the killings. Although Attorney General Mitchell declared that American education was experiencing the "saddest semester" in its history—"There can be no greater evidence of disorder in society than the sound of gunfire on a college campus," he said—and though an investigation by three hundred FBI agents concluded that the Guardsmen had been in no physical danger, and that they conspired afterward to blame the incident on a threatening mob which never existed, the Justice Department declined even to convene a federal grand jury. Long afterward this was done, but not until March of 1974 were eight indictments handed down.

At the time, an Ohio grand jury exonerated the troopers—and indicted instead twenty-five others, including the president of the student body. Although none of them were convicted, there was a widespread feeling that the victims had got what was coming to them. It was strengthened when President Nixon implied that violent protest had brought violence in return; the incident, he said, "should remind us once again that when dissent turns to violence it invites tragedy." The Scranton Commission said that "61 shots by Guardsmen certainly cannot be justified." Vice President Agnew called their report "pablum for permissiveness," and added that responsibility for what had happened lay with the students, "on the steps of the university administration, and at the door of the faculty lounge." Any other interpretation, he said, would be "scapegoating of the most irresponsible sort."

The campus disorders which greeted Nixon's announcement of the Cambodian adventure formed a key link in the chain of events which led, ultimately, to the burglarizing of the Democratic National Committee's offices in the Watergate complex in Washington two years later. The first link had been a story in the *New York Times* of May 19, 1969, under the byline of William Beecher, who covered the Defense Department for the paper. It began: "American B-52 bombers in recent weeks have raided several Vietcong and North Vietnamese supply dumps in Cambodia for the first time, according to Nixon administration sources, but Cambodia has not made any protest."

Nixon was dismayed. He felt that his worst fears about the irresponsibility of the eastern establishment press had been confirmed, and believed them reconfirmed when the *Times* published technical details of American preparation for the Strategic Arms Limitation Talks (SALT) talks with Russia. Under the Constitution there was little he could do about Beecher and his paper, but he could at least hunt the unknown informants in his administration who were leaking classified information to newspapermen. He consulted Henry Kissinger, who drew up a list of thirteen officials, including five of his own National Security Council aides, who knew about the secret Cambodian bombing. On orders from the President, their telephones were tapped by the FBI; so were the phones of four journalists who had published leaked material: Beecher; Hedrick Smith, the *Times* man at the State Department; Marvin Kalb of CBS; and Henry Brandon of the London *Sunday Times*.

It was the White House's first incursion into the twilight zone of questionable activity, and it was fruitless; Beecher's source was never found.

The President began to entertain misgivings about the efficiency of both Hoover's FBI and Richard Helms's CIA. His doubts deepened after the events of May 1970. Nixon was convinced that the campus outbreaks were the work of foreign instigators, probably Cubans, Egyptians, and eastern Europeans. He asked the CIA to identify them. After an extensive investigation the agency reported that all the agitators were native Americans. The President gave the FBI the same assignment; the bureau brought back the same explanation. Still dissatisfied, the oval office ordered more wiretaps and—something new—house break-ins to search suspected offices and homes. The programs were to be directed by a new domestic security panel consisting of the country's top intelligence men: Hoover, Helms, and the directors of the Defense Intelligence Agency and the National Security Agency. Their marching orders were to be drawn up by a twenty-nine-year-old Hoosier lawyer and presidential speech writer named Tom Charles Huston.

On June 5, 1970, the four intelligence chiefs met in the President's office, were photographed with him, and were told that he wanted them to form a committee supervising national security, with Hoover as chairman. They were to go into action on August 1. Meantime Huston would draft operational plans with the FBI director. During one of their early meetings Hoover tried to dampen the young lawyer's enthusiasm for illegal schemes by explaining the historical development of objective intelligence. Huston replied impatiently, "We're not talking about the dead past; we're talking about the living present." In addition to electronic surveillance and surreptitious entry, his plan envisaged opening mail, recruiting more FBI informers on campuses, and CIA spying on students and other Americans living abroad.

As an attorney, the Indianan was aware that second-story jobs and what he called "mail coverage" were felonies, but he wanted to go ahead anyway. He wrote: "Use of this technique is clearly illegal; it amounts to burglary. It is also highly risky and could result in great embarrassment if exposed. However, it is also the most fruitful tool and can produce the type of intelligence which cannot be obtained in any other fashion." He argued that the advantages "outweigh the risks." Hoover disagreed. In a footnote to the Huston report the director said he didn't want to be chairman of the panel and didn't even want to be a member of it. Huston felt wounded. He sent Haldeman a memorandum in early July commenting on the FBI director's comment: "His objections are generally inconsistent and frivolous—most express concern about possible embarrassment to the intelligence community (i.e., Hoover) from public exposure." On July 23 Nixon signed a "decision memo," drafted by the young lawyer, approving the plan, but when Hoover saw it he protested to Mitchell, who discussed it with the President, who dropped the whole thing. Embittered, Huston resigned that fall and went home to practice law in Indianapolis. His intelligence duties were assigned to a White House newcomer, presidential counsel John Wesley Dean III.

The following spring the *Times* began publishing fresh Pentagon leaks, and Nixon concluded that his administration had become a sieve, that something must be done, that he would have to bypass Hoover. Accordingly, the President established a Special Investigations Unit whose job, as he himself later explained, was to "stop security leaks and to investigate other sensitive security matters."

Unknown to one another then, the men who would make presidential burglary the prelude to the American scandal of the century had been emerging from governmental careers, thus becoming available for new employment. E. Howard Hunt, whose CIA career had been going downhill since the American ambassador in Madrid refused to approve his assignment as deputy station chief there, on the ground that he was an intriguer, had retired at the time of the Kent State tragedy. Four months later James W. McCord Jr. resigned from the CIA, and eight months after that G. Gordon Liddy was fired by the Treasury Department because of an unauthorized speech praising gun ownership at a National Rifle Association rally.

David Young, a thirty-two-year-old lawyer from Kissinger's staff, opened the Special Investigations Unit's headquarters in room 16 in the basement of the Executive Office Building. The *New York Times* carried a brief item reporting that Young and a colleague, Egil Krogh Jr., were doing something about leaks. One of Young's relatives read it and said to him, "Your grandfather would be proud of you, working on leaks at the White House. He was a plumber." David put a sign on the door of his new office: "Mr. Young— Plumber."

The off-year elections of 1970 were waged by the GOP leadership on the basis of a principle laid down by Murray Chotiner, Richard Nixon's first campaign mentor. It was, quite simply, that Americans vote against candidates, not for them. An aspirant for office following Chotiner's precept gave only nominal attention to his own program. Instead he blazed away at the least attractive aspects of his opponent's record, ideas, mannerisms, and private life. If the aspirant couldn't find anything, he invented something. These tactics were what the President's critics had in mind when they spoke of the Old Nixon. The GOP strategy that autumn was to convert all the party's nominees into Old Nixons. It was to be the first hundred-million-dollar congressional election, and the chief Republican firehorse would be the Vice President, or, as presidential adviser Bryce Harlow called him, "Power-pack Agnew."

Certainly the party needed a boost of some sort. The previous November Nixon's approval rating in the Gallup poll had touched 68 percent, but since then it had been eroded by worsening inflation, Cambodia, the Calley case, and rising unemployment. Early in the year Nixon told GOP leaders that they would lose in November if the jobless rate touched 5.5 percent. It went to 5.8 and hit 6 percent before the end of the year. The SALT talks were going well, and in March the nuclear nonproliferation pact was signed, yet neither these nor the administration's plan for revenue sharing generated much interest in the electorate. Its welfare reform plans also lacked appeal. Nixon's vow to preserve "neighborhood schools" without busing was well received in the South, but it angered Negroes in the North, and with the emergence of the black middle class the Negro vote was becoming formidable. By November the country would have thirteen black congressmen, 81 black mayors, 198 black state legislators, and 1,567 local black officeholders.

In the White House the Vice President was regarded as admirably suited to campaign under Chotiner's colors. During his first year in Washington he had been remarkably active at the lectern, delivering seventy-seven major speeches, and his audiences had been large and appreciative. A Gallup poll in 1970 placed him third among America's most respected men, just behind the President and Billy Graham. To be sure, eleven faculty members at the University of Minnesota had appealed to him to stop "driving moderates into the hands of the extremists." Senator George McGovern had called him "a divisive, damaging influence," and Republican Governor Francis

Sargent had announced that he was unwelcome in Massachusetts. But college professors and McGovern were already recognized as the administration's natural enemies, while Sargent's state, with 300,000 students among its inhabitants, had become identified as the most liberal in the union. In any event, Agnew had been among the first members of the administration to spurn the President's inaugural plea to Americans to "stop shouting at one another" ("I intend to be heard over the din," the Vice President had said, "even if it means raising my voice"), and Middle Americans delighted in the choicer passages of Agnewian bombast:

> Some newspapers dispose of their garbage by printing it.
> Asking Senator Fulbright's advice on foreign policy is like asking the Boston strangler to massage your neck.
> If, in challenging, we polarize the American people, I say it is time for a positive polarization.
> Violence rewarded breeds further violence and perpetual violence ultimately produces a brutal counterreaction.
> The disease of our times is an artificial and masochistic sophistication—the vague uneasiness that our values are false, that there is something wrong with being patriotic, honest, moral, and hardworking.

Agnew covered 32,000 miles while stumping thirty-two states in the fall of 1970. He set the tone for his campaign in a Palm Springs, California, press conference on September 13, when he called on the electorate to reject the Democrats as "radical liberals." Subsequently he capsulized this as "radic-libs," explaining that the politicians he had in mind could be "depended upon to vote against the interests of law and order and against the interests of a representative society and against the foreign policy of the United States virtually every time." While not endorsing all aspirants in his own party—"I would have to put one Republican senator who seeks election in that group. That's Senator Goodell of New York"—he condemned all opposition nominees: "The Democratic candidates are a team of permissive candidates who have a penchant for indulging the disorderly and fawning upon lawbreakers." His sesquipedalian prose was enlivened by two presidential speech writers, William Safire and Pat Buchanan. With them as phrasemakers, he denounced senatorial doves as "solons of sellout" and "pampered prodigies." All Democratic nominees were lumped together as "nattering nabobs of negativism," "pusillanimous pussyfooters," "vicars of vacillation," "troglodytic leftists," and "hopeless, hysterical hypochondriacs of history" catering to "foolish fads of phony intellectualism." Of his fustian rhetoric he said he liked metaphors and alliteration, "but I don't need gimmicks to get my message across. I am simply stating what America is all about."

Agreeing with him, the President sounded much the same theme while campaigning 17,240 miles in twenty-two states over twenty-three days. In all of them he was on the attack. Like Agnew, he defended no record, described no goals, acclaimed no ideals; that would have violated Chotiner's rule. Instead he stumped against students, narcotics, the SDS, rioters, draft dodgers, flag burners, homosexuals, criminals, promiscuity, and pornography, identifying all of them with the Democrats. The climax came the night before the election, when the Republicans rebroadcast on television one of the President's most strident speeches. The previous Thursday evening in San Jose, California, demonstrators had pelted his limousine with eggs and rocks, tried to smash the windows, and hammered on the doors. "You had to see their faces," an aide who was with him said later; "the hate in those faces—it got to him." *Time* noted that the episode had been "condemned in all responsible and even quasi-responsible quarters." Nevertheless, speaking after it in Phoenix, the President had seemed to blame all his critics for what had happened. He pledged that "No band of violent thugs is going to keep me from going out and speaking with the American people" —the implication was that Democrats were out to stop him—and said of the dissenters, "They're not romantic revolutionaries. They're the same thugs and hoodlums that have always plagued the good people." He concluded: "Our approach, the new approach, demands new and strong laws that will give the peace forces new muscle to deal with the criminal forces in the United States."

The quality of the election eve rebroadcast, like the message it bore, was scratchy, and at times all but incoherent. It lasted fifteen minutes. The next quarter-hour was given over to a paid reply from Senator Edmund Muskie of Maine, speaking for the other party. Muskie was calm, measured—and devastating. Noting that Nixon and Agnew had maligned Democrats and accused them of disloyalty, he said: "That is a lie, and the American people know it is a lie. . . . There are only two kinds of politics . . . the politics of fear and the politics of trust. One says: you are encircled by monstrous dangers. . . . The other says: the world is a baffling and hazardous place, but it can be shaped to the will of men. . . . Thus in voting for the Democratic Party tomorrow you cast your vote for trust . . . for trusting your fellow citizens . . . and most of all for trust in yourself."

Everyone, Muskie pointed out, believes in law and order; the Democrats had voted for the administration's bills to control crime. But what about racial tension, the environment, the economy? And what about national unity? He said: "There are those who seek to turn our common distress to partisan advantages, not by offering better solutions but with empty threat and malicious slander." He called on the voters to repudiate them.

They did. The Democrats gained twelve House seats, widening their margin to 255-180. The Republicans lost eleven governorships. They had led, with 32 statehouses to 18; now they trailed 29-21. The average Democratic candidate ran three percentage points ahead of 1968. Early in the campaign the GOP had entertained hopes of winning eight Senate seats and regaining control there. It had seemed possible, for the Democrats had twice as many Senate seats at stake. After the smoke had cleared, the Republicans had picked up just two of them, and one was of doubtful value; in Connecticut a conservative Democrat, Thomas J. Dodd, had been replaced by a liberal Republican, Lowell P. Weicker Jr.

Trying to put the best possible face on the results, Nixon claimed an "ideological victory," pointing to the defeat of Albert Gore in Tennessee, Joseph Tydings in Maryland, and Charles Goodell in New York, where Conservative party candidate James Buckley had won a three-way race with only 39 percent of the vote. But these gains were offset by the successes of Adlai Stevenson III in Illinois and John V. Tunney in California, and the Texas defeat of George Bush, whom the administration had strongly backed. Most discouraging for the White House were omens for the 1972 election. Apart from Tennessee, the celebrated GOP southern strategy had achieved nothing. Elsewhere Republicans had lost several key legislatures. Special Nixon-Agnew efforts had failed in New Jersey, Wisconsin, North Dakota, Florida, Nevada, and New Mexico, and they had done badly in big states—California, Pennsylvania, Ohio, and Michigan—where the next presidential race would probably be decided.

The president of the liberal Republican Ripon Society summed up the outcome as the GOP's "worst showing since 1964," and said of Nixon's interpretation that "to the degree he claims he has a working ideological majority now, he cannot use Congress as a scapegoat in 1972." The standing joke among Republican governors assembling after the election in Sun Valley, Idaho, was that they should have met in Death Valley. The governor of Indiana, which had given the President his biggest plurality two years earlier, said he was in trouble even there; the governor of New Mexico warned his fellow Republicans that the GOP had "lost the election because the strategy was completely negative." "In November 1970," wrote columnists Rowland Evans and Robert Novak, "the Presidency of Richard Nixon . . . hit bottom." In fact it sank lower. That winter Gallup showed the percentage of Americans who approved of the President dropping from 56 percent to 51 to 50 to 49. In the Harris poll Muskie surged ahead of Nixon by three points, and in subsequent months his margin widened to five points and then to eight points—47 to 39. *Newsweek* raised the possibility that Nixon might be a one-term President.

It was against this background that Nixon and his chief political advisers gathered in Key Biscayne for a postmortem—one of them, reflecting their host's fondness for sports cant, called it "going over the game plan." Mitchell, who was particularly gloomy, said the President had acted as though he had been "running for sheriff." All agreed that they could not afford a repeat performance two years hence. Starting now, Nixon must appear to be aloof from partisan politics, doing his job as President. The new chairman of the Republican National Committee would be Senator Robert Dole of Kansas, a GOP stalwart and a hard-liner.

But that wasn't the most important decision at the meeting. As one who was there put it afterward, "We knew we were in a damn tough fight, and we weren't going to entrust it to a bunch of cautious old hacks down at the committee." Another said later, "The decision was to get politics the hell out of the White House and across the street"—across the street being the steel and glass tower at 1701 Pennsylvania Avenue, a hundred and fifty yards from the White House. There the independent Citizens Committee for the Reelection of the President opened its second-floor offices in March 1971 amid new furniture, fashionable interior decoration, and deep orange pile carpeting. Until John Mitchell resigned from the Justice Department and took it over, it would be run by a protégé of Haldeman's, Jeb Stuart Magruder. Magruder's director of security was to be James W. McCord Jr. His counsel was G. Gordon Liddy. The committee itself was to become known to all, Republicans and Democrats alike, as CREEP.

Early Seventies Montage

IS MOTHER'S MILK FIT FOR HUMAN CONSUMPTION?

AT&T UP 1000% SINCE 1932

Hello darkness, my old friend
I've come to talk with you again
Because a vision softly creeping
Left its seeds while I was sleeping
And the vision that was planted in my brain
Still remains,
Echoing the sound of silence.
You don't need to be a weatherman
To know which way the wind blows

Masters and Johnson estimate that one-half of the marriages in the United States are threatend by sexual dysfunction

Virginia Slims

INSTAMATIC SALES HIT 50,000,000

NIXON PLEDGES SMALL STAFF, OPEN ADMINISTRATION

They Ran Out of Tear Gas

Kent State 1970

Allison Krause, 19
Sandra Lee Scheuer, 20
Jeffrey Glenn Miller, 20
William K. Schroeder, 19

Best Sellers FICTION
Love Story Segal
Islands in the Stream Hemingway
Crystal Cave Stewart
God Is an Englishman Delderfield
The French Lieutenant's Woman Fowles

SILENT MAJORITY

AMERICAN GIs SPREAD CHRISTMAS JOY TO CHILDREN AROUND WORLD

1 IN 8 AMERICANS GET SOCIAL SECURITY CHECKS

That's what it's all about
This has to be the richest country ever

— It can't be all that bad —

THE WHITE HOUSE

IKE DEAD

TO: The Staff
From: John Dean

WASHINGTON   August 17, 1971

This memorandum addresses the matter of how we can maximize the fact of our incumbency in dealing with persons known to be active in their opposition to our Administration. Stated a bit more bluntly -- how we can use the available federal machinery to screw our political enemies.

moratorium

HOMOSEXUALS MARCH IN NEW YORK

Is that all there is?
Is that all there is?
If that's not all there is, my friend,
Then let's keep dancing

Letting it all hang out

OUR AMERICAN MADNESS: WHY WE WORK SO HARD AT HAVING FUN

Portnoy's Complaint (port'-noiz kəm-plānt') *n.* (after Alexander Portnoy 1933-   ) A disorder in which strongly felt ethical and altruistic impulses are perpetually warring with extreme sexual longings, often of a preverse nature ... It is believed by Spielvogel that many of the symptoms can be traced to the bonds obtaining in the mother-child relationship.

SELL 3,000 TOPLESS SWIM SUITS *Effete Snobs for Peace*

Q: (to witness Atkins) Did there come a time when you killed Miss Tate?
A: Yes, I killed her
Q: Describe to the court what happened.
A: Well, I stabbed her, and she fell. And I stabbed her again. I don't know how many times I stabbed her and I don't know why I stabbed her . . .
Q: But how can it be right to kill somebody?
A: How can it not be right when it's done with love?

—— You better believe it ——

Raindrops keep falling on my head
But I'm not complaining
That my eyes will soon be red
Crying's not for me

Sorry about that

How's that for starters?

Go Naked

Ninety percent of all scientists who ever lived are alive now.

BLACK NATIONALISTS PICK CITY AS TARGET

Best Sellers NONFICTION

The Sensuous Woman "j"
Everything You Always Wanted to Know About Sex Reuben
Inside the Third Reich Speer
Future Shock Toffler
Zelda Milford

Thirty-six

THE DIVIDED STATES
OF AMERICA

T HAT WINTER NOSTALGIA became big business. Wooden cigar store Indians were bringing as much as $4,000 each; *Superman* comic books issued in 1938, $400. An Italian designer reintroduced the Rita Hayworth look, and his models, showing the shirt dresses and the flaring skirts, strolled to the piped rhythms of swing music. Coeds, reaching even farther back into the past, wore ankle-length turn-of-the-century frocks and steel-rimmed granny glasses. Arrow Shirts were displayed in 1906 layouts; Hertz advertisements featured sepia-toned prints and obsolete Victorian type faces. Hippies wore Mickey Mouse watches. Over three hundred radio stations observed Halloween by rebroadcasting Orson Welles's *War of the Worlds*. One of the most remarkable—and profitable—shows on Broadway was a revival of the 1920s *No, No, Nanette*. In its first week it earned $35,000; tickets went for $25 apiece; "I Want to Be Happy" became a hit again. The choreography was by Busby Berkeley. The star was sixty-year-old Ruby Keeler. When she skipped into her first tap dance to the tune of "Tea for Two," the opening night audience leaped to its feet to give her a roaring ovation.

Among the extraordinary examples of yesterday's appeal was the 1971 reissue of Sears, Roebuck's Catalogue No. 104, for 1897, with new introductions by S. J. Perelman and Richard Rovere. The publishers expected it to be bought only by libraries for reference shelves. Instead it sold 200,000 copies at $14.95. Presently a Nostalgia Book Club opened offices, offering books of old movie ads, collections of pulp magazine stories, and the adventures of Dick Tracy,

Little Orphan Annie, and Buck Rogers. Nancy Drew and Hardy
Boys mysteries were selling briskly. The Longines Symphonette Recording Society was reaching millions with albums of 1930s songs
and radio broadcasts under such titles as *Remember the Golden
Days of Radio, The Great Vocalists of the Big Band Era, Thanks
for the Memory, The Years to Remember, Those Memory Years,*
and *Theme Songs of the Big Band Era.* The most ambitious project
along these lines was a series of Time-Life albums which re-
recorded, in stereo sound, the great swing hits of Glenn Miller, Harry
James, Artie Shaw, Tommy Dorsey, Les Brown, Woody Herman,
Charlie Barnet, Jimmie Lunceford, Claude Thornhill, Lionel Hampton, and, of course, Benny Goodman.

The message was clear: Americans were yearning for the past because they were fed up with the present. Though 1971 was an event-
ful year, the character of the events was no improvement over 1970.
Later inflation would make that of 1971 seem mild, but at the time
it seemed outrageous. In February wholesale prices took their sharpest jump in seventeen years. Overall, the cost of living had risen 25
percent in five years. At the same time, FBI figures indicated that
serious crimes had increased 176 percent in the 1960s. During the
previous year there had been 5.5 million of them in the United
States, and whereas one crime in three had been solved in 1960,
the rate now was only one in five. Venereal disease had spread dis-
mayingly. The incidence of gonorrhea had attained the proportions
of a nationwide epidemic—with no vaccine to prevent infection.

Change continued to alter the country at a startling pace. The
figures from the new census, now becoming available, showed
among other things that the flight from U.S. farms in the 1960s had
reduced the population living on the land by another 40 percent.
Rootlessness was up again; six million Americans now lived in trailers. One useful measure of the shifting patterns in urban life was
the growth of shopping centers. The first one had been built outside
Portland, Maine, in 1959, and over the next decade retail business
in the central city there plunged 71 percent. By the second year
of the Nixon administration the nation had more than thirteen thousand shopping centers, with more devastating consequences for the
stores of downtown America. Another set of figures with ominous
implications—which were unappreciated by the Nixon administration—foretold the energy crisis. Since 1945 the consumption of gaso-

line in the United States had increased fourfold, and the use of electricity sixfold.

It was a rough year for tradition. Rolls-Royce went into receivership. The Army declared that henceforth married WACs and nurses could have babies and remain in uniform. Capitol Hill was rocked when a Weatherman bomb exploded in a men's lavatory just below the Senate chamber. The Roman Catholic Church announced that 1,400 parochial schools had closed their doors in the past five years. *Look* observed National Magazine Week by folding. The Bon Vivant Company, makers of fine soups, collapsed when New Jersey health authorities discovered that what they were selling was botulism; over 1.2 million cans of its vichyssoise had to be destroyed. Radicals won three of four available seats on the Berkeley City Council. The judgment "Thirty dollars or thirty days" was heard for the last time when the Supreme Court ruled that a defendant could not be imprisoned because he was unable to pay a fine.

Campuses were quiet in 1971. The impact of Kent State was obvious. A *Playboy* survey of student opinion found that only 36 percent said, "I would protest now," and even they added, "but not violently." A contributor to the *Daily Californian* wrote: "The level of life in Berkeley has degenerated. The despair of the junkie pervades much of the community. We sit around smoking dope or drinking or thinking of new stereos . . . all too many people are just waiting for life rather than living." John L. Erlich, professor of social work at the University of Michigan, said that "large numbers of students have become discouraged and alienated." Erlich also noted that "larger numbers are still committed to change," however. The chief difference was that activists had stopped demonstrating on campus. The zealots, and there were still a lot of them, were now concentrating on Washington. The cause of their loudest clamor—the war—was drearily the same. If 1970 had been the year of Cambodia in Indochina, 1971 was the year of Laos. In addition it marked an end to any lingering illusions that South Vietnam, under President Nguyen Van Thieu, was on its way to becoming a democracy.

The Gilbert and Sullivan character of South Vietnam's 1971 presidential campaign could be traced to the 1967 election. The Thieu-Ky ticket had won then, but because eleven candidates had been running, the winners had carried only 35 percent of the vote. Thieu hadn't liked that. It still rankled; he felt he had lost face. This time would be different. At his direction the Vietnamese assembly required future nominees who wanted a place on the ballot to secure the signatures of either forty assemblymen or a hundred provincial and municipal councilors (under the second option, each councilor's endorsement must be countersigned by his province chief).

Thieu had two serious challengers: Ky and the popular General Duong Van Minh. Ky and Minh reached a gentleman's agreement: they would stay out of each other's way. Minh also said that he would withdraw if he suspected electoral fraud. Fraud followed; Thieu's supreme court threw out Ky's candidacy on a technicality. Angered, Minh called at the U.S. embassy with proof of other Thieu measures showing that the president was rigging the election, among them written instructions to province chiefs to buy votes, to shift "unfriendly civil servants to other jobs," and to stuff ballot boxes. Minh then quit the race, explaining that he could not "put up with a disgusting farce that strips away all the people's hope of a democratic regime and bars reconciliation of the Vietnamese people."

That left Thieu without opposition, a situation which delighted him but alarmed Washington. After U.S. Ambassador Ellsworth Bunker had protested, the Vietnamese supreme court obligingly reversed itself, ruling that Ky was a valid nominee and that his name could be printed on the ballot. But Ky had pride, too. In addition he suspected that Thieu's orders to the province chiefs had effectively fixed the race. Thereupon *he* withdrew, naming the president as "the principal actor in the farce." The election was held as scheduled, and the principal actor in the farce received 94.3 percent of the vote, the balance representing mutilated ballots. Thieu announced that he was gratified by this "astounding" display of confidence in his leadership, but this was no time for him to be winning Pyrrhic victories. By the end of the year the American troop level there would be down to 158,000, and the ability of his army to stand on its own was in grave doubt.

A South Vietnamese campaign in Laos multiplied the doubts, which was ironic, because it was supposed to do the opposite. To prove the effectiveness of Vietnamization, 16,000 ARVN troops were ordered to cross the demilitarized zone (DMZ), penetrate Laos along route 9, and cut the Ho Chi Minh Trail, that legendary spiderweb of supply paths which by now was fifty miles wide at some points. Few planners in military history had been so careless of secrecy. For weeks in advance confident U.S. officers in Saigon briefed the press on the Hobson's choice which lay ahead for the enemy: the North Vietnamese would either have to abandon their Laotian bases or stand and fight, and if they fought they would be annihilated. To advertise the native character of the drive, a billboard was erected on route 9 two hundred yards from the border of Laos, reading NO U.S. PERSONNEL BEYOND THIS POINT. When reporters pointed out that the operation bore an American code name—Dewey Canyon II—the name was hastily changed to Lam Son 719.

Lam Son 719 was launched on February 8, 1971, to the accompaniment of the continuing drumbeat of publicity. The first reports claimed success. War correspondents knew only that the troops were moving slowly against no apparent opposition. An armored column took two weeks to move eleven miles. Then disaster struck. The enemy attacked with tanks, heavy rockets, massed artillery, and four of North Vietnam's best divisions. In Saigon the deputy U.S. commander, Major General Frederick Weyland, acknowledged that South Vietnam's losses were "worse than Tet." Stalled, the battalion commanders of Thieu's supposedly elite 1st Division asked permission to fall back. They were turned down because, Frances Fitz-Gerald wrote in *Fire in the Lake*, "The American command and the White House had claimed that the ARVN would stay in Laos and occupy the trail until the end of the dry season in May, and the ranking ARVN officers did not dare contradict the Americans."

Infantrymen of the 1st Division panicked, abandoned their positions, blew up their artillery, and desperately hacked their way through jungle to clearings where U.S. helicopters could rescue them. Americans watching televised evening newscasts that week saw terrified ARVN soldiers clinging to the helicopters' skids. Only the intervention of American air power averted total catastrophe. At the end of the forty-five-day campaign the South Vietnamese units had suffered over 50 percent casualties—3,800 killed and 5,200 wounded. Eight battalions were unable to take the field. Traffic on the trail actually increased. When Nixon told the nation in early April, "Tonight I can report that Vietnamization has succeeded," his critics accused him of insulting the country's intelligence.

A response from America's antiwar movement was inevitable. On April 18 the Vietnam Veterans Against the War encamped below Capitol Hill and picketed the Supreme Court. Presidential counsel

Charles W. Colson hurriedly organized the Veterans for a Just Peace, and the Reverend Carl McIntire formed another countergroup, the Patriots for Victory, which called on Nixon to jettison his timid Vietnam policy and "use the sword as God intended." Administration officials accused commentators of exposing their leftist sympathies by failing to give the VJP and the PFV sufficient publicity, but events were moving too fast for both the government and the press. On April 24 a peaceful Washington march was held by some 200,000 protesters. The next week a "People's Lobby" swarmed over the Hill and into draft headquarters, buttonholing congressmen and Selective Service authorities, and the end of the month brought the climax of the capital demonstrations—the arrival of the "Mayday Tribe," which invoked the international distress call on behalf of its avowed objective: "stopping the government."

Just how violent the Tribe's intentions were later became a matter of some controversy. The leaders pointed out that their symbol had been the image of Mohandas Gandhi. It adorned their pamphlets, posters, buttons, and the cover of their tactical manual, which explained the principle of organized civil disobedience. Yet some of their methods were rougher than Gandhi's. Techniques included throwing junk in the street, abandoning autos at key intersections, and lying in front of cars. The Washington police force, which was known as one of the most relaxed in the nation, decided to adopt a strategy of killing the protesters with kindness. It was never given a chance to work. The President sent new instructions from San Clemente. He wanted the government to react more aggressively.

As coordinator of law enforcement tactics he chose Attorney General Mitchell. At the time of the November 1969 demonstrations, Mitchell had told his wife Martha that the peace marchers reminded him of Russian revolutionaries. More recently he had argued before a group of attorneys that the government's right to protect itself must override the right of individuals to privacy. The example he had chosen then was the need, as he saw it, for wiretaps without court orders. The Mayday disorders provided another illustration of the Mitchell approach to law enforcement in a time of political dissent. Under normal procedures, a policeman making an arrest must complete a form, filling in the name of the person charged, the offense, the arresting officer, and the time and place of the alleged infraction. Confronted by an invasion of 12,000 to

15,000 youths, many of them bent upon disrupting Washington traffic, Mitchell decided to cut through what he regarded as red tape.

On the evening of May 1 the vanguard of the Tribe was listening to a rock concert in West Potomac Park, near the Lincoln Memorial, when 750 helmeted officers swinging riot sticks drove them into the streets. Two days later the main battle was joined. Law enforcement officials had been given an overriding mission: keep the traffic flowing. Policemen, National Guardsmen, and regular Army troops broke up large concentrations of demonstrators with tear gas and truncheons. Assault units hovered overhead in military helicopters, ready to pounce. On that first day of the dragnet 7,200 were arrested, many of them peaceful pickets and spectators. It was a record. Altogether 12,614 were taken into custody over a four-day period. The jails wouldn't hold them; the overflow was penned in an open-air stockade at Robert F. Kennedy Memorial Stadium.

There they sang "God Bless America"—derisively—and "We all live in a con-cen-tra-tion camp," to the tune of the Beatles' "Yellow Submarine." Among them was Dr. Spock, shivering in a light raincoat. Abbie Hoffman was arrested in New York and accused of being a Mayday conspirator. He said, "I had about as much to do with the demonstrations in Washington as the Capitol bombing or the earthquake in Los Angeles, which I also expect to be indicted for." He had been picked up after a scuffle, and his nose was injured and taped. He said, "Like, man, that's defacing a national monument."

Congressional doves were appalled by the demonstrations. Tunney of California told reporters that the "foolish and useless" disorders "might well have ruined several months of hard work by the real advocates of peace." As it turned out, the courts rejected the arrests as clear violations of the prisoners' civil rights. The American Civil Liberties Union had anticipated that outcome, but it had been by no means certain at the time. The administration thought the law enforcement officers had performed admirably. Returning from California, Nixon told Republican leaders that he thought the Washington police chief had done "a magnificent job." He said, "John Mitchell and the Department of Justice did a fine job, too. I hope you will all agree to make that point when you leave here." Mitchell said, "I am proud of the Washington city police. I am proud that they stopped a repressive mob from robbing the rights of others." Then he compared the peace demonstrators to Hitler's Nazi brownshirts.

Six weeks after the great Mayday bust the *New York Times* of Sunday, June 13, carried on its first page the dull head: "VIETNAM ARCHIVE: PENTAGON STUDY TRACES 3 DECADES OF GROWING U.S. INVOLVEMENT." The story jumped to six inside pages, where column after column of dense type reprinted U.S. communiqués, recommendations, position papers, cables, and presidential orders, all concerning American activity in Indochina. It was perhaps the most extraordinary leak of classified documents in the history of governments, and it was only a beginning. Subsequent installments, the editors promised, would reveal more.

What the *Times* had acquired was a copy of a massive study commissioned by Robert S. McNamara shortly before his resignation as Secretary of Defense. The Pentagon Papers, as the newspaper called the archive, had been assembled by thirty-five scholars, including analysts from the Rand Corporation think tank, in an office adjoining McNamara's. Altogether there were forty-seven volumes of typescript—4,000 pages of records and 3,000 pages of explication, a total of 2.5 million words. It was all secret, but the secrets were not military. None of it compromised American troops still in Vietnam, and there was nothing from the Nixon years. McNamara had wanted to know how the United States had become entangled in Vietnam's swamps. The papers told how. Some of the documents went back to the Truman administration. They made a lot of officials look inept, foolish, or worse. Among other things the documents revealed that Lyndon Johnson had ordered the drafting of the Tonkin Gulf resolution months before the alleged incident there. Worse, on the very day in 1965 that he had decided to commit American infantry in Vietnam he had told a press conference that he was aware of "no far-reaching strategy that is being suggested or promulgated."

Clark Clifford, McNamara's successor as Secretary of Defense, had never found time to read the study. Henry Kissinger had been one of its researchers, but he hadn't seen the completed project. President Nixon didn't even know of its existence until that fateful Sunday morning that the *Times* began publishing it. Although it affected neither him nor his conduct of the war, he was infuriated. He felt that the ability of a government to keep secrets was vital. The fact that none of his own confidences were involved here was, he thought, beside the point; next time could be different. Furthermore, at a time when he and Kissinger were carefully defining their own Vietnam policy, these documents opened old wounds and raised again the ugly issue of the government's credibility.

On Monday, June 14, the *Times* published its second installment of the papers. Mitchell called the White House and suggested that the administration tackle the newspaper in the courts. Nixon agreed. Mitchell telegraphed the paper, "respectfully" suggesting that it print no more. If the editors went ahead, he warned, they could be convicted under the espionage statute, fined $10,000, and sentenced to ten years in prison. And the government would prosecute; the leak was causing "irreparable injury to the defense interests of the United States." The *Times* ran a front-page account of the attorney general's threat, and published the third installment of the papers alongside it.

That was a wild fortnight in city rooms and courtrooms. A team of government lawyers under Assistant Attorney General Robert Mardian went into federal court in New York on Tuesday, asking for an injunction against the editors. The judge, who had been on the bench exactly five days, scheduled a hearing for Friday and issued a temporary restraining order. The *Times* obediently stopped publication, but on Friday the *Washington Post* began running its own account of the papers. Clearly the *Post's* editors had access to the same source. Four days later the *Boston Globe* began printing the documents. Meantime the Associated Press had begun sending the *Post* version around the world. Among the papers printing it was the *New York Times*.

Mardian took the *Post* to court, but the federal judge in Washington refused to hand down even a temporary order. The government, he found, could not "impose a prior restraint on publication of essentially historical data." The U.S. Appellate Court voted 2 to 1 to restrain the *Post*. The New York judge refused a permanent injunction against the *Times* but extended his temporary order until appeals courts could rule. Finally, on the following Friday, the two cases—numbers 1873 and 1875—came before the U.S. Supreme Court, which found for the press 6 to 3. Then nine justices handed down no fewer than six opinions. Along with John Harlan, Nixon appointees Burger and Harry A. Blackmun were in the minority.

Mardian had taken the position that the Justice Department was merely attempting to recover stolen papers necessary for national security. The identity of the putative thief was unmentioned then, but the FBI knew. He was Daniel Ellsberg, a summa cum laude graduate of Harvard who had written his doctoral dissertation on the decision making process, worked for Rand, become a McNamara protégé, and helped put the Pentagon Papers together. A hawk at first, he had, like so many others, been transformed by events into a dove. Resigning from Rand because he had become an embarrassment to it, he had become a fellow at the Massachusetts Institute of Technology. He had brooded long over whether to make the papers public. The invasion of Cambodia had finally decided him.

On June 23 Ellsberg, still in hiding, appeared on television at an undisclosed location and identified himself as the source of the documents. The United States, he declared, was to blame for the Vietnam tragedy: "There has never been a year when there would have been a war in Indochina without American money." He said, "I felt as an American citizen, a responsible citizen, I could no longer cooperate in concealing this information from the American people. I took this action on my own initiative, and I am prepared for all the consequences." On June 28 he surrendered to authorities in Boston and was released on $50,000 bail. That same day he was indicted in Los Angeles for stealing government property and violating the Espionage Act. Six months later twelve more criminal charges, including conspiracy, were leveled against him. A former Rand colleague, Anthony J. Russo Jr., was also indicted, together with a Los Angeles advertising woman and a former South Vietnamese ambassador to the United States. Ellsberg said: "I stole nothing and I did not commit espionage. I violated no laws and I have not intended to harm my country."

Surveying the Watergate wreckage in 1973, a team of London *Sunday Times* reporters concluded that "The Pentagon Papers tipped the Nixon administration over the edge." The White House Special Investigations Unit—the Plumbers—acquired the services of two former New York cops, a Runyonesque pair named Jack Caulfield and Tony Ulasewicz. They had been hired by John Ehrlichman two years earlier for political investigations; their assignments, first from Ehrlichman and then from John Dean, had included inquiries into Chappaquiddick, My Lai critics, the drinking habits of anti-Nixon senators, the private life of a Washington columnist, and reports that the brother of an eminent Democrat was a homosexual. In the aftermath of the Pentagon Papers case they received their first assignment as Plumbers.

Anyone who had worked with Ellsberg had a lot of explaining to do in those days, and a man high on everyone's list of possible co-conspirators was Morton B. Halperin, who had directed the assembly of the Pentagon Papers. Halperin had been an Ellsberg friend and later a Kissinger aide. Leaving the government, he had moved to the Brookings Institution, a liberal think tank in Washington. Charles Colson believed that Halperin had been a source of leaks and probably still had classified material. If so, it might be in his Brookings office. Colson sent Ulasewicz on a reconnoitering mission; the ex-cop returned to report that there was no way to burglarize the institution. According to a subsequent account by John Dean, Colson, a hard man to discourage, told Caulfield that "if necessary he should plant a fire-bomb in the building and retrieve the documents during the commotion that would ensue."

That was too much for the New Yorkers. Someone, they felt, should restrain the impulsive Colson. They took the story to Dean, who caught the next plane to San Clemente. He laid the tale before Ehrlichman; Ehrlichman phoned Washington, and no more was said about fire-bombs. It was a costly triumph for Caulfield and Ulasewicz, however. The White House suddenly lost interest in their talents. Jobs which would have come their way in the past now went to the two rising stars in the Plumbers unit: E. Howard Hunt and G. Gordon Liddy. After three months in the cold, Caulfield decided to devise a master plan for political espionage. He hoped to sell it to the Committee for the Reelection of the President. Its code name was Operation Sand Wedge. On November 24 Dean secured an appointment for him with Mitchell. The presentation was not a success. Caulfield had a hunch that someone else was going to get the work, and as he left he knew he was right; sitting in the attorney general's outer office was Gordon Liddy.

During the spring and summer of 1971, when Richard Nixon was secretly having his White House offices wired for sound, his popularity rating in public opinion polls continued to sag. Presidential aides were agonizing over the refractory nature of the Vietnam War, still the most important issue before the country, and debating among themselves how best to reverse the electorate's political mood, so discouragingly expressed in the previous autumn's off-year election. This much was clear to them: they were going to need a lot of money. Fortunately, they were in much better shape than the debt-ridden Democrats. Herbert Kalmbach, the President's personal attorney, had custody of nearly two million dollars in unspent campaign funds from 1968. In January 1971 Kalmbach deposited the first $500,000 of the 1972 war chest in the Newport Beach, California, branch of the Bank of America. It is a matter of some interest that the money was in the form of cashier's checks which he had bought, with cash, in the Security Pacific National Bank branch just across the street. Even then he was taking steps to see that contributions could not be easily traced, because even then he knew that much of the means for the coming campaign would be coming from dubious sources.

Some of those sources emerged during the next few months. The first, in March, was the dairy industry. Early in the month Secretary of Agriculture Clifford Hardin announced that price supports for "manufacturing milk"—used to make cheese and butter—would be $4.66 per hundredweight, unchanged from the year before. The milk manufacturers took steps to reverse the decision. On March 22 they formed a GOP slush fund called the Trust for Agricultural Political Development and put $10,000 in it. The next day sixteen leaders of dairy cooperatives were invited to meet Nixon and Hardin in the oval office. They told the President and the secretary that they wanted a higher federal subsidy. The following day they gave the Nixon war chest another $25,000. The day after that Hardin changed his mind and pegged milk supports at $4.93. The dairy leaders then poured a total of $527,500 into Republican bank accounts.

Another lode was opened a few weeks later. Since the early days of the Nixon administration Harold S. Geneen, president of the International Telephone and Telegraph Corporation (ITT), had been trying to block a Justice Department task force which was working to prevent a merger of ITT and the Hartford Fire Insurance Corporation. Department career lawyers were determined to establish the principle that business competition is illegally crippled by huge sprawling conglomerates like ITT. The government's campaign was being directed by Richard W. McLaren, head of Justice's antitrust division. McLaren was reporting to Deputy Attorney General Kleindienst; Mitchell had supposedly withdrawn from the case because

his New York law firm had represented ITT. On April 19, 1971, Mc-
Laren and Kleindienst conferred and agreed to carry an appeal to
the Supreme Court. Kleindienst telephoned ITT's lawyer to tell him
of the decision.

Later that same day Kleindienst received a call from John
Ehrlichman, who told him that President Nixon was "directing"
Kleindienst to drop the ITT case entirely. The deputy attorney general said that was impossible; he, McLaren, and Solicitor General
Erwin Griswold were committed. "Oh?" Ehrlichman said curtly.
"We'll see about that." A few minutes later Kleindienst's phone rang
again. It was Nixon, who began by saying, "You son of a bitch, don't
you understand the English language?" He ordered Kleindienst not
to appeal. Disturbed, the deputy attorney general told Mitchell that
he would resign rather than capitulate, and he thought McLaren
and Griswold would go with him. Shortly thereafter Mitchell told
his deputy that he had talked to Nixon and "He says do anything
you want on antitrust cases."

The President and the attorney general were being less than candid with Kleindienst. In a subsequent memo to Haldeman, Colson
said he was trying to suppress all White House-ITT correspondence
because it "would lay this case on the President's doorstep." And
Mitchell, for all his talk of having turned the whole thing over to his
deputy, had been holding regular meetings with Geneen for the
past year. As early as September 1970 Ehrlichman had written to
Mitchell criticizing McLaren's attitude and mentioning an "understanding" with Geneen.

Bargaining between the administration and the conglomerate was
apparently concluded at a lunch given by the governor of Kentucky
at the Kentucky Derby the month after Kleindienst and McLaren
thought they had committed the government to a Supreme Court
trial. The mediators were Mitchell and Dita Beard, ITT's salty
Washington lobbyist. ITT agreed to pay $400,000 and the adminis-
tration agreed to forget about the antitrust action. In a highly incriminating memorandum dated June 25, 1971, Mrs. Beard told her
immediate superior that the only Republicans to know "from whom
the 400 thousand commitment had come" were Nixon, Mitchell,
Haldeman, and the lieutenant governor of California. She said: "I
am convinced that our noble commitment has gone a long way toward our negotiations on the mergers eventually coming out as Hal
[Geneen] wants them. Certainly the President has told Mitchell to

see that things are worked out fairly. It is still only McLaren's mickeymouse we are suffering. . . . Mitchell is definitely helping us, but it cannot be known."

She ended the memo, "Please destroy this, huh?" It wasn't destroyed, and when it surfaced in a Jack Anderson column the following February 29, ITT's response was to shred all other documents relating to the case and claim that this one had been a forgery. But the Dita Beard note does not stand alone. It is braced by the Ehrlichman correspondence, including a May 5 letter to Mitchell referring to a talk between the President and the attorney general in which they had settled the "agreed-upon ends" in the ITT case. Certain events of that time are also supportive. On May 15 Geneen pledged the $400,000 to the GOP, and at the end of July the Justice Department and the government settled their differences without an appeal to the Supreme Court. ITT was allowed to keep Hartford Fire. "Quite clearly," *Fortune* commented, "Harold S. Geneen has achieved something of a victory."

The key figure in a third deal between the administration and people trying to solve legal problems was Robert L. Vesco, a controversial financier with several ties to the Nixon family. Vesco had given $50,000 to the 1968 Republican campaign through the President's brother, F. Donald Nixon. He was close to the President's other brother, Edward, and beginning in the summer of 1971 he employed the President's nephew Donald as his personal assistant. "He is the one person who has never lied to me, ever," Donald once said of Vesco, a strange statement from a young man with such an eminent relative, and one not many people would make; within two years Vesco would be a fugitive from American justice, living in Costa Rica rather than face Securities and Exchange Commission charges that he had looted Investors Overseas Services, a mutual fund, of 224 million dollars.

Vesco was already in trouble in the early summer of 1971, when, according to the indictment against him, he involved Mitchell and Nixon's Secretary of Commerce, Maurice Stans, in an attempt to buy his way out of the SEC accusations. The understanding was that Vesco would give Stans $250,000 in cash and Mitchell, according to the charges, would "exert his influence on the SEC on behalf of Robert L. Vesco." Edward Nixon later acted as bagman, delivering to Stans $200,000 in a brown attaché case. (The remaining $50,000 came in a second installment.) Mitchell set up meetings between Vesco, the SEC chairman, and the commission's general counsel. The SEC continued to prosecute anyway.

While cash began to accumulate in the GOP war chest, the White House was engaging in various parapolitical activities in 1971, most of them with a view toward the next year's presidential election. One was the compilation of a list of political enemies, which under Colson's guidance expanded to fill a file four inches thick. It included the names of Jack Anderson, James Reston, Jane Fonda, Barbra Streisand, Paul Newman, Gregory Peck, and Carol Channing. The president of the Otis Elevator Company was there—apparently because the Otis elevator in Nixon's San Clemente house didn't work properly—and so was Detroit's black Congressman John Conyers. A notation after Conyers's name read, "Has known weakness for white females." On September 9, 1971, Colson designated twenty names for "go status," but no one on the presidential staff could think of an effective method of attack. Daniel Schorr of CBS ("a real media enemy," Colson called him) was subjected to an FBI check that summer, but the sole consequence was frustration for the White House. Ronald Ziegler put out the explanation that Schorr had been investigated because he was being considered for a government job.

Various Nixon aides—Huston, Dean, Caulfield—tried to talk the Internal Revenue Service into harassing selected taxpayers. All failed, and Commissioner Randolph Thrower resigned for reasons which, he said at the time, were "between me and the President." The White House was driven to the absurd lengths of writing anonymous letters to the IRS hinting at tax evasions by people on Colson's list. It was perhaps an inevitable outgrowth of this malicious foolishness that at some point the conspirators should conclude that someone was conspiring against *them.* The someone, they thought, was J. Edgar Hoover, who kept in his office safe logs of wiretaps he had carried out on White House orders. Robert Mardian persuaded one of Hoover's assistants to steal the logs, and they were locked up in Ehrlichman's safe. Hoover missed them in July 1971. He was enraged.

Men who did not shrink from doing a bag job on the director of the FBI had no qualms about playing rough with Democratic presidential candidates, and it was in these months that what later became famous as Republican "dirty tricks" made their appearance. Mailings critical of Ted Kennedy went out in fake Muskie envelopes; a spurious Muskie aide phoned the Associated Press bureau in Boston with charges that Kennedy was a "divisive influence"; Rowland Evans and Robert Novak were gulled into printing counterfeit Muskie memos which seemed to suggest that he was engaging in questionable activities. On December 1, 1972, Donald H. Segretti gave fifty dollars to the president of the Tampa Young Republicans Club with the understanding that it would be used to discredit the primary campaigns of Senators Muskie and Jackson in Florida. It was the first installment on a project which would eventually lead to Segretti's disbarment, conviction, and imprisonment.

Some tricks were intricate. On the assumption that a third-party Wallace candidacy would hurt Nixon more than any Democratic candidate, various projects were undertaken to sabotage Wallace's American Independent Party. One of the more fantastic of them, masterminded by Mitchell and Jeb Magruder, involved paying the American Nazi Party $10,000 to persuade AIP voters in California to change their registration. The rationale behind this was that if enough voters switched, Wallace's party would have too few registrants to qualify for the ballot. It failed; the AIP actually gained 6,500 members during the period.

Another plot was directed at Ted Kennedy, the most formidable vote getter among President Nixon's possible challengers. Here the reasoning was that since young Kennedy's popularity was a reflection of John Kennedy's charisma, reducing the late President's appeal would hurt Ted. At a press conference on September 16, 1971, Nixon was asked about a recent statement by Senator Henry Jackson to the effect that the Saigon regime would be stronger if it were more democratic. Nixon replied, "If what the senator is suggesting is that the United States should use its leverage now to overthrow Thieu, I would remind all concerned that the way we got into Vietnam was through overthrowing Diem, and the complicity in the murder of Diem, and the way to get out of Vietnam, in my opinion, is not to overthrow Thieu." This was the first time anyone in the government had accused the Kennedy administration of connivance in Diem's death, and it gave Howard Hunt an idea.

Hunt had been poring over the Pentagon Papers. He told Colson that a Kennedy role in the Diem assassination might be assumed "inferentially" from State Department cables of the time. According to Hunt, Colson suggested that he "improve on them"—doctor them. Using a razor blade and a photocopier, Hunt forged two cables.

One, dated three days before the Diem assassination, began: AT HIGHEST-LEVEL MEETING TODAY, DECISION RELUCTANTLY MADE THAT NEITHER YOU NOR HARKINS SHOULD INTERVENE IN BEHALF OF DIEM OR NHU IN EVENT THEY SEEK ASYLUM. Colson referred a *Life* reporter to Hunt, saying of Nixon's accusation, "There's a big story there," but the reporter suspected duplicity and didn't bite.

The failure of this intrigue was Hunt's second disappointment that month. The other, the more bitter of the two, dated back to the previous April. On the tenth anniversary of the Bay of Pigs Hunt had flown to Miami for lunch with a Cuban-American named Bernard L. Barker who had been his principal subordinate then and was now a successful Florida real estate man. It was the opening link in a historic chain of events. The second was Ellsberg's massive leak of the Pentagon Papers. The third began with four men— Nixon, Kissinger, Haldeman, and Ehrlichman—on a helicopter ride between Los Angeles and San Clemente. The four leaders raged over the leak, which the President equated with the Alger Hiss case, and discussed bypassing the FBI with an undercover operation to learn more about it. The decision was made to detach David Young from Kissinger's National Security staff to work full-time with the Plumbers. Young then put the Ellsberg ball in Hunt's court; Hunt put it in Barker's.

But not right away. In the beginning the Plumbers explored what appeared at the time to be an innocent area. Toward the end of July they discovered, from an FBI report which was routinely routed through their office, that for two years Ellsberg had been psychoanalyzed by a Dr. Lewis B. Fielding of Beverly Hills. Two of Hoover's agents had attempted to grill the psychiatrist, but he had demurred, invoking the sanctity of the doctor-patient relationship. Hunt remembered that the CIA had a psychiatric section which drew up analytic profiles of men whose personalities were of special interest to the government. Under the CIA's congressional mandate the subjects were supposed to be foreigners—the most successful had been an analysis of Nikita Khrushchev, prepared just before President Kennedy's Vienna summit with him—but there had been one exception: Captain Lloyd Bucher of the *Pueblo*. Young asked CIA Director Richard Helms to make Ellsberg a second exception. Helms agreed. Early in August the finished profile was forwarded to the CIA.

Nobody there liked it. It wasn't at all what the Plumbers had in mind. The CIA psychiatrists seemed to admire Ellsberg. ("There is no suggestion that the subject [saw] anything treasonous in his act. Rather he seemed to be responding to what he deemed a higher order of patriotism.") On August 11 Young and Egil Krogh sent a minute on the study to Ehrlichman, rejecting it as "very superficial" and underscoring their belief that the CIA could do a better job. They wrote: "We will meet tomorrow with the head psychiatrist, Dr. Bernard Malloy, to impress upon him the detail and depth we expect." They then crossed the line into contemplation of criminal activity. "In this connection," they continued, *"we would recommend* that a covert operation be undertaken to examine all the medical files still held by Ellsberg's psychiatrist covering the two-year period in which he was undergoing analysis." At the bottom of the memorandum were the words "Approve _____ Disapprove _____." After "Approve" Ehrlichman scrawled his initial. He added: "If done under your assurance that it is not traceable."

It was this condition, stipulating that the Plumbers must use undercover operatives with no White House ties, which prompted Hunt to recruit Barker and, through him, two fellow Cubans, Felipe DeDiego and Eugenio R. Martinez. All Hunt told Barker was that he needed him to explore a "national security matter" on authorization from officials "above both the CIA and the FBI." The job, he said, concerned a traitor who was passing information to the Soviet embassy. Except for the fact that the Russians subscribe to the *New York Times*, this was untrue. Later, in prison, Barker found the deception unforgivable. Morality apart (and none of the principals seemed to see any moral issue at the time), Hunt was guilty of incredible carelessness. He failed to tell Barker not to carry in his pocket a telephone number and abbreviated address ("W.H." and "W. House") linking him with Hunt. He didn't even check to be certain that Barker's men were free of government connections. In fact one of them, Martinez, was on the CIA payroll as a Cuban informant.

Meanwhile Hunt and Liddy, his partner in this strange venture, were being outfitted by the CIA—another violation of the provision in the agency's charter forbidding domestic activity. Ehrlichman phoned Marine General Robert E. Cushman Jr., Helms's deputy, asking him to do all in his power to help Hunt, whom he identified as "a bona fide employee, a consultant on security matters." Ehrlichman didn't specify the nature of the mission. During their subsequent meeting Hunt told Cushman that he had been "charged with quite a highly sensitive mission by the White House to visit and elicit information from an individual whose ideology we aren't entirely sure of" and that he needed "flash alias documentation," "pocket litter of some sort," and "some degree of physical disguise, for a one-time op—in and out."

With the approval of Helms, the CIA's technical services division provided Hunt with a social security card and a driving license, both made out to "Edward Joseph Warren." Liddy was given identification in the name of "George Leonard." Hunt was issued a reddish-brown wig and a device, resembling false teeth, to alter the sound of his voice when telephoning. In addition Liddy received a tiny camera hidden in a tobacco pouch. On August 25, 1971, the two Plumbers flew to California on a preliminary reconnaissance mission. They didn't achieve much. After taking a picture of Liddy standing outside Dr. Fielding's office at 450 North Bedford Drive in Beverly Hills, Hunt entered the office, told a cleaning woman that he was a physician, and photographed the room. Both men timed a drive from there to the doctor's home. Then they flew back to Washington, where the plane was met by a CIA messenger who took the films from Hunt and had them developed. At the White House the two Plumbers persuaded their superiors that burglarizing the psychiatrist's office was justifiable. Young brought Ehrlichman up to date and proposed in a new minute that a committee on Capitol Hill be persuaded to look into the leak of the Pentagon Papers: "We have already started on a negative press image of Ellsberg. If the present Liddy/Hunt project is successful, it will be absolutely essential to have an overall game plan developed for its use in conjunction with the congressional investigation."

D-day for the Beverly Hills break-in was September 3, 1971; H-hour was 9 P.M. The operation was staged with all the meticulous attention to detail which had marked Hunt's participation in the Bay of Pigs, and it was just about as successful. Shortly before zero the Cubans checked in at the Beverly Hilton Hotel under assumed names. Two of them donned delivery men's uniforms and took a huge suitcase plastered with labels reading "Rush to Dr. Fielding" to North Bedford Drive. The cleaning woman admitted them and they left the bag with her, unlocking the door as they departed. Liddy was driving around outside, watching for suspicious policemen. Hunt was outside the Fielding home with a walkie-talkie to flash the alarm if the psychiatrist emerged and headed for his office.

At about midnight the Cubans returned to the office, only to discover—an omen of what was to come at the Watergate offices of the Democratic National Committee—that the cleaning woman had relocked the door. Forcing it, they removed a camera and a spotlight from the suitcase. The plan was to photograph Ellsberg's medical history. Unfortunately they couldn't find it. They dumped Dr. Fielding's files on the floor, but there was nothing for them there. All they turned up was an address book with Ellsberg's name in it. They took pictures of that and of the strewn files, to show that they had done their best. After four frustrating hours the team returned to the hotel, where Liddy phoned Washington to tell Krogh that it had been a "clean job"—Dr. Fielding would have disagreed, but Liddy meant only that they hadn't been caught. That was putting the best possible face on it. Back in the capital Hunt had to tell the White House that the mission had been a failure. Ehrlichman, according to his subsequent testimony, said he didn't want them to try again. Ehrlichman had another piece of bad news for Hunt. On instructions from Helms, General Cushman had called to say that while the CIA had been glad to help out, a repetition would be out of the question. The Plumbers were on their own now, and the pressure to produce something to justify their jobs was mounting.

The week after the first second-story job masterminded from the White House a tragic episode pointed up one of the issues deeply dividing Americans during the Nixon years. It lay between the holders of one set of values, who regarded their critics as illiberal and inhumane, and the critics, who scorned the liberals as "permissivists." The incident was the bloodiest prison revolt in the country's history. It occurred in an unlikely setting, amid the white clapboard homes, red barns, and tall silvery silos of western New York's Wyoming County. There, surrounded by dense fields of sweet corn and goldenrod, stood a fifty-five-acre penitentiary compound enclosed by thirty-foot turreted gray concrete walls. Christened after the nearby town, it bore the classical name of the ancient Athenian plain: Attica.

The state called Attica a "correctional facility," but not much correcting was done there. Under the stern administration of Superintendent Vincent Mancusi there was little vocational training and less compassion. Solitary confinement—"the box"—was the penalty for the slightest infraction of the rules, and inmates were systematically beaten in the elevator on the way there. They were allowed one bar of soap and one roll of toilet paper a month. If they worked in the hundred-degree heat of the metal shop, known to them as "the Black Hole of Calcutta," they were paid as little as 25 cents a day. Ugliest of all was the regime's naked racism. Of the 2,254 convicts, 75 percent were black or Puerto Rican, while all 383 guards were white. The keepers openly favored white prisoners, taunted the Negroes, and called their clubs "nigger sticks."

Warden Mancusi's reply to civil libertarians was that he was running a maximum security institution and that Attica's inmates included some of the country's most hardened criminals. It was true. It was also true, and an ill omen, that among them were many of a new convict breed, black militants who regarded themselves as victims of an imperialist society. Attica was, in fact, where other wardens shipped self-styled revolutionists who gave them trouble. Arriving, they smuggled in books by George Jackson and Eldridge Cleaver, held secret rallies when they were supposed to be at sports or in chapel, and circulated inflammatory pamphlets which they wrote in their cells. "If we cannot live as people, we will at least try to die like men," wrote a convict named Charles "Brother Flip" Crowley, and a poem being passed around began:

> If we must die—let it not be like hogs,
> Hunted and penned in an inglorious spot,
> While round us bark the mad and hungry dogs,
> Making their mock at our accursed lot.

In July 1971 an organization of militant inmates calling themselves the Attica Liberation Faction sent a proclamation demanding reforms to State Corrections Commissioner Russell G. Oswald. It was a clever move. Oswald had been appointed by Governor Rockefeller because his sweeping improvements in Wisconsin's prison system had been widely acclaimed by penologists, and though he had been in office only six months, he and Mancusi were already at odds on almost every administrative question. After Labor Day Oswald taped a message to the convicts asking for time to make profound changes. Among other things he pledged "meaningful rehabilitative methods, evening vocational programs, better law libraries."

He may have been too late. After the revolt guards found enormous circles drawn around the date September 9 on cell calendars. In July the militants had told Oswald that they felt there was "no need to dramatize our demands," but they changed their minds the following month. The decisive event seems to have been the death of George Jackson in San Quentin on August 21. At breakfast next morning Attica's Negroes protested by fasting. "It was the weirdest thing," a turnkey said afterward. "Nobody picked up a tray or a spoon, and nobody took any food. They just walked through the line and went to their seats and they sat down. They looked straight ahead and nobody made a sound . . . Then we noticed that almost all had some black on them. . . . It scared us because a thing like that takes a lot of organization, a lot of solidarity, and we had no idea they were so well organized."

The evangelical rhetoric of two revolutionists who were later identified as the key leaders, Herbert X. Blyden and "Brother Richard" Clarke, became more strident. Both were New Yorkers and Black Muslims; both had been convicted of armed robbery. Like George Jackson, Blyden was self-taught, a reader of history and philosophy who had been sent to Attica after leading a prison riot in the Tombs, Manhattan's House of Detention. Clarke had been transferred to Attica from a medium security prison whose warden said he had been advocating "the violent overthrow of the institution." His family had noticed that in Attica he was becoming increasingly bitter. Once when his wife was visiting him he said, "Feed the animals, feed the animals. That's what they treat us like here—animals."

On Wednesday, September 8, eighteen days after Jackson had been killed on the other side of the country, an Attica guard was punched by a convict while breaking up a fight in one of the prison exercise yards. That night the two who had been fighting were put in "the box." Other inmates said they were abused as they were dragged away, and a Puerto Rican prisoner threw a tumbler at one of the guards, cutting his face. The riot exploded the following morning. Precisely what touched it off is unclear. According to one account, a work party refused to line up at the rap of keepers' clubs. Another story put the responsibility on guards who, as a reprisal for the previous day's events, arbitrarily canceled the prisoners' exercise period. In a third version, Brother Richard led five convicts who were on their way to breakfast on a rampage, freeing Blyden, who was working in the metal shop, along the way.

However it started, the results were spectacular. Fewer than one hundred guards were on duty. They were overwhelmed, and many were captured. The prison school, the chapel, and the machine shop were put to the torch. While they were being reduced to smoldering debris, raiding parties of inmates raced through the galleries, gates, and catwalks of three of the four rectangular cellblocks —B, C and D. According to a Wyoming County deputy sheriff, they were armed with pipes which they had hidden under loaves of bread on trays in the mess halls. That may be apocryphal; the credibility of Attica's authorities was to be severely damaged before the uprising was over. But even if the inmates lacked weapons at the outset, they soon equipped themselves with them. Using grinding wheels acquired while looting the shops, some of them fashioned spears from scissor blades and broom handles. Others turned out clubs and knives which, when the keepers tried to extinguish the fires, were used to shred the hoses. With tear gas, guards managed to regain control of cellblock C and part of B, but the prisoners retained the rest, locking gates and even welding some of them shut with shop equipment.

Four hours after the revolt had begun, the battlefront hardened along lines which would remain substantially unchanged over the next four days. Cellblock D, the farthest from the administration building and the nearest to the shop, was the rebel stronghold, commanded by Blyden and Clarke. Wearing football helmets or turbans, the rebels—there were 1,280 of them—sprawled under makeshift tents in D yard, and a crude bench at one end of the yard was the epicenter of the revolt. There a rebel secretariat, the People's Central Committee, sat in continuous session, assigning work details, dictating defense measures, and even confining unruly prisoners in a "people's jail." Contacts between the convicts and state authorities were made in negotiating sessions at the table and in an A block corridor, a kind of no-man's-land dubbed the DMZ. A point of special interest was the geographical center of the prison, "Times Square," where catwalks leading to all four cellblocks met. It was held by the rebels. They had wrested it from a twenty-eight-year-old guard, William Quinn, who had battled them with a nightstick and had been overcome only after his skull had been fractured in two places. Some guards swore that they had seen him being brutally thrown from a high catwalk. There was no question that he had been gravely injured. When Clarke saw blood dripping from the unconscious guard's ear he ordered him passed through the DMZ to the authorities. Quinn's condition was a matter of great interest to both sides; if he died, every inmate participating in the uprising could be tried for murder.

Around noon Captain Henry F. Williams of the state police mustered two hundred and fifty troopers with riot equipment and told them: "If somebody on the other side gets killed, well, that's the way it's got to be. You're to take no crap from anybody. Don't lose your weapon and don't lose your buddy." That was tough talk, but it was deprived of much of its force by the fact that precipitate action was likely to lose them thirty-nine buddies—guards being held by the rebels as hostages. The captive keepers had been dressed in convict uniforms, blindfolded, and tied up in D yard. An inmate shouting through a megaphone warned that the hostages would be the first to suffer if the troopers charged, and no one in a position of responsibility, not even Superintendent Mancusi, was eager to call their bluff.

The man with the legal responsibility of dealing with the situation was Commissioner Oswald, who flew in at 2 P.M. Against Mancusi's advice, Oswald decided to enter D yard with Herman Schwartz, a Buffalo law professor trusted by the leaders of the revolt, and confront the rebels in person. He intended to tell them that he could not discuss their complaints until the hostages had been released, an unbreakable rule in penal administration. He did demand their release, but he also listened while Blyden dictated a list of fifteen demands to him. The rebels wanted, among other things, permission to hold political meetings "without intimidation," "religious freedom" for Muslims, an end to mail censorship, the right to communicate with anyone they wished, regular grievance procedures, more recreation and less time in cells, more exercise yards, a full-time physician, a better school, more fruit and less pork, the removal of Warden Mancusi, a committee of outsiders to "oversee" the behavior of the authorities during the revolt, and a federal court injunction against any "physical and mental reprisals" for the inmates' acts during the revolt. To the end of the list Blyden added that some of the convicts, at least, insisted upon "Speedy and safe transportation out of confinement to a nonimperialist country." He said: "We are men. We are not beasts, and do not intend to be beaten or driven. What has happened here is but the sound before the fury of those oppressed."

Oswald's personal courage in entering D yard was considerable. Even as he sat before the secretariat of rebel leaders, some of them were suggesting that he be added to the group of hostages, and though state police sharpshooters atop the prison walls were lining up the inmates around him in their sights, his chances of surviving a real row were negligible. His wisdom in going was another matter. Once he had heard them out and concluded that many of their points were reasonable, the pressure on him to open negotiations was almost irresistible. He yielded to it. As proof of his good faith he agreed to appoint a committee of overseers and to dispatch Schwartz to Federal Judge John T. Curtin, who was at a Vermont judicial conference, in pursuit of the injunction. Oswald did something else which was deeply resented by Mancusi and his staff. He signed a pledge of "No administrative reprisals against prisoners for activities of Sept. 9, 1971." The rebels interpreted this as a guarantee of clemency. The governor's office quickly pointed out that exoneration for criminal acts was out of the question; the commissioner didn't have the power to grant that. But the seeds of misunderstanding had been sown and were bound to bear bitter fruit.

That night Oswald returned to the floodlit prison yard, now further illumined by convicts' campfires. With him he brought a contingent of reporters—a concession to another rebel demand. Much of the time was spent putting together the panel of overseers. The inmates' choices included William Kunstler, Huey P. Newton, Bobby Seale, State Senator John R. Dunne, Tom Wicker of the *New York Times,* who had written sympathetically of George Jackson; Herman Badillo, the first Puerto Rican elected to Congress; and Clarence Jones, Negro publisher of Manhattan's *Amsterdam News.* Later Rockefeller added a number of selections of his own: his secretary, a school superintendent, a retired general, and various legislators and penologists. At one point there were thirty overseers. That was too many to be effective, and the ideological splits among them further weakened the committee.

Schwartz brought back the injunction signed by Judge Curtin. It had been drafted by one of the white prisoners, Jerome S. Rosenberg from Brooklyn, murderer of a policeman, but now the rebels rejected it as inadequate. The overseers were off to a lumbering start. Wicker, Jones, and Julian Tepper of the National Legal Aid and Defenders Association breakfasted with Wyoming County District Attorney Louis James; the best they could wangle from him was a written promise of no "indiscriminate mass prosecutions"— an assurance hardly likely to diminish the fears of the edgy convict secretariat. Another shaky agreement was broken at 4 A.M. Saturday, as the revolt approached the end of its second twenty-four-hour period, when the press pool was barred from the prison. Police hostility toward the reporters had been growing, a grim sign which usually foreshadows actions that policemen do not want outsiders to watch.

Yet Oswald was optimistic that morning. The inmates' demands had grown to thirty, but he had agreed to twenty-eight of them, drawing the line only at complete amnesty, which he now called "nonnegotiable," and the firing of Mancusi. Just as he was expressing confidence that these could be resolved, however, new developments shriveled hopes for a peaceful end to the riot. Quinn died, ending any possibility of leniency for the rebel leaders. Then Bobby Seale arrived. Before entering the prison he told fifty cheering radical demonstrators outside the walls that "If anything happens to those guards, the state and the governor should be charged with murder." Then his entourage passed out copies of a statement from the Panther Central Committee: "The prison guards, called 'hostages,' have actually in reality been placed under arrest by the 1,280 prisoners who are rightly redressing their grievances concerning the harassing, brutal, and inhuman treatment to which they are constantly subjected. . . . A promise of amnesty is the first thing that must be done to start negotiations of the prisoners' . . . demands. This is the only bail the arrested guards can have, from the analysis of the Black Panther party."

Obviously Seale had no interest in a resolution of the crisis. Inside, he told the inmates that they must make their own decisions in dealing with Oswald. In a pathetic display of trust, they begged him for advice. He replied that he could offer them no counsel without the approval of Huey P. Newton. After participating briefly in the overseers' deliberations he left, telling newspapermen that their questions and the armed state troopers were upsetting him. To cap this, Kunstler, in an act of extraordinary irresponsibility, told the rebel secretariat that representatives of "Third World nations are waiting for you across the street." Presumably he meant the fifty demonstrators, but he didn't explain, and the prisoners, now hoping for total victory, lost interest in bargaining with Oswald.

Sunday was a day of mobilization for both sides. Throughout the afternoon trucks arrived to disgorge National Guardsmen, powerful fire hoses, and crates of gas cylinders and gas masks. The overseers issued a statement warning that they were "now convinced that a massacre of prisoners and guards may take place at this institution." Wicker, Jones, Badillo, and Dunne spent over a half an hour on the telephone pleading with Rockefeller to come to Attica, but the governor issued a statement of his own saying that "In view of the fact that the key issue is total amnesty . . . I do not feel that my physical presence on the site can contribute to a peaceful settlement." He and Oswald had already agreed that if the convict leadership did not respond to a final ultimatum, they would have to resort to force. They were not sanguine. Plainly the mood of the prisoners was turning uglier. Gates were being wired to make them electrically hot, trenches were filled with gasoline. Booby traps of peat moss and oil were wired with time charges. Crude rocket catapults were fixed in position; the spears were resharpened. Barricades of metal tables were built along the main catwalk leading from A block to Times Square—a route invading troopers would have to follow. That afternoon rebels paying off old scores stabbed two white convicts to death.

The point of no return was reached early Monday. At 7 A.M. teams of policemen were assigned to specific functions: marksmanship, rescue, barricade demolition, and reserve strength. Two helicopters hovered overhead reporting on the disposition of convict forces and the situation of the hostages. At 8:35 Oswald met Richard Clarke in the DMZ. Brother Richard insisted that the rebels must be assured of "complete, total, unadulterated amnesty" and the dismissal of "that guy Mancusi." He said he wanted another half-hour to confer with other members of the secretariat. Oswald gave it to him. At 9:05 an inmate shouted through a megaphone that all the hostages would be killed by inmate "executioners" if rebel positions were attacked. An Oswald aide called back, "Release the prisoners now. Then the commissioner will meet with you." The convict yelled, "Negative." That was, literally, the last word in the negotiations. Only savagery was left.

Minutes later one of the helicopters radioed that four hostages were "at each corner of Times Square with knives at their throats."

It was a chilling sight: each captive's head was yanked back by the hair, arching his neck; the blades, held by cocked hands, were biting into the flesh. Actually this looked more desperate than it really was. What officials could not know was that they were witnessing a prime example of militant overstatement. The hostages weren't going to die at the rebels' hands. Like the demand for resettlement in "a nonimperialist country" (which had been withdrawn the first time Oswald had raised an eyebrow), the grisly gestures with the homemade daggers were a kind of rhetoric, designed to impress the world and, perhaps, the convicts themselves. There have always been men prepared to die for acts of bravado. Some were about to fall here now, and they were going to take helpless victims with them.

Convinced that the hostages were in grave peril, that they might be massacred anyway—that the danger was imminent and time was of the essence—Oswald said to his aides, "There's no question now—we've got to go in." More than five hundred local law enforcement officers and yellow-clad state troopers were coiled at the doors leading to the catwalks as *Jackpot Two*, a CH-34 helicopter, swooped down on Times Square with a load of tear gas, pepper gas, and mustard gas. The radio dispatcher's voice crackled: "Move in! Move in! The drop has been made! Base to all posts—move in. Launch the offensive!"

Troopers burst through the doors and blasted away at the barricades; marksmen on the gray walls began picking off inmates. Clearing the catwalks of obstacles took ninety minutes. Then the main attack went in. With clouds of turbid gas drifting across Times Square and D yard, it was difficult to see what was going on, and the fact that the hostages were wearing convict uniforms didn't help. Troopers insisted afterward that strong resistance persisted for about two and a half minutes. One said, "They came at us like a banzai charge, waving knives and spears. Those we had to shoot." Another said, "The ones that resisted—throwing spears and Molotov cocktails—were cut down. We caught some men with arms extended to throw weapons. Anybody that resisted was killed."

But some who didn't resist were killed, too. Sporadic firing continued for almost an hour. The New York State Special Commission on Attica (the McKay Commission) later found that the police assault had been "marred by excesses," which included "much unnecessary shooting." Some of the needless violence was attributable

to carelessness, possibly even to a contempt for human life. Rockefeller had specifically forbidden prison guards to participate in the
assault, but they went in anyhow and were responsible for at least
two homicides. Some of the policemen fired shotguns loaded with
"oo" buckshot which spread at distances exceeding thirty yards, hitting "unintended targets," the McKay investigators found, and
creating "a high risk of injury and death to unresisting inmates and
hostages." An attending physician, Dr. Lionel Sifontes of Buffalo,
reported afterward that "Many of the ringleaders were approached
by guards and shot systematically. Some had their hands in the air
surrendering. Some were lying on the ground."

More than 120 men lay wounded or dying. Counting Quinn and
the convicts who had been murdered by other prisoners during the
uprising, Attica's death toll was 32 inmates and 11 guards or administrative officers—a total of 43. Compounding the confusion in the
hours after the recapture of the prison were highly inaccurate reports about how the hostages had died. One Oswald aide said that
a guard had been found emasculated, his testicles stuffed in his
mouth. Another aide told reporters that "Several of the hostages
had their throats slashed." Stories that the guards had been butch-
ered by their captors gained credence from the fact that their blood-
stained blindfolds had fallen around their necks. In fact, three
surviving guards had suffered throat wounds, but when the medical
examiner issued his report the following morning, he found no cas-
trations and no mutilations among the dead. All had been killed
from gunfire. And only policemen had carried guns.

Governor Rockefeller said the hostages had "died in the crossfire."
Oswald lamely suggested that they "could very well have been used
as shields." The rescued hostages vigorously endorsed the police assault, and in Washington President Nixon said that the "painful,
excruciating" decision to storm Attica had been the only thing the
authorities "could possibly do." The conflict of opinion over what
had happened was rapidly becoming ideological. Those who distrusted liberals, penal reforms, "bleeding hearts" and "do-gooders"
rejected all criticism of the troopers. They blamed the convicts—
in a fierce editorial the *Atlanta Constitution* denounced "the animals
of Attica" for trying to impose "kangaroo justice" on the hostages—
and many also blamed the overseers. As an exhausted Wicker left
Attica a guard at the door hissed at him, "You people will never
again be allowed inside this facility under any circumstances."

The other side was also vehement. Newark Mayor Kenneth Gibson called the crushing of the prison revolt "one of the most callous and blatantly repressive acts ever carried out by a supposedly civilized society." Wicker later noted that although sixty inmates had been indicted on some 1,300 counts, not a single law enforcement officer had been charged with anything, despite "evidence of official negligence, official brutality, official indiscipline, official excess—possibly even official murder." After the rebellion had been suppressed, the McKay Commission found there had been "widespread beatings, proddings, kickings." Prisoners had been stripped and forced to run a gauntlet of guards with hickory billy clubs. Wounded guards had been swiftly treated, their families quickly notified. Wounded inmates had been left without medical attention for four hours, their bodies tagged "P1, P2, P3." Four days later the families of some prisoners were still frantically trying to learn whether their sons or husbands were alive or dead. Often Attica wouldn't tell them even that. Those who did hear received curt wires: REGRET TO INFORM YOU THAT YOUR HUSBAND RAYMOND RIVERA NUMBER 29533 HAS DECEASED. THE BODY REPOSES AT THIS INSTITUTION.

"All right we are two nations," John Dos Passos had written bitterly of the chasm between the rich and the starving in an earlier America. The rupture was along different lines now, but it cut equally deep. Three years earlier a new occupant of the White House had vowed to "bring us together." He hadn't done it. The people were as far apart as ever, unable to agree on the most elementary issues—justice and mercy, war and peace, right and wrong —and with a new presidential election a year away Americans were beginning to eye anew Richard Nixon's standings in the polls. Here, however, there was a change. As late as early August pollster Albert Sindlinger found that only 27 percent of the voters wanted to see Nixon reelected, but before the month was out his popularity curve paused, leveled out, and slowly rose. The decisive factor was resolute executive action at home and abroad.

The thirty-first world table tennis championships were held in Nagoya, Japan, that April, and the composition of the U.S. team was a tribute to the sport's widespread appeal: a Chrysler personnel supervisor, a Du Pont chemist, an editor of *Sports Illustrated*, a college professor, a black federal employee, an IBM programmer, an immigrant from the Dominican Republic, an employee of a Wall

Street bank, two teen-age girls, two housewives, and two college undergraduates. One of the students, Glenn Cowan of Santa Monica, was the most flamboyant member of the party; he wore tie-dyed purple bell-bottoms and a shirt with a peace symbol, and he kept his shoulder-length hair under control during play with a headband. Possibly because the headband was red, possibly because he was alert and extroverted, Cowan was singled out by players from the People's Republic of China for a historic proposal. How, he was asked, would he and his teammates like to make an all-expenses-paid tour of Red China?

They were delighted—"To quote Chairman Mao," Cowan said after consulting his teammates, "I seem to have struck the spark that started a prairie fire"—and a formal invitation to them from Secretary General Sung Chung of the Chinese table tennis delegation quickly followed. Washington had no objection; just a few weeks earlier the State Department had lifted all restrictions on Americans who wanted to travel in the People's Republic. Everyone concerned, including the ping-pong players, knew that the relationship between the two events was not coincidental. It was generally interpreted as an opening move toward detente, a reflection of the new confidence in Peking since the violent three-year power struggle there, known as the Great Proletarian Cultural Revolution, had ended in the final triumph of Mao and Premier Chou En-lai two years earlier. When seven western newspapermen were granted permission to enter China and cover the tour, it was clear that the world had reached a historic turning point. Obviously the Chinese, like the Russians before them, were using sport for diplomatic purposes. Table tennis acquired a new status overnight. Even President Nixon told his staff that "I was quite a Ping Pong player in my days at law school. I might say I was fairly good at it." Moscow sulked. The Kremlin called Peking's overture to the Americans "unprincipled."

On April 10 the U.S. team crossed from Hong Kong to the border station of Lo Wu via a short, steel-trussed bridge and continued on over another, tin-roofed bridge to the Chinese city of Shumchun. There smiling Communist officials led them to an immaculate cream and blue train. Their first destination was Canton, which since the rupture between Washington and Peking twenty-one years earlier had been rechristened Kwangchow. Along the twenty-three-mile journey there they saw banana groves, lichee trees, rice paddies, and, at strategic intervals, gigantic billboards bearing pictures of Mao. At Canton's new airport they boarded a Soviet-built Ilyushin-18 airliner while loudspeakers blared military marches and quotations from *The Thoughts of Chairman Mao*. An exhortatory sign in the terminal read PEOPLE OF THE WORLD UNITE AND DEFEAT THE U.S. AGGRESSORS AND THEIR RUNNING DOGS. It wasn't meant as an insult to the visitors. Mao's government at that point was drawing a fine line between the American people, whose friendship it wanted, and its government, which Peking Radio continued to excoriate as a conspiracy of "bloodthirsty gangsters."

Even in April Peking's climate retains the bite of winter, but apart from that the capital's reception for the U.S. ping-pong group was all hospitality. Quartered in the elegant Hsinchiao Hotel, they were entertained at banquets and taken on a tour of the nineteenth-century summer palace of the Manchu emperors and the Great Hall of the People. They saw a "revolutionary ballet," *The Red Detachment of Women*, and heard an opera celebrating the victory of Communism over capitalism, *Taking Tiger Mountain by Strategy*. Arriving at Peking's Indoor Stadium for an exhibition match with members of the Chinese team, they were greeted by 18,000 cheering fans and a huge banner reading WELCOME TO THE TABLE TENNIS TEAM FROM THE UNITED STATES. A band struck up the stirring strains of "Sailing the Seas Depends on the Helmsman, Making Revolution Depends on the Thought of Mao Tse-tung." Cowan did the frug.

Chinese tact continued in the table tennis competition. Holding back their first team, which could have crushed the Americans, they sent in second-string players who only won the men's matches 5–3 and the women's 5–4. The hosts called the contests "friendly games." They were not the most striking act of friendship. The following day Chou En-lai met China's ping-pong guests in the red-carpeted reception room of the Great Hall. The members of the United States delegation weren't the only table tennis visitors that week, and since Chinese protocol is rigidly alphabetical, they were preceded by players from Canada, Colombia, England, and Nigeria. But Chou spent most of his time—one and three-quarter hours—with them. He told them, "We have opened a new page in the relations of the Chinese and the American people." To the U.S. newsmen he said that now American correspondents could "come in batches."

That same day, as the Americans left for Hong Kong, President Nixon eased the twenty-year U.S. embargo on trade with China and

Peking resumed telephone contact with Washington and London. There was a lot to talk about; less than two weeks later a presidential commission headed by Henry Cabot Lodge recommended that the People's Republic be admitted to the United Nations provided a way could be found for Nationalist China to retain its seat. Already plans were being laid for a secret visit to Peking by National Security Adviser Henry Kissinger at which the chief topic of conversation would be a state visit by the President himself.

Early in July Kissinger flew to Asia, officially for conferences in Saigon, Thailand, India, and Pakistan. After a ninety minute talk with Pakistani President Agha Muhommad Yahya Khan, Kissinger announced a change in his schedule; he would spend a brief working holiday in the mountain resort of Nathia Gali, thirty-eight miles north of Rawalpindi. The trip wasn't turning out to be particularly newsworthy, and the curiosity of newsmen covering it was unstirred when the Yahya Khan government announced that Kissinger would have to spend an additional day in the resort because of a slight indisposition. He was thought to be suffering from Asian dysentery—"Delhi belly"—and the U.S. embassy encouraged the assumption by putting out word that a doctor had been dispatched to examine him. A correspondent suggested that the presidential adviser would be more comfortable in an air-conditioned Rawalpindi hotel. The embassy spokesman replied that the visitor did not want to embarrass anyone in the capital by his illness.

Actually Kissinger had driven to the Rawalpindi airport with three aides and boarded a Pakistan International Airlines plane for Peking. At noon on July 9 they landed on a deserted field outside the Chinese capital. Driven to a villa on a nearby lake, they lunched and were then joined, at mid-afternoon, by Chou En-lai. Chou and Kissinger conferred late that Friday night, Saturday evening, and Sunday morning. Five pounds heavier because of Chinese hospitality, the presidential adviser—who was still believed to be laid low by a stomach ailment—flew back to Pakistan and rejoined his party after a two-and-a-half day absence. Nothing more was heard from Peking Radio about American officials being gangsters or running dogs. Five days after the Kissinger mission President Nixon flew by helicopter from San Clemente to a Burbank television studio and delivered a four-minute address which astounded the world. He had been invited to visit Red China, he announced, and he was accepting with pleasure. He said: "I have taken this action because of

my profound conviction that all nations will gain from a reduction
of tensions and a better relationship between the United States and
the People's Republic of China." In a reference to Nationalist China
the President added that "seeking a new relationship" with Peking
would not be "at the expense of our old friends."

It was a promise he could not keep. His plan to seat both Chinas
in the United Nations was doomed. Each year the U.N. had come
closer to expelling the Taiwan delegation, and this was enough to
put it over the top. On October 25 the General Assembly voted
Peking in and Chiang Kai-shek's representatives out. American conservatives watching television that day beheld a spectacle of humiliation which would have been unbelievable in the days when
Dean Acheson and John Foster Dulles ran U.S. foreign policy; the
Algerians and the Albanians embraced, and the Tanzanians danced
a jig in the aisles. The reaction in Washington was sharp and angry.
Barry Goldwater demanded that the United States quit the U.N.
and consign the General Assembly to "some place like Moscow or
Peking." Hugh Scott of Pennsylvania spoke contemptuously of "hotpants principalities" like Tanzania, and presidential press secretary
Ronald Ziegler condemned "the shocking demonstration and undis-
guised glee among some of the delegates following the vote." But
these were mere political rituals. The fact was that Chiang's continuing pretensions to great-power status had been doomed from
the moment of the first conciliatory gesture toward Glenn Cowan
in Nagoya.

One month to the day after his telecast announcing that he would
be flying to Peking, Nixon went on the air again with news of another momentous step, this one to rescue the American economy.
It badly needed help. The country was sliding into its worst money
crisis since the Depression. Then the nation's crippled finances had
been further hobbled by Hoover's rigid faith in the economic gos-
pels of Adam Smith and John Stuart Mill. Nixon paid them lip service, but in practice he was anything but inflexible. Hugh Sidey of
Time observed that the President "clings to what is familiar until
the last moment. Then, when the evidence overwhelms him or
something happens in his gut, he decides to act, and nothing stands
very long in his way. He abandons his philosophy, his promises,
his speeches, his friends, his counselors. He marches out of one life
into a new world without any apologies or glancing back." At times

this could be disconcerting, but in that August of 1971, with the dollar tottering on the brink of disaster, it was heartening.

At the close of World War II the United States had been the wealthiest country in the history of civilization, holding 35 billion of the world's 40-odd billions of monetary gold. The structure of postwar finance had been established the year before at Bretton Woods, New Hampshire, where gold and dollars had been established as the reserves behind the money of every major nation outside the Communist bloc. There wasn't enough gold to support the anticipated flow of foreign trade, so the dollar, the world's strongest money, was made equal to gold. Debts between countries could be paid with either one. America pledged to redeem all available dollars with an ounce of gold for every $35, and other countries expressed the value of their currency in dollars. It worked. Trade prospered. Whenever a country managed to tip the balance of its U.S. trade in its favor—exporting more goods to America than it imported from there—its surplus dollars were used to back new issues of its own money.

Since the United States was rich and the rest of the world was comparatively poor, large sums went overseas to help the needy. It didn't matter; there was so much. Then came the Korean War and the revival of European commerce. By 1961, the end of the Common Market's first year, U.S. gold reserves were down to 17 billion dollars. In 1962 they dropped to 16 billion, in 1963 to 15 billion. At the beginning of the 1970s the reserves stood at 11 billion —almost the bare minimum, since American law required a dollar's worth of gold in Fort Knox for each four dollars in circulation, and the nation's business needed 40 billion in paper and silver. Meantime the balance of trade had become less and less favorable to the United States. In 1960 the country had imported 15 billion dollars' worth of goods and sold 20 billion abroad, leaving a surplus of five billion. By 1970 this margin was down to two billion. In May 1971 it vanished. The nation was trading in the red, and with the Pentagon still hemorrhaging wealth in Vietnam there was no hope of a quick turnaround. Secretary of Commerce Maurice Stans warned that the U.S. faced its first trade deficit since 1893.

That month economists received anxious signals from Germany. The *Wirtschaftswunder* had transformed the Federal Republic into a heavy exporter. Twice during the previous decade the deutsche mark had been revalued upward, altering its value vis-à-vis the dollar and enriching speculators who accumulated reserves of it. Now the pressure was mounting for another revaluation. As a member of the International Monetary Fund established at Bretton Woods, Bonn was obliged to maintain the relationship between the dollar and the mark, buying dollars and selling marks as the mark became more valuable. Because of the unfavorable balance in American trade, speculators had a lot of dollars—or "Eurodollars," as dollars owned abroad were called—to invest. In the first four months of 1971 the stocks of Eurodollars on the continent had taken a frightening jump, from five billion to between 50 and 60 billion, and the German central bank was being flooded with them.

Die Zentralbank bought and bought until Bonn, recognizing early signs of inflation, notified the International Monetary Fund on May 9 that it wouldn't buy any more, Bretton Woods or no Bretton Woods. Instead the Germans proposed to let their currency find its own level under the law of supply and demand. In the idiom of economists they would "float" the mark. It floated up from 25 cents to 27 cents and hung there, relieving the pressure on their central bank and, incidentally, improving the U.S. balance of trade with the Federal Republic, since American goods were now cheaper there. But the respite was brief. Because of what Larry Stuntz of the Associated Press called "that huge pool of Eurodollars sloshing around Europe"—it amounted to the equivalent of all the money circulating in America—speculators were bound to turn elsewhere. They built a fire under the French franc, but Paris, which had been watching the German agony, quickly cut loose from the International Monetary Fund and limited dollar trades. The wildcatters went after the Swiss franc next. Bern followed the example of Paris. It was becoming increasingly hard to unload dollars. Bretton Woods was coming unstuck; *Barron's* was predicting a worldwide panic by fall. Then, early in August, came an authoritative forecast that the U.S. trade deficit for the second quarter would exceed seven billion dollars. This was swiftly followed by a report of the Joint Congressional Economic Committee which declared that the dollar was overvalued, that other currencies should be revalued upward, and that if this wasn't done the United States should stop buying gold. The stock market dove; the Dow Jones industrial average dropped 100 points from its April high. There was virtually no market for Eurodollars now. American tourists in Europe found that the once mighty dollar had become unacceptable currency. World trade was at a standstill; merchants could no longer be sure what their money would buy next week, or even tomorrow.

Americans were getting bad economic news at home, too. Nixon, predicting that 1971 would be a good year and 1972 a bad year, had based his budget on an anticipated Gross National Product of 1,065 billion dollars. It came in at 1,050 billion, and half the gain was inflation. Production was down; unemployment, at 6 percent, was nearing the recession level. At the end of June the administration ended the fiscal year with an appalling 23.2-billion-dollar deficit, just two billion less than Johnson's record-breaking 1968 shortfall and an incredible 24.5 billion below Nixon's expectations. The President had alarmed his conservative supporters by talking in terms of a "full employment balance," a Keynesian concept which holds that a budget is "balanced" if the amount of spending does not exceed the amount which would be collected in taxes if everyone had a job. But even with that yardstick the administration was eight billion in the red. And the future was glum. New labor contracts promised rail workers a hike of 42 percent in 42 months; steelworkers would get 30 percent in three years. Inflation would jump accordingly.

Congress had given the President the Economic Stabilization Act of 1970, authorizing him to "issue such orders as he may deem appropriate to stabilize prices, rents, wages, and salaries." Nixon had opposed the bill. He had been forced to sign it because it set aside basic resources needed for national defense, but he had vowed he would never use it. His plans excluded controls. He didn't even believe in voluntary guidelines or jawboning—using presidential prestige to persuade labor and management to forego wage or price increases.

All this changed in one short weekend at Camp David with his economic advisers. Summoned on twenty-four hours' notice, they drafted an economic message invoking the very powers he rejected, and on Sunday, August 15, he was on television with it. He called the program his New Economic Policy. Among the measures he ordered, or asked Congress for, was a closing of the "gold window"— the United States would no longer exchange dollars for gold. Most imports would be subjected to a 10 percent surtax, designed to make American goods more competitive at home with those from abroad, and in some cases Americans would receive tax breaks if they bought U.S. merchandise. Industry would get tax credit for new investment. The 7 percent excise tax on automobiles would be repealed, an average saving of $200 per car. With few exceptions, all U.S. prices, wages, rents, and dividends would be frozen for ninety days at their present levels. A Cost of Living Council headed by Treasury Secretary John Connally would preside over the freeze.

Nixon had floated the dollar, and the effect was the same as devaluation. In money markets it amounted to 2 percent in the first two weeks. Foreign bankers were understanding; they indicated that they were prepared to revalue their currencies if the U.S. would drop the surcharge. Meanwhile there was little retaliation abroad. The Danes did introduce a surcharge of their own, and the French muttered about imposing one, but there were few threats to build tariff walls against American goods which had suddenly become cheaper. Connally was not a popular man in foreign chancelleries; his insistence that the United States must quickly achieve a 13-billion-dollar swing in its balance of payments provoked protests that so rapid a reversal would destroy the Common Market. But at a September meeting of the International Monetary Fund, financiers from the "Group of Ten" wealthiest nations continued to be sympathetic to the U.S. position. Connally, in turn, hinted that America might reopen the gold window and raise its price—direct devaluation. Subsequent talks in Rome led to an agreement, announced at the Smithsonian Institution in Washington, under which the U.S. surcharge was canceled, the value of other currencies was raised, and the price of gold was provisionally boosted to $38.

On Wall Street the day after Nixon's announcement of the freeze —or Phase One, as it was already being called—the Dow Jones industrial average jumped 32.93 to 888.95 on what was then the busiest day in its history; 31,720,000 shares were traded. In September, the first full month of Phase One, the nation's rise in living costs was held to 2.4 percent and the wholesale price index posted its biggest decline in five years. A few holes were poked in the wage and price ceilings, and inevitably there was a great deal of confusion in some industries, but for the most part the thing worked. Unfortunately it was, by definition, only the first step. On November 13 it would expire. Before then the administration had to find guidelines which provided hope of preserving relative stability while rectifying the injustices which had been frozen into the system.

On October 8 Nixon spoke to the nation again, this time setting up the machinery for Phase Two. The challenge was greater now. Economist Herbert Stein, the chief planner of the new stage, had anticipated the difficulties at the time of the first message. He said, "I knew immediately the problem would not be the freeze, but the unfreeze, the thaw." The goal of this second program was to hold inflation to between 2 and 3 percent a year. Controls would be administered by a seven-man Price Commission and a fifteen-member pay board. There would be no ceiling on profits, the President said, and the success or failure of the plan would depend upon "the voluntary cooperation of the American people."

Fear that both labor and capital might withdraw their representatives from the supervisory panels doomed hopes of keeping inflation below 3 percent. "If the President doesn't want our membership on the Pay Board on our terms, he knows what he can do," Meany told delegates to an AFL-CIO convention in Miami Beach. Nixon boldly flew to the convention hall to reply: "I know exactly what I can do. And I am going to do it." Nevertheless, the board capitulated to Meany in the last week of Phase One, announcing full recognition of deferred wage increases and establishment of 5.5 percent as the annual norm for new raises. Even that line wasn't held; in its first decision under Phase Two the board granted a 15 percent pay boost for coal miners. The price commission was no more effective. It began by approving 7 percent increases in the cost of tinplate manufactured by two steel companies. Within three weeks one-third of the country's 1,500 largest corporations had applied for endorsement of price hikes, and acceptances surpassed rejections by a ratio of 20 to 1.

In December the stock market plunged again. The board continued its conciliatory treatment of labor, but three months later Meany and two other top union leaders pulled out anyway, accusing the majority of bias. The next day Leonard Woodcock of the UAW also quit. That left only one labor member: Frank E. Fitzsimmons, the Teamsters president. Since Nixon's Christmas Week pardon of Jimmy Hoffa, the Teamsters had been in the President's pocket. That clemency had been universally attributed to politics, but few blamed Nixon. Though his standing in the polls had improved somewhat since the lows of summer, it was generally believed that if he was going to be reelected he would need all the help he could get.

Portrait of an American

RALPH NADER

IN THE CONNECTICUT MANUFACTURING CITY of Winsted his Lebanese immigrant father was the local populist, a familiar American type. Customers at Nadra Nader's Highland Sweet Shop, a restaurant and bakery, complained that the proprietor never let them eat in peace. Nadra was always lecturing them about the wrongs, the inequities, the injustices of the system. Like many immigrants, he was a more ardent Democrat than the natives. He went on about the crimes of the Interests and was forever threatening to sue them. In time nearly everyone there tuned him out, with one exception: his youngest son Ralph.

In 1938, at the age of four, Ralph Nader was a tiny spectator when lawyers harangued juries in the local courthouse. At fourteen he became a daily reader of the *Congressional Record.* He won a scholarship to Princeton, where he refused to wear white bucks or other symbols of sartorial conformity and staged a protest against the spraying of campus trees with DDT. He was locked so often in the university library after hours that he was given a key. Characteristically he responded by denouncing the administration for callous disregard of other students' legal rights. In 1955 he was elected to Phi Beta Kappa, graduated magna cum laude, and admitted to Harvard Law School, which he described as a "high-priced tool factory" turning out servants of power.

His reputation as a puritan grew. He foreswore the reading of novels; they were a waste of time. So were movies; he would limit himself to two a year. He scorned plays, tobacco, alcohol, girls, and parties. At Harvard he also quit driving automobiles, but here his motive was different. He had become interested in auto injury cases, and after some research in car technology at nearby MIT he wrote an article for the *Harvard Law Record* entitled "American Cars: Designed for Death."

The problem continued to bother him. Throughout his career he was to be concerned with the protection of the human body—from unsafe natural gas pipelines, food additives, tainted meat, pollution, mining health hazards, herbicides, unwholesome poultry, inadequate nursing homes, and radiation emission from color TVs—but the auto threat was basic. He opened a private law practice in Hartford (which rapidly became a source of free legal advice for the poor) and continued to urge stronger car safety regulations on local governments. Early in 1964 he took his campaign to Washington, where Assistant Secretary of Labor Daniel Patrick Moynihan hired him as a fifty dollar-a-day consultant to the Labor Department.

Working with Connecticut's Senator Abraham Ribicoff, Nader turned out a two-hundred-page brief calling for auto safety legislation with teeth. A General Motors engineer became the first of his many secret contacts in industry by pointing out the Chevrolet Corvair's tendency to flip over. In November 1965 Nader's first book, *Unsafe at Any Speed: The Designed-in Dangers of the American Automobile,* called the Corvair "one of the nastiest-handling cars ever built" and charged that the industry had taken "four years of the model and 1,124,076 Corvairs before they decided to do something."

Unsafe at Any Speed, which sold 450,000 copies in cloth and paper, brought its author before a Ribicoff committee on February 10, 1966, as an expert witness on hazardous autos. Three weeks later Nader became a national figure when he accused General Motors of harassing him with private detectives, abusive telephone calls, and women who tried to entice him into compromising situations. A GM operative admitted under oath that he had been instructed by his superiors "to get something somewhere on this guy . . . get him out of their hair . . . shut him up." Nader filed suit for 26 million dollars and collected $280,000. Like his book royalties, the money went to the cause; when the National Traffic and Motor Vehicle Safety Act was passed that summer the *Washington Post* declared that "Most of the credit for making possible this important legislation belongs to one man—Ralph Nader . . . a one-man lobby for the public prevailed over the nation's most powerful industry."

Nader set himself up as a watchdog of the National Traffic Safety Agency and then went after the meat packers; the result was the Wholesome Meat Act of 1967. He broadened his attack on exploiters of the consumer to include the Food and Drug Administration, Union Carbide smokestacks, think tanks, unsafe trucks, pulp and paper mills, property taxes, bureaucrats, consumer credit, banks, and supermarkets. One observer said, "Ralph is not a consumer champion. He is just plain against consumption."

Unlike the muckrakers of the Lincoln Steffens era, Nader acquired a conservative constituency. At a time of anarchy and disorder he believed in working within the system. He was a linear thinker, an advocate of law and industrial order. Stockbrokers contributed to his causes. Miss Porter's School sent him volunteer workers. He was acquiring lieutenants now—"Nader's Raiders," a reporter dubbed them—and they were mostly white upper-middle-class graduates of the best schools, with names like Pullman cars: Lowell Dodge, William Harrison Wellford, Reuben B. Robertson III, and William Howard Taft IV. One of them, Edward F. Cox, became a son-in-law of President Nixon.

He installed them in cubbyhole offices in the National Press Building furnished with secondhand desks, chairs bought at rummage sales, apple crate files, and shelves made from planks and bricks. He worked them a hundred hours a week and paid them poverty-level salaries. Royalties from the books they turned out went into his campaigns. They didn't complain; he himself was earning $200,000 a year and spending $5,000.

He lived in an $80-a-month furnished room near Dupont Circle, paid $97 a month office rent, and had no secretary. People gave him briefcases; he turned them into files and traveled instead with his papers in a sheaf of manila envelopes. His black shoes were scuffed, the laces broken and knotted. He wore a gray rumpled suit, frayed white shirts, and narrow ties which had been out of style for years. Standing six feet four inches, with wavy black hair and a youthful face, he was compared by *Newsweek* to a "Jimmy Stewart hero in a Frank Capra movie." His only unusual expense was his telephone bill. It was enormous. He was paying for calls from all his volunteer spies in industry.

Most of his income came from lecture fees. Each week he received fifty invitations to speak; he accepted 150 a year, charging as much as $2,000. He became known as the most long-winded speaker since Walter Reuther, rarely relinquishing the lectern before an hour and forty-five minutes. There was never any flourish at the end. He would simply stop talking and pivot away. College audiences gave him wild ovations, but he never turned back to acknowledge them. If asked to autograph a book he would curtly reply, "No." A friend said, "Ralph is so afraid of being turned into a movie star, of having his private life romanticized, that he has renounced his own private life."

He was an impossible customer. To a waitress he would say when ordering, "Is the ham sliced for each sandwich? Is that genuine or processed cheese? Do *you* eat sugar? You do? Let me tell you something—it's absolutely useless, no food value." To an airline stewardess he said, "The only thing you should be proud to serve on this whole plane is the little bag of nuts. And you should take the salt off the nuts." When Allegheny Airlines had the temerity to bump him from a flight on which he had a confirmed reservation, he filed suit and was awarded $50,000 in punitive damages, half for him and half for the consumer group he had been unable to address because of the missed flight.

Asked by Robert F. Kennedy why he was "doing all this," he answered, "If I were engaged in activities for the prevention of cruelty to animals, nobody would ask me that question." His ultimate goal, he said, was "nothing less than the qualitative reform of the industrial revolution," and he refused to be lured from it by any bait. Nicholas von Hoffman and Gore Vidal proposed him for the Presidency. He said, "I'm not interested in public office. The biggest job in this country is citizen action. Politics follows that."

Yet for all his evangelism, his devotion to the public good, and his monastic life, Nader's impact on society was questionable. At times he seemed to know it. "We always fail," he said once. "The whole thing is limiting the degree of failure." His audiences appeared to regard him as a performer. They applauded him, but it was as though they were applauding an act. Few of them felt compelled to get involved, to follow his example or even his advice. They went right on driving big Detroit cars, eating processed foods, coating themselves with expensive cosmetics and smoking poisonous cigarettes.

In a pensive moment he reflected that "A couple of thousand years ago in Athens, a man could get up in the morning, wander around the city, and inquire into matters affecting his well-being and that of his fellow citizens. No one asked him 'Who are you with?'" Americans of the 1970s did not inquire about him; they knew. Yet they themselves remained uncommitted. The painful fact —excruciating for him—was that however loud their cheers for Ralph Nader, however often they said that they were for him, in this Augustan age of materialism they were not really with him.

Thirty-seven

PRIDE GOETH

THE AGE OF PUBLICITY, as Louis Kronenberger called it, may be said to have begun in the 1920s with flagpole sitting and the ordeal of Floyd Collins, an unlucky youth whose entrapment and eventual death in a Kentucky cave-in was page one news for two weeks in 1925. Ballyhoo became increasingly conspicuous after World War II with the emergence of such exhibitionists as those who took their marriage vows on carnival carrousels, spent their honeymoons in department store windows, bore children under floodlights, and hired halls to celebrate their divorces. "The trouble with us in America," Kronenberger wrote in 1954, "isn't that the poetry of life has turned to prose, but that it has turned to advertising copy." He suggested that next to Marx and Freud, the ideologue with the greatest impact on U.S. lives was Phineas Taylor Barnum.

As American influence spread abroad, so did the Barnum spirit. Among the bizarre stunts overseas which put their perpetrators on front pages in 1972 was a telephoned threat to blow up the luxury liner *Queen Elizabeth 2* and the defacing of Michelangelo's *Pietà* in St. Peter's Basilica by an Australian geologist with a twelve-pound hammer, a perverted sense of theater, and the conviction that he was the son of God. They were outrageous, but at least they weren't homicidal, which was more than could be said for many foreign self-promoters. That year was memorable for what might be called the hoopla of death. Murders committed abroad for their publicity value included those of three NATO electronics experts executed by Turkish leftists, twenty-six travelers in Tel

Aviv's Lod Airport by a squad of Japanese terrorists, eleven Israeli athletes at the Munich Olympics by Palestinian Arabs of the Black September ring, and 469 Ulster Catholics and Protestants by Ulster Protestants and Catholics. In addition, Japan's Yasunari Kawabata, the 1968 Nobel Prize winner in literature, took his own life. He thereby followed the example of Yukio Mishima, a young colleague who had protested western influence in his homeland by committing ritualistic hara-kiri in the good old way, eviscerating himself and submitting to decapitation by his best friend.

Americans had no reason to feel smug about this lengthening roll of dishonor overseas. It was Lee Harvey Oswald of Dallas who had first demonstrated to his countrymen in the 1960s that attention must be paid to a daring murderer, and his example had been followed in the United States by, among others, Sirhan Sirhan, of Los Angeles, Charles Whitman of the Austin bell tower, and Robert Benjamin Smith, who had committed mayhem in the Mesa, Arizona, beauty school. In 1972 they were joined by others with similar motivation. Mobster "Crazy Joe" Gallo was gunned down in New York's Little Italy. His sister told reporters, "He changed his image, that's why this happened." When George Jackson's two Soledad colleagues were acquitted in the death of a prison guard, Angela Davis managed to transform it into a public relations triumph; "It's beautiful," she said. The end of *Life* magazine on December 29, closing a big publicity artery, was treated by some politicians as a death in the family. The name of four-star Air Force General John D. Lavelle began appearing on reference books after he had been reprimanded and reduced in rank for unauthorized bombing raids in North Vietnam; his name had been in the papers. Most memorable was Arthur Herman Bremer, who gunned down George Wallace in a Laurel, Maryland, shopping center on the eve of the presidential primary there. On the way to jail Bremer asked officers, "How much do you think I'll get for my memoirs?"

While these malefactions were drearily familiar, some Americans did break new publicity ground that year. Two police cases deserve special recognition because, unlike the Soledad, Gallo, and Wallace incidents, they displayed remarkable imaginative powers on the part of criminals or accusers. The first was the skyjacking of a Southern Airways DC9 jet by pirates who lifted extortion from the realm of the ordinary by threatening to crash the plane into the nuclear research plant at Oak Ridge unless their demands were met.

Though the airliner's tires were shot out by FBI agents, the sky-jackers collected two million dollars at the Chattanooga airport and landed in Havana, where, like so many of their predecessors, they were dismayed to find themselves under Cuban arrest and their loot confiscated. The other episode followed a charge by J. Edgar Hoover that peace workers were plotting to kidnap Henry Kissinger and blow up steam pipes beneath Washington, D.C., which carried heat to all federal buildings in the capital. Indicted for conspiracy, six Catholics and a Moslem were tried. The government lost the case, and nine months afterward two of the defendants, Father Philip Berrigan and Sister Elizabeth McAlister, startled their associates at, respectively, the Society of St. Joseph and the Sacred Heart of Mary community, by getting married.

That was thought strange by practitioners of traditional religion, but an even zanier approach to piety was that of the "Jesus people," also known as the "Jesus freaks" or the "street Christians." In reality they represented the latest stage in the youth movement, which had evolved from the beats to the hippies and was searching for a new kick. "Jesus, am I ever high on Jesus!" was one of their rallying cries. Three years earlier Theodore Roszak had declared in *The Making of a Counter Culture* that the movement had clearly defined spiritual aspects. He meant Zen and even odder sects; Christianity was then considered hopelessly square and establishmentarian. Now, however, the cats were wearing crucifixes and Christ T-shirts—"You Have a Lot to Live," read one, echoing a Pepsi-Cola jingle, "And Jesus Has a Lot to Give." They established communes called God's Love, Zion's Inn, and Soul Inn, attended Jesus rock concerts and Christian nightclubs, and made some parents yearn for the days when kids got stoned on old-fashioned marijuana.

As the colleges continued to be almost serene in 1972, peace militants talked about a public relations failure, but administrators of state universities were relieved; taxpayers had been rejecting school bond issues by lopsided votes. President Nixon's press office claimed that he had "scored points" with his constituents by a colorful turn of phrase; he had said he planned to spend more time at Camp David because "I find that up here on top of a mountain, it is easier for me to get on top of the job." On November 14 the New York Stock Exchange achieved a breakthrough in good publicity when the Dow Jones industrial average closed at 1006.16, above 1,000 for the first time in history. (It was, though no one knew it then, a good time to sell.) The public image of Jacqueline Kennedy Onassis shone more brightly, and that of one of her tormentors more dully, after a federal judge in New York ruled that a freelance photographer named Ronald E. Galella had "relentlessly invaded" Mrs. Onassis's privacy. In the future, the court ruled, Galella would be required to stay 50 yards from her, 75 yards from her children, and 100 yards from the family's homes and schools.

These varied events in the Age of Publicity, while noteworthy, were, however, rendered pallid by the accomplishments of two giants of the age. Both were American, both were passionately devoted to advertisements of themselves, and both achieved international recognition in 1972. One was an outlaw, the other merely ill-tempered.

Robert James Fischer, the irascible one, played chess. It is not recorded that he ever did anything else except insult his opponents, fail to make scheduled appearances, alienate his supporters, display greed, break his word, deliver ultimatums, throw temper tantrums, disappear at crucial moments, and become, after a classic tournament with Russia's Boris Spassky in Reykjavik, Iceland, the first U.S. winner of the world chess championship. His countrymen agreed that it couldn't happen to a worse competitor. He stalked off angrily counting a record $156,000 in prize money.

The desperado was named Clifford Irving.

Shortly before Christmas 1971 the publishing firm of McGraw-Hill dispatched a 550-word publicity release of special interest to the New York offices of major editors, newscasters, and wire services. After nearly fourteen years of refusing to be interviewed, photographed, or even seen by members of the press, Howard Hughes, America's reclusive billionaire, had apparently completed, with the help of a collaborator, a 230,000-word account of his life. The clothbound edition of the work would be issued on March 27, 1972, and *Life* would publish three 10,000-word installments from it. "Call this autobiography," the announcement quoted Hughes as saying. "Call it my memoirs. Call it what you please. It is the story of my life in my own words." Also attributed to Hughes in the release were phrases singing the praises of his assistant in the project, Clifford Irving. In the billionaire's putative words, Irving had been picked "because of his sympathy, discernment, discretion and, as I learned, his integrity as a human being."

Hughes's recollections, it seemed, had been taped: "The words in this book—other than some of the questions which provoked them—are my own spoken words." At first editors assumed that the taping sessions had been held in the Bahamas hotel where he had been hiding out for the past year, but the truth seemed to be more dramatic than that; the two men had held over a hundred meetings "in various motel rooms and parked cars throughout the Western Hemisphere."

That was the claim advanced in the publisher's announcement. It would be accepted by the public for a month, and another month would pass before it was withdrawn. In the meantime the story was to become one of the most sensational in the history of the book trade. At one point it drove news of the President's inspection of the Great Wall of China off tabloid front pages. More newspapermen were covering Hughes and Irving than the Vietnam War—nine reporters from the *Los Angeles Times* alone. Thirty postal inspectors were tracking clues in the mails. Paramount reissued *The Carpetbaggers*, a thinly disguised fictional account of Hughes's life. An X-rated film entitled *Helga and Howard* was being shown in Manhattan, Hughes T-shirts were selling well at two dollars apiece, and people were wearing pins which said, "This is a genuine Howard Hughes button."

The genuineness of the autobiography was first questioned in the wake of the December announcement. A spokesman for the Hughes Tool Company denied "the existence of a Hughes autobiography." But the recluse was celebrated for his furtiveness with his closest associates; those who knew him best thought the disclaimer was completely in character, and in fact the editors of the book had expected it. When Managing Editor Ralph Graves of *Life* showed his staff a handwritten letter from Hughes approving serialization of the text, one of them asked, "How do we know the letter's not a forgery?" Graves replied, "It's authentic, all right. We've had it checked by an expert." Albert Leventhal, a McGraw-Hill vice president, told the *New York Times*, "We have gone to considerable efforts to ascertain that this is indeed the Hughes autobiography," and Donald M. Wilson, a *Life* vice president, told another newsman, "Oh, we're absolutely positive. Look, we're dealing with people like McGraw-Hill, and, you know, we're not exactly a movie magazine! This is Time, Inc. and McGraw-Hill talking. We've checked this thing out. We have proof."

To another questioner Wilson said, "We never dealt with the Hughes Tool Company. It doesn't surprise us that they know nothing of this, since Mr. Hughes was totally secretive about the project." The person they had dealt with was Irving, who had been a McGraw-Hill author for twelve years. He had written four unsuccessful novels and, more recently, *Fakel*, an account of Elmyr de Hory, an art forger and Irving's neighbor on the Spanish island of Ibiza. In retrospect it seems that his publishers should have taken a closer look at the author's preoccupation with fraudulence and his story that Hughes insisted upon discussing the matter with no one but him. The truth was that the book was a complete fabrication. Irving had never met Hughes, let alone taped him, and Hughes had never heard of the man who claimed to be his ghost. At first glance McGraw-Hill and *Life* seem to have been inexcusably gullible. But in fact the hoaxer had shown remarkable cunning, and he had also been lucky.

The plot had begun a year earlier with the reproduction in *Newsweek* of an eleven-line handwritten note by Hughes. A month later *Life* published the letter in color. Irving was the son of a cartoonist; he had inherited his father's clever fingers, and he found that with a little practice he could produce whole pages of writing which looked like that of Hughes. The tycoon was in the news that season, and much was being made of his secrecy. Some writers suggested that he might even be dead; no one in the outside world would know. It struck Irving that a book of reminiscences purporting to bear Hughes's imprimatur might go unchallenged by him, especially since he might already be in his grave. He persuaded Richard Suskind, a fellow hack living on the neighboring island of Majorca, to collaborate with him. Later, when the names of both men had become household words, their photographs would be familiar on front pages around the world—Irving, tall and ruggedly handsome, and Suskind, "built," as a friend put it, "like an avalanche with a gargoyle on top." Ultimately their likenesses would represent the ultimate in literary chicanery. In the beginning, however, they appeared to the editors at McGraw-Hill as a writer known for reliability if not talent and his diligent researcher. The editors had no way of knowing that Irving proposed to share the swag with his crony, 75 percent for himself and 25 percent for Suskind. A third member of the conspiracy was Irving's wife Edith, an attractive Swiss painter and the mother of his two children.

Irving played McGraw-Hill with consummate skill, forwarding them apparently genuine letters from Howard Hughes in which the billionaire expressed growing interest in the collaboration. At the appropriate time Hughes's signature appeared on a contract, clause 22 of which specified that "The Publisher agrees that it shall undertake no advertising or promotion or sale of the Work prior to 30 days after acceptance by the Publisher of a complete and satisfactory manuscript for the Work." *Life*, which bought first serial rights for $250,000, also agreed to stay mum. Taking what seemed to be reasonable precautions, the publisher submitted specimens of Hughes's supposed handwriting to an expert, who compared it with samples of the real thing and reported: "The chances that another person could copy this handwriting even in a similar way are less than one in a million." Later another firm of analysts concurred, declaring that it was "impossible, based on our years of experience in the field of questioned handwriting and signatures," that anyone except Howard Hughes could have written the material which had come from Irving.

Most ingenious of all, Irving told his publisher that the eccentric tycoon insisted that checks made out to him bear only his initials: "H. R. Hughes." When the author got them, he turned them over to his wife. Edith, wearing a wig and carrying an altered passport and a stolen identity card, flew to Zurich and opened a Swiss Credit Bank account in the name of "Helga R. Hughes." Into this account, number 320496, she ultimately deposited nearly a million dollars of McGraw-Hill money, which she then withdrew and put in the Swiss Banking Corporation across the street. Meanwhile her husband and Suskind had also been traveling, researching Hughes's life in the New York Public Library, the Library of Congress, Palm Springs, California, the morgues of the *Houston Chronicle* and the *Houston Post*, and—the unkindest cut of all—the files of Time-Life. Their most valuable acquisition was the unpublished manuscript of the memoirs of Hughes's retired chief lieutenant. Irving borrowed it from one of the man's associates and photocopied it. Pooling their information, he and Suskind took turns being "Hughes" and interviewing one another on tape. The tapes were then transcribed, and Irving wrote marginal comments on the resulting thousand-page manuscript in the billionaire's hand. The result seemed so authentic that it fooled men who had known Hughes intimately years earlier.

The conspiracy began to come apart on the afternoon of January 7, 1972, when Hughes, speaking from the Bahamas, held a two-and-a-half-hour press conference over the telephone with seven journalists who had covered him before his withdrawal into seclusion. He branded Irving's book a humbug and, while he was at it, denied reports that his fingernails were six inches long, that he was emaciated, and that his hair hung to his waist. All seven of his listeners agreed that the voice was his. Irving called it a fake, but time was beginning to run out for him. Edith's end of the plot had begun to come to light. A Hughes lawyer had asked his client to fill out a questionnaire, establishing its authenticity with his fingerprints. One of the questions was: "When is the last time you personally endorsed a check for any reason?" Hughes answered in his own hand: "More than ten years ago." The conspirators had assumed that numbered accounts in Swiss banks were inviolate under all circumstances. Not so: in cases of suspected crime details could be revealed, and when the Swiss learned that checks meant for Howard R. Hughes had been cashed by a German-speaking woman calling herself Helga R. Hughes, they knew something was rotten in Zurich. A worldwide search for the mysterious Helga began.

On Thursday, January 20, the day word of this sensational new development reached New York, Irving attended a conference of McGraw-Hill and Life executives. Coolly he advanced three possible explanations for it: that he had taped a charlatan pretending to be Hughes, that Hughes had used a "loyal servant" to deposit the checks, and that he, Irving, was a mountebank. Searching the eyes of everyone there, he said in his most sincere voice, "The last of these possibilities I intend to discard, and I hope that you do, too." His presence was superb; they all nodded. Flying back to Ibiza—to the indignation of Life, whose editors thought he should stay in New York until the crisis had been resolved—he replied to reporters pointing out the resemblance between Edith and the Swiss descriptions of Helga: "Do you really think I'd involve my family in an enterprise like this?" Back in Manhattan his lawyer, whose suspicions had not yet been aroused, confided to reporters that he thought his client had been duped by a gang of impostors, two of them gifted forgers and the third a six-foot-three beanpole who looked like Howard Hughes.

This was a crucial moment in the conspiracy, and a grasp of it is essential to an understanding of what was happening to Clifford Irving. He had a large part of the money in cash, he had his freedom, and he could have kept both. Other fugitives from justice were living comfortably on Ibiza and Majorca. He, Edith, and Suskind might have remained where they were or flown to any one of several South American countries where their crimes were not extraditable. Expense was no problem; they could have afforded almost anything. The alternative was grim; exposure was now inevitable. Why, then, did Irving fly back to New York and into the trap? The answer, in the opinion of those who were close to him, was that he couldn't resist the publicity. All his life he had craved attention. His books hadn't brought it, but this caper had, and the knowledge that an eager press corps awaited him at Kennedy Airport drew him as though he were helpless. The moth simply could not resist the flame. It is one of the sad little ironies of his story that when he landed there he couldn't answer their questions. He had laryngitis. "Gentlemen, this is a horrible experience," he whispered to them. For once one believes him.

Another irony followed swiftly. Two reporters believed that Irving had been in touch with a former Hughes aide named John Meier. Calling to see him at his lawyer's house, they sent in word: "Just tell Cliff we know all about Meier." Irving had never heard of Meier, but when the message reached him he was stunned. He thought they meant *Meyer*, which sounded the same. The man who had slipped him the unpublished memoirs of Hughes's retired assistant was named Stanley Meyer. If the newsmen had been tipped off to Meyer's role, the plotters were finished, and Irving might as well own up to it. He went out to the district attorney's office, made a partial confession there, and then returned to confront the two waiting newspapermen. "There's something I have to tell you guys," he said, "but it's got to be off the record, O.K.?" Under the circumstances an off-the-record confidence was impossible, but they nodded. He took a deep breath and said, "Well, you may have guessed it and you may not. Helga Hughes is Edith. Edith is Helga."

That should have been the end of it, but it wasn't. Improvising, he said that his wife had been acting at Hughes's direction, and so convincing was the manuscript—and the opinions of the handwriting experts—that the hoax limped along for a few more days. Then two blows demolished it. The manuscript of the retired Hughes assistant's unpublished memoirs surfaced, and the story of Irving's taping sessions with Hughes in various exotic settings was unmasked. He had in fact traveled to those places, sending back picture postcards to McGraw-Hill, but he had made the mistake of mixing pleasure with business. One of his companions had been a willowy blonde scuba diving instructor who had accompanied him to St. Croix in the Virgin Islands; she told the *Chicago Tribune* that she had grown very fond of Irving, whom she had thought was separated from his wife, but that neither of them had encountered Howard Hughes. The second and more damaging of the hoaxer's playmates was a beautiful Danish baroness and entertainer named Nina Van Pallandt. Irving had been indiscreet enough to brag about Nina to a McGraw-Hill editor and reveal her name. Located by postal inspectors, Nina admitted that she had traveled with Irving and said they had, in fact, copulated their way across Mexico. Since Cliff had been constantly at her side, she said, he couldn't possibly have kept any rendezvous with Hughes.

That was the end for Irving. But not for Nina. It is a provocative comment on the value of publicity—*any* publicity—that it was only a beginning for her. For years she had been limping along as an obscure folksinger. Now, suddenly, she was in demand everywhere. She appeared twice on the *David Frost Show*, twice on the *Mike Douglas Show*, twice on the *Dick Cavett Show*, once on the *Today Show*, once on the *Johnny Carson Show*, and on a television special. Manhattan's St. Regis Hotel booked her for three weeks, and she was signed up for appearances in Miami, Dallas, San Juan, and San Francisco. Her manager said the Irving happening was "worth five hit records and an Academy Award." Without doubt she was the most distinguished fornicatrix of 1972.

Howard Hughes was not so fortunate. The uproar had become so great that the Bahaman government began to investigate the fact that his staff lacked work permits and immigration clearance, whereupon he fled to Nicaragua accompanied by six television sets, several crates of Poland water, a document shredder, blood plasma, a refrigerator, a hospital bed, mattresses, office furniture, pots and pans, various boxes of film, several hundred yards of cable, an old electric stove, a heater, and a cheap vinyl couch.

Life was reimbursed by McGraw-Hill, which got most of its money back from the Irvings and Suskind, all three of whom briefly went to prison. But that wasn't the extent of McGraw-Hill's disasters that year. The publisher suffered a long streak of bad luck. After Irving had been led away the publishers had just begun to patch up their image with the success of a book about Indians, *The*

Memoirs of Chief Red Fox, when an awkward truth emerged: *Red Fox* was plagiarized from a work published in 1940. Next the editor of the Irving book was accused of an unethical practice: borrowing money from two other authors, the sum amounting to 10 percent of their advances from the publisher. Then a final touch assured the firm's wretched situation as the laughingstock of the New York communications industry that year. Before the hoax the first floor of the new McGraw-Hill Building on the Avenue of the Americas had been leased to a branch bank. Now the tenant was moving in. Horrified publishing executives saw the gilt lettering going up on the plate-glass windows and realized that there was absolutely nothing they could do about it, because the contracts had long been executed and filed. The signs read: THE IRVING TRUST COMPANY.

On the frosty morning of February 21, 1972, the silver, blue and white fuselage of the *Spirit of '76,* as Nixon called the presidential aircraft, flitted across the muddy ribbon of the Yangtze, headed northward, and entered its glide pattern over Peking. American reporters who had covered China a quarter-century earlier were amazed by the changes in the landscape below: paved roads, irrigation canals, huge collective farms, and trees ("Trees in China!" wrote Theodore H. White) lining the highways. On this historic day the masters of Red China would once more grasp the hands of American leaders in friendship. Anti-Communism would cease to be the dominant note in U.S. foreign policy. It was an occasion for good omens, the eve of George Washington's birthday in the United States and, in Peking, the seventh day of the Year of the Rat, an auspicious time on the Chinese calendar.

The presidential jet touched down at 11:30. A moment of consternation followed. Except for U.S. correspondents and TV technicians, the airport was almost deserted. There were placards, but they had nothing to do with Nixon—LONG LIVE THE CHINESE COMMUNIST PARTY and LONG LIVE THE GREAT SOLIDARITY OF ALL THE WORLD'S PEOPLE. Fewer than four hundred troops were on hand; they were singing a Red Army ballad of the 1930s, "The Three Rules of Discipline and the Eight Points of Attention." America's peripatetic thirty-seventh President had greeted the rulers of Romania, Pakistan, Yugoslavia, Spain, Canada, Brazil, Australia, Japan, India, Ireland, Italy, Germany, Belgium, France, Britain, Austria, and the Vatican. Always there had been crowds. Here there were none.

Dismayed aides wondered what to do if he were left in the lurch. Could they fly home and say it had all been a mistake? At the last moment the inscrutable Chinese became scrutable. Premier Chou En-lai appeared with a handful of officials. Nixon extended his hand, and as millions of Americans watched on television, Chou took it.

The Chinese people were not watching. News of the visitors had been kept from them. The presidential motorcade entered the city on silent streets. All the inhabitants seemed to be elsewhere. But five hours later, when Nixon was still settling down in a two-story buff brick guesthouse, he was unexpectedly summoned to the private study of seventy-eight-year-old Mao, the living legend of the new China. The President and the Chairman chatted for a full hour, accompanied only by Chou and Henry Kissinger. The substance of the conversation remained secret, but obviously there was rapport; at one point the No. 1 International Bandit reached across the tea table and softly held the hand of the No. 1 Imperialist Dog, and next morning a picture of the meeting, with the principals smiling, appeared on the front page of the *People's Daily*. The message was clear: the visit had the Chairman's blessing. Now there was excitement in the streets. When Nixon appeared there, people clapped hands—in unison, to be sure, but that was how things were done here—and Mao designated his fourth wife, the revolutionary firebrand Chiang Ching, to be the President's official hostess.

Each day for five days Nixon and Chou conferred for four hours at a long green table. There was less there than met the eye, as the vague communiqué at the end made clear; it mostly dealt with the need for more friendship among the Chinese and American peoples, and the only real concession came from the President, a promise to withdraw U.S. military forces from Taiwan. But the real significance of the talks is that they were held at all. The President and the First Lady were determined to be amicable. It showed, and was appreciated. Every evening they sat through a three-hour ceremonial banquet in the Great Hall of the People, pluckily grappling their way through eight courses with ivory chopsticks and drinking toasts with *mao tai* while a Chinese orchestra played such tunes as "Billy Boy" and "She'll Be Coming 'Round the Mountain." They watched exhibitions of ping-pong, badminton, and gymnastics, and one evening Chiang Ching took them to a ballet, *The Red Detachment of Women*, which was all about cruel landlords. Nixon, who was trying to reduce the taxes landlords paid in the United States, nevertheless applauded heartily, and next morning his wife gamely continued her inspections of nursing homes, kitchens, agriculture communes and acupuncture clinics, though she was squeamish about needles.

After a visit to Peking's Forbidden City and a walk along the ramparts of the twenty-two-hundred-year-old Great Wall of China, the Nixons left the *Spirit of '76* behind and flew to Hangchow with Chou on a white Ilyushin airliner. There, in the city which Marco Polo had proclaimed as the greatest in the world seven centuries earlier, the President roamed through parks and cruised on historic West Lake with the premier. From Hangchow the presidential party flew on to Shanghai, their last stop, where the communiqué was issued, and then home for a report to the American people.

On the whole his countrymen gave Nixon high marks for his performance, though some thought that at times he had been obsequious. In his Peking speeches he had proposed that the two nations "start a Long March together," and he repeatedly quoted Chairman Mao, saying that "so many deeds cry out to be done, and always urgently," and recommending that his audience "Seize the day, seize the hour." He had also been banal. Shown the elaborately carved sedan chair on which each Ming emperor was carried from the Hall of Supreme Harmony to the red gates of the Forbidden City, the President remarked, "He didn't get much exercise if he was always carried on the chair." Of the Great Wall he said, "A people that can build a wall like this certainly have a great past to be proud of, and a people who have this kind of a past must also have a great future." Then: "As we look at this wall, we do not want walls of any kind between people."

Among the people on the far side of this particular wall were the Russians, and they were uneasy about possible implications of the visit. Tension between Moscow and Peking had been growing since Stalin's death nineteen years earlier. It had reached a peak the previous autumn when Lin Piao, vice chairman of the Chinese Communist Party and Mao's designated successor, had tried to fly to the USSR in a military plane. On orders from Mao and Chou, the craft had been shot down. The Soviets had regarded that as a slur on their hospitality, and now they suspected that the Chinese and the Americans were up to no good. In a Mandarin language broadcast beamed to Mao's subjects, Radio Moscow declared that nothing was "more shameless and hypocritical" than the Shanghai communiqué. China, said the Muscovite commentator, was entering into a "dangerous plot with the ruling circles of the U.S.A."

This was less a sign of anti-Americanism than of the growing friction within the Communist world. The Russians were jealous—unreasonably so, since the Nixons were going to visit them three months later. The prospect of that summit, in turn, had aroused Radio Hanoi, which called it "dark and despicable." Here there was a difference, however. Unlike Peking and Moscow, Hanoi was not interested in detente. On the contrary, the North Vietnamese were prepared to sabotage friendly relations between Washington and the two Communist capitals to the north. They didn't succeed, but they tried hard, and for a time it seemed that they were going to prevail.

News of the Peking talks reached troops of South Vietnam's 3rd Division, just south of the DMZ, over the small Japanese transistor radios then popular among ARVN forces. Not much was happening in that sector, and with the Americans and the Communists sitting down together, Thieu's men had let their guard down. There was another reason for their complacency. Since Nixon's submission of a new eight-point peace plan to the North Vietnamese there seemed to be a real movement toward peace. Thus the 3rd Division didn't feel threatened by the reports of a fresh buildup of Democratic Republic of (North) Vietnam (DRVN) forces across the 17th Parallel. As the sullen gray clouds of the northeast winter monsoon began to clear in March there was a noticeable increase in artillery fire from the north, but the South Vietnamese were unalarmed. They remained in their bunkers and sent out few patrols. Better troops would have been warier, but the 3rd Division was not a crack unit, which was precisely why the DRVN's General Vo Nguyen Giap had marked them as the first target of a new offensive, his biggest drive since Tet four years earlier.

Led by tanks, infantrymen of Giap's 304th Division bounded across the DMZ on March 30 in a savage attack which was the exact opposite of Tet—a power play, a blitz meant to overwhelm Saigon's forces with sophisticated Soviet weapons and the sheer weight of numbers. The assault units quickly captured fifteen border outposts. Over the next five weeks they advanced twenty-two miles in heavy fighting, taking ground which had been successfully and bloodily defended by U.S. Marines. The 3rd Division was virtually destroyed and the provincial capital of Quang Tri was lost. It was, as Defense Secretary Laird called it, a "massive invasion," and it was to be only one of four major North Vietnamese thrusts into South Vietnamese territory.

On April 6, four days after Easter, a DRVN tank column struck from Cambodia, driving ARVN forces from Loc Ninh. In less than a week the attackers had surrounded the provincial capital of An Loc, sixty miles north of Saigon, penning up the entire South Vietnamese 5th Division, which was one of the key units assigned to the defense of Thieu's capital. On April 18 another Red drive routed defenders in the coastal province of Binh Dinh, threatening to cut South Vietnam in half across its narrow waist. Finally, on April 22, four DRVN divisions burst into the Central Highlands, seizing Dak To and virtually encircling the provincial capital of Kontum.

Nixon responded by sending the B-52s north, pounding Hanoi and Haiphong in the first raids there in over three years. Antiwar senators reacted swiftly; Muskie of Maine introduced a resolution calling for an immediate end to all American military activity in North Vietnam. Laird, unmoved, warned Hanoi that the B-52 sorties would continue until all DRVN forces were withdrawn from South Vietnam. He said that the administration regarded the offensive as a "flagrant" violation of the 1954 Geneva accords and that Washington would spare nothing in its determination to turn the invaders back. In reality the White House mood was compounded of as much embarrassment as outrage. For three years the President had been proclaiming the success of Vietnamization, and the dispatches from Saigon strongly suggested that that policy was a failure.

The prospect of humiliation made Nixon a dangerous adversary. On May 8 he took a breathtaking step which he called Operation Linebacker. To cripple the DRVN's war-making capacity he ordered a massive air-sea blockade; the U.S. Navy would mine the waters of Haiphong and other North Vietnamese ports, and U.S. aerial sorties would smash rail lines leading out of southern China. This took him to the brink of confrontation with the very men in Peking and Moscow that he and Kissinger were wooing. He acknowledged the conflict with the Russians. In his televised address he said: "I particularly direct my comments tonight to the Soviet Union. We respect the Soviet Union as a great power. We recognize the right of the Soviet Union to defend its interests when they are threatened. The Soviet Union in turn must recognize our right to defend our interests. . . . Let us and let all great powers help our allies for the purpose of their defense—not for the purpose of launching invasions against their neighbors."

The President's aggressive response to Giap's drive gave new life to the antiwar movement, and the Committee for the Reelection of the President spent thousands of dollars to fake support for it which did not, in fact, exist. So many bogus telegrams were sent that the White House could announce with complete honesty a five-to-one ratio in favor of the move. In addition, a *New York Times* editorial critical of it was answered by a spurious ad headed "The People vs. the *New York Times*," the "People" being Charles Colson and a few aides. That was illegal, and, as it turned out, unnecessary. By the end of that month the North Vietnamese offensive had begun to falter. After laying waste 75 percent of Binh Dinh the DRVN forces there melted away. An Loc and Kontum held out, and a widely heralded Giap attempt to capture Hue never materialized. Abruptly the Hanoi menace seemed diminished. The Communists had committed all but two training divisions to the push, had lost one hundred thousand men, and had won little of strategic value. Their all-or-nothing gamble had failed. Le Duc Tho, a member of North Vietnam's politburo and Hanoi's chief negotiator, sent word to Kissinger that he was ready to reopen the talks in Paris. He still insisted that a cease-fire would be conditional upon Thieu's dismissal, but a genuine suit for peace appeared to be very near.

Moscow had something to do with that. In early May the blockade had made the likelihood of a Nixon-Brezhnev summit seem remote, but the Russians were determined to make the detente work. This became clear when Nikolai S. Patolichev, the Soviet foreign trade minister, called at the White House to exchange a few ideas about world trade. Reporters summoned to the oval office were astonished to find Nixon, Patolichev, and Ambassador Anatoly Dobrynin grinning, laughing, and bantering over how to say "friendship" in the two languages. A correspondent asked the minister whether the President's May 22 visit to Moscow was still on. "We never had any doubts about it," Patolichev replied. "I don't know why you asked." The Russians were simultaneously urging Hanoi to break off hostilities and readying a Kremlin apartment which had once belonged to the czars for occupancy by the President. The North Vietnamese were outraged by the prospect of Soviet and American leaders feasting on caviar and champagne with Giap's dead still warm in their graves, but nothing could stop deals between the world's two dominant powers—which was one of the points the Soviets wanted to make.

Improbable as it seemed to anyone aware of the history of the past two decades, American flags were waving beside the hammer and sickle when the *Spirit of '76,* arriving from Austria, descended over the glittering domes of the Kremlin churches and taxied to a stop beside the waiting figures of the Soviet president, premier, and foreign minister. Brezhnev was not there; like Mao he postponed his reception of Nixon until after the President had unpacked. That evening the Americans were guests of honor at a welcoming banquet in the Grand Kremlin Palace. In the morning the First Lady was off on tours of Soviet schools, Red Square, the famous Moscow subway, and the state-run GUM department store. Her husband's picture was on the front page of *Pravda;* it would be there every day throughout the week of talks. Appearing on the "blue screen," as Russians call their television, Nixon greeted viewers with *"Dobry vecher"* (Good evening), and parted at the end with *"Spasibo i do svidaniya"* (Thank you and goodbye). In between, another voice translated his cordial message, which was rich in the earthy Russian maxims that they cherish.

Unlike the Peking trip, this summit was more than symbolic. The banquets, the toasts, and the ballet performances were lavish, but the real meaning of the visit emerged in conferences beneath the huge gilt chandelier of the Kremlin's St. Vladimir Hall. The White House described the sessions as "frank and businesslike"; Brezhnev, bluff and hearty all week, called them "businesslike and realistic." A routine developed. The two national leaders would reach an agreement, or endorse a Russo-American understanding which might have been negotiated over a period of months or even years. Kissinger and Foreign Minister Andrei Gromyko would settle the details. Then protocol aides would appear with blue and red leather folders, and Nixon and Brezhnev would sign the documents. The two agreed to collaborate in space exploration, achieving a joint docking of a manned spacecraft in 1975. Joint research projects would examine problems of public health, cancer, heart disease, and pollution. Each consented to stop molesting the other's ships on the high seas. Both acknowledged the need to reduce troop strength in central Europe and the necessity for a conference on European security. Most important, they concurred on missile control. The two nations would limit their deployment of ABMs and freeze offensive missiles at current levels for five years.

There were some disappointments. There was no meeting of minds on the Middle East. Nixon wanted the Russians to talk Hanoi into a cease-fire; they wouldn't do it. Brezhnev was eager for a trade pact; the issue had to be referred to a commission for further discussion. The Soviet World War II lend-lease debt of 10.8 billion dollars was unresolved; they offered 300 million, Nixon wanted 800 million, all attempts at a compromise failed. On the other hand, the talks had yielded a dividend, a twelve-point statement of principles to establish rules of diplomacy for great powers, a breakthrough in international law. "We have laid out a road map," said Kissinger. "Will we follow this road? I don't know. It isn't automatic." But unless all signs failed, the implications for the future were vast. The difference between the two great systems of government were now likely to be expressed in treaties, not ideological jehads. Russia, through the coming European security conference, would draw closer to the continent and away from Asia. Trade and technology would continue to draw the two superpowers together, and understandings between them, not the fissioning of a multipolar world, which had been widely predicted, would be the paramount fact of world politics for a long time to come. The cold war was over, ended in large part through the efforts of an American President who had been one of the most resolute of the cold-warriors.

Not the least of its attractions for Nixon was the fact that it had occurred in an election year. In Peking, and then in the Kremlin, he had taken two giant steps toward four more years in the White House. Each passing day now seemed to bring him closer to victory in November. Unfortunately for his place in history, some of those around him weren't satisfied with that. They wanted to be absolutely sure. It was to be his tragedy that they were prepared to go to any lengths to guarantee a second Nixon term. Their attitude was summed up by one of them, Charles Colson, when he posted over his bar the slogan, "If you've got 'em by the balls, their hearts and minds will follow," and said, "For the President I would walk over my grandmother, if necessary." There was a word for the more extreme measures they were taking in pursuit of their goal: criminal. It was about to acquire a synonym: Watergate.

The 1972 campaign had begun to simmer in January, when a Harris poll showed Edmund Muskie running neck and neck with the President in public favor—42 percent for him, 42 percent for Nixon, and 11 percent for George Wallace. The Maine senator was clearly the strongest Democratic candidate; that same month Gallup reported that in a trial free-for-all Muskie emerged with 32 percent, Edward Kennedy with 27, Humphrey with 17, and McGovern with 3. Whoever their opponent, Republicans were preparing to come on strong. Appearing on the *Today Show*, H. R. Haldeman said that critics of the war were "consciously aiding and abetting the enemy," and the White House moved swiftly to exploit suburban indignation over the January decision of Federal Judge Robert R. Merhige Jr., who ordered busing of white schoolchildren in the two counties surrounding Richmond, Virginia, to achieve racial balance in the city's 70-percent-black schools. Judge Merhige would be reversed in June, but by then Muskie's potential adversaries would have rung all the changes on his support of busing.

In Florida Republican zealots were putting the finishing touches on a bogus letter to the Manchester, New Hampshire, *Union Leader* charging that while campaigning in the South Muskie had referred to French Canadians as "Canucks"; this would cripple him in the New Hampshire primary. Other Nixon operatives were taking similar steps to torpedo the senator's campaign, or—in the case of Howard Hunt—planning to burglarize the safe of a Las Vegas editor which was supposed to contain anti-Muskie dirt. At 1701 Pennsylvania Avenue in Washington CREEP was fleshing out its staff. Within a month John Mitchell would resign as attorney general to become in title what he already was in fact: CREEP's director.

Meanwhile the Republican war chest was rapidly being filled while that of the Democrats remained six million dollars in debt. There had always been some truth in the Democratic charge that the GOP was the party of big business. This year there would be no doubt of it. A bill requiring the naming of big donors would become law on April 10. The two chief GOP fund raisers, Secretary of Commerce Maurice Stans and Herbert Kalmbach, the President's personal attorney, were crisscrossing the country in a successful pursuit of contributions from the wealthy before the deadline. As the Nixon men warmed to their task they began to skirt the borders of indiscretion, and sometimes to cross them. Gifts totaling $114,000 were deposited in the Miami bank account of Bernard L. Barker,

Hunt's chief burglar. And although political donations from corporations were illegal even under the old law, the fund raisers solicited them and got them—$100,000 from Ashland Oil, $100,000 from Gulf, $100,000 from Phillips Petroleum, $55,000 from American Airlines, $40,000 from Goodyear, $30,000 from Minnesota Mining and Manufacturing. Ultimately they refused sums of less than $100,000; smaller donations were not worth the trouble. A list of two thousand secret donors was kept in the desk of Rose Mary Woods, the President's secretary, at the White House, where it was known as "Rose Mary's baby."

As the amounts collected mounted into the tens of millions, fertile minds brooded over ways to use them. By far the boldest ideas were the brain-children of Gordon Liddy, and he outlined them at 4 P.M. on January 27, 1972, in the office of the attorney general at the Department of Justice. His audience consisted of Mitchell, Magruder, and John Dean, special counsel to the President. Displaying colored diagrams with such code names as Target and Gemstone, Liddy lectured for a half-hour on a million-dollar operation which included the tapping of Democrats' phones, bludgeoning anti-Nixon demonstrators, and kidnapping antiwar leaders, who would be held in Mexican camps during the Republican national convention, then scheduled to be held in San Diego. One of the more imaginative aspects of the plan called for leasing a yacht and hiring prostitutes during the Democratic convention in Miami Beach. The girls (who would be "the best in the business," Liddy promised) would elicit important information from lusty Democrats and lure them into lewd positions. They would then be photographed by hidden cameras.

It is impossible to say what effect all this had on Liddy's eminent listeners. He himself never talked to federal prosecutors afterward, preferring to remain in jail. Mitchell later told congressional investigators that the submission had been "beyond the pale," Magruder said he was "appalled," and Dean called it "mind-boggling." All that can be said with certainty is that Liddy was invited back the following week for another try, and on the afternoon of February 4 he presented a cheaper, $500,000 version, featuring the clandestine cameras and wiretaps. He passed around eight-by-ten-inch charts describing proposed breaking-and-entering operations at the Fontainebleau Hotel in Miami Beach, McGovern's campaign offices on First Street in southwest Washington, and the Washington headquarters of the Democratic National Committee in the Watergate complex. According to Magruder, the attorney general "didn't feel comfortable" with this rendition either, and Liddy was told to try once again.

The winter wore on, the President flew to China and back, and Liddy still hadn't received a green light for the project. Early in March he and Hunt approached Colson, asking him to intercede with the Republican high command. Phoning Magruder, Colson said, "Gordon Liddy's upset. He's trying to get started on an intelligence operation, and he can't seem to see anybody." He urged Magruder to "get off the stick and get the budget approved for Liddy's plans." The undertaking was now budgeted at $250,000. There were no provisions for assault, abductions, or prostitution, but the proposal to burglarize and bug Democratic and McGovern headquarters remained. On March 30 Magruder flew down to Key Biscayne, where Mitchell was taking a brief holiday in the sun, and laid this final presentation before him. Three men were present—Magruder, Mitchell, and Fred LaRue, a southern Republican strategist—and later each had a different recollection of what transpired. Whatever the precise words used, the plan was accepted, and only Mitchell had the power to do that. Liddy had his green light.

The following week Magruder authorized CREEP's treasurer, Hugh Sloan Jr., to pay out $83,000 to Liddy. Of this, $65,000 was turned over to McCord on April 12; he spent most of it in New York on electronic surveillance equipment. McCord added another man to the assembling Watergate cast on May 1 when he contacted Alfred C. Baldwin III, whose name he had found in the register of the Society of Former Agents of the FBI. All the recruit was told then was that he was wanted as a temporary bodyguard for Martha Mitchell—no plum, as Baldwin realized, but he was assured that if he did a good job it might be "a stepping-stone to a permanent position." Martha didn't think much of her new escort. She later said that he deliberately led her into a hostile demonstration, told all her friends that he was a Democrat, and "walked around in front of everybody in New York barefoot." He was, she said, "the most gauche character I have ever met." But McCord liked Baldwin. He promoted him, moved him into room 419 of Washington's Howard Johnson motel, just across Virginia Avenue from the Watergate, and told him he would be doing some undercover surveillance of radicals in the capital. Returning to the room on the afternoon of Friday, May 26, the former FBI man was surprised to find McCord there, twirling the dials of an elaborate radio receiver. "We're going to put some units over there tonight," McCord said, gesturing across the street, "and you'll be monitoring them." To show how bugs worked, he dismantled the phone in the motel room, inserted a device, and tested it by dialing a local number for a recorded message. If Baldwin handled this job well, he was told, he would be given a similar assignment at the Democratic national convention.

Four days earlier a team of Cuban exiles led by Barker had flown to Washington from Miami and registered at another hotel under assumed names. Now they were moved into the Watergate Hotel. Baldwin's motel room had the advantage of providing a view of Democratic headquarters on the sixth floor of the Watergate complex, but the Cubans' new rooms were closer to the objective. Closer still was the Continental Room of the Watergate Hotel, and it was there, that evening, that Hunt, Liddy, and the Cubans opened the first act of what would turn out to be a classic comedy of errors. With wealthy Republican campaign contributors paying the bill, they ordered $236 in food and wine—almost $30 per man. After the meal everyone left the Continental Room except Hunt and Virgilio Gonzales, Barker's locksmith. These two hid in an adjoining room until waiters had locked up; then Gonzales tried to open a door at the end of the hall which would have let them into a stairwell leading to the sixth floor and the offices of the Democratic National Committee, or, as those familiar with it called it, the DNC. But the latch there was too difficult for Gonzales. So, to their dismay, was the other lock, leading to their escape route through the dining room. Left with no alternative, they settled down for a long and uncomfortable night while their gastric juices gently broke down their share of the banquet.

The others hadn't been idle, but they had been just as ineffectual. Led by Liddy, they had left Virginia Avenue for First Street and McGovern headquarters. The entrance was bathed in light from a nearby street lamp. Opening a dispatch case, Liddy produced a high-powered pellet pistol wrapped in a towel. "Shall I take that out?" he asked, gesturing at the bright light. He was capable of it; a few days earlier he had fired it in a toilet at the staid Hay-Adams Hotel, just across Lafayette Square from the White House. This time McCord discouraged him. The mission had to be aborted anyway. A drunk was loitering in the entrance of the building. He wouldn't leave, and at 5 A.M. they gave up and returned to their beds on Virginia Avenue.

The next evening Hunt took an elevator to the DNC headquarters and walked down through the building, taping door locks open as he went so that McCord and the Cubans could reach their goal from the garage in the Watergate basement. Wearing rubber gloves and carrying walkie-talkies, cameras, and flashlights, the raiding party reached the target area at 1:30 A.M. Two hours later McCord had planted taps in the telephones of Lawrence F. O'Brien's secretary and of R. Spencer Oliver, a party official. Barker, who was under the impression that they were looking for proof that Castro was financing the Democrats, found no evidence of it. In fact, this night was as unproductive as the one before. They were again unable to penetrate McGovern's offices. And the bugs were a disappointment. One didn't work at all, and the other phone, Baldwin discovered, was largely used by secretaries to arrange assignations with married politicians. According to Magruder, Mitchell, after reviewing some two hundred conversations that Baldwin had monitored, said that the information was "worthless," that the money had been wasted, and that he wanted them to try again.

The second and final act of the farce was played out on the night of Saturday, June 17. It began when the Cubans checked into rooms 214 and 314 in the Watergate Hotel and sat down to another banquet. McCord taped the garage door and then crossed to Baldwin's room at Howard Johnson's, where he checked new equipment—soldering irons, batteries, wires, and screwdrivers—which he had purchased earlier in the day. At 12:45 A.M. an important new actor appeared onstage. His name was Frank Wills, and he was a Negro watchman at the Watergate. Discovering the tape, he concluded that it had been left by a maintenance man; removing it, he crossed to Howard Johnson's for a cup of coffee. At about the same time McCord, looking out of Baldwin's window, saw the lights go off in the DNC offices. He phoned Hunt, who was in Watergate room 214 with Liddy, to say that the coast was clear. Patting the radio receiver, McCord said to Baldwin, "Any activity you see across the street, you just get on this unit and let us know." Then he joined the Cubans—Barker, Gonzales, Frank Sturgis, and Eugenio R. Martinez—in the garage. Aghast at finding the door again fastened, they appealed to Gonzales, and this time the locksmith was able to pick the lock open. There was some discussion over whether continuing with the job was an unacceptable risk. They decided to go ahead and mounted steps to the sixth floor, taping latches on the way. At 1:50 A.M. watchman Wills, finishing his coffee, returned to find the garage door taped for the second time. He telephoned the police, and at 1:52 A.M. his call was relayed to Metropolitan Police Car 727, an unmarked cruiser. Inside were three members of the District's "Bum Squad"—plainclothes men wearing T-shirts, windbreakers, and cheap slacks.

It is now 2 A.M., a historic hour. The Bum Squad parks and enters the Watergate, observed by Baldwin, who is standing on the little balcony outside his Howard Johnson's room, enjoying, in his later words, the "beautiful night." Since the three policemen are in informal clothes, he is unalarmed, but when lights begin appearing across the way he quickly radios: "Base headquarters, base one, do you read me?" In room 214 of the Watergate Hotel Hunt replies: "I read you; go on; what have you got?" Baldwin: "The lights went on on the entire eighth floor." Hunt: "We know about that. That is the two o'clock guard check. Let us know if anything else happens." At this point the thrifty Barker, who has been listening to the exchange, turns off his walkie-talkie to save the batteries. Minutes later lights start flickering on and off on the sixth floor, and Baldwin sees two of the plainclothesmen there. One of them is holding a pistol. Baldwin: "Base one, unit one, are our people in suits or are they dressed casually?" Hunt: "Our people are dressed in suits. Why?" Baldwin: "You have some trouble, because there are some individuals out there who are dressed casually and have got their guns out." Hunt—sounding, according to Baldwin, "a bit frantic"—tries to rouse the raiding party, yelling: "Are you reading this? Are you reading this?" Because of the economy-minded Barker, there is no response. It is probably too late anyway. McCord is in the process of dismantling O'Brien's phone when one of the officers sees an arm. He shouts: "Hold it! Stop! Come out!" Baldwin and Hunt hear a walkie-talkie switched on; a hoarse voice whispers into it: "They got us." Then the officers see ten rubber-gloved hands go up. McCord asks: "Are you gentlemen the Metropolitan Police?" The plainclothesmen affirm it, and the Watergate Five are placed under arrest.

Hunt called Howard Johnson's: "Are you still across the street?" Baldwin replied, "Yes I am," and Hunt told him, "Well, we'll be right over." Looking down from his balcony, Baldwin saw Hunt and Liddy emerge. Shortly thereafter Hunt burst into his room. Distraught, he asked, "What is going on, what is going on?" Baldwin said, "Come and see." The street below was swarming with uniformed patrolmen, motorcycles, and police cruisers; McCord, Barker, Gonzales, Sturgis, and Martinez were being led off in handcuffs. Hunt moaned, "I have got to use the bathroom," ran into the toilet, used it, ran out, called a lawyer, and asked Baldwin for McCord's address. They looked about at the electronic litter. Logs of previously intercepted conversations lay around; McCord's wallet and keys were on the bed. "Get all the stuff out of here and get yourself out of here!" Hunt said. "We will be in touch. You will get further instructions." As he dashed for the door Baldwin called after him, "Does this mean I won't be going to Miami?"

The *Washington Post's* account of the break-in appeared on the front page of its Sunday edition, but few papers gave it that much prominence. The *New York Times* carried thirteen inches inside under the head FIVE CHARGED WITH BURGLARY AT DEMOCRATIC QUARTERS, and most other editors played it down even more. Nevertheless, it was the most interesting story in the papers for certain high officers of the U.S. government and the Republican party, among them H. R. Haldeman, John Ehrlichman, John Mitchell, Maurice Stans, Charles Colson, Gordon Strachan, John Dean, Jeb Magruder, Fred LaRue, and, probably, the President of the United States.

A year later, during the hearings of the Senate Select Committee on Presidential Campaign Activities, chaired by Sam J. Ervin Jr. of North Carolina, Magruder was asked when this glittering array of outlaws decided to cover its tracks, and he answered in a puzzled tone, "I don't think there was ever any discussion that there would not be a cover-up." It was an involuntary reaction, and it began that morning of June 18 in Los Angeles, where several of them were holding meetings on campaign strategy. They were at breakfast in the Beverly Hills Hotel when, at about 8:30 A.M., Magruder took a call in the dining room from Liddy. "Can you get to a secure phone?" Liddy asked. Magruder said he couldn't and asked what was wrong. Liddy said, "There has been a problem." Magruder asked, "What kind of problem?" Liddy told him: "Our security chief has been arrested at the Watergate." "Do you mean Jim McCord?" "Yes." Hanging up, Magruder muttered to LaRue,

"You know, I think last night was the night they were going into the DNC." LaRue told Mitchell, who said, "This is incredible."

Their first response was to protect McCord, then the only one of the five captives known to them. According to Magruder, Mitchell proposed that Liddy approach Richard Kleindienst, the new attorney general, and ask him to spring McCord. Mitchell denied it, but someone at the Beverly Hills Hotel phoned Liddy at 9 A.M. California time—noon in Washington—and told him to do just that. Liddy found Kleindienst at the Burning Tree Country Club and put it to him in the locker room. Kleindienst not only refused to go along; he ordered his visitor to leave the club at once and then called Henry Petersen, who headed the Justice Department's criminal division, and instructed him that under no circumstances would he tolerate special treatment for the Watergate Five.

The FBI had already entered the case, which was beginning to develop unusual aspects. The papers implicating Hunt had been found in Barker's pocket. The prisoners had been carrying $1,300 in $100 bills, and another $3,200 in $100 bills had been discovered in the Cubans' rooms at the Watergate Hotel. Liddy, trying to destroy all evidence of his involvement, had used the shredder at CREEP headquarters to get rid of all documents in his possession, including his $100 bills. Strachan was searching Haldeman's White House files on his instructions and removing everything linking him to the burglars. Magruder phoned an assistant and directed him to take home a Gemstone file because, he said, he was afraid Democrats might raid his office in retaliation. And Howard Hunt was on the lam.

Dean, Colson, and Ehrlichman had held a hurried council of war over what advice they should give to Hunt. According to Dean, Ehrlichman proposed that he be told to leave the country. Dean made the call and then began to worry. Is it, he asked the others, really wise for the White House to give orders of that sort? "Why not?" Ehrlichman replied. "He's not a fugitive from justice." But Colson agreed with Dean, who made a second call canceling the instruction. Hunt decided to flee anyway. He cleaned out his desk, leaving only an empty whiskey bottle and a few Librium tablets. Then he flew to California, where he holed up in the home of a friend until he could no longer resist the pressure to turn himself in. The FBI was on his trail. They had already found Liddy, who had aroused suspicion by refusing to talk to them. Mitchell fired him for that, which seems hypocritical of him, but Liddy understood; he had told Magruder and Dean that he had "goofed," that "I am a good soldier and will never talk," and that "if anyone wants to shoot me on the street I am ready."

Meantime the presidential staff had been agonizing over the fact that disowning Hunt was almost impossible, since he was still on the White House payroll. Dean ordered Hunt's safe in room 552 of the Executive Office Building cleaned out. An aide brought him the contents: a black briefcase or dispatch case and a cardboard box containing, among other things, four walkie-talkies, a tear gas canister, four shoulder harnesses, the forged State Department Vietnam cables from 1963, evidence of his attempt to persuade *Life* that the forgeries were genuine, a folder of the Pentagon Papers, the CIA's Ellsberg profile, and Hunt's reports on Chappaquiddick. Dean looked over this extraordinary accumulation and gasped, "Holy shit!"

In California, meantime, Mitchell had issued a hurried statement trying to explain away McCord, who, he said:

> . . . is the proprietor of a private security agency who was employed by our committee months ago to assist with the installation of our security system. He has, as we understand it, a number of business clients and interests, and we have no knowledge of those relationships. We want to emphasize that this man and the other people involved were not operating either on our behalf or with our consent. I am surprised and dismayed at these reports. There is no place in our campaign or in the electoral process for this type of activity, and we will not permit or condone it.

Among the people who knew that this was a lie was Mitchell's wife. When he returned to Washington on Monday he persuaded her to stay in Los Angeles, where, she said afterward, she was held as a "political prisoner" by Baldwin's successor as her bodyguard. According to her, the guard yanked the phone wires out of the wall when she was telling a UPI reporter that "they don't want me to talk"; then he held her down while another man injected a sedative into her buttocks. There was no way to keep Martha Mitchell quiet, though. Three days later she was calling the reporter again, saying, "I'm not going to stand for all those dirty things that go on." It made a good story, but Martha's credibility was low, and most Americans accepted the official line, which was that the administration had not known anything about those dirty things. Tuesday morning Ronald Ziegler, the former adman who served as Richard Nixon's press secretary, spelled it out. In a scornful mood, he declined even to add to Mitchell's statement. "I am not going to comment from the White House on a third-rate burglary attempt," Ziegler said. "This is something that should not fall into the political process." However, when a handful of *Post* men continued to pursue the story, Ziegler did comment from the White House. He said, "I don't respect the type of journalism, the shabby journalism, that is being practiced by the *Washington Post*." And Mitchell, referring to the paper's publisher, told one of its reporters, "Katie Graham is going to get her teat caught in a big fat wringer."

In a sense the campaign which followed was the story of Richard Nixon's growing invincibility. Early trial heats had suggested a standoff. Then, as the summer progressed, the President moved ahead until all the polls conceded him about 60 percent of the vote. From then on he was beyond reach. CREEP's tremendous financial advantage—60 million dollars compared to 25 million for the Democrats—had little to do with the outcome. Watergate had even less. He had been elected four years earlier on a tide of protest against the Vietnam War. Ending the hostilities seemed to take him forever, and some 17,000 Americans had been killed there while he was doing it, but by the beginning of 1972 he had reduced the U.S. troop commitment in Vietnam from 549,500 to 139,000, and the Pentagon's weekly casualty list, which had been running at about 300 when he entered the White House, would on September 21, 1972, reach zero and remain near there. Being a political animal, he was quick to exploit this and other opportunities as they arose. In the Florida Democratic primary, for example, George Wallace campaigned on the slogan, "Send them a message," promising that if Floridians voted for him, "President Nixon will do something to halt this busing within thirty days." Wallace knew his Nixon. The President didn't wait thirty days. He demanded a busing moratorium just two days after the returns from there.

The sum of Nixon's skills was a united party led by a nominee who, his past notwithstanding, was now identified as the candidate of peace and detente. His only two rivals for the Republican nomination were Congressman Paul N. McCloskey Jr. of California on the left and John M. Ashbrook of Ohio on the right. They merely served to point up the President's preemption of the GOP center.

McCloskey arrived at the Republican convention—switched to Miami Beach after Dita Beard and ITT had made San Diego too embarrassing—with a single vote, pledged to him by New Mexico's primary law. He expected to have his name placed before the convention, thereby giving critics of Nixon's racial and military policies a chance to be heard, but the Rules Committee limited nominations to candidates controlling the delegations of at least three states. The final vote on the first ballot was: Nixon 1,347, McCloskey 1. The lone New Mexican apologized to the hall.

As a piece of stage management it was awesome. The President had eliminated any possibility of suspense by announcing his intention to keep Agnew on the ticket. Everyone in the party seemed eager to do his bidding. Ronald Reagan chaired the convention, Nelson Rockefeller put Nixon's name in nomination. Knowing the President's passion for order, floor managers limited the demonstration in his behalf to exactly twenty minutes, and to refute claims that the Democrats represented young America, 3,000 conservatively dressed youths were brought to Miami Beach on chartered buses. The boys wore their hair so short that they appeared to belong to another era—which was, of course, the idea.

To be sure, they were not the only young Americans there. Over 5,000 scruffy antiwar militants had camped in the city's Flamingo Park. During the Democratic week they were relatively quiescent, but when the GOP arrived they erupted, and 1,200 were arrested for slashing tires, blocking traffic, smashing store windows, setting bonfires in the streets, and trying to prevent delegates from attending the convention. The Republicans were elated. This, they seemed to be saying to those who objected to their tidy sessions, is what happens when you allow untidiness in politics. During the campaign which followed (in which Nixon hardly participated; he left most of the politicking to surrogates and never mentioned his opponent's name) GOP speakers spoke proudly of their unity and hammered away at the disarray on the other side.

They had a point. Riven in Chicago four years earlier, the Democrats were still absorbed in savage internecine feuds. The new presidential sweepstakes opened all their old wounds and inflicted new ones. At one time or another during the primary months the party's nomination was being sought by Muskie, McGovern, Humphrey, George Wallace, Eugene McCarthy, Fred Harris of Oklahoma, Vance Hartke of Indiana, Henry Jackson of Washington, John Lindsay of New York, Sam Yorty of Los Angeles, Wilbur Mills of Arkansas, Shirley Chisholm of New York, and Edward T. Coll, a young poverty worker from Connecticut who scared the pants off a Democratic National Committeewoman by dangling a rubber rat in front of her during a televised debate. The battle to head the ticket was a melee. Harry Truman, who had called the primaries "just so much eyewash," was vindicated. Like the Republican struggle in 1964, this one routed promising candidates and left the field in the possession of a nominee who would prove hopelessly weak in the general election and whose vulnerability had, in fact, been demonstrated in the very process which had brought him the prize.

Speaking in New Hampshire early in the year of his ill-starred race, Barry Goldwater had sunk a nail in his own coffin by calling, in effect, for the end of social security. On January 13, 1972, eight years later almost to the day, George McGovern told a college audience in Ames, Iowa, that he favored giving every American $1,000 from the federal treasury and limiting inheritances to $500,000 each. The speech didn't attract much attention at the time because McGovern was still a minor figure; in one recognition poll a few months earlier he had scored exactly 2 percent. But later it would return to haunt him, alienating millions who thought the government was too generous already and vast numbers of others who dreamed that one day they would hit the lottery, or something, big.

Part of McGovern's strength lay in the skill with which his organization exploited his obscurity. In New Hampshire, the first test, they successfully established the line that since Muskie was the front runner and from a neighboring state, any showing below 50 percent would be a defeat for him and a McGovern victory. That put the pressure on the Maine senator, who was hurt by the spurious "Canuck" letter and by the *Manchester Union Leader*'s tasteless charge that Mrs. Muskie told dirty jokes. In a televised speech outside the newspaper's office Muskie called its publisher William Loeb a "gutless coward," said "It's fortunate for him he's not on this platform beside me," and wept—perhaps the most expensive tears ever shed by a public man. Even so, Muskie won 46.4 percent of the vote on March 7 as against McGovern's 37 percent. The margin was a sweep, if not a landslide, yet so adroitly had the South Dakotan's aides depicted him as a dark horse that the spotlight was on him.

Florida, the next joust in the primary tournament, had eleven entries. McGovern sensibly said that it was not a state where he "expected to do well," and in fact he did poorly, receiving 6.1 percent of the vote. Wallace was the big winner, surprising everyone, including himself—"We beat the face cards of the Democratic deck," he crowed—and he was trailed by Humphrey, Jackson, and Muskie. The following week Muskie won in Illinois, taking 63 percent to McCarthy's 37 percent. Wisconsin came next. McGovern's troops were superbly organized there, and he led the pack of twelve candidates with 30 percent, followed by Wallace, Humphrey, and Muskie. McGovern won in liberal Massachusetts; Humphrey took Ohio and Indiana; in Nebraska McGovern beat Humphrey by six percentage points; Humphrey walloped Wallace in West Virginia 67 to 33 percent, and North Carolina went to Wallace.

By the middle of May Muskie was out of it and the marathon was settling down to a three-way contest between Wallace, Humphrey, and McGovern. Support for the Alabaman was generally interpreted as a protest vote; he said he would use it to win concessions at the national convention. Then came May 15 in Maryland. Wallace was successively hit by a rock in Frederick, eggs in Hagerstown, popsicles in Salisbury—and six bullets in Laurel. Next day he won both the Maryland and Michigan primaries, but for him, wounded and paralyzed, it was all over. It was, in fact, the end for all the Democratic candidates; without the third-party threat of Wallace siphoning off votes on the right, a Nixon victory was assured. But few realized that at the time, and the winner-take-all California primary on June 6 loomed as a titanic battle between the two survivors. The results were 1,527,392 votes, or 47.1 percent, for McGovern; 1,352,379, or 41.7 percent, for Humphrey. After that plums began toppling into the South Dakotan's lap, and he went to Miami Beach with 1,492.75 delegates—for all practical purposes, the nomination.

What was unappreciated at the time was the impact of the California campaign on McGovern's popularity. Until then no one had cast a harsh light on his program. He was seen as a handsome, decent, plainspoken man who was outraged by the Vietnam War. In three bruising televised debates, Humphrey had destroyed that image, pointing to McGovern's sometimes inconsistent and often quixotic stands on Israel, defense spending, welfare, labor law, unemployment compensation, taxation, and even, in the beginning, on Vietnam. "It was Hubert Humphrey who put McGovern away; no other Democrat could have done it to him like Hubert," pollster

Robert M. Teeter said afterward. "Not only did Hubert give it to him, but it was the first time McGovern got adversary treatment." The second time was at Miami Beach, when the watching nation saw what had happened to the Democratic party. Four years earlier, on the humid night of August 27, 1968, the Chicago convention had approved by voice vote a Credentials Committee resolution calling for a reform of the process by which convention delegates were chosen. Under the chairmanship of George McGovern, a reform commission had approved by a 10-9 vote a resolution which established a quota for blacks, and then—on a motion from a member who said, "There is no reason why our national convention shouldn't have 50 percent women, 10 to 15 percent young people"—quotas for women and youth. A majority of the commission thought that made sense, but it didn't. The quotas were a denial of the whole principle of representation. Worse, they had the effect of legitimatizing discrimination against all classifications who had no quotas —for example, the elderly, ethnic groups, and organized labor, three traditional sources of the party's strength.

In his keynote address Governor Reubin Askew of Florida declared, "It is impossible to look upon this group without feeling that one has seen the face of America." Certainly he was looking at newcomers to politics. Eight of every ten delegates were attending their first convention; 15 percent were black, 36 percent were women, and 22 percent were under thirty years of age. "Don't pass up any hitchhikers, they might be delegates," said one candidate. There were some hitchhikers—and some others. In their anxiety to assure representation to the underprivileged, the California delegation had included eighty-nine people who were on welfare. McGovern was so determined to offend no minority that he ordered kid-glove treatment of Gay Liberationists, who chanted—on television—"Two-four-six-eight, we don't overpopulate" and "Three-five-seven-nine, lesbians are mighty fine." At the same time an extraordinary number of elected Democrats were being excluded from the floor: 225 of the party's 255 congressmen and the Democratic mayors of Philadelphia, Detroit, Boston, San Francisco, Los Angeles, and Chicago.

Inevitably, the amateurs committed blunders which professionals would have avoided. The few politicians left in the hall were painfully aware of them. "I think we may have lost Illinois tonight," Frank Mankiewicz said glumly when that state's elected delegation was expelled from the convention by McGovern enthusiasts, and on the platform committee Ben Wattenberg sighed, "They just lost Michigan to the Republicans today with their busing plank. No one seemed impressed by the fact that in Macomb County they voted against busing in a referendum last fall by fourteen to one." Hugh Scott chided McGovern as a "triple A" champion who advocated "Acid, amnesty, and abortion." That was unfair, but at one time or another various McGovern supporters did speak well of all three, despite the anguished remonstrations of observers like David Riesman, who pointed out that the floor of a national political convention is not the best place to discuss so sensitive an issue as abortion. The impact of all this on the national television audience cannot be determined with precision, but subsequent events suggest that the number of blacks, women, and youths won over by the requirement that delegations "reasonably" reflect their constituencies by race, sex, and age was overwhelmed by the swarms of voters who were offended by the spectacle in Miami Beach. Of the three groups, only the Negroes went for McGovern in November, and they had been for him long before.

By the time McGovern won the nomination it was probably not worth much. He further devalued it by delivering his acceptance speech at 3 A.M., when most voters were asleep. The first in a series of disasters came less than twelve hours later at a meeting of the Democratic National Committee in the Fontaine Room of the Fontainebleau. McGovern began by announcing that Larry O'Brien had "reached a judgment that he will not stay on as the chairman of the party." That was false—O'Brien was willing to remain—and a number of people there knew it. Mrs. Jean Westwood was chosen as the new chairman. McGovern nominated Pierre Salinger as vice chairman. Charles Evers rose to say that "inasmuch as we are going to try to stay in line with the McGovern rules, I would . . . strongly urge that if we are going to have a female chairman . . . I would like to place in nomination a black man to be co-chairman or vice chairman." He then nominated an unknown Negro—whereupon McGovern said that was fine with him, thus publicly scuttling Salinger.

Unlucky Pierre was betrayed a second time. Later that same day, McGovern asked him to serve as his representative in talks with the North Vietnamese in Paris. Salinger flew to France, the story leaked to UPI, and McGovern issued a statement to the press saying, "Pierre Salinger had no instructions whatsoever from me. He told me he was going to Paris, and he said while he was there he might try to make some determinations of what was going on in the negotiations. But there wasn't the slightest instruction on my part to him." Once again there were people who knew better, among them David Dellinger, who had acted as liaison between McGovern and Hanoi. The nominee challenging Nixon's integrity was himself losing credibility fast.

Then the Eagleton affair exploded. McGovern had just begun a pre-campaign holiday in the Black Hills when reporters learned that Senator Thomas Eagleton of Missouri, his running mate, had twice been hospitalized for psychiatric care, including electroshock therapy. Up to that point the nominee could scarcely be held responsible for that calamity. He hadn't known about Eagleton's medical history at the time he picked him, and when Mankiewicz had asked Eagleton if there were any skeletons in his closet, the reply had been that there were none. The Missourian was at fault there. American ignorance of mental health being what it is, even a mild history of depression disqualifies a politician from running for national office, and the problems of a patient subjected to electroshock treatments are not mild. The obvious solution was to let Eagleton resign gracefully. McGovern didn't do it.

Instead he issued a statement saying that he was "1,000 percent for Tom Eagleton" and had "no intention of dropping him from the ticket." The mimeograph machine in the Black Hills was still warm when the *New York Post,* the *Washington Post,* and the *New York Times*—the most liberal papers in the country—said Eagleton had to go. Matthew Troy, a prominent New York Democrat whose support for McGovern had been unwavering, was quoted as saying, "I have nine kids. I don't want to see them destroyed because some unstable person might become President." Democratic headquarters were deluged with mail, wires, and calls demanding that the vice-presidential nominee quit, and the head of the ticket decided that his support of him wasn't 1,000 percent after all. He agreed to let Mrs. Westwood say on *Meet the Press* that it would be "a noble thing" for the Missourian to withdraw. Then, greeting Eagleton, he told him, "Tom, believe me I had no idea what she was going to say." His running mate replied, "Don't shit me, George." According to Eagleton, "George smirked. Not a smile of faint amusement. Not a frown of slight irritation. A smirk, that's what it was." Eagleton retired from the ticket on July 31, and after five Democrats, including Muskie, had declined to replace him, Sar-

gent Shriver consented. The episode had been one of the most disastrous in the history of presidential politics. McGovern would
never recover from it.

From that moment on the Democratic campaign was on the skids.
The nominee belatedly courted LBJ, Mayor Daley, organized labor,
and the Jewish vote; all were cool. His Washington headquarters
disintegrated. Important letters were unanswered. Speaking schedules disappeared. Distinguished Democrats who called with offers
to help were insulted by shaggy young volunteers and turned away.
At one time—in May—McGovern had been within five percentage
points of Nixon. By July, the month of the Democratic convention,
he was twenty points behind. After the Eagleton debacle he slipped
farther behind. In October, as he furiously rushed back and forth
across the country, logging 65,000 miles in the air, he gained
slightly. It didn't last. Both Gallup and Harris predicted on election
eve that the vote would split 61 percent for Nixon and 39 percent
for McGovern. Actually it was 60.7 to 37.5, with splinter candidates
getting 1.8.

Nixon had carried forty-nine states; Massachusetts and the District of Columbia went to McGovern. But that was not the full story.
The voter turnout was the lowest in twenty-four years. Only 55 percent of the country's registered voters went to the polls; the rest,
presumably, rejected *both* candidates. And while the President had
forged a historic electoral triumph, his party hadn't done at all well.
Democratic congressional candidates had held the GOP to a 12-
seat gain in the House—rather than the 41 they needed for control—
while gaining two Senate seats, making their margin there 57 to 43,
and picking up one statehouse.

McGovern said he was not disheartened. His central issue had
been the Vietnam War, and he believed he had done much to end
it. In conceding defeat he told his workers, "I want every one of
you to remember that if we pushed the day of peace just one day
closer, then every minute and every hour and every bone-crushing
effort in this campaign was worth the entire effort." That was putting the best possible face on it. Not everyone agreed. Marquis
Childs said it had been "one of the most unhappy campaigns in
American history." Understandably, Richard Nixon took a different
view. Greeting his supporters in Washington's Shoreham Hotel, he
said, "I've never known a national election when I could go to bed
earlier." As he turned away to retire there, they set up a terrific

din, chanting, *"Four more years!"* It was a top-drawer Republican crowd, well-barbered and expensively dressed. The television audience had no way of knowing that some of the most eminent chanters were felons.

In a reference to Watergate, McGovern had described the Nixon administration as "the most corrupt in history," but Gallup had reported in October that barely half the voters had heard of the break-in. Of those, four out of every five did not see it as a reason to vote Democratic. Teeter had found that only 6 percent thought the President was involved. The others tended to blame CREEP— a tribute to the party leadership's wisdom in establishing a reelection headquarters outside the White House. It was an illusion. The big campaign decisions were made at 1600 Pennsylvania Avenue. The men around Nixon continued to be deeply involved in the Watergate cover-up, which, according to subsequent testimony before the Ervin committee, took the following course.

John Dean's immediate problem, once he had seen the contents of Hunt's safe, was how to get rid of it. He took the matter up with Ehrlichman, who suggested he "shred the documents and deep-six the briefcase." Ehrlichman said, "You drive across the river on your way home at night, don't you? Well, when you cross over the bridge, just toss the briefcase in the river." Dean pointed out that it wasn't that simple; too many White House employees, including his own assistant, had seen at least part of what had been in the safe. Ehrlichman's solution was to summon to his office L. Patrick Gray, who had been acting director of the FBI since J. Edgar Hoover's death in May. On June 28, eleven days after the Watergate burglary, Dean gave him the sensitive material there, calling it "political dynamite" which "should never see the light of day." Gray kept it until the end of the year—possibly to blackmail the White House should the President fail to recommend him as permanent director—and then burned it with the Christmas trash, thereby assuring his eventual resignation in disgrace.

That same week the White House made an effort to cloak at least part of the Watergate incident with the mantle of "national security." The President himself was involved in this; later he justified his intervention by saying, "I was advised that there was a possibility of CIA involvement in some way." His concern included the possibility that Hunt's role in the Plumbers might be revealed, exposing other sensitive "national security matters," including, presumably, the burgling of Ellsberg's psychiatrist's office. CIA director Richard Helms and his new deputy, General Vernon Walters, were called to the White House, where Haldeman told him that the DNC break-in was embarrassing Nixon. He said it was "the President's wish" that Walters suggest to Gray that the arrest of five housebreakers "should be sufficient," and that it was not useful to press the investigation any farther, "especially in Mexico"—a reference to the route political contributions had followed in finding their way into Barker's bank account.

At meetings on June 26 and June 28 Dean proposed to Walters that the CIA furnish bail and pay the salaries of the five prisoners. The general said he didn't think that was a good idea, that it might hurt the "apolitical" reputation of the agency. Walters did approach Gray, but not to carry out White House suggestions; instead he warned him that presidential aides were trying to exploit both the agency and the bureau for questionable purposes. Gray already knew this. In addition to his own personal experience he was beginning to feel heat from below; FBI subordinates were telling him that a cover-up had begun and urging him to alert the President. On July 6 he did it with a phone call, cautioning Nixon that "people on your staff are trying to mortally wound you by using the CIA and the FBI and by confusing the question of CIA interest in, or not in, people the FBI wishes to interview." After a pause the President said, "Pat, you just continue to conduct your aggressive and thorough investigation," and hung up.

It was now nearly three weeks since the Watergate arrests, and efforts to conceal the trail of those behind the break-in were in full swing. Gray, having sent up his rocket and seen it sputter into nothing, allowed himself to be duped by Dean. The presidential counsel was permitted to kibitz at FBI interviews with eight White House aides and was given copies of some eighty FBI reports on Watergate. In addition he persuaded Petersen not to call five members of the staff—Colson, Young, Krogh, Strachan, and Dwight Chapin —before the federal grand jury that was looking into Watergate. Instead they testified in a separate room, where jurors could not question them. It was at this time that Kleindienst, Petersen's superior, assured the public that the Justice Department's pursuit of the truth about the break-in was "the most extensive, thorough, and comprehensive investigation since the assassination of President Kennedy."

On August 29 Nixon did some reassuring of his own. He told the country that besides giving all assistance required by the FBI, he had launched his own inquiry: "Within our own staff, under my direction, Counsel to the President, Mr. Dean, has conducted a complete investigation of all leads which might involve any present members of the White House or anybody in the government. I can say categorically that his investigation indicates that no one in the White House staff, no one in this administration, presently employed, was involved in this very bizarre incident." Dean heard this on a newscast and was astonished. He had only been following orders from Haldeman and Ehrlichman. He had conducted no investigation, had written no report, and had not even seen the President. (A year later the White House acknowledged this, saying that Nixon's confidence had been inspired by "assurances" from Ehrlichman.)

In that same statement the President said: "What really hurts in matters of this sort is not the fact that they occur, because overzealous people in campaigns do things that are wrong. What hurts is if you try to cover it up." This, of course, is precisely what was happening. John Mitchell was presiding over cover-up strategy sessions in his office, and, after July 1, when he resigned from CREEP at the importuning of Martha, in his apartment in the Watergate complex. Among those who attended were LaRue, Assistant Attorney General Mardian and Jeb Magruder. At one point Magruder volunteered to take the rap for all of them. This received serious consideration, but in the end it was decided that since he had lacked authority to approve the vast sums Liddy had spent, a guilty plea from him would merely lead to Mitchell and jeopardize Nixon's reelection.

Instead it was decided to make Liddy the cutoff point. Though an eccentric, he was reliable; he wouldn't talk, and they could build a plausible story around him, exaggerating the sums of money given to him for legitimate purposes and saying he had decided on his own to spend it on the burglary. Bart Porter, a Magruder aide, agreed to perjure himself. He would testify that he had given Liddy $100,000 to infiltrate organizations of antiwar radicals. There was one difficulty. Hugh Sloan Jr., CREEP's treasurer, was an honest man. In April he had asked Stans about Liddy's huge budget. ("I don't want to know," Stans answered, "and you don't want to know.") Now, when Magruder told him they were going to alter the figures, saying that Liddy had received only $75,000 or $80,000, Sloan replied, "I have no intention of perjuring myself." Magruder said, "You may have to."

Sloan, under the mistaken impression that he was not the only scrupulous man in the leadership of the reelection campaign, tried to warn several presidential aides that something was terribly wrong at 1701 Pennsylvania Avenue. He went to Chapin first and was advised to take a vacation. Chapin said that "the important thing is that the President must be protected." Then Sloan went to Ehrlichman, recommending that an outsider investigate the committee. "Don't tell me any details," Ehrlichman said, and, like Stans, "I do not want to know." Finally, with FBI agents waiting in his office to question him, Sloan appealed to Mitchell for guidance. The former attorney general said, "When the going gets tough, the tough get going." Sloan got going. He had no choice; Stans told the FBI that he had already resigned.

On September 15 the grand jury indicted Hunt, Liddy, the five men who had been captured in the DNC—and no others. The trail had stopped with them, and the President was greatly relieved. Late that afternoon Dean was summoned to the oval office, where Nixon and Haldeman greeted him warmly. As Dean later testified before the Ervin committee, Nixon said he hoped there would be no trial before the election and that he wanted Dean to keep a list of people giving the administration trouble, because he meant to make life difficult for them after the election. The principal thorn here continued to be the *Washington Post*, which on October 10 reported that the Watergate burglary was part of "a massive campaign of political spying and sabotage . . . directed by officials of the White House and the Committee for the Reelection of the President." The reelection high command reacted swiftly and angrily. Clark MacGregor, Mitchell's successor at CREEP, called the story "vicious and contemptible." Another committee spokesman described it as "a collection of absurdities." To Stans it was "a senseless pack of lies"; to Ron Ziegler, "the shoddiest type of journalism." Their indignation was widely accepted as righteous. The Fourth Estate had fallen sharply in public esteem during the Nixon Presidency. Symbolically, that summer the Supreme Court had ruled 5 to 4—with the administration's four appointees in the majority—that newspapermen could be required to reveal confidences by judges and grand juries. The American Civil Liberties Union declared that "in a relatively short time the press in the United States has moved from what many considered a position of extreme security to one of extreme vulnerability." The men responsible for that were now threatened by vigorous reporting. They responded by stirring the suspicion of "the media" which they themselves had planted in the public mind. Their reward was a short-term success—at the expense of ultimate disgrace.

One plank of the scaffold which awaited them fell into place at 2:27 P.M. on the foggy afternoon of December 8, when United Airlines Flight 553, approaching Chicago's Midway Airport, crashed a mile and a half short of the runway, killing thirty of its forty-five passengers. Among the dead was Mrs. E. Howard Hunt, in whose purse investigators of the accident found $10,000 in cash. A relative said she had been on her way to make a down payment on a Holiday Inn franchise. But where, the authorities wondered, did she get the money? The Hunts had always been strapped. He had wanted badly to buy a partnership in a Washington public relations firm but had been unable to round up the $2,000 required for a down payment. Now his wife's body had been found with a small fortune in $100 notes—just like the Watergate Five.

The money was hush money, and there was a lot more of it. Eleven days after the Watergate arrests the council of war over which Mitchell was presiding had decided, in Dean's words, to raise funds "in exchange for the silence of the men in jail." Herbert Kalmbach was the first to be given the assignment, though apparently he wasn't told the full story. He had arrived the next morning on a night flight from Los Angeles, and after being sketchily briefed by Dean at a rendezvous in Lafayette Park he phoned Stans, who produced $75,100 in campaign funds, all of it in the ubiquitous $100 bills. Over the next two months Kalmbach rounded up between $210,000 and $230,000, of which $154,000 went to Dorothy Hunt. The Californian had qualms over the propriety of this, and on July 26 he went to Ehrlichman with them. "John," he began, "I am looking right into your eyes." He said he wanted to know whether Dean had the authority to give him these instructions, and whether it was right. According to him, Ehrlichman answered, "Herb, John Dean does have the authority, it is proper, and you are to go forward."

At the end of August Kalmbach quit anyway and LaRue became

the new paymaster. Altogether between $423,000 and $548,000 was paid to the Watergate defendants, most of it channeled through Mrs. Hunt. Tony Ulasewicz, who actually delivered the cash, or "the laundry," as he called it, said he came to the conclusion that "something here is not kosher." Not to put too fine a point on it, CREEP was being blackmailed. Shortly after the arrests Hunt had sent Dean a dark message: "The writer has a manuscript of a play to sell." Later, according to McCord, Hunt said that unless his wife's demands were met he would "blow the White House out of the water" and produce "information which could impeach the President." Not only did he want money; he insisted on pledges of presidential clemency. Colson sent him a "general assurance" of this through Hunt's lawyer. In exchange, Hunt agreed to plead guilty and tell the press he knew of no involvement of "higher-ups."

The cover-up strategy seemed to be working. Actually it was about to unravel. The key to the imminent exposure was McCord, who felt a continuing loyalty to his old organization, the CIA, or, as he and other insiders called it, "the company." On June 30, the week presidential aides began trying to involve the agency in the toils of the cover-up, McCord sent Helms an unsigned letter promising to keep him informed and ending: "From time to time I will send along things you may be interested in." It was the first of seven anonymous letters he mailed to the director, and was followed, on December 22, by a warning to an old friend in the agency's security office: "There is tremendous pressure to put the operation off on the company." That same week he wrote John J. Caulfield:

> Dear Jack,
>   I am sorry to have to tell you this but the White House is bent on having the CIA take the blame for the Watergate. If they continue to pursue this course, every tree in the forest will fall and it will be scorched earth. The whole matter is at the precipice right now. Pass the message that if they want it to blow, they are on exactly the right course. I am sorry that you will get hurt in the fallout.

There was no signature, but none was necessary. Caulfield spread the word that McCord was planning to confess everything, and frantic efforts were made to change his mind—pledges of financial support for his family, executive clemency, rehabilitation and a job when he got out; even what McCord construed as a threat on his life from Caulfield: "You know that if the administration gets its back to the wall, it will have to take steps to defend itself." McCord answered, "I have already thought through the risks and will take them when I'm ready. I have had a good life and my will is made out." Caulfield said, "Everybody is on track but you. You are not following the game plan. Keep silent." But the old spy didn't want any part of this game plan. His mind was made up. In a letter to Judge John J. Sirica, which was read from the bench at the end of the court proceedings, he said that "Others involved in the Watergate operation were not identified during the trial," that "perjury occurred during the trial," and that "there was political pressure applied to the defendants to plead guilty and remain silent." It was a sensational moment, and one of the most fateful in the history of American jurisprudence. With it, the collapse of the Nixon Presidency began.

The President's reelection campaign had been enormously enhanced in its last days by electrifying news from Henry Kissinger: he and Le Duc Tho, Hanoi's chief negotiator, had achieved a breakthrough in their Paris talks. On October 8 the North Vietnamese had dropped their insistence that Thieu be ejected and a coalition government installed in Saigon. Eighteen days later Kissinger told a televised press conference that a final accord could be reached in one more meeting. "Peace," he said, "is at hand."

But it wasn't. On October 23 the White House announced that the signing of the cease-fire agreement was being postponed pending new sessions needed to "clarify" some matters. At least part of the difficulty seemed to lie in Saigon. South Vietnamese Foreign Minister Tran Van Lam attacked the imminent agreement as "unacceptable," and Thieu said it would amount to "a surrender of the South Vietnamese people to the Communists." If necessary, Thieu vowed, his nation would continue the war alone.

When Kissinger tried to reopen certain sensitive topics, Hanoi accused Washington of bad faith and demanded that the settlement be signed as negotiated. The Americans refused, and Le Duc Tho, furious, began advancing counterproposals on such matters as the size of the international truce supervision team and—the most vital subject for the United States—the return of U.S. prisoners of war. Kissinger announced that the other side was raising "one frivolous issue after another," that the team from Hanoi was trying to make substantive alterations "in the guise of linguistic changes."

The President was reported to be angry with both Vietnams; with

Saigon for being mulish and with Hanoi for, as he saw it, going back on its word. On December 14 Kissinger left Paris in despair and Nixon cabled North Vietnam's Premier Pham Van Dong, warning him that unless serious negotiations were resumed within seventy-two hours he would reseed Haiphong harbor with mines and unleash America's aerial might: B-52s, F-4 Phantoms, and Navy fighter-bombers. General Curtis LeMay had once proposed bombing the North back into the Stone Age, and clearly the President had something like that in mind. It was no light threat; his Air Force generals assured him that in two weeks they could saturate the enemy homeland with more tonnage than in virtually all the great raids of World War II. Furthermore, this would be terror bombing on a scale never known before. The B-52 guaranteed that. Pinpoint attacks by them were impossible. Each carried forty tons of bombs in its belly. Flying in "cells" of three, each cell laid its missiles in "boxes" a mile and a half long by a half-mile wide. Until now they had never assailed a city. If they unloaded over Hanoi, massive civilian casualties would be unavoidable.

The seventy-two hours passed, Pham Van Dong did not reply, and Nixon sent the word to U.S. air bases on Guam and in Thailand and carriers in the Gulf of Tonkin: start the blitz. The result was the most savage chapter in the long history of American involvement in Vietnam. Hanoi was pounded around the clock by every type of American aircraft in every kind of weather. Using 100 of the huge green and brown B-52s, U.S. airmen flew over 1,400 sorties in the first week alone. Americans were stunned. Only a few days earlier—until mid-December, in fact—they had been expecting total U.S. disengagement in Indochina, with the prospect that American POWs, some of whom had been in captivity for nearly ten years, might be home for Christmas. Now they were confronted by this bewildering volte-face. And they were offered no presidential explanation. In the past, Nixon, like Johnson before him, had appeared on television to announce new developments in Vietnam. Now he made no attempt at justification. The only White House official to comment was Ziegler, who told reporters that the bombing "will continue until such time as a settlement is arrived at."

The Pentagon briskly ticked off the military targets: truck parks, communications towers, power plants, warehouses, bridges, railways, shipyards, factories, roads, barracks, supply points, landing fields, and antiaircraft and surface-to-air missile (SAM) installations. But most of the objectives were in heavily populated parts of North Vietnam's cities. The Hanoi thermal power plant, for example, was only a thousand yards from the center of the capital. Diplomats and foreign newsmen stationed there sent out descriptions of a stricken city, lacking electricity and often water. Vast neighborhoods were cratered and pocked by explosives. Schools were reduced to smoking sockets in the ground. Torn copybooks lay in the rubble. Parents frantically searched for their children among jagged chunks of shattered concrete.

In the Hanoi suburb of Thai Nguyen almost a thousand civilians were dead or wounded. Coffins were stacked on street corners. The Bach Thai hospital for tuberculars was razed. So was Bach Mai general hospital; doctors carried patients piggyback from the debris. A dispensary was destroyed. One bomb hit a POW camp—incensing Nixon, who reportedly blamed the North Vietnamese for putting prisoners where missiles might fall. The Polish freighter *Josef Conrad* was sunk in Hanoi harbor, killing three of her crew; a Russian and a Chinese ship were mangled. Men in the State Department, which was charged with apologizing for these outrages, were bitter. "The way things are going," one American diplomat said gloomily, "we'll hit the cathedral in Hanoi on Christmas Eve."

In fact Nixon declared a thirty-six-hour truce over Christmas, but the moment it was over the deluge of death resumed. On walls still standing North Vietnamese chalked, "We will avenge our compatriots massacred by the Americans," and "Nixon, you will pay this blood debt." These were gestures of helplessness; the White House was over seven thousand miles away, and soon the last American ground troops would have left Indochina. North Vietnam's only real hostages against the terror were captured U.S. fliers. In the seven years before this blitz B-52s had flown 100,000 sorties and only one had been lost to enemy gunners. Now Hanoi had the strongest antiaircraft defenses in the world, and in these last two weeks of 1972 their fuming muzzles brought down sixteen of the aerial dreadnoughts, each representing fifteen million dollars. More important, ninety-eight crewmen had been captured. The American onslaught over Tonkin had increased the stakes in Paris. There was more pressure on Kissinger as well as on Le Duc Tho.

Other incentives for peace had appeared. Nixon had, not for the last time, misjudged the public's capacity for moral indignation. James Reston called the massive raids "war by tantrum," and Republican Senator William Saxbe of Ohio, who had supported the President's Vietnam policy, now came out against it, saying he was troubled "as an American" and thought most of his countrymen felt "the same way." In Europe the reaction was sharper. London's *Daily Mirror* said, "The American resumption of the bombing of North Vietnam has made the world recoil in revulsion." In Paris *Le Monde* compared the air offensive to the Nazi leveling of Guernica in the Spanish Civil War. Premier Olof Palme of Sweden went farther, equating it with the German extermination of the Jews. That angered the administration, which called the Swedish ambassador to protest, but the feeling in all western chancelleries was almost as strong.

If Washington had underestimated the depth of allied resentment, Hanoi had overestimated the wrath of the Communist world. Comment in Moscow and Peking was perfunctory. Speaking on the fiftieth anniversary of the Soviet Union, Leonid Brezhnev made the mildest of references to the B-52 strikes, and he pointedly sent his children to meet Tricia Nixon Cox and her husband at a U.S. embassy reception there. Both the Russians and the Chinese were urging the North Vietnamese to settle with the Americans. The United States had lost its enthusiasm for opposing "wars of liberation," but the eagerness of the USSR and the People's Republic of China to support them had also diminished. This, perhaps more than the bombing, led Hanoi to send out urgent signals calling for new talks. On December 30 the White House announced a bombing halt and the rescheduling of talks between Kissinger and Le Duc Tho for January 8. It was a sign of the American determination to find a solution that when Thieu sent two South Vietnamese diplomats to Washington with a threat to fight any treaty that did not meet his requirements, Nixon responded by dispatching General Alexander Haig to Saigon with a letter to Thieu telling him, in effect, to shut up.

Soon Kissinger was commuting between Paris and Key Biscayne with a briefcase containing fresh proposals. The break came in late January when the two bargainers met for their twenty-fourth round of talks in forty-two months. Two more days of dickering had been anticipated, but a final understanding was reached in just four hours. The formal end of the war came in the silk-walled conference room of Paris's old Majestic Hotel; simultaneous announcements were broadcast in Washington, Hanoi, and Saigon. (Just working

out that process, said Kissinger, had "aged us all by several years.")
President Nixon led the nation in prayer, praising the 2.5 million
Americans who had served in Vietnam "in one of the most selfless
enterprises in the history of nations." He declared that he had
achieved "Peace with honor."

But honor had little to do with it. Kissinger appreciated that. In
his thoughtful press briefing he observed that "it should be clear
by now that no one in the war has had a monopoly of anguish
and that no one has had a monopoly of insight." He made no reference to honor, or valor, or glory, or any of the other martial concepts which had become irrelevant to this conflict. "Together with
healing the wounds in Indochina," he said, "we can begin to heal
the wounds in America." That was the right note to strike, because
that was the issue for Americans. After some 46,000 U.S. battle
deaths, 300,000 wounded, and the expenditure of 110 billion dollars, they were left, as a direct result of the war, with a grave
domestic problem, a spiritual malaise. In the McLuhanesque global
village it was not possible to lay waste a distant land without inflicting hideous scars on the United States. Among the casualties had
been public esteem for the Presidency, which had led the country
into the war; for Congress, which had continued to appropriate vast
sums for it; for the courts, which had failed to find it unconstitutional; and for the institution of democracy itself, which, having
proved ineffectual in attempting to influence the makers of policy,
had degenerated into chaos in the streets. "There has been a sharp
decline in respect for authority in the United States as a result of
the war," Reston wrote on the occasion of the cease-fire, "a decline
in respect not only for the civil authority of government but also
for the moral authority of the schools, the universities, the press,
the church, and even the family . . . something has happened to
American life—something not yet understood or agreed upon, something that is different, important, and probably enduring."

The week of the truce there was an ugly row at Madison Square
Garden over whether "The Star-Spangled Banner" should be played
before athletic events. At the same time a fresh epidemic of teacher
strikes was disrupting classrooms across the country. Neither would
have been conceivable during the Depression, the last great trial
of the American spirit. The flag had flown over a poorer land then;
there had been a great deal of physical suffering in the United
States. Teachers had been among the greatest victims of the eco-

nomic crisis. Often they had been paid in worthless scrip or not at all, and some had shared the little food they had with starving children. But in that tightly disciplined society strikes by them, like disrespect for the national anthem, would have been inconceivable. That does not mean that America was a better country then; plainly it was not. It does mean that it was a different country, inhabited by other people facing challenges wholly unrelated to those of the 1970s.

Perhaps this was what Henry Adams meant when he wrote, in the early years of this century, that the test of twentieth-century Americans would be their capacity for adjustment. Change is a constant theme in the American past. The United States is the only nation in the world to worship it for its own sake, and to regard change and progress as indistinguishable. "We want change. We want progress," Lyndon Johnson said in 1965, "and we aim to get it."

But if that is one aspect of the American national character, there is another, the reverse of the same coin, which reemerged with the end of the Vietnam War. It is the yearning to renounce the present and find restoration in the unconsummated past. "America," John Brooks observed, "has an old habit of regretting a dream just lost, and resolving to capture it next time." The theme is a familiar one in American literature. One thinks of Willa Cather's lost lady and Robert Frost's "The Road Not Taken." Thomas Wolfe wrote: "Remembering speechlessly we seek the great forgotten language, the lost lane-end into heaven, a stone, a leaf, an unfound door. Where? When? O lost, and by the wind grieved, ghost, come back again." So it was that after intervening in foreign conflicts for a third of a century, the people of the United States turned inward once more, seeking comfort in insularity and renewal in isolation. "So we beat on, boats against the current," F. Scott Fitzgerald wrote at the end of his finest novel, "borne back ceaselessly into the past."

Epilogue

ECHOES

SURROUNDED BY HAPPY PERJURERS, Richard Nixon celebrated his second inauguration in a three-day, four-million-dollar extravaganza directed by up-and-coming young Jeb Stuart Magruder. The rhetoric of the January 20 inaugural address, in keeping with the retreat from far-flung world commitments, was less a promise of what the government would do than what it wouldn't. Twelve years earlier another President of the same generation had vowed that "we shall pay any price, bear any burden, meet any hardship, support any friend, oppose any foe, in order to assure the survival and the success of liberty." Now Nixon declared that "the time has passed when America will make every other nation's conflicts our own, or presume to tell the people of other nations how to manage their own affairs." At the same time he prepared to liquidate the domestic programs of liberal administrations with a paraphrase of President Kennedy's most memorable line. Nixon said, "Let each of us ask, not just what will government do for me, but what I can do for myself."

As he paused for effect, a faint sound could be heard from several blocks away. A group of youths was chanting: "Murderer!" "Out now!" "End racism!"

"It's disgusting," a woman from Iowa told a *New York Times* reporter. "Just disgusting. I don't see why we can't do something about these kids." Certainly it was indecorous. Yet counterdemonstrations, like the counterculture, were an expression of the continuing divisions in America, and they had to be endured. There is really no effective way to stifle dissent in an open society; if there were one, Magruder and his employer would have been the first to use it. The chanters—five hundred to a thousand Yippies, SDS militants, and members of the Maoist Progressive Labor Party— were the smallest and rudest band of protesters in the multitude of demonstrators roaming Washington that weekend. With them they carried a loathsome effigy—a ten-foot-long papier-mâché rat with Nixon's face, bearing in its teeth a bloodstained baby doll. That was too much even for the indulgent District police, and they confiscated it. But apart from that group the only really ugly gesture at the inaugural was the lowering of American flags around the Washington Monument and the hoisting of Viet Cong banners in their stead.

The stateliest protest had been held in the Washington Cathedral on Wisconsin Avenue at 9 P.M. the previous evening. After brief remarks by Dean Francis B. Sayre Jr. and former Senator Eugene McCarthy, Leonard Bernstein led a pickup orchestra of local musicians in the gentle, contemplative strains of Haydn's *Mass in Time of War*, with its urgent kettledrums and its final plea, "*Dona nobis pacem*" (Give us peace). In counterpoint, across the city Eugene Ormandy and the Philadelphia Orchestra were saluting the President with Tchaikovsky's bombastic *1812 Overture*. Sixteen of Ormandy's musicians had been excused because they felt it would be demeaning to play before such an audience. Presumably their absence removed any threat to Nixon's life. Even so, the firing of blanks in a cannon, usually the climax of the overture, was omitted at the request of the Secret Service. It was one of the service's less expensive suggestions under that President.

That same evening, critics of Nixon's record in Vietnam delivered to a White House guard a petition setting forth their views. On the sidewalk outside, Father Philip Berrigan performed in a crude skit meant to show how the authorities had mistreated those who had dared to speak out against them. Berrigan pretended to manhandle a woman carrying a peace placard. Lest anyone miss the point of the drama, the priest wore a large sign around his neck reading POLICE. The next day Daniel Ellsberg, who at that time faced possible conviction and sentences totaling 115 years for publishing the Pentagon Papers, addressed a testimonial dinner held by the National Peace Action Coalition. Ellsberg ridiculed the President's inaugural promise of a generation of peace, saying, "He's winding down the war like he's winding down my indictment," and comparing the manufacturers of Vietnam war matériel to the designers of the Nazi death camp at Auschwitz.

Berrigan and Ellsberg were seen by few, but most of the counter-inauguration events were well attended. The Bernstein concert was heard by 3,000 people in the cathedral and another 12,000 to 15,000 who stood in the dank night outside and listened to it over loudspeakers. The petition had been signed by 50,000. And the largest demonstration of all, timed, like the SDS march, to coincide with the President's address on Capitol Hill, drew between 75,000 and 100,000. It began when 2,500 members of the Vietnam Veterans Against the War marched from Arlington National Cemetery to the Washington Monument, continued with the signing of a mock peace treaty there, and ended with an address by New York Congresswoman Bella Abzug, who had been listening to Nixon's speech over a transistor radio and bellowed out her opinion of it.

Some youths in the audience carried obsolete signs reading STOP THE BOMBING. That was ludicrous. The blitz had been stopped three weeks earlier. Other gestures of protest also bordered on the ridiculous. Some of them were wholly unrelated to Vietnam; as Nixon spoke, a tiny biplane, rented by a disgruntled millionaire and closely shepherded by police and Air Force helicopters, trailed a banner which read LEGALIZE GOLD. But there was nothing absurd about the concept of protest. It was far truer to the American spirit than the inaugural address, the cannonless Tchaikovsky overture, and the 1,976 saucily dressed Virginia high school musicians who paraded past the White House, a tribute to Jeb Magruder's vision of what the nation's second centennial would be all about.

In the darkest year of Joe McCarthy a West Virginia college president, testifying in behalf of an embattled liberal, was asked by counsel what America represented to him. He replied that it was "the right to be different." He did not mean merely the eccentric and the whimsically wrong, though there will always be room in the United States for, say, the astrologists, the believers in flying saucers, and the Republican statesmen who bought big Washington houses in 1948 for occupancy during the first Dewey administration. But if liberty is to signify anything substantive, it must also be extended to the last limits of the endurable, shielding under its broad tent the genuinely unpopular champions of causes which the majority regards as reprehensible. Any people can cheer an Eisenhower, a MacArthur, a John Glenn, a Neil Armstrong; it takes generosity of spirit to suffer the Weathermen who hated LBJ, the Birchers who baited JFK, the Liberty Leaguers who heckled FDR.

In the lengthening memories of Americans who were entering their fifties in the Nixon years, the strains on the nation's tolerance had been great. Sometimes it had been too much, and the names of the places where patience was exhausted stain the pages of U.S. history with shame: Attica, Kent State, My Lai, Birmingham, Oxford, the Republic Steel plant in Chicago, the California camps where Americans of Japanese descent were penned up during World War II; and the Bonus Army camp on Anacostia Flats whose destruction was described in the first pages of this book.

Yet they were exceptions. A list of examples of forbearance would be many times longer, and might be regarded as a national roll of libertarian honor. It would include the names of Angela Davis, the Berrigans, Stokely Carmichael, Dr. Spock, the Chicago Seven, Woodstock, Ti-Grace Atkinson, the American Nazis who carried "Free Gas for Peace Creeps" signs, the captain of the *Pueblo*, the Fair Play for Cuba Committee, Edwin Walker, SANE's Linus Pauling, Rosa Parks, the America Firsters, Earl Browder, the Shrine of the Little Flower, William Dudley Pelley, Huey Long, Gerald L. K. Smith, and the emaciated wraiths who greeted the 72nd Congress, on its return to Washington in December 1932, by singing "The International."

Defiers of the popular will, like those who give it voice, deserve remembrance; but so do the silent witnesses who kept the key figures alert and honest and strengthened the country's democratic institutions simply by their presence. In time of crisis they gathered quietly in Lafayette Park, just across Pennsylvania Avenue from the White House; a President had but to look out a window and there they were, reminding him that his employers were watching. They were conspicuously in attendance at the great congressional hearings in which the country's temper was being tested, and often its policy forged, through the past forty years, weighing the Vietnam War, Sherman Adams and Bernard Goldfine, the Bricker Amendment, the Army-McCarthy controversy, the hoodlums exposed by Estes Kefauver, Hiss and Chambers, the five-percenters, Pearl Harbor, Roosevelt's plan for Supreme Court reform, and the part played by Wall Street in the Great Depression. They were the spectators when the Taft bell tower was dedicated, they mourned when Roosevelt and Eisenhower lay in state, and they stood in stricken silence on November 25, 1963, as a caisson bearing the body of John Kennedy clattered across Memorial Bridge toward Arlington and the eternal flame.

There is a school of historians which holds that great events may tell us less about the past than the trivia accumulated by ordinary people—the letters, pressed flowers, prom programs, cherished toys and the like saved by those who loved them and could not bear to throw them away. From time to time construction workers will stumble across such caches, sometimes entombed in old mansions. Occasionally they may find something almost as elaborate as the Westinghouse time capsule which was buried at the New York World's Fair of 1939. Such discoveries always excite curiosity, and the older ones stir speculation over what this or that article meant to people at the time it was put away. With the growing mobility of Americans the accumulation of such troves is rarer, but if members of the swing generation had one—put away, perhaps, in a storeroom the size of Fibber McGee's fabled closet—it might provide insight into what they had been like, what they had endured, what their dreams had been, and which had been realized and which dashed.

Envisaging such a cupboard, we see in front on the top shelf a steel tennis racket, several dieting books, a wide necktie, and a pantsuit broad in the beam. Just behind them are a "Welcome Home POWs" bumper sticker, one for MIAs ("Only Hanoi Knows"), and a peace decal; then a brass-colored PT boat tie clip, and cassette recordings of *Camelot*, Arlo Guthrie's *Alice's Restaurant*, and Carol Channing's *Hello, Dolly*. Behind them, well hidden in a corner beneath a pile of tie-dyed jeans, are well-thumbed copies of *Fanny Hill* and *The Autobiography of a Flea*.

Various items of clothing occupy much of the space on the second shelf: a sheath dress, a gray flannel suit, a man's narrow-brimmed felt hat, several incredibly narrow neckties, a child's coonskin cap, and a straw boater with the legend I LIKE IKE on the hatband. Concealed beneath them is an obsolete item of female apparel: a diaphragm in a white plastic case. Beyond is a curious little silver lapel pin. It resembles the bottom of a man's shoe with a hole in the sole. Nearby are a *My Fair Lady* album, a record of Edith Piaf singing *"Il Pleut,"* a Winky Dink kit, a Mouseketeer cap, and a collapsed Babee-Tenda. Copies of *Fireman Small* and *Peyton Place* lie on top of miscellaneous papers: a pamphlet on how to stop smoking, a Fish House Punch recipe, an *Around the World in Eighty Days* program, a batch of bills from a diaper service, and an envelope containing plans for a home bomb shelter (never opened).

Near the front of the third shelf is a Dior New Look skirt, an Eisenhower jacket which appears to have been worn by a slender man, early nylons, a freshman beanie, a copy of *Tropic of Cancer*, and under it a packet of three Trojans. (They sold for a dollar.) Various certificates: military discharge, marriage license, college diplomas. A ruptured duck pin. An Army divisional patch. Rationing stamps. Navy dog tags, long tarnished. A packet of V-letters. A Nazi helmet; a samurai sword. A Kate Smith Columbia record: "God Bless America." A rhinestone V-for-Victory pin.

The bottom shelf is rather junky. A pair of Thom McAn saddle shoes, very dirty, stand on top of an equally soiled reversible raincoat, beneath which is a sport coat with a belted back. A dead corsage is pressed between two 78 rpm records—"Deep Purple" and "Stardust." Beside them lie campaign pins reading "We Want Willkie" and "FDR." A third pin is shaped like a sunflower. Then: a shabby Philco radio in the form of an arch, a tattered copy of *Gone With the Wind*, a copy of *Ulysses* in which only the last forty pages seem to have been read, Boy and Girl Scout handbooks, and several square Big Little Books. There is a dusty Lionel train transformer, a jump rope, several marbles and one steelie, a splintered hockey stick, a well-oiled first baseman's mitt, a Shirley Temple doll, a sheaf of bubble gum cards, a G-man cap gun. Two Post Toasties box tops. A box of cherry bombs. A Bolo ball attached by elastic to a paddle. A pair of brown corduroy knickers. A hair ribbon. An old stand-up telephone.

Lastly, on the floor of the closet, are a batch of snapshots taken with a box Brownie. There are automobiles in them: a Model A Ford with the windshield down in some, a Chevy sporting a sassy rumble seat in others, and in the older ones, brown with age, a Model T. People are posing by the running boards. It is summer, yet the adults look very formal. The men are wearing stiff collars, the women vast hats and shapeless cotton dresses. But it is the children who seem oddest. Like their parents they are quaintly dressed. There is something else, though. It takes a moment to realize why they look so peculiar. Then you see it. There is an intensity in their expressions. They are leaning slightly forward, as though trying to see into the future. And they are smiling.

Acknowledgments

Harry Sions, the editor of this book, died in Philadelphia on March 26, 1974, when the manuscript was in the final stages of preparation for the press. He had completed his final review of the text just a few days earlier. For over seventeen years he was a colleague and a cherished friend; his skill and high intelligence left their mark on every page of this volume, as well as on much of my earlier work.

Don Congdon, my literary agent for a quarter-century, planted the seed for the book by suggesting a study of the American national character. Together with Harry and J. Randall Williams of Little, Brown, he was an unfailing source of encouragement and sound advice. The support of Don and Randy Williams was immense, and is most gratefully acknowledged.

Several other associates and acquaintances were generous with suggestions and insight. I am particularly indebted to Henry Anatole Grunwald, Herman Kahn, Louis Lasagna M.D., Daniel Patrick Moynihan, Arthur M. Schlesinger Jr., and Eric Sevareid. In addition, Harry McMahan of *Advertising Age* was a treasure of information in his special field.

My invaluable assistant, Margaret Kennedy Rider, was loyal, resourceful, and tireless during the long years of research and writing. Epsey Farrell was of great help in her role as researcher, and I am appreciative of the assistance of Ellen G. D'Oench in annotating the manuscript.

No expression of thanks to Wyman Parker, Librarian of Wesleyan

University, and the staff of the university's Olin Library, can really be adequate. For fifteen years they have sheltered me, cheered me, guarded my privacy, and given unstintingly of their considerable technical skills. At a time when their stacks are crammed, all I can give them in return is another book, and an outsize one at that. Moreover, it is imperfect, as all books are. It is true, insofar as diligence and research can establish truth, but it is not the whole truth. No volume, nor even a whole library, can provide that. All an author can offer is a fragment of reality—that, and the hope that it will endure.

CHAPTER NOTES

In these Notes, works are generally cited by the author's name only; for full listings see the Bibliography. If the note is citing an author with more than one work in the Bibliography, a brief title for the work cited is also given in the note. Other forms of citation are:

Fab Time-Life series *This Fabulous Century* (see entries at Maitland A. Edey and Jerry Korn in the Bibliography)

NYT *New York Times*

TA Time Annual *1969: The Year in Review*

T *Time* magazine

TC Time-Life series *Time Capsule* (see entry at Maitland A. Edey in the Bibliography)

W Associated Press series *The World in—* (see listing at Keith Fuller in the Bibliography)

WA *World Almanac* (cited with the year)

WM Author's interviews

The words identifying each note are the *end* of the paragraph which the note covers.

PROLOGUE: ROCK BOTTOM
(*pages 1–32*)

1 "Bonus Expeditionary Force": NYT 1/31/32; T 8/15/32; Schlesinger *Crisis* 256; *Baltimore Sun* 7/17/32. 2 off to jail: Fab IV 25. and multiplying misery: *Baltimore Sun* 7/17/32. to the country: *Baltimore Sun* 7/27/32; WM/Herman Kahn 6/5/70; *Washington* 29; Acheson 16–17, 91. *3* on ruling them. Mullett 3–8; "Who's in the Army Now?", elaborate buzzer system: Daniels 181; Gene Smith 12, 48; *Washington* 11. *4* Ike came scurrying: *Saturday Evening Post* 12/20/30; Gene Smith 48; *Washington* 11; NYT 12/25/29, 7/27/41; WM/Herman Kahn; *Foreign Service Journal* February 1955; Eisenhower *Ease* 210; WM/Eisenhower 8/27/64. *5* was rich: *Ease* 219–20; "Who's in the Army Now?"; Rovere *Years* 13; NYT 10/2/43; Mellor 129–30; Farago 105; *Washington* 601. colonies in 1776: T 2/8/32; "Who's in the Army Now?". "an ungraceful angle": "Who's in the Army Now?" *6* trolley car. NYT 9/1/43; WM/Eisenhower; Adams 155. a cottage industry: WM/Herman Kahn; *Washington* xix; Phillips *Blitz* 294–95. "Dat's de propolition": *Washington* xxi, 3, 83, 87; Schlesinger *Upheaval* 428. 7 great god macadam: NYT 5/15/48; Van Camp. *8* D.C., was like: Sylvia Porter "The Vanishing Trains" *Middletown Press* 12/9/69. to American business: NYT 4/29/32, 5/11/32, 4/24/32, 1/17/32; *Washington* 945; "Washington Through the Years"; NYT 2/4/32, 11/9/32; *Washington* 117, 918. 9 scheduled for razing: "Washington Through the Years"; NYT 2/4/32, 11/9/32; *Washington* 117, 918; Shuster 64, 105. exactly what he did: Galbraith *State* 359; *Baltimore Sun* 7/27/32; NYT 7/29/32; Daniels 193. *10* "anywhere in the world": NYT 7/21/32; *Baltimore Sun* 6/5/32, 6/8/32, 6/9/32, 6/10/32, 6/19/32, 6/27/32; T 6/13/32; Gene Smith 136. *11* "their individual cases": NYT 6/19/32; *Ease* 209; Gene Smith 135. about patriotism: NYT 7/29/32; Daniels 192; Gene Smith 152. *12* Chicago's southwest side: NYT 8/17/32, 8/2/32, 7/29/32; T 8/8/32. *13* chief of staff: NYT 7/29/32; *Baltimore Sun* 7/29/32; *Boston Herald* 7/29/32; T 8/8/32; Gene Smith 156. bitterly resented it: Congdon 117; Rovere and Schlesinger 31–33; *Ease* 159, 212. *14* solicitude toward civilians: Gene Smith 159. suit, and all: *Baltimore Sun* 7/29/32; Walter Johnson 3–5; Gene Smith 161. "his mouth again": T 8/8/32. *15* drove him out: Gene Smith 161. *16* his next move: *Ease* 213. disobey a President: Walter Johnson 3–5; *Ease* 213; Fab IV 25–26; *Ease* 213. *17* "feel for them": Fab IV 25–26; T 8/8/32; *Ease* 213; Gene Smith 162. George S. Patton Jr.: Daniels 194; *Crisis* 263; NYT 7/30/32; T 8/8/32; Mellor 103–28. *18* "heroes just now": T 8/8/32. "would surprise me": NYT 7/29/32, 8/4/32; T 8/8/32; Gene Smith 164, 166. "law and order": NYT 7/30/32; Congdon 119; *New Republic* 11/2/32; *Crisis* 263–64. *19* a difficult task: *Baltimore Sun* 7/29/32; "Who's in the Army Now?". "the Bonus marchers?" *Crisis* 261; Daniels 193. *20* "in terrible shape": Gene Smith 169. land in 1932: NYT 7/30/32; Bird 56; *Nation* 8/17/32. *21* "the next station": *Blitz* 40–41; Congdon 102; *Crisis* 251; T 2/6/33; *Blitz* 285; Mowry 75; Walter Johnson 16; WM/Eric Sevareid; Congdon 102, 110. far from home: Sevareid *Dream* 49; *Nation* 8/24/32; Walter Johnson 23; NYT 12/11/32. *22* his old menus: NYT 5/4/32. "real estate company": NYT 9/19/31. *23* "with very pity": *Esquire* June 1960; Bird 24; Wolfe 413–14. "Yes, sir": Goldman *Tragedy* 377; *Time* editors 24; *Tragedy* 274; *Relief for Unemployed Transients* 35–38. *24* venereal infection: Minehan 67–71. and, later, militancy: NYT 3/26/31, 1/20/32; *Upheaval* 428–29; Congdon 171; Bird 130; T 4/10/33, 4/17/33, 12/11/33. day was inevitable: Minehan 18–83. *25* for a quarter: NYT 8/2/41; T 5/12/41. "them at night": Congdon 152; Gene Smith 80; NYT 3/5/29; Gene Smith 206. return of prosperity: Gene Smith 66. *26* such incredible speed: Wolff 198; Gene Smith 97. "both of them": NYT 3/2/32. *27* might be softened: *Years* 78; Walter Johnson 27. people be tabled: Galbraith *Affluent* 15; NYT 1/5/32; Isabel Leighton 277. *28* legislatures, not Congress: Fab IV 25; Leary; Bird 208–209. the building trades: *Crisis* 57; Childs "Main Street"; Sulzberger 27. "make things worse": NYT 1/20/32; *Crisis* 164; *Affluent* 16; Gene Smith 76. *29* would win: Schwartz xiii, xiv; *Affluent* 45; Gene Smith 68. "political log-rolling!": T 5/30/32. "grandiloquent egotists": Mowry 57; *Crisis* 80. *30* "Depression is over": Bird 13. "spare a dime": NYT 12/3/30; Bird 58; *Crisis* 241; T 4/4/32. *31* Business Confidence Week: *Crisis* 177. "worn-out private belongings": Fab IV 76; NYT 1/4/32; Isabel Leighton 222. on American newsstands: *Middletown Press* 7/27/32; headlines T 8/8/32.

I THE CRUELEST YEAR
(pages 35–82)

35 could not understand: Gene Smith 103. "protect my children?": NYT 9/6/29; Mowry 68; Gene Smith 81. *36* "to the community": *Commonweal* 9/3/54; Bird 41. overextension of credit: Allen *Change* 144. *37* "got too little": Mowry 64. without historical precedent: Bird 115. *38* jobs was $16.21: Shannon 73; Phillips *Blitz* 32, 34. Howard Johnson, survived: Allen *Since* 132; *Time* editors 63; NYT 3/2/33, 2/6/32; *Theatre Arts* April 1931. *39* "off my pants": *Time* editors 65; Bird 12; T 12/19/32; *Since* 108. *40* a peculiar gait: Bird 226; Schlesinger *Crisis* 167. she could imagine: Bird 227. and an undertaker: Fab IV 46; Bird 40, 116; Shannon 12, 26. *41* dunes of garbage: Shannon 10; Bird 21. an entire family: *Crisis* 167; Bird 36. of their own: *Fortune* September 1932. *42* of two hundred: Gene Smith 174; NYT 1/19/33; Shannon 23. "the Depression, huh?": *Blitz* 34; Fab IV 54; Shannon 23. *43* called starvation wages: Bird 68; Shannon 26. until after sunset: Congdon 36, 45, 47. *44* began to disintegrate: *Crisis* 248; T 3/13/33. and the indigent: Bird 63. game called Eviction: ibid 27. *45* population of 600,000: *American Academy* January 1933. "bill before delivery": Bird 134. excluded from churches: ibid 26. *46* filthy old sheepskin: Schlesinger *Coming* 268; *Blitz* 257. began to disappear: Shannon 93–103 passim. *47* twenty million dollars: ibid 94. thin pocketbooks: ibid 99. "poor people were": NYT 3/8/32. *48* "to our children?": *Crisis* 3; Shannon 53; Fab IV 53. dying of hunger: *Fortune* September 1932; Bird 32. *49* "days of 1932":

Crisis 250; Wolfe 412. might be misunderstood: Bird 19. *50* "mighty vaults": Wolfe 414. "went to hell": *Newsweek* 2/17/33; NYT 2/6/32; Gene Smith 24. *51* "of the lowest": NYT 3/30/32; Congdon 612. couldn't help them. *Crisis* 190; NYT 3/11/32; Daniels 189. "policeman searches you": NYT 6/29/32, 4/14/32; T 10/17/32, *Crisis* 118. *52* taxes in full: *Blitz* 134; Bird 10; NYT 4/26/33; Daniels 183. "ammunition for radicals": NYT 5/12/33, 2/11/32; *New Republic* 5/29/35; T 1/25/32. *53* from trusting investors: T 3/21/32; NYT 3/13/32. "completely shattered": NYT 5/21/33; T 6/19/33; *Time* editors 31. *54* it had become: NYT 6/7/32, 7/29/32; *Crisis* 109; John Brooks *Golconda* 137. he liked it: Mowry 55; NYT 11/8/28; *Crisis* 280. "economic pyramid": NYT 4/8/32. "rich against poor!": NYT 4/14/32; T 4/25/32. *55* "have another Hoover": *Crisis* 175, 280, 288; NYT 7/10/32, 6/11/32; T 7/4/32. "still a Hoover": Rovere *Years* 18; *Crisis* 290. *56* were very direct: NYT 4/27/32, 5/5/32, Gene Smith 116. "here again!" Gene Smith 114. *57* campaign had begun: *Crisis* 309; T 8/8/32. *58* to "brain trust": NYT 7/3/32, 5/23/32; *Since* 78. danger of accidents: T 7/31/33; Fab IV 141. *59* endorse any candidate. *Crisis* 428; Mowry 86. General MacArthur: Gene Smith 178; NYT 11/11/32, 10/16/32. "this extraordinary hour". *Crisis* 434; *Nation* 7/13/32. *60* four years later: T 11/21/32; NYT 9/24/32, 6/17/33; *Crisis* 413, 416. *61* "of lost children". *Crisis* 428. Johnson of California NYT 9/13/32; Walter Johnson 37, *62* phoned Calvin Coolidge *Crisis* 194, 199, 204; NYT 11/6/32. would be dead: *Crisis* 201; NYT 10/12/32; T 10/24/32 *63* words had become. Walter Johnson 37; T 11/7/32; NYT 11/8/32; *Crisis* 437 Franklin Delano Ragin: NYT 11/9/32; *Crisis* 218, 437; *Blitz* 73. "do this job": Gene Smith 214 *64* was right: Walter Johnson 45; NYT 11/13/32; Bird 78. "world's in birth". NYT 12/6/32, *Crisis* 448; Shannon 120. *65* "and farmers' republic": NYT 11/8/32; Congdon 148. *66* smashed her face: NYT 1/15/33; *Blitz* 5; *Crisis* 166. "the American system": NYT 3/23/32; Shannon 114; *Coming* 22 *67* "left-wing state". *Crisis* 208; NYT 8/30/32; Bird 116. *68* of Columbia University: *Crisis* 204, 460; NYT 1/26/32, 1/6/32; Schlesinger *Upheaval* 82 "one now" NYT 11/11/32; *Crisis* 266. in Sioux City: Bird 131; *Crisis* 266. *69* "was illegal too". NYT 8/14/32; Daniels 195; Shannon 123, 125. "of other days". NYT 8/22/32; Shannon 121 "eat their gold" *Crisis* 174, *Time* editors 32. *70* about mortgage foreclosures: NYT 8/26/32. press prosecution afterward: *Crisis* 459, T 5/8/33. *71* "than twelve months". T 1/16/33, 2/6/33, NYT 2/12/33; *Crisis* 459. *72* thirty-four years. Bird 4. these. O Pioneers! ibid 2. *73* before a bath *Gold 1940–41* 7. aluminum juice extractor: T 4/27/42. *74* about hair "coloring". *Gold 1940–41* 9, 12 *59* million dollars: *Science* 5/12/33; WM/Louis Lasagna; *Blitz* 433. best friend's thoughts: Sevareid *Dream* 4. *76* Lindbergh's *We*: NYT 8/7/27. "destined to encounter": *Gold 1940–41* 11. *77* "coal beds" "in a monarchy": Theodore White *1968* 99, 97. *78* clearly visible: T 10/10/32. palms of his hands: NYT 6/16/32; *Since* 16. and cherry bombs: *Gold 1940–41* 10. *80* R.N. stewardesses: Bird 2. service improves: Bird 264. "ten years ago": NYT 5/4/37, 11/10/32; T 4/4/32. *81* "my band, son": Bird 30; *Gold 1940–41* 48. paper victory: NYT 8/20/32, 9/23/32; Fab V 66. *82* death or even illness: NYT 2/28/32, 8/24/32; T 4/11/32.

II ROOSEVELT!
(pages 84–111)

84 the outgoing President: Schlesinger *Crisis* 440; NYT 2/5/53, 7/31/32; Gene Smith 222. *85* "in the future": NYT 11/23/32, 1/8/33; *Crisis* 441. it a holiday: NYT 2/14/33. *86* was "a madman": NYT 2/16/33; *Crisis* 474. had gone under: *Crisis* 466. *87* song for children: Bird 92, NYT 3/2/33, 2/5/33. "could not be greater": *Holiday* February 1960. *88* fog, toward Washington: NYT 3/6/33, 3/2/33. barometer was falling: NYT 3/3/33, 3/2/33. *89* two financial strongholds. NYT 3/3/33. "don't want to": NYT 3/4/33. "must go now": Gene Smith 225. *90* "we can do": NYT 3/3/33, 3/4/33; Fab IV 116. with a cameraman: Schlesinger *Coming* 424; NYT 3/1/33, 3/5/33. *91* "a foreign foe". NYT 3/5/33. *92* tell him so: Walter Johnson 49; Isabel Leighton 275; *Coming* 1. without moneychangers: NYT 3/5/33, 3/6/33; Bird 96. *93* "going any lower": *Holiday* February 1960. they had done: ibid. *94* going into action: NYT 3/10/33. *95* "Are Here Again": NYT 3/9/33; Phillips *Blitz* 120; John Brooks *Golconda* 155. "bit shell-shocked": NYT 3/10/33, 6/17/33; Gunther 139. *96* "Hitler much more": *Blitz* 106. one vast classroom: *Coming* 555. President's own wife: NYT 3/9/33; *Blitz* 473. *97* "wheels turning around": NYT 3/13/33; *Coming* 557. *98* had won it: *Coming* 530, 574. "is the President": ibid 511; NYT 3/5/33; T 7/31/33. *99* One note ran: Gunther 147; NYT 1/22/61. "President like you": Fab IV 136. "and in itself": ibid; *Coming* 424; T 3/13/33; NYT 3/19/33. "why they left": WM/Herman Kahn. *100* Kleberg's constituents: NYT 5/9/33; Bird 111; *Blitz* 234. "Lord, God Almighty": Acheson 151. them, especially Hiss: WM/Herman Kahn. those of congressmen: NYT 3/7/33, 2/27/33; T 8/21/33. *101* Texas to Canada: NYT 3/25/33; *Coming* 338; Fab IV 130. "the deflationary forces": *Golconda* 154, 155. *102* control for hogs: Isabel Leighton 284; NYT 5/13/33; T 8/21/33. "the United States!": NYT 5/21/33; TC 1930 145. *103* and Ickes achieved: *Coming* 264; NYT 11/8/33. the Florida mainland: NYT 11/9/33; Bird 108. first Nixon administration: NYT 7/12/36, 9/12/36, 5/7/46. *104* anything was possible: NYT 1/22/33. "ax won't work": NYT 6/17/33; Isabel Leighton 291. *105* "authority of government": NYT 6/17/33, 5/8/33; *Coming* 98. "restraint of competition": *Blitz* 218; NYT 11/2/33. *106* it looked real: NYT 8/14/33; T 7/31/33. "on the nose": Walter Johnson 68; T 8/7/33; *Blitz* 48. "back good times": NYT 7/25/33; *Blitz* 220. *107* "American economic life": *Coming* 119, 123; T 11/13/33. *108* had saved capitalism: Fab IV 116; *Blitz* 128. to ask him: T 8/14/33; Schlesinger *Upheaval* 451. *109–111* Eleanor Roosevelt portrait: *Current Biography* 1949, 1963; NYT 11/8/62.

III STIRRINGS
(*pages 112–147*)

112 "am for Johnnie": NYT 10/26/34; Fab IV 100, 109. *113* in her purse: NYT 7/23/34, 2/8/34; Daniels 240. and Clyde Barrow: NYT 7/26/34. *114* he had left: NYT 6/5/34, 6/10/34; Schlesinger *Coming* 294. *115* nascent Liberty League: NYT 9/26/34, 7/3/34; *Coming* 153, 463; John Brooks *Golconda* 198. "virtually terminated": T 4/3/33. concern was espionage: *Coming* 53; NYT 4/6/34. *116* left he could get: Kendrick 136. do the job: NYT 11/7/34. *117* New Year's Day: NYT 5/20/34, 8/30/34, 1/11/34, 8/8/34, 2/23/33. get some rain: NYT 5/29/34. was blowing away: NYT 1/27/37, 9/22/38; *Coming* 70; Brogan 82. *118* threatened with famine: Brogan 81; Walter Johnson 67; Shannon 131. on their floors: NYT 6/21/34; *Coming* 69; Fab IV 60. *119* at 108 degrees: Fab IV 61; NYT 8/13/34; Congdon 289. "off the earth": Phillips *Blitz* 240. *120* of Upton Sinclair: Daniels 247; Sevareid *Dream* 11; NYT 4/14/39; Fab IV 64. a generation later: Schlesinger *Upheaval* 117. the regular Democratic organization: *Upheaval* 111; Daniels 248. "going on before": NYT 9/2/34; *Upheaval* 34. *121 I Got Licked:* NYT 2/24/35; Daniels 248; *Upheaval* 118. New York City: NYT 9/10/36, 11/6/36, 11/8/33. *122* or his effectiveness: NYT 9/17/33; Congdon 195. "support for reaction": NYT 11/18/34; *Upheaval* 176, 182. *123* "be USSA then": NYT 10/29/50; Schulberg 20; Allen *Since* 251. *124* "TAKE IT CLUB": NYT 8/23/34. his own good: NYT 10/25/34. *125* Days of 1935: NYT 10/16/34, 4/1/36, 6/5/35. *126* "perturbed at developments": NYT 1/5/35; *Upheaval* 391, 226. response was a fraud: NYT 4/2/35; *Upheaval* 311. *127* "hand, Mr. Chairman": NYT 8/9/35; Burns *Soldier* 362; *Blitz* 289. cents an hour: NYT 6/20/35. *128* bosses, and Negroes: NYT 5/30/34. "other crime bills": NYT 6/14/34, 7/5/34. *129* the early 1970s: NYT 1/23/35, 1/10/35, 2/5/35, 4/1/35. claim was undisputed: NYT 12/1/35; *Upheaval* 4; Isabel Leighton 242. *130* "let me know": Spivak 6. "toes against eternity": *Upheaval* 20; NYT 12/26/35; T 4/10/33. *131* ground between them: Carlson 58. the political center: NYT 6/9/36, 4/29/34. *132* "the labor problem": Isabel Leighton 241. "we will win": NYT 7/20/35; T 4/10/33; Carlson 57; Isabel Leighton 248. *133* "a holy war": Carlson 58. "unbalanced college professors": Daniels 253. *134* William Howard Taft: NYT 8/18/46. in American politics: NYT 2/1/35. *135* "still weep here": Daniels 204. "of my path": NYT 1/26/32. *136* Avenue in Washington: *Upheaval* 56. "lead the mob": NYT 9/22/35; Daniels 240–43; *Upheaval* 66. *137* his own constituents: Walter Johnson 83–86; Congdon 315. "you want it": *Upheaval* 243–44. "honestly conducted election": Isabel Leighton 357. *138* "has an intellect": NYT 6/26/35; *Upheaval* 249. over the country: NYT 3/8/35. "man a king": *Upheaval* 65. *139* "in knee breeches": NYT 9/29/35. *140* "kill Huey Long": NYT 9/9/35; *Blitz* 302; NYT 9/10/35, 9/15/35; *Upheaval* 340. been dramatically different: *Upheaval* 341. *141* resembling a sermon: NYT 6/17/36. "in the scale": Schlesinger *Thousand* 720. a chain reaction: *Blitz* 296; NYT 7/5/36. *142* a familiar form: *Blitz* 420. *143* King of Swing: Gold *1936–37* 4. in the future: Gold *1940–41* 21. *144* "censorship as possible": Fab IV 180; Mowry 25; *Time* editors 151; T 2/20/33. United States in 1935: Mowry 5. *145* "their Bewildering Offspring": ibid 3. *146* introduced to him: *Blitz* 442. *147* the New Deal: *Time* editors 63; Mowry 112.

IV THE ROOSEVELT REFERENDUM
(pages 149–178)

149 to threats overseas: NYT 12/31/33. *150* America was chickenhearted: NYT 7/4/37. aggression in Manchuria: NYT 9/1/35. *151* "is fairly certain": NYT 6/5/34; Gunther 300. was forty-three: NYT 7/27/34; "Who's in the Army Now?" *152* Swarthmore '32; NYT 4/13/35; Schlesinger *Upheaval* 199; Simon 157, 168–69. *153* abolished it: Sevareid *Dream* 59. "right-minded students here". Phillips *Blitz* 477; T 10/3/32. desperately needed cash: NYT 11/9/35. *154* "starving by degrees". Simon 155; *Fortune* June 1936; Simon 155. the university library: Bird 242, Congdon 400. of juvenile distinction: *New Republic* 10/9/35. *155* and roller skates. Gold *1940–41* 21; Fab V 48. suits and white bucks: Gold *1940–41* 4. *156* all Duke dances: Fab IV 241; Gold *1940–41* 21. yet to come. Bird 238. progressive union policies: Fab IV 164; NYT 1/28/32. *157* "return their blows": Schlesinger *Coming* 138, 413. "of his youth": NYT 12/8/35; *Coming* 143. *158* "a quieting influence": Fab IV 164; *Coming* 394. "mines without them": *Coming* 385, NYT 7/17/34; Fab IV 162. *159* "dinkey parlezvous": Bird 149; NYT 2/16/36; *Blitz* 516. "just join up!". NYT 12/8/35. *160* over 400,000: NYT 9/28/34, 11/5/34. time for persuasion. NYT 12/1/34, 3/13/35, 5/17/35. *161* "their goddam heads": Daniels 255; Graham and Gurr 332; *Coming* 396; Bird 152. "of the race": Graham and Gurr 336 ff, 387, NYT 5/22/34; *Coming* 388. *162* underpaid, and sweated: NYT 7/1/34, 2/15/35; *Coming* 406. *163* of Industrial Organizations: Simon 107; NYT 10/20/35, 11/24/35, 12/8/35. "makes us strong!". *Coming* 415. *164* it was illegal: *Upheaval* 448, 451; Mowry 116, 118; NYT 10/30/35. *165* regulate interstate commerce. NYT 5/28/35. issuing a warning: NYT 5/30/35. *166* problems was forbidden. NYT 1/7/36, 5/19/36, 5/26/36; *Upheaval* 488. ceiling over hours. NYT 6/2/36. "of the Court". NYT 10/31/36. *167* one-term President. NYT 12/15/36 from the President; *Upheaval* 633. *168* than half that: Gunther 300; NYT 3/24/35; Daniels 305. OF COUNTRY LEADS. *Upheaval* 571. political assets, luck: ibid 502, 590. *169* the American temper. NYT 1/26/36. died before November. NYT 6/12/36, 6/14/36. paused for breath: NYT 6/11/36. *170* "for to free!". *Blitz* 484. Bell was cracked: Spivak 32; NYT 8/16/36; *Upheaval* 629. for a prayer: NYT 10/16/36. *171* "within the gates": NYT 6/24/36. "you ever saw": Congdon 435; NYT 6/28/36; *Upheaval* 584. *172* in New Orleans: NYT 6/1/36, 11/3/36. was a Communist. NYT 10/16/36. Landon didn't win. *Upheaval* 616. *173* social security number. NYT 10/24/36; *Upheaval* 635. bonfire in him: Congdon 439, 442; NYT 1/1/36. *174* after his departure: NYT 11/1/36; *Upheaval* 639. "campaign manager's prophecies?": WM/DPMoynihan; *Blitz* 488; Bird 181; *Upheaval* 608. out to *Time*: NYT 12/15/36, 11/4/36, 2/19/37; Wish 471; Daniels 275. *175* "known conservative tendencies": *Upheaval* 656. *175–178* Whitney portrait: John Brooks *Once in Golconda* 210–29; T 11/23/36, 3/21/38, 5/9/38, 5/16/38.

V THE CONSERVATIVE PHOENIX
(pages 179–207)

180 Dutch East Indies: NYT 6/23/37, 6/8/37. oxygen bomb calorimeter: Congdon 615 and passim. *181* (were Gap-Free): NYT 5/24/37. awaited television: Jack Goodman 279; NYT 3/19/37. kind of year: NYT 1/21/37. *182* "with muffled oars". Schlesinger *Upheaval* 494; Gunther 61; Schlesinger *Thousand* 869. "Chief Justice understood". NYT 1/7/37, *Time* editors 36. *183* the "Court pack". NYT 2/4/37. the same decision. NYT 3/11/37; Phillips *Blitz* 501. *184* "rendezvous with death". *Blitz* 501; NYT 3/10/37, 3/5/37. "the caucus room": *Blitz* 503; Simon 205. in his hand: NYT 3/30/37, 7/7/37, 7/15/37; Congdon 468. *185* was now acceptable. NYT 7/22/37; WA 1937; Congdon 475. including Johnson himself: Goldman *Tragedy* 258. *186* be kept moving: Daniels 285; NYT 3/21/34. "that's the trouble": NYT 3/6/37; Fab IV 164. *187* burst into tears. NYT 12/19/36, 12/29/36; Daniels 266. past the police: NYT 3/25/37. *188* major GM stockholder: NYT 1/1/37; Gunther 147. issuing a statement: Spivak 110; NYT 8/1/37; Gunther 147. SHALL NOT PASS. NYT 2/3/37. *189* "the right thing?": Fab IV 167; Bird 155. outside the plants: *Time* editors 70; Allen *Since* 82; NYT 2/7/37. he was underpaid: Fab IV 170; NYT 4/7/37. *190* "is nothing there": T 5/15/39, 12/2/40. meant to change: NYT 5/16/37; Fab IV 172; Daniels 267. *191* another conversation: NYT 10/27/37; *Since* 292. "Yes, Mr. Fairless": NYT 3/8/37. *192* meet workers' demands: *Blitz* 522–23; Bird 147; NYT 5/28/37. Court, was unmentioned: NYT 5/27/37; Fab

IV 172, 175. *193* "Solidarity Forever": NYT 5/31/37; Isabel Leighton 383 ff. *194* "women doing there?": NYT 6/20/37; Isabel Leighton 386 ff; Fab IV 176. much for them: Isabel Leighton 398; NYT 7/28/37. "intimidate the strikers": NYT 6/16/37; Fab IV 176. *195* except Bethlehem Steel: Isabel Leighton 396. "in our history": NYT 5/27/37. expanding middle class: Walter Johnson 159; NYT 10/29/37. *196* ideals to work: NYT 9/23/37, 2/28/37, 9/25/37. *197* "fifty times more": Bird 183; NYT 9/29/37. of 1929–30: *Since* 305 ff; NYT 10/20/37. was on relief: Mowry 295. *198* days, lay ahead: Galbraith *Affluent* 16; *Thousand* 626; NYT 5/1/38, 4/15/38; *Since* 311. "you would wish": Bird 184. *199* not party lines: *Saturday Evening Post* 9/22/34; Schlesinger *Coming* 483. "Grand!" across it: Daniels 301; *Coming* 569. *200* businessmen, was battoning: NYT 12/5/38. "that man's skin": Gunther 56. (Colonel van Rosenfeld): Daniels 300; John Brooks *Golconda* 215. *201* businessmen to Washington: Gunther 50. *202* had syphillis: Simon 111; *Golconda* 216. breathe freely again: NYT 8/15/39. in the fall: *Since* 232. *203* "the New Deal": NYT 7/13/38. could sense it: Mowry 120, 122; *Fortune* January, 1939. for Roosevelt's signature: *Time* editors 37. *204* ugly overture: *Blitz* 507–508. "my own name": NYT 6/25/38. *205* "a commanding position": Burns *Lion* 363, 365. *206* had been committed: NYT 7/9/38, 7/14/38, 7/17/38. New Deal legislation: NYT 7/8/38; *Lion* 363. "a working majority": NYT 9/18/40; *Thousand* 708. *207* "to the forest": *Lion* 366. "President's foreign policy": Childs "They Hate" and "They Still Hate." Empire of Japan: NYT 12/13/37.

VI A SHADOW OF PRIMITIVE TERROR
(pages 209–253)

209 convoying anybody: NYT 12/13/37. *210* to declare war: NYT 2/16/32. "remembered the *Maine*": NYT 4/20/38; Fehrenbach 294; Phillips *Blitz* 532. *211* Depression become comprehensible: T 5/29/39; NYT 2/2/37, 7/15/38; *Blitz* 532. doted on Europe: Rovere and Schlesinger 229. *212* "find no one there": NYT 10/6/37; Daniels 295; *Time* editors 292. "less given up": NYT 2/9/37; Daniels 295. Canada were attacked: NYT 12/22/37; *Blitz* 548; Cooke 2; Fehrenbach 294. *213* eight thousand casualties: NYT 7/22/37; Spivak 137; T 3/6/39. *214* United States with impunity: NYT 4/30/37, 1/11/38; Congdon 606. Americans in 1914–18: Daniels 295; NYT 10/9/38. *215* "two-ocean" Navy: NYT 1/29/38. for June 6: NYT 3/22/38, 10/16/38. to the dictators: NYT 10/7/38. *216* a ringside seat: NYT 9/13/37. "you do it?": NYT 5/13/37; *Time* editors 173; *Atlantic* September 1940. said they would try: Kendrick 157 ff. *217* American public opinion: ibid. *218* "'Heils' ('Hail Victory')": NYT 9/13/38. the Siegfried Line: Congdon 574. *219* the United States: ibid 575. *221* were still preferred: ibid 578. "basely betrayed": NYT 9/21/38. *222* "on its way": ibid. say about it: McCarthy *Hurricane* 3. *223* anything after all: NYT 9/20/38. out to sea: NYT 9/21/38, 9/20/38, 9/22/38. *224* that same night: NYT 9/22/38. *225* house blew away: *Hurricane* 14. only that morning: ibid 3. *226* twenty-nine corpses: NYT 9/23/38. in a nightmare: ibid. *227* was carried away: *Hurricane* 63. "in smoking ruins": ibid 57. U.S. Weather Bureau: ibid 141. *228* of American history: NYT 9/22/38, 9/23/38. "a social power": NYT 9/30/38. "will bring peace": Daniels 303; Fab IV 39. *229* Halloween in 1938: NYT 10/31/38. *230* Sunday prime time: *Blitz* 383; T 11/20/44. *231* everyone agreed: NYT 9/26/38, 10/31/38. *232–236* Quotations from the script are from Cantril. *236* "lot to do": Congdon 589. "Jersey and fire": Cantril 67, 112. *238* time would come: T 4/10/39; NYT 6/29/39. *239* had in mind: Fab IV 112. voice was changing: T 3/13/39; Gold *1940–41* 54. *239–240n Harper's* March 1933. *240* him "Mr. Christian": NYT 7/30/39. had ever known: *Time* editors 124. no Grover Whalen: NYT 2/19/39. *241* American society: NYT 2/5/39; Fab IV 268. own food: NYT 5/17/39. *242* fourteen-lane turnpikes: Fab IV 280. "of Hell": NYT 5/15/39. to Hyde Park: NYT 6/11/39. *243* was "half-caste": NYT 6/12/39. tried to retire: T 7/24/39. of bad weather: NYT 9/16/39, 7/6/39; Rovere and Schlesinger 130. *244* "in my belt": NYT 7/19/39. *245* the experimental stage: NYT 5/24/39. *246* "Bullitt, Mr. President" (and next three paragraphs): T 9/11/39; NYT 9/1/39. "Deutschland über Alles": T 9/18/39, 9/25/39. *247* "about salt water": Fehrenbach 29. meant by neutrality: NYT 9/4/39, 9/14/39; T 9/18/39. *248* "willing to answer": NYT 11/3/40. epithet stuck: Fehrenbach 45. *249* however, sleep long: NYT 4/21/39, 5/14/39.

VII THROUGH THE NIGHT WITH A LIGHT FROM ABOVE
(pages 254-287)

254 was Viennese: Saturday Evening Post 9/7/40. life in ruins: Laurence 32. 255 "that so long?": NYT 11/11/38, 1/29/39. destroy the world: Jungk 71, 75. 256 powerful as TNT: NYT 1/3/39, Laurence 34. 257 on the blackboard: Laurence 35, 44. 258 spread the news: NYT 4/30/39, Laurence 37. ahead of them: Laurence 48. 260 "surrounding territory": Burns Soldier 249; Laurence 85. and two glasses. Laurence 83. 261 "requires action". ibid 86. on another ship: ibid, 88. 262 across the Atlantic. NYT 1/20/40; Scholastic 10/14/40. by Reynaud himself: NYT 5/15/40, 6/1/40. "liberation of the Old": NYT 6/23/40, 8/23/40. "shall never surrender": NYT 11/16/40. 263 hundred feet below. Fehrenbach 210. "to fight alone": NYT 6/14/40. "wish to live": NYT 12/18/40. 264 "them all dead": NYT 9/8/40. "talk about that": NYT 6/19/40. 265 movements ever since: NYT 7/14/40, 6/5/42, 11/27/42. diamonds, for $5,000: T 7/28/41. United States intervened: ibid. 266 Air Corps colonel: NYT 4/26/41, 4/29/41. 267 the speech "inexcusable": NYT 5/13/42; Fehrenbach 272. "name in Indochina": T 7/8/40; Fehrenbach 84. 268 on their hands: Fehrenbach 59, 101. the American people: NYT 3/1/40. 269 freighters to England: NYT 2/24/42. planes a year: Fab V 22. "the two deals": NYT 6/11/40. 270 board of directors. Fehrenbach 175; NYT 1/21/41. booed Churchill's name. NYT 4/24/41. Washington Times-Herald: NYT 9/4/40. 271 Training and Service Bill: NYT 9/17/40, 9/2/40. as U.S. citizens: American Mercury April 1940. was Lewis B. Hershey: Life 9/30/40; NYT 9/30/40. 272 "have been selected": Vital Speeches 9/1/40. Roosevelt was skating. Life 8/18/41. "rendered in this": Fehrenbach 267. 273 them Wendell L. Willkie: John Brooks Leap 307, T 7/8/40. after the election: T 9/23/40. "the White House!": Daniels 309, 319. 274 the Nazis' choice: Fehrenbach 109; Daniels 317. Superintendent of Sewers: Fab V 23. "any foreign wars": NYT 10/31/40. the White House: Walter Johnson 137. 275 Wall Street Journal: NYT 11/7/40. the same boat: T 8/26/40. 276 "are at war": T 6/24/40. 278 "to the bone"?: NYT 12/4/40. as lend-lease: Burns Soldier 25. it "in kind": NYT 12/18/40; Soldier 26. 279 "the United States": Soldier 45. to start now: NYT 12/30/40. "devoutly hope not": Fab V 25; Christian Century 2/19/41. 280 Duce any more?: T 3/3/41, 3/24/41. the western hemisphere: NYT 12/13/41, 4/11/41. 281 "North Atlantic war". Fehrenbach 227. policy, was inevitable: NYT 6/29/41. 282 "OK FDR": Soldier 91. "probably the time": NYT 7/8/41. 283 dangerous Murmansk run: NYT 6/22/41, 6/24/41. (he said wryly): NYT 2/19/41. 284 the Atlantic Charter: T 4/28/41. "no formal document": NYT 8/22/41. 285 that they approved: NYT 9/5/41. "of our nation": NYT 10/18/41; Soldier 147. "good Reuben James?" NYT 11/1/41. 286 on Japan, too: Life 10/7/40. the American Navy: Soldier 142. in the theater: Soldier 149. 287 December 10, 1941: NYT 12/7/41.

VIII AMERICA ON THE BRINK
(pages 289-317)

289 for sheer survival: NYT 7/14/40; Newsweek 4/28/41. 290 $832 a year: Burns Soldier 53; T 5/12/41, 9/22/41. rheumatic heart disease: T 5/12/41. times a week: American Journal of Sociology November 1942; Lifton 199. friend five cents: NYT 1/13/42, 4/15/42, 6/30/42, 9/22/42, 12/11/42. 291 condoms than haircuts: Bird 213; Fortune December 1937. 292 on a battlefield. John Brooks Leap 30, NYT 5/21/40. cost a quarter. Leap 29; NYT 6/13/34. 293 in "illicit relations": Gold 1940-41 31, American Magazine August 1941; Leap 28. no longer used: Chapman 28. 294 separate fraternities: NYT 2/23/41. 295 fighting this war: T 10/28/40; Soldier 266. "straight to hell": Fortune June 1942; Soldier 463; Bird 46; T 6/16/41; Current Biography 1943. in the North: Leap 276; Bird 45; Time editors 153; Soldier 463. 296 1960s were born: Leap 279. "next Brown Bomber": T 9/29/41; Gold 1940-41 10. "NAACP-type production": Gold 1941-42 25, 27. 297 her own people: ibid 27. American Presidents: Survey November 1942; Soldier 123. 298 in Constitution Hall: Leap 275; NYT 2/23/29. outdoor concert possible: NYT 3/31/39. "I can, too": NYT 2/28/39; Congdon 622. 299 the assembly line: NYT 6/26/40; T 1/6/41. and Virginia Woolf: T 1/27/41, 2/10/41, 4/7/41, 4/14/41. "unmolested by authority": Time editors 155; Life 5/12/41; NYT 5/4/48, 5/9/41; Eisinger 235, 240. 300 December 7, 1941; NYT 7/21/41, 5/3/41. "from behind": Allen Since 138. 301 sharp hostesses: T 1/31/44; Gold 1940-41 21 and passim.

substitute "outlets": *Leap* 238. *302* "on beaches": ibid 10; NYT 9/11/41. demanding private showers: T 4/1/40. "he is mad": T 3/4/40. *303* "and moral views": NYT 3/11/40; T 3/11/40. won round two: T 3/25/40. and "narrow-minded": T 4/8/40. happier about it: WA 1940. *304* the United States: T 4/8/40. *305* urgent, inexplicable request: WA 1941; NYT 10/6/41, 8/12/41, 8/17/41; Daniels 336. cruises to Hawaii: Daniels 336. kill 2,403 Americans: NYT 12/9/41. armed forces—oil: Fehrenbach 297. *306* vehemently anti-Japanese: NYT 12/7/41. Germany and Italy: *Life* 10/7/40; *Soldier* 20. "are no taxicab": T 8/4/41, 9/22/41. *307* neighboring countries: *Soldier* 135–36; Fehrenbach 304. in the Orient: NYT 10/17/41; *Soldier* 146. "at Pearl Harbor": T 11/26/45. *309* know about war?: *Soldier* 78; T 12/10/45. "on Pearl Harbor": T 12/31/45. *310* NOT A DRILL: Daniels 341. *311* bow them out . . . toward the door: *Soldier* 162–63. ATTACK PEARL HARBOR: Sulzberger 144. *312* THE STATE DEPARTMENT: ibid. would be back: NYT 12/18/41; Fab V 71. *313* "fishy to me": Fab V 71. treacherous Orientals: NYT 12/8/41. a Pacific Fleet: Gunther 330. *314* "in Valdosta, Georgia": Daniels 343. "Come anyway" . . . "of peace": Kendrick 239. "On the *ground!*": Fab V 71. *315* "fog of battle": ibid. *316* would dive: ibid. *317* "national interest required": Acheson 37.

IX COUNTERATTACK
(*pages 321–351*)

General source for WWII in the Pacific: William Manchester "Our War in the Pacific" *Holiday* November 1960 pp. 110–11, 152–67. *321* lost a war: NYT 11/29/45. *322* the sky then: T 1/12/42. offensive at once: NYT 1/2/42. coastal waters: NYT 1/2/42, 1/17/42, 1/15/42, 1/20/42, 3/4/42. *323* and San Francisco: NYT 2/3/43, 4/29/42; *Life* 8/10/42; *Time* editors 43; Burns *Soldier* 212. Malaya: NYT 12/15/41. *324* couldn't be turned: NYT 12/8/41, 1/28/42, 1/3/42. "gives a damn": NYT 12/11/41, 3/18/42; T 3/30/42; Rovere and Schlesinger 56. *325* to their fate: NYT 9/27/42, 2/22/42. Abandon Ship: NYT 3/14/42, 3/15/42. the New Hebrides?: NYT 9/30/42. *326* lovely flame trees: NYT 11/2/43. *327* unearthly splendor: *Newsweek* 3/30/42. actually drowned: *Life* 3/22/43; NYT 1/30/43. *328* "come, the better": T 7/9/45. "time to die": NYT 5/7/42. *329* planes and killed him: *Newsweek* 2/1/43; NYT 5/21/43. after he was dead: *Current Biography* 1942; NYT 5/21/43. sealing off China: NYT 2/16/42. *330* "States Marines hiding?": NYT 2/16/42, 2/2/41. and troop movements: NYT 5/6/42, 12/18/42. "men, still unafraid": NYT 1/15/42, 5/6/42. *331* time for Midway: NYT 5/8/42, 6/13/42, 7/15/42, 9/17/42. "Seattle by air": NYT 7/18/42, 9/17/43, 6/5/42; T 6/15/42. *332* patched-up *Yorktown*: NYT 6/5/42; *Life* 11/16/42. sipping rice broth: NYT 6/5/42; T 6/22/42, 6/7/43. *333* hospitalized by October: NYT 8/9/42, 11/22/42; WM/Dr. Louis Lasagna 8/4/70. hundred one night: *Soldier* 284. *334* could win all: Fab V 75; NYT 10/31/42. *335* U-boat challenge: *Soldier* 183. off to combat: NYT 8/11/42, 11/5/43, 8/11/42. *336* "work to do": Fab V 198; T 6/22/42, 2/22/43. as Los Alamos: Jungk 133. *337* "of October 3": T 5/4/42, 6/22/42; NYT 10/4/42. *338* couldn't remember it: Mazo 36. "him to bed": NYT 11/22/42. ready to move: NYT 7/10/42, 9/27/42; T 11/9/42. *339* operation was Torch: Walter Johnson 173. "a cruel initiative": *Scholastic Magazine* 1/11/43; T 11/16/42; NYT 11/9/42; T 11/16/42; *Soldier* 291. "are striking back": *Soldier* 291. *340* through Kasserine Pass: *Saturday Evening Post* 5/29/43; NYT 2/22/43. just 18,500 casualties: *Collier's* 11/9/43. Italians and Sicilians: NYT 5/9/43, 6/12/43. *341* of Axis troops: NYT 8/18/43; *Soldier* 394; NYT 7/26/43; T 9/20/43. "another Dunkerque": NYT 9/16/43, 7/18/43, 7/21/46. toward Naples: NYT 9/11/43. *342* pitiless as ever: NYT 10/2/43, 2/16/44. winters in memory: NYT 2/18/44, 1/19/44. *343* water, and time: NYT 1/3/43. *344* warmth of socks: Mauldin *Front* 36. *345* gasoline called napalm: ibid 93; *Soldier* 344. "deadpan face": NYT 11/21/48; Walter Johnson 156. "a little superfluous": *Front* 32. *346* over to Hitler: NYT 10/2/43. and David Niven: T 6/7/43; NYT 2/21/42. *347* Hopkins's youngest boy: NYT 1/10/42, 11/17/43, 12/25/44, 11/13/44, 4/12/44, 8/19/44, 8/15/44, 2/13/44; John Brooks *Leap* 286. *349* "killed same": *Soldier* 271. *350* to GI prurience: NYT 12/31/43. "einst Lilli Marlene": NYT 10/17/43.

X THE HOME FRONT
(*pages 353–400*)

353 "boy on Bataan": T 3/23/42. *354* the same again: Sevareid *Dream* 215. those of 1929: Burns *Soldier* 460; Jack Goodman 19. "so do comforts": NYT 5/3/45, 4/28/65; Walter Johnson 157; Fab V 148. *355* "in the black": T 3/15/43; Brogan 164. "a hothouse growth": NYT 12/14/60; Allen *Change* 188–90. *356* dismissed as "eggheads": NYT 4/13/38; *Soldier* 461. an overstatement: NYT 3/23/44. *357* "Win-the-War": NYT 12/29/43, 12/8/41. permitted to vote: NYT 12/29/43, 12/8/41. One *World:* NYT 11/4/42; *Soldier* 280; Walter Johnson 165; *Soldier* 337; T 2/7/44, 3/6/44; NYT 2/25/44, 6/16/43, 4/8/43. *358* to the Army: NYT 2/28/43; T 6/26/44. knew, but still: T 4/13/42. *359* "sergeant over there": NYT 2/6/44. (brands as Fleetwoods): T 7/3/44. by 22 percent: T 7/17/44; NYT 2/7/42. *360* on the West Coast: NYT 4/28/44; T 12/21/42; Jack Goodman 50. admirals wanted them: Liddell Hart 384. *361* loss of quality: NYT 2/20/41; *Soldier* 244; *Time* editors 45. of the profits: NYT 8/1/42, 8/24/42; T 8/31/42. *362* and overwhelming them: Sulzberger 418. 44,000,000,000: Fab V 150. *363* country was fighting: NYT 6/20/43; *Soldier* 213 and passim. *364* "the alien Japanese": Walter Johnson 156; NYT 2/1/42, 10/6/53. next three weeks: Fab V 201. "welcome in Kansas": ibid 204. *365* "American or not": ibid 201, 206. it to Washington: NYT 4/23/41. "elder statesman": NYT 11/3/43. *366* "or all persons": NYT 6/19/42, 3/19/42, 2/21/42; Fab V 201. *367* in horse stalls: T 4/6/42; Fab V 204. 1,862 funerals: NYT 11/4/42; Fab V 206. could go hang: *Soldier* 216. *368* were "disloyal": NYT 12/19/44, 12/20/44. more than sing: Fab V 205. *369* "rates were appalling": NYT 10/14/43; Fab V 206. overt outrages subsided: Mauldin *Home* 168. said a word: ibid 170. *370* victory gardens: NYT 1/23/42. *371* asylum and tranquillity: NYT 1/2/42, 2/6/42, 5/1/42, 5/10/42, 5/3/42, 9/7/44, 9/6/42, 10/18/42, 11/22/45, 12/3/45, 11/27/42, 11/1/42; Jack Goodman 467. *372* in Broadway alleys: NYT 7/1/42, 5/2/44, 1/28/45; T 1/15/45. they sold well: NYT 7/23/42, 3/21/42, 9/13/42, 1/21/43, 4/8/43, 10/28/43, 11/21/44. 2/29/44. frustrated women: Jack Goodman 418 *373* pajamas at night: Rovere *Years* 8; Fab V 256. Walter Annenberg's *Seventeen:* Jack Goodman 594. *374* called bobby-soxers: Fab V 27. quietly died: NYT 11/12/44. *375* were at peace: T 8/21/44; Fab V 46–49. "they're nice kids": T 7/5/43. *376* her feet, shrieking: NYT 12/10/43. twenty squad cars: NYT 10/13/44. *377* later, Mia Farrow: NYT 10/31/51, 11/8/51. "my lifetime?": Jack Goodman 379. "Sinatra is baffling": *Reader's Digest* January 1945. *378* bobby-soxer rite: NYT 3/6/45; Fab V 47. "like the Paramount": NYT 6/22/45, 6/11/45; Fab V 48. *379* Allies with nothing: Jungk 131; *Soldier* 249. the three tons· Laurence 68–69. *380* might reach 1.07: ibid 70. liquid at it: ibid 76–77. *381* technological problem: ibid 74; NYT 8/7/45. "realistic traditions": *Soldier* 550. *382* "to the project": NYT 11/4/44. *383* whole-souled Communist: NYT 6/16/50, 5/24/50, 6/17/50, 2/4/50. just been formed: NYT 7/18/50; West 217–21. *384* in fact killed: NYT 8/19/50. *385* history greatly altered: NYT 5/25/46. was Klaus Fuchs: Jungk 193; NYT 6/29/46. desert remains obscure: NYT 8/7/45. *386* criminal investigation: NYT 12/7/45. and Winston Churchill: NYT 1/8/43; *Soldier* 316. great battles ahead: *Soldier* 389. *387* "triumphant success": ibid 17, 298, 300, 546. *388* their prewar dreams: ibid 302, 489. "was once white!": ibid 498; NYT 7/27/43. *389* three heart attacks: NYT 10/2/43, 10/8/44; T 4/17/44; *Soldier* 274, 511. "the United States": *Soldier* 453; NYT 7/12/44; Walter Johnson 166. *390* "to the convention": Gunther 360; NYT 7/19/44. would be Truman: NYT 7/19/44, 7/20/44; Phillips *Truman* 37–40. *391* "Senator from Missouri": NYT 7/22/44; T 7/31/44. "about my dog": NYT 11/8/44; *Soldier* 168. *392* value was doubtful: *Soldier* 525. " 'the *Chicago Tribune!* ": NYT 10/29/44. *393* "an old man": T 10/23/44, 5/22/44. "they are not true": NYT 10/13/44; T 10/23/44. utterly wretched: NYT 10/22/44. *394* image of vitality: *Soldier* 525. been forever laid: NYT 11/8/44, 11/10/44, 11/12/44; T 11/13/44; Gunther 92. *395* with no scars: *Soldier* 530. seemed so robust: NYT 11/20/44. *396* battery of specialists: T 10/23/44; NYT 4/5/44. a frequent visitor: *Soldier* 448; NYT 4/11/44. *397* "killed himself trying": NYT 4/27/44, 2/25/44; Gunther 340. deliver a speech: *Soldier* 507. *398* "goddamned ghouls": ibid 509. "close to nonsense": ibid 508–509; Acheson 102; Gunther 38. *399* been "a sellout": NYT 2/8/44. his first inaugural: *Soldier* 594.

XI LILACS IN THE DOORYARD
(pages 402–443)

402 "was beyond us": NYT 1/23/44, 1/31/44. *403* act of war: NYT 4/17/45, 2/14/44. "the Fifth Army": NYT 5/13/44, 6/5/44. D-Day in Normandy: NYT 6/6/44, 6/7/44. *404* "is mine alone": NYT 6/6/44. "up and consolidated": NYT 7/10/44. *405* stubborn defenders: Burns *Soldier* 475. "O.K. We'll go": NYT 7/11/43; *Soldier* 475. *406* "our united crusade": *Soldier* 475; NYT 6/6/44. sunk off Arromanches: NYT 6/27/44. *407* "men at arms": NYT 7/10/44, 7/19/44, 8/8/44; T 7/3/44. "working for Vichy": NYT 8/26/44, 8/24/44; T 10/16/44. *408* "Fatherland and Führer!": NYT 9/7/44, 9/12/44, 10/21/44; T 10/25/44. "American soldier myself": NYT 12/28/44; T 1/15/45. to celebrate it: NYT 3/9/45, 4/2/45, 4/12/45. *409* U.S.-RUSS JUNCTURE: NYT 4/12/45; *Soldier* 599. Lucy's daughter: *Soldier* 599. *410* "cause for alarm": ibid 595. atom armaments race; Jungk 179. *411* this was done: NYT 8/13/45, 9/28/45, 10/1/66. *412* sharply changed: Speer 227. with the enemy: Jungk 163. uranium research: ibid. "an atom bomb": ibid 164, 166. *413* a textile mill: NYT 9/28/45; Jungk 167. *414* "going to use it": NYT 8/13/45, 9/28/45; Jungk 171. "politics or physics?": Jungk 174. *415* or be annihilated: NYT 11/28/45. "agreed to that": NYT 4/9/46; Jungk 175. *416* began a counteroffensive: NYT 7/23/42. no military significance: NYT 1/3/43, 1/10/43, 1/20/43. *417* range of Rabaul: NYT 7/2/43, 8/29/43. unloaded overhead: NYT 12/28/43. *418* anticipated a Tarawa: NYT 12/4/44. 75 percent casualties: NYT 11/25/43, 2/22/44. *419* approaching Tarawa's: NYT 4/25/44, 5/28/44. were cut off: NYT 6/21/44, 8/11/44. *420* "God protect you": NYT 7/26/44; *Soldier* 489. *421* was to come: NYT 10/20/44. of all time: NYT 10/21/44. *Banzai:* NYT 10/26/44. *422* moments of daylight: NYT 10/28/44. power was finished: NYT 10/26/44. early March, Manila: NYT 12/16/44. *423* Japs on Iwo: NYT 12/25/44. bee in the face: NYT 3/10/45. *424* GIs at leisure: NYT 3/30/45, 4/2/45, 4/13/45. absolutely secure: *Soldier* 599. *425* "laundry to dry": ibid 600; NYT 4/16/45. state documents: Asbell 33. "expert in explosives": NYT 2/13/45. *426* Outer Mongolia: T 2/26/45. "fifteen minutes more": NYT 4/16/45. filling in colors: T 6/4/45. *427* "beautiful woman": Asbell 36. 1:15 P.M.: NYT 4/13/45; *Soldier* 600. on the couch: NYT 4/13/45. *428* anguished snores: Asbell 41. "3:35 o'clock": ibid 44. *429* reach Eleanor Roosevelt: ibid 46. "concert is finished": NYT 4/13/45; *Soldier* 602. Truman at once: NYT 4/13/45; Asbell 53. *430* "was talking about": Truman I 6. "when you can": ibid. "in trouble now": T 4/23/45; Asbell 63. *431* "WARM SPRINGS, GA.": Asbell 78. "man at Warm Springs": ibid 81. *432* with her hands: ibid 84, 91, 99. "So long—out": ibid 93, 150. *433* "most clearly": ibid xi. "lost a friend": ibid 94, 117. *434* "the great man": ibid 94. "the White House": T 4/23/45; Asbell 87. the man's cheek: Asbell 91. "the next curve": Gunther 144. *435–436* "Hi, Dad" . . . to be vacated: Asbell 105–106. *436* Early drew up: ibid 124. *437* chief improviser: ibid 113. to view it: ibid 128, 134; NYT 4/14/45. *438* clasped hands: Asbell 156. "Lincoln home again": ibid 158, 160. passed overhead: NYT 4/15/45. *439* "be any man's": Asbell 170. President's widow: NYT 4/14/45. *440* Executive Mansion: Asbell 178. sealed forever: NYT 4/15/45; Asbell 183. *441–442* said his son . . . "remember it": *New Yorker* 4/21/45. *443* "Thy servant sleeping": Margaret Truman 90; Asbell 194. "is over": T 4/30/45.

XII A NEW WORLD, UNDER A NEW SUN
(pages 445–479)

445 "single moment": Phillips *Truman* 62; Asbell 136. *446* return to obscurity: T 4/23/45; *Truman* 62–63. in history: NYT 11/7/34, 9/15/40. "the President": Asbell 136–37. "for me now": ibid 137. *447* "have ever done": NYT 4/14/45; Asbell 111. *448* "son and bro": NYT 4/13/45; *Truman* 65. *449* "through her teeth": NYT 4/21/45; Margaret Truman 91, 95, 96; *Truman* 62, 144; Asbell 166. "supporter below": T 12/18/50. with greater dignity: ibid. "be game, too": *Truman* 140; T 9/24/45, 9/18/50. *450* "what they meant": *Truman* 63, 71, 169, 79; T 6/4/45; NYT 4/19/45. *451* "the new President": *Truman* 80. "not Henry Wallace": Acheson 104; NYT 7/1/45. "he died?" . . . "it just now": NYT 4/18/45; Asbell 168. *452* of the question: NYT 5/2/45, 5/3/45, 5/5/45, 5/8/45, 5/9/45, 5/10/45; T 5/14/45. *453* larger than Newark: NYT 8/9/45, 7/27/45, 12/16/45. a hand grenade?: Manchester "Our War in the Pacific"; NYT 5/4/45. *454* on Allied losses: NYT 1/28/47; Stimson "The

Decision to Use the Atomic Bomb." *455* been even greater: NYT 6/2/45, 6/8/44; Truman I 332; NYT 6/6/45, 7/23/45. "the gadget": NYT 6/6/45; Burns *Soldier* 459, 251; Jungk 175. "do something different" Jungk 178. *456* "have come in": NYT 12/7/45. *457* "winning the war": Laurence 201. stadium in Chicago: Jungk 192. *458* of a second: Laurence 168–70. as yet undetermined: NYT 8/1/45; *Soldier* 558. *459* same conclusions: NYT 4/26/45; *Truman* 53. "The Fat Man": Jungk 180. *460* greatest war criminals. *Reader's Digest* March 1947; NYT 1/28/47; *Harper's* February 1947, Compton "If the Atomic Bomb Had Not Been Used." no one said much: Jungk 198 and passim. *461* perfecting the mesh. *Current Biography* 1947. *461–462* right microsecond . . . "there be light": NYT 8/7/45; Laurence 10. *462* their window-panes: Laurence 12. *463* blown away. ibid 195. instant peace: Jungk 197, 202. "the Japanese": Truman I 416. *464* "Japanese home islands": ibid 417. "utter destruction": NYT 7/28/45; *Truman* 58. had been passed: *Truman* 59; T 8/13/45. *465* intelligence officer: NYT 8/8/45; Laurence 196, 202–206. *465–466* "of TNT" . . any of them: Laurence 208–11. *466* "from the Empire": NYT 8/18/45; Laurence 220. "long now, folks": Laurence 221; NYT 11/22/45. *467* "do with it": T 8/13/45, 8/20/45. *468* "I don't": T 10/22/45; NYT 8/9/45; Laurence 225, 228. "devised by man": NYT 7/28/45; *Truman* 68; Laurence 242. *469* turning somersaults: Jungk 211. *470* "such devastation": ibid 213; NYT 11/24/45. of his doing. NYT 8/9/45. *472* countermanded the order. *Harper's* February 1947. formalities of capitulation: NYT 8/15/45; T 8/20/45. *473* followed his example: NYT 8/15/45. "very fragile arch": Morison *Two-Ocean* 572. *474* the United States: NYT 9/2/45. war against Japan: T 7/30/45. *475* *General Henry Taylor:* NYT 8/19/45; T 8/27/45. *475–479* Reuther portrait: *Holiday* November and December 1959; NYT 3/28/46, 5/10/70; *Hartford Courant* 5/16/70.

XIII THE FRAYING FLAGS OF TRIUMPH
(*pages 480–509*)

480 in trusting them: NYT 5/13/45; Phillips *Truman* 132, 156. *481* "his own death": NYT 4/23/61, 4/4/61. *482* U.N. General Assembly: NYT 2/20/45. *483* the other leg: NYT 3/17/46; Rovere *McCarthy* 95–98. their way there. NYT 11/6/46; Fab V 221. "Richard M. Nixon": NYT 11/7/46; Mazo 41. *484* "police the world". NYT 7/18/46. *and Child Care:* NYT 9/22/46. from the hills: T 9/9/46. political war chests: NYT 8/15/45. *485* "little fellow there": T 9/3/45; Goldman *Decade* 16. *486* rapid extinction: *Decade* 7; NYT 2/9/40, 9/26/45, 8/14/46; Bird 255; Jungk 341. the black market. *Truman* 101; NYT 8/22/45; *Decade* 251; NYT 1/7/46. *487* "about inflation?" . . . Truman called back: T 9/24/45. postwar inflation: *Decade* 14. *488* in his refrigerator: T 5/6/46; *Decade* 27. "campaign of 1946": NYT 9/6/45; *Truman* 103–104. *489* had ruined them: NYT 1/15/46. "below the belt": NYT 3/11/46. dipped in the polls: NYT 7/26/46; Truman I 487 ff; NYT 1/22/46, 11/10/46. *490* collars than blue: NYT 7/22/44. was intolerable: NYT 9/2/46. *491* of his Presidency: *Commonweal* 2/8/46; T 10/8/45. their heads stubbornly: NYT 1/12/46, 4/26/46; WA 1946. "of the government": T 6/3/46. *492* was deplorable: NYT 5/18/46, 5/24/46. "sons of bitches": *Decade* 23. "do the job!": *Truman* 114 ff. *493* to General Hershey: *U.S. News and World Report* 5/3/46. "has been settled": NYT 5/26/46. *494* "coal with bayonets": *Decade* 25. burned coal: T 6/28/46. *495* and Wagner Acts: NYT 5/22/46; *U.S. News and World Report* 10/11/46. was $3,510,000: NYT 11/22/46, 12/4/46. *496* work at once: NYT 12/6/46. "his balls clank": NYT 12/8/46; *Truman* 124. *497* a heavy blow: NYT 1/8/46. *498* out of uniform: T 6/18/45. stars could, too: NYT 9/18/45, 4/11/51; Acheson 127. point freeze: NYT 7/4/46. *499* TO SPEED SAILINGS: NYT 1/7/46. *500* "wanna go home": NYT 1/12/46. "the nation accepted": NYT 1/10/46. *501* and other instigators: NYT 1/9/46, 1/8/46. "Manila and Le Havre": NYT 9/13/45. departments to himself: NYT 6/16/46. *502* "out of Army": NYT 6/6/46; T 10/22/45; *Newsweek* 1/28/46. "some other country": NYT 11/2/46. *503* in the Ruhr Acheson 86; Mowry 163. "my way home": NYT 7/10/45; Truman I 334, 337, 411, 412. *504* "not be I": NYT 7/27/45; *Truman* 92, 98. "a great pity": NYT 7/25/46, 11/15/46; Acheson 130, 634. would warn them: Walter Johnson 163. *505* and his President: ibid 226; NYT 9/21/46, 2/14/46. to his speech: NYT 3/6/46, 9/11/46; *Truman* 150. *506* "of his administration": ibid 151; NYT 9/13/46. "my resignation immediately": T 9/23/46. *507* "exactly in line": ibid; Acheson 192. "this subject again": Acheson 191; NYT 9/22/46. *508* "I'm right". Truman I 560. sometime in 1946: *Life* 11/26/45. *509* "Had enough?": NYT 1/11/47; Mazo 47; *Truman* 128; *Decade* 45. "a Republican country": NYT 11/4/48. returned to them: Walter Johnson 228.

XIV LIFE WITH HARRY
(pages 511–529)

512 "come to responsibility": Schlesinger *Thousand* 287. *513* bowed your head: NYT 6/11/50; *Business Week* 1/22/49, 2/21/49. as a Red: NYT 12/31/49. teachers looked on: NYT 5/20/56. *514* bipartisan support: NYT 12/23/41; Burns *Soldier* 184, 515; T 2/28/44, 6/28/43, 7/23/45; NYT 5/26/44, 1/22/44, 8/7/45, 12/11/46. "requires it": T 12/10/45; NYT 1/11/45; Eisinger 487. *515* serious uprising: NYT 10/2/45. *516* started to go: NYT 1/3/42. (expensive) New Look: Gold *1940–41* 31; Fab V 248. *517* on the roads: Fab V 251, 253. he didn't know: *Life* 3/1/48. *518* Stalin had become: NYT 1/27/45, 4/24/45, 12/22/45. *519* the absolute limit: Allen *Change* 263; Fab V 221, 260. *520* presidential campaign: NYT 6/23/46, 9/30/47; Kendrick 40. *521* ran one headline: Fab V 210. *522* "after the war?" . . . "most astonishing": O'Neill 3–4. all-time high: O'Neill 4; NYT 10/18/45, 6/17/43, 6/16/45, 4/22/45, 1/1/48, 11/10/46; Fab V 212; WA 1946. *523* game was security: T 6/18/45. *524* was blushing: Friedan 174; Bird 259; Kinsey 194. *525* their enthusiasm: O'Neill 13. Spock had begun: NYT 7/14/46; Gold *1940–41* 31. *526* finding a home: NYT 11/2/47, 6/15/45; Mauldin *Home* 48. "understand our problems": Mauldin *Home* 65; T 12/24/45. *527* "pla-ace to stay": T 1/15/45. well under $10,000: *Newsweek* 10/6/69; O'Neill 38 ff. *528* standard specifications: O'Neill 41; T 7/3/60. *528–529* "think big" . . . much choice: Kimball "Dream Town."

XV A LITTLE TOUCH OF HARRY IN THE NIGHT
(pages 530–577)

530 wait until Monday?: NYT 2/23/47; Acheson 217. *531* own silk hat: NYT 2/28/47, 3/2/47, 3/18/47. after September 1945: Acheson 217; Walter Johnson 203, 207; T 12/31/45. *532* no viable alternative: NYT 5/13/45; T 10/1/45. not much else: NYT 7/14/46; T 9/25/44. *533* unprecedented scale: NYT 2/8/47, 3/18/46; Acheson 212; Phillips *Truman* 174. "give the conquered": Goldman *Decade* 33, 34. "it back again": NYT 4/2/47; Rovere and Schlesinger 241. *534* "it at all": NYT 4/17/47; *Decade* 60; T 5/29/50. only as "X": Walter Johnson 208; NYT 7/8/47. under its spell: *Truman* 258, 262. *535* "do the same": ibid 305; Acheson 219. Muehlebach Hotel: NYT 3/13/47, 5/23/47; Mowry 922; *Truman* 171, 176. Kennan's reasoning: NYT 3/14/47; Rovere and Schlesinger 238. *536* "strategic monstrosity": NYT 11/30/47; Lippmann 16–23. strategic nightmare: NYT 10/17/49. *537* few sparks there: Acheson 226. "human beings": NYT 5/9/47; Acheson 227, 229. *538* "in his hand": NYT 6/6/47; George Marshall *European Initiative* 494. could take hold: Walter Johnson 209; *Truman* 184. *539* or foreign bases: NYT 4/14/48, 4/4/48; WA 1952; Mowry 76; *Truman* 192. *540* blockade on Berlin: NYT 2/24/48, 6/25/48. complete rupture: Acheson 260. on either side: ibid 262. *541* be done—yet: NYT 9/11/48; T 9/27/48. French fliers: *Newsweek* 7/12/48; NYT 7/1/48; Clay 381–86. *542* blew it up: ibid; NYT 12/17/48. they were beaten: NYT 4/17/49. grace and generosity: NYT 5/12/49; Walter Johnson 217. *543* their own money: Clay 381–86; NYT 1/25/48. "who owned it": Sevareid *Dream* 392. *544* across the water?: Walter Johnson 221. "colonial empire": NYT 7/16/45, 3/1/50; T 3/12/50. *545* "elsewhere rejected?": Kronenberger 216. *546* "in the night": Acheson 730, 731. could hardly wait: NYT 11/4/48. *547* MacArthur, or Vandenberg: Ross 95. he would lose: *Washington Post* 7/7/48. *548* in the ring: NYT 3/2/48, 3/9/48; Ross 72. General Eisenhower!: Nation 11, 64, 66, 75; *Truman* 946; NYT 11/7/46; *Nation* 3/13/48; T 3/13/48. *549* Draft Eisenhower Committee: *N.Y. Herald-Tribune* 7/10/48. to lead them then: ibid; NYT 7/10/48. issues in November: Ross 33. *550* trial run: NYT 4/18/48; Ross 77. problems with Congress?: NYT 9/7/48. like a debacle: *Washington Post* 6/4/48. *551* presidential politics: NYT 6/4/48. "growing entertainment value": Ross 84. *552* "and Czechoslovakia?": ibid 85 ff. "the biggest whistle-stop!": NYT 6/12/48. "what I'm doing!": NYT 6/19/48; T 6/28/48; *Truman* 215. *553* that was something: NYT 7/11/48; Ross 92. this convention year: NYT 9/27/48; John Brooks *Leap* 288. *554* "Federal payrolls": Ross 54. "to dislike him": NYT 1/17/48; Ross 38, 53. their little jokes: NYT 3/29/48; Rovere and Schlesinger 231. *555* "within ourselves": NYT 5/23/48, 6/25/48; *N.Y. World-Telegram* 6/14/48. bargain prices: NYT 9/20/48. *556* run the race: NYT 7/13/48, 7/15/48; Ross 109. to the door: NYT 7/15/48; Ross 116. alone, and waiting: T 7/26/48; NYT 7/15/48. *557* "for real": NYT 7/15/48. fouler than that: ibid; T 7/26/48.

558 "in the world!": T 7/26/48; NYT 7/15/48; Ross 125. "run for office": T 7/26/48. "what they say!": T 7/26/48. *559* "in the stocks!": *Truman* 222; T 7/26/48. "political courage": T 7/26/48. the Democratic South: NYT 7/18/48. to be flourishing: NYT 12/30/47, 9/11/48, 12/31/47; *Truman* 204. *560* "announce his candidacy". NYT 6/13/48; Ross 136. He refused: NYT 8/9/50, 9/11/48; Ross 145, 149. *561* "Christian martyrs": NYT 7/26/48; T 8/2/48, 7/26/48. independent center: NYT 8/30/48, 8/21/48; *Washington Post* 10/22/48. hastened their victories: NYT 11/3/48. *562* "end of it": NYT 7/27/48; Ross 132. judgment of it: NYT 7/28/48. Congress in history: NYT 8/13/48. *563* espionage hearings?: NYT 8/1/48, 8/4/48. always quotable: NYT 9/6/48. *564* "do exactly that": *Truman* 230 ff. "the farmer's back": NYT 9/17/48. *565* have written it: *Truman* 243. wished to say: Ross 180 ff; *Truman* 242. *565–566* "Democratic incumbent" . . . "and irrigation": Ross 182–85. *566* "of the world": NYT 9/21/48. over the country: Ross 206; *Truman* 242. *567* water, and faith: NYT 6/27/48; Ross 203. have a chance: Ross 167; NYT 10/30/48. *568* "that they cherish": Ross 12. would win handily: ibid 196; *Life* 11/1/48, 11/15/48; NYT 10/31/48. *569* "the poorhouse": *Detroit Free Press* 11/3/48. Dewey's inaugural: *Life* 11/15/48. *570* one instance, arrogant: ibid. *571* hedge his bet: NYT 9/10/48. almost hourly: NYT 11/25/48; *N.Y. World-Telegram* 9/24/48, Ross 226. *572* drama outside: Ross 227 ff; Rovere *Years* 48; *Truman* 245 ff. almost instantly: *Life* 11/15/48. *573* DEWEY DEFEATS TRUMAN: NYT 11/15/48. 574 back to sleep: Truman II 220 ff. *575* stared at him: NYT 11/4/48. had some sleep: T 11/8/48. "claims," he said: Ross 227. *576* governor of Illinois: NYT 11/4/48; *Truman* 247. "in American politics": *Truman* 251; Walter Johnson 233. *577* "out of this": NYT 11/6/48, 11/4/48; Ross 230; T 11/15/48. him he shouldn't: NYT 11/23/48; Ross 235.

XVI THE AGE OF SUSPICION
(pages 579–632)

579 1648 Pennsylvania Avenue: NYT 4/14/45. *580* Great Society: Phillips *Truman* 163, 164. *581* "of underdeveloped areas": NYT 11/4/64, 1/6/49, 1/21/49; *Truman* 272. was coming from: *Truman* 273. *582* "first proposed it": NYT 6/6/50. on the Hill: NYT 12/1/48, 3/4/49. Secretaries of State: Acheson 249; NYT 1/22/49. *583* suburbia themselves: Whyte 312. *584* amaze the country: NYT 3/14/48. *585* "took up sex": T 9/3/56. *588* "lack of opportunity": Fab V 217; Gold *1940–41* 15 *589* even to society: Eisinger 153; Kronenberger 197. *590* into Bloomington's computers: Guiles 90. solvent of custom: Goldman *Decade* 119. *591* bottle of Hadacol: NYT 1/23/48. *592* "loved in return": Gold *1940–41* 32. "double-breasted suits": ibid. professional athlete: Fab V 221 *593* kill a President: NYT 7/4/46, 11/2/50. lordly spaniel: Fab IV 240. *594* "who like it": Fab V 342. *595* (at the Sorbonne): NYT 9/16/50; Fab V 218. *596* the new decade: NYT 2/5/50. *597* died with it: NYT 4/4/49, 4/25/49, 12/9/49. "but could not": NYT 8/6/49; Acheson 303. *599* "nations having it": Jungk 260; NYT 9/24/49, 3/29/49; *Decade* 100. *601* be heard again: Ross 134. "frittered away": NYT 3/3/48. *602* "down the river": Walter Johnson 214. *603* "I deeply believe": NYT 11/2/46. *604* its Canadian allies: NYT 3/5/46, 2/11/50. *605* for International Peace: NYT 7/30/48, 8/4/48, 8/1/48, 2/11/49, 8/4/48. "bad security risks": NYT 12/5/47. *606* rulings were final: NYT 11/18/49; *Truman* 360. *608* nine years old: NYT 8/19/49. with orthodoxy: NYT 11/9/47. "was sacked anyway": *Truman* 351; NYT 11/18/48. *609* "their reliability": *Truman* 352. *610* the vigilantes: ibid. "question of espionage": ibid 364. plain paper wrappers: NYT 12/10/49. *612* "smoke, there's fire": *Truman* 373. "be all right": NYT 5/20/50, 5/24/50, 7/18/50; West 224. *613* both of them: NYT 6/17/50, 7/18/50, 8/12/50. *615* "Russian code": NYT 8/3/48, 8/1/48. *616* "of the hearings": *New Yorker* 9/4/48. was Alger Hiss: NYT 8/18/48, 11/25/54. *617* him a liar: Acheson 250. heavily lidded eyes: NYT 6/7/49. *618* could prove it: NYT 12/12/48. face to face: NYT 8/4/48. *619* than he knew: Cooke 71. a committee investigator: NYT 8/18/48. *620* "until I return": Cooke 80. *621* anyone named Crosley: NYT 8/26/48. *622* to the Russians: NYT 9/28/48, 11/4/48. he was trapped: NYT 12/7/48, 6/7/49. *623* had the story: NYT 12/11/48, 12/5/48. "expense of Austria": Cooke 92. "the United States": NYT 12/19/48. *624* were chagrined: NYT 12/10/48, 12/16/48. "looks like faltering": Mazo 65–66. *625* on both counts: NYT 11/18/49, 1/22/50, 3/6/49. was a mystery: NYT 12/15/49. *626* it to him: *Truman* 369. had Priscilla Hiss: Cooke 298. he had been: NYT 1/22/50. *627* "with verse 34": NYT 5/13/47, 1/26/50; Acheson 360. "was not easy": ibid 359. *628* "America can do?": NYT 2/13/50, 2/4/50. "do it again": Griffin 28. *628–632* Murrow portrait: *Current Biography* 1953; NYT 4/8/65; *Cue* 2/21/53; Kendrick passim.

XVII INTO THE ABYSS
(pages 633–674)

633 "sensible course": Acheson 354. from Hoover: Rovere and Schlesinger 213. 634 "for that purpose": NYT 12/17/49, 2/4/50, 5/24/50; Acheson 355. "chain to Alaska": NYT 3/2/49. January 12, 1950: NYT 1/13/50. 635 the United Nations: Acheson 354; NYT 1/13/50. fend for themselves: NYT 1/13/50. 636 " 'back in there' ": NYT 12/30/49; Acheson 293. "long road back": NYT 1/21/50; Acheson 358. 637 seven years left: NYT 11/6/46, 5/3/57. "recognizes me": Harper's August 1950. 638 "shape our policy": NYT 5/4/50. New Yorker: Harper's August 1950; Rovere McCarthy 128. 639 speak of traitors: NYT 2/23/50. "the State Department": McCarthy 126. 640 the fugitive list: ibid 127. "curtain of secrecy": NYT 2/20/50; McCarthy 130. 641 "not a Communist?": McCarthy 132. "in the Department": ibid. 642 "reckless performance": NYT 2/21/50. except McCarthy himself: NYT 2/23/50, 2/26/50. 643 see him discredited: NYT 5/21/50. Levine's Plain Talk: NYT 1/27/50, 4/7/50, 5/11/50. 644 "contact you later": McCarthy 144. mud-bespattered buckets: ibid 12. "its sleeves rolled": ibid 11. 645 to be told: NYT 4/26/50; Griffith 72. 646 "the State Department": NYT 3/22/50, 3/27/50; McCarthy 151, 152. with laughter: NYT 3/27/50, 4/2/50; McCarthy 153. 647 "as a Communist": NYT 4/7/50, 4/12/50. all the headlines: NYT 4/2/50, 4/21/50, 4/26/50, 5/2/50. 648 general election: NYT 6/2/50, 6/25/50, 5/3/50, 11/8/50. "the United States": Griffith 73, 100; NYT 4/19/50. 649 "half months ago": McCarthy 55. "but Russia's": NYT 6/25/50. 650 "the United States": NYT 1/20/50, 7/6/50. "shine their boots": NYT 3/24/50. 651 around the clock: NYT 8/16/50; Acheson 402. 652 before Monday: NYT 6/25/50; Phillips Truman 289. Forest Hills: NYT 1/11/50. "like a cobra": NYT 6/25/50. 653 of their lives: ibid. "Republic of Korea": Acheson 402. White House switchboard: NYT 6/26/50. 654 Success, New York: Acheson 404; NYT 6/26/50. passed 9 to 0: NYT 9/7/50. neutrality impossible: NYT 6/26/50; Truman 291. 655 in Indochina: NYT 6/27/50. an earlier Vietnam: NYT 6/29/50, 6/26/50. 656 was unanimous: NYT 6/28/50. "with the subject": NYT 6/29/50. 657 "the Armed Forces": NYT 7/1/50; Acheson 410. in June 1950: NYT 7/6/50. 658 "it amounts to": NYT 6/27/50; Truman 302. negative aim: NYT 6/30/50. 659 "battle area": ibid; Truman 302. at once: NYT 7/1/50. for an opinion: ibid; Truman 311. 660 the high command: NYT 7/21/50. "want from me?": NYT 7/21/50, 9/1/50. 661 the country's pride: NYT 7/12/50. other U.N. members: NYT 8/1/50. NKPA rear: NYT 9/16/50. a little talk: NYT 10/1/50. "fight communism": NYT 7/31/50. Wake Island: Truman 318; NYT 8/29/50. 663 "greatest slaughter": NYT 10/15/50; Truman 321. to move north: NYT 10/15/50. 664 "Kim Buck Too?": NYT 10/21/50. history of warfare: NYT 11/10/50. 665 other was doing: NYT 11/24/50, 10/25/50; Truman 323. it in Korea: NYT 11/1/50; Mazo 141. 666 "Little Big Horn": NYT 11/3/50. had found five: NYT 11/5/50. 667 "of my command": NYT 11/6/50. and power installations: Truman 325. 668 Monroe Doctrine: Rovere and Schlesinger 149. "intervention in Korea": Truman 322; NYT 10/12/50. 669 "extraordinarily light": NYT 11/10/50, 11/24/50. 670 outcome was different: NYT 12/1/50. help, at Hungnam: NYT 12/7/50. 671 was evacuated: NYT 12/11/50, 12/25/50. "military matters": Truman 327. "publicly announced": Acheson 47; NYT 11/29/50. 672 win the war: Acheson 474. 673 "is concurred in": NYT 12/13/50; Rovere and Schlesinger 156; Truman 329. 674 along the Yalu: NYT 12/28/50. the U.N. lines: NYT 1/1/50.

XVIII A HOUSE DIVIDED
(pages 679–732)

679 "spiritless defeat": NYT 1/4/51; Acheson 489. of the war: NYT 1/24/51, 3/2/51, 3/15/51, 3/31/51. 680 short of treason: Rovere and Schlesinger 245; Walter Johnson 239. balancing the budget: NYT 12/13/50, 12/21/50. the Great Debate: NYT 1/8/51; Mowry 177. 681 Roosevelt's Hundred Days: NYT 1/6/51, 1/9/51, 2/10/51, 1/16/51; WA 1951. "rebuilding of Europe": Truman II 380. 682 to future increases: NYT 12/20/50, 2/2/51; Acheson 494. his doing it: NYT 4/5/51; Walter Johnson 243. 683 "tolls for thee": NYT 11/8/50; Griffith 126. some time ago: NYT 3/3/51; Mazo 141. twelve years later: NYT 4/11/51. 684 STILL SEEN POSSIBLE: NYT 4/11/51; Phillips Truman 346; Rovere and Schlesinger 172. 685 "commander in chief": NYT 10/15/50; U.S. News 9/1/50; Truman 330, 334;

Acheson 518; Truman II 435. Joe Martin: Truman II 442; NYT 4/24/51, 4/6/51. "discussion would be": NYT 4/10/51, 4/6/51; *Truman* 340; Acheson 520. *686* "foregoing message": NYT 4/11/51, 4/9/51; Truman II 448; Acheson 523. *687* Magnuson of Washington: Rovere and Schlesinger 174. daylight in Tokyo: NYT 4/12/51; *Truman* 345. *688* THE PRESIDENTIAL CHAIR: Rovere and Schlesinger 8. might be tried: ibid 8, 12; NYT 4/22/51; *Truman* 345. "God Bless America!": *Truman* 347; NYT 4/14/51, 4/18/51, 4/19/51. *689* "Douglas MacArthur": NYT 4/19/51, 4/20/51. "could not answer": NYT 4/20/51. "duty. Good-bye": NYT 4/20/51. *690* "in my heart": NYT 4/13/51; Rovere and Schlesinger 15; NYT 4/20/51. "just fade away": NYT 4/21/51, 4/20/51; Rovere and Schlesinger 9. *691* Republican national convention: NYT 4/22/51, 6/11/52. village of Panmunjom: NYT 5/19/51, 5/24/51. *692* "one big boom": Goldman *Decade* 181. "lot of money": Michener 49. *693* the United States: NYT 12/25/52. "irreducible minimum": NYT 7/10/51, 10/10/51; Acheson 532, 538. *694* most persuasive: NYT 4/7/49, 2/4/52. "just as stupid": NYT 8/3/47, 2/12/50, 11/5/50, 5/13/51, 8/5/51. *697* increasingly resentful: WA 1952. other people's wars: NYT 1/6/51; Acheson 281. *698* growing much bigger: NYT 8/7/45; Rovere *Years* 244. "Atomic Bombers": Jungk 242. "the hydrogen bomb": *Life* 9/6/54. *699* Super, the better: Jungk 265. leave it to him: ibid 270. "saner than Hitler?": ibid 270 ff. *700* fissionable materials: ibid 274; NYT 9/25/49; Mowry 192. "or super bomb": NYT 1/22/50, 2/4/50, 2/1/50. *701* of a button: NYT 2/5/50, 1/26/64; Jungk 265, 288. *702* it was MANIAC: Jungk 300 ff; NYT 2/28/52. *703* two, and sank: NYT 11/17/52; WA 1952. reporters, "beckons": Fab VI 30; Jungk 305; NYT 8/9/53; *Decade* 137. *704* "militarily acceptable": Jungk 307. came of it: Fab VI 30. *705* "play in, too": Fab VI 25. five days underground: ibid 30, 72. of this one: ibid 1; NYT 8/12/51. *706* themselves in it: John Brooks *Leap* 232; T 3/30/59. *707* "they could picket!": Bird 259; Kluckhohn "Mid-Century"; Schlesinger *Thousand* 740. and stayed there: Fab V 44; O'Neill 19. part of him: NYT 12/9/56; Whyte 147. *708* "on company time": Whyte 74, 81; Riesman 273. largest undergraduate group: Whyte 93. *709* "spot for you": NYT 11/12/52, 7/17/55. *710* what to do: Kronenberger 184. economic security: quoted in Kluckhohn "Evolution." "than he knows": *Decade* 291. *711* on American campuses: Rovere *McCarthy* 9; NYT 12/17/52, 12/21/52, 10/8/54, 6/29/55. *712* torn asunder: Stanley Walker "Book Branding." *713* free enterprise: NYT 10/8/51. "(group-forming) society": *NYT Magazine* 5/25/58; O'Neill 83; Kluckhohn "Evolution." in Dwight, Illinois: T 3/23/70, 3/30/70. *715* his own blood: NYT 3/27/49; Wertham 369. he could get: ibid 365, 377; Fab V 215. *716* larger than radio's: Fab V 215; *Leap* 161; T 5/15/50. *717* "barefoot voice": *Time* editors 176; T 2/27/50. television began: NYT 9/5/51; T 1/16/50. Milton Berle: T 11/20/50. *718* working for pay: Theodore White *1960* 279. toilets in unison: NYT 2/3/54; *Leap* 163; *Decade* 266; Wertham 369. "program or that": Kronenberger 81. *719* Murrow retired: NYT 11/19/51, 7/2/52, 5/12/55. "the . . . the paper": NYT 7/4/41. *720* or documentary film: T 7/23/56. *Break the Bank*: NYT 12/19/52, 6/19/56, 6/29/62. *721* of peeping Toms: T 2/27/56; Kronenberger 24; Tate "The Man of Letters." and Louis Kronenberger: Allen *Change* 272; Kluckhohn "Evolution." *722* went into eclipse: *Time* editors 127; T 1/2/56; *Leap* 168. and used contraceptives: Bird 51. prewar constellations: NYT 10/18/56, 6/28/56, 12/16/55, 10/6/55, 5/21/56, 12/19/57. *723* in the millions: *Leap* 168. a ghost town: NYT 1/10/54. *724* would come later: T 12/24/56; Hechinger and Hechinger 142; NYT 9/5/56. American experience: NYT 12/31/46. *725* *Without a Cause*: NYT 12/27/55; Howe "Notes on Popular Culture." regional speech: Goldman *Tragedy* 528; Steinbeck 106. *726* political campaigns: *Leap* 57. *727* crucial shopping moment: T 8/14/44. "off at Westport": NYT 5/26/46. consumer dollar: Fab V 209. motivational research: *Leap* 86; Kendrick 480. *728* among your creditors: *Decade* 302. credit card living: ibid 303. *729* American Gas Association: T 4/27/59. in the USSR also: NYT 4/13/55. Pets in Chicago: NYT 3/10/50, 8/15/51; WA 1950. *730* "name of style": Kronenberger 106. "the money is": WA 1952; Acheson 658; WM/Louis Lasagna; NYT 3/18/55; WA 1952. "get seasick": NYT 11/21/48; WA 1952. *731* a free press: NYT 3/11/52. U.S. had tripled: NYT 11/15/55; T 6/5/50. *732* Hammarskjöld of Sweden: NYT 10/4/51, 12/4/52, 4/8/53.

733 nationwide crime: Walter Johnson 247–48. *734* Mayor William O'Dwyer: NYT 3/18/51, 3/13/51. already been developed: NYT 5/8/50. *735* mean treatment: Fab VI 96; NYT 3/15/51. "to walk out": Fab VI 100–101. autumn's World Series: NYT 8/16/52. "*do about it?*":

NYT 3/22/51; Goldman *Decade* 198–99. *736* University of Kentucky: NYT 12/1/51. cheating on examinations: NYT 3/17/53, 1/4/52; Walter Johnson 247–48. *737* five hundred dollars: NYT 4/17/51. *738* a $520 Deepfreeze: NYT 2/6/51; Phillips *Truman* 406. *739* a $9,540 mink coat: NYT 2/3/51, 7/26/51, 2/28/51. "discriminating taste": *Decade* 188. literally wicked: NYT 2/3/51. *740* he hung on: NYT 12/5/51; *Truman* 408–11; NYT 12/5/51, 12/6/51, 12/16/51. appointments secretary: NYT 10/24/51, 7/28/51; *Truman* 409. *741* McGrath and Justice: NYT 7/7/51, 12/23/51, 1/11/52. dismissed McGrath: NYT 2/2/52, 4/4/52, 4/6/52. *742* trying to avert: NYT 4/9/52, 6/3/52. honorable objectives: NYT 12/20/50; Acheson 400. *743* "living American?": NYT 9/24/50; Rovere *McCarthy* 172; Griffith 115–16. "history of man": NYT 6/15/51; *McCarthy* 178–79. between the parties: Acheson 435. *744* " 'done his damnedest' ": Neustadt 96; NYT 4/18/52. Adlai E. Stevenson: NYT 1/24/52; Truman II 490; *Truman* 417. *745* "has any politics": NYT 7/23/52; Adams 13. Eisenhower jacket: Rovere *Years* 13–20. *746* "respect to me": NYT 1/7/52; Kenneth Davis 258. "from Dwight Eisenhower": NYT 1/24/52; *Truman* 415. *747* "was flabbergasted": Truman II 491–92. Democratic nominee: *Years* 342. *748* of that inconceivable: T 1/28/52. "seek the nomination": Kenneth Davis 236; Truman II 492. *749* "seemed thin": NYT 3/30/52; Acheson 632. "Good": NYT 3/31/52; Kenneth Davis 240. "No": Kenneth Davis 240. *750* "beside Alger Hiss": ibid. *750n* misspelled "Stephenson": Mazo 86. "ultimate timidity": NYT 3/31/52. "doesn't inhale": Kenneth Davis 263. he was packing: NYT 3/13/52, 3/20/52. *751* for the nomination: NYT 3/20/52, 4/3/52, 4/2/52, 4/9/52, 4/16/52, 4/23/52; Pusey 16–17. had to say: NYT 6/20/52; *Years* 22. *752* to stamp out: Fab VI 108; *Years* 33. to its hangar: NYT 7/8/52. *753* cattle prod: NYT 7/10/52. a nice point: Mazo 84–86; *Years* 61–62; *Life* 7/19/52. *754* "of another man": NYT 7/11/52; *Years* 27. be turned back: *Years* 27. the national convention: Pusey 15. *755* demanded "fair play": NYT 7/2/52; Walter Johnson 249–50. *756* "that road again!": NYT 7/11/52; Adams 35. *757* Ike had it: NYT 7/7/52, 7/8/52, 7/12/52. "in his administration": NYT 7/12/52. "of the party": Mazo 66–68. *758* on television, too: Adams 34; Mazo 97. *759* chosen their nominee: NYT 11/1/50. friends and admirers: Mazo 100. the White House: *Years* 105. *760* was badly divided: ibid; *Chicago Tribune* 7/13/52. "to his nomination": NYT 4/17/52; Kenneth Davis 264. "should be nominated": NYT 7/21/52; Kenneth Davis 268. *761* "and fair contest": NYT 7/22/52. "for the carnage": Kenneth Davis 269. "be too late": *Years* 342; NYT 7/22/52. "Stevenson of Illinois": NYT 7/23/52. *762* "it embarrass me?" Truman II 496. choice of 1952: NYT 7/26/52. " 'Thy will be done' ": Walter Johnson 260; NYT 7/26/52. "rest of them": Hughes 196. *763* "consequences of each": Kenneth Davis 273–75. "misgovern the people": ibid. and Stevenson friend: NYT 7/27/52, 7/29/52; Kenneth Davis 276–77. "I do not know": Acheson 699–700. proud of it: Kenneth Davis 314; *Decade* 234. *764* "often rather thin": *Years* 36–37. "about his back-bone": NYT 9/13/52; Donovan 103. *765* "well concede defeat": *Decade* 222; Walter Johnson 257. next five years: Kronenberger 157. *766* "eggheads are there?": WM/John Alsop 3/23/74. "psychopathic instability": *Decade* 224. of Governor Stevenson: *Truman* 427–28; Walter Johnson 225. *767* his dander up: NYT 9/4/52; *Years* 38; Hughes 493. "his family life": Walter Johnson 259. "discussed them": Hughes 41–43; Pusey 29–32. *768* "few weeks ago": NYT 10/4/52; Pusey 31; Hughes 41–43; Donovan 244; Adams 31–32. *769* state ticket: Griffith 195; *McCarthy* 184. "apply to method": NYT 10/28/52; *McCarthy* 182–83; Pusey 29; NYT 10/4/52. "Stevenson's part": Mazo 66–67; NYT 10/14/52. *770* "was revealed today": *N.Y. Post* 9/18/52. "the beneficiaries": Mazo 118. *771* "to smear me": NYT 9/21/52, 9/19/52; Mazo 117. *772* out of the question: Mazo 116; Nixon 85–87. "hound's tooth?": *Decade* 227. "out all right": Mazo 119–20. *773* seat of power: ibid 120–21. the Ambassador Hotel: Nixon 100. *773–774* "common people" . . . "to be said": Mazo 124; Nixon 108. *774* "television and listen": Mazo 124–25. *775* against the wall: Adams 37; Mazo 126. up the receiver . . . "about politics, too!": Nixon 110; Adams 40–41; Nixon 110–11. *776* "has been questioned": NYT 9/24/52. "everything I own" . . . "is honestly ours": Nixon 115. *777* "to keep it": NYT 9/24/52. *778* "Irish never quit": Nixon 117. "your $75,000 worth": Mazo 132. burst into tears: ibid 131. *779* "beyond expectations": Nixon 118. "dog world, anyhow": Hughes 40. from Dwight Eisenhower: Adams 38–39; Nixon 119. *780* "any time thereafter": NYT 9/25/52. *780n* "genre of weepers": Mazo 136. *781* "Nixon rejoices us": ibid. *782* "ended that night": NYT 10/17/52; Hughes 32–33; NYT 10/25/52; Adams 44. "not much": Adams 44. would be defeated: Kenneth Davis 289–90. *783* went Republican: NYT 11/3/52; 11/5/52. 69.4 percent: Whyte 332. Senate, merely one: *Years* 112–15. *784* said Stevenson: Kenneth Davis 290. "much to laugh": ibid 291. the Secret Service: NYT 11/6/52; Donovan 200–201.

XX WHAT WAS GOOD FOR GENERAL MOTORS
(pages 786–845)

786 audience laughed: Fab VI 136. 787 "fallow period": ibid 152; Donovan 202, 203; Davis 320; Acheson 694. sold at $5.95 . . . from her mother: Fab VI 70–71; NYT 4/9/56, 4/23/56; Life 6/25/56; T 3/19/56, 6/18/56. 788 as Vitaphone: Fab VI 222, 58; NYT 11/28/52. great as ever: Fab VI 68. 789 frame was plastic: ibid 182–83. sharp, chill wind: NYT 12/6/52; Donovan 17–18. 790 fateful one: NYT 12/6/52; Donovan 17; NYT 11/21/52. "massive retaliation": Donovan 19; NYT 5/13/53; Goldman Decade 248–49. 791 "since my return": NYT 12/6/52, 12/10/52; Donovan 19–20. outgoing administrations: Donovan 20; NYT 12/11/52. 792 January 12 and 13: NYT 11/25/52; Adams 5; Hughes 52. Labor Department: NYT 1/17/53; Donovan 105; NYT 9/11/53. do the same: NYT 4/8/53, 4/3/53; Donovan 77; Hughes 77; NYT 2/11/53. 793 "grocery store": Rovere Years 111; Donovan 25; NYT 1/24/53; Fab VI 43, Hughes 75–76. "free economy": Hughes 76; NYT 8/28/52; Decade 280, 243. 794 times as large: Hughes 67; Years 74. "illustrious ruler": Hughes 134; NYT 1/22/53; Mazo 150; NYT 10/1/53; Mazo 251. 795 "East issues settled": Hughes 134–35; Donovan 9; Hughes 76; Adams 99. "except to kids": Donovan 20–21; NYT 1/19/53, 1/25/53, 1/21/53; Donovan 23. senator's fire: Acheson 707; NYT 3/5/53. 796 into history: Phillips Truman 431–32; NYT 1/21/53. it every morning: NYT 1/22/53, 1/25/53; Adams 71; Donovan 206. 797 is his reward: NYT 1/22/53. in "deportment": Donovan 69–70; T 1/9/56; Donovan 61. his famous grin: Donovan 3; Hughes 103. 798 "rock the boat": Donovan 200; NYT 2/12/53; Donovan 204–205; Adams 73; New Republic 2/18/57. "not to interfere": Donovan 69, 207, 208. 799 "every other individual": Adams 74; NYT 1/22/53; Walter Johnson 321, 319. "Sincerely, DE": Donovan 207, 195; Adams 426. 800 Bernard Baruch: Years 315. with Sherman Adams: Donovan 196; Adams 427. 801 "do any harm": NYT 1/3/53; Mowry 329; Years 103; Rovere McCarthy 188. be reckoned with: NYT 2/8/53, 1/11/53. had to lose: NYT 3/19/53; Griffith 101–102. 802 only seem worse: NYT 3/21/53; Adams 94; Hughes 93; Griffith 202; Donovan 89. "of Mr. Bohlen": Adams 95; NYT 3/26/53. votes to 13: NYT 3/28/53. 803 Joseph R. McCarthy: Adams 95; McCarthy 33; Donovan 89; Griffith 204; NYT 3/31/53; McCarthy 33–34. half of 1954: NYT 4/26/53, 2/7/53; Walter Johnson 280. "this is done": NYT 6/28/50. 804 applauded vigorously: Hughes 109. IS RESCINDED: Donovan 28. 805 "releasing Chiang": NYT 2/3/53; Years 266; Walter Johnson 301. extremely awkward: Years 91; Donovan 86–87. 806 and the Russians: Adams 91–92. was deadlocked: Donovan 87. "horse of containment": McCarthy 240–41; Donovan 70–71. 807 stricken in Moscow: Schlesinger Thousand 187; Years 106; NYT 3/6/63. "his death makes": Donovan 41; NYT 3/6/53; Hughes 99–101. "their own toil": Hughes 103–104. 808 "speech about it": ibid. at the end: Hughes 112; NYT 4/17/53; Hughes 110, 105, 112; Adams 97–98. 809 "out to be": Adams 117–18. of the talks: NYT 5/8/52. 810 "with the Communists": Adams 98. a major offensive: Fontaine 66–67; Adams 96; Donovan 122–23. 811 Rhee gave in: Fontaine 67; Adams 101–102; NYT 7/12/53; Donovan 124. "present agreement": Years 149. "has been implemented": T 8/10/53. "against Communism": Years 145. 812 "Eisenhower's appeasement": Donovan 119, 126. "noticed no change": ibid 125–26. Robert A. Taft: T 10/3/53. 813 further reductions: NYT 1/10/53. strategy followed: Adams 21–22; Donovan 110. counsel despair: NYT 6/5/53. 814 in ill health: T 6/22/53, 8/10/53. "Howard Roberts": NYT 6/14/53. "back in January!": NYT 6/11/53; Adams 25. 815 postponed indefinitely: NYT 7/5/53. "futile battle": NYT 7/27/53. he was dead: NYT 8/1/53. "beyond calculation": NYT 8/1/53. 816 "man, go on": NYT 1/4/53, 8/4/53. "now under discussion": NYT 1/25/54; Donovan 239. 817 "into their business": NYT 8/5/53; Hughes 28–29. "to the ministry": Donovan 85; NYT 3/31/53; Donovan 87. 818 for the demagogue: Hughes 132. "nearly impotent": Walter Johnson 279; Washington Post 7/20/53; Donovan 143–44. 819 the House 265-2: Hughes 119–20; NYT 6/2/53; Donovan 133; Years 216. 820 late Joseph Stalin: NYT 10/21/53, 10/25/53; Kendrick 36–37; NYT 9/24/53. other Radulovichs: NYT 11/25/53. and the press: NYT 4/16/54; Donovan 287–88. 821 Communists in Asia: NYT 12/19/54; Donovan 285–86, 297–98. "national security": NYT 4/29/53. from the payroll: Donovan 289; NYT 10/24/53; Adams 150, 152; NYT 1/8/54; Mazo 155–56. 822 side down: Donovan 298; NYT 4/29/53. Bricker amendment: Donovan 105, 239; NYT 8/19/53. 823 half-million Americans?: Donovan 238–39; Hughes 144. "for this amendment": NYT 2/18/54, 4/7/53; Hughes 144. 824 "of Almighty God": Years 206. listening to him yet: NYT 1/31/54. 825 executive agreements: Donovan 240–41. individual states: Hughes 142–44. 826 "treated that way!":

Adams 410. "forty-eight governments": NYT 7/15/53; Donovan 237. and 42 opposed: NYT 2/26/54, 2/27/54. 827 to resist it: NYT 2/4/54; Donovan 241; Adams 108–109. rejected as unconstitutional: NYT 2/27/54. 828 lost India's friendship: Donovan 309; Hughes 205; Kenneth Davis 343–44; NYT 5/12/53. 829 "embrace this principle": Hughes 147; NYT 7/18/53. "their captivity": Hughes 147–48; Adams 88–89; NYT 7/2/53, 12/1/53. "of this country": Walter Johnson 298; Hughes 285; *Parade* 9/28/69; *N.Y. Herald Tribune* 8/12/58. 830 "enemy attack": Adams 399–400. it would be: ibid. 831 "and then some": NYT 7/7/57; Walter Johnson 309; *Years* 199. "does not happen": NYT 2/11/54. "war may go?" . . . "with large units": Donovan 263. 832 "not look back": NYT 12/31/49, 2/8/50; Acheson 672, 674. 833 Roy 194–95, 172. 834 declare war: Donovan 263. force in Korea: Burns *Soldier* 379. "totalitarian sea": Rostow "The American National Style." 835 and he did: Acheson 677–78. ask for it: NYT 5/16/54; Roy 225, 240; NYT 3/23/54. 836 "resolute today": Jungk 310; NYT 3/30/54. "power in Indochina": *Years* 193. 837 London and Paris: Donovan 259; Adams 122–23. "profound influences": NYT 4/8/54; Adams 120. Congress could act: Roy 271. 838 "such a decision": NYT 4/17/54; Mazo 255–56. was "unlikely": NYT 4/20/54. 839 fire upon himself: NYT 4/17/54. honor of France: T 5/8/72; Roy 340. 840 "may prove inescapable": Kendrick 359. "with a crash": Donovan 267. Cambodia, and Laos: ibid 268. 841 "relations as now": Adams 126–27. "blessing in disguise": Hughes 208. 841–845 Norma Jean Baker portrait: Guiles passim; *Current Biography* 1962; NYT 8/6/62; T 8/17/62.

XXI MR. CHAIRMAN, MR. CHAIRMAN
(*pages 847–893*)

847 "rolling readjustment": NYT 1/3/54, 2/7/54, 3/2/54, 3/18/54. St. Lawrence Seaway: NYT 5/7/54, 5/8/54. 848 in September: NYT 6/20/53; Donovan 247; NYT 9/1/54. heart disease: NYT 10/8/54, 12/22/54, 7/3/54. called a *hippy*: Fab VI 80. 849 staying in Hollywood: NYT 5/21/54, 4/16/54. 850 telecast March 7, 1955: NYT 10/21/54, 2/26/54; Kendrick 374–75; NYT 7/8/55, 12/26/51, 9/13/54, 11/30/55. morning sickness: NYT 1/16/53; Goldman *Decade* 266. 851 any previous year: Mazo 155. "H-bomb program": NYT 2/7/54; *Decade* 260; NYT 4/13/54; Donovan 294. "except Communists": NYT 6/17/54; Kendrick 41. 852 Hall of Fame: NYT 6/11/54. behind Borden: NYT 6/16/54; Schlesinger *Thousand* 457. 853 he knew it: NYT 7/1/54, 11/11/54; Jungk 317. Joseph R. McCarthy: Donovan 295. refused to take it: Jungk 318. 854 "for the occasion": NYT 4/13/54; Jungk 322, 324. "the devil's work": ibid 324. 854–855 interrogation of Oppenheimer: Jungk 325–26. 855 "interests of security": Donovan 296; Jungk 330. not be overlooked: NYT 7/2/54, 6/30/54. 856 had already formed: Jungk 229–38; NYT 12/3/63, 2/19/67, 6/16/54. flying over India: NYT 2/16/55; Jungk 310; NYT 3/16/54, 4/26/55. 857 everyone on earth: NYT 10/16/55. named Irving Peress: NYT 1/8/55. 858 investigative powers: NYT 2/20/54; Adams 145; NYT 1/31/54. "from him, too": T 3/22/54. 859 Permanent Investigations Subcommittee: ibid; NYT 9/5/52; 1/3/53. "directions please": *Harvard Crimson* 5/7/54. 860 he met McCarthy: T 3/22/54; Rovere *Years* 130. they might go: Rovere *McCarthy* 191. 861 "Cohn Schines best": T 3/22/54; *McCarthy* 200. "issue in 1954": NYT 11/17/53, 11/25/53. " 'of American money' ": NYT 11/25/53. 862 "friendly countries": Donovan 247; NYT 12/2/53. the President: NYT 12/5/53, 12/4/53. 863 Joseph R. McCarthy: *McCarthy* 23; NYT 2/3/54; *Years* 97. McCarthy support: *McCarthy* 22. 864 needed Schine: ibid; NYT 11/5/53. Reber about that: Griffith 245; NYT 3/12/54. Reber-Welch exchange: *McCarthy* 208–209. 865 of the Navy: Straight 30–31. "routine step": ibid 27. 866 "unreasonable about": *McCarthy* 206. "of the Army": Adams 143–45. "to regret it": Donovan 250; Walter Johnson 292; NYT 2/21/54; Straight 200. 867 "will be available": NYT 2/25/54; Straight 61; NYT 2/24/54, 2/25/54. "on his knees": *McCarthy* 31; Griffith 247–48. 868 "known Communists": NYT 3/4/54; Griffith 248–49; NYT 3/5/54. "wreck the Army": NYT 3/5/54, 3/10/54; Griffith 273; NYT 3/11/54, 2/28/54. 869 in the chair: Walter Johnson 292–93; NYT 3/13/54, 3/17/54. "point of order": NYT 4/23/54, 7/11/53. 870 "be so named": Straight 9. "of the Army": Straight 12. 871 "the Communist party": NYT 4/23/54; Straight 235–36. "any place, anywhere": *McCarthy* 221. 872 "to the end": NYT 11/14/54; Straight 84–85. 872–877 Welch-Cohn-Mundt-McCarthy: NYT 6/10/54; Straight 249–53; Transcript of the Hearings 2428–30. 873 "not get the information": ibid 125; NYT 5/5/54; *McCarthy* 216–17. "from a pixie?": NYT 4/28/54. 878 and the CIA: NYT 6/18/54; Transcript 2973–77; NYT 6/19/54. with disfavor: Griffith 264; NYT 11/4/54, 7/20/54. they had won: *Congressional Record* 83rd Congress

2nd Session 6/11/54 8032–33; NYT 7/1/54, 8/1/54. *879* the previous January: *McCarthy* 227; NYT 12/3/54; *McCarthy* 229. "is McCarthywasm": *McCarthy* 231. *880* with a sling: NYT 7/20/54, 11/30/54; *McCarthy* 235–36; NYT 11/18/54. "in the United States": Donovan 280. *881* "of the United States": ibid 277; Adams 164–66; Mazo 152; NYT 9/16/54; Donovan 280–81; Kenneth Davis 300. cheered him accordingly: Walter Johnson 285. exposed as myth: Donovan 274–75. the jitters: NYT 10/12/54; Hughes 75–76. *882* "through with politics": Mazo 138, 152–57; NYT 6/13/54; Mazo 157. "at the polls": NYT 11/5/54; *Years* 230; *Washington Post* 11/4/54. *883* "that goddamned drum": Donovan 282–84. *884* withering "Hardeeharhar": Fab VI 81. *885* bombing or spooking: Hechinger and Hechinger 82; Fab VI 80. *886* "highly emotionalized child": Hechinger and Hechinger 144, 147. "women of means": ibid 148, 154. *887* "her life": ibid 125, 126. "by their families": John Brooks *Leap* 233; Hechinger and Hechinger 126. a billion dollars: *Leap* 233. *888* "the wild frontier!": *Newsweek* 12/27/54; Fab VI 58–59; NYT 6/1/55. *889* carried too far: Hechinger and Hechinger 142–43. of the 1950s: Fab VI 86. "beautiful to feel!": quoted in Fab VI 89. *890* "just your glassy flesh": NYT 3/2/50; quoted in Fab VI 88. *891* "to the wheel": NYT 9/5/57; quoted in Fab VI 89. *892* SMOKE POT: Fab VI 90; *Leap* 237. *893* "everybody goes 'Awww!'": quoted in Fab VI 84.

XXII WITH ALL DELIBERATE SPEED
(pages 895–944)

895–899 American Institute of Public Opinion *The 1954 Pocket Almanac. 899* "to see me?": Schlesinger *Thousand* 924. *900* in states' rights: NYT 9/9/53, 5/17/54; T 10/12/53, 5/24/54. are inherently unequal: NYT 5/18/54. *902* "just plain nuts": Hughes 241–47, 201. *903* expected of others: Walter Johnson 273; Donovan 159, 154–55. the white South: Walter Johnson 273–74. expanding rapidly: Lerner 78; Donovan 390; Graham and Gurr 389. *904* permanent expulsion: T 2/20/56; John Brooks *Leap* 289; T 3/12/56. closed its file: NYT 9/2/55. *905* "and us white": T 9/10/56. *906* nearly three to one: T 12/10/56, 12/17/56. *907* "machinery had shifted": NYT 12/6/55; T 1/16/56. *908* "to their demands": T 2/6/56. "to hate them": NYT 3/20/56; T 3/5/56. *909* "boycotting the buses": T 2/6/56. "black ape": NYT 3/23/56; T 3/5/56. roared, "No!": T 4/2/56. *910* for civil rights: T 11/26/56. "humility and meekness": T 11/26/56. "That's right": T 12/31/56. *911* "interest demands it": Phillips *Truman* 399. *912* "Chinese civil war": Kenneth Davis 303; Donovan 301. and for all: Adams 131; Donovan 303. *913* "seven-thousand-mile frontier": Donovan 302. Eisenhower's message: NYT 1/25/55. *914* "or anything else": Rovere *Years* 264. offshore islands: Adams 130; Donovan 305; Hughes 166. "of this resolution": Donovan 306. *915* had been removed: NYT 1/30/55; Donovan 307; Kenneth Davis 303. as the Soviets: Walter Johnson 303; *Years* 269–75. in the past: Donovan 75. *916* he said grimly: NYT 6/23/55. "what they're doing": Adams 114, 91. in his briefcase: ibid 177. *917* Parc des Eaux-Vives: *Years* 280; NYT 7/18/55. in helicopters overhead: NYT 7/19/55; *Years* 287. *918* democratic Germany: NYT 7/19/55; Donovan 350. *919* "all our peoples": Donovan 349; NYT 7/22/55; Donovan 344; NYT 7/22/55. just stared: Donovan 344. have proposed it: ibid 345. *920* with MIGs: *Years* 290–91. it didn't melt: Adams 179; Donovan 350. *921* vacation in Denver: NYT 7/25/55; Donovan 352. to Open Skies: NYT 9/25/55; Donovan 359–60. across the hall: NYT 9/25/55; Donovan 360–61; Adams 183. "better come over": Donovan 362–63. *922* President's chances: NYT 9/25/55; Donovan 363; Adams 183. oxygen tent: Adams 154; Donovan 363–65. "to the car": Donovan 366. *923* "My God!": Mazo 189; NYT 9/25/55. into the car: Mazo 190. *924* for some time: Adams 181–82. since the Crash: NYT 9/26/55. chief's absence: Donovan 369; NYT 9/26/55. due until January: *Years* 319–28; Donovan 370 71; Adams 186. *925* "some other guy": Adams 187–88; Donovan 378. accompanied recovery: NYT 10/15/55; Donovan 376; NYT 10/23/55; Donovan 376. *926* "agreeably surprised": NYT 11/12/55, 11/15/55; Donovan 385; Adams 191. to think about: Hughes 174–76; Donovan 397. of this term: NYT 1/9/56; T 1/16/56. "his own appointees": Donovan 393–95; Adams 226. *927* vote for him: Adams 224–26; NYT 2/15/56. "that is, affirmative": T 1/2/56; NYT 3/1/56. *928* hearing aid: T 3/26/56. "in this matter": NYT 3/1/56. "an egghead": T 3/12/56. "Secretary of Agriculture": T 3/19/56. future President: T 1/2/56 (Man of the Year). *929* ribbons of concrete: Chapman 38. six cents to seven: NYT 5/6/56, 7/7/56. year for humor: T 2/27/56. *930* "Aw rutti!": NYT 12/10/56, 8/12/56, 10/18/56, 4/22/56. a million copies: NYT 11/16/56. "through the fence?": T 5/14/56. "the same response": NYT 5/14/56. *931* of American culture: NYT 10/2/58. implications then: NYT 4/21/56, 7/20/56. criminal irresponsibility: NYT 5/5/56,

3/19/56, 4/10/56, 1/13/56, 7/27/56; T 11/12/56. things personally: T 7/2/56. *932* "just plain loaf": *Ladies' Home Journal* October 1960. "came back with": *Redbook* September 1960; NYT 4/22/56, 4/20/56, 8/5/55; T 1/16/56. *933* a million francs: T 1/16/56, 1/23/56. "like the Kellys": NYT 4/5/56, 4/16/56, 4/19/56, 4/20/56; T 4/23/56. *934* IN FEBRUARY: NYT 4/19/56, 4/20/56; T 4/30/56; NYT 8/3/56; T 8/13/56. campaign for reelection: NYT 6/25/56. *935* "Egyptians!": NYT 7/20/56, 7/27/56; T 8/6/56. Eden in 1956: NYT 8/1/56. *936* "quite a combination": TC 1956 106; Hughes 212. "may be necessary": NYT 10/30/56. "honor our pledge": Hughes 214. *937* "the Hungarian people": NYT 11/1/56, 11/4/56; Adams 258–59; NYT 11/6/56; Hughes 220. without outside help: NYT 11/2/56, 11/4/56, 11/3/56. "how are you?": NYT 11/7/56. *938* "involved answer": Adams 259. a major issue: NYT 7/18/56. "known and respected": *Years* 368. *939* operating table: NYT 9/25/55, 6/9/56. Walter Reed Hospital: NYT 6/9/56; T 6/18/56. *940* SAY DOCTORS: NYT 6/10/56. him gingerly: Kenneth Davis 327–28. be a catastrophe: NYT 10/12/56; T 11/5/56, 10/29/56; Kenneth Davis 256–57; Mazo 179, 169, 180; NYT 8/14/56. "presidential timber": NYT 7/24/56; Hughes 173. *941* "the Vice President": Mazo 165; NYT 4/27/56, 6/27/56. a major issue: *Thousand* 596; NYT 8/23/56; Kenneth Davis 335. of his "image": McGinniss 27; Kenneth Davis 323. *942* "need to win": NYT 8/12/56; Kenneth Davis 332–35; Hughes 190; NYT 4/22/56; Davis 343. *943* for the challenger: Kenneth Davis 340; NYT 9/6/56. against odds: NYT 10/24/56, 11/6/56. Hoover's in 1928: NYT 11/7/56; Walter Johnson 285–86. "the way I feel": Hughes 224–28. *944* "across the nation": NYT 8/18/56; *Thousand* 8–9; Adams 253; McCarthy *Kennedys* 119; Burns *Kennedy* 190. "for President": McCarthy *Kennedys* 119.

XXIII THE PURSUIT OF HAPPINESS
(pages 945–961)

945 as cloudless: NYT 10/5/57. *946* Auto Buy Now: Steinbeck 95; Goldman *Decade* 305; NYT 10/1/58. *It's gone:* NYT 1/2/58; Steinbeck 47. *947* size of Poland's: John Brooks *Leap* 53. "in Detroit": Walter Johnson 263; *Fortune* May 1954. handling their credit: NYT 9/4/57; Galbraith *Affluent* 171–72; Whyte 360. *948* "apparatus of it": Whyte 354–55, 362, 363. "importance of thrift": Bird 259; Whyte 353; Riesman 18; Whyte 19–20. *949* sense of identity: Galbraith *State* 49; Whyte 78, 338. *950* week to spend: Spectorsky 7–8; Whyte 401. *951* "lead the bland": *Affluent* 135, 193–94; Mowry 222; *Affluent* 4–5. community playgrounds: Whyte 350. *952* "policemen, and rats": *Leap* 104–105, 108, 114–15. "well-adjusted": Riesman 16, 26. *953* "and weakness": ibid xviii; Whyte 5. they liked it: *Leap* 138; Whyte 3–4. only natural: Eisinger xiv–xvi; *Leap* 53–54. *954* "fundamental decency": Steinbeck 183; Whyte 321, 319; NYT 12/2/56. her own party: Whyte 316, 368, 389, 315–16. *955* "Man-Trap Set": Spectorsky 191; NYT 11/16/56; Whyte 337; NYT 9/16/55; Friedan 12. "feminist ideology": Friedan 13, 17; Lifton 203. *956* luck elsewhere: Friedan 12; Lifton 202; Friedan 154. *957* considered worse: Packard *Wilderness* 22–23; Walter Johnson 266. coalition faltered: Whyte 332. "his problem?": ibid 389. *958* and resented Kronenberger 120, 122–23, 223–24. *959* the next generation: Spectorsky 197, 248; Murray "Individuality." *960* "less than ninety": Whyte 428. polled one another: ibid 429. *961* "dreams into reality": *Decade* 307; T 10/21/57; NYT 10/6/57.

XXIV BEEP BEEP
(pages 963–1000)

963 "their achievement": NYT 10/1/57; T 10/14/57. *964* "if they did": NYT 10/5/57. ("of the de-emphasis"): Hughes 246; Adams 415. "too late": Adams 416–18; T 11/18/57. *965* "windshield wipers": T 10/21/57; Walter Johnson 313; Hughes 247. "book was home": Goldman *Decade* 313; T 10/21/57; Galbraith *Affluent* xxviii. *966* "be successful": T 10/21/57. source of power: T 11/4/57. *967* coup in itself: T 10/21/57. from outer space: T 10/14/57. *968* the reason why: T 10/14/57. tail-twitching cheerleaders: Rovere *Years* 124. *969* the national income: T 10/14/57; NYT 10/3/57; T 11/18/57. "as we are": T 10/21/57, 11/18/57. *970* of the language: T 10/21/57. or entertain, pupils: ibid; Lynd and Lynd 23. *971* "it the better": T 12/2/57; NYT 11/23/57; T 12/2/57. "or *with* information?": T 11/4/57. *972* survive in space: NYT 10/27/57; T 10/28/57; NYT 11/3/57, 11/14/57. to Columbus: NYT 11/2/57. MOON, IKE: T 11/11/57. *973* would vanish: NYT 10/10/57. a U.S. ICBM: NYT 6/6/57, 8/27/57, 11/29/58. *974* "to the good": Adams 415; Hughes 429. of a solution: Adams 414–15; NYT 12/21/57. *975* "on the moon": Adams 416–18; NYT 11/8/57. "into its interior":

T 10/28/57. *976* U.S. IGY committee: T 3/17/58. *977* starcrossed Edsel: 9/30/54. across the skies: T 10/21/57, 11/18/57. would tell him: NYT 10/10/57. *978* "at this moment": ibid. "err, bollix": T 10/7/57. *979* promises of glory: T 9/26/57. by local police: T 9/16/57. possible demonstrations: NYT 8/31/57. *980* "become a deluge!": T 9/16/57. delay of integration: NYT 9/5/57, 9/16/57, 9/8/57. *981* "at my command": NYT 9/21/57; Adams 345–46. a federal court: NYT 9/15/57; Adams 349–53; T 9/23/57, 9/30/57; NYT 9/25/57. "and judgment": NYT 9/21/57. *982* "got up and bowed": T 9/30/57. *983* phone booth: NYT 9/25/57; T 10/7/57. "do my job": T 10/7/57. to be hostile: ibid. *984* "good judgment": NYT 9/24/57; T 10/7/57. "the Federal Court": Adams 332, 351; NYT 9/24/57; Adams 354. *985* "read it": Adams 354–55; T 10/7/57. "anarchy would result": Adams 355; NYT 9/25/57. *986* Army rule: NYT 9/25/57. *986–987* "Roadblock Alpha" . . . "base of the neck": T 10/7/57. *988* "in America?": NYT 9/27/57; T 10/7/57. government $4,051,000: T 5/19/58. *989* called into service: Adams 356; T 10/7/57. *989n* "of free government": Adams 356. *990* "at random": T 10/14/57, 11/11/57. he retired: T 10/14/57, 5/19/58; NYT 7/31/58. *991* felt shame: NYT 8/2/62, T 10/7/57. *992* ("was working"): NYT 11/10/57; T 11/18/57; *Saturday Review* 11/2/57; T 11/4/57. stood vigil: T 10/4/57; NYT 11/8/57. a major recession: T 11/14/57. *993* was a stroke: T 11/27/57. "wrong with him": Adams 195; T 12/9/57; NYT 11/26/57. "is to it": Adams 196–97. *994* there, he wept: T 12/9/57; NYT 11/27/57; Adams 198. "to be excellent": NYT 11/29/57, 11/30/57. *995* "First ignition!" . . . "explosion occurred": NYT 12/7/57; T 12/16/57. *996* "Custer's last stand": T 12/16/57. *997–1000* Edsel portrait: John Brooks *Edsel*; Cone; Galbraith *Affluent*; Goldman *Decade*; *Consumer Reports* January and April 1958; *Life* 7/22/57, 8/5/57, 8/21/57; NYT 11/20/56, 8/27/57, 8/29/57, 10/5/57, 10/6/57, 11/28/57, 11/20/59; T 10/21/57, 11/30/59.

XXV THE CRUSADE FALTERS
(*pages 1001–1034*)

1001 ICBM attack: NYT 7/22/59; T 12/7/59; NYT 6/10/59. *1002* called "compacts": T 4/6/59. crew cuts: NYT 1/3/59; TC 1959; NYT 3/3/59; Adams 311; NYT 7/16/58, 11/22/59, 4/10/59. *1003* opened fire: NYT 7/10/59; T 7/20/59. old for her: NYT 5/3/57, 9/6/61, 4/10/59, 10/15/59, 10/8/59, 5/7/59, 3/1/59, 1/15/60, 7/25/61. *1004* the hula hoop: T 9/15/58; NYT 8/11/57. sixty-second birthday: T 12/1/58; NYT 12/7/58. *1005* through East Germany: T 12/1/58. *1006* "intolerable situation": Adams 271. armed forces anywhere: NYT 1/6/57. "this battle": Adams 274. *1007* the warships: ibid 289; NYT 4/26/57. "Eisenhower Doctrine": Adams 289. *1008* Eisenhower consented: NYT 7/15/58, 7/4/58. Lebanese move: T 7/28/58; Adams 291. was expanding: NYT 9/24/58; Adams 293. *1009* in world affairs: NYT 7/16/58; *Time* editors 75. a light cruiser: DeMott 172. *1010* western Europe: Servan-Schreiber 59, 36. "a dear friend": Walter Johnson 266. and Panama City: John Brooks *Leap* 339. *1011* intolerable gloating: *New Republic* 10/27/58. "classless society": Nixon 259. *1012* stayed home: NYT 4/28/58. rocking the boat: Schlesinger *Thousand* 189. *1012–1020* Nixon trip: Mazo 206–46; Nixon 183–228. *1013* "irrational state": NYT 5/9/58; Mazo 233; Nixon 219. *1014* to Nixon's aid: NYT 5/14/58. *1015* was preposterous: Mazo 222. "of this mob": Mazo 225. *1017* Nixon's limousine: NYT 5/14/58. *1018* wobbled toward him: ibid. *1020* against possible attack: ibid. "assistance is requested": ibid. had been friendly: NYT 5/16/58. *1021* he was, too: Nixon 231; T 6/23/58. vicuña story: NYT 1/12/58. tax returns: T 7/14/58; NYT 6/11/58. *1022* "that he had": T 7/7/58. *1024* like Bernard Goldfine?: T 6/30/58. *1025* Washington bureaucracies: Adams 440; T 7/14/58. "as they are": T 6/23/58. *1026* "would be gone": T 6/30/58. "and tirelessly": NYT 6/19/58; Hughes 266–67; Adams 445–46. *1027* should be fired: T 6/30/58. all these years (and following paragraphs): T 7/14/58. *1029* collateral for loans: NYT 7/4/58. "told about it": T 7/14/58. a lot of that: NYT 6/19/58. *1030* White House roster: NYT 6/23/58. *1031* was political: NYT 8/14/58. *1032* "on November 4": NYT 9/10/58; WA 1959 120. lowered upon him: Adams 446–47. *1033* "I can give you": NYT 9/28/58. last cigarette: Adams 447. agreed to go: Hughes 269; Adams 451. "twenty-five states": Nixon 232–33. *1034* "your money": NYT 10/14/58, 10/16/58, 10/17/58, 10/21/58, 10/22/58, 10/23/58. "the White House": NYT 11/6/58, 11/5/58; Nixon 233. "do with Nixon": NYT 11/5/58; Nixon 234; NYT 11/5/58, 11/10/58.

XXVI TATTOO FOR THE GENERAL
(*pages 1036–1085*)

1036 proof of it: Mencken 264. dead ahead: NYT 12/19/58. "be any riots": Fab VII 28. accept contraception: NYT 11/26/59. *1037* "these questions": Kendrick 410; Goldman *Decade* 319; NYT 8/28/58. got their coffee: NYT 10/1/58, 1/3/60. *1038* on restricted beaches: NYT 2/24/60. visible at last: NYT 5/11/60, 6/16/60, 7/19/60, 6/6/60, 7/19/60, 7/26/60, 10/20/60; WA 1962 251. *1039* to do it: NYT 5/14/60; Fab VII 28–29. *1040* facts of life: NYT 5/10/60; WA 1961 168; W 1966 163; NYT 11/26/59. ("Bashfull"): Kendrick 429–30; *Decade* 318; Fab VI 44; NYT 8/29/58; T 10/19/59. "coached or tutored": NYT 11/3/59. *1041* its hearing room: *Decade* 319; NYT 10/15/59. *1042* "intellectual life": Fab VI 44; *Decade* 321–22; NYT 11/3/59. smiled at him: *Decade* 322. *1043* five to one: NYT 11/5/59, 11/6/59. every week: Kendrick 440. *1044* named Truman Capote: NYT 3/11/60; Kendrick 437; *Chicago Daily News* 9/20/58; Nixon 304; NYT 1/5/60, 5/3/60, 11/16/59; T 11/30/59. "matter anyway": T 2/23/59. *1045* "hand of Eisenhower": NYT 4/16/59; Hughes 342. *1046* "will break it": NYT 1/27/59. what it was: T 6/1/59; NYT 5/25/59; T 3/2/59. Soviet officials: WA 1960 108; T 8/3/59; NYT 7/24/59; Hughes 287; NYT 7/24/59. *1047* the "Sokolniki Summit": NYT 7/25/59; Nixon 255–58; T 8/3/59. *1047–1048* "we are stronger" . . . "no free elections": WA 1960 111; Nixon 255–58; T 8/3/59. *1048* Berlin ultimatum: NYT 8/6/59. *1049* in his eyes: NYT 8/26/59, 8/27/59; WA 1960 117; T 9/7/59; NYT 8/8/59. "going splendidly": NYT 9/3/59; T 9/14/59; NYT 9/5/59, 9/8/59. *1050* as their host: NYT 9/16/59. "than his backside": NYT 9/20/59. to a detente: NYT 9/26/59; T 10/5/59. Soviet Union next year: NYT 9/28/59. them and Khrushchev: T 10/5/59. *1052* "our friends abroad": NYT 11/5/59, 12/4/59. in Casablanca: T 12/14/59, 12/15/59. *1053* 1960, in Paris: NYT 12/23/59, 12/24/59. to join them: T 1/12/59; NYT 8/2/53. *1054* Castro's Trotsky: Schlesinger *Thousand* 220. next to impossible: T 1/12/59, 1/25/59. and they said so: T 1/12/59. *1055* bogeymen everywhere: T 4/27/59; Nixon 351–52; Haynes Johnson 25. to invade Cuba: T 11/9/59, 3/16/59; NYT 2/21/59, 1/22/59; Haynes Johnson 49. "a Communist government": NYT 1/6/59. *1056* suspicions were allayed: Haynes Johnson 30–31, 37. *1057* battle flag: ibid 76. *1058* in the camp: ibid 38. around in slime: ibid 44. *1060* "we will win": ibid 81, 75–76. *1061–1067* general sources: see under Powers in the Bibliography. *1062* Francis Gary Powers: NYT 5/6/60. *1063* "have had any": Adams 455. of his magazine: Hughes 303. *1067* weeks of pandemonium: NYT 5/8/60. *1067–1070* general sources: WA 1961 171; Hughes 300–302; *Decade* 335–38. *1068* complete confession: NYT 5/8/60. flights will continue: NYT 5/10/60. *1069* "planes over here": NYT 5/12/60. is frigid: NYT 5/17/60. *1070* world conciliation: T 5/30/60. no punishment: NYT 5/18/60. before the summit: NYT 5/26/60. "keeping busy?": NYT 5/20/60. *1071* "all of us": Hughes 306. marine helicopter: NYT 6/11/60. eighty-thousand-gun salute: NYT 6/17/60. "all of it": Theodore White *1960* 117; Hughes 310–11. *1072* years in prison: NYT 8/20/60. "us in 1952?": Adams 453. *1072n* was laid off: NYT 2/10/62. *1073* munitions. Then . . . "and will persist": Galbraith *State* 399–400; Adams 325–30; WA 1962 90; NYT 1/18/61. "it is directed": *State* 317–19. *1074* sheriff's, side: NYT 9/27/60; McGinniss 32. *1076* public explanation: Hughes 319, 250; NYT 8/25/60; Nixon 339. margin held steady: NYT 3/10/60. *1077* on and on: NYT 7/14/60. *1078* to Kennedy's 46: NYT 7/27/60. Kennedy 50: NYT 8/27/60. circumstances for him: Nixon 326; NYT 8/30/60. They applauded: NYT 9/8/60, 9/13/60; Sorensen 190–91. *1079* percent undecided: Theodore White *1960* 320. "September 26": Nixon 336; NYT 9/27/60. beard growth: NYT 10/8/60, 10/14/60, 10/22/60. *1080* "fathers, don't we?": NYT 10/13/60, 10/20/60; Nixon 363; *Thousand* 73–74. *1081* reversed the result: Sorensen 209. *1082* "will all support": Nixon 409; Theodore White *1960* 304; Nixon 376–79. Wednesday morning: NYT 12/16/60. "early yet": White *1960* 18. *1084* to be governed: NYT 12/16/60. "in the distance": Nixon 417. *1085* "to all men": Nixon 402.

XXVII A NEW GENERATION OF AMERICANS
(*pages 1089–1131*)

1089 in Cleveland Park: NYT 1/20/61; Schlesinger *Thousand* 1–2. *1090* new administration . . . "our ancient heritage": NYT 1/21/61. "what a day!": Fab VII 37; *Thousand* 5. with greater confidence: Gold *1940–41* 27. *1091* three years earlier: NYT 12/16/60; Manchester

Death 505. and pulling away: Manchester *Portrait* 11–12; NYT 12/18/60; Neustadt 94. typical early days: NYT 1/22/61. *1092* "what you told him": Agronsky 9; NYT 1/22/61; *Portrait* 12–13. rid of it: NYT 2/19/61; WM/Ronald L. Ziegler; Agronsky 9; NYT 12/16/61. *1093* as big as Ike's: NYT 2/26/61; *Portrait* 15. each morning: NYT 2/26/51; *Portrait* 15–16. *1094* cultural coordinator: Halberstam 41; *U.S. News and World Report* 5/1/61; *Thousand* 144; NYT 1/22/61, 6/27/61. Bay of Pigs: NYT 4/21/61; Haynes Johnson 67. *1095* "ill-starred an adventure": Halberstam 66, 69; *Thousand* 292. base was covered: *Thousand* 238; WM/John F. Kennedy October 1961. from the President: Sorensen 296; *Thousand* 239–40. *1096* "the United States?": Sorensen 295–96; NYT 4/21/61. "share their confidence": Sorensen 296; NYT 4/21/61; Haynes Johnson 65; *Thousand* 239, 267. *1097* "little as possible": *Thousand* 249, 259, 246. force were committed: Haynes Johnson 82, 70; NYT 4/17/61. miles away: Haynes Johnson 69, 84. *1098* "the Cubans themselves": *Thousand* 247; NYT 4/13/61; Sorensen 298. fire a rifle: *Thousand* 250; Haynes Johnson 69. chance of winning: NYT 4/21/61. *1099* "would be available": *Thousand* 269, 250; *U.S. News and World Report* 1/7/63; *Thousand* 281; NYT 5/28/61. *1100* on one ship: *Thousand* 270; NYT 4/16/61; Haynes Johnson 94; *U.S. News and World Report* 1/14/63; Haynes Johnson 113. enemy aircraft: Haynes Johnson 77–79; *U.S. News and World Report* 1/14/63. "and rebellion": Haynes Johnson 128–29; *Thousand* 274–75. *1101* by the CIA: Haynes Johnson 95. *1102* "fish is red": NYT 4/26/61; *U.S. News and World Report* 1/14/63; Haynes Johnson 100. and executed: Haynes Johnson 60, 120–22. *1103* "these people there?": ibid 100, 83, 105, 295; *Thousand* 295. *1104* had been lost: Haynes Johnson 103. *1105* back that night: ibid 111, 113. *1106* "air force fields": NYT 4/18/61; *Thousand* 271; Haynes Johnson 92; NYT 4/18/61. "off for Cuba": Haynes Johnson 93. the United States: *Thousand* 291; Haynes Johnson 152. *1107* a thousand wounded: Johnson 136–38. "the main business": ibid 143; *Thousand* 276. *1108* "popular I get": John Kennedy 112; Sorensen 291; *Thousand* 292. "alongside Fidel Castro": *Reader's Digest* November 1964; *Thousand* 285; NYT 4/23/61; *Militant* 5/1/61. *1109* WE NEED YOU: Haynes Johnson 129–30. *1110* Americans were killed: ibid 154–56; *Thousand* 278. WAIT FOR YOU: Haynes Johnson 161, 167. to ransom them: ibid 349; NYT 4/22/61, 12/24/62. "streets of Budapest": Haynes Johnson 174; NYT 4/21/61, 4/19/61. *1111* "nuclear armaments": NYT 4/21/61; *Thousand* 287–88. from the Comintern: NYT 3/2/61. *1112* "of the peril": NYT 4/21/61; Haynes Johnson 175. never forget: *Thousand* 297. *1113* and an interpreter: Halberstam 72; NYT 5/20/61; Fontaine 413. "beginning of the end": NYT 5/8/60, 9/24/60, 9/30/60, 10/13/60. immediate removal: Fontaine 390; NYT 2/14/61. *1114* divided Berlin: NYT 8/31/61; Fontaine 315, 423. intelligence activities: NYT 6/27/48, 5/15/60, 10/23/60. *1115* laugh it off: Fontaine 412–13, 314–15; T 6/9/61; Halberstam 74–75. "Jacqueline Kennedy to Paris": T 6/9/61; NYT 6/3/61. "in my life": *Thousand* 367; Halberstam 76; NYT 6/4/61. *1116* "and blackmailed": NYT 11/15/64. only straitjackets: NYT 6/6/61, 6/11/61; Fontaine 416. "cold winter": Fontaine 416. *1116n* "war over Berlin": Khrushchev 458. *1117* "have to act": Halberstam 76. chauvinistic speeches: WA 1962 113. "it's all over": WA 1962 113; Fontaine 418. Walter Ulbricht: WA 1962 115; NYT 8/6/61. *1118* in East Berlin: T 8/25/61; NYT 8/13/61, 8/16/61; *Thousand* 395. for the "mistake": WA 1962 121; NYT 9/8/61, 9/28/61, 9/2/61; *Thousand* 460–61; Fontaine 425; NYT 10/18/61. *1119* since V-J Day: Fontaine 421–22; NYT 9/19/61. "December 31, 1961": Fontaine 423–25; *Thousand* 400; NYT 10/18/61. *1120* "like the place": *Thousand* 548; Halberstam 76. of real power: NYT 3/19/61. for it—unimportant: NYT 3/1/61. *1121* "White House lawn": NYT 2/24/61; Carpenter 50; Goldman *Tragedy* 388–90; NYT 10/23/61. deeply affected: *Thousand* 396; NYT 8/21/61. *1122* "got out here": NYT 5/10/61; Halberstam 135. "will fly in": NYT 5/13/61; *Life* 10/26/62. *1123* eighteen months: NYT 10/27/72; *Thousand* 322, 539, 541; NYT 5/5/61. *1123n* draftees to Vietnam: WA 1972 88. *1124* not "lose" Indochina: *Thousand* 321; NYT 1/13/51. "your free people": Sorensen 651; *Thousand* 536. "he had inherited": T 1/29/73; Sorensen 652; *Thousand* 537–38. *1125* "matter of time": Theodore White *1968* 16; *Thousand* 542; T 8/4/61. was "essential": Halberstam 173; Sheehan 81. *1126* included troops: Sorensen 650; NYT 5/13/61, 11/10/61; Halberstam 129. "in this period": NYT 3/15/61, 3/16/61, 5/5/61, 5/9/61; Sheehan 80. chance of success: Sheehan 81, 97. *1127* imbued with it: Langer 1271; NYT 10/17/61; *Tragedy* 399; *Thousand* 544. "technological capacity": NYT 1/10/62; *Thousand* 542. political considerations: Sorensen 655. *1128* Viet Cong as heroes: NYT 10/16/61; Sorensen 655; Sheehan 142–43. "to take another": Sorensen 653; *Thousand* 547. *1129* "crazier than hell": Halberstam 177; NYT 11/10/61; Sorensen 655; Halberstam 174. making headway: NYT 2/9/62, 2/14/62; Halberstam 186. *1130* also glowed: NYT 3/27/62; *Current Biography* 1969; Langer 1271; Sheehan 111; NYT 7/25/62. *that* would mean:

Thousand 548–49; Halberstam 203. *1131* (MACV): *Thousand* 549–50; NYT 7/24/62; Fitz-Gerald 165.

XXVIII NOW THE TRUMPET SUMMONED US AGAIN
(pages 1133–1194)

1133 hundred years earlier: NYT 5/26/61. *1134* "was always time": O'Donnell and Powers 16–17; Halberstam 286. in the Kremlin: T 4/21/61, 4/28/61. the year before: Sidey 112; NYT 4/12/61. *1135* pre-eminence particularly: Sorensen 524 ff. *1136* "rocket thrust": Sidey 114–15. at 18,000 mph: NYT 4/11/61; Sidey 111–12; NYT 4/12/61. *1137* " 'the Mother-land Knows' ": NYT 4/12/61, 4/15/61; T 4/21/61. "of the world": NYT 4/13/61; T 4/21/61. *1138* "Can we leapfrog?": Sidey 129–32; NYT 4/14/61. "nothing more important": NYT 4/14/61; *Newsweek* 7/7/69; Sidey 131. *1139* "Spacetown, U.S.A.": NYT 5/6/61. "safely to earth": NYT 5/26/61; T 6/2/61; Armstrong et al 18. on its way: Sorensen 526. *1140* "taken care of": WA 1963 150; NYT 7/22/61, 8/6/61; WA 1962 128; NYT 2/21/62, 3/4/62; T 3/2/62. "I am go": NYT 2/21/62. *1141* "will you?": T 3/2/62, 2/22/62, 2/21/62. "saw of it": NYT 2/21/62, 2/24/62. *1142* they prayed: NYT 2/22/62. "hot in there": NYT 2/24/62, 2/21/62. *1143* "person ever is": NYT 2/24/62. "needed boost": NYT 2/23/62, 2/27/62, 3/2/62. *1144* into orbit: T 5/12/61; Armstrong et al 17; T 3/12/62. Houston he said: NYT 8/6/61. "peace are there": Sorensen 527–28. freedom riders: NYT 5/5/61. *1145* "the right road": ibid; *Alabama* 221. at the riders: NYT 5/5/61, 5/15/61. *1146* very advanced: NYT 3/6/61. the blacks ask?: Guthman 157; NYT 6/25/60. *1147* "We will move": NYT 5/7/61; Guthman 162. *1148* It did: NYT 5/9/61; Guthman 166–67; NYT 5/14/61; T 5/26/61. *1149* rescued the others: NYT 5/15/61. *1150* was a joke: NYT 5/20/61; Guthman 167; WM/David E. Swift; T 5/26/61. in their credit: NYT 5/16/61. *1151* of the President: NYT 5/20/61, 5/16/61. than Birmingham: NYT 5/21/61, 6/1/61. *1152* heard him say: NYT 5/21/61. "are there now": Guthman 171. "had broken down": NYT 5/21/61; T 6/2/61. *1153* simply proved wrong: NYT 5/21/61. again. Then: NYT 5/22/61. "these people are": Guthman 172–73. *1154* law enforcement officers: NYT 5/22/61. *1155* "survive politically": Schlesinger *Thousand* 936; Guthman 178. succeed Patterson: NYT 11/7/62. in waiting rooms: NYT 5/30/61; *Thousand* 936; NYT 9/23/61; Sorensen 478. *1156* time by then: Angoff and Mencken; NYT 6/25/61. of the century: Guthman 180–81. *1157* of Mississippi: *Thousand* 940; NYT 9/28/62. "of tyranny": NYT 6/26/62, 9/13/62, 9/11/62, 9/14/62. *1158* or make one: NYT 11/4/59. "about a year": Guthman 185. "take a judge?": *Thousand* 941; NYT 9/26/62. *1159* "to believe that": NYT 9/14/62, 9/21/62; Guthman 189. "rights of one": NYT 9/25/62. *1160* "Communists!": NYT 9/26/62. "how it goes?": NYT 10/1/62. "will be there": NYT 9/30/62; *Thousand* 943. *1161* turned back again: NYT 9/28/62; Lord 165–66. point of violence: Guthman 93. *1162* $5,000 a day: NYT 11/16/62. " 'poultry program' ": *Thousand* 944. *1163* broken his word: NYT 10/1/62. in "this afternoon": Lord 196. a campus booth: NYT 10/1/62; Sorensen 287. *1164* "had no choice": NYT 10/1/62, 10/5/62; Lord 209. "uphold that honor": NYT 10/1/62. *1165* "to those fellows": NYT 10/1/62; T 10/12/62; NYT 10/5/62. "trigger-happy" marshals: NYT 10/2/62; T 10/12/62; NYT 10/2/62. *1165n* Guthman 204. *1166* "lives, nigger?": Guthman 203; T 10/12/62; *Thousand* 948. Franklin Roosevelt: NYT 10/2/62, 10/7/62, 1/21/63, 4/12/63, 12/7/62. *1167* "of hate": NYT 6/14/69. "joined chapters": NYT 5/14/61; T 2/16/61. *1168* "muzzle the military": *Thousand* 743; NYT 7/21/61; *Thousand* 1020; *Life* 2/9/62. official proclamation: *Thousand* 1020. "against Communism": *Life* 2/9/62; NYT 10/29/61. *1169* "mental breakdown": DeMott 72, 77. "afternoon comes": *Thousand* 752, 753; NYT 11/17/61, 10/28/61. *1169n* "passersby notice it": NYT 4/4/65. *1170* "the Promised Land": *Thousand* 755. about the President: NYT 9/18/62: *Thousand* 755. *1171* *Air Force One:* Sidey 272–73. do it, too: NYT 1/23/61. *1172* backed down: Sidey 289–90. *1173* didn't believe her: ibid 272; *Thousand* 643; NYT 6/21/62. "is from within": Sorensen 335. Soviet technicians: Abel 6, 929–30. *1174* on the island: NYT 10/11/62. to worry about: Abel 1 *1176* "days ahead": ibid 17. the next morning: ibid 21. calls his brother: ibid 32. *1177* "planning Pearl Harbor": Robert Kennedy 31; Abel 31–42 passim. *1178* are under way: NYT 10/18/62; Abel 43–53 passim. *1179* American tradition: Robert Kennedy 36; *Thousand* 806–807. blockade of Cuba: NYT 11/3/62; Abel 54–68 passim. taken first: NYT 10/20/62. *1180* the stations why: Abel 69–75 passim. weapons in Cuba: Robert Kennedy 48–49. *1181* until Tuesday: NYT 10/23/62. on alert: Abel 76–83 passim. *1182* "flaming crisis": Abel 84–94 passim. "greatest urgency": NYT 10/23/62. six days ago: Robert Kennedy 55. *1183* "Western Hemisphere": NYT 10/23/62. hastily disperses them:

Abel 95–109 passim. *1184* the Security Council: NYT 10/24/62. *1185* "caught the burglars": *Thousand* 817; Abel 123–38 passim. before noon: NYT 10/24/62. ready for war: NYT 10/27/62. is unimportant: NYT 10/25/62, 10/27/62. *1186* "have been impeached": Robert Kennedy 17. "just blinked": ibid 71; Abel 123–38 passim. *1186n* "strain and hurt": Robert Kennedy 69–70. *1187* "of the sites": NYT 10/26/62; Abel 139–51 passim. submit to searches: NYT 10/27/62. *1188* be found: NYT 10/28/62; Abel 152–64 passim. *1189* "very hazardous course": NYT 10/28/62; Robert Kennedy 96–97. committed to Castro: Robert Kennedy 109; NYT 11/3/62. capital be evacuated: Abel 165–79 passim. 40,000 to 50,000: *Thousand* 831. "the Soviet Union": NYT 10/29/62. *1190* "nuclear test ban": Abel 180–86 passim. "go with you": Abel 186; Robert Kennedy 110. *1190–1194* Goldmark portrait: *Current Biography* 1940, 1950; *Newsweek* 1/28/48; T 12/4/50; NYT 12/17/67, 11/27/70, 7/26/71, 8/2/71, 8/3/71.

XXIX DON'T LET IT BE FORGOT
(*pages 1195–1235*)

1195 star role: Fab VII 139; Sorensen 489–90. *1196* ready for him: WA 1963 102; NYT 4/3/63. King's, followed: NYT 4/13/63, 4/14/63, 5/10/63, 4/13/63. *1197* for reinforcements: NYT 5/3/63, 5/8/63, 5/4/63, 5/8/63. base he wished: T 5/24/63; NYT 5/13/63, 5/24/63, 5/19/63. *1198* southern jails: NYT 5/16/63; Sidey 396; NYT 5/16/63, 5/1/63, 5/13/63; Sorensen 489; Schlesinger *Thousand* 964. way of thinking: Guthman 207–208; NYT 1/5/63. *1199* "hands in despair": Guthman 207–10. "risk I take": NYT 5/19/63, 5/22/63, 6/6/63. *1200* on television: NYT 6/10/63. obstruct them: Guthman 215; WA 1963 106, 109–10; Sidey 399–403; *Thousand* 964; Sorensen 493. *1201* "central government": NYT 6/12/63. Wallace walked away: Sidey 401; NYT 6/12/63. "suspected were there": NYT 6/13/63; Guthman 217–18. *1202* "life or law": *Thousand* 965; NYT 6/12/63. "can treat them": NYT 6/12/63; *Thousand* 966. encourage violence: Fab VII 144; Sidey 405; Sorensen 504–505; *Thousand* 969. *1203* HOUSING—NOW!: NYT 8/29/63. Lincoln Memorial . . . "of their character": ibid. *1204* didn't regret it: Sorensen 505. "nonviolent talk": NYT 5/10/63; Fab VII 154; NYT 5/15/63. *"fire next time!"*: Guthman 219–20. *1205* meeting deteriorated: NYT 9/19/63. youth repeated it: Guthman 220–21; *Thousand* 962–63. fire next time: Guthman 221, *1206* the *Honey Fitz*: Sidey 405; NYT 5/30/63. "than I have": NYT 5/14/63. *1207* pay that price: Sidey 416; *Thousand* 978; Halberstam 295. "our own attitude": *Thousand* 891; NYT 6/11/63; Sorensen 733. "since Roosevelt": Sorensen 733. *1208* "beneficial to all": *Thousand* 920. in 1964, either: Sidey 388. to the 88th: *Thousand* 713. *1209* "serves his nation": NYT 6/29/63, 6/6/63; *Thousand* 881; NYT 10/27/63; John Kennedy 817. *1210* he said Texas: NYT 9/4/63, 9/9/63, 10/4–11/63, 10/13/63. "guarded optimism": John Kennedy 11; NYT 1/15/63; *Thousand* 982–86; NYT 4/23/63. *1211* "McNamara says so too": *Thousand* 983. struggle between them: Halberstam 250. a "barbecue show": NYT 5/10/63, 6/11/63; Sorensen 657. *1212* "for all time": NYT 6/16/63, 7/8/63; John Kennedy 459–64. shocking treachery: NYT 6/28/63. *1213* "Binh Xuyen in 1955": Halberstam 261; *Thousand* 989–90; NYT 8/16/63. he tell them?: NYT 8/23/63. "afraid to die": Halberstam 264–65. *1214* "same country?": ibid 266–67; *Thousand* 993. "promptly as possible": Halberstam 283–84; NYT 10/3/63; Goldman *Tragedy* 399. *1215* "people of Vietnam": T 11/8/63; Sorensen 658–59; NYT 9/3/63; Halberstam 272. were reporters: NYT 10/8/63; *Thousand* 966; Halberstam 283; T 11/8/63; NYT 11/1/63; T 10/25/63. *1216* was imminent: NYT 11/3/63, 11/2/63, 11/13/63; T 11/8/63. "fatherland's interests": NYT 11/2/63, 11/3/63. *1217* stabbed repeatedly: NYT 11/2/63; T 12/6/63. but not here: NYT 11/14/63; *Thousand* 997; T 12/6/63; Halberstam 291–93. stable government: NYT 11/3/63. "so could he": NYT 12/3/63; Halberstam 286. *1218* Thursday, November 21: NYT 11/25/63. January 1, 1964: Rose Mary Woods to the author 8/4/64. *1219* effete snobs: NYT 11/20/62; T 11/22/63. (would end publication): NYT 10/16/63; Fab VII 130. "foe of Communism": T 11/22/63. "waning confidence": NYT 5/5/63, 11/16/63. *1220* "been an assassin": NYT 11/16/63. "Spindle, or Mutilate": NYT 9/4/63, 9/4/64; Customer Relations Office, U.S. Post Office, New York City; NYT 7/1/63; Sally Morgan to the author 4/10/63. ("I got screwed"): *Life* 8/23/63; NYT 4/21/63; Greene 115. *1221* in Bryan, Texas: T 6/21/63, 12/6/63, 11/22/63, 1/21/73. *1222* "break up anyway": T 11/22/63, 10/20/63. "of a man": T 10/5/63. in fact ignored: NYT 11/17/63; T 11/22/63. *1223 in the Rain*: NYT 4/14/64. by its publisher: NYT 8/25/63, 5/27/63, 8/9/63, 1/31/63, 8/25/63, 1/31/63, 9/8/63. *1224* (ten inches) reason: NYT 11/18/63, 12/30/63, 11/11/63, 4/25/63; T 11/22/63. and "Standing There": NYT 12/1/63; T 11/15/63; DeMott 78. of self-destruction: NYT 11/3/63. *1225* heavily chaperoned: NYT 11/22/63, 12/7/63, 2/2/63.

the labor movement: John Brooks *Leap* 157–58. nearly ten million: Bird 257. "that is rising": ibid 267. *1226* dollars a year: Servan-Schreiber 83–90. upper middle class: *Leap* 138. million Americans: Theodore White *1964* 365. *1227* political potency: *Leap* 11; NYT 4/16/63; *Leap* 104. across state lines: *Leap* 120–21. *1228* those with it: Manchester *Death* 189–91. in guerrilla warfare: T 9/10/73, 11/22/63. British prostitute: Sidey 390–91; NYT 11/13/63, 6/7/63. *1229* "the New Frontier": *Reader's Digest* November 1963; NYT 11/24/63. at his funeral: NYT 11/14/63; T 11/22/63. *1230* "a stiller town": *Death* 462. *1231* Arlington National Cemetery: ibid 190. *1232* DEAD JT135PCS: NYT 11/23/63; *Death* 221. began to build: NYT 11/23/63. field of stars: *Death* 442. *1233* "one more awful": NYT 11/25/63. "separate and apart": NYT 11/26/63; *Death* 572, 627. *1234* "deep for tears": NYT 11/29/63, 12/25/63, 12/4/63, 12/11/63, 5/5/65. "for their own": NYT 11/30/63; *Death* 642.

XXX THE LONG ARM
(pages 1237–1274)

1237 "domestic policy": WM/Dwight D. Eisenhower 8/27/64. *1238* "his administration": Goldman *Tragedy* 20–21, 523; NYT 1/30/67, 10/15/64, 10/3/68. as he spoke: NYT 1/5/65, 11/1/64, 8/20/64. *1239* the United States: NYT 1/21/64; T 1/5/68; NYT 8/28/64; Theodore White *1964* 413. of its region: NYT 2/4/64; *Tragedy* 525. *1240* over a thousand: NYT 1/19/66, 4/28/64; Theodore White *1968* 103–104. *1241* much more damaging: NYT 11/18/67, 4/23/64. "comfort the country": Carpenter 31, 331. *1242* to the men's: NYT 6/20/64, 7/7/64. proved nothing: NYT 9/15/64; *Tragedy* 228–29; NYT 9/25/64. *1243* "after the Kennedys": *Tragedy* 78–79. his calendar: NYT 7/31/64; Theodore White *1964* 315–16, 317. *1244* "side with me": NYT 7/31/64; *Tragedy* 199. American provocation: White *1964* 328; W 1964 152–56. supporting hostilities: NYT 8/8/64, 8/5/64. *1245* one of them: W 1968 46; NYT 8/3/64. *1246* from the coast: NYT 8/2/64, 8/4/64, 8/3/64. North Vietnamese forces: NYT 2/21/68; W 1964 152–56, 1968 46. "no wider war": Halberstam 413–14; *Tragedy* 175; NYT 3/6/64. *1247* "jungles of Vietnam": NYT 7/16/64; WA 1965 41. Fulbright agreed: NYT 8/6/64. *1248* "a fisheries bill": NYT 8/6/64, 8/8/64. *1249* "historic mistake": Fab VII 204; *Tragedy* 181–83; Halberstam 442; NYT 8/7/64; Halberstam 419. stimulate backlash: Theodore White *1964* 281; NYT 5/6/64, 5/20/64, 7/20/64; WA 1965 166. *1250* killing him instantly: White *1964* 266–68; NYT 7/17/64. million dollars: NYT 7/21/64. and white policemen: White *1964* 278; Graham and Gurr 51; *Collier's* 86. *1251* "Burn, baby, burn!": *Tragedy* 172–73. "Freedom Summer" of 1964: NYT 8/3/64, 8/29/64, 8/17/64, 4/3/64. *1252* "television sets": White *1964* 269; John Brooks *Leap* 291–92; *Economist* 5/10/69; White *1964* 277. reached Jackson: NYT 11/8/64; White *1964* 220–22; NYT 6/21/64. had been burned: NYT 6/23/64; W 1964 233–35. in the North: NYT 11/8/64. *1253* rounds of ammunition: NYT 7/9/64. *1254* being murdered: NYT 7/11/64; W 1964 233–35. any trouble: W 1967 210–11; T 10/27/67; NYT 12/5/67, 1/17/65, 2/26/65, 10/29/66, 10/21/67. defense challenges: NYT 2/26/65, 12/14/64; W 1967 220–21. *1255* "me a nigger": W 1967 211. the maximum: NYT 10/21/67; T 10/27/67; NYT 12/30/67. *1256* deep right field: NYT 7/16/64. the real thing: *Leap* 319; White *1964* 458. said he was: NYT 1/4/64, 1/28/64, 3/11/64, 1/3/64, 6/7/64. *1257* "is no virtue!": White *1964* 151, 153; NYT 5/31/64, 6/3/64, 7/17/64. *1258* no one was home: White *1964* 252. "Nazi methods": NYT 7/15/64. "it's the truth": ibid. in the black: NYT 7/18/64; White *1964* 377–79. *1259* platform with him: NYT 8/13/64. he was right: *Daedalus* Spring 1958; White *1964* 359. he was wrong: NYT 11/1/63. *1260* to the end: T 11/1/63. KNOW HE MIGHT: White *1964* 384; NYT 9/7/64; White *1964* 387. of greater interest: NYT 10/23/64; White *1964* 361. *1261* public toilet: NYT 6/19/64; White *1964* 385, 375. He declined: T 10/23/64; NYT 10/15/64; WA 1964 175–76. *1262* votes, elsewhere: NYT 10/14/64, 10/16–17/64, 8/15/64; *Tragedy* 359–61. standing ovation: *Tragedy* 245–48. *1263* "war in Asia": NYT 9/26/64. "trying to do": NYT 9/29/64; *Tragedy* 235–37, 412; NYT 10/22/64, 10/28/64. "or themselves": NYT 10/22/64. "all Americans": NYT 10/28/64. *1264* the following summer: *Tragedy* 224, 412–13. for the Democrats: NYT 11/4/64; WA 1964 40; NYT 12/15/64; W 1964 206–10. prove valuable: NYT 11/6/64, 11/11/64. *1265* seemed symbolic: NYT 9/9/64, 10/4/64, 12/30/64, 12/31/64. were under way: NYT 11/4/64, 11/5/64. lost their appeal: W 1966 38; NYT 6/16/64. *1266* House to protest: W 1966 38. "and stop it!": NYT 1/3/65, 2/14/65, 11/21/64; Raskin "Berkeley." *1267* "to our terms!": NYT 12/4/64. putting them on: W 1965 54; NYT 3/11/64. was often electrifying: Fab VII 181. *1268* "American it is": ibid 246. Laff's and Friday's: Ruffner 939; Fab VII 238. *1269* husband or wife: Fab VII 248. *of Man* (1964): T 4/8/66. going to jail: NYT 12/20/63; W 1965 96–97. *1270* in Las

Vegas: WA 1967 93; W 1965 186; Fab VII 172; W 1965 206. Soviet Aeroflot: W 1966 98; Graham and Gurr 187–89; NYT 2/4/65; Bird 235; W 1965 114, 254, 1966 234. for commuters: NYT 1/26/64; Fab VII 109; NYT 12/23/65, 3/3/65; *Life* 5/14/65. *1271 New, Pussycat?:* W 1965 252, 254; Fab VII 177. peepshow sex: Kendrick 509. director of CORE: NYT 7/15/65, 1/24/65; W 1965 24, 1967 47, 120; NYT 4/23/64. *1272* "to get known": NYT 7/17/66; WA 1967 78, 85; NYT 8/2/66; W 1966 232. "is my President": NYT 4/15/63; W 1966 208; NYT 4/28/67; W 1965 107, 264; Fab VII 178. told reporters: NYT 2/18/64, 3/15/64, 1/4/67, 3/26/64, 10/5/65; Carpenter 48; Halberstam 533. *1273* IS A JUNKIE: NYT 11/20/66, 2/4/66; W 1966 239–41; T 3/18/66, 10/10/66. "of public demand": Fab VII 132; NYT 3/22/66; W 1966 164. lost in 1964: W 1966 228–29; NYT 11/9/66; WA 1967 42; NYT 11/10/66; *Tragedy* 334. *1274* "from Saigon": *Tragedy* 498; Fab VII 204–205. the Vietnamese mire: Halberstam 630; NYT 11/28/67, 2/28/66, 4/26/66; *Tragedy* 509; NYT 4/24/66, 9/16/65, 12/15/66, 4/1/66; Halberstam 628. "kind of Presidency": *Tragedy* 378.

XXXI A DREAM OF GREATNESS—AND DISENCHANTMENT
(pages 1275–1325)

1275 the Fair Deal: NYT 1/21/61; W 1965 9; Goldman *Tragedy* 281–82; NYT 1/13/66. *1276* Truman years: NYT 9/7/45; Truman II 29. patients a week: *Tragedy* 285 ff; W 1966 136; NYT 7/31/65, 1/2/66. retired, beside him: NYT 1/13/65; *Tragedy* 307; NYT 4/12/65. *1277* since the 1930s: NYT 5/26/65, 7/3/64, 8/11/65, 4/1/65, 12/2/65; W 1965 187; *Tragedy* 332–33. seasonal workers: NYT 3/5/61; *Economist* 5/10/69; W 1966 204–205; NYT 5/19/65. *1278* in the state: W 1966 204–206, 1965 172. throughout the country: Carpenter 15; *Tragedy* 335. "and enjoy myself": NYT 11/5/64; *Tragedy* 259–60. convert his critics: NYT 10/23/65; *Tragedy* 333; W 1965 187; NYT 5/19/65. *1279* to reassure people: NYT 6/26/67; W 1967 118–21; *Life* 6/30/67; T 6/30/67. "if less briefly": *Tragedy* 439. fly at him: ibid 446. *1280* "*do* they want?": W 1965 168; NYT 10/6/65; *Tragedy* 337. "interested any more": NYT 12/1/67; Halberstam 429. "a war on?": *Tragedy* 451. do just that: NYT 11/1/64, 12/25/64. *1281* William Childs Westmoreland: Halberstam 129; NYT 11/17/61, 11/15/64. Ho Chi Minh Trail: Halberstam 355–57, 503, 507–508. *1282* rise above 100,000: NYT 2/26/64, 2/15/65; Halberstam 369–70; NYT 1/8/65. sight of blood: NYT 2/3/65. were wounded: NYT 2/6/65; W 1965 28–30. *1283* "will do that": W 1965 30; Halberstam 521. in North Vietnam: Halberstam 534, Theodore White *1968* 23; NYT 2/11/65. girls with flowers: Halberstam 237; NYT 7/4/65, 2/28/65, 3/9/65. *1284* "how to think": NYT 2/10/65, 5/16/65, 4/24/65. deputy prime minister: Fab VII 205; Halberstam 351; NYT 2/22/65; W 1965 32; NYT 6/31/65. *1285* "internal cohesion": Fab VII 205; W 1965 32; NYT 6/25/65. blacked them out entirely: NYT 5/10–12/65; W 1965 119, 223; Kendrick 16–17. number had tripled: NYT 3/31/65, 4/1/65, 6/26/65, 5/8/65, 6/17/65. *1286* do the job: NYT 6/10/65, 6/14/65; Halberstam 582–83. the White House: *Tragedy* 409; *N.Y. Herald Tribune* 5/23/65; *Washington Post* 12/5/65. *1287* like central Texas: W 1965 119; NYT 4/8/65; *Tragedy* 407–409. terms before Christmas: NYT 4/20–21/65; Halberstam 576–78. *1288* and F-111s: Halberstam 575–79; W 1965 123. "than inform it": Halberstam 584. outweighed their misgivings: NYT 7/21/65; W 1965 123; NYT 7/22/65, 7/29/65; Halberstam 597, 600. *1289* "no one else": Theodore White *1968* 23; NYT 7/24/65; Halberstam 599; NYT 7/29/65; W 1965 118. it was impossible: Halberstam 594, 595, 606, 614. *1290* "for the war": ibid 604–10. *1291* runaway inflation: NYT 5/13/68. to top 200,000: Halberstam 594, 602; NYT 8/4/65; W 1965 26. and 137 wounded: W 1965 240; NYT 12/4/65. "doesn't it?": NYT 10/9/66; Halberstam 550. *1292* in Ann Arbor: *Tragedy* 432, 433; NYT 10/17/65, 10/16/65; WA 1966 87; W 1965 222–23. "be our own": Fab VII 206. on the tracks: W 1965 222–23. *1293* into human torches: NYT 10/16/65, 9/1/65, 11/3/65. murdering children: Fab VII 218–19. "the United States": W 1965 223. *1294* author Michael Harrington: NYT 11/28/65. 66th Regiment: NYT 11/21/65; WA 1966 90–91. bring in transports: Halberstam 612–14. *1295* as the referee: NYT 8/27/66; W 1965 240; NYT 12/4/66; Halberstam 167; WA 1966 91; Halberstam 621; W 1965 238–39. "get the word": NYT 12/3/66; *Tragedy* 322; NYT 3/16/65. "*we shall overcome":* NYT 3/16/65. *1296* Negroes as equals: NYT 8/29/65, 4/20/65; W 1966 168. in "reparations": NYT 2/22/65; W 1965 35–37, 153; *Collier's* 90; W 1969 194. *1297* as a "fascist": Theodore White *1968* 102; NYT 11/25/65. revive their campaign: *Tragedy* 308–11; WA 1966 48, 52; NYT 1/2/65, 3/12/65. *1298* symbol of oppression: NYT 3/7/65, 3/8/65. "Turn Me Around": NYT 3/8/65, 3/9/65. "constitutionally permissible": NYT 3/10/65. *1299* a little garter: *Tragedy* 315; NYT 3/19/65, 3/21/65; W 1965 52–53. the second murder: NYT

3/22/65; *Tragedy* 324; NYT 3/26/65. *1300* police help: NYT 3/26/65. the maximum: NYT 8/21/65, 10/1/65, 3/11/65, 11/30/65; W 1965 196–99; NYT 8/21/65, 12/4/65. *1301* now erupted: WA 1966 57–58; NYT 3/16/65; *Economist* 5/10/69; NYT 5/27/66. "see your I.D.": NYT 6/12/66. *1302* locally as Watts: NYT 8/12/65; W 1965 138. looting the stores: NYT 8/12/65. *1303* under control: NYT 8/11/65, 8/14/65. "mutilate themselves": NYT 8/14/65; W 1965 142. *1304* 45 million dollars: NYT 8/19/65. in the South: *Collier's* 88; W 1965 154–55; NYT 7/20/65. *1305* a real torch: NYT 8/20/65, 12/7/65; *Collier's* 89; Theodore White *1968* 26–27. riots that year: *Collier's* 88–89; Theodore White *1968* 201; NYT 3/16/66; W 1966 166–71. into its own: NYT 10/17/66. *1306* in their ranks: NYT 8/27/66, 8/31/66, 1/4/66. peppered with birdshot: NYT 6/6/66; W 1966 112; NYT 6/7/66. another Selma: NYT 6/7/66, 6/8/66. *1307* "Black power!": W 1964 233–35; NYT 12/5/64. "black . . . power!": NYT 9/10/66. *1308* "Black power!": W 1966 166–67. "rights and integration": NYT 7/3/66. "I don't like": W 1966 116. *1309* were not there: NYT 6/24/66, 6/27/66. polls, he lost: W 1966 124; NYT 12/6/66, 6/1/66. was absurd: Fab VII 155; Graham and Gurr 671. *1310* "committed to error": NYT 9/22/66; W 1966 171; NYT 10/14/66, 10/15/66. "declared war": *Life: The 1960s;* W 1967 106; Theodore White *1968* 201; T 1/5/68; NYT 6/16/67. *1311* "intolerance of it": W 1966 226–29; NYT 10/15/66; *Economist* 5/10/69. years after Watts: NYT 5/27/66; T 6/14/68, 6/21/68; W 1968 119. critics at home: *Collier's* vi; W 1967 34; Sheehan 513. *1312* be 100,000 men: NYT 6/30/66; W 1966 126, 251, 249. "come in view": Sheehan 512; W 1967 248–49; NYT 4/29/67. *1313* "a good question": W 1966 249, 1967 92–94; Halberstam 641; W 1967 91; Halberstam 642. Garrison troops: W 1967 90. *1314* "11,000 miles away": W 1967 94, 1966 32, 1967 251. off in handcuffs: WA 1968 75–76; W 1967 95; Rovere *Muddy* 8, 9; *Collier's* 158; W 1967 132; NYT 6/4/67. *1315* to the war: NYT 12/11/67; W 1967 41–43; Graham and Gurr 515–16; NYT 10/22/67; W 1967 252; Fab VII 212. in Toronto: NYT 11/11/67; W 1967 252. *1316* the people were: W 1966 36; NYT 12/1/66. Viet Cong colors: *Life: The 1960s;* NYT 3/19/67, 10/18/66, 10/23/66, 10/22/66; W 1966 189; *U.S. News and World Report* 10/31/66. *1317* FBI checks: WA 1967 69; NYT 5/18/66; *Tragedy* 499–502. worse and worse: Kendrick 24; NYT 11/28/67, 1/25/67; Halberstam 640; Fab VII 30. the White House: Fab VII 97–98. *1318* obeyed them: NYT 11/7/67; *Tragedy* 511; Halberstam 640. *1319* of Minnesota: *Tragedy* 265; NYT 8/18/67; WA 1968 85. "is your enemy": *Collier's* 196, 422; NYT 5/13/67. the new goal: W 1967 143–44; NYT 7/21/67. "black revolution": NYT 8/16–21/67. *1320* "black man's resolution?": Walter Goodman "Black Power." *1321* the word Negro: ibid. snapped his picture: NYT 6/23/73, 4/17/65, 1/14/66, 1/7/66, 8/25/66, 6/14/67, 7/1/67, 12/9/67, 7/8/67, 9/22/67, 11/8/67, 9/7/67, 6/25/67; W 1966 24, 1970 137. John Bell Williams: NYT 9/27/67, 8/8/67, 1/11/67, 6/24/67, 11/8/67. *1322* "right at home": Good "Odyssey." catastophe of 1967: WA 1968 77; NYT 4/9/67. vast junkyard: NYT 1/3/67. *1323* Wednesday, July 12: W 1967 137–39; Theodore White *1968* 201. since Watts: NYT 7/13/67, 7/14/67, 7/18/67. *1324* of Negro homes: NYT 7/24/67, 8/7/67; Fab VII 148. Cambridge (Maryland): NYT 7/28/67. *1325* "as cherry pie": W 1967 142–43. Richard M. Nixon: NYT 5/23/68.

XXXII UP AGAINST THE WALL
(pages 1327–1374)

1327 "of 'The Establishment' ": Galbraith *State* 330–31. electrical power: NYT 11/10/65. *1328* oscillate wildly: Rosenthal and Gelb 17; W 1965 206–13. *1329* blackout had begun: Rosenthal and Gelb 85; W 1965 208–13; NYT 11/16/65. too, had vanished: NYT 11/13/65. *1330* led to safety: *Life* 11/19/65. increase in births: NYT 8/10–12/66. candle in his hand: Rosenthal and Gelb 37. *1331* "no electricity": ibid 66. "sharpener still worked": NYT 11/16/65; Rosenthal and Gelb 12. *1332* NED LUDD Clerk: Graham and Gurr 19. *1333* mayor was defeated: Theodore White *1968* 426–27; *Middletown Press* 10/7/70; NYT 6/11/66, 6/7/67; Fab VII 267. federal government alone: Servan-Schreiber 103, 134. *1334* in an automobile: Galbraith *Affluent* 171–72; Schlesinger *Crisis* 264. it was true: *Affluent* 171–72; Bird 150. *1335* whatever the weather: NYT 7/21/68. "Eyes of Texas": W 1965 78–81. garrison-prison state: Goldman *Tragedy* 257; Arendt 451–59. *1336* "handle current traffic": Whyte 441; Bird 262; *State* 45. now inconceivable: Servan-Schreiber 55–61. *1337* "flatulent indigestion": *Statistical Abstract of the United States 1969* table 891 p. 590; *Time* editors 73. of her mother: *Time* editors 72–73. *1338* "him to act": *State* 243, 247; Mowry 206, 207. *1339* the technostructure: *Time* editors 66; *State* 82. planned economy: NYT 1/21/68. *1340* hope of gain: Servan-Schreiber 81, 141. were expensive: Mowry 200; Servan-Schreiber 134–35. *1341* is doubtful:

Servan-Schreiber 163. of autonomy: John Brooks Leap 250; State 13, 14; Servan-Schreiber 81–82, 141. 1342 interest group: W 1965 55, 1969 122; Servan-Schreiber 69. "overthrow it": Theodore White 1968 424; "Democracy Has/Hasn't a Future." 1343 "economic goals" · Leap 269; State 20; Affluent 249. the United States: NYT 4/24/68, 7/1/68, 3/9/68. Old Wabash: NYT 6/10/68. 1344 "blasé permissivists" · New Republic 9/12/70; NYT 10/26/69; W 1970 202. "or leprosy": W 1969 122; Fab VII 59. domestic policies: New Republic 9/12/70; NYT 7/24/70; U.S. News and World Report 8/3/70. 1345 been the point: Leap 327. "stomach! Wild!": NYT 8/25/64, 10/22/67, 3/15/70. deemed nonviolent: Theodore White 1968 214. 1346 coast to coast: NYT 12/4/64, 3/11/65; W 1965 44–45; NYT 3/9/65. "today's foxhole": NYT 9/2/65, 4/15/65, 3/9/65, 2/21/65, 3/24/65, 2/23/67; Graham and Gurr 516–17; NYT 1/21/67; Leap 241. "blow is college": NYT 10/9/69. 1347 San Francisco State: NYT 11/10/66; Collier's 79; NYT 1/21/67; W 1967 128; NYT 11/27/68. "education for?": W 1969 125; NYT 3/12/67; W 1969 128. an abyss: Collier's 79. 1348 "toward youth": Life: The 1960s; Hartford Courant 11/8/69. "for self-discipline?": Hechinger and Hechinger 177. 1349 ("damn damn"): Fab V 28. "company comes": Lifton 80. "see what happens": Murray "Individuality"; Leap 145–46. "cudgels of thrift": Leap 233; Riesman 100; Packard Wilderness 25. 1350 "lunch and supper" · Leap 233, 145; Saturday Evening Post 10/28/61 "Isn't Everybody?": Hechinger and Hechinger 121; Fab V 128; Hechinger and Hechinger 116–17; Seventeen September 1961. 1351 "the puh-lain": Hechinger and Hechinger 94, 89–90; Life: The 1960s; W 1966 149. said acne: NYT 10/5/70; W 1966 150; NYT 8/5/66, 8/12/66; W 1966 163; Fab VI 148–49, V 28. 1352 Gallup reported: Lifton 111–12; T 2/23/68; Loth 15; Hechinger and Hechinger 165. would have thought: Hechinger and Hechinger 16. leisure class: W 1969 185; NYT 7/7/69. after 10 P.M.: W 1970 128. 1353 and furniture: T 2/23/68; Loth 101–102, 106–107. $3,000 and $10,000: NYT 9/5/63; T 9/13/63. 65 policemen: Leap 234; Hartford Courant 7/29/70. 1354 worth of damage: W 1969 119. girls' dormitory: Hartford Courant 3/13/70. 1355 swaying visibly: NYT 1/27/66; W 1970 192–94; Wilderness 353; W 1970 193; Hartford Courant 1/27/70; W 1970 190. Aunt Tom: W 1967 258; Wilderness 85; NYT 3/29/67; Life 2/3/67; Wilderness 81; NYT 2/10/66. 1356 higher up: W 1970 193; Friedan 249; Riesman 156; W 1967 134; NYT 6/16/67. "do we get laid?": Wilderness 144–45, 60–61. 1357 (under any circumstances): NYT 10/8/68. full body flush: NYT 1/19/68, 11/22/69, 1/14/69, 10/9/69. 1358 toddlers watched: DeMott 53; Collier's 131. lost their novelty: W 1968 186–90; NYT 7/30/68, 10/1/68, 9/23/68. 1359 is electrocuted: NYT 4/20/69, 2/12/71; DeMott 112; NYT 2/11/68. loops and coils: Wilderness 68; NYT 6/1/70. 1360 in 1965: Wilderness 250–51; W 1966 62; NYT 3/18/62, 12/20/63; Fab VII 176. key she had: W 1967 258; T 8/9/68. bedroom with whom: Middletown Press 3/6/70. 1361 "love in return": Wilderness 60. heavy drugs: ibid 149. merely a memory: NYT 9/26/43; T 6/11/45; NYT 4/13/55, 8/25/60; Phillips Blitz 358. 1362 (with benzedrine): NYT 4/12/62; T 8/10/62; NYT 12/13/62; Newsweek 8/17/70. taken a trip: W 1966 91. continued to spread: NYT 5/29/63. 1363 his mother-in-law: W 1966 91. "afraid of him": ibid; W 1967 197; NYT 5/14/67. 1364 Great Notion (1964): Collier's 76; NYT 2/4/62, 7/27/64. "nationwide avalanche": Collier's 73. 1365 a single year: W 1967 196, 1970 254. Politics of Free: Sanders 39; W 1967 197. other narcotics: Fab VII 84; Hartford Courant 8/10/70; W 1967 200. 1366 "the hard way": W 1967 196. up at dawn: ibid 198; NYT 5/5/67. 1367 deformed infants: NYT 6/28/67, 5/5/68. and up yours: NYT 6/8/66; Collier's 79. "to get in?": W 1967 201. 1368 from a cliff: NYT 5/31/67. Charles Manson: Sanders 39–40; NYT 8/19/67; Sanders 37–38. 1369 Lower East Side: NYT 10/9/69, 10/10/69. 1369–1370 in a corner . . . "anything to us": W 1967 202; T 10/20/67, 10/13/67; NYT 10/16/67. 1370 "the flowers gone?": T 10/13/67; NYT 10/5/67. 1370–1374 Hess portrait · NYT 9/28/69; Theodore White 1968 32; Stan Lehr and Louis Rossetto Jr. "The New Right Credo—Libertarianism" New York Times Magazine 1/10/71; Newsweek 9/29/69; Murray Kempton "Karl Hess: Goldwater Finds His Sorensen" New Republic 8/8/64, James Boyd "From Far Right to Far Left—and Farther" New York Times Magazine 12/6/70.

XXXIII THE YEAR EVERYTHING WENT WRONG
(pages 1375–1410)

1375 was assassinated: T 12/13/68; NYT 12/31/68, 1/10/68, 6/2/68, 4/17/68, 12/21/68, 8/17/68, 1/17/68. Biafra starved: NYT 7/16/68, 8/2/68, 1/23/68, 12/13/68. 1376 "cease and desist?": NYT 9/19/68; Fab VII 176; NYT 9/13/67, 2/15/68, 7/16/68, 7/19/68; T 5/17/68. straight or sick: NYT 9/13/68. the runner-up: NYT 5/5/68, 5/8/68, 12/24/68. off North

Korea: NYT 11/21/68, 5/28/68. *1377* and hand grenades: W 1969 110; NYT 1/24/68. He failed: W 1968 22; NYT 1/25/68. *1378* possible to forget: NYT 1/25/68, 1/27/68. "to the coast": W 1968 84. in South Vietnam: NYT 2/5/68; W 1968 84. million dollars: NYT 1/30/68. *1379* "not been achieved": T 3/1/68; NYT 1/25/68; W 1968 28–35. now this: *Life: The 1960s.* by Clark Clifford: Halberstam 647–48; NYT 4/26/68, 1/19/68. *1380* even want it: W 1968 35, 88; T 4/12/68. three years earlier: T 4/19/68; NYT 4/11/68; T 5/10/68. Complete Victory: W 1968 247–48. *1381* "clean for Gene": Theodore White *1968* 79. "the United States": NYT 3/16/68, 3/17/68. said. Then . . . "as your President": NYT 4/4/68, 4/1/68; T 3/22/68, 4/5/68. *1382* Republican vote: NYT 4/3/68. "civil rights progress": NYT 4/28/68, 5/29/68; W 1967 97. for his head: NYT 4/5/68, 1383 defending Khe Sanh: NYT 4/6/68. "free at last": W 1969 74; NYT 4/10/68. *1384* never discovered: NYT 4/20/68; T 7/26/68, 7/9/68, 3/11/69; WA 1970 913. primaries, California: TC 1968 34; NYT 5/8/68; W 1968 119; NYT 5/15/68, 6/5/68. *1385* "struggle for it—": NYT 6/6/68. a bear hug: TC 1968 34. little Arab had: ibid; W 1968 118, 115; NYT 6/6/68. *1386* trembling voice: NYT 6/5/68, 6/7/68; T 6/14/68; NYT 6/9/68. "to shining sea!": NYT 6/9/68. University of Miami—: W 1968 100. *1387* especially wicked: TC 1968 227–33; NYT 4/24/68; T 5/24/68. They were wrong: W 1968 101–103; TC 1968 227–33. *1388* able to muster: NYT 5/18/68, 5/12/68. "humanistic society": W 1968 101. *1389* as the Nazis: NYT 4/25/68, 4/30/68. *1390* to be tidy: NYT 4/27/68, 4/28/68. the United States: NYT 10/6/68. "revolutionary America": W 1968 101, 1970 58; NYT 3/8/68. *1391* vending machine: T 3/23/70. *1392* "catastrophe happens": Servan-Schreiber xvi; W 1968 53. *1393* remained aloof: T 4/19/68; NYT 5/26/68. compromise with him: NYT 1/4/66; T 2/4/66; W 1966 15–19. deliberate slowdown: T 2/16/68; NYT 2/3/68, 11/2/68; T 11/1/68; NYT 10/20/68, 10/24/68, 9/10/68, 10/15/68, 7/4/68. *1394* and San Francisco: NYT 3/20/70, 3/18/70, 3/20/70. their grievances: NYT 3/27/70, 4/3/70. take Fortas's place: NYT 6/22/68, 6/27/68. *1395* remained in office: NYT 7/17/68. *1396* before the Court: NYT 7/20/68, 9/14/68. be less liberal: NYT 10/3/68; *Life* 5/9/69; W 1968 210–12, 1969 77–79. *1397* the fans laughed: NYT 2/22/68. among the suggestions: NYT 10/18/68. 1.2 million dollars: NYT 10/21/68; W 1968 201. *1398* "marriage, and death": W 1968 201. eyes of God: NYT 11/25/68, 11/7/68, 10/24/68. Agnew of Maryland: NYT 3/14/68, 2/29/68, 3/22/68, 5/1/68. *1399* "shipbuilding firm": NYT 8/9/68; T 8/16/68. IS ROSEMARY'S BABY: T 10/25/68. *1400* "driving dream": W 1968 151; Theodore White *1968* 243; NYT 8/6/68; McGinniss 77; NYT 8/12/68. in Chicago: W 1968 151. confront them: NYT 8/21/68, 8/26/68. *1401* too risky: NYT 8/29/68. "accept the truth": ibid. *1402* North Side traffic: W 1968 161–66. "no march today": NYT 8/24/68. had parents, too: NYT 8/26/68: *New Republic* 9/7/68. *1403* of the suite: Theodore White *1968* 308–309; NYT 8/31/68. elated Richard Nixon: Theodore White *1968* 320. "cries too much": T 9/20/68; *Columbia Journalism Review* Winter 1969. *1404* Johnson and Daley: T 9/20/68. "the world": NYT 9/10/68. "of a box!": McGinniss 31. *1405* Thomas E. Dewey: NYT 10/1/68; WA 1972 19. *1406* Houses on the Hill: NYT 11/6/68, 11/7/68. *1407* could be shelved: T 7/25/69; NYT 8/17/73. "survival itself": *Middletown Press* 1/28/70; WM/Eric Sevareid 6/24/70. *1408* powder and dirt: Theodore White *1968* 196. ever lay ahead: W 1968 181. *1409* seemed inevitable: T 6/21/68; NYT 1/19/68, 10/17/68, 7/24/68. nothing happened: W 1968 181; NYT 5/23/68; T 10/4/68, 9/20/68; NYT 9/28/68. *1410* was a heroine: T 9/13/68; Theodore White *1968* 200; T 5/24/68. into the middle class: T 3/1/68; NYT 6/24/73.

XXXIV THE RISE OF THE SILENT MAJORITY
(pages 1415–1457)

1415 ten times: NYT 12/12/68; T 12/20/68. *1416* doubted their integrity: T 12/20/68. *1417* 528 million people: NYT 7/21/69. "decade is out": TA 180–81; NYT 1/28/67. miles away: NYT 7/17/69. picking up speed: W 1969 141–46. *1417–1420* general sources: W 1969 141–52; TA 180–89. *1418* had made it: NYT 7/25/69. July 20, 1969: NYT 7/21/69. *1419* "fine, sandy particles": NYT 7/21/69. "for all mankind": ibid. on the moon: NYT 7/22/69. *1420* on their horns: W 1969 147; NYT 7/25/69. "erode its dignity": NYT 7/23/69, 7/26/69; W 1969 188; TA 11. *1421* where they lay: NYT 8/3/69. "and dignity": NYT 8/4/69, 2/7/69, 3/22/69, 6/24/69. quiet good taste: TA 10. *1422* "have described it": W 1969 189. *1423* "was a success": NYT 2/6/69, 8/7/70; TA 10–11; NYT 11/22/69, 5/15/72. presidential seal: TA 18; NYT 1/19/69, 4/28/69, 6/15/69. heating systems: T 8/20/73, 9/10/73; *Middletown Press* 10/18/73. *1424* "government will listen": NYT 1/21/69. violent contention: TA 11; NYT 6/17/70; *Economist* 5/10/69. *1425* city commissioners: NYT 11/5/69; *Hartford Courant*

5/4/70; NYT 5/28/69. hundred billion dollars: TA 22. *1426* "throughout the land": NYT 2/5/69; W 1969 246–48; Chayes and Wiesner 2; NYT 6/5/69. Carswell of Florida: NYT 6/4/69, 11/22/69, 12/5/69; W 1969 237. *1427* "we want to": NYT 1/22/70, 3/17/70; W 1970 96–99. "the Constitution": NYT 4/9/70. "can do that": NYT 11/4/69; Pater and Pater 244. *1428* his first target: WA 1970 40; NYT 11/14/69. "absolute loyalty": NYT 11/14/69, 11/21/69. Vietnam War: NYT 4/5/69. than an hour: NYT 3/11/69, 4/18/69, 3/1/69. *1429* she vanished: NYT 6/18/69, 8/30/69, 8/23/69, 8/22/69, 8/23/69, 11/11/69, 11/13/69, 12/1/69, 5/15/69. a huge toilet: NYT 3/22/69; TA 134. very far away: *Middetown Press* 10/6/69; NYT 10/6/69. *1430* Vietnam War: WA 1970 907; W 1969 122–28; NYT 3/23/69. university budget: NYT 2/14/25. *1431* poor man's Harvard: NYT 4/23/69, 5/10/69, 6/3/69. ROTC at Harvard: NYT 4/10/69, 4/11/69, 5/12/69. Perkins quit: NYT 6/1/69. *1432* student riots: NYT 2/18/69, 2/28/69. "a good man": NYT 5/7/69; TA 32; NYT 6/5/69. school integration: NYT 8/27/69. *1433* "for the law": TA 12; NYT 10/30/69. called Woodstock: Theodore White *1972* 149. dollars a ticket: *Life: The 1960s;* W 1969 180–85; TA 112–23; NYT 7/17/69. *1434* a disaster: NYT 8/16/69, 8/17/69. "police work": *Life: The 1960s;* NYT 8/18/69. Woodstock Nation: NYT 8/17/69. Iron Butterfly: NYT 8/31/69, 9/1/69. *1435* in the black: W 1969 181. to death: NYT 8/10/69, 12/3/69; Sanders 356. *1436* one hundred pounds: T 1/27/67; W 1969 31–35; TA 112–23; Galbraith *State* 354. *1437* a ski resort: TA 113; NYT 4/28/69, 1/28/69. desert country: NYT 1/16/70; W 1969 125–26, 35; NYT 1/18/70, 4/29/69. a wide area: W 1969 33–34; TA 113–15; NYT 1/31/69. *1438* "black crayon": NYT 2/5/69. at three million· NYT 2/9/69. runaway well: NYT 2/8/69. *1439* House of Pancakes: TA 176. *1440* huge, flag-draped coffins: NYT 11/16/69; W 1969 220–22. "as peaceful": NYT 11/15/69; W 1969 222. *1441* leader's briefing: "The Massacre at Mylai" *Life* 12/5/69; TA 62; W 1969 257, 1971 68–72; NYT 9/7/69. loaded and ready: NYT 1/29/69. *1441–1442* in after them . . . "ditch and fired": W 1971 69–70. *1442* "this all day": W 1969 257. the killings: NYT 11/21/70. "his own safety": NYT 11/19/70, 11/24/70. *1443* "Republic of Vietnam": NYT 5/20/71; T 5/31/71; NYT 9/28/70. "of its policies": NYT 9/7/69. *1444* "go marching on": T 4/12/71; NYT 3/30/71, 4/9/71. "public clamor": NYT 4/4/71. "suffered enough": NYT 12/22/68. *1445* off the coast: NYT 5/7/69. "statement of fact": NYT 5/5/69. storm the hill: W 1969 94–95; TA 220; W 1969 95. *1446* "going to get": W 1969 95. of U.S. soldiers: NYT 5/22/69. "inflationary recession": TA 58. *1447* on June 8: NYT 2/19/70; TA 54. "election of 1972": NYT 6/20/69; W 1969 96; TA 59. at any time: NYT 10/5/69. *1448* Vietnamese din: NYT 8/26/69. "'up, and olé'": TA 13; WA 1971 78; TA 36, 37; W 1969 85–87, 240. 1449 to fly east: NYT 11/1/69. in prison: W 1970 231; NYT 11/12/70. *1450* Nantucket Sound: NYT 7/20/69; TA 212; W 1969 26; TA 29; W 1969 249–53; W 1970 74–78. turn Kennedy took: NYT 1/6/70, 4/30/70. *1451* "to the surface": NYT 1/6/70; W 1970 76. *1451–1453* "this happened" . . . "see me": TA 28–29; W 1969 249–53, 1970 75–78. *1453* senatorial duties: NYT 7/26/69. *1454* "asked of me": NYT 4/30/70. from Richard Nixon: NYT 7/22/70. *1454–1457* Spock portrait: *Current Biography* 1956, 1969; *Newsweek* 9/15/69; *Time* 5/31/68; Jessica Mitford *The Trial of Dr. Spock* New York 1969.

XXXV NATTERING NABOBS
(*pages 1458–1497*)

1458 inauspicious start: NYT 1/22/70, 2/23/70; W 1970 13–15. *1459* "Get Involved": NYT 3/8/70, 9/20/70, 11/15/70, 6/1/70, 3/29/70, 3/15/70. Satan himself: NYT 1/19/70, 1/25/70, 3/15/70. "irregular ones": NYT 10/31/69; W 1970 173–75. *1460* the Pueblo tribe; NYT 12/5/69, 12/3/70. quietly shelved: NYT 7/28/70, 1/28/70; W 1970 23. *1461* to turn back: NYT 1/13/70, 3/18/70, 6/5/70, 4/14/70; W 1970 61–68. on May 27: *U.S. News and World Report* 7/27/70; NYT 6/22/70, 5/28/70. visiting Manhattan: NYT 5/19/70; W 1970 122. *1462* seemed insatiable: W 1970 110–13; *Middletown Press* 7/3/70. "amount of money": NYT 2/19/70; W 1970 113; NYT 3/18/70. *1463* that to herself: *Newsweek* 11/12/73; WA 1958 47. "something you are": *Hartford Courant* 6/23/69; W 1970 38. by SIECUS: T 7/25/69. *1464* "Mating Toads": W 1970 39. *1465* as "counterrevolutionary": NYT 8/27/70; W 1970 193; Hargreaves 559; NYT 3/17/70. "Playboy promotes": W 1970 191. *1466* saleswoman $3,461: Hargreaves 561–63. "as men": ibid 564–65; NYT 3/23/72. *1467* buy their wares: W 1970 53–54; NYT 6/12/60, 2/26/70. "of prosperity": W 1970 54. *1468* in the closet: NYT 10/25/70, 1/1/71. Macon, and Athens: NYT 5/13/70. of the year: NYT 6/10/70, 6/17/70; W 1970 122. *1469* "of the establishment": W 1970 179. wealthy families: NYT 3/13/70; *Hartford Courant* 3/13/70; NYT 3/12/70; W 1970 58; NYT 3/7/70. *1470* in

Manhattan: NYT 3/9/70; *Hartford Times* 3/14/70; NYT 7/12/72; W 1970 58. contain the charges: NYT 3/7/70; *Life* 3/27/70. to collapse: NYT 3/18/70. *1471* no details: *Life* 3/27/70. "changed radically": NYT 10/21/70, 10/23/70. *1472* police station: T 10/17/69, 6/29/70, 8/31/70, 10/26/70, 1/4/71; W 1970 153–57, 1972 66–67, 118–21. subsequent interest: NYT 9/14/70. *1473* a boring case: NYT 8/8/70. "them off!": T 8/17/70. yelled, "Halt!": ibid. *1474* were dead: *Life* 8/21/70. in San Quentin: NYT 10/14/70. pistol from it: W 1971 168–71; NYT 8/22/71, 8/18/71, 1/6/72; W 1971 168–71. cut him down: NYT 8/22/71. *1475* "irretrievable love": NYT 9/4/71, 8/29/71; W 1971 168–71. *1476* "to be caught": NYT 6/5/72; W 1972 119. "the whole world": NYT 6/5/72. *1476–1480* general source (Chicago Seven): W 1970 34–37, *1477* said the lawyer: NYT 3/21/69. Richard G. Schultz: W 1970 34; NYT 2/7/70. judicial chaos: NYT 12/13/69. *1478* Chicago Seven: NYT 10/30/69, 10/31/69, 11/4/69, 11/6/69. *1479* "can't help yourself": NYT 9/9/73; W 1970 36. *1480* days in prison: NYT 2/16/70; W 1970 34–37. "the very beginning": NYT 2/19/70, 2/21/70; W 1972 225. "incompetently presented": NYT 9/9/73. *1481* "in new bottles": NYT 4/2/70, 7/2/70. included hospitals: W 1970 239; NYT 10/24/70. *1482* of each other: W 1970 239; FitzGerald 448–49. *1483* fourteen months: NYT 5/1/70; Chester et al 24–25. and 4,911 wounded: W 1970 236. never been any: FitzGerald 186. *1484* "mutual incomprehension": NYT 5/10/70, 5/9/70; Chester et al 29. "by five o'clock": NYT 5/7/70, 11/26/70. *1485* "reestablish order": T 11/12/73; NYT 5/16/70, 10/2/70, 7/30/70. *1486* Middlefield, Connecticut: W 1970 161. and it happened: NYT 7/17/70, 7/31/70. *1487* exchanging a word: NYT 8/2/70, 8/3/70. muggy Friday night: T 5/18/70. to the ground: NYT 5/4/70, 5/3/70. *1488* "harbor in America": NYT 5/4/70, 5/7/70. back at students: NYT 9/2/73. *1489* "on a trigger": W 1970 187. "killing us!": NYT 5/15/70. their victims: W 1970 187; NYT 5/5/70. handed down: NYT 5/19/70, 3/30/74. *1490* "irresponsible sort": NYT 10/17/70, 5/5/70; W 1970 190. "any protest": NYT 5/15/69. *1491* Tom Charles Huston: Chester et al 39–40. living abroad: ibid 41. *1492* John Wesley Dean III: W 1973 150. "security matters": NYT 6/29/71, 7/22/73. "Mr. Young —Plumber": Lukas "The Story So Far." *1493* "Power-pack Agnew": Theodore White *1972* 49. black officeholders: ibid 62; NYT 3/6/70. *1494* "and hardworking": W 1970 24, 202. *1495* "all about": NYT 12/14/70. "the United States": T 11/16/70; NYT 10/30/70; Theodore White *1972* 295. *1496* "in yourself": NYT 11/3/70; Theodore White *1972* 76. repudiate them: T 11/16/70. Lowell P. Weicker Jr.: T 11/16/70; NYT 11/5/70, 11/4/70. be decided: Chester et al 11–13; NYT 11/4/70. *1497* one-term President: Theodore White *1972* 59; Chester et al 12–13. a hard-liner: NYT 7/22/73, 1/6/61. alike, as CREEP: NYT 1/6/71; Chester et al 1; Theodore White *1972* 49; Lukas "The Story So Far."

XXXVI THE DIVIDED STATES OF AMERICA
(*pages 1499–1541*)

1499 roaring ovation: NYT 1/21/71. *1500* to prevent infection: NYT 4/4/71, 4/11/71. *1501* electricity sixfold: Theodore White *1972* 155–56, xv. pay a fine: NYT 2/5/71, 3/2/71, 9/18/71, 7/24/71, 3/3/71. becoming a democracy: W 1971 174. *1502* (his province chief): NYT 9/4/67, 6/3/71. "Vietnamese people": NYT 8/20/71, 8/6/71, 8/21/71. in grave doubt: NYT 9/2/71, 8/21/71, 8/23/71, 10/4/71. *1503* "Lam Son 719": Theodore White *1972* 58; W 1971 239–41; FitzGerald 553–55. "the Americans": NYT 2/9/71; FitzGerald 554. country's intelligence: NYT 4/8/71. *1504* "the government": NYT 4/24/71, 4/25/71, 4/27/71; Chester et al 31–34. more aggressively: NYT 4/27/71. *1505* as red tape: NYT 1/15/69; Chester et al 8. Memorial Stadium: W 1971 84–87; NYT 5/3/71, 5/4/71. "national monument": NYT 5/6/71. *1506* Nazi Brownshirts: Chester et al 34; NYT 5/11/71. reveal more: W 1971 182–85; NYT 6/13/71. "or promulgated": NYT 4/28/65. *1507* government's credibility: NYT 6/13/71. alongside it: NYT 6/15/71. *New York Times*: NYT 6/16/71. in the minority: NYT 6/27/71. *1508* finally decided him: ibid. "harm my country": NYT 6/24/71, 6/29/71, 12/31/71. *1509* as Plumbers: Chester et al 52. "that would ensue": NYT 7/5/71; Chester et al 54–55. *1510* dubious sources: NYT 7/11/71. bank accounts: *Nation* 12/20/71; NYT 9/28/71; T 12/17/73. *1511* of the decision: NYT 6/11/69, 3/2/72. "antitrust cases": T 11/12/73. "understanding" with Geneen: Chester et al 147. *1512* "cannot be known": NYT 3/1/72. "of a victory": ibid. 224 million dollars: T 5/21/73, 6/11/73; NYT 11/28/72. *1513* prosecute anyway: NYT 5/23/73. a government job: NYT 2/1/72; Chester et al 85. *1514* and imprisonment: Theodore White *1972* 89. Hunt an idea: NYT 9/17/71; Lukas "The Story So Far." *1515* it in Barker's: NYT 12/16/73. to the CIA: Lukas "The Story So Far." *1516* "not traceable": Chester et al 68. Cuban informant: ibid 70. *1517* "congressional investigation": ibid 69. *1518* for his office: Lukas "The Story So Far." was mounting: ibid. plain: Attica: T 9/27/71; W 1971 160–67; WA 1972 964; NYT 11/18/73, 9/10/71. *1519* clubs "nigger sticks": T 9/27/71. "our accursed lot": ibid. *1520* "so well organized": NYT 9/27/71, 8/22/71; W 1971 161. "like here–animals": NYT 9/17/71; T 9/27/71. *1521* along the way: T 9/20/71. *1522* tried for murder: T 9/27/71. call their bluff: NYT 9/14/71. *1523* "those oppressed": NYT 9/10/71. bitter fruit: T 9/27/71; NYT 9/11/71. the committee: NYT 9/11/71. *1524* "Black Panther party": NYT 7/13/71. *1525* with Oswald: NYT 9/12/71. to death: NYT 9/13/71, 9/14/71. *1526* victims with them: W 1971 165. "the offensive!": NYT 9/14/71; W 1971 160. "was killed": NYT 9/14/71. *1527* "on the ground": NYT 11/18/73. carried guns: NYT 9/14/71. "any circumstances": NYT 9/17/71; W 1971 167. *1528* AT THIS INSTITUTION: NYT 9/17/71; T 9/27/71. home and abroad: T 8/30/71. *1529* of Red China?: NYT 4/1/71; T 4/26/71; W 1971 62–66; WA 1972 950; NYT 4/7/71. Americans "unprincipled": NYT 4/8/71. *1530* "bloodthirsty gangsters": NYT 4/10/71. "come in batches": NYT 4/14/71, 4/15/71. *1531* President himself: NYT 4/14/71. by his illness: T 7/26/71; NYT 7/16/71. *1532* "our old friends": NYT 7/17/71; T 3/6/72; NYT 7/16/71; WA 1972 957. Cowan in Nagoya: NYT 10/27/71; W 1971 204–205; NYT 10/28/71. *1533* was heartening: NYT 8/5/71; T 8/30/71. its own money: W 1971 193. deficit since 1893: T 8/30/71. *1534* flooded with them: W 1971 194. *1535* jump accordingly: ibid 216; NYT 7/29/71. price increases: T 8/30/71. *1536* over the freeze: W 1971 217; NYT 8/15/71. into the system: NYT 8/17/73. *1537* "American people": NYT 10/8/71; WA 1972 964. he could get: NYT 3/23/72, 12/24/71. *1538–1541* Nader portrait: *Current Biography* 1966; T 4/26/71, 7/31/72, 3/14/71, 3/21/71, 10/29/73; *Life* 1/21/72; Charles McCarry *Citizen Nader* New York 1972.

XXXVII PRIDE GOETH

(*pages 1542–1588*)

1542 Phineas Taylor Barnum: Kronenberger 25. *1543* his best friend: T 5/29/72; NYT 5/22/72, 5/31/72, 9/6/72, 4/18/72, 11/36/70, 4/17/72. "my memoirs?": W 1972 71; NYT 4/8/72, 3/28/72, 12/9/72, 5/16/72. *1544* getting married: NYT 11/13/72, 11/14/72; T 6/4/73. old-fashioned marijuana: NYT 3/7/69. *1545* homes and schools: NYT 11/15/72, 7/6/72. "human being": W 1972 102–106; NYT 12/8/71, 1/10/72; Fay et al 3–4. *1546* "Western Hemisphere": Fay et al 2–3. "We have proof": Fay et al 5; NYT 12/9/72, 1/11/72. *1547* also been lucky: NYT 2/12/72. his two children: Fay et al 28. *1548* come from Irving: ibid 72. years earlier: NYT 1/29/72. *1549* Helga began: NYT 1/10/72, 1/22/72. like Howard Hughes: Fay et al 179, 181. *1550* one believes him: NYT 1/27/72. "is Helga": Fay et al 189–90; NYT 1/29/72. *1551* fornicatrix of 1972: *Life* 12/29/72; Fay et al 303. vinyl couch: Fay et al 228; NYT 6/17/72. *1552* TRUST COMPANY: Fay et al 204. Chinese calendar: NYT 2/21/72; Theodore White *1972* viii. *1553* Chou took it: W 1972 76–82; T 3/6/72; NYT 2/22/72. official hostess: NYT 2/22/72. *1554* about needles: ibid. the American people: NYT 2/24/72. "kind between people": ibid. *1555* "of the U.S.A.": W 1972 81–82. four years earlier: W 1972 230–35, 1973 1003; NYT 1/26/72. *1556* of Kontum: NYT 4/7/72, 4/20/72. was a failure: NYT 4/22/72. *1557* "their neighbors": NYT 5/9/72. *1558* wanted to make: NYT 5/12/72, 5/13/72, 5/24/72; T 5/22/72. that they cherish: NYT 5/23/72; T 6/5/72; WA 1972 1010; W 1972 82–83; NYT 5/27/72. *1559* for five years: NYT 5/27/72. of the cold-warriors: W 1972 83. synonym: Watergate: NYT 7/22/73. *1560* support of busing: Theodore White *1972* 75; NYT 1/23/72, 2/8/72, 1/11/72, 6/7/72. CREEP's director: NYT 3/5/72, 7/2/72. *1561* "Rose Mary's baby": NYT 6/11/72. by hidden cameras: NYT 6/15/72; Lukas "The Story So Far." *1562* try once again: Chester et al 136. his green light: NYT 10/23/72. *1563* national convention: Lukas "The Story So Far"; Chester et al 152; NYT 9/17/72. of the banquet: NYT 6/19/72; Lukas "The Story So Far." *1564* on Virginia Avenue: Chester et al 156. to try again: Lukas "The Story So Far." *1565* cheap slacks: NYT 6/18/72. under arrest: ibid; Lukas "The Story So Far." *1566* "going to Miami?": Lukas. of the United States: NYT 6/18/72. *1567* "is incredible": Chester et al 165. on the lam: NYT 7/2/72. *1568* "I am ready": Lukas "The Story So Far." "Holy shit!": Chester et al 176. "or condone it": ibid 168. *1569* "big fat wringer": NYT 9/13/72; Chester et al 202. returns from there: NYT 3/15/72, 3/17/72. *1570* to the hall: NYT 8/7/72, 8/23/72. course, the idea: NYT 8/23/72. the other side: NYT 8/25/72. *1571* him the prize: NYT 1/5/72, 1/11/72, 1/19/72, 2/12/72, 1/26/72, 2/12/72. something, big: Theodore White *1964* 129, *1972* 118–19; NYT 1/14/72. was on him: NYT 3/8/72, 3/14/72. *1572* went to Wallace: NYT 3/15/72, 3/22/72, 4/5/72, 4/26/72, 5/5/72, 5/11/72. the nomination: NYT 5/15/72, 5/16/72, 5/17/72,

6/7/72. *1573* "adversary treatment": NYT 5/29/72, 5/31/72, 6/5/72. party's strength: NYT 8/28/68; Theodore White *1972* 29–30. and Chicago: NYT 7/11/72, 6/3/72; Theodore White *1972* 172. *1574* him long before: Theodore White *1972* 166, 161. scuttling Salinger: NYT 7/13/72, 7/14/72, 7/15/72. *1575* credibility fast: NYT 8/17/72; Theodore White *1972* 214. didn't do it: NYT 7/26/72; W 1972 144; NYT 7/26/72. *1576* recover from it: Theodore White *1972* 203; NYT 7/31/72; White *1972* 205–206; NYT 8/6/72. getting 1.8: NYT 11/8/72. one statehouse: NYT 11/9/72. *1577* were felons: W 1972 203–204. the following course: Chester et al 207; NYT 10/5/72; Theodore White *1972* 327. in disgrace: Chester et al 183–84. *1578* and hung up: ibid 191. *1579* "of President Kennedy": NYT 8/29/72. (from Ehrlichman): NYT 8/30/72. Nixon's reelection: NYT 7/2/72; Lukas "The Story So Far." *1580* "may have to": Chester et al 196. already resigned: ibid 198. *1581* ultimate disgrace: NYT 9/16/72; Lukas "The Story So Far"; NYT 10/11/72, 6/30/72. Watergate Five: NYT 12/10/72; Szulc "The Spy Compulsion." "are to go forward": Chester et al 219. *1582* of "higher-ups": ibid 220. "in the fallout": ibid 225–26. *1583* Presidency began: ibid 229. "is at hand": W 1972 233–35; T 12/25/72, 1/1/73, 1/8/73, 1/15/73, 1/22/73, 2/5/73. the war alone: NYT 10/24/72. *1584* would be unavoidable: NYT 12/14/72. "is arrived at": NYT 12/19/72. *1585* "on Christmas Eve": NYT 12/23/72. Le Duc Tho: NYT 12/25/72; T 8/4/52. *1586* to shut up: NYT 12/31/72. *1587* "Peace with honor": NYT 1/24/72; W 1973 9, 13. "probably enduring": NYT 1/24/73. *1588* "to get it": John Brooks *Leap* 13. "into the past": *Leap* 359; Thomas Wolfe *Look Homeward Angel* (foreword); F. Scott Fitzgerald *The Great Gatsby* (conclusion).

EPILOGUE: ECHOES
(pages 1589–1594)

1589 "do for myself": NYT 1/21/73. "End racism!": ibid. *1590* in their stead: NYT 1/20/73, 1/21/73. under that President: NYT 1/20/73. *1591* camp at Auschwitz: NYT 1/21/73. opinion of it: ibid. *1592* heckled FDR: *Baltimore Sun* 12/20/51.

BIBLIOGRAPHY

Aaron, Daniel *Writers on the Left* Harcourt, Brace and World, New York 1961
Abel, Elie *The Missile Crisis* Lippincott, New York and Philadelphia 1966 (Bantam, New York 1966)
Acheson, Dean *Present at the Creation: My Years at the State Department* Norton, New York 1969
Adamic, Louis *My America* Harper, New York 1938
Adams, Sherman *Firsthand Report: The Story of the Eisenhower Administration* Harper, New York 1961
Agronsky, Martin, and others, commentary by *Let Us Begin: The First Hundred Days of the Kennedy Administration* Simon and Schuster, New York 1961
Alabama: A Guide to the Deep South, compiled by workers of the Writers Program of the Works Progress Administration in Alabama; Richard R. Smith, New York 1941
Aldridge, John W. "In the Country of the Young" *Harper's Magazine* October–November 1969
Allen, Frederick Lewis *The Big Change: America Transforms Itself 1900–1950* Harper and Row, New York 1952
—— *Only Yesterday: An Informal History of the Nineteen-Twenties* Harper, New York 1931
—— *Since Yesterday: The Nineteen-Thirties in America, September 3, 1929–September 3, 1939* Harper, New York 1940
Alsop, Stewart "The Lessons of the Cuban Disaster" *Saturday Evening Post* June 24, 1961
American Institute of Public Opinion, ed. *The 1954 Pocket Almanac* Pocket Books, New York 1953
"America's Military Decline: Where We'd Stand in a Fight" *U.S. News and World Report* March 22, 1946
Angoff, Charles, and H. L. Mencken "The Worst American State" *American Mercury* September–November 1931
Appleman, Roy E. *The United States Army in the Korean War: South to the Naktong, North to the Yalu (June–November 1950)* U.S. Government Printing Office, Washington 1961
Arendt, Hannah *The Origins of Totalitarianism* Meridian, New York 1958
Armstrong, Neil, Michael Collins, and Edwin E. Aldrin Jr. *First on the Moon* (written with Gene Farmer and Dora Jane Hamblin) Little, Brown, Boston 1970
Arnold, Thurman "How *Not* to Get Investigated: Ten Commandments for Government Employees" *Harper's Magazine* November 1948
Asbell, Bernard *When F.D.R. Died* Holt, Rinehart and Winston, New York 1961
Asch, Berta, and A. R. Magnus *Farmers on Relief and Rehabilitation* (WPA Research Monograph VIII) U.S. Government Printing Office, Washington 1937
Asch, Nathan *The Road* Norton, New York 1937
Bakal, Carl *The Right to Bear Arms* McGraw-Hill, New York 1966
Barnouw, Erik *A Tower in Babel: A History of Broadcasting in the United States* (Volume I, to 1933) Oxford, New York 1966
—— *The Golden Web: A History of Broadcasting in the United States* (Volume II, 1933–1953) Oxford, New York 1968
Barrett, George "Close-up of the Birchers' 'Founder'" *New York Times Magazine* May 14, 1961

—— "Jim Crow, He's Real Tired" *New York Times Magazine* March 3, 1957
Barrett, William "Dialogue on Anxiety" *Partisan Review* March–April 1947
Barth, Alan *The Loyalty of Free Men* Viking, New York 1951
Bell, Daniel, ed. *The Radical Right: The New American Right* Doubleday, New York 1963 (Anchor, New York 1964)
Bell, Jack *The Johnson Treatment: How Lyndon B. Johnson Took Over the Presidency and Made It His Own* Harper, New York 1965
Bendiner, Robert "Great Expectations, a Quarter of a Century Later" *New York Times Magazine* April 26, 1970
Berger, Peter L. and Brigitte "The Blueing of America" *New Republic* April 3, 1971
Bernstein, Irving *The Lean Years* Houghton Mifflin, Boston 1960
Bird, Caroline *The Invisible Scar* McKay, New York 1966 (Pocket Books, New York 1967)
Bishop, Joseph W Jr "The Warren Court Is Not Likely to Be Overruled" *New York Times Magazine* September 7, 1969
Bliven, Bruce, "Boulder Dam" *New Republic* December 11, 1935
—— "Sitting Down in Flint" *New Republic* January 27, 1937
Bohr, Niels "On Atoms and Human Knowledge" *Daedalus* Spring 1958
Brecher, Edward M. and Consumer Report Editors *Licit and Illicit Drugs: The Consumers Union Report on Narcotics, Stimulants, Depressants, Inhalants, Hallucinogens, and Marijuana—Including Caffeine, Nicotine, and Alcohol* Little, Brown, Boston 1972
Brogan, D. W. *The American Character* Knopf, New York 1944
Brooks, John *The Fate of the Edsel and Other Business Ventures* Harper and Row, New York 1963
—— *The Great Leap: The Past Twenty-five Years in America* Harper and Row, New York 1966
—— *Once in Golconda: A True Drama of Wall Street 1920–1938* Harper and Row, New York 1969
Brooks, Thomas R. "The New Left Is Showing Its Age" *New York Times Magazine* June 14, 1969
—— "Voice of the New Campus 'Underclass'" *New York Times Magazine* November 7, 1965
Brzezinski, Zbigniew "America in the Technocratic Age" *Encounter* January 1968
Burns, James MacGregor *John Kennedy: A Political Profile* Harcourt, Brace, New York 1960
—— *Roosevelt: The Lion and the Fox* Harcourt Brace, New York 1956
—— *Roosevelt: The Soldier of Freedom* Harcourt Brace Jovanovich, New York 1970
Butz, Otto "Defense of the Class of '58" *New York Times Magazine* May 25, 1958
Buxton, Frank and Bill Owen *The Big Broadcast 1920–1950* (A new, revised, and greatly expanded edition of *Radio's Golden Age*) Viking, New York 1972
Byrnes, James F. *Speaking Frankly* Harper, New York 1947
Cantril, Hadley *The Invasion from Mars: A Study in the Psychology of Panic, With the Complete Script of the Famous Orson Welles Broadcast* Princeton University, Princeton 1940
Carlson, Avis D. "Deflating the Schools" *Harper's Magazine* November 1933
Carlson, John Roy *Under Cover: My Four Years in the Nazi Underworld of America* Blakiston, Philadelphia 1943
Carpenter, Liz *Ruffles and Flourishes* Doubleday, New York 1970
Chalmers, Allan K *They Shall Be Free* Doubleday, New York 1951
Chambers, Whittaker *Witness* Random House, New York 1952
Chapman, C. C., and others *Crisis—Transportation* Caterpillar Tractor Company n.d.
Chayefsky, Paddy *Television Plays* Simon and Schuster New York 1955
Chayes, Abram, and Jerome B. Wiesner, eds. *ABM: An Evaluation of the Decision to Deploy an Antiballistic Missile System* Signet, New York 1969
Chester, Lewis, Cal McCrystal, Stephen Aris, and William Shawcross *Watergate: The Full Inside Story* Ballantine, New York 1973
Childs, Marquis "Main Street Twenty Years After" *New Republic* January 18, 1933
—— "They Hate Roosevelt" *Harper's Magazine* May 1936
—— "They Still Hate Roosevelt" *New Republic* September 14, 1938
Clark, George R "Beckerstown, 1932: An American Town Faces the Depression" *Harper's Magazine* October 1932
Clay, Lucius D. *Decision in Germany* Doubleday, New York 1950
Cohen, Morris R. "The Future of American Liberalism" in his *The Faith of a Liberal: Selected Essays* Holt, New York 1946
Cohn, David L. *The Good Old Days: A History of American Morals and Manners As Seen Through the Sears, Roebuck Catalog 1905 to the Present* Simon and Schuster, New York 1950
Collier's 1968 Year Book: Covering the Year 1967 Crowell-Collier, New York 1968
Colton, F. Barrows "The Geography of a Hurricane" *National Geographic Magazine* April 1939

Compton, Karl T. "If the Atomic Bomb Had Not Been Used" *Atlantic Monthly* December 1946

Cone, Fairfax M. *With All Its Faults: A Candid Account of Forty Years in Advertising* Little, Brown, Boston 1969

Congdon, Don, ed. *The Thirties: A Time to Remember* Simon and Schuster, New York 1962

Cooke, Alistair *A Generation on Trial: U.S.A. v. Alger Hiss* Knopf, New York 1950

Cowley, Malcolm "The Flight of the Bonus Army" *New Republic* August 17, 1932

Crane, Burton *A Century of Financial Advertising in the New York Times* New York Times, New York 1957

Daniels, Jonathan *The Time Between the Wars: Armistice to Pearl Harbor* Doubleday, New York 1966

Davis, Forrest *Huey Long: A Biography* Dodge, New York 1935

Davis, Kenneth S. *The Politics of Honor: A Biography of Adlai E. Stevenson* Putnam, New York 1967

"Democracy Has/Hasn't a Future . . . a Present" *New York Times Magazine* May 26, 1968

DeMott, Benjamin *Supergrow: Essays and Reports on Imagination in America* Dutton, New York 1969

Didion, Joan "Just Folks at a School for Nonviolence" *New York Times Magazine* February 27, 1966

Donovan, Robert J. *Eisenhower: The Inside Story* Harper, New York 1956

Dorman, Michael *We Shall Overcome: A Reporter's Eyewitness Account of the Year in Racial Strife and Triumph* Dell, New York 1964

Edey, Maitland A., ed. *This Fabulous Century: Sixty Years of American Life* (Volumes IV, 1930–1940, and V, 1940–1950) Time-Life Books, New York 1969

—— *TIME Capsule: A History of the Year Condensed from the Pages of TIME* (Volumes for 1933, 1941 and 1950, published 1967; for 1932, 1939, 1940, 1942, 1943, 1944, 1945, 1956 and 1959, published 1968; and for 1968, published 1969) Time-Life Books, New York

—— *1969: The Year in Review* Time-Life Books, New York 1970

"The Edsel" *Consumer Reports* January 1958

"The Edsel Story" *Consumer Reports* April 1958

Ehrlich, Paul R. *The Population Bomb* Ballantine, New York 1968

"Eight Scientists Protest Thomas Committee's Methods" *Bulletin of the Atomic Scientists* October 1948

Einstein, Albert, as told to Raymond Swing "Einstein on the Atomic Bomb" *Atlantic Monthly* November 1945

Eisenhower, Dwight D. *At Ease: Stories I Tell to Friends* Doubleday, New York 1967 (Avon, New York 1968)

—— *Crusade in Europe* Doubleday, New York 1948

Eisinger, Chester E., ed. *The 1940s: Profile of a Nation in Crisis* Doubleday Anchor Books, New York 1969

Evans, Rowland Jr., and Robert D. Novak "Nixonomics: How the Game Plan Went Wrong" *Saturday Review* July 1971

Farago, Ladislas *Patton: Ordeal and Triumph* Ivan Obolensky, New York 1963

Faulk, John Henry *Fear on Trial* Simon and Schuster, New York 1964

Fay, Stephen, Lewis Chester, and Magnus Linklater *Hoax: The Inside Story of the Howard Hughes-Clifford Irving Affair* Bantam, New York 1972

Federal Aid for Unemployment Relief: Hearings Before a Subcommittee of the Committee on Manufactures, U.S. Senate, 72nd Congress, 1st Session, on S.174 and S.262 U.S. Government Printing Office, Washington 1932

Federal Aid for Unemployment Relief: Hearings Before a Subcommittee of the Committee on Manufactures, U.S. Senate, 72nd Congress, 2nd Session, on S.5125 U.S. Government Printing Office, Washington 1932

Federal Cooperation in Unemployment Relief: Hearings Before a Subcommittee of the Committee on Manufactures, U.S. Senate, 72nd Congress, 1st Session, on S.4592 U.S. Government Printing Office, Washington 1932

Fehrenbach, T.R. *F.D.R.'s Undeclared War* McKay, New York 1967

Ferguson, Otis "The Spirit of Jazz" *New Republic* December 30, 1936

Fischer, John "Black Panthers and Their White Hero-Worshippers" *Harper's Magazine* August 1970

FitzGerald, Frances *Fire in the Lake: The Vietnamese and the Americans in Vietnam* Little, Brown, Boston 1972 (Vintage, New York 1973)

Fontaine, André *History of the Cold War: From the Korean War to the Present* Pantheon, New York 1969

Frady, Marshall "Gary, Indiana" *Harper's Magazine* August 1969

Friedan, Betty, *The Feminine Mystique* Norton, New York 1963

Fuller, Keith, project supervisor *The World in 1964: History As We Lived It* Associated Press, New York 1965, and similar volumes for 1965 (published 1966), 1966 (1967), 1967 (1968), 1968 (1969), 1969 (1970), 1970 (1971), 1971 (1972), 1972 (1973), and 1973 (1974)

Galbraith, John Kenneth *The Affluent Society* 2nd ed. Houghton Mifflin, Boston 1969

—— *The New Industrial State* Houghton Mifflin, Boston 1967 (Signet, New York 1968)

Garson, Barbara *MacBird!* Grove, New York 1966

Gellhorn, Walter *Security, Loyalty, and Science* Cornell University, Ithaca 1950

Glass, Remley J. "Gentlemen, the Corn Belt!" *Harper's Magazine* July 1933

Gold, Jay, ed. *The Swing Era (1936–1937: The Movies, Between Vitaphone and Video. 1940–1941: How It Was to Be Young Then. 1941–1942: Swing As a Way of Life)* Time-Life Records, New York 1970

Goldman, Eric F. *The Crucial Decade—and After: America, 1945–1960* Vintage, New York 1960

—— *The Tragedy of Lyndon Johnson,* Knopf, New York 1969

Good, Paul "Odyssey of a Man—and a Movement" *New York Times Magazine* June 25, 1967

Goodman, Jack, ed. *While You Were Gone: A Report on Wartime Life in the United States* Simon and Schuster, New York 1946

Goodman, Paul "The Chance for Popular Culture" *Poetry* June 1949

—— *Growing Up Absurd: Problems of Youth in the Organized Society* Knopf, New York 1956 (Vintage, New York 1960)

Goodman, Walter "The Question of Repression" *Commentary* August 1970

—— "When Black Power Runs the New Left" *New York Times Magazine* September 24, 1967

Goodstone, Tony, ed. *1929 Johnson Smith & Co. Catalogue* Chelsea House, New York 1970

Graham, Hugh Davis, and Ted Robert Gurr *Violence in America: Historical and Comparative Perspectives. A Report to the National Commission on the Causes and Prevention of Violence, June 1969* Signet, New York 1969

"The Great American Roadside" *Fortune* September 1934

"The Great Hurricane and Tidal Wave—Rhode Island: September 21, 1938" Providence Journal Company 1938

Greeley, Andrew N "Turning Off the People" *New Republic* June 27, 1970

Greene, Gael *Sex and the College Girl* Dial, New York 1964

Greenfield, Jeff "A Member of the First TV Generation Looks Back" *New York Times Magazine* July 4, 1971

Griffith, Robert *The Politics of Fear: Joseph R. McCarthy and the Senate* University Press of Kentucky, Lexington 1970

Grosvenor, Gilbert "Washington Through the Years" *National Geographic Magazine* November 1931

Guiles, Fred Lawrence *Norma Jean: The Life of Marilyn Monroe* McGraw-Hill, New York 1969

Gunther, John *Roosevelt in Retrospect: A Profile in History* Harper, New York 1950 (Pyramid 1962)

Guthman, Edwin *We Band of Brothers* Harper and Row, New York 1971

Halberstam, David *The Best and the Brightest* Random House, New York 1972

Hargreaves, Robert *Superpower: A Portrait of America in the 1970s* St. Martin, New York 1973

Harris, Herbert *American Labor* Yale University, New Haven 1939

Hart, *see* Liddell Hart

Hayek, Friedrich A. *The Road to Serfdom* University of Chicago, Chicago 1944

Hechinger, Grace and Fred M. *Teen-Age Tyranny* Morrow, New York 1962 (Fawcett, New York 1963)

Heffernan, Joseph L. "The Hungry City: A Mayor's Experience with Unemployment" *Atlantic Monthly* May 1932

Heinl, Robert Debs Jr. *Victory at High Tide: The Inchon-Seoul Campaign* Lippincott, Philadelphia and New York 1968

Herbers, John "Communiqué from the Mississippi Front" *New York Times Magazine* November 8, 1964

Hersey, John *Hiroshima* Knopf, New York 1946

Hersh, Seymour M. "My Lai: The First Detailed Account of the Vietnam Massacre" *Harper's Magazine* May 1970

Hicks, Granville "On Leaving the Communist Party" *New Republic* October 4, 1939

Hillman, William *Mr. President: The First Publication from the Personal Diaries, Private Letters, Papers and Revealing Interviews of Harry S. Truman* Farrar, Straus and Young, New York 1952

Hiss, Alger *In the Court of Public Opinion* Knopf, New York 1957

Holmes, Clellon "This Is the Beat Generation" *New York Times Magazine* November 16, 1952

Hook, Sidney "The New Failure of Nerve" *Partisan Review* January–February 1943

Howe, Irving "Notes on Popular Culture" *Politics* Spring 1948

Hughes, Emmet John *The Ordeal of Power: A Political Memoir of the Eisenhower Years* Atheneum, New York 1963

"Hurricane Sweeps Across Northeast, Kills Hundreds" *Life* October 3, 1938

Irving, Clifford, with Richard Suskind *What Really Happened: His Untold Story of the Hughes Affair* Grove, New York 1972

Jackson, George *Soledad Brother: The Prison Letters of George Jackson* Coward-McCann, New York 1970

Jeffries, Ona Griffin *In and Out of the White House: From Washington to the Eisenhowers* Wilfred Funk, New York 1960

Johnson, Haynes, and others *The Bay of Pigs: The Leaders' Story of Brigade 2506* Norton, New York 1964

Johnson, Walter *1600 Pennsylvania Avenue: Presidents and the People Since 1929* Little, Brown, Boston 1963

Jungk, Robert *Brighter Than a Thousand Suns: A Personal History of the Atomic Scientists* Harcourt, Brace and World, New York 1958

Kaplan, Abraham "American Ethics and Public Policy" *Daedalus* Spring 1958

Kateb, George "The Political Thought of Herbert Marcuse" *Commentary* January 1970

Kendrick, Alexander *Prime Time: The Life of Edward R. Murrow* Little, Brown, Boston 1969

Kennan, George F. *American Diplomacy 1900–1950* Mentor, Chicago 1951

—— "America's Administrative Response to Its World Problems" *Daedalus* Spring 1958

—— [X] "The Sources of Soviet Conduct" *Foreign Affairs* July 1947

Kennedy, John F. *Public Messages, Speeches, and Statements of the President, January 1 to November 22, 1963* (in *Public Papers of the Presidents of the United States*) U.S. Government Printing Office, Washington 1964

Kennedy, Robert F. *Thirteen Days: A Memoir of the Cuban Missile Crisis* Norton, New York 1969 (Signet, New York 1969)

Khrushchev, Nikita S. *Khrushchev Remembers* Little, Brown, Boston 1970

Kimball, Penn " 'Dream Town'—Large Economy Size" *New York Times Magazine* December 14, 1952

Kinsey, Alfred C. and others *Sexual Behavior in the Human Male* Saunders, Philadelphia and London 1948

—— *Sexual Behavior in the Human Female* Saunders, Philadelphia and London 1953

Kirk, Russell *The Conservative Mind* Henry Regnery, Chicago 1953

Kluckhohn, Clyde "The Evolution of Contemporary American Values" *Daedalus* Spring 1958

—— "Mid-Century Manners and Morals" in *Twentieth Century Unlimited* (ed. Bruce Bliven) Lippincott, Philadelphia 1950

Korn, Jerry, ed. *This Fabulous Century* Volumes VI (1950–1960) and VII (1960–1970) Time-Life Books, New York 1970

Kronenberger, Louis *Company Manners: A Cultural Inquiry into American Life* Bobbs-Merrill, New York 1954

Langer, William L., ed. *An Encyclopedia of World History* Houghton Mifflin, Boston 1968

Lasagna, Louis, M.D. *The Doctors' Dilemmas* Gollancz, London 1962

Lash, Joseph P. *Eleanor and Franklin: The Story of Their Relationship, Based on Eleanor Roosevelt's Private Papers* Norton, New York 1971

Lasswell, Harold D. "The Universal Peril: Perpetual Crisis and the Garrison-Prison State" in *Perspectives on a Troubled Decade: Science, Philosophy, and Religion 1939–1949* (ed. Lyman Bryson, Louis Finkelstein, and R. M. MacIver) Harper, New York 1950

Lattimore, Owen *Ordeal by Slander* Little, Brown, Boston 1950

Laurence, William L. *Dawn Over Zero: The Story of the Atomic Bomb* Knopf, New York 1946

Lear, Martha "The Second Feminist Wave" *New York Times Magazine* March 10, 1968

Leary, John L. Jr. "If We Had the Dole" *American Magazine* December 1931

Leighton, George R. "And If the Revolution Comes . . . ?" *Harper's Magazine* March 1932

Leighton, Isabel, ed. *The Aspirin Age 1919–1941* Simon and Schuster, New York 1949

Lerner, Max *Tocqueville and American Civilization* Harper and Row, New York 1966

Lescohier, Don Divance *Working Conditions* (Volume III of *The History of Labor in the U.S. 1896–1932*) Macmillan, New York 1935

Leuchtenburg, William E., ed. *Franklin D. Roosevelt: A Profile* Hill and Wang, New York 1967

Levine, Mark L., George C. McNamee, and Daniel Greenberg, eds. *The Tales of Hoffman, Edited from the Official Transcript* Bantam, New York 1970

Levinson, Leonard Louis *Wall Street: A Pictorial History* Ziff-Davis, New York 1961

Lewin, Nathan "Kent State Revisited" *New Republic* August 8 and 25, 1973

Liddell Hart, B. H. *History of the Second World War* Putnam, New York 1970

Liebling, A. J. *The Press* Ballantine, New York 1961

—— "The Red Blonde Spy Queen" *New Yorker* August 28, 1948

Life, special double issue, *The 1960s: Decade of Tumult and Change*, vol. 47, no. 13

Lifton, Robert Jay, ed. *The Woman in America* Beacon, Boston 1965

Lilienthal, David E. *This I Do Believe* Harper, New York 1949

Lilly, Doris "Jackie's Fabulous Greek" *Look* June 30, 1970

Lindley, Betty and Ernest K. *A New Deal for Youth: The Story of the National Youth Administration* Viking, New York 1938

Lippmann, Walter *The Cold War: A Study in U.S. Foreign Policy* Harper, New York 1947
Lipset, Seymour Martin, and Earl Raab "The Non-Generation Gap" *Commentary* August 1970
Long-term Economic Growth 1860–1965 (U.S. Department of Commerce, Bureau of the Census) U.S. Government Printing Office, Washington 1966
Lord, Walter *The Past That Would Not Die* Harper and Row, New York 1965
Loth, David *Crime in the Suburbs* Morrow, New York 1967
Love, Gilbert "College Students Are Beating the Depression" *School and Society* June 10, 1933
Lukas, J. Anthony "The Story So Far" *New York Times Magazine* July 22, 1973
—— "The Story Continued" *New York Times Magazine* January 13, 1974
Lynd, Albert *Quackery in the Public Schools* Little, Brown, Boston 1950
Lynd, Robert S. and Helen Merrell *Middletown in Transition: A Study in Cultural Conflicts* Harcourt, Brace and World, New York 1937
MacLeish, Archibald "The Irresponsibles" *Nation* May 18, 1940
Mailer, Norman *Miami and the Siege of Chicago: An Informal History of the Republican and Democratic Conventions of 1968* Signet, New York 1968
—— "The Steps of the Pentagon" *Harper's Magazine* March 1968
Manchester, William "The Great Bank Holiday" *Holiday* February 1960
—— *The Death of a President, November 20–November 25, 1963* Harper and Row, New York 1967
—— "Our War in the Pacific" *Holiday* November 1960
—— *Portrait of a President: John F. Kennedy in Profile* Little, Brown, Boston 1962
Marcuse, Herbert *One-Dimensional Man: Studies in the Ideology of Advanced Industrial Society* Beacon, Boston 1964
Markel, Lester *World in Review* Rand McNally, New York 1972
Marshall, E. Kennerly Jr. "Historical Perspectives in Chemotherapy" in *Advances in Chemotherapy* (Volume I ed. Abraham Goldin and Frank Hawking) Academic Press, New York 1964
—— "The Revolution in Drug Therapy" *Johns Hopkins Magazine* June 1955
Marshall, George C. *European Initiative Essential to Economic Recovery* (Department of State Publication 2882, European Series 25) U.S. Government Printing Office, Washington 1947
Mauldin, Bill *Back Home* William Sloane, New York 1947
—— *Up Front* Holt, New York 1945
Mazo, Earl *Richard Nixon: A Political and Personal Portrait* Harper, New York 1959
McCarry, Charles *Citizen Nader* Saturday Review Press, New York 1972
McCarthy, Joe *Hurricane!* American Heritage Press, New York 1969
—— *The Remarkable Kennedys* Dial, New York 1960
McGinniss, Joe *The Selling of the President 1968* Trident, New York 1969
McLuhan, Marshall *The Gutenberg Galaxy: The Making of Typographic Man* Signet, New York 1962
—— *Understanding Media: The Extensions of Man* McGraw-Hill, New York 1964
McMahan, Harry W. " 'Best of the Year' TV Commercials" *Advertising Age* December 16, 1963
Mellor, William Bancroft *Patton: Fighting Man* Putnam, New York 1946
Mencken, H. L. *Newspaper Days 1899–1906* Knopf, New York 1945
Meryman, Richard "George McGovern Talks" *Life* July 7, 1972
Michael, Paul, ed. *The American Movies Reference Book: The Sound Era* Prentice-Hall, Englewood Cliffs, N.J. 1970
Michener, James A. *America vs. America: The Revolution in Middle-Class Values* Signet, New York 1968
Millis, Walter, ed. *The Forrestal Diaries* Viking, New York 1951
Mills, C. Wright *White Collar: The American Middle Classes* Oxford, New York 1951
Milstein, Tom "A Perspective on the Panthers" *Commentary* September 1970
Minehan, Thomas *Boy and Girl Tramps of America* Farrar and Rinehart, New York 1934
Mitchell, Broadus *Depression Decade: From New Era Through New Deal, 1929–1941* Rinehart, New York 1947
Mitford, Jessica *The Trial of Dr. Spock* Knopf, New York 1969
Modell, John "American Concentration Camps" *Pennsylvania Gazette* February 1974
Moley, Raymond *The First New Deal* Harcourt, Brace and World, New York 1966
Mooney, Booth *The Lyndon Johnson Story* Farrar, Straus, New York 1956
Moorehead, Alan *The Traitors* Scribner, New York 1952
Morison, Samuel Eliot *History of United States Naval Operations in World War II* (15 volumes) Little, Brown, Boston 1947–1962
—— *The Two-Ocean War. A Short History of the United States Navy in the Second World War* Little, Brown, Boston 1963
Morris, Richard B. *Encyclopedia of American History* Harper and Row, New York 1965
Mowry, George E. *The Urban Nation 1920–1960* Hill and Wang, New York 1965
Mullett, Charles F. *The British Empire* Holt, New York 1938

Murray, Henry A. "Individuality: The Meaning and Content of Individuality in Contemporary America" *Daedalus* Spring 1958
Murrow, Edward R. *This Is London* (ed. Elmer Davis) Simon and Schuster, New York 1941
Navasky, Victor S. "Notes on Cult; Or, How to Join the Intellectual Establishment" *New York Times Magazine* March 27, 1966
Neary, John "Bombs Blast a Message of Hate" *Life* March 27, 1970
Nelson, Walter Henry *Small Wonder: The Amazing Story of the Volkswagen* Little, Brown, Boston 1965
"The Neurotic Trillionaire" *Economist* May 10, 1969
Neustadt, Richard E. *Presidential Power: The Politics of Leadership* Wiley, New York 1960
Niebuhr, Reinhold *The Children of Light and the Children of Darkness: A Vindication of Democracy and a Critique of Its Traditional Defense* Scribner, New York 1944
—— "Is There a Revival of Religion?" *New York Times Magazine* November 19, 1950
Nixon, Richard M. *Six Crises* Doubleday, New York 1962
"No One Has Starved" *Fortune* September 1932
Northeast Power Failure November 9 and 10, 1965: A Report to the President by the Federal Power Commission U.S. Government Printing Office, Washington 1965
O'Donnell, Kenneth P. "LBJ and the Kennedys" *Life* August 7, 1970
—— and David F. Powers, with Joseph McCarthy *"Johnny, We Hardly Knew Ye": Memories of John Fitzgerald Kennedy* Little, Brown, Boston 1972
One Hundred Years of Famous Pages from the New York Times, 1851-1951 Simon and Schuster, New York 1951
O'Neill, William L., ed. *American Society Since 1945* Quadrangle, Chicago 1969
Packard, Vance "Resurvey of 'Hidden Persuaders' " *New York Times Magazine* May 11, 1958
—— *The Sexual Wilderness* David McKay, New York 1968
Pater, Alan F. and Jason R. *What They Said in 1969: The Yearbook of Spoken Opinion* Monitor, Beverly Hills, California 1970
Pauling, Linus, and Edward Teller "Fallout and Disarmament" *Daedalus* Spring 1958
Phillips, Cabell *From the Crash to the Blitz* Macmillan, New York 1969
—— *The Truman Presidency: The History of a Triumphant Succession* Macmillan, New York 1966
Pound, Arthur "Bankruptcy Mill" *Atlantic Monthly* February 1932
Powers, Francis Gary "Francis Gary Powers Tells His Story" *New York Times Magazine* April 19, 1970
—— with Curt Gentry *Operation Overflight: The U-2 Spy Pilot Tells His Story for the First Time* Holt, Rinehart, and Winston, New York 1970
Pusey, Merlo J. *Eisenhower, The President* Macmillan, New York 1956
Pyle, Ernie *This Is Your War* Holt, New York 1943
Pynchon, Thomas "A Journey into the Mind of Watts" *New York Times Magazine* June 12, 1966 (Pyramid 1966)
Raskin, A. H. "The Berkeley Affair: Mr. Kerr vs. Mr. Savio & Co." *New York Times Magazine* February 14, 1965
—— "Report on the Communist Party (U.S.A.)" *New York Times Magazine* March 30, 1947
Relief for Unemployed Transients: Hearings Before a Subcommittee of the Committee on Manufactures, U.S. Senate, 72nd Congress, 2nd Session, on S.5121 U.S. Government Printing Office, Washington 1933
Report of the President's Commission on the Assassination of President John F. Kennedy U.S. Government Printing Office, Washington 1964
Report on the International Control of Atomic Energy, A (Prepared for the Secretary of State's Committee on Atomic Energy by a board of consultants) Doubleday, New York 1946
Ridgeway, James "The Cops and the Kids" *New Republic* September 7, 1968
Ridgway, Matthew B. (as told to Harold H. Martin) *Soldier* Harper, New York 1956
Riesman, David, in collaboration with Reuel Denney and Nathan Glazer *The Lonely Crowd: A Study of the Changing American Character* Yale, New Haven 1950
Roosevelt, James, and Sidney Shalett *Affectionately, F.D.R.: A Son's Story of a Lonely Man* Harcourt, Brace, New York 1959
"Roosevelt Wins" *Nation* July 13, 1932
Rosenthal, A. M., and Arthur Gelb, eds. *The Night the Lights Went Out* Signet, New York 1965
Ross, Irwin *The Loneliest Campaign: The Truman Victory of 1948* Signet, New York 1968
Rossiter, Clinton *The American Presidency* Harcourt, Brace, New York 1956 (Mentor, New York 1960)
Rostow, W. W. "The American National Style" *Daedalus* Spring 1958
Rovere, Richard H. *Affairs of State: The Eisenhower Years* Farrar, Straus, and Cudahy, New York 1956
—— *Senator Joe McCarthy* Harcourt, Brace, New York 1959
—— *Waist Deep in the Big Muddy* Little, Brown, Boston 1968

—— and Arthur M. Schlesinger Jr. *The General and the President: And the Future of American Foreign Policy* Farrar, Straus and Young, New York 1951

Roy, Jules *The Battle of Dienbienphu* Harper, New York 1965

Ruffner, Frederick G Jr., ed. *National Organizations of the United States* (Volume I of *Encyclopedia of Organizations*) Gale Research, Detroit 1968

Salisbury, Harrison E *The Shook-Up Generation* Harper, New York 1958

Sanders, Ed *The Family: The Story of Charles Manson's Dune Buggy Attack Battalion* Avon, New York 1972

Scheinfeld, Amram "Kinsey's Study of Female Sexual Behavior" *Cosmopolitan* September 1953

Schlesinger, Arthur M. Jr. *The Coming of the New Deal* Houghton Mifflin, Boston 1958

—— *The Crisis of the Old Order* Houghton Mifflin, Boston 1957

—— *The Politics of Upheaval* Houghton Mifflin, Boston 1960

—— *A Thousand Days: John F. Kennedy in the White House* Houghton Mifflin, Boston 1965

Schrag, Peter "The Forgotten American" *Harper's Magazine* August 1969

—— "Is Main Street Still There?" *Saturday Review* January 17, 1970

Schulberg, Budd *The Disenchanted* Random House, New York 1950

Schwarz, Jordan *1933: Roosevelt's Decision. The United States Leaves the Gold Standard* Chelsea House, New York 1969

Servan-Schreiber, J. J. *The American Challenge* Avon, New York 1969

Sevareid, Eric "The American Dream" *Look* July 9, 1968

—— *Not So Wild a Dream* Knopf, New York 1946

Shannon, David A., ed. *The Great Depression* Prentice-Hall, Englewood Cliffs, N.J. 1960

Shapiro, Nat, ed. *Popular Music: An Annotated Index of American Popular Songs* (Volume I, 1950–1959) Adrian Press, New York 1964

Sheehan, Neil, Hedrick Smith, E. W. Kenworthy, and Fox Butterfield *The Pentagon Papers* Bantam, New York 1971

Sherrill, Robert *Gothic Politics in the Deep South: Stars of the New Confederacy* Ballantine, New York 1968

Shirer, William L. *The Rise and Fall of the Third Reich: A History of Nazi Germany* Simon and Schuster, New York 1960

Shuster, Alvin, ed. *Washington: The New York Times Guide to the Nation's Capital* Robert B. Luce, Washington 1967

Sidey, Hugh *John F Kennedy, President* Atheneum, New York 1963

Silber, Irwin, ed. *Songs America Voted By* Stackpole, Harrisburg, Pennsylvania 1971

Simon, Rita James, ed. *As We Saw the Thirties* University of Illinois, Urbana 1967

Smith, A. Robert, and Eric Sevareid *Washington: Magnificent Capital* Doubleday, New York 1965

Smith, Gene *The Shattered Dream: Herbert Hoover and the Great Depression* Morrow, New York 1970

Smith, John M., and Tim Cankwell, eds. *The World Encyclopedia of the Film* World, New York 1972

Sorensen, Theodore C. *Kennedy* Harper and Row, New York 1965

Soule, George "Are We Going to Have a Revolution?" *Harper's Magazine* August 1932

Sparks, Fred *The $20,000,000 Honeymoon: Jackie and Ari's First Year* Dell, New York 1970

Sparrow, John *After the Assassination: A Positive Appraisal of the Warren Report* Chilmark Press, New York 1967

Spectorsky, A. C. *The Exurbanites* Lippincott, Philadelphia and New York 1955

Speer, Albert *Inside the Third Reich* Macmillan, New York 1970

Spivak, John L. *Shrine of the Silver Dollar* Modern Age, New York 1940

Spock, Benjamin, M.D. *The Common Sense Book of Baby and Child Care* Duell, Sloan and Pearce, New York 1945

Stearns, Marshall *The Story of Jazz* Oxford, New York 1956

Steinbeck, John *Travels with Charley: In Search of America* Viking, New York 1962 (Bantam, New York 1963)

Steiner, Paul *The Stevenson Wit and Wisdom* Pyramid, New York 1965

Stevenson, Adlai *Speeches of Adlai Stevenson* Random House, New York 1952

Stimson, Henry L. "The Decision to Use the Atomic Bomb" *Harper's Magazine* February 1947

Storr, Anthony *Human Aggression* Atheneum, New York 1968

Straight, Michael *Trial by Television* Beacon, Boston 1954

Streit, Peggy "Why They Fight for the P.A.T." *New York Times Magazine* September 20, 1964

Sullivan, Frank *A Pearl in Every Oyster* Little, Brown, Boston 1938

Sulzberger, C. L., ed. *The American Heritage Picture History of World War II* Simon and Schuster, New York 1966

"A Survey of Unemployed Alumni" *School and Society* March 10, 1934

Symes, Lillian "Blunder on the Left: The Revolution and the American Scene" *Harper's Magazine* December 1933
Szulc, Tad "The Spy Compulsion" *New York Times Magazine* June 3, 1973
Tate, Allen "The Man of Letters in the Modern World" *Hudson Review* Autumn 1952
Terkel, Studs *Hard Times: An Oral History of the Great Depression* Pantheon, New York 1970
Tessler, Mark A., and Ronald D. Hedlund "Students Aren't Crazies" *New Republic* September 12, 1970
Thayer, George *The War Business: The International Trade in Armaments* Simon and Schuster, New York 1969
Thompson, Hunter S. "The 'Hashbury' Is the Capital of the Hippies" *New York Times Magazine* May 14, 1967
Time, Editors of *Live Them Again: The Three Decades from Flappers to Flying Saucers, 1923-1953* Simon and Schuster, New York 1953
Tocqueville, Alexis de *Democracy in America* ed. Phillips Bradley (Vol. I) Vintage, New York 1945
Toland, John *But Not in Shame: The Six Months After Pearl Harbor* Random House, New York 1961
Truman, Harry S. *Memoirs,* volumes I (*Year of Decisions,* 1955) and II (*Years of Trial and Hope,* 1956) Doubleday, New York
Truman, Margaret, with Margaret Cousins *Souvenir: Margaret Truman's Own Story* McGraw-Hill, New York 1956
"200,000 Trailers" *Fortune* March 1937
Unemployment in the United States: Hearings Before a Subcommittee of the Committee on Labor, House of Representatives, 72nd Congress, 1st Session, on H.R.206, H.R.6011, H.R.6066 U.S. Government Printing Office, Washington 1932
Van Camp, Sarah "Growing Up in D.C. in Song and Story" (unpublished manuscript)
Vandenberg, Arthur H. *The Private Papers of Senator Vandenberg,* ed. Arthur H. Vandenberg Jr. Houghton Mifflin, Boston 1952
Vanderlip, Frank A. "What About the Banks?" *Saturday Evening Post* November 5, 1932
Villard, Oswald Garrison "An Open Letter to Governor Roosevelt" *Nation* May 11, 1932
—— "Roosevelt and Hoover Militarists Both" *Nation* October 26, 1932
Vorse, Mary Heaton "Rebellion in the Cornbelt: American Farmers Beat Their Plowshares into Swords" *Harper's Magazine* December 1932
Walker, Daniel *Rights in Conflict* Signet, New York 1968
Walker, John and Katherine *The Washington Guidebook* Metro Publishers, Washington 1969
Walker, Stanley " 'Book Branding'—A Case History" *New York Times Magazine* July 12, 1953
Warner, W. Lloyd, and others *Yankee City* Yale University, New Haven 1963
—— and others *Social Class in America: A Manual of Procedure for the Measurement of Social Status* Harper Torchbooks, New York 1960
Washington, City and Capital (Federal Writers' Project, Works Progress Administration, American Guide Series) U.S. Government Printing Office, Washington 1937
"Washington and Its Approaches" *Saturday Evening Post* December 20, 1930
Weaver, Richard M. *Ideas Have Consequences* University of Chicago, Chicago 1948
Webb, John N. *The Migratory-Casual Worker* (WPA Research Monograph VII) U.S. Government Printing Office, Washington 1937
Webbink, Paul "Unemployment in the United States, 1930-1940" *Papers and Proceedings of the American Economic Association* February 1941
Weber, Max *The Protestant Ethic and the Spirit of Capitalism* Scribner, New York 1958
Wecter, Dixon *The Age of the Great Depression* Macmillan, New York 1948
Wertham, Frederic *Seduction of the Innocent* Rinehart, New York 1954
West, Rebecca *The New Meaning of Treason* Viking, New York 1964 (Time-Life Books 1966)
White, Theodore H. *The Making of the President 1960* Atheneum, New York 1961
—— *The Making of the President 1964* Atheneum, New York 1965
—— *The Making of the President 1968* Atheneum, New York 1969
—— *The Making of the President 1972* Atheneum, New York 1973
White, William S. *The Professional: Lyndon B. Johnson* Houghton Mifflin, Boston 1964 (Crest, New York 1964)
Whitehead, Donald F. *The FBI Story: A Report to the People* Random House, New York 1956
White House Historical Association *The White House: An Historic Guide* Washington 1962
Whiteside, Thomas "Corridor of Mirrors: The Television Editorial Process, Chicago" *Columbia Journalism Review* Winter 1968/1969
"Who's in the Army Now?" *Fortune* September 1935
Whyte, William H. Jr. *The Organization Man* Simon and Schuster, New York 1956 (Anchor, New York)
Wiener, Norbert "A Scientist Rebels" *Atlantic Monthly* January 1947

Willkie, Wendell *One World* Simon and Schuster, New York 1943

Wills, Garry *Nixon Agonistes: The Crisis of the Self-Made Man* Houghton Mifflin, Boston 1970 (Signet, New York 1971)

Wilson, Sloan *The Man in the Gray Flannel Suit* Simon and Schuster, New York 1955

Wish, Harvey *Contemporary America* 4th ed. Harper and Row, New York 1966

Wolfe, Thomas *You Can't Go Home Again* Harper, New York 1934

Wolfert, Ira *American Guerrilla in the Philippines* Simon and Schuster, New York 1945

Wolff, Perry Sidney *A Tour of the White House with Mrs. John F. Kennedy* (television program) Doubleday, New York 1962

"Women in Business" *Fortune* September 1935

X [See George F. Kennan]

Yank, Editors of, selected by *The Best from Yank* World, Cleveland 1945

"Youth in College" *Fortune* June 1936

Zeiger, Henry A. *Inquest! Ted Kennedy–Mary Jo Kopechne: Prosecution or Persecution?* Tower, New York 1970

COPYRIGHT
ACKNOWLEDGMENTS

INDEX

China (cont'd)
32, 1552–55; Nixon visits, 1546, 1552–
54. See also Chiang Kai-shek; Mao Tse-
tung
China Lobby, 601, 643, 679
Chisholm, Shirley, 1571
Chmedelin, M., 269
Choate, Robert, 172
Chotiner, Murray, 758, 759, 772–75, 778,
780, 882, 1493–95
Chou En-lai, 667, 1529, 1530, 1531, 1553,
1554
Christian Science Monitor, 581
Christmas, William, 1473–74
Church, Frank, 71, 1248, 1284
church, the. See religion
Churchill, Randolph, 933
Churchill, Winston, 80, 111, 146, 175, 270,
385, 414, 433, 449, 452, 463, 598; on
Munich Pact, 228; and Battle of Britain,
262; and U.S. aid, 277, 281, 531, 539,
542, 1009; meets FDR at sea, 283; and
Pacific war, 314, 315, 324, 333–34; visits
U.S., 334, 514; and summit meetings,
386, 400, 426, 825, 848, 862, 915; loses
election, 452; and Iron Curtain speech,
502, 505; and Vietnam, 837; death, 1271
Chu Teh, Gen., 596
CIA (Central Intelligence Agency), 967,
1011, 1013, 1136, 1314; on Korea, 651,
669; and Cuban counterrevolution (Bay
of Pigs), 1054, 1056–60, 1095 1106,
1109; "Frank Bender" and, 1056, 1057,
1060, 1098, 1099; and U-2, 1061–66;
and Cuban missile crisis, 1173–76, 1179;
and Vietnam bombing, 1281, 1287,
1312; Nixon and, 1491; and Ellsberg
case, 1515–17, 1568; and Watergate,
1578. See also intelligence, military
Ciccone, Richard, 1477
Cienfuegos, Osmani, 1104
Cierva, Juan de la, 8
CIO (Congress of Industrial Organizations), 191, 391, 475, 494, 547, 771; and
AFL, 162–63, 186–88; and steel and
auto industries, 186, 187–95; and Communists, 192, 195
Citizens Committee for the Reelection of
the President (CREEP). See CREEP
City College of New York, 153
City Lights Bookshop, 889
civil defense, 313, 315, 323, 370, 704–705
Civilian Conservation Corps (CCC), 95,
100–101, 117, 128
civil rights, 133, 1196; and labor, 157–60;
World War II, 297–98, 362–69, (1948)
553, 556; Fair Deal and, 580; and segregation, 901–903, 910 (see also segregation); and Little Rock incident, 979–91;
Kennedys and, 1150–55, 1201–1205 (see
also Kennedy, John F.; Kennedy, Rob-

ert F.); in Mississippi, 1155–64; and
backlash, 1249; Acts, 1252, 1262, 1476;
J. Edgar Hoover and, 1253; (1960s)
1295–98, 1304; in North, 1304; black
power and, 1308; of rioters, 1459. See
also American Civil Liberties Union;
black groups and societies
Civil Service Commission, 906
Civil Works Administration (CWA), 103,
123
Clark, Bennett Champ, 266, 279
Clark, Chase, 364
Clark, Dick, 1043
Clark, James G. Jr., 1296, 1297, 1309
Clark, Kenneth B., 900, 1205, 1392
Clark, Mark, 1460
Clark, Gen. Mark, 340, 341, 403, 789
Clark, Ramsay, 1395
Clark, Tom C., 605, 607
Clarke, "Brother Richard," 1520, 1521,
1525
Clay, Cassius (Muhammad Ali), 991, 1269
Clay, Gen. Lucius, 541, 1117
Clayton, Will, 506, 537
Cleaver, Eldridge, 907, 1409, 1519; Soul
on Ice, 1409
Cleveland, Harlan, 1105
Cleveland Plain Dealer, 19
Clevenger, Cliff, 552
Clifford, Clark, 506; and Truman, 493,
496, 547–71 passim, 580; on Vietnam,
1288, 1447; at Pentagon, 1379, 1380,
1506
Clifton, Maj. Gen. Chester V., 684
Clutter, Herbert, 1044
Coca, Imogene, 849
Coca-Cola, 544, 1009
Coffin, Henry Sloane, 346
Coffin, William Sloane, 1457
Cohan, George M., 81
Cohen, Ben, 126
Cohen, Dr. Maimon M., 1367
Cohn, Harry, 595
Cohn, Roy, 858–79
Colbert, Claudette, 81, 239
cold war, 534, 613, 1270; Lippmann's
study of, 536; deepens, 625, 693, 732,
848; Eisenhower and, 790, 813; Dulles
and, 1045–46; and U-2 affair, 1072;
JFK and, 1110–19, 1123–24, 1135, 1173;
LBJ and, 1247; Nixon and, 1420–21,
1446, 1559
Cole, Nat King, 591
Coleman, Tom, 604
Coll, Edward T., 1571
Collier's magazine, 107, 647
Collins, Floyd, 1542
Collins, Gen. J. Lawton, 659, 684
Collins, John F., 1333
Collins, Judy, 1479
Collins, LeRoy, 1298

Duggan, Laurence, 616
Dulles, Allen, 378, 936, 1252, 1253; and Bay of Pigs, 1057, 1060, 1095, 1097. See also CIA
Dulles, John Foster, 568, 617, 662, 924, 927, 939, 1020, 1106, 1532; and America First, 267, 753; and NATO, 682; at 1952 Republican convention, 753; as Secretary of State, 790, 794, 795, 819; and "massive retaliation," 790, 1044; background and character of, 795, 828; and Bohlen appointment, 802; on "secret agreements," 805–806; policy and "brinkmanship" of, 809–11, 828–31, 1044–45, 1048, 1051; and loyalty issue, 822; and Bricker amendment, 823, 825; and Vietnam, 835–37, 838, 840; and Joseph McCarthy, 862; and Formosa crisis, 912; and Geneva conference, 915–17; and Middle East, 935, 1005–1008; illness and death, 936, 1044–46
Dumbarton Oaks conference, 357
Dun, Bishop Angus, 440
Dunham, Walter, 739
Dunne, Irene, 81
Dunne, John R., 1523, 1525
Duong Van Minh, Gen., 1215, 1502
Du Pont, Pierre S., 99, 169, 170, 189
Du Pont family, 50
Durante, Jimmy, 718
Durkheim, Emile, 36
Durkin, Martin P., 792
dust storms, 117–19
Dutch East Indies. See Indonesia
Dylan, Bob, 1350, 1435

Eagleton, Thomas, 1575, 1576
Earhart, Amelia, 150, 151
Earle, George, 206
Early, Stephen, 429, 430, 431, 436
Earp, Wyatt, 994
East Germany (German Democratic Republic). See Germany
Eastland, James O., 989, 1159
Eastman, Max, 863
Eccles, Marriner S., 126
ecology: dust storms, 117–19; movement starts, 1223; and pollution, 1334, 1425, 1436–38
Economic Stabilization Act of 1970, 1535
economy, U.S.: Hoover and, 25–32, 36, 1533; and gold standard, 27, 86–87, 94–95, 101, 149, 1533–35; Gross National Product, 38, 290, 354, 727, 929, 946, 1010, 1072, 1081, 1208, 1226, 1535; FDR and, 102–108; deficit spending, 113–14, 196; laissez-faire, 164–65; inflation, 168, 486–87, 489, 553, 580, 929, 1291, 1446, 1500, 1535, 1537; and war boom, 289, 353–56; pre-World War II, 289–90; blacks and, 296, 1146, 1251–52,

1321, 1410; civilian spending, 354, 356; and profits, 355, 1340, 1341; black market, 359, 486–87; postwar, 486–90, 494, 526, 1533; affluence and public values, 725, 727–28, 884–88, 1280, 1334, 1335; and tariff, 731, 1536; recessions, 803, 847, 881, 999; boom, 850, 938, 946–54; (1960s) 1208, 1225, 1291, 1341, 1533; (1970s) 1447, 1533; Nixon's New Economic Policy, 1532–37. See also budget, federal; business and industry; cost; Depression, Great; income; prices; stock market; wages and hours
Eddy, Nelson, 81, 181, 371
Eden, Anthony, 398, 400, 804, 917, 935–37
Edgerton, John E., 35, 44
Edison, Thomas A., 969, 1329
Edsel, the, 968, 976, 997–1000
education, 71, 80, 1225; blacks and, 6, 128, 900–901, 1146, 1156–66, 1199–1201, 1250; for veterans, 357, 396, 486; progressive, 959; (1950s) 959–60, 968–71; U.S. compared with Russian, 968–70; federal aid to, 1002, 1276; (1960s) 1270, 1342–43; parochial, 1276; and permissiveness, 1344; and busing issue, 1560, 1569. See also schools and teachers; sex education; student(s)
Edward VIII of England, 80
Edwards, Willard, 638, 643
Egan, Leo, 565
"eggheads." See intellectuals
Egypt, 280, 1174; Suez crisis, 934–37, 1005–1008
Ehrlichman, John, 1416, 1422, 1508, 1513; and ITT, 1510–12; and Pentagon Papers, 1515–17; and Watergate, 1566–68, 1577–81
Eichelberger, Gen. Robert L., 329, 416
Einstein, Albert, 82, 255, 467, 969; letters to FDR, 260–61, 410; opposes use of atomic weapons, 410, 627, 699, 703
Eisenhower, David, 1375
Eisenhower, Gen. Dwight D., 10, 151, 304, 651, 710, 750, 879, 934, 1020, 1356; early career, 4–5, 13, 16–17, 101, 283, 312, 362; and blacks, 295; as ETO commander, 336–40, 342, 386, 387, 397, 404–406, 432, 450; Crusade in Europe, 345, 730; and D-Day, 403–407; and Russia, 426, 454, 1045–46; and eastern Europe, 426; and demobilization, 500–502; Truman and, 503, 547, 551, 791; Democrats for, 548, 551, 555; and NATO, 682, 745; presidential campaigns: (1952) 682, 726, 744–45, 750–51, 754–58, 761–69, 771–75, 778–84, (1956) 942–43, (1960) 1081, (1964) 1259; and Stevenson, 746, 762–67; and Joseph McCarthy, 767–69, 802, 861–62, 879; and Korea, 781, 789–91, 808–10,

reconnaissance flights (*cont'd*)
Cuban missile crisis, 1175, 1177, 1183, 1185; EC121 shot down, 1445
Reconstruction Finance Corporation (RFC), 27, 28, 53, 124; Fulbright's investigation of, 738–39, 740
recordings, phonograph. *See* music and musicians
Redbook magazine, 932, 1455
Red Channels (blacklist), 611
Redgrave, Michael, 723
Reeb, James J., 1298, 1300
Reece, Carroll, 550
Reed, Carol, 595
Reed, David A., 68, 85
Reed, Harold W., 739
Reed, Rex, 1391
Reedy, George, 1317
Reeves, George, 715
Reilly, Mike, 398
Reinecke, Jean Otis, 519
relief. *See* welfare, public
religion, 729, 1269; and Protestant ethic, 77, 948, 1172; Father Coughlin, 129–33; and pacifism, 151; Billy Graham, 592, 727; "subversion" in, 817–18; as campaign issue, 944, 1075, 1078; (1950s) 897, 945, 950, 959; and color line, 1196; and contraception, 1358; (1970s) 1458–59; New English Bible, 1459; "Jesus people," 1544. *See also* Catholicism
Remington, William T., 563, 605, 616
Reno, Milo, 68–69
Republican National Committee, 85, 172, 273, 637, 850, 1032, 1033, 1258, 1497
Republican national conventions: (1936) 169; (1940) 273; (1948) 549, 553, 560, 717; (1952) 751–59; (1956) 940; (1960) 1078; (1964) 1247, 1249, 1257–58; (1968) 1399; (1972) 1561, 1570
Republican party, 25, 61; (1934) 120, 125; (1936) 173, 175, 206; (1940s) 207, 272–74; (1944) 389–91; (1945–48) 488–89, 508–509, 546, 555, 576; (1950s) 682, 851, 1031–34, 1075; (1952) 802–805; (1956) 943; (1964) 1255–60, 1264; (1966) 1273, 1346; (1969) 1425; (1970) 1496; (1972) 1560–62, 1566, 1569–70, 1577; and big business, 127, 938, 1560; and blacks, 128, 943; and federal judges, 164, 182, 185; campaign contributions to, 168, 770–81, 1510–12, 1560–61, 1578; and coalition, 168 (*see also* Democratic party); and loyalty issue, 599–603, 614, 618, 621; and Korea, 658, 812–13; and search for government corruption, 733, 739–43; in South, 755–56, 943; division in, 760, 815–26, 938, 1264; and Nixon, 776, 1576; and Joseph McCarthy, 878; Old Guard opposition to Soviet meeting, 915–16; and U.N., 938;

and Supreme Court, 1395; "dirty tricks," 1513–18
Reston, James, 537, 1181, 1227, 1317; on Truman, 507, 577, 581; on Eisenhower, 682, 767, 881; and Oppenheimer case, 851, 853; and Khrushchev interview, 972; and JFK, 1091, 1116, 1119–20; on Vietnam, 1288, 1585–86, 1587; and Nixon, 1406, 1513
Reuben James (destroyer), 285
Reuther, Victor, 475–76
Reuther, Walter, 475–79, 548, 560, 1050, 1203
revolution, social. *See* society
Rexroth, Kenneth, 892
Rey, Alvino, 155
Reynaud, Paul, 261
Reynolds, Jackson E., 124
Reynolds, Robert O., 1084
Rhee, Syngman, 649, 655, 658, 810–11, 815
Rhinelander, Alice, 295
Rhodes, James, 1487
Ribbentrop, Joachim von, 316
Ribicoff, Abraham, 1401, 1539
Ricco, Roger, 1370
Rich, Buddy, 375
Rich, Robert F., 500, 602
Richards, Ray, 643
Richardson, John, 1215–16, 1281
Richardson, Robert, 1303
Richardson, Seth, 608, 609–10
Richberg, Donald R., 105, 126
Rickover, Adm. Hyman G., 970
Ricks, Willie "the Reverend," 1307
Ridenhour, Ronald, 1443
Ridgway, Gen. Matthew B., 679, 686, 691, 693, 751, 835, 912
Riesel, Victor, 931
Riesman, David, 76, 706, 725, 885, 952, 1349, 1356; *The Lonely Crowd*, 36
riots and demonstrations, 1036, 1133, 1311, 1339; Bonus Expeditionary Force, 1–3, 10–21, 26, 29, 64; pacifist, 151–52; demobilization ("Wanna-Go-Home"), 497–502, 650; and Korea, 661; French, 837; bus boycott, 907–10; anti-American, abroad, 1010–20, 1071, 1181; black sit-ins, 1037–38, 1298; Berkeley, 1039, 1266–67, 1292, 1459; racist, in Mississippi, 1158–66; Birmingham, 1195–97; March on Washington, 1202–1203; in Vietnam, 1212; black, in North, 1250–51, 1271, 1322–25, 1409; against the U.S. war in Vietnam, 1271, 1284, 1291–93, 1479; draft card burning, 1292; Selma voting march, 1297–1301, 1309; Watts, 1301–1305, 1311; countrywide, 1304–1305, 1309, 1322–25, 1386; Meredith March for Freedom, 1306–1309; Roxbury, Newark, Detroit,

Chronology

1932   The Bonus Riot in Washington
15,000,000 jobless
Election of FDR
Rumors of revolution

1933   Collapse of the nation's banks
FDR's Hundred Days
Back from the brink

1934   J. Edgar Hoover and *Famous Funnies*
Black blizzards
Dr. Townsend, Father Coughlin, and Huey Long

1935   The Second Hundred Days
The birth of swing music
The rise of John L. Lewis
The Supreme Court challenges FDR

1936   The Liberty League: "Save the Constitution!"
Gone With the Wind
FDR routs Landon and the *Literary Digest*

1937   The Supreme Court "pack" plan
Birth of Congress's conservative coalition
Sit-down strikes in Detroit
Japanese sink the U.S.S. *Panay*
Isolationism at its peak

1938   Munich and H. V. Kaltenborn
New England hurricane
Orson Welles's Martian broadcast

1939   New York World's Fair
World War II starts. Lindbergh: "Keep out!"

1940   The Fall of France
America First; "God Bless America"
Einstein writes FDR a letter
Willkie vs. the Champ

1941   House Bill 1776: Lend-Lease
Nazi sub torpedoes the *Reuben James*
CCNY dismisses Bertrand Russell
Marian Anderson sings at the Lincoln Memorial
Pearl Harbor: "This is no drill"

1942   Retreat in the Pacific; Midway; Guadalcanal
GIs invade North Africa
At home: "I'll Walk Alone"
The ordeal of the Issei and Nisei

1943   Salerno, Cassino, and Tarawa
At home: Frank Sinatra and Henry J. Kaiser

1944   Anzio, Normandy, the Bulge
Saipan and Leyte Gulf

1945   Iwo Jima and Okinawa
The U.N. Charter
FDR dies; Truman is President
V-E Day
Hiroshima and Nagasaki
V-J Day

1946   Postwar inflation and strikes
"Wanna-go-home" riots
Churchill uses "Iron Curtain" in Missouri

1947   The Truman Doctrine and the Marshall Plan
A New Look in fashions

1948   The Kinsey Report
The Berlin airlift
Dixiecrats and Henry Wallace's Progressives
Truman beats Dewey

1949   William J. Levitt's first Levittown
First report of flying saucers
TV: Gorgeous George and skating derbies
China becomes Red China
Russia has the Bomb

1950   The conviction of Alger Hiss
The rise of Joe McCarthy
War in Korea; Inchon; Red China attacks

1951   Direct Distance Dialing starts
The Great Debate
MacArthur is relieved
The age of Mickey Spillane
The silent generation emerges
TV replaces radio as popular entertainment
Kefauver crime hearings

1952   The hydrogen bomb
Scandals shake Truman administration
Nixon's "Checkers" speech
Ike beats Stevenson, who is "too old to cry"

1953   Massive retaliation; bigger bang for a buck
Stalin dies; peace in Korea
The death of Taft

1954   *McCall's* coins "togetherness"
The Bricker amendment
The Army-McCarthy hearings